MAJUMDER

PLAINTS

Kolkata
Eastern Law House Private Ltd.
54 Ganesh Chunder Avenue
Kolkata 700 013

New Delhi
Eastern Law House Private Ltd.
36 Netaji Subhash Marg, Daryaganj
New Delhi 110 002

MAJUMDER
PLAINTS

CONTAINING

Principles of Pleadings with
Specimen of Plaints and Petitions

FIFTH EDITION

by

Purnendu Bhattacharyya MA, LLM
Former District & Sessions Judge and
Director, West Bengal Judicial Academy

Kolkata New Delhi
EASTERN LAW HOUSE

Published and processed by
EASTERN LAW HOUSE PRIVATE LTD.
54 Ganesh Chunder Avenue
Kolkata 700 013
Tel: (033) 2215-1989
Email: mail@elh.co.in
www.elh.co.in

First Edition 1972
Second Edition 1980
Third Edition 1995
Fourth Edition 2007
Fifth Edition 2019

ISBN 978-81-7177-349-7

Printed at
Dey's Offset, Kolkata

Preface to the Fifth Edition

The very fact of a book running into its fifth edition, albeit with revisions from time to time (following changes in the law) reveals its continued usefulness for nearly half a century. The current edition seeks to incorporate the updated position of law and to present an authentic, if illustrative, guide to drafting in civil proceedings. The true foundation of a suit lies in the pleading and as such, care has been taken to include in the specimen the essential requirements of law, substantive and procedural.

I acknowledge the assistance offered by the staff of the Eastern Law House including Mr. Somnath Chakraborty and the Director Mr. Asok De in the preparation of this edition.

I firmly believe that this thoroughly revised book will be of assistance particularly to the budding advocates. Any suggestion for improvement of the book will be appreciated.

Kolkata
19th February 2019 PURNENDU BHATTACHARYYA

Preface to the First Edition

I have attempted, within the compass of this short commentary, to set out rules of pleadings obtaining in Courts of our country. Model Forms of plaints and of major petitions have been added for the benefit of young learners.

I should express my indebtedness to authorities like *Odgers, P.C. Mogha* and *S.C. Ghosh.*

18th March 1972 A.B. MAJUMDER

Contents

FORM NO. PAGE

NEGOTIABLE INSTRUMENTS

A. Bills of Exchange (Inland)

PART ONE

Principles of Pleadings

CHAPTER

1

Introductory

SYNOPSIS

The words 'plaints' and 'complaints' are nearly synonymous. In both, the expression of grievance is predominant. Verily, when a suitor files a statement of grievance he is the plaintiff and he files a 'complaint' containing allegations and claims remedy. As days passed, we have taken up the word 'Plaint' for the civil court and the word 'complaint' for the criminal court. Plaint means a statement of grievance containing allegations and claims of remedy in the civil court.[1]

A plaint should be brief in words, rich in content, unambiguous, free from confusion, devoid of improper arguments and capable of being traversed by the defendant and it should set out the relief sought against the opponent.[2]

In Part One of the book we are concerned with the principles of pleadings as will be reflected in a 'plaint'. The present-day system of pleading in our country is based on the provisions of the Code of Civil Procedure 1908 (as amended) supplemented from time to time by Rules in that behalf by High Courts of the States. There are rules of the Supreme Court and rules by

1 Mitra's *Legal and Commercial Dictionary*, 6th Ed., p. 665.
2 S.C. Ghosh on *Principles & Forms of Pleading*, 5th Ed., p. 6.

special enactments such as rules framed under the Presidency Small Cause Courts Act 1882.

Order 6, r. 1 of CPC defines 'pleading'. It means either a plaint or a written statement.[3]

With the passing of time written pleadings supplanted archaic oral pleadings. When reduced to writing the scope of confusion, for obvious reasons, became narrower.

Pleadings are the statements of the parties in a legal and proper manner of the causes of action or grounds of defence. A pleading is the statement in a logical and legal form of the facts which constitute the plaintiff's cause of action or the defendant's grounds of defence.[4]

In this we find the object of a pleading which aims at ascertaining precisely the points for contention of the parties to a suit. The rules of pleading and other ancillary rules contained in the Code of Civil Procedure have one main object in view. It is to find out and narrow down the controversy between the parties.[5] The function of pleadings is to give fair notice of the case which has to be met so that the opposing party may direct his evidence to the issue disclosed by them.[6] Procedural law is intended to facilitate and not to obstruct the course of substantive justice. Provisions relating to pleadings in civil cases are meant to give each side intimation of the case of the other so that it may be met, to enable courts to determine what is really at issue between parties, and to prevent deviations from the course which litigation on particular causes of action must take.[7] Necessarily, a pleading is accurate only when, stripped of verbosity, it pinpoints succinctly the plaintiff's grievances giving him the right to sue for the desired relief, or when it briefly sets out the defendant's defence. When so done, there would be hardly any scope left to beat about the bush or to take the other party by surprise. What is more, a plaintiff who is purposely vague ought to be carefully examined and tied down to definite pleadings.[8] A civil court cannot adjudicate a dispute on a particular issue in the absence of a particular pleading.[9]

Pleadings should be read not by the piecemeal but as a whole[10] and should be liberally construed. Every venial defect should not be allowed to defeat a pleading, for a plaintiff's case should not be defeated merely on the ground of some technical defect in his pleadings provided he succeeds on the real issues of the case.[11]

In construing the plaint, the court has to look at the substance of the plaint rather than its mere form. If, on the whole and in substance, the suitor

3 Order 6, r. 1 of CPC For subsequent pleadings—See Or. 8, r. 9 of CPC.
4 S.C. Ghosh on *Principles & Forms of Pleading*, 5th Ed., p. 1.
5 *Kishinlal* v *Dujodwala Industries* AIR 1977 Del 19.
6 [1956] AC 218 at p. 238.
7 *Ganesh Trading* v *Mojiram* AIR 1978 SC 484.
8 AIR 1930 All 1321.
9 *State Bank of India* v *S.N. Goyal* AIR 2008 SC 2594.
10 *Ranga Vithoba* v *Rambha Dina* AIR 1967 Bom 382.
11 64 IC 517.

appears to ask for some relief as stated, the court can look at the substance of the relief.[12]

"Pleadings have to be interpreted not with formalistic rigour but with latitude or awareness of low legal literacy of poor people".[13]

Coming to construction of pleadings, Sarkaria, J. *held*: "A pleading has to be read as a whole to ascertain its import. It is not permissible to cull out a sentence or a passage and to read it out of the context in isolation. Although it is the substance and not merely the form that has to be looked into, the pleading has to be construed as it stands without addition or deletion of words, or change of its apparent grammatical sense. The intention of the party concerned is to be gathered, primarily, from the tenor and terms of his pleading taken as a whole".[14]

1 Pleading Pleading means plaint, written statement and replication to a written statement.

2 Object of pleading The object of pleading is to enable the court to decide the actual right of the parties in trial.[15] The object and purpose of pleadings and issues is to ensure that the litigants come to trial with all issues clearly defined and to prevent cases being expanded or grounds being shifted during trial.[16]

The object of a plaint is to ensure the opportunity of each party to place the relevant appropriation to the issue before the court for its consideration.[17]

Pleading is an Art, in which perfection depends on practice, and brevity is the soul of pleading as of wit. The object of pleading is definition, and a good pleading is concise, precise, relevant and comprehensive, while a bad pleading is prolix, discursive, irrelevant, vague and wanting in particulars.[18]

The whole object of pleading is that each side may be fully alive to the questions that are about to be argued in order that they may have an opportunity of bringing forward such evidence as may be appropriate.[19]

3 Interpretation A pleading has to be read as a whole and it is not permissible to consider a sentence or passage in isolation; pleadings have to be taken as a whole in order to gather what the intention of the parties is. The pleadings have to be interpreted with latitude and awareness of the low legal literacy of poor people. To gather the true spirit behind a plea, it should be read as a whole subject to the requirement of the Statute.

12 *Purushottam Dass* v *Har Narayan* AIR 1978 Del 114.

13 *Manjusri Raha* v *B.L. Gupta* AIR 1977 SC 1158.

14 *Udhav Singh* v *Madhava Rao Scindia* AIR 1976 SC 744.

15 *State of Maharashtra* v *Hindustan Construction Co. Ltd.* AIR 2010 SC 1299; (2010)4 SCC 518.

16 *Bachhaj Nahar* v *Nilima Mandal* AIR 2009 SC 1103 at p. 1105.

17 *Bachhaj Nahar* v *Nilima Mandal* (supra).

18 Mr. Justice Lort-Williams in the Foreword to the First Edition of S.C. Ghosh on *Principles & Forms of Pleading*.

19 *Lakshmi Narayan* v *State of Bihar* AIR 1977 Pat 73.

4 Facts and not law Pleadings should contain facts the party intends to rely upon and not the law. All material facts have to be stated. In a pleading the facts only but not the evidence are required to be pleaded.[20]

5 Alternative pleading Alternative pleading may be permissible and alternative plea can be taken. But the court cannot make out a third case.

6 Particulars Particulars are to be given where necessary.[1] The pleading shall give all particulars of any allegation of misrepresentation, fraud, breach of trust, wilful default, undue influence, coercion, etc.

7 Signature The pleading has to be signed by the party. The signature should be of the plaintiff or the defendant as the case may be, or of any person duly authorised by them. In case of a Corporate Body, the signatory must be properly authorised either by a Resolution or otherwise recognised by the law. The person signing should verify by reference to the numbered paragraphs of the pleading as to what is his own knowledge and what he verifies upon information received and believed by him to be true. He should sign and put the date and place. Further, in addition to the verification, he shall affirm an affidavit in support of the pleading. A defective verification is curable by an amendment of the pleading.

8 Striking out pleading Order 6, r. 16 of the Code of Civil Procedure lays down the provision of striking out pleading. The pleading may be struck out by the court if it is unnecessary, frivolous, or vexatious, or tends to prejudice, embarrass and delay the fair trial. A pleading will not be struck out only because it is unnecessary unless it is also scandalous, frivolous, or vexatious.

9 Amendment of pleadings Order 6, r. 17 of the Code of Civil Procedure 1908 provides that at any stage of the proceedings the court may allow either party to alter or amend his pleading. Such an amendment may be made even at the appellate stage, and even, in second appeal. But no application for amendment shall be allowed after commencement of the trial unless court is satisfied that in spite of due diligence the party could not have raised the matter before the commencement of trial.[2]

10 Particulars of the plaint Order 7, r. 1 of the Code of Civil Procedure 1908, provides for the particulars that should be incorporated in the plaint. Such particulars include the name of the court in which the suit is to be filed, the name, description, and place of residence of the plaintiff and the defendant, as to whether the plaintiff or the defendant is a minor or a person of unsound mind, the facts constituting the cause of action, the date and place where the cause of action arose, facts showing jurisdiction of the court, reliefs claimed by plaintiff, the amount allowed by a set-off or relinquishment of a portion of the claim, if any, and a statement as to the value of the subject-matter of the suit, for the purposes of the jurisdiction and the court-fees paid or to be paid.

20 Order 6, r. 2 of the Code of Civil Procedure 1908; *Ranjit Construction Co. Ltd.* v *National Highways Authority of India* AIR 2014 Del 64.

1 Order 6, r. 4 of the Code of Civil Procedure.

2 Order 6, r. 17 of the Code of Civil Procedure as amended by the CPC (Amendment) Act 2002 (w.e.f. 1.7.2002).

11 Rejection of the plaint Order 7, r. 11 of the Code of Civil Procedure 1908 provides for the circumstances under which the competent court can reject a plaint. In rejecting a plaint, the court shall record the reasons for such rejection. Order 7, r. 13 provides that rejection of plaint shall not preclude the plaintiff from presenting a fresh plaint in respect of the self-same cause of action. Even where an earlier plaint has been rejected a subsequent suit on the same cause of action is not liable to be dismissed on the ground of being barred by order rejecting the plaint in the earlier suit. But non-mentioning or wrong mentioning of a provision in pleading or application cannot be a ground for rejection.[3]

12 Written statement A defendant shall, within thirty days from the date of service of summons on him, present a written statement of his defence.[4] In the written statement, the defendant can deny the whole or some essential part of the averments made in plaint. The defendant may admit some facts and deny the rest and take objection in point of law. Order 8 provides as to how the defendant should raise the plea of "set-off". It is the duty of a defendant to produce documents upon which relief is claimed or relied upon by him.[5]

13 Claim of set-off and counter-claim Order 8, r. 6 of the Code of Civil Procedure 1908, provides for set-off, which the defendant can claim in the written statement against the plaintiff's demand, and if the amount of set-off is more than the claim of the plaintiff, the defendant can claim a decree for the excess amount of set-off claim. The rules relating to written statement shall also apply to the plaintiff's answer to the claim of set-off.

A written statement shall have the same effect as a plaint in a cross suit so as to enable the court to pronounce a final judgment in respect of both the original claim and the set-off.[6]

14 Court-fees The written statement claiming a set-off must bear the court-fees on the full amount and not only on the difference between the plaintiff's claims and the defendant's claims. Section 3 of the Limitation Act 1963 provides that set-off shall be treated as a separate cross suit for the purpose of limitation. For the limitation the set-off is treated as filed on the date of filing of the suit in which the set-off is claimed.

15 Counter-claim Order 8, r. 6A of the Code of Civil Procedure 1908 provides for a counter-claim. The counter-claim will be treated as a cross-suit. Rule 6B, provides that the defendant in the written statement must specifically state that he is making a counter-claim. Rule 6C provides that the plaintiff may contend that the counter-claim should be by an independent suit and that the counter-claim be excluded from the suit. Rule 6D provides that if the suit of the plaintiff is stayed, discontinued, or dismissed, the counter-claim

3 *Challamane Hucha Gowder* v *Tirumala* (2004)4 SCC 453.

4 Order 8, r. 1 of the Code of Civil Procedure as amended by the Code of Civil Procedure (Amendment) Act 2002 (w.e.f. 1.7.2002).

5 Order 8, r. 1A, *inserted* by Code of Civil Procedure (Amendment) Act 1999 (w.e.f. 1.7.2002).

6 Order 8, r. 6(2) of the Code of Civil Procedure.

may nevertheless be proceeded with. Rule 6E provides that in default of the plaintiff to reply to such counter-claim, the court may dispose off the counter-claim on merits. Rule 6F provides that if the counter-claim succeeds the court may give a judgment in favour of the party entitled to the balance amount between the plaintiff's claim and the defendant's counter-claim. Rule 6G provide that the rules relating to written statement by a defendant shall apply to the plaintiff's written statement in answer to counter-claim.

16 Limitation for the counter-claim If the cause of action arose before or after the suit, but continued upto the date of filing of the written statement, then such counter-claim may be made in the written statement or after filing of the written statement. Even if the counter-claim arose outside the territorial limits of the court, in which the said suit has been filed, the court entertaining such a suit will have the jurisdiction to decide the counter-claim.

17 Without written statement The defendant can participate in the suit or the proceedings and contest the same even without filing the written statement, but on such statement of the defendant the plaint cannot be rejected.

18 Joinder of parties Order 1, r. 1 provides for joinder of plaintiffs and Or. 1, r. 3 for joinder of defendants. The court may allow addition of parties or deletion of parties in proper cases and give its judgment for or against one or more of the joined parties. Without impleading a party, an order issued against him without giving him an opportunity of being heard is bad in law.[7]

19 Representative suit Order 1, r. 8 provides for representative suit where the parties are numerous having common interests and permission of court is obtained and notice is given to the parties sought to be represented. In granting leave to file the representative suit the court must be fully satisfied that there is sufficient community of interests as between the plaintiffs and the defendants.

20 Misjoinder and non-joinder of parties Order 1, r. 9 provides that non-joinder or misjoinder of the parties will not defeat the suit. The court may strike out or add parties to the plaint, and require amendment of the plaint. In proper cases, and averments, a person may be added as a party, name of a party may be struck out and a party can be transposed to do justice to parties.

21 Appearance of the parties The parties are entitled to appear at the hearing of the suit. If a party is not represented by any pleader, the court may request any pleader to address the court in respect of the particular matter. The court may give the conduct of the suit to such person as it deems proper. Where there are more than one plaintiffs, any one or more of them may authorise any one of them to plead or to act in any proceedings. Such authority will be given in writing, signed by the party giving it and shall be filed in court. Where neither of the parties appears on the date of hearing the court may dismiss the suit.[8]

7 *Ramrao* v *All India Backward Class* AIR 2004 SC 1459; (2004)2 SCC 76.

8 Order 9, r. 3 of the Code of Civil Procedure 1908.

CHAPTER

2

On Pleadings Generally

SYNOPSIS

1 Rules of pleading To adjudicate the grievances of a person against another person certain procedure has to be followed for convenience of disputing parties and the authority administering justice and to enforce the order. This process requires certain writings and furnishing of particulars for the purposes of records.

The fundamental rule of pleadings is contained in provisions of Or. 6, r. 2 of the CPC which enjoins:

"(1) Every pleading shall contain, and contain only, a statement in a concise form of the material facts on which the party pleading relies for his claim or defence, as the case may be, but not the evidence by which they are to be proved.

(2) Every pleading shall, when necessary, be divided into paragraphs, numbered consecutively, each allegation being, so far as is convenient, contained in a separate paragraph.

(3) Dates, sums and numbers shall be expressed in a pleading in figures as well as in words."[1]

To quote the Earl of Halsbury: "The sole object of it is that each may be fully alive to the questions that are about to be argued in order that they may have an opportunity of bringing forward such evidence as may be appropriate to the issues". The rules of pleading and other ancillary rules contained in the Code of Civil Procedure have one main object in view. It is to find out and narrow down controversy between the parties.[2]

1 Order 6, r. 2 of the Code of Civil Procedure 1908.

2 *Kishan Lal Gupta* v *Dujodwala Industries* AIR 1977 Del 19.

"The pleadings are not to be considered as constituting a game of skill between the advocates. They ought to be so framed as not only to assist the party in the statement of his case but the court in its investigation of the truth between the litigants".[3]

The pleading shall contain:

(*i*) material facts;

(*ii*) not law;

(*iii*) not evidence; and

(*iv*) immaterial facts to be discarded.

(i) ***Material facts.*** What are material facts? A fact that makes a difference in the result to be reached in a given case.[4] Facts which gave the plaintiff his cause of action or the defendant his defence are, briefly speaking, material facts which he must prove or fail. It, therefore, stands to reason that facts which are not required to support the plaintiff's or the defendant's case are not material. Whether a fact is material or not depends on the facts and circumstances of each case and can be held so or otherwise only in the context of relevant situation. It is proper to remember the observations of Cotton, LJ., quoted in *Matilal* v *Judhisthir*:[5] "It is absolutely essential that the pleading, not to be embarrassing to the defendants, should state those facts which will put the defendants on their guard and tell them what they have to meet when the case comes on for trial".

It is a well settled rule that matters of law or mere inferences of law should not be pleaded; for it is the duty of the courts to declare the conclusions and of the parties to state the premises.[6] A pleading shall contain only material facts. The readers are only reminded of the observations of P.C. Mogha:[7] "The rule is hardly appreciated in the Moffusil, and if it is possible to say that one rule of pleading which is more neglected than others, it is certainly this rule". Material facts are the entirety of facts which would be necessary to prove to succeed in the suit.[8] Any fact which is not material should be avoided. Slackness in pleadings is unfair both to the court in which they are filed and to the litigants. Material facts should be pleaded concisely. There is hardly any scope for showing literary genius in a pleading. If a factual base is not maintained in the plaint, legal argument arising thereform cannot be entertained.[9] Material facts have to be alleged and proved and evidence produced cannot be substituted for the pleading and material facts have to be alleged and then proved.[10] An order in favour of the petitioner can be

3 [1868] LR 2 A&E 265.
4 Black's *Law Dictionary*, 10th Ed.
5 *Attorney-General of the Colony of Fiji* v *J.P. Bagly Ltd.* AIR 1950 PC 73.
6 S.C. Ghosh on *Principles & Forms of Pleading*, 5th Ed., p. 323.
7 Mogha's *Law of Pleadings in India*, 12th Ed., p. 15.
8 AIR 1954 VP 53.
9 *Rohit Dhaman* v *G.K. Malhotra* AIR 2002 Del 151.
10 *Mayar (H.K.) Ltd.* v *Owners & Parties, Vassel M.V. Fortune Express* AIR 2006 SC 1828; (2006)3 SCC 100.

passed only if he sets out his case with precision supported by averments of material facts.[11]

When commencing a suit, the plaintiff is required to state only material facts, but such facts must constitute his cause of action as well. Absence of material facts will put the party to discomfiture, for no amount of evidence can be taken into consideration or regarded as sufficient in proof of any fact if specific mention of it is not made in the pleadings. Therefore, if a party omits to state a material fact, he will not be allowed to give evidence of the fact at the trial unless the pleading is amended under Or. 6, r. 17, CPC. The rule is based mainly on principles that no party should be prejudiced by change in the case introduced by this method.[12] A party can only succeed according to what was alleged and proved 'secundum allegate et probata'. No relief can be granted on facts not disclosed in the plaint.[13] Similarly, if a claim is never made in the defence, no amount of evidence can be looked into upon a plea which is never put forward.[14] When we say that the pleading should contain only material facts we mean that unnecessary facts have to be discarded altogether. It is often noticed that during the trial of a suit, some fact is sought to be introduced in evidence which does not find mention in the plaint or in the written statement, as the case may be. Then follows a heated arguments when the court intervenes and rejects any attempt of introduction of any new fact. To avoid discomfiture, the pleading should be carefully drafted so as not to miss any material fact which may subsequently be found to be so material as to decide the fate of the case this or that way. In the absence of any issue or plea no evidence can be considered to be relevant or be taken into consideration. The judicial pronouncement on the point is: "No amount of evidence can be looked into upon a plea which was never put forward. The ordinary rule of law is that evidence is to be given only on a plea properly raised and not in contradiction of a plea".[15]

VARIANCE BETWEEN PLEADINGS AND PROOF. A party cannot be allowed to adduce evidence for setting up a case inconsistent with one alleged in pleadings.[16]

Evidence cannot be allowed to be led on a point not made out in the plaint.[17] Court cannot made a new case not made out in pleadings.[18]

11 *Arikala Narasa Reddy* v *Venkata Ram Reddy Reddygari* AIR 2014 SC 1290 at p. 1296.
12 *Indermal Tekaji* v *Ramprosad* AIR 1970 MP 40.
13 *Allam Gangadhara Rao* v *Gollapalli Gangarao* AIR 1968 AP 291.
14 *Hajarkhan Kalubaya* v *Kesharkhan* AIR 1968 Guj 229.
15 *Bhagwan Datta Shastri* v *Ram Ratanji Gupta* AIR 1960 SC 200; *Om Prabha* v *Abinash Chand* AIR 1968 SC 1083. A party cannot travel beyond pleadings so as to make out a new case. The rule, however, is not inflexible (*Dalim Kr. Sain* v *Smt. Nandarani Dassi* AIR 1970 Cal 292). Claim on entirely new grounds is not maintainable. Claim implicitly founded in pleadings is, however, maintainable (*Bhagwati Prasad* v *Shri Chandramul* AIR 1966 SC 735; AIR 1970 Guj 184). Also see *Baidyanath Mandal* v *The Coal Purchase & Inspection Agency (P) Ltd.* AIR 1971 Pat 229.
16 *State of West Bengal* v *Mir Fakir Mahammad* AIR 1977 Cal 29.
17 *Md. Yunus* v *Alabi Hossain* AIR 1982 Cal 488; *Sri Venkataramana Devaru* v *State of Mysore* AIR 1958 SC 255; 84 CWN 221; *Vinod Kumar* v *Surjit Kaur* AIR 1987 SC 2179.
18 *Jugal Kishore* v *Narayan Chandra* AIR 1982 Cal 342; also see *Sheodhari* v *Suraj Prasad* AIR 1954 SC 758 at p. 760.

If material facts constituting cause of action are not averred in the plaint, the suit must fail.[19] In a petition material facts that constitute the cause of action should be stated.[20]

At times a preamble may be necessary to introduce material facts in a pleading. Such a preamble contains matters technically known as 'matters of inducement' and is permissible in a pleading. At times such matters are no less important than what follows those. To a man uninitiated in this profession 'matters of inducement' may often verge on unnecessary surplusage which is neither desirable nor permissible. There can be no hard and fast rule on the introduction of matters of inducement in a pleading. Let experience and age teach the rule.

When a pleading was partly vague but all the facts necessary for determination of a point were before the court, pleading was correct.[1] Material facts, however, do not include facts to anticipate the opponent's answer. In *Niaz Ahmed Khan* v *Abdul Latif*,[2] it was held: "A party should not plead to facts which have not become material at the stage of filing his pleading. He need not allege reply to probable defences. In other words, he is not to anticipate answers of his opponent".

(ii) ***Not law.*** In a pleading, there is no scope of pleading a provision of law or conclusion of law. It is the intention of the framers of the Code that a pleading should state facts, and the position as in law shall be inferred if such facts are capable of raising any legal inference. The pleading should present facts in such a way that those would irresistibly and spontaneously draw a legal inference. Herein lies the art of pleading. To find out the law is the duty of the court.[3] Legal effects are not to be stated by the party. In India, as in England, the duty of a pleader is to set out the facts upon which he relies and not the legal inference to be drawn from them. Likewise, the conclusion of law or a mixed question of law and fact should not be pleaded.

It is not clear how legal pleas can be absolutely avoided. When in a written statement we state that the suit was barred by principles of *res judicata* or under Or. 23, r. 1 or Or. 2, r. 2, CPC or that the suit was barred by principles of estoppel or that the suit was barred by limitation or because of non-service of statutory notices—those are really questions of law that we plead. The pleading of law may be against the rules, but this is done and is largely approved. Call it with Mogha "Objections in point of law", the fact remains that what is incorporated in a written statement is a pleading.

(iii) ***Not evidence.*** In like manner evidence has to be avoided in pleadings. We have noticed the wording of the rule of Or. 6, r. 2 to wit, a statement in a concise form of the material facts on which the party pleading relies for his

19 *H.D. Vasistha* v *Glaxo Laboratories* AIR 1979 SC 134.

20 *Hari Shankar Jain* v *Sonia Gandhi* AIR 2001 SC 3689; (2001)8 SCC 233.

1 *Union of India* v *K. Karonpura Colliery* AIR 1969 SC 125.

2 AIR 1923 Lah 475.

3 *Kedar Lal* v *Hari Lal* AIR 1952 SC 47; every legal ground of challenge need not be stated in the plaint—*State of UP* v *Satya Narain* AIR 1970 SC 1199.

claim or defence as the case may be, but not the evidence by which they are to be proved.

A pleading should not contain facts which are merely evidence to prove the material facts.

(iv) ***Immaterial facts to be discarded.*** Unnecessary details are the facts which are not material and, therefore, should be discarded.

DEFICIENCY IN PLEADING. Parties are related to each other and know everything. No element of surprise has been caused to the other party. Parties understood the case and led evidence accordingly. Deficiency in pleading would not affect case of the plaintiff.[4]

2 Particulars in pleading (Or. 6, r. 4) A pleading, to be precise, has to state all necessary particulars. It will tell the adversary what the latter has to meet when the case is heard. Particulars here refer to particulars which go to constitute a material fact to be introduced in a pleading.

Particulars in pleadings are sometimes objective and sometimes subjective. When a party to a suit is out to allege misrepresentation, fraud or breach of trust, those are objective facts and are known to the party who alleges such. He is, therefore, required to state particulars of such fraud, breach of trust, etc., with sufficient clarity. When again, a party alleges only a state of mind, such as malice, wrath, etc. of the opposite party, he cannot be expected to give particulars which is impossible.

Order 6, r. 4 of CPC covers the former case while provisions in Or. 6, r. 10 covers the latter case. Where fraud, misrepresentation, undue influence, etc., are alleged as a matter of an objective fact, the rule under Or. 6, r. 4 applies, but where a mental condition is alleged such as fraudulent intention etc. r. 10 will apply.[5]

(i) ***Fraud.*** A mere mention of fraud in a pleading is not sufficient. A party pleading fraud is obliged under Or. 6, r. 4, CPC, to give particulars of the pleaded fraud with date and items, in the pleading.[6] Fraud must be specifically pleaded and proved by the plaintiff.[7]

It is not mere use of the general words such as fraud or collusion that can serve as a foundation for the plea. Such expressions are quite ineffective to form a legal basis denuded of particular statement of facts which alone can furnish the requisite basis for the action. If the plaint averments do not set out with reasonable precision the particulars so as to constitute allegations of fraud and mirepresentation the plaint would be bad in law.[8]

Order 6, r. 4 enjoins: "In all cases in which the party pleading relies on any misrepresentation, fraud, breach of trust, wilful default, or undue influence,

4 *Kailash Chandra* v *Vinod* AIR 1994 NOC 267 (MP).
5 *Lady Dinbai Dinshaw Petit* v *The Dominion of India* AIR 1951 Bom 72.
6 *Karan Madaan* v *Nageshwar Pandey* AIR 2015 NOC 86 (Del).
7 *S.P. Gaekward* v *S.P. Gaekward* AIR 2005 SC 809.
8 *Ranganayakamma* v *K.S. Prakash* AIR 2005 Kant 426.

and in all other cases in which particulars may be necessary beyond such as are exemplified in the forms aforesaid, particulars (with dates and items if necessary) shall be stated in the pleading."[9] A strong averment in the plaint or in the written statement of fraud will not do. Fraud, undue influence or coercion must be separately pleaded and full particulars are to be separately given.[10] While it is true that 'undue influence', 'fraud', 'misrepresentation', are cognate vices and may, in part, overlap in some cases, they are in law distinct categories and are, in view of Or. 6, r. 2, required to be separately pleaded, with specificity, particularity and precision. A party can succeed only by what he alleged and proved. He cannot be allowed to travel beyond what was pleaded by him and put in issue.[11]

Allegations of collusion imply some kind of fraud. It is not enough to state in general term that there was 'collusion' without more particulars.[12] The same applies to undue influence and coercion.[13] A plea of undue influence must be precise and all necessary particulars in support of the plea must be embodied in the pleading.[14] But in *Joseph John Peter Sandy* v *Veronica Thomas Rajkumar*[15] the apex court held that the omission to make an allegation of undue influence specifically, is not fatal to the plaintiff being entitled to relief on that ground. All that the court has to see is that there is no surprise to the defendant. Allegation of fraud must be clear, definite and specific.[16] General allegation of fraud, however strong the words in which they are stated may be, if unaccompanied by particulars, are insufficient to amount to an averment of fraud of which any court ought to take notice.[17] The importance of stating the material facts cannot be gainsaid as the other party will be required to meet out allegation.

(ii) ***Conspiracy***. In the case of conspiracy, full particulars are to be stated. When facts are alleged, the party must be restricted to the particulars in his pleadings.[18]

(iii) ***Undue influence***. In the case of undue influence, it must set out that the person alleged was in fact in a position to dominate the other party's will and must also set out how that was so.[19] Particulars of undue influence are needed. Undue influence being a species of fraud must be pleaded with

9 Vide Or. 6, r. 3 speaks of Forms in Appendix A of the Code.

10 *Bishnudeo* v *Seogeni Rai* AIR 1951 SC 280; *Pt. Ram Avtar Sharma* v *Pt. Chakradhar Saran Sharma* AIR 1971 All 157; *Kasturi Lakshmibayamma* v *Sabnivis Venkoba Rao* AIR 1970 AP 440.

11 *Afsar Shiekh* v *Soleman Bibi* AIR 1976 SC 163. Also see *Kunhamina Umma* v *Special Tahsildar* AIR 1977 Ker 41.

12 *Bishnudeo* v *Seogeni Rai* AIR 1951 SC 280.

13 *Varanasya Sanskrit Viswavidyalaya* v *Dr. Rajkishore Tripathi* AIR 1977 SC 615.

14 *Bishnu Priya Dei* v *Brusabhani Mahapatra* AIR 1976 Ori 163.

15 AIR 2013 SC 2028.

16 *Bishunath Tewari* v *Mst. Mirchi* AIR 1955 Pat 66.

17 *Atul Chandra Sarkar* v *East Bengal Commercial Bank* AIR 1960 Cal 309; *Chiranjilal* v *Jaihind Investment* AIR 1978 Cal 177; *R.A. Sharma* v *C.C. Sharma* AIR 1971 All 157.

18 *Indramani Pyerelal Gupta* v *W.R. Natu* AIR 1956 Bom 518.

19 AIR 1952 Nag 85; *Dr. Lakhi Prasad Agarwal* v *Nathmal Dokania* AIR 1969 SC 583.

precision and unless it is supported by particulars, it will not be investigated by court.[20] Allegation of undue influence must be accompanied with particulars in the pleading.[1]

(iv) ***Misrepresentation.*** When misrepresentations are alleged, the party pleading them should state as to each misrepresentation, its date and whether it was made in writing or verbally, and as to each verbal misrepresentation, the occasion thereof.[2] Though pleas of undue influence and coercion may overlap in part in some cases, they are separable categories in law and must be separately pleaded. Full particulars must be stated and the case can be decided on the particulars as laid.

(v) ***Coercion.*** In the allegation of coercion, full particulars must be given.[3] Though undue influence and coercion may overlap in part in some cases, they must be separately pleaded.

(vi) ***Negligence.*** Negligence is not correlated to the state of mind. Therefore, particulars of acts constituting negligence are necessary in the plaint.[4] So also in the case of a breach of trust, the plaintiff has to aver the terms of trust as also full details of acts which constituted the breach of trust.

In respect of the expression "and in all other cases in which particulars may be necessary" in Or. 6, r. 4, we may cite some illustrations of a few such "other cases":

(*a*) CUSTOM. Where a custom is set up, the particulars of the custom with the essential requisites to its validity and binding effect must be stated.[5] It is incumbent upon a party relying upon a custom to allege that custom in unambiguous terms in his pleading and prove it: for, the presumption which can be made with regard to law cannot be made with regard to custom. Therefore, a party who relies upon custom ought to plead it clearly in his plaint so that the opposite party may know his case and may have opportunity to meet it.[6]

(*b*) CUSTOMARY RIGHT. A customary right is recognised even by the Easement Act (s. 2). But it can be claimed not as a mere personal right of the plaintiff *vis-a-vis* the particular defendant. It is the right of the community or the right recognised by the community as a whole. Normally, a custom has to be immemorial, in the sense that its origin is not traceable. In any event it has got to be of very long duration, and of very remote and distant origin. In all such cases members of the community must be examined to prove the existence of such a long-standing custom as the community's custom. The beneficiary of a custom may be a particular member of a family. But the point

20 *Bihsundeo* v *Seogini Rai* AIR 1951 SC 280; *Narayana Bhatta* v *Narsimha Bhatta* AIR 1965 Ker 189; *Misrilal Jalanchand* v *Sobhachand Jalanchand* AIR 1956 Bom 569.

1 *Ranganayakamma* v *K.S. Prakash* AIR 2005 Kant 426.

2 *Debi Prasad* v *Chhotely Lal* AIR 1966 All 438; AIR 1924 PC 180.

3 *Sales-Tax Officer, Circle 1* v *Hanuman Prasad* AIR 1967 All 565.

4 *Sahu Vanaspati Traders* v *Union of India* AIR 1966 All 333.

5 *Nathu* v *Anandilal* AIR 1953 MB 32; *Iabal Hasan* v *Sunni Central Board* AIR 1972 All 123.

6 *Mt. Gulab* v *Devilal Gokalchand* AIR 1951 Raj 136.

is that the custom is recognised by the community as a whole and that is why it partakes the character, in a sense, of customary law applicable for the people governed by that custom.[7] Proof of customary right.[8] Nature of evidence required.[9] Local custom and family custom.[10] Special custom.[11] Custom in general.[12]

Where a customary right is not specifically pleaded in the plaint but sufficient facts to form foundation of a customary right are stated in plaint—customary right could be decreed by the court.[13]

(*c*) CUSTOMARY RIGHT AND CUSTOMARY EASEMENT—DISTINCTION BETWEEN. A customary right is not an easement. An easement belongs to a determinate person or class of persons in respect of his or their land. A fluctuating body like the inhabitants of the locality cannot claim an easement. Easements are private right belonging to particular persons while customary rights are public rights annexed to the place in general. It is also well settled that the customary right is also different from customary easement. An easement is always appurtenant to the dominant tenement and inseparably attached to it and cannot be severed from it.[14]

(*d*) EASEMENT. A party setting up a plea of easement should clearly indicate in his pleading all the facts connected with such plea.[15] Mere assertion of the right of easement will not do. The plaintiff has to state the nature of easement, circumstances under which and the time when such easement was acquired.

A case of lost grant. The enjoyment of right to irrigate the land with the water of the tank for over 65 years gives rise to a presumption of immemorial user which again, would give rise to a presumption of lost grant. In such circumstance the plaintiffs cannot be expected to prove as to how the right originated. Acquisition of the right of easement by lost grant has been abundantly established.[16]

(*e*) BENAMI—CHANGE IN LAW. The Prohibition of Benami Property Transactions Act 1988. Section 4 of the Act enjoins—

(1) No suit, claim or action to enforce any right in respect of any property held *benami* against the person in whose name the property is held or against any other person shall lie by or on behalf of a person claiming to be the real owner of such property.

(2) No defence based on any right in respect of any property held *benami*, whether against the person in whose name the property is

7 *Radha Krishna* v *Tukaran Pundalik* AIR 1991 Bom 119.
8 *Mohammad Baguer* v *Naim-un-Nisa* AIR 1956 SC 548.
9 *Kumar Satya Narain* v *Raja Satya Niranjan* AIR 1924 PC 5.
10 *Raj Kishan* v *Ramjoy* (1876) ILR 1 Cal 186.
11 *Harihar Prasad Singh* v *Balmiki Prasad Singh* AIR 1975 SC 733.
12 *Mirza Raja Puspavathi* v *Sri Puspavathi* AIR 1964 SC 118.
13 AIR 1956 AP 235.
14 *Ram Chandra Sha* v *Abdul Hannan* AIR 1984 Pat 313.
15 AIR 1956 Bhup 41.
16 *Bhaskar Ghosh* v *Santosh Ghosh* AIR 1988 Cal 320.

held or against any other person, shall be allowed in any suit, claim or action by or on behalf of a person claiming to be the real owner of such property.

In *Mithilesh Kumari* v *Prem Behari Khara*[17] the question about the applicability of s. 4 of the Act to pending proceedings arose. It was held that the said provision would apply to proceedings pending on date of commencement of the Act and provisions were held applicable to an Appeal that was pending in the Supreme Court.

Following the decision in AIR 1989 SC 1247, defence raised by contesting defendants/respondents that the sale deed executed in favour of the Appellants was a *benami* transaction must be held to be prohibited in view of s. 4(2) of the Act.[18]

The burden of proof lies on the person who asserts it. The mere assertion that property was purchased *benami* is not sufficient to dismiss the suit at preliminary stage.

Benami transaction means any transaction in which property is transferred to one person for a consideration paid or provided by another person [*Vide* s. 2(*a*) of the Prohibition of Benami Property Transactions Act 1988].

Distinction between *benami* and sham transactions. In *benami* transaction title passes to *benamdar* instead of real vendee. In sham transaction there is no intention to convey property at all.[19]

Prohibition of right to recover property held in *benami*. The Prohibition of Benami Property Transactions Act coming into force during pendency of suit. Defence that suit-property was held in *benami* by wife is not permissible.[20]

Benami transaction—proof (ss. 101-104, Evidence Act). See *Radhysham Agarwala* v *Maharaj Bahadur Singh*.[1] Burden of proof is on the person asserting so.[2] Burden is always upon the person who sets up *benami* character.[3]

Prohibition of Benami Property Transactions Act 1988 is retrospective.[4]

(*f*) CONTRACT. A claim under s. 65 of the Contract Act must be specifically pleaded. If the essential facts constituting the cause of action have not been pleaded, the court will decline to entertain the claim.[5] In a suit for specific

17 AIR 1989 SC 1247.

18 *Duvuru Jaya Mohana Reddy* v *Alluru Nagi Reddy* AIR 1994 SC 1647; *Chaliloth Theroth Mahanan* v *Chaliloth Yesoda* AIR 1989 Cal 253. [In the instant case the suit of the Appellants was dismissed by the High Court on the view that said transaction was a benami transaction. The Supreme Court did not uphold the judgment and set aside the same].

19 *Rajesh Kumar* v *Virendra Kumar* AIR 1994 All 135.

20 AIR 1994 NOC 136 (MP).

1 AIR 1982 Cal 571.

2 *Krishnanand Agrihotri* v *State of M.P.* AIR 1977 SC 796.

3 *Kaddeeranbi* v *Fatimabi* AIR 1981 Bom 406; *Mahinder Singh* v *Mr. Pardaman Singh* AIR 1992 Del 357.

4 (1992)1 CLJ 512.

5 *Anath Bandhu Deb* v *Dominion of India* AIR 1955 Cal 626.

performance of the contract, there should be specific allegation that the plaintiff has been and is still ready and willing to perform his part of contract.

(*g*) AGREEMENT. Particulars as to the date of agreement, the names of contracting parties, whether the agreement was oral or in writing, consideration and terms have to be stated. There cannot be parol evidence to ascertain terms. Mr. Chagla, J. *held*: "Once the parties reduce the terms of their contract into writing, the same cannot be ascertained by parol evidence as to what transpired antecedent to the contract or what the parties did subsequent to the contract".[6]

(*h*) TORTIOUS LIABILITIES. In an action for negligence, the plaintiff must give full particulars of the negligence complained of and of the damages he has sustained.[7] When in action for public nuisance special damages are necessary to be proved, the plaint should state the full particulars of such damages.

All the provisions in Or. 6, r. 4, CPC apply to defence as well. In other words, the defendant, as much as the plaintiff, is subject to this rule.

Now, coming to subjective facts, we may recall provision in Or. 6, r. 10 of the Code of Civil Procedure:

> "Wherever it is material to allege malice, fraudulent intention, knowledge or other condition of the mind of any person, it shall be sufficient to allege the same as a fact without setting out the circumstances from which the same is to be inferred."

The circumstances from which malice, etc., may be inferred need not be pleaded in a plaint as these really constitute evidence of those facts. When a party complains of the state of mind of another, e.g. *mala fides*, it is not possible to give particulars.[8] Where a certain condition of mind, such as insanity, is relied on by a party for his claim or defence, he must allege it as a fact in his pleading and where he does not do so, and fact of existence of such state of mind is only brought out in the evidence, the court should not act on such fact.[9]

Bias must be pleaded and proved.[10]

There is no fixed rule as to how particulars are to be delivered in a court of law. The general principle is that particulars should be contained in the body of the plaint (Or. 6, r. 4). If the plaintiff or the defendant intends to submit further particulars or is called upon by the court to submit further particulars, the court may prescribe the mode as to how the same should be delivered. Where no such direction is given, the same may be furnished either in an annexure to the pleading or in suitable cases by amendment of the pleading.

6 *Dinkarrai Lalit Kumar* v *Sukhdayal Rambilas* AIR 1947 Bom 293.
7 *Sahu Vanaspati Traders* v *Union of India* AIR 1966 All 333.
8 *Lady Dinabai Dinshaw Petit* v *Dominion of India* AIR 1951 Bom 72 (but see *Indramani Pyerelal Gupta* v *W.R. Natu* AIR 1956 Bom 518).
9 AIR 1958 Nag 204.
10 *S. Venkatachalam Iyer* v *State of Madras* AIR 1957 Mad 623.

Non-compliance with the court's order when particulars were called for may entail dismissal of the suit. The court often prescribes time-limit within which the plaintiff has to submit particulars. Should the order be contumaciously disobeyed, the defendant may pray for dismissal of the plaintiff's suit. In *Vasudevan* v *Nedungatheripad*,[11] the plaintiff did not comply with the court's orders and the suit was dismissed. Where the defendant fails to comply, he is debarred from giving evidence in support thereof. Judicial views are divergent on the point whether the defence should be struck out or not. The cases referred to below[12] may be seen. Where particulars are not furnished in spite of the court's orders to that effect, the party in default runs the risk of his pleading being struck off.

3 Departure in pleading (Or. 6, r. 7) A 'departure in pleading' is not allowed as a rule.

Once the parties have submitted their pleadings, they cannot depart from the grounds or raise any new ground nor can plead any new fact inconsistent with the pleading already submitted. If anything new has to be stated, the party has to amend the plaint under Or. 6, r. 17, CPC or to file an additional statement under Or. 8, r. 9 of the Code.

Order 6, r. 7 of the Code enjoins:

> "No pleading shall, except by way of amendment, raise any new ground of claim or contain any allegation of fact inconsistent with the previous pleadings of the party pleading the same."

Where pleadings contravene Or. 6, r. 7 the court shall be justified in ignoring those. So, where there is variation between the pleading and proof, the party can only succeed according to what is alleged and proved. Suit based on one cause of action cannot be decreed on another cause of action.[13] The same principle applies in the case of a written statement as well. There is no provision in the Code to enable the court to permit the substitution *in toto* of one written statement for another already filed.[14]

The exception contained in this rule allows an amendment of the previous pleading of a party but does not allow amendment of his subsequent pleadings which would have the effect of converting that subsequent pleading into a pleading which, if originally pleaded, would have infringed this rule.[15] Therefore, a party cannot in subsequent pleading make any allegation inconsistent with what he has alleged originally.[16]

(i) ***Raising of inconsistent defence vis-a-vis mutually destructive pleas.*** Raising of mutually destructive pleas is not permissible but inconsistent defence are permissible.

11 *(Taiyyati) Vasudevan Nambiyar* v *(Unnikatungi) Nedungathiripad* AIR 1932 Mad 316.
12 *(Taiyyati) Vasudevan Nambiyar* v *(Unnikatungi) Nedungathiripad* AIR 1932 Mad 316; *Ganba Paiku* v *Ganpatisao* AIR 1937 Nag 376.
13 *Allam Gangadhara Rao* v *Gollapalli Gangarao* AIR 1968 AP 291.
14 *Kallampudi Narayanappa* v *Kaligotla Suryanarayana* AIR 1950 Mad 46.
15 AIR 1947 Bom 149.
16 *Hardial Singh* v *Jaswant Kaur* AIR 1943 Lah 159.

So, if the tenant denies the title of the respondent landlord yet he can also raise the plea seeking the protection of the rent control legislation. But the landlord cannot raise inconsistent pleas which are mutually destructive.[17]

Regarding the payment of interest, the respondent state took a contradictory stand in their counter affidavit before the Supreme Court. Such contradictory stand cannot be entertained.[18] Even though the defendant cannot take inconsistent pleas which are mutually destructive, yet if the said inconsistent pleas are not mutually destructive, such pleas can be taken. So, the defendant in the written statement raised the plea of deriving title through a person not being the owner and also raised the plea of adverse possession for more than twelve years against the real owner. It is held that when the first plea failed, he could fall back upon the plea of adverse possession for more than twelve years against the real owner.[19]

(ii) ***Denial of contract.*** When the plaintiff has alleged in the suit for redemption of mortgage that three deeds executed on the same date constituted a mortgage by conditional sale under s. 58(*c*) of the Transfer of Property Act, the defendant in written statement maintained a blissful silence. Even he did not mention that understanding of the defendants as to what transpired between the parties where not true. So, the failure of the defendant appellant to deny averments made in the plaint as to the character of the transaction and to plead a specific defence contrary to the plaintiff's would preclude him from pleading that the transaction does not fit in with s. 58(*c*) of the Transfer of Property Act.[20]

4 Forms of pleading (Or. 6, r. 3) Order 6, r. 2 enjoins that all material facts have to be stated in a 'concise form'. By application of the word 'concise form' the framers of law intended that unnecessary details should not be encouraged. The correct reading, of course, is that material facts have to be pleaded, it may be long, it may be short. Concise form suggests avoidance of unnecessary details.

It is not desirable to place undue emphasis on form; instead substance of pleadings should be considered.[1]

The framers of law have provided us with a few specimen forms in Appendix 'A' to the Code of Civil Procedure. Order 6, r. 3 speaks: "The forms in Appendix 'A' when applicable, and where they are not applicable, forms of like character, as nearly as may be, shall be used for all pleadings".

The forms may not be found always convenient and/or sufficient. Model forms given in Appendix 'A' to the Code would show their insufficiency. We

17 *Devasahayam* v *P. Savithramma* (2005)7 SCC 653.

18 *Darshan Singh* v *State of Punjab* (2007)14 SCC 262; (2007)113 FLR 493; (2007)3 LLN 34.

19 *L.N. Aswathama* v *P. Prakash* (2009)13 SCC 229; see also *Biswanath Agarwalla* v *Sabitri Bera* (2009)15 SCC 229.

20 *C. Raghunandan* v *K. Nageswar Rao* AIR 2009 AP 205.

1 *Ram Sarup* v *Bishun Narain Inter College* AIR 1987 SC 1242.

would remember that Mr. J. Lort William in *Ramprasad* v *Hazarimal*,[2] observed: "The forms in Appendix 'A' must be used with caution. They seem to have been drafted by someone with an imperfect knowledge of pleading and sometimes are in direct conflict with the Code. For example, where they prove that original documents which are part of the evidence should be annexed to the plaint, they are to be taken as the standard of the requisite brevity and also no doubt as specimen of the character of pleadings required. But they are not to be adhered to slavishly; they are in fact not perfect by any means". A suit for specific performance of contract cannot be dismissed on the ground that it was not reproduced as Forms 47 and 48 to Appendix A of the Schedule.[3]

Section 16(*c*) of the Specific Relief Act 1963 provides that the petitioner that the plaintiff must aver that he has performed or has always been ready and willing to perform his part of contract. The readiness and willingness has to be in spirit and substance and not in letter and form.[4]

5 Alternative and inconsistent pleadings We know that inconsistent facts can be pleaded. A plea that the document was a gift-deed is not defeated if the defendant also pleads that the document could also be construed as a release-deed of the undivided share of the plaintiff in favour of the other sharers and the strict conditions of a valid gift under the Mohammadan law need not be insisted upon.[5]

The Supreme Court has observed in *Firm Srinivas Ramkumar* v *Mahabir Prasad*:[6] "A plaintiff may rely upon different rights alternatively and there is nothing in the Civil Procedure Code to prevent a party from making two or more inconsistent sets of allegations and claiming relief thereunder in the alternative. Ordinarily, the court cannot grant relief to the plaintiff on a case for which there was no foundation in the pleadings and which the other side was not called upon or had an opportunity to meet. But when the alternative case, which the plaintiff could have made, was not only admitted by the defendant in his written statement but was expressly put forward as an answer to the claim which the plaintiff made in the suit, there would be nothing improper in giving the plaintiff a decree upon the case which the defendant himself makes. ... Thus, where in a suit for specific performance of the contract, in part performance of which the plaintiff alleges to have paid the defendant some money, the defendant denies the contract and pleads that the money was taken by him as a loan, the court can pass a decree for recovery of the loan in favour of the plaintiff on his failure to prove the contract even though the plaintiff had failed to plead and claim relief, on this alternative case". But we must remember that if the inconsistent pleas will lead to the prejudice and embarrassment of the trial they cannot be allowed.[7] All new and inconsistent pleas cannot be allowed. An employee alleges absence of any

2 AIR 1931 Cal 458.
3 *Baldev Singh* v *Chhota Singh* AIR 2002 P&H 47.
4 *Diwakar Mullick* v *Kumari Ganga Khandelwal* AIR 2016 Chh 53.
5 *Thakkadi Syed Mohamed* v *Ahmed Fathumml* AIR 1973 Mad 302.
6 *Firm Sinivas Ram Kumar* v *Mahabir Prasad* AIR 1951 SC 177.
7 *Onkarmal Agarwalla* v *Bireswar Hazra* AIR 1959 Cal 195; 61 CWN 970.

domestic enquiry. He cannot be allowed to contend that no proper procedure was followed.[8] The proper course for the court in such a case would be to require the party pleading to remove the inconsistency either by giving further or better particulars or by setting out his pleas in the alternative.

Inconsistent claim can be made in written statement by amendment.[9]

The plaintiff similarly can make alternative claims. The object of permitting alternative reliefs to be claimed in one litigation is to obviate the necessity of another litigation, to dispose of the same controversy or the subject-matter of the same relief though the ground upon which the relief is claimed may be different. Where there is no inconsistency in the facts alleged, alternative pleas in law are always permissible. If one of such claims is proved, the relief should be granted on that basis. But a plaintiff suing for a declaration that a certain contract against him is void and inoperative having been obtained by undue influence cannot in the same suit, in the alternative, ask for relief of specific performance of the same contract.[10]

This does not of course mean that variance between pleadings and proof can be encouraged. Though every variance between pleading and proof is not necessarily fatal to the suit or defence but a party will not be allowed to succeed in a case not so set up by him and cannot be allowed at the trial to change his case or set up a case inconsistent with what he has alleged in his pleading, except by way of amendment of the plaint under Or. 6, r. 17 of the Code.[11]

To sum up: A plea not pleaded or not raised in issue can be entertained at a later stage, even sometimes in appeal, provided the party concerned is not prejudiced, and provided further that all materials and facts to supply the basis for such a plea are already on record. Alternative pleas in such circumstances can be entertained.

6 Effect of a document (Or. 6, r. 9) Wherever the contents of any document are material, it shall be sufficient in any pleading to state the effect thereof as briefly as possible, without setting out the whole or any part thereof, unless the precise words or any part thereof are material.

If, when stating some material facts, it is necessary to mention a document in which it is contained, its legal effect should be stated concisely,[12] e.g. "the plaintiff has thereafter purchased the said property in Schedule. A, appended below, by a Kobala dated 2.5.1963 (duly registered) executed by the defendant in his favour and has acquired right, title and interest in the said property by such purchase".

8 *Factory Manager, Model Mills* v *State Industrial Court, Nagpur* AIR 1967 Bom 147.

9 *Prasant Chandra Sen* v *United Commercial Bank* AIR 1982 Cal 555 (*Nrisingh Pal* v *Steel Products Ltd.* AIR 1953 Cal 15).

10 *Prem Raj* v *The DLF Housing & Construction (P) Ltd.* AIR 1968 SC 1355.

11 *Sheodhari Rao* v *Suraj Prasad Singh* AIR 1954 SC 758; *Firm Srinivas Ram Kumar* v *Mahabir Prasad* AIR 1951 SC 177; *Board of Directors, YMCA* v *R.H. Niblet* AIR 1957 All 219; *Gostha Behari Bera* v *Haridas Samanta* AIR 1957 Cal 557; *Trojan & Co.* v *Nagappa* AIR 1953 SC 235; *Murlidhar Chatterjee* v *International Film Co. Ltd.* AIR 1943 PC 34.

12 20 CWN 310; AIR 1916 Cal 658.

Where, again, precise words of the document or part thereof are material the said words or part thereof may be averred in the pleading, e.g. "in the said contract dated 3.1.1963 the plaintiff expressly agreed that in case the defendant paid back to the plaintiff a sum of ₹5,000 within the 31st day of December 1967, the plaintiff should not claim specific performance of the said contract".

7 Verification of pleadings [s. 26(2) and Or. 6, r. 15(4), CPC] Save as otherwise provided by any law for the time being in force, every pleading shall be verified at the foot by the party or by one of the parties pleading or by some other person proved to the satisfaction of the court to be acquainted with the facts of the case.

The person verifying shall specify, by reference to the numbered paragraphs of the pleading, what he verifies of his own knowledge and what he verifies upon information received and believes to be true.

The verification shall be signed by the person making it and shall state the date on which and the place at which it was signed.

The person verifying the pleading shall also furnish an affidavit in support of his pleadings.[13]

Sub-rule (4) of r. 15 of Or. 6, inserted by the Code of Civil Procedure (Amendment) Act 1999 (w.e.f. 1.7.2002), is procedural in character and thus is only directory in nature. Non-compliance with the provision of Or. 6, r. 15(4) would not automatically render the suit *non est*.[14]

Omission of verification of a defective verification can be cured at a later stage as it is a mare irregularity[15] and the plaint should not be rejected.[16] Such defect is curable.[17]

Pleadings not verified—effect. Non-verification of a pleading is not fatal and the court is to consider the objection relating to defects at the earliest in view of Or. 6, r. 15 of the Code of Civil Procedure.[18]

Sub-rule (4) which was inserted to Or. 6, r. 15 of the Code of Civil Procedure stipulates that the person verifying the pleading should furnish an affidavit in support of his pleadings.[19]

8 Striking out of pleadings (Or. 6, r. 16) Pleadings may be struck out at the instance of the court at any stage of the proceeding when such pleadings are:

(*i*) unnecessary;

(*ii*) scandalous, frivolous or vexatious; or

13 As amended by the Code of Civil Procedure (Amendment) Act 1999, w.e.f. 1.7.2002 see also s. 26(2).

14 *Vidyawati* v *Bhakti* AIR 2006 SC 1194.

15 *Kanakeswar Narzary* v *Deputy Commissioner, Kokrajhar* AIR 2005 NOC 2005 (Gau); *Dashrath Khunte* v *Sammelal Jangde* AIR 2011 Chh 191.

16 *Bal Mukund Persad Gupta* v *Mathura Prasad* AIR 2002 All 363.

17 *P.A. Mohammed Riyas* v *M.K.I. Raghavan* AIR 2012 SC 2784; (2012)5 SCC 511.

18 *K. Krishnaraj* v *Anil C. Lobo* AIR 2015 Kant 152.

19 *Barendra Biswal* v *Rama Roy* AIR 2015 Ori 125.

(*iii*) may tend to prejudice, embarrass or delay the fair trial of the suit;

(*iv*) otherwise an abuse of the process of the court.

The relevant provision is enjoined in Or. 6, r. 16 of the CPC which runs as follows:

> The court may at any stage of the proceedings order to be struck out or amended any matter in any pleading—
>
> (*a*) which may be unnecessary, scandalous, frivolous or vexatious, or
>
> (*b*) which may tend to prejudice, embarrass or delay the fair trial of the suit, or
>
> (*c*) which is otherwise an abuse of the process of the court.

The object of Or. 6, r. 16 of the Code of Civil Procedure is to ensure that the plaintiff should present his pleading in an intelligible form without causing embarrassment to the defendant.[20]

When allegations which were made were scandalous as well as unnecessary as the question to *mala fides* could be made on the basis of other averments in the plaint, the court has every power to direct the deletion of such averments from the plaint.[1]

The court can *suo motu* compel striking out or amendment of portions of the pleading if those appear unnecessary to satisfy the reasons for so doing. Parties to a suit can also invoke the assistance of the court to take action. But the power should be sparingly used. The power is there, but the power under the rule should be exercised with great care and caution.[2] Though the court has unfettered power to take action 'at any stage of the proceeding', the greater the delay the chance more feeble. The court may decline to exercise its jurisdiction unless objection is taken at the earliest opportunity.

The power of the court to strike out pleadings is extraordinary in nature and must be used by the court sparingly and with extreme care, caution and circumspection.[3]

Pleadings include a plaint as well as a written statement. But in the case of a written statement striking out a portion thereof may be a tough job, for a written statement ought not to be struck out unless it is clear beyond all reasonable doubt that the allegations in it are such as cannot afford a defence to the action and which, if not struck out, would unnecessarily delay the suit. Allegation in a written statement offering no defence and made for the purpose of protracting trial—defence must be struck out.[4]

Statements which are indecent or offensive, insinuations on character, imputations of a scandalous nature, having no bearing with the case are to be struck out. Scandalous allegations can be expunged from any record or

20 *Sathi Vijay Kumar* v *Tota Singh* (2006)13 SCC 353.

1 *Sk. Illias* v *Co-operative for American Relief Everywhere, India* AIR 2007 Ori 9.

2 *All India Reporter Ltd.* v *D.D. Datar* AIR 1951 Nagpur 412; *Anant Balkrishna Naik* v *Govind Datta Gaunderkar* AIR 1976 Goa 74.

3 *Sathi Vijay Kumar* v *Tota Singh* (2006)13 SCC 353.

4 *Singhai Karelal Kundanlal Trust* v *Kesri Dal Mill* AIR 1976 MP 54.

proceeding.[5] A pleading is embarrassing if it is too general and does not give a clear idea of the case the opponent is required to meet or of how much of the statement of claim is admitted and how much is denied. A claim for alternative relief is not, however, embarrassing.

(i) ***Unnecessary pleadings.*** When a plaint contains unnecessary matter such unnecessary portion may be struck out. If it is harmless, it need not be struck out. An unintelligible pleading may be ordered to be struck off or ordered to be amended.

(ii) ***Scandalous pleadings.*** Nothing, however, can be scandalous which is relevant, e.g. allegations of adultery in a divorce petition.

It is absolutely essential that a plaint, not to be embarrassing to the defendants, should state those facts which will put the defendant on his guard, tell him what he will have to meet when the case comes on for trial.[6]

9 Amendment of pleadings (Or. 6, r. 17) Law sometimes makes a provision for an erring litigant. Through mistake or inadvertance, there may be pleading which requires amendment and/or alteration. Order 6, r. 17 is a provision to the point. It reads:

> "The court may at any stage of the proceedings allow either party to alter or amend his pleadings in such manner and on such terms as may be just, and all such amendments shall be made as may be necessary for the purpose of determining the real questions in controversy between the parties:
>
> Provided that no application for amendment shall be allowed after the trial has commenced, unless the court comes to the conclusion that in spite of due diligence, the party could not have raised the matter before the commencement of trial."

This provision is to be read along with r. 18:

> Rule 18. *Failure to amend after order.* If a party who has obtained an order for leave to amend does not amend accordingly within the time limited for that purpose by the order, or if no time thereby limited then within fourteen days from the date of the order, he shall not be permitted to amend after the expiration of such limited time as aforesaid or of such fourteen days, as the case may be, unless the time is extended by the court."

The object of making a provision like the present one is to afford an opportunity to correct pleadings with an eye to avoid multiplicity of suits and to shorten litigation. Normally, amendments are allowed in the pleadings to avoid multiplicity of litigations.[7] If the nature of proposed amendment neither changes the nature and character of the suit nor does it introduce any fresh ground, such amendment is to be allowed.[8]

5 *Amalgamated Commercial Traders* v *C. Hariprasad* AIR 1966 Mad 161. See *Roop Lal Sathi* v *Nachattar Singh* AIR 1982 SC 1559; (1982)3 SCC 487.
6 *Mati Lal Poddar* v *Judhistir Das Teor* 31 IC 181.
7 *Rameshkumar Agarwal* v *Rajmala Exports (P) Ltd.* (2012)5 SCC 337.
8 *Gurbakhsh Singh* v *Buta Singh* AIR 2018 SC 2635.

Rules of procedure have no other aim than to facilitate the task of administering justice. The powers under this rule are discretionary[9] and the discretion is to be exercised according to judicial principles and not in any arbitrary, vague or fanciful manner, or so as to cause injustice to the other side. The discretion is wide and is to be liberally exercised. We would remember that a court should allow the amendment of a pleading where there has been a clerical error, or a *bona fide* misdescription of property or where there has been a mistake of law or fact.[10] Description of a party to a suit can be amended.[11]

In a suit for partition, plaintiff by way of proposed amendment wants to plead that his father held the property in question in fiduciary capacity in trust for benefit of plaintiff and his mother. Delhi High Court held that fiduciary capacity in such transaction arises on account of relationship which father has with the minor child. Proposed amendment is merely an elucidation to plead the cause more specifically and in express words. No prejudice would be caused to opposite party by allowing proposed amendment and so amendment should be allowed.[12]

There is no provision in the Code of Civil Procedure authorising the court to direct *suo motu* a party to amend his pleadings. Hence, where no application under Or. 6, r. 17 is made for leave to amend, but the court *suo motu* directs amendment of written statement to include a new defence not already raised in his pleadings the direction is erroneous.[13]

Amendment when refused. As a general rule amendment which converts a suit of one character into a suit of another character[14] or which alters the fundamental character of a suit, e.g. the foundation over which the suit is based, shall not be allowed.[15] This is different from a proposed amendment seeking to introduce a new ground of claim, for "an amendment may be allowed even if it introduces a new ground of claim or an allegation of fact inconsistent with the original pleading where the court thinks it just and necessary[16] but cannot be allowed after expiry of limitation.[17] Amendments in elucidation or amplification of plaint averments are allowable.[18] If, however, the plaint is unambiguous, no amendment to clarify the claim can be allowed.[19] Therefore,

9 *Batoo Mal* v *Rameshwar Nath* AIR 1971 Del 98. Amendment to be allowed in the interest of justice *Mohammed Mustafa* v *Sri Abu Bakar* AIR 1971 SC 361; (1970)3 SCC 891.

10 *SRM Ars. Sp. Sathappa Chettiar* v *SRM Ars. Rm. Ramanathan Chettiar* AIR 1958 SC 245.

11 *Ramagouda* v *Gouhal Basangouda* AIR 1969 Mys 111; *Jai Jai Ram Monohar Lal* v *National Buildings* AIR 1969 SC 1267.

12 *Adesh Kanwarjit Singh Brar* v *Babli Brar* AIR 2011 Del 187.

13 *Siri Chand Prasad* v *Lakshmi Singh* AIR 1969 Pat 107.

14 *Harish Chandra Bajpai* v *Triloki Singh* AIR 1957 SC 444.

15 AIR 1952 Ass 10.

16 *Jamnalal Ramlal Kintee* v *Kishendas, State of Hyderabad* AIR 1955 Hyd 1.

17 *Ram Dayal* v *Brijraj Singh* AIR 1970 SC 110 (contra *Charan Das* v *Amir Khan* AIR 1921 PC 50; *Bisweswar Bajpai* v *Jagneswar Bajpai* AIR 1968 Cal 213).

18 AIR 1970 Cal 8.

19 *Parma Nand Ahuja* v *Satya Dev Ahuja* AIR 1973 Del 190.

it should be remembered that the court cannot, by way of amendment, substitute one distinct cause of action for another. The court shall not allow amendment which is forbidden by law.[20] Consequential amendment ought to be allowed.[1]

Amendment can be made at any stage of the proceeding.[2] Delay simpliciter is no ground for refusal.[3] Amendment in plaint for enhancement of compensation may be granted at any stage of the proceeding even in appeal.[4] Delay in filing the petition for amendment should be compensated by cost and it should not be a ground for rejecting the application.[5] An amendment may be allowed before or at, or after, the trial, or before the final decree, in appeal, in second appeal,[6] in revision. A prayer for amendment of plaint was made to claim preferential right under s. 22 of the Hindu Succession Act 1956 after 13 years. Ordinarily such a preferential right can be claimed within one year. Such prayer cannot be granted.[7] Closure of case for judgment. Court can consider application for amendment of pleadings even thereafter, before pronouncement of judgment.[8]

An application for amendment of a plaint so as to make the suit a representative one must be made within the time allowed for the suit.[9] Amendment to take a plea after eight years should not be allowed on account of gross delay and laches.[10] But the rule that a petition for amendment of pleadings is liable to be rejected on the ground of unusual delay is not an inflexible one.[11] Amendment of plaint or written statement cannot be allowed after commencement of trial.[12] But if application for such an amendment is made after commencement of trial, the applicant should prove that in spite of due diligence he could not raise the matter before commencement of trial.[13] It has been held that mere framing of issue does not amount to commencement of trial.[14] Amendment of plaint by introducing a case not set up in original plaint: amendment once allowed by the court cannot be objected to in subsequent stages of the proceeding.[15] All amendments will be generally permissible when they are necessary for determination of the

20 *Sant Ram* v *Abdul Haq* AIR 1971 J&K 81.
1 *Bikram Singh* v *Ram Baboo* AIR 1981 SC 2036.
2 *Roe* v *Davies* [1876]2 ChD 729.
3 *South India Corporation* v *State Trading Corporation* AIR 1970 Ker 138. Amendment prayed for after 22 years was rejected (AIR 1970 SC 42).
4 *State of Maharashtra* v *Sitaram Narayan Patil* AIR 2010 NOC 986 (Bom).
5 *B.K.N. Pillai* v *P. Pillali* (2000)1 SCC 712; AIR 2000 SC 614.
6 AIR 1971 SC 361.
7 *Ashutosh Chaturvedi* v *Prano Devi* AIR 2008 SC 2171; (2008)15 SCC 610; *South Kokan Distilleries* v *Prabhat Gajanan Naik* AIR 2009 SC 1177; (2008)14 SCC 632.
8 *Narendra Singh* v *Srimati Malti Devi* AIR 1993 MP 248.
9 *Chinnaswami Naicker* v *Kandesami Gouder* AIR 1970 Mad 81.
10 *Gauri Shanker* v *Hindusthan Trust Pvt. Ltd.* AIR 1972 SC 2091.
11 *Dr. Mrs. Sarojini Pradhan* v *Khirode Chandra Prodhan* AIR 1973 Ori 214.
12 *Jaiwant Singh Negi* v *Man Mohan Singh* AIR 2010 Utr 100.
13 *Abdul Rehman* v *Mohd. Ruldu* (2012)11 SCC 341.
14 *Dibya Prasad Pradhan* v *State of Sikkim* AIR 2011 Sikk 1.
15 *Jogesh Chandra Sen* v *Sm. Kiron Bala Saha* AIR 1977 Cal 167.

real controversy in the suit. All the same, substitution of one cause of action or the nature of the claim for another in the original plaint or change of the subject-matter or of controversy in the suit is not permissible. Introduction by amendment of inconsistent or contradictory allegations in negation of the admitted position of facts or mutually destructive allegations of facts are also impermissible though inconsistent pleas on the admitted position can be introduced by way of amendment. In general, the amendments should not cause prejudice to the other side which cannot be compensated in costs. Amendment of a claim or relief, which is barred by limitation when the amendment is sought to be made, should not be allowed to defeat a legal right accrued except when such consideration is outweighed by the special circumstances of the case.[16] Inadvertent omission to raise alternative plea—amendment for inclusion of such plea should be allowed even if it is time-barred.[17]

Where by the proposed amendment, the respondent sought to negate his own admission in the written statement, it should not be allowed.[18] A party is not allowed to set up a new case or a new cause of action by amendment particularly when a suit on the new case or cause of action is barred.[19]

Belated application for amendment is not liable to be rejected merely for the delay if the court finds that by allowing the application real controversy between the parties may be resolved. In such a situation the court may allow application where opposite party can be compensated by cost or otherwise.[20] Such cost should not be exemplary but reasonable.[21]

In a suit for eviction on the ground of rebuilding, amendment of plaint for adding grounds of sub-letting and wrongful user was allowed.[22]

The court may allow amendment in the petition or compliance filed under the Protection of Women from Domestic Violence Act.[23]

16 *Kanailal Das* v *Jiban Kanai Das* AIR 1977 Cal 189.
17 *Ganga Prasad Sarraf* v *Smt. Sukra* AIR 1977 All 210.
18 *Shaik Masthan Sahib* v *Palayani Balarami Reddi* AIR 1953 Mad 958; *Biva's Pvt. Ltd.* v *West Bengal Khadi & Village Industries Board* AIR 1977 Cal 333.
19 AIR 1957 SC 96.
20 *Surender Kumar Sharma* v *Makhan Singh* (2009)10 SCC 626.
21 AIR 1974 Pat 18.
22 *Dr. R.D. Anklesaria* v *Mrs. Kamala Roy* AIR 1977 Cal 464.
23 *Kunapareddy* v *Kunapareddy Swarna Kumari* AIR 2016 SC 2519.

CHAPTER 3

Structure of a Plaint

SYNOPSIS

1 Particulars in a plaint (Or. 7, r. 1) The provision of Or. 7, r. 1 of the CPC lists the particulars of a plaint. The relevant rule reads:

"The plaint shall contain the following particulars:

(*a*) the name of the court in which the suit is brought;

(*b*) the name, description and place of residence of the plaintiff;

(*c*) the name, description and place of residence of the defendant, so far as they can be ascertained;

(*d*) where the plaintiff or the defendant is a minor or a person of unsound mind, a statement to that effect;

(*e*) the facts constituting the cause of action and when it arose;

(*f*) the facts showing that the court has jurisdiction;

(*g*) the relief which the plaintiff claims;

(*h*) where the plaintiff has allowed as set-off or relinquished a portion of his claim, the amount so allowed or relinquished; and

(*i*) a statement of the value of the subject-matter of the suit for the purposes of jurisdiction and of court-fees, so far as the case admits."

2 Formal parts of a plaint Some of the particulars listed above constitute formal parts of a plaint,

(*a*) heading;

(*b*) cause title or title of suit;

(*c*) body of the plaint.

The heading of a plaint contains the name of the court where the suit is brought. In appropriate cases, a statement of particular jurisdiction of the court, below the name of the court in which the suit is brought, has to be furnished. The serial number of the suit comes to be written after filing. Classification of the suit together with the year of filing of the suit is also to be mentioned.

The Cause Title contains name, description and place of residence of the plaintiff or plaintiffs and of the defendant or defendants in their respective arrays. Where the plaintiff or the defendant is a minor or a person of unsound mind, a statement to that effect has to be added. Further, gist of valuation of the suit in terms of money may, in proper cases, have to be noted. In other words, the particulars mentioned in items (*b*) to (*d*) of Or. 7, r. 1, CPC are inserted in the Cause Title.

And the body of a plaint consists of particulars in items (*e*) to (*i*) of Or. 7, r. 1, CPC.

3 Heading of a plaint

Illustrations. (*a*) In the Court of the Civil Judge (Junior Division) (Sadar), Cooch Behar.
Title Suit No. 12/18.

(*b*) In the Court of the Civil Judge (Senior Division), Jalpaiguri.
Other Class Suit No. 18/18.

(*c*) In the Court of the District Judge, Burdwan.
Matrimonial Suit No. 12/18.

(*d*) In the Hon'ble High Court at Calcutta.
Ordinary Original Civil Jurisdiction.

(*e*) In the Hon'ble High Court at Calcutta.
Testamentary and Intestate Jurisdiction.

And, so on.

4 Cause title—Name, description, place of residence of the plaintiff, or the defendant

The Title of Suit follows next. Below the heading (i.e. the name of the court) of a plaint we find the name of the plaintiff and the name of the defendant with their description together with the place of residence of each of such plaintiffs or the defendants along with a statement to the effect when such plaintiff or the defendant is a minor or a person of unsund mind. It may be noted here that the name, description and place of residence of the plaintiff must be given fully as enjoined by the provision in Or. 7, r. 1(*b*). The law, however, is lenient so far as those particulars of the defendant are concerned. In the latter case, the plaint should contain such particulars as could be ascertained prior to filing of the suit.

When the plaintiffs and the defendants are more than one, they have to be numbered serially.[1]

1 *Vide* Civil Rules & Orders, vol. 1, Calcutta High Court.
Rule 18(1). "In every pleading, petition, etc., names of parties should bear consecutive numbers and a separate line should be allowed to name and description of each person."

An individual has to sue or to be sued in his own name. But where the plaintiff or the defendant is a body corporate, they must sue or be sued in its corporate name unless there be statutory instructions in the statute forming a corporation. Partner of a firm may institute a suit or be sued in the firm name when registered. A person who carries on business in a name or style other than his own may be sued in such name or style as if it were a firm name (see Or. 30, r. 10, CPC). In cases of a person of unsound mind or where the plaintiff or the defendant is a minor, the name of the next friend or guardian or where there is a certificated guardian of a minor or a mentally ill person his name should be stated in the Cause Title after naming the plaintiff or the defendant. A Hindu idol is a juristic person and may sue or be sued in his own name by or through its *shebait*.

5 Title suit by a deity—dismissal with costs *Shebait* is personally liable to meet decretal costs,[2] unless in view of all the facts of the case the court directs him to be indemnified out of the trust estate.[3]

6 Suit relating to administration of temple Idol is not a necessary party. Suit by Idol represented by next friend is maintainable.[4]

In a Cause Title the main features are:

(*i*) Name.

(*ii*) Description.

(*iii*) Place of residence of both parties to a suit.

(i) ***Name.*** The title (surname) by which the defendant is generally known should be given in a plaint for personal actions.

(ii) ***Description.*** The description[5] of parties in a plaint has had the only object of securing correct identification of the party suing and the party sued. There cannot be, for obvious reasons, any dogmatic rules as to what would constitute a proper description. It differs in varying circumstances.

Generally speaking, father's name, occupation and caste are sufficient description of an individual. It may include the age.

Rule 18(2). "These numbers should not be changed, and in the event of death of a party during pendency of the suit or proceeding, his heirs or representatives, if more than one, should be shown by sub-numbers. Where fresh parties are brought in, they are to be numbered consecutively to the plaintiffs or defendants, as the case may be, already in the suit ....".

2 *Pannalal Paik* v *Indubala Haldar* AIR 1988 Cal 323.

3 *Sri Sri Sridhar Jew* v *Manindra K. Mitter* AIR 1941 Cal 272.

4 *Sakanacan* v *Akamala Sree Dharma Saystha* AIR 1992 Ker 406.

5 Opinion of the Judicial Committee—The term 'description' includes all those titles by which a person is known, and that, if plaintiff from animosity, pique, or anything in fact but a *bona fide* dispute as to the right to title, obstinately refused to give his adversary that title by which he is generally recognised, the court ought not to permit or sanction that species of insult, but will exercise a sound discretion in first requiring the plaintiff to amend his plaint and afterwards in rejecting the plaint, should be first order to be contumaciously disobeyed.

When the description is defective, it is a case of misdescription. Misdescription of parties can be corrected at any stage.

In a suit by a joint family firm, the suit was instituted in the firm name. Amendment seeking addition of individual partners can be allowed as the case is one of misdescription. X suing as proprietor of 'Todi Financing Corporation'—amendment sought by describing 'X' as partner of the Corporation and by impleading the retired partner as defendant should be allowed.[6]

Where a suit for recovery of money due under a promissory note was filed by a firm through one of its partners the amendment of the plaint on the ground that the partnership firm already stood dissolved on the date of filing the suit, such amendment cannot be refused.[7] Where a party is wrongly described as minor but was actually a major, and the court orders amendment giving a correct description and in spite of it the amendment is not carried out; the court can strike out the name of such party who was wrongly described.[8] Addition of word 'minors' to the description of minor defendants not to be disallowed normally.[9] Where one person sues or is sued and another person is sought to be substituted in his place, the case is not one of misdescription of parties but clearly a case of substitution of the parties. Such amendment can be allowed only if there is no question of limitation.[10] In a suit by a firm, plaintiff suing by mistake as owner of the firm, such mistake can be set at right, the suit cannot be said to be not-maintainable on the technical ground that the plaintiff sued in his own name.[11] A suit was filed by a firm through an individual, and in amendment substituted the name of sole proprietor of the firm for the name of the individual. It was allowed after rejecting the plea of limitation put forward by the defendant.[12] Company wrongly described as a company incorporated under the Companies Act, such wrong description will not take away jurisdiction of the court to try the suit.[13] Describing the defendant as the State of Vindhya Pradesh instead of the Union of India is merely a case of misdescription of the defendant, amendment was allowed to join the Union of India as a defendant.[14] Where a foreign firm institutes a suit in its firm name which it cannot do in view of Or. 30, r. 1, and the maintainability of the suit being objected on the ground the plaint is amended by the substitution of the names of the partners, there is no addition of new plaintiffs but merely a clarification on the individuals already on record.[15] Amendment of a plaint by seeking to delete the word 'limited' affixed to the

6 AIR 1979 Cal 10.

7 *Vishnu Agencies (Pvt.) Ltd.* v *Commercial Tax Officer* AIR 1978 SC 484.

8 AIR 1928 Oudh 428 (per Simp).

9 AIR 1978 Punj 100.

10 AIR 1958 J&K 20.

11 *Purushottam & Co.* v *Manilal Sons* AIR 1961 SC 325. Also see *Ranagouda* v *Gonhal Basangouda* AIR 1969 Mys 111.

12 *Mohinder Singh* v *Chawa Commission Shop, Chawa* AIR 2003 NOC 103 (P&H).

13 *Babulall Choukhani* v *Caltex (India) Ltd.* AIR 1967 Cal 205.

14 AIR 1956 VP 16.

15 *Mura Mohiden* v *V.O.A. Mohomed* AIR 1955 Mad 294.

defendant company so as to make suit one against firm—case held one of misdescription of the defendant and could not be allowed.[16]

To sum up: If, however, imperfectly and incorrectly a party is designated in a plaint, the correction of the error is not the addition or substitution of the party but merely clarifies and makes apparent what was previously shrouded in obscurity by reason of the error or mistake. The question in such a case is one of the intention of the party and if the court is able to discover the person or persons intended to sue or to be sued a mere misdescription of such a party can always be corrected provided the mistake was *bona fide*. Such an amendment does not involve the addition of a party so as to attract s. 22(1) of the Limitation Act.[17]

(iii) *Place of residence of both parties to a suit.* Order 7, r. 1(*b*) and r. 1(*c*) enjoin that the place of residence of the plaintiff and that of the defendant have to be mentioned in a plaint.

In personal actions and in suits against individuals, the place of residence is required for service of processes as also for identification of the party. The place of residence of the plaintiff and also the defendant have to be given accurately. "It is not sufficient to make vague statements as to the defendant's place of residence as 'carrying on business in Calcutta'.[18]

In suits against corporate bodies, association of persons, firms, Government, etc., the place of residence is a misnomer and necessarily the place of residence in such cases is the place of business, place of registered office.

Some illustrations are given as to name, description and place of residence of parties to a suit.[19]

The plaintiff or the defendant when

(*i*) The Government of India[20]	The Union of India
(*ii*) The Government of India in Railway Claim cases[21]	The Union of India, owning and representing:

16 *National Industries* v *Sasson Rice Mills Ltd.* AIR 1953 Cal 381.

17 *Mura Mohiden* v *V.O.A. Mohomed* AIR 1955 Mad 294.

18 *Ramprasad Chimanlal* v *Hazarimull Lalchand* AIR 1931 Cal 458.

19 See Appendix 'A'—Pleadings—Titles of Suits of the Code of Civil Procedure 1908.

20 Article 300 of the Constitution of India reads: "The Government of India may sue or be sued by the name of the Union of India and the Government of a State may sue or be sued by the name of the State". Section 79 of the CPC states: "In a suit by or against the Government the authority to be named a plaintiff or defendant, as the case may be....." Again, Or. 27, r. 3 of CPC enjoins: "In suits by or against the Government, instead of inserting in the plaint the name and description and place of residence of the plaintiff or defendant, it shall be sufficient to insert the appropriate name as provided in s. 79. A petition for writ of *mandamus* against the Collector and the Assistant Collector cannot be interpreted as directed against the State Government (*Lal Chand* v *The Collector of Sirmur* AIR 1952 HP 16).

21 It is not necessary that the Railway administration as such through the Manager or anybody else should be impleaded as a party defendant to the suit. (*Chandra Mohan Saha* v *Union of India* AIR 1953 Ass 193; *Natwarlal Gowardhandas* v *Union of India* AIR 1957 MP 157).

	(*i*) N.F. Railway Administration, Maligaon, Guwahati-11.
	(*ii*) N.E. Railway Administration, Gorakhpur, Uttar Pradesh.
(*iii*) Any State Government	(*i*) The State of West Bengal.
	(*ii*) The State of Meghalaya.
(*iv*) Advocate General[1]	The Advocate-General of (Assam)
(*v*) Karta or Manager[2] of a joint Hindu family	(*i*) Sri 'A' son of Sri 'B' for self as Karta of the joint Hindu family consisting of himself and other members residing at .... P.S. .... Dt. ....
	(*ii*) Sri 'A' son of Sri 'B' for self and as the managing member of the joint Hindu family consisting of himself and other members residing at .... P.S. .... Dt. ....
(*vi*) Hindu joint Family[3] business concern	(1) Sri A son of Sri B
	(2) Sri C son of Sri B carrying on a joint family business under the business name and style as 'Samagri Bhandar' at .... P.S. ..... Dt. ......
(*vii*) Individuals in personal actions	(*i*) Md. Ajabuddin Mia, son of late Tasar Mahmud Mia, by caste Muslim, by occupation—agriculturist, residing at village X P.S. Y Dt. Z.
	(*ii*) Mohonlal Sethia, son of the late Dulichand Sethia of 10, Armenian Street, P.S. Barabazar, Calcutta, at present

1 See ss. 92 and 93 of CPC.

2 A joint family trading business is not a partnership. A suit by or against a firm owned by a joint family cannot be brought in the name of the firm under which the business is being carried. It must be brought by or against the plaintiff.

3 Order 30, CPC does not apply to a joint Hindu family firm. A joint Hindu family firm must sue and be sued in the name of its members. A joint Hindu family firm is not entitled to bring a suit in its business name (*Motilal Chhajulal* v *Giridharilal Rameshwarlal* AIR 1942 Cal 613).

A joint Hindu family firm when registered is governed by the Partnership Act (AIR 1949 Ass 71).

A joint Hindu family business may be sued in its trade name (*Jamunadhar Poddar Firm* v *Jamnuram Bhakat* AIR 1944 Cal 138).

	residing at Cooch Behar town, P.S. Kotwali, District Cooch Behar.
(*viii*) Partnership firm[4]	(*i*) M/s. H.L. Pal & Sons, a firm registered under the Indian Partnership Act with its principal place of business at .... P.S. ...... Dt. ....
	(*ii*) Sri A.B. and Sri C.D. carrying on business in partnership under the name of XY at .... P.S. .... Dt. ....
(*ix*) Company[5]	M/s. A & Co. Ltd. having its registered Office at .... Calcutta-1.
(*x*) Company in liquidation[6] Voluntary liquidation Official Liquidation	(*i*) M/s. A.B. Company Ltd. in Liquidation by Liquidator Sri 'A' having office at .... P.S. .... Dt. ....
	(*ii*) M/s. X Company Ltd. (in liquidation) by the Official Liquidator having office at .... P.S. .... Dt. ....
(*xi*) Official Receiver	Sri 'A' son of Sri 'B' Official Receiver to the estate of the late 'C' of .... P.S. .... Dt. ....
(*xii*) Minor	(*i*) Sri 'A' son of 'B'—minor, by father and natural guardian 'C' son of 'D' of .... P.S. .... Dt. ....
	(*ii*) Sm. A, daughter of the late B—minor, represented by next

4 A partnership firm not registered is not entitled to sue being hit by provisions of s. 69(1)(2) of the Partnership Act except under circumstances in s. 63(3)(4) of the said Act. But a partnership which is not registered may be sued in the firm name.

Suit by a firm.—Plaintiff suing through mistake as owner of the firm. Mistake is curable and the suit can be maintained (*Ranagouda* v *Gonhal Basangouda* AIR 1969 Mys 111).

5 Suit filed by or behalf of unregistered firm not maintainable (*Shivraj Fine Art Litho Works* v *Purushottam* AIR 1993 Bom 30).

6 *In case of official liquidator*—The word "Official" has to be added before the word 'Liquidator'. Individual name of the Official Liquidator need not be given.

	friend Sri 'C' son of Sri 'D' residing at .... P.S. .... Dt. ....
(*xiii*) Person of unsound mind	Sri 'A' son of Sri 'B' residing at .... P.S. .... Dt. .... a person of unsound mind represented by his guardian/ next friend Sri 'C' son of late 'D' of .... P.S. .... Dt. ....
(*xiv*) Corporation[7]	(*i*) North Bengal State Transport Corporation, Hq. Cooch Behar. (*ii*) The Food Corporation of India, established and constituted under the Food Corporation Act 1964, having its registered office at .... P.S. .... Dt. ...... (*iii*) State Bank of India, a body corporate constituted by the State Bank of India Act 1955, having its central office at Bombay and a branch office at .... P.S. .... Dt. .... in the State of West Bengal.
(*xv*) Co-operative Society	Cooch Behar Co-operative Rice Mills Ltd. a co-operative society registered under the W.B. Co-operative Society Act and having its registered office at .... P.S. .... Dt. ....
(*xvi*) Individual carrying business in the name other than own[8]	Sri Vithalbhai Patel son of late 'B' carrying on business under the trade name "Hind Tobacco Co." at .... Town. P.S. .... Dt. ....

7 *Corporation.*—A legal body with the quality of perpetual existence and succession except as limited by statute effecting the incorporation. These are examples of incorporated associations and are to be distinguished from other associations and societies which are unincorporated associations, namely, registered societies, firms, clubs, etc.

8 An individual carrying on business in firm name must sue in his own name (*Bhagwan Manji* v *Hiraji Premaji* AIR 1932 Bom 516). His position is that of a person with an alias, if he dies, substitution has to be made to avoid abatement of the suit.

A plaint filed by an unregistered firm would not be a plaint at all. All proceeding upon such a plaint would be non-existent and without jurisdiction in the eye of law—*Sunderlal & Sons* AIR 1976 Cal 471. A person suing in his trade name, brings about in the plaint a case of misdescription of his ownself—*Jai Jai Ram Manoharlal* v *National Building Material Supply* AIR 1969 SC 1267; (1969)1 SCC 869.

(*xvia*) Proprietory concern	Sri Pradip K. Sen son of Late Ajoy Kumar Sen carrying on business under the name and style of 'SEN & Co.' at B.B. Ganguly Street, Kolkata.
(*xvii*) Administrator	Sri 'A' son of Sri 'B' by caste—by occupation— residing at .... P.S. .... Dist. .... Administrator to the Estate of late "X" deceased.
(*xviii*) Executor	Sri 'A' son of late 'B' by caste .... by occupation .... Executor of 'X' deceased, residing at .... P.S. .... Dt. ....
(*xix*) Official Assignee	Sri 'A' Official Assignee and the Assignee of the estate of 'X' an insolvent, having office at .... P.S. .... Dt. ....
(*xx*) Reversioner	Sri 'A' son of Sri 'B' by caste— by occupation .... Revisioner to the estate of late 'X' deceased, residing at .... P.S .... Dt. ....
(*xxi*) Constituted Attorney[9]	Sri 'A' by his constituted Attorney Sri 'B' son of late 'C' residing at .... P.S. .... Dt. ....
(*xxii*) Idol[10]	(*i*) 'A' an idol in the temple at .... P.S........... Dt. .... through Sri 'A' son of Sri 'B' the Manager of the temple.

Though a plaint in the name of an unregistered firm is legally *non-est* for all purposes yet, a plaint or a proceeding instituted in the trade or businessname of a sole owner is not similarly deemed to be void for all future purposes. In case of a *bona fide* error where the mistake has been made not for any ulterior purpose the court permits a rectification of the same so that the person suing is permitted even at a late stage to show himself as the claimant on record.

Amendment of decree allowed—*J.D. Singh* v *The Calcutta Port Trust* (1993)1 CLJ 139. Suit by sole proprietor in trade name amounts to institution of the suit in the name of wrong person. Such mistake can be amended, at any stage subject to law—*Oriental Coal Co. Ltd.* v *Mohonlal Kishanlal* AIR 1984 Bom 174.

A person can be sued in his trade name but he cannot sue in his trade name (*Samrathrai Khetsidas* v *Kasturbhai Jagabhai* AIR 1930 Bom 216).

9 For signature by a constituted attorney see provisions of Or. 6, r. 15 of CPC. A petition supported by an affidavit or a verified petition seeking permission of the court to sign the verification to the plaint is a legal pre-condition.

10 A suit should be brought in the name of the idol. But the idol should be represented by the *shebait*/manager etc.

	(*ii*) A, an idol in the temple at .... P.S. .... Dt. .... through the shebait Sri .... son of .... residing at .... P.S. .... Dt. ....
(*xxiii*) Shebait	Sri A, son of Sri B residing P.S. .... Dt. .... shebait of idol 'X' in the temple at .... P.S. .... Dt. ....
(*xxiv*) Mutawalli[11]	A, Mutawalli of the *Auqaf* estate of .... etc.
(*xxv*) Trustees	M/s. 'A' & 'B' Managing Trustee of the Cooch Behar Welfare Organisation with office at .... P.S. .... Dt. ....
(*xxvi*) Registered Society[12]	Sri 'A' President of the Bazar Samity, a society registered under the Act of having its office at .... P.S. .... Dt. ....
(*xxvii*) Unregistered Society[13]	(*a*) The Unknown Club, an unregistered society with its office at .... P.S. .... Dt. .... having its members as follows: (*i*) "A" (*ii*) "B" (*iii*) "C"

11 A waqf may be public or private. As regards public waqf, the Mutawalli is merely a manager of the waqf estate, the right in property is vested in the God. But in a private waqf the estate vests in the beneficiaries. A Mutawalli both in public and private waqf can sue and be sued.

12 Societies registered may sue or be sued in the name of the President, Chairman, Secretary, as is prescribed by the rules of the society. In suits by or against unregistered societies, all members of the society shall have to join (*Bhagwandas Singh* v *Pinjra Pole Pashu* AIR 1927 All 789; 103 IC 45). Also *Parul Das Roy* v *Anath Das* AIR 1991 Cal 1.

13 A suit by an unregistered body—it must be instituted in the names of all the members of the company (*Hriday Nath Roy* v *Akhil Chandra Roy* AIR 1929 Cal 445). Names of all the members must be disclosed (*Board of Directors, YMCA* v *R.H. Niblett* AIR 1957 All 219). When defendant, all members must be impleaded as defendants. CPC, Or. 1, r. 28—Suit on behalf of society. Suit was filed by the Secretary in his own name, Rules of society authorising Secretary to conduct legal proceedings. Suit properly instituted. *Parul Das Roy* v *Anath Das* AIR 1991 Cal 1.

A suit by a club through or represented by its Secretary is not maintainable even though there was an arrangement that the Secretary should sue. The suit must be brought by all the members or by one or more of such members as a representative suit under Or. 1, r. 8 of CPC.

(*b*) A, B, C, D—Members of the 'X' club of .... an unincorporated society with office at .... P.S........... Dt. ....

(*c*) A & B—on behalf of themselves and other members of the 'Vyabasai Samity', an unincorporated society.

(*xxviii*) In representative suits[14] — Sri 'A' son of Sri 'B' suing on behalf of himself and of the Hindu villagers of village .... P.S. .... Dt. ....

(*xxix*) Municipality[15] — The Municipal Commissioners of Cooch Behar having their office at Cooch Behar Town, P.S. Kotwali, Dt. Cooch Behar.

Title of the suit cannot be treated as part of the plaint as it is not covered by verification appended at the foot of the plaint.[16]

7 Body of a plaint A body of the plaint has to contain (*vide* Or. 7, r. 1) the following particulars and aspects.[17]

(*a*) Preamble—matters of inducement.

(*b*) Facts constituting the cause of action.

(*c*) Date of cause of action.

(*d*) Reliefs claimed—prayer portion.

(*e*) Facts showing jurisdiction of the court.

(*f*) Statement of the value of the subject-matter of the suit for the purposes of pecuniary jurisdiction and of court-fees.

(*g*) Statement of a representative capacity in a suit (Or. 7, r. 4).

14 A suit for recovery of property which is claimed by the defendant as belonging to an idol can be properly maintained in the name of the *shebait* (*Bidhu Sekhar Banerjee* v *Kuloda Prosad Deogharia* 50 IC 525).

A suit against executors, which contains a claim against them personally, should not be dismissed merely because in the title portion of the plaint the executor defendants have not been described as such when in the body of the plaint they have been so described (*Srimati Jagattarin Dasi* v *Prafulla Chandra Ghose* 35 IC 792).

15 Municipality is a Corporation aggregate and shall be sued in its name. Section 13 of the West Bengal Municipal Act enjoining that there shall be established for each Municipality a Board of Councillors having authority over the Municipality.

13(2). Such Municipality shall be a body corporate of the place by reference to which the Municipality is known, having perpetual succession and a common seal, and by that name shall sue and be sued.

16 *Mehboob Ullah* v *Jwala Prasad Kajriwal* AIR 1974 All 413.

17 But in an Interpleader suit some more particulars are required. See Or. 35, r. 1, CPC—see Chapter IX.

(*h*) Grounds of exemption from law of limitation (Or. 7, r. 6).

(*i*) Statement of set-off or relinquishment of a portion of plaintiffs' claim.

(*j*) Rejection and/or return of a plaint.

(*k*) Preliminary issue.

(*l*) Abandonment of plea.

(a) ***Preamble—matters of inducement.*** After the phraseology "the plaintiff states" introducing the body of the plaint generally a few lines are devoted (as are required by circumstances of the case) to serve as introductory to setting of the facts leading gradually to cause of action, e.g.:

"The plaintiff is a registered partnership and Sri A.B. is a partner of the firm".

Or, "That the defendant No. 1 is a businessman of Cooch Behar town, P.S. Kotwali, Dt. Cooch Behar and the defendant No. 2 is a businessman of Kolkata having his office at Kalakar Street, Kolkata 700 007, P.S. Barabazar and a branch business at Cooch Behar town, P.S. Kotwali, District Cooch Behar. The parties hereto are known to each other".

Thus a plaint is commenced with statements as to who the parties are, their relative position and circumstances leading to the cause of action.

Technically, such matters are known as "matters of inducement".[18] The matters may not have direct bearing on the cause of action but ensures a good beginning and irresistibly leads to cause of action in so subtle a way as when it appears that introduction of such matter was just a necessity. For obvious reasons, pleading is not an essay and, therefore, there is no scope for literary workmanship. Matter of inducement should be brief and just what was necessary—not a word more.

(b) ***Facts constituting the cause of action.*** Under Or. 7, r. 1(*e*), the plaint is to contain the facts constituting the cause of action and the time when such cause of action arose.

'Cause of action' means "rights which can be enforced, or liabilities which can be redressed, by the legal procedings...."[19] "Cause of action" means the bundle of essential facts which is necessary for the plaintiff to prove before he can succeed in the suit, or to put it differently, it refers to the media upon which court arrives at a conclusion in his favour.[20] The expression 'cause of action' means every fact which it would be necessary for the plaintiff to prove if traversed, in order to support his right to the judgment of the court, but it does not comprise any piece of evidence which is necessary to prove each fact, but every fact which is necessary to be proved. In the restricted sense, the expression means the circumstances forming the infringement of the right or the immediate occasion for the action. In its wider sense it means the necessary conditions for the maintenance of the suit, including not only the

18 Odger, *Principles of Pleading and Practice* (21st Ed., 1975), Chapters 6 and 7.

19 *Sugden* v *Sugden* [1957]1 All ER 300 (CA).

20 Re, *Lakshminarayan Chettiar* AIR 1954 Mad 594 (FB).

infraction of the right, but the infraction coupled with the right itself; in other words, in its wider sense it means the whole bundle of material and essential facts which it is necessary for the plaintiff to prove in order to entitle him to succeed in the suit.[21]

One and the same transaction may give rise to several distinct causes of action and the plaintiff may bring as many separate suits as there are causes of action, but not more than one suit can be brought in respect of a single cause of action.

No cause of action has been established against one of the defendants but the trial court passed a decree against him—can be set aside by the Appellate Court in exercise of power under Or. 41, r. 33.[22]

JOINDER OF CAUSES OF ACTION. Land let out on different rate of rent on different dates. Tenancy is in favour of some persons. Suit for eviction—cause of action arising as a result of notice under s. 106 of the Transfer of Property Act. There is no question of misjoinder of causes of action (Or. 2, r. 3, CPC).

The objection as to misjoinder of causes of action when not raised either in written statement or even at the time of framing of issues or subsequently during pendency of suit—cannot be allowed to be raised in appeal.[1]

Where the plaint does not disclose 'cause of action' dismissal of the plaint under Or. 7, r. 11 is permissible.[2]

(c) ***Date of cause of action.*** The date of cause of action should be clearly stated in a plaint[3] unless the date can be ascertained from the statement of facts constituting the cause of action. It is the date on which the event constituting the cause of action happened or the infringement of the plaintiff's right is full and complete and gives him the right to institute a suit.

Illustrations below will explain it better.

In a case of contract—the date of breach of contract.

Khas possession—the date of dispossession of the defendant.

Wrongful dismissal—the date in the order of dismissal and/or when the order reached the plaintiff.

Partition—when demanded but refused.

Tortious liabilities—when tortious acts committed.

Recovery of loan—date of loan unless acknowledged subsequently.

Handnote/pronote—date of execution of handnote etc.

Bond—date of bond/or date of agreed payment.

Railway claims case—date of short-delivery.

21 *Md. Kahil* v *Mahboob* AIR 1942 All 122.
22 *Bihar Supply Syndicate* v *United Salt Wroks* AIR 1993 SC 2054 following *Mahant Dhanjir* v *Madan Mohan* AIR 1988 SC 54.
1 *Devesh Chandra Gupta* v *Dinanath* AIR 1992 All 115.
2 *Jagannath Prasad* v *Smt. Chandrawati* AIR 1970 All 309.
3 *Sm. Kalyani Dasi* v *Ganesh Chandra Sreemany* AIR 1932 Cal 259.

The primary object of mentioning the date of cause of action in a plaint is to satisfy the court and the opponent that the suit was filed in time. The statement as to when the cause of action arose need not be made in a separate paragraph if it is clear from other facts alleged in the plaint. It may be noted here that the plaintiff cannot be tied down to the date of accrual of cause of action mentioned in the plaint. The court is entitled to determine the date on which the cause of action arose from the facts alleged and proved.[4] It is appropriate to quote here the observations of Lord Williams, J. in *Ramprasad* v *Hazarimull*: "Rule 1(*e*) and (*f*), require not that a statement should be made that the plaintiff has a good cause of action or that it arose on such and such a date, or that it arose partly or wholly within the jurisdiction but that particulars should be given of facts constituting the cause of action and when it arose, and facts showing that it arose partly or wholly within the jurisdiction .... The plaintiff must give such particulars as will enable the defendant and the court to ascertain from the plaint whether in fact and in law the cause of action did arise as alleged or not. The plaintiff's mere statement that it did is useless for this purpose just as it would be useless to state merely that he had a good cause of action .... Whether these necessary facts appear in their appropriate places in the plaint or in a separate paragraph at the end is a matter for choice."[5]

(d) *Reliefs claimed—prayer portion (Or. 7, r. 7)*

(*i*) General or other reliefs;
(*ii*) Relief on separate grounds;
(*iii*) Alternative reliefs;
(*iv*) Relief for events happening after institution of suit, when law changes;
(*v*) Reliefs not claimed;
(*vi*) More than one relief.

In a suit the plaintiff claims reliefs as are expedient. Reliefs sought for may be of various kinds depending on facts of individual cases. In any case, the plaintiff has to state specifically the relief or reliefs he claims.[6]

Order 7, r. 7, enjoins: Every plaint shall state specifically the relief which the plaintiff claims either simply or in the alternative, and it shall not be necessary to ask for general or other relief which may always be given as the court may think just to the same extent as if it had been asked for. And the same rule shall apply to any relief claimed by the defendant in his written statement.

The relief which is appropriate to the facts found and the legal position determined should be awarded. The court is not tied down to the actual relief claimed. Any appropriate relief which can be granted should be granted.[7] If

4 *Fatch Ali Shah* v *Mahomed Bakhsh* AIR 1928 Lah 516.
5 *Ramprasad Chimanlal* v *Hazarimull Lalchand* AIR 1931 Cal 458 (460). Contra, see ILR 59 Cal 448 by Buckland, J.
6 AIR 1971 Punj 21; *Furkan* v *Mst. Mumtaz Begam* AIR 1971 Raj 149.
7 *Mistra Nand Kaushik* v *State of UP* AIR 1968 All 204.

a party makes a case which he fails to prove in its entirety, but still if he is entitled to relief on what he has been able to prove, he would get such relief as may be allowed to him in the circumstances.[8] A relief cannot be granted if it is not claimed.[9] The relief which is not prayed for, cannot be granted.[10] If a relief which was specifically prayed for is not granted, it shall be deemed to have been declined.[11] Where the plaintiff is held entitled to a decree on admission of the defendant, the decree should be allowed, but he should be deprived of costs for false pleas.[12]

(I) GENERAL OR OTHER RELIEFS. A general or other reliefs need not be specifically asked for in the plaint but can always be granted by the court as if it has been asked for.[13] On the basis of subsequent events, the court can mould the relief for complete and full justice.[14] So, where through mistake the plaintiff omits to pray for the proper relief or if the relief claimed in the plaint is not wholly sufficient or appropriate, the court has always the power to grant the proper relief according to the circumstances of the case.

The test in such cases is to see whether the defendant will not be taken by surprise or be embarrassed by such relief being granted,[15] e.g.:

(*i*) A court can always award future interest on the sum found to be due to the plaintiff, even though the latter has not claimed it.[16]

(*ii*) The court may, in a suit for exclusive possession, pass a decree for joint possession.[17] In a suit for ejectment, a plaintiff can be given a decree for a share of a part of the property if he is found entitled to it, even if he has not made an alternative case in his plaint.[18] But no relief for partition can be granted in a suit for ejectment at any rate without amendment.

(*iii*) In a suit for recovery of possession of disputed lands—no claim of *mesne profits* made in the plaint. Held, *mesne profits* cannot be granted.[19]

(II) RELIEF ON SEPARATE GROUNDS. Order 7, r. 8 of CPC enjoins: "Where the plaintiff seeks relief in respect of several distinct claims or causes of action founded upon separate and distinct grounds, they shall be stated as far as may be separately and distinctly".

A plaintiff may in a proper case rely upon one set of material facts for his relief and also on another and even inconsistent set of material facts for relief

8 *Makhan Lal Ghose* v *Mahaluxmi Bank Ltd.* AIR 1968 Cal 90.
9 *Om Prakash* v *Ram Kumar* AIR 1991 SC 409.
10 *Union of India* v *Ibrahim Uddin* (2012)8 SCC 148; (2012)4 SCC (Civ) 362.
11 *Jaspal* v *State of Haryana* (2001)1 Punj LR 684 (P&H).
12 AIR 1942 Nag 4; *State of Rajasthan* v *Associated State Industries* AIR 1971 Raj 128.
13 *Kaushal Singh* v *Ghanshiam Singh* AIR 1956 All 639; *Pandohi Ahir* v *Faruq Khan* AIR 1954 All 191.
14 *S.K. Parthasarathy Naidu* v *K. Rama Naidu* AIR 2001 Mad 399.
15 *Kaushal Singh* v *Gharshiam Singh* AIR 1956 All 639; AIR 1916 Cal 820.
16 *Rup Ram* v *Harphul* AIR 1921 Lah 125.
17 *Pandohi Ahir* v *Faruq Khan* AIR 1954 All 191.
18 *Vishwanathaswamy Naicker* v *Kamu Ammal* 21 IC 724.
19 *Lakhia Singh Patra* v *Jotilal Aditya Deo* AIR 1968 Pat 160.

in the alternative; but where such alternative cases are alleged, the facts belonging to them respectively should not be mixed up but should be stated separately so as to show on what facts each alternative relief is claimed.

(III) ALTERNATIVE RELIEFS. It is open to the plaintiff to pray for alternative reliefs which may be inconsistent with one another but not mutually destructive. In a plea for declaration that particular contract is void plaintiff cannot alternatively pray for specific performance of the same contract.[20] In a suit based on tenancy, the plaintiff can claim damages for use and occupation in the alternative.[21] We are to remember that in all such cases of alternative relief, the plaintiff has set out the facts relied on him in his alternative claims distinctly and separately. Therefore, if the facts are not stated in the plaint, the plaintiff cannot claim the alternative relief without amending the plaint.[22] But where alternative case, which the plaintiff could have made, but did not make, in the plaint, is admitted by the defendant in a written statement, it is possible to grant the plaintiff relief on that basis.[23] A suit for declaration of title and permanent injunction has been prayed for and has been dismissed. No plea of easement was raised in the plaint as an alternative claim. While rejecting the relief of declaration of title and permanent injunction, court could not grant the relief of injunction on the basis of the easement right.[24]

(IV) RELIEF FOR EVENTS HAPPENING AFTER INSTITUTION OF SUIT. It is well settled that ordinarily the decree in a suit accords with the rights of the parties as they stood at the date of the institution,[25] but this principle is not of universal application and the court may, in appropriate cases, depart from this rule and take notice of events which have happened since the institution of the suit and pass the decree according to the circumstances at the time the decree is passed.[1]

Sir Ashutosh observed: "A suit is to be tried in all its states on the cause of action as it existed at the date of its commencement. An exception to this rule, namely, that a court may take notice of events which happened since the institution of the suit and afford a relief to the parties on the basis of the altered conditions, is applied in cases where it is shown that the original relief claimed has, by reason of subsequent change of circumstances become inappropriate or that it is necessary to base the decision of the court on the altered circumstances in order to shorten litigation or to do complete justice between the parties".[2]

20 *Prem Raj* v *DLF Housing & Construction* AIR 1968 SC 1355.
21 AIR 1954 Assam 156.
22 *Prahlad Mohanti* v *Prahlad Chandra Das* AIR 1944 Pat 276.
23 *Indermal Takaji Mahajan* v *Ramprosad Gopilal* AIR 1970 MP 40; *Firm Sriniwas Ram Kumar* v *Mahabir Prasad* AIR 1951 SC 177.
24 *Bachhaj Nahar* v *Nilima Mandal* AIR 2009 SC 1103.
25 *Nabbobai* v *Hassan* AIR 1954 MB 181; *Ramdayal* v *Maji Devji* AIR 1956 Raj 12; *Porkrakutty* v *Attancheri Velappil* AIR 1954 Mad 381; *Doorga Prasad* v *Secretary of State* AIR 1945 PC 62.
1 *Chandravati* v *Rameshwar Kaviraj* AIR 1968 Pat 422.
2 *Rai Charan Mondal* v *Biswanath Mondal* AIR 1915 Cal 103 (followed AIR 1971 Cal 716; *Lachmeshwar Prasad* v *Keshwarlal* AIR 1941 FC 5).

It is the duty of the court (per Bejoyesh Mookerjee, J.), which still retains control of the judgment, to take notice of subsequent events, post-suit events as they are called, and to mould its decree so as to shorten litigation, preserve the rights of the parties and thus best subserve the ends of justice. What to say of the primary court, even a court of appeal is to take notice of facts which may have arisen subsequently provided that such action causes no prejudice to either party.[3] A court can always take notice of cause of action arising subsequent to the presentation of the plaint.[4] The court has power to take notice of subsequent events and grant reliefs on that basis.[5] In a suit for recovery of rent during pendency of appeal lease itself expired by efflux of time. Appellate court can take subsequent events into consideration.[6]

For events happening after institution of a suit, the plaintiff files a petition to amend the plaint to include fresh cause of action. The amendment so prayed should be allowed to shorten litigation and best subserve the ends of justice.[7] Where pending a suit for a declaration of title the defendant takes possession of the property in dispute, the plaintiff may amend the plaint by adding a prayer for possession instead of bringing another suit. Where again, in a suit for money, the real cause of action arose only after the institution of the suit, the court should not reject the plaint and drive the plaintiff to a fresh suit, but should pass a decree on the basis of such subsequent cause of action.[8]

When law changes. Where the facts are not in dispute and the accrual of cause of action subsequent to the suit is under the terms of a statute of which the court must take notice, a formal amendment of the plaint is unnecessary, for the court is bound to administer the law of the land at the date when it gives its decision on a dispute.[9] Change of law effected during the pendency of the suit or appeal can be taken cognizance of by appropriate court.[10] It is worth recalling what Mr. Hughes, CJ. *held* in *Paterson* v *State of Alabama* (quoted in AIR 1941 FC 5): "We have frequently held that in the exercise of our appellate jurisdiction, we have power not only to correct error in the judgment under review but to make such disposition of the case as justice requires. And in determining what justice does require the court is bound to consider any change either in fact or in law, which has supervened since the judgment was entered".

3 *Kiran Bala Saha* v *Bankim Chandra* AIR 1967 Cal 603.
4 *S.P. Narayaswami Pillai* v *Dhanakoti Ammal* AIR 1967 Mad 220. Also see *Bhushan Ch. Pal* v *Bengal Coal Co. Ltd.* AIR 1966 Cal 63.
5 *Ramanugrah Jha* v *State of Bihar* AIR 1966 Pat 97.
6 *Ranvijaya Shahi* v *Bala Prasad Motani* AIR 1978 Pat 91.
7 *Pangoti Mangarao* v *Chinnadi Kishan Rao* AIR 1965 AP 98.
8 *Ramdayal* v *Maji Devji* AIR 1956 Raj 12.
9 *Lakshmi Ammal* v *Narayanswami Naicker* AIR 1950 Mad 321; *Lachmeshwar Prasad* v *Keshwarlal* AIR 1941 FC 5.
10 *Punjab Co-operative Bank* v *Amrik Singh* AIR 1966 All 216; *Bhushan Ch. Paul* v *Bengal Coal Ltd.* AIR 1966 Cal 63; *Jitnath Singh* v *State of Bihar* AIR 1974 Pat 28.

(v) Reliefs not claimed. Relief not claimed may also be granted.[11] But the Supreme Court held that a relief cannot be granted if it is not claimed.[12] An alternative prayer not claimed may be granted if such relief had foundation in the pleading,[13] but the court cannot grant relief when there is no foundation for it in the pleadings.[14] The trial court can mould relief and grant decree as required by merits of the case.[15]

(vi) More than one relief. Where a plaintiff is, in the facts of the case, entitled to more than one relief in respect of the same cause of action, he is at liberty to sue for any or all of such reliefs under the condition that if he omits, without the permission of the court, to sue for all of such reliefs he shall be precluded from suing for the reliefs which he omitted.

Order 2, r. 2 of CPC enjoins:

"(1) *Suit to include the whole claim*— Every suit shall include the whole of the claim which the plaintiff is entitled to make in respect of the cause of action, but a plaintiff may relinquish any portion of his claim in order to bring the suit within the jurisdiction of any Court.

"(2) *Relinquishment of part of claim*— Where a plaintiff omits to sue in respect of, or intentionally relinquishes, any portion of his claim, he shall not afterwards sue in respect of the portion so omitted or relinquished.[16]

"(3) *Omission to sue for one of several reliefs*— A person entitled to more than one relief in respect of the same cause of action may sue for all or any of such reliefs, but if he omits, except with the leave of the court, to sue for all such reliefs, he shall not afterwads sue for any relief so omitted. "

But Order 34, r. 14(1) is an exception:

"Where a mortgagee has obtained a decree for the payment of money in satisfaction of a claim arising under the mortgage, he shall not be entitled to bring the mortgaged property to sale otherwise than by instituting a suit for sale in enforcement of the mortgage, and he may institute such suit notwithstanding anything contained in Order II, rule 2."

It is not necessary for the plaintiff to pray for general relief such as 'costs of the suit' or 'other relief' which may always be given as the court may think just to the same extent as if it had been asked for (*vide* Or. 7, r. 7 of CPC), e.g. in the prayer portion, prayers—

(*i*) 'All costs of suit.'

11 *Union of India* v *Jotirmoyee Sharma* AIR 1967 Cal 461; AIR 1971 P&H 21.

12 *Union of India* v *Ibrahim Uddin* (2012)8 SCC 148; (2012)4 SCC (Civ) 362; *Om Prakash* v *Ram Kumar* AIR 1991 SC 409.

13 *Khali Panigrahi* v *Kamala Devi* AIR 1967 Ori 100.

14 *Dula Dei* v *Jadi Bewa* AIR 1965 Ori 113.

15 *Bhondoo* v *Udatro* AIR 1970 All 307. On admission of defendant without amendment of plaint—*State of Rajasthan* v *Associated Stone Industries* AIR 1971 Raj 128.

16 *Chhotabhai Jethabhai Patel* v *Union of India* AIR 1971 Cal 221; *Governor-General in Council* v *Mussaddi Lal* AIR 1961 SC 725.

(*ii*) 'Such other and further relief, as law and equity would allow the plaintiff in the facts and circumstances of the case'

are quite unnecessary though it is largely the practice.

Where the plaintiff claims a larger relief, the court will not dismiss the suit but give the plaintiff only such smaller relief involved in that larger one, if he is so entitled to.[17] But where the plaintiff claims less than what he is entitled to, the court will not grant him any relief he has not specifically claimed unless the plaint is amended before the judgment. But the court should not refuse to grant a relief not specifically asked for in the plaint, if such relief is obviously required by the nature of the case and is not inconsistent with the relief claimed or with the case raised by the pleadings.[18]

(e) ***Facts showing jurisdiction of the court.*** We have acquired a habit to insert in a plaint a bare statement "the court has jurisdiction to try the suit". But under provisions of Or. 7, r. 1(*f*) we are required to state facts which would show that the court has jurisdiction to try the suit.

For questions on jurisdiction, provisions in ss. 16, 19 and 20 of the Code of Civil Procedure may be referred to. Briefly speaking, a suit shall be instituted either where the cause of action or any part thereof arose or where all the defendants reside or carry on business or personally work for gain. Accordingly, the plaintiff has to show which of the above positions attracts jurisdiction in the particular suit. Parties cannot by agreement confer jurisdiction on the court not possessed by it under the Code. But an agreement that one of the courts having such jurisdiction shall alone try the dispute is not contrary to public policy and does not contravene s. 28 of the Contract Act.[19] If there are more than one court having territorial jurisdiction over the subject-matter, agreement conferring it on one court, neither is violative of s. 28 of the Contract Act nor against public policy.[20]

CONSIGNMENT NOTE LIMITING JURISDICTION. Third party is not bound by such terms.[21] The condition is consignment note restricting the jurisdiction to certain court alone would not in any way create bar to the filing of the suit for loss or damage of goods when the consignor or any person duly authorised by him had not signed the consignment note. It cannot be assumed that there is an agreement which would constitute estoppel creating a bar in maintaining the suit in any other court than the court mentioned in the consignment note. Mere printing on the consignment note will not constitute an agreement.[1] Written hire-purchase agreement providing for filing of suits in courts in particular place alone—objection to territorial jurisdiction of courts at that

17 *Khanta Mandalani* v *Hem Kumari Debi* AIR 1941 Pat 29.

18 *Gulabgir* v *Nathmal* AIR 1932 Nag 23; *Imam Din* v *Nizam Dian* AIR 1933 Lah 267.

19 *Hakam Singh* v *Gammon (India) Ltd.* AIR 1971 SC 740. Also see *Tulasi Ram* v *Jeet Goods Carrier Branch* AIR 1977 NOC 189 (All). Also see *Patel Roadways* v *Bata India Ltd.* AIR 1982 Cal 575.

20 *Thakral & Sons* v *Indian Petro Chemicals* AIR 1994 Del 226.

21 *East India Tpt Agency* v *National Ins. Co. Ltd.* AIR 1991 AP 53.

1 *South Eastern Road Ways* v *United India Insurance* AIR 1991 Ker 41.

place cannot be sustained.[2] The court arriving at a conclusion that it has no jurisdiction to try the suit the proper order to pass is not dismissal of suit but return of plaint for presentation to proper court.[3]

Words 'subject to Kolhapur jurisdiction' on the Goods Forwarding Note (Consignment Note of the Carriers). Suit filed against carriers at Poona (destination). The argument that the Kolhapur court had no inherent jurisdiction and, therefore, merely by incorporating such words as 'subject to Kolhapur jurisdiction' in the Goods Forwarding Note the jurisdiction to entertain a suit could not be conferred on Kolhapur court was therefore untenable. 'A person who signs a document which contains contractual terms is normally bound by them even though he has not read them and even though he is ignorant of their precise legal effect. It is only when the document is not signed but is merely delivered to him that the question would arise whether the terms of the contract were adequately brought to his notice.[4] Subject to jurisdiction of court at particular place'—the parties could not by any private agreement confer or take away the jurisdiction, but the courts could compel the parties to abide by their contract if there is such a contract and if there is no circumstance indicating otherwise, the courts would compel the parties to abide by their contracts.[5]

'Subject to Anand jurisdiction' in the endorsement of the receipt does not contain the ouster clause using the words like 'alone', 'only', 'exclusive' and the like. It did not exclude the jurisdiction of all other courts who were otherwise competent to entertain the suit.[6]

Dismissal of suit for want of pecuniary jurisdiction is not proper. Court should have returned the plaint under Or. 7, r. 10 for presentation to the proper court.[7]

The opposite view may also be noticed. Calcutta firm 'B' supplying goods to Rajahmundry firm 'A' on A's indent. Goods received at Rajahmundry in bad condition. A filed a suit for damages at Rajahmundry. Held, Rajahmundry court had jurisdiction to try the suit. Words 'subject to Calcutta jurisdiction' in B's bill did not exclude jurisdiction.[8]

When two courts have jurisdiction, choice of forum is with the plaintiff and not with the defendant.[9] Court lacking inherent jurisdiction to try a suit—consent, waiver or acquiescence by parties to the suit cannot confer it.[10]

2 *Vasireddi Seetharamaiah* v *Srirama Motor Finance* AIR 1977 AP 164.
3 *RSDV Finance Co.* v *Shree Vallabh Glass Works* AIR 1993 SC 2094.
4 *Ghatge & Patil* v *Madhusudan Ramkumar* AIR 1977 Bom 299.
5 *Bhagatram Goyal* v *Gupta Cables* AIR 1977 Cal 451; AIR 1962 AP 452.
6 *RSDV Finance* v *Shree Vallabh Glass Works* AIR 1993 SC 2094 at p. 2098 relying on *A.B.C. Laminart* v *A.P. Agencies* AIR 1989 SC 1239.
7 *Vijay Kumar* v *Ballav Raj* AIR 1992 Del 233.
8 *Grandhi Pitchaiah* v *Palukuri Jagannadhan* AIR 1975 AP 32; *Patel Bros.* v *Vadilal Kashidas* AIR 1959 Mad 227; *Kanpur Sugar Supply* v *Harsukh Lal* AIR 1971 All 502 relied on AIR 1962 AP 452 and *Jhun Jhunwala Bros.* v *NKM Subbaramier* AIR 1968 Mad 194.
9 *Narayan Pillai* v *Gopala Pillai* AIR 1974 Ker 27.
10 *Chandra Bhushan Khanna* v *Brij Nandan Singh* AIR 1978 All 459.

But when the court passing decree lacks territorial jurisdiction, the decree would not be totally a nullity. Defect as to territorial jurisdiction can be waived.[11]

Some illustrations are given below:

(*i*) In a suit for khas possession— "That the suit property lies at village .... P.S. .... Dt. ....

(*ii*) In a suit for recovery of loan— "That the defendant took loan of ₹ .... at ...... Cooch Behar, within the jurisdiction of this court."

The plaint allegations alone and not the defence or evidence let in by parties should decide the question of jurisdiction.[12] Therefore, all the facts showing that the court has jurisdiction should be set out in the plaint, and if any special jurisdiction vested in the court by law is invoked, all the facts which call for the exercise of that jurisdiction should be set out.[13]

To sum up: It is for the plaintiff to allege specifically and prove how the court has jurisdiction. A bare statement in the plaint that the cause of action arose within its jurisdiction is certainly not enough.[14]

(f) ***Statement of the value of the subject-matter of the suit for the purposes of jurisdiction and of court-fees.*** Valuation of the subject-matter[15] of a suit has twofold purposes:

(*i*) Pecuniary jurisdiction.

(*ii*) Payment of court-fees.

Where the valuations in a suit are twofold and such valuations are different, they have to be stated specifically, to wit, (*i*) valuation for the purpose of jurisdiction, and (*ii*) valuation for the purpose of court-fees. No harm if stated in one and the same paragraph (*see* exception in West Bengal—Footnotes).[15]

In a case where more reliefs than one, based on the same cause of action are sought either jointly or in the alternative, the fees shall be paid according to the value of the relief in respect of which the largest fee is payable [s. 17(2) of the Court-fees Act].

Where again, the plaintiff claims separate and distinct reliefs in respect of two or more separate and distinct causes of action, he is called upon to state the valuation of each cause of action separately, the court-fees being

11 *Chandra Bhushan Khanna* v *Brij Nandan Singh* AIR 1978 All 459; *Nandarani Bose* v *Ranchhoddas Muldani* AIR 1981 Cal 275.

12 *Madan Lal L. Rajaram v Munsidatu* AIR 1956 Pepsu 80.

13 *Jakhu* v *Dhanji Pasu* AIR 1952 Kutch 77.

14 *Ramaswami* v *Velayathan Pillai* AIR 1938 Mad 496.

15 In the State of West Bengal, Civil Rules & Orders, issued by the Calcutta High Court, is followed. Rule 22: "It should be clear in every plaint how the valuation has been calculated".

Rule 254 (Notes). "Valuations for purposes of jurisdiction and for payment of court-fee shall be separately shown".

payable in respect of each (*vide* s. 17 of the Court-fees Act), i.e. he shall be chargeable with the aggregate amount of the fees with which plaints would be chargeable under the Court-fees Act in separate suits instituted in respect of each such cause of action.

Again, where the plaintiff claims relief in the alternative of different values, he should state his valuation in respect of two reliefs and pay the court-fees on the value of the larger relief, i.e. the court-fees on one yielding higher court-fee need be paid.[16]

DEFICIT PAYMENT OF COURT-FEES. Deficiency of court-fees paid in High Court on Plaint and on Memo of Appeal. No exception can be taken thereafter with regard to maintainability of suit (s. 149, CPC).[17] The court is empowered to grant time for payment of additional court-fees under ss. 151 and 152 of the Code of Civil Procedure 1908.[18]

JURISDICTION OF CIVIL COURT. Section 9, CPC. Statutory authority acting in violation of rules—Civil Court can interfere.[19]

SUIT INSTITUTED WITHIN LIMITATION. The plaint was rejected for non-payment of proper court-fees but was restored to original file and number on payment of deficit in fees in exercise of inherent jurisdiction of the court—suit cannot be said to have been time-barred. Suit would be deemed to have been filed on the date it was filed.[20]

For choice of forum by agreement.[21]

Plaint comprising causes of action within territorial jurisdiction of the court as well as causes of action outside its jurisdiction—court cannot return plaint solely on ground that some of causes of action are not triable by it. In such a case the court can call upon the plaintiff to amend his plaint by striking out all such causes of action as are beyond its jurisdiction and then proceed with the plaint in respect of remaining causes of action which are within its jurisdiction. If the plaintiff does not amend the plaint, the court has to proceed to judgment with the plaint as it stands unamended on all such causes of action as are within its cognizance and to dismiss the suit in respect of the causes of action outside its jurisdiction.[22]

SUIT FOR DAMAGES AGAINST CORPORATION. Corporation has its subordinate office in place where cause of action arose. The court at such place would have jurisdiction. Parties cannot confer jurisdiction on court where Corporation has its principal office.[1]

(I) *VALUATION FOR THE PURPOSE OF PECUNIARY JURISDICTION*. Valuation of a suit is required to be given in a plaint to determine the pecuniary jurisdiction of

16 AIR 1932 Mad 158.
17 *Mst. Saimunissa* v *Sk. Mohinddin* AIR 1991 Pat 183.
18 *Shaikah Habibullah* v *Md. Sultan Khan* AIR 2001 Cal 22.
19 *Bimal Sahoo* v *Gauri Rani Pahari* AIR 1991 Cal 120.
20 *Sk. Nafel Ali* v *Sm. Nihar Bala Das* AIR 1981 Cal 273.
21 *Biswanath Chowdhury* v *U.P. Forest Corporation* AIR 1986 Cal 334.
22 *Sheela Adhikary* v *Rabindra Nath Adhikary* AIR 1988 Cal 273.
1 *Patel Roadways* v *Prasad Trading Co.* AIR 1992 SC 1514.

a court, i.e. whether the suit according to the value of the subject-matter shall have to be filed in this court or that court.

(II) VALUATION FOR PURPOSES OF COURT-FEES. The Court-fees Act provides rates of court-fees to be paid on a suit according to the value of the subject-matter. The rates are not uniform in all the States and different charts are there with different scales of fees and then again on different reliefs.The object of inserting valuation for court-fees is to see that the plaint is sufficiently stamped with reference to valuation of the subject-matter of the suit.

Where the value of the property is the basis that value should be given, e.g. "the suit property is valued at ₹3,000 and *ad valorem* court-fees are paid". In a suit for declaration the valuation is given: "that the suit is valued at ₹3,000 for purposes of jurisdiction of the court and for reliefs of declaration fixed court-fees of ₹20 are paid". And, so on.

One point more in respect of valuation: if no objection is made to the valuation given in the plaint, that matter must be deemed to be final between the parties and the parties cannot be allowed to take up that question.[2] In a suit for declaration with consequential relief valuation by plaintiff is ordinarily to be accepted.[3]

(g) Statement of representative capacity in a suit (Or. 7, r. 4). When a suit is brought in representative capacity, say, under Or. 1, r. 8, the plaint shall contain a statement to that effect. If leave of the court is necessary to commence a suit of the said character and the leave has been obtained that should find place in the body of the plaint. The plaint should show that the plaintiff is qualified to do so whenever such is the case.[4] A suit would not be dismissed on the ground that the plaint has been signed by the Director of a company not properly authorised.[5]

Order 7, r. 4 enjoins: "Where the plaintiff sues in a representative character, the plaint shall show not only that he has an actual existing interest in the subject-matter, but that he has taken the steps (if any) necessary to enable him to institute a suit concerning it."

Under Or. 7, r. 4 the plaintiff has to satisfy two conditions:

(*i*) that the plaintiff has an actual existing interest in the subject-matter; and

(*ii*) that the plaintiff has taken the steps (if any) necessary to enable him to institute a suit concerning the same 'subject-matter'.

Where the plaintiff has no existing interest in the subject-matter, he is not entitled to sue in a representative character. A *shebait* can bring suit for protection of the interest of the idol. An administrator with Letters of

2 *Deonath Missir* v *Chandraman Missir* AIR 1958 Pat 430.

3 *Tara Devi* v *Thakur Radha Krishna Maharaj* AIR 1987 SC 2085 (*Sathappa Chettiar* v *Ramanathan Chettiar* AIR 1958 SC 245 and *Meenakshisundaram* v *Venkata Chalam* AIR 1979 SC 989 relied on).

4 AIR 1925 Nag 183.

5 *Private Eye (P) Ltd.* v *Hind High Vaccum Co. Pvt. Ltd.* AIR 2003 Kant 95.

Administration can successfully bring a suit. At the beginning we have submitted that the plaintiff should show that he is qualified to do so. Not only that, it is to be seen that the plaintiff has, before institution of the suit, taken steps to qualify him.

Order 7, r. 9 provides for procedure on admitting plaint. "Where the court orders that the summons be served on the defendants in the manner provided in r. 9 of Or. 5, it will direct the plaintiff to present as many copies of the plaint on plain paper as there are defendants within seven days from the date of such order along with requisite fee for service of summons on the defendants".

'Executor' not described as such in title of suit but in the body of the plaint is described as such—suit should not be dismissed.[6] Where a suit brought by or against a person in a representative capacity, it is not necessary to state in the cause title of the plaint the representative capacity in which the plaintiff or the defendant sues or is sued, although no doubt that is the convenient place to make such a statement. At any rate the failure to make such a statement in the Cause Title of the plaint would not be a defect of the party but would merely be a matter which the court might allow to amend by adding a statement to the plaint that the plaintiff or the defendant was suing or was being sued in his representative capacity.[7]

To illustrate—in a suit by a person, as an administrator, the plaint should state that the plaintiff has obtained the Letters of Administration. An idol can sue and be sued only through its *shebait.* The right of suit is vested in the *shebait* (Practice: Idol is allowed to sue). In a suit of representative character it is sufficient if the plaint shows that the plaintiff is a *shebait.*

(h) *Grounds of exemption from law of limitation (Or. 7, r. 6).* Order 7, r. 6 enjoins: "Where the suit is instituted after the expiration of the period prescribed by the law of limitation, the plaint shall show the ground upon which exemption from such law is claimed:

Provided that the court may permit the plaintiff to claim exemption from the law of limitation on any ground not set out in the plaint, if such ground is not inconsistent with the grounds set out in the plaint."

The language is clear. The plaintiff has to show that his cause of action accrued within the period of limitation.

Where the claim is barred by limitation but the plaintiff intends to proceed with the claim by pleading an exemption from the law of limitation on the basis of some exemption, the plaint has to contain the facts by which exemption is sought for.[8] We would recall here the provisions of Or. 7, r. 11(*d*)—if the claim is barred by the general rule of limitation, and the ground of exemption is not alleged, the plaint is liable to be rejected".

6 *Smt. Jagattarini Dasi* v *Prafulla Chandra Bose* 35 IC 792.

7 *Bidhu Sekhar Banerjee* v *Kutoda Prasad Deogharia* 50 IC 525.

8 *Krishna Ch. Bhaumick* v *Pabna Dhanabhandar* AIR 1935 Cal 225; *Rameswami Chetti* v *Anaiya Padayachi* AIR 1936 Mad 545.

If a suit was filed after expiration of limitation period, the suit may be rejected if the ground of exemption from limitation was not pleaded.[9] If a plaint does not show ground of exemption, the plaintiff cannot be allowed to raise it[10] at the time of trial by putting in evidence and document, such as acknowledgment of liability. A plainitff claiming exemption from any rule of limitation on the ground of fraud must allege it in the plaint, stating when such fraud became known to him.[11] The plaintiff must show in his pleading the grounds upon which an exemption from limitation is claimed.[12]

The judicial pronouncements are worth consideration: It is sufficient that the grounds of exemption are apparent on the face of the plaint. It is not necessary that the plaint should specifically, and in so many words, claim the ground of exemption.[13] Mere technical non-compliance is not fatal when facts on which exemption from law of limitation is claimed appear from the face of the record.[14]

Let us refer to a few illustrations:

(*i*) Where the fact of minority is apparent on the face of the record, it is not necessary that the ground of exemption should be specifically pleaded; for, "the courts are bound to apply the law of limitation to suits, whether it is pleaded or not, and to dismiss a suit which is apparently out of time. Conversely, they are bound not to dismiss as barred a suit which, on the face of it, is not barred".[15]

(*ii*) If the facts referring to the acknowledgment are sufficiently set out in the plaint, it would suffice and the plaint would be considered as embodying sufficient averments which would take the claim from the bar of limitation.[16]

(*iii*) Where a plaint is presented on the reopening date after court holidays, and the period of limitation has expired during the holidays, the fact that the ground of exemption was not specifically mentioned in the plaint will not entail the dismissal of the suit, inasmuch as the court is bound to take judicial notice of holidays.

(*iv*) Where a plaint presented to a wrong court is returned for presentation to the proper court, the endorsements on the plaint will show the applicability of s. 14 of the Limitation Act 1963, and, therefore, it is not necessary to specifically allege that ground of exemption.[17]

BENEFIT OF S. 14, LIMITATION ACT. Expression 'good faith' qualifies prosecuting proceeding in court having no jurisdiction. Error in valuing suit or wrong

9 *T.K. George* v *Dr. T.K. Koshy* AIR 2002 NOC 6 (Ker).

10 *Jogeshwar Roy & Binod Behari* v *Ram Narain Mitter* ILR 31 Cal 195.

11 *Kalyanmal* v *Ahmed Uddin Khan* AIR 1934 PC 208.

12 *Shah Manmall Missimall* v *K. Radhakrishnan* AIR 1972 Mad 108.

13 *Shiv Dayal* v *Ramrikh* AIR 1955 Raj 188; *Halsnad Madappaya* v *P. Mahabala Rao* AIR 1937 Mad 826.

14 *Chowa Mahato* v *Jnani Ram* AIR 1967 Pat 301.

15 *Gangadhar Sarkar* v *Khaja Abdul Ajij* 2 IC 77.

16 *N. Subramanian* v *S. Kalyanarayana* AIR 1958 Ker 243.

17 *Binodilal* v *Satyendrasingh* AIR 1956 MB 97.

computation of court-fees cannot be grounds for denying benefits of s. 14 to the plaintiff.[18]

If the grounds of exemption from limitation law are not taken in the plaint and if there is no application to amend the plaint, the suit ought to be dismissed as barred by limitation.[19] This is an age old law.

SECTION 5 OF THE LIMITATION ACT 1963—CONDONATION OF DELAY. Courts should adopt liberal approach as a principle for the following reasons:

(1) Ordinarily a litigant does not stand to benefit by lodging an appeal late.

(2) Refusing to condone delay can result in a meritorious matter thrown out at the very threshold and cause justice being defeated. As against this when delay is condoned the highest that can happen is that a cause would be decided on merits after hearing the parties.

(3) 'Every day's delay must be explained' does not mean that a pedantic approach should be made. Why not every hour's delay? every second's delay? The doctrine must be applied in a rational commonsense pragmatic manner.

(4) When substantial justice and technical considerations are pitted against each other, cause of substantial justice deserves to be preferred for the other side cannot claim to have vested right in injustice being done because of a non-deliberate delay.

(5) There is no presumption that delay is occasioned deliberately, or on account of culpable negligence or on account of *mala fides*. A litigant does not stand to benefit by resorting to delay. In fact, he runs a serious risk.

(6) It must be grasped that judiciary is respected not on account of its power to legalize injustice on technical grounds but because it is capable of removing injustice and is expected to do so.[20]

Application for condonation of delay made by the State Government. Treatment similar to any other litigant ought to be accorded to the State. The fact that it was the State which was seeking condonation and not a private party was irrelevant. The doctrine of equality before law demands that all litigants, including the 'State' as a litigant are accorded the same treatment and the law is administered in an even-handed manner. There is no warrant for according a step-motherly treatment when the State is the applicant praying for condonation of delay.[21] Case of delay when Government is applicant for condonation.[1]

The legislature has conferred the power to condone the delay in enacting s. 5 of the Limitation Act in order to enable the courts to do substantial justice to parties ... "sufficient cause" was adequately elastic to enable the courts to

18 *Vijay Kumar Rampal* v *Dewan Devi* AIR 1985 SC 1669.

19 *Palani Chetti* v *Sevugan Chetti* AIR 1933 Mad 395.

20 *Collector, Land Acquisition, Anantnag* v *Mst. Katiji* AIR 1987 SC 1353.

21 *Ibid*, p. 1354.

1 *G. Ranegowda, Major* v *Special Land Acquisition Officer, Bangalore* AIR 1988 SC 897; *State of Nagaland* v *Lipak* AIR 2005 SC 2191; (2005)3 SCC 753.

apply the law in a meaningful manner which subserves the ends of justice, which is the life purpose of the existence of the institution of courts.[2]

Leading of oral evidence while adjudicating an application under Or. 41, r. 3A (2), CPC or s. 5 of the Limitation Act is not permissible. The question of limitation has to be decided on the basis of affidavits filed on record.[3]

Section 3, Limitation Act. *One word more*: There cannot be waiver of limitation or estoppel against plea of Limitation.[4]

(i) ***Statement of set-off or relinquishment of a portion of plaintiffs' claim [Or. 7, r. 1(h)].*** The plaintiff has to state in a suitable place in the plaint the amount set-off or relinquished, if any.

"The amount set-off or relinquished should be specified with precision or at least should be stated in such a manner that the amount may be inferred from the other allegations in the plaint". *P* sued *D* stating that ₹1,191 was due to him, that he relinquished ₹491 thereof and that a decree should be passed for the balance ₹700. It was found that something less than ₹1,191 but more than ₹700 was due to *P* from *D*. Held that *P* was entitled to a decree for ₹700.[5]

(j) ***Rejection and/or return of a plaint.*** Order 7, CPC, provisions of rr. 10 and 11 of Or. 7 have their own fields of operation and should not be intervened. The scope of r. 10 is confined only to jurisdictional defect and in case the court finds that the particular suit is not entertainable by it and that it should have been filed in some other court the only course open to it, is to direct its return for being filed in the proper court.

Rule 11 will, however, come to the picture when the plaint on being presented is admitted and found to be within the cognizance of that court. But despite this the plaint, on the face of it, may suffer from some defect of the nature mentioned in cls. (*a*), (*b*) and (*d*) r. 11 of rule because of which the same cannot be sustained. It is in those circumstances that the court can exercise the power to reject the plaint.

No doubt cases of jurisdictional defect can also arise under cl. (*d*) of r. 11 only if recourse to r. 10 is not possible for want of another court where the plaint could be presented or where there is a statutory bar. In either of these cases the plaint can be rejected for defect of jurisdiction also.[6]

The plea that there is no cause of action for suit is not a ground of rejection of a plaint.[7] If application for return or rejection of plaint under Or. 7, rr. 10 and 11 is not filed, court cannot order for return of the plaint.[8] A court has power to reject a plaint at any stage of proceeding even without an application by a party, if it finds that the conditions under Or. 7, r. 11 exist.[9]

2 *Collector, Land Acquisition, Anantnag* v *Mst. Katiji* AIR 1987 SC 1353.
3 *Birendra Nath Singh* v *Santa Devi* AIR 1992 Pat 146.
4 *Ajab Enterprises* v *Jyant Vegoiles* AIR 1991 Bom 35.
5 8 IC 943.
6 *Governing Council of Kayastha Pathsala* v *Ram Chandra Srivastav* AIR 1992 All 158.
7 *British Airways* v *Art Works Export* AIR 1986 Cal 120.
8 *Exphar SA* v *Eupharma Laboratories Ltd.* AIR 2004 SC 1682.
9 *Vithalbhai (P) Ltd.* v *Union Bank of India* AIR 2005 SC 1891; (2005)4 SCC 315.

A civil court under Or. 6, r. 17 can allow the plaint to be so amended as to result in ousting its own jurisdiction in the matter and in case the amendment is allowed and carried out the proper course to be followed is to return the amended plaint to the plaintiff for presentation in the proper court under Or. 7, r. 10, CPC.[10] Court's power to allow amendment of the pleadings cannot be restricted or controlled by the provision of Or. 7, r. 11, CPC.[11]

Where a suit is filed in a court not having pecuniary jurisdiction the suit should not be dismissed. Court should have returned the plaint under Or. 7, r. 10 for presentation to proper court. The remedy of appeal under Or. 43, r. 1(*a*) is available.

The rejection of the plaint on any of the grounds mentioned in rr. 10 and 11 of Or. 7 shall not of its own force preclude the plaintiff from presenting a fresh plaint in respect of the same cause of action.

(k) *Preliminary issue.* Under Or. 14, r. 2, the court is to pronouncc judgment on all issues. But under sub-rule (2)(*a*) where issues both of law and of facts arise in the same suit, and the court is of opinion that the case or any part thereof may be disposed of on an issue of law only, it may try that issue first if that issue relates to—

(*a*) the jurisdiction of the court, or

(*b*) a bar to the suit created by any law for the time being in force,

and for that purpose may, if it thinks fit, postpone the settlement of other issues until after that issue has been determined, and may deal with the suit in accordance with the decision on that issue.

We have the legal position explained in the reported decision in *Manager Bettiah Estate* v *Bhagawati Saran Singh*.[12] Only an issue of law can be decided as a preliminary issue only where it is such that its decision does not necessitate investigation into facts and it relates either to jurisdiction of the court or to the suit being barred under any prevailing law, and that, in the opinion of the court, the decision of the issue will result in the decision of the whole or a part of the suit. The discretion in this regard must always be exercised on the basis of sound judicial principles. It may, however, be made clear that even if an issue of law can be decided as a preliminary issue as aforesaid the court is not always bound to decide it as a preliminary issue and can in its discretion postpone its decision also along with other issues whether of law or fact. The whole purpose behind the provision is to restrict piecemeal decision and unnecessary multi-tier Appeals at intermediate stages on preliminary issues only and thus avoid procrastination of litigation.

"The new provision justly aims at abridging the proceeding in the suit rather than permitting prolongation thereof. Territorial jurisdiction of court is a mixed question of law and fact involved and cannot be decided as a

10 *Benisham Mohonlal* v *Mahadeo Tukaram* AIR 1985 Bom 462.

11 *Lok H&C Ltd.* v *Everest Indu Ltd.* (2005)1 Mah LJ 700 (Bom).

12 AIR 1993 All 2.

preliminary issue.[13] [Contra: Issue regarding territorial jurisdiction should be tried as a preliminary issue.[14]]

When a bar to suit is created by law, e.g. *res judicata* is a question of law it constitutes a bar to suit created by law. A suit on be disposed of on this preliminary issue [Or. 14, r. 2(2)(*b*)], CPC.[15] It is no longer obligatory to try a preliminary issue first. Discretion lies with the court. Only those issues falling under cls. (*a*), (*b*) and (*d*) of r. 2(2) can be tried as preliminary issue.[16]

(l) ***Abandonment of plea (Or. 14, r. 1).*** Whenever a party raises a plea and does not have the issue raised in this regard and goes to trial and has the matter decided without having an issue raised on the plea, the party must be deemed to have given up such a plea.[17]

13 *Naresh Das* v *Gopal Das* AIR 1991 Cal 237.

14 *Femina Handloom* v *M.R. Verma* AIR 1993 Ker 210.

15 *Sri Laxmimone Dasi* v *Manik Ch. Das* AIR 1991 Cal 231; see *Smt. Sulochana Devi* v *Govinda Nag* 1986(1) CHN 58; AIR 1986 Cal 430.

16 *Sunni Wakf Board* v *Gopal Singh* AIR 1991 All 89.

17 *B.R. Mulani* v *Dr. A.B. Aswathanarayana* AIR 1993 Kant 257.

CHAPTER

4

Structure of a Written Statement

SYNOPSIS

1 Introductory—nature and purport of a written statement 'Written statement' is a term of specific connotation ordinarily signifying a reply to the plaint by the plaintiff.[1] A written statement is the defence of the defendants, an answer to the claim of the plaintiff in a suit.

Order 8, r. 1. provides that—

> *Written statement.* The defendant shall, within thirty days from the date of service of summons on him, present a written statement of his defence:
>
> Provided that where the defendant fails to file the written statement within the said period of thirty days, he shall be allowed to file the same on such other day, as may be specified by the court, for reasons to be recorded in writing, but which shall not be later than ninety days from the date of service of summons.
>
> In its application to commercial disputes of a Specific Value in Or. 8, r. 1, the proviso runs as follows:
>
> Provided that where the defendant fails to file the written statement within the said period of thirty days, he shall be allowed to file the

1 *Food Corporation of India* v *Yadav Engineer & Contractor* AIR 1982 SC 1302; (1982)2 SCC 499; *Rachappa Guruadappa, Bijapur* v *Gurusiddappa Nuraniappa* AIR 1989 SC 635; JT 1988(4) SC 497.

written statement on such other day, as may be specified by the court, for reasons to be recorded in writing and on payment of such costs as the court deems fit, but which shall not be later than one hundred twenty days from the date of service of summons and on expiry of one hundred twenty days from the date of service of summons, the defendant shall forfeit the right to file the written statement and the court shall not allow the written statement to be taken on record.[2]

Order 8, r. 1A. *Duty of defendant to produce documents upon which relief is claimed or relied upon by him.* (1) Where the defendant bases his defence upon a document or relies upon any document in his possession or power, in support of his defence or claim for set-off or counter-claim, he shall enter such document in a list, and shall produce it in Court when the written statement is presented by him and shall, at the same time, deliver the document and a copy thereof, to be filed with the written statement.

(2) Where any such document is not in the possession or power of the defendant, he shall, wherever possible, state in whose possession or power it is.

(3) A document which ought to be produced in Court by the defendant under this rule, but, is not so produced shall not, without the leave of the Court, be received in evidence on his behalf at the hearing of the suit.

(4) Nothing in this rule shall apply to documents:

(*a*) produced for the cross-examination of the plaintiff's witnesses, or

(*b*) handed over to a witness merely to refresh his memory.

Filing of a written statement is not discretionary. There has been a change in law the defendant. If, it is that the time to file written statement has been fixed or upto the date allowed by the court. First hearing signifies the day on which the court proceeds to frame and record the issues. The right to file a written statement at or before the first hearing can only be exercised until the date which is fixed for the first time for the final hearing of the suit and does not extend beyond that stage up to the adjourned date of the hearing.[3] The amended Code of Civil Procedure prescribes the period of limitation for filing a written statement as 90 days which would not strictly apply to the proceeding before Motor Accident Claims Tribunal.[4] Filing of a written statement by the defendant is obligatory when the defendant is so required by the court. Failure of the defendant to file a written statement on the day fixed by the court or before issues are framed, will not entitle him as of right, thereafter to file it.[5] It does not mean that the defendant will be shut out once for all. He may be permitted by the court to file it on a later date on sufficient

2 Section 16 of the Commercial Courts, Commercial Division and Commercial Appellate Division of High Courts Act 2015 (Act 4 of 2016) (w.r.e.f. 23.10.2015).

3 *Bihar State Electricity Board* v *New Gobindpur Coal Co. Pvt. Ltd.* AIR 1973 Pat 191.

4 *New India Assurance Co. Ltd.* v *Sanjoy Devshri* AIR 2005 NOC 574 (Guj).

5 AIR 1957 All 283.

grounds shown for not filing the same in time. If written statement is not filed despite several adjournments granted for the same may be order passed that the defendant may contest without it. If subsequent application for filing it before commencement of *ex parte* hearing is submitted, the court has power to entertain it under Or. 8, r. 9.[6]

> Order 8, r. 10. *Procedure when party fails to present the written statement called for by a court.* Where any party from whom a written statement is required under r. 1 or r. 9 fails to present the same within the time permitted or fixed by the Court, as the case may be, the Court shall pronounce judgment against him, or make such order in relation to the suit as it thinks fit and on the pronouncement of such judgment a decree shall be drawn up.

Written statement not filed within time permitted by trial court. It can be admitted by trial court under Or. 8, r. 10 even at the stage when *ex parte* hearing was concluded and the matter was adjourned for delivery of judgment.[7] When a written statement was not filed within 90 days, right to file is not lost, court may condone the delay.[8]

The time limit can be extended only in exceptionally hard cases. While extending time, it has to be borne in mind that the legislature has fixed the upper limit of ninety days. The discretion of the court to extend the time shall not be so frequently and routinely exercised so as to nullify the period fixed under Or. 8, r. 1, CPC.[9] A court has no power to time beyond 90 days in filing written statement.[10]

2 Condonation of delay A petition for condonation of delay in filing the written statement must reveal sufficient cause. When filing of the suit was followed by miscellaneous petition and the defendants were prevented from filing the written statement in time in view of the intervening application including appeal, it would constitute sufficient cause for condoning the delay.[11] When the defendant has valid reason for not filing the written statement within 90 days, the right to file the written statement is not lost, and the court would condone the delay.[12]

When there is negligence on the part of the defendant in filing written statement and the delay was not properly explained, the defendant should not be allowed to file written statement.[13]

For non-compliance we may refer to r. 10 which reads as follows: "Where any party, from whom a written statement is required under r. 1 or r. 9 fails

6 *Kali Pado Sharma* v *Surendra Nath Mahatha* AIR 1975 Pat 24.

7 *Ramesh Chandra* v *Corporation of Calcutta* AIR 1987 Cal 111; AIR 1974 Del 35 and AIR 1978 MP 39 relying on.

8 *S.G. Narayana Swamy* v *Ramkrishnappa* AIR 2003 NOC 378 (Kant).

9 *Salem Advocate Bar Association* v *Union of India* AIR 2005 SC 3353.

10 *A. Satyapal* v *Yasmin Banu Ansari* AIR 2004 Kant 246; *Liyakhath Ali* v *H.N. Lolitheswar* AIR 2004 Kant 271.

11 *Prakash Bishu Chettri* v *Rabin Rai* AIR 2010 Sikk 24.

12 *Ashok Kadermani* v *State of Karnataka* AIR 2005 Kant 124.

13 *Branch Manager, Hazaribagh Branch National Insurance Co. Ltd.* v *Anand Prakash Handa* AIR 2012 Jhar 6.

to present the same within the time permitted or fixed by the court, as the case may be, the court shall pronounce judgment against him, or make such order in relation to the suit as it thinks fit, and on the pronouncement of such judgment a decree shall be drawn up".

When the written statement has not been filed by the defendant within the time stipulated in r. 1 or r. 9 of Or. 8, CPC, the court can exercise its option either to pronounce the judgment or to make such order as it thinks fit. The court need not necessarily pronounce the judgment but make such order in relation to the suit as it thinks fit.[14]

Omission to file a written statement does not necessarily mean admission of facts in the plaint. But, according to a decision of the Bombay High Court, "such failure means only that he admits the allegations in the plaint, and he is entitled to appear and submit any argument open to him on the plaint".[15] Under this rule, the court has the right to pronounce a judgment but before pronouncing a judgment, "the court should go into the case and pronounce a decision upon the facts so far as they are before it."[16]

If the defendant admits and relies on such facts as are asserted in the plaint, those need not be repeated in the written statement. The whole object of pleadings is that each side may be fully alive to the questions that are about to be argued in order that they may have an opportunity of bringing forward such evidence as may be appropriate.[17]

Evidentiary value of admission in a written statement. True, the general rule is that pleading is no part of evidence. But where a defendant made an admission in his written statement against his own interest and none of the co-defendants who were claiming through the defendant in question and to whose interest the admission, was detrimental, did not examine the defendant who made the admission, the adversary was entitled to use the admission to his advantage when the co-defendants did not state that the defendant making admission was not able to come to court and depose and there was no evidence that the defendant was in collusion with the adversary-plaintiffs.[18]

3 Defendant may participate even without written statement If the court after refusing to extend time to file written statement, directs that the defendant though not filing is entitled to take part in the proceeding, such order is valid. The defendant without filing a written statement cannot challenge the maintainability of the suit and cannot pray for rejection of the plaint. If the court at that stage allows such prayer and rejects the plaint such order is bad in law and is liable to be set aside.[19]

4 Contents of a written statement

(*i*) Heading;

14 *Kailash* v *Nanhku* AIR 2005 SC 2441; (2005)4 SCC 480.
15 AIR 1938 Bom 470.
16 15 IC 212.
17 *Lakshmi Narain Ram Narain* v *State of Bihar* AIR 1977 Pat 73.
18 *Sita Ram* v *Droupadi Devi* AIR 1984 Pat 35.
19 *Nishit M. Prabhu* v *Chandranath* AIR 1986 Bom 46.

(*ii*) Body of a written statement; and

(*iii*) Signature and verification.

(*i*) The heading of a written statement contains—

Name of the court, suit number, names of parties with their respective places of residence. Then: "The written statement on behalf of the Defendant No. 2" etc.

The Defendant No. 2 states—

....

(*ii*) *Body of a written statement* contains objections on fact and on points of law.

(*iii*) The written statement has to be signed and verified (*see* Chapters 6 & 7 *infra*).

5 Doctrine of traverse—non-traverse—result When a defendant denies the facts alleged in the plaint, he is said to traverse.

Three fundamental rules of traverse are:

Order 8, r. 3. *Denial to be specific*. "It shall not be sufficient for a defendant in his written statement to deny generally the grounds alleged by the plaintiff, but the defendant must deal specifically with each allegation of fact of which he does not admit the truth, except damages". Denial must be clear, explicit and unambiguous. A general statement that the plaintiff's allegations are not admitted will not be enough or a proper compliance with the rule.

Order 8, r. 4. *Evasive denial.* "Where a defendant denies an allegation of fact in the plaint, he must not do so evasively, but answer the point of substance. Thus, if it is alleged that he received a certain sum of money, it shall not be sufficient to deny that he received that particular amount, but he must deny that he received that sum or any part thereof, or else set out how much he received. And if an allegation is made with diverse circumstances, it shall not be sufficient to deny it along with those circumstances".

Again, Or. 8, r. 5 enjoins:

Specific denial. (1) Every allegation of fact in the plaint, if not denied specifically or by necessary implication, or stated to be not admitted in the pleading of the defendant, shall be taken to be admitted except as against a person under disability.[20]

Provided that the Court may in its discretion require any fact so admitted to be proved otherwise than by such admission.

(2) Where the defendant has not filed a pleading, it shall be lawful for the Court to pronounce judgment on the basis of the facts contained

20 What has been alleged in the plaint, but has not been denied in the written statement, must be deemed to have been admitted by the defendant for all practical purposes—*South India Corporation (Agencies) Pvt. Ltd.* v *State Trading Corporation of India* AIR 1970 Ker 138.

in the plaint, except as against a person under a disability, but the Court may, in its discretion, require any such fact to be proved.

(3) In exercising its discretion under the proviso to sub-rule (1) or under sub-rule (2), the Court shall have due regard to the fact whether the defendant could have, or has, engaged a pleader.

(4) Whenever a judgment is pronounced under this rule, a decree shall be drawn up in accordance with such judgment and such decree shall bear the date on which the judgment was pronounced."

The simple meaning of this rule is that every allegation of fact in the plaint will be deemed to be admitted if in the written statement it is neither specifically denied nor specifically stated to be not admitted.[21]

Denial must be specific or by necessary implication. A general denial cannot mean a denial by implication. Each and every fact alleged in the plaint has to be traversed. Otherwise, the plaintiff is relieved from the onerous task of proving his allegations in the plaint as are neither specifically denied nor stated to be not admitted in the written statement. But in *Edmuond Francis Heberlet* v *Mustt. Fatima Khatoon*[1] it is held that specific denial is not necessary in all cases. When it is denied that the defendant has made *any* construction on roof at the premises, word 'any' is good enough to cover all situations and all descriptions. It is not necessary to state that the defendant denies that he made construction of any room or other construction.

The rule has application when the defendant files a written statement. If the defendant did not file a written statement at all, the question of admission is irrelevant. In a suit filed against two Railway administrations, one of them did not enter appearance. The suit as filed was bad for want of notice under s. 77, Indian Railways Act (now s. 192 of the Railways Act 1989). It was contended that since no specific objection was taken by the Railway that did not appear, the objection as to want of notice must be deemed to have been impliedly waived under Or. 8, r. 5. *Held,* Or. 8, r. 5 applies where the defendant resists the suit and files a written statement. This rule specifically refers to 'pleading of the defendant'. Where a written statement is not put in, r. 5 is not attracted.[2] The court may proceed to pronounce a judgment on the allegations in the plaint or may like the plaintiff to prove his allegations in the plaint. The proviso to Or. 8, r. 5(1) adds: "Provided that the court may, in its discretion, require any fact so admitted to be proved otherwise than by such admission". A court is not justified in passing a decree on no evidence.

The rule of admission by non-denial, as contemplated in Or. 8, r. 5(1) however, does not apply where the defendant is a person under disability. A minor, a person of unsound mind are persons under disability.

6 Factual objections The defendant may like to admit facts alleged by the plaintiff, but may avoid effects thereof showing justification, e.g. in a suit for defamation he may admit the allegation but plead justification.

21 AIR 1958 Pat 430.
1 AIR 2011 Cal 13.
2 *Tahsil Co.-op. Agricultural Association* v *Union of India* AIR 1968 MP 185.

The defendant may as well deny facts.

7 Legal objections or objections in point of law Those are:

The defendant may raise:

(*i*) the suit is not maintainable for want of statutory notice etc.;

(*ii*) the plaint does not disclose cause of action;

(*iii*) the plaintiff has no right to sue;

(*iv*) the suit barred by principles of *res judicata;*

(*v*) the suit barred by principles of waiver, estoppel, acquiescence;

(*vi*) the suit is barred by special enactment;

(*vii*) the court has no jurisdiction;

(*viii*) the suit is barred by limitation;

(*ix*) the suit is barred under Or. 23, r. 1, CPC, s. 34 of Specific Relief Act; Or. 2, r. 2, CPC etc.;

(*x*) the suit is bad for misjoinder of parties and causes of action;

(*xi*) the suit is premature,

and so on.

These are just illustrative and not exhaustive.

Some of these are known technically as 'special defences'. In a suit on the basis of a contract, the defendant may admit that he made the contract, but may avoid the effect of that admission by pleading performance, fraud, release, limitation etc.[3]

Order 8, r. 2, enjoins: "The defendant must raise by his pleading all matters which show the suit not to be maintainable, or that the transaction is either void or voidable in point of law, and all such grounds of defence as, if not raised, would be likely to take the opposite party by surprise, or would raise issues of fact not arising out of the plaint, as, for instance, fraud, limitation, release, payment, performance, or facts showing illegality."

Order 8, r. 2 is the special defence which takes any of the following forms, namely:

(1) All the matters which show that the suit is not maintainable must specifically be pleaded;

(2) That the transaction is either void or voidable in point of law to be specifically pleaded in the written statement;

(3) All such grounds of defence which, if not raised would likely take the plaintiff by surprise require to be specifically pleaded;

(4) If the defendant wants to raise the issue of facts not arising out of plaint, as for instance fraud, limitation, released, payment, performance or facts showing illegality has to be specifically pleaded.[4]

3 AIR 1955 Pepsu 51.

4 Ganguly, *Civil Court Practice and Procedure*, 14th Ed., p. 338.

A defendant's written statement should contain all particular defences whether in points of fact or in points of law, for he will not be allowed, as of right, to rely on any ground of defence which he has not taken in his written statement. Further, no amount of evidence can be looked into upon a plea which was never put forward.[5] It is the duty of the defendant to produce documents upon which relief is claimed or relied upon by him.[6] Alternative defence, if any, should be specifically raised.[7] Failure to raise all pleas shall indicate waiver.[8] In other words, what has been alleged in the plaint but has not been denied in the written statement must be deemed to have been admitted by the defendant for all practical purposes. That is, what is indicated under Or. 8, r. 5. Again, where a written statement merely rests content with the statement that the suit is bad for defect of parties without giving any reason as to why it is bad for defect of parties and the point is not specifically raised therein, the defect, if any, on this ground should not be allowed to defeat the whole suit.[9] This rule is of importance when facts are concerned but the defendant will not be shut out if the dispute is of law; for, the question of law can be raised without any pleading. Courts are bound to take notice of any ground of illegality appearing on facts stated in a party's pleadings or disclosed otherwise, though his opponent does not raise it in his pleadings.

When the suit is barred by limitation on the very allegation of the plaint, the defendant is entitled to raise such plea of limitation without taking such specific plea. It is also the duty of the court to see as to whether the suit was within limitation or not.[10]

8 Set-off—legal and equitable The essence of a set-off is that the defendant should have a cause of action against the plaintiff apart from the suit and not merely as a defence to the plaintiff's claim. To put it differently, the set-off is in the nature of a cross action which would be separately entertained.[11]

The relief of set-off is contained in provision of Or. 8, r. 6 of CPC which enjoins: "(1) Where in a suit for the recovery of money the defendant claims to set-off against the plaintiff's demand any ascertained sum of money legally recoverable by him from the plaintiff, not exceeding the pecuniary limits of the jurisdiction of the Court, and both parties fill the same character as they fill in the plaintiff's suit, the defendant may, at the first hearing of the suit, but not afterwards unless permitted by the Court, present the written statement containing the particulars of the debt sought to be set-off."

Following conditions must be satisfied for a claim of set-off:

(i) Suit must be for recovery of money. For example, a suit for arrears of rent, a suit for refund of consideration of kobala, a suit on a negotiable instrument and

5 AIR 1930 PC 57; AIR 1957 Pat 586.
6 Order 8, r. 1A of the Code of Civil Procedure 1908, as inserted by the CPC (Amendment) Act 1999 (w.e.f. 1.7.2002).
7 AIR 1964 SC 1254; *Biswanath Panda* v *Gadadhar Panda* AIR 1971 Ori 115.
8 *K.N. Ramakrishnan* v *C. Keral Chand* AIR 1971 Mad 150.
9 AIR 1956 Cal 625.
10 *Food Corporation of India* v *Babulal Agrawal* AIR 2004 SC 2926; (2004)2 SCC 712.
11 AIR 1954 Pat 439.

so on. A 'suit for ejectment of a tenant on ground of default but without adding a claim for recovery of a sum of money as arrears of rent is not a suit for money'.[12]

(ii) ***Defendant's claim must be for an ascertained sum of money.*** The defendant cannot plead set-off for an unascertained sum. Illustration (*c*) appended to the rule may be seen. The defendant's claim for set-off may be rejected if the defendant did not claim any ascertained specific sum by way of set-off and no court-fees was paid.[13]

(iii) ***It must be legally recoverable.*** The rule does not apply where the plaintiff is not bound by law to pay to the defendant, e.g., where the debt is barred by limitation. The plea of adjustment to which Or. 8, r. 6 will not be applicable can be raised only where prior to the date of the suit an adjustment had already been effected.[14]

(iv) ***Both parties must fill same character as they fill in plaintiff's suit.*** In order to entitle a defendant to plead a set-off it is necessary that parties should fill the same character as they fill in the plainitff's suit. An amount due to the defendant as a trustee cannot be claimed in set-off in a personal action against the defendant.

(v) ***The sum claimed by way of set-off should not exceed the pecuniary limits of jurisdiction of court.*** The value of the claim of set-off must be within the pecuniary jurisdiction of the court. Where the plaintiff brings a suit for recovery of ₹2,000, the court has pecuniary jurisdiction of ₹5,000, the defendant can claim set-off up to ₹5,000. Where the amount of set-off exceeds the pecuniary jurisdiction of the court, the defendant can reduce his claim and bring it within the jurisdiction of the court. When he so reduces his claim, he will be barred by Or. 2, r. 2, from claiming the balance afterwards by a separate suit.[15]

9 Set-off to be specifically claimed When the claim for set-off was neither raised in the written statement nor was any court-fee paid therefor, such a claim for set-off at the time of hearing is not maintainable.[16]

Order 8, r. 6(3) reads:

> "The rules relating to a written statement by a defendant apply to a written statement in answer to a claim of set-off."

The right of set-off being a ground of defence must be pleaded as part of a written statement and the court has to adjudicate a plea of set-off, even if the plaintiff fails in his claim.

As distinguished from legal set-off, discussed above, there may be equitable set-off. Where in a suit for an ascertained sum of money by way of damages for breach of contract, the defendant sets up a claim in respect of an unascertained sum by way of damages for breach of the same contract on the

12 AIR 1956 Punj 120.
13 *State Bank of India* v *Bihar Central Trading Co.* AIR 2005 Jhar 33.
14 *Durga Prasad Sharma* v *Sadasib Biswal* AIR 1969 Ori 171.
15 AIR 1942 Mad 580.
16 *Bank of Rajasthan* v *Pala Ram Gupta* AIR 2001 Del 58.

part of the plaintiff roughly estimating it to a certain amount, the set-off claimed is an equitable set-off and not a legal set-off.[17] The right of equitable set-off has always been made available to the defendant in our country, though the same cannot be claimed as a matter of right. Order 8, r. 6 does not preclude what is called an equitable set-off.[1]

In cases of mutual debits and credits, and in cases where cross demands arise out of the same transaction, or are so connected in their nature and circumstances as to make it inequitable that the plaintiff should recover and the defendant driven to a cross suit, Court of Equity in England has allowed a plea of set-off even though the amount may be unascertained. This set-off is known as an equitable set-off[2] and such a right is recognised by Indian courts.[3]

A plea of set-off could be entertained and given effect to independent of r. 6, of Or. 8.[4]

The distinction between a legal set-off and an equitable set-off is that while in the former case the court is bound to entertain and adjudicate upon the plea when raised, the defence of an equitable set-off cannot be claimed as a matter of right, but the court has discretion to adjudicate upon it in the same suit, or to order it to be dealt with in a separate suit.[5]

It is essential for a valid claim to an equitable set-off that the cross demands should have arisen out of the same transaction. A plea of equitable set-off will not be available where it relates to a different transaction.[6] The two conditions for allowing a claim of an equitable set-off are that it must arise out of the same transaction which is the basis of the plaintiff's claim and that it would be inequitable to drive the defendant to a separte suit for the purpose.[7]

To sum up: Set-off is a plea in defence, a plea available to the defendant only. It is a defence and a counter-claim combined, defence to the extent of wiping out the plaintiff's claim and a claim by the defendant in the suit itself for the balance.

10 Counter-claim Where the defendant in a suit claims an amount from the plaintiff therein below and up to the plaint-claim it is a claim for set-off *stricts sensu*; but when the claim is for an amount larger than the plaint-claim, the claim for the excess over the plaint-claim is a counter-claim which is really in the nature of another suit by the defendant against the plaintiff.[8]

Here a short discussion of rr. 6A to 6G of Or. 8, CPC may not be irrelevant:

> 6A. *Counter-claim by defendant.* (1) A defendant in a suit may, in addition to his right of pleading a set-off under rule 6, set up, by way of counter-

17 AIR 1954 Pat 30.
1 AIR 1952 Pat 73.
2 AIR 1956 Pat 199.
3 AIR 1925 Mad 830.
4 AIR 1954 Trav. Co. 243.
5 *Munshi Ram* v *Radha Kishan* AIR 1975 P&H 112.
6 AIR 1952 SC 201.
7 *M.M. & M. Refinery* v *M.S.S.I. Corpn.* AIR 1974 Mad 39.
8 *Govindji Jevat & Co.* v *C.S. & W. Mills* AIR 1968 Ker 310.

claim against the claim of the plaintiff, any right or claim in respect of a cause of action accruing to the defendant against the plaintiff either before or after the filing of the suit but before the defendant has delivered his defence or before the time limited for delivering his defence has expired, whether such counter-claim is in the nature of a claim for damages or not:

Provided that such counter-claim shall not exceed the pecuniary limits of the jurisdiction of the Court.

(2) Such counter-claim shall have the same effect as a cross-suit so as to enable the Court to pronounce a final judgment in the same suit, both on the original claim and on the counter-claim.

(3) The plaintiff shall be at liberty to file a written statement in answer to the counter-claim of the defendant within such period as may be fixed by the Court.

(4) The counter-claim shall be treated as a plaint and governed by the rules applicable to plaints.

6B. *Counter-claim to be stated.* Where any defendant seeks to rely upon any ground as supporting a right of counter-claim, he shall, in his written statement, state specifically that he does so by way of counter-claim.

6C. *Exclusion of counter-claim.* Where a defendant sets up a counter-claim and the plaintiff contends that the claim thereby raised ought not to be disposed of by way of counter-claim but in an independent suit, the plaintiff may, at any time before issues are settled in relation to the counter-claim, apply to the Court for an order that such counter-claim may be excluded, and the Court may, on the hearing of such application make such order as it thinks fit.

6D. *Effect of discontinuance of suit.* If in any case in which the defendant sets up a counter-claim, the suit of the plaintiff is stayed, discontinued or dismissed, the counter-claim may nevertheless be proceeded with.

6E. *Default of plaintiff to reply to counter-claim.* If the plaintiff makes default in putting in a reply to the counter-claim made by the defendant, the Court may pronounce judgment against the plaintiff in relation to the counter-claim made against him, or make such order in relation to the counter-claim as it thinks fit.

6F. *Relief to defendant where counter-claim succeeds.* Where in any suit a set-off or counter-claim is established as a defence against the plaintiff's claim, and any balance is found due to the plaintiff or the defendant, as the case may be, the Court may give judgment to the party entitled to such balance.

6G. *Rules relating to written statement to apply.* The rules relating to a written statement by a defendant shall apply to a written statement filed in answer to a counter-claim.

A counter-claim may be set up only in respect of claim as to which the party can bring independent action in the court in which the counter-action is brought, yet the counter-claim need not be an action of the same nature as the original action or analogous thereto. The court has the power to treat the counter-claim as a cross-suit and hear the original suit and the counter-claim together if the latter is properly stamped.[9] Order 8, r. 6A(2). The counter-claim shall be treated as a plaint and is governed by the rules applicable to plaints.

A counter-claim, as distinguished from a set-off, is in the nature of a cross-action. A counter-claim may be set up only in respect of claims as to which the party could bring an independent action in the court in which the counter-claim is brought. Where the defendant could not put forward a claim as a plaintiff, the plea of counter-claim was not entertainable.[10] The plaintiff filed a suit for pre-emption. The defendants in their written statement pleaded that they had spent a certain amount in making improvements to the property and the plaintiff's suit for pre-emption should not be decreed without making the plaintiff liable for that amount. *Held,* the defendant has no cause of action against the plaintiff, and no separate action could be maintained on the basis thereof. The claim could only be put forward as a defence to the suit and it could not be called a counter-claim.[11]

Whether plea of counter-claim is competent when there is no provision in the Code?

Yes.[12]

Though there was no provision the CPC for making a counter-claim, a court had got the power to treat the counter-claim in the plaint as a cross-suit and hear the two together if the counter-claim is properly stamped.[13]

Limitation in the case of a counter-claim runs from the date of institution of the plaintiff's suit, not from the date of filing a written statement by the defendant.[14]

A reading of r. 6A, CPC makes it clear that the counter-claim has to be treated as a cross-suit and it has to be tried along with the original claim made in the suit.

When the counter-claim has to be tried along with the original claim and all the rules of pleading apply to a counter-claim—it becomes a plaint in the cross-suit and the plaintiff is entitled to file a written statement in answer to the counter-claim of the defendant, it necessarily follows that a counter-claim, if not set up in the written statement, it has to be set up before the issues are framed, at any rate before recording of the evidence commences.

9 *Munshi Ram* v *Radha Kishan* AIR 1975 P&H 112.

10 AIR 1949 Mad 630.

11 AIR 1950 All 201; *Uthandarama Pillai* v *M.A. Pillai* AIR 1971 Mad 215—When the defendant's claim is not a counter-claim, no court-fees is payable on it.

12 The rules of the High Court Original Side do not provide for a relief by the defendant by way of a counter-claim—47 CWN 421. But see: counter-claim is recognised—AIR 1964 SC 11.

13 AIR 1955 Pat 320; AIR 1950 J&K 39; AIR 1952 Pat 73.

14 AIR 1942 Cal 559.

Once recording of evidence commences, counter-claim cannot be filed. When cause of action arose after filing of the written statement or after the expiry of date of filing, it would not come within the scope of Or. 8, r. 6A(1) of the Code of Civil Procedure 1908.[15]

"If a counter-claim is permitted to be set up after the evidence is adduced, it would cause great prejudice to the plaintiff in the suit because at the time of adducing evidence, he will not be aware of the counter-claim, as it will not be on record. Therefore, he cannot be expected to, and he is not required to, adduce evidence having a bearing on the counter-claim.

"Further, allowing the counter-claim to be set up after the evidence is recorded would be doing nothing but ignoring rr. 6A to 6G of Or. 8 of the CPC."[16]

Dismissal of counter-claim in a Title Suit as not maintainable is a decree. Revision under s. 115, CPC against such dismissal order is not maintainable.[17]

Counter-claim can be filed in a suit for specific performance. Filing of counter-claim is not restricted to money suits only.[18]

Counter-claim can be raised even after written statement is filed. It need not satisfy conditions which govern claim in the nature of set-off under Or. 8, r. 6.[19] But see: cause of action accruing after filing of written statement. Filing of counter-claim is not permissible.[20]

A counter-claim can be raised against the plaintiff not against the co-defendant.[1]

11 Right of counter-claim Right of counter-claim is an additional right. Discretion of court has to be exercised in a judicious manner and cannot be used contrary to the statutory interdiction contained in Or. 8, r. 6A, CPC.[2] The counter-claim filed by the defendant who has not filed the written statement but had the right to file the written statement is not maintainable.[3]

Setting up of a counter-claim by plaintiff to a counter-claim of defendant is not barred.[4]

To sum up: A set-off is a statutory defence to a plaintiff's action, a counter-claim is substantially a cross-action. The plea of set-off is a weapon of defence, up to the amount of the plaintiff's claim, but it is one of attack so far as the amount is in excess of the claim. The essence of a counter-claim is that the defendant should have a cause of action against the plaintiff. A counter-claim must be of such a nature that the court would have jurisdiction to entertain

15 *Santilata Tripathy* v *Krushanapriya Pani alias Tripathy* AIR 2005 NOC 316 (Ori).

16 *Parvathamma* v *K.R. Lokanath* AIR 1991 Kant 283.

17 *Narayan Chandra De* v *Pratirodh Sahini* AIR 1991 Cal 53.

18 *Kavindra Jain* v *Anil Lal* AIR 1992 MP 131; *Mahendra Kumar* v *State of M.P.* AIR 1987 SC 1395 relied on.

19 *Datta Bandu Sadale* v *Sridhar Payagonda* AIR 1992 Bom 422.

20 *Prem Narayan* v *Ram Vilash* AIR 1992 MP 29; AIR 1985 SC 1395.

1 *Jaiwant Singh Negi* v *Man Mohan Singh* AIR 2010 Uttar 100.

2 *Bollepanda P. Poonacha* v *K.M. Madapa* AIR 2008 SC 2003; (2008)13 SCC 179.

3 *Ramesh Chand* v *Anil Panjwani* AIR 2003 SC 2508; (2003)7 SCC 350.

4 *The Nav Samaj Ltd.* v *Shavrao Tukaramji* AIR 1984 Bom 23.

it as a separate action. A counter-claim is, therefore, to be treated for all purposes, for which justice requires it to be so treated, as an independent action.

As to jurisdiction of the court in cases where counter-claim is pleaded Or. 8, r. 6(1) will govern. No counter-claim can be successfully pleaded when pecuniary jurisdiction of the court is exceeded.

Set-off and counter-claim may be made without payment of court-fees by an indigent person. This is as *per* Or. 33, r. 17 of the CPC which enjoins that rules contained in Or. 33 shall, so far as may be, apply to him as if he were a plaintiff and his written statement were a plaint.

Where in a suit for recovery of certain amount on the basis of 'khata', the defendant by his additional written statement puts forward a counter-claim for accounting arising out of transactions between him and the plaintiff on the basis of an agreement, the written statement can be treated as a cross-claim.[5]

12 New defences Order 8, r. 8. "Any ground of defence which has arisen after the institution of the suit or the presentation of a written statement, claiming a set-off or counter-claim may be raised by the defendant or plaintiff, as the case may be, in his written statement".

The plea of invalidity of notice was not taken in the written statement so the defendant cannot be allowed to raise such plea at the time of argument.[6]

13 Additional written statement and subsequent pleadings The defendant is permitted, with the leave of the court, to file an additional written statement incorporating new defences. When the plaintiff amends his plaint, the defendant is entitled to file an additional written statement.

A written statement (or reply) of the plaintiff by way of defence to a set-off or counter-claim or an additional written statement from the defendant subsequent to the filing of a written statement by the defendant are subsequent pleadings as contemplated in Or. 8, r. 9, CPC. Except in the case of set-off, a replication can be filed by the plaintiff with the leave of court.[7]

Under r. 9 leave of the court is essential before any party can present a further pleading after the written statement has been filed. But the court itself may require at any time a written statement or an additional written statement from any of the parties to a suit. If the pleadings of either party are too vague, the court may require such party to file a further and fuller statement. When a defendant intends to bring in additional defence he may, with leave of the court, file an additional written statement.

The only subsequent pleading that may be filed without the leave of the court is the written statement filed by way of defence to a set-off, or a counter-claim.

5 *Mohinder Singh Jaggi* v *Data Ram Jagannath* AIR 1972 SC 1048.
6 *Kadavandi Krishnachari* v *Diocese of Guntur Society, R.C.M.* AIR 2003 AP 340.
7 *M.L. Gupta* v *Kripal Singh* 2002 AIHC 3616 (Del).

In this connection Or. 8, rr. 9 and 10 are important.

9. *Subsequent pleadings.* No pleading subsequent to the written statement of a defendant other than by way of defence to set-off or counter-claim shall be presented except by the leave of the Court and upon such terms as the Court thinks fit; but the Court may at any time require a written statement or additional written statement from any of the parties and fix a time of not more than thirty days for presenting the same.

10. *Procedure when party fails to present written statement called for by Court.* Where any party from whom a written statement is required under rule 1 or rule 9 fails to present the same within the time permitted or fixed by the Court, as the case may be, the Court shall pronounce judgment against him, or make such order in relation to the suit as it thinks fit and on the pronouncement of such judgment a decree shall be drawn up.

14 Amendment of written statement Amendment of a written statement availing a new legal stand deserves to be allowed.

Where a plaintiff files a suit for damages on the ground that the defendant has terminated the agreement between them and the defendant seeks to amend the written statement alleging that the suit is hit by s. 69 of the Partnership Act as the agreement is not registered, the amendment should be allowed.[8] Written statement was amended to clarify and elucidate facts already in the pleadings and to formulate new questions of law from such facts or decisions by the court. Amendment after seven years, *held,* did not cause injustice to the plaintiff.[9]

The rigid principle of amendment of plaint under Or. 6, r. 17 cannot be applied in the case of receiving additional written statement.[10]

Original plea of the defendant was that the property was gifted to her. By amendment of the written statement a plea was sought to be introduced that even if the gift was not proved, she being in continuous possession of the property she became absolute owner by adverse possession. Amendment should be allowed.[11] When there is no change in the cause of action, amendment in written statement which takes plea contrary to or inconsistent with the plea already taken would be allowed.[12]

As a result of the amendment of the written statement, case has to be opened afresh. Defendant's interest is not in any way injured either by granting or by refusing amendment. Amendment should not be allowed.[13]

Admission of certain facts by mistake in written statement can be corrected by amendment.[14]

8 *Sarojini Pradhan* v *K.C. Pradhan* AIR 1973 Ori 214.
9 *Iswar Jagannath* v *Fatik Chandra* AIR 1972 Cal 372.
10 *P. Saraswathi* v *C. Subramaniam* AIR 2014 Mad 50.
11 *Gulwant Kaur* v *Mohinder Singh* AIR 1972 Punj 260.
12 *Pramendra Kr. Mitra* v *Amarendra Kr. Mitra* AIR 2004 NOC 423 (Cal).
13 *Inder Singh* v *Chhaju Singh* AIR 1972 Punj 255.
14 *Dileep Singh Mehta* v *Macknion Mackenzie* AIR 1993 Cal 25.

15 Written statement by legal representatives Order 22, r. 4(2), CPC provides its own horizon. Order 22, r. 4(1), speaks of substitution of legal representatives. The court on an application made in that behalf shall cause the legal representative of the deceased defendant to be made a party and shall proceed with the suit.

Sub-rule (2) of r. 4 of Or. 22, CPC enjoins:

> "Any person so made a party may make any defence appropriate to his character as legal representative of the deceased defendant."

As stated above, sub-rule (2) of r. 4 provides its own horizon and prescribes its own limitations. It allows a person made a party under Or. 22, r. 4 to make 'any defence', the only limitation being that the defence so made must be "appropriate to his character as legal representative of the deceased defendant". Besides all these distinguishing features, it may be notified that Or. 8, r. 9 invests the court with the discretion to either allow or reject the request of the defendant for additional written statement. Its natural corollary is that a party cannot raise, as a matter of right, any fresh plea by way of additional written statement without first obtaining the leave of the court which the court in its discretion, may or may not grant. A legal representative can and may, as a matter of right, raise any defence which is appropriate to his character as legal representative of the deceased defendant. And, if he chooses to raise any defence, he being entitled to do so, the court has no discretion to stop or debar him from so doing.[15]

15 *Saiyal Sirajul Hasan* v *Syed Murtaza Ali Khan* AIR 1992 Del 162; *J.C. Chatterjee* v *S.K. Tandon* AIR 1972 SC 2526.

CHAPTER

5

Registered Address of the Party

SYNOPSIS

1 The registered address—object for furnishing Simply speaking, a registered address is the party's address for service. A registered address shall be deemed to be the address of a party for the purpose of service of all processes in the suit or in any appeal from any decree or order therein made and for the purpose of execution proceedings. Service of any process may be effected upon a party at his registered address. And, that indicates the object of furnishing a registered address by a party to the legal proceedings.

Rule 14A lays down 'Address for service of notice'. Furnishing registered address of the party is essential as such address shall be deemed to be the address of the party for the purpose of all processes in the suit or in any appeal and for the purpose of execution.

Order 6, r. 14A. *Address for service of notice.* (1) Every pleading, when filed by a party, shall be accompanied by a statement in the prescribed form, signed as provided in rule 14, regarding the address of the party.

(2) Such address may, from time to time, be changed by lodging in Court a form duly filled up and stating the new address of the party and accompanied by a verified petition.

(3) The address furnished in the statement made under sub-rule (1) shall be called the "registered address" of the party, and shall, until duly changed as aforesaid, be deemed to be the address of the party for the purpose of service of all processes in the suit or in any appeal from any decree or order therein made and for the purpose of execution, and shall hold good, subject as aforesaid, for a period of two years after the final determination of the cause or matter.

(4) Service of any process may be effected upon a party at his registered address in all respects as though such party resided thereat.

(5) ....

(6) ....

(7) ....

(8) Nothing in this rule shall prevent the court from directing the service of a process at any other address, if for any reason, it thinks fit to do so.

2 Contents of a registered address We may refer to r. 15 of the Civil Rules & Orders, vol. I, published by the Calcutta High Court which enjoins:

"The registered address for service filed with every pleading (whether by the plaintiff or the defendant) under Or. 6, r. 14A shall state the following particulars:

(*i*) the name of the street, lane or section and number of the house (if any);

(*ii*) the name of the town or village;

(*iii*) the Post Office;

(*iv*) the district; and

(*v*) the Munsifi (if in West Bengal) or the district court (if outside West Bengal).

A specimen registered address as current in West Bengal—

In the Court of the Civil Judge (Senior Division), Cooch Behar.

Title Suit No. 11 of 20 .....

Sri .... Plaintiff

versus

Sri .... Defendant.

Registered Address of the Plaintiff:

Harendra Narayan Road, Cooch Behar Town, P.S. Kotowali

P.O. Cooch Behar, Dt. Cooch Behar

Within the jurisdiction of Sadar Munsiff, Cooch Behar.

Requisite particulars in a registered address of a party are identical throughout India. We would refer to rules under different High Courts of our country which are almost identical in their nature, object and purpose.

3 Rules with regard to registered address under different High Courts in India There have been High Court amendments so far as r. 14 of Or. 6, CPC is concerned.

(a) *Calcutta, Assam and Orissa High Court Amendments*

In Calcutta and Assam after r. 14, there has been introduced r. 14A which reads:

"Every pleading, when filed, shall be accompanied by a statement in a prescribed form signed as provided in Rule 14 of this Order, of the party's address for service. Such address may from time to time be changed by lodging in court a form duly filled up and stating the new address of the party and accompanied by a verified petition. The address so given shall be called the registered address of the party and shall, until duly changed as aforesaid, be deemed to be the address of the party for the purposes of service of all processes in the suit or in any appeal from any decree or order therin made and for the purposes in the suit or in any appeal from any decree or order therein made and for the purposes of execution, and shall hold good subject as aforesaid for a period of two years after the final determination of the cause of matter. Service of any process may be effected upon a party at his registered address in like manner in all respects as though such party resided thereat."

There has been similar amendment under the Orissa High Court. Amendments by insertion of r. 14A almost identical in nature and purpose. On the occasion of filing a plaint in the courts subordinate to Calcutta, Assam and Orissa High Courts, the plaintiff and on the occasion of submitting written statement the defendant has to file separately a "Registered Address" of the`party.

But in the amendments under other High Courts, as follows, Or. 7 has been amended by adding some other rules after r. 18.

(b) ***Allahabad High Court***

After Or. 7, r. 18, the Allahabad High Court, amendments—Rules 19 to 25.

19. Every plaint or original petition shall be accompanied by a proceeding giving an address written in Hindi, written in Devnagri script at which service of notice, summons or other process may be made on the plaintiff or the petitioner. Plaintiffs or petitioners subsequently added shall, immediately on being so added, file a proceeding of this nature.

20. An address for service filed under the preceding rule shall be within the local limits of the District Court within which the suit or petition is filed, or of the District Court within which the party ordinarily resides, if within the limits of the State of Uttar Pradesh.

21. Where a plaintiff or petitioner fails to file an address for service, he shall be liable to have his suit dismissed or his petition rejected by the court *suo motu* or any party may apply for an order to that effect, and the court may make such order as it thinks just.

22. Where a party is not found at the address given by him for service and no agent or adult male member of his family on whom a notice or process can be served, is present, a copy of the notice or process shall be affixed to the outer door of the house. If on the date fixed such party is not present another date shall be fixed and a copy of the notice, summons or other process shall be sent to the registered address by registered post, and such service shall be deemed to be as effectual as if the notice or process had been personally served.

23. Where a party engages a pleader, notices or processes for service on him shall be served in the manner prescribed by Or. III, r. 5, unless the court directs service at the address for service given by the party.

24. A party who desires to change the address for service given by him as aforesaid shall file a verified petition, and the court may direct the amendment of the record accordingly. Notice of such petition shall be given to such other parties to the suit as the court may deem it necessary to inform, and may be either served upon the pleaders for such parties or be sent to them by registered post, as the court thinks fit.

25. Nothing in these rules shall prevent the court from directing the service of a notice or process in any other manner, if, for any reasons, it thinks fit to do so.

(c) *Bombay High Court*

Order 7, rules 19-26 for Bombay and Gujarat by H.C. Amendment in 1930.

19. *Address to be filed with plaint or original petition.*—(1) Every plaint or original petition shall be accompanied by a memorandum in writing giving an address at which service of notice or summons or other process may be made on the plaintiff or the petitioner. Plaintiffs or petitioners subsequently added shall, immediately on being so added, file a memorandum in writing of this nature.

(2) This address shall be called the "registered address", and it shall, subject to rule 24 of this Order, hold good in all proceedings in the suit and in appeals and also for a further period of six years from the date of final decision for all purposes including those of execution.

20. *Nature of address to be filed.*—The registered address filed under the preceding rule shall be within the local limits of the District Court within which the suit or petition is filed, or if he cannot conveniently give an address as aforesaid at a place where a party ordinarily resides.

21. *Consequence of failure to file address.*—Same as r. 21 under Allahabad High Court.

Rules 22 and 23 speak of the mode of service.

24. Almost similar to r. 24 under Allahabad High Court.

25 and 26. Not relevant for our purpose.

(d) *Madhya Pradesh*

Order 7, Rules 19-23.

19. *Registered address.*—Every plaint or original petition shall be accompanied by a memorandum giving an address at which service of process may be made on the plaintiff or the petitioner. The address shall be within the local limits of the Civil District in which the plaint of the original petition is filed or, if an address within such Civil District cannot conveniently be given within the local limits of the Civil District in which the party ordinarily resides.

This address shall be called "registered address" and it shall hold good throughout interlocutory proceedings and appeals and also for a further period of two years from the date of final decision and for all purposes including those of execution.

20. *Registered address by a party subsequently added as plaintiff or petitioner.*—Any party subsequently added at the plaintiff or petitioner shall in a like manner file a registered address at the time of applying or consenting to be joined as plaintiff or petitioner.

21. *Consequences of non-filing of registered address.*—If the plaintiff or the petitioner fails to file a registered address as required by r. 19 or r. 20, he shall be liable, at the discretion of the court, to have his suit dismissed or his petition rejected.

An order under this rule may be passed by the court *suo motu* or on the application of any party.

Rule 22 speaks of mode of service of notice.

23. *Change of registered address.*—A plaintiff or petitioner who wishes to change his registered address shall file a verified petition and the court shall direct the amendment of the record accordingly. Notice of such petition shall be given to such other parties to the suit or proceedings as the court may deem it necessary to inform.

(e) *Patna High Court*

Order 7, Rules 19-22.

19. Every plaint or original petition shall be accompanied by a statement giving an address at which service of notice or summons or other process may be made on the plaintiff or the petitioner and every plaintiff or petitioner subsequently added, shall, immediately on being so added, file a similar statement.[1]

20. An address for service filed under the proceeding rule shall state the following particulars:

(1) the name of the street and number of the house (if in a town),

(2) the name of the town or village,

(3) the Post Office,

(4) the district, and

(5) the Munsifi (if in Bihar) or the District Court (if outside Bihar).

21. Where a plaintiff or petitioner fails to file an address for service, he shall be liable to have his suit dismissed or his petition rejected by the court *suo motu*, or any party may apply for an order to that effect, and the court may make such order as it thinks fit.

22. A party who desires to change the address for service given by him as aforesaid shall file a verified petition, and the court may direct the amendment of the record accordingly. Notice of such petition shall be given to such other parties to the suit as the court may deem it necessary to inform, and may be either served upon the pleaders for such parties or be sent to them by registered post as the court thinks fit.

1 Order 8, r. 11. Failure to file statement of address. Defence need not be struck out (AIR 1976 Pat 399).

(f) *Rajasthan*

Order 7, Rules 19 to 25.

19. (1) Every plaint or original petition shall be accompanied by a memorandum giving an address at which service of process may be made on the plaintiff or the petitioner. Plaintiffs or petitioners subsequently added shall, immediately on being so added, file a memorandum of this nature.

(2) This address shall be called the registered address and it shall hold good throughout interlocutory proceedings and appeals and also for a further period of two years from the date of the final decision and for all purposes including those of execution.

20. Same as r. 20 in Allahabad, for State of Uttar Pradesh read 'Rajasthan'.

21.(1)—Same as r. 21—Allahabad.

22.(1)—Same as r. 21(2)—Madhya Pradesh.

Rule 22 speaks of mode of service of notice, etc., r. 23 speaks of the mode of service and same as r. 23—Allahabad. Rule 24 speaks, of the change in registered address and is the same as r. 24—Allahabad. Rule 25—Same as r. 25 of Allahabad.

(g) *Punjab High Court*

Order 7, Rules 19 to 25.

19. Every plaint or original petition shall be accompanied by a proceeding giving an address at which service of notice, summons or other process may be made on the plaintiff or petitioner. Plaintiffs or petitioners subsequently added shall, immediately on being so added, file a proceeding of this nature.

20. An address for service filed under the preceding rule shall be within the local limits of the District Court within which the suit or petition is filed, or of the District Court within which the party ordinarily resides, if within the limits of the territorial jurisdiction of the Punjab High Court.

21. Where a plaintiff or a petitioner fails to file an address for service, he shall be liable to have his suit dismissed or his petition rejected by the court *suo motu* or any party may apply for an order to that effect and the court may make such order as it thinks just.

22 and 23. Speaks of mode of service of notice and summonses etc.

24. A party who desires to change the address for service given by him as aforesaid shall file a verified petition, and the court may direct the amendment of the record accordingly. Notice of such petition shall be given to such other parties to the suit as the court may deem it necessary to inform, and may be either served upon the pleader for such parties or be sent, to them by registered post as the court thinks fit.

25. Nothing in these rules shall prevent the court from directing the service of a notice, summons or other process in any other manner, if, for any reasons, it thinks fit to do so.

To sum up: Law as to filing of a registered address is uniform throughout India save that (1) In West Bengal, Assam and Orissa the pleading shall be accompanied by the registered address, i.e., both the plaint and the written statement shall be accompanied by a registered address. But in other States, aforesaid, only the plaint and petition shall be accompanied by a registered address. No registered address is required to be filed along with the written statement.

(2) In West Bengal, Assam and Orissa for filing petitions, filing of registered address is not necessary as in other States as aforesaid.

(3) In West Bengal, Assam and Orissa for failure suit is not to be dismissed, but in other States a suit will be dismissed for failure unless the court otherwise directs.

4 Law regarding 'registered address' Sub-rule (1) of r. 14A of Or. 6 enjoins that every pleading, when filed by a party, shall be accompanied by a statement in the prescribed form, signed as provided in r. 14, regarding the address of the party. And, as a 'pleading' shall mean plaint or written statement (*vide* r. 1 of Or. 6), the party has to file, along with the plaint or with the written statement, as the case may be, a statement as to the address of the party in the prescribed form.

Such address shall be known as the registered address of the party. It may, however, from time to time be changed by lodging in court a form duly filled up and stating the new address of the party and accompanied by a verified petition.

5 Incomplete, false or fictitious 'registered address'—consequences thereof—remedy Sub-rule (5) of r. 14A of Or. 6, CPC enjoins:

"Where the registered address of a party is discovered by the Court to be incomplete, false or fictitious, the court may, either on its own motion, or on the application of any party, order—

(*a*) in the case where such registered address was furnished by a plaintiff, stay of the suit, or

(*b*) in the case where such registered address was furnished by a defendant, his defence be struck out and he be placed in the same position as if he had not put up any defence."

The above penal provisions are not altogether without any remedy. In appropriate cases, the order of stay or the order of striking out defence may be vacated by the court on application to the court for setting aside the order after furnishing his true address [vide Or. 6, r. 14A(6)].

"The court, if satisfied that the party was prevented by any sufficient cause from filing the true address at the proper time, shall set aside the order of stay or order striking out the defence, on such terms as to costs or otherwise as it thinks fit and shall appoint a day for proceeding with the suit or defence, as the case may be [Or. 6, r. 14A(7)]."

6 'Registered address' and service of process Sub-rules (3), (4) and (8) of r. 14A of Or. 6, become relevant in connection with service of process.

Sub-rule (3) reads: The address furnished in the statement made under sub-rule (1) shall be called the 'registered address' of the party, and shall, until duly changed as aforesaid be deemed to be the address of the party for the purpose of service of all processes in the suit or in any appeal from any decree or order therein made and for the purpose of execution, and shall hold good, subject as aforesaid, for a period of two years after the final determination of the cause or matter.

Sub-rule (4) reads: "Service of any process may be effected upon a party at his registered address in all respects as though such party resided thereat.[2]

But the court's hands are not tied. Process may be served at any other address. There may of course be reason for that; for, sub-rule (8) enjoins: "Nothing may in this rule shall prevent the court from directing the service of a process at any other address, if, for any reason, it thinks fit to do so".

2 In suits to be tried in summary procedure the provision for filing address of the defendant for service of notices on him is contained in Or. 37, r. 3(1) of CPC.

CHAPTER

6

Signature in Pleadings

SYNOPSIS

1 Rules of signature (Or. 6, r. 14) Signature on a pleading indicates authenticity of the same. Law enjoins that a pleading has to be signed before presentation in a court of law. Order 6, r. 14, CPC reads:

"Every pleading[1] shall be signed by the party and his pleader (if any):

Provided that where a party pleading is, by reason of absence or for other good cause, unable to sign the pleading, it may be signed by any person duly authorised by him to sign the same or to sue or defend on his behalf".

2 Object of signature in pleadings Signature indicates knowledge, confirms authenticity, ensures *bona fides* of a pleading. The object of requiring every pleading to be signed by the party is to prevent, as far as possible, disputes as to whether a suit was instituted with the plaintiff's knowledge and authority.[2]

3 Competency A pleading shall be signed by the party and his pleader, when appointed. Where there are several plaintiffs, the plaint should normally be signed by every one of them. But where several persons institute a suit, it is sufficient that one of them signs the plaint with the other plaintiffs' knowledge and authority.[3] There is no rule providing that a person named as a co-plaintiff is not to be treated as a plaintiff unless he signs and verifies the plaint.[4]

1 Procedure of signature is same whether it is an affidavit, or a Vakalatnama or pleadings—AIR 1928 Mad 175—Per Wallace, J.
2 AIR 1925 Sind 275.
3 AIR 1951 Pat 323; AIR 1950 Ajmer 30.
4 (1890)17 Cal 580 (PC) followed in AIR 1924 Pat 104 (106).

This provision is excepted where "by reason of absence" or "for other good cause" the plaintiff is unable to sign the plaint it may be signed by any person duly authorised by him to sign (*vide* Or. 3, r. 2; by a constituted attorney[5]) the same, or to sue or defend on his behalf. It, therefore, stands to reason that a pleading can be signed by a person duly authorised by the plaintiff in that behalf or duly authorised by the plaintiff or the defendant to sue or defend on his behalf. Oral authorisation may do.[6] Even authority given after the institution of the suit to a servant who had signed the plaint originally without a formal authority was held to be normally sufficient.[7] (In this case plaint was signed and verified by a servant of the plaintiff. Objection was raised by the defendant. Plaintiff then signed a power of attorney authorising the servant to sign and verify for him and for ratifying his previous acts).

Whether a person is duly authorised or not depends on the facts of each particular case. Again, the question when a particular person can be said to be duly authorised that also depends upon the circumstances of each case.

Words "other good cause" are of wide significance and leave the matter to the discretion of the court. There is nothing in law to prevent a corporation from suing by its agent as provided under Or. 3, r. 1, CPC. Order 29, r. 1 is only permissive and does not preclude a corporation from taking advantage of Or. 3, r. 1 and Or. 6, r. 14 and having its pleadings signed by a duly constituted agent.[8]

A pleading signed by an unauthorised person is invalid.[9] But in such a case, the court may permit the party himself to sign a pleading at a subsequent stage.[10]

Though a plaint may in above circumstances be signed by any person other than the plaintiff, yet a plaint containing scandalous statements should be signed and verified by the plaintiff himself. Again, where material facts depend on the personal knowledge of the plaintiff, the plaint shall be signed and verified by him.

4 Irregularity, omission and defective signatures An irregularity in the signature of a plaint is a mere defect of procedure and does not affect the jurisdiction of the court.[11] It is remediable at any stage of the litigation. Nor it is fatal for a suit. Where it appears that a suit was filed with the knowledge of the plaintiff, absence of signature in the plaint may be cured by an appropriate amendment at any stage of the suit.[12] Let us incidentally refer to s. 99 of the CPC introduced in the Code of Civil Procedure in the light of reported cases

5 AIR 1967 All 487.
6 46 CWN 957; AIR 1971 All 229.
7 104 IC 747.
8 AIR 1957 Ker 164.
9 Note Rule 14(2) of Civil Rules & Orders, vol. 1 (Calcutta High Court)—"All pleadings .... presented to the court shall be dated and signed by the person presenting and also, where necessary, by such other person as may be law be required to sign them".
10 16 IC 225; AIR 1922 Bom 113.
11 AIR 1956 Hyd 133; AIR 1941 Nag 159.
12 ILR 22 All 55. Also see 104 IC 747.

in ILR 26 Bom 259 and ILR 27 Mad 80. It reads: "No decree shall be reversed or substantially varied, nor shall any case be remanded, in appeal on account of any misjoinder or non-joinder of parties or causes of action or any error, defect or irregularity in any proceedings in the suit, not affecting the merits of the case or the jurisdiction of the court".[13]

Erroneous signature or an irregularity in signature in a pleading of defective frame or signature is a mere irregularity, falling within s. 99.[14] The defect, if any, is one of form and not of substance.

Omission to sign or defect in the signature or verification may be cured at any stage by amendment.[15] If a plaint is not signed by plaintiff or his authorised agent for *bona fide* mistake, such defect can be cured by the trial court before judgment.[16] In fact, the proper course is not to dismiss the suit or reject the plaint but to get the plaint amended.[17] It is immaterial whether the signature was made by the plaintiff himself or someone else on his behalf as signing is merely a matter of procedure.[18] Use of a mere stamp bearing the name of the party is sufficient even when a party is able to sign.[19] It is not the requirement of law that a party to a court proceeding cannot sign his name in the mode his fancy or humour dictates. [One Madhav Upendra Shenvi Talaulicar (also known as Madhav Talaulicar, U.S. Talaulicar in public and private life) signed as U.S. Talaulicar—there was nothing illegal or irregular].[20]

5 Signature—modes thereof—special cases

In suits by or against a corporation. Order 29, r. 1 is permissive and not mandatory. A plaint by a company may be signed by one or the other of the persons mentioned in the rule. But this does not exclude Or. 6, r. 14, and as a company is unable to sign itself, the words 'good cause' in the latter rule enable a company to authorise a person to sign a plaint on its behalf. Therefore, even if the officer is not the principal officer of the company, he may still validly sign a pleading provided he is a person duly authorised to sign it or to sue on behalf of the plaintiff. A statement in the plaint or a written statement of the company that a person is the principal officer and able to depose to the facts of the case is sufficient.[21]

Signing on behalf of a corporation under Or. 29, r. 1 is not mandatory but permissive and does not preclude a corporation from presenting a plaint

13 Referred to in AIR 1977 Pat 257.
14 AIR 1944 Oudh 37.
15 *Om Prakash* v *Ashalata* 2002(1) Bom LR 843 (Bom); *Union Bank of India* v *Naresh Kumar* AIR 1997 SC 3; (1996)6 SCC 660.
16 *Uday Shankar Triyar* v *Ram Kalewar Prasad Singh* AIR 2006 SC 269; (2006)1 SCC 75.
17 AIR 1915 Cal 444.
18 *Anantha Ram* v *Addl. Civil Judge* 2001 All LJ 2620.
19 AIR 1928 Mad 175.
20 *Madhav Upendra Talaulicar* v *Yashwant Sitaram Dessai* AIR 1968 Goa 53.
21 AIR 1970 Ker 138.

signed by the duly constituted agent.[22] When under the Articles of Association of a company a suit on behalf of a company has to be filed with the consent of the Directors but when the same has been filed by the Secretary without such consent the suit is not maintainable even though the Secretary held the general power of attorney from the Directors. Subsequent ratification by the Directors is not sufficient to cure the defect.[23] Local Manager of a bank is competent to sign and verify the plaint as he is the principal officer of the bank.[24] Order 6, r. 14 also applies to companies. There is nothing in law to prevent a corporation from suing by its agent as provided by Or. 3, r. 1; and Or. 29, r. 1, being only permissive pleadings can be signed by a duly constituted agent.[25]

Suits by a shebait. Signature and verification can be made by agent of the *shebait*.[26]

6 Waiver of signature Can there be waiver of a signature in a pleading? Yes, in proper cases. The absence of signature in the plaint may be waived by the defendant. An objection as to signature, if not taken by the defendant at the earliest possible opportunity, cannot be allowed to be raised for the first time .... in appeal; for, we must remember that the court should not make a technical fetish of Or. 6, r. 14 but apply it according to reason and common sense.[27]

22 *Judhisthir* v *Koshal Transport* (1971)37 Cut LT 108.
23 *Turner Morrison* v *Hungerford Investment* AIR 1972 SC 1311; (1972)1 SCC 857.
24 *United Bank of India* v *Probhas* AIR 1977 Cal 55; 81 CWN 48; *Umesh* v *State Bank of India* AIR 1987 Ori 67.
25 AIR 1957 Ker 164. But see AIR 1969 Cal 496.
26 AIR 1952 Cal 352.
27 AIR 1967 Cal 486.

CHAPTER

7

Verification of Pleadings

SYNOPSIS

1 Rules of verification under the Code of Civil Procedure We have noticed that pleadings have to be verified. As a matter of fact, all statements in a court of law requiring judicial determination should be verified.[1]

Order 6, r. 15, CPC enjoins:

"15. *Verification of pleadings*. (1) Save as otherwise provided by any law for the time being in force, every pleading shall be verified at the foot by the party or by one of the parties pleading or by some other person proved to the satisfaction of the court to be acquainted with the facts of the case.

(2) The person verifying shall specify, by reference to the numbered paragraphs of the pleading, what he verifies of his own knowledge and what he verifies upon information received and believed to be true.

(3) The verification shall be signed by the person making it and shall state the date on which and the place at which it was signed.

(4) The person verifying the pleading shall also furnish an affidavit in support of his pleadings."

Sub-section (2) of s. 26 of the CPC provides that "in every plaint, facts shall be proved by an affidavit".

The provision of Or. 6, r. 15 is not mandatory and any defect can be cured at any stage. Therefore, where there were allegations that the plaint was not

1 Civil Rules & Orders (vol. 1), Calcutta High Court Rule 16: "All petitions requiring judicial investigation or determination unless filed with an affidavit in support thereof should be verified in the manner prescribed by Or. 6, r. 15, CPC.

signed and verified as per provisions of Or. 6, rr. 14 and 15 but the plaintiff, while in his deposition was found to have made out the case in the plaint, the plaint was not liable to be rejected merely on the ground that the plaint was not signed and verified properly.[2] A defect in verification is curable.[3]

2 Verification of election petition In case of election petition a separate affidavit as required under Or. 6, r. 15(4) cannot be insisted upon,[4] but defect in verification of the pleading because the petitioner failed to furnish separate affidavit in support of pleadings is a curable defect.[5]

3 Rules in different High Courts in India

(i) ***Calcutta High Court (O.S.) Rules of verification.*** "Where any person, other than a party pleading, verifies a pleading under Or. 6, r. 15, CPC his fitness to so verify shall be proved by his affidavit at the time the pleading is presented. In a pleading on behalf of a company, the fitness of the person purporting to verify it, even though that person be a director or other principal officer, must be proved by affidavit". Ch. VII, r. 8 of the Rules.

> "Where in a suit by a company registered under the Indian Companies Act, the plaint was signed and verified by the Secretary, and the plaint stated that he was authorised by the Articles of Association of the Company to do all acts in connection with suits, and it appeared that the Articles of Association empowered the Secretary to verify pleadings, it was held that the requirements of Or. 14, r. 1 of CPC were satisfied and no affidavit testifying to the fitness of the Secretary to verify was required".

(ii) ***Bombay High Court (Original Side) Rules of verification.*** "All plaints and written statements shall be verified before one of the Assistant Masters or Associations of the Court appointed in that behalf and elsewhere in India before the officer, indicated in the Code of Civil Procedure, s. 139. The verification shall be in Form No. 1".

(*Vide* Ch. 6, r. 95, Ch. 7, r. 123).

The Bombay High Court amendment of Or. 6, r. 15:

After sub-rule (1) of r. 15, in so far as it applies to the Bombay City Civil Court, insert the following:

Provided that in respect of pleading to be filed in the Bombay City Civil Court such verification shall within the local jurisdiction of the court, be made before one of the officers of the said court empowered to administer oath and elsewhere, before any other mentioned in s. 139 of the Code of Civil Procedure 1908.[6]

(iii) ***Madras High Court (Original Side) Rules.*** "The plaint of a corporation, or incorporated company, or of a company authorised to sue and be sued in the

2 *Kailash Singh* v *Hiralal Dey* AIR 1994 Gau 12 (Aid of s. 99 of CPC is there).
3 *Gurjant Singh* v *Krishan Chander* AIR 2001 Raj 211.
4 *Prasanna Kumar* v *G.M. Siddshewar* AIR 2010 Kant 113.
5 *Devinder Singh* v *Deputy Commissioner, Simla* AIR 2010 HP 33 (DB).
6 Section 139, CPC prescribes persons competent to administer oath on affidavit.

name of an officer or trustee, may be subscribed and verified on behalf of the corporation or company by a director, or other principal officer of the corporation or company, who states in the verification of the plaint that he is acquainted with the facts of the case".

The plaint of a firm may be subscribed and verified by any of the partners who states in the verification of the plaint that he is acquainted with the facts of the case.

"The next friend of a minor plaintiff or other plaintiff under disability may subscribe and verify the plaint on behalf of a minor subject to his presenting together with the plaint an affidavit stating the age of the minor and that the next friend has no interest directly or indirectly adverse to that of the minor, and is otherwise a fit and proper person to act as a next friend. (M. High Court O.S. Rules, Or. 2, r. 3)".

4 Object and requirements of verification In all probability the intention of the framers of law to secure verification at the bottom of pleadings is that statements making a pleading should not be false or irresponsible statements. On the contrary, the party verifying a pleading is made responsible for his statements which must be true to his knowledge or information as the case may be. The main object of verification of pleadings is:

> "A verification has been described as possessing the security of being made under the sanction of a declaration for which the person making it would be liable to the penalties attaching to the crime of giving false evidence, if the declaration were false to his knowledge."

As it stands, a verification, therefore, is of great consequence. It is intended to afford some guarantee that a false or totally trivial claim should not be put before the court. It is not a formality simpliciter; for, it is the business of the court to see that the provision in Or. 6, r. 15, CPC is carried out. The object of verification is to fix responsibility for the allegations made in a plaint on the verifier and to ensure that no false allegations are made freely and recklessly.[7] The court is bound to see in every case that the pleadings are verified in the manner prescribed and that the verifications are not treated as mere formalities.

Admission made in plaint, not properly verified. In a subsequent suit admission in the said plaint could not be used as against the defendant in the subsequent suit.[8]

5 Competency of verifier Next comes the question as to who is required to sign the verification. Normally, the party or one of the parties to the suit verifies. An agent authorised to sign the pleadings is competent to sign the verification; and if it is proved to the satisfaction of the court that some other person is acquainted with the facts of the case, he may be permitted to verify. Where there are several plaintiffs, verification by one of them is enough.[9] It is open

7 *Rajkumar Dhar* v *A Stuart* AIR 1958 Cal 104; ILR (1958)1 Cal 136.
8 AIR 1977 NOC 157 (Cal).
9 AIR 1951 Pat 323; AIR 1950 Ajmer 30.

to the opposite party to insist on the party himself verifying the pleading in important cases.[10] Where the plaint contains serious allegations of fraud, falsification of account, culpable negligence, etc., against the defendants and the verification is sought to be made by an agent under a power of attorney, by merely putting on record the power of attorney, it is wholly insufficient for the purpose, as the plaintiff's agent simpliciter holding an authority to sign the verification under the power of attorney would be incompetent to verify the plaint.[11] The requirement in rr. 14 and 15 (Or. 6 of CPC) that a plaint should be signed and verified by a party is surely procedural and the party can make good the deficiency at a later stage and, therefore, the rejection of a plaint on the ground that it was not signed and verified by the plaintiff or his Mukhtiar, but was signed by the plaintiff's pleader, would not be valid and the proper course for the court would be to give an opportunity to the plaintiff or his Mukhtiar to sign and verify the plaint.[12]

Authority competent to verify pleadings: Special cases under the Code of Civil Procedure

(A) IN SUITS BY OR AGAINST FIRMS. In a suit by or against a firm pleadings "required to be signed, verified or certified may be signed, verified or certified by any of the partners constituting the firm". (Or. 30, r. 2, CPC).

(B) IN A SUITS BY OR AGAINST CORPORATIONS OR COMPANY. "In suits by or against a corporation, any pleading may be signed and verified on behalf of the corporation by the secretary or by any director or other principal officer of the corporation who is able to depose to the facts of the case." (Or. 29, r. 1, CPC).

Order 6, rr. 14 and 15 do not apply to companies but Or. 29, r. 1 does not exclude the operation of Or. 6, rr. 14 and 15, CPC. Therefore, an agent holding a power of attorney is entitled to sign and verify the plaint on behalf of a corporation. The signing and verification of the written statement by a constituted attorney of the company is indicative of the appearance of the company in suit.[13]

General Manager can delegate the duty of signing and verifying although there is no such express provision in the power of attorney.[14] The Official Liquidator of a registered company in liquidation is competent to verify.[15] Principal officer of a corporation need not verify plaint from actual personal knowledge. He may verify upon his information and belief.[16] Plaint signed and verified by the authorised agent of bank. Plaint held properly signed and verified.[17]

10 ILR 9 All 505; ILR 8 Cal 885; ILR 6 Cal 268.
11 AIR 1958 Cal 104.
12 *All India Reporter Ltd., Bombay* v *Ramchandra Dhondo Datar* AIR 1961 Bom 292; *Karanshingh* v *Ram Rachhpal Singh* AIR 1977 HP 28.
13 AIR 1969 Cal 496.
14 AIR 1937 Nag 379.
15 AIR 1956 Nag 204.
16 9 CWN 608.
17 *United Bank of India* v *P.C. Deb* AIR 1977 Cal 55.

(C) IN SUITS BY OR AGAINST GOVERNMENT

Order 27, r. 1 provides:

> "In any suit by or against the Government, the plaint or written statement shall be signed by such person as the Government may, by general or special order, appoint in this behalf, and shall be verified by any person whom the Government may so appoint and who is acquainted with the facts of the case".

The appointee from the Government shall be competent to sign. The person competent to verify a pleading shall also be an appointee by the Government besides such person shall have appointment who is acquainted with the facts of the case. Authority to sign and authority to verify may be given to one and the same person. A written statement filed on behalf of the Government in reply to a writ petition is not exempt from the provisions of this rule and must be verified by a responsible officer of the Government who is acquainted with the facts of the case.[18]

(D) IN PROBATE AND LETTERS OF ADMINISTRATION PROCEEDINGS. (See s. 281 of the Indian Succession Act).

Verification of application by the party:

> "I .... the petitioner in the above petition declare that what is stated therein is true to the best of my information and belief."

Verification of one of the witnesses to the will in the application for probate.

"I (C.D.) one of the witnesses" to the last will etc.

(E) IN SUCCESSION CERTIFICATE. Written statement filed by objectors is not proper in the eye of law if not verified and supported by affidavit.[19]

(F) BY AN ILLITERATE PERSON. 'A', 'B' by the pen of "C.D".

(G) ORDER 6, R. 15 READ WITH OR. 29, R. 1 OF CPC. Principal officer—Plaint signed and verified by the authorised agent of bank acquainted with the facts of the case—plaint held properly signed and verified.[20]

6 Modes of verification By a verification, the person verifying has to state with reference to the contents of a plaint or of a written statement what, amongst others, of such he verifies on his own knowledge and what he verifies upon information received and believed by him to be true. It may be that every averment in the plaint or in the defence is not within his knowledge. He may have received information from sources which he believes to be true.

A much used form of verification reads as follows:

> "I ...., the plaintiff in the above suit do hereby declare that contents of paras ..... to ..... are true to my knowledge and contents of paras ...... to ......are true to the best of my information and belief and I sign this verification this the ...... day of .... 20 ...... at my lawyer's chamber at Cooch Behar."

18 AIR 1953 HP 95.
19 *National Bank Ltd.* v *Devi Dayal* AIR 1968 Punj 292.
20 *United Bank of India* v *Prabhash Ch. Deb* AIR 1977 Cal 55.

Law does not require that the verifier has to disclose the source of his information. A verification is not faulty in form merely because it does not state the source of information.[1]

A verification in the form "the contents of the plaint are true to the best of my knowledge and belief" is not strict compliance with the Code though it substantially complies with it.[2] It goes against the principle enumerated in Or. 6, r. 15. Again, in a verification stating "to the limit of my knowledge the purport of this is true" is not a verification that can be said to have complied with the rule.[3]

7 Omission, irregularities and defective verification The want of verification does not have the effect of making the plaint void. It does not affect the merits of the case and can be rectified by permitting the party concerned to make good the deficiency by amending the pleading under Or. 6, r. 17, CPC.[4] Even if the plaint or an application is not properly verified, the court has the jurisdiction to exercise its discretion to allow or to refuse proper verification by the plaintiff or the applicant.[5] In case of such amendment where allowed, the plaint should be deemed to have been presented on the date of actual presentation and not on the date of its verification. The question of limitation does not arise.

Suit filed in the name of sole proprietary firm. Plaint verified not by the sole proprietor but by the manager—power of attorney produced during the trial. Rules are substantially complied with and the suit is maintainable.[6]

A defect in verification is a mere irregularity and may be cured at any stage of the suit.[7] In case of defects in verification and affidavits, an opportunity should be given to rectify the defects.[8] A defect in verification should be brought to the notice of the court at the early stage.[9] When an application for leave to sue as pauper was rejected for defective verification, the High Court remanded the application for correction. Defective frame or signature or verification of a plaint or petition can be corrected.[10] Where the petitioner has verified the whole body of the petition with reference to his own knowledge, non-reference to paragraphs is not improper. The law does not prohibit that form of verification.[11] Defective verification is cured when the defendant admits execution of hand-note on which the suit is based.[12]

A verification can be amended even after the period of limitation.[13] And where a defective verification of the plaint is amended, the plaint must be taken to have been presented on the date of the actual presentation. There

1 AIR 1934 Cal 632.
2 AIR 1949 Ajmere 37.
3 ILR 15 All 59.
4 AIR 1950 Mys 70; AIR 1931 All 507; AIR 1925 All 79.
5 *Ram Gopal* v *Surendra Kumar* AIR 1970 All 221.
6 AIR 1976 Mad 151.
7 *Mukhtiar Kaur* v *Ghulab Kaur* AIR 1977 Punj 257.
8 *Suman Jain* v *Jaimala Jain* AIR 2008 Del 91 (DB).
9 *Pushpalata Parshuram Bowkar* v *Madhanlal N. Pittie* 2005 AIHC 1084 (Bom).
10 ILR 55 All 216.
11 *Madhav Upendra* v *Yashwant Sitaram* AIR 1968 Goa 53.
12 *B.R. Sharma* v *Nanak Chand* AIR 1967 All 486.
13 ILR 54 Cal 380.

is a difference between a defective verification in a plaint and that in a winding-up petition under the Companies (Court) Rules. Defect in verification in such a petition is not a mere irregularity—leave cannot be granted to rectify.[14]

In the case of an election petition under the Representation of the Peoples Act, it would be a wrong exercise of discretionary power to dismiss an application on the sole ground of absence of date of verification. The applicant should normally be called upon to remove the lacuna by adding a supplementary verification.[15]

Again, verification of a petition required under s. 281 of the Indian Succession Act is similar to verification required of pleadings under Or. 6, r. 15, CPC. Omission to verify, or defective verification of a pleading is a mere irregularity within s. 99, CPC. An omission to verify, or a defective verification of a petition for probate, cannot have a more serious effect than that of a plaint.[16] But an affidavit in support of the pleadings is required to be furnished under r. 15(4) of Or. 6.

8 Waiver of a defect All objections as to defect, omission, irregularity in verification of a pleading may also be taken. If not taken at the earliest opportunity the plea of waiver may be successfully raised.

Lack of verification as regards some paragraphs—not a defect which affects merit of case or jurisdiction of court.[17]

9 Authority under a power of attorney A power of attorney cannot go beyond the principal. But the general principle of this Rule is that a principal must be in a position to make an authorisation and continue to exert his or her authority so that the agent binds the principal. Where the principal was found to be old, feeble, weak and mentally infirm and not in a position to think independently for herself the power of attorney executed by her would become worthless. Such an agent would be committing an immoral and an unethical act by acting on a power of attorney of a principal whom he knows is mentally unsound, weak, suffers from mental infirmity and has no legal capacity to authorise. This is like continuing to act on a power of attorney of a dead man. If the agent continues to act on the power of attorney his action will be writ large with fraud, misappropriation, cheating and criminal breach of trust. In the instant case[18] the power of attorney was declared null and void.

It, therefore, stands to reason that signature and verification by a constituted attorney needs close scrutiny. Execution of a document by holder of General power of attorney of vendors. Subsequent revocation of authority of executant by vendors. This cannot be a ground for refusal by the Registrar for registration of the deed.[19]

14 *In the matter of Gaya Textiles Pvt. Ltd.* AIR 1968 Cal 388.
15 AIR 1955 SC 610.
16 AIR 1958 All 329.
17 *I.T.C. Ltd.* v *Phurba Lama* AIR 1992 Sikkim 34.
18 *Mahendra Pratap Singh* v *Padam Kumari Devi* AIR 1993 All 143.
19 *Kishori Devi* v *The State of Rajasthan* AIR 1992 Raj 24. (The case of *Goswami Malti* v *Purushottam Lal* AIR 1984 Cal 297 foll.).

CHAPTER

8

On Parties to Suits—Generally

SYNOPSIS

Section 26 of the Code of Civil Procedure lays down that every suit shall be instituted by the presentation of a plaint or in such other manner as may be prescribed. But before a suit is filed, the plaintiff has to decide as to who may be joined as plaintiffs or who may be joined as defendants. The parties so joined, either as plaintiffs or as defendants, are the original parties to the suit. Over and above to cure the defect of non-joinder of necessary parties or of mis-joinder of parties, the plaintiffs by amendment either add some other person as plaintiff or defendant or may delete the name of any person from the category of the plaintiff or of the defendant. The court has also power to strike out or add parties in the suit. Where there are numerous persons having the same interest in one suit, one person may sue or may defend the suit on behalf of all in the same interest. These provisions are contained in Or. 1 of the CPC.[1]

1 Parties to a suit Parties to a suit are normally such persons who figure either as a plaintiff or the defendant in a suit, i.e. parties on record. It may be that no relief is claimed against one or some of such persons and that no decree is passed. Even then, since he was impleaded he shall be deemed to be a party to the suit.

There is, however, the important exception when a person or persons, not actually on record, be regarded as parties to a suit. This arises particularly in suits of representative character, e.g. where a suit is filed against the *Karta* of a joint Hindu family or a trustee or in a suit under Or. 1, r. 8 of CPC. Persons represented by the party on record in such suits are also parties to

1 Ganguly, *Civil Court Practice and Procedure*, 14th Ed., p. 255.

the suit. They, though not formally mentioned in the cause-title of a suit, have to abide by the decision of the court that may be passed in the suit.

A party, whose name is struck off from the record, ceases to be a party to the suit. A minor who is not properly represented by a guardian *ad litem* is not a party to the suit.[2] So also a person of unsound mind not properly represented by a guardian *ad litem* is not a party.[3] But in such cases neither the next friend nor the guardian *ad litem* is a party to the suit.[4] A *benamdar* is not a party to the suit.

2 Classification of parties Parties to a suit may be classified under eight major heads, to wit:

(*a*) Necessary party;
(*b*) Proper party;
(*c*) Intervener;
(*d*) Quasi party (or party for watching proceedings);
(*e*) Pro forma plaintiff;
(*f*) Pro forma defendant;
(*g*) Parties in dual capacity;
(*h*) Unnecessary party.

We would deal with each class of party one after another with reference to laws governing them in the light of latest reported cases.

(a) *Necessary party.* Necessary party is a person who must be included in action either as plaintiff or defendant, unless there is a valid excuse for his nonjoinder.[5] A necessary party is a person without whom no order can effectively be made and whose presence is necessary for a complete and final decision of a proceeding.[6] Persons who are directly interested in the suit should appear as plaintiff or defendants—is the general rule governing selection of parties. Their presence is essential and they are, therefore, necessary parties to a suit. To put it otherwise, persons who ought to be joined as parties are called necessary parties, i.e., persons in whose absence no effective decree can be passed at all. A representative suit was brought by villagers of village 'A' for declaration that they were entitled to take water by means of sluice at a certain point from a supply channel before it reached the tank in village 'B'. The Government was the permanent owner of the channel in question. Held, there could be no effective and complete adjudication in the absence of the Government since any declaration given or injunction granted in favour of the plaintiffs could be rendered inoperative if the Government refused to

2 AIR 1942 Lah 129.
3 AIR 1917 Cal 844. As to who is a necessary party see AIR 1947 All 18; AIR 1953 SC 521; AIR 1970 Raj 167.
4 *Rup Chand* v *Dasodha* ILR (1908)3 All 55.
5 *City of Hutchinson for Human Relations Commission of Hutchinson* v *Hutchinson, Kansas Office of Kansas State Employment Service* 517 P 2d 117.
6 *Mumbai International Airport (P) Ltd.* v *Regency Convention Centre & Hotels (P) Ltd.* AIR 2010 SC 3109; (2010)7 SCC 417.

carry it out and that, therefore, the Government was a necessary party to the suit, even if no relief was asked for against them.[7] In a suit for partition *bona fide* purchasers of suit property are necessary parties.[8] A person only indirectly or remotely interested is not a necessary party. In a suit on promissory note after death of the holder—his right passes by devolution to his heirs—all of them must join in a suit to enforce that entire right as a whole. If any of them refuses to join as a plaintiff, he must be impleaded as a defendant.[9] A third party who has no direct interest in the suit is not a necessary party.[10]

A son is not a necessary party to a suit against his father on a mortgage of his joint family property as he can bring a suit for declaration that the mortgage decree is not binding on his share. But when he himself applies to be made a defendant contending the binding nature of the mortgage, he should be joined as a proper party to the suit under Or. 1, r. 10, CPC to effectually and completely settle the questions involved in the suit and to avoid multiplicity of proceedings[11] (*per* Pollock, J. in *Motiram* v *Lalchand*). Doctors and Nurses of a hospital are not necessary parties in a suit against that hospital for compensation on account of negligence or lapse in treatment.[12]

Unless written statement is filed the question whether the defendant is a necessary party cannot be decided.[13]

A few illustrations may appear useful:

(*i*) PARTITION SUITS. All persons interested in properties are necessary parties to a suit for partition.[14] Third person claiming title to property adverse to the plaintiff in a partition suit is a necessary party and is entitled to be joined in the suit.[15]

(*ii*) PARTNERSHIP. In a suit for dissolution of partnership and accounts—all the partners should be on record.[16] Suit for accounts by one partner against some only of the others is not maintainable. Order 30, r. 4 of the CPC does not sustain such action.[17] In a suit against firm for binding partnership property, all or any of the partners need not be joined by name—Individual partners have to be joined only when they are to be bound personally.[18]

(*iii*) PRE-EMPTION SUIT. (*a*) In a suit for pre-emption in respect of a joint purchase by several co-vendees, all of them are necessary parties.

7 *Champalal* v *Padam Chand* AIR 1971 MP 133.
8 *Dhanalakshmi* v *P. Mohan* AIR 2007 SC 1062.
9 AIR 1949 Mad 161.
10 *Bank of Rajasthan* v *Transocean Bulk Carriers Ltd.* AIR 1999 Mad 105.
11 AIR 1937 Nag 121.
12 *Savita Garg* v *Director, National Heart Institute* AIR 2004 SC 5088.
13 *Gunendra Kumar Das* v *Dwra Steamship* AIR 1989 Cal 398.
14 AIR 1956 Bom 625.
15 *Daitari Prasad* v *Umakanta* AIR 1971 Ori 44.
16 58 Mad LJ 613.
17 AIR 1971 P&H 186.
18 *Vraj Kuwar Bai* v *Kunjbiharilal* AIR 1971 MP 109.

(*b*) A second vendee is necessary party (ILR 35 All 385; AIR 1970 Raj 167).

(*c*) Vendor is not a necessary party (AIR 1943 Lah 252).

(*d*) A rival pre-emptor is a necessary party to a suit for pre-emption (AIR 1948 Nag 32).

(*iv*) SUIT BY CO-OWNERS. All co-owners are necessary parties to a suit to recover joint property, but one of the several co-owners can maintain an action in ejectment against a trespasser without impleading other co-owners (AIR 1965 SC 271; AIR 1971 Cal 252; AIR 1970 Pat 1; AIR 1967 Mys 143) though it may be desirable to add them as proper parties (AIR 1956 MB 35; AIR 1953 All 331).

(*v*) JOINT PROMISEES. (Section 45 of the Contract Act). Section 45 deals with devolution of joint rights in the case of joint promisees, but it does not deal with a case where a joint promisee does not want to join as a co-plaintiff and is arrayed as a pro forma defendant with the specific plea that no relief is claimed against him. The judgment and the decree in such a case, in fact, enures to his benefit also.

A person cannot be compelled to be a plaintiff for, as is obvious, he cannot be compelled to bring an action at law if he does not want to do so. At the same time, it is equally true that a person cannot be prevented from bringing an action, by any rule of law or practice, merely because he is a joint promisee and the other promisee refuses to join as a co-plaintiff. The proper and the only course in such cases is to join him as a pro forma defendant. Therefore, where two parties contract with a third party a suit by one of the joint promisees making the other as co-defendant, is maintainable even if the plaintiff does not prove that the other joint promisee has refused to join him as a co-plaintiff (*Jahar Roy* v *Premji Bhimji Mansata* AIR 1977 SC 2439).

(*vi*) ADMINISTRATION SUIT. In an administration suit, the legal personal representatives of the deceased are necessary parties (AIR 1932 PC 146).

(*vii*) SUIT ON TORTS. All persons jointly injured need not be impleaded as parties to a suit on Torts (ILR 25 Cal 285; AIR 1932 Mad 583).

(*viii*) AGAINST GOVERNMENT. (*a*) Where any act of the Government is questioned or the proprietary right or right to revenue of the Government is likely to be affected, the Government is a necessary party to the suit (AIR 1950 Ori 257; AIR 1943 Cal 114).

(*b*) Where the Government has no interest of any kind in the suit it is neither a necessary party nor a proper party.[19]

19 AIR 1947 Cal 332; AIR 1936 PC 150.

(c) Revenue sale for realisation of Government dues—Suit to set aside sale. Government is a necessary party.[20]

(b) *Proper party*. A proper party is one in whose absence an effective order can be made, but whose presence is necessary for a complete and final decision on the question involved in the proceeding.[1] The distinction between a necessary party and a proper party lies in the comparative utility of the parties at the trial. In the absence of a necessary party, the court cannot pass any effective decree at all,[2] but in the absence of a proper party the decree can be passed so far it relates to parties who are before the court.

In some cases it may be expedient to join other persons as parties whose presence before the court may be necessary in order to enable the court effectually and completely to adjudicate upon and settle all questions involved in the suit. Plaintiff sought for declaration that she was the legally wedded wife of the defendant. The defendant's earlier wife and son filed a petition to the court for being added as defendants, and they were interested to deny the marriage of the defendant with the plaintiff. The petitioner satisfied conditions of Or. 1, r. 10(2), CPC. They were added as proper party.[3] Such persons when joined constitute a proper party. It means a party who may be interested in the result of the suit and who may have a right to seek assistance of court in coming to a decision on point of issue.[4] In an application for grant of letter of administration the resondent registered society is a proper party.[5]

The object of adding proper parties to a suit is to ascertain the truth or otherwise of the pleadings by eliciting confirmation or objection, if any, from the parties so added and brought on record. The procedure avoids multiplicity of suits and protects interest or interests of a party already on record. Obviously, there is some reference to proper parties in the plaint in all cases where proper party is added.

It is, therefore, correct to say that a necessary party is always a proper party, but a proper party may not always be a necessary party.

A few illustrations may serve an inquisitive reader:

(*i*) Whenever there are allegations of bad faith, misconduct and impropriety and not merely illegality made against the Returning Officer in an election petition, the Returning Officer is a proper party (AIR 1969 Mad 116).

(*ii*) Divorce petition filed by wife against husband—Adulteress joined as correspondent. She is neither a proper party nor a necessary party under rr. 11 and 12(*a*) of the rules framed under the Hindu Marriage Act (AIR 1966 Punj 337). Under the Special Marriage Act (Calcutta

20 AIR 1967 MP 150.
1 *Udit Narayan Singh* v *Board of Revenue* AIR 1963 SC 786.
2 *Ruma Chakraborty* v *Sudha Rani Banerjee* AIR 2005 SC 3557.
3 AIR 1958 MP 195.
4 AIR 1953 Hyd 170. (See AIR 1925 Cal 1257).
5 *Anantanand* v *Pragatisheet Jotiyiar (Raiger) S.S. Sansthan* AIR 2014 Raj 95 (DB).

High Court) Rules, 1955 (printed under r. 340A of Civil Rules and Orders, Vol. I), Rule 10 enjoins:

> "In every petition for divorce on the ground of adultery, the alleged adulterer shall be impleaded as a co-respondent:
>
> Provided that the court may, on being satisfied that the petitioner has not been able to ascertain the name and identity of the alleged adulterer, excuse the petitioner from so impleading him:
>
> Provided further that if after the court has so excused the petitioner, the identity of the alleged adulterer is discovered, the fact must be brought to the notice of the court, and the court shall thereafter pass such order as it may think fit."

The order contemplated therein, it is submitted, is an order under Or. 1, r. 10 to implead the alleged adulterer as a co-respondent.

To sum up: A person would be a necessary party if he ought to have been joined, that is to say, in whose absence no effective decree can be passed at all. He would be a proper party to be impleaded if his presence is necessary for an effectual or complete adjudication[6] to bind them as well by the decree and avoid thereby multiplicity of suits.

(c) *Intervener.* An intervener is a person who is not a party to the suit, but who intervenes either on his own behalf or on behalf of the public or a section thereof, or an intervener is a person who voluntarily interposes in an action or other proceeding with the leave of the court.[7] We have seen above that under Or. 1, r. 10 of the CPC, the court is empowered to add parties at any stage of the proceeding *suo motu* or on application of a person seeking to be made a party, i.e., seeking to intervene in the proceeding. Such a person is an intervener.

To put in the language of Wharton: "Interveners are third persons, not originally parties to a suit, who claim an interest in the matter and right to interpose at any stage of the suit in defence of their own interest, whenever affected either as to person or property" (*Law Lexicon*—pp. 431-432).

If a third party files a petition seeking intervention, the court is called upon to consider whether there are just grounds to entertain the petition; for, it is not generally the province of the court to force the plaintiff in a case to implead particular persons as plaintiffs. The power contemplated in Or. 1, r. 10(2), CPC is a discretionary power and, as in all cases, the discretion should be judicially exercised. "What the court ought to see, when a person applies to be made a party, is whether there is anything which cannot be determined owing to his absence, or whether a third person will be prejudiced by his not being joined as a party" (*per* Kumaraswamy Sastri, J. in *Vattam Ramakrishnayya* v *Vattini Satyanarayana*).[8]

We would refer to certain conditions when intervention should be allowed or disallowed:

6 AIR 1941 FC 16.
7 Mitra's *Legal and Commercial Dictionary*, 6th Ed.
8 AIR 1929 Mad 291.

(i) WHEN INTERVENTION IS ALLOWED. If on construction of a plaint it appears that a necessary party has been left out and if such person seeks intervention it should be forthwith allowed.

The matter hinges on a true and correct interpretation of the powers contemplated in provisions under Or. 1, r. 10(2) of the CPC. The court has been granted power to add plaintiff(s) or defendant(s) "whose presence before the court may be necessary in order to enable the court effectually and completely to adjudicate upon and settle all the questions involved in the suit". The expression "all the questions involved in the suit" refers to questions on record and between parties already on record. Persons whose interests would be affected by the litigation are entitled to come on record to protect their interests when those are jeopardised by the persons already on record.[9]

Therefore, an intervener who is not considered as necessary party should not be allowed to intervene. The opinion is divergent on this point. According to latter view,[10] the expression "all the questions involved in the suit" may mean questions which have been mentioned in the pleadings by the parties as also which may be raised by any of such parties and third persons. When a court is to completely adjudicate upon and settle all such questions once for all, thereby the court's hands are not fettered to add such third persons either *suo motu* or on their seeking. This will rule out fresh litigation over the same question. Though it is not the province of the court, as we have submitted hereinbefore, to force the plaintiff to implead a third person against his wishes, the court will not hesitate to order addition of intervener if his presence is considered necessary keeping the above principle in view.

Everything is permissible up to a certain length. A court has to exercise the power judicially. Instead of effectual and complete adjudication, if such addition tends to embarrassment of the plaintiff the procedure should not be adopted.

Intervention under Special Rules.[11]

(ii) WHEN INTERVENTION IS DISALLOWED. Before succeeding in a petition for intervention the applicant has to establish that he has personal interest in the reliefs of the suit. If he has had no interest he is neither a necessary nor a proper party and his prayer for intervention will be, for obvious reasons, rejected. Again, when such applicant has had interest adverse both to the plaintiff and the defendant on record he has the right to intervene.

Again, "where by allowing a person to be impleaded as a party the nature of the suit will be altered, the application should not be allowed (*per* Haveliwala, A.C.J. in *Mukhi Jeramdas Jethanand* v *Tikamal Mulchand*).[12]

9 *P.R. Nallathambi* v *V. Raghavan* AIR 1973 Mad 25.

10 AIR 1929 Mad 443 (In this case Government applied to be made party-defendant to which both plaintiff and defendant opposed—Government being proper party should be added).

11 For Intervention under Special Rules—See Calcutta High Court Original Side Admiralty Rule No. 12, Non-domiciled Divorce Rule No. 12. Matrimonial Suits Rule No. 8 etc.

12 AIR 1935 Sind 194.

Thus, whether intervention shall be allowed or not depends on the merits of each particular case. In dispensing justice the court's powers are unfettered in the matter of adding parties.

Rule 8A under Or. 1 permits a court to allow a person or a body of persons to intervene and to take part in the proceedings of the suit.

Rule 8A reads: While trying a suit, the court may, if satisfied that a person or body of persons is interested in any question of law which is directly and substantially in issue in the suit and that it is necessary in the public interest to allow that person or body of persons to present his or its opinion on that question of law, permit that person or body of persons to present such opinion and to take such part in the proceedings of the suit and the court may specify.

This provision, however, does not militate against general power in Or. 1, r. 10(1) and r. 10(2).

(d) *Quasi party*. In some cases courts of law have allowed third parties to watch the proceedings in order that they may be bound by such proceedings. Under s. 283 of the Indian Succession Act 1925, persons claiming to have an interest in the estate of the deceased, to whom citations are issued, are entitled to come and see the proceedings before grant of probate or letters of administration.

Section 283, Indian Succession Act reads: (1) In all cases the District Judge or the District delegate may, if he thinks proper,—

(*a*) .....

(*b*) .....

(*c*) ..... issue citations calling upon all persons claiming to have any interest in the estate of the deceased to come and see the proceedings before the grant of probate or letters of administration.

The object of special citation is to give notice to persons interested in the estate of the deceased of the proceedings for grant, for it is obligatory upon the court, when it is brought to its notice that there is a person entitled to special citation, to issue such citation and it is the bounden duty of a propounder to have special citation served upon a person who, under the law, is entitled thereto.[13] In a petition for appointment of guardian of a minor under s. 10(1) of the Guardians and Wards Act, the petitioner has to state what near relations the minor has. If the court thinks expedient, notice is served on them to elicit their objection, if any. The provision in s. 31(4) of the Guardians and Wards Act may also be seen in this connection. The court is competent to hear "any person" in connection with a petition for purposes referred to in ss. 28 and 29 of the Act.

In partition suits, mortgagees of co-sharers are sometimes given leave to watch the proceedings in order to safeguard their interests.[14]

In no case, however, ought anybody to be added as a party to the suit merely for the purpose of watching proceedings. "It appears to me to be a

13 AIR 1931 Cal 497.
14 35 CWN 296.

mistake to make an order for a person to be a party for watching the proceedings. I see neither meaning nor purpose in such an order. The applicants who have no interest to the extent of 15/16th share to the property ought not to be allowed to become parties to the proceedings."[15]

(e) *Pro forma plaintiff.* Adding a pro forma plaintiff is to burden the plaint practically for nothing. The idea of pro forma plaintiff is repugnant[16] to law.

Order 1, r. 1 provides: "All persons may be joined in one suit as plaintiffs where (*a*) any right to relief in respect of, or arising out of, the same act or transaction or series of acts or transactions is alleged to exist in such persons, whether jointly, severally or in the alternative; and (*b*) if such persons brought separate suits, any common question of law or fact would arise." Accordingly, when a suit is commenced all parties should unite leaving scarcely any scope for a plaintiff to be joined with plaintiffs on record as a pro forma plaintiff. However, some persons, though very rare, are joined as pro forma plaintiffs. They have no relief to claim nor any relief is claimed for such pro forma plaintiffs even.

(f) *Pro forma (or, nominal) defendant.* When a person is made a nominal party to a suit but in which no relief is asked for against him, he is known as a pro forma defendant.

In the language of Mr. Rankin, J.: "It does happen sometimes that a person is impleaded merely for the sake of conformity, as for example, the plaintiff's co-sharers. A person may be impleaded to represent the legal interest although he is a bare trustee having no real interest in the matter, or he may be impleaded because he has a right or title which is affected by the order sought though not prejudicially affected. There are circumstances under which it is not improper in ordinary language to describe a defendant as being pro forma.[17]

Even so, "Pro-defendant is not a term that ought ever to appear in the Cause Title of any suit or proceeding."

The expression pro forma defendant is not known to law.[1] There is not necessarily a conflict of interest between a pro forma defendant and other defendants.

A person may be added as a pro forma defendant even after the period of limitation. "Rules of limitation apply only to claims. The fact that a claim is barred against a particular defendant does not prevent that defendant being impleaded pro forma."[2]

On the death of a pro forma defendant omission to bring on record his legal representatives does not cause the suit to abate.[3]

(g) *Parties in dual capacity.* A person suing and a person sued can have more capacities than one ... Thus a person may sue and be sued in his personal as

15 ILR 56 Cal 447, 451, 452.
16 8 CWN 408.
17 ILR 55 Cal 590.
1 41 IC 468.
2 AIR 1937 All 502.
3 44 IA 218.

well as representative capacity. (Case of a plaintiff against a handful of fishermen under Or. 1, r. 8, CPC).[4]

It is not necessary that when a person is sued in two capacities, his name should be repeated twice in the Cause-title. It is sufficient if the two capacities are indicated in the body of the plaint, and if that is done, he will be considered to be a party in the suit in both the capacities.[5]

Even where it is permissible to sue in different capacities, the court has a discretion to order separate suits to be filed or separate trial of the claims made in such capacity. Thus, where a plaintiff in his individual capacity sought to recover possession of properties B, C, D & E and as *shebait* of the deity Nandadulal Thakur sought to recover possession of property 'A', it was held in a Calcutta case, that the plaint should be treated as comprising two suits—one at the instance of the plaintiff as *shebait* and the other at the instance of the plaintiff in his personal capacity—and the two suits should be separately tried.[6]

Order 2, r. 5 is an exception to this rule which reads: "No claim by or against an executor, administrator or heir, as such, shall be joined with claims by or against him personally, unless the last-mentioned claims are alleged to arise with reference to the estate in respect of which the plaintiff or the defendant sues or is sued as executor, administrator or heir, or are such as he was entitled to, or liable for, jointly with the deceased person whom he represents."

(h) *Unnecesary party*. Strictly speaking, no person should be impleaded in a suit if he is neither a necessary party nor a proper party. Party introduced having no connection with reliefs claimed in the plaint—it is a case of improper joining, technically known as 'mis-joinder'. To put it otherwise, when a person is impleaded in a suit contrary to provisions of the Code of Civil Procedure, there arises a case of misjoinder. And, in a case of improper joinder, the proper course is to strike out names of parties so joined.

A person wrongfully or unnecessarily made a party is entitled to costs. Therefore, before impleading a party it has to be considered whether a person should be impleaded at all, e.g., in a pre-emption suit vendor is not a necessary party to the suit.

Order 22, r. 10. *Lis pendens transferee*. The plaintiff is not bound to implead him. However, he is vitally interested in litigation. The court in its discretion can implead him as a proper party under Or. 22, r. 10(1), CPC.[7]

3 Misjoinder of parties The objection as to misjoinder of parties shall have to be taken at the earliest possible opportunity and in all cases where issues are settled, at or before such settlement unless grounds of such objection have subsequently arisen.[8] If no such objection is taken it will be deemed to have

4 AIR 1940 Pat 247.
5 AIR 1943 Cal 319.
6 AIR 1928 Cal 199.
7 *Jagannath Mahaprabhu* v *Pravat Chandra Chatterjee* AIR 1992 Ori 47.
8 *Sri Ram* v *Jagannath* AIR 1976 SC 2335.

been waived. Similar is the case of the objection regarding misjoinder of cause of action.[9]

4 Misdescription of parties Where a party has been wrongly described in the title of a suit, it is a case of misdescription. Where it is clear who the person is who intends to sue or who is intended to be sued but is described wrongly, it is a case of misdescription of parties which can be corrected by the court at any time.[10]

This correction is allowed under s. 153 of the Code of Civil Procedure which reads: "The court may at any time, and on such terms as to costs or otherwise as it may think fit, amend any defect or error in any proceeding in a suit, and all necessary amendments shall be made for the purpose of determining the real question or issue raised by or depending on such proceeding." For example, a defendant in a suit was described as a manager of a firm by mistake, amendment describing defendant individually allowed.[11] Plaintiff suing through mistake as owner of a firm—mistake is curable.[12]

But the amendment sought purportedly to remove misdescription cannot be resorted to as a camouflage for substitution. Where one person sues or is sued but another person is sought to be substituted in his place, the case cannot be treated as one of misdescription. Such substitution can be allowed provided it is not barred by limitation.

5 Party when dead at the time of institution of suit The matter is to be considered (*i*) when there is sole plaintiff or sole defendant, (*ii*) when there are several plaintiffs or several defendants.

When a suit is instituted in the name of a sole plaintiff or a sole defendant who is dead at the time of the institution of the suit, the same is a nullity. The plaint cannot be amended by bringing legal representatives of the deceased on record.[13] (For contrary view see AIR 1938 Nag 458).

A suit, filed by or against a dead person being a nullity, the legal representatives of such a dead person cannot be added.[14] If a suit is brought against a dead person who was already dead prior to the filing of the plaint, institution of such suit is not void *ab initio* and the plaintiff can be permitted to implead the legal representatives when the dead person had been impleaded due to *bona fide* mistake.[15] In a writ petition filed before the High Court the name of a party who was long dead had been wrongly included as one of the applicants by *bona fide* mistake. The court may permit the legal representatives of the deceased party to be impleaded.[16]

9 *R.M.A.L. Visalakshmi Achi* v *R.M. Sreenivasan* 2000 AIHC 3827.
10 AIR 1914 Mad 636.
11 AIR 1924 Sind 144.
12 AIR 1969 Mys 111.
13 *Khaja Begum* v *Gulam* AIR 1976 AP 65.
14 *Cuttack Municipality* v *Shyam Sunder Behara* AIR 1977 Ori 137.
15 *R. Rajalakshmamma* v *R. Kankaiah* AIR 1978 AP 279.
16 *Jaswant* v *Financial Commissioner* AIR 1993 P&H 111 (DB).

Where, however, there are several plaintiffs or several defendants and one of them died, the suit cannot be said to be void *ab initio*. The name of the deceased should be struck out and the suit shall proceed. It cannot be said that in such a case the suit was not validly instituted against any one.[17]

Suit filed against a dead person. Plaintiff becomes aware of defendant's death from remarks on returned summons. Plaintiff sought for impleadment of L/R's of defendant property thereafter. Plaintiff is entitled to invoke proviso to s. 21(1) of the Limitation Act.[18]

Suit filed against more than one defendant. One of the defendants is dead at the time of institution of suit. *Held*, death of defendant renders the suit a nullity. Provisions in Or. 1, r. 10, CPC could be invoked for bringing heirs on record.[19]

When a suit or appeal was preferred against several respondents and one of them was dead, the suit/appeal was proper and maintainable. It was not so much a question of substitution. Order 1, r. 10 comes into play.[20]

Misjoinder and non-joinder. "No suit shall be defeated by reason of the misjoinder or non-joinder of parties, and the court may in every suit deal with the matter in controversy so far as regards the rights and interests of the parties actually before it.

Provided that nothing in this rule shall apply to non-joinder of a necessary party." [Or. 1, r. 9].

6 Addition or substitution of plaintiff [Or. 1, r. 10(1)] A court has power to add parties to a suit. It has power to strike out parties from the suit. The power is contemplated under Or. 1, r. 10, CPC which reads:

> "Order 1, r. 10(1). Where a suit has been instituted in the name of the wrong person as plaintiff or where it is doubtful whether it has been instituted in the name of the right plaintiff, the court may at any stage of the suit, if satisfied that the suit has been instituted through a *bona fide* mistake, and that it is necessary for the determination of the real matter in dispute so to do, order any other person to be substituted or added as the plaintiff upon such terms as the court thinks just."

The rule contemplates two different types of cases—(*i*) where a suit is brought by a plaintiff who subsequently discovers that he cannot get the full relief he seeks without the joinder of some other person as co-plaintiff, (*ii*) where in a suit it is found that some other person, and not the original plaintiff, is entitled to the relief claimed.[1] In the former contingency, a new party has to be added and in the latter a new party has to be substituted as the plaintiff.[2]

17 AIR 1934 All 25.
18 *Karnappa Swamy* v *C. Rammurthy* AIR 1993 SC 2324.
19 *Nevandroar Javernal* v *Debikabai* AIR 1982 Bom 589.
20 *Alabhai* v *Bhura Bhya* AIR 1937 Bom 401 see also *Muswant Ashgani Bibi* v *Shamal Kumar Basu Mallick* AIR 1986 Cal 227.
1 AIR 1939 PC 170.
2 8 IC 87; AIR 1934 Nag 159; 13 IC 350.

Conditions required:

(*i*) The suit may have been instituted in the name of wrong person as plaintiff.

(*ii*) The suit may have been instituted in the name of person where there is doubt if the suit was instituted in the name of the right man.

(*iii*) The court has to be satisfied that such suit was instituted through a *bona fide* mistake, and

(*iv*) Addition and/or substitution was necessary for the determination of the real matter in dispute.

Therefore, unless the first two conditions are satisfied, a defendant is entitled to dismissal of a suit brought by an unauthorised person and the defect cannot be cured by addition or substitution of persons who might have brought the suit.[3] Another equally important condition for applicability of the sub-rule is that the action was commenced in the name of the original plaintiff by a *bona fide* mistake. The mistake may be of fact, may be of law, but it must be an honest mistake and not a deliberate one to bring it within the class *'bona fide'*. 'A', agent of 'B', files a suit in his own name by a *bona fide* mistake. Court can substitute name of Principal 'B' for that of original plaintiff 'A'.[4]

Finally, the substitution or addition should be necessary for determination of real matter in dispute. This may be done at any stage, and even in appeal.[5] When, however, a party seeks to add a new party after the expiry of the period of limitation the court may refuse such prayer.[6] While no addition can be allowed after limitation[7] for substitution of one plaintiff for the other under Or. 1, r. 10(1) limitation does not apply.

7 Addition and striking out of parties [Or. 1, r. 10(2)] Order 1, r. 10(2). The court may at any stage of the proceedings, either upon or without the application of either party, and on such terms as may appear to the court to be just, order that the name of any party improperly joined, whether as plaintiff or defendant, be struck out, and that the name of any person who ought to have been joinded, whether as plaintiff or defendant, or whose presence before the court may be necessary in order to enable the court effectually and completely to adjudicate upon and settle all the questions involved in the suit, be added.

Impleading of a party. Power of court to do so does not depend solely on the question whether the party has interest in the suit property. The question to be considered is whether the right of the party may be affected if he is not added as a party.[8]

Under r. 10(2) of Or. 1, CPC the court has power:

(*i*) to proceed *suo motu*,

3 AIR 1957 Cal 688.
4 AIR 1927 Bom 424.
5 *Conugunta Subbarayudu* v *E. Brahmananda* AIR 1970 AP 211.
6 *K.C.S.F. Ltd.* v *R.P. Mills* AIR 1984 All 143.
7 *Bihar Co.-op. Motor Vehicles Insurance Society Ltd.* v *Rameshwar* AIR 1970 Pat 172.
8 *Torai Tea Co.* v *Kumkum Mittal* AIR 1994 Cal 191.

(*ii*) to proceed on the application of either party to a suit,

(*iii*) to proceed at any stage of the proceeding,

(*iv*) to proceed on any just term,

(*v*) to strike out any party improperly joined whether as plaintiff or as defendant,

(*vi*) to add name of any person who ought to have been joined whether as plaintiff or defendant,

(*vii*) to add name of any person whose presence before the court may be necessary in order to enable the court effectually and completely to adjudicate upon and settle all questions involved in the suit before the court.

Order 1, r. 10(2) gives a wide discretion to the court to meet every case of defect of parties. But this discretion should be exercised in a reasonable manner so as not to cause inconvenience or embarrassment.[9] The principles governing the power of the court under Or. 1, r. 10, CPC are that as a rule the court should not add a person as defendant in a suit when the plaintiff is opposed to such addition. The reason is that the plaintiff is the '*dominus litis*'. He cannot be compelled to fight against a person whom he does not wish to fight and against whom he does not claim any relief. The word 'may' in sub-rule (2) imports a discretion. In exercising that discretion, the courts will invariably take into account the wishes of the plaintiff before adding a third person as a defendant to his suit.[10]

(I) ADDITION OF PARTIES. Where a person is neither a necessary nor a proper party, the court has no jurisdiction to add him as a party under this sub-rule. If a petitioner is neither a necessary nor a proper party, his application for addition of parties should be rejected.[11] Otherwise, the power may be exercised at any stage. Party can be added before decree is actually drawn up.[12] Where an application was made at a late stage, the court will refuse to exercise its discretion under sub-rule (2). Apart from this rule, the court has power to add parties on general principles where such addition is expedient.[13]

A court has power to act under this rule after a preliminary decree and add a party and thus reopen the proceedings.

For obvious reasons the plaint has got to be amended where a defendant is sought to be added under the court's orders.

ADDITION OF PARTY IN APPEAL. Order 41, r. 20(2). The court has jurisdiction to implead a person as a respondent in appeal if he was a party in a suit even though the period of limitation has expired.[14]

9 AIR 1956 Cal 263.

10 AIR 1968 Mad 287; *Gonsalo De Filomena Luis* v *I.P.H. Fernandes* AIR 1977 Goa 4.

11 *Paras Nath* v *Additional District Judge* 2016(3) All LJ 311 (All).

12 61 IC 378.

13 AIR 1954 All 11.

14 *Paramjit Singh* v *A.D.J., Ludhiana* AIR 1993 P&H 122.

(II) STRIKING OUT PARTIES. Party introduced having no connection with relief claimed in suit is a case of improper joinder. In case of improper joinder of defendants the proper course is to strike out names of such defendants and not to dismiss the suit as against them.[15] This improper joinder is, technically speaking, a case of mis-joinder and names of unnecessary parties are to be struck out.

Parties whose names are struck out cease to be parties to a suit and must be treated as persons who have been dismissed from suit and not as persons against whom the suit has been dismissed.[16] They are discharged, not that they have been defeated.

If a party is found to have been unnecessarily impleaded the court has always the power to delete his name. Such striking out of the name of the defendant who has been unnecessarily impleaded in the suit can be done at any stage of the proceeding.[17] But only because a defendant has not filed written statement his name should not be deleted if he is really a necessary party.[18]

In a divorce petition filed by the wife against her husband, the adulterer is neither a necessary party nor a proper party. Her application to remove her name from divorce petition must succeed.[19] But see Note 2(*b*) proper party ante at pp. 95-96.

Order 1, r. 10(4) enjoins: "Where a defendant is added, the plaint shall, unless the court otherwise directs, be amended in such manner as may be necessary, and amended copies of summons and of the plaint shall be served on the new defendant and, if the court thinks fit, on the original defendant". The amendment referred to in this sub-rule is such amendment as is necessitated by addition of a defendant and not such as would add to or alter the nature of the suit as originally brought.

Coming to the question of limitation where a new party is added:

Order 1, r. 10(5) reads: Subject to the provisions of the Limitation Act 1963, s. 21, the proceedings as against any person added as the defendant shall be deemed to have begun only on the service of the summons.

Section 21 of the Limitation Act 1963. "(1) Where, after the institution of a suit, a new plaintiff or, defendant is substituted or added, the suit shall, as regards him, be deemed to have been instituted when he was so made a party:

Provided that where the court is satisfied that the omission to include a new plaintiff or defendant was due to a mistake made in good faith it may direct that the suit as regards such plaintiff or defendant shall be deemed to have been instituted on any earlier date.

(2) Nothing in sub-section (1) shall apply to a case where a party is added or substituted owing to assignment or devolution of any interest during the

15 AIR 1955 Nag 234.
16 AIR 1938 Mad 435.
17 *International Air Transport* v *Aziz Fatima* AIR 1985 Del 381.
18 *Ajodhya Dei* v *Braja Mohan* (1987)1 Cur Civ Cas 1073 (Ori).
19 *Sarla Sharma* v *Shankuntala* AIR 1966 Punj 337.

pendency of a suit or where a plaintiff is made a defendant or a defendant is made a plaintiff."

8 Transposition of parties A transfer of parties from one side to the other, i.e. from the side of the plaintiffs to the defence and *vice versa*, is known as transposition of parties.

Wherever the ends of substantial justice require a transfer of parties from one side to the other, this power is exercised *suo motu* or on application of either party. "The course of adding pro forma defendants as co-plaintiffs should always be added where it is necessary for a complete adjudication upon the questions involved in the suit and to avoid multiplicity of proceeding.[20] Again, in *Nirod Chandra Banerjee* v *Prafulla Chandra Banerjee*, it was held: "Transfer of parties from one side to the other should be granted where refusal would prejudicially affect the applicant" (*per* Mookherjee and Rankin, JJ).[1]

The Supreme Court reaffirmed the principle and observed as follows: "The power under the provision [Or. 1, r. 10(2), CPC] is exercisable by the court even *suo motu*. As pointed out by the Privy Council in *Bhupendra* v *Rajeswar* (AIR 1931 PC 162), the power ought to be exercised by a court for doing complete justice between the parties."[2] Transposition was allowed by amendment enabling the court to effectually and completely adjudicate all questions involved in the suit.[3] The power is inherent in the court[4] under s. 151, CPC. Transposition is generally resorted to in partnership suits and partition suits.

We would hereunder discuss—

(*i*) Transposition of defendant as plaintiff;

(*ii*) Transposition of plaintiff as defendant.

(i) *Transposition of defendant as plaintiff.* The transposition of a defendant as a co-plaintiff should always be allowed "where it is necessary for a complete adjudication upon the questions involved in the suit and to avoid multiplicity of proceedings. But such a transposition of defendant as a plaintiff should not be granted if it results in changing the character of the suit.[5] It was held: Court has jurisdiction to make the transposition of a defendant into a plaintiff after the expiry of the limitation period within which the suit by the transposed defendant could have been brought, where the claim is identically the same whether preferred by one plaintiff or the other.[6] A plaintiff can be transposed to the category of defendant and *vice versa*.[7] In a partition suit transposition of defendant as plaintiff is always permissible.[8] Before allowing a party to be

20 AIR 1931 PC 162. (Also see AIR 1939 Pat 397).
1 AIR 1925 Cal 421; AIR 1941 Mad 364.
2 AIR 1965 SC 1812.
3 *Bhismadev Taria* v *Radhakishan Agarwalla* AIR 1968 Ori 230.
4 AIR 1937 Mad 563.
5 AIR 1922 Cal 454.
6 AIR 1935 Mad 95.
7 *Kiran Tandan* v *Allahabad Development Authority* AIR 2004 SC 2006.
8 A. *Thakurdas* v A. *Venilal* AIR 1977 Kant 60.

transposed as a plaintiff, the court can insist that it should be *prima facie* satisfied about (*i*) the *bona fides* of the applicant, (*ii*) the plausibility of the applicant's claim and (*iii*) the genuineness of his interest in the litigation.[9] No order of transposition as a plaintiff or addition of a new plaintiff should ordinarily be passed where it is *prima facie* patent that if the newly added party or the transposed plaintiff had originally filed the suit on the date when the suit in question was in fact filed, it would have been doubtlessly barred by time.[10] Transposition of defendant to the array of plaintiffs cannot be permitted if it alters the nature of the suit.[11]

When the company petition is filed with the consent of the other shareholders, the same must be treated in a representative capacity and therefore, the making of an application for withdrawal by the original petitioner in the company petition would not render the petition under s. 397 or s. 398 of the Companies Act 1956, non-existent. The other shareholders who have given their consent to file the suit can be transposed as petitioners in the said case.[12]

Under Or. 1, r. 11 read with Or. 1, r. 10, the court has power to transpose a defendant as plaintiff and give him the conduct of the suit.

The law as to the transposition of a defendant to the category of plaintiff is well settled. Where it is necessary for a complete adjudication of the question involved in the suit, parties may be added or transposed. But where by the court's order, character of the suit may be altered by the addition or transposition of the intervener defendant and the party sought to be transposed does not wish to adopt the plaintiff's case transposition can never be permitted.[13]

(ii) ***Transposing plaintiff as defendant.*** Under Or. 1, r. 10 one of the plaintiffs can be transposed as a defendant if his original joinder was improper. The court has, apart from provisions in Or. 1, r. 10, inherent power to transpose one of the plaintiff's as a defendant.[14]

9 *Arjan Singh* v *Kartar Singh* AIR 1975 P&H 184.
10 *Manphool* v *Surja Ram* AIR 1978 P&H 216.
11 *Kalyan Singh* v *Kagdi Ram* AIR 1977 HP 73.
12 *B.D. Pvt. Ltd.* v *Peerless General Finance Investment Co. Ltd.* AIR 2013 SC 1690.
13 *Durga Prasad* v *Lal Babu Sha* AIR 1984 Pat 310.
14 AIR 1925 Cal 328.

CHAPTER

9

On Parties to Suits—In Particular

SYNOPSIS

1 Administrator Code of Civil Procedure provides under Or. 31 a comprehensive set of rules regarding suits by or against Trustees, Executors and Administrators.

Rule 1 (states)— "In all suits concerning property vested in a trustee, executor or administrator, where the contention is between the persons beneficially interested in such property and a third person, the trustee, executor or administrator shall represent the persons so interested, and it shall not ordinarily be necessary to make them parties to the suit. But the Court may, if it thinks fit, order them or any of them to be made parties.

Rule 2.—"Where there are several trustees, executors or administrators, they shall all be made parties[1] to a suit against one or more of them."

But administrators outside India need not be made parties. For an infant, administrator guardian *ad litem* has to be appointed to avoid non-joinder.

Beneficiaries need not be joined in such a suit, but they may be added. We should remember that the suit contemplated in Or. 31 of the Code must be with regard to a contention not in between beneficiaries themselves nor in between beneficiaries and administrators but in between beneficiaries and third person/s.

Finally, an Administrator may commence a suit for administration where there are disputes between heirs and legatees and when he is in doubt as to how the estate should be administered.

2 Administrator-General Under s. 5 of the Administrator-General's Act, the Administrator-General shall be a corporation sole by the name of the Administrator-General of the State for which he is appointed and as such Administrator-General shall have perpetual succession and an official seal, and may sue and be sued in his corporate name.

The Administrator-General is in the position of an inter-pleader plaintiff and is entitled to recover his costs from the losing claimant.[2] Again, s. 40 of the Act provides that a creditor suit the Administrator-General shall be liable to pay costs unless he had applied in writing to the Administrator-General in the manner required by the section.

Nothing in s. 80, CPC shall apply to any suit against the Administrator-General in which no relief is claimed against him personally. (See s. 41 of the Administrator-General's Act 1913).

3 Advocate-General In special proceedings like those contemplated in ss. 91 (public nuisance) and 92 (public charities) of the Code of Civil Procedure and under the Mental Health Care Act, the Advocate-General is entitled to initiate and intervene in any proceedings in civil courts.

Under s. 93 of the Code, the powers conferred by ss. 91 and 92 on the Advocate-General may, outside the Presidency towns, be, with the previous sanction of the State Government, exercised also by the Collector or by such officer as the State Government may appoint in the behalf.

Under Or. 27A, r. 1 in any suit in which it appears to the court that any such question as is referred to in cl. (1) of Art. 132 read with Art. 147 of the Constitution, is involved, the court shall not proceed to determine that question until after notice has been given to the Attorney-General for India if the question of law concerns the Central Government and to the Advocate-General of the State if the question of law concerns a State Government.

1 AIR 1934 All 1.
2 ILR 10 Bom 350.

4 Agent An agent is entitled to bring a suit on behalf of his principal in the latter's name under certain conditions. Again, if he files a suit in his own name by a *bona fide* mistake, the name of the principal may be substituted under Or. 1, r. 10(1) of the CPC. Under Or. 3, r. 1 of the Code a recognised agent is entitled, save where otherwise expressly provided by law, to make appearance, file application or act in or to any court.

Persons holding powers of attorney, authorising them to make and do such appearances, applications and acts on behalf of parties, are recognised agents. Again, persons carrying on trade or business for and in the name of parties not resident within the local limits of the jurisdiction of the court within which limits the appearance, application or act is made or done, in matters connected with such trade or business only are also recognised agents.

Service of process on recognised agents will be deemed service on the party. Under Or. 3, r. 3(2) "the provisions for the service of process on a party to a suit shall apply to the service of process on his recognised agent."

Any service of summons on agent who at the time of service of summons, personally carries on business or work for such person within such limits, shall be deemed good service.[3]

An agent has, however, no right of audience. He cannot plead or examine witness. He cannot be a substitute for a lawyer which he can engage on behalf of the party to a suit. He can sign and verify a plaint under Or. 6, rr. 14/15 of the Code on application to and permission from the court.[4]

A decision against an agent binds the principal.

Holder of power of attorney cannot give evidence on behalf of his principal. Principal becoming old, weak, mentally infirm and not in a position to think independently—power of attorney becomes worthless.[5]

5 Airman Airman when serving under the Government in such capacity is to commence a suit or to defend him and cannot obtain leave of absence for the purpose of prosecuting or defending the suit in person; he may authorise any person to sue or defend in his stead.

The authority in question must be in writing and shall be signed by the airman before his Commanding Officer. The person authorised may prosecute or defend the suit or may engage lawyer on behalf of his principal. The authority shall be countersigned by the competent officer[6] which shall be filed in court.

This rule applies to a suit by or against military or naval men equally.

6 Alien—(i) Alien Enemies, (ii) Alien Friends Section 83 of the Code of Civil Procedure provides circumstances when alien enemies and alien friends may commence a suit in courts in the States of India.

3 Order 5, r. 13, CPC.

4 For signature and verification by an Agent see Note 1 of Chapter 6 & Note 5 of Chapter 7 *ante*.

5 *Mahendra Pratap Singh* v *Padam Kumari* AIR 1993 All 143.

6 See Or. 27, r. 1, CPC.

Alien enemies residing in India with the permission of the Central Government, and alien friends may sue in the courts in the States, 'as if they were citizens of India'; but, alien enemies residing in India without such permission, or residing in a foreign country, shall not sue in any such court.

No matter whether cause of action arose before or after the war, an alien enemy can be sued in Indian courts.[7] When war broke between the plaintiff's country and India and the plaintiff was not an alien enemy, his right to prosecute could not be affected.[8] An alien enemy cannot file a writ petition, such a writ petition is not maintainable.[9]

Section 83, CPC does not preclude suits against aliens not residing in India or affect their right of defence in such suit.[10] A resident of Pakistan cannot be said to be an alien enemy within the meaning of s. 83 as is clear from the Explanation to the section (quoted below). The Pakistan Government is not at war with India. Such a person can maintain a suit for restitution of conjugal right in an Indian court even though he may have come to India casually.[11]

Analysis of s. 83 of CPC:

(*i*) Alien enemies residing in India, with the permission of the Central Government, may sue in the courts in the States;

(*ii*) Alien friends may sue in the courts in the States as if they were citizens of India;

(*iii*) Alien enemy residing in India, without permission, cannot sue in any of such courts;

(*iv*) Alien enemy residing in a foreign country cannot sue in any of such courts.[12]

Permission of residence may be express. It may be inferred as well from circumstances. "An alien enemy residing in a foreign country" has been described in the Explanation to s. 83 which reads:

> "Every person residing in a foreign country, the Government of which is at war with India and carrying on business in that country without a licence in that behalf granted by the Central Government, shall, for the purpose of this section, be deemed to be an alien enemy residing in a foreign country."

7 Ambassadors and Envoys (of a foreign State) Any Ambassador or Envoy of a foreign State may, with the consent of the Central Government, be certified in writing by a Secretary to that Government, but not without such consent be sued in any competent court [s. 68(1) of CPC (since omitted)].

7 20 CWN 691.
8 *Feroza* v *Daulat* AIR 1975 Del 1.
9 *ACC Ld.* v *Pakistan PLD* 1972 Lahore 201.
10 *Prem* v *Jagat* AIR 1944 All 97.
11 *Nizamuddin* v *Husseni* AIR 1960 MP 212.
12 AIR 1920 Lah 4.

Consent is to be obtained prior to institution of the suit. Subsequent consent is of no avail. There can be no waiver of consent as provisions are imperative.[13]

Special provisions regarding suits against foreign Rulers, Ambassadors and Envoys may be referred to, s. 86 of the Code enjoins:

"86. *Suits against foreign Rulers, Ambassadors and Envoys.* (1) No foreign State may be sued in any Court otherwise competent to try the suit except with the consent of the Central Government certified in writing by a Secretary to that Government:

Provided that a person may, as a tenant of immovable property, sue without such consent as aforesaid a foreign State from whom he holds or claims to hold the property.

(2) Such consent may be given with respect to a specified suit or to several specified suits or with respect to all suits of any specified class or classes, and may specify, in the case of any suit or class of suits, the Court in which the foreign State may be sued, but it shall not be given, unless it appears to the Central Government that the foreign State—

(*a*) has instituted a suit in the Court against the person desiring to sue it, or

(*b*) by itself or another, trades within the local limits of the jurisdiction of the Court, or

(*c*) is in possession of immovable property situate within those limits and is to be sued with reference to such property or for money charged thereon, or

(*d*) has expressly or impliedly waived the privilege accorded to it by this section.

(3) Except with the consent of the Central Government, certified in writing by a Secretary to that Government, no decree shall be executed against the property of any foreign State.

(4) The preceding provisions of this section shall apply in relation to—

(*a*) any Ruler of a foreign State;

(*aa*) any Ambassador or Envoy of a foreign State;

(*b*) any High Commissioner of a Commonwealth country; and

(*c*) any such member of the staff of the foreign State or the staff or retinue of the Ambassador or Envoy of a foreign State or of the High Commissioner of a Commonwealth country as the Central Government may, by general or special order, specify in this behalf,

as they apply in relation to a foreign State.

(5) The following persons shall not be arrested under this Code, namely:

13 AIR 1940 Cal 244.

(*a*) any Ruler of a foreign state;

(*b*) any Ambassador or Envoy of a foreign State;

(*c*) any High Commissioner of a Commonwealth country;

(*d*) any such member of the staff of the foreign State or the staff or retinue of the Ruler, Ambassador or Envoy of a foreign State or of the High Commissioner of a Commonwealth country, as the Central Government may, by general or special order, specify in this behalf.

(6) Where a request is made to the Central Government for the grant of any consent referred to in sub-section (1), the Central Government shall, before refusing to accede to the request in whole or in part, give to the person making the request a reasonable opportunity of being heard."

8 Army (*See* No. 5 "Airman" *supra*).

9 Associations Associations, broadly speaking, may be divided into two classes:

(a) *Incorporated Associations* and (b) *Unincorporated Associations*.

(a) *Incorporated Associations*. It means the formation of a legal body with the quality of perpetual existence and succession except as limited by the Royal Charter or statute effecting the incorporation.

Examples of incorporated associations:

(1) Registered Companies
(2) Registered Trade Unions
(3) Medical Council
(4) Red Cross Societies
(5) Universities
(6) Bar Councils
(7) Co-operative Societies
(8) Cantonment Authority
(9) State Bank of India
(10) Insurance Companies
(11) Municipalities
(12) Anchal Panchayet
(13) Corporations, etc.

Incorporated Associations are Corporations.

(b) *Unincorporated Associations*. There may be associations and societies that are not corporations. Those come under the classification of "unincorporated associations" where a group of persons associate together in a body for the fulfillment of some common purpose (such as literary, cultural etc.). Such a body takes the shape of an unincorporated association. Unregistered association is sued through its Secretary. Suit though not properly constituted can be allowed to proceed with in representative capacity.[14] The purpose is obviously not for acquisition or gain. Societies formed with a view to profits are of two kinds:

(*i*) Firms

(*ii*) Other unincorporated bodies.

Mode of Suing

As to how they will sue or be sued see under Headings—Companies—No. 17 *infra*

Trade Unions—No. 49 *infra*

Co-operative societies—No. 45 *infra*

Municipalities—No. 37 *infra*

Corporations—Nos. 15, 16 *infra*.

10 Attorney-General (See No. 3 "Advocate-General" *supra*) The Advocate-General in our country corresponds to the 'Attorney-General' in England[15] (*per* Mr. Justice Beaman in the *Advocate-General of Bombay* v *Haji Esmail Hassan*).

11 Benamdar A *benamdar* (name-lender) represents the real owner. He can commence a suit in his own name. He can be sued in his own name. The real owner need not be added as a party to the suit.

A real owner has of course the right to apply to the court to be joined in the suit after the *benamdar's* death either under s. 151 or under Or. 1, r. 10(2).[16] The court can add the real owner *suo motu*. Where the suit is by a *benami* holder upon a promissory note, the court may add the real creditor as plaintiff. Where in a proceeding between a *benamdar* and third party the *benamdar* dies and his legal heirs are brought on record, the decree against the heirs of *benamdar* binds the real owner.[17] A decision in a proceeding against *benamdar* binds a real owner even though he does not join in the proceeding.[18]

A *benamdar* possesses ostensible title. He holds and represents the property for all practical purposes to the entire world except the real owner. Section 66 of CPC does not create any legal bar of a *benamdar* to recognise the title of a real owner. He can do so by an instrument which constitutes a deed of release. It is well settled that the purchaser of a property from an ostensible owner (*benamdar*) is protected from the real owner save for their want of knowledge of a real owner and *benamdar* can transfer a valid title in favour of a purchaser.[19]

14 AIR 1974 Pat 158.
15 5 IC 213. (On the authority of *Attorney-General* v *Brodie* 4 MIA 190).
16 AIR 1941 Nag 178; AIR 1918 PC 140.
17 AIR 1969 SC 316. [See: Limitation imposed by the Benami Transactions (Prohibition) Act].
18 *Chandran* v *Venkata Subramanya* AIR 1977 Mad 292.
19 *Satyabhamabai* v *Pandurang* AIR 1990 Bom 194; AIR 1978 Mad 244 following.

12 Clubs A club is a voluntary association of persons, an unincorporated body of persons.

Truly speaking, clubs are societies not for gain but for objects mainly social in character. Members of a club are required to pay subscription for their membership together with enrolment or admission fee, if any, as and when demanded under rules of the club. Cessation of membership is voluntary. There is also procedure for termination of membership under certain conditions.

A club is the most anomalous group of human beings that is known to law. It is a union of persons for social intercourse or for the promotion of certain pursuits which are closely allied to social intercourse, and the members usually regulate their conduct to which they subscribe. A club has no existence apart from its members. It differs from a corporation in that respect.[20]

A club is not a body corporate of any description. A club like other unincorporated body of persons cannot institute a suit in the club name nor it can defend a cause in the club name. The suit by a club has to be brought in the names of or against all the members of the body.[21]

An unregistered society can hold property. It can sue or be sued. There are, no doubt, great difficulties about suing it because it is necessary to sue it as a joint body and to implead all the members thereof—Mr. Walsh and Mr. Banerjee, JJ.[22] A suit against any member of an unregistered club when bad for non-joinder of parties.[1]

An unregistered club cannot commence a suit in the name of its Secretary or President. A suit by a club through or represented by its Secretary or other office-bearer is not maintainable even though he or they may have authority in that behalf of the association.[2] The suit must be brought by all the members[3] or by one or more of such members by obtaining permission under Or. 1, r. 8, CPC.

When a defendant, the Secretary of a club cannot be sued personally for a contract which he entered into on behalf of the club. If, however, he undertook liability the position is different.[4]

A member of a club may seek interference of the court to restrain the committee from violating its own rules. Therefore, where the plaintiff was expelled from the club on the basis of a resolution of the general committee of the club, he was entitled to sue for an injunction restraining the committee from excluding him from the club if he could show that action on the part of the members offended against elementary principles of natural justice and that there was reason so as to justify interference by a civil court.[5] Rules, bye-

20 Mitra: *Legal & Commercial Dictionary*, 6th Ed., p. 149.
21 AIR 1925 All 337; ILR 21 All 346.
22 AIR 1927 All 789.
1 *Laxminarayan* v *Vithaldas* AIR 1962 MP 31.
2 AIR 1922 Bom 109.
3 ILR 46 Bom 132; AIR 1940 Sind 63.
4 ILR 20 All 497.
5 AIR 1939 Bom 35.

laws framed by corporate bodies like Trade Unions, Societies are contractual in nature. For breach thereof the court can grant remedies like cancellation of expulsion order, invalidation of resolutions of meetings. But the civil suit is barred when alternative remedy is available before domestic forum. The domestic forum refusing to decide the matter or exercising jurisdiction illegally or failing to exercise it, civil suit shall not be barred by existence of alternative remedy.[6]

Where a club consists of numerous persons and names of members are unascertained, in such a case procedure under Or. 1, r. 8 of CPC is advisable. In the case of clubs, the Secretary or any other office-bearer, though authorised by the members cannot sue or be sued without obtaining leave.[7]

13 Collector A Collector is the Chief Officer-in-Charge of the revenue administration of a district. [Cf. General Clauses Act, s. 3(11)].

Power conferred by ss. 91 and 92, CPC on the Advocate-General may outside the Presidency Towns, be, with the previous sanction of the State Government, exercised also by the Collector (*vide* s. 93 of the CPC).

14 Deputy Collector A Deputy Collector can depute his officer to examine a witness on commission provided the place where the witness is sought to be examined is within his jurisdiction.

15 Corporation From the standpoint of composition, corporations[8] may be divided into two classes:

(a) *Corporation sole*;

(b) *Corporation aggregate*.

(a) *Corporation sole*. "A Corporation sole is a body politic having perpetual succession, constituted in a single person ..." [*Vide* Halsbury's *Laws of England*, 4th Ed., vol. 9, p. 719, para 1206]. In our country, the Administrator- General (*vide* s. 5 of the Administrator-General's Act) and the Official Trustee (*vide* s. 6 of the Official Trustees Act) are corporations sole.

He has had the right to sue and be sued in the corporate name.

(b) *Corporation aggregate*. A corporation aggregate is a "collection of many individuals united into one body under a special denomination having perpetual succession under an artificial form, and vested by the policy of the law with the capacity of acting in several respects as an individual", particularly of taking and granting property, of contracting obligations and of suing and being sued, of enjoying privileges and immunities in common, and of exercising a variety of political rights, more or less extensive, according to the designs of its institutions, or the powers conferred upon it. Corporations are created

6 *State Bank of India Staff Association* v *Manindra Bhattacharjee* AIR 1991 Cal 378.

7 *Mathura Bhuvan Co.-op. Hsg. Scty. Ltd.* v *Official Liquidator* AIR 2004 Bom 14.

8 Viewed from the standpoint as to the nature and functions, corporations are either (*i*) ecclesiastical or (*ii*) lay. Ecclesiastical Corporation Sole, e.g. Bishop. Ecclesiastical Corporation Aggregate, e.g., Dean of a Cathedral Church—vide Halsbury's *Laws of England*, 3rd Ed., vol. 8, p. 304. In India we have no Ecclesiastical Corporation.

by (*i*) prescription, (*ii*) Letters Patent and (*iii*) Act of legislature[9] (*vide* Halsbury's *Laws of England*, 4th Ed., vol. 9, p. 719, para 1204).

Lay Corporation (Aggregate) may again be divided into:

(*i*) Trading Corporation (Aggregate):

(*a*) Chartered Companies;

(*b*) Companies incorporated by Special Act of Parliament, e.g. Railway Co.

(*c*) Companies incorporated under the Companies Act.

(*ii*) Non-Trading Corporations (Aggregate) comprise:

(*a*) Corporations having statutory powers of Local Government such as Municipalities, Anchal Panchayet etc.

(*b*) Trade Unions.

(*c*) Co-operative Societies for self-help.

(*d*) Charitable or benevolent institutions like Indian Red Cross Society.

(*e*) Institutions for promotion and research such as Universities.

(*f*) District School Board, and so on.

(Based on Halsbury's *Laws of England*, 3rd Ed., vol. 8, pp. 303-305).

Order 29, r. 1, CPC enjoins that in suits by or against a corporation any pleading shall be signed and verified on behalf of the corporation by the secretary or by any director or other principal officer of the corporation who is able to depose to the facts of the case.[10]

Corporation includes not only statutory corporation but also a company registered under Companies Act.[11] If a corporation has more than one branch, suit against such corporation may be filed in any of the court having jurisdiction over the place where the branch is situated notwithstanding that no cause of action has arisen therein.[12]

A corporation for the purposes of Or. 29, CPC means a body authorised by law to act as one individual and constituted either by prescription, by the Letters Patent, or by an Act of the Legislature, e.g. Calcutta State Transport Corporation.

A registered company under the Companies Act is a corporation. The word 'Corporation' in Expl. of s. 20 of the CPC includes not only statutory corporation but also the company registered under the Companies Act.[13] A

9 Corporation by prescription—A corporation which is of such antiquity that the consent of the sovereign may be presumed is a corporation by prescription (ILR 20 All 167, 169). Corporation by Act of Legislature—A registered company is a corporation by the Act of Legislature (say, by the Indian Companies Act 1956).

10 See Chapters 6 and 7 "Verification" of and "Signature" in pleadings.

11 *Indian Performing Rights Society Ltd.* v *Sanjay Dalia* AIR 2015 SC 3479.

12 *Surinder* v *Bengal National Textile* AIR 1978 P&H 156.

13 AIR 1971 SC 740.

corporation as a plaintiff has to sue and as defendant has to be sued in its own corporate name unless such a corporation is specially authorised by law to sue and be sued in some other name,[14] for a statutory corporation maintains its separate juristic entity even where it exercises statutory powers or is controlled by the Government.[15] A corporation should not sue or be such in the names of its agents or servants. Ordinarily, the directors of a company are the only persons who can conduct litigation in the name of the company, but when they are the wrong-doers against the company and have acted *mala fide*, the majority of the shareholders can sue in the name of the company,[16] if there be no provision in the articles of the association to meet the contingency.

Head office of a Bank which had sanctioned loan is at Shrinagar. Loan documents were executed at Jammu and the loan was disbursed at Jammu. Loan repayment notice on behalf of Jammu and Kashmir Bank was issued by the branch of the Bank. It is held that the cause of action arose within the territorial jurisdiction J&K and the court at J&K had territorial jurisdiction to try the suit.[17]

In some cases the Act itself provides that the corporation shall sue or be sued in its corporate name:

For example—Section 4 of the Indian Red Cross Societies Act;
Section 18 of the Co-operative Societies Act;
Section 32 of the Madras Hindu Religious Endowment Act;
Section 13 of the Indian Trade Unions Act;
Section 3 of the Indian Universities Act;
and so on.

A corporation as distinguished from a firm—the firm has no existence in law; it is a mere abbreviated name for the partners of which it consists, and not a legal entity as a corporation.[18]

16 Foreign corporation In the matter of suing foreign corporations in India, the rules obtaining in England in a like situation have been followed. It is not necessary that such foreign corporation should be registered in India. A State Bank of "Native State" was held not entitled to sue in a British Indian Court.[19]

A foreign corporation is competent to sue in its corporate name, without being registered under the Companies Act or an Act of Parliament (here, Singer Manufacturing Company incorporated in USA).[20]

14 AIR 1962 AP 20. In the cause-title, name, description and place of business of such corporation should be given. The particulars of the person who signs and verifies the pleading are not required.
15 AIR 1966 SC 1364; AIR 1969 Cal 95.
16 AIR 1950 FC 133.
17 *BBF Industries Ltd.* v *Union of India* AIR 2015 J&K 1.
18 AIR 1940 All 81.
19 AIR 1933 Lah 456.
20 10 LC 141. (See also provisions of s. 83 of CPC under heading 'Aliens').

Company incorporated outside India—it is still liable to be sued in India.[21]

17 Companies Suits by or against a company must be instituted in the name of the company. A company registered under the Companies Act has a legal entity of its own separate from that of its shareholders whoever they may be.[22] It makes no difference where the entirety of the capital is subscribed by the Government or the company is controlled by the Government and run, in substance, as a Government department[23] ... Even where a company is a 'Government company' within the meaning of s. 617 of the Companies Act 1956 the juristic character of the company does not change and it is not identified with the State.[24]

Where under the articles of association of a company a suit on behalf of the company has to be filed with the consent of the directors, a suit filed by the Secretary holding a general power of attorney from the company would be maintainable even if the action taken by the Secretary is approved by the directors subsequently.[25]

Majority members of a company may also commence proceedings in the name of the company if there be no provision in the constitution of the company. Company in liquidation retains its corporate powers including the power to sue. So such a suit must be in the name of the company, not in the name of liquidator.[1]

The cause-title in the like suit is,

The A.B. Company Ltd., having its registered office at .... P.S. .... Dt. .... *Plaintiffs*.

versus

C.D. etc. .... *Defendants*.

(*Vide* Appendix A, 1st Schedule of CPC) (Title of suits).

We would now refer to provisions with regard to a company in liquidation. Section 457 of the Companies Act 1956 (now s. 290 of the Companies Act 2013) defines powers of a liquidator.

The section reads: "The liquidator in a winding-up by the Tribunal shall have power, with the sanction of the Tribunal,—

(*a*) to institute or defend any suit, prosecution, or other legal proceeding, civil or criminal, in the name and on behalf of the company ...."

Thus, when a company is wound up by the Tribunal or under control of the Tribunal, the Official Liquidator shall institute or defend any suit,

21 *Babulall Choukhani* v *Caltex (India) Ltd.* AIR 1967 Cal 205.
22 AIR 1963 SC 1811.
23 AIR 1963 SC 1890; AIR 1964 SC 1486.
24 AIR 1969 Cal 95.
25 *Turner Morrison and Co. Ltd.* v *Hungerford Investment Trust Ltd.* AIR 1972 SC 1311.
1 *Globe United* v *H.B. Bovari* AIR 1974 Del 200; ILR (1974)1 Del 398.

prosecution and/or other legal proceedings in the name and on behalf of the company.

In the case of voluntary liquidation, the voluntary liquidator shall have similar powers. In the cause-title of a plaint the official liquidator shall be described by the style of "The official liquidator" of the particular company in respect of which he acts and not by his individual name (*vide* s. 452 of the Companies Act 1956).

The official liquidator is entitled to exercise some of his powers only with the sanction of the Tribunal. (See s. 457 of the Companies Act now s. 290 of the Companies Act 2013).

The cause-title showing names of parties should be written as follows:

The 'X' 'Y' Tea Co. Ltd. (in liquidation) by the Official Liquidator having office at ...... Dt. ...... *Plaintiff*

versus

'A' 'B' (add description and residence) ... *Defendant*

Individual name of the Official Liquidator not to be given.

In case of voluntary liquidation—

M/s. A.B. Co. Ltd., in liquidation by the Liquidator[2] having office at ...... Dt. .... Plaintiff/Defendant.

18 Unregistered Company A suit by an unregistered company shall be brought in the name of all the members of the company. Similarly, an unregistered company shall be sued in the name of all the members of the company. Such an unregistered company is not authorised to sue in the name of its secretary or such other principal officer. Order 29 of the CPC is not available to an unregistered company.

Where such a company consists of numerous persons the plaintiff may proceed under Or. 1, r. 8 of the CPC with prior permission of the court.

19 Government pleader Under Or. 27, r. 4, the Government pleader in any court shall be the agent of the Government for the purpose of receiving processes against the Government issued by the court.

20 Executors (See No. 1 "Administrator" *supra*) Order 31, r. 1, CPC enjoins—"In all suits concerning property vested in a trustee, executor or administrator, where the contention is between the persons beneficially interested in such property and a third person, the trustee, executor or administrator shall represent the persons so interested, and it shall not ordinarily be necessary to make them parties to the suit. But the court may, if it thinks fit, order them or any of them to be made parties."

Necessarily, the rule does not apply where the contention is between the beneficiaries *inter se*.[3]

2 The epithet 'Voluntary' need not be added but in case of Official Liquidation the epithet 'Official' must be added before the word 'Liquidator'—Section 452 of the Companies Act 1956.

3 39 IC 779.

Where there are several trustees, executors or administrators all of them shall be sued whether the suit is against one or more of them (Or. 31, r. 2) provided that the Executors who have not proved their testator's will, and trustees, executors and administrators outside India, need not be made parties. Where a suit is between the persons who are beneficially interested in the suit property and a third party, in such case, making all the trustees party in the suit is not necessary.[4]

Executor can be sued personally or in representative capacity.[5]

Before we pass on to next we would remember the provisions of Or. 31, r. 3 which says: "Unless the court directs otherwise, the husband of a married trustee, administratrix, or executrix shall not as such be a party to a suit by or against her."

21 Firm There are six kinds of firms such as: Registered Partnership; Foreign firm; One man firm; Dissolved firm; Hindu joint family firm and Unregistered firm.

Registered partnership. A firm is a mere abbreviated name for the partners of whom it consists, a compendious mode of describing the partners composing the firm. It is a legal fiction to describe a group of persons but having no legal entity[6] or, as such, any legal existence.

Order 30, r. 1 of the CPC enjoins that a partnership can sue or be sued in the name of the firm. But the rule is merely permissive. A plaintiff may bring a suit impleading all the individual partners of a firm without naming the firm as one of the defendants. Similarly, members of a firm can sue jointly in their individual names.[7] The proper mode of commencing a suit under Or. 30, r. 1 is, however, to commence in the name of the firm. It is not necessary that all the partners should be named as plaintiffs in a plaint; for it was held:[8] "In describing the cause-title of such suit the name of the plaintiff should be the name of the firm only without addition of the names of the partners suing although addition of such name does not matter in the least." It is true that a firm does not have legal entity but Or. 33, r. 1, CPC permits that two or more persons claiming as partners may sue or be sued in the name of the firm. Appendix 'A' to the Code shows that in a suit against a firm description of the defendant should be "A.B., a firm carrying on the business in partnership at ..." It is not necessary to give the names of the partners or to sue the firm through the partners.[9]

Foreign firm. Provisions in Or. 30, r. 1 applies to foreign firms as well. We have seen that Or. 30, r. 1 is applicable to firms when persons carry on business in India. Therefore, when a foreign firm carries on business in India, even though the partners themselves are residing outside India, Or. 30, r. 1 applies

4 *Sainath Mandir Trust* v *Vijaya Mandale* (2004)106(1) Bom LR 259.
5 AIR 1949 Cal 690.
6 AIR 1957 AP 658; AIR 1954 Bom 423; AIR 1954 Assam 111.
7 63 CWN 21.
8 AIR 1936 Cal 353.
9 AIR 1978 All 123.

to suit by or against such firms.[10] Where the partners of a foreign firm do not carry on any business in India they cannot sue or be sued in the firm name.[11]

One-man firm. One-man firm is a misnomer. Where a single individual carries on business in the name of a firm or a Company, he practically uses an assumed or trade-name. He should sue in his own name.[12]

If he dies during pendency of a suit his legal representatives shall have to be substituted.[13]

(See No. 23 "Persons carrying on business in names other than their own" *infra*).

Dissolved firm. A dissolved firm is not entitled to sue in the firm name.[14] Suit against firm, filed after the death of a partner, firm dissolved in the meantime—cause of action accruing before its dissolution. Suit held valid.[15] Under Or. 30, r. 4 legal representatives of a deceased partner of a firm, against whom a suit is filed under Or. 30, r. 1 need not be brought on record as parties. This is so whether the partner died before or after the institution of such suit.[16] Decree passed in a suit filed by an unregistered firm is not a nullity. Plea of non-registration was not raised in suit itself. It cannot be raised in a separate suit.[17]

Hindu joint family firm. The firm meant in Or. 30, r. 1 of the Code does not include an undivided Hindu family or a joint family business. And a Hindu joint family firm is not entitled to bring a suit in its business name.[18] (See exception with regard to joint family firm in Punjab—Where it may sue and be sued in the firm name—AIR 1940 Lah 425). But where a joint family firm is registered under the Partnership Act, it can have the benefit of Or. 30, r. 1 of the Code.[19]

Unregistered firm. An unregistered firm, i.e. a partnership which is not registered under the Partnership Act cannot be treated as a legal entity and a suit cannot be brought without joining all the partners.[20] Suit for recovery of money by a partnership firm. Firm not registered on date of institution of suit. *Held*, suit is not maintainable. Subsequent registration during pendency of suit—does not cure the defect.[1] Bar to sue does not operate against suit for recovery of debt due and payable to an unregistered dissolved firm.[2]

10 AIR 1932 Nag 114.
11 AIR 1945 PC 71.
12 AIR 1932 Bom 516.
13 34 CWN 36.
14 AIR 1945 Oudh 284.
15 *Rajindra Prasad Sinha* v *K.C. Thapar & Co.* AIR 1975 Pat 265.
16 *Jaichand Lal* v *Gopal Prasad* AIR 1973 Pat 441.
17 *Jalal Mohd.* v *Kakka Mohd.* AIR 1972 Mad 86.
18 AIR 1938 Lah 563; AIR 1942 Cal 613; AIR 1936 Nag 292.
19 AIR 1949 Assam 71.
20 AIR 1954 Assam 111.
1 *Annapurna Fertilisers* v *Arunodays Fertilisers* AIR 1994 AP 157.
2 *Kantilal Jathalal* v *Ghanoshyam Ratilal* AIR 1994 Guj 56.

If in a suit by firm, the plaintiff suing through mistake as owner of the firm, such a mistake is curable and the suit can be maintained.[3]

22 Partners For suits between co-partners—see provisions of Or. 30, r. 9, CPC.

23 Persons carrying on business in names other than their own Any person who carries on a business in a name or style other than his own may be sued in such name or style as if it were a firm name. The rule applies not only to a single individual carrying on business under a firm name or assumed name but it also applies to a number of individuals carrying on business either under a firm name or an assumed name when those individuals do not constitute a partnership in law.[4] When any person or persons carry on business under an assumed or trading name, which may be the name of the firm, or an individual or anything else Or. 30, r. 10 applies.

He may carry on business in the name of an individual—A,

carrying on business in the name of B.

the plaintiff should be described as A .... s/o ....

of .... P.S. Dt. ....

carrying on business in the name of "B".

Where the plaintiff is aware that a person is carrying a business in the trading name of an individual, the defendant should be described as

A .... s/o ....

Carrying on business in the trading name of "B" .... Defendant.

The rules also applies when a joint Hindu family carries on business in an assumed name. Benefits of Or. 30, r. 10 can be availed of even by a limited company carrying on the business in name or style other than its own.[5]

A person can be sued in his trade/firm name, but he himself cannot sue in his firm/trade name.[6]

A suit after the death of the sole proprietor thereof must be brought against his legal representatives and not against him in the name of the firm, for, if after his death the suit is brought against the firm name, such suit was against a dead person. During the pendency of a suit, substitution of legal representatives is advisable when the proprietor dies.

24 Foreign Ruler—Foreign Prince [See ss. 85, 86, 87, 87A and 87B.] A plaintiff Ruler shall sue in the name of his State.

Under s. 87. "The Ruler of a foreign State may sue, and shall be sued, in the name of his State".

If the Central Government so directs, the Ruler may be sued in the name of an agent or in any other name.

3 *Ramangouda* v *Firm G. Basangouda* AIR 1969 Mys 111.
4 AIR 1956 Ori 186; AIR 1944 Cal 138.
5 *Rajendra Prasad Oil Mills* v *Chunni Devi* AIR 1969 All 1.
6 AIR 1932 Bom 516.

A foreign State means any State outside India which has been recognised by the Union Government. The head of the State is its Ruler—"Who is for the time being recognised by the Central Government to be the head of that State."

A Ruler of a foreign State shall not be sued in Indian courts except with the consent of the Central Government in writing in the manner and circumstances as described in s. 86(2) of the Code. The only exception is that a tenant of immovable property may sue a Ruler without such consent if he holds the property from the Ruler. Sanction is to be obtained prior to institution of the suit. Without previous sanction the suit should be dismissed or allowed to be withdrawn with liberty to bring a fresh suit duly sanctioned.[7]

25 Native Prince, Rulers of former Indian States Section 87B of the Code makes provisions of s. 85 and s. 86 [sub-secs. (1) and (3)] applicable to Rulers of former Indian States. By virtue of s. 87B, the Rulers of former Indian States have been given exemption against being sued. But the Code makes no provision with regard to any rights or privileges of such Rulers when they file a suit in a court in any State in India.[8]

Government's consent to sue a former Ruler is no consent to sue his successor—the plaintiff has to obtain the consent afresh.[9] Application made to sue the former H.E.H. Nizam the VII cannot be proceeded with against H.E.H. Nizam the VIII.

26 Foreigner (see No. 6 "Alien" *supra*).

27 Government, Government Officer, Public Officer Order 27, r. 3 of the Code enjoins:—"In suits by or against the Government instead of inserting in the plaint the name and description and place of residence of the plaintiff or defendant, it shall be sufficient to insert the appropriate name as provided in s. 79."

Again, Art. 300(1) of the Constitution of India reads: "The Government of India may sue or be sued by the name of the Union of India and the Government of a State may sue or be sued by the name of the State and may, subject to any provisions which may be made by an act of Parliament or of the Legislature of such State enacted by virtue of powers conferred by this Constitution, sue or be sued in relation to their respective affairs in the like cases as the Dominion of India and the corresponding provinces or the corresponding Indian States might have sued or been sued if this Constitution had not been enacted."

7 AIR 1935 Oudh 164. The provisions in s. 86 applies to—
- (*i*) any Ambassador or Envoy of a foreign State;
- (*ii*) any Commissioner of a Commonwealth country;
- (*iii*) member of staff or retinue of Ruler, Ambassador, Envoy, High Commissioner as Central Government may by general or special order specify in this behalf.

8 AIR 1955 Bom 275.

9 *Behhood Ali Khan* v *Secretary to Govt.* AIR 1969 AP 106.

Section 79 of the Code of Civil Procedure reads:

"In a suit by or against the Government, the authority to be named as plaintiff or defendant, as the case may be, shall be—

(*a*) in the case of a suit by or against the Central Government—the Union of India, and

(*b*) in the case of a suit by or against a State Government—the State".

In Railway claim cases: Union of India owning and representing—

(*i*) N.F. Rly., Maligaon, Gauhati-II,

(*ii*) N.E. Rly., Gorakhpur, (Uttar Pradesh) etc.

In a case where a railway is administered by a Government or State, a suit can be brought against the Government or the State concerned. It is not necessary that the railway administration, as such, through the manager or any body else, should be impleaded as a party—defendant to the suit.[10]

Prior to institution of a suit against any of the Governments, Central or Provincial or against any officer of the Government, a notice under s. 80 of the CPC is imperative. Calcutta Improvement Act—a notice under s. 156 of the Act is a must.[11]

The Government of India or Government of a State may sue or be sued by the name of the Union of India or the Government of a State, respectively.[12] If in a suit claim for relief is made against the Union of India or any State, Union of India or the State must be impleaded as a party otherwise such a suit is not maintainable for want of necessary party.[13]

28 Hindu joint family A Hindu joint family may commence a suit by or through the *karta* or manager of the family. In a suit by a member of the joint family to recover property belonging to a joint family—suit must be instituted by or on behalf of all the members, where the plaintiff is the manager of the joint family he need not add other members as parties.[14] The defendants, however, to protect their interest, are at liberty to pray for addition of individual member as a co-plaintiff.

Where there are two or more managers all should join in commencing a suit.

A suit cannot fail merely because of the absence of description in the cause title that the plaintiff is the head or *'karta'* of the joint family, when it is actually found that the plaintiff was *karta* and it has been definitely alleged that he and his minor sons were proprietors of the firm.[15]

Existence of two *kartas* of a joint Hindu family is not contemplated by Hindu law: of course there may be two managers of the property. The *karta* of the joint Hindu family is certainly the manager of the family property, but

10 AIR 1957 MP 157; AIR 1956 Pat 511.
11 *B.K. Saha & Co.* v *C.M.D.A.* AIR 1993 Cal 249.
12 Article 300 of the Constitution of India.
13 *Chaman Lal* v *State of Punjab* AIR 2014 SC 3640.
14 *Allam Gangadhara Rao* v *Gollapalli Gangarao* AIR 1968 AP 291.
15 AIR 1954 Assam 111.

he undoubtedly possesses powers which the ordinary manager does not possess. The *karta*, cannot, therefore, be just equated with the manager of property .... The latter would be two persons entitled to represent the family and their power to represent would depend on the terms of authority conferred on them by the members of the joint Hindu family. Their authority to act for the family is not divided under any principle of Hindu law, but is based on the members of the joint family conferring certain authority on them. Therefore, on the death of one of such, the other cannot continue to represent the joint family when the authority given by the joint Hindu family was to the effect that both of them were to act jointly.[16]

29 Idol A Hindu idol is a juristic person and can sue and be sued in his/her name.

There is no specific provision in the Code as to how a Hindu idol has to be impleaded in a court of law. Nevertheless, suits have been many and some conventional procedure on the analogy of r. 1 of Or. 32 of the Code has been adopted and recognised by courts of law with so much uniformity that departure therefrom will hardly be accepted. The manager or the *shebait* of an idol can sue on behalf of the idol which is considered to be a perpetual minor in the eye of law. The rules of procedure relating to a minor should, for the purpose of proceeding, be applied by analogy as far as possible to a Hindu deity.[17] A deity can sue through any person. If the right of suit in such a case be in the idol and not in the *shebaits*, such a suit is maintainable on the ground that an idol can sue through any person as a next friend who has no interest adverse to it and it is immaterial that such a next friend happens to be one of the *shebaits*.[18] Suit by a worshipper representing an idol for recovery of its property from the alienee is maintainable even though the trustee continues in office.[19]

Idols may be: (*i*) Family idol;
(*ii*) Public idol.

(i) ***Family idols.*** They may have property or may not have property. Idols having property raise complications as would be discussed below.

Idols not having property hardly leads to dispute; for, property is the source of all disputes and rancours. Still in such cases dispute arises due to wounded sentiments. All suits in such cases generally relate to the right of worship of the idol. When this right is denied, the aggrieved member or members can bring a suit for the right to worship and joint possession of the idol. In such a suit,[20] the idol and female members of the family are not necessary parties. No harm if the idol is made a pro forma defendant.

Where idols have property and the property is dedicated absolutely to the idol, the *shebait* (entrusted with the management and possession of the property)

16 *Union of India* v *Sree Ram Bohra* AIR 1965 SC 1531.
17 51 CWN 383; AIR 1929 All 887.
18 *Nirmal* v *Jyoti Prosad* 45 CWN 709.
19 *Bishwanath* v *Radha Ballabhji* AIR 1967 SC 1044; *Periyaguruswamy* v *Mahalingam* AIR 1971 Mad 278.
20 33 CWN 96.

of the idol is competent to bring suits.[21] The right of suit respecting the property of the idol was declared to be "vested in the *shebait* and not in the idol", though the procedure of courts allows a suit in the name of the idol or deity.[22]

All suits in respect of the property dedicated to the idol ought to be brought by or against *shebaits*, and the idol need not be joined in any such suit unless "the result might conceivably vitally affect its interests".[23] Where a *shebait* declines to institute a suit for the protection of the property of the idol, it can sue through its next friend appointed by the court,[1] or where the interest of the *shebait* is adverse to that of idol.

So far as the *shebait's* rights to commence a suit or to defend, the following should be remembered:

(1) A *de facto shebait* is competent, like a *de jure shebait*, to sue and be sued respecting the idol.

(2) A future *shebait*, i.e. one who in future is entitled to succeed to the office of the *shebait* or the founder or any member of the family for whose spiritual benefit the idol was established can maintain a suit for a declaration that the alienations of properties made by the *shebait* are unauthorised and are not binding on the *debuttar* estate,[2] for removal of the *shebait*, for administration of the *shebait*, for administration of the *debuttar* estate and for appointment of a Receiver.[3]

Coming to the question whether all the *shebaits* would join in a suit where there are several *shebaits* we would note that in suits by or against *shebait*, all *shebaits* are necessary parties.[4] Those who refuse to join as plaintiffs ought to be made defendants.

(ii) ***Public idols.*** An idol of a public religious institution is an idol whose worship is available to members of the public and the endowment in favour of such a public idol is known as a Hindu public religious endowment. A public religious endowment may be created by an individual or by the public by raising of subscription.

Except where there are statutory provisions in that behalf (as mentioned below), the procedure to commence a suit relating to a public religious endowment is the same as in the case of a private idol. Where *R*, acting as *pujari* or manager of a private Hindu temple, raises in residential buildings of his own in the temple premises and converts them to his own use and asserts a proprietary title to them. *R* commits acts of mismanagement and

21 45 CWN 932; AIR 1941 Cal 272.
22 AIR 1940 PC 116.
23 ILR 33 All 735 following reported case may also be seen—AIR 1936 All 653; AIR 1934 Pat 531.
1 44 CLJ 522.
2 35 CWN 768.
3 AIR 1934 Pat 584; AIR 1930 Cal 583.
4 AIR 1935 Cal 623; but see AIR 1971 Ori 15—in certain special circumstances suit by some of the *shebaits* is maintainable.

misappropriation of the temple and its properties ... A person who has made large donations for the maintenance of the temple has clearly a substantial interest to maintain a suit for possession of the temple and its properties against the *pujari* or manager, on behalf of the deity to protect the property from mismanagement and misappropriation. Section 92, CPC has no application to the suit and the sanction of the Advocate-General is not a condition of its initiation.[5]

The following statutory enactments are relevant in so far as they modify the right to sue and be sued—

(*i*) The Religious Endowments Act 1863.[6]

(*ii*) The Charitable and Religious Trusts Act 1920.

(*iii*) Section 92 of the CPC.

(See Chapter 10 *infra* for details).

Suit by a deity through next friend—previous suit for the same relief by next friend in his own name. Suit by deity not barred.[7]

30 Local board Section 3(31) of the General Clauses Act 1897, defines local authority—which "shall mean a municipal committee, district board, body of Port Commissioners or other authority, legally entitled to, or entrusted by the Government with, the control or management of a municipal or local fund."

Port trust is thus a local authority.[8]

31 Persons of unsound mind By Or. 32, r. 15 of the CPC the provisions contained in rr. 1-14 of the said Order, so far as they are applicable, have been sought to be extended to persons adjudged to be of unsound mind[9] and to persons who, thought not so adjudged, are found by the court on enquiry, by reason of unsoundness of mind or mental infirmity, to be incapable of protecting their interests when suing or being sued.

Therefore, a suit on behalf of a person of unsound mind has to be filed by a next friend. Where such person is a defendant, the court has to appoint a guardian *ad litem*. A man who is not of unsound mind but because of mental infirmity is not capable of protecting his interest, he also should have the benefits of the above provision. The rule applies to the deaf and dumb as well.[10]

Suit by next friend on behalf of mentally unsound plaintiff. Enquiry by court under Or. 32, r. 15 to ascertain plaintiff's mental state not held at the time of plaintiff's filing the suit but subsequently. Plaintiff is found to be of unsound mind. Omission to hold enquiry at the initial stage does not vitiate the suit. It is a curable irregularity.[11]

5 AIR 1970 SC 532.
6 In Orissa, the Act has been repealed by Orissa Religious Endowments Act.
7 *Sri Ramjee* v *Biswanath Pd. Sah* AIR 1978 Pat 129.
8 AIR 1936 Mad 789.
9 A person can be adjudged to be of unsound mind under the Mental Health Act 1987.
10 AIR 1930 Lah 425.
11 *Clara Auroro* v *Sylvia Angela* AIR 1985 Bom 372.

While during pendency of the suit a person develops insanity, the court should see that his interests are protected by a suitable next friend.[12] He cannot go unrepresented.

Under Or. 32, r, 15 the court is empowered to appoint a guardian for a person of unsound mind, when the court is satisfied that the person is incapable of protecting his interest for any mental infirmity.[13] When any decree for specific performance was passed without any inquiry and without appointing a guardian for the defendant, such a decree is not sustainable.[14]

When a person of unsound mind is not represented by a guardian in the suit, the decree is of no effect.[15] It is a void decree.

(For further treatment see No. 32 "Minors" *infra*).

32 Minors Where the plaintiff or the defendant in a suit is a minor, the suit shall be instituted or defended in his name by his next friend. Order 32, r. 1 of the CPC enjoins:

> "Every suit by a minor shall be instituted in his name by a person who in such suit shall be called the next friend of the minor".

The provisions in Or. 32 are meant to protect the interest of minors and to see that they are represented in the suit by qualified persons fit to look after minor's interests.

A suit by a minor without a next friend should not be summarily dismissed, but an opportunity should be given to constitute the suit in regular manner.[16]

33 Suit by or against the minors and persons of unsound mind Order 32, rr. 1 to 14 apply to the suits by or against the minors.

Rules 1 to 15 apply to suits by or against the persons of unsound mind except r. 2A of the said Or. 32.

Every suit by a minor shall be instituted in his name by his next friend and without the next friend, the suit is not maintainable. The court may ask the next friend to furnish requisite security for payment of necessary costs that might be incurred by the defendant. The court may also appoint a guardian on behalf of the minor for the suit.

Further, the next friend or the guardian should not receive any consideration or benefit out of the estate of the concerned minor. Any compromise by next friend or guardian without leave of the court will be declared invalid. On the retirement of the next friend or the guardian, the appointment of a new next friend or new guardian in the proceedings of the suit should be with the consent of the court.

12 AIR 1936 Lah 7.
13 *Kasturi Bai* v *Anguri Chaudhary* AIR 2003 SC 1773; *Jai Prakash Goel* v *State* AIR 2005 Del 83.
14 *Krishnakutty Madhavan* v *Veena M.G.* AIR 2012 Ker 166.
15 *Ibid.*
16 AIR 1928 Cal 537.

Until a suitable next friend or guardian is appointed on behalf of the minor, the suit cannot be proceeded with in the court.

Rule 15 provides that the rr. 1 to 14 as applicable to a minor shall also equally apply to a person of unsound mind except that no order for furnishing of security could be passed against a person of unsound mind.

Title of suit: X, a minor by his next friend Y ...... *Plaintiff*

versus

A. B. etc. .... *Defendant*

When the minor is a defendant, the court, "on being satisfied of the fact of his minority, shall appoint a proper person to be the guardian for the suit for such minor." The procedure for appointment of a guardian *ad litem* is contained in Or. 32, r. 3(2-4) of the Code. Suit against minor—No notice given to guardian. *Ex parte* decree against minor can be set aside.[17]

Title of suit—A.B. etc. .... *Plaintiff*

versus

X, a minor by his father and natural guardian Y residing at etc. ....

.... *Defendant*

A decree passed against a minor not properly represented is without jurisdiction; it is null and void. A suit was filed against the mother and her minor son through her as guardian. The mother did not enter her appearance. There was failure to appoint court-guardian. *Ex parte* decree was passed against both. *Held*, the decree is nullity as against the minor.[18] Similarly, a decree against a minor impleaded as a major or against a major impleaded as a minor is not binding.

The next friend may retire with permission from the court. He may be removed by the court (see Or. 32, rr. 8, 9, 11). On attainment of majority, a minor may elect to proceed with the suit. He shall apply to the court for an order discharging the next friend and for leave to proceed in his own name. He may also abandon the suit. His name may be a struck off, when a co-plaintiff, by orders of the court. On attaining majority a minor plaintiff cannot take the plea that he would continue to be represented by his guardian.[19]

34 Math, Mohant An "Asthal" or a "Mutt" is an institution of monastic nature and is established for the service of a particular cult, the instruction in its tenets, and the observance of its rites ...... The Mohant is the head of the institution, sits upon the gadi, initiates candidates into the mysteries of the cult, superintends the worship of the idol and the accustomed spiritual rites, manages the property of the institution and administers its affairs, and the whole assets are vested in him as the owner thereof in trust for the institution

17 *Md. Hasan* v *Md. Abbas* AIR 1984 Pat 170.
18 AIR 1957 Pat 260; AIR 1955 All 584; *Manoranjan* v *Brundabati* AIR 1969 Ori 52.
19 *Bajranglal* v *Umesh Kumar* AIR 2000 MP 326.

itself.[20] In case of a Math, while the ownership in the general case is with the spiritual head of the institution, still the property may be held on different conditions and subject to different incidents, and that there are varieties of circumstances and tenure and in respect of these the use and custom are clear. They form the law of the Math.[21]

A suit on behalf of a Mutt has undoubtedly to be instituted in the name of a Mohunt, but the person in whose name the suit is brought has in relation to the suit a distinct capacity of its own. He is therein a stranger to himself in his personal and private capacity.[22]

The question as to the position of the head of a Mutt must be determined in each case upon the conditions on which they were given or which may be inferred from long-established usage[23] and customs of the institution. Opinion is divergent on the issue. *Acharya, Sevaks*—they are liable to render accounts as trustees.[24]

For properties vested in a Mohant the suit shall be commenced by the Mohant. In the absence of a legal Mohant, a *de facto* Mohant can commence a suit to recover possession of the idol's property.[1] Again, a *de facto* trustee of an endowment can sue for the benefit of the deity and also be sued in his capacity as the representative of the deity.[2]

A Mohant can acquire personal properties with his funds.[3]

Where the secular and religious duties of a Mohant are interdependent and inseparably blended and the two capacities are closely intermingled so that a proper and efficient discharge of the one depends on the control of the other, the civil court has in a fit case and, if need be, jurisdiction to remove the Mohant not only from his secular but also from the religious office.[4]

35 Military (See No. 8 "Army" *supra*).

36 Mosque The question whether a British Indian Court will recognise a mosque as having a *locus standi in judicio* is a question of procedure. In mosque known as *Masjid Shahid Ganj* v *Shiromoni Gurdwara Prabandhak Committee*,[5] Sir George Rankin, J. held: "Suits cannot completely be brought by or against such institution (mosque) as artificial person in the British India Courts."

20 AIR 1916 PC 256; 33 IC 583—(In ILR 27 Mad 435 it was held that the Mohant was not a mere trustee but a "Corporation Sole" having an estate for life in the permanent endowments of the Math—in a word 'life tenant'. But in ILR 33 Mad 265 held otherwise). A Mohant is incompetent to create any interest in respect of the Math property to endure beyond his life (AIR 1922 PC 123).
21 AIR 1919 PC 62; 53 IC 288.
22 B.K. Mukherjea, *The Hindu Law of Religious and Charitable Trusts*, 5th Ed., p. 365.
23 AIR 1933 Bom 276; 84 IC 759 may be seen.
24 55 IC 956.
1 AIR 1936 Cal 215.
2 AIR 1933 PC 75; AIR 1949 Mad 721; AIR 1952 Ori 312.
3 58 IC 900.
4 AIR 1940 PC 24.
5 The expression "Juristic personality" whether may be extended for any purpose to a Muslim institution generally or to mosque in particular. See AIR 1940 PC 116.

(But see mosque—a juristic person—AIR 1928 Lah 372 and 24 IC 100).

37 Mutawalli A permanent dedication by a person professing Islam of any movable or immovable property for any purpose recognised by the Muslim law as pious, religious or charitable is a waqf. It includes—

(*i*) A waqf by user;

(*ii*) *mashrut-ul-Khidmat*;

(*iii*) a *waqf-al-aulad*.

The donor of a waqf is "Waqif". There may be a Shia waqf and a Sunni waqf governed by Shia law and Sunni law respectively.

The Waqf Act 1995. In s. 3(*i*) "Mutawalli" means, any person appointed, either verbally or under any Deed or Instrument, by which a waqf has been created, or by a competent authority, to be the mutawalli of a waqf and includes any person who is a mutawalli of a waqf by virtue of any custom or who is a Naib-Mutawalli, Khadim, Mujawar, Sajjadanashin, Amin, or other person appointed by a Mutawalli to perform the duties of a Mutawalli save as otherwise provided in the Waqf Act any person, Committee, or Corporation for the time being managing or administering any waqf or waqf property. Provided that no member of a Committee or Corporation, shall be deemed to be a Mutawalli, unless such member is an office-bearer of such a Committee or Corporation. Provided further that the Mutawalli shall be a citizen of India. Board of Waqf is the controlling authority of the waqfs. Every waqf has to be registered at the office of the said Board who shall maintain a Register of Waqfs. The powers and duties of Mutawalli are specified in the Act. State Government shall constitute Tribunals, for particular area to hear all disputes relating to waqfs, Mutawalli Management of waqf property and to hear all complaints of persons interested in the waqf. Civil courts who have no jurisdiction in respect of any dispute, question or other matters relating to any waqf, waqf property or other matters which is required by the said Act to be determined by a Tribunal. The Board may file a suit in a civil court and the court may appoint Receiver on the wakf property. In any suit or proceeding, in respect of a waqf or waqf property, the Board may appear and plead as a party to the suit or proceeding. The Central Government may regulate secular activities of all waqfs. The Central Government may establish a Central Waqf Council for the purpose of advising on matters concerning working of Waqf Boards and the due administration of waqfs.

A waqf may be public or private. In a public waqf, the Mutawalli is in the position of a quasi-trustee.[6] The property of the waqf vests in the God, the Mutawalli having no right in the property. But in the case of a private waqf, the right in the property vests in the beneficiaries.

A Mutawalli, both in public and private, can commence a suit and be sued. If there be several Mutawallis all must join as plaintiffs. They must exercise the powers of their office jointly.[7] Such of them as refuse to join as plaintiffs

6 48 IA 302.
7 AIR 1935 Cal 623.

must be made defendants. A decree of rent against one of two Mutawallis of a waqf estate is bad. The decree is not binding on the waqf or the other Mutawalli particularly where there is nothing on record to show that the waqf or the other Mutawalli was represented by the contesting Mutawalli.[8] A *de facto* Mutawalli[9] is entitled to act on behalf of the trust and sue for recovery of the rent of the shops belonging to the trust.

A Mutawalli, unlike the *shebait* or Mohant, has no power, without the permission of the court, to mortgage, sell or exchange waqf property, unless he is expressly authorised by the deed of waqf to do so. A mortgage, however, made by a Mutawalli without the previous sanction of the court is not void if made for a justifying necessity and may be retrospectively confirmed by the court.[10]

In fine, the office of Mutawalli is not heritable or transferable in the absence of a provision in *waqfnama*. He has no power to nominate his successor in his office unless he is given such power to do by the deed of waqf.

38 Municipality Municipality is a corporation aggregate with a body of Commissioners. Like other corporations aggregate a municipality can sue and be sued in the name of the Commissioners of the municipality of the particular place.[11] Names of the Chairman, or of the individual Commissioners need not be given in the Cause-Title of the plaint. Where in a suit by a municipal body the plaintiff was described as "A.B. Chairman of the Municipal Board of ......" but the intention was clear that it was the Municipal Board that was suing, it was held that the defect was merely one of form.[12] During the pendency of the suit, a municipality was superseded by the Administrator—decree against the municipality without bringing the Administrator on record was a nullity.[13]

Before institution of a suit a notice is required. Such notice is mandatory. A similar provision is noticeable in almost all the State Acts. In particular, the West Bengal Municipal Act 1993 s. 407(1) provides:

> "No suit shall be instituted in any court having jurisdiction against any municipal authority or any officer or other employee of the Municipality or any person acting under the direction of any municipal authority or any officer or other employee of the Municipality in respect of any act done or purporting to be done under this Act or the rules or the regulations made thereunder until after the expiration of one month next after a notice in writing has been delivered or left at the office of such authority or at the office or the residence of such officer or other employee or person, stating—
>
> (*a*) the cause of action,

8 65 IC 592.
9 AIR 1929 All 518.
10 AIR 1932 Cal 356.
11 For Kolkata—See the Kolkata Municipal Corporation Act 1980.
12 AIR 1924 Oudh 309.
13 AIR 1938 Lah 83.

(*b*) the name and residence of the intending plaintiff, and

(*c*) the relief which such plaintiff claims."

39 Official assignee An official assignee is a public officer within the meaning of "Public Officer" under s. 2(17) of the Code of Civil Procedure.

40 Official liquidator The official liquidator of a company is merely an agent of the court for the purposes of liquidation of the company. The official liquidator of a company, though not a pauper himself, may file a suit in *forma pauperis* on behalf of a pauper company.

41 Official trustees The Government appoints official trustee for each State. The same person may be appointed official trustee for two or more States. Under s. 6 of the Official Trustees Act 1913, an official trustee is a Corporation Sole (see No. 15 "Corporation" *supra*) and by the name of the official trustee of the State may sue and be sued.

In a suit against the official trustee in which no relief is claimed against him personally, notice under s. 80 of the CPC has been held inapplicable. (See s. 16 of the Official Trustees Act).

The official trustee shall not administer of estate of a deceased person unless he is expressly appointed the sole executor of and sole trustee under the will of such person. Again, the official trustee shall always be the sole trustee, and it shall not be lawful to appoint the official trustee along with any other person.

42 Political agent In pre-independence days political agents were appointed by the Government to manage the estate of a 'Chief' (Ruling Chief). But such Political Agent was not really the agent to act on behalf of a Prince or a Chief or to prosecute or defend any suit on his behalf. They are to be distinguished from 'recognized agents' specially appointed by order of the Central Government at the request of the Sovereign Prince or the Ruler's Chief as contemplated in s. 85 of the Code.

43 Public body (See Public Charities, Public Trusts—Provisions of s. 92 of CPC—Chapter 10 *infra*).

44 Society At pages 115-116 *ante* we have referred to unincorporated body of persons. Illustrations of such associations are,—

(*i*) Societies;

(*ii*) Clubs etc.

(For "Clubs" see No. 12 *supra*).

Any seven or more persons associated for any literary, scientific or charitable purpose, or for any such purpose as is described in s. 20 of the Societies Registration Act 1860, may form themselves into a society for the purposes of the said Act.

Societies may be registered as well as unregistered. A society when registered under s. 3 of the Societies Registration Act, it is a registered society.

Order 29 of the Code has no application to unregistered or unincorporated society. A suit by an unregistered society must be brought in the names of, or against all the members of the body.[14] Names of all the members must be disclosed.[15] Therefore, a suit when commenced in the names of some of the members of the society or in the name of its Secretary, the suit is liable to be dismissed. In proper cases provisions under Or. 1, r. 8 of the Code may be adopted and one or more of such persons may sue on behalf of all.[16]

The position is different with regard to societies registered under the Societies Registration Act 1860.[17] Under s. 6 of the Societies Registration Act, a registered society can sue or be sued in the name of the President, Chairman or Principal Secretary or other principal officer of the institution[18] as shall be determined by rules and regulations of the society. In default of such determination the registered society may sue and be sued in the name of such person as shall be appointed by the governing body of the society for the occasion. When a society is registered under a particular name, the society can validly adopt different name for institution of a suit by and against it. Suit instituted in that different name is maintainable.[1]

A third party intending to sue a registered society may sue the President, etc., when he applies to the society for nominating any officer to be the defendant but none is nominated; for, the proviso to s. 6 of the Societies Registration Act reads,—

> "Provided that it shall be competent for any person having a claim or demand against the society, to sue the President or Chairman, or the Principal Secretary or the trustees thereof, if on application to the governing body some other officer or person be not nominated to be the defendant.[2]

A registered society has been rendered a continuity, some sort of perpetual succession. In case of change of office or death the suit does not abate. Section 7 reads:

> "No suit or proceeding in any civil court shall abate or discontinue by reason of the person, by or against whom such suit or proceedings shall have been brought or continued, dying or ceasing to fill the character in the name whereof he shall have sued or been sued, but the same suit or proceeding shall be continued in the name of or against the successor of such person."

In a Calcutta case it was held that s. 7 is only a corollary (though a necessary corollary) to s. 6, providing for the continuation of the suit in

14 AIR 1929 Cal 445.
15 AIR 1935 All 872; AIR 1957 All 219.
16 *Saraf and Swarnkar Samiti* AIR 1973 MP 216.
17 For West Bengal—See the West Bengal Societies Registration Act 1961.
18 AIR 1950 All 480; AIR 1960 AP 605.
1 *Krishna Kumar Sinha* v *Kayastha Pathshala* AIR 1966 All 570.
2 AIR 1960 AP 605.

certain contingencies and prescribing the mode therefor.[3] We should remember that neither the provisions contained in s. 7 nor those contained in s. 6 militate against a registered society suing or being sued in its registered name.[4] The provisions of ss. 7 and 6 are not mandatory. The best course is to sue the registered society by the name of the Chairman representing the society.

In suits between members of the same society, provisions in s. 10 of the Societies Registration Act will apply. They are liable to be sued as strangers. Section 10 of the Societies Registration Act reads:

> "Any member who may be in arrear of a subscription which, according to the rules of the society, he is bound to pay, or who shall possess himself of or detain any property of the society in a manner or for a time contrary to such rules, or shall injure or destroy any property of the society, may be sued for such arrear or for the damage accruing from such detention, injury or destruction of property in the manner hereinbefore provided."

Under s. 10, any member who is, *inter alia*, in arrears with his subscription or who is wrongfully in possession of the society's property may be sued by the society as though he were a stranger.[5]

45 Soldier (See No. 8 "Army" *supra*).

46 Summary procedure Order 37, r. 1 of the Code of Civil Procedure 1908 provides that:

Courts and classes of suits to which the order is to apply.

High Court, City Civil Court and any other civil court are enumerated as Court of Small Causes.

The courts' jurisdiction will be determined by the High Court by a Gazette Notification to the effect that the Summary Procedure will apply to the suits upon the Bills of Exchange, Hundis, Promissory Notes, for recovery of the debts due or liquidated demand to be payable by the defendant under a written contract, under any Act or on the guarantee.

In the plaint below the number of Suit in the Cause Title of the Suit, there should be written "Under Order 37 of the Code of Civil Procedure 1908". [*Vide* Or. 37, r. 2(1)(*c*)].

The summons of the suit shall be in Form No. 4 in Appendix "B" or any such other form as may be prescribed by the authorities concerned. [*Vide* Or. 37, r. 2].

47 Surety Under s. 145 of the CPC, where any person has become liable as surety (*a*) for the performance of any decree or any part thereof, or (*b*) for the restitution of any property taken in execution of a decree, or (*c*) for the payment of any money, or for the fulfilment of any condition imposed on any

3 AIR 1959 Cal 361.
4 AIR 1959 Cal 361; AIR 1946 Bom 516.
5 AIR 1950 All 480.

person, under an order of the court in any suit or in any proceeding consequent thereon, the decree or order may be executed against him, to the extent to which he has rendered himself personally liable."

Judgment-debtor released from arrest on execution of surety bond by surety that on failure of the judgment-debtor to pay within certain period, he would be liable for it—execution can be taken out against surety.[6] Section 145 of the CPC applies only when the surety rendered himself personally liable.

48 Trustees Trust is defined as confidence reposed in some other with respect to property of which he is in possession or over which he can exercise the power for the benefit of some other person or object.[7] "A 'trust' is an obligation annexed to the ownership of property, and of a confidence reposed in and accepted by the owner, or declared and accepted by him, for the benefit of another, or of another and the owner."

Trusts are— (*a*) Private trust,

(*b*) Public trust.

The Indian Trusts Act 1882, relates to private trusts and trustees.[8] "The person who accepts the confidence is called the 'trustee'."

(a) ***Private trust.*** When the beneficial interest is limited to specified individuals or definitely ascertainable individuals, it is a private trust.[9]

In Private trusts—

(*i*) the property may be vested in the Official Trustee; or

(*ii*) the property may be vested in others.

Unless the trust property (except where the trust is declared by will or the author of the trust is himself the trustee) is transferred to the trustee no trust is created.

When the property is vested in the official trustee—he shall always be the sole trustee. "It shall not be lawful to appoint the official trustee to be the trustee along with any other persons (see the Official Trustees Act). No one is bound to accept a trust. The intended trustee may disclaim it and such disclaimer shall prevent the trust property from vesting in him. But under s. 10 of the Indian Trusts Act "a disclaimer by one of two or more co-trustees vests the trust property in the other or others, and makes him or them the sole trustee or trustees from the date of the creation of the trust." But a trustee who has accepted the trust cannot afterwards renounce it except under conditions in s. 46(*a*)(*b*) of the Act. The office of a trustee is, however,

6 AIR 1934 Mad 186.

7 B.K. Mukherjea, *The Hindu Law of Religious and Charitable Trusts*, 5th Ed., pp. 4-5.

8 Rules of Mohammedan law as to Waqf, public or private, religious or charitable endowments are exempted from application of the Indian Trusts Act—See s. 1 of the Act; AIR 1949 Mad 721.

9 Goyle's *The Law of Trusts*, 3rd Ed., p. 7.

vacated by his death or by his discharge from his office. A trustee may apply to the court for his discharge under s. 72 of the Act on grounds mentioned in s. 71 of the Act.

A trustee is required to take steps for preservation of trust property and the assertion or protection of the title thereto, if necessary, by maintaining and defending suits. In case of a private trust if there is a breach of trust or mismanagement on the part of the trustee, a suit can be brought in a civil court by any person interested for the removal of the trustee and for the proper administration of the endowment.[10] "Where there are more trustees than one, all must join in the execution of the trust, except where the instrument of trust otherwise provides."

(For Official Trustees)—see No. 41 "Official Trustees" *supra*).

(b) *Public trust.* In a public trust beneficial interest vests in an uncertain and fluctuating body of persons, either the public at large or some considerable portion of it answering a particular description.[11]

In suits where the property is vested in a trustee or trustees and the contention is between the persons beneficially interested in such property and a third person, the trustee shall commence a suit representing the persons so interested for the benefit of beneficiaries. The beneficiaries need not be joined ordinarily as co-plaintiffs. But the court may add the beneficiaries.

Where there are several trustees—all should jointly commence suit. An unwilling trustee or a trustee who has done some act precluding him from the plaintiff should be made a defendant in the suit.[12] In suits against trustees all the trustees, except those who reside at the time of suit outside India, should be joined as co-defendants (*vide* Or. 31, r. 2, CPC). Order 31, r. 2 deals with suits against trustees but not by trustees.

Where one of several co-trustees dies or is discharged, the trust survives and such trustees may sue or be sued unless the instrument of trust expressly declares otherwise (s. 76 of the Indian Trusts Act).

Again, when one of them dies or disclaims, the authority may be exercised by continuing trustees (s. 44 of the Act).

A minor trustee can sue by his next friend and be sued by the guardian *ad litem*[10] lest the suit should be dismissed for defect of parties.

49 Trade Unions A Trade Union[14] registered under the Indian Trade Unions Act 1926, shall be a body corporate by the name under which it is registered and shall sue or be sued by its registered name (s. 13, Trade Unions Act 1926). Suit by the Vice-President is held bad.[15]

10 *Thenappa Chettiar* v *Karuppan Chettiar* AIR 1968 SC 915.
11 *Shanti Devi* v *State* AIR 1982 Del 453.
12 AIR 1938 Mad 982.
13 Section 10 of the Trusts Act read with Or. 31, rr. 1 & 3 CPC; ILR 35 Cal 182. In private trust—AIR 1968 SC 915.
14 The Societies Registration Act 1860, the Co-operative Societies Act 1912, and the Companies Act 1956 shall not apply to any registered Trade Union.
15 AIR 1933 Lah 203.

A suit filed by a Trade Union is not a representative suit and such suit is not within the ambit of Or. 1, r. 8, CPC.[16]

The name of a registered trade union may change but a legal proceeding is not affected thereby. Section 26(1) of the Trade Unions Act reads:—"The change in the name of a registered Trade Union shall not affect any rights or obligations of the Trade Union or render defective any legal proceeding by or against the Trade Union, and any legal proceeding which might have been continued or commenced by or against it by its former name may be continued or commenced by or against it by its new name."

What is perhaps most important in our study for the present is that the trade unions are immune from civil suit in certain cases.

Section 18(1) of the Trade Unions Act enjoins: "No suit or other legal proceeding shall be maintainable in any civil court against any registered Trade Union or any office-bearer or member thereof in respect of any act done in contemplation or furtherance of a trade dispute to which a member of the Trade Union is a party on the ground only that such act induces some other person to break a contract of employment, or that it is in interference with the trade, business or employment of some other person or with the right of some other person to dispose of his capital or of his labour as he wills."

But for tortious liabilities of an agent of the trade union a suit in a civil court shall lie provided he acted with the guilty knowledge of the executive of a trade union; for s. 18(2) says:

> "A registered Trade Union shall not be liable in any suit or other legal proceeding in any civil court in respect of any tortious act done in contemplation or furtherance of a trade dispute by an agent of the Trade Union if it is proved that such person acted without the knowledge of, or contrary to express instructions given by the executive of the Trade Union."

Once a Trade Union is dissolved it is no longer a corporate body. It then loses its right to sue or be sued in its corporate name.

50 The Waqf Act 1995 (Central Act) The word "waqf" means the permanent dedication by any person, of any movable or immovable property for any purpose recognised by the Muslim law as pious, religious or charitable [s. 3(*r*)]. Section 6 of the said Act of 1995, *inter alia*, provides that—

(1) If any question arises, whether a particular property specified as waqf property in the list of auqafs is waqf property or not or whether a waqf specified in such list is a Shia waqf or Sunni waqf, the Board or the Mutawalli of the waqf or any person aggrieved may institute a suit in a Tribunal for the decision of the question and the decision of the Tribunal in respect of such a matter shall be final.

16 *Nagar Vikas Pradhikaran Kamgar Sangh* v *Jaipur Vikas Pradhikaran* 1990 Lab IC 764; (1990)2 LLJ 581.

The limitation for filing such a suit is one year from date of publication of the list of waqfs. Only the Tribunal will have jurisdiction.

Sub-section (5) of s. 6 of the said Act provides that—

> "On and from the commencement of this Act no suit or other legal proceeding shall be instituted or commenced in a court in that State in relation to any question referred to in sub-section (1)".

Under s. 13 of the said Act of 1995, the State Government shall establish a Board of Auqafs which shall be a body corporate having perpetual succession and a common seal with power to acquire and hold such property and to transfer such property and shall sue and be sued in its own name.

Section 36 of the Act requires every waqf to be duly registered with the Board of Waqfs.

Section 83 of the Act provides for constitution of the Tribunal:

> (1) The State Government shall by Notification in the Official Gazette constitute as many Tribunals as it may think fit, for the determination of any dispute, question or any other matter relating to a waqf or waqf property eviction of a tenant or determination of rights and obligations of the lessor and the lessee of such property, under this Act and define the local limits and jurisdiction of such Tribunals.
>
> (2) Any Mutawalli, person interested in a waqf or any other person aggrieved by an order made under this Act or Rules made thereunder, may make an application within time specified in this Act or where no such time has been specified, within such time as may be prescribed, to the Tribunal for the determination of any dispute, question or other matter relating to the waqf.

Sub-section (5) of s. 83 of the Act of 1995 provides that the Tribunal shall be deemed to be a civil court under the Code of Civil Procedure 1908 while trying a suit or executing a decree or order.

Sub-section (9) of section 83 provides that no appeal shall lie against any decision or order whether interim or otherwise, given or made by the Tribunal. Provided that a High Court may, on its own motion or on the application made by the Board of Waqfs, or any person aggrieved, call for and examine the records relating to such dispute, question or other matter which has been determined by the Tribunal for the purpose of satisfying itself as to the correctness, legality or propriety of such determination and may confirm, reverse or modify such determination or pass such other order as it may think fit.

Section 85 provides that no suit or other legal proceeding shall lie in any civil court, Revenue Court and any other authority in respect of any dispute, question or other matter relating to any waqf, waqf property or other matter, which is required by or under this Act to be determined by a Tribunal.

Section 92 of the said Act of 1995, provides that in every legal proceeding in respect of a waqf or waqf property the Board may appear and plead as a necessary party in such suit or legal proceeding.

A proceeding in a court under s. 18 of the Land Acquisition Act is a proceeding within the meaning of s. 92 of the Waqf Act and the Board is entitled to apply for impleading itself as a party in those proceedings.[17]

Section 107 of the said Act of 1995, provides that suit for possession of waqf immovable property or for possession of any interest therein, the Limitation Act of 1963 shall not apply.

17 *Madras State Wakf Board* v *Revenue Divisional Officer, Madurai* (1966)1 MLJ 212.

Chapter

10

Pleadings and Special Rules in Respect of Some Particular Types of Suits

SYNOPSIS

1 Interpleader suits It means a suit to determine a right to property held by a usually disinterested third party (called a *stakeholder*) who is in doubt about ownership and who therefore deposits the property with the court to permit interested parties to litigate ownership.[1]

Section 88 of the Code of Civil Procedure provides:

> "88. *Where interpleader suit may be instituted.* Where two or more persons claim adversely to one another the same debt, sum of money or other property, movable or immovable, from another person, who claims no interest therein other than for charges or costs and who is ready to pay or deliver it to the rightful claimant, such other person may institute a suit of interpleader against all the claimants for the purpose of obtaining a decision as to the person to whom the payment or delivery shall be made and of obtaining indemnity for himself:
>
> Provided that where any suit is pending in which the rights of all parties can properly be decided, no such suit of interpleader shall be instituted."

Where a person deposits in a bank and subsequently there is a dispute between the depositor and another regarding ownership of money deposited, the bank can bring an interpleader suit.[2]

Therefore, in an interpleader suit, the dispute is not between the plaintiff and the defendant but between the defendants. The plaintiff must not have

1 Black's *Law Dictionary*, 10th Ed.
2 AIR 1957 Mad 745.

any interest in the claim except his interest for charges and costs and to obtain indemnity for himself against rival claimants. Order 35, r. 1, enjoins: "In every suit of interpleader the plaint shall, in addition to the other statements necessary for plaints, state—

(*a*) that the plaintiff claims no interest in the subject-matter in dispute other than for charges or costs;

(*b*) the claims made by the defendants severally; and

(*c*) that there is no collusion between the plaintiff and any of the defendants".

The plaintiff is impartial. He must be in a position to walk out of the suit with a mere claim for costs.[3] Where the defendants do not claim adversely to each other, nor does the plaintiff admit the title of one of the defendants or is willing to pay or deliver the property to him, the suit is not an interpleader suit. A suit by a tenant against two sets of landlords for a declaration which defendant has what right and such other prayer is not by way of interpleader.[4] Collusion between the plaintiff and any of the defendants is a condition against an interpleader suit. If the plaintiff has in some way identified himself with one of the parties in the sense that it will make a difference to him which of the two succeeds, an interpleader suit will not lie.[5] The defendants must claim the money or property adversely to one another from the whole of the subject-matter of the suit, but the rival claims must be with reference to the same debt, sum of money or other property. An interpleader suit against the landlord cannot be filed by the tenant.[6] An amendment of plaint in an interpleader suit can be made by inclusion of new properties and by joinder of new parties.[7]

There are two major restrictions, except that contained in r. 1, Or. 35 with regard to interpleader suit. Order 35, r. 5 reads: "Nothing in this Order shall be deemed to enable agents to sue their principals or tenants to sue their landlords, for the purpose of compelling them to interplead with any persons other than persons making claim through such principals or landlords". In order to bring the case under the above exception, it has to be shown that the plaintiff is an agent of the defendant and has instituted the suit for the purpose of compelling the defendant to interplead with person other than persons making claims though him.[8]

2 Representative suits Where in a suit the parties represent themselves and others and again where they represent solely others, the suit takes the character of a representative suit. As such, representative suits are of two types:

(*a*) where the parties represent themselves and others; and

(*b*) where the parties represent exclusively others.

3 AIR 1938 Cal 287.
4 14 CWN 784.
5 AIR 1952 Mad 564.
6 *Sushila Mehta* v *Chandrakala* AIR 2005 NOC 412 (Raj).
7 *Raja Bhagwati Baksh Singh* v *Civil Judge* AIR 1961 All 559.
8 AIR 1954 Punj 103.

(a) ***Where the parties represent themselves and others.*** It is usual that parties to a suit would represent themselves. But there may be occasions when they represent others as well, when permitted to do so under the provisions of law, e.g.

(*i*) Suits by or against the *karta* (or the managing member) of a joint Hindu family.

(*ii*) Suits under s. 14 of the Religious Endowments Act 1863.

(*iii*) Suit under s. 91 of the CPC.

(*iv*) Suit under s. 92 of the CPC.

(*v*) Suits under Or. 1, r. 8 of the CPC.

(I) SUITS BY OR AGAINST THE KARTA OF A JOINT HINDU FAMILY. When *karta* of a joint Hindu family files a suit, he files it on behalf of himself and other members of the family. Similarly, where he is sued as a representative of a joint Hindu family, other members of the family shall be deemed to have been represented through him. The rule applied when a manager was sued in respect of a joint family liability.[9]

(II) SUIT UNDER S. 14 OF THE RELIGIOUS ENDOWMENTS ACT 1863.[10] Any person or persons interested in any public religious trust (mosque, temple or religious establishment or in the performance of worship or of the services thereof or the trust relating thereto) may bring a suit under s. 14 of the Religious Endowments Act 1863, against the trustee, manager, superintendent or a member of any committee appointed under the Act for any misfeasance, breach of trust or neglect of duty committed by him in respect of the trust after obtaining the previous leave of the court under s. 18 of the said Act.

Any person or persons interested may bring the suit. Under s. 15 of the Religious Endowments Act, the word "interest" has been described as—"Any person having a right of attendance, or having been in the habit of attending at the performance of the worship or service of any mosque, temple or religious establishment or of partaking in the benefit of any distribution of alms".

Such person or persons may bring a suit by him or themselves without joining other persons interested.

The suit cannot be instituted without the previous leave of the court. Section 18 of the Act enjoins: "No suit shall be entertained under this Act without a preliminary application being first made to the court for leave to institute such suit".

Persons to whom such leave is granted must join as plaintiffs. Where leave was granted to three persons, all of them should unite together to bring the

9 AIR 1937 Mad 610.

10 The Act does not apply to the Presidency of Bombay nor to any Presidency Towns. For Madras, see the Madras Hindu Religious Endowments Act 1927.

suit. One of them is not competent to bring a suit without getting the sanction amended.[11]

Legal opinion is divergent as to who is to be sued in such actions. A suit contemplated by this section is generally against the trustee,[12] manager, or superintendent of any mosque, temple or religious establishment or the member of any committee appointed under s. 7 of the Act.

A suit under s. 14 of the Act is a representative suit[13] and the right of suit is not personal to the plaintiff. Therefore, upon the death of one of the plaintiffs the suit does not abate. Any one of the persons interested may get himself substituted and continue the suit without fresh leave.[14]

Where a suit is brought against the trustees or members of any committee, the right to sue survives against the surviving defendants alone.[15]

In a private trust temple, misappropriation and mismanagement was made by the *pujari*. Persons who have made large donation for the maintenance of the temple have the right to sue on behalf of the deity to protect the property of the temple. Such suit is maintainable under Or. 7, r. 4 of the Code of Civil Procedure. A person who has made large donations for the maintenance of the temple has clearly a substantial interest to maintain a suit for possession of the temple and its properties against the *pujari* or manager on behalf of the deity to protect the property from mismanagement and misappropriation. Section 92 of the CPC has no application.[16] Section 92 applies to public trusts and public charities.

(III) SUIT UNDER S. 91 OF CPC AGAINST PUBLIC NUISANCES.

(IV) SUIT UNDER S. 92 OF CPC AGAINST PUBLIC CHARITIES.

(See suits relating to public matters below).

(V) SUITS UNDER OR. 1, R. 8, CPC.

The provision contained in Or. 1, r. 8, CPC is what is required for cross-actions.

11 AIR 1915 Mad 127—For West Bengal—"Notwithstanding anything contained in this Act, the powers of the Civil Court under ss. 5 and 10 shall be exercised in respect of any Wakf property in Bengal by the Board of Wakfs appointed under the Bengal Wakf Act 1934.

12 According to Allahabad High Court—it applies to the trustee, manager or superintendents appointed under the Act, i.e. under s. 3(7) of the Act (AIR 1935 All 273). According to Madras High Court, s. 14 applies to both classes of trustees, managers or superintendents.

According to Calcutta High Court—words 'trustee, manager or superintendent' refer only to hereditary trustees under s. 4 (ILR 40 Cal 323).

But this view was dissented in some other cases where it was held that s. 14 applied to trustees whether hereditary or selected (see ILR 62 Cal 125; ILR 34 Cal 584, 595).

13 AIR 1928 Mad 614.

14 ILR 41 Mad 237; 61 Cal 80.

15 ILR 53 Mad 790.

16 *Ramchand (dead) by LRs v Thakur Janaki Ballabhji Maharaj* AIR 1970 SC 532.

Order 1, r. 8 enjoins: (1) "Where there are numerous persons having the same interest in one suit, (*a*) one or more of such persons may, with the permission of the court, sue or be sued, or may defend such suit, on behalf of, or for the benefit of all, persons so interested; (*b*) the court may direct that one or more of such persons may sue or be sued, or may defend such suit, on behalf of, or for the benefit of, all persons so interested.

(2) The court shall, in every case where a permission or direction is given under sub-rule (1), at the plaintiff's expenses, give notice of the institution of the suit to all persons so interested, either by personal service, or, where, by reason of the number of persons or any other cause, such service is not reasonably practicable, by public advertisement, as the court in each case may direct.

But the court shall in such case give, at the plaintiff's expense, notice of the institution of the suit to all such persons either by personal service or, where from the number of persons or any other cause such service is not reasonably practicable, by public advertisement, as the court in such case may direct.

(3) Any person on whose behalf or for whose benefit a suit is instituted the defendant under sub-rule (1) may apply to the court to be made a party to such suit".[17]

Order 1, r. 8, CPC does not prescribe any stage at which the application can be filed. Such application can be filed at any stage of the proceeding but after getting permission from the court.[18] Order 1, r. 8 is an enabling provision and lays down the procedure how a suit by numerous persons having interest in common may be commenced. This provision, however, does not debar a person from suing in his own right although the act complained of has injured other persons also.[19] The rule presupposes that each one of the numerous persons by himself has a right of suit. A person who has no right of suit on behalf of himself cannot, therefore, be allowed to sue in a representative capacity.[20]

Conditions for application of these rules are:

(*i*) Parties must be numerous and that they should have the same interest in the suit.

17 Local Amendments—(*a*) Calcutta—In sub-rule (1) for the first sentence commencing with the words "where there are" and ending with "persons so interested", the following substitution was made—"Where there are numerous persons having the same interest in the suit, the court may direct that one, or more such persons may sue or be sued, or may defend, in such suit, on behalf of, or for the benefit of all persons so interested."
(*b*) Assam—same as Calcutta.
(*c*) Bombay—In Or. 1, r. 8, sub-rule (1) after the first sentence ending with the words "so interested" the following sentence shall be inserted, namely,—"the court may in suitable cases direct what two or more persons having the same interest in the suit may sue or be sued or may defend, in such suits, on behalf of, or for the benefit of, all persons so interested."

18 *Krishna Vasudevan* v *Shareef* (2005)12 SCC 180.

19 101 IC 500.

20 AIR 1942 Cal 360.

When one or two persons having an interest common with numerous others may sue or be sued with the permission of the court, on behalf and for the benefit of all persons so interested. By the term "numerous"—no number is meant, nor there is any limitation for number, e.g., the Sadgope caste of A.B. Town, the inhabitants of village XY, the Hindu community of village C.B. etc.. Club and other associations can sue or be sued under Or. 1, r. 8 after obtaining previous permission under this rule (see No. 12 of Chapter 9 'Clubs' *supra*). Under this rule a suit is permissible on behalf of a body against some of its own members.[1] It is well settled law that provisions of Or. 1, r. 8, CPC are mandatory in nature but it may apply where the parties are numerous. But if there is absence of numerous parties, provisions of Or. 1, r. 8, CPC would not apply.[2]

(*ii*) Prior permission of the court is required. The permission of the court, contemplated in Or. 1, r. 8 of the Code, should be taken before institution of the suit. When commencing a suit the plaint shall be accompanied by a petition to the court for permission. But permission granted afterwards is not an illegality. Even if permission was given after the publication of the notice, that would not vitiate the proceedings.[3] There cannot be waiver of the necessity of permission and the suit without leave of the court shall be dismissed. Nevertheless, the permission need not be express. It is sufficient if it can be gathered from proceedings of the court. Application for amendment of plaint so as to make the suit a representative one must be made within the time allowed for institution of the suit.[4] If after obtaining permission to sue in representative capacity, some more persons are added as parties, in such a case fresh permission is not necessary. Earlier permission is good for any number of persons added as party.[5] Separate application for permission to sue in representative capacity is not needed.[6]

(*iii*) Notice is to be given to the parties who are sought to be so represented.

The court is required to give notice of the institution of a suit under Or. 1, r. 8 of the Code to all such persons either personally or by public advertisement. The latter mode can be resorted to only when personal service is not 'reasonably' feasible due to the number of such persons or for any other sufficient cause. Failure to issue notice sometimes vitiates proceedings and the suit is not a representative suit then. When a plaint contains an averment that the plaintiffs are filing the suit in a representative capacity and later, an application under Or. 1, r. 8 is made, the court may either grant a conditional permission subject to objections being raised by the parties to whom notice is issued or may immediately issue notice even without expressly granting any such conditional permission. After the service of notice either by personal delivery or public advertisement, when either objections have been filed and

1 AIR 1929 Mad 623; AIR 1971 Mad 274.
2 *Balunkeswar Mahadev* v *Smt. Brajeswari Mohapatra* AIR 2004 Ori 42.
3 AIR 1943 Mad 161; AIR 1952 Kutch 92; AIR 1965 Ker 200.
4 AIR 1940 Mad 789; AIR 1970 Mad 81.
5 *V.N. Jayaraman* v *Commercial Tax Officer* 2001 AIHC 4649 (Mad).
6 *Nakuleswar Paul* v *State of Tripura* AIR 2005 Gau 54.

an application for impleadment is made or no objections are filed and no application for being impleaded is made, the court must, after disposing of such objections, if any, pass the final order granting or refusing permission. Thereafter the court shall have jurisdiction to enter into the merits of the case and proceed with the trial. If, however, no express order granting permission is made at any stage whatsoever, the suit would not acquire a representative character.[7]

In a suit of representative capacity, a notice under r. 8(2) of Or. 1, CPC is mandatory.[8] When no notice is given, it is nothing but non-compliance of the provisions of Or. 1, r. 8(2), CPC and the suit would not be deemed to have been filed in representative capacity.[9]

Suit filed in a representative capacity. Death of one of the plaintiffs during pendency of second appeal—the appeal does not abate.[10]

From Note 7(*g*) of Chapter 3 at p. 49 *ante* we have seen that in cases where the suit is brought in representative capacity the fact should be stated not only in the body of the plaint but also in the cause-title of the suit.

"But it is not necessary that the cause-title should show that the suit is representative though it is a convenient place for stating the fact."[11]

If during the pendency of a representative suit, one of the plaintiffs dies no substitution is necessary. The other plaintiff can go on with the suit.[12] When one of the representative defendants dies there is no abatement.[13]

(b) *When the parties to a suit represent exclusively others.* There may be a case where a plaintiff has had no personal interest in the suit. But under the exigency he or they have to file a suit only to represent others, e.g. (*a*) *shebait* of an idol, (*b*) receiver of a property, (*c*) executor to a will, (*d*) administrator to the estate of a deceased, (*e*) *benamdar* for real owner, and so on.

3 Suits relating to public matters (As provided for in ss. 91 and 92 of the Code).

Such suits are: (*i*) Suits relating to public nuisances (s. 91);
(*ii*) Suits relating to public charities (s. 92).

(*i*) *Suits relating to public nuisances and other wrongful acts affecting the public.* The provision in the Code of Civil Procedure relating to cases of public nuisances is contained in s. 91 of the Code which reads:

7 *Sri Ram Krishna Mission* v *Paramanand* AIR 1977 All 421.
8 *Kusasan Samal* v *Chandramani Pradhan* AIR 2003 Ori 157.
9 *Subhash Market Association* v *Municipal Corporation of Delhi* AIR 2005 Del 209 (DB).
10 AIR 1976 SC 371.
11 AIR 1919 Cal 245 (ILR 46 Cal 877).
Order 7, r. 4 enjoins: "Where the plaintiff sues in a representative character, the plaint shall show not only that he has an actual existing interest in the subject-matter but that he has taken steps (if any) necessary to enable him to institute a suit concerning it."
12 AIR 1935 Cal 413.
13 AIR 1940 Lah 272.

91. (1) In the case of a public nuisance or other wrongful act affecting, or likely to affect, the public, a suit for a declaration and injunction or for such other relief as may be appropriate in the circumstances of the case, may be instituted,—

(*a*) by the Advocate-General, or

(*b*) with the leave of the Court, by two or more persons, even though no special damage has been caused to such persons by reason of such public nuisance or other wrongful act.

(2) Nothing in this section shall be deemed to limit or otherwise affect any right of suit which may exist independently of its provisions.

A private individual cannot sue in respect of a public nuisance without sustaining a special damage by such nuisance. Section 91 is an exception to that. Under this section a suit can be maintained even 'without proof of special damage' provided the suit is brought by the Advocate-General of a State or with the leave of the court by two or more persons and the other conditions of s. 91 are satisfied.[14] This does not mean that a private person cannot commence a suit; for, "the section does not deprive any person of any right which he may have independently of its provisions". The said right is safeguarded under sub-sec. (2) of s. 91: for, e.g. on proof of special damage he can bring a suit independently of provisions of s. 91.[15]

Section 91 applies to public nuisances. Public nuisance means an unreasonable interference with a right common to the general public, such as a condition dangerous to health, offensive to community moral standards, or unlawfully obstructing the public in the free use of public property.[16] Words 'public nuisances' have not been defined in the Code of Civil Procedure. For definition we are to refer to s. 268 of the Indian Penal Code. The nuisance must affect the people in general.[17]

Therefore, acts adversely affecting particular persons or caused to a given set of persons are not public nuisances, obstruction of a village pathway is not a public nuisance. Suit for removal of public nuisance (removal of wall built within 10 feet of his house depriving the plaintiff of the enjoyment of basic rights and amenities—special damage inferred)—suit is maintainable only on special damage shown.[18] If any act causes obstruction and trespass on land used by the public for children's burial place is a public nuisance.[19]

14 AIR 1942 Cal 360; AIR 1958 AP 586; also see AIR 1937 Pat 54; AIR 1939 All 586; AIR 1940 Pat 449.

15 AIR 1949 Nag 314; *Sri Ram Singh* v *Smt. Patti* AIR 1968 All 18; *Chandrawati Devi* v *Rameshwar Kaviraj* AIR 1968 Pat 422.

16 Black's *Law Dictionary*, 10th Ed.

17 Instances of public nuisance—Obstruction of public highway, pollution of public waterways, storage of inflammable articles likely to endanger human life, acts of interference with the right of the public to freely navigate in a navigable river, building of a construction over any part of a public street and so on.

18 AIR 1973 All 310.

19 *LRs of Bhatkaran* v *Vijay Singh* AIR 2015 NOC 43 (Raj).

Any person who has a house abutting on a public road or lane is entitled to access to the road or lane from the house and no person or authority can destroy that right. This right does not emanate from prescription or long user but from the fact that the house abuts on the public way. Hence, if an obstruction is made by any person or authority of such public way which affects the ingress or egress, special damage to the owner of the property must be presumed and the plaintiff is entitled to maintain the suit for demolition of the obstruction.[20] If any nuisance affects the neighbourhood and this nuisance has affected the public in general, a suit for removal of such nuisance is maintainable.[1]

A person whose right to pass along a highway is obstructed or interfered with can maintain a suit in respect of public nuisance without proving any other damage.[2]

Who can bring a suit as contemplated in s. 91, CPC.?

(*i*) The Advocate-General;[3]

(*ii*) Two or more persons with the leave of the court.

In a suit of the above nature reliefs that may be prayed for:

(*i*) *Declaration*—that the place involved is a public thoroughfare etc.

(*ii*) *Injunction—restraining nuisance*. The plaintiffs filed a suit[4] in representative capacity on behalf of the villagers of a certain village to restrain the defendants from lying salt-pans in the bed of the suit tank belonging to the Government, thereby making the water in it useless to the people for bathing, drinking and other purposes. It was found that the villagers had an immemorial right to the use of the water in the tank for their drinking and bathing purposes as also for the use of their cattle. *Held:* As the plaintiffs-villagers had a common right over the water in the tank, any interference with that right gave them a cause of action even though interference was not in respect of the land belonging to the plaintiffs. The action of the defendants amounted to a nuisance and the plaintiffs were entitled to an injunction prayed for.

SUIT AGAINST PUBLIC TRUST. Leave of court for its institution is the condition precedent.[5]

20 *Bhagwanti* v *Jiuti* AIR 1975 All 341.

1 *Dilip Kaushal* v *State of MP* AIR 2008 MP 324 (FB).

2 *Pyarelal* v *Santlal* AIR 1972 Raj 103.

3 "The powers conferred by ss. 91 and 92 on the Advocate-General may, outside the Presidency towns, be, with the previous sanction of the State Government, exercised also by the Collector or by such officer as the State Government may appoint in this behalf" (vide s. 93 of CPC). Rules of a legal department of the Government authorising the Collector etc., does not make the Advocate-General *functus officio*—AIR 1949 Nag 183. When the Collector refuses consent, the Advocate-General may grant the same.

4 *Pakkle* v *V.P. Aiyasami* AIR 1969 Mad 351.

5 *N. Anandan* v *Ayyanna Gounder* AIR 1994 Mad 43.

DEDICATION OF PRIVATE PROPERTY FOR A RELIGIOUS OR CHARITABLE PURPOSE. Dedication need not be made in writing and can be made orally or can be inferred from conduct.[6] In respect of a public temple, the law is well-settled that the true beneficiaries of religious endowments are not the idols but the worshippers and that the purpose of the endowment is the maintenance of that worship for the benefit of worshippers.[7]

PROPERTY BELONGING TO TEMPLE—SALE BY MANAGER. Suit by worshippers for declaration that the sale-deed executed by manager was null and void. The suit is maintainable.[8]

CHARITABLE PURPOSE. Purpose must not involve carrying on of activity of profit. Fact that monies for accomplishment or implementation of the purpose is obtained by carrying of an activity for profit is immaterial.[9]

(ii) Suits relating to public charities. Institution of a suit under s. 92, CPC—Grant of leave for:

Although as a rule of caution, court should normally give notice to the defendants before granting leave under s. 92 to institute a suit, the court is not bound to do so. If a suit is instituted on the basis of such leave, granted without notice to the defendants, the suit would not thereby be rendered bad in law or non-maintainable.

The grant of leave cannot be regarded as defeating or seriously prejudicing any right of the proposed defendants because it is always open to them to file an application for revocation of the leave which can be considered on merits and according to law.

Although cl. (*ffa*) of s. 104(1) of the Code provides that an appeal shall lie against the refusal of grant of leave, that cannot lead to the conclusion that it is obligatory on the part of the court to give notice to the proposed defendants before granting leave because an appeal lies only against refusal of leave and not against grant of leave. Before refusing leave the proposed plaintiffs are bound to be heard and it is the plaintiffs and not the defendants who could be prejudiced by refusal to grant such leave.[10]

The main purpose of s. 92(1) is to give protection to public trusts of a charitable or religious nature from being subjected to harassment by suits being filed against them. That is why it provides that suits under that section can only be filed either by the Advocate-General or by two or more persons having an interest in the trust—suit to remove existing trustee-plaintiff having remote relationship with the founder of the trust. His interest in the trust held not sufficient to maintain the suit[11] with the leave of the court. The

6 *Tilkayat Sri Govindlalji* v *State of Rajasthan* AIR 1963 SC 1638.
7 *Deoki Nandan* v *Murlidhar* AIR 1957 SC 133 at p. 137.
8 *Kapoor Chand* v *Ganesh Dutt* AIR 1993 SC 1145.
9 *Victoria Technical Institute* v *Addl. Commissioner of Income Tax, Madras* AIR 1991 SC 997 (*Addl. Comm. of Income-tax* v *Surat Art Silk* AIR 1980 SC 387 foll.).
10 *R.M. Narayana Chettiar* v *N. Lakshmanan Chettiar* AIR 1991 SC 221.
11 AIR 1978 Mad 205.

object is that before the Advocate-General files a suit, he would satisfy himself that there is a *prima facie* case either of a breach of trust or of the necessity for obtaining directions of the court.[12]

Section 92(1) of the CPC enjoins:

> 92. *Public charities.* (1) In the case of any alleged breach of any express or constructive trust created for public purposes of a charitable or religious nature, or where the direction of the Court is deemed necessary for the administration of any such trust, the Advocate-General, or two or more persons having an interest in the trust and having obtained the leave of the Court may institute a suit, whether contentious or not, in the principal Civil Court of original jurisdiction or in any other Court empowered in that behalf by the State Government within the local limits of whose jurisdiction the whole or any part of the subject-matter of the trust is situate to obtain a decree—
>
> (*a*) removing any trustee; (*vide* reliefs in paras (*a*) to (*h*) under s. 92(1) of the Code) etc. Relief claimed in the suit seeking to prevent a breach of trust by a trustee. The suit could fall within general cl.(*h*) of s. 92(1).[13]

Section 92[14] applies under four conditions:

(*i*) There should be an express or constructive trust for public purposes[15] of a charitable or religious nature. In case of a private Hindu temple for a suit against the *pujari* for mismanagement, s. 92 has no application;[16]

(*ii*) There should be breach of trust;[17]

or, the direction of the court is deemed necessary for the administration of such trust;

(*iii*) The suit is to be filed by the Advocate-General or by two or more persons having an interest in the trust and they should have obtained the leave of the court;

(*iv*) The suit must be a representative suit on behalf of the public and not for own interest of the plaintiffs.

Section 92, CPC applies to public religious trust only and it has no application to private *debuttar*.[18]

12 *Madappa* v *Mahanthadevaru* AIR 1966 SC 878.

13 *Jathedar Sadhu Singh* v *Charan Singh* AIR 1972 Punj 347.

14 Cognate Legislation—Proceedings under s. 142 of the Sikh Gurdwaras Act are analogous to those under s. 92 of CPC.

15 The suit contemplated by s. 92 is directed against trustees. Existence of a public trust as required by s. 92, is essential—AIR 1965 AP 143.

16 *Ramchand (dead) by LRs.* v *Thakur Janaki Ballabhji Maharaj* AIR 1970 SC 532.

17 A suit for rendition of accounts by co-trustees against trustee who was in day-to-day change of trust-properties. The suit does not come within scope of s. 92 (AIR 1969 Del 75).

18 *Subhash Chandra Banik* v *State of West Bengal* AIR 2011 Cal 125 (DB).

In s. 92(1), 'leave of the court' has been substituted by 'consent of the Advocate-General'. Leave for institution of suit under s. 92. The court is not bound to give notice to defendants before granting leave although as a rule of caution it should normally give such notice.[19]

Section 92(2), CPC—Court finds the suit to be incompetent for want of leave of Advocate-General under s. 92. The court's findings on other issues were no findings at all, and at such would not operate as *res judicata*. In such a case the court ought not to have considered the other issues and instead, it should have rejected the plaint.[20]

A suit under s. 92 is a suit of special nature which presupposes the existence of a public trust of a religious or charitable character. Such a suit can proceed only on the allegation that there was a breach of such trust or that the direction of the court is necessary for the administration of the trust and the plaintiff must pray for one or more of the reliefs that are mentioned in the section.[1] If the allegation of breach of trust is not substantiated or if the plaintiff has not made out a case for any direction by the court for proper administration of the trust, the very foundation of a suit under the section would fall. If it is clear that the plaintiffs are not suing to vindicate the right of the public but are seeking a declaration of their individual or personal rights or of any other person or persons in whom they are interested, then the suit would be outside the scope of s. 92.

It is not every suit claiming the reliefs specified in the section that can be brought under the section but only the suits which, besides claiming any of the reliefs, are brought by individuals as representatives of the public for vindication of public rights and in deciding whether a suit falls within s. 92 the court must go beyond the reliefs and have regard to the capacity in which the plaintiffs are suing and to the purpose for which the suit was brought. When the right to the office of a trustee is asserted or denied and relief is asked for on that basis, the suit falls outside s. 92.

There is no reason to think that whenever a suit is brought by two or more persons under s. 92, the suit is to vindicate the right of the public.[2]

(*a*) The first condition of application of s. 92 is that it should be a trust and the trust must be a public one of a charitable and religious nature. If an Waqf has been created substantially for public purpose, it is a public charity and s. 92 applies.[3] Where a property is dedicated to a mosque and the property is in possession of the wife of the deceased executant of the Waqf—suit by the plaintiff-mosque to recover possession—*Held*, s. 92 has no application and consequently

19 *R.M. Narayana* v *N. Lakshmanan* AIR 1991 SC 221.

20 *Ambiah* v *J. George* AIR 1992 Mad 265.

1 *Mahant Pragdasji Guru* v *Patel Iswarlal Bhai* AIR 1952 SC 143.

2 *Swami Paramatmanand Saraswati* v *Ramji Tripathi* AIR 1974 SC 2141.

3 Waqf in favour of family members of the founder and in favour of the public—suit for removal of Mutawalli and appointment of new trustee. *Held*, provisions of s. 92 were attracted and the suit filed without the consent of the Advocate-General was not maintainable (AIR 1969 SC 884).

consent of the Advocate-General for filing the suit is not necessary.[4] A trust for the purposes of s. 92 may be either a express or a constructive trust.

A suit of this nature may be on the grounds:

(*i*) that there has been a breach of trust;

(*ii*) that the direction of the court is required for the administration of the trust.

In the former case, when a trustee sets up his own title in the trust properties, it is a case of breach. In the latter case, breach is not necessary, but there may be necessity of the court's orders for a scheme or otherwise for the administration of the trust.[5]

(*iii*) Persons suing must have an interest in the trust. Mere leave of the court will not entitle a party to sue unless he has an interest in the trust. In other words, persons seeking relief must be persons interested in the trust.[6] They may exercise the power separately or jointly.

The Advocate-General has had the power to bring a suit by himself, i.e. he can himself initiate proceedings as well as grant sanction for others. He may intervene in a suit at any stage.

Leave of the court is a condition precedent to institution of a suit. Without leave, the suit is to be dismissed and cannot be rectified by any subsequent amendment. Where addition or amendment alters the nature of the suit, a fresh sanction is necessary.[7] Old law—the object of the sanction is to protect the trust property as well as the trustees from an indefinite number of reckless and harassing suits being brought against the trustees.[8]

"Where the consent in writing of the Advocate-General or Collector has been given to a suit by three persons as plaintiffs, the suit cannot validly be instituted by two only. The suit as instituted must conform to the consent. (*per* Rankin).[9]

(*b*) Under s. 92[10] of the CPC, the suit brought is of a representative nature. Where a person seeks relief against a particular infringement of his individual right in a public trust, the suit is not a suit under s. 92. The section is not intended to adjudicate upon conflicting rights of private individuals. Here, the suit is brought by two or more persons as representing the general public in order to secure the proper administration of a trust.

4 AIR 1941 PC 1; *Amir Bai* v *Management, Nitasandra Mosque* AIR 1969 Mys 103.

5 AIR 1928 Cal 368.

6 51 IA 282; ÅIR 1948 EP 49; AIR 1957 Mad 597; AIR 1965 AP 143.

7 AIR 1944 Cal 163.

8 AIR 1947 Oudh 22.

9 AIR 1938 PC 184.

10 In Madras the Madras Hindu Religious Endowments Act will govern. Cognate Legislation—Bihar Hindu Religious Trusts Act 1950.

Section 92 is limited in its application to suits for reliefs specified in s. 92(*a*) to (*h*).[11] If a suit does not contain the prayer for reliefs specified in that section, s. 92 shall not apply. The words 'such further reliefs' in s. 92(1)(*h*) mean reliefs of the same nature as in (*a*) to (*g*) of the said section. The court has power under Or. 1, r. 10(2) to add parties in a suit under s. 92 of the Code as in any other suit. Thus in a suit under s. 92 to remove a trustee, the son of the trustee on his own application was added as a party even against the wishes of the plaintiffs, in order to enable him to establish his rights in any scheme that might be framed.

Defence—The principle under s. 92, cls. (1) and (2) is equally applicable to defence also.[12]

A suit under s. 92 not being a suit which is presented by individuals for their own interest does not abate by the subsequent death of one of the plaintiffs. Personal heirs cannot be brought on record as legal representatives in such suits.[13] Such a suit does not become defective or incompetent.[14] A suit instituted against a trustee or a Sajjadanaihin of a religious institution for his removal for breach of trust and framing a scheme, does not abate by the death of the trustee or Sajjadanaihin. But the cause of action survives against the representatives of the deceased, in so far as the framing of the scheme is concerned. In a suit under s. 92 where the question is whether the property is private or public and the defendant contends that the property is a private one and pending the suit the defendant dies, the action does not abate but survives[15] as against the sons of the defendant and the action does not abate.

Finally, referring to the question of jurisdiction, we must remember that a suit under s. 92 must be brought in the 'principal civil court of original jurisdiction or in any other court empowered in that behalf by the State Government within the local limits of whose jurisdiction the whole or any part of the subject-matter of the trust is situate'. Section 92 of the Civil Procedure Code is not governed by the provisions of ss. 16, 17 and 20 of the Code. The court's jurisdiction to entertain a suit under s. 92 of the Code depends only upon the existence within its jurisdiction of property which is the subject-matter of the trust.[16] It was held: "By creating special jurisdiction in regard to suits of that class, the general jurisdiction of a Civil Court cannot be invoked and non-compliance with the specific provision would be fatal to the maintainability of the suit.[17] Section 92 overrides Letters Patent, cl. 12.

Section 92, CPC specifies the courts which shall have jurisdiction to entertain the suit relating to public trust. District Courts and subordinate courts shall have concurrent jurisdiction without pecuniary limits. Section 92 is a self-contained provision and conferment of the jurisdiction in regard

11 AIR 1952 SC 143.
12 *Manadeo* v *Yaduvansh* AIR 1969 All 571.
13 *Bishambhar* v *Raghunath* AIR 1971 All 207.
14 AIR 1938 PC 184.
15 AIR 1934 All 315.
16 AIR 1955 Bom 55.
17 AIR 1957 AP 10.

to suits under s. 92 does not depend upon the value of the subject-matter of the suit. Even if the State Government by notification conferred the jurisdiction on the District Court or other court, the word "or" denoting an alternation giving a choice, even if the State Government notifies any other court, the jurisdiction of the District Court does not stand substituted.[18]

Comparative scope of s. 92 of the Civil Procedure Code and Religious Endowments Act 1963.

(*i*) Suits in respect of religious endowments which do not charge trustee, manager, etc. with misfeasance, breach of trust or neglect of duty are outside the scope of Religious Endowments Act. They fall within the provisions of s. 92 of the Code.

(*ii*) Religious endowments alone come within the purview of Religious Endowments Act while charitable trust fall within the ambit of s. 92 of the Code.

(*iii*) Suits with respect to public religious trusts charging trustee, manager etc., fall both within s. 14 of Religious Endowments Act and s. 92 of the Code.

(*iv*) In both the cases prior permission of the Court is necessary.

(*v*) A suit under Religious Endowments Act and that under s. 92 of the Code—both are representative suits.

(*vi*) In the case of a private trust for breach of trust or mismanagement on the part of trustee a suit can be brought under Religious Endowments Act for the removal of the trustee and for the proper administration of the endowment (AIR 1968 SC 915).

4 Special case (*i*) Contents; (*ii*) Form; (*iii*) Jurisdiction and (*iv*) Registration.

Section 90 of the Civil Procedure Code reads:

"Where any persons agree in writing to state a case for the opinion of the court, then the court shall try and determine the same in the manner prescribed".

The manner is prescribed in rr. 1 to 5 under Or. 36 of the Code. Rules 1 and 2 speak of the form and contents of an application for opinion. Rule 1 enjoins:

(i) *Contents*

Rule 1. (1) Parties claiming to be interested in the decision of any question of fact or law may enter into an agreement in writing stating such question in the form of a case for the opinion of the court, and providing that, upon the finding of the court with respect to such question,—

(*a*) a sum of money fixed by the parties or to be determined by the court shall be paid by one of the parties to the other of them; or

18 *Sri Seyaram Educational Trust* v *A.G. Syed Mohideen* AIR 2010 SC 671.

(*b*) some property, movable or immovable, specified in the agreement, shall be delivered by one of the parties to the other of them; or

(*c*) one or more of the parties shall do, or refrain from doing, some other particular act specified in the agreement.

The above are the contents of an agreement to state a case. Again r. 2 of Or. 36 provides: "Where the agreement is for the delivery of any property, or for the doing, or the refraining from doing, any particular act, the estimated value of the property to be delivered, or to which the act specified has reference, shall be stated in the agreement".

(ii) *Form*

Order 36, r. 1(2) reads: "Every case stated under this rule shall be divided into consecutively numbered paragraphs, and shall concisely state such facts and specify such documents as may be necessary to enable the court to decide the question raised thereby."

Material facts have to be stated and documents should be referred to and their effects stated (as under Or. 6, r. 9 of CPC). The agreement, obviously, would pose a question to be answered by the court. The agreement should be signed by the parties to the agreement. The right to state a case for the opinion of the court is not intended to enable parties to refer to the court academic questions. For, r. 1 "would prevent the court from being burdened with mere academic discussions or other matters in which the parties had no substantial interest".[19]

(For Cause-Title of a Special Case, see Notes below).

(iii) *Jurisdiction*

"The agreement has to be filed in the ordinary local jurisdiction. Order 36, r. 3(1) reads:

> "The agreement, if framed in accordance with the rules .... may be filed with an application in the court which would have jurisdiction to entertain a suit, the amount or value of the subject-matter of which is the same as the amount or value of the subject-matter of the agreement".

(iv) *Registration of a Special Case*

Order 36, r. 3(2) enjoins:

> "The application when so filed, shall be numbered and registered as a suit between one or more of the parties claiming to be interested a plaintiff or plaintiffs, and the other or the others of them as defendant

19 AIR 1930 Bom 232.
Notes: Title of a special case:
In the Court of the Munsif(s) ....
Other Class (Special Case)/Suit No. ... of 20...
A.B. etc. .... 1st Party/Plaintiff.
C.D. etc. .... versus .... 2nd Party/Defendant.
Special case for opinion of the court on questions of law under Or. 36, r. 1 of CPC.
Valued at ₹4,000.

or defendants; and notice shall be given to all the parties to the agreement, other than the party or parties by whom the application was presented."

5 Cross-suit (or cross-action) We have seen in Chapter 4, Note 10 *ante* that a defendant is entitled to set-off (both legal and equitable) as also to plead a counter-claim. While set-off is a statutory defence to a plaintiff's action, a counter-claim is substantially a cross-action.[20]

Where the defendant in a suit claims an amount from the plaintiff therein below and up to the plaint claim it is claim for set-off in a strict sense; but when the claim is for an amount larger than the plaint claim, the claim for the excess over the plaint claim is a counter-claim which is really in the nature of another suit by the defendant against the plaintiff.[21]

Except the provision in Or. 8, r. 6 of the Code, there is no provision for entertaining a counter-claim but the court has inherent power to treat a counter-claim as a plaint in a cross-suit. The defendant has to pay court-fees on that. In other words, a cross-suit has to be properly stamped".

A cross-suit is to be distinguished from cross-objection as provided for in Or. 41, r. 22 of the Code.

It is open to a court to convert to treat a counter-claim as a plaint in a cross-suit. The plaintiffs had set up a case on the basis of their title over the suit land. The defendants in their written statement denied the title of the plaintiffs and contended that they were the owners and the plaintiffs were the tenants of the suit land and also paid court-fees on the relief sought by them. *Held,* to avoid multiplicity of suits it would be in the interest of justice to treat the counter-claim of the defendants as a cross-suit and try it as such.[22]

20 AIR 1941 Nag 258.

21 *Govindji Jevat & Co.* v *Cannanore Spinning and Weaving Mills Ltd.* AIR 1968 Ker 310.

22 AIR 1964 SC 11; AIR 1977 NOC 219 (MP).

Part Two

Specimen of Plaints and Petitions

Accounts

1. Suit for accounts

In the Court of District Judge at ....

Suit No. .... of 20.........

Mrs. P., residing at ...., Alipore, Kolkata

.... *Plaintiff*

versus

Mr. X., residing at .... Alipore, Kolkata

.... *Defendant*

Suit for Accounts valued at ₹ ....

The plaintiff states as follows:

1. Mr. Q the owner of several houses died on 10.1.20........... after making his last Testament and Will on 15.12.20..... appointing the plaintiff, Mrs. P his wife as the sole executrix.

2. On 15.6.20....., the plaintiff applied for probate of the said Will. But, the deceased's brother who was actually looking after the deceased contested such grant of Probate of the said Will, pursuant to which the said matter was fixed for hearing as a Contentious Matter and it was numbered as Suit No. 5 of 20.....

3. After hearing, this learned court was pleased to issue Probate of the said Will to the plaintiff, Mrs. P., as the rightful legal Executrix of the Estate of the deceased.

4. After taking charge as Executrix of the Estate of the deceased covered by the said Will, the plaintiff found that the defendant had already collected the rents of the house properties of the said deceased after his death till filing of application for grant of necessary Probate.

5. The defendant did not, however, deposit the rents collected by him to the account of deceased or to the account of the Executrix of the said Estate properties. The defendant did not furnish any statement of account of rents collected of the Estate covered by the said Will.

6. Ultimately the plaintiff vide his letter dated 5.1.20..... demanded payment of the said rent amounts collected in respect of the Estate covered by said Will of the deceased and also complete statements of accounts in relation to the said Estate and/or rents collected pursuant thereto in respect of said Estate property. The defendant was requested to furnish the said full particulars within 3 weeks therefrom.

7. The defendant received the said letter by signing on copy of the same but did not comply with the said request of plaintiff.

8. In the premises, the plaintiff is entitled to and claims full statements of accounts in respect of rents collected and any disbursements made therefrom and a decree for payment of balance amount of rents collected and/or in his hands for payment to plaintiff.

9. No part of the plaintiff's claims is barred by law of limitation.

10. The plaintiff's cause of action for this suit arose within the jurisdiction of this learned court, *inter alia*, pursuant to said demand letter. The plaintiff's cause of action is still continuing from day to day as the defendant is still committing defaults in complying with the request and not furnishing full statements of accounts and wrongfully withholding the rent amounts in respect of the said properties which are to be handed over to the plaintiff as the Sole Executrix of the said deceased.

11. For the purposes of jurisdiction and court-fees, the suit is valued at ₹.............. on which court-fees in stamps have been paid.

12. In the premises, this learned court has the jurisdiction to entertain, try and determine the suit and no part of the plaintiff's claims is barred by limitation.

The plaintiff, therefore, claims:

(*a*) Decree directing the defendant to submit full statements of accounts of rents collected by him during the period from the date of death of Testator till date of grant of probate of said Will;

(*b*) Decree for payment of rents collected according to such statements of accounts with interest at 12% per annum;

(*c*) Costs;

(*d*) Further and other order and reliefs as the plaintiff is entitled to in the law and equity.

Verification

Affidavit

2. Suit by principal against agent for account

In the Court of .... at ....

Suit No. .... of 20 ....

AB, residing at .... within the said jurisdiction.

...... *Plaintiff*

versus

CD, residing at .... within the said jurisdiction.

...... *Defendant*

The plaintiff states:

1. On .... 20 .... the plaintiff (orally or in writing, as the case may be) employed the defendant as his agent, to collect the rents of the plaintiff's various house properties from the tenants, to discharge and pay the taxes and rates

relating thereto and duly to account to the plaintiff therefor. Particulars of the said properties are set out in Schedule 'A' hereto annexed.

2. The defendant acted as such agent for six months namely from .... 20......... to .... *inclusive* and during that time collected, but has not accounted for any of the said rents, nor has paid over any moneys in his hands to the plaintiff, although requested in writing dated .... so to do within a fortnight from the date of such request.

3. The plaintiff has in consequence been unable to ascertain how much the defendant has realised as rent and, if, and what, taxes and rates he had paid (You may 'add, and is therefore unable to sue for a sum certain').

4. The parties are residing at their respective addresses within jurisdiction of this Learned Court.

5. The breach of agreement and/or obligations by defendant took place lastly on .... when in spite of several requests, the defendant failed to furnish the accounts and to make payment of collections made by him.

6. For the purposes of jurisdiction and court-fees, the suit is valued at ₹................ on which court-fees in stamps have been duly paid.

7. No part of the plaintiff's claim is barred by Law of Limitation.

The plaintiff claims—

(1) To have a full and true account of the receipts of such rents and of the payments, if any, of such taxes and rates.

(2) Payment of such sum as may be found due from the defendant upon the taking of accounts.

(3) Interest by way of damages.

(4) Costs.

(5) Further and other reliefs as the plaintiff is entitled to in law and in equity.

Verification

I, AB, son of XY, aged about..... years do hereby solemnly affirm and say as follows:

1. I am the plaintiff above-named and I am fully acquainted with the facts and circumstances of this case.

2. The statements contained in paragraphs 1 to 7 hereinabove are true to my knowledge and the rest are submissions before the Ld. Court.

Signed before me on this ....
day of .... 20 .... Advocate/Notary.

Affidavit

3. Suit by a principal against an agent for rendering of accounts (Another Form)

In the Court of the Civil Judge (Senior Division) at Alipore

Mr. P., residing at ...., 7, Alipore Road, Kolkata

.... *Plaintiff*

versus

Mr. X, residing at ..., 32, Alipore Road, Kolkata

...... *Defendant*

Suits for Accounts and Decree valued at ₹...........

The plaintiff states as follows:

1. That the plaintiff owns various properties as described in the Schedule given hereunder and marked 'A'.

2. That the plaintiff had appointed the defendant by a writing dated ... (or, orally, as the case may be, on ......) as the plaintiff's duly authorised agent with a view to collect rents etc. in respect of the plaintiff's properties and to render proper accounts to the plaintiff every month and to make payment of collections of such rent to the plaintiff less the expenses directly incurred in relation to such collection of rent.

3. That the said agency of the defendant was terminated with effect from .... by the plaintiff by a notice dated ...., served on the defendant by Registered Post with A/D, (or, that the said agency is still subsisting, or that the defendant had given up the agency by writing with effect from .... or that the said defendant acted as the plaintiff's agent for the period from .... to ....).

4. That during the subsistence of the said agency, the defendant had collected rents, etc. but did not deliver up the moneys to the plaintiff. The defendant did not also meet the taxes and other statutory dues as required and did not account for the receipts and for expenditure (or the defendant did not render any accounts at all for the said period of the agency).

5. That the plaintiff had sent a notice dated .... by Regd. Post with A/D, to the defendant requesting him to submit the accounts and deliver up the moneys lying in his hands within a period of seven days from the date of receipt of such notice. The defendant duly received the said notice on .... but did not comply with the request made therein.

6. That the plaintiff in the circumstances of the case pleads his inability to sue for a specific sum and tentatively claims a sum of ₹2,00,000 from defendant.

7. That the cause of action for the suit arose at 7, Alipore Road, 24-Parganas (South) where the plaintiff entered into an agency with defendant (or at 10, Alipore Road, Kolkata where the defendant was required to perform his statutory obligations of the aforesaid agency) all within the jurisdiction of this learned court on .... till the date of termination of the said agency (or when the agency is still subsisting) or generally when the plaintiff demanded for rendering of accounts from defendant but the defendant refused to do so, all within jurisdiction of this learned court.

8. For the purposes of jurisdiction and court-fees, the suit is valued at ₹2,00,000 on which *ad valorem* court-fees have been paid.

9. No part of the plaintiff's claims is barred by Law of Limitation.

The plaintiff, therefore, prays for and claims:

(*a*) Judgment and Decree directing the defendant to furnish full accounts of receipts and expenditure for the said period (state particulars of the period).

(*b*) A Decree against the defendant for such moneys as may be found due upon taking such accounts on payment of necessary court-fees.

(*c*) Costs of the suit.

(*d*) Such further and other reliefs as the plaintiff is entitled to in law and equity.

SCHEDULE

Verification

In the Court of the Civil Judge (Senior Division) at Alipore

Suit No. .... of 20...

Mr. P residing at 7, Alipore Road, Kolkata

.... *Plaintiff*

versus

Mr. X residing at 32, Alipore Road, Kolkata

...... *Defendant*

Affidavit verifying the plaint

I, Mr. P, son of the Mr. Q, residing at 7, Alipore Road, District: 24-Parganas (South), Kolkata do hereby solemnly affirm and say as follows:

1. I am the plaintiff in the Plaint and I know the facts and circumstances of the case and I am able to depose thereto.

2. The plaintiff owns various properties described in the schedule given hereunder:

SCHEDULE

....

....

This is true to my knowledge.

3. The plaintiff appointed the defendant as the plaintiff's duly authorised agent with a view to collect claims, etc. in respect of plaintiff's properties mentioned in the schedule annexed hereto marked "A" and to render proper accounts to the plaintiff every month and to make payment of collections of such rents to the plaintiff loss the expenses directly incurred in relation to such collection of claims. The statements are correct and true to my knowledge. The particulars in the Schedule "A" are correct.

4. The said agency of the defendant was terminated with effect from .... by the plaintiff by a Notice dated .... served on the defendant by Registered Post with A/D. This is true to my knowledge. This Acknowledgment due receipt was signed by the defendant. I know his signature.

5. During the period of the said agency the defendant collected rents, etc. but did not deliver up the moneys in his hands to the plaintiff. The defendant did not pay the taxes and other statutory dues as required and did not account for the receipts or expenditures. This is true to my knowledge.

6. The plaintiff had sent a Notice by Registered Post with A/D to the defendant requesting him to submit the accounts and pay the money in hands within 7 days. The defendants received the said Notice but did not comply with the request. These are true to my knowledge.

7. The plaintiff is unable to specify the particular sum payable by the defendant but claims a sum of ₹2 lakh. This is true to my knowledge.

8. The cause of action for the suit arose at ...., Alipore Road, Kolkata where the plaintiff entered into the Agency Agreement with the defendant. The defendant was required to perform his contractual obligations at ...., Alipore Road, Kolkata. The defendant committed breach of the agreement at ...., Alipore Road, Kolkata

within the jurisdiction of this Learned Court. This is true to my knowledge. As such the cause of action of the plaintiff arose within the jurisdiction of this learned court. This is my submission.

9. For the purpose of jurisdiction and court-fees the suit has been valued at ₹2,00,000 on which *ad valorem* court-fees have been paid. This is true to my knowledge.

10. No part of the plaintiff"s claim is barred by the Law of Limitation. This is true to my knowledge of facts and law and also submissions to this learned court.

11. The plaintiff has made several prayers for Judgment and Decree for the amount found due or owing and payable by the defendant to the plaintiff and costs and other reliefs. These are my humble submissions to this learned court.

12. The aforesaid statements in paragraphs 1 to 11 are true to my knowledge.

Solemnly affirmed by the said Mr. P.
in the court promises at Alipore on this
5th day of April, 2006.

Before me
Magistrate/Notary

N.B. : Every pleading has to be verified. In every plaint facts shall be proved by affidavit [s. 26(2), CPC]. The person verifying the pleading shall also furnish an affidavit in support of his pleading [Or. 6, r. 15(4), CPC].

The plaint, petition, application and affidavit should also comply with and follow the rules and practice of the court/Tribunal and those followed by the learned lawyers.

SCHEDULE "A"
State here that claim

NOTES: 1. See ILR 7 Cal 89; For conditions required—See AIR 1971 J&K 71; AIR 1971 J&K 140; AIR 1971 Punj 186.

2. Accounts cannot be demanded from heirs of a deceased agent—42 CWN 1157. Heirs can be sued for recovery of a specific amount due from such agent—17 CWN 5.

3. Valuation for appeal—original valuation in the plaint (All and Mad High Court)—amount decreed by the court (Cal, Punj and Bom High Courts).

4. Jurisdiction—where contract of agency entered, where agency is performed or refusal to render account takes place—94 IC 287.

5. Section 213 of the Indian Contract Act enjoins that an agent is bound to render proper accounts to his principal on demand. The principal prior to institution of suit must, therefore, demand for accounts—AIR 1947 Bom 135 and the deemed of the principal for rendition of accounts is recognized by the Contract Act.

6. Article 2 of the Limitation Act shall govern the period of limitation.

7. Court-fees in West Bengal s. 7(*e*)—according to the amount at which the relief sought is valued in the plaint (West Bengal Court-fees Act 1970).

8. Cause of action arises when demand is made and refused. Where there is no demand when the agency terminates.

9. Procedure—Or. 20, r. 16 of the CPC enjoins that the court shall, before passing its final decree, pass a preliminary decree directing such accounts to be taken as it thinks fit.

10. Suit for accounts [Court-fees Act, s. 7(*iv*)(*f*)]. In a suit for accounts the plaintiff is not obliged to state the exact amount which would result after

taking all the accounts and he may, therefore, put a tentative valuation upon the suit, but he is not permitted to choose an unreasonable and arbitrary figure for that purpose—*Abdul Hamid* v *Abdul Majid* AIR 1988 SC 1150. The plaintiff cannot arbitrarily and deliberately undervalue the relief—*Meenakshi Sundam* v *Venkatachalam* AIR 1979 SC 989 at p. 993. The plaintiff has not been given the absolute right or option to put any valuation whatever on such relief and where the plaintiff manifestly and deliberately underestimates the relief the court is entitled to examine the correctness of the valuation given by the plaintiff and to revise the same if it is patently arbitrary or unreasonable—*Smt. Tara Devi* v *Thakur Radha Krishna Maharaj* AIR 1987 SC 2085 at p. 2086.

For special direction as to accounts—See Or. 20, r. 17 of the Code.

4. Suit by a principal against a defaulter-agent

In the Court of .... at ....

Suit No. .... of 20 ....

(Set out cause title)

The plaintiff states as follows:

1. That the plaintiff owns various properties as described in the Schedule below.

2. That the plaintiff had appointed the defendant by a writing dated .... (or, orally on ....,) as his agent to collect rent (set out here particulars of job) and to render accounts to the plaintiff duly.

3. That the defendant acted as the agent of the plaintiff for the period from ...... to ...... when his agency was terminated by a deed (or, by a notice as the case may be, dated .... duly served on the defendant by registered post).

4. That the defendant was negligent all through and defaulted to collect rent, etc., for which recovery of a sizable amount of rent became barred by limitation (state the period with amount when known).

5-8. (Same as in paras 4 to 8 in Form No. 2).

Verification

Affidavit

NOTES: 1. Plaint must contain an averment in respect of wilful default with illustrations of default. For consequences of neglect, want of skill or misconduct, an agent is liable to his principal for loss or damage—See s. 212 of the Indian Contract Act.

2. Limitation—Three years under Art. 2 of the Limitation Act 1963.

5. Suit by principal against agent for account, with allegations of wilful default

In the Court of .... at ....

Suit No. .... of 20.............

(Set out cause title)

The plaintiff states as follows:

1. By a registered power of attorney dated .... 20.........., the plaintiff employed the defendant as his paid agent to apply for and collect the rents of the

various house properties of the plaintiff from the tenants and duly to account to the plaintiff therefor. Particulars of the said properties are set out in Schedule 'A' hereto.

2. The defendant acted in pursuance of the agreement from .... to .... and during that time conducted his business so recklessly and negligently that the plaintiff has suffered damage (here specify some acts of negligence of the defendant) and nature & quantum of damage.

3. Tenants of some of the houses quitted the same. The defendant, who knew or ought to have known about their impending departure, was guilty of negligence and wilful default in allowing the said tenants to depart without realising the rents due from them.

4. The plaintiff is unable to ascertain the whereabouts of the said tenants and cannot take steps to recover the arrears of rent due from them. The plaintiff is unable to give full particulars of the amounts due from the said tenants until after discovery and the following particulars are all that the plaintiff can give:

Premises	*Tenant*	*Monthly rent*	*Date of departure*	*Months in arrears*

5. The defendant, without any authority from the plaintiff, accepted reduced rent from some of the tenants.

PARTICULARS:

Premises	*Tenant*	*Rate of rent*	*Reduced rent*

6. By a notice in writing dated .... 20........., the plaintiff terminated the defendant from the said employment with effect from ....

7. The defendant has not rendered any account to the plaintiff although requested in writing dated .... 20.........., so to do and has not paid any sum to the plaintiff in respect of the rents actually realised by him.

The plaintiff claims—

(1) An account of what is due to the plaintiff from the defendant in respect of moneys received by the defendant for or on account of the plaintiff or which might have been so received but for the defendant's breach of duty, wilful default or neglect.

(2) Payment of the sum to be found due upon taking such account.

Verification

Affidavit

6. Suit against an agent by the principal for not using due care and for negligence

In the Court of .... at ....

Suit No. .... of 20.........

(Set out cause title)

The above-named plaintiff states as follows:

1. That the defendant was engaged by a letter in writing dated ...... by the plaintiff to act as the latter's agent to induct a tenant in his house premises situated at .... P.S. .... District ....

2. That in the said letter the defendant was granted a reward of ₹100 as his commission. Discretion was granted to the defendant in the matter of choice of a possible tenant but with caution that the plaintiff should not suffer in respect of damage to the said premises or in respect of the rent therefor.

3. That the defendant had inducted one Sri ...... as a monthly tenant in the said premises at a rent of ₹........ per month with effect from the (date) .... according to Bengali calendar month.

4. That the said Sri .... occupied the premises and paid rent for the first three months. On ...... the plaintiff learnt that said Sri ...... vacated the premises surreptitiously with all his belongings and removed electrical fittings and three Belgian mirrors valued at ₹........ from the premises.

5. That the plaintiff could not trace out the said ...... in this town.

6. That due to the defendant's negligence the plaintiff has lost

(*i*)	rent for 5 months @ ₹ 600 p.m.	₹3,000
(*ii*)	Electrical fittings (description)	₹ 120
(*iii*)	3 Belgian mirrors bound in frame of size .... ft. x ...... ft.	₹1,500
		₹4,620
	(in words)	

7. That the defendant was careless in the matter of selection of the tenant in the premises and was thoroughly negligent to keep the plaintiff posted of his movements and suffered damage for his carelessness and negligence.

8. That the cause of action for this suit arose on ...... at ...... when the plaintiff knew of the defendant's negligence.

9. Suit valuation—(damage and loss as above).

The plaintiff, therefore, prays:

(*i*) For a judgment and decree for ₹...... as per a/c below.

(*ii*) Costs.

(*iii*) Other and further reliefs.

Account of loss

(State particulars)

Verification

Affidavit

NOTE: In suits by the principal against an agent for neglect and misconduct—limitation is three years when neglect or misconduct becomes known to the plaintiff—*vide* Art. 4 of the Limitation Act 1963.

7. Suit by principal against agent for damages for negligence

In the Court of .... at ....

Suit No. .... of 20.........

(Set out cause title)

The above-named plaintiff states as follows:

1. The plaintiff was the owner of a house .... in .... Street, which was let to one C.D., a shopkeeper, for the term of .... years subject to the *proviso* that the lessee should not assign the demised premises without the written licence or consent of the lessor first had and obtained.

2. On .... 20.........., C.D. contracted to sell his lease and business to one A.G. and, accordingly, applied to the plaintiff for his consent in writing to the transfer of the lease to the said A.G., whereupon the plaintiff placed the matter in the hands of the defendant, who was an auctioneer and house agent, and gave him a consent or license in writing to the said transfer and instructed him not to hand over the license to C.D. until he had paid ₹ .... the rent in arrear.

3. Thereafter, on .... 20.........., the defendant, C.D. and the said A.G. met at .... and the purchase was completed, and the defendant then handed over the license to C.D. on receipt of a cheque drawn by C.D. to the order of the defendant and crossed "& Co." for the amount of the rent in arrear, together with a small sum for the defendant's charges.

4. The defendant sent the said cheque to his Bank for credit to his account and himself gave the plaintiff a cheque for .... which was dishonoured as a result of the cheque given by C.D. to the defendant being dishonoured.

5. C.D. has disappeared and the plaintiff has lost the chance of recovering the rent from him.

6. The defendant has not made good the loss to the plaintiff.

The plaintiff claims—

₹................

Verification

Affidavit

8. Suit by an agent against a principal for accounts of profit

In the Court of .... at ....

Suit No. .... of 20.............

(Set out cause title)

The above-named plaintiff states as follows:

1. That the plaintiff is a carpenter.

2. That the defendant owns a cabinet-firm and he supplies furniture on contract.

3. That the plaintiff was engaged by the defendant by an agreement in writing dated ...... to construct some pieces of furniture (specify) in respect of a contract secured by the defendant. That under Clause No. ...... of the contract of agency with this plaintiff, the defendant agreed to pay to the plaintiff $^1/_2$ share of the net profits for the contract.

4. That the plaintiff had duly built the said furniture and made over to the defendant on ....

5. That the defendant did not pay to the plaintiff his share of profit.

6. That the plaintiff demanded his share of profit orally on .... but the defendant avoided payment. The plaintiff thereafter issued a notice dated .... to the defendant by registered post demanding his share of profit but to no effect.

7. That the plaintiff is ignorant of the profits derived by the defendant for the said contract and all papers and accounts thereof are in possession of the defendant.

8. That the cause of action for this suit arose first on .... when the plaintiff had demanded his share of profits and then on .... when after expiry of the period given in the notice the defendant did not render accounts of profit and pay accordingly.

The plaintiff, therefore, claims:

(*a*) An account of profits of the said contract;

(*b*) Payment to the plaintiff of such sum as may be found due in the plaintiff's share upon the taking of accounts;

(*c*) Costs of suit.

Verification

Affidavit

9. Suit for secret profit by a principal against an agent

In the Court of .... at ....

Suit No. .... of 20...........

(Set out cause title)

The above-named plaintiff states as follows:

1. That the defendant was engaged by the plaintiff on .... as the latter's agent to negotiate sale of his firearm to any intending purchaser and was offered commission at 10% on the value which may be had by sale of the firearm.

2. That through the defendant the plaintiff had on .... sold his firearm at ₹......... to one A.B. and duly paid to the defendant commission at the agreed rate.

3. That on the occasion of talks, the defendant had entered into a separate agreement with the said A.B. that in case he could purchase the firearm from the said A.B. at .... said A.B. would pay to the defendant extra profit of ₹......... The defendant did not disclose to the plaintiff the situation. The plaintiff sold his firearm at ₹......... to A.B. whereby the defendant gained profit of ₹......... secretly.

4. That the plaintiff is entitled to recover the said sum of ₹......... earned secretly by the defendant.

5. Cause of action—date of sale.

The plaintiff, therefore, prays:

(*i*) For a decree of ₹.........

(*ii*) Costs.

Verification

Affidavit

NOTES: 1. See s. 211 of the Contract Act. In a transaction acting on behalf of the principal, if any profit accrues, the agent must account for it.

2. A suit for accounts arises where there is liability on the part of one for rendition of accounts—65 CWN 1067. In a like suit, the plaintiff is to pay court-fees on the amount which he shows to be the value of the relief sought.

10. Suit for accounts against a co-sharer

In the Court of .... at ....

Suit No. .... of 20.........

(Set out cause title)

The above-named plaintiff states as follows:

1. That one A.B. .... since deceased, held vast landed properties at Moujas ...... and .... within P.S. .... Dt. ...., more fully described in the Schedule below.

2. The said A.B. died intestate in the .... 20... leaving as his only heirs three sons, namely, the plaintiff and the defendants of this suit and, properties in the Schedule below devolved on the plaintiff and the said defendants in equal shares.

3. That the defendant No. 1 is the eldest brother of the plaintiff and the defendant No. 2. On the death of the plaintiff's father, the parties hereto held the said properties in the Schedule below in *Ejmali* and the defendant No. 1 managed the properties in the Schedule below and collected yields thereof.

4. That the defendant No. 1 for some time past has been neglecting to provide the plaintiff with necessaries of life on the pretext of low income. Thereupon the plaintiff had requested defendant No. 1 on .... to disclose to the plaintiff the savings from the income of the *Ejmali* properties together with account of receipts and expenses of the *Ejmali* property since the plaintiff's father's death on .... 20... but the defendant No. 1 did not show any interest.

5. That the plaintiff is entitled to (*i*) an account of the income and expenditure of the properties in the Schedule below and (*ii*) to payment of the plaintiff's share from savings, if any.

6. That the cause of action for the suit arose on .... when the plaintiff had demanded from the defendant No. 1 accounts.

7. That for the purposes of jurisdiction and court-fees the suit is tentatively valued at ₹1,000 and *ad valorem* court-fees are paid thereon.

The plaintiff, therefore, prays:

(*a*) For a judgment and decree for accounts of the receipts and expenditure of the property in the Schedule below since .... 20 ....

(*b*) For payment to the plaintiff his share from the savings of the said property, if any.

(*c*) Costs of suit.

Verification

Affidavit

11. Suit by a coparcener for accounts against the managing member of a Joint Hindu Family

In the Court of .... at ....

Suit No. .... of 20 ....

(Set out cause title)

The plaintiff states as follows:

1. The plaintiff and the defendant are brothers and, at all material times, were members of a joint Hindu family governed by the Dayabhaga school of Hindu law.

2. The plaintiff was 12 years when his father died.

3. Since his father's death, which took place on .... the defendant has been managing the joint family properties in which the plaintiff has an undivided one-half share. The plaintiff is unable to give full particulars of the said properties until after discovery. Such particulars as the plaintiff can give are set out in Schedule 'A' hereto.

4. The plaintiff attained majority on or about ....

5. On .... 20.........., the plaintiff verbally requested the defendant to inform him what the joint family properties consisted of at the time of the death of their father and what they consisted of then, and also what portion of the family income had been actually saved but the defendant refused to disclose any information to the plaintiff.

6. Since .... 20........., the defendant is in possession and enjoyment of the joint family property to the exclusion of the plaintiff.

The plaintiff claims—

(1) An account of the receipts and disbursements of the joint family properties since ....

(2) Ascertainment of the plaintiff's share of the income derived from the joint family properties.

(3) Payment to the plaintiff his half-share of the net profits of the joint family properties in the hands of the defendant.

(4) Discovery.

(5) Appointment of a Receiver.

Verification

Affidavit

12. Suit for accounts against a certificated guardian

(After his discharge from office)

In the Court of .... at ....

Suit No. .... of 20............

(Set out cause title)

The plaintiff states as follows:

1. That the defendant was appointed a guardian of the plaintiff during the latter's minority in respect of the minor's properties, described in the Schedule below on .... by the order of the District Judge of Cooch Behar in Misc. (Guardianship) Case No. ...... of ......20....

2. That the plaintiff attained majority on .... and he is now 22 years old.

3. That the defendant had applied for resigning his office of guardianship on ...... before the District Judge .... whereupon he was directed to submit accounts till .... which, it is learnt, the defendant did. The said accounts were audited and the defendant was discharged from his office by the District Judge on ....

4. That on enquiry the plaintiff has learnt that during the period from ...... to .... the defendant had collected rents of house properties, mentioned in item No. .... of the Schedule below. The defendant deliberately suppressed the said receipts in his accounts filed before the court. Nor the defendant let the court know that the said property in item No. .... of the Schedule was let out to a tenant.

5. That the plaintiff estimates a sum of ₹......... to be due from the defendant on account of such receipt.

6. That the cause of action for this suit arose on .... when the defendant was discharged from office.

7. That the plaintiff values his suit at ₹...... and pays *ad valorem* court-fees thereon.

The plaintiff prays:

(*a*) For a judgment and decree—

(*i*) directing the defendant to render a faithful and true account regarding receipts from the tenant during the period from ...... to ......

(*ii*) for payment to the plaintiff of a sum of ₹........... or such sum as may be found due on accounting.

(*b*) Costs of suit.

SCHEDULE

(Description of property)

Verification

Affidavit

NOTE: A certificated guardian may apply for discharge under s. 41(4) of the Guardianship and Wards Act.

13. Suit for accounts against the Karta of a Joint Hindu Family

In the Court of .... at ....

Suit No. .... of 20........

(Set out cause title)

The plaintiff states as follows:

1. The plaintiff, AB, is the brother of defendant CD, and the plaintiff's father died on .... at .... leaving no legal heirs except plaintiff and defendant being his two sons.

2. The deceased father of the plaintiff did not make any Testamentary Will at the time of his death or create any Family Trust in respect of his properties and as such, after his death, the properties mentioned in a Schedule described below devolved upon plaintiff and defendant in equal proportionate shares for plaintiff and defendant.

3. After the death of plaintiff's father, the plaintiff and the defendant have been jointly enjoying the said Joint Family properties, but the said properties are being looked after by defendant as the Karta of Joint Family.

4. The defendant as the elder brother was looking after the Joint Family properties and collected the rents, issues and related profits out of the same as the Karta of Joint Family for purpose of running the Joint Family.

5. For the last several months, the defendant in breach of his legal and moral obligations has been wilfully and negligently failing to pay the requisite amounts to meet the necessary expenses to maintain the Joint Family.

6. The plaintiff requested the defendant to make proper arrangement and to make adequate amounts available out of the Joint Family property to the plaintiff but the defendant did not mend his ways and failed to provide proper amount for maintaining the Joint Family.

7. The plaintiff states that the defendant out of the income in the Joint Family property has accumulated vast sums of moneys and has deposited the same in his Savings Bank Account No. .... with .... Bank at .... as will appear from statement of account received by post, a copy whereof is annexed hereto marked 'A'.

8. In the circumstances, the plaintiff demanded a reasonable explanation from the defendant as to how the defendant could accumulate the huge sum of ₹40 lakh in his Bank account, inasmuch no other visible source of income was there of the defendant to run family except the income from Joint Family property of which he is the Karta. But the defendant failed to give any satisfactory explanation to the plaintiff's query.

9. The plaintiff, in the circumstances, therefore claims half of the share of the total credit balance in the said Bank account of the defendant being the total collection of income out of Joint Family properties and credited to the defendant's account.

10. In spite of demands, the defendant failed to give any satisfactory explanation or to deposit 50% of the amount in his said Bank account with said Bank.

11. In the premises the plaintiff claims a decree for payment of ₹20 lakh with applicable interest from .... to ....

12. The cause of action for this suit arose at .... within the jurisdiction of this learned court. The said cause of action arose from .... and is still continuing as the defendant is wilfully withholding the legitimate half share out of the income of Joint Family property without paying the said share to the plaintiff.

13. For purposes of jurisdiction and court-fees, the suit is valued at ₹20 lakh on which *ad valorem* court-fees in stamps have been paid and the plaintiff undertakes to pay any additional court-fees on the decretal amount if found payable in excess of the court-fees already paid.

14. No part of the plaintiff's claims herein in barred in by Law of Limitation:

The plaintiff, therefore, prays for and claims:

(*a*) Decree for rendering of accounts by the defendant in respect of the Joint Family properties as detailed in the Schedule below.

(*b*) Decree for ₹20 lakh out of the moneys lying in the said Bank account of defendant in .... Bank.

(*c*) Further decree for rendering of accounts of dealings and transactions by defendant in respect of Joint Family properties and monies lying in the said Bank Account.

(*d*) Costs of the suit.

(*e*) Further reliefs as the plaintiff is entitled to in law and in equity.

Schedule mentioned above

Verification

Affidavit

14. Written statement to the above plaint

In the Court of .... at ....

Suit No. .... of ....

(Set out cause title)

The defendant states as follows:

1. The suit is not maintainable.

2. This learned court has no jurisdiction over the said suit.

3. The suit does not disclose any cause of action.

4. In any event it is barred by the principles of estoppel, waiver and acquiescence.

5. It is barred by the Law of Limitation.

6. Save and except what are specifically admitted the defendant denies all other allegations made in the said plaint.

7. With reference to the paragraphs 1 and 2 of plaint I say that by mutual agreement the plaintiff and the defendant would possess the ancestral property in different specific portions and in fact, they have been enjoying such different portions of this properly left by their father.

8. The statements and allegations in paragraphs 3 and 4 of the plaint are not correct. The defendant was not the Karta as wrongly alleged. The defendant never dealt with the paternal property as the Karta of the Family. By amicable arrangement the plaintiff and defendant have been occupying specific portions of the said property since their father's demise. The defendant was requested by plaintiff for equal division of the properties left by their father. The plaintiff did not agree to do so and wrongfully has filed the said suit to harass the defendant.

9. The plaintiff has no cause of action and the suit is liable to be dismissed.

10. The defendant prays that the said suit be dismissed with costs.

Verification

Affidavit

15. Suit on khata accounts

In the Court of the Assistant District Judge at ....

S.C.C. No. ...... of 20 .....

M/s. ....
a firm registered under the Partnership Act
with its principal place of business at ....

P.S. .... District .... *Plaintiff*

versus

....
Son of ....
by caste .... by occupation—business.
residing at ....
P.S. .... District .... *Defendant*

Suit on Khata accounts.

Claim valued at ₹............

The above-named plaintiff states as follows:

1. That the plaintiff is a firm, registered under the Indian Partnership Act, carrying on business of cloth at .... and Sri .... is one of the partners.

2. That the defendant used to purchase cloth from the aforesaid plaintiff firm on credit and to sign Credit Memo issued by the plaintiff-firm covering such sales. The defendant had an account opened for such transactions in the plaintiff's shop.

3. That the defendant was making part payments of his dues on account of purchases from time to time in his said running account.

4. That the defendant made his last purchase on credit on .... and he last paid in his running account on ....

5. That the plaintiff firm files herewith account Khatas of the firm showing such transactions along with true copy of accounts.

6. That the dues of the defendant to the plaintiff firm, after adjustment with payments made from time to time, stands at ₹...... as per Schedule of accounts appended below.

7. The defendant did not pay to the plaintiff-firm their dues though repeated demands were made.

8. The plaintiff firm's transactions with the defendant ceased on the .... corresponding to .... from which date the cause of action for the present suit arose at .... within the jurisdiction of this court.

9. The plaintiff firm is entitled to damages at the rate of 12% on the claim above noted according to business practice and the plaintiff claims a sum of ₹......... as damages as per Schedule of account appended below.

The plaintiff, therefore, prays:

(*i*) That the suit be decreed for ₹........... as per account shown in the Schedule of account below.

(*ii*) Costs.

SCHEDULE OF ACCOUNTS

Verification

Affidavit

Typed under my dictation.

Advocate ....

NOTES: 1. Person suing must have been shown in Register of Firms—AIR 1971 AP 63; AIR 1971 J&K 109 (See s. 69(2) of the Partition Act).

2. Suit by unregistered firm is incompetent and should be simply dismissed—AIR 1971 Punj 212.

16. Suit for an account of profits made out of moneys paid to the defendant

In the Court of .... at ....

Money Suit No. .... 20 ...

(Set out cause title)

Suit for account of profits: Claim laid at ₹.............

The above-named plaintiff states:

1. By an agreement dated the .... day of .... 20 ...... between the parties hereto, it was agreed:

(*a*) That the plaintiff would pay to the defendant the sum of ₹10,000 to be utilised by the defendant for purchase and sale of jute in the name of and for and on behalf of the plaintiff;

(*b*) that the defendant should be entitled to 15% of the net profits made on such transactions and pay the balance 85% thereof to the plaintiff at monthly intervals on the first day of each month;

(*c*) that the defendant, when requested by the plaintiff so to do, shall render a true and faithful account of how he utilised the plaintiff's money together with the nature and particulars of transactions and profits earned; and

(*d*) that the defendant shall repay to the plaintiff on the latter's demand all moneys of the plaintiff that might be in his hands.

2. Pursuant to the said agreement, referred to above, the plaintiff had paid to the defendant on .... the sum of ₹10,000 against a receipt of the same date. The defendant used the said sum or part thereof for purchase and sale of jute, particulars whereof are not known to the plaintiff.

3. By a letter dated the .... day of .... 20 ..., the plaintiff had requested the defendant to render a true and accurate account to the plaintiff as to how he utilised the said sum of ₹10,000, of all purchases and sales of jute made by him, of the amount of profits. The said letter was sent per registered post with A.D. and was received by the defendant on the .... day of .... 20....

4. In breach of the agreement dated the .... day of .... 20 ... the defendant failed to render accounts and did not pay to the plaintiff profits at the above agreed rate.

5. By a notice dated the .... day of .... 20..., the defendant was instructed to return to the plaintiff all moneys then in the hands of the defendant within 15 days from the receipt of the said notice. The defendant has failed to comply with the instructions made therein.

6. The plaintiff tentatively values this suit at ₹.........

7. The cause of action arose on .... when the first default was made.

The plaintiff claims:

(*i*) An account of how the defendant utilised the said sum of ₹10,000 or part thereof together with the account of purchases and sales of jute;

(*ii*) an account of profits made on such transactions;

(*iii*) a decree for payment by the defendant to the plaintiff of all money found to be payable to the plaintiff on accounting;

(*iv*) costs of suit; and

(*v*) any other relief as may be admissible.

Verification

Affidavit

17. Suit for an account of goods delivered to the defendant for sale

In the Court of .... at ....

Suit No. .... of 20.............

(Set out cause title)

The plaintiff A.B. states:

1. That the plaintiff is a manufacturer of ....

2. By an agreement in writing dated the .... day of ...... 20 ..., the defendant agreed with the plaintiff that he would, on commission, act as an agent for the plaintiff for sale of .... and shall render a true and accurate account to the plaintiff of all such sales when requested by the plaintiff so to do and further to pay to the plaintiff all moneys received by him by such sales after deducting his commission.

3. That the defendant, as agent of the plaintiff, has made sales of ...., particulars whereof are not known to the plaintiff.

4. By a letter dated the .... day of .... 20 ..., the plaintiff had requested the defendant to render to the plaintiff a true and accurate account of sales effected by him and/or to pay to the plaintiff all moneys as may be due to the plaintiff. The said letter was sent to the defendant under registered post with A.D. and was received by the defendant on the .... day of .... 20 .... In breach of the aforesaid agreement, the defendant failed to render an account as also to pay up any of the moneys received by him.

5. In the premises, the plaintiff has suffered loss.

6. Cause of action.

7. Suit valuation.

The plaintiff, therefore, prays for:

(*a*) a judgment and decree

(*i*) that an account be taken of all sakes effected through the defendant and of sale proceeds received by him;

(*ii*) amount of commission on all sales;

(*iii*) payment to the plaintiff of all moneys deducting commission of the defendant; and

(*iv*) damages for wrongfully withholding accounts and payment;

(*b*) costs of suit;

(*c*) further or other relief.

Verification

Affidavit

18. Suit for value of goods purchased on credit

In the Court of the Civil Judge (Junior Division) (Sadar), at ....

Money Suit No. .... of 20 ....

.... *Plaintiff*

versus

B ....

C ....

.... *Defendants*

Suit for goods purchased on credit valued at ₹..................

The above-named plaintiff states as follows:

1. That the plaintiff is a partner of a registered partnership firm dealing in wholesale and retail sale of yarn at .... Bazar .... town and Sri .... is one of the partners of the said firm.

2. That the defendant No. 2 is an employee of the defendant No. 1. That the defendant No. 1 purchased through his agent and employee said defendant No. 2 from the plaintiff's shop on .... on credit, ... bundles of yarn valued at ₹............ and the defendant No. 2 signed a Credit Memo No. .... dated .... of the plaintiff firm while taking delivery of the said yarn for and on behalf of defendant No. 1.

3. That the plaintiff files herewith the Credit Memo (in original) No. .... dated ....

4. That the defendant No. 1 did not pay the value thereof in spite of demands made in that behalf.

5. That the plaintiff is entitled to recover the said sum of ₹........... plus interest thereon @ 10% per annum on the said sum, according to usage of trade, amounting to ₹......... making a total of ₹......... as per account in the Schedule of claim below.

6. That the cause of action for this suit arose on .... when the defendant No. 1 purchased the said goods on credit at .... town within the jurisdiction of this court.

7. That for the purpose of jurisdiction the suit is valued at ₹........... and *ad valorem* court-fees are payable.

The plaintiff files this suit with court-fees of ₹.......... and shall deposit the balance of court-fees within the time specified by the court.

That the Credit Memo book filed herewith may please be returned after verification on condition of refiling.

The plaintiff, therefore, prays:

(1) For a decree of ₹...... as per account in the Schedule of claim below.

(2) Costs.

SCHEDULE OF CLAIM

Verification

Affidavit

19. Suit for price of goods sold

In the Court of Civil Judge (Sr. Division) at ....

Suit No. .... of 20...

Mr. P., carrying on business at ...... Alipore Road, Kolkata

...... *Plaintiff*

versus

1. Mr. X., residing at .... Alipore Road, Kolkata

2. Mrs. Z, wife of Mr. X residing at .... Alipore Road, Kolkata

.... *Defendants*

Suit for recovery of the price of goods sold and delivered valued at ₹......... .

The plaintiff states as follows:

1. The plaintiff carries on business as a Grocer dealing in all kinds of consumer goods under the name and style of "Grocery Stores".

2. Defendant No. 1 is a service-holder and resides at the aforesaid address and occasionally purchased goods from the plaintiff.

3. Defendant No. 2 is the wife of defendant No. 1.

4. During the temporary absence of defendant No. 1 in connection with his business affairs, defendant No. 2 managed the affairs of their family with their two children.

5. During the absence of defendant No. 1 in the month of December, 20... defendant No. 2 purchased certain foodstuffs and other necessary articles for daily use from the plaintiff's shop valued at ₹...... on credit with promise to pay price of goods purchased by her within the next following month on return of her husband from tour.

6. The defendant No. 1 delayed his return to Kolkata for two months and the plaintiff had to supply goods on credit of the first defendant to his wife, being defendant No. 2 during the husband's absence so that defendant No. 2 could maintain their family during the absence of her husband from Kolkata.

7. The plaintiff in the meantime raised certain bills as and when goods were supplied to the defendant No. 2 and the defendant No. 2 duly acknowledged receipt of such supplies of goods by signing on the back of the said bills. After return of defendant No. 1, to Kolkata after three months, the plaintiff demanded payment of the outstanding bills for supplies of goods to his wife, defendant No. 2. The total price of goods sold and delivered to defendant No. 2 but on account of defendant No. 1 from time to time and due and owing by the defendants being an aggregate sum of ₹6,000.

8. The plaintiff raised a consolidated bill stating therein all the bills for supply of goods duly signed and acknowledged by defendant No. 2 and in return demanded a payment of ₹6,000 from defendant No. 1. But defendant No. 1 failed and neglected to pay the said sum of ₹6,000 in spite of demands made by the plaintiff.

9. Defendant No. 1 from time to time promised to pay the said sum to the plaintiff but failed to keep the said promises.

10. There is now due from and owing by the defendants jointly and severally to the plaintiff for goods sold and delivered on their account a total sum of ₹6,960 with interest calculated upto 30th September 20....... The plaintiff claims further interest at 16% per annum from 1st October 20...... till payment.

11. In spite of demands, the defendants have and each one of them has failed to pay the plaintiff's claims herein. Copies of the demand letters are annexed hereto and collectively marked "A".

12. In spite of such demands, the defendants have not paid the said sum or any portion thereof to the plaintiff.

13. The plaintiff's cause of action for this suit arose at the address of the plaintiff from where the goods were sold and delivered to the defendants and whereto the defendants were required to make payment therefor, but the defendants have failed to pay the same to plaintiff. Further, the defendants are both residing within the jurisdiction of this Learned Court. In the premises, this Learned Court has the necessary jurisdiction to entertain, try and determine this suit.

14. For the purposes of jurisdiction and court-fees, the suit is valued at ₹6,960 on which the necessary court-fees in stamps have been duly paid.

15. In the premises, the plaintiff claims a decree for payment of ₹6,960 claimed herein and in the meantime, an order of injunction be issued restraining the defendants from encumbering, or transferring their assets and properties without first paying the claims of the plaintiff.

The plaintiff, therefore, prays for and claims:

(*a*) Decree for payment of ₹6,960 with interest at 16% per annum from 1st October 20... by the defendants jointly and severally to the plaintiff;

(*b*) Interest at 16% per annum from 1st October 20... till realisation of ₹6,960;

(*c*) Costs;

(*d*) Further orders be made as the plaintiff is entitled to in law and equity.

Verification

Affidavit

20. Suit to reopen a settled account

In the Court of .... at ....

Other Suit No. .... of 20 ....

(Set out cause title)

The plaintiff states as follows:

1. That the defendant was appointed an agent of the plaintiff by a Power-of-Attorney (General) executed by the plaintiff and registered on .....

2. That by the said power-of-attorney the defendant was conferred authority, amongst others, to realise plaintiff's dues from various debtors.

3. That the defendant acted under the said power as constituted attorney for the plaintiff for the period from .... to .... when the power was cancelled and revoked and agency terminated.

4. That the defendant submitted on .... an account of receipts from various debtors and deposited a sum of ₹...... with the plaintiff, representing such collections. The plaintiff had accepted the said statement of accounts in good faith and without verification.

5. That on ...... the plaintiff learnt that the defendant made false entries in the said statement by omitting to mention a sum of ₹...... received from 'X' on ...... and falsely entering ₹...... against true receipt of ₹...... from 'Y' under the dates .... and .... respectively.

6. That the cause of action for this suit arose on ...... when the defendant submitted a false statement of accounts and thereafter on ..... when such false entries were detected by the plaintiff at .... within the jurisdiction of this court.

7. That the plaintiff values his suit at ₹...... and has paid court-fees thereon.

The plaintiff prays:

For a decree of ₹......... or such sum as may be found due together with costs of suit.

Verification

Affidavit

21. Suit on balance due on open, mutual and current account

In the Court of .... at ....

Suit No. .... of 20.............

(Set out cause title)

The above-named plaintiff states as follows:

1. That the plaintiff-firm is a registered partnership with its principal place of business at ...... P.S. ...... Dt. .... and Sri .... is a partner competent to sign and verify the plaint.

2. That the defendant is a businessman with his shop at .... P.S. ...... District ......

3. That in or about .... 20 ......, the plaintiff-firm represented by its partner Sri .... and the defendant came to an agreement that the plaintiff would supply to the defendant (*name the commodity*) as may be required by the defendant and that the defendant would supply to the plaintiff .... (*name the commodity*) as may be required by the plaintiff and that accounting would be made by the first week of January, 2002 and in the first week of January every year until the arrangement was bilaterally stopped, and on such accounting the balance due from one party to the other shall be paid by the second week of January every year.

4. That transactions in the manner as agreed between the parties began from .... and it continued till .... Accounting was made on ....January, 20 ......, and it appeared that during the period of preceding 12 months in 20 ...... a sum of ₹......... became due to the plaintiff and a sum of ₹...... became due to the defendant. After adjustment a sum of ₹...... stood due to the plaintiff-firm.

5. That the plaintiff has submitted hereinbelow copies of accounts showing mutual transaction and craves leave of the court to submit relevant account books in the court in time.

6. That the defendant did not pay to the plaintiff-firm their dues in spite of oral demand.

7. Cause of action.

8. Suit valuation.

The plaintiff-firm, therefore, prays:

(*i*) For a decree of ₹.........

(*ii*) Interest ₹......... @ 10% on the amount due.

Verification

Affidavit

NOTES: 1. Article 1 of the Limitation Act 1963—3 years from the close of the year bearing last admitted or proved item in the account.

2. There must be independent dealing between the parties which can be duly set off against each other—AIR 1959 SC 1349; AIR 1963 Ass 11.

3. Open, mutual and current account—meaning and principles—*Chanbey Sushil Chandra* v *Raj Bahadur* AIR 1977 All 259.

4. Nature of account on either side has to be shown in the plaint together with date of last item and the date of the close of the year of account should be stated—which indicate the cause of action.

22. Suit on an account stated

In the Court of .... at ....

Suit No. .... of 20............

(Set out cause title)

The plaintiff states as follows:

1. That the plaintiff runs a business of grocery articles under the trade name of "........." The defendant has had a business of .... at ....

2. On an account stated between the parties hereto in writing on the ...... day of .... 20 ...... a sum of ₹......... is found to be due to the plaintiff, particulars whereof is given in the Schedule of claim below.

3. In spite of repeated demands, the defendant has not paid the amount due any part thereof till date.

4. Cause of action.

5. Suit valuation.

The plaintiff claims:

(*a*) a judgment and decree for ₹.........;

(*b*) costs of suit.

SCHEDULE OF CLAIM

(State here particulars of account stated)

Verification

Affidavit

NOTES: 1. 'An acknowledgment on admission of liability is in itself a new cause of action; and for want of a better name, it also is called an account stated'—*Odgers' Principles of Pleading and Practice*, 21st Ed. at p. 171.

2. Account stated gives a cause of action. Limitation is three years from the date of account, if made in writing and signed by the defendant.

23. Suit on an account stated (Another Form)

In the Court of .... at ....

Money Suit No. .... 20...

M/s. A .... *Plaintiff*

versus

M/s. B .... *Defendant*

The plaintiff states as follows:

1. That the plaintiff firm, is a registered partnership with its principal place of business at .... and Sri .... is a partner of the firm, competent to sign and verify the plaint.

2. That the plaintiff firm carries on business of edible oil.

3. That the defendant firm is also a registered partnership dealing in wholesale business of grocery.

4. That upon terms of business, the plaintiff firm had supplied to the defendant firm on credit during the period from .... to .... mustard oil and the defendant firm during the same period and a few months thereafter supplied to the plaintiff firm soap-cakes, packing materials.

5. That the parties hereto, represented by their partners, agreed on .... that the dues of the plaintiff firm on account of supply of mustard oil be adjusted by a set-off against the defendant's dues on account of supply of soap-cakes and packing materials and the plaintiff's dues, if any, shall be paid.

6. That on .... accounting was done and the plaintiff's dues were found at ₹...... from the defendant firm. Sri ...., a partner of the defendant firm had signed under the accounts in the plaintiff firm's 'Jama Kharach Bahi'.

7. That the plaintiff firm had requested the defendant to meet up the dues but to no effect.

8. The defendant firm has not paid the dues or any part thereof till date.

9. That the cause of action arose on .... when the account was stated at .... within the jurisdiction of this court.

10. That for the purposes of jurisdiction and court-fees, the suit is valued at ₹........ and *ad valorem* court-fees have been paid.

11. That the plaintiff firm submits herewith a true account of the plaintiff firm for the relevant period showing the transactions together with account books.

The plaintiff firm, therefore, prays:

For a decree of ₹......... and costs of the suit.

Statement of accounts:

Verification

Affidavit

NOTES: 1. When an account is stated and signed by the debtor, Art. 64(15) applies. But when the account is not signed, Art. 115 shall apply.

2. Suit on a Moblok Bundi in West Bengal. In a case of 'account stated' there are usually two cross accounts (AIR 1932 All 461) and cause of action arises when accounting is made.

24. Suit for reopening of settled accounts under Or. 7, r. 1 read with s. 26 of the CPC 1908

In the Court of Civil Judge (Senior/Junior Divisions) at ....

Suit No. .... of ....

Mr. X., son of Mr. Y, carrying on business at .... within the jurisdiction of this Ld. Court.

...... *Plaintiff*

versus

Messrs Z & Co. Ltd. a company registered under the Companies Act 1956 and carrying on business at .... within the jurisdiction of this Ld. Court.

... *Defendant*

The plaintiff states as follows:

1. The plaintiff carries on business as whole-saler of different kinds and items of building materials and as a contractor for construction of building.

2. The defendant carries on business as stockist and supplier of all sorts of building materials.

3. The plaintiff had dealings and transactions with the defendant in building materials and a Current Mutual Account was maintained for all supplies made by the defendant to the plaintiff and all payments made by the plaintiff to the defendant from time to time.

4. The transactions by and between the parties herein continued for more than 2 years.

5. On an audit of the accounts of the plaintiff it was found that the plaintiff had paid substantially more amount for the bills submitted by the defendant for supplies of goods by the defendant.

6. On further scrutiny it was found that certain duplicate bills were submitted by the defendant and the plaintiff, in good faith, without proper checking had paid the same.

7. On further scrutiny of the transactions by and between the parties, it was discovered that the plaintiff paid a total sum of ₹.......... in excess of legitimate dues of the defendant for supplies of building materials.

8. Several sets of statements of accounts were also submitted by the defendant and the plaintiff in good faith signed the same as true and correct.

9. After more than 2 years and on scrutiny of the plaintiff's accounts it transpired that such settled accounts were incorrect and contrary to the actual transactions by and between the plaintiff and the defendant. From Auditors' Report it was revealed that the plaintiff had paid in excess more than ₹........... during the last two years due to ignorance of the actual accounts pertaining to transactions by and between the plaintiff and the defendant.

10. The plaintiff stated that due to fraudulent entries made by the defendant and the plaintiff being unable to detect such fraudulent entries made payment to the defendant and also signed the Statement of Accounts to be true and correct. Now after more than 2 years and on scrutiny of the accounts by plaintiff's Chartered Accountant recently appointed it appears that the plaintiff had actually paid an excess of ₹.......... and that whatever accounts were settled, were due to ignorance of the plaintiff about the actual entries of the transactions between them. The plaintiff annexes hereto different statements of accounts contained in a schedule and duly signed as true and correct mainly due to ignorance of the plaintiff of the real transactions are annexed hereto marked 'A'. After such accounts were audited by the Chartered Accountant appointed for this purpose it appears to the plaintiff from the report submitted by Chartered Accountant that such accounts between the parties herein are totally incorrect and the fraudulent entries in respect of the transactions have been included in such accounts.

11. The plaintiff issued a legal notice to the defendant stating such discrepancies in the accounts and claimed reopening of such accounts but the defendant has refused to do so.

12. The plaintiff states that there is now due from and owing by defendant to plaintiff a total sum of ₹......... including a principal of ₹............. plus interest of ₹......... from the date of such excess payment made by plaintiff and given in a Schedule annexed hereto marked 'B'.

13. The plaintiff, therefore, is entitled to reopening of the Settled A/cs. and decree against the defendant for payment of ₹.......... with further interest due thereon. The defendant is also liable to pay the costs in respect of this proceeding.

14. No part of plaintiff's claims is barred by the Law of Limitation.

15. For the purposes of jurisdiction and court-fees, the suit is valued at ₹......... on which court-fees in stamps have been paid.

The plaintiff, therefore, prays for and claims:

(*a*) Reopening of the Settled Accounts;

(*b*) Decree for payment of ₹.......... against the defendant in favour of the plaintiff;

(*c*) Costs of the suit;

(*d*) Further and other orders be made and other reliefs be granted to the plaintiff as this learned court may deem fit and proper.

SCHEDULE 'A'

SCHEDULE 'B'

Verification

Affidavit

25. Suit on an account stated with an alternative claim based on original debt

In the Court of .... at ....

Suit No. .... of 20..........

(Set out cause title)

The plaintiff states as follows:

1. That the plaintiff runs a business of grocery articles under the trade name of "...........". The defendant has had a business of ...... at ....

2. State mutual transactions.

3. On an account stated between the parties hereto in writing on the .... day of .... 20 ...... a sum of ₹...... is found due to the plaintiff.

4. In the alternative, the plaintiff is entitled to recover the said sum of ₹ .... being the balance of the price of goods purchased by the defendant from the plaintiff on credit as per account below.

5. Cause of action.

6. Suit valuation.

The plaintiff claims:

Account

(Purchased by the defendant on credit)

Verification

Affidavit

26. Suit on an account stated in respect of cross-demands

In the Court of .... at ....

Suit No. .... of 20........

(Set out cause title)

The plaintiff A.B. states:

1. In between the parties hereto, there were a number of dealings ....

2. (State here in brief mutual dealings). The said transactions resulted in claims and demands upon both sides.

3. On an account stated in writing on the .... day of ...... 20...... and signed by ...., a partner of the defendant firm a sum of ₹ ...... was agreed due to the plaintiff from the defendant firm.

4. That the defendant firm has failed to pay up the said sum of ₹ .... or any part thereof to the plaintiff in spite of the latter's repeated demands.

5. The plaintiff is entitled to recover the said sum of ₹ ..... together with damages thereon at $12^1/_2$% per annum, as per business practice, for the period from .... till realisation.

6. Suit valuation.

7. Cause of action (date when account is stated and signed).

The plaintiff claims:

(*a*) a decree for ₹ .... together with damages thereon at $12^1/_2$% per annum from ...... till realisation;

(*b*) cost of suit.

CLAIM

(State here the claim and how worked out)

Verification

Affidavit

ACKNOWLEDGMENT

27. Suit on an acknowledged debt

In the Court of the Civil Judge (Junior Division) at ....

Money Suit No. .... of 20 ....

A,
Son of B
residing at .... *Plaintiff*

versus

C,
father's name not known
of .... P.O. ....
P.S. .... District .... *Defendant*

Suit on an acknowledgment of debt

Valued at ₹ ....

The plaintiff states as follows:

1. That the plaintiff and the defendant had a joint business of cloth at ...... The business was separated and after accounting a sum of ₹...... stood payable to the plaintiff by the defendant. The defendant was short of fund and he acknowledged in writing on ...... his loan of ₹........ which he promised to pay within a month from date.

The said deed of acknowledgment is filed herewith and be treated as a part of the plaint.

2. That the defendant did not pay the sum within the stipulated period in spite of demands made by the plaintiff. Thereupon the plaintiff issued a registered notice of demand dated ...... to the defendant demanding the sum through his lawyer, but the registered notice was refused. A true copy of the original notice, along with the refused envelope containing the said notice, postal regn. coupon are filed herewith.

3. That the plaintiff is entitled to recover from the defendant a sum of ₹ ....

4. That the cause of action for the suit arose on .... at ...... within the jurisdiction of this court.

5. That for the purpose of jurisdiction the suit is valued at ₹........ and *ad valorem* court-fees are paid thereon.

The plaintiff, therefore, prays:

(1) For a decree of ₹ ....

(2) For such other relief or reliefs as law and equity would allow.

Verification

Affidavit

NOTES: 1. For acknowledgment of debt—see s. 19 of the Limitation Act.

2. Receipt in lieu of old debt—receipt can be an acknowledgment within the meaning of s. 19 on the satisfaction of the following conditions.

(*i*) The acknowledgment must have been made before the expiration of the period prescribed for the suit;

(*ii*) it must be a clear and unambiguous acknowledgment specifically admitting liability in respect of the debt sued upon—see AIR 1971 Pat 229;

(*iii*) it must be signed by the party or his authorised agent.

—AIR 1968 All 316. Entry in chitha of creditor signed by debtor signifying unconditional acknowledgment of liability not time-barred at the time—gives cause of action to the plaintiff—AIR 1968 Pat 203. But acknowledgment or payment beyond prescribed period of limitation would not attract fresh period of limitation—AIR 1968 Pat 245.

3. Loan taken by defendant from Bank. Deposit of large amounts in Bank by him towards part repayment of loan—amounts to acknowledgment of debt—*S.B.I.* v *Tarlok Singh* AIR 1992 Del 76.

28. Suit on a Moblokbandi

In the Court of the Civil Judge (Senior Division) at Cooch Behar

SCC No. .... 20 ...

A. .... *Plaintiff*

versus

1. B.
2. C.

Son of late D

Carrying on a joint family business under the name and style of ......

.... *Defendant*

Suit for instalment Moblokbandi
Claim laid at ₹.........

The above-named plaintiff states as follows:

1. That the defendants, at all material times, ran a joint family business under the name and style of ...... of ...... P.S. ...... District .... and the said B was the Karta of the said joint family business.

2. That a sum of ₹......... was due to the plaintiff from the defendants in or about 20..... S.Y. On the 28th Agrahayan, 14....... B.S. (corresponding to Migsar Sudi 3, 20....... S.Y.) there was an accounting and the defendant No. 1 as Karta of the defendant concern had executed a Moblokbandi in the pucca khata of the plaintiff on the 28th Agrahayan, 14.......B.S. acknowledging the liability of the defendants for that sum of ₹......... and further agreed to pay the said sum by 9 yearly instalments to wit, 8 yearly instalments of ₹......... each beginning with Chait Sudi 20...... S.Y. and the 9th instalment of ₹......... within Chait Sudi 20...... S.Y.

3. That the defendants have not paid any instalment thereafter in spite of repeated requests.

4. That the plaintiff is entitled to recover the said sum of ₹.............. from the defendant.

5. That the cause of action arose first on Chait Sudi 9th (......) on expiry of Chait Sudi 8th, 20...... S.Y. and on each succeeding Chait Sudi 9th at ...... within the jurisdiction of this court.

6. That for the purpose of jurisdiction and court-fees the suit is valued at ₹......... and *ad valorem* court-fees are paid thereon.

The plaintiff, therefore, prays:

(*a*) For a judgment and decree of ₹.........

(*b*) for all costs of suit.

Verification

Affidavit

Typed under my dictation Sd/- .... Advocate Typed by me: Sd/- .... Prof. Typist	I, A, the plaintiff of the above-noted suit do hereby declare that the statements made in paras 1 to 4 are true to my knowledge and I sign this verification today the .... day of ..... December 20 ...... at .... Cooch Behar.

Acknowledgment (s. 18) of debt must be of subsisting liability which is not already barred—*P. Sreedevi* v *P. Appu* AIR 1991 Ker 76.

ADMINISTRATION

29. Suit for administration by a creditor

In the Court of .... at ....

Other Suit No. .... of 20......

(Set out cause title)

The plaintiff states as follows:

1. That one Mr. A son of .... of (address) .... since deceased took a loan of ₹...... (prior to his death) on .... from the plaintiff.

2. That the said 'A' had executed a will on ...... and in the said will named the defendant as the executor of the will.

3. That the plaintiff has learnt that the defendant has on ...... obtained probate of the said will in Act XXXIX Case No. ...... of ...... of the court of the District Judge of all the properties of the deceased, described in Schedule 'A' appended below, have come to the hands of the defendant.

4. That the defendant, in spite of requests from the plaintiff in that behalf, did not pay up the plaintiff's loan.

5. That the plaintiff is entitled to recover from the defendant the said loan with interest till recovery at 10 per cent per annum or for administration of the estate of the deceased.

6. That the plaintiff has submitted particulars of his claim in the Schedule 'B' appended below.

7. Cause of action.

8. Valuation.

The plaintiff, therefore, prays:

For a decree of ₹...... as per a/c. in the Schedule 'B' below (Or, for administration of the property of the deceased).

SCHEDULE 'A'

(Set here particulars of property)

SCHEDULE 'B'

(Set here particulars of claim)

Verification

Affidavit

NOTE: A suit for administration of estate is to be treated as a suit for accounts within the meaning of s. 7(*iv*)(*f*) of the Court-fees Act. Its valuation for jurisdiction should be the same as that for court-fees—AIR 1970 Cal 479.

30. Suit by a creditor for self and on behalf of all other creditors for administration and for appointment of a receiver

In the Court of .... at ....

Suit No. .... of 20............

G.H. residing at .... for self and on behalf of all other creditors of A.B., deceased, late of ....

... *Plaintiff*

Versus

1. C.D.
2. E.F.

—executors of the said A.B., deceased, residing at ....

... *Defendants*

The plaintiff states as follows:

1. The plaintiff is a creditor of A.B., deceased in the sum hereinafter mentioned.

2. The said A.B. died on ...., 20 ..... having made his last will dated ...., 20 ..... and appointed the defendants his executors.

3. The defendants proved the will on 8th April, 20 ...., and possessed themselves of the movable and immovable property of the deceased, and yet have not paid the plaintiff his debt.

Particulars of claim:

Principal sum due on the promissory note (or bond) of the testator dated	₹......................
Interest from .... 20 .... at 6 per cent. per annum	₹......................
TOTAL	₹......................

4. The said A.B. was, and his estate still is, indebted to various other unsecured creditors. A list of the said creditors together with their respective claims is set out in Schedule hereto annexed and marked "A".

5. The estate is not of the value of more than ₹............... which is insufficient to pay all the debts of the estate.

6. The defendants are guilty of wilful default and waste in administering the estate.

Particulars:

(*a*) The defendants wilfully omitted to get in a debt due to the testator from one K. N. on a promissory note dated .... for ₹5,000 and allowed the same to be time-barred.

(*b*) The .... Bank Ltd., had a claim of ₹15,000 against the testator on an overdraft account. The defendants, although they had sufficient funds of the estate in their hands within six months of the testator's death, did not pay off the said debt until .... whereby the testator's estate has been diminished by the amount of interest which would have been saved if the debt had been paid sooner.

The above particulars are all that the plaintiff can give before discovery.

7. For the purpose of jurisdiction and court-fees, the suit is valued at ₹...... on which court-fees in stamps have been duly paid.

The plaintiff claims—

(1) That an account be taken of what is due to the plaintiff and all other creditors of the deceased.

(2) That an account be taken of the dealings of the defendant with the estate of A.B. deceased, on the footing of wilful default or neglect.

(3) That the estate of the deceased be administered.

(4) That a Receiver be appointed of the said estate.

SCHEDULE 'A'

Verification

Affidavit

31. Suit for administration by specific legatee

In the Court of .... at ....

Suit No. .... of 20.......

(Set out cause title)

The plaintiff states as follows:

1. That one ...... of ...... executed his last will on ...... and died at ...... on ...... within the jurisdiction of this court.

2. That by the said will the said ...... had bequeathed to the plaintiff all immovable properties the said testator held at the time of his death.

3. That in the said will the testator appointed the defendant as his executor.

4. That the defendant brought an action, Case No. ...... of 20 ...... in the Court of the District Judge (of the place), proved the will and obtained a probate of the said will and all the properties and the legacy of the plaintiff came to his hands.

5. That the plaintiff has furnished in the Schedule below a list of properties that was bequeathed to the plaintiff as far as the plaintiff could know.

6. That the defendant has not delivered to the plaintiff peaceful possession of the properties that was bequeathed to the plaintiff even now, in spite of requests made therefor.

7. Cause of action arose on ... when the legacy became deliverable to the plaintiff.

8. Valuation.

The plaintiff, therefore, prays:

(*a*) For direction to the defendant for

(*i*) delivery of properties that fell to the plaintiff by the will;

(*ii*) showing inventory of the properties;

(*iii*) administration of the estate of ...... (testator)

(*b*) All costs of suit.

SCHEDULE

(Particulars of properties bequeathed to the plaintiff)

Verification

Affidavit

NOTE: For a legacy against an executor or administrator—limitation is 12 years from when legacy becomes payable or share deliverable under Art. 106 of the Limitation Act 1963.

32. Suit for administration by a pecuniary legatee

In the Court of .... at ....

Suit No. .... of 20..........

(Set out cause title)

The plaintiff states as follows:

1. That one A.B., of .... Town, P.S. ...... District .... executed a will on .... and died on .... at ...... within the jurisdiction of this court.

2. That by the said will the said A.B., appointed the defendant as his executor.

3. That said A.B., had bequeathed to the plaintiff a legacy of ₹......... by the said will out of his estate.

4. That the defendant proved the said will before the District Judge .... in Probate Proceedings No. .... of 20........ and was granted probate together with a certified copy of the will by the said court on ......

5. That the defendant has been in possession of the estate of the said A.B., since then.

6. That the plaintiff had requested the defendant to pay to the plaintiff the said sum of ₹........ but the defendant has been avoiding.

7. That the plaintiff is entitled to recover the said sum of ₹........ from the defendant and/or alternatively, orders for administration of the estate.

8. That the cause of action for this suit arose on .... when the defendant was granted probate and thereafter on ...... when legacy was demanded by the plaintiff at ...... within the jurisdiction of this court.

9. Suit valuation.

The plaintiff, therefore, prays:

(*a*) For a judgment and decree for ₹........ against the defendant.

(*b*) Alternatively, for an account of the estate of the said A.B. and for administration of the same by the court's order.

Verification

Affidavit

33. Suit by residuary legatee against executors for administration and for account on the basis of wilful default

In the Court of .... at ....

Suit No. .... of 20.........

(Set out cause title)

The plaintiff states as follows:

1. The plaintiff is the residuary legatee of A.B., ... who died on .... 20....... having made his will dated .... 20....., and appointed the defendants his executor.

2. The defendants proved the will on .... 20.........., and have possessed themselves of the movable and immovable property of the deceased.

3. The defendants as executors have been guilty of wilful default in not getting in certain properties of the testator. The plaintiff is unable to give full particulars under this paragraph until after discovery and the following particulars are all that the plaintiff can give:

Particulars:

B.C. owned the testator ₹5,000 on a promissory note dated .... 20......... repayable on demand with interest at 6 *per cent per annum*. The defendants were aware of the said fact but they never applied to B.C. for payment or acknowledgment, whereby the sum due on the said promissory note was time-barred and was lost.

The plaintiff claims—

(*a*) An account of the dealings of the defendant with the testator's estate on the footing of wilful default.

(*b*) Administration of the estate.

Verification

Affidavit

ADMIRALTY

34. Suit for wages by a master of a steamship

In the High Court at Calcutta

Money Suit No. .... of 20 ....

(Set out cause title)

The plaintiff states as follows:

1. That the defendant owns a steamship SS (*name the ship*).

2. That the plaintiff was appointed 'master' of the said steamship by the defendants under an agreement dated ...... temporarily with effect from ...... at a salary of ₹...... plus allowances (if any) (*State nature and amount*) *per mensem* payable according to English calendar.

3. That following the said agreement the plaintiff acted as the master of the aforesaid steamship for the period from .... to ....

4. That the plaintiff was paid his wages up to ...... The defendant did not pay to the plaintiff his wages for the period which amounts to ₹...... as per account in the Schedule of claim below.

5. That the plaintiff made several requests to the defendant and last on ...... by a notice served by registered post with A/D.

6. That the cause of action for this suit arose on the 1st of ...... for the salary of the month of ...... and thereafter on the first day of each subsequent month at (place of appointment) within the jurisdiction of this court. (Or, on ...... when the voyage

ended during which voyage the plaintiff earned wages as per account in the Schedule of claim below).

The plaintiff claims:

(*i*) A judgment and decree for ₹........ as per account in the Schedule below.

(*ii*) Costs of suit.

SCHEDULE OF CLAIM

Salary/wages for the period from
...... to .... at the rate of ₹......
per month

Add Allowances

....

₹.....................
(in words)

Verification

Affidavit

NOTES: 1. For limitation of recovery of seaman's wages—three years from the end of the voyage during which the wages are earned—vide Art. 6 of the Limitation Act 1963.

2. Admiralty Jurisdiction—Admiralty Courts Act (1861).
Section 6: Consignment entrusted to one vessel for shipment and delivery at Indian Port, brought to that port by another vessel. The mere fact that consignment was brought to Indian Port by another vessel cannot direct Admiralty Court from proceeding against vessel on which initially consignment was loaded—*CNA Peejay Exports* v *A.V. Nikolay Maksinov* AIR 1993 Bom 286.

35. Admiralty Jurisdiction

In the High Court at Calcutta
Admiralty Suit No....... of 20........

In the matter of:

Mr. P., carrying on business at 3 Brabourne Road, Kolkata 700 001 within the said jurisdiction.

...... *Plaintiff*

versus

Owners and Parties interested in the Motor Vessel "Navigator".

.... *Defendant*

The plaintiff states as follows:

1. The plaintiff carried on and is still carrying on business as the Steamship Agent, Stevedore and Ship Chartering Brokers at Mumbai, New Delhi and at 3 Brabourne Road, Kolkata.

2. The Motor vessel *M.V. Navigator* is a Motor Vessel of ... Tonnes Gross and ... Tonnes Net Registered ...... in Length and .... Beam, fitted with Engines of .... BHP Nominal Horsepower and of .... hands all told.

3. While the said *Motor Vessel Navigator* was at Calcutta Port and/or while the said vessel arrived at the Sandheads during the months of July and August 20....... the plaintiff at the request of and/or order of defendants and/or their agent agreed to supply and supplied certain necessaries and rendered services. The particulars of the dates and the nature of charges for the said supply of necessaries and rendering of the services by way of necessaries will appear from the bills of the plaintiff, copies whereof are annexed hereto as part of this plaint and collectively marked with the Letter 'A'. The statements contained in the said Bills are true and correct.

4. By a writing dated 6th September 20........ signed by defendants and/or its Agents, duly authorised in that behalf, the defendants had acknowledged supply of the said necessaries and rendering of the services by way of necessaries and the liability to pay to the plaintiff but wrongly disputed certain items therein. A copy of the said letter is annexed hereto and marked with Letter 'B'.

5. There is now due from and owing by the defendants to the plaintiff a sum of ₹......... particulars of which will appear from a Schedule filed herewith and marked with the Letter 'C'.

6. The plaintiff claims the said sum of ₹......... from the defendants for supplying the necessaries and also rendering of the services by way of such necessaries elsewhere than in the Port to which the said Motor Vessel belongs, and the same are "necessaries" within the provisions of s. 5 of the Admiralty Courts Act 1861, and/or the Law of Admiralty.

7. The plaintiff is entitled to interest at 6% per annum from the respective dates of sale and/or supplies of the said necessaries. The plaintiff claims alternatively interest at 6% per annum by way of damages.

8. In spite of demands, the defendants have failed and/or neglected to pay the said sum of ₹........ or any portion thereof to the plaintiff.

9. The aforesaid necessaries were supplied and are essential and/or necessary services were rendered to the said vessel in the Port of the said vessel and/or of the defendants as owners of the said vessel.

10. The said vessel is presently lying at Port of Calcutta in the State of West Bengal within the Admiralty Jurisdiction of this Hon'ble Court. The said vessel is a foreign vessel plying under the Flag of X country and is not registered in India and defendants are not at the time of institution of this suit domiciled in India.

11. The cause of action having arisen within the territorial jurisdiction of the Admiralty Jurisdiction of this Hon'ble Court and the said vessel Navigator is now within the territorial limit of the Admiralty Jurisdiction of this Hon'ble Court.

12. For the purpose of court-fees, the suit is valued at ₹......... and as such is triable within the jurisdiction of this Hon'ble Court as a Court of Admiralty and/or Vice Admiralty and/or as a Colonial Court of Admiralty. This Hon'ble Court has and the City Civil Court has not the jurisdiction to entertain, try and determine this suit.

13. The plaintiff prays for leave to pay additional or excess court-fees, if any, at the time of decree on the sum found due by this Hon'ble Court in respect of amount of principal and interest.

The plaintiff, therefore, claims for:

(*a*) Decree for ₹.........

(*b*) Interest from ...... till filing of the suit, interim interest and interest on Judgment at 6% p.a.

(*c*) Arrest of the said vessel *M.V. Navigator* and its tackles, apparel, and furniture.

(*d*) Declaration that the said vessel is remaining charged for payment of ₹ .... due and owing by the defendants to plaintiff.

(*e*) Declaration that the plaintiff has a lien on the said vessel *M.V. Navigator* for the said sum of ₹..........

(*f*) Costs.

(*g*) Such further and other orders and/or reliefs as to this Hon'ble Court may seem fit and proper to afford complete relief to the plaintiff.

Annexures:

A—Copy of bills

B—Letter of acknowledgment

C—Particulars of dues

Verification

Affidavit

ADOPTION

36. Suit for setting aside an adoption

In the Court of .... at ....

Suit No. .... of 20........

(Set out cause title)

The plaintiff states as follows:

1. The plaintiff is the only legal heir of A.B. since deceased and had right, title and interest over the properties described below which were left by the said A.B.

2. That in collusion with the Settlement Department of the Government of ...... the defendant managed to record his name for the said properties in the Schedule below as an adopted son of the said A.B., being allegedly taken in adoption by ......, widow of the said A.B. on or about the ...... day of ...... 20.........

3. The defendant was never adopted as a son by the said .... (name the widow of A.B.).

4. Even if, without conceding, there was an adoption of the defendant by the said .... the same is invalid as because [state here reasons such as (*as the case may be*)]:

(*a*) the defendant was an orphan at the material date and no prior permission of the court was obtained by the guardian who gave in adoption;

or

(*b*) the defendant was married at the material date, and there is no custom in the community which the defendant belongs to, permitting adoption of married persons;

or

(*c*) the defendant was aged 17 years at the material date, and there is no custom in the community to which the defendant belongs, permitting adoption of boys aged more than 15 years;

or

(*d*) neither any dattok homam nor any giving and taking ceremony was took place;

or

(*e*) the widow of the said AB was not older by 21 years than the defendant at the time of adoption.

5. The plaintiff is entitled to declaration:

that the defendant is not the adopted son of A.B.; alternatively, adoption of the defendant by the widow of A.B., is void *ab initio*.

6. Cause of action—(date when the story of adoption came to the knowledge of the plaintiff).

7. Suit valuation—(Value of relief).

The plaintiff, therefore, prays:

(*i*) for a decree declaring:

(*a*) that the defendant is not the adopted son of A.B.;

(*b*) alternatively, adoption of the defendant by the said widow of A.B., is void and for setting aside the adoption by an appropriate order,

(*ii*) any other relief to which the plaintiff is entitled in law and equity.

(*iii*) Costs of suit.

Verification

Affidavit

NOTES: 1. No convincing evidence of the giving and taking ceremony. Further no evidence on record to show that widow had the authority of her husband to take anybody in adoption. Alleged adoption held bad—AIR 1963 SC 185; AIR 1978 Ori 199.

2. Execution of adoption deed proved by production of one attesting witness. No burden is cast on the party to doubly prove the adoption deed by producing the other attesting witness—AIR 1978 All 472.

3. Adoption of person over 15 years of age—valid only if recognised by custom —*Kondiba Rama Papal* v *Narayan Kondiba Papal* AIR 1991 SC 1180; (1991)2 SCC 218.

4. Adoption by two co-widows is invalid—AIR 1977 Bom 298.

5. For proof & nature of evidence—*Vandabasi Kartikaya* v *S. Kamalamma* AIR 1994 AP 102.

6. Adoption of destitute or abandoned children by foreigner or Indian parents—See *Laxmikant Pandey* v *Union of India* AIR 1987 SC 232. Direction by the Supreme Court in AIR 1984 SC 469 and AIR 1986 SC 272 have been modified in AIR 1987 SC 232.

See *Laxmikant Pandey* v *Union of India* AIR 1992 SC 118; AIR 1984 SC 469 referred to.

7. Foreign adoption—Adoption by foreign couples. Recommendation by council set up pursuant to guidelines in AIR 1984 SC 469 and AIR 1986 SC 272, though not final or conclusive must be given great weight.

Broad principle that only legislative guidelines under s. 7 of the Guardians and Wards Act be followed is improper—*Karnataka State Council for Child Welfare* v *Society of Sisters of Charity* AIR 1994 SC 658.

8. Proof—No giving and taking ceremony of child established. Adoption not proved—*Urmila Devi* v *Hemanta Kumar* AIR 1993 Ori 213. Also see *Lakshman Singh* v *Rup Kanwar* AIR 1961 SC 1378.

   Leading case on Adoption—*Kishorilal* v *Md. Chattibai* AIR 1959 SC 504. But, when a registered document of adoption is produced that gives rise to the presumption that adoption was made in compliance with the provisions of the Act unless disproved. Proving of giving and taking of adopted child is not necessary—*Pathivada* v *Korada Singh* AIR 1993 AP 336.
9. Inter-country adoption—Procedure has been laid down by Supreme Court in AIR 1984 SC 469 (See Notes 6 above)—*Laxmikant Pandey* v *Union of India* AIR 1992 SC 118.
10. In some cases to complete adoption *'dattok homam'* is necessary but in the case of twice-born classes no such ceremony is needed if the adopted boy belongs to the same gotra as of the adoptive father—*Madhusudan Das* v *Narayanibai* AIR 1983 SC 114.
11. A mentally ill person can be adopted. In s. 10 of the Hindu Adoptions and Maintenance Act there is no bar—*Devgonda Raygonda Patil* v *Shamgonda Raygonda Patil* AIR 1992 Bom 189.
12. Cogent and reliable evidence as regards fact of adoption. Mere absence of registered document is not sufficient to reject adoption—*Sm. Chandrani Bai* v *Pradeep Kumar* AIR 1991 MP 286.

AGENCY

37. Suit by a creditor against a principal for money borrowed by agent

In the Court of .... at ....

Suit No. .... of 20........

(Set out cause title)

The plaintiff states as follows:

1. That the defendant No. 2 was and is at all material times a constituted attorney and an agent of the defendant No. 1.

2. That the defendant No. 1 owns a business of wholesale and retail sale of tea at ...... The defendant No. 1 lives away from ...... (name the place of business). The defendant No. 2 runs and manages the said business in the name of the defendant No. 1 under the power of attorney as agent of the defendant No. 1.

3. That the defendant No. 2 had borrowed from the plaintiff on ...... a sum of ₹........ for retiring a P.W.B. of a consignment of tea of the said business of the defendant No. 1 and executed the same day a handnote for the said sum as agent of defendant No. 1 promising to liquidate the loan on demand together with interest at 10% per annum.

4. That defendant No. 2 has not paid the dues of the plaintiff under the said handnote in spite of demands made by the plaintiff.

5. That the plaintiff is entitled to recover his dues under the handnote from defendant No. 1, alternatively from defendant No. 2, as per account below.

6. Cause of action—(On the date of handnote).

7. Suit valuation—(Principal together with interest up to date of suit) *ad valorem* court-fees paid thereon.

The plaintiff prays for a decree of ₹........ as per account below from defendant No. 1, alternatively from defendant No. 2.

Statement of account

Principal	₹...........
Add interest @ 10% per annum from ...... to 20	₹...........
Total:	₹...........

(In words)

Verification

Affidavit

NOTES: 1. For principal's liability to third person—the principal is liable for acts done by agent in course of his employment and within the scope of his authority—see s. 237 of the Indian Contract Act. Liability of a pretended agent—see s. 23 of the Indian Contract Act.

2. See s. 235 of the Indian Contract Act—a person untruly representing himself to be the authorized agent is liable to make compensation.

3. Third person can sue the principal, or the agent or both alternatively.

38. Suit by an agent for commission against his principal

In the Court of .... at ....

Suit No. .... of 20.........

(Set out cause title)

The plaintiff states as follows:

1. That the defendant employed the plaintiff by a letter in writing as his agent on .... for securing orders for .... manufactured by the defendant and orally agreed to pay to the plaintiff 25% of the value of orders as may be secured by the plaintiff, as commission.

2. That during the period from ...... to .... the plaintiff had secured for the defendant orders for ...... valued at ₹........ only and the plaintiff's commission payable by the defendant is ₹........ only.

3. Despite repeated demands the defendant did not pay to the plaintiff said commission.

4. That the cause of action for this suit arose on ...... at ...... where the defendant carries on work for gain, within the jurisdiction of this court.

5. That the suit is valued at ₹........ and *ad valorem* court-fees are paid thereon.

The plaintiff claims:

(*i*) A decree of ₹........

Verification

Affidavit

NOTES: 1. See ss. 211 to 225 of the Indian Contract Act for duties of the agent to his principal and *vice versa*.

2. Though there is no statutory provision entitling the agent to sue his principal for accounting, in exceptional circumstances such a right is available to the agent on equitable considerations. Where the agent knew about the actual state of affairs of the accounts agent's plea of special circumstances was ruled out—AIR 1967 SC 333; AIR 1977 All 259.
3. Relationship between the principal and the agent, terms of agency material for the cause and breach of duty have to be stated.
4. In suits between principal and agent limitation is for three years under Arts. 1, 2, 3, 4, 23 and 55 of the Limitation Act 1963, as the case may be.

39. Suit by an agent for money paid on behalf of the principal

In the Court of .... at ......

Suit No. .... of 20.......

(Set out cause title)

The above-named plaintiff states as follows:

1. That the plaintiff is a commission agent at Kolkata. The defendant has had his business of ...... at Cooch Behar.

2. That the defendant had engaged the plaintiff by a letter in writing dated .... to work as his commission agent for purchase and sale of ...... at Kolkata. The defendant further agreed to pay to the plaintiff commission on each transaction at 5% over the value.

3. That the defendant had instructed the plaintiff on ...... in writing to purchase ...... tonnes of ...... (name the commodity) and to sell until further instructions. In compliance the plaintiff has purchased ..... tonnes of .... on ...... at a cost of ₹........ from his fund.

4. That the defendant had sent a sum of ₹........ to the plaintiff. The plaintiff is entitled to recover from the defendant the balance of ₹........ together with commission of ₹........ at the aforesaid agreed rate.

5. Cause of action—on date of purchase at the place where purchased.

6. Suit—valuation—(balance, commission, interest).

The plaintiff claims:

(*i*) A decree for ₹........

(*ii*) Interest @ $6^1/_2$% per annum till date of payment.

Verification

Affidavit

40. Suit by a principal for damages against an agent for latter's negligence

In the Court of .... at ....

Suit No. .... of 20..........

(Set out cause title)

The above-named plaintiff states as follows:

1. That the defendant was at all material times a Constituted Attorney and an agent of the plaintiff with authority to sue in the name of the plaintiff, attend and look after court-cases on behalf of the plaintiff.

2. That the defendant as Constituted Attorney of the plaintiff had instituted a Money-Suit No. ...... of the year 20...... in the court of ...... against one A.B. for recovery of a sum of ₹........ due to the plaintiff on a promissory note. The said suit was fixed for peremptory hearing on ....

3. That the defendant did not appear when the case was called on for hearing and the suit was dismissed on ...... for default. The fact of dismissal was not reported to the plaintiff nor the defendant filed any petition for restoration of the Money-Suit and/or for setting aside order of dismissal within the period of limitation.

4. That the said sum of ₹........ and interest thereon is lost to the plaintiff for gross negligence of the defendant.

5. That the defendant did not compensate the loss.

6. The cause of action arose on ...... when the said Money-Suit was dismissed and loss occurred to the plaintiff.

7. That the suit is valued at ₹........ (principal plus interest which could have been recovered in the suit together with costs of suit) as per account below and *ad valorem* court-fees are paid thereon.

The plaintiff claims

₹........ as per a/c below.

Account of claim

Money due on handnote	₹........
Interest claimed in Money-Suit	₹........
Cost of court-fees paid in Money-Suit	₹........
Loss of Advocate's fees	₹........
	₹........

(in words)

Verification

Affidavit

41. Suit by a principal against a del credere agent for the price of goods sold

In the Court of .... at ....

Suit No. .... of 20........

(Set out cause title)

The above-named plaintiff states as follows:

1. That the plaintiff had engaged the defendant No. 1 on the ...... day of ...... 20...... orally as his *del credere* agent (or, by an agreement in writing on ......) to sell imitation pearls for the plaintiff.

2. That by the said agreement defendant No. 1 agreed that possible buyers would perform their contractual obligations and defendant No. 1 would remain answerable to the plaintiff for the payment of the price thereof. It was further agreed that defendant No. 1 would get 25% *del credere* commission on all sales effected through him.

3. That the defendant No. 1 had instructed the plaintiff in writing on .... to despatch by registered parcel/Insurance to the pro-defendant No. 2 one hundred

imitation pearls, valued at ₹........ only. In compliance the plaintiff had sent to the pro-defendant No. 2 one hundred imitation pearls under insured cover.

4. That the pro-defendant No. 2 did not pay the plaintiff's dues.

5. That the plaintiff is entitled to recover from defendant No. 1 the said sum of ₹........ together with damages at $6^1/_2$% till realisation.

6. That the plaintiff has furnished below details of all transactions.

7. Cause of action.

8. Suit-valuation.

The plaintiff claims (*i*) Decree for ₹.......
(*ii*) Costs.

Verification

Affidavit

NOTES: 1. ILR 46 Bom 489.
2. ILR 49 Mad 156.

42. Suit by a principal against his agent for acting contrary to instructions

In the Court of .... at ....

Suit No. .... of 20........

(Set out cause title)

The plaintiff states as follows:

1. That the plaintiff had appointed the defendant as his agent by a letter dated ...... (or by an agreement executed on ...... /or on ...... verbally) to purchase, if practicable, for the plaintiff woollen goods at Ludhiana during the period from ...... to ....

2. That from Ludhiana the defendant wrote back to the plaintiff quotations of price and quality of ready-made woollen garments. The price of certain varieties appeared to the plaintiff exorbitant whereupon the plaintiff sent in instructions to the defendant not to purchase items Nos. (*i*) and (*iv*) of the price-list. The defendant received the said instructions.

3. That the defendant contrary to instructions of the plaintiff, had purchased the said varieties of woollen garments in items Nos. (*i*) and (*iv*) at the rate of ₹........ per piece.

4. That the plaintiff did not find market of the same at ...... at the above rate and the same are lying in stock as blocked capital.

5. By reason of the matters aforesaid the plaintiff has suffered damage as under:

(State here nature and quantum of damage)

6. Cause of action.

The plaintiff therefore prays for a decree of ₹.......... against the defendant as damages.

Verification

Affidavit

43. Suit by principal against agent for acting contrary to instructions (Another Form)

In the Court of .... at ....

Suit No. .... of 20........

(Set out cause title)

The above-named plaintiff states as follows:

1. In July, 20 ...., the plaintiff verbally employed the defendant as his agent to sell one hundred bales of cotton lying at ....

2. On 1st August, 20.........., the defendant wired to the plaintiff enquiring if he could sell the goods on that date at the rate of ₹........ *per* bale. The plaintiff replied by wire the same day instructing the defendant to wait and not to sell unless the price reached ₹........ *per* bale.

3. The defendant in breach of his duty sold the goods on the said date at ₹......... per bale.

4. By reason of the premises the plaintiff has suffered damage.

Particulars of claim ....

Value of 100 bales at ₹........ per bale	....	₹ ....
Price of 100 bales at ₹........ per bale	....	₹ ....
Difference	....	₹ ....

The plaintiffs claim—

₹........ damages.

Verification

Affidavit

NOTES: 1. See s. 211 of the Indian Contract Act and s. 189 of the Indian Contract Act.

2. When the principal sustains loss that should be the amount of damages but when no apparent loss only nominal damages may be claimed.

44. Suit by a principal against an agent for accounts

(See Form No. 1)

45. Suit by a principal against a defaulter-agent

(See Form No. 3)

46. Suit by an agent against a principal for accounts of profit

(See Form No. 5)

47. Suit for secret profit by a principal against an agent

(See Form No. 6)

48. Suit by principal against sub-agent for recovery of secret profits

In the Court of .... at ....

Suit No. .... of 20........

(Set out cause title)

The plaintiff states as follows:

1. The plaintiffs, a Company incorporated under the Companies Act 1956, are shipowners carrying on business at ....

2. In ...... 20..., the plaintiffs were engaged in the formation of a steamship company and were desirous of raising money on debentures to be secured on certain ships.

3. By letter dated .... 20.........., the plaintiffs employed P. & T. brokers, to procure for the plaintiffs a loan of ₹........ on a commission of 2% on the transaction.

4. The said P. & T. with the assent of the plaintiffs employed the defendant as sub-agent on the terms that the defendant and the said P. & T. should share between them the commission payable by the plaintiffs.

5. In July 20........, the defendant introduced Mr. ...., the representative of the plaintiffs, to the L. G. & T. Society of ...... as being likely to advance the money required; and ultimately was successful in getting the advance made and the debentures issued on .....

6. On .... 20........., the plaintiffs paid the said P. & T. and the defendant the agreed commission.

7. On or about .... 20.........., the plaintiffs discovered that the defendant had entered into an arrangement with the said L. G. & T. Society, without the knowledge of the plaintiffs or of the said P. & T., by which the said L. G. & T. Society agreed to pay the defendant on the completion of the transaction ₹........ and also five *per cent* on the annual premiums payable upon a sinking fund policy of insurance which had to be taken out by the plaintiffs with the L. G. & T. Society to insure the ultimate payment of the amount of the said debentures.

8. On .... 20.........., the defendant secretly and corruptly received from the said L. G. & T. Society the said sum of ₹........ and ₹........ being five *per cent* on the annual premia paid up to that date.

The plaintiffs claim—

(*a*) To recover from the defendant the said sum of ₹........

(*b*) A declaration that the plaintiffs are entitled to recover from the defendant such further sums which the defendant may receive by way of commission from the said L. G. & T. Society in respect of future annual premia on the aforesaid policy of insurance.

Verification

Affidavit

49. Suit by agent against principal for breach of implied term in a contract to supply goods in a merchantable state

In the Court of .... at ....

Suit No. .... of 20.........

(Set out cause title)

The plaintiff states as follows:

1. The plaintiffs are fruit brokers of Mumbai.

2. The defendants are purchasers of oranges and shippers in Palestine, whose branded goods are well known in the Mumbai market as of standard quality.

3. By a contract in writing dated .... 20.........., and made at .... the plaintiffs agreed to sell in Mumbai 40,000 cases of the defendants' oranges of the Ophir brand during the season ...., shipment 30 *per cent.* November-December 20 ...., 70 *per cent.* January-March, 20.........., on the following terms:

(*a*) The defendants to ship and, after shipment, to draw upon the plaintiffs for 7*s.* 6*d.* *per* case of oranges f.o.b. Palestine ports, which was to be treated as an advance made by the plaintiffs.

(*b*) The plaintiffs to obtain delivery of the goods from the ship by paying the freight and to pay the duty and expenses such as landing charges and haulage from the docks.

(*c*) The plaintiffs to sell the oranges and, after sale, to account to the defendants, deducting from the sale proceeds first of all $7^1/_2$ *per cent.* on the gross sales as brokerage, 6*d.* *per* case covering repacking expenses and haulage, freight, duty, and then the advance, and to pay the balance, if any, to the defendants.

4. It, was an implied term of the said contract that the oranges, should reach Mumbai in a merchantable state.

5. The defendants began to make shipments on account of these 40,000 cases on .... by the Steamship V, and went on shipping at ten different ships down to ....

6. Thereafter, the consignment of 5,000 cases which arrived on .... by the Steamer .... were oranges that were abnormally wet and in process of deterioration, and the plaintiffs were unable to sell the said oranges as merchantable oranges of the Ophir brand. Large numbers of oranges had to be sold as wet, wasty and slack, because their condition was such as to make it impossible to repack them, and such as were saleable, required an excessive amount of repacking.

7. In the premises, the plaintiffs have suffered damage.

Particulars:

The plaintiffs claim—

₹........ damage.

Verification

Affidavit

50. Suit by agent against principal for indemnity against damage for breach of contract

In the Court of .... at ....

Suit No. .... of 20.........

(Set out cause title)

The plaintiff states as follows:

1. The plaintiffs are brokers at Mumbai. The defendants are merchants of Kolkata.

2. On .... 20........, the plaintiffs, under instructions in writing dated .... from the defendants, contracted in writing with B, a merchant of Mumbai,

to sell and deliver to him 20 bales of woollen socks (here state description) within one month from the date of contract at the price of ₹........ *per* bale.

3. The defendants did not supply the goods and, accordingly, the plaintiffs could not fulfil the contract, whereupon in .... 20..........., B, sued the plaintiff in the High Court at Mumbai (Suit No .... of ....) for recovery of ₹........ as damage for breach of contract.

4. By letter dated .... the plaintiffs informed the defendants of the suit, and by their letter dated .... the defendants authorised the plaintiffs to defend the suit.

5. The plaintiffs defended the suit, but on .... the said suit was decreed for ₹........ with costs and interest on judgment at 6 *per cent.*

6. On .... the plaintiffs paid ₹....... to B. in satisfaction of the said decree and also paid ₹...... to his own solicitors as taxed costs as between attorney and client.

Particulars:

The plaintiffs claim—

₹........ for such damages, costs and expenses.

Verification

Affidavit

51. Suit by agent for breach of contract of employment

In the Court of .... at ....

Suit No. .... of 20..........

(Set out cause title)

The plaintiff states as follows:

1. At all material times the defendant company (hereinafter referred to as 'the company') carried on business in ....

2. By an agreement in writing dated .... 20........., and made between the plaintiff and the company, in consideration of the plaintiff subscribing ₹........ in shares of the company, and in consideration of the plaintiff having suggested introducing to the company certain classes of cotton goods to be manufactured by them, the company appointed the plaintiff their sole agent in West Bengal, Bihar and Assam for the sale of those goods for the term of seven years, and thereafter until the agreement should be determined by six months' notice on either side.

3. The said agreement *inter alia* provided that—

(*a*) the plaintiff was to use his best endeavours to obtain orders for the said goods of the company at prices to be from time to time agreed upon between them and to communicate to the company all orders to be obtained by the plaintiff, and the company were to accept and execute all orders sent by the plaintiff unless they had reasonable grounds for refusal;

(*b*) the company were to pay to the plaintiff, so long as he should continue to be their agent, a commission of 4%. upon the invoiced price of all goods delivered by the company and duly paid for by the respective purchasers thereof.

4. In pursuance of the said agreement the plaintiff subscribed ₹........ in the capital of the company and acted as the sole agent for the company for the sale of the above-mentioned goods until such time as is hereinafter mentioned.

5. After January 20........, the plaintiff obtained and duly communicated to the company diverse orders for the aforesaid goods, yet the company in breach of the agreement unreasonably refused to accept some of the said orders.

6. By reason of the premises the plaintiff lost the commission which he would have earned upon the orders not accepted by the company as aforesaid.

PARTICULARS:

Date	*Name of the intending purchaser*	*Quantity of goods*	*Value of goods*	*Commission*

7. On .... the company sold their business without making provision for the plaintiff's agreement being taken over by the purchaser, thereby treating the agency and agreement as terminated.

8. By reason of the premises the plaintiff has lost the benefit of the said agreement for the remainder of the term of seven years and has suffered damage.

Particulars:

(Here set out the number of orders that would probably be obtained during the remainder of the period of the agency and the value of the said orders).

The plaintiff claims—

(1) ₹........ damages in respect of the orders specified in ....

(2) ₹........ damages for loss of the benefit of the said agreement.

AGISTMENT OF CATTLE (BAILEE OF CATTLE)

52. Suit for agistment of cattle

In the Court of .... at ....

Suit No. .... of 20..........

(Set out cause title)

The plaintiff states as follows:

1. That the plaintiff runs a dairy at ...... in the district of ...... The defendant at all material times owned five heads of milch cow with calves.

2. That in or about the ...... day of ......20... the defendant left ...... on transfer and left those cows and calves in the care of the plaintiff with a request to feed them and take care of them.

3. That the plaintiff took those in his care and custody in his dairy and spent a sum of ₹........ for the agistment of feeding and taking care of those.

4. On return of the defendant the plaintiff had returned (the heads of cattle) on the ...... day of ......20... and demanded from the defendant the said sum of ₹........which the defendant did not pay.

The plaintiff claims—

Particulars (state here dates, amounts etc.)

For upkeep .... ₹........
Fodder .... ₹........
Total ₹........

Verification
Affidavit

ALIENATION

53. Suit by a creditor under s. 53 of the Transfer of Property Act for declaration that alienation by the debtor is void

In the Court of .... at ....
Suit No. .... of 20......
(Set out cause title)

The above-named plaintiff states as follows:

1. That the defendant was indebted to the plaintiff for which the plaintiff commenced a Money Suit No. ...... of 20... against the defendant in the court of .... and obtained a decree for ₹........ with costs on ......

2. That the plaintiff has not put the decree in the said Money Suit No. ...... of 20..... in execution as yet and decretal dues have not been paid.

3. That the plaintiff has learnt that the defendant was and is indebted to Mr. X and Mr. Y for a total sum of ₹........ as mentioned below in Schedule 'A', at the time of the transfer mentioned in para 4 below.

4. That the defendant had transferred on .... by a deed of sale (Regd. on ....) his properties worth about ₹........ to his brother. That no consideration passed and the transaction was collusive, a sham transaction. Particulars of the said properties are described in Schedule 'B' below.

5. That the cause of action for the suit arose on ...... (date of sale by defendant of his properties) at ...... within the jurisdiction of this court.

6. Suit valuation (amount of consideration in the kobala).

The plaintiff, therefore, prays for:

(*a*) A declaration that the sale effected by the defendant in favour of the pro-defendant No. 2 on ...... is not binding upon the creditors of the defendant including the plaintiff.

(*b*) All costs of suit.

SCHEDULE 'A'

Nature of debt:	*Amount*	*Name with address of creditors*
By handnote	₹........	Mr. 'X' residing at ...... P.S. ...... District ....
By unpaid khata accounts	₹........	Mr. 'Y' residing at ...... P.S. District ....
	₹........	

SCHEDULE 'B'

Date of transfer:

Consideration:

Particulars of property transferred:

Verification

Affidavit

NOTES: 1. See s. 53 of the Transfer of Property Act 1882.
2. Limitation—three years vide Art. 58 of the Limitation Act 1963.
3. A like suit is to be instituted on behalf of and for the benefit of all the creditors of the defendant.

ALLUVION

54. Suit for possession of diluviated land reformed in situ

In the Court of .... at ....

Suit No. .... of 20............

(Set out cause title)

The plaintiff states as follows:

1. That the plaintiff owned and possessed 3.00 acres of land at Mouja ...... P.S. ... District—Cooch Behar, described more particularly in Schedule 'A' below.

2. That to the south of the plaintiff's land in Schedule 'A' there was the river Torsa.

3. That in the year 20 ...., the river Torsa shifted its course and in June and July, 20 ......, nearly two acres of land, being southern portion of the land in Schedule 'A', were diluviated. Only recently the river receded and the said lands of the plaintiff were reformed *in situ*. Lands thus reformed *in situ* is described more particularly in Schedule 'B' below.

4. That the said land in Schedule 'B' below is the subject-matter of the suit and will hereinafter be referred to herein below as the suit property.

5. That the plaintiff got into possession of the suit property in early January, 20 ......, but the defendant dispossessed the plaintiff from the suit property towards the end of January, 20......

6. That the plaintiff is entitled to khas possession of the suit property after finding the plaintiff's title thereto.

7. That the cause of action for this suit arose in January, 20......, when the plaintiff was dispossessed from the suit property at village .... within the jurisdiction of this court.

8. That for the purpose of jurisdiction and court-fees the suit is valued at ₹........ (market value of the suit property) and *ad valorem* court-fees are paid.

The plaintiff, therefore, prays:

(*a*) For a decree a khas possession of the suit property in Schedule 'B' below after finding the plaintiff's title thereto.

(*b*) *Mesne profits* (if desired).

SCHEDULE A

SCHEDULE B

Verification

Affidavit

NOTE: See 56 CLJ 263.

APPRENTICESHIP

55. Suit by an apprentice against his master for wrongful dismissal

In the Court of .... at ....

Suit No. .... of 20..........

(Set out cause title)

The above-named plaintiff states as follows:

1. That the defendant is a partnership firm engaged in repairs of automobiles with its workshop at ... P.S. ...... Dt. ...... within the jurisdiction of this court.

2. That by an indenture of apprenticeship dated the ...... day of January, 20 ...... between the plaintiff and the defendant firm, the defendant agreed to take in the plaintiff as an apprentice for three years from the said date, to teach the plaintiff repair works of automobiles and to pay to the plaintiff at ₹........ p.m. for the first year, ₹........ p.m. during the second year and at ₹........ for the third and the final year.

3. In terms of the said indenture of apprenticeship, the plaintiff became an apprentice under the defendant firm and worked for 20 .... On the 10th day of January, 20 ......, the defendant firm dismissed the plaintiff without just cause and wrongfully refused to continue the plaintiff's apprenticeship in the defendant-firm.

4. The plaintiff has suffered damage for such wrongful dismissal.

5. Cause of action (date of dismissal).

6. Suit valuation (aggregated value of loss of earnings, training for the rest of the apprenticeship period, loss of future prospects, loss of status).

The plaintiff claims (*i*) damages of ₹........ as per below:

(*ii*) costs of suit.

Claim

For loss of earnings from 1.1 .... to 31.12		₹........
Loss of training	...	₹........
Loss of future prospects	...	₹........
Loss of status	...	₹........
	... Total	₹........

Verification

Affidavit

NOTE: See Apprentices Act (52 of 1961).

Section 22(1) and 22(2)—Appointment of person as apprentices—Reciprocal obligations of employer and employee after completion of apprenticeship. Clause in contract that apprentice shall be absorbed in the department if there are vacancies—It creates reciprocal obligations on both parties—*Narinder Kumar* v *State of Punjab* AIR 1985 SC 275.

56. Suit by apprentice for breach of covenant in an apprenticeship deed

In the Court of .... at ....

Suit No. .... of 20.............

(Set out cause title)

The above-named plaintiff states as follows:

1. The defendant Company (hereinafter referred to as 'the Company') is a Company Limited whose registered office is at ....

2. By a deed of apprenticeship dated .... 20......., made between the plaintiff and the Company, the plaintiff put himself as apprentice to the Company, in their business carried on by them at .... aforesaid for the term of five years from the date thereof and the Company, in consideration of the plaintiff so put and bound himself, and also in consideration of the sum of ₹........ then paid to the Company by the plaintiff, convenanted and agreed with the plaintiff to teach him the art, trade and business of .... to board and lodge him and to pay him the weekly wages of ₹........ during the said term.

3. The plaintiff accordingly on .... 20......, entered upon his duties as such apprentice, but the Company refused to keep, teach and maintain the plaintiff after 31st December 20...........

4. By reason of the premises the plaintiff has suffered damage.

Particulars:

(State special damage if any)

The plaintiff claims—

(1) ₹........ damages.

(2) Alternatively, refund of the said sum ₹........ or so much thereof as was not exhausted by keeping, teaching and maintaining the plaintiff.

Verification

Affidavit

57. Defence by employer to claim for breach of covenant in an apprenticeship deed

In the Court of .... at ....

Suit No. .... of 20.........

(Set out cause title)

The above-named defendant states as follows:

1. The defendant Company admits having agreed to take in the plaintiff as an apprentice in their business for the term of five years, but states that by the deed of apprenticeship referred to in paragraph 2 of the plaint, the plaintiff was bound to order and behave himself as a true and faithful apprentice and not to steal or waste the defendant Company's goods.

2. Ever since the plaintiff entered upon his duties as apprentice, that is, from ...., his conduct was disreputable. He frequented singing rooms and theatres, smoked cigars and stayed out till late hours of the night and persisted in his conduct in spite of repeated warnings given to him by the manager of the defendant Company.

3. Prior to 31st December, 20.................., the plaintiff was detected having stolen ₹........ from the defendant Company's till.

4. By reason of the premises it became unsafe for the defendant Company to continue the plaintiff in their service, wherefore the defendant Company dismissed him on ....

5. Hence the suit be dismissed with costs.

Verification

Affidavit

ASSIGNMENT

58. Suit by an assignee of a debt under an absolute assignment

(Debt secured by a simple Bond)

In the Court of the Sub-Judge, ... at ......

S.C.C. No. .... of 20 .....

(Set out cause title)

The plaintiff states as follows:

1. That the defendant No. 1 had taken loan of a sum of ₹...... from the defendant No. 2 on ...... by executing a Money Bond in favour of the defendant No. 2 of the same date and agreed to liquidate the said loan together with interest at ...... % per annum over the principal within six months from date.

The said Money Bond is submitted herewith which may be treated as a part of the plaint.

2. That thereafter the defendant No. 2 assigned the said debt entirely with interest due on the bond from the defendant No. 1 to the plaintiff by executing a deed of sale on ...... (registered on ......) for consideration.

3. That the defendant No. 2 did not issue any notice of assignment to the defendant No. 1 whereupon the plaintiff had issued a notice of assignment dated .... to the defendant No. 1 by registered post with A/D. The said notice was received by the defendant No. 1 on ......

4. That, as far as the plaintiff could learn, defendant No. 1 paid nothing to the defendant No. 2 under the said Bond.

5. That the defendant No. 1 did not pay to the plaintiff the debt due from him even after receipt of the said notice dated ......

6. That the plaintiff had issued a notice of demand dated ...... by registered post with A/D on defendant No. 1 asking him to pay up the plaintiff's dues, but to no result.

7. That if it transpires that the defendant No. 2 received any money under the bond prior to or after the said assignment, the plaintiff is entitled to recover such sum of money from the defendant No. 2 as he may have taken from the defendant No. 1 under the Bond.

8. That the cause of action for this suit arose at ...... within the jurisdiction of this court on ...... (state here the date following the date of expiry of the time for repayment given in the Bond) and thereafter on ... (state here the date of assignment).

9. That the suit is valued at ₹........ for the purposes of jurisdiction and court-fees.

The plaintiff prays:

(*a*) For a judgment and decree for a sum of ₹........ against the defendant No. 1 as per account in the Schedule below.

(*b*) For a judgment and decree for such sum with interest at the above rate against the defendant No. 2 which he may have received from the defendant No. 1.

(*c*) Costs of suit.

Verification

Affidavit

59. Suit by an assignee of a debt under an absolute assignment (Simple Form)

In the Court of .... at ....

Money suit No. .... of 20.........

(Set out cause title)

The plaintiff states as follows:

1. That a sum of ₹........ was due to Sri *XY* from the defendant on the ....day of............20...... for the latter's purchase from said Sri *XY* a wrist-watch on credit and delivered to the defendant by the said Sri *XY*.

2. That the said *XY* absolutely assigned the said debt due to him from the defendant to the plaintiff by an assignment in writing on the said..............day of..................20.......

3. That the plaintiff issued a notice of such assignment to the defendant by his letter dated the ... day of ...... 20... with a request to pay up the said sum to the plaintiff.

4. The defendant received the notice on.........but did not pay.

5. Cause of action.

6. Suit-valuation.

The plaintiff claims—

(*i*) ₹........

(*ii*) Costs of suit.

Verification

Affidavit

NOTES: 1. See s. 130 of the Transfer of Property Act 1882—Transfer of actionable claim.

2. Transfer can be effected by an instrument in writing, though not registered. A negotiable instrument can be transferred by simple endorsement.

3. Notice of assignment—see s. 131 of the Transfer of Property Act—Not a must obligation of the plaintiff.

4. Assignor may be impleaded when there is doubt that some amount under the claim might have been paid to the assignor.

5. Limitation is the same as in a suit for recovery of money under a Money Bond.
6. Agreement for reconveyance—specific performance at the instance of assignee of vendor is maintainable—AIR 1978 Cal 443.
7. Assignee of a part of a debt cannot sue for that part only. He must sue for the whole—AIR 1940 Lah 96, the assignor or transferees of other part must be impleaded—AIR 1941 Lah 337.

60. Suit by an assignee of a promissory note

In the Court of .... at ....

Suit No. .... of 20.............

(Set out cause title)

Suit on a promissory note with interest

Claim laid at ₹........

The plaintiff states as follows:

1. The defendant had executed a Promissory Note on .... for ₹........ (in words) in favour of Sri 'A' and agreed to liquidate the loan with interest at 8% per annum when demanded.

2. That the defendant has not paid any amount to the said 'A' either towards the principal or by way of interest.

3. That the said 'A' by a registered deed against a proper consideration dated ...... assigned the said Promissory Note dated ...... to the plaintiff.

4. That the plaintiff informed the defendant of the said assignment by a notice dated ...... to the plaintiff.

5. That the plaintiff informed the defendant of the said assignment by a notice dated ...... sent per registered post with A.D. and requested payment of the loan but the defendant did not comply with the demand.

6. That the cause of action arose on ...... (date of execution of the Promissory Note) at ... (place of execution of the Promissory Note) within the jurisdiction of this court.

7. That the cause of action arose on ...... (date of execution of the Promissory Note) at ...... (place of execution of the Promissory Note) within the jurisdiction of this court.

8. The plaintiff values his suit at ₹........

The plaintiff claims a decree for ₹........ as per account in the Schedule of claim below:

SCHEDULE

(Statement of claim)

Principal—	₹........
Add interest from ...... to	₹........
Total	₹........

(In words)

Verification

Affidavit

NOTES: 1. When property in promissory note is transferred by partition, the transferee is entitled to maintain the suit. His right cannot be defeated on ground of non-endorsement—AIR 1969 Pat 215.

2. Suit on a promissory note by a assignee. Assignor—Original payee is a proper party—AIR 1978 Mad 310; AIR 1954 Mad 960.

61. Suit by an assignee of a promissory note (Another Form)

In the Court of .... at ....

Money Suit No. .... of 20...

(Set out cause title)

The plaintiff states as follows:

1. That the defendant executed a promissory note dated ...... 20... for ₹........ in favour of one A.B. agreeing to repay the loan on demand with interest at 10 per cent per annum.

2. That by a registered deed of assignment dated .... 20... said A.B. assigned the said promissory note in favour of the plaintiff.

Particulars of Claim

Principal sum	₹ ....
Interest up to .... 20......	₹ ....
Total	₹ ....

The plaintiff claims ....

₹ ....

Verification

Affidavit

62. Defence of set-off to claim by assignee of debt

In the matter of ....

(Set out]cause title)

The defendant states as follows:

1. The defendant says that the plaintiff's assignor .... at the time of commencement of this suit, was and is indebted to the defendant in the sum of ₹........ for goods sold and delivered, particulars of which are set out in schedule "A" hereto and the defendant claims to set-off this amount against the plaintiff's claim.

2. The suit be dismissed with costs.

SCHEDULE 'A'

Verification

Affidavit

63. Suit by an assignee of a debt under an equitable assignment

In the Court of the Sub-Judge at ....

Money Suit No. .... of 20...

1. A.B.

2. C.D.

.... *Plaintiff*

versus

X.Y.

.... *Defendant*

Suit for recovery of debt valued at ₹8,000.

The above-named plaintiffs state:

1. That the defendant took a loan of ₹8,000 from the second-named plaintiff C.D. by executing a handnote in his favour on the ....day of .... 20.... The loan was not liquidated.

2. On the .... day of .... 20... the second-named plaintiff assigned in writing to the first-named plaintiff the said debt due to him from the defendant.

3. That the first-named plaintiff gave a notice of such assignment to the defendant by a letter dated ...., sent to the defendant by registered post with A/D.

4. The defendant received the notice on ....but did not pay the money.

5. The first-named plaintiff, or alternatively, the second-name plaintiff, is entitled to recover the said sum of ₹8,000.

6. Cause of action (first on date of handnote and thereafter on the date of assignment).

7. Suit valuation.

The plaintiffs claim—

(*i*) Decree for ₹8,000 in favour of the first-named plaintiff, alternatively, in favour of the second-named plaintiff.

(*ii*) Costs of suit.

Verification

Affidavit

64. Suit by the assignee of a life policy

In the Court of .... at ....

Money suit No. .... of 20........

(Set out cause title)

The plaintiff states as follows:

1. That the defendant is a Life Insurance Corporation, a statutory body corporate with its registered office and H.Q. at...........

2. On the...........day of...........20 ......, the plaintiff's uncle...........since deceased, insured his life with the defendant corporation for the sum of ₹............

3. In considerations of premium paid by the said .... till death as and when fell due, the defendant corporation had granted the said ...... a policy bearing No. ....

4. The said .... assigned the said policy during his life-time by an endorsement thereon on the .... day of .... 20 ... in favour of the plaintiff. The plaintiff duly gave a notice of such assignment to the defendant corporation at the above address by his letter dated the .... day of .... 20 ....

5. The said .... died on .... at .... District .... His death being reported by a letter, the plaintiff was instructed by the defendant corporation to submit claim forms together with a Death Certificate. The plaintiff complied with all such instructions. The claim in the policy has not been met as yet.

6. Cause of action (date of assignment and finally on date of death of the insured).

7. Valuation (claim in the policy).

The plaintiff claims,—

(*a*) decree for ₹.........

(*b*) Costs.

Verification

Affidavit

NOTE: Under Art. 44(*b*) time would start running when the company denies its liability—AIR 1978 Cal 298.

ARBITRATION AND CONCILIATION

Autonomy The parties may determine the number of arbitrators, the procedure to be adopted by the arbitrator, the rules governing disputes, place of arbitration. The language of the arbitral proceedings and rules of procedure governing the same and in absence of an arbitration agreement between the parties, the Arbitral Tribunal has the autonomy as regards the rules of procedure and the rules governing the substance of the disputes involved, the place of arbitration and the language of the proceedings of arbitrators.

Interpretation In *Sundaram Finance Ltd.* v *M/s. NEPC (India) Ltd.* AIR 1999 SC 565; (1999)2 SCC 499, Hon'ble Supreme Court of India has said that—

> "1996 Act is very different from that of the Arbitration Act 1940. The provisions of this Act have therefore to be interpreted and construed independently and in fact, reference to the 1940 Act may actually lead to misconstruction. In other words, the provisions of the Act of 1996 has to be interpreted being uninfluenced by the principles underlying the 1940 Act. In order to help in construing this provision, it is more relevant to refer to UNCITRAL Model Law rather than to the provisions of the 1940 Act."

An arbitration agreement may be in a clause under a contract in writing or it is specifically contained in a document signed by the parties or contained in letters, telexes, telegrams or in exchange of statements of the claim and defence or a reference to a document which contains an arbitration clause.

"*Scott* v *Avery Clause*" means a clause making an award a condition precedent to any right of action or a suit.

Where a party has taken any proceedings before any court the other party may make an application stating that the subject-matter of disputes is covered by the arbitration clause, and in that case the court may refer the parties to arbitration (s. 8).

Interim order Before or during the arbitral proceedings a party may make an application to a court for any interim order (s. 9).

Where the arbitrators have been appointed a party may make an application to them for an interim measure of protection (s. 17).

A person may apply to the Chief Justice of the High Court or to the Chief Justice of the Supreme Court for appointment of an arbitrator, where there is an agreement for arbitration between the parties and the parties have failed to agree upon or to appoint arbitrators (s. 11).

A person who is appointed to act as an arbitrator should disclose before-hand in writing any circumstances liable to give rise to justifiable doubts as to the independence or impartiality of the arbitrator so appointed (s. 12).

The appointment of an arbitrator may be challenged on the grounds mentioned in s. 12. A party intending to challenge the competence of the arbitrator appointed may within fifteen days of such appointment of arbitrator or on becoming aware of any reasonable ground for challenging the competence and constitution of the Arbitral Tribunal and this challenge has to be filed before the arbitrator and not before any court (s. 13).

If the arbitrator becomes unable to perform his functions or subsequently withdraws from his office or the parties agree to terminate his mandate, then the arbitrator will cease to act as such and in case any dispute arises in respect of the mandate of the arbitrator a party may apply to the court to decide as to whether the mandate of the arbitrator stands terminated (s. 14).

Under s. 9 a party to the arbitration may apply before or during the arbitral proceedings or after making of the final Arbitral Award but before execution to the court for grant of interim order or measures (s. 9).

The rules of procedure for the conduct of the arbitral proceedings will be governed by the terms and conditions of agreement between the parties and in absence thereof will be decided by the arbitrator himself. The arbitrator will not be bound by the provisions of Code of Civil Procedure 1908 or the Indian Evidence Act 1872 in this regard (s. 19).

The claimant shall file the Statement of Claim and the respondent shall file the Statement of Defence and Counter-claim, if any, within the time stipulated by the arbitrator. In some cases, the arbitrator may extend the time for filing the said pleadings (s. 23).

The arbitrator will hear the parties unless the parties otherwise agree when the arbitrator shall decide whether it would be oral hearings for presentation of evidence or oral arguments or the proceedings shall be conducted on the basis of documents and other materials made available. Unless the parties otherwise agree the arbitrator may hold oral hearings where both the parties should be given sufficient notice for such hearings, presentation of documents, inspection of documents as well as proof of documents, for expert evidence with connected matters (s. 24).

If the claimant fails to submit statement of claim in spite of direction to do so, the proceedings should be terminated. If the respondent fails to submit statement of defence in spite of opportunity being given, the arbitrator should continue with the proceedings and give his award (s. 25).

Experts may be appointed by the Arbitral Tribunal at the request of a party and necessary assistance may be obtained on an application being made to the court (ss. 26-27).

The arbitrator in conducting the proceedings may apply the law and rules as prevailing in India. In International Commercial Arbitration, the arbitrator shall apply the rules of law according to agreement between the parties as regards the substance of disputes. If the parties have not designated the law applicable thereto, the Chief Justice shall apply the rules of law appropriate in the circumstances and the arbitrator is bound to give his award according to terms and conditions of the agreement and the law applicable thereto, and not on any principles of equity (s. 28).

Where there are more than one arbitrators, the majority view will be the decision of the Tribunal (s. 29).

In many cases an award may be made on terms agreed to between the parties (s. 30).

Forms and contents of the arbitral award have been mentioned in s. 31.

The arbitral proceedings being terminated by final arbitral award or by an order of the arbitrator where the claimant withdraws his claim or the parties agree or the arbitrator finds any reason for continuation of proceedings unnecessary or impossible the arbitrator issues an order accordingly (s. 32).

The arbitrator may, on the application of a party, make any correction or give suitable interpretation or make an additional award on an application made by a party within a specified period of 30 days from the date of receipt of the arbitral award (s. 33).

Any party aggrieved by the award may make an application for setting aside the award on the grounds mentioned in s. 34 of the said Act of 1996. Where the time-limit for making such application for setting aside the award has expired the award shall be executable as a decree of the court. The time-limit for making an application for setting aside of an award, is three months. An application may be made for condonation of delay upto 30 days. Where the notice of the award was not served on the appropriate officer of the respondent, on an application to the Supreme Court for condonation of delay of several months the prayer was granted and the delay was condoned. [See *Union of India* v *Tecco Trichy Engineers and Contractors* AIR 2005 SC 1832 (para 12)].

If the application under s. 34 does not succeed the award may be executed as a decree of the court (s. 36).

An appeal will lie for granting or refusing to grant any relief under s. 9 of the Act of 1996 or against an order setting aside the award or refusing to set aside an award or for an order of the arbitrator regarding the competence of and jurisdiction of the arbitrator or granting or refusing to grant an interim order by the arbitrator (s. 37).

From a District Court order though there may not lie an appeal to the High Court, but an application for revision under s. 115 of the Code of Civil Procedure 1908 may be maintainable. [*Shyam Sunder Agarwal & Co.* v *Union of India* AIR 1996 SC 1321 (s. 37)].

Where with respect to the arbitration agreement any application has been made before the court the said court alone shall have necessary jurisdiction to hear the arbitral proceedings and all subsequent applications in the matter shall be made in that particular court only (s. 42).

The Limitation Act 1963 shall apply to arbitration proceedings and that the time shall be deemed to have commenced on the date of request for reference of the disputes to the arbitration. The arbitration agreement provides for any limitation period for taking steps to commence the actual arbitral proceedings. The court may extend such period of time as it thinks fit and proper on consideration of facts and circumstances of the case. Where the court sets aside an award, the period between commencement of arbitral proceedings and the date of such order of the court setting aside the award shall be excluded in computing the period of limitation for commencement of the arbitration proceedings with respect to the said dispute included in arbitration proceedings (s. 43).

Foreign award. Enforcement of a foreign award may be refused on an application of the respondent on ground of his incapacity or in absence of proper notice of appointment of the arbitrator or the award deals with matters not previously contemplated under the agreement and for not falling within the terms submitted to the arbitrator or the award contains decisions on matters beyond the scope of submissions to arbitrator or the composition of the Arbitral Tribunal, or the procedure followed by arbitrator was not in accordance with the agreement or was not in accordance with law of the country where the arbitration took place, or the award has not yet become binding on the parties or it has been set aside or suspended by a competent authority of the foreign country under whose law the award was made. However, enforcement of the award may be refused if the subject-matter of the disputes is not capable of settlement by arbitrator under the laws of India or enforcement of the award would be contrary to the public policy of India. Where an application for setting aside of an award or for suspension of the award has been made or is pending before a competent authority, the High Court may adjourn the application for enforcement of the award and on the application of the award-holder the court may direct the respondent to give suitable security (s. 48).

If the foreign award is enforceable then it can be executed as a decree of the court (s. 49).

An appeal shall lie from an order refusing to refer the parties to arbitrator or refusing enforcement of the foreign award to the appropriate court. There cannot be any second appeal (s. 50).

A foreign award if it is enforced, can be resisted on the grounds mentioned in s. 57 of the Act of 1996 (s. 57).

Such award can be executed as a decree of the court. An appeal shall lie from such an order refusing to refer the parties to arbitration or refusing to enforce a foreign award by the appropriate court and in that case no second appeal except to the Supreme Court of India will lie (ss. 58-59).

65. Application for referring the disputes to arbitration

Application No. .... of 20...

Suit No. ... of 20...

In the High Court at Calcutta

Ordinary Original Civil Jurisdiction

In the matter of:

An application under s. 8 of the Arbitration and Conciliation Act 1996;

And

In the matter of:

M/s. P. Co. Ltd., a company registered under the Companies Act 1956 and carrying on business at Mission Row, Kolkata, within the said jurisdiction.

...... *Plaintiff*

versus

M/s. X Co. Ltd., a company registered under the Companies Act 1956 and carrying on business at Ezra Street, Kolkata, within the said jurisdiction.

...... *Defendant*

To
The Hon'ble Chief Justice and His Companion Justices of the said Hon'ble Court.

The humble petition of M/s. X. Co. Ltd. the defendant above-named most respectfully sheweth:

1. Your petitioner carries on business as Producer, Manufacturer and Dealer in Finished Teas. The plaintiff carries on business as Wholesaler and Distributor of Finished Teas.

2. Your petitioner sold and delivered certain quantities of teas to the plaintiff on stipulated terms and conditions which had specified that any disputes between the parties will be referred to arbitration of a sole individual as agreed to by both the parties and in the absence of any agreement the defendant's Sales Manager would be the Sole Arbitrator to decide and resolve the disputes.

3. Disputes and differences arose between the parties and your petitioner requested the plaintiff to refer the matter for arbitration of Mr. Y, the Sales Manager of the petitioner. The plaintiff did not reply to such request.

4. Your petitioner states that the subject-matter of the suit is covered by arbitration clause in the agreement dated .... entered into between the parties.

5. The plaintiff has wrongly filed the present suit in which your petitioner has not filed any defence or any written statement or taken any steps to defend the suit. The present application is the first step your petitioner has taken in the present suit.

6. In view of the aforesaid your petitioner submits that the parties be referred to arbitration as contained in the arbitration agreement between the parties and competent person be appointed as the Sole Arbitrator to adjudicate and resolve the disputes and to give his award.

7. This application is being made *bona fide* and in the interests of justice.

Your petitioner, therefore, humbly prays Your Lordships for the following orders:

(*a*) Suit No. .... of 20 .... filed by the plaintiff be dismissed and the disputes covered by the said suit be referred to the Ld. Sole Arbitrator, for proper adjudication;

(*b*) stay of all further proceedings in the suit;

(*c*) costs of this application be paid by plaintiff;

(*d*) further and other orders be made and directions be given as the Hon'ble Court may deem fit and proper so as to afford complete relief to your petitioner.

And your petitioner as in duty-bound shall ever pray.

Verification

Affidavit

66. Application for referring the dispute to arbitration (Another Form)

Application No. .... of 20........

In the High Court at Calcutta

Civil Appellate Jurisdiction

Insolvency Jurisdiction

Matter No. ...... of 20........

In the matter of:

An application under s. 41 of the Arbitration and Conciliation Act 1996 for referring the dispute to Arbitrator

And

In the matter of:

AB, son of .... residing at ....Kolkata.

...... *Claimant-Petitioner*

versus

Official Assignee, High Court, Calcutta of the Estate of XY, the insolvent

...... *Respondent*

To
The Hon'ble Chief Justice and His Companion Justices of the said Hon'ble Court.

The humble petition of the petitioner above-named most respectfully sheweth:

1. Your petitioner states that your petitioner and XY both residing in Kolkata entered into a contract under which the petitioner agreed to supply certain goods to the said XY from time to time and XY agreed to pay the price on delivery of the goods. The said contract contained an Arbitration Clause to the effect that any disputes between the parties would be referred to the Learned Arbitrator, Mr. M. A copy of the contract is annexed hereto and marked 'A'.

2. Your petitioner states that during the course of dealings disputes arose between the parties which were referred to arbitration.

3. In the meantime, XY was declared insolvent and the estate vested in the Official Assignee, the respondent herein.

4. Your petitioner states that the said Official Assignee of the estate in question has not adopted the contract and he advised the petitioner to obtain an order of the Hon'ble High Court.

5. Your petitioner states that the matter in dispute should be submitted to arbitration as the said XY was bound by arbitration agreement and Official Assignee is only representing the estate of the said XY.

6. Your petitioner prays for reference of disputes between the parties to arbitration.

In the premises your petitioner most humbly prays Your Lordship for the following orders:

(*a*) an order be made directing that the matter in dispute be submitted to arbitration in accordance with arbitration agreement;

(*b*) cost of this application be paid by respondent;

(*c*) further and other orders be made and directions be given as this Hon'ble Court may deem fit and proper to afford complete relief to your petitioner.

And your petitioner as in duty bound shall ever pray.

Verification

Affidavit

67. Application for interim orders

Application No. ... of 20...

In the High Court at Calcutta

Ordinary Original Civil Jurisdiction

In the matter of:

An Agreement dated .... containing an arbitration clause;

And

In the matter of:

A petition under s. 9 of the Arbitration and Conciliation Act 1996 for interim measures of protection and preservation;

And

In the matter of:

M/s. P. Co. Ltd., a company registered under the Companies Act 1956 and carrying on business at Ezra Street, Kolkata;

...... *Claimant-Petitioner*

versus

M/s. X Co. Ltd., a company registered under the Companies Act 1956 and carrying on business at Ezra Street, Kolkata.

...... *Respondent*

To
The Hon'ble Chief Justice and His Companion Justices of the said Hon'ble Court.

The humble petition of M/s. P. Co. Ltd., the petitioner above-named most respectfully sheweth:

1. Your petitioner sold and delivered finished teas to the respondent company at agreed price and the respondent duly received the same, and appropriated the goods but did not make payment for the same.

2. Your petitioner has observed that all the said teas have not yet been sold by respondent and the same have been lying in the godown of the respondent company.

3. The said godown is situate at the said address where the respondent carries on its business.

4. Under the agreement the respondent was to make full payment of the goods delivered within 24 hours of receipt of same.

5. The respondent duly acknolwedged receipt of the said goods in good condition and without any objection or complaint whatsoever, and appropriated the same.

6. In spite of repeated demands, the respondent has failed to pay any portion of price of the goods sold and delivered to respondent on ....

7. The claim of the petitioner is ₹30 lakh as will appear from copies of invoices duly received and signed by the respondent annexed hereto collectively marked 'A'.

8. In the premises your petitioner states that it is a fit case for issue of an order of injunction restraining respondent from dealing with or disposing of the said teas without first paying claims of your petitioner.

9. Your petitioner states that to prevent further wrongful disposal of said teas sold and delivered to the respondent without making payment, a receiver be appointed over the said teas which is lying in the godown of the respondent situated at the said address where the respondent's office is situate.

10. Your petitioner states that orders as prayed for herein are necessary for protection and preservation of teas which have been sold and delivered to the respondent but did not get any payment therefor.

11. In order to prevent the teas from being disposed of by the respondent without making payment to your petitioner, an order of injunction and appointment of receiver be made and the orders, as prayed for, are necessary for the protection of the petitioner's legal rights.

12. This application is made *bona fide* and in the interest of justice.

Your petitioner, therefore, humbly prays Your Lordships for the following orders:

(*a*) An order of injunction be issued restraining the respondent, its servants and agents from disposing of or wrongly dealing with the said goods sold and delivered by the petitioner to the respondent;

(*b*) Receiver be appointed over the said teas lying in the godown of the respondent which teas your petitioner had sold and delivered to the respondent but did not get any payment for the price of the said teas sold and delivered;

(*c*) Receiver be directed to take possession of the tea, make an inventory and submit reports to this Hon'ble Court with copies to the petitioner;

(*d*) Cost of this application be paid by respondent;

(*e*) Further orders be made and directions be given as to this Hon'ble Court may deem fit and proper so as to afford complete relief to your petitioner.

And your petitioner as in duty bound shall ever pray.

Verification

Affidavit

68. Application for appointment of Arbitrator

Application No. ...... of 20...

In the High Court at Calcutta

Ordinary Original Civil Jurisdiction

In the matter of:

An application under s. 11 of the Arbitration and Conciliation Act 1996 for appointment of an arbitrator by Hon'ble Chief Justice

And

In the matter of:

Mr. P. Co. Ltd., a company registered under the Companies Act 1956 and carrying on business at 1, Ezra Street, Kolkata 700 001

...... *Petitioner*

versus

X Co. Ltd., a company registered under the Companies Act 1956 and carrying on business at Ezra Street, Kolkata 700 001

...... *Respondent*

To

The Hon'ble Chief Justice and His Companion Justices of the said Hon'ble Court.

The humble petition of M/s. P. Co. Ltd., the petitioner above-named most respectfully sheweth:

1. Your petitioner carries on business as grower and wholesale dealer in teas.

2. The respondent carries on business and deals in finished teas.

3. Your petitioner sold and delivered five quintals of teas on .... to the respondent on terms and conditions specified in an agreement dated .... which specifically contained an Arbitration Clause. A copy of the Agreement is annexed hereto marked 'A'.

4. The respondent had in breach of the agreement failed to pay the price of the said goods sold and delivered by petitioner to the respondent and as such disputes and differences arose between the parties.

5. In spite of repeated requests, the respondent did neither pay the amount nor refer the matter to arbitration. Copies of letters are annexed hereto collectively marked 'B'.

6. Your petitioner states that no special or technical or legal knowledge is required or necessary to decide the disputes in this case as it is a normal and ordinary case of goods sold and delivered but payment not forthcoming from the respondent for such teas.

7. A copy of the last letter requesting the respondent to appoint its own sole arbitrator within 30 days from date of receipt of the said letter is annexed hereto marked 'C'. The respondent did not give any reply to such a letter and kept silent all the while.

8. In spite of several requests the respondent has failed to appoint its own arbitrator. Your petitioner, in the meantime, has named an arbitrator but he cannot alone act as arbitrator as the said Arbitration Agreement specifically provides that each one of the parties will appoint its own arbitrator and two arbitrators so appointed will appoint the third arbitrator.

9. In the premises, to settle the disputes and differences between the parties, appointment of an arbitrator in terms of the Arbitration Clause in the said Agreement is very much necessary.

10. The petitioner prays that Your Lordship will be pleased to appoint an arbitrator on behalf of the respondent so that the two arbitrators so appointed will appoint a third arbitrator and they will adjudicate the disputes between the parties.

11. This application is made *bona fide* and in the interest of justice.

Your petitioner, therefore, most humbly prays Your Lordships for the following orders:

(*a*) Appointment of an arbitrator on behalf of the respondent;

(*b*) Costs of this application be paid by the respondent;

(*c*) Further and other orders be made and directions be given as the Hon'ble Court may deem fit and proper to afford complete relief to your petitioner.

And your petitioner as in duty bound shall ever pray.

Verification

Affidavit

69. Affidavit relating to application for appointment of Arbitrator

Application No. ...... of 20...

In the High Court at Calcutta

Ordinary original civil jurisdiction

In the matter of:

An application under s. 11 of the Arbitration and Conciliation Act 1996 for appointment of arbitrator

And

In the matter of:

M/s. P. Co. Ltd., a company registered under the Companies Act 1956 and carrying on business at ...... Kolkata.

...... *Petitioner*

versus

M/s. X Co. Ltd., a company registered under the Companies Act 1956 and carrying on business at .... Kolkata

...... *Respondent*

Affidavit as required by r. 3(*h*) of the Notification of the High Court at ...... dated .... 20... framing the Scheme for Appointment of Arbitrators 1996.

I, ... son of ...., working for gain at .... do hereby solemnly confirm and say as follows:

1. I am the Managing Director of M/s. P. Co. Ltd. of ...., Kolkata and a principal officer and constituted attorney thereof. I know and I have made myself acquainted with the facts and circumstances of this case and I am authorised and able to depose thereto.

2. I say that an agreement was entered into by and between the petitioner and the respondent for sale of jute goods by the petitioner to the respondent according to the specifications and at the price mentioned in the agreement. The said agreement contains a clause for settling disputes between the parties by Arbitrators, one to be appointed by each party and that the said two Arbitrators will appoint the third Arbitrator. A copy of the agreement is annexed hereto marked "A".

3. Disputes and differences arose between the parties and the petitioner appointed Mr. EF as the Arbitrator in terms of the said agreement and this was informed to the respondent. A copy of the letter is annexed hereto marked "B". The respondent duly received the said letter as will appear from a receipt duly signed by the respondent annexed hereto marked "C".

4. I say that the petitioner in terms of the said Arbitration Agreement appointed its Arbitrator and requested the respondent to appoint the respondent's Arbitrator so that the two Arbitrators can appoint the third Arbitrator. The respondent duly received the said letter which will appear from the signature of the officer of the respondent on a copy of the letter which is annexed hereto marked "D".

5. The respondent has failed to respond to the request of the petitioner and has failed to appoint an Arbitrator even though more than 30 days have passed.

6. I say that in view of the aforesaid the petitioner has become entitled to make the application praying for appointment of an Arbitrator so that the two Arbitrators can appoint a third one and they can settle the disputes in accordance with the Arbitration Agreement contained in the contract, a copy whereof is annexure "A" hereof.

7. I say that the petitioner is entitled to make the application requesting the Hon'ble Chief Justice to appoint the second Arbitrator as the respondent has failed to appoint an Arbitrator in spite of requests and in spite of provisions in the contract.

8. The statements in paragraphs 1 to 7 hereinabove are true to my knowledge based on information derived from records maintained by the petitioner and I believe them to be true.

Solemnly affirmed by the said Mr. ....
in the Court House at Calcutta on
this..... day of ... 20....

Before me

Commissioner

Verification

Affidavit

70. Application to Arbitrator

Before the Learned Arbitrator Mr. R

In the matter of:

An application under s. 12 of the Arbitration and Conciliation Act 1996

And

In the matter of:

Challenging appointment of Mr. R as the Arbitrator.

...... *Petitioner*

And

In the matter of:

M/s. P. Co. Ltd., a company registered under the Companies Act 1956 and carrying on business at ......, Kolkata

...... *Claimant-Petitioner*

versus

M/s. X Co. Ltd., a company registered under the Companies Act 1956 and carrying on business at .... Kolkata

...... *Respondent*

To
The Learned Arbitrator, Mr. R.

The humble petition of the petitioner M/s. P. Co. Ltd., most respectfully sheweth:

1. In the arbitration proceedings between the claimant and the respondent Your Honour has been appointed arbitrator for deciding the disputes between the claimant-petitioner and the respondent. Such an appointment was made on January 7, 20....

2. Your petitioner states that after appointment of Your Honour as an Arbitrator, the petitioner M/s. P. Co. Ltd., through its Director and from the records in possession of the claimant came to know of the circumstances existing at the time of such appointment which gave rise to justifiable doubt as to Your Honour's independence and impartiality. According to the arbitration agreement dated .... the parties agreed to have an arbitrator who possesses the qualifications of an aeronautical engineer. Your special knowledge about the proper working of the engine and the electrical

fittings for safe operation of the aeroplane in the international route does not appear from your curriculum vitae.

3. As the settlement of the disputes between the parties requires special and technical aeronautical knowledge both theoretical and practical the petitioner humbly requests you to consider this aspect of the matter and give your decision before Your Honour commences or continues the arbitral proceeding.

4. This request is being made to avoid future complications and prolongation of the disputes between the parties.

Your petitioner, therefore, humbly prays Your Honour for a decision as to whether Your Honour will be pleased to commence and continue with the arbitration proceedings.

And your petitioner, as in duty bound shall ever pray.

Verification

Affidavit

71. Application for claim for award (Statement of Claim)

Before the Learned Arbitrator Mr. ....

(Set out cause title)

Statement of claim of Builder Co.

The claimant states:

1. On 10th June 20......... the Claimant entered into an Agreement with the Owner Company to construct a building on the land of the Owner Company according to specifications and sanctioned plan made available to the claimant at a total cost of ₹............. A copy of the Agreement is annexed hereto marked "A".

2. The Claimant took possession of the land, brought on the land labour and materials. The Claimant requested the Respondent to make the land fit for construction by clearing the site of all obstructions.

3. The Respondent failed to take any step to clear the site. The Claimant at extra cost made the site fit for construction thereon and demanded payment of ₹.......... as costs thereof. A copy of the bill is annexed hereto marked "B".

4. The Claimant started construction. There were disturbances at the site created by some locals and the work was delayed causing additional expenses for idle labour and plant and machinery. A claim therefor was made. A copy of the bill for ₹........ is annexed hereto marked "C".

5. The Respondent made part-payments from time to time against the bills submitted by the Claimant. The Claimant made claims for certain extra work and for escalation of labour charges and material costs for ₹............... Copies of the bills are annexed hereto marked "D".

6. In January, 20 ...... the Claimant requested the Respondent to take over possession of the building which was complete and asked for payment of its bills.

7. The Respondent made certain payments and took possession of the building but complained that some small fittings and fixtures were required to be made to make the building habitable.

8. As the outstanding claims of the Claimant were not paid the said minor repairs, fittings and fixtures could not be done.

9. In spite of several demands from time to time the Respondent delayed the matter and the Claimant requested the Respondent on 15th June 20.......... for referring the matter to arbitration.

10. The disputes were ultimately referred to this Learned Arbitrator for settlement.

11. The Claimant claims an Award for ₹......... the particulars of which are given in a schedule annexed hereto marked "E" and interest and costs.

12. The Claimant is entitled to and claims interest @ .... per annum on the Awarded amount.

The Claimant, therefore, claims an Award for ₹........... with interest at .... per annum against the Respondent and costs of the present proceedings.

Further and other orders/awards be made as the Claimant is entitled to.

Verification

Affidavit

72. Claimant's statement of claim

Before the Learned Arbitral Tribunal

In the matter of:

A Statement of Claim made under s. 23 of the Arbitration and Conciliation Act 1996

and

In the matter of

M/s. P. Co. Ltd., of Kolkata

...... *Claimant*

versus

M/s. X Co. Ltd., of ...., Kolkata

...... *Respondent*

Statement of Claim

The claimant states as follows:

1. The claimant is a company duly registered under the Companies Act 1956 and *inter alia*, carrying on business as the Manufacturer and Dealer in Teas. The respondent is a company duly registered under the Companies Act 1956 and carrying on business, *inter alia*, as dealer in, *inter alia*, in teas.

2. The claimant entered into a contract dated .... with the respondent whereby and whereunder the claimant agreed to sell and the respondent agreed to buy the tea produced and processed by claimant at an agreed fixed rate.

3. The said agreement contained an arbitration clause, covering the condition that all the disputes and differences arising out of or in connection with the said transactions in teas and related matters would be settled by arbitration. A copy of the said agreement is annexed hereto marked 'A'.

4. Pursuant to the said agreement the claimant had sold and delivered from time to time diverse quantities of teas of various grades and quality to the respondent.

5. The respondent had duly received the said quantity of teas, and appropriated the same. In this connection copies of relevant challans and copies of receipts of the said goods by the respondent together with copies of bills raised by claimant on the respondent for the goods sold and delivered to the respondent are annexed hereto collectively marked 'B'.

6. The respondent received the goods in good condition and appropriated the same towards the contract and sold the same and made certain small payments from time to time to the claimant. A copy of statement of such transactions is annexed hereto marked 'C'.

7. The relevant debits in connection with goods sold and delivered to the respondent and relevant credits issued by the claimant containing the statement of part payments made by respondent from time to time by respondent to claimant are annexed hereto collectively marked 'D'.

8. The claimant from time to time demanded payment from the respondent for the outstanding balance price of teas sold and delivered to the respondent by the claimant. The respondent duly acknowledged receipt of such demand letters and promised to pay as soon as the respondent was able to realise the total balance price of goods sold and delivered by the respondent to its customers.

9. The respondent failed and neglected to keep its promises and from time to time prayed for some time to pay, the outstanding balance amount of the claimant as soon as the respondent was able to realise the bills from its customers. Copies of such letters of acknowledgment of liabilities and promise to pay are annexed hereto collectively marked 'E'.

10. After giving credits for all sums of moneys paid and/or realised on behalf of the respondent there is now due from and owing by respondent to the claimant an aggregate sum of ₹... in respect of the outstanding price of goods sold and delivered to the respondent by the claimant upto 30th September 20.... The claimant is entitled to and claims interest at 16% per annum from the date of each bill till 30th September 20....

11. There is now due from and owing by the respondent to claimant an aggregate sum of ₹...... with interest calculated upto 30th September 20.... Statements of accounts are annexed hereto collectively marked 'F'. The claimant claims further interest from 1st October 20...... at 16% per annum till realisation.

12. In spite of demands, the respondent failed and neglected to pay the claims of the applicant being a sum of ₹...... or any portion thereof.

13. The respondent is bound by the Arbitration Agreement dated ....

14. As the respondent has failed to pay the claims of the claimant in spite of demands for payment of the same being raised, several disputes have arisen, the claimant referred the matter to this Learned Arbitral Tribunal, and pursuant to directions, the claimant has filed the present Statement of Claim.

15. No part of the claim of the claimant is barred by the Law of Limitation.

16. The respondent has no valid defence to the claims of claimant.

17. The claimant, therefore, claims an Award for payment by respondent of ₹...... with interest at 16% per annum from 1st October 20... till payment.

The claimant, therefore, prays for and claims:

(*a*) an award for payment of ₹...... in favour of he claimant and against respondent;

(*b*) interest from 1st October 20... at 16% per annum on the claimed amount till payment by respondent to claimant;

(*c*) costs of the present arbitration proceedings and incidentals thereto be paid by the respondent;

(*d*) further and other orders be made as the claimant is entitled to in law and in equity.

Signature of Claimant

Signature of Claimant's Advocate

Verification

Affidavit

73. Statement of defence and counter-claim of respondent

Before the Learned Arbitrator Mr. ....

(Set out cause title)

The respondent states:

1. This reference for Arbitration has been made on ....

2. I have read a copy of Statement of Claims filed by the Claimant and I have understood the contents and purport thereof.

3. The disputes between the parties arose on .... when the Claimant submitted bill for labour and materials escalation charges. The contract does not provide for labour and material escalation charges.

4. The Claimant slowed down the progress of the work of the building. The Respondent paid on protest several bills of the Claimant particulars whereof are given in a Schedule annexed hereto marked "A".

5. The Claimant wrongfully slowed down the construction work of the building in spite of repeated requests to expedite the work and complete the same. In this connection a copy of the letter dated .... is annexed hereto marked "B".

6. The Claimant from time to time raised bills for the work and the Respondent paid most of the bills.

7. All the bills of the Claimant were paid by the Respondent excepting the bill for escalation of labour and materials.

8. On notice to the Claimant the Respondent got the unfinished work done by workers under supervision of the Respondent's Manager.

9. In view of the breaches of contract by the Claimant and as a direct result thereof the Respondent has suffered loss and damages of ₹........... details whereof are annexed hereto collectively marked "C".

10. By a letter dated .... the Respondent gave reminder to Claimant to pay to the Respondent a sum of ₹........ with interest at 18% per annum. The Claimant received the said demand letter and by its letter dated .... stated that the matter was receiving attention. A copy of the letter is annexed hereto marked "D".

11. The Respondent states that alleged claims of the Claimant are not sustainable on facts and further the same are barred by the law of Limitation.

12. The Claimant is not entitled to any of its claims made in the Statement of Claims either under the contract or otherwise and the same are barred by the Law of Limitation.

13. No part of the Respondent's counter-claims is barred by the Law of Limitation in view of implied admission of liability by the Claimant, *inter alia*, in its letter dated .... a copy whereof is annexure "D" hereof.

14. The Respondent states that the Claimant's claims be rejected as not sustainable and barred by the Law of Limitation.

15. In view of the aforesaid an Award for ₹............. be given in favour of Respondent with interest at 18% per annum on the awarded amount till payment and the claim of Claimant be rejected.

It is, therefore, claimed that the Claimant's claims be rejected and the respondent's counter-claim be allowed and an Award be given in favour of respondent for ₹............ with interest at 18% per annum and costs and further and other orders be made as to this Learned Tribunal may deem fit and proper to afford complete relief to the respondent.

Signed

Verification

Affidavit

74. Statement of defence with counter-claim (Another Form)

Before the Learned Arbitral Tribunal

In the matter of:

M/s. P. Co. Ltd. of ...., Kolkata

..... *Claimant*

versus

M/s. X Co. Ltd., of ...., Kolkata

..... *Respondent*

Defence: Written Statement of the respondent to the Statement of Claim of Claimant.

The respondent states as follows:

1. The claimant had supplied teas at stipulated price and warranted and guaranteed that the tea supplied would be of top superior quality with good flavour. But the claimant on the other hand delivered the said goods to the respondent which were of substandard stuff with foul flavour and several customers of the respondent to whom the said goods were supplied had rejected the same on the complaint of foul flavour omitting from the teas when they were used for drinking purpose and complained of the same to the claimant.

2. The respondent rejected the entire balance quantities of tea being of inferior quality and not fit for human consumption by the customers of respondent and consumers of such teas.

3. In spite of such complaints made to the claimant by the respondent the claimant did not replace the said rejected teas with good quality tea.

4. In this connection the respondent annexes copies of the various complaints received from its customers as also copies of a various letters issued by the respondent to the claimant requesting for replacement of such substandard teas with good quality tea immediately. Copies of said documents are annexed hereto and marked 'A'. In spite of several reminders, the claimant has failed and neglected to replace the said defective teas supplied by claimant to the respondent.

5. In the premises the claimant is not entitled to any payment in respect of teas sold and delivered to respondent and specially after the various complaints received by the respondent from its customers regarding bad quality of tea and on that plea the respondent rejected the entire balance quantity of teas and requested the claimant to replace the same with good quality of standard tea fit for human consumption.

6. In spite of several requests made, the claimant failed to replace the said teas rejected by respondent's customers. The claimant thus failed and neglected to take back the balance quantity of rejected teas and replace the same with good standard quality teas. Copies of the various complaints of the customers received by the respondent are annexed hereto marked 'B'.

7. In view of the aforesaid, the claimant is not entitled to receive any payment as the price of goods sold and delivered by claimant to respondent inasmuch as the said bad quality teas stood rejected by its customers being unfit for human consumption as will appear from the various complaints received from its customers.

8. In the premises the respondent prays that the claimant's statement of claim be rejected. The claimant is not entitled to claim any payment from the respondent and the statement of claim of the claimant may be dismissed with costs.

9. The respondent further states that due to wrongful acts of claimant, the respondent had suffered loss and damages which the respondent is entitled to claim from the claimant by way of compensation.

10. The respondent has suffered loss of business as well as reputation and also loss due to incidental expenses incurred by respondent in receiving the teas and storing the same in its godowns and making appropriate arrangements for sale of teas to its various customers.

11. Further, due to bad quality of teas received and delivered by the claimant and supplied by the respondent to its customers who rejected the same, the respondent has suffered loss and damages in money and also suffered in business reputation in the market.

12. Further the customers of the respondent had to be duly compensated for such supply of defective teas unfit for human consumption.

13. In the premises, the claimant is liable to pay to the respondent by way of compensation the loss and damages suffered by respondent which loss and damages the respondent has assessed at ₹......... with interest thereon from 1st November 20... till realisation at 16% per annum.

14. The respondent further states that the claimant is not entitled to any payment as claimed by claimant or otherwise or at all. On the other hand, the respondent is entitled to claim an amount of ₹...... with interest payable from 1st November 20... at 16% per annum till payment relating to the claims of the respondent due to loss and damages suffered by the respondent caused by the claimant.

15. In spite of demands, the claimant has not paid the said sum of ₹......... or any portion thereof with further interest thereof to the respondent.

16. In the premises, the respondent claims by way of an Award of ₹...... in favour of the respondent and against the claimant with interest at 16% per annum from 1st November 20... till the award is passed and from the date of award on the awarded amount till payment by the claimant.

17. The respondent also claims the costs of the present proceedings to be paid by the claimant.

18. The respondent prays that the claimant's claim be dismissed with costs.

19. Further, the counter-claim of the respondent be allowed and an award be made for the said sum of ₹...... in favour of the respondent against the claimant.

20. No part of the respondent's claims is barred by Law of Limitation.

In the premises, the respondent claims for following orders:

(*a*) The statement of claim of claimant be rejected;

(*b*) an award be made for payment of ₹.......... payable by claimant to the respondent with interest at 16% per annum from 1st November 20.......... till payment;

(*c*) costs of the present proceedings and incidentals thereto be directed to be paid by the claimant to the respondent;

(*d*) further and other orders be made and directions be given as the respondent is entitled to in law and equity.

And respondent as in duty bound shall ever pray.

Verification

Affidavit

75. Application for termination of mandates of Arbitrator

In the High Court at Calcutta

Ordinary Original Civil Jurisdiction

Misc. case Arbitration No. ..... of 20...

In the matter of:

An application under ss. 14 and 15 of the Arbitration and Conciliation Act 1996 for substitution of Arbitrator

And

In the matter of:

Arbitration proceedings.

Between

P. Co. Ltd., a company registered under the Companies Act 1956 and carrying on business at .... Kolkata.

..... *Claimant-Petitioner*

versus

M/s. X Co. Ltd., a company registered under the Companies Act 1956 and carrying on business at .... Kolkata

...... *Respondent*

To
The Hon'ble Chief Justice and His Companion Justices of the said Hon'ble Court

The humble petition of M/s. P. Co. Ltd., the petitioner above-named most respectfully sheweth:

1. Your petitioner states that in the arbitration proceedings between the petitioner and the respondent regarding sale of goods, Mr. Z was appointed as Arbitrator.

2. Subsequent to the appointment it has come to the knowledge of the petitioner that the said Mr. Z, the Arbitrator, has become *de jure* or *de facto* unable to perform his functions (or, for other reasons he fails to act without undue delay) (or, he has withdrawn from his office).

3. Your petitioner states that for the purpose of proceeding with the arbitration it is necessary that this Hon'ble Court will decide as to whether the mandate of the Learned Arbitrator is required to be terminated.

4. Your petitioner states that this Hon'ble Court has the jurisdiction to hear the matter and give its decision that the Learned Arbitrator is incapable of further acting as Arbitrator.

5. This application is made to expedite the settlement of disputes between the parties.

Your petitioner, therefore, prays Your Lordships for the following orders:

(*a*) The mandate of the Arbitrator, Mr. Z, be terminated with immediate effect;

(*b*) Further and other orders be made as this Hon'ble Court may deem fit and proper to afford complete reliefs to your petitioner.

And your petitioner, as in duty bound, shall ever pray.

Verification

Affidavit

76. Application to Arbitrator to determine his jurisdiction

Before the Learned Arbitrator Mr. R

In the matter of:

An application under s. 16 of the Arbitration and Conciliation Act 1996

And

In the matter of:

A Ruling on the competency and jurisdiction of the Learned Arbitrator and as to the existence of Arbitration Agreement.

And

In the matter of:

M/s. P. Co. Ltd., a company registered under the Companies Act 1956 and carrying on business at ……, Kolkata

…… *Claimant*

versus

M/s. X Co. Ltd., a company registered under the Companies Act 1956 and carrying on business at ……… Kolkata

…… *Respondent-Petitioner*

To

The Learned Arbitrator, Mr. R.

The humble petition of the respondent M/s. X. Co. Ltd., most respectfully.

States:

1. Your Honour has been appointed as the Arbitrator in the aforesaid proceeding to decide the disputes between the parties.

2. Your petitioner states that a reasonable objection exists as to the validity of the arbitration agreement and as to the competence of your own jurisdiction to decide the matter.

3. You were approached by the claimant and you as the Advocate of the claimant carried on prolonged negotiation with the petitioner and expressed your views but failed to settle the matter. In view of this, the question of your competency and jurisdiction to decide the said matter as an Arbitrator exists.

4. The objection is raised along with the submissions of the petitioner's defence, wherein specific objections and grounds thereof have been stated, a copy whereof is annexed hereto for your ready reference.

In the circumstances your petitioner prays for a decision as to your competence to decide the matters in dispute.

And your petitioner, as in duty bound, shall ever pray.

Verification

Affidavit

77. Application for assistance to direct a person to give evidence before Arbitrator

Application No. ……… of 20…

In the High Court at Calcutta

Ordinary Original Civil Jurisdiction

In the matter of:

An application under s. 27 of the Arbitration and Conciliation Act 1996; for court assistance in the form of adducing evidence by a person

And

In the matter of:

M/s. P. Co. Ltd., a company registered under the Companies Act 1956 and carrying on business at ...... Kolkata.

...... *Petitioner*

versus

M/s. X Co. Ltd., a company registered under the Companies Act 1956 and carrying on business at ...... Kolkata.

...... *Respondent*

To
The Hon'ble Chief Justice and His Companion Justices of the said Hon'ble Court

The humble petition of M/s. P. Co. Ltd., the petitioner above-named most respectfully sheweth:

1. Your petitioner entered into a contract which contained an arbitration clause. The said contract provided for supply of tea by the petitioner to the respondent at an agreed price.

2. The petitioner-claimant sold and delivered the goods produced in its tea gardens to respondent at an agreed price. The agreement contained an arbitration clause.

3. Disputes and differences arose between the parties and pursuant to invocation of arbitration clause, arbitrators were appointed to resolve such disputes.

4. In court of arbitration proceedings it appeared that in order to verify the exact quantity and quality of teas supplied by the petitioner-claimant evidence of the principal consumer of tea who purchased the teas supplied by the claimant-petitioner to the respondent is necessary as they will be in a position to state the nature and extent of defect of tea purchased by said customer from the respondent as the tea was refused and rejected by them and payment of such teas was withheld on the plea of bad quality tea which was found unfit for human consumption.

5. Your petitioner requested the said consumer of teas but he has refused to co-operate and comment in any manner whatsoever.

6. Your petitioner states that the evidence of the said consumer of tea is very important and essential inasmuch as the said consumer is a leading tea merchant in the market with long experience in the trade and capable in certifying the quality of the tea properly. In the premises, the petitioner states that it is seeking the assistance of this Hon'ble Court to adduce evidence in the pending arbitral proceedings between the parties.

In this connection, the required particulars are as given below:

(*a*) Name and address of the claimant M/s. P. Co. Ltd. of ......, Kolkata.

(*b*) Name and address of the respondent M/s. X Co. Ltd. of ...... Kolkata.

(*c*) Name and address of arbitrator: Mr. M, son of ...... residing at ......

(*d*) The general nature of the claim is for recovery of price of goods that is teas sold and delivered by claimant to respondent.

(*e*) The Ld. Arbitrator has countersigned this petition as is indicated by his approval.

(*f*) Name and address of the person to be heard and examined as witness and statement of his testimony required:

(*i*) Name and address of witness to be examined:

Mr. ...... wholesale consumer, son of .... carrying on business at ......, Kolkata.

7. Your petitioner states that this Hon'ble Court has the jurisdiction to hear the present petition and to direct the said consumer to give evidence regarding the exact quality of tea produced by the claimant and sold to and/or through the respondent to Mr. .... wholesale consumer of tea who is the witness to be examined in the proceedings.

8. Your petitioner states that the petition has been made *bona fide* and in the interest of justice.

Your petitioner, therefore, most humbly prays Your Lordships for the following orders:

(*a*) Mr. ...... of ...... be directed to be present before the arbitrator Mr. .... at ...... on .... and his evidence be adduced directly to the Ld. Arbitrator;

(*b*) cost of the present proceedings regarding adducing of evidence given by the said Mr. ....shall be borne by the claimant-petitioner in the first instance;

(*c*) further orders be made as this Hon'ble Court may deem fit and proper so as to afford complete relief to the petitioner.

And your petitioner, as in duty bound shall ever pray.

Approved

....

(Arbitrator)

Verification

Affidavit

78. Application to Arbitrator for correction, interpretation, additional award

Before the Learned Arbitral Tribunal

In the matter of:

An application under s. 33 of the Arbitration and Conciliation Act 1996 for correction and interpretation of award and for additional award

And

In the matter of:

M/s. P. Co. Ltd., at .... Kolkata

...... *Claimant-Applicant*

versus

M/s. X Co. Ltd. of Kolkata

...... *Defendant*

The humble petition of the Claimant-Applicant above-named most respectfully sheweth:

1. The Learned Arbitrator has given the award dated 1st September 20.... This application is made on this 15th day of September 20... within the period prescribed in s. 33 of the Arbitration and Conciliation Act 1996.

2. The claimant states that in the award the following infirmities have been noticed:

(*a*) There is a computation error in the 2nd paragraph of the award where the total will come to ₹5,00,000 and not ₹3,50,000;

(*b*) In the fourth paragraph of the award there is a clerical error and/or typographical error such as the claims of the applicant allowed by the award will be ₹31,000 and not ₹13,000 as wrongly typed.

3. The fourth paragraph of the award appears to be vague and clarification and/or interpretations are required in respect of the following matters:

(*a*) ....

(*b*) ....

The applicant states that the aforesaid modifications and/or clarifications are required in the said award.

4. The applicant states that additional award is required to be made in respect of the following claims though made in the Statement of Claim and evidence adduced but the award is silent in respect of those claims and the applicant is entitled to an award in respect of the said claims

Particulars of the claims omitted from the award

(*a*) ....

(*b*) ....

(*c*) ....

5. The applicant has given notice of this application and served a copy on the respondent three days prior to moving this application.

6. This application is made within the period of limitation and in accordance with the provisions of s. 33 of the Arbitration and Conciliation Act 1996.

The applicant, therefore, prays for:

(*a*) necessary corrections be made as prayed for in paragraph 2 above;

(*b*) interpretations be given as stated in paragraph 3 hereinabove;

(*c*) an additional award be made as claimed in paragraph 4 above;

Signature of Claimant

Signature of Claimant's Advocate

Verification

Affidavit

79. Appeal from the order of a single Judge refusing to make interim order for protection of subject matter of arbitration

Appeal No. ……… of 20…

In the High Court at Calcutta

Civil Appellate Jurisdiction

In the matter of:

An appeal under s. 37(1) of the Arbitration and Conciliation Act 1996

And

In the matter of:

An appeal under s. 37(1) of the Arbitration and Conciliation Act 1996 from the original order dated 15th September 20… passed by the Hon'ble Judge, Mr. J. of this Hon'ble High Court

And

In the matter of:

M/s. X Co. Ltd., carrying on business at ……… Kolkata

…… *Respondent-Appellant*

versus

1. M/s. P. Co. Ltd., registered under the Companies Act 1956 and carrying on business at ……… Kolkata

…….. *Claimant-Respondent*

2. Mr. M. the Learned Arbitrator, residing at …… Kolkata

……… *Respondent*

MEMORANDUM OF APPEAL

Being aggrieved by and/or dissatisfied with the Order dated 10th September 20…, passed by the Hon'ble Mr. Justice J. in the appeal No. 5 of 20….., the appellant begs to prefer this appeal from the said order dated 10th September 20….., *inter alia*, on the following:

GROUNDS

I. For that the Hon'ble Judge erred in not appreciating and not granting an order of sale of the goods being the subject-matter of the Arbitration Agreement in spite of the fact that the said goods are of wasting nature.

II. For that the Hon'ble Judge failed to make an interim order for the proper preservation and custody of the goods being subject-matter of the Arbitration Agreement.

III. For that the Hon'ble Judge failed to make an order for sale of goods being the subject-matter of the Arbitration Agreement and being of wasting nature.

IV. For that the Hon'ble Judge erred in not directing the respondent to furnish security for the amount in dispute in the Arbitration Agreement.

V. For that the Hon'ble Judge failed to appreciate and erred in not doing so that in the facts and circumstances of the case the respondent should have been asked to furnish security for the amount in dispute being subject-matter of Arbitration Agreement.

VI. For that the Hon'ble Judge should have directed the respondent and erred in not doing so for detention and preservation of the subject-matter of disputes.

VII. For that the Hon'ble Judge failed to appreciate the need for appointment of Receiver and erred in not appointing Receiver over the subject-matter of disputes being the disputed goods covered by the Arbitration Agreement.

VIII. For that the impugned order appealed from is otherwise bad in law and in fact and the same be set aside and quashed.

The above are in my opinion, good grounds of appeal.

80. Appeal from the order of arbitrator about his jurisdiction (Another Form)

Appeal No. .... of 20...

In the High Court at Calcutta

Civil Appellate Jurisdiction

In the matter of:

An order dated 15th September 20... passed by the Ld. Arbitrator, Mr. M. on 15th September 20...

And

In the matter of:

An appeal under s. 37(2) of the Arbitration and Conciliation Act 1996

And

In the matter of:

An order of the learned Arbitral Tribunal represented by Mr. M.

And

In the matter of:

M/s. X Co. Ltd., carrying on business at .... Kolkata

...... *Defendant-Appellant*

versus

M/s. P. Co. Ltd., a company registered under the Companies Act 1956 and carrying on business at .... Kolkata

...... *Claimant-Respondent*

Memorandum of Appeal from the order of the Arbitral Tribunal dated 10th September 20... passed by Learned Arbitrator Mr. M.

Being aggrieved by and dissatisfied with the Order dated 10th September 20…, of the Learned Arbitrator, the appellant begs to prefer this appeal on, *inter alia*, on the following:

GROUNDS

I. For that Learned Arbitrator failed to appreciate and erred in doing so that in the facts and circumstances of the case. He had no jurisdiction to entertain and decide the disputes referred to him.

II. For that the Learned Arbitrator failed to appreciate and erred in doing so as the Learned Arbitrator exceeded the scope of his authority.

III. For that the Learned Arbitrator was otherwise wrong both in facts and in law in refusing to grant an interim measure of protection in respect of subject-matter of the disputes.

IV. For that the Learned Arbitrator failed to direct the respondent to furnish proper security in respect of the subject-matter of disputes.

V. For that the Learned Arbitrator was otherwise wrong both in facts and in law and therefore the said order of the Learned Arbitrator be set aside and quashed.

The above are in my opinion, good grounds of appeal.

81. Application for referring the parties to arbitration under the New York Convention Award

Application No. …… of 20…
In the High Court at Calcutta
Extraordinary Jurisdiction

In the matter of:

An application under s. 45 of the Arbitration and Conciliation Act 1996 for referring the parties to arbitration

And

In the matter of:

M/s. P. & Co. Ltd., carrying on business at ………., Kolkata.

………… *Claimant-Petitioner*

versus

M/s. X Co. Ltd., carrying on business at ………., Kolkata

…… *Respondent*

To
The Hon'ble Chief Justice and His Companion Justices of the said Hon'ble Court

The humble petition of M/s. P. & Co. Ltd., the petitioner above-named most respectfully sheweth:

1. Your petitioner states that an agreement for settlement of disputes between the parties herein arising out of a legal relationship considered as commercial under the law in force in India was made after October 1960. The said agreement was made in writing for arbitration to which New York Convention Awards as mentioned in the 1st Schedule to the Arbitration and Conciliation Act 1996 applies. The said agreement has been entered into in a territory on which the Central Government has by Notification in Official Gazette declared to be a territory to which the said New York Convention Award applies.

2. Your petitioner states that the petitioner and respondent have jointly entered into an agreement for the said arbitration.

3. Your petitioner states that the parties herein be referred to arbitration for the settlement of their disputes.

4. Your petitioner states that the said Agreement for Arbitration as per the said Act is operative and capable of being performed.

5. Your petitioner states that this is a matter under the provisions of New York Convention Awards as set forth in the 1st Schedule of the Act of 1996 applies and it is therefore necessary to refer the matter in dispute to Arbitration.

6. A copy of the said Agreement is annexed hereto marked 'A'.

7. This application is being made *bona fide* and in the interest of justice.

Your petitioner, therefore, humbly prays Your Lordships for the following orders:

(*a*) an order be made directing the matter in question be referred to arbitration in accordance with the said Agreement;

(*b*) costs of this application be the cost in the arbitration proceedings;

(*c*) further and other orders be made and directions be given as this Hon'ble Court may deem fit and proper so as to afford complete relief to your petitioner.

And your petitioner as in duty bound, shall ever pray.

Verification

Affidavit

82. Application for referring disputes to arbitration under Geneva Convention Awards

Matter No....... of 20...

In the High Court at Calcutta

Extraordinary Jurisdiction

In the matter of:

An application under s. 54 of the Arbitration and Conciliation Act 1996 disputes to be referred under the Geneva Convention Awards for arbitration

And

In the matter of:

M/s. P. Co. Ltd., carrying on business at .... Kolkata

...... *Claimant-Petitioner*

versus

M/s. X & Co. Ltd., carrying on business at ...., Kolkata

...... *Respondent*

To
The Hon'ble Chief Justice and His Companion Justices of the said Hon'ble Court

The humble petition of M/s. P. Co. Ltd., the petitioner above-named most respectfully sheweth:

1. Your petitioner states that the parties herein have entered into an agreement dated .... to refer the matter in dispute to which the Geneva Convention Awards is applicable to arbitration. A copy of the said agreement is annexed hereto marked 'A'.

2. The said arbitration agreement under which the disputes between the parties arose is valid and operative under s. 54 of the Act of 1996 and is capable of being carried into effect.

3. Your petitioner claims that the parties herein be referred to the Arbitrator for decision of their disputes.

4. Your petitioner states that the said matter of dispute be referred to arbitration which is valid under s. 53 of the said Act of 1996. Your petitioner states that the disputes between the parties herein be referred to arbitration according to the statutory provisions of s. 54 of the said Act of 1996.

5. Your petitioner states that the said agreement in still valid and operative and enforceable and could be always referred to arbitration under the provisions of s. 54 of the Arbitration and Conciliation Act 1996.

6. Your petitioner states that the disputes between the parties herein be referred to arbitration under the said Geneva Convention Awards for the necessary settlement of the disputes between the parties.

7. This application has been made *bona fide* and in the interest of justice.

Your petitioner, therefore, humbly prays Your Lordships for the following orders:

(*a*) disputes between the parties herein be referred to arbitration under provisions of the s. 54 of the Arbitration and Conciliation Act 1996;

(*b*) cost of the application be the costs in the said arbitration;

(*c*) further orders be made and directions be given as to this Hon'ble Court may deem fit and proper to afford complete relief to your petitioner.

And your petitioner as in duty bound, shall ever pray.

Verification

Affidavit

83. Appeal for setting aside award

Application No. .... of 20...

In the High Court at Calcutta

Ordinary Original Civil Jurisdiction

In the matter of:

An application under s. 34 of the Arbitration and Conciliation Act 1996

And

In the matter of:

An application for setting aside an arbitral award dated 1st November 20...

And

In the matter of:

M/s. X Co. Ltd., a company registered under the Companies Act 1956 and carrying on business at .... Kolkata

...... *Defendant-Petitioner*

versus

M/s. P Co. Ltd., a company registered under the Companies Act 1956 and carrying on business at .... Kolkata

...... *Claimant-Respondent*

To
The Hon'ble Chief Justice and His Companion Justices of the said Hon'ble Court

The humble petition of M/s. X. Co. Ltd. the petitioner above-named most respectfully sheweth:

1. Your petitioner states that disputes and differences arose between the petitioner and the respondent in connection with a contract containing arbitration clause. The matter was referred to the arbitration of Mr. M.

2. After statement of claim and statement of defence were filed the parties adduced evidence, examined witnesses and thereafter made submissions before the learned Tribunal.

3. On 15th September 2005 the learned arbitrator gave and published his award, a copy whereof is annexed hereto marked "A".

4. Your petitioner states that the said arbitral award be set aside, *inter alia*, for the following reasons:

The arbitral award was passed *ex parte* due to absence of the petitioner for some unavoidable reasons. Due to total strike your petitioner could not avail of any conveyance to reach the place of arbitration and the award was given *ex parte*.

5. Your petitioner states that the Arbitration Agreement is not valid under the law governing the parties.

6. Your petitioner states that the arbitral award deals with a dispute not contemplated and not falling within the terms of the submissions to arbitration.

7. The said award contains decisions on matters beyond the scope of submission to arbitration.

8. Your petitioner states that the arbitral proceeding was not in accordance with the agreement between the parties.

9. Your petitioner further submits that the dispute is not capable of settlement by arbitration under the law in force.

10. Your petitioner states that the said award is in conflict with the public policy of India inasmuch as the award was induced and affected by fraud, corruption as also it violated the provisions of ss. 75 and 81 of the Arbitration and Conciliation Act 1996. The Learned Arbitrator acted as a conciliator which conciliation proceeding failed and the knowledge acquired by him was utilised in giving the Award.

11. The learned arbitrator wrongly used and took advantage of the views expressed, admission made and the willingness of the petitioner to accept the proposal for settlement made by the conciliator. The Learned Arbitrator was not entitled to admit the evidence given in the said conciliation proceedings in giving the Award.

12. Your petitioner states that the said Award taken as a whole is in conflict with the public policy of India and is liable to be set aside and be set aside.

13. This application for setting aside the award is made within three months from the date of receipt of the award.

14. Your petitioner states that the said arbitral award be pronounced void and unenforceable and be set aside.

15. This application is made *bona fide* and in the interest of justice.

Your petitioner, therefore, humbly prays Your Lordships for the following orders:

(*a*) The Award dated 15th September 20....... given by Mr. M, the Learned Arbitrator, be set aside on the grounds mentioned;

(*b*) costs of this arbitration proceedings be paid by the respondent to the petitioner;

(*c*) further and other orders be made as this Hon'ble Court may deem fit and proper to afford complete relief to your petitioner.

And your petitioner as in duty-bound shall ever pray.

Verification

Affidavit

BAILMENT AND PLEDGE

84. Suit by a pawnee for money and sale of pledged ornaments

In the Court of .... at ....

Money Suit No. .... of 20.......

(Set out cause title)

The above-named plaintiff states as follows:

1. That the defendant borrowed from the plaintiff on........... a sum of ₹............ agreeing to repay the said loan with interest at...............% per annum and as a security for repayment of the loan had pledged with the plaintiff his gold ornament, as described below.

2. That there was no specific period mentioned for repayment of the loan.

3. That the plaintiff is entitled to recover from the defendant a sum of ₹....... inclusive of interest at ....% calculated till this date against the said loan.

4. That the plaintiff had made a demand in writing from the defendant for payment of a sum of ₹.......... by a notice dated .... served on the defendant by registered post with A/D., but the defendant did not comply with the terms of the notice.

5. That the plaintiff seeks sale of the pledge for satisfaction of his claim.

6. That the cause of action for this suit arose on............(date of refusal after demand) at.................. within the jurisdiction of this court.

7. Suit valuation:

The plaintiff, therefore, prays:

(*i*) For a judgment and decree for ₹........... together with interest @..........% per annum making a total of ₹.................

(*ii*) For sale of the pledged ornament and application of sale proceeds, less costs and expenses of conducting sale, towards satisfaction of the plaintiff's decree.

(*iii*) (*When necessary*) For permission to apply for a personal decree against the defendant for balance of plaintiff's dues in case the sale proceeds did not satisfy the plaintiff's claim fully.

(*iv*) Costs of suit.

Description of pledged article

Verification

Affidavit

NOTES: 1. For recovery of movable property from a depository or pawnee by a pledge limitation is three years from the date of refusal after demand—see Art. 70 of the Limitation Act 1963.

2. When no specific period for repayment, there must be an express demand by the pawnee for the amount due.

85. Suit by a pawnee for balance after sale of a pledged property

In the Court of................. at ....

Suit No. .... of 20 ....

(Set out cause title)

The plaintiff states as follows:

1. That the defendant borrowed from the plaintiff on................ a sum of ₹......................... and promised to repay the loan with interest at 8% per annum. The defendant further deposited with the plaintiff on................an ornament as a security against repayment of the loan.

2. That particulars of the ornament pledged with the plaintiff is described in the Schedule below.

3. That the defendant did not liquidate the loan in spite of repeated demands made in that behalf. The plaintiff last issued a notice dated.......... on the defendant by registered post with A/D demanding payment of the loan within.........days from the date of receipt of the notice. The defendant was warned in the said notice that in case the defendant failed to liquidate the loan within the period allowed, the plaintiff would sell the pledged ornament and appropriate sale proceeds thereof towards his dues. The defendant received the said notice on .... but did not comply with the notice.

4. That the plaintiff thereafter issued a notice dated........... of sale of the pledged ornament to the defendant by registered post with A/D and sold the ornament for ₹............on.........

5. That after recovery of ₹...........through sale of the pledged ornament the plaintiff is entitled to a further sum of ₹.........from the defendant on account of the loan.

6. That the cause of action for this suit arose on...........(date of pledge) at..............within the jurisdiction of this court.

7. That the suit is valued at ₹.............(balance due together with interest, if any) and *ad valorem* court-fees are paid thereon.

The plaintiff claims—

(*a*) ₹.............

(*b*) ₹............. as interest at the above rate for the period from................ to.................

Verification

Affidavit

NOTES: 1. Limitation—three years from the date of loan—Art. 19 (Old).

2. Notice of sale—must be a reasonable notice—see s. 176 of the Contract Act.

3. Return of pledged articles (Contract Act, s. 174) loan taken by loanee by pledging gold articles. Articles bequeathed to legal representatives by a will. Loan was discharged by legal representatives. Bank demanded production of Succession Certificate before returning pledged articles. *Held*, the Bank has no jurisdiction, as under s. 370 and s. 214 of the Indian Succession Act; pledged articles are not security and Bank is not a debtor of the deceased—*Branch Manager, S.B. of Hyderabad* v *Gadiraju Rana* AIR 1993 AP 337.

86. Suit by a bailor for recovery of money bailed

In the Court of .... at ....

Money Suit No. .... 20 …… .

(Set out cause title)

The plaintiff submits:

1. That the plaintiff had made over to the defendant on..............a sum of ₹...... to be kept in deposit until withdrawn.

2. That on.....................the plaintiff had requested the defendant to refund the deposit but the defendant avoided. Thereafter the plaintiff has served a notice dated........... on the defendant by registered post with A/D requesting him to refund the deposit but the defendant refused to refund the deposit.

3. That the cause of action arose on........... when demand for refund was made.

The plaintiff claims:

(*i*) for a decree of ₹......... against the defendant;

(*ii*) for costs of suit.

Verification

Affidavit

87. Suit by a bailor against a bailee for injury to goods bailed

In the Court of......................... at ....

Suit No. .... of 20 ....

(Set out cause title)

The plaintiff states as follows:

1. That the plaintiff and the defendant have been known to each other for long.

2. That before proceeding to New York the plaintiff had delivered his refrigerator to the defendant on.............. with a request to keep the same in good condition while in his custody and to return the same to the plaintiff on demand in working condition.

(When the bailee is not a gratuitous bailee add for a reward of ₹.............. payable to the defendant when the defendant redelivers the article on demand).

3. That the plaintiff had purchased the refrigerator on.............. at a sum of ₹............. and the article was almost new when the same was left with the defendant.

4. That the plaintiff returned to India on.................... and demanded redelivery of the said article from the defendant. The defendant delivered back the article to the plaintiff on................... in a completely damaged and improper condition and the said refrigerator is now beyond repairs and rendered worthless.

5. That for the negligence of the defendant, the plaintiff has suffered damages of ₹..........

6. That the cause of action arose on.............. when the said refrigerator was redelivered to the plaintiff in a completely damaged condition at............. within the jurisdiction of this court.

7. Suit valuation (value of refrigerator).

The plaintiff claims a decree of ₹............. as damages.

Verification

Affidavit

88. Suit by a bailor for negligence and failure to redeliver goods bailed

In the Court of........................ at ....

Suit No. .... of 20 ....

(Set out cause title)

The plaintiff states as follows:

1. That the defendant has been known to the plaintiff for long and he enjoyed reliance of the plaintiff.

2. That on............... the plaintiff had delivered to the defendant his TV set before he left for the continent to be retained by the defendant (or to be safely kept and taken care of by him) until demanded back. The defendant agreed that he would take due care of the TV set and would return the same to the plaintiff when requested.

3. That the plaintiff returned in the month of.............. and demanded from the defendant to return the set on................ The defendant has not returned the TV set to the plaintiff and the same has been lost to him.

4. That the said TV set was valued at ₹..................

5. By reason of the matters aforesaid, the plaintiff has been deprived of the said goods and has suffered loss and damages.

6. That the cause of action arose on .... when demand for redelivery was made at.................

The plaintiff claims:

(*a*) Return of the TV set from the defendant or in lieu thereof a decree for a sum of ₹....................... being value thereof in case the defendant fails to redeliver the same;

(*b*) a decree for ₹ .... as damages or for wrongful detention.

Verification

Affidavit

NOTES: 1. See s. 8 of the Specific Relief Act 1963.
2. Limitation—three years.

89. Suit by bailor against bailee for unauthorised dealing with goods bailed

In the Court of........................ at ....

Suit No. .... of 20 ....

(Set out cause title)

The plaintiff states as follows:

1. By a contract in writing dated .... 20......., the defendant agreed for reward to warehouse certain drapery goods for the plaintiff at the defendant's depository No. 5 .... Road, and on .... 20......., the plaintiff, in pursuance of the said agreement, entrusted the defendant with the said goods.

2. In breach of the said agreement and without the plaintiff's knowledge or consent, the defendant deposited a portion of the said goods at No. 6, ... Street. Particulars of the said goods are set out in Schedule 'A' hereto annexed.

3. On .... 20....., a fire occurred on the said premises No. 6 .... Street, and the said goods were destroyed.

4. The plaintiff had insured the goods with ......, giving No. 5, ... Road as the place where they were deposited, and as a result of the aforesaid unauthorised dealing with the goods by the defendant, the plaintiff has lost the benefit of the insurance.

5. The said goods were worth ₹..........

The plaintiff claims—

₹............. damages.

SCHEDULE 'A'

Verification

Affidavit

90. Suit by a bailor against warehouseman for damages for conversion

In the Court of............................ at ....

Suit No. .... of 20 ....

(Set out cause title)

The plaintiff states as follows:

1. That the plaintiff had engaged on.............. the defendant, a warehouseman to store in his warehouse at .... 20 bales of jute for reward and to redeliver the said articles to the plaintiff on demand.

2. That the parties entered into the said transaction by an agreement dated .... in writing.

The plaintiff craves leave of the court to produce the said agreement on call.

3. That pursuant to the said agreement the defendant had lifted 20 bales of jute, valued at ₹ ...., from the plaintiff's premises at .... P.S. .... District .... and stored the same in his aforesaid warehouse.

4. That the plaintiff had made his own arrangement for storing jute and requested the defendant by a letter dated ...., served on him duly, to redeliver the said 20 bales of jute at plaintiff's cost by ....(date when return desired). The defendant did not deliver back the same.

5. That on enquiry the plaintiff has learnt that the defendant delivered the said bales of jute to one A.B., once a partner with the plaintiff in a firm. The plaintiff was kept in the dark and the defendant had no justification to do that way.

6. That the plaintiff is entitled to return the said 20 bales of jute or value thereof as damages for wrongful conversion.

7. That the cause of action arose on .... (when demand was made and there was default).

The plaintiff, therefore, prays:

(*a*) For return of 20 bales of jute.

(*b*) In the event of the defendant's failure to return the same, then for a decree of ₹ .... as damages for conversion.

Verification

Affidavit

91. Suit against a workman for failure to redeliver goods bailed

In the Court of...................... at ....

Suit No. .... of 20 ....

(Set out cause title)

The plaintiff states as follows:

1. That the defendant runs a jewellery shop at .... in the town of...........

2. That the plaintiff delivered to the defendant on................ a pair of golden bangles for effecting repairs thereon. Since then reasonable time has elapsed.

3. That on .... the plaintiff had requested the defendant to redeliver the same (as required) but the defendant failed.

4. That the said pair of bangles weighed .... grams and is approximately valued at ₹....................

5. By reason of the matters aforesaid, the plaintiff has suffered loss and damages.

6. That the cause of action for this suit arose at .... within the jurisdiction of this Court on ....

The plaintiff prays:

(*a*) Return of the said pair of bangles or, in the alternative, damages for a sum of ₹.................

(*b*) ₹.................. for detention.

Verification

Affidavit

NOTE: Limitation—three years.

92. Suit by a bailee (borrower) against a bailor for injuries caused by undisclosed defects of things bailed

In the Court of...................... at ....

Suit No. .... of 20 ....

(Set out cause title)

The plaintiff states as follows:

1. That on......... the defendant had lent to the plaintiff a horse for riding for a reward.

2. That the defendant knew that the horse was vicious and would not tolerate a new rider and was quite unfit for the purpose for which the same was lent to the plaintiff.

3. That the defendant did not caution the plaintiff as to its nature.

4. That while riding the said horse on .... it jumped so high that the plaintiff was thrown down and as a result the plaintiff was severely injured.

5. That the nature of injury sustained by the plaintiff has been described below.

6. That the plaintiff has suffered damage as per account in Schedule "A" below.

7. That the cause of action arose on .... (date of hiring and accident if separate dates, on the date of accident).

8. Suit valuation (damages).

The plaintiff prays:

(*i*) Decree for ₹..............

(*ii*) Costs.

Particulars of injuries sustained by the plaintiff:

(State nature of injuries).

SCHEDULE—A.

Account of claim

₹....................

₹....................

₹....................

Total : ₹....................

Verification

Affidavit

NOTE: See s. 150 of the Contract Act.

93. Suit by a bailee against a bailor for injuries caused by faults of things bailed

In the Court of.................... at ....

Suit No. .... of 20 ....

(Set out cause title)

The plaintiff states as follows:

1. That the plaintiff had hired on .... for reward from the defendant his taxi and driver thereof for a journey from Cooch Behar to Siliguri.

2. That the taxi barely crossed 10 miles when the right front wheel of the vehicle went off, the vehicle dashed against a tree by the side of the road and turned turtle. That the plaintiff sustained severe injuries on his person in the impact. The driver also sustained injuries.

3. That there was a motor accident case and on investigation by an M.V. Inspector, on.................... it came to light that the vehicle was not fit when it was let out on hire.

4. That the defendant failed to provide the plaintiff with a suitable vehicle for the purpose for which the same was hired by the plaintiff.

5. That the plaintiff has suffered damages, valued at ₹.............as under.

(State here particulars of injuries and special damages, if any)

6. Cause of action.

7. Valuation.

The plaintiff, therefore, prays for a decree of ₹..........as damages.

Verification

Affidavit

NOTE: See s. 150—*Illustration* (*b*) of the Indian Contract Act.

94. Defence by gratuitous bailee to claim for injury to goods bailed

In the Court of .... at ....

Suit No. .... of 20 ....

(Set out cause title)

The defendant states as follows:

1. The defendant admits that he received the picture referred to in paragraph 1 of the plaint from the plaintiffs but says that the picture was already moth-eaten and injured by damp when received by the defendant.

2. The defendant did not keep the said picture in a damp place or in a place open to or infested by moths.

3. The defendant took all reasonable care of the said picture and has not been guilty of the alleged or any negligence.

Verification

Affidavit

BANK AND DEPOSITS

95. Suit by a (non-trader) customer against his banker for dishonouring a cheque

In the Court of....................... at ....

Suit No. .... of 20 ....

(Set out cause title)

The plaintiff states as follows:

1. That the plaintiff has a Savings Account No. .... with the defendant bank at its .... branch.

2. That the plaintiff drew a cheque No. .... dt. ....for ₹ .... on the said branch of the defendant bank payable to Sri..................

3. That at all material times the defendants had money of the plaintiff in their hands in the said Savings Account to cover up the amount in the said cheque.

4. That on .... said Sri .... payee of the cheque presented the same for payment at the defendant bank but the cheque was dishonoured without just cause.

5. That the plaintiff, by such act of dishonour, has been insulted and injured in reputation.

6. That the cause of action arose on .... (date when the cheque was dishonoured).

The plaintiff, therefore, prays:

For a decree of ₹ ....as damages.

Verification

Affidavit

NOTE: When a customer of a bank is a non-trader, he has to prove special damage to recover substantial damage. Otherwise he is entitled to a nominal damage—see AIR 1939 Cal 63.

96. Suit by a customer (trader) against his bankers for dishonouring a cheque

In the Court of.................... at ....

Suit No. .... of 20 ....

(Set out cause title)

The plaintiff states as follows:

1. That the plaintiff is a trader and carries on business in.................. under the name of......................

2. That in the course of his said business the plaintiff used to purchase goods from the market on credit.

3. That on ....20 ...., the plaintiff drew a bearer cheque for ₹....... on the defendant bank in favour of one (name the payee). The plaintiff usually made part payment of the price of goods supplied by the said payee, to the plaintiff on credit.

4. That on ....20 ...., he drew another bearer cheque for ₹...................... on the defendant bank in favour of one (name of payee) with whom also the plaintiff was in the habit of dealing, in payment of the price of goods supplied by him to the plaintiff on credit.

5. That the said cheques were duly presented for payment by the respective payees at the defendant bank on .... 20 .... and although the defendant bank had sufficient funds to the credit of the plaintiff's said account, they wrongfully dishonoured the said cheques.

6. That for non-payment of the said cheques, the said (payee) and (payee), have refused to supply any further goods to the plaintiff on credit and have threatened him with criminal prosecution whereby the plaintiff has suffered humiliation and his business credit has been greatly injured.

7. Cause of action (on the date of dishonour of cheques).

8. Suit valuation (on damages *ad valorem*).

The plaintiff claims ....

₹....................... damages.

Verification

Affidavit

97. Suit by a (trader) customer against his banker for dishonouring a cheque (Another Form)

In the Court of .... at ....

Suit No. .... of 20........

(Set out cause title)

The plaintiff states as follows:

1. That the plaintiff is a businessman and has had an account with the defendant bank at its .... Branch.

2. That the plaintiff issued a cheque No. ....dt. ....on the defendant bank for ₹................, payee being M/s. A.B. of .... against the latter's supply of three bags of ....(articles) on credit.

3. That the said payee of the cheque M/s A.B. had presented the cheque at the bank on .... but the defendant dishonoured the cheque though there was sufficient money of the plaintiff in their hands in the said account.

4. That for such dishonour of the cheque the said M/s. A. B. has stopped supply of further articles to the plaintiff on credit. The plaintiff has been injured in his reputation and business credit.

The plaintiff, therefore, prays for a decree of ₹........... as damages.

Verification

Affidavit

98. Bank's suit for recovery of its claims and enforcement of equitable mortgage against borrower and the guarantor

In the Court of............................ at ....

Title suit No. .... of 20 ....

"A Bank" a Body Corporate constituted under the Banking Companies (Acquisition and Transfer of Undertakings) Act 1970, and, *inter alia* carrying on business at .... within the jurisdiction of this learned court.

... *Plaintiff*

versus

1. Traders Co. Ltd., a company duly registered under the provisions of the Companies Act 1956 and carrying on business, *inter alia*, at within the jurisdiction of this learned court.
2. Mr. G, residing at .... within the jurisdiction of this learned court.

... *Defendant*

The plaintiff states as follows:

1. The plaintiff carries on business of banking having one of its branches at .... within the jurisdiction of this learned court.

2. The first defendant is carrying on business as a trader in diverse goods and obtained credit facilities from the plaintiff Bank in a Cash Credit Account with a limit which varied from time to time against hypothecation of all its movable assets and mortgage of its immovable property situate at .... all within the jurisdiction of this learned court. The defendant No. 2 guaranteed payment of all the present and future indebtedness and liabilities of the first defendant to the plaintiff.

3. At the request of the defendants, the plaintiff on .... sanctioned credit facilities to the first defendant in a Cash Credit Account with a limit of ₹5,00,000 on terms and conditions contained, *inter alia*, in the plaintiff's said sanction letter a copy whereof is annexed hereto marked 'A'. The first defendant duly accepted the said terms and conditions of the said sanction letter by duly signing on duplicate copy of the said sanction letter as will be apparent from the annexure 'A' hereof.

4. The plaintiff granted the said credit facilities to the first defendant in the said Cash Credit Account with a limit of ₹5,00,000 on the terms and conditions contained therein, and *inter alia* on the following terms and conditions:

(*a*) The advances would be granted and continue to be granted at the sole discretion of the plaintiff;

(*b*) The outstanding amount in respect of the said advances would be payable by the defendants on demand being made by plaintiff;

(*c*) Interest would be charged on the outstanding balance amount at 12% per annum with quarterly rates with liberty to the plaintiff to enhance the rate at any point of time at the discretion of the plaintiff, including the rates thereof;

(*d*) All the first defendant's present and future goods, produce, merchandise, bills, moneys receivable, book debts, plant machinery, stores, and spare parts and all other assets would remain hypothecated with the plaintiff as security for payment of all present and future indebtedness and liabilities of the first defendant to the plaintiff;

(*e*) The first defendant would deposit its Title Deeds relating to its immovable properties with the plaintiff at its said office with intent to create security thereon for payment of all present and future indebtedness and liabilities of the first defendant to the plaintiff;

(*f*) The first defendant would submit regularly all necessary statements and other information as might be required from time to time by the plaintiff;

(*g*) The first defendant would exhibit at its godown the name and address of the plaintiff's relevant Branch declaring that the first defendant's goods stored therein are remaining charged to the Bank.

(*h*) The first defendant would maintain a margin that might be required by the plaintiff from time to time in respect of the hypothecated assets as also in respect of the said credit facilities granted to the first defendant;

(*i*) The first defendant would not operate with any other Bank or Branch any other Bank Account without prior written consent of the plaintiff;

(*j*) The bills that might be deposited for collection at any point of time and the relevant securities would be collected by the plaintiff at the sole risk and responsibility of the first defendant and if such bills are not paid by the drawees thereof, then the first defendant would return the same forthwith and on any default thereof, the plaintiff would be compelled to debit the relevant amount of the bills in the relevant account of the defendant No. 1. Such bills would be collected at the sole risk and responsibility of the first defendant;

(*k*) On any default on part of the first defendant in observing any of the terms and conditions of the said agreement, the plaintiff would be entitled to call up the loans, demand payment and enforce the securities without giving any further notice to the first defendant.

The said and other terms and conditions will appear, *inter alia*, from the following banking documents:

(*i*) Promissory Note for ₹5,00,000 dated ....

(*ii*) D. P. Note Delivery Letter dated ....

(*iii*) Agreement of Hypothecation of Goods dated ....

(*iv*) Agreement of Hypothecation of Plant and Machinery dated ....

(*v*) Agreement of Hypothecation of Book Debts dated ....

(*vi*) Letter of Lien and Set-off dated ....

Copies of the aforesaid documents are annexed hereto marked "B" to "B 5".

5. In consideration of the plaintiff having agreed to grant, granting and/or continuing to grant the said credit facilities to the first defendant, at the request of the said defendant No. 2, the said defendant No. 2 guaranteed to the plaintiff due payment of all present and future indebtedness and liabilities of the first defendant with interest, costs, charges and expenses, waived its rights as a surety and agreed to remain liable as a principal debtor and declared that the said guarantee would be continuing and binding on his heirs and successors. The terms and conditions of the Guarantee will appear from a Letter of Guarantee a copy whereof is annexed hereto and marked "B-6".

6. The said charge and/or modifications thereof created by the first defendant in respect of its movable assets and immovable properties were duly registered with the Registrar of Companies and accordingly copies of relevant Forms Nos. 8 and 13 were duly certified by the Registrar of Companies, as duly registered, and copies of the said Forms 8 and 13 duly registered as such are annexed hereto and marked collectively as Annexure "C".

7. The first defendant availed of the said credit facilities in the said Cash Credit Account with a limit of ₹ 5,00,000 hypothecated all its present and future movable assets and created an equitable mortgage in respect of its immovable properties by deposit of Title Deeds and defendant No. 2 guaranteed the same by executing a Letter of Guarantee in favour of the plaintiff for due payment of all present and future indebtedness and liabilities of the first defendant to the plaintiff.

8. The first defendant availed of the said credit facilities in the said Cash Credit Account with a limit of ₹ 5,00,000 but failed to strictly observe the terms and conditions on which the said cash credit facilities were granted to the first defendant inasmuch as the said Cash Credit Account became and continued to be irregular, and in spite of several requests, the first defendant failed to regularise the said Cash Credit Account.

9. In view of the aforesaid, the plaintiff called up the loans and demanded payment from the defendants.

10. After giving credits for all the sums of moneys paid by and/or realised on behalf of the first defendant and after the necessary adjustments, there is now due from and owing by the first defendant to the plaintiff Bank in the said Cash Credit Account a sum of ₹ 7,00,000 with interest calculated upto .... The plaintiff claims further interest from .... till realisation at 12% per annum with quarterly rates. A Statement of Accounts, duly certified under Bankers Books Evidence Act is annexed hereto marked "D".

11. In spite of demands, the first defendant has not paid the said sum or any portion thereof. In spite of notice of such default and in spite of demands, the second defendant has failed and neglected to pay the plaintiff's claims herein. Copies of the relevant demand letters are annexed hereto collectively marked 'E'.

12. Under the circumstances, and in view of the aforesaid, the plaintiff Bank claims a decree for payment of ₹ .... with interest calculated at 12% per annum with quarterly rates till payment. Further, the plaintiff Bank claims a declaration that the movable assets mentioned in a schedule annexed hereto marked 'F' are remaining hypothecated to the plaintiff as security and the immovable properties mentioned in a schedule annexed hereto and marked 'G' are remaining mortgaged to plaintiff for

payment of all present and future indebtedness and liabilities of the first defendant to the plaintiff.

13. The defendants are residing at .... within the said jurisdiction of this learned court, the mortgaged immovable properties are situate at .... within the jurisdiction of this learned court.

14. This learned court has the necessary jurisdiction to entertain, try and determine this suit.

15. The plaintiff Bank now claims a decree for the said sum of ₹ .... with interest and costs, as applicable, liberty to sell and realise the hypothecated assets and to appropriate the proceeds in *pro tanto* satisfaction of the plaintiff's claims herein and a Preliminary Mortgage Decree in respect of the mortgaged immovable properties mentioned in Annexure "G" hereof with interest and costs as applicable thereof.

16. No part of the plaintiff's claims herein is barred by the Law of Limitation.

17. The plaintiff Bank has duly paid proper court-fees in stamps in respect of the claims of the plaintiff.

In the premises, the plaintiff prays for and claims:

(*a*) A decree for payment of ₹ .... against the defendants jointly and severally to the plaintiff;

(*b*) Interest from .... till the date of passing of the decree and thereafter on the decretal amount at 12% per annum with quarterly rates;

(*c*) A declaration to the effect that movable assets mentioned in annexure "F" hereof are remaining hypothecated with the plaintiff as security for payment of the plaintiff's claims hereof;

(*d*) A declaration to the effect that immovable properties mentioned in Annexure "G" hereof are remaining mortgaged with the plaintiff as security for payment of the plaintiff's claims herein;

(*e*) A preliminary mortgage decree for payment of ₹......... in respect of the said mortgaged immovable properties;

(*f*) Receiver;

(*g*) Injunction;

(*h*) Costs;

(*i*) Further and other reliefs as the plaintiff is entitled to in law and in equity.

Verification

Affidavit

99. Written statement of the defendants to the suit of the plaintiff for enforcement of claim and mortgage

In the Court of .... at ......

Title suit No. .... of 20.......

(Set out cause title)

The defendants state as follows:

1. The instant suit is not maintainable.

2. The plaintiff has no valid cause of action for this suit.

3. This learned court has no jurisdiction to entertain, try or determine the present suit and it is liable to be and be dismissed with costs.

4. Without prejudice to the aforesaid but strongly relying thereon the defendants now deal with the allegations and contentions contained in the plaint in the following paragraphs.

5. The statement contained in paragraph 1 of the said plaint is a matter of record.

6. With reference to paragraph 2 of the plaint, these defendants do not admit that any of the assets were hypothecated or any immovable properties were mortgaged to the plaintiff. It is denied and disputed that movable assets of the first defendant are situate at .... within the jurisdiction of this learned court. The immovable properties mentioned in the plaint are situate outside jurisdiction of this learned court. Further defendant No. 2 did not execute any Letter of Guarantee. But, the plaintiff however, got several documents to be signed by the defendant No. 2 and defendant No. 2 signed at blank spaces in those documents without knowing the purport, meaning and effect thereof as these documents were blank in several portions. Further, defendant No. 2 never intended to guarantee payment to the plaintiff as a Guarantor.

7. With reference to paragraph 3 of the plaint these defendants state that the said sanction letter is vague and the plaintiff did not act in terms of the said sanction letter.

8. With reference to paragraph 4 of the plaint, these defendant do not admit that the first defendant ever obtained any credit facilities in a Cash Credit Account with a limit of ₹5 lakhs or on any of the said terms and conditions mentioned in the said paragraph. These defendants further deny and dispute that the purported terms and conditions mentioned in the said sanction letter were ever agreed upon. The said purported claims are therefore not at all binding on these defendants. Further the several banking documents relied upon by the plaintiff as mentioned in the plaint, were not signed by the first defendant and the said documents were got signed without knowing the terms and conditions contained therein. The said documents are therefore not binding on these defendants.

9. With reference to paragraph 5 of the plaint defendant No. 2 was never given any opportunity to know about the nature, contents and effect of the documents as those were signed along with several other documents and the defendant No. 2 never knew the contents, purport, and effect thereof and these defendants never knew and never admitted their liability or guarantee to make payment of any amount as wrongly claimed by plaintiff from the first defendant. The purported Letter of Guarantee is not therefore binding on defendant No. 2 who merely signed the same with blanks in various places without actually knowing the true meaning, purport, and effect thereof.

10. With reference to paragraph 6 of the plaint these defendants state that the said Forms 8 and 13 were not clearly explained to these defendants inasmuch as the plaintiff got signed the said Forms Nos. 8 and 13 without explaining to either of the defendants, true meaning, purpose and effect thereof.

11. With reference to paragraph 7 of the plaint, these defendants deny and dispute that the first defendant availed of the said credit facility from the plaintiff in the said Cash Credit Account as alleged. The plaintiff did not disburse a substantial portion

of the said amount of credit facilities in the said Cash Credit Account with a limit of ₹5 lakhs and had committed breaches of the agreement as a result of which business of these defendants suffered heavily. The alleged irregularities in the said Cash Credit Account was hence caused by the wrongful acts of the plaintiff and not due to any failure or act of these defendants.

12. With reference to paragraph 9 of the plaint, these defendants state that they did not enter into any contract or agreement with the plaintiff and did not commit any breaches of the alleged contract and hence the plaintiff was not entitled to call up the loans or demand any payment and as such the demands are wrongful.

13. With reference to paragraph 10 of the plaint, these defendants do not admit the correctness, validity and legality of the entries in the Statement of Accounts annexed to the plaint. The plaintiff also failed and neglected to collect several bills from first defendant's customers the total amount of bills was more than ₹7 lakh. The plaintiff also did not return those bills deposited with the plaintiff for collection and against which plaintiff wrongly claims to have exercised its right of lien. Such act of the plaintiff was wrongful, illegal and contrary to agreement. Further Statement of Accounts as relied upon by plaintiff was not properly certified under the provisions of the Bankers Books Evidence Act and the entries are not correct and valid.

14. With reference to paragraph 11 of the plaint these defendants state that the alleged demand for payment is invalid and wrongful and illegal and the said claims are not due or payable by these defendants to plaintiff. Hence the plaintiff's letters were all wrongful and illegal and the contents thereof are incorrect. The plaintiff has not given any credit for several amounts being the proceeds of the bills drawn by the first defendant on its customers from time to time and thereafter handed over to the plaintiff for collection. The plaintiff has not given any correct and valid account for such bills as to the exact amount the plaintiff had collected. These defendants do know the total amounts realised out of the proceeds of each such bills. Hence these defendants claim a true and correct up-to-date Statement of Accounts showing the amount of bills deposited with the plaintiff for collection and the correct amounts that the plaintiff has actually collected including details of amounts yet to be collected. If the bills have been collected then there cannot be any amount outstanding and hence there cannot be any subsisting claim of plaintiff against these defendants. These defendants deny and dispute the correctness and legality of the said demand letters of the plaintiff and also deny their liabilities to the plaintiff to pay any amount to the plaintiff.

15. With reference to paragraph 12 of the plaint it is denied and disputed that the plaintiff is entitled to a decree for payment of ₹........ from these defendants or any interest at 12% per annum with quarterly rests or otherwise or at all. The plaintiff is not entitled to any declaration of mortgage of immovable property of the defendant No. 1 mentioned in annexure .... to plaint and denies that the erection of mortgage of any immovable property as mentioned in annexure 'G' to the plaint. These defendants state that the said land was never mortgaged and therefore the purported mortgage of the said immovable property is invalid and illegal. Further to the knowledge of the plaint, the said landed property is a Debuttar Property and it could not be mortgaged as wrongly claimed by the plaintiff in the said paragraph, for obtaining the said credit facility in the said account for the purpose of carrying on the business of the defendants.

16. With reference to paragraph 13 of the plaint, it is denied and disputed that no portion of the plaintiff's claims or cause of action is not withing the jurisdiction of this court.

17. With reference to paragraph 14 of the plaint, these defendants deny and dispute that mortgaged immovable property is situate at .... or within said jurisdiction of this learned court.

18. With reference to paragraph 15 of plaint, these defendants deny and dispute that the plaintiff is entitled to a decree for payment of ₹........ or any other sum. It is further denied and disputed that plaintiff has any right to sell or realise the proceeds of the landed property for appropriation to this account in *pro tanto* satisfaction of its claims. It is denied and disputed that the plaintiff is entitled to a Preliminary Mortgage Decree inasmuch there is no valid legal or equable mortgage created and as such the question of any payment of any interest thereon does not and cannot arise at all.

19. With reference to paragraph 16 of the plaint, it is further denied and disputed that no part of plaintiff's claim or cause of action is barred by the law of limitation.

20. With reference to paragraph 17 of the plaint, it is denied and disputed that proper court-fees in stamps have been paid in respect of the purported alleged claims of the plaintiff.

21. These defendants state that the plaintiff has no valid cause of action as against these defendants and the present suit is liable to be and be dismissed with costs.

Verification

Affidavit

100. Suit by a customer against banker for money paid by the bank on a forged cheque

In the Court of .... at ......

Suit No. .... of 20........

(Set out cause title)

The plaintiff states as follows:

1. At the time material hereto, the plaintiff had a current deposit account with the defendant bank.

2. In .... 20..., the defendant Bank sent to the plaintiff his pass book duly filled up. From the said pass book, the plaintiff found that he had been debited with a sum of ₹........ under date .... 20....

3. The plaintiff did not draw the cheque for which it was debited with the said sum.

4. The said cheque was a forged one and if the defendant bank had exercised due care and caution it could have detected the forgery.

5. The defendant bank is wrongfully refusing to make good the loss caused to the plaintiff as aforesaid in spite of demand made in writing on .... 20....

The plaintiff claims—

₹.................

Verification

Affidavit

101. Suit for recovery of money deposited with a bank

In the Court of .... at ....

Suit No. .... of 20........

(Set out cause title)

The plaintiff states as follows:

1. That the plaintiff made a fixed deposit with the defendant bank of India at its Dharmatala branch for ₹............. for a period of ....years.

2. That the defendant bank under the scheme of fixed deposit of the bank agreed to repay the deposit on expiry of the said period of .... years with interest at ....% per annum.

3. That the plaintiff requested the defendant bank on .... to pay back the deposit with interest.

4. That the defendant bank did not pay the money. The plaintiff is entitled to get back the amount deposited together with interest till the date of payment.

5. The cause of action arose on .... when demand was made on expiry of the ...... day of .... 20 ...... till which the money was kept in fixed deposit.

6. The plaintiff values his suit at ₹........ as per account in the Schedule below.

The plaintiff, therefore, prays for a judgment and decree for ₹............

Schedule.

Amount deposited in fixed deposit A/C No.	₹....................
Interest @ the rate of ....% p.a. on the said amount for the period from............... to	₹.....................
Add interest @ the rate of ₹.............. p.a. till	₹.......................
Rupees (In words)	₹.................

Verification

Affidavit

NOTES: 1. Amount deposited with bank for due performance of contract with the Government. In the absence of any contractual relationship with the officer of the Government with whom the deposit was meant to be kept as security, the banker is liable to pay to the depositor—AIR 1968 SC 1115.

2. Limitation for recovery of deposit—three years when the demand is made —vide Art. 22 of the Limitation Act 1963.

102. Suit to recover deposit from a private body

In the Court of the Civil Judge (Junior Division) at ....

Money Suit No. ....of................

(Set out cause title)

Suit for recovery of deposit

Claim valued at ₹...........................

The above-named plaintiff states as follows:

1. That A.B. deceased was the father of the plaintiff. The said A.B. was the Head Clerk of the .... Tea Estate, P.S. .... District ....

2. That the defendant No. 2 is a partner of the defendant No. 1 firm and was intimately known to the said A.B. who used to keep in deposit his moneys with the defendants from time to time. That on .... the said A.B. had sent to the defendant No. 2 per bearer four cheques for a total sum of ₹..................... duly endorsed and one thousand rupees cash with instructions to keep the same in deposit in the name of the plaintiff. The defendant No. 2 encashed the cheques and kept the same in deposit in the name of the plaintiff in the account of defendant No. 1 making a total of ₹........ only.

3. That by a letter dated .... the plaintiff had demanded refund of the deposit from the defendant No. 2. The said notice was sent per registered post with A/D. and was received by the addressee on............. but the money was not paid. A fresh demand was made by the plaintiff by his notice dated .... addressed to the defendant No. 2 by registered post with A/D. The latter notice came back with the endorsement 'refused'.

4. That the plaintiff is entitled to recover the deposit of ₹.......... only.

5. That the cause of action for this suit arose on .... when the demand for refund of deposit was made at .... within the jurisdiction of this court.

6. That for the purpose of jurisdiction and court-fees, the suit is valued at ₹ .... and *ad valorem* court-fees are paid thereon.

The plaintiff, therefore, prays for:

(*a*) recovery of the amount in deposit, and

(*b*) interest @ 10% p.a.

Verification

Affidavit

NOTE: Suit for repayment of deposit can be filed at the place of the defendant's business headquarters in India even though the deposit may have been made at the defendant's branch office outside India—*Alagappa Chettiar* v *A. Venkatachalam Chettiar* AIR 1973 Mad 162.

103. Suit for recovery of deposit

(See Form No. 102)

104. Suit for recovery of security deposit from Government

In the Court of the Sub-Judge .... at................

S.C.C. No. .... of 20 ....

(Set out cause title)

Suit for recovery of security deposit valued at ₹........... .

The plaintiff states as follows:

1. That the plaintiff-firm is a partnership business and Sri A.B. is one of the partners of the plaintiff-firm and is competent to sign and verify plaint.

2. That the then Sub-Divisional Controller of Food & Supplies .... by his Memo No. .... dated .... addressed to the plaintiff-firm, had instructed that as per Memo No. .... dated .... of the Deputy Commissioner of .... each trader seeking allotment of wagon, was to make a floating cash security deposit of ₹....... in favour of the Deputy Commissioner of .... under the head "Revenue Deposit" lest no consideration should be made for allotment of wagon.

3. That the plaintiff had accordingly deposited with the .... Treasury a sum of ₹.......... under the head "Revenue Deposit" on ....under Challan No. .... dated ....in favour of the Deputy Commissioner of ....The duplicate challan, duly signed by the Treasurer and the Accountant of the .... Treasury, is with the plaintiff.

4. That the aforesaid sum of ₹....... was retained by the defendant State as floating cash security and was a deposit to be held with the Deputy Commissioner of ....

5. That the aforesaid sum is lying in deposit with the State of West Bengal and the plaintiff is entitled to withdraw and/or to recover the same.

6. That several requests were made for refund of the said deposit but to no effect.

7. That the plaintiff firm thereafter has served a notice under s. 80, CPC dated ...... on the Collector of the district of .... by registered post with A/D through their authorised lawyer Sri .... Advocate.

8. That the cause of action for this arose on .... when demand for refund and/or withdrawal was first made by the plaintiff.

9. That for the purpose of jurisdiction the suit is valued at ₹....... and *ad valorem* court-fees are paid thereon.

The plaintiff, therefore, prays:

(*a*) For a decree enabling the plaintiff to recover the deposit of ₹........ by appropriate order to the defendant.

(*b*) For costs of the suit.

Verification

Affidavit

105. Suit for recovery of moneys wrongfully dealt with

In the Court of .... at ....

Suit No. .... of 20......

AB, son of late 'F' residing at .... within the jurisdiction of this learned court.

... *Plaintiff*

versus

1. Bank, a Body Corporate constituted under Banking Companies (Acquisition & Transfer of Undertakings) Act 1970 and carrying on business, *inter alia* at .... within the jurisdiction of this learned court.
2. CD son of late 'S' residing at .... within the jurisdiction of this learned court.

... *Defendants*

The plaintiff states as follows:

1. The plaintiff is the son of late 'F'. The said 'F' owned several properties both movable and immovable and by executing a Will appointed "CD" being defendant No. 2 as the Sole Executor of the said Will and the Trustee of the assets and properties of the late deceased 'F'.

2. The plaintiff is the only son, heir and sole beneficiary of the said Will of his father late 'F'. The said Will is dated ....

3. After the death of said 'F' the defendant No. 2 being 'CD' applied for and obtained a Probate of the said Will of the plaintiff's late Father 'F'. Thus the defendant No. 2 was appointed as the Trustee of the assets and properties of late 'F' and Executor of the said Will.

4. Defendant No. 2 after obtaining the Probate of the said Will has been managing the assets and properties covered by the said Will left by the said late 'F' the plaintiff's father, and defendant No. 2 has been acting as the Sole Executor as well as the Trustee of the assets and properties left by the Plaintiff's late Father 'F'.

5. Recently the plaintiff has come to know that the defendant No. 2 is a registered member of a club known as "Entertainment Club" in that locality and the plaintiff further came to know that the defendant No. 2 has opened an account with defendant No. 1 bank and at the time of opening of such account he submitted a copy of the said Probate of the said Will of plaintiff's father, being late 'F' and further stating that he is also the Trustee of the said assets left by the said testator of the said Will. On the basis of this contention of defendant No. 2 and the relevant documents produced by him copies whereof were duly delivered to the defendant No. 1 the said defendant No. 1 opened a current account in the name of defendant No. 2 as the Sole Trustee and Executor of the Estate, assets and properties of the said late 'F', the father of the plaintiff.

6. The plaintiff has recently come to know that the defendant No. 2 has been issuing regularly every month several cheques in favour of the said "Entertainment club" drawn on the said account opened by defendant No. 2 with defendant No. 1 bank in respect of all the assets and properties left over by the said Will of the late 'F' on which defendant No. 2 obtained a probate and thus became the Sole Executor of the said Will and Sole Trustee of the assets and properties left by the said late 'F' being father of the plaintiff.

7. The plaintiff states that the defendant being the Sole Trustee and Executor of the said Will cannot wrongfully utilise the assets and moneys left behind by the said late 'F' under the said Will inasmuch as the defendant No. 2 is bound to utilise the funds belonging to the said trust or held by defendant No. 2 as the Sole Executor and Trustee for the sole benefit of the plaintiff only as the plaintiff is sole beneficiary of the assets and properties left by his father late 'F' under the said Will of which defendant No. 2 has obtained a Probate and has been since acting as the Sole Executor and Trustee of the assets and properties left over by the said late 'F' and has to further administer the said assets and properties as Trustee and is bound to pay towards all receipts and income arising out of the estate, assets and properties left under the said Will to the plaintiff only.

8. The plaintiff has recently ascertained from reliable sources that defendant No. 2 has deposited with defendant No. 1 Bank different sums of moneys amounting to ₹ .... and further the said defendant No. 2 out of the said amount of ₹ .... has paid his club's bills to the extent of a total of ₹ ...., which sum the plaintiff states are the trust property to be utilised for the sole benefit of the plaintiff only inasmuch as defendant No. 2 cannot utilise such moneys to pay for his Entertainment

Club's bills as he is only the Sole Executor and Trustee of the said Will left by the late 'F' being father of the plaintiff.

9. Thus the plaintiff is entitled to and claims a sum of ₹ .... from the defendant No. 1 for wrongfully allowing the defendant No. 2 to utilise the trust funds for payment of personal Clubs bills of defendant No. 2. Defendant No. 2 is also liable to pay to plaintiff a total sum of ₹ .... on account of the moneys utilised by defendant No. 2 in criminal breach of his duties as the Sole Trustee and Executor of the said Will of late 'F' being father of plaintiff.

10. In this case, the plaintiff's cause of action arose within the territorial jurisdiction of this learned court and the defendants Nos. 1 and 2 are respectively carrying on business and/or residing at their respective addresses as stated above within the jurisdiction of this learned court.

11. No part of the plaintiff's claims herein is barred by the Law of Limitation, and this learned court has the necessary jurisdiction to entertain, try or determine this suit.

12. For the purposes of jurisdiction and court-fees, the instant suit is valued at ₹ .... on which the requisite court-fees in stamps have been duly paid.

The plaintiff, therefore, prays for and claims as follows:

(*a*) Decree for payment of ₹ .... against the defendants Nos. 1 and 2 jointly and severally with interest @ 15% per annum.

(*b*) Receiver;

(*c*) Injunction;

(*d*) Costs;

(*e*) Further reliefs as the plaintiff is entitled to in law and equity.

Verification

Affidavit

BOND

106. Suit on a simple Money Bond

In the Court of the ....

Money Suit No. .... of 20......

(Set out cause title)

The plaintiff states as follows:

1. That the defendant by executing a bond on ...... (and registered on ......) in favour of the plaintiff took loan of ₹ ...... from the plaintiff the same day at (name of the place of transaction) agreeing to repay the loan with interest at ...... % per annum on or before .... (or bound himself to pay to the plaintiff the sum of ₹ ...... together with interest at .... % per annum on or before ....). The said bond was subject to a condition that if the defendant paid to the plaintiff the sum of ₹ .... together with interest at .... % per annum the bond should be void). The plaintiff files the said bond herewith which may be treated as a part of the plaint.

2. That the defendant had paid on .... a sum of ₹ .... on account of principal and interest. The said payment has been noted at the back of the bond by the defendant himself. (Or, that the defendant did not pay any sum thereafter either towards principal or interest, as the case may be).

3. That after adjustment with payments so made by the defendant, the plaintiff is entitled to recover from the defendant a sum of ₹ .... as per account in the Schedule below under the said bond.

4. That the defendant did not pay the outstanding amount in spite of demands made by the plaintiff from time to time.

5. That the cause of action for this suit arose on .... (the date when the bond became payable) at .... (Place of transaction) within the jurisdiction of this court.

6. That for the purpose of jurisdiction and court-fees the suit is valued at ₹........ and *ad valorem* court-fees are paid thereon.

The plaintiff claims:

(*i*) For a judgment and decree for ₹...... as per account in the Schedule below.

(*ii*) All costs of suit.

SCHEDULE OF CLAIM

Verification

Affidavit

NOTES: 1. In an action on the bond with other conditions, it should set out the terms of the bond and its conditions and state each breach and claim damages as though the bond were an express covenant by the defendant to do the various acts specified in the conditions—*Odgers' Principles of Pleading and Practice* at p. 173 (21st Ed.).

2. Distinction between registered and unregistered bonds is no longer thereafter the Limitation Act 1963. Limitation is three years for both kinds of bond.

3. Where a day is specified in the bond the cause of action arises on the day so specified and limitation is three years from the day so specified under Art. 28 of the Limitation Act. But where no such day is specified, the cause of action arises on the date of execution of the bond. Limitation is three years from the date of the bond under Art. 29 of the Limitation Act 1963. Again, in a bond which is subject to a condition, the cause of action will arise when the condition is broken and suit is to be filed within three years from such date under Art. 30 of the Act.

107. Suit on an Instalment Bond (Simple Form without a default clause)

In the Court of .... at ....

Suit No. .... of 20...

(Set out cause title)

The above-named plaintiff states as follows:

1. That the defendant owed the plaintiff a sum of ₹......... only.

2. That the defendant in consideration of the said loan had executed on ..... an Instalment Bond promising therein to liquidate the said loan by 10 equal annual

instalments payable by the 31st December each year and beginning with December, 20... together with interest at 10% per annum on the principal sum then remaining due and in case the defendant paid instalments as agreed, the bond in question shall become void.

3. That the defendant paid instalments falling in December, 20 ...... to December, 20 ... and the instalment due in December, 20 ...... has not been paid. Remaining instalments have not become due as yet.

4. That the plaintiff is entitled to recover from the defendant a sum of ₹....... plus interest on ₹........ from 1.1.20 ...... up to the date of suit amounting to ₹......

5. That the cause of action for this suit arose on 1.1.20... on expiry of 31.12.20 ... (when the instalment fell due) at .... within the jurisdiction of this court.

6. Suit valuation (as per claim).

The plaintiff claims:

A decree for ₹...... as per account in the Schedule below.

Account of Claim

Instalment due in December, 20...	₹ ....
Interest on instalment due in December, 20... and remaining instalment @ 10% per annum	₹ ....
Total	₹ ....

Verification

Affidavit

NOTES: 1. Unless there be express promise in the bond to sue for the entire amount—suit may be instituted for defaulted instalments.

2. Article 36 of the Limitation Act 1963 will apply when a bond is payable by instalments. Limitation is three years from the expiration of the first term of payment as to the part then payable; and for the other parts, from the date of expiration of the respective terms of payment. It applies only to those cases when the plaintiff claims recovery of the instalment in respect of which there was default and not for the whole amount in the bond which case is governed by Art. 37 of the Act—AIR 1963 All 273. Instalment Decree—Decree-holder not exercising option under default clause—Art. 136 of the Limitation Act governs—*Champalal Jajodia (ex parte)* v *LIC* AIR 1984 Cal 158.

108. Suit based on an Instalment Bond with default clause

In the Court of .... at ....

Money Suit No. .... of 20...

(Set out cause title)

The plaintiff states as follows:

1. The defendant was indebted to the plaintiff in the sum of ₹ .... for the price of goods sold and delivered to the defendant by the plaintiff and in consideration of the plaintiff, at the defendant's request, forbearing to sue the defendant for the time being, the defendant executed a bond on ...... 20 ...... whereby he became bound to the plaintiff in the said sum of ₹......... subject to the condition—

(*a*) that the said bond should be void in case the defendant paid to the plaintiff on the .... day of ...... and ...... day of ...... 20 ...... the .... day of .... 20 ...... the sum of ₹...... per annum until the whole of the said sum of ₹ .... should be fully paid, but

(*b*) in case any of the said payments should from any clause whatever, not be paid upon the days hereinbefore mentioned then the whole balance then remaining unpaid, of the said sum of ₹........ with interest forthwith become due and payable.

2. The defendant paid the first instalment on the due date, but paid the 2nd and the 3rd instalments after they became due, that is, on .... 20 .... and .... 20 .... respectively, and the plaintiff accepted the said payments at the verbal request of the defendant and upon the understanding that the plaintiff was not waiving thereby the right to claim the entire balance in case of default in payment of any of the subsequent instalments.

3. The defendant has not paid any other instalment. The entire balance has been recoverable.

The plaintiff prays for and claims:

(*a*) a decree for the principal amount,

(*b*) interest @ 10% p.a.

Particulars of claim:

Principal amount of instalments unpaid ₹ ....

Interest upto ₹ ....

Net amount due ₹ ....

Verification

Affidavit

109. Suit on an Instalment Bond with a default clause (Alternative Form)

In the Court of .... at ....

Suit No. .... of 20...

(Set out cause title)

The plaintiff states:

1. That the defendant on ...... took from the plaintiff a loan of ₹........ and promised to repay the said loan with interest at 10% per annum.

2. That on the occasion of taking loan the defendant on the said date had executed in favour of the plaintiff an Instalment Bond agreeing to liquidate the loan with interest by six (or number as agreed) annual instalments beginning with January, 20....

3. That in the said bond, the defendant agreed that on default in any one of such instalments, the entire money then due should be payable at once and the plaintiff shall be competent to recover the same, if necessary, by a suit.

4. That the defendant paid two annual instalments in time but defaulted to pay the third instalment which fell due in January, 20.... The plaintiff is entitled to recover all moneys together with stipulated interest as per statement of claim in the Schedule appended below.

5. That the cause of action for this suit arose at ...... within the jurisdiction of this court on ...... (the date of loan) and thereafter on the first day of February, 20....., on expiry of January, 20....., when the defendant defaulted in payment of the third instalment.

6. That the plaintiff values his suit at ₹......... and pays court-fees on such.

The plaintiff, therefore, prays:

(*i*) For a decree for ₹........ as per statement of claim in the Schedule below.

(*ii*) For cost of suit.

SCHEDULE

Statement of Claim

Verification

Affidavit

NOTES: 1. In a bond which is payable by instalments and which provides that if default be made in payment of one or more instalments, the whole shall be due—Art. 37 of the Limitation Act will govern. Period of limitation is three years from when the default is made unless where the payee or obligee waives the benefit of the provision and thus when fresh default is made in respect of which there is no such waiver.

2. There must be clear averment in the plaint as to waiver. 'Demand' need not be pleaded. If, however, the bond provides a clause for 'demand' a demand prior to institution of suit is necessary and should be pleaded in the plaint.

110. Suit by employer against employee for breach of condition of a bond not to engage in business in competition with the employer

In the Court of .... at ....

Suit No. .... of 20......

(Set out cause title)

The plaintiff states as follows:

1. The plaintiff carries on business in .... at ....

2. On .... 20......., the plaintiff took the defendant into his employment as a travelling agent and agreed in writing to continue to employ him in connection with the said business at a salary of ₹....... *per month*, for a period of 5 years.

3. In consideration thereof the defendant by his bond of even date bound himself to pay to the plaintiff the sum of ₹ .... as and for liquidated damages, subject to the condition that the said bond should be void if the defendant should not during the term of his employment, whether in his present or any other capacity, carry on or be engaged or concerned or take part in the business of .... within the city of .... except on behalf of or with the consent of the plaintiff in writing.

4. The plaintiff discovered on ...., that since .... 20......, the defendant had been carrying on or taking part in the said business of .... within the said city of .... on his own account and without the knowledge or consent of the plaintiff.

The plaintiff claims—

₹........ as and for liquidated damages.

Verification

Affidavit

111. Suit by executors of a deceased partner against surviving partners on a bond to secure payment by instalments of the share of the deceased partner and for indemnity against the partnership liabilities

In the Court of .... at ....
Suit No. .... of 20.....
(Set out cause title)

The plaintiff states as follows:

1. One A.B. since deceased, and the defendants carried on business in partnership under the style of "..............."

2. The said A.B. died on the .... day of .... during the subsistence of the said partnership having by his will dated .... appointed the plaintiffs his executors who duly proved the said will on .... day of ....

3. On ...., the accounts of the said partnership were examined by the parties and the amount then owing to the plaintiffs as such executors on account of the share and interest of the said A.B. deceased, was ascertained and agreed to be the sum of ₹ ....

4. The defendants were unable to pay the said sum and executed a bond on the .... day of ...., whereby they became bound to the plaintiffs in the said sum of ₹ .... subject to the condition that the said bond should be void in case the defendants or either of them should pay to the plaintiffs on the .... day of .... and .... day of .... in every year commencing with the .... day of .... the sum of ₹ .... together with interest on the said sum of ₹ .... or such part thereof as would for the time being remain unpaid, at the rate of 6% *per annum*, until the whole of the said sum of ₹ .... should be fully paid.

5. By the said bond the defendants also agreed to keep fully and effectually indemnified the legal representatives of the said A.B. deceased, his estate and effects from all debts, liabilities, claims and demands which then were or might at any time thereafter be or become due to or be made by any person or persons, from or against the said legal representatives of the said A.B., his estate and effects, by reason of the said A.B. having been a member of the said partnership.

6. The defendants paid the first instalment of ₹ .... on the due date but have not paid any other instalment.

7. On ...., one J.D., a creditor of the partnership, executed his decree dated .... for ₹ .... in Suit No. .... of .... of this court, in respect of partnership debts incurred before the death of A.B. and on .... the plaintiffs were obliged to pay to the said J.D. the said sum in satisfaction of his decree.

PARTICULARS OF CLAIM:

Balance of instalments due	...	₹ ....
Interest at 6 *per cent. per annum*	...	₹ ....
Amount paid to J.D.	...	₹ ....
Interest on the said sum at 6 *per cent. per annum* by way of damages	...	₹ ....
Total Amount	...	₹ ....

The plaintiffs claim—

(1) ₹............

(2) Further interest at 6%.

Verification

Affidavit

112. Suit on a Security Bond

In the Court of .... at ....

Suit No. .... of 20.........

(Set out cause title)

The plaintiff states as follows:

1. That the plaintiff had appointed in the month of ...... 20 ...... one A.B., as his agent for sale of ...... manufactured by the plaintiff. The said A.B. was introduced to the plaintiff by the defendant.

2. That a Security Bond executed by the defendant on ...... the defendant had agreed *inter alia* that if the said A.B. failed to discharge his responsibilities as an agent or failed to account for all moneys received by him for and on behalf of the plaintiff and if the plaintiff suffered any loss for acts of omission by the said A.B., the defendant shall compensate such loss on reference being made to the defendant.

3. That the said A.B., acted as the plaintiff's agent for the period from ...... to ...... 20 ...... The plaintiff has learnt reliably that the said A.B. collected from the market a sum of ₹ .... as sale proceeds of ...... but did not make over the money to the plaintiff. Thereupon the plaintiff had intimated the defendant in writing by a notice dated ......, sent by registered post with A/D, that the said A.B., as agent of the plaintiff, collected on behalf of the plaintiff a sum of ₹ ...... within the period from ...... to ...... 20 ...... but did not pay to the plaintiff. In the said notice the defendant was held responsible for the money on the basis of the aforesaid Security Bond. The defendant received the notice but neither A.B., nor the defendant paid the money.

4. That the plaintiff is entitled to recover the said sum of ₹ .... together with interest as per account below.

5. Cause of action.

6. Suit valuation.

The plaintiff, therefore, prays for recovery of ₹ ...... as per account below.

ACCOUNT OF CLAIM

Verification

Affidavit

NOTES: 1. In a suit like the above, the conditions of security and breaches thereof should be specifically pleaded in the plaint.

2. Limitation—three years from the date.

113. Suit on a Fidelity Bond

In the Court of .... at ....

Suit No. .... of 20...

(Set out cause title)

The plaintiff states:

1. That the plaintiff is a manufacturer of cosmetic goods, the same having a good market in diverse districts of West Bengal.

2. Before entering into the service under the plaintiff, the defendant executed on the ...... day of ......20 a bond to the plaintiff of a sum of ₹ .... The condition of

the bond was that if the defendant would faithfully discharge the duties of collection of the sale proceeds of cosmetic goods from different markets and honestly account for and pay over to the plaintiff all moneys coming to his hands for and on behalf of the plaintiff, the bond should be void, otherwise the same should remain in full force.

3. That the defendant had collected during the period from ...... to ...... a sum of ₹ .... from different markets in Jalpaiguri and West Denajpore but did not credit the moneys so received to the plaintiff. It follows that the defendant has misappropriated the said sum of ₹........

4. Cause of action.

5. Suit valuation.

The plaintiff, claims,—

(*a*) Decree for ₹....... with damages thereon at $12^1/_2$% per annum (from the date of collection) till realisation; and

(*b*) Costs.

Verification

Affidavit

114. Suit by employer against guarantor on a Fidelity Bond

In the Court of .... at ....

Suit No. .... of 20...

(Set out cause title)

The plaintiff states that:

1. On 5th July 20..........., the plaintiff, at the request of the defendant, took one G.H. into his service and employment as his managing clerk upon certain terms and conditions contained in an agreement in writing dated .... and made between the plaintiff and the said G.H., in consideration whereof the defendant executed a bond dated .... for the payment to the plaintiff of the sum of ₹.........

2. The conditions of the bond were to the effect:

(*a*) That the said G.H. at all times during the continuance of his service and employment as aforesaid should honestly, diligently and faithfully discharge his duties as the managing clerk to the plaintiff.

(*b*) That the defendant will indemnify the plaintiff against all losses, damages and expenses which the plaintiff may sustain or incur by reason of any dishonesty, want of diligence or of faithfulness on the part of the said G.H. towards the plaintiff during the course of his service and employment.

(*c*) That the guarantee shall be a continuing guarantee to the plaintiff up to but not exceeding altogether the sum of ₹...... for the whole ultimate balance that shall be due to the plaintiff from the said G.H. in respect of any of the losses, damages and expenses aforesaid with interest thereon at 6 *per cent. per annum.*

3. The said G.H. did not during the continuance of his service and employment, honestly, diligently and faithfully discharge the duties of the managing clerk to the plaintiff and did not honestly account for, nor pay over, to the plaintiff all moneys received by him for and on behalf of the plaintiff.

PARTICULARS:

(*a*) On ...., the said G.H. received ₹....... from one K.D. for and on behalf of the plaintiff and dishonestly appropriated the same to his own use.

(*b*) The said G.H. colluded with one B.D., who owed the plaintiff ₹......, and did not take any steps to realise the said amount from the said B.D., which it was his duty to do, with the result that the said debt became time-barred on ...., and the plaintiff has lost the said sum.

PARTICULARS OF CLAIM:

.... 20.........	Amount misappropriated	...	₹ ....
	Interest at 6% from .... to	...	₹ ....
.... 20..........	Amount allowed to be time-barred	...	₹ ....
	Interest at 6% from .... to	...	₹ ....
	Total	...	₹ ....

The plaintiff claims—

(1) ₹.......

(2) Further interest at the rate of 6% until payment or judgment.

Verification

Affidavit

115. Suit on Bond

In the Court of .... at ....

Suit No. .... of 20...

(Set out cause title)

The plaintiff states that:

1. On ...... 20 ...., the defendant borrowed ₹ .... from the plaintiff and executed a bond by which he bound himself to pay to the plaintiff the said sum on the ...... day of ...... 20 ...... (or on demand) with interest for the same at the rate of 9 per cent per annum.

2. The defendant has not made any payment towards the said loan on repeated demands.

PARTICULARS OF CLAIM

Principal sum	...	...	₹......
Interest at 9 per cent per annum from date of default, till date of suit		...	₹......
		Total	₹......

The plaintiff claims .... ₹......

and further interest @ 9% p.a. till payment.

Verification

Affidavit

BROKER

116. Suit by a broker for commission and expenses

In the Court of .... at ....

Money Suit No. .... of 20...

(Set out cause title)

The plaintiff states as follows:

1. That the plaintiff is a broker on commission for sale of house premises.

2. That the defendant intended to sell his house premises situate at .... and engaged the plaintiff on .... orally as his broker and agent for sale thereof to any intending purchaser and agreed that the defendant would pay to the plaintiff a commission at the rate of 3% on the price of the house premises in case the transaction materialized.

3. That the plaintiff by negotiation had settled the sale of the defendant's house premises to Sri ...... son of ...... at a consideration of ₹ ...... And, on ...... the defendant sold to the said ...... the defendant's house premises by a registered deed of sale for a consideration of ₹ ......

4. That out of the said transaction the plaintiff is entitled to a commission of ₹ ...... at the above agreed rate.

5. That the plaintiff requested the defendant on .... to pay to the plaintiff his commission but the defendant avoided payment of the same on flimsy pretexts.

6. That the cause of action arose on ...... (the date of sale) when the money became payable to the plaintiff at ...... within the jurisdiction of this court.

7. That the plaintiff values his suit at ₹ .... (the amount of commission) and pays court-fees thereon.

The plaintiff, therefore, prays for—(*a*) a decree of ₹ ....

(*b*) interest at the rate of......... till realisation of the plaintiff's dues (if desired).

Verification

Affidavit

CANCELLATION OF A DEED

117. Suit for setting aside a transfer effected by a certificated guardian

In the Court of District Judge at ....

Suit No. .... of 20...

(Set out cause title)

The plaintiff states as follows:

1. That the defendant No. 1 was appointed a guardian of the property of the plaintiff, when he was minor in Misc. (Guardianship) Case No. .... of 20... by the District Judge of ....

2. That the plaintiff owned, among others, the property described in the Schedule below, which is the subject-matter of the suit and will hereinafter be referred to as suit-property.

3. That the plaintiff has attained majority on .... 20....

4. That the defendant No. 1 as the certificated guardian of the plaintiff sold for a consideration of ₹ ...... only to one A.B. defendant No. 2 the suit-property by a registered sale-deed on ...... by obtaining permission of the District Judge ...... on ...... on false representation that the money was required for maintenance of the plaintiff.

5. That the plaintiff at the material time had enough properties by which his maintenance could be well-afforded and there was absolutely no necessity to sell the suit-property for a paltry sum of ₹ .... The said sale was not for the welfare and benefit of the plaintiff. The plaintiff further believes that the consideration money, received by the defendant No. 1, was not applied to the plaintiff's maintenance.

6. That the cause of action for this suit arose on .... (date of sale) and subsequently on .... when the plaintiff attained majority.

7. That for the purpose of jurisdiction and court-fees the suit is valued at ₹ ...... (amount of consideration).

The plaintiff, therefore, prays:

(*a*) For a judgment and decree for setting aside the sale dated .... in respect of the suit-property.

(*b*) For khas possession of the suit-property by evicting the defendant No. 2

SCHEDULE

(State here description of the suit-property)

Verification

Affidavit

NOTES: 1. Cancellation of instrument is provided for under s. 31 of the Specific Relief Act 1963—Limitation Art. 59 of the Limitation Act 1963.

2. A transfer by a legal guardian (*de jure*) as for example a transfer by a natural guardian is valid.

3. A transfer of the Hindu minor's property by his *de facto* guardian being in the nature of *ultra vires* act it is open to the minor when he attains majority to repudiate it if it was not for his benefit or for his necessity—*Hari Satya Banerjee* v *Mahadev Banerjee* AIR 1983 Cal 76.

Legal necessity—The recital in the sale-deed that sale was executed for legal necessity is not by itself evidence either of the existence of the legal necessity or adequacy of the enquiry by the alienee. The alienee must adduce some independent evidence to establish the legal necessity for transfer or of the adequacy of enquiry—*Hari Satya Banerjee* v *Mahadev Banerjee* AIR 1983 Cal 76 at p. 80.

But under s. 8 of the Hindu Minority and Guardianship Act a Hindu Guardian's contract for purchase of immovable property binds a minor—*Manik Chand* v *Ramchandra* AIR 1981 SC 519.

4. A transfer may be set aside by a minor if it was not for any legal necessity or for the benefit of the minor.

5. Any transfer by a *de facto* guardian of a minor Hindu after commencement of the Hindu Minority and Guardianship Act 1956 (i.e. 25.8.1956) would be void *ab initio*—*Madhegowda* v *Ankegowda* AIR 2002 SC 215.

6. A transfer by a certificated guardian, with prior permission of the court, is valid but a transfer by a certificated guardian without permission or in contravention of permission is void.
7. When a transfer of a minor's property is by a legally competent guardian (such as natural guardian, *de facto* guardian, certificated guardian) a minor may sue to set aside the transfer within three years of attaining majority (*vide* Art. 60 of the Limitation Act). But when a transfer was made by an incompetent person—the sale being void, a minor can sue for possession within 12 years (*vide* Art. 65 of the Limitation Act). Prayer for setting aside the sale is not required for a void transaction.
8. An instrument may be partially cancelled (when rights or obligations are separable) under s. 32 of the Specific Relief Act 1963.

118. Suit for setting aside a transfer effected by a natural guardian

In the Court of .... at ....

Suit No. .... of 20...

(Set out cause title)

The plaintiff states as follows:

1. That the pro-forma defendant No. 2 is the mother and was natural guardian of the plaintiff at all material times.

2. That the plaintiff was born in ...... and has attained majority on ......

3. That the plaintiff owned amongst others the property described in the Schedule below. The said pro-forma defendant No. 2 has sold to the defendant No. 1 the said land, on .... by executing a sale-deed in favour of the defendant No. 1 for a consideration of ₹ ....

4. That the said sale by the pro-forma defendant No. 2 in favour of the defendant No. 1 was not for any legal necessity. There were a number of landed properties fetching considerable income in the name of the minor.

5. That the cause of action for this suit arose on ...... (date of sale) and thereafter on ...... when the plaintiff attained majority at ...... within the jurisdiction of this court.

6. Suit valuation (amount of consideration).

The plaintiff claims:

(*i*) That the sale by the pro-defendant No. 2 in favour of the defendant No. 1 be set aside.

(*ii*) Possession of the said property.

SCHEDULE

(State here description of suit-property)

Verification

Affidavit

NOTES: 1. See under Form No. 117.
2. For setting aside—Art. 60 of the Limitation Act providing three years when the ward attains majority.

119. Suit by a Muslim minor (after attaining majority) for setting aside a transfer effected by a de facto guardian

In the Court of .... at ....

Suit No. .... of 20...

(Set out cause title)

The above-named plaintiff states as follows:

1. That the plaintiff owned, amongst others, the property described in the Schedule 'A' below.

2. That the plaintiff was born in .... and was a minor till ...... when he attained majority.

3. That the plaintiff lost his father and grandfather at his early age and had been living in care and protection of his mother A.B. Bewa, who is defendant No. 2 in this suit and was a *de facto* guardian of the plaintiff during his minority.

4. That the pro-forma defendant No. 2 by executing a sale-deed on ... has sold the said property which is described in the Schedule 'A' below to the defendant No. 1.

5. That the said sale by A.B. Bewa, is void and not binding on the plaintiff.

The plaintiff claims:

(*a*) A declaration that the sale-deed dated .... executed by A.B. Bewa (the mother) is void;

(*b*) Khas possession of the property in the Schedule 'A' below.;

(*c*) Mesne profits of ₹ .... as per account, in the Schedule 'B' below.

SCHEDULE 'A'

(State here description of the land)

SCHEDULE 'B'

Mesne profits.

Yield of ...... valued at ₹ ....

Verification

Affidavit

120. Suit for cancellation of a sale-deed by a minor or by a person of unsound mind

In the Court of .... at ....

Suit No. .... of 20...

(Set out cause title)

The plaintiff states as follows:

1. That the plaintiff, at the instance of A.B., a relation of the defendant, had executed a kobala on .... intending to sell the land in the Schedule below, for a consideration of ₹ .... in favour of the defendant.

2. That the plaintiff was born on the ...... and on the date of execution of the aforesaid kobala (sale-deed) the plaintiff was a minor and the said kobala is void (or, that the plaintiff was a person of unsound mind at the material date).

3. That the defendant is trying to have the land in the Schedule below in his possession. (When possession to vendee has been delivered, there should be a prayer for recovery of possession).

4. That the plaintiff is entitled to have the sale-deed dated ...... adjudged void and cancelled. (*Add, if necessary*).

5. Cause of action.

6. Suit valuation.

The plaintiff, therefore, claims a decree holding the kobala dated .... void and for cancellation of the same.

(*If necessary*, for recovery of possession of the land sold)

SCHEDULE

(State here description of the property)

Verification

Affidavit

NOTES: 1. See s. 31(1) of the Specific Relief Act 1963.
2. For property which the plaintiff has conveyed while insane, limitation is three years under Art. 102 from the date when the plaintiff is restored to sanity and has knowledge of the conveyance.
3. Mere prayer for declaration that the sale-deed is void is not sufficient. There should be a prayer for cancellation of the deed too. If possession has been delivered on the basis of the deed, it is submitted, there should also be a prayer for recovery of possession.
4. A suit of this nature can be brought by the Legal Representatives of the executant (100 IC 932) or even by a person not a party to the deed (1938 MLJ 54).
5. A minor, inducing others to think that he was of age, cannot take advantage of his own fraud. But see 102 IC 449 (Pat).

121. Suit for setting aside a deed obtained by fraud

In the Court of the Civil Judge (Senior Division) at ......

Title Suit No. .... 20...

A.B. ... ... *Plaintiff*

versus

C.D. ... ... *Defendant*

Suit for setting aside fraudulent kobala and for khas possession

[Valued at ₹ 10,000]

The above-named plaintiff states as follows:

1. That the plaintiff's sister ...... "S" ...... held in her exclusive right a piece of land in Dakhaliswatta interest measuring .... centimal acres as, described in item (1) of the Schedule "A" and another piece of land in Dakhaliswatta interest measuring ...... centimal acres .... as, described in item (2) of the Schedule "A" below at .... P.S. .... District ...... The said "A" had several structures on the said lands as described in items (1) and (2) of Schedule "A" below.

2. That while owning and possessing the properties in Schedule "A" below the said "S" had made a gift to the plaintiff, by executing a registered deed of gift on ...... out of the properties in Schedule "A" portions thereof which are more specifically described in items (1) and (2) of Schedule "B" below, by partition with separate boundary and gave the plaintiff delivery of possession of the gifted properties and the plaintiff accepted the gift and has been possessing the said properties in Schedule "B" since the time of gift exclusively in his own right and interest.

3. The defendant has been living since two/three months prior to death of the said "S" on ...... on a portion of the premises in Schedule "A", because of relationship he had with "S". The said portion of land is described in particular in Schedule "C" below and falls under the property in Schedule "B".

4. That the plaintiff unlike the defendant is a helpless, illiterate man and is not adept in worldly ways. On the other hand, the defendant is an intelligent, shrewd and crooked man. The plaintiff was often engaged by the defendant as a day labourer under the latter. The plaintiff used to seek advice from the defendant from time to time and he had at all material times no one other than the defendant to take the plaintiff into confidence. The plaintiff in turn placed his full reliance on the defendant and was at his beck and call. In a word, the plaintiff was under the thumb of the defendant.

5. That the plaintiff has no wife or children. His own relations (namely, 'S's husband's brother's sons to wit, B and C) were cherishing ill-feelings against the plaintiff as 'S' gifted away her properties in Schedule "B" to the plaintiff in preference to them.

6. The plaintiff in the circumstances was thrown in the care of the designing defendant who was then living in the property in Schedule "C" who spared no moment to take the opportunity and by exploiting the plaintiff's simplicity and faith had suggested to the plaintiff in the 1st part of Bhadra, 14 .... B.S. that the plaintiff would be required to submit a petition for mutation in respect of the properties he received by way of gift from his sister lest he should lose his rights therein. The plaintiff believed in the defendant whereupon the defendant, along with his associate one X, took the plaintiff on that date to the Kachari premises and obtained from the plaintiff his thumb impressions on some blank sheets of papers and also on a stamp, already written out by a scribe engaged by the defendant holding out the same to the plaintiff as the petition for mutation. The matter that was written on the stamp was not read over to the plaintiff by anybody nor contents thereof were explained to the plaintiff. The plaintiff understood that he was putting his thumb impressions on the petition for mutation and accordingly put his L.T.I.'s on the stamp at the dictation of the defendant and his engaged scribe and persons present there.

7. That the plaintiff never for a moment till then could entertain an idea that the defendant would betray him or that the stamp paper with writings thereon was in reality a kobala purporting a sale of the "B" Schedule properties in favour of the defendant.

8. That the defendant by exercising fraud on the plaintiff has, with the assistance of his own men, created a kobala in respect of the "B" Schedule properties, beyond the knowledge of the plaintiff, got the plaintiff's L.T.I.'s thereon on false representation and has got the same registered. No consideration passed for the said kobala as recited therein and the plaintiff did not receive a single farthing as consideration. The defendant has no capacity to pay a consideration of ₹ ...... The plaintiff did not intend to sell the "B" Schedule properties to the defendant nor he had any necessity to sell the same.

9. That the said properties in Schedule "B" is located within the municipal area of .... and are the subject-matter of the suit and will hereinafter be referred to as suit property.

10. That the aforesaid kabala, in the circumstances, is a fraudulent deed, collusive in character and bogus in nature. It is a sham transaction and has not been acted upon. The defendant did not acquire any right, title and interest in suit property on the strength of the said fraudulent deed. On the contrary, the plaintiff has been possessing the properties sought to be conveyed by the aforesaid fraudulent deed, excepting a portion thereof described in Schedule "C" below.

11. The plaintiff did not know of the alleged kobala. The defendant kept it secret and was awaiting an opportune moment. In the early part of Poush, 14 .... B.S., the defendant one day told the plaintiff that sold plaintiff the suit property and was required to make over possession of the same to the defendant. The plaintiff got bewildered to hear it and immediately reported the matter to one P, a man of the locality. Thereafter the plaintiff with the assistance of the said P made shifting enquiries and at last took certified copy of the fraudulent kobala and came to learn from P for the first time precisely that the defendant got a kobala executed by the plaintiff in his favour in respect of the suit property fraudulently, on the pretext of filing a petition for mutation, on .... by false recital as to consideration of ₹ .... etc.

12. That the plaintiff has further learnt that the defendant in collusion with the said B and C have got their names mutated in respect of properties in Schedule "A" (inclusive of suit properties) at the back of the plaintiff on 30.8.20......., by pleading his title on the strength of the aforesaid fraudulent kobala. The plaintiff knew nothing of the said mutation proceedings and is not bound by the findings and orders in the said mutation case. The defendant did not acquire any title to suit properties by said findings of the mutation case.

13. The plaintiff had asked the defendant about the fraudulent kobala and demanded possession of the "B" Schedule property in .... which the defendant refused.

14. That the plaintiff is entitled to a declaration that the aforesaid kobala dated 22.8.20..... in favour of the defendant, allegedly executed by the plaintiff, is a void, fraudulent, invalid and inoperative deed and the same is liable to be set aside. The plaintiff is further entitled khas possession of the property in Schedule "C" below.

15. [Add: If and when necessary]. That the plaintiff before now had instituted this in court against the defendant a Title Suit No. ...... for declaration that the said kobala was fraudulent. There was formal defect in the plaint of the said suit in respect of framing of the suit and reliefs prayed for. The plaintiff has withdrawn the suit on ...... with liberty to sue the defendant afresh over the same subject-matter. The plaintiff has deposited costs of the suit on ....

16. The plaintiff files herewith a challan showing deposit of costs of ₹ .... and a certified copy of the order sheet dated ...... of the title suit ...... of this court and those may be treated as part of the plaint.

17. That the cause of action for this suit arose first on ...... when the fraudulent kobala came into being and thereafter in the middle of ...... 20 ...... when he defendant first divulged the fact of kobala and demanded possession of suit properties at .... town within the jurisdiction of the court.

18. That for the purpose of jurisdiction and court-fees the suit is valued at ₹........... and *ad valorem* court-fees are paid thereon.

The plaintiff, therefore, prays for:

(*a*) A judgment and decree declaring that—

(*i*) the kobala deed dated .... in favour of the defendant and allegedly executed by the plaintiff is a fraudulent, invalid and inoperative deed.

(ii) The defendant did not acquire any right, title and interest by the said kobala dated ......

(b) Setting aside the aforesaid kobala and directing the District Sub-Registrar, ... accordingly.

(c) For khas possession of the property in Schedule "C".

(d) Costs.

(e) Such other relief or reliefs as law and equity would allow the plaintiff.

SCHEDULE "A"

SCHEDULE "B" *(Suit property)*

SCHEDULE "C" *(Khas possession)*

Verification

Affidavit

NOTES: 1. Limitation—Art. 95 of the Limitation Act 1963. The starting point of limitation is not the date of execution of the deed but time when fraud became known to the party wronged—*Ningawwa* v *Byrappa* AIR 1968 SC 956.

2. When the plaintiff is not a party to the deed, he need not pray for setting aside the deed; for a declaration that the deed is null and void is sufficient.

3. For declaration of forgery of an instrument—limitation is three years under Art. 56 of the Act from when registration becomes known to the plaintiff.

4. On plaint allegations that the plaintiff was in possession of disputed property and the only thing she needed was declaration that impugned documents were null and void and of no effect—court-fee need not be paid under s. 7(*iv*)(*c*) of the Court Fees Act—*Gita Debi Bajoria* v *Harish Chandra Saw Mill* AIR 1971 Cal 202.

122. Suit for declaration of title alleging non-execution of a will

In the Court of Civil Judge (Senior Division) at ....

or

Family Court at ....

Suit No. .... of 20.........

(Set out cause title)

The plaintiff states as follows:

1. That one A.B. held vast landed properties at Moujas ...... within P.S. ...... District ......, more particularly described in the Schedule appended below:

2. That the said A.B. died on .... leaving the plaintiff his only son as heir. The defendant is the first cousin of the plaintiff being father's brother's son.

3. That the defendant has been demanding 50%, share by partition of the properties in the Schedule below claiming the said A.B. bequeathed 50% of his properties to the defendant by a will dated ......

4. That the said A.B. did not execute any will. If there be any will in the custody of the defendant, allegedly executed by A.B., the same is a forged and fraudulent document.

The plaintiff claims for a decree:

(*i*) declaring the absolute title of the plaintiff upon a further declaration that the alleged will in the custody of the defendant was never executed by the said A.B.

(*ii*) alternatively, to have the will adjudged fraudulent and, therefore, void and cancelled.

Verification

Affidavit

NOTES: 1. Execution of the will under suspicious circumstances. Immediately after execution the executant died. Only one of three attestors was examined and said attestor was closely related to the beneficiary under the will. Facts create doubt on genuineness of will. Such will cannot be acted upon—*Addepalli Venkata Laxmi* v *Ayinampudi Narasimha Rao* AIR 1994 AP 72.

2. Muslim Will (WASEEAT)—Consent of heirs. It is for the person who claims under a Will to establish that other heirs had consented to bequest. Bequest in excess of $^1/_3$rd of estate cannot take effect unless such bequest is consented to by heirs after death of testator—*Yasin Imambhai* v *Hajarabi* AIR 1986 Bom 957.

CHARGE

123. Suit for cancellation and return of promissory note executed on misrepresentation and recovery of outstanding amount

In the Court of .... at ....

Suit No. .... of 20....

Mr. A, son of Mr. B, carrying on business at .... within the jurisdiction of this learned court

... *Plaintiff*

versus

Mr. C, son of Mr. D, carrying on business at ...... within the jurisdiction of this learned court

... *Defendant*

The plaintiff states as follows:

1. The plaintiff carries on business as a retailer in diverse goods.

2. The defendant carries on business as a wholesaler in diverse goods.

3. The plaintiff had dealings and transactions with the defendant both on cash and on credit basis from time to time.

4. The plaintiff was busy in his dealings with some of his customers and the defendant, in the meantime, had approached the plaintiff for payment of ₹...... said to have been outstanding just as on the date and demanded payment forthwith as the defendant's auditors required such a declaration for payment for closing the Yearly Accounts. The plaintiff expressed his inability to make such down payment of the said outstanding sum and asked for credit for some time.

5. The defendant, however, insisted on such payment and ultimately suggested that a Demand Promissory Note be issued for ₹....... so that the accounts of the defendant could be closed to the full and final satisfaction of the Auditors of defendant. The plaintiff without properly examining the position of the accounts of defendant but simply relying on the statement of accounts of the defendant with whom the plaintiff had long-standing relationship & dealings and in good faith executed a Promissory Note for ₹........ with interest at 16% per annum. The said Promissory Note was payable on demand being made but the defendant verbally agreed not to enforce the said Promissory Note before expiry of 6 months.

6. On examination of the accounts of the plaintiff by the Auditors for the purpose of preparing Annual Profit and Loss Account and Balance Sheet for the relevant period it was found that in the Ledger account in name of the defendant there was no outstanding amount as on the date of execution of the said Promissory Note and that the said Promissory Note was executed without consideration by plaintiff on misrepresentation of the defendant. The plaintiff stated the above facts in a letter and also annexed a statements of accounts upto relevant date showing that there was no amount due and payable by plaintiff to the defendant as on the date when the said Promissory Note was issued and executed and there was also no amount due to the defendant by the plaintiff as on the relevant date of the closing of such accounts, a copy whereof was annexed to the said letter.

7. The defendant, however, failed to reply to the said letter of plaintiff or to return the said Promissory Note obtained by such misrepresentation and without consideration for execution of the said Promissory Note.

8. The plaintiff requested the defendant to return the said Promissory Note for cancellation inasmuch as the plaintiff issued the said Promissory Note on misrepresentation of the defendant. The plaintiff further stated that as on date of execution of the said Promissory Note there was nothing at all due by the plaintiff to the defendant and as such the said Promissory Note was issued without any consideration and by taking undue advantage of the plaintiff being busy with other customers.

9. In spite of said requests to return the said Promissory Note for cancellation, the defendant failed to return the said Promissory Note and also did not give any reply to the said letter of the plaintiff, a copy whereof is annexed hereto marked "....".

10. In the premises, the plaintiff claims immediate delivery and return of the said Promissory Note for cancellation.

11. The plaintiff claims a declaration that no amount is due or payable by plaintiff to defendant in respect of the transactions concerning the said Promissory Note which was obtained without any consideration and wrongfully by misrepresentation by the defendant.

12. The plaintiff's cause of action for this suit arose at .... where the defendant carried on business within the jurisdiction of this learned court, and no part of the plaintiff's cause of action is barred by the Law of Limitation and the plaintiff has paid proper court-fees on the plaint.

The plaintiff, therefore, prays for and claims:

(*a*) Decree for cancellation of the Promissory Note dated .... for ₹ ....

(*b*) Decree directing the defendant to deliver the said Promissory Note to plaintiff for cancellation;

(c) Injunction;

(d) Costs;

(e) Further and other reliefs.

Verification

Affidavit

124. Written statement of Mr. C, the defendant to the plaint claiming return of the promissory note

In the Court of .... at ....

Suit No. .... of 20...

(Set out cause title)

The defendant states as follows:

1. The suit is not maintainable.

2. It is barred by the Law of Limitation.

3. It is barred by the principles of waiver and acquiescence, and the suit be dismissed with costs.

4. The statements contained in paragraphs 1, 2 and 3 of the plaint are substantially truc and correct.

5. With reference to paragraph 4 of the plaint it is denied and disputed that the plaintiff was busy in his dealings with some of his customers when the defendant approached the plaintiff for payment of outstanding amount. The defendant duly explained the correct position of his accounts and the plaintiff was absolutely satisfied as regards the genuineness of claims of defendant.

6. With reference to paragraph 5 of the plaint, the defendant states the plaintiff on his own voluntarily executed the said Promissory Note and undertook to pay the balance amount after examining the accounts in regard to all transactions therein.

7. With reference to paragraph 6 of the plaint, the defendant denies that there was in fact no outstanding amount as on the date of execution of the said Promissory Note. The contentions of the plaintiff in his letters as also in the statements annexed to the said letters are incorrect and invalid. A Statement of Account as on .... the date of execution of the said Promissory Note is annexed hereto marked 'A' which clearly shows that there was due from or owing by the plaintiff to the defendant the said sum of ₹ ....

8. With reference to paragraph 7 of plaint, the defendant states the said letter of the plaintiff was duly replied to but the plaintiff is now denying receipt of the said letter. A copy of the said reply is annexed hereto marked 'B'.

9. With reference to the paragraph 8 of the plaint, the defendant denies that the defendant was liable to return the said Promissory Note without payment to defendant by the plaintiff. It is denied that on the date of execution of the Promissory Note, there was nothing due or owing by plaintiff to defendant.

10. With reference to paragraph 9 of the plaint, the defendant states that the plaintiff was not entitled to return of the Promissory Note or cancellation thereof. The letter of the plaintiff to the defendant is annexed hereto and marked 'C'.

11. With reference to paragraph 10 of plaint, the defendant denies that the plaintiff is entitled to return of the said Promissory Note or that the said Promissory Note is liable to be cancelled.

12. With reference to paragraph 11 of the plaint, the defendant denies that the plaintiff is entitled to any declaration as prayed for therein. It is further denied that no money is due or payable by the plaintiff to defendant as wrongly contended.

13. With reference to paragraph 12 of plaint, the defendant states that the plaintiff has no valid cause of action as against the defendant and as such, the suit be dismissed with costs.

Verification

Affidavit

125. Suit for declaration and enforcement of a charge on property

In the Court of .... at ....

Suit No. .... of 20...

(Set out cause title)

The plaintiff states as follows:

1. That the defendants Nos. 1 and 2 and the plaintiff are respectively son and widow of one 'A' since deceased.

2. That the defendant No. 1 brought a partition suit (Title Suit No. .... of 20......) in the court of the .... at ...... against the defendant No. 2 and the plaintiff and the said T. Suit was compromised on ...... and a decree was passed in terms of the compromise petition filed by the parties hereto.

3. That the compromise decree provided *inter alia* that—

(*i*) the first defendant would get the properties in Schedule A, and the second defendant would get the properties in Schedule B mentioned in the said above, in their respective shares;

(*ii*) that the plaintiff would be entitled to a maintenance of ₹ ...... per month and a charge was created on the properties in Schedules A and B of the defendants Nos. 1 and 2 for due payment of the said maintenance to the plaintiff.

State here particulars of charge, namely:

(*i*) When and how created;

(*ii*) Particulars of the property charged;

(*iii*) Amount for which charged;

(*iv*) By whom payable and

(*v*) In whose favour charge was created.

4. That the plaintiff has not been paid her maintenance since the month of..........

5. That the defendants sold portions from their allotted shares in Schedules A and B below to one .... defendant No. 3 by a registered kobala (who is not a *bona fide* transferee for value and without notice of the charge to be averred where necessary—see s. 100, T.P. Act).

6. That the plaintiff is entitled to ₹ ...... as arrears of maintenance from the defendants Nos. 1 and 2.

7. Cause of action on .... when the money sued for became due.

8. Suit valuation.

The plaintiff, therefore, prays:

(*i*) For a decree of ₹ ...... against the defendants Nos. 1 and 2 as arrears of maintenance at the rate of ₹ ...... per month for ...... months from ..... to ......

(*ii*) A declaration that properties purchased by the defendant No. 3 are subject to a charge in the plaintiff's favour for due payment of her maintenance.

(*iii*) Decree under Or. 34, r. 4, CPC in Form No. 5A of Appendix D the 1st Schedule of the CPC.

Verification

Affidavit

NOTES: 1. See 36 CWN 153; AIR 1934 Lah 756—for conditions of a valid charge.

2. Limitation: Art. 62 will govern enforcement of payment of money charged upon immovable property—12 years.

3. Charge on property created by consent decree—charged property can be brought to sale in execution without filing fresh suit—AIR 1968 Guj 156.

4. When a charge is created by the Arbitrator in his award and the charge is not one by act of parties, provisions of s. 100 of the T.P. Act are not attracted. Such a charge can be enforced by execution of decree on award—AIR 1968 Cal 336.

5. Charge and mortgage—for difference see 163 IC 69.

6. Even without being a party to the agreement any one in whose favour a charge is created may bring a suit.

COMMISSION

126. Suit by an estate agent against the principal for commission for introduction of purchaser of property

In the Court of .... at ....

Suit No. .... of 20...

(Set out cause title)

The plaintiff states:

1. That the plaintiff is a broker and estate agent dealing in purchase and sale of, house properties for others on commission basis/brokerage.

2. That the defendant had engaged the plaintiff on .... the .... day of .... 20 .... orally (or by a letter dated the .... day of .... 20 ....) to act as his agent in introducing an intending purchaser of the defendant's house situate at .... and agreed that in case the plaintiff did so, the plaintiff would be entitled to a commission/brokerage of 10% on the sale price of the said property.

3. That the plaintiff had introduced one A.B. to the defendant who intended to purchase the said house property of the defendant and, as a matter of fact, the defendant sold the said property to the said A.B. on the ..... day of ..... 20 ..... for ₹ ....

4. That the plaintiff is entitled to a sum of ₹ .... as commission being 10% of the sale price.

5. Cause of action.

6. Suit valuation.

The plaintiff claims:

(*a*) decree for ₹6,000,

(*b*) costs.

Verification

Affidavit

127. Suit by an agent against his principal for an account of commission for introduction of customers

In the Court of .... at ....

Suit No. .... of 20...

(Set out cause title)

The plaintiff states:

1. That the defendant is and was at all material times a manufacturer of T-shirts with his principal place of business at 17, Sooterkin Street, Kolkata 700 002.

2. That by an agreement dated the .... day of ......20 ...., the defendant engaged the plaintiff as his agent (*i*) to introduce to the plaintiff customers for T-shirts manufactured by the defendant and to secure order from such customers (*ii*) in such event, to pay to the plaintiff a commission of 25% on the amount of all such orders and a commission of 5% on introduction of customers.

3. From time to time the plaintiff introduced to the defendant several customers who themselves placed orders for T-shirts as also secured orders himself. The plaintiff has submitted below names of customers so introduced together with particulars of orders secured by him. The plaintiff has furnished below also names of customers introduced but who themselves placed orders. The plaintiff does not know the nature of orders placed in the latter case.

4. It is reliably learnt that all such orders have been executed by the defendant from time to time.

5. By a notice dated the .... day of ...... 20 ...., the plaintiff had requested the defendant to render to the plaintiff a true account of orders received and executed by the defendant and to pay to the plaintiff his dues as commission. The defendant avoided the same on flimsy pretexts.

6. Cause of action.

7. Suit valuation.

The plaintiff claims:

(*a*) an account be taken of all orders secured to the defendant within the period from .... to .... and of the amount of commission due to the plaintiff.

(*b*) payment of commission as may be found due on accounting; and

(*c*) damages at 10.5% on the same for withholding the same without just cause.

Particulars

(*i*) Introduction of customers—(names and other particulars of customers).

(*ii*) Orders secured (date, quantum, names and other particulars) by the plaintiff himself.

Verification

Affidavit

128. Suit by an agent for commission against his principal

(See Form No. 38 *ante*)

129. Suit for profits by a principal against his commission agent

(See Form No. 9 *ante*)

COMPANY

130. Suit by a director of a company for his fees

In the Court of .... at ....

Suit No. .... of 20...

(Set out cause title)

The plaintiff states:

1. That the defendant is a company with its registered office at ......

2. That the plaintiff was appointed on the ...... day of ...... 20............ a director in the defendant company and is so now.

3. On the strength of a resolution of the defendant company at its general meeting held on the .... day of ...... in conformity with Article No. ...... of the Articles of Association of the defendant company, the fees of each director were fixed at ₹ ...... per year.

4. That the plaintiff is entitled to his fees for the period from ...... to ...... for his services rendered to the defendant company which remains unpaid.

5. Cause of action.

6. Valuation.

The plaintiff claims:

(*a*) The sum of ₹......

(*b*) Costs.

Verification

Affidavit

131. Suit by a company against shareholders for allotment money and calls

In the Court of .... at ....

Suit No. .... of 20...

(Set out cause title)

The plaintiff states:

1. The plaintiff is a company registered under the Companies Act 1956 with its registered office at ......

2. By Article No. ...... of the Articles of Association of the plaintiff the directors of the company are competent to make call on all shares not fully paid up together with interest at the rate of .... % per annum on all moneys due to the plaintiff till the date of payment.

3. The defendant applied to the plaintiff company for five ordinary shares of ₹10 each in the capital of the plaintiff company and paid ₹10 per share agreeing to pay another ₹10 per share on allotment. The defendant was allotted five shares on the .... day of .... but he did not pay the money due from him on allotment of shares.

4. The directors made a call on all the members on the ...... day of ...... for ₹ 10 per share payable within seven days from the date of call.

5. The defendant did not pay the said call or any money due from him.

6. Cause of action.

The plaintiff company claims:

(*a*) Allotment money ₹50.

(*b*) Call money ₹10.

(c) Interest thereon at ...... % from due date till realisation.

Verification

Affidavit

CONTRACT

[*Suit for specific performance of a contract—See Sale of land*].

132. Suit by actor against theatrical company for breach of contract and damages for loss of publicity

In the Court of .... at ....

Suit No. .... of 20...

(Set out cause title)

1. The plaintiff carries on the profession of an actor.

2. The defendant company are theatrical producers.

3. By a contract contained in two letters dated .... 20.......... and .... 20........, the defendant company agreed to engage the plaintiff to play one of the three leading parts in the musical comedy to be produced at .... Theatre, the foremost theatrical house in the city of ...., called ...., for six weeks certain from .... 20........, at a salary of ₹ .... *per* week of nine performances.

4. The defendant company cast the plaintiff for the part of ...., and on reading the first Act of the play, the plaintiff found that the part assigned to him was not a leading but a minor part and he therefore requested the defendant company to give him a leading part.

5. The defendant company refused to recast the plaintiff and alleged that the part assigned to the plaintiff was a good performance of the contract.

6. Therefore the plaintiff declined to appear in the production and was compelled to forego the opportunity of displaying his talent and abilities before the public and thereby suffered damage ....

7. The plaintiff obtained service at an equivalent remuneration elsewhere.

The plaintiff claims—

₹........... as damages for loss of publicity.

Verification

Affidavit

BREACH OF CONTRACT

133. Suit for prohibitory injunction to restrain a breach of contract

In the Court of .... at ....

Suit No. .... of 20...

(Set out cause title)

The plaintiff states:

1. That the defendant took on lease the premises, described in the Schedule hereunder, following a registered deed of lease executed by the parties hereto on ...... and registered on ......

2. That under terms of the said deed of lease the defendant was/is obliged to occupy the said premises solely and exclusively for godown purpose.

3. That the defendant in violation of Clause No. ...... of the said deed of lease began digging earth from the open courtyard of the premises intending to .... (state the object of digging, if known). The plaintiff came to know of the defendant's activities on ...... and immediately protested. The defendant appeared not to pay heed to the plaintiff's request. On the contrary, the defendant threatened to continue digging of earth and, as a matter of fact, the defendant was continuing digging of earth through his hired labour as before.

4. Cause of action—date of digging and date of plaintiff's knowledge.

5. That for the purpose of jurisdiction and court-fees the suit is valued at ₹50 only.

The plaintiff prays for a judgment and decree granting perpetual injunction restraining the defendant, his agent, labour and/or servants from digging earth from the premises in suit, and for compensation of costs of refilling of the land.

SCHEDULE

(State here description of the premises)

Verification

Affidavit

NOTES: 1. Limitation is three years for compensation for the breach of any contract, express or implied, under Art. 55.

2. Plaintiff in order to succeed in a suit for damages for premature cancellation of a contract by the defendant must establish that such cancellation was wrongful—*G.L. Kilikar* v *State of Kerala* AIR 1971 SC 1196.

3. Suit for damages for breach of contract (s. 73). Quantum of loss. Principle of mitigation of loss. The principle of mitigation of loss does not give any right to the party who is in breach of the contract but it is a concept that has to be borne in mind by the court while awarding damages—*M. Lachia Shetty* v *The Coffee Board* AIR 1981 SC 162.

134. Suit to rescind a contract of sale on the grounds of fraud and misrepresentation

In the Court of .... at ....

Suit No. .... of 20...

(Set out cause title)

The plaintiff states as follows:

1. That the defendant represented to the plaintiff on .... that he held a piece of land measuring 3.20 acres at Mouja ...... P.S. ...... District .... more particularly described in the Schedule below, and that he had saleable interest therein. The plaintiff did not entertain any doubt and placed reliance on his words.

2. The plaintiff agreed to purchase the said land for a consideration of ₹ .... and plaintiff and the defendant entered into a contract on .... for sale of that land.

3. That lately on .... the plaintiff on examination of the defendants' title-deeds found that the said land stood vested in the State of West Bengal from before the contract of sale and purchase as aforesaid and that the defendant had no saleable interest in the said land.

4. That the representations made by the defendant on .... were fraudulent and by such fraudulent representation induced the plaintiff to enter into the aforesaid contract of purchase.

5. That the plaintiff is entitled to rescission of the said contract.

6. That the cause of action for this suit arose on .... (the date of contract) and thereafter on .... when the plaintiff came to know of the defendant's fraudulent representation at .... (the place where the property is situated).

7. Suit valuation (value of the land).

The plaintiff, therefore, prays for:

(*i*) a decree for rescission of the contract,

(*ii*) costs.

Verification

Affidavit

NOTES: 1. See s. 19 of the Indian Contract Act 1872 and s. 27(1) of the Specific Relief Act 1963.

2. Limitation—three years from when rescinded *vide* Art. 59 of the Limitation Act 1963.

3. Court-fees—on the value of the relief sought.

4. Nature of the contract and grounds for rescission of the same should be specifically pleaded in the plaint.

5. Section 7—Where no time is given for acceptance of offer, acceptance has to be communicated within reasonable time. Offer could not be kept open indefinitely—*Shree Jaya Mohal Cooperative* v *Zenith Chemical Works* AIR 1991 Bom 211.

135. Suit to rescind a contract on the ground of fraudulent misrepresentation and recovery of money paid under it

In the Court of .... at ....

Suit No. .... of 20...

(Set out cause title)

The plaintiff states as follows:

1. In .... 20....., the defendants entered into a contract with D.S. Ltd., shipbuilders, for building a steel screw steamer of .... tons at the price of ₹ .... to be paid for in five instalments of ₹ .... each (1) when the keel was laid; (2) when the vessel was framed; (3) when the vessel was plated and ready for riveting; (4) when the vessel was launched; and (5) when the vessel was completed.

2. In the month of .... 20....., negotiations took place between the plaintiffs and the defendants through their respective brokers for the sale to the plaintiffs of the vessel then in the course of construction.

3. On or about .... the defendants by their brokers, Messrs. T.M. & Co., represented to the plaintiffs that the keel of the vessel had been laid, that the frames had been bent, and that the erection of the same had been started. These statements were also made in e-mail sent by the defendants to the plaintiffs and were repeated in a letter of the same date.

4. The defendants through their brokers offered the ship at ₹ .... and the plaintiffs on the good faith of the representations aforesaid accepted this offer.

5. Accordingly, by an agreement in writing dated .... made between the plaintiffs and the defendants, the defendants assigned to the plaintiffs the benefit of their contract of .... with D.S. Ltd. in consideration of a cash payment of ₹ .... the plaintiffs undertaking to pay the subsequent instalments amounting to ₹ .... in the manner aforesaid.

6. Shortly afterwards, the plaintiffs decided to resell their rights under the contract, and accordingly entered into negotiations with the B.H.L. Ltd., and passed on to that company copies of the e-mail and letter mentioned in paragraph 3 hereof containing the information as regards the state of progress of the building of the vessel. The said B.H.L. Ltd., are hereinafter referred to as 'the said company'.

7. In reliance on these representations the said company, by an agreement dated .... agreed to purchase from the plaintiffs all their rights and benefits under the agreement of ...., at the price of ₹ .... and covenanted to pay the several instalments which should thereafter become due.

8. On .... the said company sent a representative to .... to inspect the ship and it was then discovered that the representations contained in the aforesaid e-mail and letter of .... with regard to the state of construction of the vessel, were with the exception of the statement that the keel was laid, untrue, and that nothing had been done except the laying of the keel.

9. Thereupon by a letter dated .... the said company complained to the plaintiffs and on .... the plaintiffs asked for explanation from the defendants but the latter disclaimed all responsibility.

10. By a letter dated .... the said company informed the plaintiffs that if they had known the position and had any knowledge that the plaintiffs' statement with regard to the state of construction of the vessel was incorrect, they would not have accepted the assignment of the contract and gave notice that they repudiated their contract on the ground of misrepresentation.

11. On .... the plaintiffs having satisfied themselves about the facts, wrote to the defendants a letter saying that the said company had repudiated their contract with the plaintiffs and were applying to the court to rescind the same and that the plaintiffs likewise claimed rescission of their contract with the defendants.

12. The said company have since commenced an action against the plaintiffs for rescission.

The plaintiffs claim—

1. Setting aside of the contract dated........
2. Recovery of the money paid under it.
3. Interest by way of damages on the said sum.

Verification

Affidavit

136. Suit to rescind a contract and for recovery of money paid under it

In the Court of .... at ....

Suit No. .... of 20...

(Set out cause title)

The plaintiff states as follows:

1. That the defendant had entered into a contract in writing on .... with the plaintiff for .... after negotiations on ....

2. That the plaintiff had relied on the representation of the defendant and advanced to the defendant on .... a sum of ₹ .... for performance of the contract. The defendant issued a receipt therefor.

3. That the defendant was not performing his contract whereupon the plaintiff entertained a doubt about the defendant's honesty and made enquiries and learnt that the defendant had made false representations (state the nature of fraud and false representation) to the plaintiff with a view to obtaining some money.

4. That the plaintiff thereupon rescinded the contract with the defendant by a letter dated .... and demanded back the aforesaid money paid to the defendant as advance.

5. Cause of action arose—on the date of contract and subsequently on .... when the contract was rescinded.

The plaintiff, therefore, prays for:

(*i*) setting aside of the contract dated .... with the defendant.

(*ii*) Recovery of ₹ .... paid to the defendant on ....

(*iii*) Costs.

Verification

Affidavit

137. Suit for price for supply of goods (on document)

In the Court of Civil Judge (Junior Division) at ....

Money Suit No. .... of 20 .....

A ....
son of B.........
residing at ....
P.S. ....
District— .... *Plaintiff*

versus

C ....
son of D ....
by caste .... by occupation
of ....
P.S. ....
District ....

Suit for recovery of price for supply of goods

Claim laid at ₹ ....

The plaintiff states as follows:

1. That the plaintiff had supplied to the defendant at the latter's seeking 10 truckload 'boulders' at ₹ .... per each truckload within the period from .... to .... and the defendant owes the plaintiff a sum of ₹ .... on that count.

2. That the defendant executed a document on .... agreeing to pay the said dues to the plaintiff within one month and a half from the date of execution of the said document and, failing to pay within the stipulated period, to pay the same together with interest thereon @ .... per annum till the date of payment. The said document is annexed herewith and the plaintiff prays that the same may be treated as a part of the plaint.

3. That the defendant failed to pay the said amount of ₹ .... within the stipulated date though repeated demands were made.

4. That the cause of action for this suit arose on the .... after expiry of one month and a half from (date of demand) .... at .... within the jurisdiction of this court.

5. That the value of the subject-matter of the suit for purpose of jurisdiction and court-fee is laid at ₹ ....

The plaintiff claims:

(*a*) A decree of ₹ ....

(*b*) Interest at 10% per annum from the date of suit till realisation.

(*c*) Costs.

Verification

Affidavit

NOTES: 1. Contract for sale of goods—suit for recovery of damages for breach of contract the cause of action consists of the contract and its breach. Such a suit can therefore be filed either at the place where the contract was made or at the place where it should have been performed and the breach occurred. In such a contract performance of the contract consists not only of delivery of the goods but also of payment of price. Cause of action, therefore, for a suit on breach of contract would arise not only where the goods were to be delivered but also where the price would be payable on such delivery—*Sreenivasa Pulvarising Industries* v *Jai Glass & Chemicals* AIR 1985 Cal 74.

2. In a suit for price of goods sold and delivered to be paid for after the expiry of a fixed period of credit, the suit cannot be brought until the period of credit expires; the cause of action arises when the period of credit expires. Under Art. 15, limitation is three years when the period of credit expires.
3. Compensation for supply of goods—Compensation would normally be market price of goods with interest at 6%—AIR 1970 SC 1201.

138. Suit for price for supply of goods on credit

In the Court of the SCC Judge at ....

SCC No. .... of 20 ......

A ....

.... *Plaintiff*

versus

1. State of .... represented by ....
2. B. (State official designation with address).

.... *Defendants*

Suit for recovery of price for goods purchased on credit.

The above-named plaintiff states as follows:

1. That the plaintiff, is a registered firm dealing in petrol, mobil oil, distilled water, etc., from its petrol pump at .... and Sri .... is a partner of the firm.

2. That the defendant No. 2 is a public officer of the State Government of .... The defendant No. 2 purchased and received through his employees, within the period from .... to .... ltrs. of petrol .... ltrs. of mobil oil and .... bottles of distilled water from the plaintiff's petrol pump on credit, valued at ₹ .... On each occasion of purchase, the defendant No. 2 had issued requisition (slips) in writing. On various dates bills together with such requisition slips were submitted to the defendant No. 2 in his office for payment by Peon Book of the plaintiff. Particulars of transactions, bills, value, etc., are described in the Schedule below and are duly entered in the Daily Sales Register of the plaintiff as also in the ledger maintained in regular course of business. A true copy of the ledger along with extract from the Daily Sales Register is filed herewith.

3. That the plaintiff is entitled to the said sum of ₹ .... together with interest at the rate of ....% p.a. over the said sum according to the usage of trade, as mentioned in the Schedule of claim below.

4. That the plaintiff made repeated demands for the plaintiff's dues, but the defendant No. 2 did not pay. The plaintiff has served notice dated .... (registered on ....) under s. 80 of the CPC on the Collector, ... and on the defendant No. 2 under registered post with A/D through their authorised lawyer Sri .... Advocate, Cooch Behar.

5. That the cause of action for this suit arose at ...., within the jurisdiction of this court on .... when the first purchase on credit was made and thereafter on each date of subsequent transactions.

6. That for the purpose of jurisdiction and court-fee, the suit is valued at ₹ .... and *ad valorem* court-fees are paid thereon.

The plaintiff, therefore, prays:

(*a*) for a judgment and decree for ₹ ....

(*b*) Costs of suit.

SCHEDULE

Verification

Affidavit

NOTE: Suit for the price of goods supplied—no fixed period of credit was agreed—Transaction including various items though falling under different heads treated as parts of single transaction—moneys were payable on demand—Article 120 of the old Limitation Act applied—AIR 1970 Guj 284.

139. Application for setting aside ex parte decree

In the Court of .... at ....

Miscellaneous Case No. ....of 20 .... arising out of

M/s. P. & Co. Ltd, a company registered under the Companies Act 1956 and carrying on business at .... Kolkata within the said jurisdiction

...... *Plaintiff-Opposite Party*

versus

Mr. M, working for gain at .... Kolkata within the said jurisdiction

...... *Defendant-Petitioner*

The petitioner-defendant states:

1. The defendant is carrying on business in various consumer goods.

2. The plaintiff is a supplier of ready made garments to the defendant for the defendant's business on certain terms and conditions agreed to between the said parties.

3. According to the said agreement, the defendant used to pay the defendant's bills from time to time for supply of goods either by cash or sometimes by account payee cheque after endorsement of proper receipt of such payment by the plaintiff on the back of such bills.

4. In spite of such regular payments on 18th September 20 ...., the plaintiff informed defendant that a sum of ₹ .... was due and owing by the defendant to plaintiff and the plaintiff demanded payment of the said sum.

5. The defendant informed the plaintiff that the said sum of ₹ ...... has already been paid in cash on presentation of the relevant bill and the plaintiff's authorised agent collected the said payment on due receipt of the said payment by signing on the back of the relevant bill. A copy of the said receipted bill is annexed hereto marked 'A'.

6. Thereafter the defendant did not take any further supplies from the defendant as the goods offered were of much inferior quality and were not of the required standard for sale by the defendant.

7. Subsequently the defendant was surprised to learn on 15th October 20... that the plaintiff by fraudulently suppressing due legal process of the court had obtained an *ex parte* decree for payment of ₹........ plus interest which was allegedly payable

by the defendant because of the fact the plaintiff suppressed the fact of Summons by fraudulent means.

Particulars of Fraud

(*i*) The plaintiff has not received payment of ₹ .... while the said payment has been already made by the defendant and the same duly acknowledged by the plaintiff's Agent, on the reverse of the relevant bill on presentation.

(*ii*) The plaintiff had deliberately suppressed the Summons for the suit in collusion and conspiracy with the officers entrusted to serve such summons on the defendant.

8. In the premises, the defendant is apprehensive that the plaintiff may wrongfully put the said decree for execution any day.

9. The defendant prays that the said *ex parte* decree be set aside and as the decree was obtained by fraud.

The plaintiff, therefore, prays for and claims:

(*a*) Declaration that the said *ex parte* decree dated ...... obtained by the defendant was by practising fraud and is void and inoperative.

(*b*) Restore the suit to its original file and number.

(*c*) Such other reliefs as are due in law and in equity.

Verification

Affidavit

140. Suit for specific performance

In the Court of Civil Judge (Senior Division) at Alipore

Suit No. .... of 20..........

Mr. P., residing at .... Alipore, Kolkata

...... *Plaintiff*

versus

Mr. X, residing at .... Alipore, Kolkata

...... *Defendant*

Suit for specific performance valued at ₹ ....

The plaintiff states:

1. The plaintiff is the Presiding Shebait of Sri Sri Durga Mata installed in the temple many years ago where large number of devotees come to worship the said deity from different places.

2. The defendant is the owner of a piece of vacant land adjacent to the temple premises. The said vacant land is measuring 3 cottahs and is shown in a map annexed hereto marked 'A'.

3. After negotiations with the defendant, owner of vacant land of 3 cottahs, an agreement was entered into in writing on 5.9.20...... whereby the defendant agreed

to sell and transfer the said land measuring 3 cottahs at ₹ .... being full consideration money for sale and transfer of said land. At the request of the defendant the plaintiff paid by a cheque No. .... dated 10th June 20........ for ₹ .... by way of advance.

4. In consideration of the said payment of amount of ₹ .... and with a promise to pay the balance amount of ₹ ...., the defendant agreed to execute and register a Deed of Sale of such land within 60 (sixty) days from the date of agreement on payment of the balance amount of ₹ ....

5. The plaintiff states that the said land is necessary for construction of certain additional rooms including a Prayer Room/Hall and several other small rooms for stay of devotees who may come from distant places.

6. Subject to completion of all necessary formalities, the possession of land would be made available to plaintiff and the plaintiff could start construction according to sanctioned plan on the said land.

7. The plaintiff requested the defendant to execute and then register the deed of sale of the said land. The plaintiff offered to pay balance sum of ₹ .... and requested the defendant to execute the deed of sale of said land and the plaintiff showed his readiness and willingness to pay the balance purchase price. The plaintiff is still ready and willing to pay the agreed purchased price of ₹ .... less the amount advanced by it on the defendant executing and registering the necessary sale deed of the said land.

8. In spite of several requests, the defendant has failed to execute the said sale deed and the defendant failed to give any valid reasons for not executing the said sale deed and also delayed the matter unnecessarily on some pretext or the other.

9. The plaintiff is still ready and willing to perform his part of the said agreement but the defendant is wrongfully avoiding the execution of sale deed even after accepting the advance of ₹ .... and in spite of the readiness and willingness of the plaintiff to pay the balance sum of ₹......... on defendant executing the said sale deed.

10. The plaintiff states that there is no other land available for sale in the area adjacement to the temple building of the said deity.

11. No part of the plaintiff's cause of action for this suit herein is barred by the Law of Limitation.

12. The plaintiff claims specific performance of the agreement entered into on .... between the parties for execution of the sale deed a copy whereof is annexed hereto marked "B".

13. The receipt for payment of ₹ .... is annexed hereto marked 'C'. All copies of the letters addressed to the defendant in this connection are annexed hereto collectively marked 'D'.

14. The plaintiff is entitled to claim specific performance of the contract for execution of agreement and deed of sale and delivery of and giving possession of the said land to the plaintiff.

15. The plaintiff's cause of action for this suit arose within the jurisdiction of this learned court where the said subject-matter being the said 3 cottahs of land is situate all within the jurisdiction of this learned court.

16. The plaintiff's cause of action arose on .... within the jurisdiction of this learned court and the same is still continuing from day to day.

17. For the purposes of jurisdiction and court-fees, the suit is valued at ₹ .... on which court-fees in stamps have been duly paid.

The plaintiff, therefore, claims:

(a) Specific performance of the contract directing defendant to execute the sale deed of land on payment of balance consideration money in respect of said property and register the same.

(b) Injunction restraining the defendant from entering into any contract for sale of said land or transfer to anybody except to plaintiff.

(c) Receiver be appointed over the said suit property with direction to take possession, make inventory and take steps for protection of the said land.

(d) Cost of the suit be paid by defendant to plaintiff.

(e) Further and other orders and reliefs as the plaintiff is entitled to in law and equity.

Annexures

A—Map

B—Agreement

C—Receipt of payment

D—All copies of letters

Verification

Affidavit

141. Suit for recovery of money (following breach of trust)

In the Court of Civil Judge (Senior Division) at Alipore

Suit No. .... of 20........

Mr. P., residing at ...., Kolkata

...... *Plaintiff*

versus

1. Mr. X Bank carrying on business, *inter alia*, at .... Kolkata

2. Mr. Y, son of Mr. Z residing at .... Kolkata

...... *Defendants*

Suit for recovery of money valued at ₹ ....

The plaintiff states:

1. Mr. W left a Will dated 5th September 20.... Under the said Will defendant No. 2 was appointed Executor of the Will and Trustee of the properties left by the said deceased. The plaintiff is the sole beneficiary under the said Will.

2. The defendant No. 2 obtained probate of the Will and realised the assets left by the Testator. The value of the assets was estimated at ₹ ....

3. The defendant No. 2, the Trustee, opened an account with the defendant No. 1 Bank intimating that the money so deposited in the account was trust money of which the defendant No. 2 was the Trustee and the plaintiff was the beneficiary.

4. The defendant No. 2 on opening the said account was authorised to withdraw money from the trust fund only for the necessaries of the beneficiary, the plaintiff, and that the Bank should be informed as to how the money has been utilised. The Bank was furnished with a copy of the Will and the probate by the Trustee.

5. In spite of the aforesaid facts known to the defendant bank, the defendant No. 1 wrongfully allowed the respondent No. 2, the Trustee, to withdraw moneys from the said account for his personal use and benefit.

6. The plaintiff, the sole beneficiary, came to know from the Statement of Account that from the Trust Account with the Bank the defendant No. 2 withdrew ₹......... for his personal use and not for the purpose of the Trust.

7. In view of the wrongful withdrawal allowed by the Bank and utilised by the defendant No. 2, Trustee, the said sum for his personal use, the plaintiff beneficiary has suffered a loss of ₹ .... due to negligence of defendant No. 1 Bank. The defendant No. 2 in breach of trust wrongfully withdrew the said sum of ₹ .... and wrongfully misappropriated the said sum being the trust money for the purpose of his own use causing loss and damages to the plaintiff, the sole beneficiary.

8. In the premises the plaintiff has suffered loss and damages to the extent of ₹ .... due to breach of trust by defendant No. 2 and breach of obligation by defendant No. 1.

9. The defendant No. 1 is liable to compensate the plaintiff to the extent of ₹ .... with interest at 12% per annum for its negligent act of allowing the trust money to be withdrawn for the personal use of the trustee. The defendant No. 2 is liable to pay the said sum of ₹ .... with interest at 12% per annum for breach of trust and wrongful enrichment of himself. Defendant No. 2 is also liable to compensate the plaintiff for breach of trust and failure to act in accordance to his obligations.

10. The plaintiff claims ₹ .... with interest from the date of wrongful withdrawal and misappropriation of the said sum at 12% per annum from the date of withdrawal of the said sum from the bank.

11. The defendants Nos. 1 and 2 are jointly and severally liable to compensate the plaintiff by payment of ₹ .... with interest at 12% per annum from the date of withdrawal of the said sum by the trustee from the Bank.

12. The plaintiff's cause of action arose for this suit on .... when the Bank allowed withdrawal of the said sum of ₹ .... and defendant No. 2 wrongfully withdrew the said sum for his personal use in breach of trust.

13. The cause of action for this suit arose at the address of the Bank wherefrom the money was wrongfully withdrawn or allowed to be withdrawn at the said branch within the jurisdiction of this learned court.

14. In spite of demand the defendants have and each one of them has failed to pay the plaintiff's claims.

15. For the purposes of jurisdiction and court-fee the suit is valued at ₹ .... and *ad valorem* court-fees have been paid thereon.

The plaintiff, therefore, prays for and claims:

(*a*) Decree for ₹ .... against the defendants jointly and severally with interest at 12% per annum from ....

(*b*) Interest at 12% per annum on the decretal amount till recovery thereof.

(*c*) Cost of the suit be paid by the defendants jointly and severally to the plaintiff.

(*d*) Further and other orders be made as to this learned court may deem fit and properties afford complete relief to the plaintiff.

Verification

Affidavit

NOTE: Mr. P should also affirm an affidavit in support of the facts stated in the plaint as required under Order VI, Rule 15 of the Code of Civil Procedure.

142. Suit to set aside sale deed

In the Court of Civil Judge (Senior Division) at Alipore

Suit No. .... of 20.........

Mr. P., son of Q, residing at ...., Kolkata

.... *Plaintiff*

versus

1. Mr. X, son of .... residing at ...., Kolkata
2. Mr. Y, son of Z, residing at ...., Kolkata

.... *Defendants*

Suit to set aside sale deed valued at ₹ ....

The plaintiff states:

1. The plaintiff was born on .... out of the wedlock of Q and R.

2. The plaintiff states that both his parents died on 15th March .... as a result of a train accident and at that time the plaintiff was only 10 years old.

3. The plaintiff's father had two properties, one in which the plaintiff resides and the other at ...... Chetla Road, Kolkata which was let out to tenants. The plaintiff being the only heir and legal representative of his parents who have since died, the plaintiff has inherited both the immovable properties.

4. As the plaintiff was a minor, on an application made before the District Judge, Alipore the defendant No. 1 was appointed as the certified guardian of the plaintiff.

5. The plaintiff was being maintained during his minority out of the rents and profits of the immovable property situate at ...... Chetla Road, Kolkata.

6. The defendant No. 1 was bound to obtain permission from the District Judge for dealing with the properties of the plaintiff during his minority. However, the defendant No. 1 without obtaining any permission from the learned court sold and transferred the immovable property of the minor by a registered deed of sale dated .... to defendant No. 2 when the plaintiff was a minor. Such sale was not for the benefit of the plaintiff. The sale price was only ₹........ when the property was worth ₹.......

7. The defendant No. 2 purchased the property at an under value fully knowing that the property belonged to a minor and that without the consent of the learned court the defendant No. 1 had no right to dispose of the said immovable property.

8. The plaintiff has attained majority on 5th January 20 .... The plaintiff is entitled to and claims cancellation of the said sale deed made in favour of defendant No. 2.

9. In the premises, the plaintiff claims a declaration that the said sale is void as the minor's property was sold without the consent of the learned court which appointed defendant No. 1 as certified guardian of the plaintiff, then a minor.

10. The cause of action for this suit arose on 2nd March 20 .... when the said property was sold to defendant No. 2 and on 5th January 20 .... when the plaintiff attained majority.

11. For the purposes of jurisdiction and court-fees the suit is valued at ₹ .... on which proper court-fees in stamps have been paid.

The plaintiff, therefore, claims:

(*a*) Decree declaring that the sale of the immovable property as described in the sale deed to defendant No. 2 is null and void and the said sale deed be set aside and that the said sale is not binding on the plaintiff.

(*b*) Defendant No. 2 be directed to produce the said sale deed so that this learned court may cancel the same as invalid.

(*c*) Direction on defendant No. 2 to make over possession of the said property to the plaintiff.

(*d*) Cost.

(*e*) Further and other orders be made as to this learned court may deem fit and proper to afford complete relief to the plaintiff.

Verification

Affidavit

143. Suit for recovery of money for contractual works done

In the Court of .... at ....

Suit No. .... of 20 ....

(Set out cause title)

The above-mentioned plaintiff states as follows:

1. That the plaintiff is a contractor by occupation.

2. That the defendant wanted in January, 20 ......, to effect repair works and whitewash of his premises at ...... Town P.S. ...... within the jurisdiction of this court by using materials and employing labour at the cost of the defendant. The entire work was estimated at ₹ .... and is specifically described in the Schedule below. The plaintiff agreed and it was settled in January, 20 ......, that the plaintiff would complete the work within February, 20 ...., and shall be paid his dues by the first week of March, 20 ....

3. That between the 5th and the 25th day of February, 20 ...... the plaintiff has executed the work and not gratuitously.

4. That the plaintiff demanded from the defendant the said sum of ₹ .... on the 4th of March, 20 ...... but the defendant did not pay. The plaintiff had thereafter requested the defendant in writing by a notice dated ...., sent to the defendant per registered post with A/D, for payment of the said sum but to no result.

5. That the cause of action arose in the first week of March, 20 ......, when the aforesaid sum stood payable on completion of the work.

6. That for the purpose of jurisdiction and court-fees the suit is valued at ₹ .... and *ad valorem* court-fees are paid thereon.

The plaintiff, therefore, claims:

(*a*) A decree for ₹ ....

(*b*) Costs of the suit.

SCHEDULE OF WORKS DONE

Verification

Affidavit

NOTES: 1. When remuneration is fixed—suit is for the agreed sum. But when no remuneration is fixed—suit is for a reasonable sum or the market rate for the services rendered. See s. 70 of the Indian Contract Act.

2. When no time is fixed for remuneration—limitation is three years from the time when the work is completed—*vide* Art. 18 of the Limitation Act.

3. When a work is done under a contract pursuant to the terms thereof no amount can be claimed by way of *quantum meruit*—*Puran Lal* v *State of UP* AIR 1971 SC 712.

CONTRIBUTION

144. Suit by a lessee against co-lessees for contribution

In the Court of .... at ....

Suit No. .... of 20 ....

Mr. X .... *Plaintiff*

versus

Mr. A .... *Defendant* No. 1

Mr. B. .... *Defendant* No. 2

The plaintiff states as follows:

1. That the defendants are first cousins of the plaintiff. The plaintiff and the said defendants are lessees in respect of the premises described in the Scheduled below and are jointly liable to pay to the lessor ₹ .... annually as rent for the said premises according to English calender year.

2. That the defendants did pay their share in the rent so also the plaintiff. Thereupon the lessor of the premises brought a Money Suit No. .... of the year .... in the court of .... at .... impleading the plaintiff and the defendants as defendants in the said Money Suit No. .... of .... and got a decree on .... for ₹ .... as rent for the years 20 ...... to 20 .... both inclusive, with costs.

3. That the decretal amount was not paid whereupon the lessor brought a Money Execution Case No. .... of the year .... against the plaintiff and the defendants and the house property of the plaintiff was sought to be sold in the said Execution proceedings.

4. That to save the property, the plaintiff was constrained to meet the decretal dues of the said Money Suit No. .... of .... together with costs of execution amounting to ₹ ....

5. The plaintiff requested the defendants to pay the proportionate amount payable by them towards the rent for the years for which the Money Decree was passed. But they have refused to pay their share.

6. That the plaintiff is entitled to recover from the defendant the proportion amount due to be borne by them.

7. That the cause of action for this suit arose on .... when the plaintiff paid dues in the share of the defendants at .... within the jurisdiction of this court.

8. Suit—valuation (share of the defendant in the money paid by the plaintiff).

The plaintiff claims a decree of ₹ .... from the defendants being the share in the dues of the lessor paid by the plaintiff.

SCHEDULE

(State here description of the premises)

Verification

Affidavit

NOTES: 1. See s. 69 of the Contract Act—for joint liability.

2. Co-lessees are liable to contribution once a decree for rent is passed against lessees jointly—See *Sashti Gopal Samui* v *Haridas Bagdi* AIR 1938 Cal 415.

3. Contribution suits are to be instituted within three years of the date of payment—Art. 48 of the Limitation Act 1963.

4. Contribution suits generally occur amongst co-debtors, co-partners, co-owners, co-sureties, co-tortfeasors etc. But joint wrong-doers are not entitled to sue for contribution—*Dharni Dhar* v *Chandra Shekhar* AIR 1951 All 774—Dissenting. See AIR 1936 Pat 49 and *Rama Krushna Mohanty* v *Radha Krushna Mohanty* AIR 1970 Ori 237. Co-owner of property carrying out repairs and claiming share in cost from other co-owner enjoying benefits of repairs—Principle of contribution supports such claim—*Ganga Saran* v *Narayan Das* AIR 1971 All 43.

5. Section 69—Reimbursement of person paying money due by another in payment of which he is interested (Contract Act). The section deals with reimbursement and not with contribution, whereas s. 43 of the Contract Act enjoins that any one of joint promisors may be compelled to perform.

Each of two or more joint promisors may compel every other joint promisor to contribute equally with himself to the performance of the promisee, unless a contrary intention appears from the contract.

145. Suit by manager of a joint Hindu family for contribution in respect of money borrowed for joint family purposes

In the Court of .... at ....

Suit No. .... of 20 ....

(Set out cause title)

The plaintiff states as follows:

1. The plaintiff and the defendant A.B. and C.D. at all times material hereto were and are members of a joint Hindu family governed by the Dayabhaga. The relationship between the parties will appear from the pedigree set out hereunder:

Pedigree:

2. At all material times the plaintiff was the managing member of the said family.

3. In .... 20 ...., money was required for payment of Government revenue and other joint family expenses and on or about .... 20......., the plaintiff borrowed ₹ .... repayable with interest at the rate of 6 *per cent.* from one X.Y. of .... on a promissory note and expended the amount for the said purposes.

Particulars of expenses:

(Here give particulars with dates)

4. In .... 20 ...., the defendant C.D. brought a suit for partition against the plaintiff and the defendant A.B. herein (Suit No. .... of .... on the file of ....).

5. By the decrees made in the said suit the joint family properties were partitioned and the money due under the said promissory note was declared to be a joint family debt.

6. In .... 20 ...., the plaintiff paid the said X.Y. the whole amount then due on the said promissory note for principal and interest, namely, ₹ ....

The plaintiff claims—

₹ .... from each of the defendants as his share of the amount paid by the plaintiff as aforesaid.

Verification

Affidavit

146. Suit by a partner against other partners for contribution

In the Court of .... at ....

Suit No. .... of 20 ....

(Set out cause title)

The above-named plaintiff states as follows:

1. That the plaintiff and the defendants Nos. 1 to 3 were at all material times partners of M/s. Saha Brothers, a partnership firm with its registered office at ...... P.S. ...... District ....

2. That during subsistence of the partnership the plaintiff and the defendants jointly borrowed for the interest of the said partnership from Sri A.B. a sum of ₹ .... on .... by executing a handnote the same day agreeing to repay the said loan together with interest at 8% per annum on demand.

3. That the said loan was not repaid. Thereupon the said A.B. brought a Money Suit No. .... of 20 ...... in the court of the ...... at .... against this plaintiff and the defendants for his dues under the said handnote and the suit was decreed for ₹ .... inclusive of costs.

4. That the plaintiff met from his own fund the entire decretal dues on ...... and is entitled to recover from the defendants 3/4th share of the money he so paid.

5. That the cause of action for this suit arose on ...... when the plaintiff paid the entire decretal amount at .... within the jurisdiction of this court.

6. That the suit is valued at ₹ .... for the purposes of jurisdiction and court-fees and *ad valorem* court-fees are paid thereon.

The plaintiff, therefore, prays:

(*a*) A decree of ₹.............

(*b*) Costs.

Verification

Affidavit

NOTES: 1. A partner is entitled, to contribution from co-partners in a like case—43 CWN 1214.

2. Limitation—three years *vide* Art. 48 of the Limitation Act 1963.

147. Suit by a partner against his co-partner for contribution

In the Court of .... at ....

Suit No. .... of 20 ....

(Set out cause title)

The plaintiff states as follows:

1. That at all material times the plaintiff and the defendant carried on business in partnership under the name of .... at ....

2. That on ...... 20 ...... the plaintiff and the defendant borrowed ₹ .... from M/s. (Name the Bank) on their joint promissory note, repayable on demand with interest at 16 per cent per annum, and applied the money for partnership purposes.

3. That the said Bank instituted a suit in the court of .... on the said promissory note (being Money Suit No. .... of ....) and on .... obtained a decree for ₹ .... with costs.

4. That to avoid execution of the decree in the said Money Suit No. .... of ...... the plaintiff paid out of his personal fund the said Bank ₹ .... in full satisfaction of their claims under the decree.

5. The defendant has refused to pay one-half of the amount to the plaintiff even after demands.

The plaintiff claims—

₹ .... as half share of the amount paid as aforesaid.

Verification

Affidavit

148. Suit for contribution between co-judgment-debtors

In the Court of .... at ....

Suit No. .... of 20 ....

(Set out cause title)

The above-named plaintiff states as under:

1. That the plaintiff and the defendant jointly took a loan of ₹ ...... from the .... Bank of India, Cooch Behar branch, on ...... by executing jointly a handnote the same day agreeing to repay the loan on demand with ...... % interest per annum thereon.

2. That the loan was not liquidated in spite of requests made by the said bank in that behalf. Thereupon the .... bank commenced and SCC. Suit No. .... of 20... in the court of .... at .... The plaintiff and the defendants entered their appearance in the said SCC suit and on admission of claim of the plaintiff of the said SCC suit the same was decreed for ₹ ...... without costs on ....

3. That the said .... bank next brought SCC Execution Case No. ...... of 20... against the plaintiff and the defendant for recovery of decretal dues and sought to attach the household articles of the plaintiff by process of the court.

4. That the plaintiff to avoid discomfiture paid to the decree-holder. Bank on .... the entire decretal amount together with costs of execution amounting to ₹ .... out of his personal funds and is entitled to recover from the defendant $^1/_2$ of the said amount.

5. Cause of action—(on date of payment by the plaintiff in excess of his own share).

6. Suit—valuation (demand—amount of the plaintiff).

The plaintiff claims a decree of ₹ ....

Verification

Affidavit

NOTES: 1. See AIR 1950 Pat 212; 45 CWN 357.

2. Limitation—Art. 23 of the Limitation Act 1963.

149. Suit for contribution by an executant of a promissory note who paid the whole of the judgment debt

In the Court of .... at ....

Suit No. .... of 20 ....

(Set out cause title)

The plaintiff states as follows:

1. That the plaintiff and the defendant jointly executed a promissory note on ...... for ₹ ...... in favour of one (name the promises) each receiving ₹ .... out of the consideration.

2. That the money having not been paid back the said (promisee) sued both the plaintiff and the defendant on the said promissory note in Money Suit No. .... of .... in the court of .... and obtained a decree against the plaintiff and the defendant for ₹ ...... with costs.

3. That the decree being not satisfied, the said promisee executed the decree against the plaintiff alone by causing a warrant to be issued for his arrest, and on .... 20 .... whereupon the plaintiff paid the said promisee ₹ ...... in full satisfaction of his claim under the decree aforesaid.

4. The plaintiff demanded from the defendant the amount due to be paid by him under the promissory note but the defendant has refused to pay.

The plaintiff claims ....

(*a*) A decree for ₹ .... (half of the amount paid by the plaintiff as aforesaid) against the defendant.

Verification

Affidavit

150. Suit for contribution between parties (co-plaintiff or co-defendants) in a suit

In the Court of .... at ....

Suit No. .... of 20 ....

(Set out cause title)

(i) *When co-plaintiffs*

The plaintiff aforesaid states as follows:

1. That the plaintiff and the defendant jointly brought a Title Suit No. ...... of the year .... in the Court of the Civil Judge (Junior Division) at .... claiming their right, title and interest therein and for khas possession of the suit-property, mentioned as such in the plaint of the said Title Suit, against one A.B.

2. That the said Title Suit No. .... of .... was dismissed with costs on .... after hearing.

3. That the said A.B. realised costs of the suit amounting to ₹ .... on .... from the plaintiff.

4. That the plaintiff is entitled to recover $^1/_2$ of the said sum from the defendant.

5. Cause of action—(on date of payment by the plaintiff).

(ii) *When co-defendants*

1. That one A.B. commenced a Title Suit No. .... of the year ...... in the Court of the Civil Judge (Junior Division) at .... impleading this plaintiff and the defendant as defendants in the said title-suit.

2. That the plaintiff and the defendant jointly entered their appearance in the said Title-Suit, submitted a joint written statement and contested the suit.

3. That after hearing the said Title-Suit was decreed on ...... with costs.

4. That the said A.B. realised costs of the said Title-Suit amounting to ₹ .... on .... from this plaintiff alone.

5. The plaintiff demanded from the defendant the amount of costs due to be paid by him under the decree of the court but the defendant refused to pay.

6. Cause of action—(as above).

The plaintiff claims a decree of ₹ .... being $^1/_2$ of the amount paid by the plaintiff to the said A.B.

Verification

Affidavit

NOTES: 1. Limitation—three years *vide* Art. 48 of the Limitation Act 1963.

2. In a case reported in AIR 1970 Ori 237—'A' deposited in court for 'B' on behalf of himself and others—A filed a suit for contribution against others—Period of three years commences to run not from the date of deposit but from the date of appropriation of the deposit by 'B'.

151. Suit by a surety against a co-surety for contribution

In the Court of .... at ....

Suit No. .... of 20 ....

(Set out cause title)

The above-named plaintiff states as follows:

1. That the plaintiff and the defendant had by executing a bond on .... stood sureties for payment by one A.B. of a sum of ₹ .... to C.D. by the ...... day of ...... 20 ...... and bound themselves for payment of the said sum to C.D. in case A.B. defaulted in payment.

2. That the said A.B. did not pay the money to C.D. within the stipulated period whereupon the C.D. had brought a Money Suit No. ...... of the year .... against the said A.B. and the plaintiff in the court of .... at .... and obtained a decree on .... for ₹ .... inclusive of costs.

3. That the plaintiff as surety had paid to the said C.D. the said decretal amount on ....

4. The plaintiff demanded from the defendant the amount of costs due to be paid by him under the decree of the court but the defendant refused to pay.

5. That the cause of action for this suit arose on ...... when the plaintiff paid the decretal amount at .... within the jurisdiction of this court.

6. Suit valuation .... ($^1/_2$ of the amount paid by the plaintiff).

The plaintiff, therefore, claims:

I. A decree for ₹ .... being $^1/_2$ of the money paid by the plaintiff.

II. Costs of suit.

Verification

Affidavit

NOTES: 1. For liability of a co-surety see s. 146 of the Indian Contract Act.
2. Limitation—three years *vide* Art. 43 of the Limitation Act 1963 from the date when the surety pays anything in excess of his own share.

152. Suit by a trustee against his co-trustees for contribution

In the Court of .... at ....

Suit No. .... of 20 ....

(Set out cause title)

The plaintiff states as follows:

1. The plaintiff and the defendant are the trustees, and one C.D., the beneficiary, under the will of A.B., late of ....

2. In .... 20 ...., the said C.D. instituted a suit in this Court (No. .... of ....) against the plaintiff and the defendant herein for accounts and administration of the trust estate.

3. On .... 20 ...., the preliminary decree for administration was made in the said suit and an account was directed to be taken of the dealings of the defendant thereto with the trust estate.

4. The sum of ₹ .... was found due from the said defendants on the taking of accounts, and on .... a final decree was made in the said suit against them for the said sum together with all costs of the suit and of the reference and interest on judgment at 6 *per cent.*

5. The costs aforesaid were duly taxed and the party costs amounted to ₹ .... as *per* allocation issued on ....

6. The said C.D. threatened to execute the decree against the plaintiff alone, whereupon the plaintiff deposited into Court to the credit of the said suit ₹ .... on .... out of his personal funds in full satisfaction of the decree aforesaid.

7. The plaintiff demanded from the defendant the amount of costs due to be paid by him under the decree of the court but the defendant refused to pay.

The plaintiff claims—

₹ ...., one half share of the amount paid by the plaintiff as aforesaid.

Verification

Affidavit

CONVERSION

153. Suit for conversion of goods by failure to deliver

In the Court of .... at ....

Suit No. .... of 20 ....

(Set out cause title)

The plaintiff states:

1. That one A.B. owned a Telerad Television set. A.B. died on ...... and on his death the plaintiff became the owner of the said television set and was entitled to the possession thereof.

2. That the defendant is a distant relation of the said A.B. Towards the last days of A.B. the defendant removed the television set to his house and has been wrongfully possessing the same.

3. That the plaintiff had requested the defendant to deliver up the same to the plaintiff. The defendant avoided. Thereafter the plaintiff had issued a notice dated the ...... day of .... 20 .... through his authorised lawyer requesting the defendant immediate delivery of the same. The defendant received the said notice on .... but failed to deliver up the same and has thereby converted the same to his own use.

4. In the premises, the plaintiff has been deprived of the use of the same and the plaintiff has suffered loss and damage.

5. Cause of action.

6. Suit valuation.

The plaintiff claims:

(*i*) delivery of the said Telerad Television set with accessories;

(*ii*) alternatively, value of the same; and

(*iii*) damages of ₹ ...... for conversion.

Verification

Affidavit

NOTES: 1. The tort of conversion consists in an act of wilful interference, without lawful justification, with any chattel in any manner inconsistent with the right of another, whereby that other is deprived of the use and possession of it. Two elements are combined in such interference (1) dealing with a chattel in a manner inconsistent with the right of the person entitled to it, and (2) an intention in so doing to deny that person's right or to assert a right which in fact is inconsistent with such right—*Namor Ali* v *C.I.W.T. Corpn.* AIR 1978 SC 274.

2. There are three distinct methods in which one may be guilty of conversion (1) by wrongly taking a chattel, (2) wrongfully detaining it, (3) by wrongfully disposing of it. In the first case, the wrong-doer acquires a possession which is wrongful *ab initio*. In the second, he acquires possession rightfully but retains it wrongful. In the third case, he neither takes it wrongfully nor retains it, but so acts that it is lost to the true owner—*Paramananda Mohanty* v *Bira Behera* AIR 1978 Ori 114.

154. Suit for conversion by destruction

In the Court of .... at ....

Suit No. .... of 20 ....

(Set out cause title)

The plaintiff states:

1. That the plaintiff was the owner of a gold wrist watch, described below and was entitled to possession thereof.

2. The defendant, while in possession thereof, tried his hand in repairing the same. He is/was never a watch-maker and being a novice destroyed and damaged the watch beyond repairs.

3. The plaintiff, by reason of matters aforesaid, has been deprived of the same and he has suffered loss and damage.

The plaintiff claims:

(*i*) value of the watch ₹ ....

(*ii*) Costs.

Description of the watch

Verification

Affidavit

155. Suit for detention and conversion of goods

In the Court of .... at ....

Suit No. .... of 20 ....

(Set out cause title)

The plaintiff states as follows:

1. That the plaintiff is and was the owner of a gold wrist watch, described below and was/is entitled to possession thereof.

2. That the defendant has been wrongfully possessing the same since the .... day of ...... 20 ...... (here describe how the defendant came to possess it).

3. The defendant was instructed by a notice dated the ...... day of ...... 20 ...... sent to him by registered post with A/D to deliver up the same to the plaintiff but the defendant did not. The defendant is wrongfully detaining the same depriving the plaintiff of its use and benefits.

4. In the premises, the plaintiff has suffered loss and damage.

5. Cause of action.

6. Suit valuation (value of the watch).

Description of the watch

The plaintiff claims:

(*i*) Value of the watch ₹ ......

(*ii*) Damages for detention ₹ ......

(*iii*) Damages for conversion ₹ ......

(*iv*) Costs of suit.

(*v*) Any other relief.

Verification

Affidavit

COPYRIGHT

156. Suit for infringement of copyright in a dramatic work

In the Court of .... at ....

Suit No. .... of 20 ....

(Set out cause title)

The plaintiff states as follows:

1. The plaintiff is the author and the owner of the copyright in a play in one act entitled "The Rogue" and of the sole right of performance of the said work.

2. The defendant at all material times was the President of The Young Women's Dramatic Society of .... and she authorised or permitted the members of the said society to represent or perform the said play on 5th February 20 ...., at the .... Hall.

3. The said performance was without the plaintiff's consent and licence and was in public and constituted an infringement of plaintiff's copyright.

The plaintiff claims—

₹ .... damages.

Verification

Affidavit

157. Suit for infringement of copyright in a book

In the High Court at Calcutta

Suit No. .... of 20 ....

Ordinary Original Civil Jurisdiction

M/s. P. Co. Ltd., a company registered under the Companies Act 1956 and carrying on business at............... Kolkata within the said jurisdiction.

.......*Plaintiff*

versus

M/s. X & Co. Ltd., a company registered under the Companies Act 1956 and carrying on business at .... Kolkata within the said jurisdiction.

.........*Defendant*

The plaintiff states:

1. The plaintiff carries on business as the printers and publishers and is the owner of copyright of the book called "DREAM" edited by Mr. M. but the copyright has been sold to plaintiff.

2. The defendant is owner of a Theatrical Party and performs Jatras in public halls and in open spaces and sells tickets for the audience who desire to attend such functions.

3. The defendant has not obtained any written consent or licence from the plaintiff for using or performing drama for the purpose of using contents or any portion thereof of the said "DREAM" of which the plaintiff is the sole owner.

4. The defendant is thus infringing the plaintiff"s copyright of the said literary work "DREAM" and by adaptations and conversion of the said work in a dramatic play for performance in public styled as "IMAGINATION".

5. For this wrongful infringement of copyrights of the plaintiff in the said "DREAM" during performance of the drama under the name "IMAGINATION" the defendant has violated the copyrights of the plaintiff in the said "DREAM" inasmuch as the theme and contention of the said "DREAM" and the said "IMAGINATION" are indentical.

6. The defendant is in possession of the manuscript of conversation and adaptation thereof and intends to publish the same by only changing the title of the book to "IMAGINATION", as edited and authored by the defendant himself.

7. For such wrongful exhibition of play of the "DREAM" work with changed name of "IMAGINATION", the defendant has infringed upon copyright of the said literary work "DREAM" play by adaptation and conversion thereof for performance in public but styled as "IMAGINATION".

8. For such wrongful violation by the defendant by acts of adaptation and conversion of the said work "DREAM" of the plaintiff and utilising the same by the heading "IMAGINATION" the plaintiff has suffered loss and damages which plaintiff is assessing at ₹ ....

9. The plaintiff by its lawyer"s regd. letter dated 15th September 20....... demanded the defendant to forthwith surrender the manuscript of the said converted and adapted work "IMAGINATION" and to pay an amount of ₹ .... for the damages suffered by the plaintiff due to wrongful infringement of the plaintiff"s copyrights.

10. In spite of demands made, and also the said letters including the one dated 2nd October 2005, the defendant failed to pay the compensation as required by

plaintiff and to resist from exhibiting any such drama or any other form under the name "IMAGINATION" and/or using the contents of the said literary work "DREAM" without proper consent of the plaintiff. The plaintiff also claims damages for ₹......... for infringement of copyrights of the plaintiff by staging the play in the form of literary work "DREAM".

11. The plaintiff claims surrender of original manuscript of IMAGINATION copied or adapted from the literary work "DREAM" and all other printed copies thereof and also an undertaking not to use any other material of the literary work entitled "DREAM".

12. The plaintiff also claims compensations from the defendant for the wrongful infringement of the copyright of the plaintiff in his work "DREAM" without proper permission of the plaintiff.

13. The plaintiff also claims surrender by the defendant of the manuscript of the book entitled "IMAGINATION" and payment of ₹ .... by way of damages suffered by the plaintiff due to wrongful infringement of the plaintiff"s copyright by defendant.

14. The plaintiff's cause of action for this suit arose within the jurisdiction of this learned court on or about 15th September 20 .... in terms of demand notice and the cause of action is still continuing day to day.

15. For the purposes of jurisdiction and court-fees, the suit is valued at ₹ .... on which court-fees in stamps have been duly paid.

16. No part of the plaintiff"s claims is barred by Law of Limitation.

17. In the premises, this Hon"ble Court has the jurisdiction to entertain, try and determine this suit.

The plaintiff, therefore, prays for and claims:

(*a*) Decree for payment of ₹ .... by way of damages suffered by plaintiff due to wrongful infringement of copyright of plaintiff;

(*b*) Decree directing the defendant to surrender manuscript of the work "IMAGINATION" within 7 days of service of the said order to be made herein;

(*c*) Order of injunction be issued restraining defendant, his agents and servants from staging performance of the drama originating from work "DREAM" but in the name of "IMAGINATION" or in any form whatsoever;

(*d*) Receiver;

(*e*) Injunction;

(*f*) Costs;

(*g*) Such further orders be made or other reliefs be given as this Hon"ble Court may deem fit and proper to afford complete relief to plaintiff.

Verification

Affidavit

158. Suit for surrender of manuscript infringing copyright

In the High Court at Calcutta

Suit No. .... of 20 ....

Ordinary Original Civil Jurisdiction

Mr. P., residing at ...., Kolkata
.... *Plaintiff*

versus

Mr. X., residing at ...., Kolkata
.... *Defendant*

The plaintiff states:

1. The plaintiff is the writer and owner of the copyright in the original literary work "DREAM" since 20 ....

2. The defendant is the owner of a Yatra Party and performs Yatras in public places at different locations from time to time.

3. The defendant without obtaining any prior consent either written or oral, from the plaintiff has infringed the plaintiff's copyright in the said literary work "DREAM" by suitable adaptation and conversion of the said literary work "DREAM" by performing in public under the style of "IMAGINATION" in the last few weeks.

4. The defendant is in possession of the original manuscript of the converted work "IMAGINATION" and intends to publish the same as the original book edited by the defendant.

5. For such wrongful adaptation and conversion of the ideas and matters contained in the said literary work of the plaintiff being "DREAM" and changing the title of the book to "IMAGINATION" and performing Jatras in public using the same for his purpose has been causing loss and damages to the plaintiff.

6. The plaintiff by his letter dated 18th September 20..., demanded from the defendant to surrender the original manuscript of the converted and adapted book "IMAGINATION" and also to pay an amount of ₹ .... as compensation for the damages suffered by plaintiff due to wrongful and illegal acts of the defendant. The defendant was required to respond within 15 days of receipt of the said letter.

7. The defendant received the said letter on 1st October, 20 ...... but has failed and neglected to comply with the demand or to further retrain from staging dramatic performances in public of the said work "IMAGINATION" by adapted version of the plaintiff's literary work "DREAM".

8. In view of the said wrongful acts and infringement of the copyright by the defendant, the plaintiff has suffered damages which the plaintiff assesses at ₹ .... lakhs and demanded payment of the said sum and surrender of the adopted work "IMAGINATION".

9. The plaintiff claims surrender of the original manuscript of the book "IMAGINATION" which has infringed upon the copyright of the plaintiff's original literary work "DREAM" and also a decree for ₹ .... by way of damages with interest and costs thereon.

10. The plaintiff's cause of action for this suit arose on .... within jurisdiction of this learned court and the same is continuing day to day.

11. For the purposes of jurisdiction and court-fees, the suit is valued at ₹ .... on which *ad valorem* court-fees in stamps have been duly paid.

12. No part of the plaintiff's claims is barred by Law of Limitation.

The plaintiff, therefore, prays for and claims:

(*a*) Decree for ₹ .... with interest @ 15% per annum till payment by the defendant;

(*b*) Injunction restraining the defendant, his servants and agents from performing any Yatras or any other drama or shows under the name "IMAGINATION" which is really an adaptation and conversion of the plaintiff's literary work "DREAM";

(*c*) Injunction restraining defendant from performing Yatra under the name "IMAGINATION";

(*d*) Decree directing the defendant to forthwith surrender the original manuscript of the book "IMAGINATION" which is in infringement of the plaintiff's original literary work "DREAM";

(*e*) Injunction restraining the defendant from in any way infringing the plaintiff's copyright in the play "DREAM";

(*f*) Receiver;

(*g*) Costs;

(*h*) Further and other reliefs.

Verification

Affidavit

159. Suit for infringement of copyright in a plan

In the Court of .... at ....

Suit No. .... of 20 ....

(Set out cause title)

The plaintiff states as follows:

1. The plaintiff is a designer and fitter of shop fronts and the like and carries on business at .... in the town of ....

2. The defendants are partners who carry on business as .... at .... in the town of ....

3. On .... 20 ...., the plaintiff sent to the defendant at his request, a blue-print which was a plan and elevation for a shop front at .... and also a detailed specification of the work on the said shop front. A copy of the said blue-print is marked "A' and annexed hereto.

4. In October 20 ...., the plaintiff saw the shop front erected at .... by the firm of .... The said work was a reproduction of a substantial part of the said plan and elevation.

5. The plaintiff is the author and the owner of the copyright in the said plan and elevation and the defendants infringed the said copyright by authorising the reproduction of the said plan and elevation in the construction of the said shop front, without the consent of the plaintiff first had and obtained.

The plaintiff claims—

₹ .... damages.

ANNEXURE

Verification

Affidavit

160. Suit for infringement of copyright in industrial design

In the Court of the Civil Judge (Senior Division) at ....

Suit No. .... of 20 ....

Mr. P., residing at ....

.... *Plaintiff*

versus

Mr. Z, residing at ....

...... *Defendant*

Suit for claim of damages and injunction for an infringement of copyrights valued at ₹ ....

The plaintiff states as follows:

1. The plaintiff is a Registered Owner of an Industrial Design No. V for Shirts, printed on the back as "GOOD LUCK WITH PICTURE" which is the Registered Design. The said registered design is printed both on cotton and silk shirts and Ganjees/Vests.

2. The plaintiff is enjoying the said copyright in the said Industrial Design for the last several years ever since the said Industrial Copyright Registered Design was first registered.

3. The defendant without any written consent of the plaintiff or any authority of law made certain half-sleeved Shirts/Ganjees with the substantially same design as that of and sold the same plaintiff on the back of which the said plaintiff's Registered Design has been printed and registered thus infringing the said copyright of the plaintiff.

4. The defendant by using the same Registered Copyright/Industrial Design of the plaintiff and the defendant selling the said products in the market without any lawful authority is infringing upon the plaintiff's patent and property rights as a result of which the plaintiff has suffered damages due to huge reduction in sale of plaintiff's products in the said design and the defendant has illegally earned huge profits out of such sale of wearing materials passed off as the product of the plaintiff. The plaintiff thus claims loss and damages suffered by plaintiff due to wrongful infringement of the plaintiff's Copyrights and Industrial Design Rights. The plaintiff assesses such loss and damages at ₹ .... and claims the same from the defendant and also prays for an order of injunction restraining the defendant and his servants from infringing the Copyright or Industrial Design of the plaintiff's products.

5. In spite of demands, the defendant has not paid the claims of the plaintiff. In spite of requests, the defendant has not refrained from selling his products in the market by wrongfully imitating and using the Copyrights and Industrial Design of the plaintiff wilfully and wrongfully in selling defendant's products.

6. The plaintiff's cause of action for this suit arose within the jurisdiction of this learned court on or about 10th January 20 .... and the same is continuing from day to day thus causing further loss and damages to the plaintiff.

7. For purpose of jurisdiction and court-fees, the suit is valued at ₹ .... on which the necessary court-fees in stamps have been paid.

8. No part of the plaintiff's claims is barred by the Law of Limitation in view of the continuing breaches and infringement of the plaintiff's Copyrights and the Industrial Design and other wrongful acts of the defendant.

Particulars of Copyright and Industrial Design

"GOOD LUCK WITH PICTURE" on Shirts are annexed hereto marked "A'.

The infringement of plaintiff's copyrights by defendant in garments in which the plaintiff's Copyrights and Industrial Design have been imitated and used is annexed hereto and marked "B'.

The plaintiff, therefore, prays for and claims:

(*a*) Decree for payment of ₹ .... with interest at 10% per annum;

(*b*) Injunction restraing the defendant, his agents and servants from using or imitating the plaintiff's Copyright or Industrial Design being "GOOD LUCK WITH PICTURE" on any product of the defendant without prior written consent of plaintiff;

(*c*) Decree for furnishing full statements of accounts of sales of the products of defendant using the plaintiff's Copyright/Industrial Design or design not substantially different from plaintiff's said registered design or copyright;

(*d*) Decree for the damages for wrongful and illegal acts of the defendant causing loss of sales and business of plaintiff as might be assessed by this learned court;

(*e*) Direction for delivering and surrendering of design prepared by defendant on imitation of the said Copyright/Industrial Design of the plaintiff to this learned court for necessary destruction;

(*f*) Costs;

(*g*) Further orders be made and directions be given as this learned court may deem fit and proper to afford complete relief to the plaintiff.

ANNEXURES

Verification

Affidavit

161. Suit for injunction restraining infringement of copyright in a book

In the High Court at Calcutta

Ordinary Original Civil Jurisdiction

Suit No. .... of 20 ....

Mr. P., residing at .... Kolkata

.... *Plaintiff*

versus

Mr. X., residing at .... Kolkata

.... *Defendant*

Suit for injunction restraining the infringement of copyright valued at ₹ ....

The plaintiff states as follows:

1. The plaintiff is the author and owner of copyright as depicted in his original literary work entitled "THE HUMAN NATURE".

2. The defendant is the owner and conductor of a Theatrical party and performs various dramas in the public in the city.

3. The defendant any without obtaining, permission of the plaintiff in writing or orally, infringed upon the plaintiff's copyright of the said literary work by adaptation and conversion of the said literary work for his dramatic work for performance in the public styled as "INSTINCT".

4. The defendant is in possession of the original manuscript of the said converted literary work and intends to publish the same by changing title of the said book as edited by defendant.

5. The original adaptation and conversion of the plaintiff's literary work by the defendant and incorporating the same in the instinct resulted in the plaintiff suffering loss and damages which is estimated at ₹ ....

6. The plaintiff vide his letter dated 10th September, 20..., demanded from the defendant to surrender the manuscript of the said converted and adapted book "INSTINCT" and demanded payment of ₹ .... as value of the damages suffered by the plaintiff due to such infringement of the copyrights of the plaintiff's work within 3 weeks.

7. The defendant received the said letter of the plaintiff but has failed and neglected to comply with the said demand of plaintiff.

8. The plaintiff, therefore, claims immediate surrender of the manuscript of the said book "INSTINCT" and also payment of ₹ .... being the compensation for loss and damages suffered by the plaintiff due to the wrongful act of infringement of copyright of the plaintiff's book.

9. The plaintiff states that the present suit's cause of action arose at .... Kolkata within the jurisdiction of this Hon'ble court and such wrongful act by the defendant is still continuing day by day.

10. For the purposes of jurisdiction and court-fees, the suit is valued at ₹ .... on which court-fees in stamps have been paid.

11. No part of the plaintiff's claims herein is barred by the Law of Limitation.

The plaintiff, therefore, prays for and claims:

(*a*) Decree directing the defendant to surrender the original manuscript instinct copied from the plaintiff's original literary work "The Human Nature" within a period of 10 days from the date of order to the plaintiff;

(*b*) Decree for payment of ₹ .... by way of compensation towards the loss and damages suffered by plaintiff due to infringement of the copyright;

(*c*) Injunction restraining the defendant, his agents and representatives from committing any act further infringing the copyright of the plaintiff's literary work;

(*d*) Costs;

(*e*) Further and other orders be issued and directions be given as this Hon'ble court may deem fit and proper so as to afford complete relief to the plaintiff.

Verification

Affidavit

162. Suit by assignee of copyright for infringement of the performing right in a song

In the Court of .... at ....

Suit No. .... of 20 ....

(Set out cause title)

The plaintiff states as follows:

1. The plaintiffs, The P.R. Society, Ltd. (hereinafter referred to as "the society,") are a company incorporated under the Companies Act 1956, as a company limited by guarantee, the members of which consist of composers, authors, publishers and proprietors of musical, literary and dramatic works.

2. The objects for which the society was established, as stated in the Memorandum of Association, were "to exercise and enforce on behalf of the members of the society, being the composers of any musical works or the authors of any literary or dramatic works, or the owners of dramatic works, or the owners or publishers of or being otherwise entitled to the benefit of or interested in the copyrights in such works, all rights and remedies under the Copyright Act 1957 or otherwise in respect of the public performance of their works."

3. By Article .... of the Articles of Association, "every member who was a publisher, should during his period of membership assign to the society his interest, whether present or future, in the right to perform any musical or dramatic work which had been or which might thereafter be published by him, and to invest the society with the sole right during the period of his membership to authorise or to forbid the public performance of any works published or to be published by him."

4. In the year 20.........., the plaintiffs Messrs. C. & Co. Ltd. music publishers, became members of the society and by an indenture dated ...., they in accordance with the Articles of Association, assigned to the society (among other things) "the right of performance in all parts of the world of each and every song with words thereof or musical work (not being a musical play) the right of performance of which they belonged to, or should thereafter be acquired by or be or become vested in the assignor during the continuance of the assignor's membership of the society" such rights to be held by the society for the period of the assignor's membership.

5. Thereafter on .... 20 ...., one Mr. W.H.F., the author and composer of a song called "The Wedding," assigned the copyright and sole right of representation of that song to the said C. & Co. Ltd., in consideration of a cash payment.

6. On .... 20 ......, the defendants, proprietors of the Music Hall at .... authorised the public performance of the said song in the said Music Hall without having obtained the consent of the plaintiffs.

7. The defendants threaten and intend to continue the said infringement.

The plaintiffs claim—

1. A decree of perpetual injunction restraining the defendants from permitting their Hall to be used for public performance of the song without the consent of the plaintiffs.
2. ₹ .... damages for infringement.

Verification

Affidavit

163. Suit for damages for infringement of a registered trade mark and for injunction

In the Court of .... at ....

Suit No. .... of 20 ....

(Set out cause title)

The plaintiff states as follows:

1. The plaintiff firm is a registered partnership with its registered office at .... P. S. .... District ....

2. The plaintiff firm is a manufacturer of shampoo, having its workshop at .... P. S. .... District ....

3. That the plaintiff firm registered a trade mark on .... for such shampoo manufactured by them in their workshop by the name "Hair Queen" and have exclusive right to the use of the said trade mark for shampoo manufactured by the plaintiff firm.

4. That the defendant has lately liberated in the market for sale shampoo under the name of 'Black Queen' and has thus infringed the plaintiff's trade mark (state here particulars of infringement—identical mark, confusing resemblance etc.).

5. That the plaintiff firm is suffering loss and is likely to suffer loss unless the defendant be restrained from infringing the trade mark.

6. Cause of action.

7. Suit valuation.

The plaintiff, therefore, prays:

(*a*) For a decree of ₹ .... as damages for infringement of the plaintiff's trade mark.

(*b*) For a perpetual injunction restraining the defendant from infringing plaintiff's aforesaid trade mark.

(*c*) Costs.

Verification

Affidavit

NOTES: 1. Trade mark is to be registered under the Trade Marks Act 1999; for infringement of unregistered Trade Mark the aggrieved person has no right to go to a court of law—See s. 27(1) of the Trade Marks Act 1999. Saving clause s. 27(2)—remedy for "passing off goods" not affected.

2. Suit under s. 142(4) is to be filed in the District Court alone—when a person is wrongly threatened with suit for infringement of a trade mark.

3. Reliefs in a suit for infringement to be sought for—

(*i*) an injunction

(*ii*) at the option of the plaintiff, either damages or an account of profits, together with or without any order for the delivery-up of the infringing labels and marks for destruction or erasure—See s. 135 of the Act; AIR 1965 Mad 250.

4. What constitutes infringement of a Trade Mark—See s. 29 of the Act. Savings—See ss. 35, 36 of the Act.

5. Suit for passing off—See *East End Hosiery Mills* v *Agarwal Textiles* AIR 1971 Cal 3; *National Bell Co.* v *Metal Goods Mfg. Co.* AIR 1971 SC 898; *Ruston & Hornby Ltd.* v *Zamindara Engineering Co.* AIR 1970 SC 1649.

6. Tests of fraudulent imitation of Trade Mark—See *Hariprasad Lalchand* v *Nanoo Khan Hussain Bux* AIR 1968 MP 234. Deceptive similarity in carton, get up and colour scheme with that of the registered Trade Mark constitutes infringement under s. 29(1) of the Trade and Merchandise Marks Act—*Kedar Nath* v *Monga Perfumery & Flour Mills* AIR 1974 Del 12. Deceptive similarity—*Astra IDL Ltd.* v *TTK Pharma Ltd.* AIR 1992 Bom 35; AIR 1990 Cal 225.

   Expression 'deceptively similar'—in deciding the question of similarity of two marks, the following well established principles are to be followed—

   (*i*) Marks are remembered by general impressions or by same significant detail rather than by a photographic recollection of the whole;
   (*ii*) overall similarity is the touchstone;
   (*iii*) marks must be looked at from the first impression of a person of average intelligence and imperfect recollection;
   (*iv*) overall structure, phonetic similarity and similarity of idea are important and both visual and phonetic tests are to be applied;
   (*v*) marks must be compared as a whole, microscopic examination being impermissible; and
   (*vi*) the board and salient features must be considered for which the marks must not be placed side by side to find out difference in design.

   In addition, the nature of the commodity, the class of purchasers, the mode of purchase and other surrounding circumstances must also be taken into consideration—*Hiralal Prabhudas* v *Ganesh Trading Co.* AIR 1984 Bom 218. What one has to see is overall impression given by mark in minds of members of general public—*National Chemicals* v *Reckitt & Colman* AIR 1991 Bom 76 (case of *F. Hoffimann La Roche* v *Geoffry Manners* AIR 1970 SC 2062 followed).

7. Suit for passing off—jurisdiction of court—court where plaintiff has substantial market for his product has jurisdiction. The suit is not required to be filed only where plaintiff resides—*Cadila* v *Kamath* AIR 1991 Kant 303.

DAMAGES

164. Suit for damages caused by negligent driving of a car

In the Court of the Civil Judge (Senior Division) at Alipore,
District 24 Parganas (South)

Suit No. .... of 20 ......

1. Mr. P residing at ...., 7, Alipore Road, Kolkata
2. Mrs. Q, wife of Mr. P, residing at ...., Alipore Road, Kolkata

.... *Plaintiffs*

versus

1. Mr. X residing at ...., Alipore Road, Kolkata.
2. Mr. Y residing at ...., Alipore Road, Kolkata.

3. Z Insurance Co. Ltd. having its Branch Office at ...., Alipore Road, Kolkata.

...... *Defendants*

Suit for damages valued at ₹..........

The plaintiff's state as follows:

1. The plaintiffs are serviceholders and each one of them earns ₹.......... per month apart from other amenities provided by their employers.

2. Defendant No. 1 is a neighbour of the plaintiffs and is the owner of a car which he occasionally makes available to the people including the plaintiffs for pleasure trips at different places including Puri for consideration.

3. The said car has been comprehensively insured with defendant No. 3 who has issued a policy covering all risks including damages to the car and/or the person who is driving including defendant No. 2 as also any guests, friends and acquaintances carried in the said car either for consideration or otherwise.

4. At the invitation of defendant No. 2 the plaintiffs agreed to have a trip in the car of defendant No. 1 from 7, Alipore Road, Kolkata to Hotel Resort at Puri, Orissa and back on payment of ₹........... and the cost of petrol and all other expenses to be borne by defendant No. 2.

5. Such a trip and arrangement for it by the plaintiffs were covered by the Insurance Policy issued by defendant No. 3. from its Alipore office. The said policy also included all risks including injury to people in the car, damage to the car and injury to members of the public irrespective of the fault or negligence that might be in driving the car.

6. On the basis of the aforesaid and on the assurance of defendant No. 1 for safe journey the plaintiffs paid ₹............ in advance, agreed to pay the petrol bills as and when required. The said contract and/or arrangement was effective for 28 days from the date of departure from 7, Alipore Road, Kolkata till return thereto.

7. The aforesaid arrangements were covered by the Insurance Policy issued for consideration by defendant No. 3 in favour of defendant No. 1 covering the same car.

8. On 5th January 20..... according to the arrangement the defendant No. 1 came with the car and the plaintiffs boarded the car including the luggages to spend their holidays in Puri.

9. The owner of the said car defendant No. 1 was driving the car following the route best suited to him.

10. The first defendant took the usual route to Puri *via* Kharagpur.

11. While the car driven by the first defendant was nearing Kharagpur it developed certain defects and making noises which on complaint the first defendant ignored the same and assured that there is nothing to be afraid of. The first defendant's car was proceeding towards Kharagpur when suddenly defendant No. 2 driving a car emerged from the lane at a high speed and collided with the car of the first defendant causing serious damages to the right leg of plaintiff No. 1 and the right arm of plaintiff No. 2 a part from damages to first defendant's head, arm and leg.

12. The local people gathered and took particulars of the incident and the cars and took the wounded persons to the local hospital.

13. At the hospital the plaintiffs were treated and after 7 days were discharged with bandages as the plaintiffs were not in a position to walk and as such special arrangements had to be made to reach them home at extra cost.

14. As a result of the said accident the plaintiffs could not attend their respective offices for three months during which they did not get any salary and in the facts and circumstances of the case.

15. The plaintiffs had to suffer physical pain and injury and disablement from attending to their ordinary work apart from suffering financial damages and loss for payment of medical expenses and non-receipt of remuneration for the period of absence apart from physical pain and agony.

16. The plaintiffs have suffered damages of a total sum of ₹ .... each particulars of which are given in a schedule annexed hereto. Such claims are supported by relevant certificates and receipts for payment, copies whereof are annexed hereto marked ......

17. The plaintiffs state that defendants Nos. 1, 2 and 3 are liable to pay the claims of the plaintiffs.

18. The first defendant is liable to pay the plaintiff's claims under the contract of carriage as also for negligent driving of the car wherein the first defendant had special responsibilities to take special care so that the plaintiffs did not suffer any injury.

19. The defendant No. 2 is liable to pay the compensation to the plaintiffs for his negligent driving. The defendant No. 2 came out of the lane at a high speed without caring for any traffic on the main road and failing to stop his car when he saw the first defendant's car going towards Kharagpur in normal speed. Defendant No. 2 for his negligent driving and thereby causing damage to the plaintiffs is liable to pay compensation as claimed herein jointly and severally with defendants Nos. 1 and 3.

20. In the premises the plaintiffs claim a decree for ₹......... against the defendants jointly and severally and interest and costs.

21. The particulars of negligence on the part of the first defendant and also of defendant No. 2 are given in a Schedule annexed hereto marked ....

22. For the purposes of jurisdiction and court-fees the suit is valued at ₹ .... on which court-fees in stamps have been paid.

23. As the defendants are residing and/or carrying on business within the jurisdiction of this Learned Court this Learned Court has the jurisdiction to entertain, try and determine the suit.

The plaintiffs, therefore, pray for and claim:

(*a*) Decree for ₹............ against the defendant Nos. 1, 2 and 3 jointly and severally;

(*b*) Alternatively, an enquiry into the damages suffered by the plaintiffs and a decree for the sum found due against the defendants jointly and severally;

(*c*) Cost;

(*d*) Further and other orders be made as this Learned Court may deem fit and proper to afford complete reliefs to the plaintiffs.

And the plaintiffs as in duty bound shall ever pray.

SCHEDULES

Verification

Affidavit

165. Suit for recovery of movables wrongfully detained or their value and for damages for detention

In the Court of .... at ....

Suit No. .... of 20............

(Set out cause title)

The above-named plaintiff states as follows:

1. That the plaintiff had lent to the defendant at latter's seeking on .... wardrobe, valued at ₹............ only. The defendant promised to return the said furniture within two months from the date.

2. That the defendant did not return the furniture within the time agreed and despite plaintiff's request therefor has wrongfully detained the same.

3. That the cause of action arose on .... (on the date following the date within which the same was to be returned) at .... within the jurisdiction of this court.

4. Suit valuation (value of the wardrobe and amount of damages).

The plaintiff claims:

(*a*) Decree directing delivery of the wardrobe within a time specified by the court or for ₹ .... being its value in the event of non-delivery.

(*b*) ₹............. as damages (or, compensation) for detention of the wardrobe.

Verification

Affidavit

NOTE: Limitation three years under Art. 91(*b*) of the Limitation Act 1963 from when the detainer's possession becomes unlawful.

166. Suit for recovery of goods lent to the defendant

In the Court of .... at ....

Suit No. .... of 20............

(Set out cause title)

The above-named plaintiff states as follows:

1. That the defendant is the plaintiff's neighbour. At the seeking of the defendant the plaintiff had lent to the defendant on .... his gold wrist-watch. The defendant promised to return the same within three days.

2. That the defendant did not return the watch within the time agreed and despite plaintiff's request therefor has wrongfully detained the watch.

3. That the said watch was gifted to the plaintiff by his father, since deceased and is associated with his memory and, therefore, is of special value to the plaintiff.

4. That the plaintiff is not interested in its money-value and pecuniary compensation will not be adequate for the watch.

5. Cause of action.

6. Valuation of the suit (money value).

The plaintiff, therefore, prays:

For a decree directing the defendant to return the said watch within a time specified by the court, failing which for issue of a writ for seizure of the article and delivery to the plaintiff.

Verification

Affidavit

NOTES: 1. See Or. 20, r. 10, CPC.
2. See Or. 21, r. 31, for execution.

167. Suit for damages for breach of agreement

In the City Civil Court, Calcutta

Suit No. .... of 20.....

M/s. P & Co. Ltd., a company registered under the Companies Act 1956 and carries on business *inter alia* at .... Kolkata within the said jurisdiction

...... *Plaintiff*

versus

M/s. X & Co. Ltd. a company registered under the Companies Act 1956 and carries on business, *inter alia* at .... Kolkata

.... *Defendant*

Suit for damages for breach of agreement valued at ₹..........

The plaintiff states:

1. That the plaintiff is a company registered under the Companies Act 1956 and carries on business, *inter alia*, in plant and machinery including consumer goods.

2. The defendant carries on business as the Auctioneer at a reasonable remuneration based on the percentage of sale price.

3. That the plaintiff engaged the defendant as the Auctioneer to sell at auction certain plant and machinery of plaintiff lying in the plaintiff's godown subject to a reserve price.

4. That it was agreed by and between the plaintiff and defendant that the defendant would sell specified plant and machinery at an auction to the successful bidder and on condition that the said purchaser would deposit 25% of the bid price immediately and undertake to pay the balance price before taking delivery of the goods sold at auction within 7 days.

5. That the plaintiff agreed to pay to auctioneer 5% of the price paid by the purchaser as remuneration by way of commission to auctioneer.

6. That the defendant auctioneer advertised and held the auction and sold the plaintiff's articles at the highest price of ₹.......... on which the said bidder paid 25% of the value of goods on the spot itself. The auctioneer, however, failed to obtain the

contract signed by purchaser at the time of the auction in violation of instructions of the plaintiff.

7. That the purchaser issued a cheque for the balance amount being the price of the goods and took delivery of the same purchased in the auction.

8. That the cheque for ₹............... issued by the said purchaser on presentation for collection was dishonoured for want of sufficient funds in the account of the purchaser.

9. That the plaintiff demanded the said payment from defendant by a letter which was duly received by the defendant by signing on a copy of the said letter. The said letter of the plaintiff returned the dishonoured cheque and requested for immediate cash payment from the said bidder/purchaser. The defendant duly received the said letter but failed and neglected to collect and deliver the said payment covered by the said cheque.

10. That in view of the said, the plaintiff claims from the defendant/auctioneer and aggregate amount of ₹................ with interest at 12% per annum from the date of the sale till realisation.

Particulars

11. That the plaintiff claims a decree for ₹.............. with further interest at 12% per annum from .... till the date of decree and on the decretal amount till payment.

12. That in spite of demands, the defendant auctioneer has not paid the said sum or any portion thereof to the plaintiff.

13. That for the purpose of jurisdiction and court-fees, the suit is valued at ₹............ on which court-fees in stamps have been duly paid.

14. No part of the plaintiff's claims is barred by the law of limitation.

The plaintiff, therefore, claims:

(*a*) Decree for ₹........ with interest at 12% per annum from .... till the date of decree and interest on decretal amount at 12% per annum till payment;

(*b*) Cost;

(*c*) Injunction;

(*d*) Receiver;

(*e*) Further and other orders be made as the plaintiff is entitled to.

Verification

Affidavit

168. Suit for return of motorcycle duly repaired

In the Court of the Civil Judge (Sr. Division) at Alipore

Suit No. .... of 20...........

Registered under the Companies Act 1956
M/s. P. & Co. Ltd. carrying on business at
.... Kolkata

.... *Plaintiff*

versus

Mr. X & Co. Ltd., registered under the Companies Act 1956 and carrying on business at .... Kolkata

............*Defendant*

Suit valued at ₹.............. on which court-fees in stamps have been paid

The plaintiff states:

1. That the plaintiff purchased a motorcycle (here state the particulars of the motorcycle) from the defendant on 15th July 20...... by paying the full consideration money of ₹................

2. That the defendant guaranteed proper functioning of the said motorcycle and undertook to carry out monthly service of the said motorcycle for a period of one year from the date of purchase.

3. That the plaintiff took possession of the said motorcycle and obtained licence for driving the same on payment of full consideration money to the defendant.

4. That the defendant gave possession of the said motorcycle and also gave a guarantee for a period of one year for proper functioning of same and undertook to carry out monthly service the said motorcycle for a period of one year free of cost.

5. That after using the said motorcycle for three months, the cycle developed some troubles and there were frequent breakdowns of the said motorcycle due to which plaintiff had to suffer hardships in coming to and from office by doing some minor repairs on his own account.

6. That on complaints being made to the defendant, the defendant through its authorised representative took back the said defective motorcycle for the purpose of repairing the same and promised to return the same within 30 days after proper repairing of the said motorcycle.

7. That on expiry of the said one month, the plaintiff requested the defendant to deliver the said motorcycle after proper repairs and in good working condition. But the defendant did not deliver back the motorcycle on some pretext or other in spite of repeated requests and visits made by the plaintiff to the workshop of the defendant.

8. That the plaintiff through his Advocate wrote several letters to defendant for immediate return of the said motorcycle duly repaired and, in the alternative, to pay the full price of the motorcycle valued at ₹................. plus interest at 12% per annum calculated from the date of taking delivery on purchase of said motorcycle from the defendant. The plaintiff in thus entitled to interest on the said sum of ₹............. from 15th July 20..... till payment at 12% per annum.

9. That the plaintiff's cause of action for this suit arose within jurisdiction of this learned court, the defendant is carrying on business at its said address at Kolkata within the jurisdiction of this learned court. The plaintiff's cause of action arose on 15th July 20..... and in October 20..... and the same is still continuing because of refusal of the defendant to return the said motorcycle after repairs.

10. That for purposes of jurisdiction and court-fees, the suit is valued at ₹.......... on which appropriate court-fees in stamps have been paid.

11. No part of the plaintiff's claims is barred by law of limitation.

The plaintiff, therefore, prays for and claims:

(*a*) Immediate delivery of the said motorcycle in good working condition by the defendant to the plaintiff;

(*b*) Alternatively, a decree for payment of ₹............... plus interest at 12% per annum from 15th July 20..... till payment;

(*c*) Further interest at 12% per annum on the decretal amount;

(*d*) Cost;

(*e*) Further and other orders and/or reliefs to granted as this learned court may deem fit and proper to afford complete relief to the plaintiff.

Verification

Affidavit

169. Application for compensation under s. 166 of the M.V. Act 1988

(See Rule 329 of the West Bengal Motor Vehicles Rules 1989)

To
The Motor Accidents Claims Tribunal at ....
Constituted under s. 165(1) of the M.V. Act 1988

A .... Petitioner

versus

1. B .... (owner of the vehicle)

2. C .... (Insurance Co.)

I, ... son/daughter/wife/widow of .... residing at .... P.S. .... District .... having been injured in motor vehicle accident, hereby apply for the grant of compensation for the injury sustained. Necessary particulars in respect of the injury, vehicle, etc. are given below:

I, ... son/daughter/wife/widow of .... residing at .... hereby apply, as a legal representative/agent for the grant of compensation on account of death/injury sustained by/Sri/Kumari/Srimati .... son/daughter/wife/widow of Sri/Srimati .... who died/was injured/in a motor vehicle accident.

Necessary particulars in respect of the deceased/injured/the vehicle etc. are given below:

1. Name and father's name of the person injured/dead (husband's name in the case of married woman and widow).
2. Full address of the person injured/dead.
3. Age of the person injured/dead.
4. Occupation of the person injured/dead.
5. Name and address of the Employer of the deceased, if any—
6. Monthly income of the person injured/dead.

7. Does the person in respect of whom compensation is claimed pay income-tax? If so, state the amount of income-tax (to be supported by documentary evidence).
8. Place, date and time of accident.
9. Name and address of Police Station in whose jurisdiction the accident took place or was registered.
10. Was the person in respect of whom compensation is claimed travelling by the vehicle involved in accident? If so, give the names of places of starting of journey and destination.
11. Nature of injury/injuries sustained/ and continuing effect, if any, of the injury/injuries.........
12. Name and address of the Medical Officer/if any, who attended on the injured/dead.
13. Period of treatment and expenditure, if any, incurred thereon (to be supported by documentary evidence).
14. Nature of the injury and whether if caused permanent disablement or not.........
15. Registration number and the type of the vehicle involved in accident.
16. Name and address of the owner of the vehicle.
17. Name, and Policy Number, insurance particulars address of the insurer of the vehicle.
18. Has any claim been lodged with the owner/insurer? If so, with what result?
19. Name and address of the applicant.
20. Relationship with the deceased.
21. Title to the property of the deceased.
22. Amount of compensation claimed.
23. Any other information that may be necessary or helpful in the disposal of the claim.

Or

I wish to claim compensation under s. 140 of the Motor Vehicles Act 1988 only.

Or

I wish to make a claim for compensation under the said Act and also in pursuance of the right on the principle of fault.

Verification

I, ... solemnly declare that the particulars given above are true and correct to the best of my knowledge and belief and that no claim in respect of the said accident has been filed or is pending before any other Court.

NOTES: 1. This form is for West Bengal as per West Bengal M.V. Rules 1989.

2. The period of limitation for filing an application under s. 166 of the M.V. Act 1988 is six months of the occurrence of the accident. The tribunal may entertain an application after the expiry of six months, but not later than 12 months if it is satisfied that the applicant was prevented by sufficient cause from making the application in time (cf. s. 5 of the Limitation Act)—See AIR 1969 Raj 316. Since then by M.V. (Amendment) Act 1994 sub-sec (3) of s. 166 has been deleted. No limitation. Delay not condoned—appeal lies—AIR 1969 Mad 316.

3. The application under s. 140 of the M.V. Act 1988 is to be filed in the prescribed form. Court-fees ₹10 for West Bengal vide r. 331 of M.A. Claims Tribunal Rules. Application for compensation under r. 329 of the W.B.M.V. Rules 1989 claim upto

₹ 5000	—	₹ 10
₹ 5000 to 50,000	—	$^1/_4$% of the amount of claim.
₹ 50,001 to 1 lakh	—	$^1/_2$% of the amount of claim.
Exceeding 1 lakh	—	1% of the amount of claim.

4. Right to file an application—(*i*) by the injured, (*ii*) where death has resulted from the accident, by the legal representatives of the deceased (AIR 1970 Mys 67), cause survives to heirs—AIR 1969 Cal 394. Legal representatives in West Bengal shall have the meaning assigned to it under cl. (11) of s. 2 of the Code of Civil Procedure—vide Notification No. 6367 dated 5.9.61 of the Home Department, Government of West Bengal; (*iii*) or, by an agent duly authorised by the person injured or the legal representatives of the deceased, as the case may be. Petition filed by one of the legal representatives as Karta of H.U.F. maintainable—AIR 1970 Pat 172. In a proceeding under s. 166 the person assured is necessary party—AIR 1969 AP 390.

5. In every application under s. 140 of the M.V. Act 1988 are to be appended (*a*) a report containing description of the accident, (*b*) First Information Report, (*c*) Injury Certificate or in cash of death, Post Mortem Report or Death Certificate, and (*d*) a certificate regarding ownership and Insurance particulars of vehicle involved in the accident from the Regional Transport Officer in form (COMPC), issued free of charge—See Rule 330 of the W.B.M.V. Rules 1989.

6. In deciding a claim the tribunal is a court within s. 3 of the Evidence Act. Judgment of Criminal Court determining guilt or innocence of the driver is not binding on Claims Tribunal—AIR 1970 Punj 137. Tribunal has power to have evidence recorded on commission—AIR 1970 Mad 259.

7. Where during pendency of proceedings substitution is necessary the court has the power to order substitution—AIR 1969 Cal 394.
8. For scope of ss. 110 to 110C (under Act of 1939) see AIR 1969 Punj 172 and forms of other States.

170. Application for grant of solatium from solatium fund by the victim of hit and run Motor Accident

FORM I

[Clause 20(1)]

Form of application for compensation from solatium fund

I, ... son of/daughter of/widow* of Shri .... residing at .... having been grievously injured in motor vehicle accident hereby apply for grant of compensation for the grievous injuries sustained. Necessary particulars in respect of the injury sustained by me are given below:—

I, ... son of /daughter of/widow of* Shri .... residing at .... hereby apply as a legal representative/agent for the grant of compensation on account of death/injuries sustained by Shri Shrimati/ Kumari .... son of/widow of/daughter of Shri .... who died/had sustained injuries in a motor vehicle accident on .... at. Particulars in respect of accident and other information are given below:

1. Name and father's name of person injured (husband's name in case of married woman or widow).
2. Address of the person injured/dead:
3. Age .... Date of Birth ....
4. Sex of the person injured/dead:
5. Place, date and time of the accident:
6. Occupation of the person injured/dead:
7. Nature of injuries sustained:
8. Name and address of Police Station in whose jurisdiction accident took place or was registered.
9. Name and address of the Medical Officer/Practitioner who attended on the injured/dead:
10. Name and address of the claimant/claimants:
11. Relationship with the deceased:
12. Any other information that may be considered necessary or helpful in the disposal of the claim:

I hereby swear and affirm that all the facts noted above are true to the best of my knowledge and belief.

Signature of the Claimant

* Strike out whichever is not applicable.

FORM II

[Clause 20(i)]

Annexure-Sanction Order No.

Dated:

Discharge receipt

Received with thanks from .... Insurance Co. Ltd. sum of Rs. .... being the compensation under hit and run provisions of the Motor Vehicles Act in full and final settlement of my claim for the accident occurred to me/ to the deceased person .... (name of decease) on .... (date of accident) at .... (name of place).

Signature of revenue stamp
by beneficiary/victim

Witness.

NOTES: 1. In exercise of the powers conferred by sub-sec. (1) of s. 163 of the M.V. Act 1988 the Central Government has framed the Solatium Scheme 1989 for payment of compensation to the victims of hit and run motor accident. Effective from 1.7.1989.

2. Limitation for application 6 months from date of accident in form No. 1 along with daily filled in discharge receipt in form II (as above) along with an undertaking in form V before the claim Enquiry Officer.

3. On receipt of request of the claims Enquiry Officer, the claims Settlement Commissioner shall sanction the claim, as per as possible within a period not exceeding 15 days from date of receipt of request.

4. The sanction has to be communicated to the nominated office of the Insurance Company for payment.

5. See Solatium Scheme 1989—Vide Gazette of India Extra Pt. II, s. 3(*ii*) dt. 12.6.1989 S.O. 440(E).

DECLARATION

171. Suit for declaration

In the Court of Civil Judge (Senior Division) at ....

Suit No. ....of 20 ....

1. Mrs. P, wife of M (since deceased) residing at .... Kolkata

2. Miss Q being the unmarried daughter of M (since deceased) residing at ...., Kolkata

.... *Plaintiffs*

versus

Mr. X residing at ...., Kolkata

.... *Defendant*

Suit for declaration valued at ₹ ....

The plaintiff states as follows:

1. That late Mr. M, husband of plaintiff No. 1 and father of plaintiff No. 2, purchased a property by a Registered Deed of Sale dated 20th August 20 .... in the joint names of his wife and unmarried daughter, being premises No. 5, Blue Lane, Kolkata. The property is fully described in the schedule hereunder. The property was purchased for the benefit of the plaintiffs.

2. The defendant, the son of late Mr. M, is claiming a share in the said house property which was purchased by the said Mr. M (since deceased) in the name of the plaintiffs on the ground that such transaction was Benami Transaction within the meaning of s. 2(9) of the Prohibition of Benami Property Transaction Act 1988 as the consideration money was advanced by Mr. M, since deceased.

3. The plaintiffs claim for a declaration that the plaintiffs are the lawful owners of the said house property covered by the Sale Deed and that the defendant has no right, title or interest in the said property.

4. The plaintiffs state that the provisions of the said Prohibition of Benami Property Transaction Act 1988 have no application in the present case and the allegations of the defendant that the said purchase was a Benami Transaction is wrongful and untenable.

5. The plaintiffs' cause of action for this suit arose within the jurisdiction of this learned court on or about the 10th of September 20... when the defendant wrongfully demanded from the plaintiffs a share in the said house property wrongfully contending that the purchase by his father was a Benami Transaction and was not valid.

6. In the premises the plaintiffs claim a declaration that the plaintiffs are the lawful owners of the said house property and that the defendant has no right, title or interest therein.

7. The cause of action arose within the jurisdiction of this learned court on or about 10th September 20... and it is continuing from day to day.

8. The suit is valued at ₹ .... on which court-fees in stamps have been paid.

Schedule of property

All that piece and parcel of land with structures measuring 3 cottahs situate at being premises No. 5, Blue Lane, Kolkata and as described in the Title Deeds.

9. The suit has been filed within the period of limitation.

The plaintiff, therefore, claims:

(*a*) Declaration that the said property mentioned in the Schedule above belongs to the plaintiffs and they are the lawful owners having equal shares and that the defendant has no right, title or interest in the said property;

(*b*) Injunction restraining the defendant from interfering with the right, title and interest and possession of the plaintiffs in the said property;

(*c*) Costs;

(*d*) Further and other orders be made so as to afford complete relief to the plaintiffs.

Verification

Affidavit

172. Suit for declaration of tenancy right and for injunction

In the Court of Civil Judge (Junior Division) at ......

Title Suit No. .... of 20 ......

(Set out cause title)

Suit for declaration of plaintiff's tenancy right and for injunction upon the defendants not to interfere with possession of the plaintiff in the tenanted premises.

Claim laid at ₹ .... only.

The plaintiff states as follows:

1. That the plaintiff entered into an agreement in writing on .... with the defendants to take out the premises, described in the Schedule 'A' below, on rent at ₹ .... per month according to English calendar month.

2. That pursuant to the said agreement, the plaintiff took possession of the demised premises as a monthly tenant under the plaintiff and paid rent for the same month by month up to the month of .... 20 ......

3. That the plaintiff has been running a shop dealing in .... in the said premises. The plaintiff has engaged a salesman who is living in the said premises at night.

4. That the defendant sprang a surprise when he along with two others forcibly ousted plaintiff's salesman Sri .... from the said premises and locked up the same and drove away the plaintiff's salesman .... at night about .... on .... with show of force and got signature of the said salesman upon a piece of paper previously written out by the defendant and took the keys of the premises.

5. That within the premises the plaintiff had valuable pieces of furniture, electrical goods, documents, rent receipts, trunks containing cash of ₹ .... and personal account books of the current and for back periods as described in the Schedule "B" below. Those articles are perhaps under lock and key, the keys remaining under the custody of the defendants from the night of .... the .... 20 ......

6. That the plaintiff's tenancy in the demised premises not being lawfully terminated, the said tenancy right in the premises is still subsisting. Be it noted that the plaintiff did never surrender his tenancy right in favour of the defendants. Nor the plaintiff committed any act for which he was liable to eviction.

7. That the plaintiff lodged an Ejahar (FIR) in the local P.S. for the unauthorised and illegal interference by the defendant on ...... with the plaintiff's tenancy right. The enquiry in the said matter is pending with the police.

8. That the defendant, it is learnt, is going to open the premises very soon with the intention to start a similar business as that of the plaintiff as the police is not up and doing and taking charge of the premises and the cash and other valuables of the plaintiff remaining inside the said premises.

9. That it is now extremely necessary and urgent that the defendant be restrained to do acts which will cause great loss and harassment to the plaintiff and will entail multiplicity of proceedings.

10. That, in the facts and circumstances of the case, the plaintiff is entitled to a decree declaring that the plaintiff has a subsisting tenancy right in the demised premises and to a decree of perpetual injunction restraining the defendant from interfering with his tenancy right and possession till tenancy is lawfully terminated.

11. That the cause of action for this arose on .... when the defendant forcibly took away the key of the tenanted premises at ...... town .... P.S. ...., within the jurisdiction of this court.

12. That for the purpose of jurisdiction the suit is valued at ₹ ...... and for reliefs of declaration with consequential relief of injuries fixed court-fees of ₹ ...... are paid.

Therefore, the plaintiff prays:

For a judgment and decree declaring:

(*a*) That the tenancy of the plaintiff in the demised premises is subsisting.

(*b*) That the defendant be restrained by a decree of injunction from interfering with the plaintiff's possession of the demised premises until the said tenancy is lawfully terminated.

(*c*) That a mandatory injunction be granted directing the defendant to make over the keys of the premises to the plaintiff within a specified time.

(*d*) A temporary mandatory injunction to the same effect as prayer (*c*).

SCHEDULE 'A'

(Description of premises)

SCHEDULE 'B'

Verification

Affidavit

173. Suit for declaration of plaintiff's right and for injunction

In the Court of the Civil Judge (Junior Division) at Alipurduar

Other Class Suit No. .... of 20 .....

(Set out cause title)

The plaintiff states as follows:

1. That the plaintiff became a contractor with effect from ...... for the Refreshment Room at ...... railway station, a station in the defendant's railway after deposit of security, etc., to the tune of ₹ .... on .... with the Station Superintendent, Alipurduar Junction. An agreement was entered into by the defendant then represented by the Deputy Chief Commercial Superintendent, NF Railway and the plaintiff on .... The said agreement is in the custody of the defendant Railway Administration.

2. That since .... the plaintiff was thus engaged in catering to the travelling public foodstuff etc. at .... railway station.

3. That under clause 1 of the said agreement, the contract with the plaintiff can be terminated by a three calendar months' prior notice in writing intimating the intention to terminate the agreement. In the instant case, no notice of termination of the agreement has been served on the plaintiff and the said contract is still subsisting.

4. That the plaintiff did not violate any term and condition of the said agreement by which the agreement could be unilaterally terminated and without notice.

5. That further the plaintiff (licensee of the Refreshment Room) did not commit any act of refusal in agreeing to payment of enhanced rent, water and electric charges. Accordingly, the defendant Railway Administration was not entitled to terminate the contract. No notice contemplated in clause .... of the agreement was ever complied with and thus the said contract is still alive.

6. That since the contract has not been terminated up till now the plaintiff is still the contractor of the said Refreshment Room at .... railway station.

7. That in the meantime the water charge and vending fees of the said Refreshment Room was enhanced by the defendant. The plaintiff paid enhanced water charge and vending fees (otherwise known as licence fee) for the year 20 ......, on .... and was granted a money receipt therefor.

8. That the plaintiffs' contract has been renewed from time to time. Last renewal was made upto .... by a letter No. .... dated of the General Manager (Commercial) .... Railway. The plaintiff is expecting renewal for further period.

9. That only the other day a letter No. .... dated .... has been sent by the General Manager (Commercial) .... Railway, to the plaintiff asking him to hand over vacant possession of the Refreshment Room to the Station Master .... Station.

10. That the plaintiff has learnt that a copy of the said letter has also been addressed to the Station Master, ... Railway Station and attempt is being made by the defendant Railway Administration to enter into a contract in respect of the said Refreshment Room with others and to oust the plaintiff immediately, if necessary, by force.

11. That the cause of action for this suit arose at .... within the jurisdiction of this court on .... when the plaintiff received letter No. .... dated .... asking the plaintiff to hand over the vacant possession of the Refreshment Room.

12. That for the purpose of jurisdiction, the suit is valued at ₹ .... and for reliefs of declaration with consequential relief of injunction *ad valorem* court-fees are paid.

The plaintiff, therefore, prays:

(*a*) That the suit be decreed declaring:

the contract of Refreshment Room at ...... Railway Station with the plaintiff not being determined the plaintiff is still the contractor for the same.

(*b*) That the suit be decreed granting orders of injunction restraining the defendant.

(*i*) from entering into Agreement with anybody else during the period of subsistence of the contract with the plaintiff, regarding the contract of the said Refreshment Room.

(*ii*) from ousting the plaintiff from the said Refreshment Room during subsistence of the said contract with the plaintiff.

(*c*) Costs.

Verification

Affidavit

174. Suit for declaration of legitimacy

In the Court of Civil Judge (Senior Division) at ....

Suit No. .... of 20 ....

Mr. P, son of Mr. Q, residing at .... Kolkata

.... *Plaintiff*

versus

1. Mr. X, son of Mr. Q, residing at .... Kolkata

2. Ms. Y, daughter of Mr. Z, residing at ...., Kolkata

.... *Defendants*

Suit for declaration of legitimacy valued at ₹ ....

The plaintiff states as follows:

1. The plaintiff is the son of defendant No. 2 and her late husband Mr. Q, born on .... during the subsistence of their marriage.

2. The plaintiff states that the marriage between the defendant No. 2 and Q was declared null and void on .... within the meaning of s. 11 of the Hindu Marriage Act 1955.

3. However, the plaintiff should be deemed to be the legitimate son of Q. The plaintiff is entitled to the properties left by the said putative father Q.

4. The plaintiff claims for a declaration that he is the legitimate son of defendant No. 2 and her late husband Q and is entitled to their personal properties. Particulars of the properties left by the said Q are given in a schedule annexed hereto marked "A".

5. The defendant No. 1 is the son of plaintiff's father Mr. Q by his second wife. The defendant No. 1 wrongfully declined to give due share of the personal properties left by Mr. Q. In this connection, pursuant to the request made by the plaintiff the defendant No. 1 in reply dated 15th March 20 .... wrongfully contended that the plaintiff was not entitled to any share in the properties left by Mr. Q but without assigning any reason for such contention. A copy of the said letter is annexed hereto marked "B".

6. The plaintiff claims determination of the respective rights of the plaintiff and defendant No. 1 in the properties left by their father, Mr. Q.

7. For the purposes of jurisdiction and court-fees the suit is valued at ₹ .... on which court-fees in stamps have been paid. The assets and properties in question are situate at .... Kolkata within the jurisdiction of this learned court.

The plaintiff, therefore, prays for and claims:

(*a*) Declaration that the plaintiff is the legitimate son of Mr. Q and is entitled to the properties left by Mr. Q;

(*b*) Decree for delivery of possession of the properties left by Mr. Q;

(*c*) Costs;

(*d*) Further and other reliefs as the plaintiff may be entitled to in law and in equity.

SCHEDULE

ANNEXURE

Verification

Affidavit

175. Suit for declaration of a legal character of the plaintiff

(By an expelled member of a club)

In the Court of .... at ....

Suit No. .... of 20 ....

(Set out cause title)

The above-named plaintiff states as follows:

1. That the plaintiff was at all material times a member of the registered club, known as ...... with office at ...... P.S. ...... District ....

2. That the said club has had its Constitution and the defendants Nos. 1 to 12 are members of the governing body of the said club.

3. That the defendants are sued as representing themselves and other members of the said club.

4. The provisions as to the procedure for expelling a member from the club are contained in Rules 2(*a*) to (*d*) of the said Constitution. Relevant provisions read as follows:

2(*a*) ....
2(*b*) ....
2(*c*) ....
2(*d*) ....

5. That the plaintiff was expelled from the club on .... by a resolution of a meeting of the said governing body held on .... in absence of the plaintiff on the allegation ....

6. That in so doing the defendants violated provisions contained in said Rules Nos. 2(*a*) and 2(*c*) of the said Constitution. The plaintiff made an attempt to move the domestic tribunal and the same having failed the plaintiff files this suit.

7. That the cause of action for this suit arose on .... at .... when the impugned resolution was passed by the defendants casting a cloud of doubt over the legal character of the plaintiff as a sitting member of the said club.

8. That for the purpose of jurisdiction, the suit is valued at ₹.......... and for reliefs of declaration and consequential relief of injunction *ad valorem* court-fees are paid.

The plaintiff, therefore, prays for a decree:

(A) Declaring (1) That he is still a member of the said club.

(2) That the Resolution No. .... dt. .... passed in the meeting of the defendants on .... expelling the plaintiff is void.

(B) Granting perpetual injunction restraining the defendants from debarring the plaintiff of his rights and privileges of a member of the said club except in accordance with law.

Verification

Affidavit

176. Suit for declaration that dismissal of the plaintiff from office is illegal

In the Court of .... at ....

Suit No. .... of 20 ....

(Set out cause title)

The plaintiff states as follows:

1. That the plaintiff was appointed as a .... under the defendant on the .... day of ...... 20 ...... by a letter of appointment bearing No. ...... dated the .... day of .... 20 .... The plaintiff joined his service under the defendant on the .... day of .... 20 ......

2. That at all material times, the plaintiff was a .... in the establishment of the defendant.

3. That on the .... day of ...... 20 ...... the defendant served a notice bearing No. ...... of the day of .... 20 ...... purporting to dismiss the plaintiff from his said office on the grounds:

(*a*) ....

(*b*) ....

4. That the plaintiff denies all the allegations. The order of dismissal of the plaintiff is arbitrary, without jurisdiction, illegal and void.

5. The plaintiff is entitled to declarations—

(*i*) that his dismissal from the said office is arbitrary, without jurisdiction, illegal and void;

(*ii*) that the plaintiff should be deemed to be continuing in his service;

(*iii*) that the plaintiff is entitled to and be paid consequential reliefs of disbursement of his pay and allowances as per account below.

6. Cause of action—(date of dismissal).

7. Suit valuation—for the purposes of jurisdiction of the court the suit is valued at ₹ .... and for relief of declaration with consequential relief of disbursement of pay and allowances *ad valorem* court-fees are paid thereon.

The plaintiff, therefore, prays:

(*i*) For a decree declaring that [(*i*), (*ii*) of para 5 above];

(*ii*) for an order for payment [(*iii*) of para 5 above];

(*iii*) costs;

(*iv*) further relief.

Claim of Pay and Allowance

₹ ....

₹ ....

Verification

Affidavit

DECREE

177. Suit for setting aside a decree on grounds of fraud

In the Court of .... at ....

Other Suit No. .... of 20 ....

A.B. .... *Plaintiff*

versus

C.D. .... *Defendant*

The above-named plaintiff submits as under:

1. That the defendant is a cunning fellow and is sort of a tout. He obtained a decree against the plaintiff on......... *ex parte* for specific performance of a contract (Or as the case may be) in Other Suit No. .... of 20 ...... in the court of .... at ....

2. That the defendant put into execution the said decree in O. Execution Case No. ...... of 20 .... notice whereof was served on the plaintiff by the court peon on ......

3. That the said decree in the aforesaid Suit No. .... of ...... was fraudulently obtained by the defendant by fraudulent suppression of the summons. The plaintiff did not receive any summon, nor any court peon even went to the plaintiff's place of residence. The alleged 'refusal' of summons is a collusive endorsement on the writ of summons by the court peon.

4. That the plaintiff did not enter into any contract with the defendant for sale of his lands and the defendant's contention in the suit was false to his knowledge.

5. That the plaintiff had no knowledge of the said suit, far less of the decree. The plaintiff came to know of the same on .... only on receipt of a notice of the aforesaid O. Ex. Case. The plaintiff gathered particulars by an information slip attached herewith.

6. That the said decree is liable to be set aside.

7. That the cause of action for this suit arose first on the (date of decree) and subsequently on .... when on service of notice of the Ex. Case the plaintiff had knowledge of the decree.

8. That for the purpose of jurisdiction and court-fees the suit is valued at ₹ .... (value of the suit decree of which is questioned) and *ad valorem* court-fees are paid thereon.

The plaintiff, therefore, prays:

(*i*) For a judgment and decree setting aside the decree of the Other Suit No. .... of .... of this court,

(*ii*) for permanent injunction restraining the decree-holder from proceeding with the O. Execution Case No. .... of 20 .... of this court, and

(*iii*) costs.

Verification

Affidavit

NOTES: 1. In a suit for declaration that decree is null and void and is not binding on the plaintiff without any other consequential relief—court-fee is fixed under Act—21 CWN 375. But where in a suit a decree is sought to be set aside, or in addition to a declaration that the decree is void, a consequential relief such as possession or injunction is also sought for *ad valorem* court-fees will have to be paid.

2. Unless a party to the suit, decree of which is challenged, the plaintiff need not add a prayer for setting aside the decree. Section 34 of the Specific Relief Act—Proviso will not be a bar.
3. When a plaintiff sues for a declaration that the decree is fraudulent he, to avoid the bar of the proviso of s. 34 of the Specific Relief Act, must pray for consequential relief:
   (*i*) to set aside the decree;
   (*ii*) to a perpetual injunction restraining the decree-holder from executing the decree.
4. Decree sought to be set aside on ground of fraud in service of summons. Particulars of fraud should be pleaded—AIR 1977 NOC 344 (Ori). Particulars of fraud must be given. General allegations, however strong, are not sufficient—AIR 1974 Cal 393. Decree cannot be set aside as fraudulent merely on ground of perjured evidence—AIR 1974 Cal 393.

178. Suit for setting aside a decree on the ground of fraud (Another Form)

In the Court of .... at ....

Suit No. .... of 20 ....

(Set out cause title)

The plaintiff states:

1. That the defendant obtained a decree against the plaintiff from the court of the Civil Judge (Junior Division), ... on the .... day of .... 20 .... in Title Suit No. .... of ... 20 ....

2. That the said decree was obtained by the defendant by exercising fraud on the plaintiff, a defendant in the said Title Suit. Particulars of the fraud are given below:

(*a*) ....

(*b*) ....

3. That because of such fraud, the plaintiff could not take up his legitimate defence and was unable to contest the suit.

4. The plaintiff came to know of such fraud on inspection of the case record of the said Title Suit after a notice of T. Execution Proceedings No. .... of this court was served on the plaintiff on the .... day of .... 20 ... .

5. Cause of action (date of knowledge of the fraudulently obtained decree).

6. Suit—valuation (as in the decree).

The plaintiff claims:

(*a*) setting aside of the decree in Title Suit No. ...... of ... 20 ... of the court of Civil Judge (Junior Division), Cooch Behar;

(*b*) permanent injunction restraining the decree-holder from proceeding with T. Ex. Proceedings No. .... of 20 ....

(*c*) costs; and

(*d*) any other or further relief.

Verification

Affidavit

NOTE: Decree obtained against a minor by fraudulently describing him as a major. Decree is voidable and a civil suit for cancellation of such decree is maintainable —AIR 1975 All 463.

179. Suit for setting aside a consent decree or for amendment therein

In the Court of .... at ....

Suit No. .... of 20 ....

(Set out cause title)

The plaintiff states as follows:

1. That the defendant had instituted as plaintiff SCC Suit No. ...... of 20 ...... in this court against this plaintiff. The plaintiff had entered his appearance in the said SCC Suit No. ...... of 20 ...... and submitted a written statement denying claim of the plaintiff in the said suit.

2. That the said SCC suit was fixed for peremptory hearing on .... The parties hereto effected a compromise in respect of the claim of the said suit on the terms appearing as under:

(*i*) That the plaintiff's suit shall be decreed for ₹........ only;

(*ii*) That the defendant shall pay the decretal amount by three equal annual instalments commencing with January 20 ......; in default of any instalment the entire dues under the decree shall be payable at once;

(*iii*) parties do bear their costs.

3. That on ...... the plaintiff depended on the defendant to engage his law-clerk for writing out the compromise petition. It was written and the plaintiff and his lawyer signed the compromise petition so also the defendant and his lawyer in the Bar Library at a distance of .... yds. from the court-room. The signed compromise petition was then made over to the defendant for submitting in the court. The plaintiff did not, however, accompany the defendant.

4. That in January 20 ......, the plaintiff obtained a certified copy of the decree and found to his surprise that the said copy did not reflect the terms of compromise as was agreed upon on .... Rather the same indicated that the terms of compromise were altered. The plaintiff, then, through his lawyer, found that the original compromise petition was fraudulently altered in the amount of decree and number of instalments. ₹ .... was changed by ₹ .... and term of three instalments was changed by a term of four instalments.

5. That the defendant on the basis of the said fraudulently tampered compromise-petition obtained a consent decree for ₹ .... on ...... 20 ....

6. That the plaintiff is entitled to a decree vacating the said consent-decree and/or for amendment thereof in terms of the actual terms of compromise as in para 2 above.

7. That the cause of action for this suit arose on .... the date of consent-decree and thereafter in January 20 ...... when the plaintiff discovered the fraud in the decree.

8. That for the purpose of jurisdiction and court-fees the suit is valued at ₹ .... and *ad valorem* court-fees are paid thereon.

The plaintiff, therefore, prays for:

(*a*) Judgment and decree setting aside the consent-decree in SCC Suit No. ...... of 20 ...... passed on ....

(*b*) Alternatively, orders amending the decree in said SCC Suit No. .... of 20...... to conform with the terms of compromise stated in para 2 hereinbefore.

Verification

Affidavit

NOTES: 1. A suit for declaration that the compromise-decree was void shall be valued at the amount of the decree. And the decree should be prayed to be set aside—court-fees are under s. 7(*iv*)(*c*) of the Court-fees Act.

2. Suit for setting aside a decree with consequential relief—*Ad valorem* court-fees on the amount of the liability imposed by the decree to be paid—AIR 1957 Nag 53.

180. Suit for declaration that decree of dissolution of marriage is void

In the Family Court at ....

Suit No. ...... of 20......

1. Mrs. P., Wife of Mr. X, residing at 7, Ezra Street, Kolkata 700 001 within the jurisdiction of this Hon'ble Court.

2. Miss R, daughter of Mr. X, a minor represented by the plaintiff No. 1 her mother and natural guardian residing at 7, Ezra Street, Kolkata 700 001

.... *Plaintiffs*

versus

Mr. X, son of Mr. Z, residing at 22, Mount Road, London

.... *Defendant*

The plaintiffs state:

1. That the plaintiff No. 1, Mrs. P, was married to the defendant under provisions of the Hindu Marriage Act 1955 on 6th January 20... at Delhi, where the plaintiff resided at that point of time. Out of the said wedlock a daughter was born to them on 6th February 20.......

2. That the plaintiff No. 2 is the minor daughter of the plaintiff No. 1 and the defendant and she is being represented by her natural guardian the plaintiff No. 1.

3. That after about 6 months, a daughter was born, the defendant permanently left India for London after getting a lucrative employment there, promising that after 3 months, he would make necessary arrangement to take the plaintiffs to London for settling there.

4. That the defendant, however, did not make the necessary arrangement to take the plaintiffs to London to his place of residence in spite of several requests.

5. That after about 3 years, from the date the defendant had left India for London the plaintiff No. 1 received a letter from the defendant to the effect that he had obtained a decree of divorce against her (Plaintiff No. 1) and he would pay her a monthly maintenance of ₹ .... for her and the daughter.

6. That plaintiff No. 1 states that the decree and judgment for divorce obtained by the defendant in England, i.e. from a Foreign Court is void and inoperative in India, where the marriage has been solemnised. The plaintiff claims for a declaration that marriage solemnised is still subsisting and that the defendant is liable to maintain the plaintiffs as per provisions of the Indian Laws.

7. That the plaintiff states that a reasonable cost of maintenance to the plaintiffs including the cost of her daughter's education would be ₹ .... per month and that the defendant obtaining decree and judgment for payment of ₹ .... per month is null and void and the same be set aside and quashed.

8. That the decree of divorce is a nullity in view of the fact that no notice has been served by the Court of England on the plaintiff in respect of the proceedings and that the said court had no jurisdiction.

9. That the cause of action for this suit arose within the jurisdiction of this learned court, in which the plaintiff is at present residing and the marriage was duly solemnised.

10. That for purpose of jurisdiction and court-fees, the suit is valued at ₹ .... on which court-fees in stamps have been paid.

The plaintiff, therefore, prays for and claims:

(*a*) A declaration that the decree and judgment of divorce obtained by defendant in a Foreign Court in London to the effect that the marriage between plaintiff No. 1 and defendant had been dissolved, is void and inoperative in India;

(*b*) Declaration that the marriage between plaintiff No. 1 and the defendant still subsists and the defendant is liable to pay maintenance allowance to the plaintiff as per provisions of law prevalent in India;

(*c*) Costs;

(*d*) Further and other reliefs be granted as the plaintiff is entitled to in law and in equity.

Verification

Affidavit

Deposit

181. Suit for recovery of deposit

In the Court of .... at ....

Suit No. .... of 20 ....

(Set out cause title)

The plaintiff states as follows:

1. The plaintiff had kept in deposit with the defendant a sum of ₹........... on the .... day of .... 20 ...... on condition that the defendant would return the same on demand by the plaintiff.

2. The defendant is not a banker and there was no stipulation for interest.

3. The plaintiff demanded back from the defendant the said sum of ₹............., but the defendant avoided (state here the date of demand).

4. Cause of action (date of demand).

5. Suit—valuation the said sum of ₹ .... (plus, if thought proper, damages for withholding the deposit causing loss to the plaintiff).

The plaintiff claims:

(*i*) Payment of ₹ ....

(*ii*) Damages at 8% per annum (from the date of deposit till the date of payment) over the said sum amounting to ₹ ....; and

(*iii*) Costs of suit.

Verification

Affidavit

NOTES: 1. Condition under which deposit was made, deposit demand and refusal have to be stated.

2. A demand is necessary before institution of suit—AIR 1936 PC 171; 162 IC 454.

3. Article 22 of the Limitation Act 1963 applies.

182. Suit to recover money deposited (Another Form)

In the Court of .... at ....

Suit No. .... of 20 ....

(Set out cause title)

The plaintiff states:

1. That on .... 20 ...... the plaintiff had deposited with the defendant firm ₹ .... and on the same day the defendant firm issued to the plaintiff the following memorandum addressed to him evidencing the deposit and the terms thereof:

> "The sum of ₹ .... that you have deposited with us will be handed over to you whenever you demand the same and we will pay you interest thereon at the rate of 12 per cent per annum".

2. That by a letter dated .... 20 ......, the plaintiff demanded payment of the money so deposited with accrued interest, but the defendant firm have failed to make any payment.

Particulars of claim

Principal amount	...	₹ ....
Interest upto	...	₹ ....
Net amount due		₹ ....

The plaintiff claims:

(1) ₹ ....

(2) Further interest till the date of actual payment.

Verification

Affidavit

183. Suit for recovery of specific goods deposited

In the Court of .... at ....

Suit No. .... of 20 ....

(Set out cause title)

The plaintiff states as follows:

1. Before he sailed for Europe in March 20........, the plaintiff left the following articles belonging to him with the defendant for safe custody. The defendant verbally promised to take particular care of the said articles and to return the same to the plaintiff when he would return to India.

Particulars of articles:

(*i*) An original painting of .... by ...., a famous artist.

(*ii*) Six ancient gold coins of the Moghul period.

2. The plaintiff returned to India in September 20......... and on .... demanded return of the aforesaid articles from the defendant but the defendant disowned having received any of the said articles from the plaintiff.

3. The defendant wrongfully detains the said articles from the plaintiff.

4. The said articles are of unusual beauty, rarity and distinction and are of special value to the plaintiff and no pecuniary compensation will be an adequate compensation to the plaintiff for the said articles.

The plaintiff claims—

(*a*) Return of the said articles.

(*b*) Costs.

Verification

Affidavit

DISTRESS

184. Suit for illegal distress

In the Court of .... at ....

Suit No. .... of 20 ....

(Set out cause title)

The plaintiff states:

1. That the plaintiff is the owner of the .... Municipal Holding No. .... of Ward No. .... within the district of .... The plaintiff has had his furniture in his said holding.

2. On the .... day of .... 20 .... at about .... p.m. the defendant by his employees/agents entered the plaintiff's said holding and wrongfully seized and took possession of the plaintiffs furniture, described below, alleging execution of a distress warrant for non-payment of municipal tax for the said holding.

3. That the claim for the municipal tax was false and the issue of distress warrant was absolutely illegal.

4. The plaintiff has suffered damage and loss.

5. Cause of action (date of seizure).

6. Suit valuation (aggregate of the reliefs).

The plaintiff claims:

(*a*) Return of the furniture, wrongfully seized;

(*b*) Damages for trespass;

(*c*) Damages for wrongful seizure;

(*d*) Damages for illegal distress; and

(*e*) Costs.

Description of furniture seized

Verification

Affidavit

185. Suit for recovery of the value of goods distrained and sold

In the Court of .... at ....

Suit No. .... of 20 ....

(Set out cause title)

The plaintiff above-named states as follows:

1. That the plaintiff is a grocer. His gross annual turnover is less than ₹ .... The plaintiff is not liable to sales tax.

2. That the defendant No. 1 is the Sales-tax Officer of the district of .... while the defendant No. 2 is the Certificate Officer of the .... sub division of .... district.

3. That on requisition by the defendant No. 1 the defendant No. 2 started a Certificate Proceeding No. Sales-tax .... of 20 .... against the plaintiff and served a notice under s. 7 of the P.D.R. Act demanding from the plaintiff a sum of ₹ ...... The plaintiff had entered his appearance and duly submitted his objection under s. 9 of the said Act denying the plaintiff's liability for the certificate dues.

4. On the .... day of .... 20 .... the defendant No. 2 by himself and his subordinates wrongfully distrained in the premises of the plaintiff the undermentioned household articles of the plaintiff as a distress for pretended claim of certificate dues and later, on the ...... day of .... 20 .... wrongfully sold the said articles as such distress.

5. The plaintiff is entitled to recover from the defendants the value of the articles distrained and sold as aforesaid.

6. Cause of action (date of distress and subsequent date of sale).

7. Valuation (value of articles sold and damages).

The plaintiff claims:

(*a*) ₹ .... being value of articles sold;

(*b*) ₹ .... as damages for illegal distress;

(*c*) Costs of suit; and

(*d*) Any other or further relief.

List of articles seized and sold with respective value

Verification

Affidavit

DOWER

186. Suit by a Muslim wife for (i) Prompt dower; (ii) Deferred dower; (iii) Both prompt and deferred dower

In the Court of the .... at ....

Money Suit No. .... of 20 ....

(Set out cause title)

Suit for prompt dower

Deferred dower

Prompt and deferred dower

Claim laid at ₹ .... (state here the amount of dower).

The plaintiff states as follows:

1. That the defendant was married to the plaintiff in the month of ... 20 ... at village ..... P.S. .... District .... within the jurisdiction of this Court.

2. That the marriage between the plaintiff and the defendant was negotiated by guardians of respective parties.

3. That at the time of marriage it was agreed in between the plaintiff and the defendant that the plaintiff shall be paid a prompt dower ₹ .... (or that the plaintiff shall be entitled to a dower of ₹ ......) on dissolution of marriage by death or divorce.

Or, that the plaintiff's dower would be ₹ .... the 1/4th of which was to be prompt while the balance deferred.

4. (*In case of prompt dower*)

That the marriage of the plaintiff with the defendant has been consummated and a son was born of the wedlock. The marriage is still subsisting. On ...... the plaintiff demanded from the defendant her said prompt dower but the defendant refused to pay.

(*Or, in case of deferred dower*)

That the marriage of the plaintiff with the defendant has been consummated. The defendant has divorced the plaintiff with effect from .... entitling the plaintiff to claim aforesaid deferred dower of ₹ .... The plaintiff by a notice of demand dated ...., sent per registered post with A/D, claimed from the defendant the said amount of deferred dower but the defendant did not pay.

(*Or, in case of prompt and deferred dower*)

That the marriage of the plaintiff with the defendant was duly consummated. The plaintiff obtained a decree of dissolution of marriage with the defendant on ...... in Matrimonial Suit No. ...... of .... of the Court of ...... at ...... within the knowledge of the defendant. The plaintiff is entitled to the whole amount of dower, both prompt and deferred, as never before the plaintiff had asked the defendant for dower. The defendant has not paid to the plaintiff the dower money in spite of repeated demands made by the plaintiff in that behalf.

5. That the cause of action for this suit arose at .... within the jurisdiction of this court.

In case of prompt dower on .... when demand for prompt dower was made but the defendant did not pay.

In case of deferred dower on .... when the plaintiff's marriage with the defendant was dissolved by Talak entitling the plaintiff to the payment of dower.

In case of prompt and deferred dower on .... when the plaintiff's marriage was dissolved by court's decree entitling her to dower.

6. That for the purpose of jurisdiction and court-fees the suit is valued at ₹ .... (state here the amount of dower).

The plaintiff prays for:

(*a*) a decree for ₹ .... as prompt dower.

(Or, a decree for ₹ .... as deferred dower.

Or, a decree for ₹ .... as both prompt and deferred dower).

(*b*) Interest @ .... per annum up to the date of institution of suit ₹ .... (where necessary).

Verification

Affidavit

NOTES: 1. Prompt dower can be demanded at any time after marriage and consummation is not a condition of its payment (11 IC 558) nor does consummation of marriage debar a wife from suing for her prompt dower—*Muhammad Taqi Khan* v *Farmoodi Begum* AIR 1941 All 181.

2. A dower can be fixed even after marriage and the amount fixed at marriage can even be varied by a post-nuptial agreement—*Mt. Fatima Bibi* v *Lal Din* AIR 1937 Lah 345; 171 IC 421.

187. Defence to claim by Shia Mahomedan wife for prompt dower, where the character of dower was not specified

In the Court of .... at ....

Suit No. .... of 20 ....

(Set out cause title)

The plaintiff states as follows:

1. The defendant admits the *Kabin Nama* mentioned in paragraph 3 of the plaint, but says that by the immemorial custom among Shia Mahomedans of ...., the locality to which the plaintiff belonged, where the contract of dower does not specify whether it is to be prompt or deferred, only one-third of the total amount of the dower is payable as prompt.

2. Between .... and .... the defendant paid the plaintiff ₹ .... in cash and purchased for her articles of jewellery of the value of ₹ .... and the plaintiff received the said amount and the said jewellery in lieu or satisfaction of her claim for prompt dower.

3. The plaintiff did not make the alleged or any demand for dower.

4. Save what is hereinbefore expressly admitted all allegations in the plaint are denied.

Verifiction

Affidavit

188. Suit by a Muslim wife for dower
(Where not specified whether dower was prompt or deferred)

In the Court of .... at ....

Suit No. .... of 20 ....

(Set out cause title)

Suit for dower

Valued at ₹ ....

The plaintiff states as follows:

1. That the defendant was married to the plaintiff in the month of .... 20 .... at . ... within the jurisdiction of this court.

2. That at the time of marriage the plaintiff's dower was settled orally [or by a 'Kabin Nama' (mention registered, if registered) executed by the defendant on ....] at ₹ ...., but it was not settled whether the dower shall be prompt or deferred.

3. That the marriage is still subsisting though the plaintiff has been living at her father's place.

4. That on .... the plaintiff had demanded from the defendant by a notice dated .... served through her authorised lawyer Sri .... Advocate the said sum of ₹ .... as prompt dower. The defendant in his reply denied to pay the dower.

5. That the cause of action for this suit arose at .... within the jurisdiction of this court on .... on expiry of the period given in the said notice for compliance.

6. The plaintiff puts the value of her suit at ₹ .... for the purposes of determination of jurisdiction and court-fees.

The plaintiff prays:

(*i*) for a judgment and decree for ₹ .... as prompt dower,

(*ii*) for all costs of suit.

Verification

Affidavit

NOTES: 1. Muslim Women (Protection of Rights on Divorce) Act 1986. Section 3. Application by divorced woman for sum of Mahr or dower. Only Magistrate concerned and not Family Court can entertain such application—*Arjun Hossain* v *Smt. Salma* AIR 1992 All 322.

2. Gift in lieu of dower-debt is not valid—*Mst. Saimunnissa* v *Sk. Mohiuddin* AIR 1991 Pat 183.

189. Suit for deferred dower

Before the Family Court at ....

Miscellaneous Suit No. ... of 20...

In the matter of

P., the widow of Q residing at ...., Kolkata

.... *Plaintiff*

versus

1. X, the mother of Q.
2. Y, the brother of Q.
3. Z, the sister of Q.

All are residing at ...., Kolkata

...... *Defendants*

Suit for deferred dower valued at ₹ ....

The plaintiff states as follows:

1. The defendants hereinabove are all Mohammedans and they are governed by Muslim Laws.

2. The plaintiff was married to Q, who died on 5.1.20... leaving behind an estate valued at ₹ .... situate at .... Kolkata.

3. At the time of the marriage of the plaintiff an agreement was entered into in writing whereby the said deceased Q undertook to pay the deferred dower to the plaintiff, an amount of ₹ .... payable upon dissolution of the said marriage either by death or otherwise.

4. Defendants are the mother, brother and sister of the deceased Q, respectively as mentioned above and they all are also heirs of the deceased Q.

5. The defendants are in possession of assets and properties left behind by the deceased Q and are enjoying the rents, profits and usufructs of the said Estate without discharging the dower debt of late deceased Q payable to the plaintiff.

6. The plaintiff demanded from the defendants payment of dower debt but defendants have refused to pay the same.

7. In the premises, the plaintiff claims a sum of ₹ .... as the deferred dower due and payable by defendants as also a declaration of charge upon the respective shares of the defendants in the assets and properties left behind by the said deceased Q.

8. The plaintiff's cause of action for this suit arose within the jurisdiction of this learned court on 5.1.20... on the death of Q and is still continuing from day to day.

9. For purposes of jurisdiction and court-fees, the suit is valued at ₹ .... and *ad valorem* court-fees in stamps have been paid.

The plaintiff, therefore, prays for and claims:

(*a*) declaration that the plaintiff is entitled to claim deferred dower;

(*b*) decree for ₹ .... against the defendants jointly and severally for payment of deferred dower according to their respective shares of liability;

(*c*) declaration of charge upon the estate left behind by the deceased being Premises No. ...... of Road, Kolkata for payment of the said deferred dower of ₹ .... with interest;

(*d*) receiver;

(*e*) injunction;

(*f*) costs;

(*g*) further and other reliefs as the plaintiff is entitled to.

Verification

Affidavit

190. Suit by the other heirs of a deceased Mahomedan against the widow in possession of his estate in lieu of her dower, for accounts and administration

In the Court of .... at ....

Suit No. .... of 20 ....

(Set out cause title)

The plaintiff states as follows:

1. The parties are Shia Mahomedans.

2. One G.H. died on 6th February 20........, leaving him surviving the defendant, his widow, and the plaintiffs A.B., C.H. and E.F. his mother, brother and sister respectively, as his heirs under the Mahomedan law.

3. The defendant was married to the said G.H. on ....

4. At the time of the said marriage the said G.H., settled upon the defendant a dower of ₹ .... payable upon dissolution of marriage by death or otherwise.

5. Immediately after the death of G.H. the defendants came into possession of certain immovable properties left by her husband (particulars whereof are set out in schedule "A" hereto annexed) under her claim as an heir of the deceased and for her dower, and it was then verbally agreed between the defendants and the plaintiffs that the defendants should remain in possession, and appropriate the rents and profits of the said properties until the dower debt would be discharged. The net annual income of the said properties is about ₹ ....

6. By letter dated ...., the plaintiffs called upon the defendants to account for the rents and profits realised and appropriated by them out of the said properties and offered to pay her the balance, if any, of the dower debt; but the defendant by letter dated .... refused to render any account to the plaintiffs or any of them.

7. The plaintiffs are entitled as the heirs of G.H. deceased to the undermentioned shares in the properties left by him. (Here state the shares). The remaining share in the said properties belongs to the defendant as one of the heirs of G.H. deceased.

The plaintiffs claim—

(1) An account of the dealings of the defendant with the properties specified in the schedule "A" hereto.

(2) Administration of the said properties.

(3) Appointment of a receiver.

SCHEDULE

Verification

Affidavit

191. Suit by the heirs of a deceased Mahomedan against transferee from the widow who was in possession of the property in lieu of her dower

In the Court of .... at ....

Suit No. .... of 20 ....

(Set out cause title)

The plaintiff states as follows:

1. That one A.M., a Hanafi Mahomedan, died on 6th November 20........ leaving him surviving the defendant No. 1, his widow, and the plaintiffs his heirs, under the Mahomedan law. The relationship of the plaintiffs with the deceased will appear from the pedigree set out hereunder:

(Here set out the pedigree)

2. Immediately on the death of the said A.M., the defendant No. 1 took possession of his immovable properties under her claim as an heir of the deceased and for her dower and got her name to be entered on the registry as its possessor instead of his. The said properties are fully set out in Schedule "A" hereto annexed.

3. By a sale deed dated .... the defendant No. 1 for the consideration therein mentioned, purported to transfer and convey the said properties of the defendant No. 2 absolutely. There is a recital in the said deed that the defendant No. 1 was the absolute owner of the said properties.

4. On ...., the defendant No. 2 entered into possession of the said properties on the strength of his purchase and is continuing in possession thereof and is denying the title of the plaintiffs or any of them to the same.

5. The defendant No. 1 has got .... *annas* share in the said properties as an heir of A.M. deceased and the plaintiffs have got the remaining .... *annas* share therein.

The plaintiffs claim—

(1) A declaration that the sale deed aforesaid in so far as it affects the plaintiffs share in the said properties is invalid and not binding on the plaintiffs.

(2) Possession of the properties to the extent of the plaintiffs' share therein.

(3) ₹ .... as *mesne profits* from .... up to the date of suit.

(4) Future *mesne profits* from the date of suit up to that of delivery of possession.

SCHEDULE 'A'

Verification

Affidavit

EASEMENT

192. Suit for declaration that easement right acquired is absolute

Before the Learned Civil Judge (Senior Division) at Alipore

Suit No. ...... of 20.......

In the matter of

P., son of Q residing at Alipore Road, Kolkata

.... *Plaintiff*

versus

X, son of Y, residing at Alipore Road, Kolkata

.... *Defendant*

Suit for declaration that the Easement Right acquired is absolute valued at ₹ ....

The plaintiff states as follows:

1. The plaintiff is the owner of a two-storeyed building being premises No. ... Alipore Road, Kolkata and is within the Kolkata Municipal Corporation.

2. The defendant is owner of a one-storeyed building just adjacent to the plaintiff's building on the eastern side being premises No. .... Alipore Road, Kolkata within the Kolkata Municipal Corporation.

3. The plaintiff states that although the said premises of the plaintiff and defendants were built more than 22 years ago. Since then the plaintiff has been enjoying access to and use of light and air from and over the defendant's building to the plaintiff's building as an easement and as of right without any interruption. The right to such access to and use of light and air has thus become the absolute indefeasible easement right of plaintiff.

4. The defendant has since been taking steps to construct another storey over their existing one thus infringing and obstructing the access to and use of light and air to the plaintiff's building situate on the western side.

5. The plaintiff by his Regd. letter dated 5.1.20......... requested the defendant not to infringe and not to obstruct the plaintiff's right of access to and use of light and air caused by the attempted construction of first floor of his building on the eastern side. The defendant received the said letter of plaintiff in due time on signing on a copy of the said letter but has not taken any step to accede to such request of the plaintiff.

6. The plaintiff's cause of action for this suit arose within the jurisdiction of this learned court under Alipore Police Station and within Kolkata Municipal Corporation on or about 15.12.20........ and the same is still continuing from day to day.

7. For purposes of jurisdiction and court-fees, the suit is valued at ₹ .... on which *ad valorem* court-fees in stamps have been paid.

The plaintiff, therefore, claims:

(*a*) Declaration that the easement right acquired to the plaintiff's aforesaid building and the right of access to light and air are absolute and indefeasible;

(*b*) An order of injunction be issued restraining the defendant, his agents and servants from infringing and obstructing the plaintiff's aforesaid easement right in any way;

(*c*) Cost;

(*d*) Such further and other orders be made and reliefs as this learned court may deem fit and proper to afford complete relief to the plaintiff.

Verification

Affidavit

193. Suit for obstruction to plaintiff's right of way

In the Court of .... at ....

Suit No. .... of 20 ....

(Set out cause title)

The plaintiff states as follows:

1. That the plaintiff owns his house premises at Mouja .... P.S. .... District .... within the jurisdiction of this court being plot No. .... and .... recorded in Khatian No. .... of the said Mouja.

2. That the plaintiff was and is at all material times entitled to a right of way, from the plaintiff's house premises, for pedestrian traffic, lying over the defendant's land in plot Nos. ...... and .... more particularly described in the Schedule below, to 'A' street, a public road.

The said way, its position, termini thereof are shown in the sketch map attached here-to which may be treated as a part of the plaint.

3. That the plaintiff enjoyed the said way peaceably openly and without interruption as an easement and as of right since the year ...... and for more than 20 years until .... when the easement was disturbed and/or obstructed as aforesaid.

4. There is no other alternative way in the locality to reach the said public road from the plaintiff's house premises and the plaintiff requires absolutely the suit land for pedestrian traffic.

5. That the defendant wrongfully obstructed the said way on his land on .... by raising barbed wire-fencing across the way on plot Nos. ....

6. That the cause of action for the suit arose on .... when the defendant obstructed the plaintiff's right of way at Mouja .... within the jurisdiction of this court.

7. That for the purpose of jurisdiction the suit is valued at ₹.......... and for reliefs of declaration with consequential relief of injunction *ad valorem* court-fees are paid thereon.

The plaintiff, therefore, prays:

(*a*) For a decree declaring that the plaintiff has an easement right on the said way, described in the Schedule below and in the sketch-map.

(*b*) For a decree of mandatory injunction directing the defendant to remove the obstruction on the said way.

(*c*) For a decree of perpetual injunction restraining the defendant from any act of future obstruction.

(*d*) Costs.

SCHEDULE

Sketch map

(State here the course of the way, termini—
East-West long etc. and such other description)

Verification

Affidavit

NOTES: 1. User of way, water course, etc., as an easement as of right openly and without interruption for 20 years renders such user absolute.

2. See s. 25 of the Limitation Act. Private individuals may have right of way by grant, or prescription or right.

3. (See Easements Act)—besides customary right originating from custom.

4. Limitation for compensation for obstructing a way or a watercourse—three years *vide* Art. 85 of the Limitation Act 1963.

5. AIR 1970 Manipur 67—the word 'peaceably' indicates that the user must be without violence (see s. 26 of the Limitation Act).

6. Easement of necessity should not be granted in absence of pleading—AIR 1969 Ori 201.

7. In a suit for injunction—the plaintiff states the amount at which he values the relief sought.
(For West Bengal: See s. 7(*iv*)(*c*) of the West Bengal Court-fees Act 1970).

8. Provisions of ss. 45 and 51 are not attracted where right of easement has not become absolute—AIR 1970 All 404.

194. Suit for obstruction of right of way (Another Form)

In the Court of .... at ....

Suit No. .... of 20 ....

(Set out cause title)

The above-named plaintiff states as follows:

1. That the plaintiff owns his house at plot No. .... of Mouja .... Town .... P.S. .... District .... and was and is entitled to a right of way from his house over plot No. .... to a public highway/road, to the north of the plaintiff's house east-west long as shown in the sketch-map enclosed herewith.

2. That the plaintiff and members of the public of the locality have been entitled to the said right of way by enjoyment thereof for more than 20 years before now as of right and without interruption (or from time immemorial without any interference from anybody).

3. That in the Records of Right and in the Town Settlement Map as well the said plot is shown as such.

4. That on ...... the defendant wrongfully raised barbed wire fencing across the said way at its east end and caused obstruction to the plaintiff's user of the said way.

5. [*If necessary add*]. That the plaintiff had called a Salish on ...... of the leading men of the locality at the plaintiff's outhouse where the defendant was also present. The defendant was requested by the plaintiff and many others assembled there to remove the obstruction but he refused.

6. That for the aforesaid obstruction, the plaintiff has been disturbed in his enjoyment of his said right of way and prevented from user of the said road/highway and the plaintiff and other members of his family have been put to difficulties.

7. The cause of action for this suit arose on .... (when obstruction was raised) at .... within the jurisdiction of this court.

8. That for the purpose of jurisdiction the suit is valued at ₹ .... and for reliefs of declaration with consequential relief of injunction *ad valorem* court-fees are paid thereon.

The plaintiff, therefore, prays:

(a) for a declaration that the aforesaid passage is a public way;

(b) for an injunction restraining the defendant from the repetition or continuance of the act complained hereinabove; and

(c) for a decree of mandatory injunction directing the defendant to remove the said obstruction within a time specified by the court.

Sketch map

Verification

Affidavit

NOTES: 1. Limitation—three years *vide* Art. 113 of the Limitation Act 1963.

2. Å distinction has to be made between a public road in which the public in general has a right of way and a village road in which the inhabitants of a particular village or villages have the right. In the case of a public road in the full sense, proof of special damage will be necessary, while in the case of a village road, that is to say a quasi-public road, even in the absence of proof of special damage the suit can be decreed—AIR 1921 Cal 271; ILR 15 Cal 460; 22 IC 916; AIR 1968 Pat 422; AIR 1968 All 18.

3. Right of way (s. 15, Easements Act).

Plaintiffs continuously using path in dispute without any objection for more than 20 years. It raises presumption that their user was as of right. Plaintiffs acquired easementary right of way over path in dispute by prescription—*Suresh Chand* v *Hindu Mal* AIR 1994 HP 56.

Village Pathway—Comes under the description of the second class of rights intermediate between the public and private roads has its origin in custom but a public highway exists for all citizens and has its origin in dedication. Suit for declaration of right to village pathway—proof of special damage is not necessary—*Harendra Nath* v *Asin Sindhu* AIR 1981 Cal 325 (Easements Act, s. 18).

4. Public way—Cart track in use for longtime. Unilateral shutting off by revenue authorities is not permissible—*Dilip* v *Executive Engineer* AIR 1993 Bom 140.

5. Easements Act, s. 28—Right of easement: House with land—House gifted to defendant and land to plaintiff after leaving a 'Gali' (strip of land) between the house and land gifted to plaintiff. Express mention in gift deed of plaintiff that Gali was left out for enjoyment by defendant of windows etc. of his house—Gali subsequently transferred by donor to defendant. Plaintiff cannot in face of transfer be said to possess easementary right in Gali by implication—*Mst. Kamla* v *Bhanwarlal Vaid* AIR 1985 SC 473.

195. Suit for obstruction to right of flow of rain water etc.

In the Court of .... at ....

Suit No. .... of 20 ....

(Set out cause title)

The plaintiff states as follows:

1. That the plaintiff owns his house properties on plot No. ...... and the defendant has had his house properties on plot No. .... and .... within the town of .... P.S. .... District .... within the jurisdiction of this court.

2. That there is a drain on the land of the plaintiff running north-south along the western boundary of the plaintiff's said house properties. The said drain carries rain water accumulated on the plaintiff's land. The plaintiff, as of right, is entitled to undisturbed flow of rain water through the said drain.

3. That the defendant had on .... obstructed the natural flow of water by depositing earth at its northern end. As a result, the entire courtyard of the plaintiff's house properties is under stagnant water, likely to affect hygienic condition of the house adversely. The defendant is continuing the obstruction in spite of protest made by the plaintiff.

4. That the plaintiff has suffered damage and will suffer so unless the obstruction is removed forthwith.

5. Cause of action (on the date when obstruction was raised).

6. Suit valuation (plaintiff's valuation of damages).

The plaintiff, therefore, prays:

(*a*) For a judgment and decree for ₹ .... as damages.

(*b*) For a decree of mandatory injunction directing the defendant to remove the obstruction within a time specified by the court.

(*c*) For perpetual injunction restraining the defendants from repeating the said or similar obstruction.

(*d*) Costs of suit.

Verification

Affidavit

NOTES: 1. See Art. 85 of the Limitation Act—three years.

2. Obstruction must be shown to be of such proportion as to cause substantial injury which may be restrained by an injunction and that the injury was caused by interference with the plaintiff's right.

196. Suit for interference with a right of privacy and for mandatory injunction

In the Court of .... at ....

Suit No. .... of 20 ....

(Set out cause title)

The plaintiff states as follows:

1. That the plaintiff is the owner of a house standing on the .... Road at .... Town P.S. .... District .... wherein the plaintiff lives with his wife for the last 25 years.

2. That the plaintiff's wife is a *pardanashin* lady and she has been living secluded from outsiders in the said house of the plaintiff for the last 25 years.

3. That the defendant has built in the month of .... 20.......... a double storeyed house to the north of the plaintiff's house. The rooms of the defendant's house in the first floor are fitted with windows overlooking the plaintiff's inner apartments ('Andarmahal') where the plaintiff's wife lives.

4. That in the above premises, the defendant has interfered with the right of privacy of the plaintiff's wife enjoyed hitherto.

5. That the cause of action for this suit arose in the month of ...... 20..... when the defendant opened windows in the rooms of the first floor invading the right of privacy.

6. Suit–valuation.

The plaintiff, therefore, prays:

(*i*) For a mandatory injunction directing the defendant to close windows overlooking the 'Andarmahal' of the plaintiff.

(*ii*) For an injunction restraining the defendant from doing any act which may or is likely to interfere with the said right of privacy.

Verification

Affidavit

NOTES: 1. A right or privacy originates from custom or from grant, prescription or express usage.

2. See under-mentioned cases (*i*) AIR 1931 Pat 280.
(*ii*) 5 CWN 147.
(*iii*) AIR 1935 All 1002.
(*iv*) AIR 1942 Bom 217.

197. Suit for compensation for diverting a water-course

In the Court of .... at ....

Suit No. .... of 20 ....

(Set out cause title)

The plaintiff states:

1. That the plaintiff owns and possesses 12 acres of land at Mouja .... appertaining to Khatian (Record of Rights, No. .... Plot No. within P.S. .... District ....).

2. That the said lands are irrigated by the natural flow of a stream known as Buri Torsha passing through the said lands of the plaintiff, specifically described in the Schedule below, and as such, the plaintiff is a riparian owner.

3. That the defendant, owner of an upper holding, diverted the water-course of the said stream on .... by (state the manner how diverted). Thus, the plaintiff has been deprived of the benefit of the said flow of water to his land and disadvantage of agriculture.

4. That the plaintiff lodged a protest with the defendant on .... but the defendant did not pay heed to the plaintiff's protest and the said diversion is continuing. That the plaintiff has suffered damage and will continue to suffer such until the defendant is restrained by an appropriate order of injunction.

5. Cause of action arose on .... when the water-course was diverted at .... within the jurisdiction of this court.

6. That the plaintiff values his suit at ₹ .... (being the amount of damages).

The plaintiff, therefore, prays:

(*i*) a judgment and decree for ₹ .... as damages.

(*ii*) a decree of injunction restraining the defendant from continuing or repeating the diversion of the water-course.

(*iii*) a decree for damages on account of loss of agricultural income.

SCHEDULE

(State here particulars of the plaintiff's land)

Verification

Affidavit

NOTES: 1. Every riparian owner is entitled to unobstructed natural flow of water—See AIR 1935 All 836.

2. Limitation—three years from the date of obstruction—vide Art. 85 of the Limitation Act.

198. Suit for injunction to prevent obstruction of right to light

In the Court of .... at ....

Suit No. .... of 20 ....

(Set out cause title)

The plaintiff states:

1. The plaintiff is the owner of a dwelling house abutting on the .... road at .... Town, P.S. .... District .... in which there are the under-mentioned ancient lights.

(Name the windows and their situations admitting light.)

2. Of late the defendant has been raising a structure to the east of the plaintiff's dwelling house. It is reasonably apprehended that if construction of the defendant's structure be not stopped immediately, the same would obstruct light coming to the plaintiff's dwelling house through those windows.

3. That the plaintiff's dwelling house shall be rendered inhabitable and the plaintiff will be deprived of the enjoyment of his dwelling house. Further, it would cause irreparable injury to the plaintiff.

4. That the defendant was requested orally on the .... day of .... 20......... to stop the construction but the defendant threatened to continue the erection.

5. That the said construction of the defendant has been a nuisance to the plaintiff.

6. Cause of action (from date when construction began and the same is continuing from day to day).

7. Suit valuation (according to value of relief).

The plaintiff claims–

(*a*) a perpetual injunction restraining the defendant by himself and/or by his contractors, workmen from continuing to erect the said building so as to obstruct light to the plaintiff's dwelling house through the said windows; and

(*b*) a mandatory injunction for pulling down the erections already made causing obstruction to light.

Verification

Affidavit

199. Suit for mandatory injunction to remove obstruction to the access of light and air to a house

In the Court of .... at ....

Suit No. .... of 20 ....

(Set out cause title)

The plaintiff states as follows:

1. That the plaintiff, was and is the owner and occupier of a dwelling house, No. ...., ... Street, in the town of Kolkata, having windows on the east side thereof, viz., 2 dining room windows on the ground floor, and one drawing room window and one bed room window on the first floor, as shown in the plan hereto annexed and marked 'A'.

2. The plaintiff and his predecessors in title enjoyed the access and use of light and air to and for the said house through the said windows peaceably as an easement and as of right without interruption for 20 years prior to the disturbance hereinafter complained of, ending within two years next before the institution of this suit.

3. The defendant, in .... 20....., erected a wall on the adjoining land belonging to him near to the said windows up to a height of .... feet and has thereby materially interfered with the access of light and air heretofore enjoyed by the occupants of the said house and has rendered the said house unwholesome and unfit for the ordinary purpose of habitation.

The plaintiff claims—

To have the said wall pulled down.

Plan 'A'

Verification

Affidavit

200. Defence to a claim for mandatory injunction for obstruction to the access and use of light and air to and for a house

In the Court of .... at ....

Suit No. .... of 20 ....

(Set out cause title)

The defendant states as follows:

1. The defendant denies that the access and use of light and/or air to and for the said house through the said windows or any of them has been enjoyed by the plaintiffs and/or their predecessors in title for the said period of 20 years within the meaning of s. 25 of the Limitation Act, as alleged or at all.

2. The alleged enjoyment during the statutory period was interrupted by the defendant erecting a ...... in ..... 20..... and maintaining the same until ....

3. The said windows are not ancient windows. In .... the plaintiff rebuilt his house and opened new windows which did not receive the same cones of light as were enjoyed through the old ones and no easement respecting the new windows has been acquired by enjoyment for the statutory period.

4. The defendant denies that the said wall has materially interfered with the access of light and/or aid to and for the said house through any of the said windows

or has rendered the said house unwholesome or unfit for ordinary purposes of habitation as alleged or at all.

5. The suit be dismissed with costs.

Verification

Affidavit

GUARANTEE, SURETY AND INDEMNITY

201. Suit on a guarantee of a debt against a surety

In the Court of .... at ....

Suit No. .... of 20 ....

(Set out cause title)

The plaintiff states as follows:

1. That the defendant No. 2, accompanied by the defendant No. 1, had approached the plaintiff on .... and requested the plaintiff to advance a loan of ₹ .... to the defendant No. 1 on the latter's executing a hand-note for the said sum.

2. That the plaintiff was hesitant to advance any loan to the defendant No. 1 as he had no means to repay and explained to the defendants the position. Thereupon the defendant No. 2 pleaded his willingness to stand a surety for the due payment. As a matter of fact, the defendant No. 2 promised in writing that he bound himself for the sum of ₹ .... to be paid back to the plaintiff by the defendant No. 1 on plaintiff's demand, with interest at 10% per annum.

3. That the plaintiff had, thereupon advanced a loan of ₹ .... to the defendant No. 1 on his executing a handnote on .... repayable on demand with interest at 10% per annum.

The plaintiff files herewith the said handnote executed by the defendant No. 1 and the written promise of the defendant No. 2, which may be treated as a part of the plaint.

4. That the defendant No. 1 did not repay the loan in spite of demands made by the plaintiff. The plaintiff then requested the defendant No. 2 for payment of the plaintiff's dues but the defendant No. 2 also did not pay.

5. That the plaintiff is entitled to recover from the defendant No. 2 a sum of ₹ .... as per account in the Schedule below.

6. That the cause of action for this suit arose on .... (date of execution of the handnote) at .... within the jurisdiction of this court.

7. That for the purpose of jurisdiction and court-fees the suit is valued at ₹ .... and *ad valorem* court-fees are paid thereon.

The plaintiff, therefore, claims:

Rupees .... as per account in Schedule below.

SCHEDULE

Accounts

Principal due on handnote	.....	₹ ....
Interest @ 10% over the sum for the period from .... to	.....	₹ ....
(In words)		₹ ....

Verification

Affidavit

NOTES: 1. The creditor can proceed against the principal debtor or against the surety at his option.

2. It is not the law that the creditor has to sue the debtor first. It is not necessary that the creditor should exhaust all remedies against the debtor or should give notice of the principal's default nor it is necessary to make a demand upon the principal before proceeding against the surety, unless such notice is stipulated in the contract.

3. Liability of the creditor and the surety is co-extensive.

4. Contract of guarantee is a tripartite agreement which contemplates principal debtor, creditor and the surety—AIR 1968 Cal 371.

5. Continuing guarantee–in the case of continuing guarantee and an undertaking by the defendant to pay any amount that may be due by a company to a bank on the general balance of its account or any other account, so long the account is a live account in the sense that it is not settled and there is no refusal on the part of the guarantor to carry out the obligation, the period of limitation for a suit to enforce the bond could not be said to have commenced running. Limitation would only run from the date of breach under Art. 30 of the Limitation Act 1963. Continuing Guarantee—Section 141 of the Contract Act. It can be for fixed period. It would only mean a guarantee which extends to a series of transactions–*Eastern Bank* v *Parts Services* AIR 1986 Cal 61.

6. Guarantee and Indemnity—for difference—See AIR 1940 Bom 315.

202. General defences by surety in a suit on a guarantee of debt

In the Court of .... at ....

Suit No. .... of 20 ....

(Set out cause title)

[The surety may take one or more of the following defences]:

1. The defendant never gave the alleged or any guarantee to the plaintiff.

2. The defendant admits that he wrote a letter to the plaintiff on .... but denies that in that letter he gave any such guarantee as is alleged in paragraph .... of the plaint.

3. The defendant admits that he gave a letter of guarantee to the plaintiff on .... but states that the contents of the said letter have not been fully set out in the plaint. By the said letter of guarantee the defendant undertook to pay the amount to the plaintiff "after attempts have been made to realise the same from the principal debtor." The plaintiff did not take any steps before bringing the suit to recover the debt by proceeding against the principal debtor or his assets.

4. The defendant denies that the plaintiff lent the alleged or any money (or supplied the alleged or any goods) to the alleged principal debtor as alleged or at all.

5. The guarantee sued on was a continuing guarantee and was by the express terms thereof revocable by notice. On .... before the plaintiff made any advances to A.B., the principal debtor, the defendant revoked the said guarantee by notice in writing dated ....

6. This defendant admits that he gave the plaintiff the said letter of guarantee but states that A.B., the principal debtor, was a near relative of his and the plaintiff

procured the signature of this defendant to the said letter by threatening that if he did not sign he would prosecute the said A.B. and have him imprisoned.

7. The consideration for the said guarantee was the withdrawal by the plaintiff of a non-compoundable criminal case against A.B., (the principal debtor).

8. The defendant was induced to give the said guarantee by the fraud of the plaintiff; (*here state particulars of fraud*) ....

9. The plaintiff discharged the defendant from all liability under the alleged guarantee by (*here state the grounds*).

10. The suit may be dismissed with costs.

Verification

Affidavit

203. Suit against a surety for payment of rent for house premises

In the Court of .... at ....

Suit No. .... of 20 ....

(Set out cause title)

The plaintiff states:

1. That the plaintiff owns his house premises at .... Town .... P.S. .... District .... more fully described in the Schedule appended hereto.

2. That the defendant proposed to the plaintiff on .... for renting out the said premises in the Schedule to one A.B. at a monthly rent of ₹ .... according to English calendar month. The defendant on the occasion had verbally guaranteed payment of the said rent by the said A.B. duly.

3. That on the basis of the said verbal guarantee by the defendant, the plaintiff let out the said premises to the said A.B. on .... The said A.B. duly paid rent for the months of January to March 20 …, but defaulted to pay rent from the months of ...., 20 .... to ……, 20…, both inclusive.

4. That the plaintiff is entitled to recover from the defendant arrears of rent for .... months as aforesaid, he being a surety for payment of the same.

5. That the cause of action for this suit arose on the 1st day of .... 20........... for rent for the month of .... 20................. and on the 1st day of each subsequent month at .... within the jurisdiction of this court.

6. That for the purpose of jurisdiction and court-fees the suit is valued at ₹ .... (......... month's rent) and *ad valorem* court-fees are paid.

The plaintiff claims:

Rupees .... as arrears of rent for .... months from .... 20....... to .... 20 .... both inclusive.

SCHEDULE

(State here description of the premises)

Verification

Affidavit

204. Suit against a principal and the surety for price of goods

In the Court of .... at ....

Suit No. .... of 20 ....

(Set out cause title)

The plaintiff states:

1. That the plaintiff owns a grocer's shop and the defendant No. 1 is known to the plaintiff for long.

2. That on or about .... 20...... the defendants came to the plaintiff's shop when the defendant No. 1 agreed with the plaintiff that in case the plaintiff had supplied the defendant No. 2 edible oil, etc., on credit as may be required by the defendant No. 1 shall remain answerable to the plaintiff for due payment of the price therefore.

3. That the plaintiff had thereafter supplied to the defendant No. 1 goods worth ₹ .... as mentioned in the Account below within the period from .... The plaintiff had submitted to the defendant No. 1 a bill for ₹ .... on .... by a peon book.

4. That the defendant No. 1 did not pay the plaintiff's dues.

5. That the plaintiff is entitled to recover from the defendants the said sum of ₹ .... together with damages at $6^1/_4$% per annum.

The plaintiff claims:

Rupees .... only

Account

Date of supply	Nature of goods with quality and quantity	Value	Concerned Bill No. with date.

Verification

Affidavit

NOTE: Filing of suit both against principal debtor and sureties. In a suit where the creditor chooses to proceed against the principal debtor and the sureties jointly and severally and the suit abates against the principal debtor, the suit cannot be decreed against sureties because in respect of the same subject-matter of the suit there will be two conflicting decrees–*T. Raju Setty* v *Bank of Baroda* AIR 1992 Kant 108.

205. Suit on an express indemnity

In the Court of .... at ....

Suit No. .... of 20 ....

(Set out cause title)

The plaintiff states as follows:

1. That the defendant by executing a sale-deed (registered) on .... had sold to the plaintiff a piece of land measuring 10 acres at Mouja .... P.S. .... District ...., more particularly described in the Schedule below.

2. That on the occasion of sale the defendant had represented that there was no encumbrance on the land sold and that the defendant had saleable right therein. The defendant further agreed in the sale-deed that in case the plaintiff could not acquire title to the land or any encumbrance was found to exist, the defendant shall indemnify the plaintiff against the loss.

3. That it now appears that the land which the defendant sold to the plaintiff on .... was hypothecated by the defendant in favour of the State of West Bengal on .... for an agricultural loan of ₹ .... (in Agri. Loan Case No. .... of 2002-03). The State of West Bengal commenced Certificate Proceedings No. .... and threatened to sell the property in auction on .... whereupon the plaintiff on .... met the entire certificate dues together with cost amounting to ₹..........

4. That thereupon the plaintiff by a notice dated ...., sent to the defendant .... by registered post with A/D. had intimated the defendant of the position and demanded from him a sum of ₹ .... to indemnify the plaintiff against his loss. The defendant paid no heed to the plaintiff's said notice and has not indemnified the plaintiff against his loss amounting to ₹ .... as per account below.

5. That the cause of action for this suit arose on .... when the plaintiff was constrained to pay the Certificate dues and on .... when after receipt of notice the defendant by breach of contract to indemnify failed to indemnify the loss.

6. That for the purpose of jurisdiction and court-fees, the suit is valued at ₹ .... and *ad valoren* court-fees are paid thereon.

The plaintiff claims:

A decree of ₹ .... as damages as per account below.

SCHEDULE OF LAND

Accounts

Payment made under Certificate Proceedings	₹ ....
Legal costs borne in Certificate Proceedings	₹ ....
Total	₹ ....

Verification

Affidavit

NOTE: For distinction between contract of indemnity and contract of guarantee–See AIR 1970 SC 1973.

206. Suit for indemnity in respect of unpaid debts (express indemnity)

In the Court of .... at ....

Suit No. .... of 20 ....

(Set out cause title)

The plaintiff states as follows:

1. As per a contract of indemnity dated .... made between the plaintiff and the defendant, the defendant agreed that in consideration of the plaintiff agreeing to work .... for A. B. as per latter's requirement, the defendant would pay to the plaintiff all moneys or such sums of money as may be due to the plaintiff by the said A. B., provided the same remains unpaid to the plaintiff.

2. That the plaintiff, pursuant to the contract with the said A.B., had completed the work as agreed. A sum of ₹ .... is payable to the plaintiff by the said A.B for the said work. The same has not been paid.

3. That the defendant being liable for the said sum, the plaintiff had requested the defendant to clear up the dues. The defendant received the notice but avoided payment.

The plaintiff claims:

(*i*) payment of the said sum of ₹ ....; and

(*ii*) interest thereon as may be admissible.

Verification

Affidavit

NOTES: 1. See s. 124 of the Contract Act.
2. For extent of damages to a promisee see s. 125 of the Contract Act.
3. Cause of action for a suit for breach of contract of indemnity arises when the plaintiff is actually damnified.

207. Suit on an implied indemnity

In the Court of .... at ....

Suit No. .... of 20 ....

(Set out cause title)

The plaintiff states as follows:

1. That the defendant by executing a sale-deed (registered) on .... had sold to the plaintiff a piece of land measuring 10 acres at Mouja .... P.S. .... District ...., more specifically described in the Schedule appended below, for a consideration of ₹ .... truly paid.

2. That on the occasion of sale the defendant has represented that the said property was free from encumbrance.

3. That the plaintiff found that the said property stood vested in the State long before the execution of the sale-deed and the plaintiff did not acquire right, title and interest by such purchase.

4. That in the premises, the plaintiff has sustained loss of ₹..... as per account below.

5. That the defendant has not indemnified the plaintiff against his loss even after repeated demands.

6. Cause of action–breach of implied covenant.

The plaintiff, therefore, prays for a judgment and decree for

(*i*) ₹ .... as damages;

(*ii*) ₹ .... interest @ 8% per annum from the date of kobala till the date of the suit.

Account:

(*i*) Consideration paid	...		₹ ....
(*ii*) Cost of stamp and registration	...		₹ ....
		Total	₹ ....

Verification

Affidavit

208. Suit by a company against a shareholder for indemnity against costs of action which he was allowed to defend in company's name

In the Court of .... at ....

Suit No. .... of 20 ....

(Set out cause title)

The plaintiff states as follows:

1. The plaintiff Company (hereinafter called 'the Company') is incorporated under the Companies Act.

2. The defendant at all material times was and is the registered holder of ..... shares in the capital of the Company.

3. In December .... 20 .... one C.D. brought a suit against the Company in this court (Suit No. .... of ....) to recover a sum of ₹ .... (state briefly the nature of the claim in the suit).

4. The Directors of the Company decided not to defend the said suit.

5. On .... the defendant requested the Directors of the Company to allow him to defend the said suit in the name of the Company and it was then agreed in writing between the said Directors and the defendant that the defendant would defend the said suit in the name of the Company and would indemnify and keep indemnified the Company against all costs, charges and expenses which the Company might be liable for, pay, incur, or sustain in connection with the defence of the said suit and also against all sums of money whether for costs, charges, expenses, or otherwise howsoever which the Company might be ordered to pay to the plaintiff in the said suit.

6. The defendant accordingly defended the said suit.

7. On .... the plaintiff in the said suit recovered judgment therein against the Company for ₹ .... for their claim and ₹ .... for costs.

8. The defendant has not indemnified the Company against any of the said costs, charges and expenses.

9. The Company incurred ₹ .... as costs and expenses in and about defending the said suit. Particulars of such costs are set out in schedule hereto.

10. On .... the Company paid ₹ .... as costs to the plaintiff in the said suit.

The plaintiff Company claims—

₹ ....

SCHEDULE

Verification

Affidavit

209. Suit for indemnity against seller of property

Before the Learned Court at ....

Suit No. .... of .... 20......

(Set out cause title)

The plaintiff states as follows:

1. The plaintiff purchased a house property from the defendant after the defendant guaranteed that the said property was free from encumbrances at a total price of ₹ ....

2. Before purchase of the said property the plaintiff searched the records of the Municipality concerned and found that the title was clean and there was no outstanding amount due to the Municipality.

3. The plaintiff also searched the office of the Registrar of Assurances and found that the said property was free from encumbrances.

4. After the plaintiff paid the consideration money in full to the defendant the plaintiff received a notice from one Mr. X. for ₹ .... for bricks supplied to the defendant. The said person also showed a decree and in execution of such decree the property had been attached by the said lender.

5. To save the property purchased from the defendant at a lump sum amount free from all encumbrances the plaintiff paid the said sum of ₹ .... In view of the facts that the plaintiff had to pay the said person the said sum of ₹ .... to save the property from the attachment and sale, it is the obligation of the defendant to compensate or indemnify the plaintiff to the extent of ₹ ....

6. The plaintiff has discharged the obligation of the defendant and as such is entitled to be reimbursed to the extent of the said ₹ .... Further, the defendant gave warranty at the time of sale of the property that the said property was free from encumbrances and as such the defendant is liable to pay the said sum of ₹ .... paid by the plaintiff to discharge the obligation of the defendant to the said claimant.

7. In the premises the plaintiff claims a decree for ₹ .... against the defendant with interest at 16% per annum.

8. No part of the plaintiff's claim herein is barred by the Law of Limitation.

9. The plaintiff's cause of action arose within the jurisdiction of this learned court and such cause of action is continuing from day to day.

10. For the purposes of jurisdiction and court-fees the suit is valued at ₹ .... on which court-fees in stamps have been paid.

11. Particulars of the property and the claim of the said third party against the defendant will appear from copies of the documents annexed hereto collectively marked "A".

The plaintiff, therefore, prays for and claims:

(*a*) Decree for ₹ .... with interest at 16% per annum from the date when the claim was paid to the claimant of the defendant.

(*b*) Receiver.

(*c*) Injunction.

(*d*) Costs.

(*e*) Further and other reliefs as the plaintiff is entitled to in law and in equity.

ANNEXURES 'A'

Verification

Affidavit

210. Written statement of defendant to the suit for indemnity

In Court of .... at ....

Suit No. .... of 20.......

(Set out cause title)

The defendant states as follows:

1. The suit is not maintainable in law and facts.

2. It is barred by the Law of Limitation.

3. It is barred by the principles of waiver and acquiescence.

4. With reference to the paragraph 1 of the plaint, the defendant denies and disputes that he ever guaranteed that the said property was free from all encumbrances.

5. With reference to paragraphs 2 and 3 of the plaint, the defendant states that the plaintiff made searches of records available in the concerned Municipality as also in the office of Registrar of Assurances and in the process was duly satisfied that the said property was free from all encumbrances and on that very basis the said sale was duly transacted and completed on "as is what is" basis.

6. With reference to paragraph 4 of the plaint, the defendant states that the defendant has no precise knowledge of the said decree alleged to have been passed or any attachment of the said property in execution of the said decree.

7. With reference to paragraph 5 of the plaint, the defendant states that the alleged attachment of the said property was illegal and wrongful and no money was therefore liable to be paid to the alleged decree-holder. The defendant does not admit that the plaintiff ever paid a sum of ₹ .... or any other sum. It is denied and disputed that the plaintiff is entitled to claim a sum of ₹ .... or any other sum from the defendant by way of compensation or indemnity or otherwise or at all.

8. With reference to paragraph 6 of the plaint, it is denied and disputed that this defendant had any obligation to pay the said sum of ₹ .... or any other sum. It is denied and disputed that the defendant ever gave any warranty that the said property was free from all encumbrances as has been wrongly alleged. It is further denied and disputed that the defendant is liable to pay the said sum of ₹ .... and any interest thereon to the plaintiff.

9. With reference to paragraph 7 of plaint, it is denied and disputed that the plaintiff is entitled to claim a decree for payment of ₹ .... or any other sum or payment of any interest at 16% per annum or at any other rate or at all.

10. With reference to paragraphs 8 and 9 of the plaint, this defendant denies and disputes that the plaintiff has any valid cause of action as against the defendant and as such, no cause of action could arise.

11. With reference to the paragraph 10 of plaint, it is denied and disputed that this learned court has any jurisdiction to entertain, try or determine this suit.

12. With reference to paragraph 11 of the plaint, this defendant denies and disputes the correctness and validity of the documents mentioned therein copies whereof are contained in annexure 'A' to the plaint.

13. In view of aforesaid, the plaintiff is not entitled to any of reliefs and prayers as made in the said plaint and the suit is, therefore, liable to be and be dismissed with costs.

Verification

Affidavit

Infringement

211. Suit for damages for infringement of patent rights

In the High Court at ....

Suit No. of .... 20 ....

Ordinary Original Civil Jurisdiction

Mr. P. carrying on business at ...., Kolkata within the said jurisdiction

.... *Plaintiff*

versus

Mr. X. carrying on business at ...., Kolkata within the said jurisdiction.

.... *Defendant*

The plaintiff states as follows:

1. The plaintiff carries on business as the manufacturer of and dealer in medicines. The plaintiff is a registered and legal owner of patents of different medicines owing a patent right of the medicine called "COLDLIFE" for the cure of cold and caugh.

2. The defendant has infringed such patent rights of the plaintiff and has wrongfully prepared and/or is selling his medicines under the name and style of "COLD RELIEF" with intent to infringing the patent right of plaintiff by taking undue advantage of the good-will of the plaintiff's patented medicine "COLDLIF".

3. By reason of such wrongful infringement of the plaintiff's patent right by defendant, the plaintiff has suffered loss and damages which the plaintiff assesses at ₹............, particulars whereof are given in a Schedule annexed hereto and marked 'A'.

4. In spite of requests, the defendant failed to refrain from infringing the patent rights of the plaintiff's medicine "COLDLIF" causing thereby continuous loss and damages to the plaintiff.

5. The plaintiff claims the said sum of ₹............. being the loss and damages suffered due to wrongful infringement of plaintiff's patent right by the defendant. The plaintiff claims an order of injunction restraining the defendant from continuing to infringe upon the patent right of the plaintiff.

6. The plaintiff's cause of action arose within the jurisdiction of this Learned Court and further the defendant is carrying on business at the said address within the jurisdiction of this Hon'ble Court.

7. The defendant has infringed and is continuing to infringe upon the plaintiff's patent right and as such, the question of limitation does not arise.

8. In spite of demands, the defendant has not paid the plaintiff's claim for ₹.......... and has not restrained himself from continuing to infringe the patent rights of the plaintiff.

9. In the premises, this Hon'ble Court has the jurisdiction to entertain, try and determine this suit.

10. The plaintiff is entitled to a decree for payment of loss and damages for a sum of ₹............ plus interest and an order of injunction restraining defendant from continuing to infringe the plaintiff's patent rights.

11. For the purpose of jurisdiction and court-fees, the suit is valued at ₹............... on which court-fees in stamps have been paid.

The plaintiff, therefore, prays for and claims:

(*a*) Decree for payment of ₹.............. by way of loss and damages for infringement of the plaintiff's patent rights by defendant.

(*b*) Interest on the said sum of ₹.......... from the date of filing of the suit till decree and on decretal amount till realisation.

(*c*) Injunction restraining the defendant its agents and servants from continuing to infringe the plaintiff's patent rights and/or selling medicine under the imitated name "COLD RELIEF".

(*d*) Delivery of all infringed articles of medicine in possession, custody and control of defendant.

(*e*) Cost of the suit.

(*f*) Further and other orders as the plaintiff is entitled to in law and equity.

SCHEDULE 'A'

Verification

Affidavit

212. Suit to restrain infringement (passing off) of trade mark

In the High Court at ....

Suit No .... of 20 ....

Ordinary Original Civil Jurisdiction

P & Co. Ltd. carrying on business *inter alia*,
at ...., Ezra Street, Kolkata

...... *Plaintiff*

versus

X & Co. Ltd. carrying on business, *inter alia*,
at ...., Ezra Street, Kolkata

.... *Defendant*

Suit to restrain infringement of Trade Mark valued at ₹......

The plaintiff states:

1. That the plaintiff is a company registered under the Companies Act 1956 and carrying on business, *inter alia*, as manufacturer of confectionery articles including biscuits. The plaintiff sells such biscuits under the registered Trade Mark "PKG". The said name is registered under the Trade Marks Act 1999. The said biscuits are of special nature, quality and size. There is in the market no other biscuits of that quality. In this respect an expert's report is annexed hereto marked "A".

2. That the defendant company has been registered about six months ago and has started a bakery. The defendant manufactures different kinds of breads, biscuits and cakes and sells the same in the market. The products of the defendant could not catch the imagination of the public. The defendant in its bakery business has been suffering losses due to quality and also for other reasons.

3. That with a view to increasing its sale, the defendant has manufactured and is selling biscuits with the mark 'PKG' on it. After the defendant brought out such biscuits with the mark of 'PKG', the public being unaware of the imitation and taking the said biscuits with the mark PKG to be the product of the plaintiff and on such assumption large number of public are purchasing the biscuits manufactured by the defendant putting the plaintiff's brand name PKG by infringing the registered Trade Mark of the plaintiff.

4. That the plaintiff appointed a surveyor who made a market survey in respect of the said biscuits with the brand name PKG and submitted a report to the plaintiff to the effect that the public are confused, they cannot distinguish between the biscuits manufactured by plaintiff with its PKG brand and the biscuits manufactured by defendant with PKG brand and that most of the public who purchase biscuits they do so believing that they are purchasing the original manufactured biscuits under the brand name PKG of the plaintiff. The report further states that the defendant's business with PKG mark not only misleads the consuming public but also infringes the Trade Mark of the plaintiff's the said brand.

5. That the biscuits under the name PKG manufactured and sold by the defendant is not a registered Trade Mark and that even if the defendant applies for registration to the Trade Mark Office, it will not register the same inasmuch as the plaintiff's biscuits are PKG embossed is already a registered Trade Mark and as such the defendant has no right to the said "PKG" name or to use same in its biscuits.

6. That the plaintiff states that there has been clear evidence that the defendant has infringed the Trade Mark of the plaintiff and is still continuing to do so and will not stop from doing so unless restrained by an order of injunction of this Hon'ble Court.

7. That the plaintiff through its Advocate's letter narrated the facts and pointed out that the defendant has been infringing the Trade Mark of the plaintiff by manufacturing and selling biscuits with PKG embossed on it and that by doing this wrongful act the defendant has been causing loss and damages to the plaintiff inasmuch as the sale of plaintiff's biscuits with PKG brand has been reduced substantially. The said advocate's letter also pointed out that unless the defendant stopped manufacture and sale of biscuits with the said PKG the brand name, the plaintiff would take appropriate steps against the defendant and also claim damages for infringement of registered Trade Mark. To this letter the defendant simply denied that it has infringed the Trade Mark of the plaintiff but could not lawfully justify its manufacturing biscuits with the brand name PKG. A copy of the plaintiff's Advocate's letter and a copy of the defendant's reply are annexed hereto collective marked "B".

8. The plaintiff states that the sale of the said biscuits with PKG mark was ₹............ per year more or less during the last three years but since the defendant's biscuits with PKG mark came into the market the sale of the plaintiff's biscuits with PKG mark came down by 50% of the previous years on an average.

9. In spite of the said advocate's letter and in spite of a further letter by the plaintiff requesting the defendant to desist from manufacturing and selling biscuits with the plaintiff's Trade Mark PKG, the defendant has not paid any heed thereto.

10. Due to the wrongful acts of the defendant and infringement of plaintiff's trade mark and defendant selling its biscuits with the plaintiff's trade mark PKG, the plaintiff has been suffering loss to the extent of ₹.............. per month which the defendant is liable to pay to the plaintiff by way of compensation.

11. The plaintiff states that it is a fit case for restraining the defendant from continuing infringement of plaintiff's trade mark by manufacturing and selling by the defendant biscuits with the plaintiff's registered Trade Mark PKG thereby passing off the defendant's inferior quality of biscuits as the biscuits manufactured by the plaintiff.

12. In spite of plaintiff's advocate's letter and plaintiff's further request the defendant has been continuing and intends to continue manufacture and sale of biscuits with the brand name of PKG thereby infringing the trade mark of the plaintiff unless restrained by an order of injunction of this Hon'ble Court.

13. The plaintiff also claims damages which the plaintiff assesses at ₹.................... for wrongfully infringing the plaintiff's trade mark by the defendant. A Statement of Account is annexed hereto marked 'C' to show the extent of loss suffered by the plaintiff due to wrongful infringement of plaintiff's trade mark by the defendant.

14. The plaintiff claims a decree against the defendant for ₹ .... with interest and costs.

15. The plaintiff's cause of action arose within the jurisdiction where the defendant sells his biscuits with the plaintiff's trade mark biscuits in and around Ezra Street within the jurisdiction of this Hon'ble Court.

16. The plaintiff has paid court-fees for the amount of damages claimed in the suit.

17. The plaintiff reserves the rights to take further proceedings against the defendant for further and other loss and damages caused by the wrongful acts of the defendant and prays for leave under Or. 2, r. 2 of the Code of Civil Procedure.

The plaintiff, therefore, prays for leave under Or. 2, rr. 2 of the Code of Civil Procedure and claims:

(*a*) Decree for ₹ .... against the defendant;

(*b*) Alternatively, an enquiry into the damages suffered by the plaintiff for the wrongful infringement of plaintiff's registered Trade Mark 'PKG' by the defendant and a decree for the sum found due on such enquiry;

(*c*) Injunction restraining the defendant from using the plaintiff's brand name on any product including biscuits manufactured and sold by the defendant;

(*d*) Direction on the defendant to submit accounts of the sale of biscuits under the plaintiff's brand name PKG to ascertain the actual damages caused to the plaintiff;

(*e*) Cost of the suit be paid by the defendant;

(*f*) Further and other reliefs as the plaintiff is entitled to in law and in equity.

ANNEXURE 'A'

ANNEXURE 'B'

ANNEXURE 'C'

Verification

Affidavit

HIRE AND HIRE-PURCHASE

213. Suit for hire-charge of goods against a hirer

In the Court of .... at ....

Suit No. .... of 20 ....

(Set out cause title)

1. That the plaintiff deals in crockery.

2. That the defendant hired from the plaintiff on .... 10 dozen of porcelain plate and 10 dozen of tumbler glass for the period from .... to .... in connection with the marriage ceremony of the defendant's daughter on .... and agreed to return the articles on .... and to pay the hire-charge of ₹ .... per diem.

3. That the defendant returned the articles on .... but did not pay the hire-charge.

The plaintiff claims:

₹ ....

Verification

Affidavit

NOTE: Limitation–three years when the hire becomes payable under Art. 12 of the Limitation Act 1963.

214. Suit for rent of goods against a hirer

In the Court of .... at ....

Suit No. .... of 20 ....

(Set out cause title)

1. That the plaintiff is a cabinet-maker.

2. That the defendant hired from the plaintiff for three months w.e.f. January to .... 20 .... some piece of furniture, detailed in the Schedule 'A' below, agreeing to re-deliver the same on expiry of .... 20............ and to pay rent therefor at the rate of ₹ .... p.m. on the 1st day of .... 20 .... and on the 10th day of succeeding months till 1.4.20...........

3. That the defendant returned the hired furniture on the 2nd day of .... 20 .... and paid ₹ .... only promising to pay the balance rent within the next seven days. But the defendant did not pay the same.

The plaintiff claims:

(*i*) ₹ .... from the defendant.

(*ii*) Costs.

SCHEDULE 'A'

Verification

Affidavit

NOTE: For limitation see footnotes under Form No. 213.

215. Suit against a hirer for damages for breach of agreement

In the Court of .... at ....

Suit No. .... of 20 ....

(Set out cause title)

The plaintiff states:

1. That the plaintiff deals in crockery.

2. That the defendant hired from the plaintiff on .... 10 dozen of porcelain plate and 10 dozen of tumbler glass for the period from .... to .... in connection with the marriage ceremony of the defendant's daughter.

3. That the defendant agreed and undertook to use the said articles in a careful and reasonable manner during the continuance of hiring and to return the articles intact at the expiration of hiring (reasonable wear and tear excepted) as also to pay hire-charge for the same at the rate of ₹ .... per diem.

4. That the defendant paid the hire-charge duly and returned the said articles to the plaintiff on .... but as many as 11 pieces of plate bore cracks and were rendered unserviceable and greatly damaged otherwise than by reasonable wear and tear (or by the negligent use by the defendant and/or his men).

5. That the plaintiff has suffered loss and damage and is entitled to damages of ₹ .... being value of 11 procelain plates.

The plaintiff claims:

₹ .... as damages.

Verification

Affidavit

NOTES: 1. The hirer is a bailor and has to take reasonable care of the goods— See ss. 151 and 152 of the Contract Act.

2. Limitation three years under Art. 53 of the Limitation Act 1963.

216. Suit for arrears of rent in a hire-purchase

In the Court of .... at ....

Suit No. .... of 20 ....

(Set out cause title)

The plaintiff states as follows:

1. That the plaintiff is a registered partnership.

2. That the plaintiff firm deals in motorcycles.

3. That the defendant by executing a hire-purchase agreement on .... agreed to hire a motorcycle from the plaintiff firm of .... (make) upon terms, amongst others, as follows:

(State here terms of hire-purchase)

4. The defendant paid the initial hire-charge on .... and obtained delivery of the motorcycle and paid moneys from time to time as agreed upon but did not pay the 10th and last instalment of ₹ ....

5. Thereupon the plaintiff firm retook possession of the motorcycle on .... on expiry of the agreed date of payment of the said instalment. The plaintiff firm was, however, agreeable to return the vehicle in case the defendant paid a sum of ₹ .... within .... as suggested in a notice dated .... issued by the plaintiff firm to the defendant by registered post with A/D. The defendant received the said notice but did not pay the money.

6. That the cause of action arose on .... when the said instalment fell due at .... within the jurisdiction of this court.

The plaintiff, therefore, prays for a judgment and decree for ₹ .... as rent.

Verification

Affidavit

217. Suit for the hire of goods on termination of contract

In the Court of .... at ....

Suit No. .... of 20 ....

(Set out cause title)

The plaintiff states:

1. The plaintiff owns an air-cooler apparatus with fittings. The defendant intended to hire the same for six months as the defendant might require.

2. By an agreement in writing dated .... 20....... between the plaintiff and the defendant, the plaintiff let the said air-cooler apparatus with fittings to the defendant on hire at a rent of ₹ .... p.m. with effect from .... 20....... The defendant agreed to pay to the plaintiff hire-rent month on the 1st day of each month following the month for which the rent fell due, so long as the said agreement should continue.

3. The defendant terminated the agreement by a notice dated ...., 20............ with effect from 1st of ...., 20.......................

4. The defendant returned the apparatus.

5. There remains due and owing to the plaintiff a sum of ₹ .... being arrears of (unpaid) hire-rent for the months from .... to ...., 20........ both inclusive.

The plaintiff claims:

(*a*) A decree for ₹ .... with damages at the rate as may appear proper; and

(*b*) costs of suit.

Verification

Affidavit

218. Suit by owner for arrears of rent payable under a hire-purchase agreement, after the owner has retaken possession on default

In the Court of .... at ....

Suit No. .... of 20 ....

(Set out cause title)

The plaintiffs state as follows:

1. The plaintiffs are dealers in motor cars.

2. By a hire-purchase agreement dated ...., (hereinafter called the agreement), the plaintiffs agreed to let and the defendant agreed to take on hire a .... horse-power .... cylinder motor car made by .... upon the terms *inter alia*:

(*a*) The hirer shall pay to the owner on the execution of the agreement the initial hire of ₹ ...., which shall become the absolute property of the owner, and punctually pay to the owner at his address for the time being and without previous demand 20 consecutive monthly rents of ₹ ...., the first payment to be made on the .... day of .... and each subsequent payment on the .... day of every subsequent month.

(*b*) The hirer may at any time terminate the hiring, on giving a week's notice, and the defendant shall return at his own cost and risk the said motor car to the owner.

(*c*) If the hirer shall make default in payment of any monthly instalment for .... days after the same shall become due, then the agreement shall immediately be determined (without any previous notice or demand on the part of the owners) and thereupon it shall be lawful for the owner without previous notice to retake and resume possession of the said motor car.

(*d*) In the event of the agreement being determined by the hirer, the hirer shall not be entitled to repayment of the said sum so paid by him on the execution of the said agreement or to any credit or allowance thereof or in respect of any other payments made by him to the owner under the terms of the said agreement but all such payments shall be considered forfeited to the owner. And the determination of the said hiring as aforesaid shall not affect or prejudice any claim the owner may have against the hirer for arrears of hire payments or for damages for breach of the said agreement.

(*e*) If the hirer shall duly perform and observe all the stipulations and conditions in the said agreement and shall duly pay to the owner monthly sums by way of rent amounting together with the said sum of ₹ .... so paid on the execution of the said agreement to the sum of ₹ .... then the hiring shall come to an end and the said motor car shall become the property of the hirer but until all such payments as aforesaid have been made, the said motor car shall remain the property of the owner.

3. The defendant duly paid the said sum of ₹ .... at the time of the execution of the agreement and obtained delivery of the said motor car from the plaintiffs.

4. Thereafter the defendant made default in payment of the 3rd and 4th instalments of monthly rent payable under the agreement, whereupon, on ...., the plaintiffs gave a notice dated .... under registered post with a/d which was duly received by the defendant who did not pay the amount due and the plaintiffs retook possession of the said motor car on ....

Particulars of rent in arrears:

The plaintiffs claim—

₹ .... rents in arrears.

Verification

Affidavit

219. Suit for arrears of instalments in a hire-purchase

In the Court of .... at ....

Suit No. .... of 20 ....

(Set out cause title)

The plaintiff states as follows:

1. That the plaintiff-firm is the owner of a scooter, bearing Registration No. ....

2. The defendant having intended to purchase the said vehicle on hire-purchase terms, the parties hereto entered into a hire-purchase agreement on the .... day of .... 20 ...., whereby the plaintiff firm let to the defendant the said vehicle at a total hire-purchase price of ₹ ....

3. Terms of hire-purchase agreement, amongst others, were:

(*i*) that the defendant would pay ₹ .... on the execution of the agreement; and

(*ii*) that the defendant would pay the balance amount by .... monthly instalments payable on the 1st day of each English calendar month thereafter.

4. The defendant, in breach of the said agreement, made defaults in the payment of instalments which fell due on .... and .... amounting to ₹ ....

5. Cause of action.

6. Suit–valuation–₹ .... (with interest as per terms in the hire-purchase agreement, if any).

The plaintiff claims:

(*i*) ₹ ....; and

(*ii*) costs of suit.

Verification

Affidavit

220. Suit for arrears of hire and return of goods

In the Court of .... at ....

Suit No. .... of 20 ....

(Set out cause title)

The plaintiff firm states:

1. That the plaintiff-firm is a registered partnership.

2. That the plaintiff-firm is the owner of a Jeep bearing Registration No. ....

3. The defendant having intended to purchase the said vehicle on hire-purchase terms, the parties hereto entered into a hire-purchase agreement on the .... day of .... 20........... whereby the plaintiff firm let to the defendant the said vehicle at the total hire-purchase price of ₹ ....

4. Terms of hire-purchase agreement, amongst other, were:

(*i*) that the hirer-defendant would pay ₹ .... on the execution of the agreement;

(*ii*) that the hirer would pay the balance by 40 monthly instalments payable on the 1st day of each English calendar month thereafter;

(*iii*) if any of the instalments should at any time be in arrear and unpaid the plaintiff shall be entitled to terminate the agreement by a notice in writing; and

(*iv*) the plaintiff, on such termination, be entitled to the possession of the vehicle forthwith.

5. The defendant has failed to clear up instalments which fell due on the 1st day of .... 20.......... and on the 1st day of................, 20..............

6. The plaintiff firm issued a notice to the defendant by registered post with A/D. on the.......... day of..............., 20................ demanding return of the vehicle as also the payment of the instalments which fell due. The defendant received the notice on the .... day of ...., 20............... but failed to return the vehicle. The defendant has wrongfully detained the vehicle to his use.

7. By reason of the matters aforesaid, the plaintiff firm has suffered loss and damage.

8. Cause of action.

9. Suit—valuation.

The plaintiff claims:

(*a*) delivery to the plaintiff of the said vehicle;

(*b*) a sum of ₹ .... being arrears of instalments;

(*c*) damages for detention of the vehicle; and

(*d*) alternatively to relief in col. (*a*) above, payment to the plaintiff value of the vehicle, less the sums paid by the defendant.

Verification

Affidavit

221. Suit for recovery of dues under hire-purchase agreement

In the Court of .... at ....

Suit No. .... of 20 ....

(Set out cause title)

The plaintiff states as follows:

1. The plaintiff carries on business as Lease Financing and hire-purchase financing of plant, machinery and car and all other types of vehicles.

2. On .... a hire-purchase agreement was entered into by and between the plaintiff and defendant in respect of a lorry. Under the said agreement, the defendant agreed to pay hire-charges of ₹ .... per month with option to purchase the said vehicle by payment of an aggregate sum of ₹ .... in due course.

3. The plaintiff under the agreement of hire-purchase with defendant under which the defendant made selection of lorry from a lorry-manufacturer and at the request of defendant, the plaintiff purchased the said lorry and delivered the same to the defendant on hire-purchase on monthly hire rental of ₹ ....

4. It was agreed that on failure of defendant to pay three instalments, the plaintiff was entitled to take possession of the said vehicle and sell it at the risk and expense of the defendant.

5. The defendant took delivery of the said lorry and made payments from time to time for a period of two years and thereafter had stopped payment of the hire rental for the said lorry and as such, a sum of ₹ .... became due and payable by the defendant by way of payment of rent and/or hire-purchase price for the said vehicle under the said hire-purchase agreement with interest.

6. The defendant was requested by a notice dated .... to return the said vehicle but he failed to do so.

7. The plaintiff therefore claims a total amount of ₹ .... being the arrears of hire-purchase rentals and/or towards total value of the purchase of the said lorry sold and delivered to defendant under the hire-purchase agreement.

8. The plaintiff demanded from the defendant a total sum of ₹ .... but the defendant has not paid the said sum or any portion thereof to the plaintiff.

9. The plaintiff therefore claims from the defendant a total sum of ₹ .... together with interest at 12% per annum till realisation and costs.

10. The plaintiff's cause of action for the suit arose at .... within the jurisdiction of this learned court and the defendant made defaults in payment at the office of the plaintiff at .... within the jurisdiction of this learned court. As such, this learned court has the jurisdiction to entertain, try and determine this instant suit.

11. For the purposes of jurisdiction and court-fees, the suit is valued at ₹ .... on which the requisite court-fees in stamps have been paid.

The plaintiff, therefore, prays for and claims:

(*a*) Decree for ₹ .... with interest at 12% per annum till realisation;

(*b*) Receiver;

(*c*) Injunction;

(*d*) Costs;

(*e*) Further and other reliefs as the plaintiff is entitled to in law and equity.

Verification

Affidavit

222. Written statement to the plaint for the recovery of dues under the hire-purchase agreement

In the Court of .... at ....

Suit No. .... of 20 ....

(Set out cause title)

The defendant states as follows:

1. The statements contained in paragraphs 1 and 2 of the plaint are matters of record and save and except what will appear therefrom the defendant does not make any admission in respect thereof.

2. With reference to the paragraph 2 of the plaint, the defendant states that the said hired car after some time did not function properly and the defendant duly made this complaint to the plaintiff.

3. With reference to paragraph 3 of the plaint, the defendant states that the plaintiff gave a specific warranty that the car will give satisfactory trouble-free service for two years.

4. With reference to paragraph 4 of the plaint the defendant states that the alleged agreement was one-sided and unilateral and that the default clause was very harsh and was not therefore enforceable against the defendant.

5. With reference to paragraph 5 of the plaint, the defendant submits that he regularly made payments of ₹ .... per month as monthly instalments in accordance with hire-purchase agreement, but after about 2 years, the car developed some defects and started giving trouble and did not give proper service. The defendant requested the plaintiff to get the car duly repaired otherwise it was not possible for the defendant to use the car and pay the monthly rental/instalments in respect of the car.

6. With reference to paragraph 6 of plaint, the defendant requested the plaintiff to replace the said defective vehicle otherwise the business of the defendant is bound to suffer heavily but the plaintiff never took any steps in the matter.

7. With reference to paragraph 7 of plaint, this defendant denies and disputes that the plaintiff is entitled to claim a sum of ₹ .... or any other sum either as unpaid arrears of hire-purchase rentals or towards payment of the total purchase value of the said car under the said Hire Purchase Agreement. As the said car failed to give satisfactory service, the plaintiff is not entitled to any payment in respect of the said car.

8. With reference to paragraph 8 of the plaint, the defendant states that the said purported demand of ₹ .... was invalid and illegal and not due and payable by defendant or receivable by the plaintiff.

9. With reference to paragraph 9 of the plaint, the defendant denies and disputes that the plaintiff is entitled to claim a sum of ₹ .... or any interest at 12% per annum or at any other rate.

10. With reference to paragraph 10 of the plaint, the defendant denies and disputes that the plaintiff has any valid cause of action or that the alleged cause of action could arise at .... within the jurisdiction of this learned court. It is further denied and disputed that the defendant committed any defaults in payment of the hire-purchase rental instalments as has been wrongly alleged. It is further denied and disputed that this learned court has any valid jurisdiction to entertain, try and determine the present suit.

11. With reference to paragraph 11 of the plaint, it is denied and disputed that this learned court has any jurisdiction to entertain the said suit and therefore payment of any court-fees in stamps is immaterial.

Hence, the suit is liable to be and be dismissed with costs.

Verification

Affidavit

223. Suit for damages for breach of hire-purchase agreement (a case of parting with possession)

In the Court of .... at ....

Suit No. .... of 20 ....

(Set out cause title)

The plaintiff states:

1. The plaintiffs are a financial concern carrying on the business of financing hire-purchase deals in electric fans (if necessary, add make, brand etc.).

2. By an agreement in writing dated the .... day of ...., 20.................. the plaintiffs had let to the defendant a 36" electric fan (add make, name, brand, etc.) on hire-purchase terms at a total hire-purchase price of ₹ ....

3. Terms of hire-purchase agreement, amongst others, were:

(*i*) that the defendant would pay ₹ .... on the execution of the agreement;

(*ii*) that the defendant would pay the balance amount by three monthly instalments on the 1st day of each English calendar month thereafter; and

(*iii*) the defendant would not, without the prior consent of the plaintiffs in writing, sell, let, assign or part with possession of the said fan.

4. The defendant paid the instalment that fell due on the 1st of .... 20. ....

5. It transpires that the defendant sold the said fan or parted with possession of the fan to a person unkown to the plaintiff on or about the .... day of .... 20..., in breach of the said agreement.

6. The plaintiff's have suffered loss.

7. Cause of action (date of parting with possession or conversion).

8. Suit–valuation (extent of damage to be stated).

The plaintiff's claim:

(*i*) Price of the said electric fan less amounts paid towards the price as rent, i.e. ₹ ....; and

(*ii*) damages for ₹ .... for breach of agreement (or, for conversion).

Verification

Affidavit

IDOL

224. Suit by an idol for administration of debuttar property

In the Court of .... at ....

Title Suit No. .... of 20.........

Sri Radha Madhav Jew, an idol installed at the Radha Madhav Temple at .... P.S. .... District .... through His next friend Sri .... son of .... residing at .... P.S. .... District ....

...... *Plaintiff*

versus

Sri .... son of .... Shebait of the plaintiff idol with residence at vill. .... P.S. .... District ....

.... *Defendant*

Suit for administration of debuttar property valued at ₹ ....

The plaintiff states as follows:

1. That one ...., a devout Hindu, since deceased, had installed the plaintiff idol at his residence at village .... P.S. .... District .... in a temple on Maghi Purnima .... B.S.

2. That by a registered deed of endowment (*Arpan-nama*) the said .... had endowed considerable properties in favour of the plaintiff, as described particularly in the Schedule below, and further provided therein that out of the income of the said properties in the Schedule the defendant Shebait would—

(*i*) perform daily worship of the idol,

(*ii*) meet expenses of periodical festivals, named in the deed of endowment.

3. That by the said deed of endowment the said .... constituted himself the first shebait of the idol and provided that after his death his first son would be the shebait and on his death the Shebaitship shall devolve on ....

4. That as per arrangement in the said deed of endowment, the defendant assumed the office of the shebait of the plaintiff idol in or about ...., 20 ....

5. That the defendant has not been attending to daily worship of the idol. He has sold away a considerable portion of the idol's properties (state here particulars of mismanagement such and otherwise) and is guilty of maladministration of the debuttar properties.

6. That in the circumstances of the case the defendant should be removed from the office of shebait and a new shebait should be appointed (or a scheme should be framed) for administration of debuttar properties.

7. That the cause of action for this suit arose on .... (when maladministration became manifest).

8. That the plaintiff is a member of the family of the said .... and is interested in the worship of the idol.

9. That for the purpose of jurisdiction and court-fees the suit is valued at ....

The plaintiff, therefore, prays:

(*a*) For a judgment and decree for administration of the debuttar properties and the framing of a scheme therefor.

(*b*) For removal of the defendant and for appointment of a shebait in terms of the deed of endowment.

(*c*) Receiver.

(*d*) Injunction.

SCHEDULE

Verification

Affidavit

NOTES: 1. Normally the deity has to be represented by the entire body of Shebaits. Suit by some of Shebaits–maintainable in special circumstances—AIR 1971 Ori 15.

2. Scheme for management of a temple–See AIR 1970 Cal 373.

225. Suit by a next friend of an idol against the shebait

In the Court of .... at ....

Title Suit No .... of 20 ....

1. Sri ....
–a Hindu idol represented by her next friend X son of late Y, by faith Hindu, of

village .... P.S. ....
District ....

2. C son of D, by faith Hindu, by occupation .... residing at village .... P.S. .... District ....

.... *Plaintiffs*

versus

P, ...
.... Son of Q, by faith Hindu, by occupation–agriculturist, shebait of the idol," ...." of Vill .... P.S. .... District ....

.... *Defendants*

Suit for removal of the present Shebait and for appointment of a new shebait.

Valued at ₹ ....

The above-named plaintiffs state as follows:

1. That one A, since deceased of village .... P.S. .... District .... had installed on the .... B.S. the plaintiff No. 1 a family deity under the name and style of .... at his residence at Mouja .... P.S. .... District ....

2. That the said A dedicated by a deed of endowment dated .... registered on .... considerable immovable properties, detailed in the Schedule "A" below, in favour of the plaintiff No. 1 for the expenses and upkeep of the 'Seva Puja' of the said deity and for periodical festivals mentioned in clause 14 and Schedule 'Kha' of the deed.

3. That by the said deed of endowment the said "A" constituted himself the shebait of the deity till his death. After him, as per terms of the deed, regarding devolution of the office of shebait, E widow of A became the shebait. E died in 14 .... B.S. After her death the defendant 'P' became the shebait since Poush, ... 14 .... B.S. of the said deity and is now in office.

4. That the deed of endowment contained *inter alia,* a list of bounden duties of the shebait as in cls. 13 and 14 of the said deed, and the qualification to hold the post of the shebait are enumerated in cl. 9, of the said deed. Besides, the said deed contains provisions for removal of a shebait in certain contingencies enunciated in cl. 6 read with cls. 11 and 12 of the said deed of endowment. Anybody interested in the debuttar property shall be entitled to cause removal of the erring shebait as enjoined in cl. 6 of the deed and, if necessary, through a court of law as enjoined in cl. 12(9) of the said deed of endowment.

5. That said 'P' (Defendant) the present shebait of the plaintiff No. 1, has been guilty of the following acts of gross misconduct, mismanagement, breach of duty, misfeasance and breach of conditions of shebaitship, to wit,

(*i*) He has been living in adultery with one 'B'.

(*ii*) The defendant has built a house for the said B out of the income of the debuttar properties at Mouja .... at an approximate cost of ₹ ....

(*iii*) The following articles are lost from the custody of the defendant-shebait due to his negligence, namely, ...

(*iv*) The C.I. sheet roofing of Bhog ghar comprising 2 pcs. of 18 ft. C.I. sheets are missing and have not been accounted for.

(*v*) That the temple itself (wherein the Vigraha) has been installed is in a dilapidated condition requiring immediate repairs which is not being attended to in spite of repeated requests.

(*vi*) That the defendant has purchased in his own name the following properties from out of the debuttar fund.

(State Particulars)

(*vii*) That the defendant took compensation from the State of West Bengal for acquisition of debuttar intermediary rights about ₹ .... and the same has not been accounted for or credited to debuttar fund.

(*viii*) The defendant is neglecting to perform the worship of the plaintiff No. 1 continually since ....

(*ix*) That for failure to submit satisfactory accounts of the debuttar property by the defendant-shebait and for failure to maintain accounts and for failure to produce account books and for the perverse statement before the .... in connection with Case No. .... of W.B. Estate Acquisition Act, the debuttar was held to be a partial debuttar and benefits of s. 6(1) read with s. 6(2) and proviso to s. 17(1) of the W.B. Estate Acquisition Act could not be drawn with consequential loss of annuity causing and resulting in a definite harm to the debuttar estate.

6. That under cl. 2 of the deed of endowment the responsibility and/or right to select and/or appoint next shebait has been granted to religious and learned members of the family of said A in consultation with religious learned villagers of Mouja.................

7. That under cl. 10 of the deed of endowment the shebait to be appointed should be eligible for the post if he has had (*i*) faith in Hinduism, (*ii*) reverence for Sri .... Debi. Disqualifications for the post of a shebait have been enumerated in cl. 11 of the deed.

8. That aforesaid X representing the plaintiff No. 1 and the plaintiff No. 2 are family members of said "A". They are interested in the said family deity and her 'Seva Puja' and they have no interest adverse to the interest of the deity. Besides they fulfil conditions of eligibility as enumerated in cl. 2(9) of the deed of endowment.

9. That the cause of action for this suit arose in 20.........., wherefrom the defendant shebait has been committing acts of misfeasance stated in para 1 above, at Mouja....... P.S. .... within the jurisdiction of this court.

10. That for the purpose of jurisdiction the suit is valued at ₹ .... and fixed court-fee of ₹ .... are paid.

The plaintiffs, therefore, pray:

(*a*) for a decree and judgment for—

(*i*) removal of the defendant shebait,

(*ii*) for administration of debuttar properties by appointing the said X and plaintiff No. 2 either singly or jointly as shebaits of the deity or by appointing such other person from the family members of the said "A" as deemed qualified and eligible as shebait for administration of debuttar property in Schedule "A" below and for 'Seva Puja' of the plaintiff No. 1.

(*b*) Costs,

(*c*) such other relief or reliefs as law and equity would allow the plaintiffs.

SCHEDULE A

(State here description of properties)

Verification

Affidavit

NOTES: 1. In a case of private trust temple alleging mismanagement and misappropriation by the *Pujari*—a suit was brought by a person making donations for temple maintenance on behalf of the deity—Held s. 92 of the C.P. Code had no application. The plaintiff had right to sue—AIR 1970 SC 532.

2. In a case of private trust temple the Civil Court has jurisdiction to frame scheme for management—AIR 1970 SC 532.

3. Public and Private Temple—Criteria indicated—AIR 1970 SC 2025.

226. Suit by a creditor against a shebait of an idol for a debt

In the Court of .... at ....

Suit No. .... of 20 ....

(Set out cause title)

The above-named plaintiff states as follows:

1. That the defendant Sri A.B. was and is the shebait of Sree Govinda Jew, a Hindu idol installed at Govinda Mandir at .... Town, P.S. .... District ....

2. That the defendant had, as such shebait, borrowed ₹ .... from the plaintiff on .... for the puja of the idol agreeing to repay the loan on demand.

3. That the defendant did not repay the loan though repeated requests were made by the plaintiff in that behalf.

4. That the plaintiff is not a money lender and the said loan was an accommodation loan.

5. Cause of action on .... (date of loan).

6. Suit valuation .... (amount of loan).

The plaintiff claims:

A decree for ₹ .... from the defendant.

Verification

Affidavit

NOTES: 1. Where there are several shebaits all of them should be joined in the suit.

2. Idol may be sued and represented by the shebait. Or, the shebait may be sued representing the idol.

3. Debuttar property is liable only when it is established that there was necessity for the loan (idols are always minors–proposition of legal necessity in case of minors should be kept in view).

227. Suit by future shebaits to have a sale of debuttar property declared void

In the Court of .... at ....

Suit No. .... of 20 ....

(Set out cause title)

The plaintiff states as follows:

1. One J.M., a Hindu governed by the Dayabhaga, died 6th February 20..........., having made his Will dated ...., whereby he dedicated the properties specified in schedule 'A' hereto for the worship of the family deity, Thakur Sri Sri Govind Jiu (hereinafter called "the deity"), installed by him in his family dwelling house No. .... and appointed his wife as the shebait of the deity.

2. By the terms of the said Will the testator provided that after the death of his wife, her adopted son, M.M. (the defendant No. 1) would carry on the sheba of the said deity out of the income of the said properties and, after him, the shebaitship would continue in his line.

3. In ...., the said M.M. mortgaged some of his personal properties to the defendants Nos. 2 and 3 who obtained a decree upon the mortgage and had the properties sold on or about ....

4. The entire debt under the mortgage not having been satisfied by the sale, the defendants Nos. 2 and 3 obtained a personal decree against the said M.M. under Or. 34, r. 6 of the Civil Procedure Code and in execution of that decree, purchased the properties mentioned in the schedule hereto which formed part of the properties dedicated to the deity by the Will of J.M. deceased. The said defendants are in possession of the said properties since ....

5. The plaintiff No. 1 is the son, and the plaintiffs No. 2, 3 and 4, are the grandsons by ...., a predeceased son, of the said M.M.

6. These plaintiffs are the members of the family for whose benefit the deity was installed and the endowment aforesaid was made and they are the future shebaits of the deity. They are interested in the maintenance of the worship, and the preservation of the property, of the deity.

The plaintiffs claim—

(1) A declaration that the properties mentioned in the schedule hereto belong to the deity.

(2) A declaration that the sale of the said properties as aforesaid is invalid.

(3) Possession of the said properties to the defendant M.M. as the shebait of the deity.

SCHEDULE

Verification

Affidavit

228. Suit for removal of shebait

In the High Court at Calcutta
Ordinary Original Civil Jurisdiction

Suit No. .... of 20........

Mr. P being a shebait of the deity Sri Sri Iswar Jagannath residing at .... Kolkata.

...... *Plaintiff*

versus

X, son of Late Y, residing at .... Kolkata.

.... *Defendant*

Suit for removal of shebait.

The plaintiff states:

1. One Mr. M. of .... Kolkata, a Hindu governed by Dayabhaga School of Hindu Law, installed the plaintiff deity "Sri Sri Iswar Jagannath" at ...., Kolkata by a deed of religious endowment. By the said document the plaintiff Mr. P and the defendant Mr. X were appointed as shebaits.

2. The said M after establishment of the said deity died. Before his death he endowed several immovable properties as described in the schedule below in favour of the said deity for its daily sheba-puja.

3. The said deed provided that the said deity would remain in the residential house of Mr. P for five years and in the residential house of Mr. X for five years alternately.

4. It was provided that for the first five years the deity would remain in the residential house of Mr. P at .... , Kolkata. The said house property was bequeathed to Mr. P by the Late Mr. M for Mr. P's separate residence. The family residential house was bequeathed to Mr. X.

5. Under the terms of the said religious endowment the shebait under whose custody the said deity would stay would offer all facilities to all relatives of the Late Mr. M. to take part in the sheba-puja of the said deity.

6. According to the terms of the said religious endowment, if any shebait fails to perform the daily sheba-puja of the said deity, he should be removed from the office of the shebaitship and the other shebait would perform the daily sheba-puja of the said deity alone.

7. It has been noticed by the plaintiff that the defendant shebait under whose custody the said deity is now staying is not taking due care and interest and is not regularly doing proper sheba-puja and thereby has made himself liable to be removed from the office of shebaitship of the deity.

8. The plaintiff through his Lawyer's letter dated 15th October, 20 .... asked the defendant to perform his duty by doing daily sheba-puja of the said deity but he has failed and neglected to take any steps in that direction.

9. The plaintiff Mr. P as shebait of the said deity claims removal of the defendant from the office of the shebaitship and to allow Mr. P to perform the daily sheba-puja of the said deity to the exclusion of the defendant Mr. X.

10. The cause of action for this suit arose within the jurisdiction of this Hon'ble Court as the situation of the said deity is at .... Kolkata within the jurisdiction of this Hon'ble Court.

11. The plaintiff's cause of action is continuing from day to day.

12. For the purposes of jurisdiction and court-fees the suit is valued at ₹ .... on which court-fees in stamps have been paid. The property involved in the present suit is given below.

The plaintiff, therefore, claims:

(*a*) A decree removing Mr. X from the office of the shebaitship of the deity Sri Sri Iswar Jagannath;

(*b*) Direction on Mr. X to hand over the deity with all puja articles and utensils to Mr. P within the date to be specified by this Hon'ble Court;

(*c*) Injunction restraining the defendant from intermeddling with the property and assets of the deity as described in the said religious endowment;

(*d*) Cost of the suit;

(*e*) Further and other orders be made so as to afford complete relief to the plaintiff.

SCHEDULE OF PROPERTY

Verification

Affidavit

229. Suit for removal of Manager of a temple

In the Court of Civil Judge (Senior Division) at Alipore

Miscellaneous Suit No. .... of 20...

Mr. P. son of Mr. Q residing at Alipore Road, Kolkata

.... *Plaintiff*

versus

Mr. X, son of Mr. Y residing at Alipore Road, Kolkata

.... *Defendant*

Suit for removal of Manager of a temple valued at ₹....................

The plaintiff states:

1. That one Mr. Z, built a Temple from his own resources and dedicated the same to the deity, Sri Sri Radha Krishna Jew. The said Mr. Z made provisions for daily seva puja of the said deity as also for daily distribution of alms to the needy persons coming to worship at the temple.

2. That the said Mr. Z transferred several properties to the said temple with direction to defray the expenses of the said deity's seva-puja and daily distribution of alms to the poor.

3. That by the said deed of dedication, and establishment of the said deity, and also transfer of properties for the benefit of the deity, the defendant was appointed as Manager for proper management and functioning of the temple and to carry out the provisions of the deed of dedication.

4. That the plaintiff is a needy person and has no regular income and visits the temple regularly and is a devotee of the said deity. The plaintiff is an interested person in the temple management and regular distribution of alms as directed by Mr. Z, and as contained in the said deed of dedication.

5. That since last few months the distribution of alms to the needy persons including the plaintiff has been substantially reduced for no lawful reason. On enquiries made from the staff of the temple and persons connected with the defendant-manager the plaintiff has come to know that the income from the assets remaining dedicated to the temple has not been at all reduced. Further, the usufructs of the property dedicated to the deity of the temple has remained the same and no known expense has increased. As such, there is no reason whatsover for curtailing the quantum of distribution of alms by the concerned manager-defendant from the income derived from properties dedicated to the temple.

6. That in this connection the plaintiff approached the manager-defendant and informed him the fact that distribution of alms has been drastically reduced and that the manager-defendant would be pleased to look into matter. The plaintiff politely informed the defendant-manager about the fact of substantial reduction in distribution of alms thereby causing serious hardship to the plaintiff along with others.

7. That the plaintiff states that the defendant as Manager of the Temple Trust property is expected to carry out the directions contained in the Trust Deed and other documents so that the distribution of alms is not jeopardised by wrongful diversion of funds.

8. That in spite of several requests, the manager-defendant has not taken any visible steps to restore the original quantum of distribution of alms for and on behalf of the said deity of the Temple to the needy persons.

9. That the plaintiff states that there has been breach in carrying out directions and intentions of settlor of the said deity as contained in the said Trust Deed and the said Manager, the defendant, is liable to account for and explain his conduct in reducing the distribution of alms to the needy and poor devotees of the said deity who regularly visit the temple including the plaintiff.

10. That the plaintiff after observing for several months the conduct of the manager-defendant in the distribution of alms to devotees who come to the temple and who used to get such alms regularly came to know that the everybody has a complaint to lodge regarding the reduced distribution of alms. In the premises, the manager-defendant be directed to show cause as to why he should not be removed forthwith and in his place a new and proper manager be appointed.

11. That further the defendant-manager be directed to render full and proper accounts and statements regarding the temple related to payments and receipts and reasons as to why distribution of alms has been drastically reduced recently. The plaintiff also claims the removal of manager from his post and a new person be appointed as the Manager as to this Hon'ble Court may deem fit and proper for the said post at a remuneration payable same as that of the existing Manager as contained in Trust Deed.

12. That the cause of action for this suit arose on .... as it will appear from the aforesaid facts and is still continuing from day to day.

13. That no part of the plaintiff's claims herein is barred by the law of limitation and in the premises this learned Court has jurisdiction to entertain, try and determine this suit.

14. That for the purposes of jurisdiction and court-fees, the suit is valued at ₹ .... on which court-fees in stamps have been paid.

The plaintiff, therefore, prays for and claims:

(*a*) The defendant be directed to render proper accounts for the last three financial years duly certified and audited by a Chartered Accountant to be appointed by this learned court;

(*b*) On such accounting being made, the defendant be directed to properly account for and give reasons for reduction in quantum of distribution of alms to the needy devotees visiting the temple;

(*c*) A decree be passed against defendant for refund of moneys wrongfully utilised for or appropriated by the defendant with interest thereon to the funds of the deity of temple;

(*d*) The defendant be removed from the post of Manager of the temple on rendering proper and full accounts;

(*e*) A suitable person be appointed as Manager of the Estate of the said deity of the temple on such conditions as this learned court may deem fit and proper;

(*f*) Cost of the present suit;

(*g*) Further and other orders be made as this learned court may deem fit and proper so as to afford complete relief to the plaintiff.

Verification

Affidavit

INJUNCTION

230. Suit for injunction

In the Court of the Civil Judge (Senior Division), Alipore

Suit No. .... of 20........

Dr. P, son of Mr. Q, by profession doctor, having his chamber and residing at 7, Alipore Road, Kolkata.

.... *Plaintiff*

versus

1. X Co. Ltd., a company registered under the Companies Act 1956 and carrying on business, *inter alia,* at 8, Alipore Road, Kolkata, where it runs a Coffee House.
2. Mr. Y, Managing Director of M/s. X Co. Ltd. and works for gain at 8, Alipore Road, Kolkata.
3. Mr. Z working for gain as Manager of M/s. X Co. Ltd. at 8, Alipore Road, Kolkata.

...... *Defendants*

Suit for Injunction valued at ₹ ......

The plaintiff states:

1. That the plaintiff is well-established and reputed doctor and carries on his profession and resides at 7, Alipore Road, Kolkata. The plaintiff has his chamber in the ground floor facing the road.

2. The first defendant carries on business as retailer of food products and has several restaurants and Coffee Houses. The first defendant has recently opened a Coffee House at premises No. 8, Alipore Road, Kolkata. The said premises has a big hall facing the road and having entrance, *inter alia,* facing and direct from the road. The first defendant has converted the big hall at premises No. 8, Alipore Road, Kolkata into a Coffee House fully air-conditioned and fitted with loud speakers and having elaborate arrangement of music.

3. The defendant No. 2 is the Managing Director of the company who sits at a corner of the Coffee House to oversee and give directions regarding the management of the Coffee House.

4. The defendant No. 3 is the Manager of the Coffee House and he looks after the functioning of the Coffee House, arrangement of music and other aspects of entertainment of the customers of the Coffee House.

5. The defendants Nos. 2 and 3 are jointly and severally responsible for carrying out the functioning of the Coffee House.

6. The defendants keep open the Coffee House till late night upto 10.30 p.m. The Coffee House opens early in morning and by 11 o'clock customers start visiting the Coffee House.

7. The defendants play music using microphones at a high pitch. Apart from that, from time to time they bring bands and other instruments of music at particular hours.

8. The plaintiff starts his chamber from 11 a.m. and continues till 1 p.m. and again the chamber is opened at 4 p.m. and continues till 10 p.m. During the said periods patients visit and the plaintiff has to examine them and has to carry out different tests for which the plaintiff has instruments, plant and machinery in his laboratory in his said premises.

9. The plaintiff complained to the defendants about the noise made by the loud music and beating of drums and playing of other instruments. The plaintiff requested the defendants to keep the pitch at a low level within a reasonable limit so that the neighbours can carry out their usual business or profession.

10. The plaintiff also complained about the noise level of the music and other instruments played in conjunction with music. The plaintiff complained that such excessive noise seriously disturbs his profession and in addition as the Coffee House is kept open till 10.30 p.m. at night the plaintiff and the neighbours are disturbed and could not sleep peacefully.

11. The plaintiff by several letters requested each of the defendants to refrain from creating excessive noise as also keeping the Coffee House open till late-night causing disturbance to the plaintiff and others. Copies of the letters are annexed hereto collectively marked "A".

12. The defendants did not give any reply in writing but orally defendants Nos. 2 and 3 assured the plaintiff that they would keep the noise within a reasonable level. In spite of such assurances the situation has not improved.

13. The plaintiff caused the noise level to be measured and also obtained a report as to the nature of functioning of the Coffee House and also the timings of its functioning. Copies of the reports of independent experts are annexed hereto collectively marked "B".

14. The plaintiff through his Advocate caused a notice to be served on the defendants giving them 7 days' time to run the Coffee House keeping usual regular

hours and not allowing the noise level to go beyond the prescribed limit. The defendants did not reply to the said Advocate's letter. A copy of the Advocate's letter is annexed hereto marked "C".

15. The plaintiff states that the plaintiff has a right to carry on with his profession without being unduly disturbed in his profession. The plaintiff has also a right to sleep without being disturbed by late-night noise and the defendants have been infringing those rights without any justification whatsoever.

16. The plaintiff states that the plaintiff is entitled to an order of injunction restraining each of the defendants, their servants and agents from using musical instruments or making noise beyond the reasonable limit which limit according to experts has been specified in their reports, copies whereof are annexures "B" hereof.

17. The plaintiff complained to the concerned authorities about the excessive noise and disturbance till late-night but with no fruitful result.

18. In the premises, the plaintiff is entitled to an order of injunction of this learned court restraining the defendants from using the Coffee House in a manner which will infringe the rights of the neighbours including the plaintiff. The normal mode of function of the Coffee House will appear from the annexures hereto.

19. The plaintiff is filing this suit as a last resort after exhausting all persuasive means.

20. The plaintiff's cause of action arose within the jurisdiction of this learned court at premises Nos. 7 and 8, Alipore Road, Kolkata.

21. For the purposes of jurisdiction and court-fees the suit is valued at ₹ .... on which court-fees in stamps have been paid.

22. No part of the plaintiff's cause of action for this suit is barred by the Law of Limitation.

The plaintiff, therefore, prays for and claims:

(*a*) Injunction restraining the defendants and each one of them, their agents, servants and nominees from using loud speakers and microphones and making noises exceeding the usual limit of .... decibels as will appear from the experts' reports being annexures hereto;

(*b*) An expert be appointed to visit the Coffee House and make report to this learned court covering the allegations made against the defendants and thereafter to suggest remedial measures;

(*c*) Cost of the present proceeding;

(*d*) Further and other orders be made as this learned court may deem fit and proper to afford complete relief to the plaintiff.

ANNEXURES

Verification

Affidavit

231. Suit for prohibitory injunction to restrain a breach of contract

(*See* Form No. 133 *ante*).

NOTES: 1. Temporary and perpetual injunctions are granted under provisions of s. 37 of the Specific Relief Act.

Temporary injunctions are regulated by the Code of Civil Procedure [see s. 37(1)]. According to Calcutta High Court a court has inherent power to grant temporary injunction apart from the authority in Or. 39 of the Code—AIR 1952 Cal 560; AIR 1933 Cal 377.

Cases where perpetual injunction may be granted are enumerated in s. 38 of the Specific Relief Act.

2. Interim injunction order—suit dismissed for default but restored. Interim injunction order would cease on dismissal of suit and would not automatically revive on setting aside of dismissal order and restoration of suit—AIR 1976 All 264.
3. The courts have inherent jurisdiction to issue temporary injunctions in circumstances which are not covered by the provisions of Or. 39, CPC if the court is of opinion that the interest of justice requires the issue of such interim injunction. The mere fact that there are certain provisions as regards the issue of injunction in Or. 39, CPC does not debar the court from passing orders of temporary injunction for doing justice in the exercise of its inherent powers under s. 151 of the Code, though the discretion has to be exercised with the extreme caution and applied only in very clear cases—AIR 1976 All 447.
4. Plaintiff must establish that he would suffer irreparable loss if injunction is not granted—AIR 1976 Pat 323.

232. Suit for injunction restraining an election

In the Court of Civil Judge (Junior Division) at ....

Title Suit No. .... of 20 ......

A, son of B, Secretary, ...
of vill. .... P.S. .... District ....
...... *Plaintiff*

versus

1\. .... High School, represented by the President of the Managing Committee of the said school, situated at village .... P.S. .... District ....
2\. The Managing Committee of the .... High School, constituted by

(*i*) C
(*ii*) D
(*iii*) E
(*iv*) F
(*v*) G
(*vi*) H
(*vii*) I
(*viii*) J
(*ix*) K
(*x*) L
(*xi*) M

(State names and respective places of residence of the defendants)

.... *Defendants*

Suit for injunction
Valued at ₹ ....

The above-named plaintiff states as follows:

1. That the .... High School, established long back at Mouja .... within P.S. .... District .... was being run and managed by a Managing Committee, duly elected in .... 20 .... and the plaintiff was at all material times and is the Secretary of Managing Committee of the said school.

2. That the plaintiff together with the defendants Nos. 2(*i*) to 2(*xi*) are members of the present Managing Committee of the defendant school. Defendant No. 2(*ii*) is the Headmaster of the defendant school, now on leave, and is *ex-officio* Assistant Secretary of the Managing Committee of the school.

3. That the defendant school is governed by Rules and Regulations framed, by the Education Department, Government of West Bengal and by the Board of Secondary Education, West Bengal from time to time, pursuant to provisions in the West Bengal Secondary Education Act. And the Rules and Regulations contained in Notification No. .... dated. .... of the Education Department, Government of West Bengal and Circular issued by the Board of Secondary Education, West Bengal, supplementing the said Notification govern the procedure for election of members to the Managing Committee of a high school like the defendant school.

4. That under relevant rules the plaintiff is a donor and is automatically a life member of the Managing Committee of the said school.

5. That the Managing Committee was directed by a letter No. .... dated .... by the Board of Secondary Education, West Bengal, to hold a general election for election of members to the Managing Committee for the said............ high school.

6. That for such election a Voters' List and a programme in details have to be prepared by the head of the institution, as per instructions of the said Board contained in Circular/Rule of the said Notification No. .... dated .... of the Education Department, Government of West Bengal, in consultation with the Managing Committee where there is any, and such a Voters' List and the programme should be approved at a meeting of the outgoing Managing Committee.

7. That the said Voters' List is to be prepared under different categories, i.e., it is to contain names, amongst others, of donors, persons interested in education and so on. Every page of such Voters' List shall have to be countersigned by the Secretary of the Managing Committee.

8. That the defendant No. 1 President has allegedly prepared a Voters' List but not in consultation with the Managing Committee nor the said Voters' List has been approved by the outgoing Managing Committee in a meeting. The Voters' List does not bear the countersignature of the Secretary of the Committee.

9. That further, the said Voters' List has not been prepared correctly inasmuch as the name of the plaintiff, a donor, does not find mention therein.

10. That under the existing Rules and Regulations such an election should be held and conducted by a person who is not in any way connected with the management of the school or is not a candidate for election and who shall be selected by the head of the institution in consultation with the Managing Committee if not otherwise directed by the Board. That in the instant case the Board has not made any specific direction. The plaintiff has learnt that no such person has been selected by the head of the institution in consultation with the Managing Committee and the defendant No. ...... himself has usurped illegally the authority to conduct the proposed election.

11. That the defendant No. .... has wrongly usurped the authority of the Managing Committee and has issued a notice (printed) dated .... for holding

the election of members to the Managing Committee on .... and has further issued a programme of election. The said defendant was not authorised by the Managing Committee in a meeting to issue the said notice. The said notice is without jurisdiction and any election on the basis of the said notice and programme is void and is liable to be set aside.

12. That the Secretary of the Managing Committee of the school has been kept in dark about the proposed election which is going to be held on ....

13. That any election of the members to the Managing Committee on the basis of the said Voters' List, prepared illegally and which is incorrect due to omission of the name of the plaintiff and of countersignature by the Secretary and on the basis of the programme not approved in a meeting will be void and without jurisdiction and is liable to be set aside.

14. That for the election of members to the Managing Committee the defendant school would for obvious reasons entail a huge expenditure from the school fund. In case the election is held void, money spent will be lost for nothing.

15. That in the circumstances the defendants should be restrained by an appropriate order of injunction from holding the proposed election on .... on the basis of the said Voters' List prepared by the defendant No .... illegally and incorrectly.

16. That the cause of action for this suit arose at Mouja .... within the jurisdiction of this court, on .... when the notice for holding the election was issued by the defendant.

17. That for the purpose of jurisdiction and court-fees the suit is valued at ₹ .... and court-fees of .... are paid.

The plaintiff therefore prays:

(*a*) that the suit be decreed granting permanent injunction, restraining the defendants to forbear from holding the election on .... of the members to the Managing Committee of the defendant school on the basis of the Voters' List prepared by the defendant;

(*b*) for cost of suit;

(*c*) for such other relief or reliefs as law and equity would allow the plaintiff.

Verification

Affidavit

233. Suit for mandatory-cum-prohibitory injunction by a landlord against a tenant

In the Court of .... at ....

Suit No. .... of 20 ....

(Set out cause title)

The plaintiff states as follows:

1. That the defendant is a monthly tenant under the plaintiff in respect of the premises, described in the Schedule below, at a rent of ₹ .... p.m., according to Bengali calendar month.

2. That there is an open courtyard within the premises let out to the defendant.

3. That the defendant without prior consent of the plaintiff began to construct a pucca well in close proximity of the eastern room (*vide* item *ii*) of the Schedule below

and has already dug earth to a considerable depth. The defendant, unless restrained by an appropriate order from a competent court of law, it is apprehended, will continue the said act of construction.

4. That the cause of action for this suit arose on .... when the defendant began digging earth for constructing a pucca well at .... within the jurisdiction of this court.

5. That for the purpose of jurisdiction and court-fees the suit is valued at ₹ .... and court-fees of ₹ .... are paid thereon.

The plaintiff, therefore, claims for a decree:

(*i*) of mandatory injunction directing the defendant to fill up the ditch forthwith;

(*ii*) prohibitory injunction restraining the defendant from digging earth or constructing a well or any structure in the said premises.

SCHEDULE 'A'

(State here the particulars and description of the premises)

Verification

Affidavit

NOTES: 1. The plaintiff is at liberty to put his own valuation.

2. Limitation Act 1963—see s. 22 of the Limitation Act 1963 providing for cases of continuing breach of contract or continuing tort.

234. Suit for a mandatory injunction by a landlord against a tenant

In the Court of .... at ....

Suit No. .... of 20 ....

(Set out cause title)

The above-named plaintiff states as follows:

1. That the defendant is a monthly tenant under the plaintiff in respect of the premises, described in the Schedule appended below, at a rent of ₹ .... p.m. according to English calendar month, hereinafter referred to as demised premises.

2. That the demised premises was let out solely and exclusively for business purpose.

3. That the defendant, without consent of the plaintiff, began raising of an improvised structure on the open inner courtyard of the premises on .... intending to use the same as a kitchen.

4. That the plaintiff came to know of the unauthorised construction only on .... and protested the same day but the defendant threatened to complete the construction.

5. That the cause of action for this suit arose on .... when the plaintiff came to know of the unauthorised construction at .... within the jurisdiction of this court.

6. Suit valuation.

The plaintiff, therefore, prays:

(*i*) For a decree of mandatory injunction directing the defendant to pull down the said unauthorised construction forthwith;

(*ii*) For an injunction restraining the defendant and his engaged labour to continue acts of construction.

SCHEDULE

(State here description of the tenanted premises
and nature of unauthorised construction)

Verification

Affidavit

NOTE: Mandatory injunction on interlocutory application—If a court is called upon to grant any relief on any interlocutory application which when granted would mean granting substantially the relief claimed in the suit, the court will be very slow and circumspect in the matter of granting any such prayer. It is indeed true that such a relief should be granted only in exceptional cases. Though exercise of such a discretion should be limited to rare and exceptional cases, still at the same time no court should think that in law there is any absolute bar to the court granting such a relief. In deserving cases, the court would not hesitate to come to the aid of a litigant and uphold the cause of justice by granting such a relief—*Indian Cable Co.* v *Sumitra Chakravorty* AIR 1985 Cal 248 at p. 253.

235. Defence to a claim by landlord for mandatory injunction

In the Court of .... at ....

Suit No. .... of 20 ....

(Set out cause title)

The defendant states as follows:

1. The defendant did the acts complained of with the plaintiff's leave:

(Set out particulars showing when and how the leave was granted).

Or,

The defendant commenced erecting the said building on .... 20 .... to the knowledge of the plaintiff. Nevertheless the plaintiff stood by and saw the defendant erecting the building and expending money in connection therewith. The plaintiff has been guilty of laches and has acquiesced in the construction of the said building.

2. The defendant did not receive the alleged or any complaint from the plaintiff.

3. The defendant has expended ₹ .... on the said building and the granting of the injunction would be oppressive and would inflict great hardship on the defendant.

4. The suit be, therefore, dismissed with costs.

Vefification

Affidavit

236. Suit by landlord against tenant for an injunction to restrain a breach of covenant

In the Court of .... at ....

Suit No. .... of 20 ....

(Set out cause title)

The plaintiff states as follows:

1. By a lease dated .... 20 ...., the plaintiff demised to the defendant a suite of rooms situate upon and forming part of the .... floor of the dwelling house known as .... in .... Street in the city of .... for a term of twenty years from .... at a monthly rent of ₹ ....

2. By the said lease the defendant covenanted, *inter alia,* to use the said premises as a private residence only and not to do or permit to be done upon the said premises anything which in the opinion of the landlord might be or become a nuisance or annoyance to or in any way interfere with the quiet or comfort of the landlord or other occupants of the said dwelling house, nor to use the same for any illegal, immoral or improper purpose.

3. The defendant has committed a breach of the said covenant by permitting the said premises to be so used as to cause annoyance and interfere with the quite and comfort of the plaintiff and the other occupants of the said dwelling house.

Particulars:

4. On .... 20 ......, the plaintiff and other occupants of the said dwelling house complained to the defendant about the said annoyance but the defendant paid no heed to their remonstrance.

5. The defendant threatens and intends, unless restrained from so doing, to continue to commit the breach of covenant complained of.

The plaintiff claims—

An injunction to restrain the defendant from further committing the aforesaid or any other breach of the said covenant.

Verification

Affidavit

237. Suit by a landlord against a tenant for a prohibitory injunction

In the Court of .... at ....

Suit No. .... of 20 ....

(Set out cause title)

Suit for injunction
Claim valued at ₹ ....

The plaintiff states as follows:

1. That the defendant is a tenant under the plaintiff in respect of the premises, described in the Schedule below, at a rent of ₹.............. per month according to English calendar month following an agreement of tenancy executed by the parties hereto on ....

2. That the defendant by Clause No .... of the said agreement covenanted not to use the premises for any purpose other than residential. The defendant, in breach of the agreement, has been storing in the said premises kerosene oil for business purpose and has rendered the premises almost a godown.

3. That the plaintiff had instructed the defendant on .... to remove barrels of kerosene oil from the premises but the defendant appeared not to pay any heed to the plaintiff's instructions, rather he threatened to continue storing of kerosene oil in the premises.

4. That the cause of action for the suit arose on .... when the defendant commenced storing of kerosene oil in breach of the agreement at .... within the jurisdiction of this court.

5. That the plaintiff values the suit at ₹ .... for the purpose of jurisdiction and court-fees and pays *ad valorem* court-fees thereon.

The plaintiff claims:

(*i*) A decree of injunction restraining the defendant from storing kerosene oil in the said premises.

(*ii*) Costs of suit.

SCHEDULE

(State here particulars of the premises)

Verification

Affidavit

NOTES: 1. Suit valuation–plaintiff own valuation of the relief—see s. 7(*iv*)(*c*)(*d*) of the Court-fees Act.

2. Limitation—three years.

3. All plaints should be verified by an affidavit in addition to verification by the same person.

238. Suit for an injunction restraining acts of waste

In the Court of .... at ....

Suit No. .... of 20 ....

(Set out cause title)

The above-named plaintiff states as follows:

1. That the defendant is a monthly tenant under the plaintiff in respect of the premises described in the Schedule below.

2. That the defendant, without permission of the plaintiff, pulled down three C.I. sheets from the roof of the veranda of the room mentioned in item No. (2) of the Schedule below and threatened to pull down the remaining C.I. sheets of the said roof, intending to raise the roof to the height of the room for widening the room in item No. (2) of the Schedule.

3. That the defendant should be restrained immediately by an appropriate order of the court.

4. Cause of action–when act of waste first began to be committed.

The plaintiff, therefore, prays:

For an injunction restraining the defendant from committing further waste in the premises in the Schedule below.

SCHEDULE

(Description of the premises)

(1) ....

(2) ....

(3) ....

etc.

Verification

Afidavit

NOTE: In a suit to restrain waste limitation is three years from when the waste begins under Art. 89 of the Limitation Act 1963.

239. Suit for an injunction against the obstruction and diversion of water-course

(See Form No. 197 *ante*–case of a riparian owner).

In the Court of .... at ....

Suit No. .... of 20 ....

(Set out cause title)

The plaintiff states as follows:

1. That the plaintiff owns a factory known as .... standing on the left bank of the river ...., within the village .... P.S. .... District .... The plaintiff had been using water of the said river for working the said factory for the last seven years when the factory first commenced manufacture.

2. That the defendant lately started a parallel factory on the left bank of the river at a distance of .... and on .... cut the bank of the said river to a considerable length and diverted water to his factory.

3. That for such reasons, the plaintiff is deprived of the flow of water of the said river and work in the plaintiff's factory has to be stopped.

4. That the plaintiff is entitled to a mandatory injunction directing the defendant to restore flow of water to the plaintiff factory and to refrain from doing acts of diversion in future.

5. Cause of action–on the date when diversion was caused.

The plaintiff, therefore, prays for:

(*a*) an order of mandatory injunction directing the defendant to restore flow of water to the plaintiff's factory,

(*b*) an order of permanent injunction restraining the defendant from doing acts of diversion of the water-course in future,

(*c*) a decree for compensation for loss caused to the plaintiff,

(*d*) costs.

Verification

Affidavit

NOTE: For compensation for diverting a water-course limitation is three years under Art. 86 of the Limitation Act 1963, from the date of diversion.

240. Suit for injunction against interference with construction of a house

In the Court of .... at ....

Suit No. .... of 20 ....

(Set out cause title)

The plaintiff states as follows:

1. The plaintiff is the owner of a plot of land measuring about 6 Cottahs, as described in a Schedule annexed hereto and marked 'A'.

2. The plaintiff has got the said property properly surveyed and the soil tested and obtained a report from surveyor as to the suitability of construction of a six-storeyed building on the said land. A copy of the said Survey Report is annexed hereto and marked 'B'.

3. The plaintiff obtained from the Construction Engineer a report as to the nature and contents and the mode of construction of the multi-storeyed building at the said premises of the plaintiff. Copy of the report is annexed hereto and marked 'C'.

4. The plaintiff applied to the concerned Municipality for sanctioning a plan for construction of the said six-storeyed building supported by the relevant documents. A copy of the said application is annexed hereto marked 'D'.

5. The plaintiff entered into a contract with a Builder Contractor for the construction of said six-storeyed building on the land of the plaintiff in accordance with the sanctioned plan.

6. The contractor started the preparation of the ground and laying down the foundation of the said six-storeyed building in accordance with plan sanctioned by Municipality. The contractor collected bricks, sand and cement, iron rods, and other building materials on the site to carry out the construction according to the plan at agreed prices. At this stage, the defendant approached the plaintiff and submitted a construction plan of the plaintiff's intended six storeyed building and offered to complete the work at a cheaper price than the existing contractor who had started construction work.

7. In view of fact that plaintiff has already entered into an agreement with existing contractor who has duly proceeded with the said work in accordance with the sanctioned plan and the progress of work was found satisfactory the plaintiff could not accept the offer of the new contractor.

8. The said nominee contractor Mr. D. after having failed to persuade the plaintiff to give the contract for such construction of the said building started doing some mischiefs.

9. The said Mr. D. threatened that as the job was not given to him, he would not allow the house to be constructed and started creating disturbances to the construction of the building by employing labour to disturb the work of the existing contractor of the plaintiff's building by various means and the defendant also threatened the plaintiff that the building would soon collapse before the construction would have been completed.

10. The plaintiff tried to settle the matter with defendant and offered to pay a lump sum of ₹ .... but the defendant claimed ₹ .... the estimated net profit if the construction was given to the defendant.

11. The plaintiff did not agree to pay the said sum of ₹ .... to the defendant and the defendant started causing mischief and disturbance to the construction of the said building. The defendant caused stoppage of the work by the existing contractor for the plaintiff's said house and thereby the contractor had to pay wages to the labourers even though due to disturbance created by the defendant, no construction work was done on some particular days when the defendant committed such mischief.

12. In spite of requests, and offering a consolation offer of ₹ .... the defendant did not refrain from causing disturbances to the said work of construction of the said premises of the plaintiff.

13. In the premises, the plaintiff by a letter dated .... informed the defendant about his wrongful acts and gave warnings that if the defendant did not stop creating mischief and obstruction to the work of said construction, the plaintiff would take legal proceedings against the defendant. A copy of said letter is annexed hereto and marked 'E'.

14. The plaintiff claims damages from the defendant for his wrongful activities and hampering the progress of construction of house thereby causing loss to the plaintiff by way of payment to the labourers wages for work which could not be done because of wrongful acts of defendant.

15. The plaintiff also claims an order of injunction restraining the defendant from creating any disturbance to the construction of plaintiff's said multi-storeyed building.

16. The plaintiff also claims appointment of a receiver/inspector, to visit the said premises of the plaintiff to watch the activities of the plaintiff's contractor and the defendant's activities in relation to construction of said house and to take appropriate action against the wrong-doer permitting the plaintiff's existing contractor to complete his job peacefully.

17. For the purposes of jurisdiction and court-fees the suit is valued at ₹ .... on which proper court-fees in stamps have been paid.

The plaintiff, therefore, prays for and claims:

(*a*) Injunction restraining the defendant from in any way interfering with the work of construction of the said multi-storeyed building at the premises of plaintiff.

(*b*) Receiver/ Inspector be appointed to look after the said construction of said house of the plaintiff and to see that no disturbance is created by the defendant or his agents to the construction of the plaintiff's building by the existing contractor.

(*c*) Costs of the suit.

(*d*) Further and other orders be made as this learned court may deem fit and proper so as to afford complete relief to the plaintiff.

SCHEDULE

Verification

Affidavit

241. Written statement to the plaint for injunction

In the Court of .... at ....

Suit No. .... of 20 ....

(Set out cause title)

The defendant states as follows:

1. The suit of the plaintiff is not maintainable.

2. The plaintiff has no valid cause of action as against the defendant.

3. This learned court has no jurisdiction to entertain, try or determine the suit.

4. The suit is barred by waiver and acquiescence and be dismissed with costs.

5. The defendant is the Secretary of a Local Youth Club and holds through out the year educational and entertainment functions for the general benefit of people of the locality.

6. For the purpose of the said philanthropic and educational activities, the club needs money and one of the modes of obtaining funds is only in the form of donations from the persons intending to construct new houses, as they are in a better position to pay immediate cash for the benefit of the general public through the defendant's said club. The defendant does not admit the statements and allegations contained in paragraphs 1, 2, 3 and 4 of the said plaint.

7. With reference to paragraph 5 of the plaint the defendant does not have any knowledge of the alleged contract with the Builder or the terms and conditions thereof and no admission is made in respect of the contents of the said contract.

8. With reference to paragraph 6 of the plaint, the defendant states that on following the usual practice, the defendant approached the plaintiff to pay a voluntary donation of ₹ .... to the local club for the benefit of the people of the locality. Further, the plaintiff will also be benefited by the activities of the club.

9. With reference to paragraph 7 of the plaint, the defendant states that the defendant approached the plaintiff for funds which he outright rejected and thereafter the defendant requested the plaintiff to give the construction work of the plaintiff to the defendant's nominee contractor to construct the said building at the same cost as the plaintiff had earlier agreed to pay to his existing contractor. But the plaintiff also wrongly refused to do so.

10. With reference to paragraphs 8 and 9 of the plaint, the defendant states that the plaintiff expressed his difficulty in changing the contractor, the plaintiff might have to pay huge amount of compensation to existing contractor.

11. With reference to paragraph 10 of the plaint, the defendant states that the defendant on considering the difficulties of the plaintiff, suggested an amicable settlement of the matter, by plaintiff paying a sum of ₹ .... as donation to the defendant as the secretary of the local club for the benefit of club members. This, the plaintiff, refused to agree to or pay the said sum of ₹ ....

12. With reference to paragraph 11 of the plaint in view of the aforesaid, the defendant, specifically denies that he created any obstruction to the construction work of the building of the plaintiff.

13. With reference to paragraphs 12, 13, 14, 15 and 16 of the plaint, the defendant states that by long practice, it has become the custom that for construction of any new building, the owner has to give some donation to the local club for benefit of its members, before he constructs a new building. In the present case, the plaintiff committed breaches of the said practice/usage of contribution to the local club before construction of any kind of building.

14. In view of aforesaid, the plaintiff has no valid cause of action and hence no injunction can be issued and the suit be dismissed with costs.

Verification

Affidavit

242. Suit for injunction in respect of construction

In the Court of .... at ....

Suit No. .... of 20 ....

(Set out cause title)

The plaintiffs state as follows:

1. Mr. Neighbour is the owner of the premises No. 1 situate at the entrance of a public lane having a one-storied building with some vacant land.

2. The plaintiffs are members of the public and they reside in their respective premises situate at the further end of the said public lane having their respective residential unit.

3. The plaintiffs also own motor cars which can enter into and exit from the said lane. The plaintiffs have their respective garages at their residences for their cars.

4. The plaintiffs have the right of free ingress to and egress from the said lane along with their vehicles.

5. Nobody has any right to obstruct the right of other citizens or the free use of public thoroughfare, road or lane.

6. Since the first week of January, 20..... the defendant has been preparing for construction of a multi-storied building on his vacant land.

7. Since 15th February, 20..... the defendant has started bringing in bricks, sand, stonechips and wooden planks by way of preparation for starting construction work on his land.

8. Apprehending wrongful obstruction of the plaintiffs' free ingress to and egress from the said public lane, the plaintiffs requested the defendant to store the materials at a convenient place within his compound and not to dump them on the side of the lane thereby obstructing free passage to and from the respective residences of the plaintiffs.

9. The defendant, it appears, has not considered the inconveniences and difficulties that would be experienced by the public including the plaintiffs who are members of the public by wrongfully storing building materials on the public lane knowing fully well that such wrongful storage occupy almost half of the area of the lane leaving the other half of the lane suitable for walking but no car can enter into or exit from the said lane, thereby causing great inconvenience to the public including the plaintiffs.

10. The plaintiffs have been unable to persuade the defendant to see reason and to carry on his construction work in a manner which will not cause great inconvenience to the public who use the lane. The defendant, however, has not been able to appreciate the inconveniences and difficulties of the public who use the public lane.

11. The plaintiffs state that the defendant has no right to obstruct the public way by storing his building materials causing great inconvenience to the public who use the public lane.

12. The plaintiffs by their Advocate's letter dated .... stated the facts and gave warning to the defendant that unless the defendant acted according to law and removed the obstruction from the public lane and stored his building materials inside the compound of the defendant there being adequate space for such storage, the plaintiffs would take legal proceedings to assert their public right and to restrain the defendant from wrongfully encroaching upon the right to use public pathway and obstruct the members of the public being the plaintiffs from exercising their right of ingress to and egress from the said public lane, the plaintiff would seek the assistance of the law.

13. The defendant received the said notice by signing on a copy thereof but failed to take any action to remove obstruction from the said public lane and as such the plaintiffs are compelled to file the present suit.

14. The plaintiffs state that the defendant has no right to store his building materials in public lane thereby obstructing the plaintiffs, members of the public, the right of ingress to their residences and egress from their residences to the main road through the lane.

15. The plaintiffs claim an order of injunction restraining the defendant from allowing obstruction to continue any further and in addition a receiver be appointed to supervise the removal of obstruction from the public lane for use of the public including the plaintiffs.

16. The defendant is residing at the said address within the jurisdiction of this learned court and is carrying on the wrongful obstruction of the public lane situate at the said address within the jurisdiction of this learned court and as such this learned court has the jurisdiction to entertain, try and determine this suit.

17. The court-fees have been paid on proper valuation of the suit.

18. No part of the plaintiffs' cause of action for the suit is barred by the Law of Limitation or the principles of waiver or acquiescence.

The plaintiffs, therefore, pray for and claim:

(*a*) Decree directing the defendant to forthwith remove the obstruction caused by storing the building materials on the public lane by the side of the defendant's premises so that the members of the public including the plaintiffs could enter the public lane by cars and go out of the public lane to the main road by cars;

(*b*) Receiver be appointed to supervise the work of clearance of obstruction by the defendant of the said public lane and, if required, to remove the obstruction by taking help of the police;

(*c*) Injunction restraining the defendant from allowing the existing obstruction to continue or to create further obstruction in the public lane regarding the use of the public lane by the members of the public including the unfettered movement of vehicles used by the plaintiffs;

(*d*) Injunction;

(*e*) Costs;

(*f*) Further and other reliefs.

Verification

Affidavit

243. Written statement of the defendant to the plaint for injunction

In the Court of .... at ....

Suit No. .... of 20 ....

(Set out cause title)

The defendant states as follows:

1. The instant suit is not maintainable, the plaintiffs have no valid cause of action against the defendant and the facts are not correctly stated in the plaint inasmuch as the defendant has not shown to have done anything wrong. As such, the plaintiffs have no cause of action against the defendant and the suit has been wrongly filed in this learned court and hence the suit be dismissed with costs.

2. Without prejudice to the aforesaid but strongly relying thereon, the defendant states that the plaintiffs are not the members of the general public and that the said lane is not a public lane and the land forming the said lane actually belongs to the owner of the premises on both sides of the said lane.

3. Save and except what are matters of record, the defendant does not admit the correctness and validity of the statements contained in the paragraph Nos. 1, 2 and 3 of the plaint.

4. With reference to the paragraph 4 of the plaint, the defendant does not admit that the plaintiffs are members of the general public or they have the right of free ingress to and egress from the said lane along with their vehicles.

5. With reference to paragraph 5 of the plaint, the defendant denies that there has been any obstruction of any public thoroughfare or road or the said lane. Further, the plaintiffs have been always using and are at liberty to use the said lane treating it as a public thoroughfare.

6. With reference to paragraphs 6 and 7 of the plaint, the defendant states that the statements contained therein are substantially true and correct.

7. With reference to paragraph 8 of the plaint, the defendant states that the plaintiffs had no cause or grievance to be apprehended about any possible obstruction to the plaintiff's right to free ingress to and egress from their respective residences through the said lane. Further, the defendant has duly complied with the requests of plaintiffs and stored materials for construction of the said building at the extreme side of the said lane in front of the defendant's premises. Further, the defendant states that actually there has been no obstruction to a free passage to and from respective residences of the plaintiffs through the said lane. Thus the free passage was not in any way obstructed as wrongly contended.

8. With reference to paragraph 9 of the plaint, it is denied that the defendant has caused any inconvenience or difficulties allegedly faced by the plaintiffs or the general public. It is denied that such storing of the building materials was in any way wrongful. It is denied that half of the area of the said lane was obstructed by the building materials or the space left in the said lane was not adequate enough for either walking or for plying of cars, etc. through the said lane. It is denied that the storing of building materials has caused any inconvenience to the public or to the plaintiffs.

9. With reference to paragraph 10 of the plaint, it is denied that the defendant's construction work is being done causing inconvenience to general public who use the said lane. It is denied that there has been any appreciable inconvenience or difficulty caused to the general public who use the said lane for their day to day work.

10. With reference to paragraph 11 of the plaint, it is denied and disputed that the defendant has in any way obstructed the general pathway by storing his building materials or that the general public who use the said lane have in any way experienced any inconvenience or difficulty.

11. With reference to paragraph 12 of the plaint, the defendant states that the plaintiff's Advocate's letter dated .... contained incorrect statements and contentions. The defendant states that, in fact, there was no obstruction caused by storing of building materials on the extreme side of the said lane. In any event, it may be noted that the said building materials were removed since .... and the construction work was started and by the time the plaintiffs have filed their present suit, all the building materials stored have been cleared from the said lane and there was, therefore, no alleged obstruction to the use of the said lane by the plaintiffs or general public, and also plying of motor vehicles to and from the respective residential premises of the plaintiffs.

12. With reference to paragraph 13 of the plaint, the defendant states that the defendant has since duly complied with the request contained in the said letter of the plaintiffs and had removed the building materials from the said lane.

13. With reference to paragraph 14 of the plaint, the defendant states that the defendant has not in any way asserted any right to store his building materials in the said lane or to cause any obstruction to the plaintiffs or members of the general public. The defendant states that there was, in fact, no obstruction caused to ingress to the plaintiffs' residences or egress from the plaintiffs' residences to the main road through the said lane.

14. With reference to paragraph 15 of the plaint, the defendant states that the plaintiffs are not entitled to any order of injunction as against the defendant inasmuch there is no obstruction by the alleged storage of building materials as wrongly complained of by the plaintiffs therein and, therefore, the question of appointment of Receiver to supervise the removal of such obstruction from the said lane due to storage of building materials does not and cannot arise inasmuch as the defendant has since already removed all building materials from the said lane and the said lane is absolutely clean and free from any building materials which might have caused the alleged obstruction of plaintiffs or general members of the public.

15. With reference to paragraph 16 of the plaint, the defendant denies and disputes that there is now any wrongful obstruction of any portion of the said lane and as such, the plaintiffs have no valid cause of action for their present suit and thus, the learned court has no jurisdiction to entertain, try or determine this suit.

16. The suit be dismissed with costs.

Verification

Affidavit

244. Suit for an injunction restraining making noises

In the Court of .... at ....

Suit No. .... of 20 ....

(Set out cause title)

The plaintiff states as follows:

1. The plaintiff is an academician, author of several text books for school children and runs a tutorial home for giving coaching to school and college students in his own premises, at .... within the jurisdiction of this learned court.

2. The defendant is the owner of the building adjacent to the building of plaintiff.

3. The defendant has recently opened a discotheque on his Ground-floor and keeps the same open throughout the day and late in the night and plays music sometimes at very high pitch.

4. The defendant is the Secretary of a Local Club and from time to time arranges gatherings of children where the defendant uses microphones to announce the programmes for the children to give lessons on music, the children sing in concert and the defendant announces from time to time the programme of the meeting and plays the correct tunes of the music sung by the children. All these are being done through microphone from time to time throughout the day and till late at night till 10.00 p.m.

5. There are several groups of children who come by batches at different times and leave the place after having some lessons over the microphone from the defendant.

6. The plaintiff complained to the defendant about the excess noise made in the discotheque disturbing the plaintiff as also other neighbours and the use of microphone throughout the day till 10.00 p.m. at night disturbing not only plaintiff but also neighbours.

7. The plaintiff requested the defendant to stop such singing in the discotheque at loud voices or making noises thus disturbing the neighbours including plaintiff but the defendant paid no heed to such requests and/or complaints.

8. The plaintiff from time to time in writing, requested the defendant to keep his activities relating to the children limited to particular hours of the day and not to use microphone at a high pitch disturbing the plaintiff as also his neighbours from carrying out their day to day work and specially disturbing the plaintiff in carrying out his tutorial work as also his activities as a writer of articles in the local newspapers and preparing text books for the students.

9. Copies of the various letters ventilating the grievances of the plaintiff and requesting the defendant to restrict his activities within such limits so that the rights of neighbours may not be seriously affected and they may carry on their daily work and take rest at home in the usual manner without being disturbed all the time by noises made in discotheque and the use of microphone at a high pitch.

10. The plaintiff claims an order of injunction restraining the defendant from making any loud noise in running his discotheque or using microphone at high pitch at the time of the gathering of children at or near premises of defendant and disturbing throughout the day from time to time till 10.00 p.m. at night.

11. This learned court has the jurisdiction to entertain, try and determine the suit. The suit has been valued at ₹ .... on which the requisite court-fees in stamps have been paid.

12. No part of plaintiff's claims herein is barred by Law of Limitation and that the cause of action is continuing from day to day.

The plaintiff, therefore, prays for and claims:

(*a*) An order of Permanent Injunction restraining the defendant from making excessive noises at his discotheque or from using microphone at a high pitch or for long hours violating the norms of noise and creating sound pollution;

(*b*) Receiver be appointed to record the performance of the defendant and to report every month to this learned court for further steps to be taken if required;

(*c*) Cost of the suit;

(*d*) Further and other reliefs be granted as this learned court may deem fit and proper to afford complete relief to the plaintiff.

Verification

Affidavit

245. Written statement to the plaint for injunction against noise

In the Court of .... at ....

Suit No. .... of 20 ....

(Set out cause title)

The defendant states as follows:

1. The suit is not maintainable as it is vexatious and against the public health and right to live in peace.

2. At the request of the plaintiff, and as a good neighbour the defendant restricted the noise in the discotheque and the activities of the discotheque cannot by any standard be complained as making excessive noise or disturb the neighbours.

3. The defendant as Secretary to the Local Club for the entertainment and education of the children from time to time holds gatherings of children where the defendant arranges for giving them lessons, *inter alia*, in music and the children sing in concert by way of practice. The defendant thereafter sings to demonstrate to the gathering of children the correct tune of the song.

4. For the all-round development of the children, the defendant also carries out different kinds of lessons for different subjects suitable for children. These activities are done through microphone as large number of children gather on every appointed day. The programme is carried on at intervals to suit the different batches of the children.

5. The defendant states that the use of the microphone is indispensable for this kind of public work. The plaintiff cannot have any grievance for the use of such microphone or causing any disturbance to the plaintiff for the gatherings of children and the consequent noises made by them.

6. It is submitted that the plaintiff's grievances are against public interest and the plaintiff living in congested area of a town and has to bear some amount of such inconvenience and allow carrying out good work in the public interest and as such, the plaintiff has no valid cause of action against the defendant.

7. The plaintiff has no valid cause of action against defendant. The suit is speculative and *mala fide* and has been filed out of sheer jealousy.

8. The suit be dismissed with costs.

Verification

Affidavit

246. Suit for an order of injunction restraining from committing nuisance at the premises of the plaintiff

In the Court of .... at ....

Suit No. .... of 20 ....

(Set out cause title)

The plaintiff states as follows:

1. The plaintiff is the owner of a house with a garden and a pond.

2. The defendant is carrying on business as a hotelier at the adjacent premises. The plaintiff has been regularly noticing that the defendant from time to time was depositing waste materials and thus polluted the water of the pond of plaintiff.

3. The water of the pond of the plaintiff is being used for house hold purposes as well as for the purpose of watering of the garden adjacent thereto for cultivation of vegetables and flowers.

4. Due to defendant's above wrongful and polluted discharge of effluents and waste garbage from the hotel premises to the pond, it became practically impossible to use the said water either for house hold purposes or for gardening.

5. The plaintiff states that the defendant is under obligation not to damage the premises of the plaintiff or to pollute the water of the pond or to cause any sort of inconvenience by wrongful discharge of the effluents from his adjacent premises.

6. The defendant is thus liable to be restrained forthwith by an order of injunction from committing any further nuisance to the premises of plaintiff.

7. The plaintiff, therefore, claims an injunction restraining the defendant from polluting the water of pond of plaintiff or discharging any effluents from his premises to any part of the premises of the plaintiff.

8. The plaintiff's cause of action arose within the jurisdiction of this learned court where the immovable property of plaintiff and the defendant are situate and the cause of action is arising from day to day.

9. For the purposes of jurisdiction and court-fees, the suit has been valued at ₹ .... on which the requisite court-fees in stamps have been duly paid.

The plaintiff, therefore, prays for and claims:

(*a*) A Decree of Permanent Injunction restraining the defendant from discharging any effluents or from depositing any articles or waste or garbage materials either in the pond or any other portion of the premises of the plaintiff;

(*b*) Costs of the suit;

(*c*) Further and other orders be made as this learned court may deem fit and proper so as to afford complete relief to plaintiff.

Verification

Affidavit

247. Written statement to the plaint claiming injunction for nuisance

In the Court of .... at ....

Suit No. .... of 20 ....

(Set out cause title)

The defendant states as follows:

1. The plaintiff has no cause of action for this suit.

2. The defendant carries on business as a hotelier at the adjacent premises of the plaintiff under a licence from the proper authorities to run the hotel.

3. The defendant has the Licence to dispose off its waste materials in the manner it has been doing for the last three years.

4. The defendant denies that any waste material has been deposited in the pond of the plaintiff as wrongly alleged. It is denied that the water of the pond is used for drinking or for the garden where vegetable and flowers are cultivated.

5. The defendant denies that effluences or waste garbage from the hotel premises are discharged to the plaintiff's pond. It is denied that for any act of the defendant it has become impossible for the plaintiff to use the water of the pond for house hold or gardening purposes.

6. The defendant denies that he has any obligation to prevent damages to the premises of the plaintiff. It is denied that any act of the defendant has polluted the water of the pond of the plaintiff or caused any inconvenience to the plaintiff. It is denied that the defendant has discharged any effluents to the premises of the plaintiff.

7. The plaintiff is not entitled to any order of injunction as prayed for inasmuch as the defendant has not committed any alleged nuisance to the plaintiff's premises.

8. The suit be dismissed with costs.

Verification

Affidavit

248. Suit for injunction restraining improper use of let-out premises

In the Court of .... at ....

Suit No. .... of 20 ....

(Set out cause title)

The plaintiff states as follows:

1. The plaintiff is the owner of premises No. .... of (address) .... consisting of three floors with compound. The plaintiff has let out to the defendant the ground floor for his residential-cum-business purposes. The ground floor let out to the defendant consisting of six rooms and a big hall is on the eastern portion of the premises.

2. The defendant in breach of the implied obligations installed in the said hall a heavy machinery for chemical processing causing damage to the building. The defendant is using the said machine for processing chemicals for manufacturing his products particulars whereof are not known to the plaintiff.

3. The defendant by such manufacturing process is causing nuisance to the occupiers of the said premises and also to the neighbours as the said machine emits smoke, steam and also emanates foul smell, all injurious to the health of the inhabitants of the said premises and also to the neighbours.

4. The plaintiff did not let out the said premises to the defendant for doing any business which would cause nuisance to other inhabitants of the premises or to the neighbours and that the defendant is acting in breach of the agreement of tenancy as also causing nuisance to the inhabitants of the premises and to neighbours by the emission of smoke, steam and bad smell from the said machine.

5. The defendant is acting in breach of the agreement of tenancy as also causing nuisance to the inhabitants of the premises and to neighbours and the defendant be restrained from continuing with the said wrongful acts causing nuisance to the inhabitants of the said premises and also to the neighbours.

6. The plaintiff is entitled to and claims an injunction restraining the defendant from operating with the said machine and to remove the said machine from the premises and in any event the defendant be restrained from allowing emission of foul smell, harmful steam and excessive noise by the defendant's machinery, thereby causing physical injury, annoyance and discomfort to the inhabitants of the said premises and immediate neighbours thereof.

7. The plaintiff's cause of action arose at .... on and from .... and the same is still continuing from day to day.

8. No part of the plaintiff's cause of action is barred by the Law of Limitation.

9. This learned court has the jurisdiction to entertain, try and determine this suit which is valued at .... on which court-fees in stamps have been paid.

The plaintiff, therefore, prays for and claims:

(*a*) Injunction directing the defendant not to operate the said machine and not to allow emission of steam from the machine harmful to the inhabitants of the said building and to the neighbours, if required, by removing the machinery from the said tenanted premises.

(*b*) Receiver;

(*c*) Injunction;

(*d*) Costs;

(*e*) Further and other reliefs.

Verification

Affidavit

INSOLVENCY

249. Suit for recovery of a debt against an insolvent

Before the NCLT/DRT ....

(Adjudicating Authority) at ....

Money Suit No. .... of 20 ....

XX .... *Plaintiff*

versus

1. PQ ....

2. The Official Assignee of the property of A.B. of .... an insolvent with Office at .... (Or the Official Receiver and Receiver of the property of A.B. of .... an insolvent of .... (address) ....

..... *Defendants*

The above-named plaintiff states as follows:

1. That one A.B. of .... (address) mortgaged his properties, described at the foot of the plaint by executing a registered deed of mortgage on .... in favour of the plaintiff.

2. That the said A.B. died on the .... day of .... 20 ….., leaving his only son who is the defendant No. 1 of this suit. All interests of the mortgagor devolved on the defendant No. 1.

3. That on seeking of the defendant No. 1 in an Insolvency Proceeding No. .... of 20 .... in the court of the District Judge at .... the defendant No. 1 by orders of the said court dt. .... was adjudged an insolvent. By the said orders dt. .... the court was pleased to appoint the defendant No. 2 a Receiver of the said defendant insolvent's estate.

4. That the plaintiff is entitled to a sum of ₹ .... together with interest of ₹ .... as per account below under the said mortgage.

5. Cause of action ....

The plaintiff, therefore, prays for:

(*i*) A judgment and decree for a sum of ₹ .... as per account below within a period specified by the court.

(*ii*) In default, for an order of the sale of the mortgaged property below and satisfaction of the plaintiff's dues from sale proceeds thereof;

(*iii*) Costs of the suit.

Verification

Affidavit

NOTES: 1. See the Insolvency and Bankruptcy Code 2016.

2. Official Assignee or Receiver in insolvency is a public officer. Hence, notice under s. 80, CPC is necessary.

INJURY

250. Suit by wife for personal injuries sustained in the act of saving her husband

In the Court of .... at ....

Suit No. .... of 20 ....

(Set out cause title)

The plaintiff states as follows:

1. On .... the plaintiff and her husband were out for shopping and happened to be in the shop of G. & Co. at .... as customers.

2. At the time material hereto the defendants by their servants were engaged in carrying out repairs to the glass roof of the said premises and they negligently allowed a piece of wood to fall on to glass roof which they had not protected as they ought to have done.

3. The result was that, while the plaintiff and her husband were there, a portion of the skylight forming part of the roof, fell and a piece of glass struck the plaintiff's husband causing him a severe shock. At the moment, the plaintiff, on seeing the glass

falling, immediately and instinctively clutched her husband's arm and tried to pull him away from the spot. In this effort to pull him out of danger, which the plaintiff reasonably believed to exist, she sustained injuries.

Particulars of injuries:

4. By reason of the premises the plaintiff has suffered damage.

Particulars of special damage:

The plaintiff claims—

₹ .... as damages.

Verification

Affidavit

251. Suit for damages for injury caused to domestic animal

In the Court of .... at ....

Suit No. .... of 20 ....

(Set out cause title)

The above-named plaintiff states as follows:

1. That the defendant had beaten up mercilessly and maimed the plaintiff's one milch cow on .... alleging damage of defendant's vegetable garden.

2. That the defendant did not keep the fence of the garden in proper repairs. In any case, even if the plaintiff's cow damaged any vegetable that was nominal and the defendant could not justify his conduct in maiming the cattle.

3. That the defendant intentionally caused injury which is permanent in nature and the cow has been rendered useless.

4. That in consequence thereof the plaintiff has suffered damage of ₹ .... (being the value of the cow).

The plaintiff prays for a judgment and decree for:

(*i*) ₹ .... as damages;

(*ii*) ₹ .... as further damages for being deprived of the milk of the cow for about .... days.

Verification

Affidavit

NOTES: 1. See s. 429 of IPC.
2. Value must be the value on the date of the wrong done.
3. Limitation–three years from the date when the injury was caused.

252. Suit for damages for felling and removal of trees

In the Court of .... at ....

Suit No. .... of 20 ....

(Set out cause title)

The above-named plaintiff states as follows:

1. That the plaintiff holds and possesses a piece of land measuring approximately 10 kathas to the contiguous west of his dwelling house at village .... P.S. .... District ....

2. That the said 10 kathas of land is described more particularly in the Schedule "A" below. The plaintiff had grown there five Mahogany trees. Those were about 12' ft. high and 18" inches in girth.

3. That the plaintiff was away from his house for a month in .... 20.......... while taking opportunity of his absence the defendant entered the said land in Schedule "A" on .... and felled three of such trees and removed the same.

4. That trees so felled and removed would value ₹ .... @ ₹ .... per each tree.

5. Suit—Valuation (value of trees).

6. Cause of action—(date of trespass and felling of trees).

The plaintiff, therefore, prays for a decree of ₹ .... as damages.

SCHEDULE 'A'

Verification

Affidavit

NOTE: Limitation–three years.

253. Suit for compensation for trespass and cutting away plaintiff's crops

In the Court of .... at ....

Suit No. .... of 20 ....

(Set out cause title)

The above-named plaintiff states as follows:

1. That the plaintiff owns and possesses a piece of land measuring .... acres at village .... P.S. .... District .... recorded in settlement Khatian No. ...., more particularly described in the Schedule "A" below.

2. That the plaintiff has grown Hemti paddy this year on the said land and the paddy was fit for harvest.

3. That the defendant had trespassed into the said land on .... with his associates and cut away paddy from the entire land in Schedule "A".

4. That the paddy would have measured .... Qls. valued at ₹ ....

5. That the plaintiff has suffered damage thereby.

6. That the cause of action arose on (date when trespass was committed) at .... (place of occurrence) within the jurisdiction of this court.

7. That the suit is valued at ₹ .... (price of paddy) for the purpose of jurisdiction and court-fees.

The plaintiff claims:

(*a*) ₹ .... as damages.

(*b*) An order of permanent injunction restraining the defendant and his associates from unlawfully entering the suit land and committing unlawful acts.

SCHEDULE 'A'

(State here description of the land)

Verification

Affidavit

NOTES: 1. Plaintiff must be in possession of the land trespassed into on the date of trespass. In case of continuing trespass injunction may be prayed for.

2. Limitation–three years from the date of trespass under Art. 87 of the Limitation Act 1963.

254. Suit for damages for theft of fish from plaintiff's tank

In the Court of .... at ....

Suit No. .... of 20 ....

(Set out cause title)

The above-named plaintiff states as follows:

1. That the plaintiff owns and possesses a tank, commonly, known as 'Sibbari Dighi', at .... town, P.S. .... District .... The plaintiff has undertaken pisciculture therein and had liberated therein fish from last year. There were big Rohu, Katla etc. fish in the tank.

2. That on the night of .... the defendant No. 1 hired a gang of fishermen and netted fish from the said tank stealthily and sold the fish so caught to the defendant No. 2 for a sum of ₹ .... The defendant No. 2 purchased the same knowing the same to be stolen.

3. That the plaintiff has suffered damages of ₹ ....

4. Cause of action.

5. Suit valuation.

The plaintiff, therefore, prays:

(*a*) For a decree of ₹ .... from the defendant No. 1 or, alternatively, from the defendant No. 2.

(*b*) Costs of suit.

Verification

Affidavit

255. Suit for damages for personal injuries caused by the defendant's dog

In the Court of .... at ....

Suit No. .... of 20 ....

(Set out cause title)

The plaintiff states:

1. That the defendant is the owner of a dog named .... which the defendant keeps unchained.

2. That on or about the .... day of .... 20............ while the plaintiff was crossing the road in front of the defendant's house, the said dog of the defendant all on a sudden rushed on and bit the plaintiff.

3. That on enquiry the plaintiff came to know that the dog in question was of a fierce nature and was habituated to bite a stranger on the road. The defendant was so callous and negligent not to keep the dog in chains.

4. The plaintiff sustained injuries, had to incur a heavy expenditure for his treatment and could not attend to his calling for three weeks from .... to .... both days inclusive.

5. Cause of action (date of bite).

6. Suit–valuation–(cost of medical expenses and loss of professional gains).

The plaintiff claims (*a*) damages:

(*i*) of ₹ .... for reimbursement of medical expenses; and

(*ii*) of ₹ .... for loss of professional gains as per account below.

(*b*) Costs of the suit.

Accounts

Cost of injections – ₹ ....

Fees of the doctor – ₹ ....

Loss of professional gains – ₹ ....

(state how loss is calculated).

Verification

Affidavit

256. Suit by a child for personal injury caused by a concealed danger

In the Court/Tribunal of .... at ....

Suit No. .... of 20 ....

C, a minor, represented by his father and natural guardian,

A, ... *Plaintiff*

versus

X, ... *Defendant*

The plaintiff states as follows:

1. The plaintiff is a minor aged about six years, represented duly by his father and natural guardian, A.

2. The defendant at the time material hereto was the owner of a motor lorry and trailer, bearing registered No. ....

3. On the .... 20......, at about 4-30 p.m., the said lorry and trailer loaded with bags of sugar was being driven by a driver of the defendant, a man named ...., and was passing in front of the gate of .... School along .... Street, Kolkata 700 032.

4. The plaintiff, aged six years, who was standing on the footpath near the said gate, on noticing that sugar was leaking from some of the said bags instinctively ran into the roadway to the side of the lorry in order to catch some of the escaping sugar, when he was injured by the rear offside wheel of the trailer running over his left foot.

Particulars of injuries:

5. At the time of the accident the driver knew that some of the bags were leaking, and that there were many children in or about the said street to whom the escaping sugar was an inducement and an opportunity to run into danger.

6. The lorry and the trailer was an allurement to the plaintiff and a concealed danger to him.

7. The defendant had done nothing to cover or protect the bags in any way or to prevent the sugar from escaping to the roadway and therefore failed in his duty to prevent such inducement or opportunity from resulting in danger.

8. By reason of the accident the plaintiff has suffered damage.

Particulars of special damage:

The plaintiff claims—

₹ .... damages.

Verification

Affidavit

INSURANCE

257. Suit on a policy of fire insurance

In the Court of .... at ....

Money Suit No. .... 20..........

(Set out cause title)

The above-named plaintiff states as follows:

1. That the defendant No. 1 is an insurance company, with registered office at .... and the defendant No. 2 is a body corporate under the Life Insurance Corporation Act 1956.

2. That the defendant No. 2 has lately purchased the interest of the defendant No. 1. Accordingly, the defendant No. 2 is impleaded as a co-defendant in the suit.

3. That under a policy (describe 'Fire' or otherwise) No. .... dt. .... the defendant No. 1, in consideration of the premiums paid by the plaintiff so far and to be paid when due, insured the plaintiff against damage of the godown known as premises No. .... at .... of the plaintiff for a sum of ₹ .... (sum assured) and agreed *inter alia.*

(*i*) that the defendant .... (state terms of policy).

4. That on the night of .... 20 .... the said godown caught accidental fire and was completely damaged and the loss of plaintiff is estimated at ₹ .... only.

5. That the plaintiff had intimated to the defendant No. 1 in writing on .... the fact and extent of damage with all available particulars and a demand was also made therein for payment of ₹ .... to the plaintiff under the said policy. The said letter-cum-demand was sent to the defendant No. 1 per registered post with A/D., at their above address.

6. That the defendant No. 1 is avoiding payment under the policy and finally denied on ....

7. That the cause of action arose at .... where the said godown was situated on .... (date of accidental damage) within the jurisdiction of this court/or on .... when the defendant No. 1 denied to meet the claim of the plaintiff on the said policy wholly.

8. Suit valuation.

The plaintiff, therefore, prays:

For a judgment and decree for ₹.....................

Verification

Affidavit

NOTES: 1. Limitation Act–Art. 44(*b*) of the Limitation Act 1963.

2. To claim under a Fire Insurance Policy the fire should be pleaded accidental and onus is on the plaintiff which may shift under proper circumstances—See AIR 1940 PC 199.

3. Limitation for recovery of a sum under a policy of insurance on the proof of death is also three years under Art. 44(*a*) of the Limitation Act 1963.

4. The insurer cannot avoid a contract of insurance containing misrepresentations not about material facts—AIR 1971 Cal 285.

5. Forum to claim payment of money under Insurance Policy–Direction for payment by High Court in a writ petition under Art. 226 of the Constitution of India. *held,* not proper. Civil suit is the only available remedy—*Life Insurance Corporation of India* v *Smt. Kiran Sinha* AIR 1985 SC 1265.

258. Suit by a plaintiff under insurance of a motor car (third party risks)

In the Court of .... at ....

Suit No. .... of 20 ....

(Set out cause title)

The plaintiff states as follows:

1. That the plaintiff owns a Fiat car No. .... registered with R.T.A., ... (name of the district).

2. That the defendant No. 1 owns a vehicle No. .... registered with R.T.A. .... and lent the vehicle on .... to the pro-defendant No. 2 for a pleasure-trip.

3. That the defendant No. 1 was insured against third party risks but the pro-defendant No. 2 as far as the plaintiff has learnt, was not.

4. That the pro-defendant No. 2 was driving the said vehicle rashly and negligently on .... and dashed against the plaintiff's said car at about .... p.m.., on the .... Road 20 yds. to the south of the crossing of ..... Road and .... Road.

5. That in the said impact the plaintiff's car .... was badly damaged, particulars of such damage being mentioned in Schedule 'A' below (or, that in the said impact the plaintiff sustained injuries on his person and the plaintiff's vehicle was badly damaged, particulars of which are detailed in Schedule 'A' below).

6. That the defendant No. 1 acted illegally in lending his vehicle No. .... to the pro-defendant No. 2.

7. That the pro-defendant No. 2 is without means and cannot afford to pay the plaintiff damages. As such the plaintiff sues the defendant No. 1 direct and is entitled

to recover from him a sum of ₹ .... as damages as per account of claim in Schedule 'B' below.

8. That the cause of action for the suit arose at .... within the jurisdiction of this court on .... when the accident occurred.

9. The plaintiff claims damages of ₹ ....

SCHEDULE 'A'

(State here particulars of damage)

SCHEDULE 'B'

(State here particulars of damages claimed)

Verification

Affidavit

NOTE: See provisions of the M.V. Act 1988 (effective from 1.7.1989).

259. Suit by an assignee of a Life Insurance Policy

(*See* Form No. 64)

260. Suit against an insurer for loss of cargo

In the Court of .... at ....

Suit No. .... of 20 ....

(Set out cause title)

The plaintiff states:

1. That the plaintiff had consigned on the .... day of .... 20...........the undermentioned cargo on board S.S. *Sindhu* ex Kolkata to Paradip, consignee thereof being M/s .... of .... under a bill of lading dated ....

2. The defendant, the Marine Insurance Corporation has had its office at .... Kolkata 700 001. On payment by the plaintiff the defendant corporation insured the said cargo, valued at ₹ .... , in the ship S.S. *Sindhu* at and from Kolkata to Paradip against perils of the seas by a Policy No. .... [State particulars].

3. The said goods were duly shipped in the said vessel and, reportedly, the same were totally lost by perils insured against, on or about the .... day of .... 20 .... when the policy was in force [State the perils and nature thereof leading to loss].

4. The plaintiff is thus entitled to payment of the said sum of ₹ ....

5. The plaintiff has served a notice dated the .... day of .... 20........... demanding ₹ .... but to no purpose.

6. Cause of action.

7. Suit-valuation.

8. Claim–sum insured [together with damages, if thought proper].

Verification

Affidavit

261. Suit by an assignee of a Life Policy against Life Insurance Corporation

In the Court of .... at ....

Suit No. .... of 20 ....

(Set out cause title)

The plaintiff states as follows:

1. That one A.B. insured his life with the defendant for ₹ .... on .... The defendant, in consideration of the premiums paid and to be paid to them as therein mentioned, granted to A.B. a Policy No. .... agreeing to pay to the executors, administrators or assigns of the said A.B., the said sum in the policy together with all bonuses which might accrue upon the said policy, within three months of notice received by him about the death of the said A.B.

2. That the said A.B., assigned on .... the said policy by an endorsement thereon (or by a separate instrument, as the case may be) to the plaintiff.

3. That on .... the plaintiff gave to the defendant at .... its principal place of business in .... a notice in writing of the said assignment, together with a copy of the said endorsement duly certified.

4. That the said A.B., died on ...., while the policy was still in force. The plaintiff gave the defendant a notice in writing of death of said policy-holder.

5. That the defendant has not paid, in spite of notice to the plaintiff, the sum payable on the said policy or any part thereof.

The plaintiff claims:

(1) ₹ ....

(2) ₹ .... for bonuses accrued on the said policy.

(3) Interest at 18%.

(4) Costs etc.

Verification

Affidavit

262. Defence that the policy was obtained by the fraudulent concealment and misstatement of material facts

In the Court of .... at ....

Suit No. .... of 20 ....

(Set out cause title)

The defendant states as follows:

1. Previous to effecting the insurance, the assured delivered to the defendant a proposal and a declaration which by the condition of the policy formed the basis of the insurance effected by the policy.

2. The said proposal and declaration contained certain untrue statements of material facts and did not disclose certain facts then material to be known to the defendant and of which it was ignorant.

Particulars:

(*a*) The deceased untruly stated that ...., and omitted to state the material fact that ......

(*b*) The deceased untruly stated that .... whereas ......

3. The deceased omitted to state, and made misstatements of, the material facts aforesaid fraudulently to induce the defendant to issue to him the policy sued upon, and the defendant upon the faith of the said false and fraudulent statements issued the said policy.

4. By reason of the premises the said policy became and is wholly void.

5. The suit is thus not maintainable and be dismised with costs.

Verification

Affidavit

263. General defences to a claim on a policy of fire insurance

In the Court of .... at ....

Suit No. .... of 20 ....

(Set out cause title)

The defendants states as follows:

(The defendants may take one or more of the following defences.)

1. The plaintiff had no interest in the subject-matter of the insurance.

2. The policy was subject to a condition that it should be void if the plaintiff made any material misdescription of the property thereby insured or made any misstatement of or omitted to give any information material to be known for estimating the risk. The proposal on the basis of which the said policy was effected contained certain untrue statements and did not disclose certain material facts then known to the plaintiff but unknown to the defendants, the particulars of which are as follows:

(*Here give the particulars*)

3. The policy was subject to a condition that if after the insurance had been undertaken by the defendants anything whereby the risk was increased be done to, in, or upon the property insured without the sanction of the defendants signified by indorsement on the policy, the insurance as to the said property should cease to attach. After the insurance was undertaken by the defendants the plaintiff without the sanction of the defendants did the following acts whereby the risk was greatly increased:

(*Here give the particulars*)

4. The policy was subject to the condition that the insurance should not be in force until, nor should the defendants be liable for any loss or damage by fire happening before, the premium or a deposit on account thereof was tendered to, and accepted by, the defendants. The said loss or damage by fire happened before any such premium or deposit was tendered to or accepted by the defendants.

5. The policy was subject to a condition that the plaintiff within fifteen days of the happening of any loss or damage by fire deliver to the defendants a claim in writing for the loss or damage containing as particular an account as might be reasonably practicable of the items of property damaged or destroyed, stating in respect each amount of the damage and the estimated value at the time of the loss or damage. The plaintiff did not comply with the said condition.

6. The policy was subject to the condition that all benefits under the said policy would be forfeited if the plaintiff or anyone acting on his behalf made any fraudulent claim or used any fraudulent or false book, account, entry, voucher etc., or any

fraudulent means or devices to obtain any benefit under the policy. On .... the plaintiff delivered to the defendants a fraudulently exaggerated claim supported by false entries in books of accounts, particulars of which are as follows:

(Particulars)

7. The policy was subject to the condition that it would cease to be in force as to any of the property thereby insured which should pass from the assured to any other person otherwise than by Will or operation of laws, unless notice thereof be given to the defendants, and the insurance be declared to be continuing in favour of such other person by a memorandum indorsed thereon by, or on behalf of, the defendants. The assured assigned the policy to the plaintiff without giving any notice thereof to the defendants.

8. The policy was subject to the condition that the defendants should not be liable for any loss or damage after the expiration of 12 months from the happening of the loss or damage unless the claim was the subject of pending action or arbitration. The suit was filed more than 12 months after the fire and there had been no reference to arbitration.

9. The policy was subject to the *proviso* that in all cases where the policy would be void or would cease to be in force all moneys paid to the defendants in respect thereof should be forfeited.

10 The suit is thus not maintainable and be dismissed with costs.

Verification

Affidavit

264. Suit against an Underwriter on a Policy of Marine Insurance on a ship for total loss

In the Court of .... at ....

Suit No. .... of 20 ....

(Set out cause title)

The plaintiff states as follows:

1. On .... 20, the defendants, in consideration of ₹ ...., paid to them by the plaintiff, issued in favour of the plaintiff a policy of marine insurance for ₹ .... on the ship called ....

Particulars:

1. Valued or Open: Valued at ₹ ....
2. Voyage:—At and from Kolkata to Rangoon.
   (or, Time: From .... p.m., of .... to .... p.m. of ....).
3. Premium to defendants: ₹ .... *per cent.*
4. Perils insured against: Of the seas, man-of-war, fire, enemies, etc.
5. Loss:—Total

2. The said ship, while on the said voyage was, on .... totally lost by the perils of the seas.

(*Here specify the perils*)

3. The plaintiff at all material times, was interested in the said ship to the amount insured.

The plaintiff claims—

₹ ....

Verification

Affidavit

265. Suit by assured on an accident policy

In the Court of .... at ....

Suit No. .... of 20 ....

(Set out cause title)

The plaintiff states as follows:

1. The plaintiff at all times material hereto was a medical practitioner of ....

2. By a policy of insurance dated .... 20......, made between the defendants and the plaintiff, the defendants, in consideration of the sum of ₹ .... paid to them as premium, insured the plaintiff in the sum of ₹............ against *inter alia*, any accidental personal injury totally disabling and incapacitating him from attending in any way to his usual business or occupation.

3. On .... 20....., at about .... p.m., the plaintiff met with an accident, that is to say, he was knocked down and run over by a tram-car at the crossing of .... and .... Streets in .... and suffered severe injuries to both his legs.

Particulars of injuries:

4. As a result of the injuries the plaintiff was removed to the .... Hospital where both his legs were amputated on .... and the plaintiff has thereby been totally disabled and incapacitated from attending in any way to his usual business or occupation.

5. In compliance with the conditions of the said policy, the plaintiff, on .... 20....., gave to the defendants notice in writing of the accident and on .... 20........, forwarded to them a full report of the accident together with a report and certificate from ...., a registered medical practitioner; yet the defendants have not paid the plaintiff the said sum or any part thereof.

The plaintiff claims—

₹ ....

Verification

Affidavit

INTEREST

266. Suit for recovery of contractual/customary interest

In the Court of .... at ....

Suit No. .... of 20 ....

(Set out cause title)

The plaintiff states as follows:

1. That the defendant had purchased on .... from the plaintiff .... piecc goods valued at ₹ .... on credit and agreed to pay the price thereof within a reasonable time together with interest on the value at 12% per annum.

2. That after repeated requests the defendant paid only the principal, i.e. the .... value of the goods on .... but did not pay the interest as agreed.

3. Cause of action (date of purchase or when interest became due).

4. Suit valuation (amount of interest payable).

The plaintiff claims ₹ .... as interest.

Verification

Affidavit

NOTES: 1. See the Interest Act 1839–Circumstances when interest is allowed.

2. Contractual interest–interest can be claimed only when there is an express contract (AIR 1966 All 129; AIR 1967 Punj 497) or implied, for its payment, or under a custom or usage of trade (9 MIA 266).

3. Interest cannot ordinarily be decreed as damages under s. 73 of the Contract Act when it is not recoverable under the Interest Act.

4. In a suit for recovery of customary interest–the plaint shall contain–

(*i*) That there is an age-old custom that on such a transaction the buyer shall pay interest @ of ₹ ....% per annum.

(*ii*) That the defendant was aware of such cumtom at the material time of aforesaid transaction. See s. 61 of the Sale of Goods Act. Interest is at the discretion of the court [*vide* s. 61(2) of the Act].

5. Limitation–three years when the interest becomes due under Art. 25 of the Limitation Act 1963.

267. Suit for recovery of interest only

In the Court of .... at ....

Suit No. .... of 20 ....

(Set out cause title)

The plaintiff states as follows:

1. That the plaintiff is a licensed money lender.

2. That the defendant took a loan of ₹ .... from the plaintiff on .... by executing a bond on the same day which will be payable after three years. The said bond contained *inter alia* a term that the defendant would pay to the plaintiff interest on the principal sum at 10% per annum at the end of every 12 months, calculated from the date of the bond.

3. That the defendant paid interest at the agreed rate on expiry of the first year but did not pay interest on expiry of the second and the third years.

4. That the cause of action arose on .... on expiry of the second year.

The plaintiff claims:

₹ .... as interest for the second and third years, at the aforesaid rate.

Verification

Affidavit

NOTES: 1. No claim for interest for period to filing of suit–such interest not claimed in Memo of appeal. Refusal to award such interest by the High Court, held was proper—*N.M. Siddique* v *Union of India* AIR 1978 SC 386.

2. All conditions in s. 1 of the Interest Act (32 of 1839) have to be fully complied with before claiming interest—*Hanuman Bux* v *Assam Oil Co.* AIR 1978 Cal 18.

INTERPLEADER SUIT

268. Suit by a bailee against rival claimants

In the Court of .... at ....

Suit No. .... of 20 ....

(Set out cause title)

The plaintiff states as follows:

1. That in or about .... Sri 'A' s/o 'B' had deposited with the plaintiff a gold watch for custody. The plaintiff as a bailee has been keeping the said watch with him.

2. That the said A, defendant No. 1, has demanded from the plaintiff re-delivery of the watch. The defendant No. 2 by a notice dated .... on the plaintiff instructed the plaintiff not to deliver the watch to the defendant No. 1. What is more, he claimed delivery of the watch to him alleging his ownership of the watch.

3. That the plaintiff is unable to ascertain the respective rights of the defendants.

4. That the plaintiff himself has no claim upon the said watch other than for charges and costs of a bailee. The plaintiff is agreeable to deliver the watch to the rightful claimant as may be directed by the court.

5. That this suit has not been instituted in collusion with any of the defendants.

6. That the cause of action arose on .... when rival claim was put by the defendant No. 2.

7. That the suit is valued at ₹ .... (value of the watch) and court-fees is paid on .... (claim of the plaintiff).

The plaintiff, therefore, prays:

(*i*) that the defendants be directed to interplead together relating to their claim on that watch.

(*ii*) that the watch be delivered to a person authorised by the court and the plaintiff be discharged from his liability upon delivery to the defendants.

(*iii*) Costs.

Verification

Affidavit

NOTES: 1. See s. 88 and Or. 35 of CPC.

2. Limitation governed by Art. 113–three years.

3. Costs–see Or. 35 of CPC.

269. Suit for recovery of jewellery sold and delivered on dishonour of cheque

In the Court of .... at ....

Suit No. .... of .... 20.....

(Set out cause title)

The plaintiff states as follows:

1. The plaintiff carries on business of manufacturing and selling jewellery and several kinds of gems and stones.

2. The defendant purchased from the plaintiff jewellery with stones the total value of which was ₹ ....

3. The defendant was a known personality and of good financial standing.

4. The defendant issued a cheque for ₹ .... on X Bank at .... within the jurisdiction of this learned court.

5. The plaintiff in due course deposited the said cheque with its banker but the said cheque was returned unpaid with a notice that the defendant did not have such funds in her account.

6. The plaintiff had good business relationship with the defendant and did not want to institute criminal case for dishonour of cheque.

7. The plaintiff wrote a letter to the defendant with a copy of the notice of the bank informing about dishonour of the cheque for insufficient funds and the plaintiff demanded payment of ₹ .... with interest at 16% per annum.

8. The defendant by her letter expressed regret for dishonour of the said cheque in spite of her having sufficient funds in her account and that the defendant would take up the matter with her banker. The defendant promised to pay the said sum of ₹ .... with interest within three months.

9. On the expiry of three months the plaintiff again reminded the defendant by a letter about the said payment of the said sum of ₹ .... with interest which letter the defendant duly received on signing on a copy thereof but did not reply thereto.

10. The plaintiff waited for three months more for payment of the said sum of ₹ .... with interest at 16% per annum as claimed by the plaintiff from the defendant but no payment was forthcoming.

11. As a last resort the plaintiff demanded payment of the said sum of ₹ .... with interest at 16% per annum and notified that if payment was not received within 7 days from the date of receipt of the letter the plaintiff would take legal proceedings for recovery of the said outstanding amount. The defendant received the said letter by signing on a copy thereof and putting date of receipt but did not make payment within the stipulated period or at all.

12. In the premises the plaintiff by its letter dated .... demanded payment of a sum of ₹ .... with further interest at 16% per annum.

13. In spite of demands the defendant has not paid the said sum or any portion thereof to the plaintiff.

14. The plaintiff annexes hereto a photocopy of the cheque with the Bank's Slip dishonouring the cheque marked "A" and "B" respectively. A copy of the demand letter is annexed hereto marked "C".

15. The plaintiff's cause of action arose within the jurisdiction of this learned court, the defendant is residing at the aforesaid address within the jurisdiction of this learned court. No part of the plaintiff's claim herein is barred by the law of limitation. For the purposes of jurisdiction and court-fees the suit is valued at ₹ .... on which court-fees in stamps have been paid.

The plaintiff, therefore, prays for and claims:

(*a*) Decree for ₹ .... with further interest at 16% per annum till payment;

(*b*) Alternatively, decree for return of jewellery;

(*c*) Receiver;

(*d*) Injunction;

(*e*) Costs;

(*f*) Further and other reliefs.

Verification

Affidavit

270. Written statement to the plaint for the recovery of jewellery on dishonour of cheque

In the Court of .... at ....

Suit No. .... of 20........

(Set out cause title)

The defendant states as follows:

1. The instant suit is not maintainable.

2. The plaintiff has no valid cause of action as against the defendant.

3. The alleged cause of action is barred by the principles of waiver and acquiescence.

4. Without prejudice to the aforesaid, but strongly relying thereon, I now deal with the allegations and contentions contained in the plaint in the following paragraphs—

5. The statements contained in paragraphs, 1, 2 and 3 of the plaint are matters of record.

6. With reference to paragraph 4 of the plaint, the defendant states that at the request of the plaintiff, the defendant issued the said cheque on the specific assurance that the cheque would not be sent for encashment or clearance to the Bank until a written prior intimation is given by the defendant to plaintiff.

7. With reference to paragraph 5 of the plaint, the defendant states that the defendant did not give his consent to the plaintiff to encash the said cheque. The plaintiff, in breach of the agreement with the defendant, had deposited the said cheque with its Bank. Hence the said cheque was returned dishonoured and unpaid inasmuch as the defendant did not have adequate funds in his account and such deposit of said cheque in the Bank was in breach of the agreement and it was hence rightly returned unpaid.

8. With reference to paragraph 6 of the plaint the defendant simply relied on his good business relationship with plaintiff and expected that the plaintiff would keep its promise not to deposit the said cheque for collection and clearance without having obtained prior written consent from the defendant.

9. With reference to paragraph 7 of the plaint, the defendant states that the said letter was wrongly written by the plaintiff and the plaintiff in breach of the agreement acted wrongly in sending the cheque for collection. Thus the demand of the plaintiff for ₹ .... with interest at 16% per annum was wrongful and runs contrary to the agreement.

10. With reference to paragraph 8 of the plaint the defendant denies and disputes that the defendant had ever expressed regret for such dishonour of the said cheque. The defendant, however, regretted that plaintiff in spite of its promise had deposited the said cheque for collection. Further, the defendant had good business relationship with the plaintiff and was never a defaulter in the past. The defendant, however, promised to pay whatever moneys which were outstanding against the defendant and in spite of conciliatory attitude of the defendant, the plaintiff unnecessarily held out threats against the defendant. The defendant states that the defendant did not want to have further transactions with the plaintiff in view of the above facts.

11. With reference to paragraph 9 of the plaint, the defendant states that she discovered items of jewellery which were imitation jewellery out of the entire jewellery purchased from the plaintiff the total cost of which came to ₹ .... and this fact was discovered only after the above dispute arose and the defendant intended to return such rejected imitation jewellery whose value was about ₹ .... of the total purchase as a result price of balance jewellery would be ₹ ....

12. With reference to paragraph 10 of the plaint, the defendant denies that the defendant is liable to pay the sum of ₹ .... with interest at 16% per annum as wrongly contended by plaintiff. However, the defendant returned to the plaintiff some of rejected jewellery purchased earlier from the plaintiff and the value of such jewellery offered to be returned was worth not more than ₹ .... The agreement with the plaintiff provided that the defendant would be entitled to return any jewellery or any part thereof within a period of one year from the date of such purchase of jewellery.

13. With reference to paragraph 11 of plaint, the defendant states that demand of the plaintiff for payment of ₹ .... with interest at 16% per annum was wrongful and such amount was not at all due or payable by defendant in view of the aforesaid jewellery rejected worth ₹ ...., and for this purpose, the defendant took such jewellery to the plaintiff's shop and offered to return the same to the plaintiff but the plaintiff refused to accept the same and on the contrary wrongfully demanded payment of the entire purchase price of ₹ .... with applicable interest thereon.

14. With reference to paragraph 12 of the plaint the defendant denies the alleged right of the plaintiff to demand a sum of ₹ .... or any interest thereon. The claim was wrongful in view of the fact the alleged sale stood cancelled to the extent of ₹ .... and the defendant was ever ready and willing to return the rejected jewellery worth ₹ .... at any point of time.

15. With reference to paragraph 13 of the plaint, the defendant denies any undertaking to make payment of demanded amount of the plaintiff. Inasmuch as the defendant was and is ever ready and willing to pay only ₹ .... being the value of jewellery retained by it out of the total jewellery purchased at a cost of ₹ .... The plaintiff is liable to take delivery of the rejected jewellery worth ₹ .... as offered by defendant.

16. With reference to paragraph 14 of the plaint, the defendant states that in view of the aforesaid facts, the defendant instructed his Banker not to pay the said cheque for ₹ .... and as such, the said cheque of the defendant was dishonoured on presentation. The plaintiff was not entitled to encash the said cheque in view of the facts stated above.

17. With reference to paragraph 15 of the plaint, the defendant states that the suit is not maintainable and the learned court has no jurisdiction to entertain, try or determine this suit.

18. The suit be dismissed with costs.

Verification

Affidavit

271. Suit by creditor against members of a joint Hindu family for money borrowed by karta

In the Court of .... at ....

Suit No. .... of 20 ....

(Set out cause title)

The plaintiff states as follows:

1. The defendants at all material times were and are members of a joint Hindu family governed by the Mitakshara school of law. Defendant No. 1 at all material times was the manager or karta of the said joint family.

2. Defendants No. 1 and 2 are full brothers, and defendant No. 3 is the minor son of defendant No. 1.

3. On .... 20......, the defendant No. 1 as such manager or karta borrowed ₹ .... from the plaintiff for payment of land revenue and taxes in respect of the joint family properties and verbally agreed to repay the said loan with interest at 9 *per cent. per annum.*

Particulars of claim:

Principal sum	...	......	₹	....
Interest up to	...	......	₹	....
		Total ...	₹	....

4. The plaintiff demanded return of the money first orally and then in writing on .... 20 ...., but the defendant No. 1 has not yet paid back the loan. The plaintiff claims—

(1) A personal decree against defendant No. 1 for ₹ ....

(2) Decree against defendants No. 2 and 3 for the said sum limited to the extent of their interest in the joint family properties.

Verification

Affidavit

272. Suit for personal decree against a junior coparcener for money borrowed by karta

In the Court of .... at ....

Suit No. .... of 20 ....

(Set out cause title)

The plaintiff states as follows:

1. The defendants at all material times were and are members of a joint Hindu family governed by the Dayabhaga school of law.

2. In .... 20......, the defendant A.B., and his brother C.B., since deceased, both Hindus governed by the Dayabhaga school of law, started a joint family business and carried on the said business for the benefit of the joint family consisting of themselves and the defendant E.B., the son of C.B.

3. On .... 20........, the defendant A.B. and the said C.B. borrowed ₹ .... from the plaintiff for paying the debts of the said business, promising to repay the loan with interest at 6 *per cent. per annum.*

4. C.B. died on .... 20......, and, on his death, the said business was continued by the defendants.

5. At all material times the defendant E.B. took an active part in the conduct of the said business.

6. The plaintiff demanded return of the money first orally and then in writing on .... 20 ...., but the defendant No. 1 has not yet paid back the loan.

The plaintiff claims—

₹ ....

Verification

Affidavit

273. Suit to enforce a mortgage of joint family properties executed by karta

In the Court of .... at ....

Suit No. .... of 20 ....

(Set out cause title)

The plaintiff states as follows:

1. One A.B. a Hindu governed by the Mitakshara school of law, died on 5th March 20 .... leaving him surviving five sons, namely, the adult defendant No. 1 and the minor defendants 2, 3, 4 and 5.

2. The defendants at all material times were and are members of a joint Hindu family.

3. At all material times the defendant No. 1 was the karta of the said joint family and carried on an ancestral business for the benefit of the said joint family.

4. On .... 20....., the defendant No. 1 as karta of the said joint family borrowed for purpose of the said business ₹ .... from the plaintiff on mortgage of certain joint family properties. The following are the particulars of the said mortgage.

5. The sum of ₹ .... is due for principal and interest on the said mortgage.

6. The plaintiff asked for return of the mortgage money first orally and then in writing but the defendant did not pay heed thereto.

The plaintiff claims—

(1) An account of what is due to the plaintiff for principal, interest and costs.

(2) Payment of the amount to be found due together with subsequent interest and costs within a time to be specified by the court.

(3) In default of such payment, the mortgaged property or a sufficient part thereof be sold and the sale proceeds, after defraying thereout the costs of and incidental to sale be applied towards payment of the plaintiff's dues aforesaid.

(4) In case of deficiency, liberty be given to the plaintiff to apply for a personal decree against the defendant No. 1 for the balance amount.

A. SCHEDULE (PROPERTY MORTGAGED—DETAIL)

B. PARTICULARS OF CLAIM:

Verification

Affidavit

274. Suit on a mortgage of joint family property executed by father for payment of antecedent debt

In the Court of .... at ....

Suit No. .... of 20 ....

(Set out cause title)

The plaintiff states as follows:

1. The defendant No. 1 and his minor sons, the defendants Nos. 2 and 3 at all material times were and are members of a joint Hindu family governed by the Mitakshara school of law.

2. On .... 20......, the defendant No. 1 as karta of the said joint family, executed a mortgage in favour of the plaintiff in respect of certain joint family properties. The following are the particulars of the said mortgage. (Here give particulars).

3. The said mortgage was executed to pay off a prior mortgage debt dated .... for ₹ .... executed by the said defendant No. 1 in favour of one .... Alternatively, the plaintiff used reasonable care to ascertain the existence of such circumstances as made him believe that such a debt existed.

4. The sum of ₹ .... is due to the plaintiff on the said mortgage executed in his favour.

5. The plaintiff claimed the amount due first orally and then in writing but the defendant No. 1 has not paid the same.

The plaintiff claims—

(1) An account of what is due to the plaintiff for principal, interest and costs.

(2) Payment of the amount to be found due together with subsequent interest and costs within a time to be specified by the court.

(3) In default of such payment, the mortgaged property or a sufficient part thereof be sold and the sale proceeds, after defraying thereout the costs of and incidental to sale, be applied towards payment of the plaintiff's dues aforesaid.

(4) In case of deficiency, liberty be given to the plaintiff to apply for a personal decree against the defendant No. 1 for the balance amount.

Verification

Affidavit

275. Suit by minor coparceners of a Mitakshara joint family to have a sale of joint family property set aside on the ground that the debt incurred by their father was immoral

In the Court of .... at ....

Suit No. .... of 20 ....

(Set out cause title)

The plaintiff states as follows:

1. The plaintiffs and their father, the defendant A.B., at all material times were and are members of a joint Hindu family governed by the Mitakshara school of law.

2. On .... 20......, the defendant A.B. executed a mortgage of a certain joint family property specified in scheme "A" hereto, (hereinafter called 'the said property'), in favour of the defendant C.D. for a consideration of ₹ ....

3. The defendant C.D. instituted a suit on the said mortgage in this court (Suit No. .... of ....) and obtained a preliminary decree and a final decree on .... and .... respectively, and purchased the said property at the court sale held in execution of the said final decree, on ....

4. The plaintiffs were not parties to the said suit or to any of the proceedings therein.

5. The defendant A.B. had borrowed the said sum of ₹ .... on the said mortgage for an immoral purpose, viz. for keeping and maintaining a concubine. Without incurring the debt it was impossible to gratify his immoral propensities.

The plaintiffs claim—

(1) A declaration that the mortgage deed aforesaid was not binding on the said joint family.

(2) A declaration that the said property was not liable to be sold in execution of the decree dated .... made in Suit No. .... of ....

(3) That the said sale be set aside.

(4) An injunction to restrain the defendant C.D. from obtaining possession of the said property on the strength of the aforesaid sale.

Schedule 'A'

Verification

Affidavit

LEASE AND TENANCY

276. Suit by landlord against tenant for rent

In the Court of .... at ....

Suit No. .... of 20 ....

(Set out cause title)

The plaintiff states as follows:

1. The plaintiff and the defendants No. 2 and 3 are joint owners of the house and premises No. ...., Street, in .... hereinafter called 'the said premises'.

2. Under a verbal agreement made on .... the defendant No. 1 became a monthly tenant to the plaintiff and to the defendants No. 2 and 3, in respect of the said premises at the rent of ₹ .... per month and has been in occupation of the said premises as such tenant since ....

3. The defendant No. 1 has not paid the rent for the months of ....

4. The defendants No. 2 and 3 refused to join as co-plaintiffs in this suit although thereunto verbally requested by the plaintiff on ....

The plaintiff claims—

Judgment for ₹ .... as rent in arrear in favour of the plaintiff and the defendants No. 2 and 3.

Verification

Affidavit

277. Suit by landlord for rent against lessee and his assignee

In the Court of .... at ....

Suit No. .... of 20 ....

(Set out cause title)

The plaintiff states as follows:

1. By a registered lease dated .... 20......, the plaintiff let to the defendant No. 1 the house and premises No. ...., Street in ...., hereinafter called 'the said premises', at a monthly rent of ₹ .... payable in advance on the .... of every month.

2. By a deed of assignment dated ...., the defendant No. 2 has been assigned with the lease by the defendant No. 1.

3. The sum of ₹ .... is due as arrears of rent in respect of the said premises.

The plaintiff claims—

₹ .... rent in arrear.

Verification

Affidavit

278. Suit by landlord against tenant for damages for breach of covenant to repair

In the Court of .... at ....

Suit No. .... of 20 ....

(Set out cause title)

The plaintiff states as follows:

1. By a registered lease dated .... the plaintiff let to the defendant the house No. .... Street .... for a term of fifteen years.

2. By the said terms of the said lease the defendant covenanted to keep the demised building in good and tenantable repair during the continuance of the said term.

3. The defendant has not kept the said building in tenantable repair.

Particulars of non-repair

4. By reason of the breach of covenant aforesaid, injury has been caused to the reversioner.

The plaintiff claims—

₹ .... damages for the breach aforesaid.

Verification

Affidavit

279. Suit by landlord for possession and mesne profits upon determination of tenancy by a notice to quit

In the Court of .... at ....

Suit No. .... of 20 ....

(Set out cause title)

The plaintiff states as follows:

1. Under a verbal agreement made on or about the 31st December 20......., the defendant occupied the dwelling house No. .... Street, in .... from the 1st day of January 20........, as a monthly tenant to plaintiff at the rent of ₹ .... per mensem, until such time as hereinafter mentioned.

2. On .... 20....., the plaintiff gave the defendant a notice in writing to quit and deliver up possession of the said house on the expiry of the 1st day of .... 20......., yet the defendant continues to be in occupation of the said house.

The plaintiff claims—

(1) Possession of the said house upon eviction of the tenant.

(2) ₹ .... as *mesne profits* at ₹ .... per diem from up to the date of suit.

(3) Further *mesne profits* until possession is delivered.

Verification

Affidavit

280. Suit by landlord for possession and mesne profits after determination of tenancy by efflux of time

In the Court of .... at ....

Suit No. .... of 20 ....

(Set out cause title)

The plaintiff states as follows:

1. By a registered lease, dated .... 20........ the plaintiff let to the defendant the house and premises No. .... Street in the town of .... (hereinafter called 'the said premises'), for a term of 25 years from .... at the monthly rent of ₹ .... payable in advance on or before the 7th day of every month. The said lease contained a covenant that at the determination of the tenancy the tenant should deliver up the demised premises to the landlord.

2. The said term expired on .... yet the defendant has not delivered up the possession of the said premises to the plaintiff.

The plaintiff claims—

(1) Possession of the said premises.

(2) ₹ .... as *mesne profits* from .... up to the date of suit.

(3) Future *mesne profits* until possession is delivered.

Verification

Affidavit

281. Suit by landlord against tenant for possession on forfeiture of lease for non-payment of rent in breach of express covenant

In the Court of .... at ....

Suit No. .... of 20 ....

(Set out cause title)

1. By a registered lease, dated .... 20......, the plaintiff let to the defendant the house and premises No. .... Street in ...., (hereinafter called 'the said premises'), for a term of three years from the .... 20......., at the monthly rent of ₹ .... payable in advance on or before the 5th day of each month.

2. The said lease contained the following *proviso* for re-entry:

> "Provided always that if the said rent or any part thereof shall be unpaid for the space of twenty one days next after the day hereinbefore appointed for the payment thereof (whether the same shall have been legally demanded or not), then it shall be lawful for the landlord or any person or persons duly authorised by him in that behalf to re-enter and repossess, and thereupon the term hereby created shall cease without prejudice to any right of action or remedy of the landlord in respect of any antecedent breach of any of the covenants by the tenant contained in the lease."

3. The defendant made default in the payment of rent for the month of ...., whereupon the plaintiff, by letter dated ...., called upon the defendant to yield up possession of the said premises forthwith, but the defendant has not complied with the said demand and is continuing in wrongful occupation thereof.

The plaintiff claims—

(1) Possession.

(2) ₹ .... rent in arrear.

(3) ₹ ...., mesne profits from .... to ......, the date of suit.

(4) Future mesne profits until possession is delivered.

Verification

Affidavit

282. Suit by landlord for possession and mesne profits upon a breach of condition, involving forfeiture, where tenant was required to remedy the breach but failed to do so

In the Court of .... at ....

Suit No. .... of 20 ....

(Set out cause title)

The plaintiff states as follows:

1. By a registered lease, dated ...., the plaintiff let to the defendant the house and premises No. .... Street in ...., (hereinafter called 'the said premises'), for a term of 21 years from .... upon terms and conditions contained therein.

2. By the said lease the defendant covenanted to paint all the external wood and iron work of the said premises in the year .... and every succeeding third year of the said term with two coats of paint mixed in oil by appointing professional persons.

3. The said lease contained a *proviso* to the effect that in case of default in the performance or observance of any of the covenants, conditions or agreements on the part of the tenant contained therein, the term of the lease thereby created should cease and determine and it should be lawful for the landlord immediately or at any time afterwards to enter upon the said premises and repossess the same.

4. The defendant committed a breach of the said covenant.

(Here specify the breach).

5. On .... 20......, the plaintiff gave the defendant a notice in writing that the term of the lease would cease and determine unless the defendant remedied the breach complained of within one month from the date of receipt of the said notice.

6. The defendant has not remedied the breach in terms of the said notice.

The plaintiff claims—

(1) Possession upon determination of lease.

(2) ₹ .... rent in arrear.

(3) ₹ ...., *mesne profits* from .... to ......, the date of suit.

(4) Future *mesne profits* until possession is delivered.

Verification

Affidavit

283. Suit by landlord for possession on forfeiture of lease upon denial of title by the tenant

In the Court of .... at ....

Suit No. .... of 20 ....

(Set out cause title)

The plaintiff states as follows:

1. The defendant was a monthly tenant to the plaintiff in respect of the premises No. .... Street in ...., (hereinafter called 'the said premises').

2. In .... 20......., the plaintiff brought a suit against the defendant in this court (Suit No. .... of ...... 20.......) for recovery of ₹ .... as arrears of rent in respect of the said premises.

3. In the written statement filed by the defendant in the said suit, he denied the plaintiff's claim alleging that the plaintiff was not his landlord. The said suit was decreed with costs on ....

4. After his denial of title as aforesaid, the plaintiff, by a letter dated ...., gave the defendant notice determining the lease and called upon him to deliver up the vacant possession of the said premises to the plaintiff. Yet the defendant has not delivered up possession of the said premises.

The plaintiff claims—

(1) Possession of the said premises upon eviction of the defendant.

(2) ₹ .... as *mesne profits* from .... up to the date of suit.

(3) Future mesne profits up to the date of delivery of possession.

Verification

Affidavit

284. Suit for arrears of rent against a tenant

In the Court of .... at ....

Money Suit No. .... of ....

(Set out cause title)

Suit for arrears of rent

Claim laid at ₹ ....

The plaintiff states as follows:

1. That the defendant is a monthly tenant under the plaintiff in respect of the premises, described in the Schedule below, at a rent of ₹ .... per month according to English calendar month.

2. That the defendant defaulted to pay rent for the said premises for 11 months beginning with .... 20 .... till .... 20 .... both inclusive.

3. That the defendant did not pay the dues in spite of requests of the plaintiff.

4. That the cause of action for this suit arose on the 1st day of .... 20........ and thereafter on the 1st day of each succeeding month at .... within the jurisdiction of this court.

5. That for the purpose of jurisdiction and court-fees this suit is valued at ₹ ....

The plaintiff, therefore, prays:

(*i*) A judgment and decree for ₹ ....

(*ii*) Costs of suit ....

SCHEDULE

(State here description of the tenanted premises).

Verification

Affidavit

NOTES: 1. Limitation–three years under Art. 52 of the Limitation Act 1963, from when the arrears become due. When under *bona fide* belief, the plaintiff was prosecuting a suit for ejectment could he claim suspension of the running of time?—See *Sunil* v *Nagendra Bala* AIR 1962 Cal 238.

2. Landlord relying on deed of purchase as regards tenanted premises. Said deed was not duly stamped—Not admissible in evidence to prove title of plaintiff-landlord—*Gita Devi v Chandramoni Karnani* AIR 1993 Cal 280.
3. Originally two separate portions were leased out, subsequently by a deed of consideration new single tenancy was entered into by parties. Suit by plaintiff-landlord claiming possession of two separate portions on expiry of demised terms of original lease. The suit is not maintainable in view of subsequent consolidated lease–*Manmatha Krishan v Dena Bank* AIR 1992 Cal 362.

285. Suit for ejectment of a tenant on grounds of default

In the Court of the Civil Judge (Junior Division) at ....

Suit No. .... of 20 ....

(Set out cause title)

Suit for ejectment, arrears of rent and damages.

Valued at ₹ ....

The plaintiff above-named states as follows:

1. That the defendant was a monthly tenant under the plaintiff in respect of the premises described in Schedule "A" (hereinafter called 'the said premises') below from ...., 20........ paying therefor rent at the rate of ₹ .... per month. The said tenancy was according to English calender month.

2. That the defendant defaulted in payment of rent for the said premises for six months from .... 20....... to .... 20 ..... and for such default the defendant became liable to be evicted from the said premises.

3. That the plaintiff through his lawyer, sent to the defendant a notice dated ...., determining the tenancy on expiry of .... and requiring him to quit and vacate the said premises on the expiry of......... 20........... The said notice was sent by registered post with A/D and was refused by the defendant on ...., and received back by the plaintiff's lawyer on .... A true copy of the said notice, the Registration receipt and the refused envelope are filed herewith and the plaintiff craves leave of the court to treat the same as part of the plaint.

4. That the defendant has not vacated the premises as yet. The plaintiff is entitled to khas possession of the premises on ejectment of the defendant. The plaintiff is also entitled to get ₹ .... being rent for the months from .... 20 ...., to ....20........, and damages for the defendant's wrongful occupation of the premises at the rate of ₹ .... per diem until the plaintiff recovers possession. The plaintiff claims for the present damages of ₹ .... up to the date of institution of the suit.

5. That the cause of action for this suit arose for ejectment and damages on the 1st of ...., 20 ...., and for arrears of rent on the 1st day of .... 20, ..., and on the first day of each subsequent month at ...., within the jurisdiction of the court.

6. That the suit is valued for the purpose of jurisdiction and court-fees at ₹ .... (being one year's rent ₹ .... for ejectment plus arrears of rent of ₹ .... and for damages up to date of suit ₹ ....) and court-fees of ₹ .... are paid.

The plaintiff, therefore, prays:

(*a*) For a decree for khas possession of the premises in Schedule "A" by ejecting the defendant.

(*b*) For a decree of ₹ .... being arrears of rent from ...., 20.........., to .... 20 ...., both inclusive at the rate of ₹ .... per month.

(*c*) For a decree of ₹ .... as damages and further damages until possession is delivered to the plaintiff at such rate as the court deems proper on payment of court-fees.

(*d*) For costs.

SCHEDULE

All that premises containing etc.

Verification

Affidavit

NOTE: In a suit by a landlord to recover possession from a tenant limitation is 12 years under Art. 67 from when the tenancy is determined.

286. Suit for ejectment of a tenant on other grounds (for forfeiture of lease for non-payment of rent in breach of express covenant)

In the Court of .... at ....

Suit No. .... of 20 ....

(Set out cause title)

The above-named plaintiff states as follows:

1. That the plaintiff let out to the defendant his house premises, more particularly described in the Schedule below, following a deed of lease executed by the parties hereto on .... at a monthly rent of ₹ .... according to English Calendar month.

2. That the defendant by the said deed of lease agreed *inter alia* (*i*) to pay rent for the premises month by month by the first week of the month following the month for which the rent was due; and (*ii*) that the plaintiff shall be entitled to re-enter the premises and resume possession of the premises in case of default in payment of rent for three consecutive months.

3. That the defendant is occupying the said house premises under the plaintiff. He paid rent up to the month of .... 20............. and defaulted to pay rent for eight months commencing from .... to ...., both inclusive.

4. That the plaintiff by a notice dated .... served on the defendant by registered post with A/D, has terminated the lease on expiry of the month of .... 20........ for aforesaid breach of express covenant.

5. That the cause of action for eviction arose on .... and for arrears of rent first on .... and thereafter on the 8th day of each subsequent month at .... within the jurisdiction of this court.

6. Suit-valuation.

The plaintiff claims:

(*a*) For khas possession of the house premises in the Schedule below by evicting the defendant.

(*b*) For recovery of ₹ .... as arrears of rent.

(*c*) For damages/mesne profits for the period from .... to the date of suit amounting to ₹ .... at the rate of ₹ .... per diem.

(*d*) For damages and/or mesne profits at the same rate, on payment of court-fees by the plaintiff, from .... till date of recovery of possession.

SCHEDULE

Verification

Affidavit

NOTE: Suit for ejectment–determination of lease should be pleaded–AIR 1970 Cal 452.

287. Suit for ejectment of a tenant on expiry of term and for damages

In the Court of .... at ....

Suit No. .... of 20 ....

(Set out cause title)

The plaintiff states as follows:

1. That the plaintiff let out his house, described in the Schedule below, on .... to the defendant for a period of 20 years with effect from .... at a rent of ₹ ...... per year, following an agreement of lease executed by the parties hereto on .... and registered on ....

2. That the period of lease expired on .... and the lease has not been renewed.

3. That the plaintiff by a notice dated .... served on the defendant by registered post with A/D., requested the defendant to quit and deliver to the plaintiff vacant possession of the same but the defendant did not deliver possession. The defendant is a trespasser in the said premises.

4. That the cause of action for this suit arose on .... on expiry of the term at .... within the jurisdiction of this court.

The plaintiff, therefore, prays:

(*i*) For khas possession of the said premises in the Schedule below by eviction of the defendant therefrom;

(*ii*) ₹ .... as damages/mesne profits for wrongful occupation at the rate of ₹ .... per diem till the date of suit;

(*iii*) damages at the same rate, on payment by the plaintiff of the court-fees, till the plaintiff gets possession of the same.

SCHEDULE

(State here particulars of the premises)

Verification

Affidavit

NOTES: 1. No notice is required when the lease is for a term certain.

2. When a tenant occupies beyond the term—it is a case of holding over under s. 116, T.P. Act—notice is required to terminate the lease.

3. A tenant after expiry of term must be sued for ejectment within 12 years.

288. Suit for ejectment of a lessee for denial of plaintiff's title

In the Court of .... at ....

Suit No. .... of 20 ....

(Set out cause title)

The plaintiff states as follows:

1. That the defendant is a monthly tenant in respect of the premises, described in the Schedule below, under the plaintiff at a monthly rent of ₹ .... according to English calendar month.

2. That the defendant to pay rent for months from .... to .... 20....... whereupon the plaintiff had instituted S.C.C. Suit No. .... of 20.......... against the defendant for arrears of rent in the court of .... at ....

3. That the defendant entered his appearance in the said S.C.C. Suit No. .... of 20........ against the defendant for arrears of rent in the court of .... at ....

4. That the defendant entered his appearance in the said S.C.C. suit No. .... of 20 .... and contested the suit by filing a written statement and stated *inter alia* that he was possessing the said premises in the schedule below in his own right and that the plaintiff had no title to the premises.

5. That the plaintiff served a notice dated .... terminating the lease.

6. That the cause of action for eviction arose on .... and for arrears of rent first on .... and thereafter on the .... the day of each subsequent month at .... within the jurisdiction of this court.

7. Suit-valuation.

The plaintiff claims:

(*a*) For khas possession of the house premises by evicting the defendant.

(*b*) For recovery of ₹ .... as arrears of rent.

(*c*) For damages/mesne profits for the period from .... to the date of suit amounting to ₹ .... at the rate of ₹ .... per diem.

(*d*) For damages and/or mesne profits at the same rate, on payment of court-fees by the plaintiff, from .... till date of recovery of possession.

Verification

Affidavit

NOTE: Evidence Act, s. 116—Principle of Estoppel.
Tenant is not permitted to deny title of the Landlord. But the Rule does not apply when the tenant is under threat of eviction by person claiming paramount title—*D. Satyanarayana* v *P. Jagdish* AIR 1987 SC 2192.

289. Suit by a landlord against a tenant for a mandatory injunction

(*See* Form 234 *ante*)

290. Suit by a landlord against a tenant for a prohibitory injunction

(*See* Form 237 *ante*)

USE AND OCCUPATION

291. Suit for damages for wrongful use and occupation of plaintiff's premises

In the Court of .... at ....

Suit No. .... 20............

(Set out cause title)

The plaintiff states as follows:

1. That the plaintiff is the owner of the house premises at ....Street, at .... Town, P.S. .... District ...., more particularly described in the Schedule below, hereinafter called the premises.

2. That the said premises was lying vacant. In or about the month of .... 20 .... the defendant trespassed into the said premises and occupied the same till the month of .... 20 .... The defendant is not a tenant and there was no agreement of tenancy.

3. That the plaintiff had requested the defendant by a notice dated .... served by registered post with A/D to quit and vacate the said premises by .... and therein intimated the defendant that the plaintiff was losing ₹............. each month in the shape of rent for the defendant's use and occupation of the said premises.

4. That the defendant left the premises only on .... and for such wrongful use and occupation by the defendant the plaintiff has lost ₹............ being .... month's reasonable rent @ ₹............. per month (or, that the defendant left the premises on .... The letting value of the said premises is ₹.............. per month.

6. Suit valuation.

The plaintiff claims:

(*i*) ₹............. or such other sum as may be adjudged admissible to the plaintiff as damages or *mesne profits* for defendant's wrongful use of the suit premises.

(*ii*) Costs.

SCHEDULE

(State here particulars of the premises)

Verification

Affidavit

NOTES: 1. Limitation—Art. 113 applies.

2. The right to recover damages for use and occupation does not arise out of anything contained in the Transfer of Property Act, but it is a right under the general law for the recovery by the owner of the damages from a person who has used the property. There is no question of any privity of contract in such a case—AIR 1978 All 423.

292. Suit for damages for (legal) occupation of plaintiff's premises

In the Court of .... at ....

Suit No. .... 20............

(Set out cause title)

The aforesaid plaintiff states as follows:

1. That the defendant was inducted on the 1st day of ...., 20 ...., as a monthly tenant at a rent of ₹ .... per month, according to English calendar month, in the house premises of the plaintiff, at .... Town .... P.S. .... District .... more particularly described in the Schedule below.

2. That there was no agreement in writing governing the tenancy and the contract of tenancy was oral.

3. That the defendant defaulted in payment of rent since his entry in the premises whereupon the plaintiff had issued a letter of demand on .... by registered post with A/D to the defendant asking him to pay up the arrears of rent. The defendant has sent in a reply on .... denying the tenancy, amongst others.

4. That the plaintiff is entitled to recover from the defendant a sum of ₹.................. as arrears of rent for eight months from ...., 20 .... to ...., 20 .... both inclusive. If, however, the defendant establishes that he is not a tenant in the said premises in Schedule A then, alternatively, for a sum of ₹............... as damages, calculated at the rate of reasonable rent of ₹.............. per month (or, calculated at the letting value of the said premises at ₹............. per month).

5. Cause of action arose on the 1st of ...., 20............, and on the 1st day of each subsequent month.

6. Valuation.

The plaintiff claims:

A decree for ₹................. as arrears of rent as per account in Schedule 'B' below or, alternatively, as damages for use and occupation of the said premises by the plaintiff for the aforesaid period or, in the alternative, as *mesne profits* for the use and occupation of the said premises.

SCHEDULE A

(State here particulars of the premises)

SCHEDULE B

Arrears of rent for .... month from ...., 20 ..... to ...., 20............... @ ₹................. per month	...	₹ ....
Or, damages @ ₹............ per month for the period from .... to	...	₹ ....

Verification

Affidavit

NOTE: The defendant may enter the premises without agreement of tenancy. In such a case he has to pay reasonable rent. A like suit may be brought even against a trespasser—97 IC 564. A defendant may enter the premises with permission but without any agreement of tenancy. His entry is legal but for want of agreement of tenancy he has to be sued for damages, calculated at the rate of reasonable letting value.

293. Suit against a licensee for use and occupation

In the Court of .... at ....

Suit No. .... 20............

(Set out cause title)

The plaintiff states:

1. That the plaintiff is the owner of the dwelling house situate at. .... P.S. .... District ....

2. On the seeking of the defendant the plaintiff orally permitted and granted to the defendant on the .... day of ...., 20 ...., a licence to use and occupy the said dwelling house of the plaintiff, described in Schedule 'A' below.

3. Terms of the said licence, amongst others, were:

(*i*) the defendant would pay to the plaintiff a sum of ₹............ per month for his use and occupation of the said dwelling house.

(*ii*) the defendant would attend to all essential repairs.

4. The defendant did not pay the sum of ₹............. for his use and occupation of the premises for the period from .... to .... as per account in Schedule 'B' below.

5. Cause of action.

6. Suit valuation.

The plaintiff claims:

(*i*) ₹........ together with damages at the rate of ₹....... per month till realisation.

SCHEDULE 'A'

Description of the dwelling house

SCHEDULE 'B'

Claim

Licence fee at the rate of ₹................ per month for .... months from .... 20........... to .... 20 .... (both inclusive).	₹............ x ... = ₹............

Verification

Affidavit

NOTE: Suit for mandatory injunction against a licensee for possession. The plea that only a suit for possession and not mandatory injunction would lie against a person in occupation of the property as licensee after termination of licence is not sustainable. The possession of the licensee for all practical purposes being of owner himself, once the licence is terminated the licensee is bound to restore the possession to the owner and in the event of default, the owner is entitled to mandatory injunction to direct delivery of possession—*Santlal Jain* v *Autar Singh* AIR 1985 SC 857; followed in *Ajab Singh* v *Shital Puri* AIR 1993 All 138.

WEST BENGAL PREMISES TENANCY

Section 21 of the West Bengal Premises Tenancy Act 1997 provides for deposit of rent with the Rent Controller.

Section 38 of the said Act provides that the State Government may appoint Controller, Additional Controller, Deputy Controller and Registrar and they will exercise the powers conferred by the said Act.

Section 35 of the said Act provides for making necessary repairs and taking measures for maintenance of essential services by the tenant from time to time on failure of the landlord to do so.

Section 17 of the said Act provides that the Controller may fix the fair rent on application either by tenant or landlord, as the case may be, in the prescribed manner.

Sections 6 and 7 of the said Act provides for protection of the tenant against the possibility of any eviction by the landlord.

294. Petition by a tenant for depositing rent with the Rent Controller

(Vide s. 21 of the West Bengal Premises Tenancy Act 1997)

In the Office of the Rent Controller (Sadar) ....
Rent Control (Deposit) Suit/Case No. .... of 20...

A, Proprietor of .... P.S. ....
.... District ....

...... *Tenant-petitioner*

versus

(1) B.
(2) C.
both sons of D, of ....
P.S. .... District ....

...... *Landlords-Opposite Parties*

Prayer for deposit of rent with the Rent Controller under s. 21 of the West Bengal Premises Tenancy Act 1997.

The applicant prays for permission to deposit the rent of the premises as per particulars furnished below:

(*i*) Particulars of the premises with description:

(*ii*) Period for which rent is deposited:

(*iii*) Amount of rent deposited—₹ ....

(*iv*) Name and address of the landlord claiming to be entitled to such rent:

(*v*) Reasons and circumstances for the application of deposit of rent:

The petitioner had been paying rent for the tenanted premises for some months together at a time in pursuance to an oral agreement of the parties hereto. The petitioner requested the landlords by two registered letters dated .... and .... to accept rent but they did not comply with the request. Thereupon the petitioner tendered rent for the months of .... 20 .... to the landlords B and C on.......... who refused to accept the rent. Thereupon the petitioner had remitted on .... by money order the said rent which has also been refused by the landlords.

To safeguard the interest of the petitioner against default, the petitioner is compelled to make deposit of rent with the Rent Controller.

Verification

Affidavit

295. Petition by tenant for repairs of rented premises

Under s. 35 of the West Bengal Premises Tenancy Act 1997

Before the Rent Controller of ....

H.R. Case No. .... of 20 ....

A.B. etc. ... ... *Tenant-Petitioner*

versus

C.D. etc. .... *Landlord-Opposite Party*

Petition under s. 35 of the West Bengal Premises Tenancy Act 1997

The above-named petitioner states as follows:

1. That following an agreement in writing dated .... entered into by the parties hereto, the petitioner is a monthly tenant under the opposite party, according to Bengali calender month at a rent of ₹............. per month, in respect of the premises described in the Schedule below.

2. That the premises containing shop room (vide item 1 of the Schedule below) have C.I. sheet roofing. Seven of C.I. sheets in the roof bear holes and during rains water percolate. The entire shop room having *kacha* floor becomes drenched with water pouring through the holes in the said C.I. sheets. The petitioner at his cost, filled the shop premises with wooden ceiling. Due to pouring of water the ceiling is damaged.

3. That the petitioner requested the Landlord before rains in .... to effect repairs which are essential but the opposite party turned a deaf ear; and, the petitioner had to hear the troubles. That at last the petitioner was compelled to issue a notice dated .... to landlord-opposite party through his lawyer by registered post with A/D to effect essential repairs. (The landlord by a reply dated .... through his lawyer .... practically declined to effect repairs and demanded enhanced rent).

4. That the landlord O.P., as is evident, is reluctant to effect essential repairs.

It is, therefore, prayed that Your Honour would be pleased to serve a notice on the opposite party requiring him to make necessary repairs of the premises, which are essential, namely, replacement of 7 C.I. sheets of the shop-room.

SCHEDULE

(Here insert the description of tenanted premises)

Verification

(As in plaint)

Affidavit

NOTES: 1. Law does not enjoin that the petition of this nature should be a verified petition. Nevertheless, such a petition, requiring judicial determination, should be a verified one.

2. If after service of notice as contemplated under s. 35(2) of the West Bengal Premises Tenancy Act the landlord fails to show cause or to make such repairs or to take within reasonable time such measures, as the case may be, the tenant is at liberty to apply afresh for permission of the Rent Controller to make such repairs or to take such measures himself, enclosing an estimate of cost of such repairs or measures see s. 35 of the West Bengal Premises Tenancy Act.

296. Petition by a tenant for maintenance of essential services and for action against disturbance thereof

Before the Controller at ....

House Rent Case No. .... of 20.....

A.B. etc. ....

.... *Tenant-Petitioner*

versus

C.D. etc. ....

.... *Landlord-Opposite Party*

Petition under s. 35 of the West Bengal Premises Tenancy Act 1997.

The above-named petitioner states as follows:

1. That the petitioner is a tenant under the landlord-opposite party in respect of the premises, described in the Schedule below, at a monthly rent of ₹............... according to English calendar month.

2. That the premises are provided with water-tap connection. The petitioner has been drawing water from such taps since inception of tenancy in the month of .... in 20....

3. That the tenant is in arrears in payment of rent to the opposite party. The landlord demanded rent on .... and threatened the petitioner that in case the rent was not cleared within the next three days he would stop water connection.

(Or, state here circumstances as the case may be).

4. That the opposite party wilfully cut off the supply of water with effect from .... and thus interfered with the supply (or service) comprised in the tenancy of the demised premises.

5. That as far as the petitioner could know, the opposite party did not obtain a previous written consent of the Rent Controller before such interference nor such interference was for the purpose of effecting repairs or in compliance with any municipal requisition.

It is, therefore, prayed that Your Honour would be pleased to:

(*i*) order immediate restoration of the supply of water which has been interfered with by the opposite party.

(*ii*) impose compensation on the opposite party of such sum as deemed necessary, after an inquiry.

SCHEDULE

(Here state the description of the tenanted premises)

Verification

Affidavit

NOTES: 1. Such a petition must be signed by the complainant. It must contain a prayer for action. A petition for restoration of supply is no complaint—54 CWN 916.

2. When there are joint-tenants one of them may file the petition—43 CWN 527.

3. Petition when dismissed for non-payment of process fees, fresh complaint may be filed—AIR 1951 Ass 129.

4. Limitation—six months vide s. 27(2) of the W.B. Premises Tenancy Act 1997.

297. Petition for fixation of a fair rent

Before the Controller at..........

A.B. ....

.... *Tenant-Petitioner*

versus

C.D. ....

.... *Landlord-Opposite Party*

Petition for fixation of fair rent under s. 17 of the West Bengal Premises Tenancy Act 1997

The humble petition of the above-named petitioner most respectfully sheweth:

1. That since ...., 20 ...., the petitioner is a monthly tenant according to Bengali calendar month under the opposite party in respect of the premises, described in the Schedule below, at a monthly rent of ₹...............

2. That other premises of the locality similar or nearly similar to the demised premises in the Schedule below carry a monthly rent of ₹............. or so.

3. That the tenant-petitioner in his utmost anxiety and due to pressing necessity had to take out the premises in the Schedule below at an exorbitant rent as aforesaid.

4. That tenant-petitioner, therefore, prays for fixation of fair rent or such rent as would be reasonable having regard to the situation, locality and condition of the premises and the amenities provided therein compared to those of similar or nearly similar other premises in the locality and having regard also to the rent payable in respect of such premises.

The tenant-petitioner begs to submit herewith an annexure showing certain comparable units.

SCHEDULE

(State here particulars of the demised premises)

Annexure

[See Note (3) below]

Verification

Affidavit

NOTES: 1. For fair rent see s. 17, notice of for increase of fair rent see s. 20 of the West Bengal Premises Tenancy Act 1997, and for revision of fair rent—see s. 18 of the Act.

2. The Controller cannot *suo motu* fix a fair rent. The Controller shall fix the fair rent on application made to him either by the landlord or by the tenant in the prescribed manner (s. 17).

3. Statement in the Annexure is not obligatory. It is a matter for inquiry. But it would facilitate an inquiry.

298. Petition by a landlord for increase of fair rent

Before the Controller, at.........

House Rent Case No. .... 20...

A.B. S/o C.D. ....

.... *Landlord-Petitioner*

versus

E.F. S/o G.H. ....

.... *Tenant-Opposite Party*

Petition under s. 17 of the West Bengal Premises Tenancy Act 1997

The above-named petitioner states as follows:

1. That the opposite party is a tenant under the petitioner at a monthly fair rent of ₹............ according to English calendar month in respect of the premises described in the Schedule below.

2. That the fair rent of ₹.......... for the premises was fixed by the Rent Controller on .... under provisions of s. 17(3) of the West Bengal Premises Tenancy Act 1997 on an application being made by the opposite party in that behalf.

3. That the said fair rent includes the tenant's share of municipal rates and taxes. On the date of fixation of fair rent the proportionate municipal tax for the demised premises was ₹......... and the rent included $^1/_2$ share of the said tax. In the assessment taking effect from 1st June 20..., the municipal tax for the demised premises has increased from ₹...... to ₹...... only.

Or,

That on seeking of .... and with the written consent of the tenant opposite party, the landlord has effected substantial improvements/or structural alterations of the demised premises in 2005 at a huge cost.

4. That in view of the aforesaid circumstances, the petitioner is entitled to increase in fair rent at the rate contemplated in s. 17 of the Act.

It is, therefore, prayed that the fair rent for the premises may be appropriately increased after notice to the opposite party.

SCHEDULE

Verification

Affidavit

NOTES: 1. Circumstances under which fair rent may be increased—AIR 1953 Mad 705.

2. Ordinary tenantable repairs are not improvements—59 CWN 491; AIR 1952 Cal 585. Installation of electricity—AIR 1955 Mad 93 and re-roofing are instances of improvements.

3. Increase of electricity duty—AIR 1957 SC 309, provides a ground for increase in fair rent.

4. Petition shall be signed and verified. Amendment of the petition is permissible—AIR 1954 Ajmer 12.

299. Petition for striking out a defence

In the Court of .... at ....

Other Suit No. ... of 20....

A.B. ....

.... *Landlord-Plaintiff*

versus

C.D. ....

.... *Tenant-Defendant*

Petition under s. 7(3) of the West Bengal Premises Tenancy Act 1997

The above-named plaintiff states as follows:

1. That the plaintiff has commenced the above suit against the defendant for khas possession of the premises in suit by eviction of the defendant on the ground of default, by the defendant, in payment of rent from ...., 20 .... till date.

2. That writ of summons of the said suit was served on the defendant on.........

3. That the defendant has not deposited in this court or with the Rent Controller nor has paid to the plaintiff landlord rent for the period of default or for the period thereafter within the time allowed in s. 7(1) of the Act.

4. (*When required*) the defendant-tenant did not file any application under sub-sec. (2) of s. 7 of the Act.

5. An affidavit in support of this petition is attached herewith.

It is, therefore, prayed that the court may be pleased to order the defence against delivery of possession to be struck out and to proceed with the hearing of the suit.

Verification

Affidavit

NOTES: 1. The court can *suo motu* strike out. Section 7(3) does not speak of making of an application. But the court must be satisfied of the situation for which an application supported by an affidavit is necessary.

2. Arrears of rent include (*i*) arrears accrued due prior to suit, (*ii*) arrears after suit—64 CWN 689. Time-barred rent need not be deposited—65 CWN 1093; 59 CWN 747; 57 CWN 801. Contra: AIR 1978 SC 287. Rent should be paid at the agreed rate unless in dispute as in s. 7(2) of the Act.

3. Delay is fatal. It cannot be extended—57 CWN 537. One day's delay is fatal—67 CWN 300. Delay due to procedural complication is condoned—64 CWN 763 so also delay due to mistake or negligence of court's officers.

4. Expression 'shall' in s. 7(3) is a Directory and not a mandatory provision—*B.P. Khemka* v *Birendra Kumar* AIR 1987 SC 1010.

LICENCE

300. Suit by licensor against licensee for possession

In the Court of .... at ....

Suit No. .... of 20 ....

(Set out cause title)

The plaintiff states as follows:

1. One A.M. died on 5th January 20........, leaving him surviving the plaintiff, his widow.

2. On .... 20....., the plaintiff obtained a grant of letters of administration to the estate of the deceased.

3. A.M., at the time he died, owned among other properties a house, No. .... Street in ...., hereinafter called 'the said house'.

4. Sometime before the death of A.M., the defendant came to live with him in the said house and was allowed to live there.

5. After the death of A.M., the plaintiff allowed the defendant at his request to continue to live in the said house.

6. On or about .... the plaintiff verbally requested the defendant to leave the said house within a week; yet the defendant is continuing to stay in the said house.

The plaintiff claims—

(1) Decree directing the defendant to quit and vacate the said house.

(2) ₹ .... as damages at the rate of ₹ .... per diem for use and occupation of the said house from .... up to the date of suit.

(3) Further damages at the aforesaid rate until the defendant delivers up possession of the said house.

Verification

Affidavit

301. Suit by licensee against licensor for revocation involving breach of contract

In the Court of .... at ....

Suit No. .... of 20 ....

(Set out cause title)

The plaintiff states as follows:

1. By an agreement in writing dated ...., the defendant agreed with the plaintiffs to allow the eastern flank wall of his building, No. .... Street in .... for bill-posting for a period of four years, at ₹ .... a year, with liberty to the plaintiffs to erect a hoarding for the said purpose.

2. By a registered lease, dated ...., the defendant let the said flank wall to one A.B. The said agreement with the plaintiffs was not referred to in the said lease and no assignment of the interest of the plaintiffs in the said building was made to the lessee.

3. On ...., the said A.B. refused, and he is still refusing, to allow the plaintiffs to post any bills upon the said wall or to erect any hoarding.

4. By reason of the facts hereinbefore complained of, the plaintiffs have suffered and are suffering damages.

Particulars of damage:

The plaintiff claims—

₹ .... as damages.

Verification

Affidavit

302. Suit by licensee against trespasser

In the Court of .... at ....

Suit No. .... of 20 ....

(Set out cause title)

The plaintiff states as follows:

1. From September .... 20....., until such time as is hereinafter mentioned, the plaintiffs were in possession of a piece of land specified hereunder with the leave and license of ...., the owners thereof, and which they used as their courtyard and over which they had cattle troughs and a platform.

2. On ...., the defendants forcibly removed the said cattle troughs and platform and took possession of the land by erecting buildings upon it.

3. By reason of the premises the plaintiffs have been deprived of the use of the said land and have suffered damages.

Particulars of damages:

The plaintiffs claim—

(1) Possession of the said land.

(2) Mandatory injunction directing the defendants to remove the buildings they have erected upon the said land.

(3) ₹ .... as damages.

Verification

Affidavit

303. Suit by a licensee for khas possession by ejecting a trespasser

In the Court of the Civil Judge (Junior Division) at ....

Title suit No............... of 20..............

1. A.B. .... *Plaintiffs*

2. etc.

versus

1. C.D. .... *Principal-Defendant*

2. State of West Bengal represented by Collector, District of ....

3. E.F. ...... *Pro-defendants*

Suit for declaration that plaintiffs have right, title and interest to and rights to occupy and possess the suit land and for khas possession thereof.

Claim valued at ₹ ....

The above-named plaintiffs state:

1. That the "Unknown Club" is a registered association of persons with its office at .... bearing Registration No. .... dated .... Plaintiff Nos. 1 to 15 constitute the present governing body of the said Club. The said governing body is also known as the Executive Committee of the Club.

2. That the pro forma defendant No. 4, the Government of .... owned, amongst others, a piece of khas land measuring 0.18 acres in plot No. .... of Mouja ...., P.S. ...., District ...., recorded in favour of the pro forma defendant in 'O' khatian in current settlement operation. The said land is described more particularly in the Schedule "A" below.

3. That the plaintiffs No. 1, 2, 4, 8, 12 and eight others, constituting the previous governing body of the said club, had applied to the State of West Bengal for settling with the said .... Club a piece of government khas land at .... with a view to erecting a building for the accommodation of the club-cum-office of the .... club as also for occupation and enjoyment thereof, pro forma defendant No. 4, the State of West Bengal by entering into a written registered instrument dated .... has licensed out to the governing body of the club, a piece of land (out of the land in Schedule A) measuring .... acres on an annual rent of ₹ .... The said .... acres of land is described more particularly in the Schedule 'B' below and is triangular in form, shown in the enclosed sketch-map which may be treated as a part of the plaint.

4. That the said .... acres of land, described in the Schedule 'B' below is the subject-matter of this suit and will hereinafter be referred to as suit property.

5. That the defendant Nos. 1 and 2 have been possessing the suit land since the year .... by raising unauthorised structures thereon in .... and have been carrying on business therein. The said defendant Nos. 1 and 2 have absolutely no right, title and interest to the suit land. The plaintiffs could not get possession of the suit land after the same was licensed out to the unknown Club on ....

6. That in circumstances of the case, plaintiffs will be deemed to have been dispossessed from the suit land from the date of execution of the aforesaid registered instrument, i.e. from ....

7. That the plaintiffs are entitled to declaration, that the plaintiff club is a licensee of the suit property and is entitled to occupy and possess the suit land to the exclusive of others;

and

further, for the matter of that, the plaintiff governing body of the .... Club an entitled to khas possession of the suit land by eviction of the defendant Nos. 1 and 2 therefrom after demolition of their unauthorised structures standing on the suit land.

8. That the governing body of the Club have served notices dated .... through their lawyer on the defendants No. 1 and 2 by registered post with A.D., requesting them to vacate the suit land and to remove their structures therefrom. The defendants No. 1 and 2 received that notice on November .... but did not comply with the request made therein.

9. That the cause of action for this suit arose on .... when the governing body of the .... Club were granted the licence by execution of the aforesaid instrument by failing to get possession thereof were deemed to have been dispossessed from suit land and thereafter in later part of .... after expiry of the notice period at .... P.S. ...., District ...., within the jurisdiction of this court.

10. That a notice under s. 80, CPC dated .... has been served on the defendant the State of West Bengal, received by the Collector, on ....

11. That for the purpose of jurisdiction the suit is valued at ₹ .... and for the reliefs of declaration with consequential relief of khas possession *ad valorem* court-fees of ₹ .... are paid.

Prayers:

SCHEDULE A

SCHEDULE B

Verification

Affidavit

NOTES: 1. Licence being revocable at the pleasure of the Licensor (except in cases mentioned in s. 60 of the Easements Act) no notice is necessary to revoke a licence—45 IC 317. Notice not required unless stipulated in the Agreement—*Subal Roy* v *Manomohan Morul* AIR 1991 NOC 106 (Gau).

2. In cases mentioned in s. 62 of the Easements Act there is implied revocation of a licence.

3. A licence is personal. The authority cannot be claimed by agents, transferee or heirs. On the death of the Licensee his heirs are trespassers—131 IC 175.

4. Deed providing user of premises on payment of per day. It is licence, not lease—*Hind Trading* v *Didi Modes* AIR 1993 Del 301.

5. Licence created by statutory tenant is legal and valid—*Mani Nariman* v *Phiroz N. Bhatina* AIR 1991 SC 1494.

6. From conduct of licensor–irrevocability of a licence may be inferred—*Ramsarup* v *Bishun Narain Inter College* AIR 1987 SC 1242 at 1243.

304. Suit for ejecting a licensee under permissive occupation

In the Court of .... at ....

Suit No. .... of 20 ....

(Set out cause title)

The plaintiff states as follows:

1. That the plaintiff is the owner of the holding known as .... Cottage at .... Town. P.S. .... District .... hereinafter called 'the premises'.

2. That the plaintiff's said plot of land is described in the Schedule below.

3. That the defendant is known to the plaintiff for long. In or about .... 20, the plot of land was lying vacant when the defendant sought for plaintiff's permission/licence to occupy the same temporarily for a month or so. On the occasion of the defendant's proposal, the defendant agreed that he would quit and deliver unto the plaintiff vacant possession of the said premises on expiry of the month of .... 20 ..... or whenever called upon by the plaintiff so to do, whichever is earlier.

4. In pursuance to such agreement, the defendants occupied the premises since .... under the said licence.

5. That the plaintiff had requested the defendant on .... to quit and deliver unto the plaintiff vacant possession of the said premises by .... but the defendant did not comply with the plaintiff's request. The plaintiff thereafter has issued a notice dated .... by registered post with A/D through his authorised lawyer Sri .... Advocate, requesting the defendant to quit and deliver unto the plaintiff vacant possession of the premises on expiry of a month after receipt of the notice.

6. That the said notice was received by the defendant on .... but the defendant did not comply with the request made therein.

7. That the defendant was allowed reasonable time. The defendant has no right to continue to occupy the said premises after the permission was withdrawn (or, licence was revoked).

8. That the cause of action for this suit arose on .... at .... within the jurisdiction of this court.

9. That for the purpose of jurisdiction and court-fees the suit is valued at .... and court-fees of ₹ .... are paid thereon.

The plaintiff, therefore, prays:

(*a*) for khas possession of the property in the Schedule below after eviction of the defendant,

(*b*) Costs.

SCHEDULE

(State here particulars of the suit-land)

Verification

Affidavit

NOTES: 1. In a suit for recovery of possession of immovable property from a licensee upon revocation or termination of his licence—the court-fees is to be paid:

(*i*) Where a licence fee is payable by the licensee–according to the amount of the fee payable for the year next before the date of presenting the plaint.

(*ii*) Where no such fee is payable—according to the amount at which the relief sought is valued on the plaint.

2. A licence is revocable any time except in circumstances under s. 60 of the Easements Act—for implied revocation—see s. 62 of the Easements Act.

3. When co-sharers are grantors of licence, one co-sharer by himself cannot revoke licence. Either all co-sharers must join or otherwise one or more of them to act on behalf of all to revoke licence—AIR 1977 All 469.

4. Notice prior to institution of a suit for ejectment of a licensee is not necessary. Heirs of a deceased licensee are not licensees.
5. A permissive possession cannot be converted to an adverse possession unless it is proved that the person in possession asserted an adverse title to the property to the knowledge of the true owners for a period of 12 years or more–AIR 1971 SC 996.

MAINTENANCE

305. Suit by a Hindu wife for maintenance against her husband

In the Court of .... at ....

Suit No. .... of 20 ....

(Set out cause title)

The above-named plaintiff states as follows:

1. That the plaintiff was married to the defendant on the .... day of .... 20......... at her father's place at .... within the jurisdiction of this court and she is still the wife of the defendant.

2. That the defendant deserted the plaintiff in .... and did not since enquire of her food and clothings. From .... the plaintiff is constrained to put up with her father at the above address.

3. That the defendant is a businessman dealing in .... at .... and has a net income from the said business of about ₹ .... per mensem.

4. That the plaintiff, in consideration of the status of the parties hereto and in consideration of the income of the defendant, is entitled to a sum of ₹ .... per month as maintenance.

5. That the cause of action for this suit arose on .... at ....

The plaintiff, therefore, prays for a judgment and decree:

(*i*) Fixing a sum of ₹ .... per month as maintenance of the plaintiff;

(*ii*) order on the defendant to pay to the plaintiff the said sum month by month;

(*iii*) maintenance, *pendente lite*.

(*iv*) decree for arrears of maintenance at the said rate since when the plaintiff has been living separate.

(*v*) litigation costs.

Verification

Affidavit

NOTES: 1. See s. 8–for suit valuation.
2. A Hindu wife is entitled to maintenance from her husband during her lifetime under situations contemplated in s. 18(2) (*a*) to (*g*) of the Hindu Adoptions and Maintenance Act 1956 and also in ss. 24/25 of the Hindu Marriage Act. For maintenance from father-in-law, see s. 19.
3. Section 22, Hindu Adoptions and Maintenance Act—Destitute widowed daughters could not get sufficient provision from deceased husband's family. She has a right of maintenance against her brothers after death of her father—*Kota Vamprasada* v *Kota China* AIR 1992 AP 1.

4. For considerations of guiding amount of maintenance—see s. 23 of the Act.
5. For maintenance of a Hindu widow—determination of quantum—see AIR 1971 Mad 282.
6. See s. 7 of the Family Courts Act 1984. Now the suitor Hindu or Muslim has to approach the Tribunal for like reliefs.

306. Defence to a claim by wife for maintenance

In the Court of .... at ....

Suit No. .... of 20 ....

(Set out cause title)

The defendant states as follows:

1. The defendant admits his marriage with the plaintiff.

2. On or about .... 20....., the plaintiff voluntarily left the defendant and has since been staying with her parents and has refused to perform her marital duties.

3. The defendant has always been ready and willing to maintain the plaintiff upon condition of her living with him.

4. The claim for maintenance is excessive as the defendant does not earn the amount as asserted by the plaintiff.

5. Save what is hereinbefore expressly admitted, the defendant denies all other allegations in the plaint.

6. The claim be dismissed.

Verification

Affidavit

307. Suit under s. 24 of the Hindu Marriage Act 1955 by Hindu husband for maintenance against wife

In the Hon'ble Family Court at

(Matrimonial Jurisdiction)

(Matrimonial Suit No. ...... of ....

A.B. (Name, description and address)

.... *Petitioner*

versus

C.D. (Name, description and address)

.... *Respondent*

Petition under s. 24 of the Hindu Marriage Act 1955

The petitioner states:

1. That the respondent has filed a petition for divorce against the petitioner on the ground of cruelty which is pending in this court.

2. That your petitioner has no independent income sufficient for his support as due to a street accident on .... he is now unable to work. The petitioner has no income of his own for necessary expenses of the instant proceeding but his wife is a Government employee, drawing ₹............ per month. So he is entitled to receive from

the respondent the expenses of the proceeding and he is also entitled to receive monthly maintenance during the proceeding having regard to the income of the respondent.

3. That it is incumbent upon the respondent to provide maintenance to the petitioner during pendency of the instant proceedings.

It is therefore, prayed that the respondent be directed to pay a sum of ₹ .... as cost of litigation and a sum of ₹ .... per month for his maintenance *pendente lite*.

Verification

Affidavit

308. Petition under s. 24 of the Hindu Marriage Act 1955 for maintenance pendente lite

In the Hon'ble Family Court at
(Matrimonial Jurisdiction)

Matrimonial Suit No .... of ....

A.B. (Name, description and address)
.... *Petitioner*

versus

C.D. (Name, description and address)
.... *Respondent*

Petition under section 24 of the Hindu Marriage Act 1955

The petitioner states:

1. That the petitioner has filed a suit for divorce against the respondent husband on the grounds of adultery and cruelty, and it is pending in this court.

2. That your petitioner has no independent income sufficient for her support and is living with her parents. The petitioner, not having any income of her own to meet necessary expenses of the instant-proceedings she is entitled to receive from the respondent the expenses of the proceedings and monthly maintenance during the proceeding having regard to the income of the respondent.

3. That the respondent is a Central Government Employee and has a monthly income of at least ₹ .... and is also leading a luxurious life.

4. That it is incumbent upon the respondent to maintain the petitioner during the pendency of the said proceedings.

It is therefore, prayed that the respondent be directed to pay a sum of ₹ .... as litigation expenses and a sum of ₹ .... per month for her maintenance *pendente lite*.

Verification

Affidavit

NOTE: The above reliefs may be obtained and Court's Order almost in every type of proceeding namely suit for—

(*i*) nullity of marriage;

(*ii*) annulment of voidable marriage;
(*iii*) judicial separation;
(*iv*) divorce;
(*v*) alimony and
(*vi*) restitution of conjugal rights.

309. Suit by a Muslim wife for maintenance

In the Court of .... at ....

Suit No. .... of 20 ....

(Set out cause title)

The plaintiff states as follows:

1. That the plaintiff was married to the defendant at the plaintiff's father's house at village .... P.S. .... in the month of .... 20.......... according to Shariat.

2. That the defendant is a man of cruel temperament and he turned the plaintiff out of his house on .... whenfrom the plaintiff has been living in the care of her father.

3. That the plaintiff's father is a poor man and he has been maintaining the plaintiff since .... with much difficulties. The plaintiff is constrained to live separately and to claim maintenance.

4. That the defendant is a permanent State Government employee, working as .... (official designation) and has been drawing a salary of ₹ .... p.m. The plaintiff, in the facts of the case and in consideration of the income of the defendant, claims ₹ .... p.m. as her maintenance.

5. Cause of action.

6. Suit-valuation.

The plaintiff claims:

(*i*) A decree of maintenance of ₹ .... p.m.

(*ii*) A decree of arrears of maintenance at the same rate commencing from ....

Verification

Affidavit

COGNATE LEGISLATION: 1. Section 125 of CrPC. On a wife's demand for maintenance, husband issued notice that she had already been divorced wife was entitled to maintenance only for three months of Iddat (AIR 1970 AP 298) from the date of notice on which divorce came into effect. She was not entitled to past maintenance for the period prior to notice, in absence of any specific agreement.

2. Court-fees—Under s. 7(*ii*) of the West Bengal Court-fees Act 1970, in suits for maintenance–according to the value of the subject-matter of the suit and such value shall be deemed to be 10 times the amount claimed to be payable for one year.

3. Muslim law—Children born out of dissolved wedlock. Father's obligation to maintain them is absolute. Right of children not affected by the provisions of s. 3(1)(*b*), Muslim Women (Protection of Rights on Divorce) Act 1986–*Siraj Sahibji* v *Smt. Roshan Siraj* AIR 1990 Bom 344.

4. *Shah Bano's* case—AIR 1985 SC 945. The right to maintenance conferred by s. 125, CrPC can be exercised irrespective of the personal law of the parties. (A divorced Muslim wife claimed maintenance).

Husband of a Muslim wife contracting second marriage or taking mistress. First wife is entitled to claim maintenance and separate residence (s. 125(3), Explanation, CrPC). It is immaterial that husband can marry again under personal law. Husband's right to take more than one wife is not affected—*Begam Subanu* v *A.M. Abdool Gafoor* AIR 1987 SC 1103.

310. Suit by a widow for maintenance

In the Court of .... at ....

Suit No. .... of 20 ....

(Set out cause title)

The plaintiff states:

1. That the plaintiff's husband .... (X) and the defendants were brothers and they were living in joint mess and having joint property at all material times. Said properties are described in the Schedule below.

2. Unfortunately for the plaintiff, her husband died on .... leaving the plaintiff as his only heiress and successor. The plaintiff has been living with her father at ..... since after her husband's death.

3. The defendants are in possession of said properties and have been wrongfully withholding maintenance from the plaintiff.

4. The expected annual income of said properties is ₹ .... or so. The plaintiff claims a sum of ₹ .... p.m. as her maintenance.

5. The plaintiff is entitled to a declaration of charge on the said properties for such payments as also to an order for payment of maintenance at the above rate month by month.

6. Cause of action.

7. Suit-valuation.

The plaintiff claims:

(*a*) A declaration of charge on the properties, described in the Schedule below, for payments of maintenance;

(*b*) An appropriate order directing the defendants to pay to the plaintiff month by month by the 1st week of each English Calendar month of sum of ₹ .... as maintenance.

SCHEDULE

(State here the description of properties with annual output) ... ₹ ....

Verification

Affidavit

311. Petition by a parent for maintenance against son

In the Court of .... at ....

Petition No. .... of 20 ....

(Set out cause title)

Petition under s. 125 of the CrPC.

The petitioner states as under:

1. That your petition is a senior citizen having no individual income sufficient for his support. The respondent is the son of the petitioner and an employee of State Government drawing a salary of ₹ .... per month.

2. That the respondent since his marriage is misbehaving the petitioner. As a result of that it is impossible for the petitioner to live with his son and his wife. Now your petitioner is living with his friend in his house.

3. That it is incumbent upon the respondent to maintain the petitioner.

It is therefore, prayed that the respondent be directed to pay a sum of ₹ .... per month for his maintenance.

Verification

Affidavit

312. Petition by a parent for maintenance against his son under the Maintenance and Welfare of Parents and Senior Citizens Act 2007

Before the Maintenance Tribunal at ....

Petition No. .... of 20 ....

(Set out cause title)

The petitioner states as under:

1. That your petition is a senior citizen having no individual income sufficient for his support. The respondent is the son of the petitioner and an employee of State Government drawing a salary of ₹ .... per month.

2. That the respondent since his marriage is misbehaving the petitioner. As a result of that it is impossible for the petitioner to live with his son and his wife. Now your petitioner is living with his friend in his house.

3. That it is incumbent upon the respondent to maintain the petitioner.

It is therefore, prayed that the respondent be directed to pay a sum of ₹ .... per month for his maintenance.

Verification

Affidavit

313. Petition by daughter for maintenance against father

In the Court of .... at ....

Suit No. .... of 20 ....

(Set out cause title)

The humble petition of petitioner above-named, most respectfully sheweth:

1. That your petitioner is the daughter of the defendent, aged 22 years. She has no independent income sufficient for her support for living with dignity.

2. That the respondent is a businessman having income of approx ₹ .... per month and has an additional income of ₹ .... per month from the rent of the house property.

3. That the respondent is neglecting the petitioner or providing any financial support to your petitioner.

It is therefore, prayed that the respondent be directed to pay a sum of ₹ .... per month for her maintenance

Verification

Affidavit

314. Petition by physically challenged adult son for maintenance against his father

In the Court of .... at ....

Suit No. .... of 20 ....

(Set out cause title)

The petitioner above-named states:

1. That your petitioner is the son of the respondent. As your petitioner is a physically challenged person, he is unable to earn his bread and medical expenses for himself.

2. That the respondent is geting ₹ .... per month as interest from Bank and additional ₹ .... per month as income from his agricultural property.

3. That the respondent is not taking care of his son though the son is unable to earn any income on his own.

It is therefore, prayed that the respondent be directed to pay a sum of ₹ .... per month for his maintenance

Verification

Affidavit

315. Application for custody of children under the Hindu Marriage Act 1955

In the Court of the District Judge at ....
Matrimonial Case No. .... of 20.........

A.B. .... *Petitioner*

versus

C.D. .... *Respondent*

Petition for maintenance and custody of children under s. 26 of the Hindu Marriage Act 1955.

The above-named petitioner states as follows:

1. That the petitioner has commenced in this court the above proceedings against the respondent praying for a decree of judicial separation from the respondent under the provisions contained in s. 10 of the Hindu Marriage Act 1955. The said proceeding is pending.

2. That the petitioner and the respondent have a son named Sriman .... born of wedlock on .... and is now aged .... years.

3. That the said boy is living with the respondent at the latter's father's place in a very wretched condition as a charity boy. Before the respondent withdrew herself with the boy to her father's place, the boy had been reading in the .... Kindergarten at .... No arrangement has so far been made by the respondent for the education of the boy. The respondent has been mixing up with anti-social elements and has been receiving them at her place. This would tell upon the morale of the boy adversely. The boy intends to put up with the petitioner.

4. That in the circumstances of the case, the petitioner is entitled to custody of the boy for the welfare and education of the boy.

It is, therefore, prayed that the court may be pleased to:

(*i*) pass necessary orders for handing over custody of the boy Sriman .... to the petitioner.

(*ii*) pass an interim order in the light of above prayer in para 1.

Verification

Affidavit

NOTES: 1. AIR 1971 Mys 69. Considerations which guide a court.

2. Maintenance cannot be granted to adult son under s. 24. Section 26 empowers court to provide for maintenance of only minor children—*Kartarchand* v *Smt. Tarabati* AIR 1982 Bom 15.

3. But a physically challenged adult son is entitled to maintenance—*Ashan Ali* v *Junagar Begum* 1999 CrLJ 4214 (Gau). Maintenance of a daughter can be claimed even after attaining majority till her marriage—*Jagdish* v *Manjulata* (2002)5 SCC 422.

316. Petition for alimony and maintenance (permanent) under the Hindu Marriage Act 1955 (s. 25 of the Act)

In the Court of the District Judge at ....

Matrimonial Suit No. .... of 20 ....

A.B. .... *Petitioner*

versus

C.D. .... *Respondent*

Petition under s. 25 of the Hindu Marriage Act 1955 for permanent alimony and maintenance.

The above-named petitioner states as follows:

1. That the petitioner has instituted the above suit against the respondent praying for dissolution of her marriage with the respondent by a decree of divorce.

2. That the case was finally heard on .... No decree has yet been passed.

(Or, a decree of divorce was passed on ....).

3. That the petitioner has had no source of income or property and is not capable of maintaining herself. She has been living with her parents.

4. That the respondent is a State Government employee drawing a salary of ₹......... p.m. (State particulars); besides, he has landed properties of about 10 acres of land at .... District ....

5. That in the circumstances of the case, the respondent should be directed to pay to the applicant month by month, not exceeding the life of the petitioner, a sum of ₹......... or such other sum which appears to the court to be just, for her maintenance and support.

It is, therefore, prayed that Your Honour may be pleased to

(*i*) direct the respondent to pay to the petitioner a monthly sum of ₹ .... or such other sum as deemed just restrospectively from the date of institution of the cause.

(*ii*) pass necessary orders securing such payment by a charge on the immovable properties of the respondent, described in the Schedule below.

SCHEDULE

(Description of the properties)

Verification

Affidavit

NOTES:
1. Consideration for grant of interim maintenance and litigation expenses—AIR 1970 MP 14.
2. Existence of unsatisfied decree for restitution of conjugal rights against the applicant is no bar to a claim—AIR 1970 Punj 341.
3. Provisions contained in s. 25 of the Hindu Marriage Act 1955, are not controlled by s. 18 of the Hindu Adoptions and Maintenance Act—AIR 1959 MP 349 (See Model Form of Plaints—Claim for maintenance).
4. Section 25(2)—Permanent alimony. Court's power to increase quantum of maintenance allowance under other circumstances—Doctrine of estoppel or *res judicata* cannot be invoked to defeat applicant's claim to a higher rate of maintenance allowance—*Ram Shanker Rastogi* v *Smt. Vinay Rastogi* AIR 1991 All 255.
5. Application under s. 25 for alimony need not necessarily be in writing, it can be oral—*Sadanand Sahader* v *Solochana* AIR 1989 Bom 220.
6. Expression proceedings under the Act in s. 24 of the Hindu Marriage Act cannot be given narrow and restricted meaning. Application for

maintenance *pendente lite* during pendency of application under Or. 9, r. 4, CPC is maintainable—*Vinod Kumar Kejriwal* v *Usha Vinod Kejriwal* AIR 1993 Bom 160. Maintainable when petition under Or. 9, r. 13 is pending—*Dipti Ghosh* v *Swapan Ghosh* AIR 1991 Cal 416.

Section 24 proceedings for maintenance *pendente lite* and expenses of proceedings—Not hit by s. 4(*b*) of the Hindu Adoptions and Maintenance Act. Provision under s. 24 is not inconsistent with provision of s. 18 of the Hindu Adoptions and Maintenance Act—*Vinod Kumar Kejriwal* v *Usha Vinod Kejriwal* AIR 1993 Bom 160.

7. Section 28(2)—No appeal lies to the High Court against interim orders passed under ss. 24, 25 or 26 of the Act—*Sunil, Hansraj Gupta* v *Payal Sunil* AIR 1991 Bom 423.
8. Husband obtaining decree of divorce on ground of adultery—Does not disentitle wife to maintenance—*Golab* v *Kamal Golab* AIR 1985 Bom 88.

317. Application for alimony during pendency of suit (under s. 24 of the Hindu Marriage Act 1955)

In the Court of the District Judge at .... or Family Court at ....

Suit No. .... of 20 ....

A.B. .... *Petitioner*

versus

C.D. .... *Respondent*

Petition under s. 24 of the Hindu Marriage Act for maintenance *pendente lite* and expenses of proceedings.

The above-named petitioner states:

1. That the above suit stands posted on .... for ascertaining contest. The respondent (petitioner herein) intends to contest the suit by submitting a written statement.

2. That the petitioner has now been residing with her father at the address mentioned in the cause title of the suit.

3. That the petitioner has had no source of income or any money by which she can maintain herself or meet the expenses in contesting the above suit properly.

4. That the petitioner of the above suit is an employee under .... and draws a salary of ₹ .... per month inclusive of all allowances.

5. The respondent (petitioner) is entitled to:

(*i*) maintenance during pendency of the suit; and

(*ii*) an ad hoc payment of a reasonable sum to meet costs of litigation.

It is, therefore, prayed that Your Honour would be pleased to direct the petitioner of the suit to;

(*i*) pay to the respondent (petitioner herein) month by month a sum of ₹........ for her maintenance during pendency of the above suit;

(ii) pay to the respondent petitioner, within a time specified by the learned court, a sum of ₹ .... to meet costs of litigation, pending in the court.

Verification

Affidavit

NOTES: 1. For alimony pending suit under the Divorce Act (Act 4 of 1869) place of residence of wife not relevant. Possession of independent means by wife would be a relevant factor—*Leelavatty* v *Sundar Athmascelan* AIR 1977 Mad 409.

2. Maintenance during pendency of proceedings (s. 24 of the Hindu Marriage Act)— Object behind s. 24 is to provide financial assistance to the indigent spouse to maintain herself (or himself) during pendency of proceedings and also to have sufficient funds to defend or carry on the litigation so that the spouse does not unduly suffer in the conduct of the case for want of funds—AIR 1977 Del 176. Powers of Court—AIR 1979 All 2.

3. Jurisdiction of the Civil Court to grant relief under s. 24 of the Hindu Marriage Act could not be ousted by mere pre-existing order under s. 488, CrPC (now s. 125 of the 1973 Act)—AIR 1978 P&H 112.

4. Order granting maintenance not supported by any reasons is liable to be set aside—*Sm. Satish Bindra* v *Surjit Singh Bindra* AIR 1977 P&H 383. Factors fixing— AIR 1979 Bom 173; AIR 1980 All 109.

5. Section 24, maintenance *pendente lite* Amount of income sufficient for her support would cover such amount as would be necessary for necessaries suited to status and station which the wife would have enjoyed as the wife of the husband-respondent—*Chitra Sengupta* v *Dhrobojyoti Sengupta* AIR 1988 Cal 98.

MASTER AND SERVANT

318. Suit for damages for wrongful dismissal

In the Court of the Civil Judge (Junior Division) at............

Other Suit No. .... of 20...............

A.B. ....

...... *Plaintiff*

versus

.... Corporation

H.Q. ....

...... *Defendant*

Suit for arrears of pay and damages for wrongful dismissal.

The plaintiff states as follows:

1. That the plaintiff was appointed by the defendant Corporation as an assistant in the scale of ₹ .... per month by an Order No. .... dated .... The plaintiff joined his said post on .... 20 ....

2. That the plaintiff while on duty was placed under suspension by the Secretary of the Corporation by an Order No. .... dated .... with effect from ....

3. That the plaintiff had been charge-sheeted by the defendant Corporation by an Order No. .... dated. .... issued by the Secretary of the defendant Corporation asking him to show cause by .... why he should not be dismissed from service. The plaintiff has been dismissed from his service in the Corporation retrospectively with effect from.............

4. That allegations contained in the aforesaid charge-sheet are baseless. That the plaintiff was orally informed that there would be an enquiry but there was no enquiry. The plaintiff has further learnt that the Secretary of the Corporation took evidence of some witnesses at the back of the plaintiff without informing the plaintiff and without allowing him to cross-examine the said witnesses.

5. That the plaintiff has not been allowed reasonable opportunity to defend himself.

6. That the said order of the Secretary of the defendant Corporation No. .... dated. .... is wrongful, against principles of natural justice and equity.

7. That the plaintiff has not been paid his salary for the months of .... to .... The plaintiff is further entitled to damages of ₹ .... being six months' pay in the above scale for wrongful dismissal as per account in the Schedule below.

8. That the cause of action for this suit arose on .... (date of dismissals/or date when communicated) for damages for wrongful dismissal and on .... for pay of .... 20............. and on the first day of each subsequent month at .... within the jurisdiction of this court.

The plaintiff claims:

(*i*) A decree for ₹ .... as arrears of pay.

(*ii*) A decree for ₹ .... as damages for wrongful dismissal.

SCHEDULE

(Details of claim)

Verification

Affidavit

NOTES: 1. Circumstances for which dismissal was wrongful have to be pleaded with reference to facts.

2. Under the Limitation Act 1963–claim for wages and declaration–both three years. In a suit to recover arrears of salary–cause of action arises on a date when the salary of a particular period becomes due under terms of employment and not when order of dismissal is set aside—AIR 1971 Raj 142.

3. Suit is governed by residuary Art. 113 of the Limitation Act 1963–*State of Punjab* v *Gurdev Singh* AIR 1991 SC 2219.

319. Petition for reinstatement in service after declaration of the order of dismissal

Before the Hon'ble State Administrative Tribunal

Petition No. .... of 20 ....

(Set out cause title)

The plaintiff states as follows:

1. That the plaintiff was appointed as an L.D. clerk in the office of the.......... State of West Bengal and at all material times was attached to ....

2. That the plaintiff was served with a charge-sheet No. .... dated .... for allegations (*i*) .... (*ii*) .... etc., and was directed to show cause within 72 hours as to why disciplinary action should not be taken against him.

3. That the plaintiff had shown cause in writing on .... denying the charges in a representation addressed to the.............

4. That nothing was heard thereafter till .... when by a Government Order No. .... dated .... the plaintiff was intimated that charges having been proved against him he was dismissed with immediate effect.

5. That the plaintiff at all material times held a civil post under the Government of West Bengal and was entitled to all reasonable opportunities to defend himself as provided in Art. 311 of the Constitution of India. That no enquiry in true sense of the term was ever held.

The plaintiff was not served with any notice to show cause against the punishment inflicted. The Enquiry Officer collected statements against the petitioner at his back. All those offended the principles of natural justice.

6. That in the facts of the case, the said Order No. .... dated .... dismissing the plaintiff is arbitrary, unjust, unconscionable, void and *ultra vires*.

7. That the plaintiff should be deemed to be in service or, in the alternative, the plaintiff is entitled to reinstatement to his post.

8. Cause of action arose when the plaintiff received the Government Order No. .... dated .... dismissing the plaintiff at .... within the jurisdiction of this court.

9. Statement showing service of notice under s. 80 of the CPC.

10. That for the purpose of jurisdiction and court-fees the suit is valued at ₹ .... and for reliefs of declaration fixed court-fees of ₹ .... are paid.

The plaintiff, therefore, prays:

(*a*) For a judgment and decree declaring that:

(*i*) The Government Order No. .... dated .... issued by .... is arbitrary, unjust, unconscionable opposed to principles of natural justice and equity and therefore void, illegal and *ultra vires*.

(*ii*) That the plaintiff is still continuing his service in the post of .... or, in the alternative, the plaintiff is entitled to reinstatement to his post.

(*b*) Costs.

Verification

Affidavit

320. Suit by a servant for wages

In the Court of Small Causes Judge at ....

S.C.C. No. .... of 20 ....

A. .... *Plaintiff*

versus

B. .... *Defendant*

Suit for recovery of arrears of pay Claim valued at ₹ ....

The plaintiff states:

1. That the plaintiff was engaged by the defendant as the latter's house-hold servant and he worked as such for the period from the month of Jaisthya, 14 .... B.S. till Baisakh, 14 .... B.S. under the defendant tending his cattle and attending his agricultural lands, ploughing etc. on a scale of pay of ₹ .... per month. The defendant agreed to pay the plaintiff his pay by the first week of every month following the month for which pay was payable.

2. That the plaintiff was dismissed from his service by the defendant some time by the first week of Jaisthya, 14 .... B.S.

3. That the defendant did not pay the plaintiff the latter's pay month by month as agreed or at all.

4. On his dismissal, the plaintiff demanded from the defendant on .... his arrears of pay. The defendant did not pay. The plaintiff thereafter arranged a Panchayeti with respectable villagers of the locality in the month of Ashar 14 .... B.S. The defendant was present in the Panchayeti and promised that he would pay to the plaintiff the latter's dues within the next 15 days.

5. That the defendant did not pay as promised.

The plaintiff is entitled to recover from the defendant a sum of ₹ .... being his pay for 12 months from Jaisthya, 14 .... B.S. to Baisakh, 14 .... B.S. both inclusive.

6. That the cause of action for this suit arose at Mouja .... within the jurisdiction of this court first in the month of Ashar, 14 .... B.S. corresponding to July, 20...................... and thereafter by the first week of each succeeding month when the wages accrued due to plaintiff.

7. That for the purpose of jurisdiction and court-fees the suit is valued at ₹ .... and *ad valorem* court-fees are paid thereon.

The plaintiff, therefore, prays for a judgment and a decree for ₹ ....

Verification

Affidavit

NOTE: Limitation—three years from the wages accrue due—*vide* Art. 7 of the Limitation Act 1963.

321. Praying for promotion and declaration of seniority in service

Before the learned West Bengal Administrative Tribunal at Kolkata

Petition No. .... of 20 ....

P, son of M residing at .... Alipore Place, Kolkata

.... *Petitioner*

versus

1. State of West Bengal, represented by Secretary to the Department of .... Nabanna, Howrah.

2. Z .... son of Mr. Y, residing at
.... Alipore Park, Kolkata

.... *Respondents*

The humble petition of Mr. P. the petitioner above-named most respectfully sheweth:

1. Your petitioner is a graduate in Commerce Stream and also in Law. Your petitioner was appointed under the Respondent No. 1 as an Asstt. Accountant in the Accounts Department being selected by way of a Competitive Examination.

2. Your petitioner's name appeared in the Promotion List at Serial No. 4.

3. Your petitioner states that the incumbents whose names were numbered at serial Nos. 1, 2 and 3 respectively were promoted and therefore your petitioner's name was next in the Promotion List due for promotion. Your petitioner states that respondent No. 1 arbitrarily promoted the respondent No. 2 hereinabove whose name appeared at serial No. 5 in the Promotion List without any reason whatsoever while your petitioner's name was at serial No. 4 above the name of the respondent No. 2.

4. Your petitioner, aggrieved by the above wrongful and arbitrary act of the respondent No. 1, made a representation to the respondent No. 1 by a letter dated 10th January 20... ventilating his complaints and grievances pointing out the illegal and discriminatory acts by wrongfully promoting the respondent No. 2 whose name was below that of the petitioner in the promotion list as item No. 5. A copy of the petitioner's representation to the respondent No. 1 is annexed hereto marked 'A'.

5. In the circumstances your petitioner preferred an appeal before the concerned appellate authorities by a Memorandum dated 15th February 20.......... which was summarily rejected by them without assigning any reason whatsoever and without giving any opportunity to the petitioner of being heard in his appeal before them. A copy of the order of rejection is annexed hereto marked 'B'. A copy of the said Memorandum of Appeal is annexed hereto marked 'C'.

6. Being aggrieved by and dissatisfied with the order of rejection by the appellate authorities and illegal action of respondent No. 1, your petitioner begs to move this appeal before this Hon'ble Tribunal on the following amongst other.

GROUNDS

I. For that it was incumbent upon respondent No. 1 to promote the eligible petitioner to the next higher scale before the respondent No. 2 could be promoted and the respondent No. 1 erred in not doing so.

II. For that the respondent No. 1 acted without jurisdiction inasmuch as he has no right or authority to supersede the petitioner and erred in doing so.

III. For that the right to promotion and consequential and incidental benefits in relation thereto comes within the fundamental rights under the Constitution of India.

IV. For that the said order of respondent No. 1 is otherwise wrong both in facts and in law and the same be set aside and quashed.

7. Your petitioner states that this appeal for due promotion is in the interest of equity and justice and it is fully assured and guaranteed under the fundamental rights of Constitution of India.

8. The principles of law and natural justice demand that the arbitrary act of the respondent No. 1 be set aside and proper justice be done to your petitioner.

In the circumstances aforesaid, your petitioner most humbly prays for the followings orders:

(*a*) This learned Tribunal will be graciously pleased to direct the respondent No. 1 to promote the petitioner to the next higher scale, as prayed for;

(*b*) An order be made directing respondent No. 1 to grant the consequential seniority in promotion and emoluments and consequential benefits as per order prayed for in prayer (*a*) above;

(*c*) Such further and other orders be made as to this learned Tribunal may deem fit and proper as to afford complete relief to your petitioner.

And your petitioner, as in duty bound, shall ever pray.

ANNEXURE 'A'

ANNEXURE 'B'

ANNEXURE 'C'

Verification

Affidavit

322. Petition for declaration of status as Research Assistants

Before the .... Industrial Tribunal at Kolkata
Miscellaneous reference Case No. ...... of 20...

In the matter of:

Declaration of Status of Research Assistants of

1. Mr. P., residing at .... Alipore Road. Kolkata

2. Mr. Q. residing at .... Alipore Road, Kolkata

Both are employees of R. Company Ltd. represented by R. Trade Union having its registered office at .... Alipore Road, Kolkata

.... *Claimants*

versus

Management of R. Co. Ltd. having its factory at ..... Alipore Road, Kolkata

...... *Respondents*

The humble petition of the claimants above-named most respectfully sheweth:

1. Your claimants state that the Government of West Bengal has made the following reference before this learned Tribunal for adjudication.

"Can the Research Assistants employed by the respondent be classified as 'Workmen' as per provisions of Factories Act?"

2. The claimants are holding M.Sc Degree and have research experience in computers and electronics.

3. The claimants are employed with respondent company as the Research Assistants in their factory for manufacture of computers and allied equipments.

4. The claimants state that the Research work has been carried out by them in another separate building of the factory premises.

5. The claimants state that the main work of the claimants is to develop proper functioning of computers and specially in the field of voice regulating Mechanism and to improve the functioning of the said voice recordings.

6. The claimants are not engaged in manufacturing process of respondents.

7. The claimants, however, are required to work on Saturdays also which is a general off-day for other employees of respondents and were treated in the category of workers.

8. The claimants state that they have been forcibly and wrongfully treated as workmen and thereby are subjected to great hardship and harassment.

9. In view of the aforesaid, the respondents are acting wrongfully and contrary to the provisions of law.

10. The claimants are entitled to a declaration that they are the employees of the respondents and they are entitled to be treated as a special category as "Research Assistants".

11. This application has been made *bona fide* and in the interest of justice.

The claimants, therefore, humbly pray that this Hon'ble Tribunal will be graciously pleased to declare:

(*a*) that the claimants are not Workmen as per provisions of Factories Act 1948.

(*b*) such other and further orders or declaration be made as this Hon'ble Tribunal may deem fit and proper to afford complete relief to the claimants.

And the claimants as in duty bound shall ever pray.

Verification

Affidavit

323. Review application

Before the Court of the

Civil Judge (Senior Division), Alipore

Application No. .... of 20...

In the matter of:

An application filed for review of the order passed under Order 47, Rule 1 of the Code of Civil Procedure 1908 in Suit No. ... of 20...

And

In the matter of:

M/s. P. Co. Ltd., a company registered under Companies Act 1956 and carrying on business at .... Alipore Road, Kolkata.

.... *Plaintiff-Petitioner*

versus

M/s. X. Co. Limited, a company registered under the Companies Act, 1956 and carrying on business at .... Alipore Road, Kolkata.

.... *Defendant-Respondent*

The humble petition of M/s. P. Co. Ltd., plaintiff-petitioner above-named most respectfully sheweth:

1. Your petitioner filed the above suit No. ... of 20... against the defendant in this Learned Court and obtained a Judgment and Decree in its favour on 5th January 20....

2. So far as the petitioner has been able to ascertain, there has been no appeal filed against the said Judgment and Decree in the said Suit.

3. Your petitioner, being aggrieved by the said Judgment and Decree dated 5th January 20... hereby prays for review of the said Judgment and Decree on, *inter alia*, the following.

GROUNDS

I. For that there has been discovery of new and important matters of evidence which were not within the due knowledge of your petitioner and could not be produced at the time of hearing of the suit upto the time the said Judgment and Decree was passed in spite of best efforts and exercise of due diligence thereof.

II. For that there are some mistakes as also errors apparent on the face of the records.

III. For that there are other sufficient causes for reviewing the said Decree and Judgment dated 5th January 20....

4. In the above context, your petitioner has affirmed an affidavit supporting the above statements and contentions which is annexed hereto.

In view of the facts stated above, your petitioner prays that this learned Court would be graciously pleased to:

(*a*) Set aside the said Order and Judgment dated 5th January 20....

(*b*) To re-hear the said suit on the basis of the grounds set forth above.

(*c*) To make such other and further order or orders as this learned Court may deem fit and proper to afford complete relief to your petitioner.

And for this act of kindness your petitioner, as in duty bound shall ever pray.

Verification

Affidavit

Money Suit

324. Suit for money lent

In the Court of the Civil Judge (Junior Division), at ....

Money Suit No. .... of 20..........

Manu Bhai Patel, carrying on business in the trade name of 'Basanti & Co.' at the ......

.... *Plaintiff*

versus

1. Roy & Dutta Constructions, a partnership firm at ....
2. "A" son of Sri "B" Partner of M/s. Roy & Dutta Construction, residing at ....

.... *Defendants*

Suit for recovery of loan

Valued at ₹ ....

The above-named plaintiff states as follows:

1. That the plaintiff is the sole proprietor of and carried on a business under the trade name "Basanti & Company" with its registered office at .... The defendant No. 1 firm and one of its partners Sri "A" are known to the plaintiff for some time past and enjoyed reliance of the plaintiff as such.

2. That on the .... Sri A approached the plaintiff at the latter's *guddee* at .... and requested the plaintiff to advance to defendant No. 1 a loan of ₹ .... (Rupees.............) only to help the firm tide over their financial crisis touching execution of a contract work then in hand. The said Sri A .... also proposed that he would immediately issue a post-dated cheque in favour of the plaintiff covering the intended loan which the plaintiff could negotiate any time after three months from date when the defendant firm would have sufficient money to their credit in the bank.

3. That the plaintiff because of his old acquaintance with the defendant firm and with Sri A in particular, a partner of the firm placed his reliance on him and advanced on .... a sum of ₹ .... as accommodation loan from the fund of .... company to the defendant firm. That on .... the said Sri "A" had then issued on behalf of M/s .... a cheque No. .... dated .... for ₹ .... in favour of the plaintiff drawn on the State Bank of India .... and requested the plaintiff to present the cheque to the bank any time after three months from the date of above transaction.

4. That in the first week of .... the plaintiff came to learn on enquiry from the bank concerned that the defendant firm had no deposit to their credit to cover the money in the said cheque. The plaintiff informed their position to the defendant firm orally when the defendant firm pleaded their inability and requested the plaintiff to present the said cheque any time in .... when he could encash the cheque.

5. That the plaintiff endorsed cheque in favour of his bearer Sri. .... who presented the cheque to the bank on .... and came to learn that the payment was stopped by the drawer. An Objection Memo was issued by the bank on ....

6. That the plaintiff had thereafter intimated the position to the defendant firm and to Sri A and requested them to clear off the debt but to no result.

7. That the plaintiff had advanced the said loan of ₹ .... from his concern Basanti & Co. and the said transaction is recorded in Rokar and ledger of the said concern. The plaintiff craves leave of the court to submit before the court the said cheque No. .... dated ...., the Objection Memo, A/C Khatas of the plaintiff showing relevant transactions.

8. That the plaintiff is entitled to recover from the defendant the said sum of ₹ ....

9. That the plaintiff is not a money lender and the above loan was an accommodation loan. The plaintiff does not claim any interest for the loan.

10. That the cause of action for this suit arose on .... at .... town within the jurisdiction of this court when the loan was advanced.

11. That for the purpose of jurisdiction and court-fees the suit is valued at ₹ .... and court-fees of ₹ .... is paid.

The plaintiff therefore prays:

(*a*) For a decree for ₹ .... against the defendant;

(*b*) Costs.

Verification

Affidavit

NOTE: Limitation— (*i*) Three years from date of loan—Arts. 19, 20.
(*ii*) If money was repayable at specified time—Art. 113.
(*iii*) If money was lent by cheque—Art. 20.

325. Suit for money paid by the plaintiff payable by the defendant

In the Court of .... at ....

Suit No. .... of 20 ....

(Set out cause title)

The plaintiff states as follows:

1. That one A.B. got attached the house premises of the plaintiff on .... through process of the Court of Civil Judge (Junior Division) at .... in Money Execution Case No. .... of 20......... brought by A.B. against the defendant.

2. That at the material time, the defendant was a tenant in the plaintiff's house premises and he was not the owner of the same. The defendant was away at Kolkata. On being informed he requested the plaintiff to meet the decretal dues with promise to repay the money on his arrival. In any case, to avoid disgrace and on the defendant's request the plaintiff paid unto the said court on .... the entire decretal amount together with costs amounting to ₹ .... which was payable by the defendant and by such payment got the house premises released from attachment.

3. That the defendant is liable to pay to the plaintiff the said sum of ₹ .... together with costs of the suit.

4. The plaintiff requested the defendant first orally on .... 20 .... and then by a letter dated .... 20 .... (received by him on .... 20..........) to pay the amount due by .... 20 .... but the defendant has refused to pay.

5. That the cause of action for this suit arose on .... when payment was made by the plaintiff at .... within the jurisdiction of this court.

The plaintiff claims:

₹ .... together with costs of suit as admissible.

Verification

Affidavit

NOTES: 1. The plaintiff shall plead (*i*) payment of money which stood payable by the defendant; (*ii*) defendant's request to pay and his promise to repay.—See ss. 69, 70 of the Indian Contract Act.

2. Limitation—three years from the date of payment by the plaintiff (old Art. 61). Article 23 of the Limitation Act 1963.

3. Unjust enrichment—s. 69 of the Contract Act–AIR 1992 SC 645.

4. Suit for contribution—the right and duty of contribution is founded on doctrine of equity and does not depend upon contract–AIR 1938 PC 169. Section 69 of the Contract Act does not apply to contribution suits—AIR 1934 Cal 709.

326. Suit for recovery of money for a consideration which failed

In the Court of Small Causes Judge at ....

S.C.C. No. .... of 20 ....

(Set out cause title)

The plaintiff states as follows:

1. That the plaintiff had on. .... made over to the defendant a sum of ₹ .... to escort on his way back the plaintiff's wife then at Delhi and to meet air passage and incidentals of his wife by the said money.

2. That the plaintiff's wife fell sick and she postponed her journey. Accordingly the plaintiff asked the defendant not to book her passage. The defendant replied in the affirmative.

3. That the said sum of ₹ .... is lying with the defendant. Despite requests of the plaintiff, the defendant did not return the money.

4. That the cause of action for this suit arose on .... when the plaintiff paid the money to the defendant at .... within the jurisdiction of this court.

5. That for the purpose of jurisdiction and court-fees, the suit is valued at ₹ .... and *ad valorem* court-fees are paid thereon.

The plaintiff, therefore, prays:

A decree of ₹ .... only and costs of the suit.

Verification

Affidavit

NOTE: For money paid upon an existing consideration which afterwards fails limitation is three years under Art. 47 of the Limitation Act, calculated from the date of failure—see AIR 1962 Raj 83.

327. Suit for money paid under a mistake of fact

In the Court of .... at ....

Suit No. .... of 20 ....

(Set out cause title)

The above-named plaintiff states as follows:

1. That the plaintiff and his brother Sri A.B., jointly executed a promissory note on .... in favour of the defendant agreeing to pay to him a sum of ₹ .... with interest at 10% per annum on demand.

2. That the plaintiff's brother, the said A.B., had liquidated the loan with interest on .... but the fact was not intimated by the said A.B. in time.

3. That the plaintiff quite ignorant of the fact, paid to the defendant once again on .... a sum of ₹ .... inclusive of interest which the defendant accepted under a mistake of fact.

4. That the plaintiff wrote to his brother A.B. of such payment when in reply he intimated that already he had met the dues. The defendant has had and received the said sum to his own use.

5. The plaintiff, thereupon, informed the defendant accordingly and requested him to return the amount paid as mistake by the plaintiff on .... 20 .... but the defendant has not heeded to the request.

6. That the cause of action for this suit arose on .... when the plaintiff paid ₹ .... to the defendant at .... within the jurisdiction of this court.

7. That for the purpose of jurisdiction and court-fees the suit is valued at ₹ ....

The plaintiff claims:

A decree for ₹ .... with interest @ 10% per annum till the date of payment.

Verification

Affidavit

NOTES: 1. See s. 72 of the Contract Act. Right to relief under s. 72 extends to money paid under mistake thinking that it was due when in fact it was not due—AIR 1971 MP 162. Money paid under a mistake induced by fraud of third party may be recovered—AIR 1963 All 450.

2. For recovery of payment made under mistake of law—AIR 1970 SC 898. Suit for refund of tax illegally collected is maintainable—AIR 1970 SC 1002.

3. It is not correct to say that every sum paid under mistake is recoverable no matter what the circumstance may be. Plaintiff may be disentitled by estoppel—AIR 1949 PC 297; AIR 1978 Cal 169.

4. Excess amount paid beyond terms of contract—This amounts to mistake within meaning of s. 72. Payment made is repayable—*Bd. of Trustees of the Cochin Port Trust* v *Ashok Leyland* AIR 1992 Ker 1; AIR 1990 Bom 239.

5 Mistake relates not only to fact but also to mistake of law. Money paid under a mistake of law is as much recoverable as money paid under a mistake of fact (*Sibaprasad's* case AIR 1949 PC 297). Terminal tax paid to the Municipality under mistake of law—comes within s. 72 of the Contract Act. Court is right in granting relief of refund—*Nagar Mahapalika, Kanpur* v *Sri Ram Mahadeo* AIR 1990 SC 274.

6. Payment of rent in excess. Payment not shown to have been made under mistake, s. 72 does not apply—AIR 1970 SC 1490.

328. Suit for money obtained by fraud

In the Court of .... at ....

Suit No. .... of 20 ....

(Set out cause title)

The plaintiff above-named states as follows:

1. That on seeking of the defendant on .... the plaintiff had advanced to the defendant a sum of ₹ .... as loan. On occasion of advancing the loan the defendant wanted to pledge a wrist-watch which he was then wearing representing that the same belonged to him and thus induced the plaintiff to advance the loan.

2. That on such representation of the defendant, the plaintiff advanced to the defendant a loan of ₹ .... (₹ ....) and took the said wrist-watch from the defendant as a security against the loan.

3. That on .... A.B., defendant's brother, claimed the wrist-watch as the same belonged to him. On enquiry the plaintiff came to know that the watch really belonged to the said A.B. and that the defendant made a false representation.

The plaintiff claims:

(*i*) ₹ .... with interest at 10% per annum till the date of realisation;

(*ii*) Costs.

Verification

Affidavit

329. Suit for money obtained by coercion

(See Form No. 328 *ante*)

NOTE: Coercion used in s. 72 of the Contract Act merely means payment under compulsion which the defendant has no right to claim—65 IC 517; AIR 1969 Mys 230; AIR 1970 Guj 59.

330. Suit for refund of money overpaid

In the Court of .... at ....

Suit No. .... of 20 ....

(Set out cause title)

The plaintiff states as follows:

1. That the plaintiff had executed on .... an instalment bond for ₹ .... in favour of the defendant.

2. That the plaintiff paid the last instalment under, the said bond, of ₹ .... on .... and was granted by the defendant a receipt therefor. It appears that an excess sum of ₹ .... was paid on .... as the last instalment due was for ₹ .... only.

(State particulars how overpayment was caused).

3. That the plaintiff detected the said overpayment on .... and requested the defendant to refund the said sum of ₹ ...., but the defendant denied over payment and refused to pay.

4. That the cause of action for this suit arose on .... at .... within the jurisdiction of this court.

5. That for the purpose of jurisdiction and court-fees the suit is valued at ₹ .... and *ad valorem* court-fees are paid thereon.

The plaintiff claims:

(*i*) A decree for ₹ .... only.

(*ii*) Costs.

Verification

Affidavit

331. Suit on a handnote

In the Court of the Small Causes Judge at ....

S.C.C. No. .... of 20 ....

Gopilal Gupta, son of late Ram Charit Gupta of Bhawaniganj Bazar, Cooch Behar town, P.S. Kotwali, District–Cooch Behar.

.... *Plaintiff*

versus

A.B. son of late .... by occupation–service residing at Cooch Behar town, P.S. Kotwali, District–Cooch Behar.

.... *Defendant*

Suit on a handnote

Valued at ₹ ....

The plaintiff states as under:

1. That the defendant borrowed from the plaintiff a sum of ₹ .... on .... by executing a handnote and agreed to pay back on demand the principal amount together with interest @ 10% per annum.

The said handnote is filed herewith and may be treated as a part of the plaint.

2. That the defendant did not pay any money in spite of repeated demands made by the plaintiff in that behalf (or, the defendant, on demand, paid a sum of ₹ .... on .... and a sum of ₹ .... is still due from the defendant).

3. A notice of demand dated .... was sent by the plaintiff to the defendant through the plaintiff's lawyer by registered post with A/D. The defendant received the notice on .... but did not meet the demand of the plaintiff.

4. That the plaintiff is not a money lender. The said loan is an accommodation loan. The plaintiff does not claim interest.

(Or, that the plaintiff is entitled to recover from the defendant the said sum of ₹ .... together with interest @ 10% per annum over the said sum till realisation).

5. The cause of action for this suit arose on .... when the defendant executed the handnote at .... within the jurisdiction of this court.

6. That for the purpose of jurisdiction and court-fees, the suit is valued at ₹ .... and *ad valorem* court-fees are paid thereon.

The plaintiff, therefore, prays:

(*a*) For a judgment and decree for ₹ ....

(*b*) Costs.

(*c*) Such other relief as law and equity would allow.

Verification

Affidavit

NOTES: 1. Limitation is three years when the demand is made—*vide* Art. 21 of the Limitation Act 1963.

2. N. I. Act (s. 118)—Suit based on promissory note. Execution proved. Presumption as to consideration arises. Burden to prove lack of consideration is on the defendant—*Marimuthu Kounder* v *Radha Krishna* AIR 1991 Ker 39.

3. Several joint promisors. Consideration paid to only one. Other promisors are equally liable to pay the amount—*Andhra Bank* v *Anathnath Goel* AIR 1991 AP 245.

4. When the owner of a single right as the holder of a promissory note dies and his right passes by devolution to his heirs, all of them must join in a suit to enforce that entire right as a whole. If any of them refuses to join as plaintiff, he must be impleaded as a defendant—AIR 1971 MP 133.

332. Suit against a Surety on a Guarantee of Debt

In the Court of .... at ....

Money Suit No. .... of 20 ....

(Set out cause title)

The plaintiff states:

1. That on or about .... one A.B. approached the plaintiff for a loan of ₹ .... on a promissory note.

2. That the defendant has been known to the plaintiff for long. On the occasion, the defendant wrote a letter to the plaintiff whereby he agreed that if the plaintiff would lend ₹ .... to said A.B. on a promissory note (bearing interest at 18% per annum) he would be responsible to the plaintiff for the repayment of the loan with interest.

3. The plaintiff in good faith had lent ₹ .... to said A.B. on a promissory note dated .... repayable on demand with interest at 6% per annum.

4. That neither A.B. nor the defendant as surety has paid any part of the sum due on the said promissory note in spite of demands both oral and written.

5. That the plaintiff is entitled to recover from the defendant a sum of ₹ .... together with interest as accrued till realisation.

6. That the cause of action for this suit arose on .... at .... within the jurisdiction of this court first on .... when demand was made said A.B. and on .... when the defendant was requested by a letter to satisfy the claim.

PARTICULARS OF CLAIM

Principal	₹ ....
Interest from .... to .... @ 18% per annum	₹ ....
Net amount due	₹ ....

The plaintiff claims—

(*i*) ₹ ....

(*ii*) Costs.

Verification

Affidavit

MORTGAGE SUIT

333. Suit by a mortgagee under a simple mortgage

(Based on personal covenant to pay)

In the Court of .... at ....

Suit No. .... of 20 ....

(Set out cause title)

The plaintiff states as follows:

1. That the defendant took a loan of ₹ .... from the plaintiff on .... and executed the same day a simple mortgage (registered on ....) in favour of the plaintiff in respect of his immovable properties described in Schedule 'A' below.

2. That the defendant by terms in the said mortgage covenanted to pay personally the mortgage money on .... together with interest thereon at the rate of .... per cent. per annum.

3. That the defendant did not pay the plaintiff his dues under the mortgage.

4. That the plaintiff is entitled to recover from the defendant a sum of ₹ .... together with interest of ₹ ....

5. Cause of action.

6. Suit valuation.

The plaintiff, therefore, claims, a decree for ₹ ....

SCHEDULE 'A'

Verification

Affidavit

NOTES: 1. A mortgagee can sue the mortgagor on the basis of the covenant. He is not required to sue for sale of martgaged property. He is, of course, well entitled to bring a fresh suit for sale thereof.
Order 2, r. 2 will not be a bar—see Order 34, r. 14 of CPC.

2. Limitation—three years *vide* Art. 55 of the Limitation Act 1963 from the date following the due date.

334. Suit by a mortgagor for redemption

In the Court of .... at ....

Suit No. .... of 20 ....

(Set out cause title)

The plaintiff states as follows:

1. That the plaintiff had borrowed from the defendant on .... a sum of ₹ .... and mortgaged his properties to the defendant by executing a deed of mortgage (registered) the same day.

2. That particulars of the said mortgage are:

(*a*) Amount with date—

(*b*) Rate of interest—

(*c*) Due date—

(*d*) Properties mortgaged—

3. That the said mortgage deed provided *inter alia:*

(*a*) that the plaintiff would deliver possession of the said properties to the defendant on the date of mortgage or on the following day;

(*b*) that the defendant would cultivate the lands either by himself or by his bargadars and would appropriate to himself the income from produce thereof in satisfaction of his dues under the mortgage after meeting costs incidental to cultivation;

(*c*) that the mortgagee would submit an account of income from mortgaged properties when called upon to do so;

(*d*) that the mortgagor would be competent to redeem at any time upon payment of balance to the mortgagee, if any.

4. That the plaintiff had delivered possession of the mortgaged property to the defendant on .... and the defendant is in possession thereof.

The plaintiff, therefore, prays:

(*a*) For a judgment and decree—

(*i*) to redeem the mortgaged property,

(*ii*) to get reconveyance and possession of the mortgaged property,

(*iii*) for a correct account of the income for the material period.

(*b*) Costs.

(*c*) Further and other reliefs.

Verification

Affidavit

NOTES: 1. Mortgagee and transferees from mortgagee can be sued for reliefs.

2. In a suit for recovery of mortgage debt in usufructuary mortgage—the suit is not maintainable in the absence of personal covenant to pay—see s. 58 of the T.P. Act—AIR 1968 Assam 10.

3. Limitation to redeem or recover possession of immovable property mortgaged is 30 years under Art. 61(*a*) of the Limitation Act 1963, from when the right to redeem or to recover possession accrues.

4. Valuation in a suit for redemption is the amount due on the mortgage—52 CWN 132.

5. The mortgagor is not required to make a tender of the amount due under the mortgage before filing a suit for redemption. If he makes such a tender then he gets entitled to certain benefits under the provisions of ss. 83 and 84 of the T.P. Act. But there is nothing in law which compels a mortgagor

to tender the amount due under the mortgage before filing a suit—*Abdur Rahim* v *Vithaldas* AIR 1981 Bom 58.

335. Suit by a mortgagee for sale or foreclosure

(Mortgage by way of conditional sale)

In the Court of .... at ....

Suit No. .... of 20 ....

(Set out cause title)

The plaintiff states as follows:

1. That the defendant had executed a mortgage by way of conditional sale in favour of the plaintiff on .... (registered on ....) and ostensibly sold the properties described in Schedule 'A' appended below for a consideration of ₹ .... paid by the plaintiff the same day.

2. That on the occasion of execution of the mortgage, the defendant agreed that he would pay back the principal sum with interest at 8% per annum till the date of payment whereupon the sale of the properties in Schedule. 'A' shall become void and that, in default of payment of the principal sum together with interest as aforesaid, the sale shall become absolute.

3. That the defendant failed to meet the dues of the plaintiff under the mortgage.

4. That the plaintiff's claim has been stated in Schedule 'B' below.

5. That the cause of action for the suit arose on .... when the money secured by the mortgage fell due at .... within the jurisdiction of this court.

6. Suit valuation.

The plaintiff claims for a judgment and decree under Or. 34, r. 2 of the Code of Civil Procedure in Form No. 3A in Appendix D to the 1st Schedule of the Code.

SCHEDULE 'A'

SCHEDULE 'B'

Verification

Affidavit

NOTES:
1. See s. 67 of the T.P. Act.
2. See s. 58(*c*) of the T.P. Act 1882 for definition of a mortgage by conditional sale. Also see AIR 1964 Pat 193.
3. Reliefs to be prayed—See Or. 34, r. 2. Forms 3 & 3A of the Appendix D of the Code.
4. For sale out and with a condition of re-purchase—See *Nana Tukaran* v *Sonabai* AIR 1982 Bom 437; AIR 1962 Pat 53.
5. For foreclosure by a mortgagee limitation is 30 years from when money secured by the mortgage became due under Art. 63(*a*) of the Limitation Act 1963.

336. Suit by a mortgagee under an equitable mortgage for charge and dues

In the Court of .... at ....

Suit No. .... of 20 ....

(Set out cause title)

The plaintiff states as follows:

1. That the defendant had borrowed from the plaintiff on .... a sum of ₹ .... and executed a promissory note on the same day for the said sum agreeing to repay the said sum with interest @ 10% per annum till the date of payment.

2. That to create a security for payment of the said loan with interest, the defendant had deposited with the plaintiffs the same day his title deeds, described below in Schedule 'A'.

3. That the defendant failed to pay the plaintiff the latter's dues under the pronote in spite of repeated requests in writing made in that behalf.

4. That the plaintiff's claim under the promissory note is stated in Schedule 'B' below.

5. That the cause of action for this suit arose on .... at .... within the jurisdiction of this court.

6. Suit valuation.

The plaintiff, therefore, prays:

(*a*) For a decree declaring that properties mentioned in the title deeds, in Schedule 'A', are charged with the payment of the loan under the promissory note.

(*b*) For a decree under Or. XXXIV, r. 4 of CPC in Form No. 5A in Appendix D of the 1st Schedule of the Code.

(*c*) Costs.

(*d*) Further reliefs as may be allowed in law and equity.

SCHEDULE 'A'

(State here particulars of title deeds and properties)

SCHEDULE 'B'

(State here particulars of claim)

Verification

Affidavit

NOTES: 1. Title deed mentioning only the land. Mortgage would operate both on the land and the building standing thereon—AIR 1978 AP 257.

2. Three requisites for an equitable mortgage are—(*i*) debt; (*ii*) deposit of title-deeds and (*iii*) an intention that the title deeds so deposited shall be security for the debt—AIR 1981 Cal 404.

3. For definition of an equitable mortgage—see s. 68(*f*) of the TP Act 1882.

337. Suit by a mortgagee bank against mortgagor with facilities to over-draw against an account in the bank

In the Court of .... at ....

Suit No. .... of 20 ....

(Set out cause title)

The above-named plaintiff states as follows:

1. That the plaintiff was and is a Banking Institution at .... and is a limited company with its registered office at .... P.S. .... District ....

2. That defendant No. 1 had a Current Account No. ..... with the plaintiff. The said defendant No. 1 intended to overdraw his said account for a sum of ₹ .... (₹ ....) only, mortgaging or keeping as security his properties against the loan prayed for.

3. That the Board of Directors of the plaintiff bank recommended overdrawal of ₹ .... (₹ ....) only and in accordance with the Resolution No. .... in the meeting dated .... of the Board of Directors of the plaintiff bank dated .... the defendant No. 1 was required to execute an agreement for overdrawing his said Current Account No. .... to the extent of ₹ .... on his agreeing to pay interest thereon at the rate of 9% per annum with six monthly rests. Defendant No. 1 executed the said- agreement on ....

4. That defendant No. 1 was further required to furnish security for the repayment of the said overdrawn account with interest at the agreed rate. Accordingly, defendant No. 1 as security for repayment of the balance of the overdraft account, that might be outstanding immediately on the termination of the said agreement with stipulated interest thereon and/or for the entire overdraft of ₹ .... together with interest thereon at the stipulated rate, mortgaged his property in Schedule 'A' hereunder by executing a mortgage deed dated .... in favour of the plaintiff-bank.

The said mortgage deed is filed herewith and may be treated as a part of the plaint.

5. That the said mortgage dated .... executed by defendant No. 1 is duly registered in the office of the Registrar of Companies, West Bengal and the plaintiff has been granted a Certificate of Registration. The plaintiff craves leave of the court to file the same in the court at the time of trial.

6. That a sum of ₹ .... is due to the plaintiff from defendant No. 1 under the said mortgage as per account is Schedule 'B' below which covers the principal together with interest up to. .... (date of filing the suit).

7. That the plaintiff has served a notice dated .... on defendant No. 1 by registered post with A/D through their lawyer Sri .... Advocate demanding the overdrawn amount with interest as admissible till the date of payment. The notice was received by defendant No. 1 on .... but he did not pay the dues.

8. That the plaintiff has learnt that defendant No. 1 has transferred the property in Schedule 'A' to defendant No. 2 by a registered deed dated ....

9. That the plaintiff is entitled to recover the dues in Schedule 'B' from the defendants.

10. That the cause of action for this suit arose on .... when the mortgage was executed by defendant No. 1 at. .... within the jurisdiction of this court.

11. That for the purpose of jurisdiction and court-fees the suit is valued at ₹ .... and *ad valorem* court-fees of ₹ .... are paid thereon.

The plaintiff, therefore, prays:

(*a*) Decree for ₹ .... against defendant No. 1 and, if it is found that defendant No. 2 has purchased the mortgaged property, then in the alternative, against defendant No. 2;

(*b*) Interim interest and interest on judgment;

(*c*) Decree in Form No. 5 or 5A of Appendix 'D' to the Code of Civil Procedure or in such other form as this court may deem fit and proper.

(*d*) Receiver.

(*e*) Injunction restraining the defendants from disposal of the property in Schedule 'A' disposal of the suit.

(f) Costs.

(g) Further and other reliefs.

SCHEDULE 'A'

(State particulars of the property mortgaged)

SCHEDULE 'B'

Principal loan	₹ ....
Interest due @ 9% per annum	₹ ....
	₹ ....

(In words)

Verification

Affidavit

NOTE: Copies of statements of accounts can be relied on to prove the bank's demands when payment of money by the bank is unchallenged and corroborated by other evidence—AIR 1978 NOC 171 (Cal).

338. Suit by a prior mortgagee against a mortgagor and a puisne mortgagee

In the Court of .... at ....

Suit No. .... of 20 ....

(Set out cause title)

The plaintiff states as follows:

1. That defendant No. 1 took a loan of ₹ .... from the plaintiff on .... and executed a deed of mortgage on the same day (registered on) .... in favour of the plaintiff in respect of the properties of defendant No. 1, described in Schedule 'A' below.

2. That defendant No. 1 in the said mortgage agreed to repay the loan within five years from the date of execution of the mortgage with interest at 8% per annum.

3. That defendant No. 1, the plaintiff has learnt, has subsequently executed another mortgage in respect of the self-same properties in Schedule 'A' in favour of defendant No. 2 on ....

4. That defendant No. 1 did not pay up the dues under the mortgage dated .... and the plaintiff is entitled to recover from the defendants a sum of ₹ .... as per account in Schedule 'B' below.

5. That the cause of action arose on .... (date following expiry of the due date).

The plaintiff, therefore, prays:

(a) Decree under Or. 34, rr. 4, 7 of the CPC.

SCHEDULE 'A'

(Description of properties mortgaged)

SCHEDULE 'B'

(Dues of the plaintiff under the mortgage)

Verification

Affidavit

NOTES: 1. Limitation—12 years from due date—*vide* Art. 62 of the Limitation Act 1963.

2. Jurisdiction—Place where mortgaged property is situated.

339. Suit by a puisne mortgagee against a prior mortgagee and the mortgagor

In the Court of .... at ....

Suit No. .... of 20 ....

(Set out cause title)

The plaintiff states as follows:

1. That defendant No. 1 took a loan of ₹ .... from the plaintiff on .... and executed a deed of mortgage on the same day (registered on ....) in favour of the plaintiff in respect of the properties described in Schedule A appended below.

2. That defendant No. 1 agreed in the said mortgage to repay the loan within five years from the date of mortgage with interest at 8% per annum.

3. That the said mortgage to the plaintiff is subject to a prior mortgage in respect of the self-same properties in Schedule 'A' by defendant No. 1 in favour of defendant No. 2. The plaintiff states below particulars of the said prior mortgage.

Date of mortgage—

Amount with rate of interest—

Due date—

Properties mortgaged—same as in Schedule 'A' below.

4. That defendant No. 1 paid nothing to the plaintiff under the mortgage dated .... and as such a sum of ₹ .... as per account in Schedule 'B' below is due to the plaintiff from defendant No. 1.

5. Cause of action.

6. Suit valuation.

The plaintiff, therefore, prays:

(*a*) For a decree under Or. 34, rr. 4, 7 of the CPC.

SCHEDULE 'A'

(Description of properties mortgaged)

SCHEDULE 'B'

(Dues of the plaintiff under the mortgage)

Verification

Affidavit

NOTES: 1. Where there several mortgagees, all should join in the suit as plaintiffs. When any co-mortgagee does not join, he is to be made a defendant—AIR 1936 Pat 439.

Similarly, all mortgagors should be impleaded and when dead all of the heirs of a deceased mortgagor shall be impleaded as defendants.

2. When a puisne mortgagee is not made a party his rights are not affected.
3. Jurisdiction—where mortgaged property is situated.

340. Suit by mortgagee for foreclosure

In the Court of .... at ....

Suit No. .... of 20 ....

(Set out cause title)

The plaintiff states as follows:

1. By a registered mortgage by way of conditional sale, dated ...., the defendant, for the consideration of ₹ .... ostensibly sold certain immovable properties situate within the jurisdiction of this court (particularly described in Schedule 'A' hereto annexed) to the plaintiff on condition that in default of payment of the said principal sum with interest at 6 *per cent per annum* and all costs and charges and expenses properly incurred or to be properly incurred by the plaintiff in respect of his claim under the said mortgage together with interest thereon at the aforesaid rate, on ...., the sale should become absolute (or, on condition that on payment etc., the sale should become void, or the buyer should transfer the property to the seller, as the case may be).

2. The defendant has made default in payment.

PARTICULARS OF CLAIM:

Principal sum	...	...	₹ ....
Interest up to date of suit	...	...	₹ ....
Costs, charges and expenses properly incurred in respect of the mortgage security together with interest thereon at the rate aforesaid as per particulars set out in Schedule 'B' hereto annexed	...	...	₹ ....
		Total	₹ ....

The plaintiff claims—

Decree under Or. 34, r. 2 of the Code of Civil Procedure in Form No. 3A in Appendix D to the First Schedule thereto.

SCHEDULE 'A'

SCHEDULE 'B'

Verification

Affidavit

341. Written statement to the suit for foreclosure of mortgaged property

In the Court of Civil Judge (Senior) Division at ....

Suit No. .... of 20 ....

Suit for foreclosure of a mortgage under section .... Order 34 of the Code of Civil Procedure 1908 valued at ₹ ....

(Set out cause title)

The defendant states as follows:

1. The suit is not maintainable in the facts and circumstances of the case and the position in law, justice and equity.

2. Save and except what are matters of record, this defendant does not admit the allegations and contentions in paragraph 1 of the plaint.

3. Save and except what will appear from the Mortgage Deed, this defendant does not make any admission in respect of the statements contained in paragraph 2 of the plaint.

4. With reference to paragraph 3 of the plaint, save and except what will appear from the Register of Mortgage, I make no admission in respect of the assertion of the plaintiff.

5. With reference to paragraph 4 of the plaint, the defendant denies that he has not paid any interest or principal of the loan. The defendant states that on several occasions the defendant offered to pay the interest as also a portion of the principal amount, but for reasons best known to the plaintiff, the plaintiff refused to accept the same.

6. With reference to paragraph 5 of the plaint, this defendant denies the correctness and validity of the purported demand letter dated ....

7. With reference to paragraph 6 of the plaint, the defendant states that it is not correct that the defendant has not offered to pay any portion of the principal amount or interest.

8. The defendant states that the plaintiff in the past has refused to co-operate with the defendant and refused to accept small part-payments and as such the mortgage money could not be paid at least in part. Now the defendant has arranged funds and he is in a position to liquidate the plaintiff's principal amount of loan with interest at the agreed rate thereon. The defendant states that this learned court will be pleased to determine the amount payable by the defendant for redemption of the mortgage and give 3 (three) months' time to the defendant to deposit the said amount in court for redemption of the said mortgage.

9. With reference to paragraph 7 of the plaint, the defendant denies that the defendant is not entitled to redeem the mortgaged property. In the facts and circumstances of the case as stated hereinabove, the defendant is entitled to and the learned court will allow to redeem the mortgaged property on payment of the amount to be fixed by this learned court.

10. With reference to paragraph 8 of the plaint, the defendant states that in view of the defendant's offer to pay by instalments the plaintiff has no cause of action for him to sue. The notice of demand was wrongful and invalid. No cause of action for this suit arose at the place where the defendant resides or where the mortgaged property is situated and inasmuch as the defendant offered to pay the mortgage debts by instalments.

11. The submissions of the plaintiff in paragraph 9 of the plaint is disputed. In view of the statements made hereinabove, the plaintiff has no cause of action for this suit.

12. With reference to paragraph 10 of the plaint, the defendant denies and disputes the allegations.

13. In view of the aforesaid, the defendant states that the plaintiff is not entitled to any of the prayers made in the plaint.

14. The defendant states that the defendant be given leave to redeem the mortgaged property on payment of the principal amount with interest and direction be given on the plaintiff to execute the necessary documents in relation thereto.

15. Directions be given to submit a report on the compliance of the order of this learned court, that is, on completion of the redemption of the mortgaged property.

Verification

Affidavit

NOTE: Separate Affidavit as required under s. 26(2) and Or. 6, r. 15(4) of the Code of Civil Procedure 1908 also is to be filed.

342. Suit by mortgagor for redemption of a usufructuary mortgage

In the Court of .... at ....

Suit No. .... of 20 ....

(Set out cause title)

The plaintiff states as follows:

1. The plaintiff is the mortgagor of lands of which the defendant is the usufructuary mortgagee. The said lands are situate within (or partly within and partly outside) the local limits of the jurisdiction of this court.

2. The following are the particulars of the said mortgage executed on ....

3. The mortgage deed *inter alia* provided—

(*a*) The mortgagee would realise and receive the rents and profits of the mortgaged property and, after defraying therefrom the costs and expenses, of and incidental to management, credit the net income thereof towards his dues on the said mortgage and submit an account of his dealings with the income of the said properties to the plaintiff whenever called upon in writing to do so.

(*b*) The mortgagor would be entitled to redeem at any time on payment of the entire balance for the time being remaining due.

4. The defendant took possession of the mortgaged properties on .... and has remained in possession thereof.

5. The defendant submitted to the plaintiff an account unsupported by vouchers on .... showing that the sum of ₹ .... that is, ₹ .... for principal and ₹ .... for interest was due on the said mortgage. The plaintiff did not accept the correctness of the said account, and pending examination of the accounts by him, and, without prejudice, he, on the same day, tendered to the defendant at his aforesaid place of residence the said sums, but the defendant refused to accept the same. The plaintiff brings the said sum into court for redemption of the mortgage.

The plaintiff claims—

1. To redeem the said property and to have the same reconveyed to him and have possession thereof.
2. ₹ .... as mesne profits from ...., the date of the tender, and further mesne profits until possession is delivered.
3. An account of the sums received and disbursements made by the defendant as mortgagee, and payment of the surplus amount to be found due to the plaintiff upon the taking of such account together with interest thereon at 6 *per cent per annum* from ....

Verification

Affidavit

343. Suit by equitable mortgagee for declaration of charge and sale

In the Court of .... at ....

Suit No. .... of 20 ....

(Set out cause title)

The plaintiff states as follows:

1. On .... 20......, having received ₹ .... as loan from the plaintiff the defendant executed a Promissory Note for ₹ .... in favour of the plaintiff agreeing to repay the said sum on .... with interest at 9 *per cent per annum.*

2. On the same day, subsequent to the said loan, the defendant deposited with the plaintiff at ...., several documents of title specified in the schedule hereto with intent to create a security on the property to which the same relate for the payment of the said loan to the plaintiff.

3. The defendant has not made any payment towards the said loan, although requested on several occasions.

Particulars of claim:

The plaintiff claims—

(*i*) A declaration that the property to which the said documents of title are charged with the payment of the said loan to the plaintiff.

(*ii*) Decree under Or. 34, r. 4 of the Code of Civil Procedure in Form No. 5A in Appendix D to the First Schedule thereto.

SCHEDULE

Verification

Affidavit

344. Suit by subrogate for enforcement of the rights of the mortgagee whose mortgage has been redeemed

In the Court of .... at ....

Suit No. .... of 20 ....

(Set out cause title)

The plaintiff states as follows:

1. By a mortgage deed, dated .... 20....., the defendant mortgaged certain immovable properties, situate within (or partly within and partly outside) the local limits of the jurisdiction of the court hereinafter called the 'said property,' to one A.B. The following are the particulars of the said mortgage.

2. By a registered instrument, dated .... made between the plaintiff and the defendant, the defendant agreed that the plaintiff would be subrogated to the rights of A.B. on payment of the amount due under the said mortgage.

3. On .... 20......, the plaintiff paid ₹ .... to A.B., in full satisfaction of his claim under the said mortgage.

Particulars of claim

The plaintiff claims—

(1) A declaration that he is the subrogate of the rights of A.B. under the said mortgage.

(2) Decree under Or. 34, r. 4 of the Code of Civil Procedure in Form No. 5A in Appendix D to the First Schedule thereto.

Verification

Affidavit

NEGOTIABLE INSTRUMENTS

A. Bills of Exchange (Inland)

345. Suit by an endorsee of a Bill of Exchange against drawer, acceptor and Indorser

In the Court of .... at ....

Suit No. .... of 20 ....

(Set out cause title)

The plaintiff states as follows:

1. That defendant No. 1 drew a Bill of Exchange on .... for ₹ .... upon defendant No. 2 requiring the latter to pay to the order of defendant No. 3 the said sum of ₹ .... 30 days after date.

2. That defendant No. 2 accepted the Bill of Exchange.

3. That defendant No. 3 endorsed the Bill in favour of the plaintiff on ....

4. That the plaintiff had duly presented the said Bill for payment to defendant No. 2, on .... but the same was dishonoured.

5. That the plaintiff has served a notice of dishonour dated .... of the said Bill on each of the defendants by registered post with A/D as contemplated in s. 93 of the Negotiable Instruments Act 1881.

6. That the plaintiff is entitled to recover a sum of ₹ .... as per account below.

7. Cause of action (on .... on expiry of time fixed for payment).

8. Suit-valuation.

The plaintiff, therefore, prays for:

(*i*) A decree of ₹ ....

(*ii*) Interest at the rate of ....% per annum till payment.

Account of claim

Principal	...	₹ ....
Interest @ 6% per annum	...	₹ ....
Total	...	₹ ....

Verification

Affidavit

NOTES: 1. For liability of the drawer—See s. 30.
For liability of the endorser—See s. 35 of the Negotiable Instruments Act 1881.
2. Liability of the drawer and the endorser arises only on service of notice of dishonour under s. 93 unless excepted under s. 98 of the Act.
3. For liability of the endorser—See AIR 1933 Mad 61.
4. In a suit by an endorsee of an instrument the principal dies pending suit—*Held,* suit not affected—AIR 1969 Mad 83.
5. Limitation—In a suit on a Bill of Exchange

(*i*)	when the bill or note falls due	3 yrs. Art. 31
(*ii*)	when the bill is presented	3 yrs. Art. 32
(*iii*)	when the bill is presented at that place	3 yrs. Art. 33
(*iv*)	when the fixed time expires	3 yrs. Art. 34
(*v*)	when the date of the bill or note	3 yrs. Art. 35

6. A draft by branch of a bank on its head office is a Bill of Exchange—AIR 1956 Cal 615; AIR 1970 Cal 503.

346. Suit by a payee of a Bill of Exchange against drawer for non-acceptance

In the Court of .... at ....

Suit No. .... of 20 ....

(Set out cause title)

The above-named plaintiff states as follows:

1. That the defendant drew a Bill of Exchange on .... for ₹ .... upon one A.B., payable to the plaintiff 30 days after date.

2. That the plaintiff had presented the said Bill to the said A.B. on .... for acceptance. But the said Bill was dishonoured by its non-acceptance.

3. That the plaintiff has served on the defendant a notice dated .... by registered post with A/D of dishonour of the said Bill.

4. That the defendant has not paid the said Bill.

5. That the plaintiff's claim is stated in the Schedule below.

6. The cause of action arose on .... (the date of refusal to accept the Bill of Exchange) at .... within the jurisdiction of this court.

7. Suit-valuation.

The plaintiff claims

₹ ....

SCHEDULE

Account of claim

Principal	... ...	₹ ....
Add interest @ $6^1/_2$ per cent per annum till date of suit	... ...	₹ ....
	Total	₹ ....

Verification

Affidavit

NOTES: 1. See ss. 61, 75 of the Negotiable Instruments Act.
2. Dishonour by non-acceptance—See s. 91 of the Negotiable Instruments Act 1881.
3. Non-presentment—See ss. 61, 75, 75(*a*) of the Negotiable Instruments Act 1881.
4. Cause of action in a like case arises on the date of the refusal to accept the Bill of Exchange and limitation is three years from such date under Art. 40 of the Limitation Act 1963.

347. Suit by a payee of a Bill of Exchange for default of payment

In the Court of .... at ....

Suit No. .... of 20 ....

(Set out cause title)

The above-named plaintiff states as follows:

1. That the defendant drew a Bill of Exchange for ₹ .... on .... upon one A.B. payable to the plaintiff 45 days after date.

2. That the plaintiff presented the Bill to A.B. on .... for payment but the same was dishonoured.

3. That the defendant, on intimation, promised to pay to the plaintiff the said money but did not pay.

4. That the cause of action for this suit arose on .... (date when drawn) at .... within the jurisdiction of this court.

5. Suit-valuation.

The plaintiff, therefore, prays for a decree of ₹ .... as per account below.

Claim

Principal	... ...	₹ ....
Add interest @ 6% per annum till date of suit		₹ ....
		₹ ....

(In words ....)

Verification

Affidavit

NOTES: 1. See s. 98 when notice of dishonour may be dispensed with.
2. For protection under ss. 85, 85A—when available—See AIR 1970 Ker 74.

348. Suit by acceptor induced by fraud of drawer to accept bill, against drawer, for cancellation and delivery up of the bill

In the Court of .... at ....

Suit No. .... of 20 ....

(Set out cause title)

The plaintiff states as follows:

1. At all material times the defendant was the manager of the plaintiff's hardware business at ....

2. On .... 20.........., the plaintiff was induced by the fraud of the defendant to accept a bill of exchange hereinafter mentioned.

Particulars:

(*a*) By his letter dated .... 20....., the defendant represented to the plaintiff that he as the agent for the plaintiff had discharged a debt in respect of the said business due to one K.D., and by the said letter he requested the plaintiff to accept the enclosed bill of exchange for ₹......... dated .... drawn by himself upon the plaintiff and payable on demand.

(*b*) Relying upon the said representation and induced thereby the plaintiff accepted the said bill of exchange on .... and sent it to the defendant by post.

(*c*) On .... 20.........., the plaintiff discovered that the defendant did not discharge the alleged or any debt as the agent for the plaintiff and that the said representation was false to the knowledge of the plaintiff and was made with the intention of inducing the plaintiff to accept the said bill.

3. On .... 20.........., the plaintiff demanded the said bill to be delivered up to him but the defendant has failed and neglected to do so.

4. The plaintiff apprehends that the instrument, if left outstanding, may cause him serious injury.

The plaintiff claims—

(1) A declaration that he was induced to accept the said bill of exchange by the fraudulent misrepresentation of the defendant.

(2) Injunction restraining the defendant, his servants and agents and each one of them from parting or otherwise dealing with the said bill of exchange.

(3) An order directing the defendant to deliver up the said bill to be cancelled.

Verification

Affidavit

B. Cheque

349. Suit by an endorsee of a cheque against the endorser

In the Court of .... at ....

Suit No. .... of 20 ....

(Set out cause title)

The above-named plaintiff states as follows:

1. That the defendant No. 1 had drawn on .... a cheque No. .... for ₹ .... on the United Bank of India, ... branch, in favour of one A.B., defendant No. 2.

2. That the said A.B., defendant No. 2 had endorsed the said cheque in favour of the plaintiff on ....

3. That the plaintiff had duly presented the cheque to the .... bank, on .... and the same was dishonoured.

4. That a notice of dishonour has been served by the plaintiff on each of the defendants by registered post with A/D on ....

5. That the plaintiff is entitled to recover from defendant No. 2, a sum of ₹ .... together with interest @ 6% per annum till recovery.

The plaintiff, therefore, prays:

(*i*) A decree for ₹ ....

(*ii*) Interest @ 6% per annum till realisation.

Verification

Affidavit

NOTE: Suit on pronote by endorsee—Forum—AIR 1973 All 368.

350. Suit by a customer (non-trader) against his bankers for dishonouring a cheque

In the Court of .... at ....

Suit No. .... of 20 ....

(Set out cause title)

The plaintiff states as follows:

1. At the time material hereto the plaintiff had a current Banking account with the defendants.

2. A cheque dated .... , for ₹ ...., drawn by the plaintiff was duly presented for payment at the defendant's Bank on ...., by one AB, the payee of the said cheque.

3. The said cheque was dishonoured by the defendants although they had sufficient funds of the plaintiff in their hands to the credit of the said account wherewith to pay the amount of the cheque. By reason of the premises, the plaintiff's credit has been injured and he has suffered damage.

(Here set out particulars of special damage, if any).

The plaintiff claims—

₹ .... damages.

Verification

Affidavit

C. Hundi

351. Suit on a Hundi

In the Court of Civil Judge (Senior Division) at ....

Money Suit No. .... of 20 ....

(Set out cause title)

Claim for money due on hundi together with interest valued at ₹ ......

The plaintiff states as follows:

1. That defendant No. 1 carries on business at .... while defendant No. 2 is a businessman of Kolkata having his office at P. .... Kalakar Street, P.S. Barabazar, Kolkata 700 007, with a branch business at .... P.S. .... District .... The parties hereto are known to each other.

2. That defendant No. 1 being in need of some money for expansion of his business he, along with defendant No. 2, approached the plaintiff at the latter's *guddee* at .... Armenian Street, Kolkata 700 001, for a loan of ₹ .... only.

3. That it was agreed in between the plaintiff and the defendants that a loan of ₹ .... would be given by the plaintiff to the defendants on two hundies of ₹ .... and of ₹ ....; such hundies being executed by defendant No. 1 in favour of the plaintiff and accepted by the defendant No. 2. Due date of repayment would be 360 days after the hundies being executed.

4. That pursuant to the above agreement and for the consideration of the said sums of money, ₹ .... and ₹ .... truly paid by the plaintiff to defendant No. 1 on .... the said defendant No. 1 executed on .... two hundies one for ₹ .... and another for ₹ .... in favour of the plaintiff. Defendant No. 2 thereafter duly accepted the said two hundies. The due date of repayment being the 360 days from ....

5. That the defendants could not repay the said ₹ .... and ₹ .... on the due date, i.e. on .... to the plaintiff as agreed upon and they requested the plaintiff to continue and allow the loan to subsist on the same terms and conditions to which the plaintiff agreed. The defendant No. 1 then executed one renewed hundi for the consolidated sum of ₹ .... instead of two hundies as before in favour of the plaintiff on ...., and defendant No. 2 accepted the said hundi. The due date of repayment being 330 days from ...., i.e. on .... The original two hundies and the renewed hundi are being filed herewith and those will form part of this plaint.

6. That defendant No. 2 the acceptor of the hundi dated ...., did not pay up the said sum of ₹ .... on the due date nor thereafter, in spite of repeated demands for the same. Neither did defendant No. 1 pay any money towards the payment of the hundi for ₹ .... Therefore, the plaintiff is well entitled to claim the entire sum of ₹ .... together with the overdue interest @ 10% p. a. from ...., up to .... as agreed upon from both the defendants which amounts to ₹ .... as per account in Schedule "A" below.

7. That the plaintiff would not have lent ₹ .... on the hundi to defendant No. 1 if the defendant No. 2 would not have accepted the said hundi. Therefore defendant No. 2 is equally liable to the plaintiff for the said sum of ₹ .... together with interest thereon.

8. That defendant No. 1 deposited his title deeds of property mentioned in Schedule "B" below with the plaintiff's solicitor, Sri A. B. M. of Calcutta High Court, in his office in Kolkata by way of further and additional security for the loan of ₹ .... and ₹ .... paid by the plaintiff to defendant No. 1 on ...., which title deeds are being filed herewith.

9. That the plaintiff hereby does forgo his right to claim mortgage charge on the said properties for the loan now due and owing by the defendants to the plaintiff and pray for simple money due on the hundi for ₹ .... as memtioned above, as per account in the Schedule below.

10. That the said transactions have been entered in the ledger of the plaintiff (against the name of defendant No. 1) regularly kept in his business.

11. That the cause of action for this suit first arose on .... i.e. due date of the hundi for ₹ .... and lastly on ...., when last demand was made at Cooch Behar town P.S. Kotwali, where defendant No. 1 usually carries on business within the jurisdiction of Your Honour's Court.

12. That for the purpose of jurisdiction and court-fees the suit is valued at ₹ .... and *ad valorem* court-fees ₹ .... are paid thereon.

13. That defendant No. 1 has got his permanent residence at .... within the jurisdiction of this court and personally works for gain within the Town of .... at N.N. Road, P.S. Kotwali, and defendant No. 2 occasionally resides in the same town. The plaintiff, therefore, prays for permission to file this suit here in this court for his claims though the cause of action for this suit arose partly in Kolkata and partly in ...., within the jurisdiction of this court.

Therefore, the plaintiff prays:

(*a*) That a decree for ₹ .... be passed against the defendants and in favour of the plaintiff.

(*b*) That a decree for interest on the decretal dues be passed at the rate of 10% p.a. till the date of realisation.

(*c*) That a decree for costs of the suit be passed.

(*d*) That any other reliefs which the plaintiff is entitled to, may be awarded unto him.

SCHEDULE A

(*Account of Loan*)

Principal—₹ ....

Interest—₹ ....

Total due for principal and interest— ₹ ....

(₹ ....) only.

SCHEDULE B

(Property covered by the title deeds deposited District .... P.S. .... Pargana ...., Thak No. ...., Taluk ...., Sheet No. ...., Dag No. ...., formerly Dag No. .... respectively Khatian No. .... Touji No. .... area being .... decimal bearing rent of ₹ .... Dakhali Satta standing in the name of the .... own occupied.

(1) On the above-mentioned Dag No. .... land there stands a pucca one-story building.

(2) On the above-mentioned Dag No. .... land there stands a C.I. Sheet house.

(3) On the above-mentioned Dag No. .... land there stands another C.I. sheet house.

1. Hundi for ₹ .... dated ....
2. Hundi for ₹ .... dated ....
3. Hundi for ₹ .... dated ....
4. Pronote dated .... for ₹ .... executed by defendant No. 1 in favour of the plaintiff.

List of documents filed along with plaint:

Verification

Affidavit

352. Suit by an endorsee of a hundi against the drawer and the endorser

In the Court of .... at ....

Suit No. .... of 20 ....

(Set out cause title)

The aforesaid plaintiff states as follows:

1. That M/s. Ashkaran Subhkaran, defendant No. 1 drew a hundi on .... for ₹ .... on M/s. A.B., defendant No. 2, at Kolkata payable to defendant No. 3, M/s. Champalal Mohonlal Sethia, or order 45 days after date.

2. That the said defendant No. 3 endorsed the said hundi to the plaintiff.

3. That the plaintiff has presented the hundi on .... to M/s. A.B. which was dishonoured on the same day.

4. That the plaintiff has served a notice dated. .... on all the defendants by registered post with A/D of dishonour of the hundi.

5. That the plaintiff is entitled to a sum of ₹ .... inclusive of interest at 6% per annum as per account below.

6. The plaintiff prays for:

A decree for ₹ .... as per account below.

Particulars of claim

Hundi money—	₹ ....
Add interest @ 6% per annum from .... to .... 20..............	₹ ....
Total	₹ ....

Verification

Affidavit

NOTES: 1. Place where a like suit has to be filed is discussed in AIR 1938 Nag 262.

2. Section 80 prescribed rate of interest 6% but more may be claimed for a hundi according to usage—See s. 1 of the Act which does not affect a hundi.

3. Notice of dishonour is optional so far a hundi is concerned—See AIR 1937 Pesh 103.

D. Promissory Note

353. Suit by a payee on a promissory note

In the Court of .... at ....

Suit No. .... of 20 ....

(Set out cause title)

The plaintiff states as follows:

1. That the defendant had executed in favour of the plaintiff on .... a promissory note for ₹ .... repayable on demand together with interest at 10% per annum.

2. That the defendant did not pay any money under the promissory note in spite of repeated demands made therefor.

3. Cause of action—(Date of pronote).

4. The plaintiff values his suit at ₹ ....

The plaintiff prays for a Judgment and decree for ₹ ....

Verification

Affidavit

NOTES:
1. For definition of a promissory note—See s. 4 of the Negotiable Instruments Act 1881.
2. A pronote is payable on demand—See s. 19 of the Negotiable Instruments Act.
3. Limitation three years under Art. 35 of the Limitation Act 1963, from the date of the note—See AIR 1940 Cal 401.
   But when a promissory note is payable at a fixed time after date—limitation is three years when the note falls due under Art. 31 of the Act 1963.
4. Essentials of a promissory note—See AIR 1970 Punj 516.
5. An improperly stamped promissory note, which also contains a statement of amounts due on a previous note, cannot be admitted in evidence in order to save limitation in respect of the promissory note previously executed—AIR 1973 AP 170.
6. Several joint-promisors, consideration paid to only one other promisors are equally liable to pay the amount—*Andhra Bank* v *Ananta Nath Goel* AIR 1991 AP 245.

354. Suit by a payee on a promissory note (based on original consideration)

In the Court of .... at ....

Suit No. .... of 20 ....

(Set out cause title)

The above-named plaintiff states as follows:

1. That the defendant had borrowed from the plaintiff on .... a sum of ₹ ..... and promised to liquidate the loan with interest at 10% per annum till payment.

2. That subsequently the defendant executed on .... a promissory note in favour of the plaintiff for the said loan of ₹ .... repayable on demand with interest at the above rate.

3. That the defendant did not repay the loan in spite of repeated demands made in that behalf. Last demand was made by a notice in writing dated .... served on the defendant by registered post with A/D.

4. That the cause of action arose on .... (date of loan independently of the pronote) at .... within the jurisdiction of this court.

5. That the suit is valued at ₹ .... as per account in the Schedule below and *ad valorem* court-fees are paid thereon.

The plaintiff, therefore, prays:

(*i*) Decree for ₹ .... inclusive of interest @ 10% per annum.

(*ii*) Costs.

SCHEDULE

Account of claim

Verification

Affidavit

NOTE: Sections 8, 78 of the Negotiable Instruments Act— Rules embodied in sections do not apply to instruments which devolve by operation of law or is assigned. After death of the holder of a promissory note, all heirs should unite in suing. If any of them refuses to join as plaintiff—he must be impleaded as a defendant—AIR 1971 MP 133.

355. Suit by an endorsee of a promissory note

In the Court of .... at ....

Suit No. .... of 20 ....

(Set out cause title)

The plaintiff states as follows:

1. That defendant No. 1 executed a promissory note on .... for ₹ .... to pay to defendant No. 2 or order the said sum on demand with interest at 6% per annum.

2. That defendant No. 2 endorsed the said promissory note to the plaintiff on .... at .... (name of the place where endorsement is made).

3. That the plaintiff presented the promissory note to defendant No. 1 but the same was dishonoured.

4. That the plaintiff has served by registered post with A/D notice of dishonour dated .... on both the defendants.

5. That the cause of action arose on .... when the promissory note was endorsed to the plaintiff by defendant No. 2 at .... within the jurisdiction of this court.

6. That the suit is valued at ₹ .... for the purpose of jurisdiction and court-fees and *ad valorem* court-fees are paid thereon.

The plaintiff claims:

A decree for ₹ ....

Particulars of claims:

Principal	...	₹ ....
Add interest 6% per annum	...	₹ ....
(In words ....)	Total	₹ ....

Verification

Affidavit

NOTES: 1. Delivery of the promissory note after endorsement is necessary.
2. Notice of dishonour has to be served prior to suit and within the time allowed.
3. Cause of action arises where the promissory note is executed and also at the place where endorsement is made.
4. For a suit against endorser limitation runs from the date of endorsement.
5. When a negotiable instrument is endorsed—endorsee can sue even after the death of the endorser. Right to sue survives on the death of endorsee to his legal representatives—AIR 1968 Mad 260.

356. Suit by payee on a lost promissory note

In the Court of .... at ....

Suit No. .... of 20 ....

(Set out cause title)

The plaintiff states as follows:

1. On .... 20........., the defendant executed in favour of the plaintiff a promissory note for ₹ .... promising to repay the said sum on demand with interest at .... *per cent. per annum.*

2. The said promissory note was lost by theft (or, destroyed by fire) on or about ....

3. By letter dated .... 20........., the plaintiff gave the defendant notice that the said promissory note has been lost and called upon him to pay the amount due on the said promissory note and offered to indemnify him against any further claim thereon, but the defendant by his letter, dated .... 20......., denied having executed the said promissory note.

4. The sum of ₹ .... is due on the said promissory note.

5. The plaintiff is ready and willing to indemnify the defendant against the claim of any other person upon the said promissory note.

Particulars of claim:

.... 20.........	Principal sum	₹ ....
Interest from .... to	...	₹ ....
	Amount due ...	₹ ....

The plaintiff claims—

₹ ....

Verification

Affidavit

357. Suit for enforcement of bill of exchange

In the Court of Civil Judge (Senior Division) at Alipore

Suit No. .... of 20 ....

Mr. P., carrying on business at ....
Kolkata

..... *Plaintiff*

versus

Mr. X, carrying on business at ——

Kolkata

.... *Defendant*

Suit on Bill of Exchange valued at ₹ ....

The plaintiff states:

1. The plaintiff has been carrying on business in consumer goods and had business deals with the defendant.

2. For goods sold and delivered to the defendant valued at ₹ .... the plaintiff drew a Bill of Exchange for the value of goods so delivered and the defendant duly accepted the same in good faith payable after 30 days.

3. The defendant duly accepted the said goods and appropriated the same and there was no complaint whatsoever in respect of the said goods.

4. On due date of payment of the said Bill of Exchange, the same was presented to the defendant for necessary payment. The defendant examined the Bill of Exchange presented to him on due date but failed to pay the amount covered by Bill of Exchange which was payable after 30 days from date of its acceptance.

5. The plaintiff by a letter dated 5th September 20 .... recorded that the said Bill of Exchange was payable on presentation by plaintiff to defendant but this was not paid. The Bill of Exchange was payable 30 days after the date of its acceptance and the said Bill of Exchange was presented to the defendant for payment 30 days after the date of presentation and acceptance of the said Bill of Exchange by the defendant.

6. When the defendant did not pay even after expiry of 30 days from the date of acceptance of the said Bill of Exchange and presentation thereof for payment, the plaintiff got the said Bill of Exchange duly noted and protested.

7. In spite of the said demand made by the plaintiff by his letter dated 6th September 20 .... a copy whereof is annexed hereto marked 'A' the defendant has not paid the amount mentioned in the said Bill of Exchange namely ₹ .... or any part thereof.

8. The plaintiff states that the defendant is bound to pay the amount of said Bill of Exchange, namely ₹ .... with interest at 12% per annum from the due date of payment of the said Bill of Exchange.

9. There is now due from and owing by the defendant to plaintiff in respect of the said Bill of Exchange a sum of ₹ .... with interest calculated upto 31st December 20 ....

Particulars

Amount due in respect of:		
Principal amount of Bill of Exchange	:	₹ ....
Interest at ...... per annum upto date of filing of the suit	:	₹ ....
Notarial expenses incurred	:	₹ ....
Total	:	₹ ....

10. In spite of demands, the defendant has not paid the sum of ₹ .... or any portion thereof to the plaintiff. The plaintiff is entitled to further interest from 1st January 20 .... till payment at .... % per annum.

11. In spite of demand, the defendant has not paid the said sum or any portion thereof to the plaintiff. A copy of the demand letter is annexed hereto and marked 'B'.

12. The plaintiff's cause of action arose at the plaintiff's said address in Kolkata within the jurisdiction of this learned court. The said cause of action arose on .... when the demand letter was received by defendant as also prior thereto when the defendant on presentation of the said Bill of Exchange has refused to pay the same.

13. No part of the plaintiff's claims is barred by the law of limitation.

14. For the purposes of jurisdiction and court-fees, the suit is valued at ₹ .... on which *ad valorem* court-fees in stamps have been duly paid.

The plaintiff, therefore, prays for and claims:

(*a*) Decree for payment of ₹ .... by the defendant with interest at ....% per annum from 1st January 20 .... till payment;

(*b*) Injunction restraining defendant, its agents and representative from disposing off, or dealing with or encumbering the assets and property without first paying the claims of plaintiff;

(*c*) Cost of the suit be paid by defendant;

(*d*) Further orders be made so as to afford complete relief to plaintiff.

ANNEXURE

Verification

Affidavit

(The person verifying the plaint shall also affirm an affidavit in support of facts stated in the plaint as required under Order VI, Rule 15 of the Code of Civil Procedure).

358. Suit for enforcement of hundi by endorsee

In the Court of the Civil Judge (Senior Division) at Alipore

Money Suit No. .... of 20 ....

Mr. P residing at .... Kolkata

..... *Plaintiff*

versus

1. Mr. X residing at .... Kolkata

2. Mr. Y residing at .... Kolkata

... *Defendants*

Suit by endorsee against the drawer and endorser of hundi valued at ₹ ....

The plaintiff states as follows:

1. The plaintiff and the defendants have business relations.

2. Defendant No. 1 drew a hundi on 5th September 20 .... addressed to Mr. Y for ₹ .... payable to defendant No. 1 or order 90 days after date. Mr. Y. defendant No. 2 duly accepted the said hundi.

3. Defendant No. 1 for consideration endorsed the said hundi to the plaintiff. On due date of payment the plaintiff presented the said hundi for payment to Mr. Y but the same was dishonoured. The notice of dishonour in writing dated 9th October 20 .... was given to each of the defendants Nos. 1 and 2.

4. The plaintiff claims the said sum of ₹ .... with interest at 16% per annum from defendants Nos. 1 and 2 jointly and severally. The defendant No. 1 is liable as endorser of the hundi and the defendant No. 2 is liable as acceptor of the hundi in favour of the plaintiff.

5. In spite of demand the defendants have failed and neglected to pay the plaintiff's claims under the said hundi.

6. There is now due from and owing by the defendants to the plaintiff in respect of the said hundi a sum of ₹ .... with interest calculated upto 5th January 20 .... The plaintiff claims further interest from 7th January 20 ...... at 16% per annum from the defendants jointly and severally. The defendant No. 1 is liable to pay the claims of the plaintiff as a drawer and endorser of the hundi and defendant No. 2 is liable to pay to the plaintiff the said sum as an acceptor of the hundi.

7. The cause of action for this suit arose within the jurisdiction of this learned court. Further, the defendants also reside at their respective addresses within the jurisdiction of this learned court.

8. The claim of the plaintiff is not barred by the law of limitation.

9. In spite of demand the defendants have and each one of them has failed to pay the plaintiff's claims herein. A copy of the hundi and copies of demand letters are annexed hereto marked "A", "B" and "C" respectively.

10. For the purposes of jurisdiction and court-fees the suit is valued at ₹ .... on which court-fees in stamps have been paid.

The plaintiff, therefore, prays for and claims:

(*a*) Decree for ₹ .... against the defendants Nos. 1 and 2 jointly and severally;

(*b*) Interest at 16% per annum from 6th January 20... till date of decree and on the amount of the decree at 16% per annum;

(*c*) Costs;

(*d*) Further and other orders be made and directions be given as to this learned court may deem fit and proper to afford complete relief to the plaintiff.

Annexures

Verification

Affidavit

[Affidavit of the person verifying the plaint in support of the facts stated in the plaint (Order VI, r. 15 of CPC)].

NUISANCE

359. Suit against carrying on a noxious trade/manufacture

In the Court of .... at ....

Suit No. .... of 20 ....

(Set out cause title)

The above-named plaintiff states as follows:

1. That the plaintiff has had his house premises on the .... Road at .... Town. P.S. .... District ....

2. That the defendant in or about .... 20 .... started a business of .... (name the noxious trade with particulars and result thereof). The nuisance has steadily continued ever since that date.

3. By reason of the matters aforesaid, the plaintiff's house has been rendered unhealthy and unhabitable. The plaintiff and the members of his family have been suffering discomfort and inconvenience.

4. The defendant would, it is reasonably apprehended, continue the said nuisance unless restrained by an appropriate order of the court.

The plaintiff claims:

(*i*) Damages of ₹ ....

(*ii*) An order of injunction restraining the defendant to .... etc.

Verification

Affidavit

360. Suit by an individual in respect of a private nuisance

(See Form No. 361)

361. Suit by an individual in respect of a public nuisance on a public road

In the Court of .... at ....

Suit No. .... of 20 ....

(Set out cause title)

The above-named plaintiff states as follows:

1. That at 'X' point on public road known as .... Street, at .... Town, P.S. .... District .... there was and is a wooden bridge over a river flowing below.

2. That the plaintiff and other pedestrians have been lawfully using the said bridge on the .... river from ....

3. That the defendant is a contractor. As far as the plaintiff could know, the defendant entered into a contract with the P.W.D. (Roads) .... for repairs of the said wooden bridge. The defendant dug a pit at the northern approach of the bridge (nearly) 3 ft. deep—state the description but did not erect any fencing nor there was any caution. This position was not known to the plaintiff.

4. That in the night of .... the, 20........, while the plaintiff was walking along the said street he fell into the said pit and broke his right leg.

5. That the plaintiff is a day labourer. By reason of the injuries he remained hospitalized for about three months from .... to .... and could not earn his living within the said period.

6. That the cause of action arose on .... (date of injury).

The plaintiff claims from the defendant a sum of ₹ .... as compensation.

Verification

Affidavit

NOTE: In the case of a public nuisance—See s. 91(1), CPC.

(*i*) The Advocate-General of a State or two or more persons with the leave of the Court may institute a suit for declaration and injunction to restrain a public nuisance or other wrongful act though no special damage was caused.

(*ii*) An individual may also bring a like suit but in such a case he has to prove that has sustained special damage—48 IC 88; see s. 91(2) of the Code.

362. Representative suit in respect of a public nuisance

In the Court of .... at ....

Suit No. .... of 20 ....

(Set out cause title)

The above-named plaintiffs state as follows:

1. That there lies a public road, the Ulick Brown Street, running north-south, at .... Town, P.S. ...., District ...., within the jurisdiction of this court.

2. That the defendant has had his house premises to the east of the said road and the plaintiffs, amongst others, have their house premises lying both to the east and west of the said road.

3. That on .... the defendant encroached a portion of the said road in front of the plaintiff No. 1's house and has raised a structure thereon. The road at that point has been narrowed and the road has been obstructed for public use.

4. That the plaintiffs and many others of the locality had requested the defendant on .... to remove the obstruction and dismantle the structure but this request proved abortive. It is apprehended from the defendant's conduct that he would not remove the obstruction.

5. That the plaintiffs pray leave of the court hereby to bring this suit to prevent the said public nuisance.

6. That the cause of action for this suit arose on .... when the defendant raised the construction and obstructed the road at .... within the jurisdiction of this court.

The plaintiff, therefore, prays:

(*a*) A declaration that the said road is a public road and the defendants cannot obstruct the road.

(*b*) An order directing the defendant for removal and dismantling of the structure.

(*c*) An injunction restraining the defendant from obstructing the road or doing any act of obstruction.

Verification

Affidavit

NOTES: 1. See s. 91 of the Code of Civil Procedure.

2. Case of common right of villagers over water in a tank—AIR 1969 Mad 351.

363. Suit for injunction restraining creation of nuisance by discharge of foul water

In the Court of .... at ....

Suit No. .... of 20 ....

(Set out cause title)

The plaintiffs state as follows:

1. The defendant is the owner of a premises at the entrance of a public lane at ...., in the town of .... The defendant has started a factory for manufacturing distilled water.

2. The plaintiffs are the members of the public and they have their respective residential premises inside but on the public lane.

3. The plaintiffs and other persons of the locality were residing quite peacefully and without any trouble.

4. Recently the defendant has installed requisite machinery and started manufacturing distilled water but has not made adequate arrangement for discharge of foul water from his machines. The defendant is discharging such water in the public lane and it takes a long time for the water to be canalised through the underground drain. The foul water discharged by the machines of the defendant travel long way by the side of the footpath and then they find way to the underground drain. During the discharge of the foul water foul smell comes out and causes nuisance to the residents of the said public lane.

5. The plaintiffs and some other residents of the said public lane from time to time requested the defendant to find ways and means to discharge the foul water in such a way that it does not travel through the lane thereby emitting foul smell but the defendant has not taken any effective steps to stop the nuisance.

6. The plaintiffs through their Advocate issued a notice dated .... to the defendant stating the facts and requesting the defendant not to continue with the nuisance otherwise the plaintiffs would take legal proceedings against the defendant to enforce the plaintiff's legal rights and to prevent the defendant from committing public nuisance. The defendant duly received the said notice but failed to take any effective steps and is continuing with the said act of nuisance.

7. The defendant is residing as also committing the nuisance at the said public lane situate within the jurisdiction of this learned court and as such this learned court has the jurisdiction to entertain, try and determine this suit. The suit is valued at ₹ .... on which court-fees in stamps have been paid.

8. No part of the cause of action of the plaintiffs is barred by waiver or acquiescence.

9. In the premises the plaintiffs pray for injunction restraining the defendant from committing any nuisance or continuing the nuisance complained of and to take alternative steps to discharge foul water in a manner not causing any inconvenience to the public including the plaintiffs.

The plaintiffs, therefore, pray for and claim—

(*a*) Injunction restraining the defendant from causing nuisance by discharging foul water in the manner complained of;

(*b*) Receiver be appointed to supervise and assist the diversion of foul water in such manner that the same does not cause any inconvenience to the members of the public including the plaintiffs;

(*c*) Cost;

(*d*) Further and other orders be made as this learned court may deem fit and proper.

Verification

Affidavit

364. Written statement to the plaint for injunction

In the Court of .... at ....

Suit No. .... of 20 ....

(Set out cause title)

The defendant states as follows:

1. The plaintiffs have no valid cause of action against the defendant.

2. Save and except what are matters of record, the defendant does not make any admission in respect of the statements contained in paragraphs 1, 2 and 3 of plaint.

3. With reference to the paragraph 4 of the plaint, the defendant states that the defendant obtained licence from the Corporation for setting up the distilled water factory unit and for discharge of water to the footpath sewerage drain. The discharge of such water is in accordance with law, and has the permission of the Corporation. The defendant states that the foul smell complained off is negligible and not felt by ordinary persons passing through the said public lane.

4. With reference to paragraph 5 of the plaint, the defendant states that the plaintiffs have *mala fide* started complaining about the setting up of said Distilled Water Manufacturing Unit as the defendant refused to pay exorbitant Puja Subscription as also donation to the local club of plaintiffs. The allegations contained in paragraph 5 of plaint are incorrect, motivated and denied and the suit cannot be based on such invented grievances.

5. With reference to the paragraph 6 of the plaint, the defendant denies that the defendant has created any public nuisance and the defendant states that the plaintiffs have no legal or moral right to prevent the defendant from running its Unit. The defendant states that the said purported legal notice of the plaintiffs is incorrect, based on wrong assumptions and does not disclose any valid cause of action and contains untrue allegations and contentions. The defendant has been discharging the waste water direct to the underground sewerage drain.

6. With reference to paragraph 7 of plaint, the defendant, denies that the defendant had committed any public nuisance at the said public lane or otherwise. The defendant further states that the valuation on the suit is not correct.

7. With reference to paragraph 8 of the plaint, it is denied and disputed that the alleged cause of action of the plaintiffs is not barred by the principles of waiver or acquiescence.

8. With reference to the paragraph 9 of the plaint the defendant states that the defendant is acting in accordance with the law and pursuant to the licence issued by Corporation committing no public nuisance as wrongly complained of, and as such, the plaintiffs have no valid cause of action as against the defendant.

9. The suit be dismissed with costs.

Verification

Affidavit

365. Suit for injunction against diversion of a water-course

(See Form No. 239)

PARTITION

366. Suit by a coparcener for partition and accounts against the karta

In the Court of .... at ....

Suit No. .... of 20 ....

(Set out cause title)

The plaintiff states as follows:

1. The plaintiff and the defendants are members of a joint Hindu family governed by the Mitakshara school of law and their relationship with each other will appear from the pedigree set out hereunder.

2. The plaintiff and the defendants jointly own and possess the properties set out in Schedule "A" hereto.

3. Since ...., when A.B., father of the plaintiff, died, the defendant No. 1 has acted as the karta of the joint family and the manager of the joint family properties.

4. The defendant No. 1 acting as such karta and manager has mis-appropriated some of the family properties and has misapplied the income thereof to purposes which are not family purposes.

Particulars:

5. The defendant No. 1 is wrongfully claiming that Items 1 and 2 of the said Schedule "A" are his self-acquired or separate property.

6. The respective shares of the parties in the joint family properties are as follows:

(Set out respective shares of the parties)

The plaintiff claims—

(1) A declaration as against defendant No. 1 that items 1 and 2 in Schedule "A" hereto form part of the joint family properties.

(2) That defendant No. 1 be directed to render a true and faithful account of his dealings with the joint family properties since ...., and payment to the plaintiff his .... shares in the sum to be found due on the taking of the accounts.

(3) Partition of the joint family properties by metes and bounds in accordance with the shares of the parties, and allotment to the plaintiff of his share in severalty.

Pedigree

SCHEDULE 'A'

Verification

Affidavit

367. Defences to a claim for partition

In the Court of .... at ....

Suit No. .... of 20 ....

(Set out cause title)

The defendants state as follows:

(The defendants may take one or more of the following defences)

1. The plaintiff is not a son or legal representative of A.B., deceased and is not entitled to the alleged or any share in any of the properties specified in schedule "A" to the plaint. The plaintiff has never been in possession of any of the said properties.

2. If, which is denied, the plaintiff is a son of A.B. deceased, the defendants say that in .... 20...., the plaintiff demanded of them a share of the profits of the said properties. By letter dated ...., the defendants denied the plaintiff's title, and they have since been in exclusive continuous possession of the said properties to the knowledge of the plaintiff (or without any attempt at concealment). Accordingly, the plaintiff's title, if any, to the said properties has been extinguished by adverse possession of the defendants.

3. No part of the properties included in Schedule "A" to the plaint is within the local limits of the jurisdiction of this court, (or, if the suit is filed on the original side of the High Court, items 1, 2 and 3 of Schedule "A" to the plaint are outside the local limits of the ordinary original civil jurisdiction of this court, and no leave to sue under Clause .... of the Letters Patent of the .... High Court, was obtained by the plaintiff at the time of the institution of the suit).

4. The suit is one for partial partition and should not be entertained. The following properties have been omitted from the list of joint family properties.

(Describe such particulars)

5. Items .... and .... of Schedule "A" to the plaint are the separate property of defendant No. 1 and do not form part of joint family properties.

6. The defendant No. 1 has spent ₹ .... out of his separately acquired money in improving item No. 5 of the Schedule "A" to the plaint and claims that on partition the same should be allotted to him.

7. There was a private partition between the plaintiff and the defendants in .... 20...., in respect of the said properties and, ever since the said partition, the plaintiff and the defendants have been in separate possession and enjoyment of the properties respectively allotted to them and the parties have acquiesced in the result of the said partition. The said partition is a bar to re-partition of the said properties.

8. The plaintiff's share in the said properties is .... and not .... The respective shares of the defendants in the said properties are as follows:

(Set out respective shares of the parties)

9. The defendants want their respective shares to be partitioned and allotted to them.

Verification

Affidavit

368. Suit for partition and for khas possession of the plaintiff's share

In the Court of the Civil Judge (Senior Division) at...................

T. S. No. .... of ....

(Set out cause title)

Suit for partition and khas possession.

Valued at ₹ ....

The plaintiff states as follows:

1. That defendants Nos. 1 to 16 together hold in *ejmali* a piece of land measuring 11.30 acres at .... Mouja .... P.S. .... District ...., more particularly described in Schedule 'A' below.

2. That the quantum of share of each of the defendants in the said property in Schedule 'A' is as follows:

Defendant No. 1	...	...	1 anna 2 gandas.
Defendants Nos. 2 and 3	...	...	each 2 annas.
Defendant No. 4	...	...	1 anna 6 g. 2 k. 2 kranti.
Defendant No. 5	...	...	15 ganda 1 kara.
Defendants Nos. 6 and 7	...	...	each 6 g. 2 k. 2 kranti.
Defendants Nos. 8, 9 and 10	...	...	each 13 g. 1 k. 1 kranti.
Defendant No. 11	...	...	14 g. 2 k. 2 kranti.
Defendant No. 12	...	...	2 annas.
Defendant No. 13	...	...	1 g. 3 k. 2 kranti.
Defendants Nos. 14 and 15	...	...	each 1 anna.
Defendant No. 16	...	...	1 anna 7 g. 2 kranti.

3. That defendant No. 1 out of his undivided 1 anna 2 ganda share has sold to the plaintiff 3 acres of land by executing a registered kobala dated .... on receipt of a consideration of ₹ .... only.

The said land is described in Schedule 'B' below.

4. That by such purchase the plaintiff has acquired right, title and interest to the land in Schedule 'B' below. The plaintiff has paid rent after his purchase.

5. That there were crops standing in the land in Schedule 'B' in ...., 14 .... B.S. and defendant No. 1 promised to deliver possession of the land by the end of Vaisakh .... 14 .... B.S., after harvest but the defendant avoided delivery of possession on expiry of Vaisakh, even after demands.

6. That the plaintiff was compelled to serve a notice dated .... on defendant No. 1 through his lawyer asking the defendant to deliver possession of the land in Schedule 'B'. But defendant No. 1 did not comply with the said request.

7. That thereafter in the last part of .... 14 .... B.S., the plaintiff met the defendants and asked them to partition the suit property and deliver possession of the 'B' Schedule property but the defendants refused.

8. That the plaintiff is entitled to partition of the property in Schedule 'A' and khas possession of his share, preferably the 'B' Schedule land after finding his title thereto.

9. That the cause of action for this suit arose in .... 20.........., when the plaintiff's request for partition was not conceded to at Mouja .... P.S. .... within the jurisdiction of this court.

10. That for the purpose of jurisdiction the suit is valued at ₹ .... and for the purpose of partition and khas possession the plaintiff's share (i.e. 3 acres of land) is valued at ₹ .... and court-fees are paid thereon.

The plaintiff therefore prays:

(*a*) A preliminary decree for partition of the property in Schedule 'A' according to the shares of parties;

(*b*) the appointment of a Commissioner for effecting the partition in terms of the preliminary decree;

(*c*) final decree embodying the Commissioner's report;

(*d*) khas possession of the plaintiff's share;

(*e*) costs;

(*f*) such other relief or reliefs as law and equity would allow the plaintiff.

SCHEDULE 'A'

SCHEDULE 'B'

Verification

Affidavit

369. Suit for partition

In the Court of .... at ....

Suit No. .... of 20 ....

(Set out cause title)

The above-named plaintiff states as follows:

1. That one A.B. owned the house premises at No. ...., N.S. Road at ...., Town, P.S. .... District ...., more particularly described in the Schedule appended hereto.

2. That the said A.B. died on .... leaving his widow, one daughter Srimati C.D. and two sons named E.F. (Defendant No. 1) and G.H. Each of them held $^1/_4$ th share in the property on the death of the said A.B., and they possessed the said property in *ejmali*.

3. That the said G.H. by executing a sale-deed on .... (registered on...........) has transferred his $^1/_4$ th share to the plaintiff. Later, said Srimati C.D. sold her $^1/_4$th share to defendant No. 2 by executing a sale-deed on .... (registered on ....).

4. That defendants No. 1 and 2 and the plaintiff are owners in *ejmali* possession of the said property in the Schedule below.

5. That the plaintiff has $^1/_4$th share in the said property in the Schedule below which is the subject-matter of the suit and will hereinafter be referred to suit-property.

6. That the plaintiff claimed for partition of his $^1/_4$th share of the said property in the month of .... but the defendants did not pay heed to the plaintiff's request.

The plaintiff prays:

(*i*) For a decree of partition of his $^1/_4$th share in the suit-property.

SCHEDULE

(State here particulars and description of the property)

Verification

Affidavit

NOTE: CP Code, s. 54 and Or. 20, r. 18:

In a suit for partition of common properties and business, the shares of the parties in the subject-matter should first be ascertained. Next, in order to make proper allotments to the parties, the subject-matters for partition should be properly assessed and valued and for that purpose and for fair valuation of the allotments for the parties, the assets and the liabilities of the estate for partition should be found out. Provision may be made for meeting the liabilities and in making allotments while considering the assets and liabilities of the joint properties; owelty money, if necessary, is to be determined for assessment of the proper valuation of the allotments. In order to achieve these purposes, accounts of profits and liabilities are to be taken up for consideration at the time of final decree so that in future after the final decree, the parties may not have any occasion to file suits in connection with the liabilities or claims in respect of the properties already partitioned and in which the parties have been given possession. There should not be any scope for future litigation over the same matters after the determination of the partition suit.

In a suit for partition of properties and businesses, the question of accounting becomes unavoidable for final determination and assessment of the valuation of the properties to be allotted to the parties—AIR 1951 Mad 938; AIR 1961 Ori 111.

In a partition suit where different properties and businesses are involved, the question of accounts and joint liabilities and assets of the estate to be partitioned becomes essential and for that no separate prayer for rendering accounts need be mentioned in the plaint—*Saraswati Devi* v *Satyanarayana* AIR 1977 Cal 99.

PARTNERSHIP

370. Suit by a partner for dissolution of partnership

(On expiry of term vide s. 42 of the Indian Partnership Act)

In the Court of .... at ....

Suit No. .... of 20 ....

(Set out cause title)

The above-named plaintiff states as follows:

1. That the plaintiff and the defendant entered into a partnership business by executing a partnership deed on .... under the name and style of .... with its registered office at .... P.S. .... District .... within the jurisdiction of this court.

2. That clause No. .... of the said partnership deed provided that the said partnership would be for a term of three years from date of commencement of partnership.

3. That the term of partnership expired on the 15th day of .... 20......., and the partnership stood dissolved on the expiry of the term.

4. That no accounting was made of the returns of the partnership for the last two years.

5. That the plaintiff is entitled to a declaration that partnership stood dissolved on .... or to dissolution by a decree of the court and to have the said business wound up.

6. Cause of action (on the date of dissolution).

7. Suit valuation.

The plaintiff, therefore, prays:

(*a*) For a decree declaring that the partnership of M/s. .... stood dissolved on expiry of ....

(*b*) Or, in the alternative, the said partnership be dissolved by a decree of the court.

(*c*) For accounts of the said partnership for 20....... and 20............

(*d*) For winding up the affairs of the said partnership.

(*e*) For appointment of a Receiver.

Verification

Affidavit

NOTES: 1. Court-fees in a like suit—see s. 7(*iv*)(*f*) of the Court-fees Act (in West Bengal s. 7(*iv*)(*e*) of the West Bengal Court-fees Act 1970).

2. Limitation—three years *vide* Art. 5 of the Limitation Act from the date of dissolution.

3. Bar under s. 69(4)(*b*) of the Partnership Act does not apply to suits of small causes nature valued at not exceeding ₹100—AIR 1978 Cal 321.

371. Suit by a partner for winding up of a dissolved partnership with an alternative prayer for dissolution

In the Court of .... at ....

Suit No. .... of 20 ....

(Set out cause title)

The plaintiff states as follows:

1. The plaintiff, under a verbal agreement made on ...., entered into a partnership at will with the defendant for carrying on a commission agency business under the name of .... upon the term that the partners would contribute equally to the capital and share equally the profits and losses.

2. Disputes and differences arose between the plaintiff and the defendant as such partners soon after the commencement of the business profits and losses and, accordingly, the said partnership was by mutual verbal agreement dissolved on .... (or, on .... the plaintiff gave notice in writing to the defendant of his intention to dissolve the firm.)

3. No settlement of account has been made between the partners since the commencement of the partnership.

The plaintiff claims—

(1) A declaration that the partnership stood dissolved on ....

(2) Alternatively, that the partnership be dissolved by decree of the court.

(3) An account be taken of the partnership business.

(4) Appointment of a receiver pending winding up.

Verification

Affidavit

372. Suit for dissolution of partnership and for accounts

In the Court of Civil Judge (Senior Division) at ....

O. C. Suit No. .... of 20 ....

(Set out cause title)

Suit for dissolution of partnership and for accounts.
Claim laid at ₹ ....

The above-named plaintiff states as follows:

1. The plaintiff and the defendants have since April 20 .... been carrying on Government contract works and other business under an oral agreement of partnership in .... 20........, followed by a formal agreement of partnership in writing executed between the parties on ....

2. Under the terms of the agreement, the defendant was to secure and conduct the business either in his name or in the name of the plaintiff or in the name of both and keep accounts and the plaintiff is to contribute ₹ .... to the capital of the partnership and both should share equally the profits thereof as also losses, if any.

3. Several disputes and differences have arisen between the plaintiff and the defendant as partners whereby it has become impossible to carry on the business in partnership with advantage to each other.

4. That defendant has violated the conditions laid down in the said agreement by misappropriating the profits realised from the partnership business and by not showing the accounts and not rendering accounts although demanded by the plaintiff.

5. Under the terms of the agreement, the plaintiff contributed ₹ .... to the capital out of which the defendant refunded ₹ .... leaving the balance of ₹ .... in the hands of the defendant.

6. The plaintiff served a notice upon the defendant by registered post on .... for rendition of accounts up to date giving one month's time for the same, but the defendant under false pretext did not comply with the notice.

7. The plaintiff tentatively values his claim at ₹ .... and claims the entire amount that may be found due from the defendant on accounting.

8. The cause of action for the present suit arises on .... the time for accounting given in the registered notice, the date of violation and other dates.

9. For the purpose of the jurisdiction of the court and for court-fees the suit is valued tentatively at ₹ .... and court-fees paid thereon.

10. The plaintiff, therefore, prays:

(*a*) for a decree for dissolution of the partnership,

(*b*) that accounts be taken from the defendant and a decree be passed in favour of the plaintiff for the amount that may be found due from the defendant,

(*c*) for a decree for costs of the suit,

(*d*) for appointment of a Receiver, if necessary,

(*e*) for such other relief as may be deemed fit.

Verification

Affidavit

NOTES: 1. Suit by partners for dissolution of partnership and accounts. Death of one of respondent sharers during appeal. In case of failure to bring legal representatives on record, appeal abates as a whole—AIR 1972 SC 1181.

2. For Limitation three years from the date of dissolution—Article 5, Limitation Act 1963.

3. See AIR 1971 P&H 186—against some of the partners not maintainable.

4. Suit by a sleeping partner for accounts of partnership—court's duty—AIR 1971 Punj 134. Suit for dissolution and rendition of accounts when barred by limitation—AIR 1971 Raj 111.
5. Firm was dissolved on date on which retirement was intimated. Suit for accounts barred as filed beyond three years from date of dissolution. Article 5, Limitation Act 1963—*Mir Abdul Khaliq* v *Abdul Gaffar* AIR 1985 SC 608.
6. Partnership Act (s. 44)

   In a suit for dissolution and accounts—Assets of firm consisting of immovable property—suit cannot be treated as a suit for land. Therefore, a suit for dissolution and accounts is maintainable though the court has no territorial jurisdiction over the assets of the firm which are immovable properties—*Tilokram Ghosh* v *Gita Rani* AIR 1989 Cal 254.

   Suit for rendition of accounts filed 3 years after dissolution would be barred under Art. 5 of the Limitation Act.

373. Suit for winding up a partnership on expiry of term and for accounts

In the Court of .... at ....

Suit No. .... of 20 ....

(Set out cause title)

The above-named plaintiff states:

1. That the plaintiff and the defendant entered into a partnership business under a partnership deed dated .... under the name and style of .... with its registered office at .... P.S. .... District ....

2. That the said partnership business was, under the terms of the partnership, for a term of five years.

3. That the said partnership business was carried on till the 31st day of .... 20......, and the partnership stood dissolved with effect from the 1st of .... 20...... on expiry of the term of partnership.

4. That there has been no accounting for the last year of the partnership business in spite of the plaintiff's request made to the defendant in that behalf.

5. That the cause of action for this suit arose on the 1st of .... 20......... at ......

6. Suit valuation.

The plaintiff, therefore, prays:

(*a*) For accounting of the partnership for the year 20.......

(*b*) For a decree for winding up the affairs of the partnership.

Verification

Affidavit

NOTES: 1. See s. 42—A partnership is dissolved on expiry of term when the term is fixed.
2. Section 46—After dissolution a partner is entitled to the winding-up of the business.
3. Limitation—when dissolved—three years *vide* Art. 5 and not yet dissolved—three years *vide* Art. 113 of the Limitation Act 1963.
4. Sections 39, 42, 46 deal with consequences ensuring after general dissolution. They do not abrogate terms of contract under which partnership is no continue between surviving partners after death of one

.... Share of the deceased partner in assets including goodwill will devolve on his legal representative in absence of anything to the contrary in the agreement—AIR 1970 SC 1147.

374. Suit against the sole surviving partner of a firm

In the Court of .... at ....

Suit No. .... of 20 ....

(Set out cause title)

The plaintiff states:

1. That M/s. "Look Well, Kolkata" was a partnership business with its registered office at 7 Sooterkin Street, Kolkata 700 013. The said partnership was constituted by partners A.B. and the defendant.

2. That the partner A.B. died on the .... day of .... 20............ and the defendant has been carrying on the business as sole proprietor thereof under the trade name of "Look Well, Kolkata".

3. That during the life-time of A.B., the plaintiff had supplied to the said partnership on credit readymade garments of different descriptions and sizes as listed below worth ₹ .... as per account below.

4. Neither the said partnership firm nor the defendant paid the value thereof. In the facts of the case the defendant is liable to pay to the plaintiff the value of the goods.

5. Cause of action.

6. Suit valuation.

ACCOUNT OF CLAIM

Date of purchase on credit	*Quantity description*	*Value*
		₹ ....

The plaintiff claims:

(*i*) ₹ .... being the value of goods purchased on credit;

(*ii*) Damages thereon at $12^1/_2\%$ per annum till realisation thereof.

Verification

Affidavit

375. Suit against partners for debts transferred from the old partnership firm to a new one

In the Court of .... at ....

Suit No. .... of 20 ....

(Set out cause title)

That plaintiff states:

1. That the defendant 'X' together with 'Y' and 'Z' carried on a business in partnership under the name and style of .... On or about the .... day of .... 20........ 'Y' died and his son 'P' was taken in as a partner in the firm. Still later, on or about the ..... day of .... 20...... 'Z' sold his share and interest in the firm to 'X' and 'P'. The said 'X' and 'P' are the present partners of the firm ".................."

2. That the plaintiff had supplied to the firm .... pieces of blankets on credit on or about the .... day of .... 20... The price thereof remains unpaid.

3. That there was an agreement amongst the parties hereto on or about the .... day of .... 20.......... that 'X' and 'P' would be answerable to the plaintiff for the liability of the old firm.

4. That the plaintiff is entitled to recover from the defendants ....(etc. ....).

Details of claim	*Quantity and nature*	*Value*
....	....	....

5. The plaintiff claims ₹ ....

Verification

Affidavit

376. Suit by a partner for partial accounts without dissolution of the firm

In the Court of .... at ....

Suit No. .... of 20 ....

(Set out cause title)

The plaintiff states that—

1. Under a deed of partnership dated ...., the plaintiff and the defendant have since the .... day of .... been carrying on business of .... at .... under the style of ....

2. The said partnership deed, *inter alia,* provided as follows:

(*a*) The plaintiff and the defendant to share the profits and the losses of the business is equal proportion.

(*b*) The defendant to be the managing partner of the business.

(*c*) The defendant as such managing partner to keep accounts and to render accounts of the business at the close of each year in the month of ....

(*d*) The net profits of the business at the close of each year to be divided among the partners.

3. The defendant has not rendered any accounts of the business for the year .... and refuses to do so in spite of demand in writing made by the plaintiff on ....

4. By reason of the premises, the plaintiff has been prevented from getting his share of profits of the business for the said year.

The plaintiff claims—

(1) To have a full and true account of the partnership business for the year ....

(2) Payment of his half of the net profits for the said year as may be found due upon the taking of accounts.

Verification

Affidavit

377. Suit for winding up of the affairs of a dissolved partnership and for appointment of a receiver and manager

In the Court of .... at ....

Suit No. .... of 20 ....

(Set out cause title)

The plaintiff states that—

1. The plaintiff on ...., entered into partnership agreement with the defendant for carrying on business in .... under the style of .... for a term of .... years.

2. By the partnership agreement the plaintiff was to do the canvassing work, and the defendant was to look after the management, and to remain in charge of the accounts and the funds of the said business, and that both were to contribute equally to the capital and to share equally the profits and losses, of the said business.

3. Accordingly, the said business was carried on until .... when the term fixed by the partnership agreement expired, and the partnership stood dissolved.

4. No settlement of accounts has been made between the plaintiff and the defendant as partners since the commencement of the partnership.

5. There are certain existing debts of the partnership which have to be paid and certain contracts with third parties which have to be performed.

(*Give particulars*)

6. There are disagreements between the plaintiff and the defendant as to the mode of discharging the said debts and executing the said contracts.

The plaintiff claims—

(1) A declaration, if necessary, that the partnership stood dissolved on ....

(2) Partnership accounts and winding-up of the affairs of the partnership.

(3) Appointment of a receiver and manager pending on winding-up.

Verification

Affidavit

POSSESSION

378. Suit for declaration of title and for khas possession

In the Court of the Civil Judge (Junior Division) at ....

Title Suit No. .... of 20 ....

A.B. ... ...
Plaintiff

versus

1. C.D.
2. E.F. sons of G.H.

... *Defendants*

Suit for title and khas possession valued at ₹ ....

The above-named plaintiff states as follows:

1. That the defendants held a 'Krishi Proja' interest measuring .... acres at Mouja .... P.S. .... District ....

2. That by executing a kobala on .... the defendants sold to the plaintiff on receipt of a consideration of ₹ .... a portion of the aforesaid land measuring .... acres, described more particularly in the Schedule. The said property in the Schedule below is the subject-matter of the suit and will hereinafter be referred to as suit property.

3. That on the occasion of sale, the defendants proposed to have reconveyance of the suit property on payment to the plaintiff the said sum of ₹ .... any time within .... The plaintiff agreed to their proposal.

4. That while the plaintiff was always willing the defendants did not exercise their option.

5. That since there was a proposal of reconveyance, the defendants proposed that they would retain possession over the suit property till the date of reconveyance. The plaintiff readily agreed.

6. That on failure by the defendants to exercise option, the plaintiff had issued a notice to the defendants dated .... by registered post with A/D through his lawyer Sri. .... by which the option of reconveyance was thrown open for 10 days from the date of receipt of notice. The defendants received the notice on .... but they did not avail themselves of the opportunity.

7. That in the said notice the defendants were warned that the offer would be withdrawn on expiry of the said 10 days and the defendants shall have to deliver vacant possession of the suit property immediately thereafter. The defendants did not comply with the notice nor vacated the suit property.

8. That the plaintiff is entitled to khas possession of suit property after finding his title thereto.

9. That the cause of action for this suit arose first on .... when the plaintiff purchased the suit property and thereafter on .... on expiry of 10 days from the receipt of notice referred to above.

10. That for the purpose of jurisdiction and court-fees the suit is valued at ₹ .... and *ad valorem* court-fees are paid thereon.

The plaintiff, therefore, prays:

(*i*) for khas possession of the suit property after finding the plaintiff's title thereto.

(*ii*) Costs.

SCHEDULE

Verification

Affidavit

379. Suit for declaration of title and for khas possession (Another Form)

In the Court of the Civil Judge (Junior Division) at ....

Title Suit No. .... of ....

(Set out cause title)

Suit for title and khas possession valued at ₹ ....

The above-named plaintiff states as follows:

1. That the defendant owned a piece of land measuring 12 acres at Cooch Behar town, Thak No. 914, P.S. Kotwali, District Cooch Behar appertaining to Hal Settlement Khanda Khatian No. 4138 more particularly described in Schedule "A" below. While owning and possessing the same, the defendant had sold therefrom a portion thereof, measuring 3 kathas 4 dhurs to one .... by executing a (registered) kobala in his favour ....

The said 3 katha 4 dhurs of land is described more particularly in Schedule "B" below and was well divided by measurements from side to side and by boundaries in the aforesaid kobala. The vendor-defendant made delivery of possession to vendee .... after such sale.

2. That the said .... possessed the property in Schedule "B" below and raised house-structures thereon but could not complete the same. Any way, the said .... while owning and possessing the said land with structures thereon had sold the land in Schedule "B" with structures thereon to one Sri. .... by executing a (registered) kobala on .... and made over the possession to the said .... after such sale.

3. The said .... possessed the land in Schedule "B" with incomplete structures thereon and thereafter had sold the same to the plaintiff on .... by executing a (registered) kobala in his favour for a consideration of ₹ .... for the land in Schedule "B" and ₹ .... (for structures) ₹ .... only. The said vendor .... made over possession of the said land in Schedule "B" together with structures thereon to the plaintiff.

4. That the plaintiff had to remain away at .... for his livelihood. He occasionally visits premises in Schedule "B" whereon construction is on progress.

5. That the plaintiff last paid a visit in .... during the Puja holidays when the plaintiff found that the defendant had encroached upon a portion of the land in Schedule "B" measuring 3 dhurs of land as described in Schedule "C" below which is the subject matter of the suit and is further shown in the sketch map which may be treated as a part of the plaint. The defendant has been raising a pucca boundary wall on the encroached land.

6. That the defendant was requested in .... to give up possession of the encroached land in Schedule "C" and to stop raising boundary wall, but the defendant paid no heed to the plaintiff's request.

7. That the plaintiff is entitled to khas possession of the land in Schedule "C" by demolition of the plaintiff's unauthorised boundary wall so far raised on the suit land.

8. That the cause of action for the suit arose in .... when the defendant dispossessed the plaintiff from the suit land at .... within the jurisdiction of this court.

9. That for the purpose of jurisdiction and court-fees the suit is valued at ₹ .... and *ad valorem* court-fees are paid thereon.

The plaintiff, therefore, prays:

(*a*) For a decree of khas possession of the land in Schedule "C" after finding the plaintiff's title thereto.

(*b*) For an order of mandatory injunction of by demolition of unauthorised boundary wall of the defendant standing to the suit land.

(*c*) For all costs of suit.

SCHEDULE "A"

SCHEDULE "B"

Side to side measurements:

In the North:

South:

East:

West:

SCHEDULE "C"—Suit land

Verification

Affidavit

NOTES: 1. Court-fees—In a suit for recovery of possession from a trespasser, where no declaration of title is prayed for or necessary for the disposal of the suit— according to the amount at which the relief sought is valued in the plaint—See s. 7 (*vi*)(*a*) of the West Bengal Court-fees Act 1970.

2. One of co-sharers not impleaded—defendant found to have no right, title over such property—suit is competent even in absence of all co-sharers as it would enure to benefit of all co-sharers—*Debahari* v *Sribatsa* AIR 1994 Ori 86.

3. Suit for recovery of possessions based on title. Section 6 of the Limitation Act has no application. Limitation prescribed in Art. 65 and not Art. 64 is applicable to such suit—*Chandra Bhan Prasad* v *Mohanlal* AIR 1987 Cal 322.

380. Suit for restoration of possession under s. 6 of the Specific Relief Act 1963

In the Court of Civil Judge (Senior Division) at ....

Suit No. .... of 20 ....

.... *Plaintiffs*

versus

.... *Defendants*

Suit for restoration of possession under s. 6, Specific Relief Act and for realisation of compensation for the damage caused by the members of the defendant club.

The above-named plaintiffs state:

1. That the plaintiffs are refugees from Bangladesh and they left hearth and home there, and have taken shelter in the Indian soil at Cooch Behar in 20 .... In .... and .... 20......., they and the pro-defendant No. 15 took possession of old plot No. .... in sheet No. .... of Cooch Behar which is commonly known as 'Kadamtola' and constructed structures thereon separately and were running their business openly since then. Subsequently, the pro-defendant No. 15 moved eastward within that plot and has been carrying on his own business in a separate structure raised by him and the plaintiffs were possessing the land described below separately from pro-defendant No. 15. The said plaintiffs jointly were running the business of bamboo and bamboo mats etc. with their side business such as contractory up till .... Be it stated here that business was the only source of income to maintain their big family.

2. That defendants No. 1 to 14 are some of the members of the defendant club, namely, "Unknown Club" situated on the road just to the east of 'Madan Mohan Bari'

of Cooch Behar. The defendants representing the defendant club, i.e. "Unknown Club" formerly in the year 20..........., brought a case numbering 21/65 T.S. in Sadar Munsif's against the present plaintiffs as defendants alleging that the lands described below, i.e. the suit-lands, have been settled with the defendant club, and thereby the said club got right in respect of the said lands for declaration that the defendant club are licensee for that land and has right, title as conferred by a deed of agreement alleged to be executed by the State of West Bengal and interest to and right to occupy and possess the said land and for recovery of possession of the same by evicting the present plaintiffs therefrom and after demolition of their structures thereon. The present plaintiffs, as defendants keenly contested that suit denying the right, title and interest to the suit-land by filing a written statement in due time but at last, when they, i.e. the defendant side (present) came to understand that they will lose the case, they withdrew the case one year ago on .... They had not the courage to bring any fresh suit or any proceeding up till now in respect of suit-lands and the suit properties against the present plaintiffs. The plaintiffs were thus in peaceful possession of the said properties up to .... When the defendants at about .... p.m. suddenly together with other 150 or 200 unknown men, being fully equipped with dangerous weapons such as lathis, daos, khantas etc., most illegally and forcibly came upon the suit-land, drove away the plaintiffs from the house standing thereon and totally dismantled their structures, i.e., tin chhapra consisting of 35 pieces of C.I. sheets, removed the fencing thereof and other belongings of the plaintiffs therein together with cash box containing the sale proceeds and hard cash altogether to the extent of ₹ .... and scattered away the stacked bamboo and bamboo mats lying thereon here and there and thereby causing a heavy loss to the plaintiffs to the tune of at least ₹ .... as roughly estimated and thus dispossessed the plaintiffs from the suit-land and took it in their illegal possession. The defendant club or the defendants who claim to be the members of the said club, had no possession at all in the suit-land before such dispossession and the plaintiffs were all along in possession of the same land to the entire exclusion of the defendant club and its members. Under the circumstances stated above, the plaintiffs are entitled to get restoration of possession in respect of the suit-land under s. 6 of the Specific Relief Act 1963 and also to get the compensation as estimated from the defendants for the damage caused by the defendants to the plaintiffs. The plaintiffs are always entitled to get those reliefs. The defendants have no right to dispossess the plaintiffs from the suit-land.

3. That defendants Nos. 1 to 15 are members of the defendant club. There are other members also. The plaintiffs do not know their names, description and places of residence. But they all have common interest. As such, it is necessary for the plaintiffs to bring this suit against the defendants in their representative character as enjoined under Or. 1, r. 8 of CPC and for that purpose, the plaintiffs are bringing this suit with the leave of the court.

4. That for the purpose of jurisdiction, the suit-land is valued at ₹ .... and for restoration of the same under s. 6 of the Specific Relief Act, half of the *ad valorem* court-fees payable for ₹ .... is paid for this suit and for the compensation the plaintiff tentatively value their claims, for the present at ₹ .... and *ad valorem* court-fees thereon are paid and claim the entire amount that may be found due from the defendants to the plaintiffs, on ascertainment by the court and pray to pay further the required amount of *ad valorem* court-fees upon the amount assessed thereafter.

5. The cause of action for this present suit on .... at about .... p.m. when the defendants forcibly and illegally dispossessed the plaintiff from this suit-land by demolition of structures, i.e. the tin chhapra thereon and caused a heavy loss to the plaintiffs by dismantling the same and by removing all movables lying therein including

the cash money and all belongings of the plaintiffs and also scattering away here and there the bamboo and bamboo mats etc. lying thereon.

6. The plaintiff, therefore, pray:

(*a*) for a decree for restoration of possession of the suit-land in favour of the plaintiffs against the defendant under s. 6 of the Specific Relief Act 1963,

(*b*) for a decree for the amount of compensation due to the plaintiff for the damage caused by the defendants to be ascertained by the court,

(*c*) for a decree for all costs of the suit,

(*d*) for such other relief or reliefs as the plaintiffs may be entitled to.

SCHEDULE OF SUIT-LAND

SCHEDULE OF THE PROPERTIES

Upon the above land:

1. One C.I. sheet chhapra. 22$^{1}/_{5}$ft. length x 21$^{1}/_{5}$ ft. breadth within 35 pcs. of C.I. sheets, 16 shal khuttis bamboo fencing, wooden frame, having three wooden chouki and wooden planking ₹ ....

2. Two Hazak lights ₹ ....

3. One cash box containing cash of ₹ .... cash in hand and ₹ .... sale proceeds and price of the said cash box ₹ ....

4. One almirah wooden—₹ ....

5. Bedding—complete one set—₹ ....

6. Tape 100 ft.—₹ ....

7. Other implements (iron) such as dao, axe, spade etc.—₹ ....

8. One account book—₹ ....

9. One stock book—₹ ....

Bamboo—450 in number of big varieties and 1,312 in number of Makla variety.

Bamboo mats— 3,755 pieces, size 3' x 4' ft. each.
748 pieces sized 4' x 5' ft. each.

Bamboo splints—in all 1,203 bundles in number.

Salwood planks— 12 pcs. size 2$^{1}/_{5}$ x 12' each.
6 pcs. size 2$^{1}/_{5}$ x 10' each.
6 pcs. size 2$^{1}/_{5}$ x 10' each.
6 pcs. size 2$^{1}/_{5}$ x 71/5' each.
15 pcs. size 2$^{1}/_{5}$ x 5' each.
3 pcs. size 2$^{1}/_{5}$ x 5' each.
45 pcs. size 5' x 1' each.

Sal posts—in length 5' fit 77 pcs.

Tarpaulin—6.

Gunny Bag screens—200 yds. and their wooden frames worth of ₹ .... in all excluding the items Nos. 1 to 9.

Verification

Affidavit

NOTES: 1. AIR 1979 Bom 405—A suit for possession on title is to be distinguished with a suit under s. 6 of the Specific Relief Act. A suit under s. 6 cannot be resisted on the ground of title. It can be maintained against a true owner if he has dispossessed the plaintiff otherwise than in due course of law.

2. Presumption in title from possession can arise only where facts disclose no title in any party—AIR 1968 SC 1165.

3. Question of title is irrelevant in a suit like this—AIR 1968 SC 620. Also see AIR 1970 SC 846; AIR 1971 Ori 135.

381. Suit for possession on the ground of possessory title

In the Court of .... at ....

Suit No. .... of 20 ....

(Set out cause title)

The plaintiff states as follows:

1. That the plaintiff had been in exclusive and peaceful possession of a piece of land measuring .... Bighas at .... Mouza .... P.S. ....District .... more specifically described in the Schedule appended below (hereinafter referred to as suit property), by cultivation for about .... years since 20........

2. That by act of possession claiming as of own, the plaintiff acquired therein a possessory title against the defendant who has nó title thereto.

3. That the defendant trespassed into the suit-property on .... and ploughed the same and thereby forcibly and wrongfully dispossessed the plaintiff from the suit-property.

4. That the plaintiff is entitled to recover khas possession of the same, at .... within the jurisdiction of this court.

5. That the cause of action for this suit arose on .... (the date of dispossession).

6. That for the purpose of jurisdiction and court-fees, the suit is valued at ₹ .... and court-fees of ₹ .... are paid.

The plaintiff, therefore, prays for a decree and judgment:

(*i*) For recovery of khas possession of the suit-property.

(*ii*) Costs.

SCHEDULE

Verification

Affidavit

NOTES: 1. Where a plaintiff has possessed the land adversely for the statutory period of 12 years, he acquires a title and can bring a suit if dispossessed to throw out a trespasser under Art. 64 of the Limitation Act 1963 but where he possessed for a period shorter than 12 years he will have to sue under s. 6 of the Specific Relief Act 1963 within six months from the date of dispossession.

2. Apart from above, a plaintiff having anterior possession can sue a trespasser under general law but the Calcutta High Court holds a different view—AIR 1934 Cal 561.

3. A trespasser can sue the rightful owner; a tenant when dispossessed by a third party can sue. According to Calcutta High Court, a landlord in the event is entitled to sue the trespasser without joining the dispossessed tenant—15 CWN 294.
4. A suit on possessory title can be filed within 12 years of dispossession (*vide* Art. 64 of the Limitation Act 1963)—AIR 1970 Bom 405. Prior possession even without semblance of title in plaintiff as against trespasser would be lawful and suit can be filed independently of s. 9 (Specific Relief Act 1877), i.e. even after a period of six months from dispossession—AIR 1971 Ori 185. Now s. 6 of the Specific Relief Act 1963.

382. Suit for possession under s. 6 of the Specific Relief Act 1963

In the Court of .... at ....

Suit No. .... of 20 ....

(Set out cause title)

The above-named plaintiff states as follows:

1. That the plaintiff held a piece of agricultural land measuring .... acres at Mouja .... P.S. .... District .... more fully described in Schedule 'A' below (hereinafter referred to as suit-property) and was in peaceful possession thereof.

2. That the defendant dispossessed the plaintiff on .... from the suit-property and has been since then wrongfully possessing the suit-property.

3. That the cause of action for this suit arose on .... (date of dispossession) at Mouja .... within the jurisdiction of this court.

4. That for the purpose of jurisdiction and court-fees the suit is valued at ₹ .... and court-fees of ₹ .... are paid.

The plaintiff, therefore, claims for a decree:

(*i*) For recovery of khas possession of the suit-property.

(*ii*) Costs.

SCHEDULE 'A'

(State here particulars of suit-property)

Verification

Affidavit

NOTES: 1. This type of suit is not maintainable against the Government—See s. 6(2)(*b*) of the Specific Relief Act 1963 but the Government may bring a suit under s. 6. Dispossession by a statutory body under statutory rules—suit is maintainable—AIR 1971 Raj 84.
2. Limitation is six months from date of dispossession—See s. 6(2)(*a*) of the Specific Relief Act 1963.
3. No other relief except restoration of possession is admissible and that can be had without reference to any question of title—AIR 1934 All 541.
4. Court-fees half of *ad valorem* court-fees on the amount or value of the subject-matter under Schedule 1, Art. 2 of the Court Fees Act.
5. AIR 1970 SC 846—In an action for ejectment against a trespasser prior possession of the plaintiff is sufficient title notwithstanding that the suit is brought more than six months after dispossession.

6. In a suit under s. 6 the plaintiff need not prove title. If the period of six months has passed the defendant is entitled to raise question of title and requires the plaintiff to prove better title—AIR 1968 SC 1165.
7. A possessory suit lies even for partial dispossession—ILR 5 Mad 250.

383. Suit for joint possession of an immovable property

In the Court of .... at ....

Suit No. .... of 20 ....

(Set out cause title)

The plaintiff states as follows:

1. That the plaintiff and the defendant are brothers, being sons of A.B., who died on ....

2. That the said A.B. held house property at .... Town, P.S. .... District .... within the jurisdiction of this court. The said property is described more particularly in the Schedule below.

3. That the plaintiff was so long living in Kolkata in connection with his service. The defendant was living with the said A.B. in the same mess in the said house premises. On the death of A.B. on 20.............., the defendant took possession of the said property to the exclusion of the plaintiff.

4. That the plaintiff is entitled to joint possession in the said property with the defendant and had requested defendant to share possession of the same with the plaintiff on .... but to no purpose.

5. That the cause of action for this suit arose on .... when the plaintiff's request for sharing possession was rejected by the defendant.

The plaintiff prays for:

(*i*) a decree for joint possession of the said property in the Schedule below to the extent of the plaintiff's share.

(*ii*) Costs.

SCHEDULE

Verification

Affidavit

NOTES: 1. Articles 64 & 65 of the Limitation Act—Mere possession even of a trespasser does not constitute adverse possession unless accompanied by open assertion of hostile title—*Premendu* v *Sripati* AIR 1976 Cal 55; *Gaya Parshad* v *Dr. Nirmal Chander* AIR 1984 SC 930 and *Jahrul Islam* v *Abul Kalan* AIR 1991 Cal 132. No evidence of open assertion of hostile title against plaintiff. No fact indicative of ouster was proved to have taken place any time 12 years before the date of suit. Plea of adverse possession is not maintainable. Burden in this behalf squarely lies upon the defendant—Merely 15 or 16 years of possession cannot be said to be indicative of presumption of ouster—*Joti Dadu Novale* v *Manukabai* AIR 1988 Bom 348. No adverse possession against a co-sharer can be inferred in the absence of evidence of open assertion of a hostile title coupled with exclusive enjoyment and possession by one of them to the knowledge the other—AIR 1971 SC 1337.

2. In order perfect title two separate ingredients are necessary—
(*i*) *Corpus possidendi* (Physical possession).
(*ii*) *Animus possidendi* (intention to exclude the adversary from possession).

The possession must be adequate in continuity and publicity.

Mere possession beyond statutory period is not sufficient—*Venkatachalaiah* v *Nanjundaiah* AIR 1992 Kant 270.

384. Suit for declaration of title by adverse possession with injunction

In the Court of the Civil Judge (Junior Division) at Mathabhanga

Title Suit No. .... of 20.........

(Set out cause title)

The above-named plaintiff states as follows:

1. That the principal defendant No. 3 and defendant No. 4 and the pro forma defendant No. 5 and defendant No. 6 together with one A.B., held a piece of land measuring 2.90 acres at Mouja Bara Simulguri, P.S. Mathabhanga, more particularly described in the Schedule 'A' appended below.

2. That the said defendant No. 3 and the defendant No. 4 each had 4 annas while the said pro forma defendants No. 5 and 6 each 2 annas and the said A.B. balance 4 annas share.

3. That in the current settlement the said land in Schedule 'A' below has been recorded in the names of the principal defendants No. 3 and 4 and the pro forma defendants No. 5 and 6 and the said A.B., with noting of their respective shares in finally published Khatian No. .... of Mouja Bara Simulguri, P.S. Mathabhanga.

4. That the said land in Schedule 'A' comprises two plots—to wit, plots No. ....

5. That the plaintiff owned land in Khatian No. .... of Mouja Bara Simulguri in *Darchukani* interest contiguous to the land in Schedule 'A' and came to possess the land in Schedule 'A' since .... 14 .... B.S. and has been possessing the land openly, adversely and to its entirety to the knowledge of the rightful owners continuously and without interruption since then.

6. That the name of the plaintiff has been entered in Col. 23 of the relevant Khatian No.................. for the said land in plots No. .... as adverse possessor since 13................. B.S. That the plaintiff gave over possession of plot No. .... to his cousin brother one year back and he is possessing the same. The plot No. .... in particular is being possessed by the plaintiff which is specifically described in Schedule 'B' and is the suit property.

7. That the said recorded defendants or any body else did not possess the suit property since .... B.S. That the principal defendants made an unsuccessful attempt on the .... 20....... to dispossess the plaintiff from the suit-property. On enquiry the plaintiff has learnt that the pro forma defendants No. 5 and 6, sold the property in Schedule 'B', i.e. the suit-property to the principal defendants No. 1 and 2.

8. That the said A.B. died leaving his only daughter, namely, the said pro forma defendant No. 6 and her 4 annas share devolved on the pro forma defendant No. 6. That the pro forma defendant Nos. 5 and 6 had no right to sell the suit-property to the principal defendant Nos. 1 and 2 as their title as well as the title of other co-sharers in the suit-property extinguished long back by 12 years' adverse possession as aforesaid.

9. That in the facts of the case the plaintiff has acquired a good and valid title to the suit-property by adverse possession for more than 12 years.

The plaintiff prays:

(*i*) For a declaration that the plaintiff acquired right, title and interest in the suit-property.

(*ii*) For injunction restraining the defendants from taking possession of the suit-property.

SCHEDULE 'A'

SCHEDULE 'B'—Suit-property

Verification

Affidavit

385. Suit for legacy

In the Court of Civil Judge (Senior Division) at Alipore

Suit No. .... of 20 ....

Mr. P, residing at ...., Kolkata

.... *Plaintiff*

versus

Mr. X, residing at ...., Kolkata

.... *Defendant*

Suit for legacy valued at ₹ ....

The plaintiff states:

1. Mr. M. residing at ...., Kolkata died on 15th July 20 .... after making his last and final Will and testatement on 10th June 20 ....

2. By the said Will the said Mr. M. bequeathed his assets and properties to the plaintiff and appointed defendant as the Executor of the said Will.

3. The defendant also applied for and obtained a probate of the said Will. The defendant was also required to take possession of all movable assets and immovable properties covered by the said Will.

4. The plaintiff has come to learn that the defendant did not intentionally take possession of certain portions of properties mentioned in annexure 'A' in respect of the Estate left behind by Mr. M., deceased, covered by the said Will.

5. By a letter dated 17th August 20 ...., the plaintiff requested the defendant to take possession of the said property, sell it and discharge his obligations stated in the said Will, but the defendant has not taken any steps so far.

6. The defendant as executor of the said Will and as he has obtained necessary probate of the said Will is bound legally to act in terms of directions contained in the said Will also by probate to protect the interests of Estate of Mr. M. as well as that of the plaintiff.

7. In spite of requests and demands made by the plaintiff the defendant has failed and neglected to take possession of some of the properties covered by the said Will and also to discharge his obligation in the said Will as the executor thereof.

8. The plaintiff claims for payment of his legacy valued at ₹ .... as also the Administration of the said estate covered by the said Will.

9. In spite of demands made and several letters written by plaintiff to defendant, the defendant has failed to reply to the said letters or to act in accordance with directions of the said Will for which the probate has been granted to the said defendant.

10. The plaintiff's cause of action for this suit arose within jurisdiction of this learned court inasmuch as the defendants as executor has committed defaults in not acting as per terms of the said Will and probate and certain properties covered by the said Will are situate within the jurisdiction of this learned court and that in spite of requests made to the defendant, the defendant has committed defaults at Alipore Road, Kolkata within the jurisdiction of this learned court.

11. In view of this, the cause of action for this suit arose within jurisdiction of this learned court.

12. No part of the plaintiff's claims or cause of action for this suit is barred by law of limitation.

13. The plaintiff states that the suit has been valued at ₹ .... being the estimated valuation of assets left behind in the said will and on which necessary court-fees in stamps have been paid.

14. This learned court has the jurisdiction to entertain, try and determine this suit in view of the cause of action arising within jurisdiction of this learned court as also in view of the fact that the defendant resides within the jurisdiction of this learned court.

15. The cause of action of the plaintiff arose within jurisdiction of this learned court and the same is continuing day to day.

The plaintiff, therefore, prays for:

(*a*) decree directing the defendant to take possession of properties mentioned in Annexure 'A' hereof and to deal with the same in terms of Will;

(*b*) decree for payment of ₹ .... by the defendant to the plaintiff being the value of legacy payable to the plaintiff under the Will;

(*c*) decree for accounts of the estate left in the said Will of which the defendant obtained the probate;

(*d*) decree for rendering accounts by the defendant in respect of the assets and properties covered by the said Will probate of which has been obtained by the defendant;

(*e*) cost;

(*f*) further and other orders be made and directions be given as this learned court may deem fit and proper to afford complete relief to the plaintiff.

Annexure A

Verification

Affidavit

PRE-EMPTION

386. Suit for pre-emption

In the Court of the Civil Judge (Senior Division) at Alipore

Suit No. .... of 20 ....

Mr. P., residing at No. .... Alipore Road, Kolkata

..... *Plaintiff*

versus

1. Mr. X, residing at No. .... Alipore Road, Kolkata.
2. Mr. Y, residing at No. .... Alipore Road, Kolkata

.... *Defendants*

Suit for Pre-emption valued at ₹ ....

The plaintiff states that:

1. The plaintiff and the defendant No. 1 are brothers. Their father, Mr. Q, was the owner of a two-storyed building being the premises No. ...., Alipore Road, Kolkata.

In the said two-storeyed building there are 5 bedrooms, 5 attached bathrooms, a kitchen including provision of all modern amenities.

2. After the death of plaintiff's father, the assets and properties left behind were equally divided between the sons, being the plaintiff and the first defendant. In this connection, there was a partition deed duly registered which provided for allocation of Ground Floor to the plaintiff and allotment of the first floor and roof rights to the first defendant. The said partition deed specifically provided that if any of the two brothers, namely, plaintiff and the first defendant had to dispose off the said property by sale or otherwise, his portion of the premises, then the said portion has to be sold or transferred by an offer made to the other brother as he will be vitally interested to possess the other portion of the property. Such partition deed was duly executed and registered and the same is still valid and enforceable.

3. The first defendant surreptitiously and without the knowledge of the plaintiff and in total breach of the said deed sold his portion of the said premises, being the entire portion of the first floor premises with all rights and appurtenances there to defendant No. 2 by a sale deed executed and registered with the Registrar of Assurances, West Bengal, Kolkata. The plaintiff states that such transfer and execution of the deed of sale was in breach of the Agreement, Partition and in violation of the covenants and undertaking given by first defendant.

4. After coming to know of such wrongful transfer of the first defendant's first floor of premises No. .... Alipore Road, Kolkata, the plaintiff requested defendant No. 2 to sell the said entire first floor portion of the said premises being .... Alipore Road, Kolkata at the price he had paid to the first defendant plus 20% thereon by way of due compensation. But the defendant No. 2 refused to accept the said offer and to sell the said first floor of premises No. .... Alipore Road, Kolkata to the plaintiff. A copy of the said letter addressed by plaintiff to defendant No. 2 is annexed hereto and marked 'A'. In view of the aforesaid and wrongful refusal of defendant No. 2 either to sell or transfer the said first floor of premises No. .... Alipore Road, Kolkata, the plaintiff hereby claims the right of pre-emption to the said property, purchased by defendant No. 2 from the defendant No. 1.

5. The plaintiff has the right of pre-emption under the law as also under the said contract contained in the deed of partition. In reply to the plaintiff's letter, defendant No. 1 admitted transferring the first floor property of premises No. .... Alipore Road, Kolkata but contended that he was not bound by the covenants contained in partition deed inasmuch as since the property was divided and registered in individual names of the plaintiff and the first defendant, the said partition deed had lost its force.

6. In view of the said refusal of the defendants to honour the said agreement contained in the said partition deed as also provisions of the law, the plaintiff has been compelled to file the present suit.

7. This learned court has the jurisdiction to proceed inasmuch as the premises in the said suit is situate within the territorial limits of this learned court and also the cause of action arose at ...., Alipore Road, Kolkata all within the jurisdiction of this learned court. Further the defendant No. 2 is residing within the jurisdiction of this learned court.

8. For the purposes of jurisdiction and court-fees, this suit is valued at ₹ .... on which court-fees in stamps have been duly paid. Further, the cause of action of the plaintiff is not barred by the law of limitation as the plaint is being presented within a period of three years from the date of wrongful transfer by the first defendant of the entire first floor premises situate at .... Alipore Road, Kolkata.

The plaintiff, therefore, claims:

(*a*) A decree for transfer to the plaintiff of the entire first floor of premises No. .... Alipore Road, Kolkata sold by first defendant to the second defendant by way of and in enforcement of the right of pre-emption on payment of the consideration money paid by second defendant to the first defendant plus 20% thereon;

(*b*) Order of injunction restraining the defendant No. 2 from selling or disposing off or encumbering in any manner whatsoever the said first floor of the premises No. .... Alipore Road, Kolkata without first offering the same to the plaintiff;

(*c*) Costs of the suit;

(*d*) Further and other orders be made and/or reliefs be granted as the plaintiff is entitled to in law and equity.

Annexure 'A'

Verification

Affidavit

387. Suit for pre-emption of the land sold

In the Court of .... at ......

Suit No. .... of 20......

(Set out cause title)

The plaintiff states that:

1. The plaintiff and the defendants are governed by the Mohammedan Sunni Law and they are residing in the same village side by side.

2. Under the said law it is the moral obligation of the person to first offer the property he intends to sell to the owner of the adjoining land and only if such offer is refused then the owner can sell it to an outsider.

3. Defendant No. 2 an adjoining landowner sold and transferred on .... 20 .... ten acres of land particulars whereof are given in schedule annexed hereto marked 'A' by a registered deed of sale.

4. The plaintiff, though he is the owner of the adjoining land had no knowledge of such sale and after coming to know of such sale from a neighbour the plaintiff made enquiries and came to know of the said fact.

5. The plaintiff states that the plaintiff being the actual owner of adjoining land was thus entitled to be first offered for sale of the said land by defendant No. 2 before sale to the defendant No. 1 and the plaintiff being owner of adjoining land under the provisions of the Sunni law was entitled to "Shuffa" meaning thereby the right of pre-emption to have the land offered for sale before offering same to an outsider.

6. The plaintiff on coming to know the fact of said transfer of land by defendant No. 2 to the defendant No. 1 without offering the same to plaintiff, the plaintiff by a letter asserted his right *talab-i-mowshibat* as per the provisions of the law in the presence of the defendant No. 1 and two witnesses who were specially called for the said purpose on the aforesaid land observing the formalities of Sunni law of pre-emption.

7. In view of the aforesaid the plaintiff claims a decree for pre-emption in respect of the said land mentioned in the schedule on payment of the sale price as paid by the purchaser defendant No. 1 and that the defendant No. 2 will not suffer any prejudice and that the defendant No. 1 would get back his money paid to defendant No. 2 at the time of purchase of said land.

8. The plaintiff's cause of action is not barred by law of limitation.

9. There has been no waiver or acquiescence on the part of plaintiff.

10. The plaintiff has paid court-fee in stamps on the valuation of the suit properties at ₹ ....

The plaintiff, therefore, prays for and claims:

(*a*) Decree directing the defendant No. 1 to transfer the said property purchased by him from the defendant No. 2 and as described in the Schedule on payment by the plaintiff a sum of ₹ .... being the price paid by defendant No. 1 to defendant No. 2 for purchase of the land plus interest;

(*b*) Receiver;

(*c*) Injunction;

(*d*) Costs;

(*e*) Further and other reliefs.

SCHEDULE 'A'

Verification

Affidavit

388. Suit for shuffa or pre-emption under Muslim law

(Sunni law—on the ground of vicinage)

In the Court of .... at ......

Suit No. .... of 20.......

(Set out cause title)

The plaintiff states as follows:

1.That by a deed of sale (registered) dated .... one Md. XY son of .... residing at village .... P.S. .... District .... had sold to the defendant 3 acres of land appertaining to Khatian No. .... of Mouja .... P.S. .... District .... More fully described in Schedule 'A' below for a consideration of ₹ .... only. The said sale was valid, complete and *bona fide*.

2. That the plaintiff owns and possesses lands in Khatian No. .... of Mouja .... P.S. .... District .... adjoining the said land in Schedule 'A' below and is *a Shafi-i-jar* and is, therefore, entitled to claim pre-emption.

3. That the plaintiff, the said Md. XY and the defendants belong to Sunni sect.

4. That the plaintiff heard on .... of the sale by Md. XY in favour of the defendants and immediately declared his intention to assert his right (*talab-i-mowashibat*) the same day.

5. On the following morning the plaintiff affirmed his intention, referring expressly to the previous *talab-i-mowashibat* and made a formal demand in presence of the defendant and witnesses specially called to bear witness to the demand being made. Thus the plaintiff observed *talab-i-ishhad.*

6. That the cause of action for this suit arose on .... (date of sale of the property).

7. That for the purpose of jurisdiction and court-fees the suit is valued at ₹ .... (consideration amount) and *ad valorem* court-fees are paid thereon.

The plaintiff therefore, prays:

(*i*) For decree for possession of the property in Schedule 'A' below on payment of ₹ .... plus interest to the defendant.

(*ii*) Costs.

SCHEDULE 'A'

(State here the particulars of the property)

Verification

Affidavit

NOTES: 1. Mohamedan laws of pre-emption have no application in Madras-Presidency. For:
Punjab—see the Punjab Pre-emption Act 1913.
For Oudh—see the Oudh Laws Act 1876.

2. See Chapter 13—Pre-emption—Principles of Mahomedan Law by F. Mulla, 22nd Ed.

3. Shiah law and Sunni law on pre-emption are slightly different. Under Shiah law no pre-emption on ground of vicinage, or participation in immunities and appendages.

4. Right of pre-emption does not arise on sale of leasehold interests in land sought to be pre-empted—AIR 1968 SC 540.

5. Whether the right is founded on law or general usage or on special contract limitation is one year under Art. 97 of the Limitation Act 1963 from when the vendee taking physical possession of the land is sought to be pre-empted.

6. Purchaser of lands is not entitled to claim compensation for improvements done since his purchase where pre-emption right is upheld—AIR 1971 Cal 169.

389. Suit for pre-emption under Muslim law (Shiah law—On the ground of co-sharership)

In the Court of .... at ......

Suit No. .... of 20.......

(Set out cause title)

The above-named plaintiff states as follows:

1. That by a registered deed of sale dated .... one Md. XY son of .... had sold to the defendant three acres of land, appertaining to Khatian No. .... of Mouja .... P.S. .... District ...., more fully described in the Schedule appended hereto, for a consideration of ₹ .... only. The said sale was valid, complete and *bona fide.*

2. That the plaintiff is the only co-sharer of the said Md. XY in respect of 8 annas share of the lands in the said Khatian No. .... of aforesaid Mouja and is a *Shafi-i-shaiek* and is, therefore, entitled to claim pre-emption.

3. That the vendor Md. XY and the plaintiff are Shiahs and governed by the Shiah law of pre-emption (or, that the vendor Md. XY is a Sunni Mahomedan and the plaintiff is a Shiah Muslim and they are guided by the Shiah law of pre-emption).

(Or, that the vendor Md. XY is a Shiah Muslim and the plaintiff is a Sunni and the right of pre-emption of the plaintiff is governed by Shiah law).

4. That the cause of action for this suit arose on .... (date of sale of the property).

5. That for the purpose of jurisdiction and court-fees the suit is valued at ₹ .... (consideration amount) and *ad valorem* court-fees are paid thereon.

The plaintiff therefore, prays:

(*i*) For decree for possession of the property in schedule below on payment of ₹ .... to the defendant.

(*ii*) Costs.

SCHEDULE

Verification

Affidavit

390. Petition of pre-emption under the West Bengal Land Reforms Act

Pre-emption Case No. .... 20..........

A. B. .... *Petitioner*

versus

C. D. .... *Opposite party*

Petition under s. 8 of the West Bengal Land Reforms Act 1955.

The petitioner states as follows:

1. That the petitioner and one A.B. held in *ejmali* an agricultural plot of land measuring 2.19 acres at Mouja .... P.S. .... District .... recorded in Hal Settlement Khatian No. .... of the said Mouja.

2. That the petitioner owns 12 annas share in the said plot of land while the said A.B. held remaining 4 annas share.

3. That out of his 4 annas share in the plot of land the said A.B. sold on .... to the C.D. (opp. party) a portion thereof measuring, 12 acres by a *kobala* for a consideration of ₹ .... The said sale-deed was registered in the office of the District Sub-Registrar of .... on .... The said, 12 acres is more fully described in the Schedule below.

4. That the C.D. is not a co-sharer in that plot of land. The petitioner, therefore has had right of pre-empting the land in the Schedule below.

5. That the petitioner has deposited on .... with the .... by challan No. .... dt. .... sum of ₹ .... with a further sum of 10 per cent of that amount.

6. That the petitioner received notice under sub-sec. (5) of s. 5 of the West Bengal Land Reforms Act 1955 and this petition is within time. (Or, that no notice as contemplated in sub-sec. (5) of s. 5 of the West Bengal Land Reforms Act 1955, was served on the petitioner and the petitioner came to know of the aforesaid sale on ....).

7. That the cause of action for this petition arose on ....when the said deed of sale in favour of the O.P. was registered at...............

The petitioner, therefore, prays:

For transfer of the property in the Schedule below to the petitioner by pre-emption.

NOTES: 1. Forum: Court of Civil Judge (Junior Division) (in West Bengal).

2. Limitation—(*i*) In the case of a co-sharer applicant—three months from the service of notice under s. 5(5).

(*ii*) When no notice served—s. 137 of the Limitation Act 1963 providing three years will apply—see 55 CWN 501.

(*iii*) In the case of contiguous raiyat—four months from the date of transfer.

Where an application under s. 8 is filed after the coming into force of the Limitation Act 1963, s. 5 thereof will be applicable to the applicant and if he can show that he had sufficient cause for not filing the application within four months, the delay may be condoned—*Chandra Sekhar Sadar* v *Baidyanath Ghosh* AIR 1982 Cal 6 (AIR 1976 SC 105 rel. on).

3. Date of accrual of right of pre-emption—date of registration of the sale deed —not the date of execution of the kabala—see 44 CWN 802; 53 CWN 107.

4. See ss. 8 and 9 of the West Bengal Land Reforms Act 1955 (effect from 22.10.1963).

5. Purchaser of land is not entitled to claim compensation of improvements done since his purchase where right of pre-emption is upheld—AIR 1971 Cal 169.

6. Application filed for pre-emption on ground of being co-sharer. Amendment application claiming pre-emption on ground of vicinage. Application cannot be refused on ground of limitation. Held, the amendment cannot be said to change the nature and character of the proceeding for pre-emption nor does it introduce a new and inconsistent case—AIR 1978 Cal 482.

7. Right of pre-emption of person having land adjoining the plot out of which a portion is sold. Held, the person having land adjoining the plot of land over of which the land was sold has every right to claim pre-emption even if his land is intervened by a piece of land held by another co-sharer—AIR 1978 NOC 194 (Cal).

8. For a non-notified co-sharer the limitation for an application in court, if there was no service of notice of sale of portion of the plot of land on the

other co-sharers as required in law, for any reason whatsoever, will be three years from the date of the completion of such sale—AIR 1978 NOC 206 (Cal).

9. Right of pre-emption—It is weak and inequitable right, can be defeated by estoppel. Failure to serve notice by vendor on pre-emptor does not render sale void—*Indira Bai* v *Nand Kishore* AIR 1991 SC 1055.
10. Homestead of agriculturist—It is to be treated as agricultural land though might not be an agricultural land—Its sale to stranger, application by co-sharer of such holding, for pre-emption is maintainable—*Abdulla Kabir* v *Md. Nasiruddin* AIR 1989 SC 931.
11. The right of pre-emption is a weak right and it can be defeated by estoppel. Even in Muslim Law which is the genesis of this right, as it was unknown to Hindu law and was brought in wake of Mohammedan Rule, it is settled that the right of pre-emption is lost by estoppel and acquiescence—*Indira Bai* v *Nand Kishore* AIR 1991 SC 1055.

391. Suit for foreclosure of mortgaged property

In the Court of the Civil Judge (Senior/Junior) Division at ....

Suit No. .... of ....

(Set out cause title)

Or. 34 of the Code of Civil Procedure 1908
Valued at ₹ ....

The plaintiff states as follows:

1. The defendant mortgaged his property particulars whereof are given in a schedule annexed hereto marked "A" and obtained a loan from the plaintiff for ₹ .... for defraying the expenses of the defendant's daughter's marriage.

2. The plaintiff gave the said loan of ₹ .... to the defendant and the defendant by way of security executed a Registered Simple Mortgage in favour of plaintiff in respect of his dwelling house.

3. The defendant agreed to repay the said sum of ₹ .... with interest at 15% per annum and committed to redeem within a period of 8 (eight) years and the interest was payable half-yearly and the plaintiff would duly issue receipt for such payment.

4. In breach of the agreement the defendant has not paid any interest or any portion of the principal amount though since the loan was given and the mortgage deed was executed more than 5 (five) years have passed.

5. The plaintiff through his lawyer issued a notice dated .... which was duly served on the defendant. A copy of the demand letter and evidence of receipt thereof are annexed hereto collectively marked "B".

6. In spite of receipt of the said demand letter the defendant has not paid any portion of the principal amount or interest.

7. The plaintiff states that the defendant is not entitled to redeem the mortgaged property in the facts and circumstances of the case.

8. The plaintiff's cause of action for this suit arose on the date when the mortgage was created and on the date when the notice of demand was served on the defendant. The cause of action arose at the place where the defendant resides and where the mortgaged property is situate, both within the jurisdiction of this learned court.

9. No part of the plaintiff's cause of action for this suit is barred by the law of limitation.

10. The plaintiff has paid court-fee on the valuation of the mortgaged property.

The plaintiff, therefore, prays for and claims:

(*a*) Preliminary decree against the defendant directing him to pay the claim of the plaintiff being ₹ .... with further interest from .... and costs within a period to be fixed by this learned court and in default of payment decree of foreclosure preventing the defendant from redeeming the scheduled property;

(*b*) Costs;

(*c*) Further and other orders be made and reliefs be granted as to this learned court may deem fit and proper in the facts and circumstances of the case.

ANNEXURE A

Verification

Affidavit

NOTE: Section 26 and Or. VI, r. 15(4) of the Code of Civil Procedure 1908 require that in every pleading (plaint and written statement) facts shall be proved by affidavit and that the person verifying the pleading shall furnish an affidavit in support of his pleadings.

In view of this provision the person who has verified the plaint shall also file a separate affidavit which is intended to be used as Examination-in-Chief and should be in greater detail.

392. Defence to a claim by a Hindu for pre-emption according to custom

In the Court of .... at ......

Suit No. .... of 20.......

(Set out cause title)

The defendant states as follows:

1. The plaintiff is not a native of the district of .... in Bihar. He is a native of the district of .... in the Uttar Pradesh and has no right of pre-emption.

2. The sale in question is only a fictitious one got up with a view to protect the property from the claims of certain creditors of the vendor.

Or

The sale in question was a sham transaction. No consideration was paid by the defendant except the sum of ₹1 and the rest of the consideration was covered by a series of bonds none of which has yet been satisfied.

3. Subject to what is hereinbefore stated, the defendant denies that the plaintiff came to know of the sale for the first time on .... He knew about the sale on ....

4. The defendant denies that the plaintiff declared the alleged or any intention to assert the right of pre-emption or that the plaintiff affirmed the said intention or performed the ceremony of *talabi-ishbad* as alleged or at all.

5. Alternatively, the defendant says that the plaintiff did not declare his intention to assert the right of pre-emption immediately on receipt of news of the sale and also

did not affirm his said intention or perform the said ceremony without delay. The suit be dismissed with costs.

Verification

Affidavit

RAILWAYS AND OTHER COMMON CARRIERS

393. Suit against common carriers for refusal to carry goods

In the Court of .... at ......

Suit No. .... of 20.......

(Set out cause title)

The plaintiff states as follows:

1. The defendants are common carriers and carry on a motor transport service from .... to ....

2. On the .... 20........, the plaintiffs tendered to the defendants as such common carriers at .... twelve cases of sundry goods to be conveyed for them from .... to ....

3. The plaintiffs were ready and willing and offered to pay to the defendants ₹ .... being reasonable reward or hire for so doing.

4. The defendants refused to receive or carry the said goods or any portion thereof, although they had then ample room in their vehicles and sufficient means and convenience to carry the said goods as aforesaid.

5. By reason of the premises the plaintiffs were obliged to engage a lorry on the said day for conveying the said goods to the place aforesaid at greater expense.

Particulars of damage:

Difference between the cost of carriage if the goods had been conveyed by the defendants and the cost of carriage actually incurred as aforesaid ... ₹ ....

The plaintiffs claim—

₹ .... damages.

Verification

Affidavit

394. Suit against a common carrier for compensation for injury or damage to goods

In the Court of the Civil Judge (Senior Division), at ....

Money Suit No. .... of 20 ....

M/s. A. B., a firm registered under the Indian Partnership Act 1932 with its registered office and principal place of business at .... Road, Cooch Behar town, P.S. Kotowali, District Cooch Behar.

.... *Plaintiff*

versus

1. C.D. Corporation Hq. Cooch Behar.
2. P.Q. Insurance Co. ....
...... *Prin. Defendant*

3. E.F. .... Armenian Street, Kolkata.
.... *Pro-defendant*

Suit for compensation
Valued at ₹ ....

The above-named plaintiff states as follows:

1. That the defendant No. 1, Corporation at all material times was and is a common carrier engaged in the business of transporting for hire goods from place to place by its carrier service.

2. That on .... the pro forma defendant No. 3 delivered .... bags of goods to defendant No. 1 and the defendant No. 1, as such common carrier, received from the said pro forma defendant .... bags of .... at Kolkata office of the defendant No. 1 Corporation for carrying safely from Kolkata to Cooch Behar for hire under a Consignment Note No. .... dated .... issued by defendant No. 1.

3. That the plaintiff was the consignee of the above consignment for valuable consideration.

4. That defendant No. 1 did not safely carry the said goods and on the occasion of taking delivery of the consignment on .... it was noticed that .... bags out of the consignment were badly water damaged as described in the Schedule of Claim below. The amount of loss (by damage) suffered by the plaintiff firm is assessed at ₹ ....

5. That such damages to the consignment is due to gross negligence, misconduct and carelessness of the defendant Corporation or its agents and/or employees.

6. That the plaintiff-firm by their letters dated .... and .... addressed to the C.D. Corporation demanded payment of ₹ .... as compensation for the damage. The said letters were sent per registered post with A/D. Since then the plaintiff received a copy of a letter No. .... from defendant No. 1 wherefrom it appeared that defendant No. 1 was seeking settlement of the claim by defendant No. 2.

7. That the plaintiff thereafter served a notice dt. .... under s. 10 of the Carriers Act on the .... of the defendant Corporation by registered post with A/D through their authorised lawyer. Defendant No. 1 in reply intimated to the plaintiff's lawyer by a letter No. .... dt. .... that the claim was forwarded to the Defendant-Insurance Co. for settlement.

8. That none of the principal defendants 1 and 2 settled the claim so far. The plaintiff is entitled to recover the said sum as compensation from the principal defendants.

9. That the cause of action for this suit arose at Cooch Behar within the jurisdiction of this court on .... when the consignment was delivered to the plaintiff in partly damaged condition.

10. That for the purpose of jurisdiction and court-fees the suit is valued at ₹ ....

The plaintiff prays:

(*a*) for a judgment and decree for ₹ .... as per account in the Schedule of claim below,

(*b*) Costs.

Schedule of Claim

40% of 7 bags .... leaves damaged valued at	......	₹	....
30% of 7 bags .... leaves damaged valued at	......	₹	....
20% of 7 bags .... leaves damaged valued at	......	₹	....
Add sales tax 2% over the value		₹	....
		₹	....

Verification

Affidavit

NOTES: 1. For a suit for compensation for loss of or injuries to goods against a carrier limitation is three years when the loss or injury occurred—*vide* Art. 10 of the Limitation Act 1963—AIR 1979 AP 41.

2. Public carrier under M.V. Act is a common carrier. The provisions of the Contract Act do not govern the liability of a common carrier nor do they override the provisions of the Carriers Act. The scope of liability of a common carrier engaged in road transport is no way different from that of other common carriers by land.

3. A common carrier is not a mere bailee of goods entrusted to him. He is an insurer of goods. He is answerable for the loss of goods even if such loss is not caused by negligence or want of care on his part. Act of God and States enemies excepted—AIR 1971 Ker 197.

4. In the absence of any special contract negativing liability for loss occasioned by events beyond his control, a common carrier engaged in road transport is liable for loss of goods destroyed on the way by unruly mob. The activity of the mob is not the act of God—AIR 1971 Ker 197.

5. See Privy Council case on liability—ILR 18 Cal 620.

6. Notice—AIR 1979 AP 41.

7. Loss of goods by common-carrier. Suit by Insurance Co. making payment to owner. Notice under s. 10 not necessary—*National Insurance Co. Ltd.* v *Omprokash Poddar* AIR 1993 Cal 26.

8. In absence of special contract carrier cannot be absolved from liability for loss or damage on basis of conditions in consignment note—AIR 1991 Ker 41.

9. Jurisdiction—Condition about jurisdiction of court—cannot be acted upon unless the consignor has signed the Note—*South Eastern Roadways* v *United India Insurance* AIR 1991 Ker 41.

10. Notice under s. 10 of the Carriers Act before institution of suit for loss or injury to goods—appropriate notice under s. 10 is not necessary where certain documents, held on facts could be construed as notice to carrier under s. 10—*Balurghat Transport Co.* v *The Laxmi Tea* Co. AIR 1987 Cal 370.

11. Notice under s. 10 is obligatory even in cases of non-delivery. Reference to non-delivery in s. 9 but not in s. 10 is immaterial—*Sharma Goods Transport* v *Vidarbha Weavers* AIR 1988 Bom 269.

395. Suit against a private carrier for damages for injury to goods/for loss of article

In the Court of .... at ......

Suit No. .... of 20.......

(Set out cause title)

The plaintiff states as follows:

1. That the defendant M/s. A.B. Transport Agency is a firm, engaged in carrying goods occasionally from place to place for reward as a private carrier.

2. That the defendant as such entered into a contract (oral or written) on ..... with the plaintiff for carrying the plaintiff's house hold effects described in Schedule 'A' below, from the plaintiff's house at .... to .... and there deliver the same to the plaintiff for reward to the defendant.

3. That pursuant to the said contract on .... the defendant had carried the plaintiff's household articles detailed in Schedule 'A', by a truck on .... and delivered to the plaintiff the same day and the defendant was paid his charges therefor.

4. That on the occasion of delivery of the articles to the plaintiff, it was found that three tables and one almirah were broken.

(Or, that a box containing valuables was missing and was consequently lost to the plaintiff).

5. That the defendant failed to exercise reasonable care and skill in the matter of transporting the said articles, while in their custody, and because of defendant's carelessness and negligent handling some of the household articles, described fully in Schedule 'B', got broken and were delivered to the plaintiff in damaged condition.

(Or, that the defendant failed to exercise reasonable care and skill in the matter of carrying the said articles while in their custody and because of the defendant's careless and negligent handling the box, containing valuable articles, was found short and consequently not delivered to the plaintiff).

6. That for such injury to goods (or, that for loss of the articles) mentioned in Schedule 'B' the plaintiff has suffered loss and damage to the tune of ₹ ....

7. Cause of action.

8. Jurisdiction and suit valuation.

The plaintiff claims from the defendant:

(1) ₹ .... as damages.

(2) Costs.

SCHEDULE 'A'

SCHEDULE 'B'

Verification

Affidavit

NOTES: 1. Contract of carriage (Contract Act, s. 148)—A contract of carriage has certain peculiar ingredients. No doubt, for all outward purposes it is a contract for the carriage of goods which were entrusted by one party to the other. But a contract of carriage is not an equation of a contract of bailment nor is the carrier liable as a bailee. On the other hand, there is in-built in such contracts the element of an insurance contract for it could reasonably be said the carrier is equitable to an insurer who undertakes the carriage of goods with all the attendant risks of such carriage—AIR 1978 Mad 112.

2. In a case of non-delivery of goods by carrier, in a suit for compensation limitation is governed Art. 11 of the Limitation Act 1963—AIR 1970 Ori 157.
3. For difference between common carrier and private carrier and their respective liabilities—AIR 1971 Ker 197 summarises different authorities and case laws.
4. Liability of common carrier (s. 6 of the Act).
   Condition in consignment Note absolving carrier from liability for any loss or damage to goods due to theft or fire etc.— carrier cannot escape liability on basis of said condition in absence of special contract signed by owner of goods—*South Eastern Railways* v *United India Insurance* AIR 1991 Ker 41.

396. Suit against a common carrier for compensation for loss of goods due to negligence

In the Court of .... at ......

Suit No. .... of 20.......

(Set out cause title)

The plaintiff states as follows:

1. That the defendant M/s. A.B. Corporation is a common carrier and carries goods from place to place for charges. The defendant has his office at Kolkata and branch office at .... amongst other places.

2. That the plaintiff had delivered to the defendant at his office at .... Kolkata, three bales of cotton cloth, valued at ₹ .... for safe carriage to .... The defendant had accepted the consignment and issued to the plaintiff a Consignment Note No. .... Dt. ....

3. That the said consignment did not reach the destination at .... even after expiry of the reasonable period of transit and was not delivered to the plaintiff.

4. That such loss of the consignment is due to negligence, carelessness and misconduct of the defendant corporation or its agents and/or employees concerned.

5. That a notice dated............... of suit under s. 10 of the Carriers Act has been served on the defendant by registered post with A/D., by the plaintiff through his authorised lawyer Sri. .... Advocate. But the defendant did not bother to answer.

6. That the cause of action for this suit arose at Kolkata within the jurisdiction of this court on .... (date of booking).

7. Suit valuation.

The plaintiff, therefore, prays:

(*i*) For a judgment and decree for ₹ .... as compensation for non-delivery.

(*ii*) Costs.

Verification

Affidavit

397. Suit by owners against common carriers for loss of goods caused by fire (where there was no privity of contract between the owners and the carriers)

In the Court of .... at ......

Suit No. .... of 20.......

(Set out cause title)

The plaintiff states as follows:

1. The defendant company at all material times were and are common carriers engaged in the business of transporting for hire goods from place to place by inland navigation.

2. On .... 20.........., the plaintiffs delivered to the .... Railway Company, hereinafter referred to as 'the Railway Company', and the Railway Company received from the plaintiffs .... packages of Assam Tea for carrying safely from Assam to Puri for hire.

3. The said goods were conveyed over the Railway Company's line from Assam to Gauhati. But in as much as a section of the Railway Company's line south of .... had broken down, the Railway Company on or about .... arranged with the defendant company, upon certain terms as to division of freight, for carriage by the defendant company of the said goods in ships or flats from Gauhati on the Brahmaputra river down to Kolkata on the Hooghly river. At the latter point the goods were again to be put on rail and carried over the Railway Company's line to Puri.

4. On or about .... the said goods were put on board the defendant company's fleet .... for carriage by river to Kolkata.

5. On .... while the vessel was still lying at Gauhati, a fire broke out and .... out of the aforesaid .... packages were destroyed.

6. By reason of the premises the plaintiffs have suffered damage.

Particulars of damage:

Value of .... packages ... ... ₹ ....

The plaintiffs claim—

(1) ₹ ....damage.

(2) Costs.

Verification

Affidavit

398. Suit against a common carrier for damages for delayed delivery of the consignment resulting in loss of the consignor

In the Court of .... at ......

Suit No. .... of 20.......

(Set out cause title)

The plaintiff states as follows:

1. That the defendant is a common carrier and carries goods for reward with their head office at Cawnpore and branch office, amongst other places, at Gauhati.

2. That on .... the plaintiff had delivered to the defendant .... tins of mustard oil for carriage ex. Cawnpore to Gauhati. The defendant accepted the consignment, issued a Consignment Note No. .... date .... to the plaintiff and realised freight, for such carriage, amounting to ₹ .... against a Money Receipt No. .... dated ...., issued by the defendant.

3. That normally it takes seven days in transit from Cawnpore to Gauhati. In the instant case, the goods were despatched on .... and were delivered to the plaintiff's agent .... only on .... i.e. 15 days after they should have been delivered in normal course.

4. That within the period from when the same should have been delivered and the time when the same were actually delivered, the price of mustard oil went down by 5 rupees paise per k.g., and the plaintiff has suffered and/or is likely to suffer loss of ₹ .... in the said consignment.

5. That delay in transit of the consignment is due to misconduct and gross negligence of the defendant.

6. That the plaintiff is entitled recover from the defendant damages of ₹ .... as per account given in the statement of claim below.

7. Cause of action arose on the date of delivery (or, on ....when the consignment should have been delivered and thereafter on .... when the consignment was delivered).

8. Suit valuation.

STATEMENT OF CLAIM

Loss due to difference in price @ ₹ 5 per k.g. in .... k.g. (........ tins) of mustard oil	₹ ....
	₹ ....

The plaintiff prays for:

(*a*) a decree of ₹ .... as damages/loss

(*b*) Costs.

Verification

Affidavit

NOTE: In a suit for compensation against a carrier for non-delivery or delay in delivery of goods limitation is three years when the goods ought to be delivered—*vide* Art. 11 of the Limitation Act.

399. Suit against a carrier for late delivery

In the Court of .... at ......

Suit No. .... of 20.......

(Set out cause title)

The plaintiff states as follows:

1. The defendants works as carrier for reward.

2. The plaintiff, having intended to open a shop at the "Jana Mela". 20......... scheduled to be held from .... to .... at the 'Maidan' Premises, entered into an agreement on the .... day of .... 20........ with the defendant that the latter would carry for the plaintiff three bales of 'sarees' from Banaras to Kolkata within the .... day of .... 20......... for the market in the said Jana Mela, 20........

3. The defendant agreed, took advance freight of ₹ .... from the plaintiff on the .... day of .... 20......... and took three bales of sarees in his custody for carriage.

4. The defendant, in breach of the said agreement dated the .... day of .... 20....... did not carry the same in time for the said market. The defendant carried and delivered the same to the plaintiff only on the .... day of .... 20 .... when the 'Jana Mela' was over.

5. As a result, the plaintiff lost the market and was compelled to undersell the same.

6. The plaintiff suffered loss of profits, loss for undersale as per account below.

7. Cause of action (date within which the goods were agreed to be carried).

8. Suit valuation—(Aggregate of estimated profit, and of loss for undersale).

Particulars of claim

The plaintiff claims damages of ₹ .... plus costs.

Verification

Affidavit

400. Suit by a common carrier for charge/freight for carriage of goods

In the Court of .... at ......

Suit No. .... of 20 ....

(Set out cause title)

The plaintiff states as follows:

1. That the plaintiff firm is a common carrier with its registered office at ............P.S. .... District ....

2. That the defendant delivered on .... to the plaintiff firm three bales of cotton piece goods for carriage ex. Kolkata to Cooch Behar by the latter's carrier service and agreed to pay ₹ .... as charge of carriage. The Consignment Note No. .... dt. .... issued to the defendant bore an endorsement "To pay" which meant that the defendant would pay the freight on arrival of the consignment at destination.

3. That the plaintiff firm had carried the consignment sefely and delivered the same to the defendant on. .... and demanded ₹ .... as charge for carriage.

4. That the defendant did not pay the freight/charge.

5. That the cause of action for this suit arose on .... when the consignment was made available to the defendant at Cooch Behar within the jurisdiction of this court.

6. Suit valuation.

The plaintiff, therefore, prays for a judgment and decree for ₹ .... only and costs.

Verification

Affidavit

401. Suit against a common carrier for damages for loss of goods

In the Court of .... at ......

Suit No. .... of 20.......

(Set out cause title)

The plaintiff states as follows:

1. That M/s. A.B. are and were at all material times common carriers of goods for hire with their office at. ....

2. That the plaintiff had delivered to the defendants on .... at their office at .... one bale of hessian goods for carrying the same ex. Kolkata to Cooch Behar by their transport service, consignee being Sri. .... of .... an agent of the plaintiff.

3. That the defendant received the bale of hessian goods and issued to the plaintiff a Consignment Note No. .... dt. .... agreeing to carry safely and securely for the plaintiff the said goods from Kolkata to Cooch Behar and thereat deliver the consignment to the consignee on production of the said Consignment Note and realise freight therefor.

4. In breach of the said agreement, the defendant did not carry the goods or deliver the same to the plaintiff but wrongfully failed to carry the said goods and failed to deliver the same even after expiry of the reasonable period of transit. In the premises the plaintiff has been deprived of the said goods and has suffered loss and damage.

5. That the plaintiff has served a notice of suit dated .... on the defendant under s. 10 of the Carriers Act (Act III of 1865) by registered post with A/D.

6. That the plaintiff is entitled to compensation for loss of the said consignment, valued at ₹ ....

7. Cause of action—Date of booking and thereafter on .... when the consignment ought to be delivered at the destination.

8. Suit valuation—(value of the consignment as per invoice or market rate).

The plaintiff, therefore, prays:

(1) ₹ .... as compensation damages for non-delivery of the bale (of hessian goods).

(2) Costs.

Verification

Affidavit

NOTES: 1. For compensation for non-delivery against a carrier—Limitation is three years *vide* Art. 11 of the Limitation Act 1963, from the date when the goods ought to be delivered.

2. Short delivery of goods. A claim petition was filed before Railway Claims Tribunal. Claim petition not being suit is governed by residuary Art. 137 and not Art. 10 of the Limitation Act.

3. Limitation of three years', Rule under Art. 137 starts from the date when open delivery of goods is granted—*Central Coal Fields* v *Union of India* AIR 1993 Pat 150.

402. Suit by consignor of goods against railway for loss of goods consigned

In the Court of .... at ......

Suit No. .... of 20.......

A.B. merchant residing at ....

... *Plaintiff*

versus

Union of India

... *Defendant*

The plaintiff states:

1. .... Railway at all material times was and is a Railway, administered by the defendant.

2. By an agreement in writing dated the .... 20.........., and made between the plaintiff and the defendant, contained in Receipt No. .... dated .... granted to the plaintiff by one C.D., the defendant's agent, in that behalf, and which incorporated and was made subject to Railway Risk Rate the defendant agreed to carry for reward .... bags of vests, the property of the plaintiff, from Howrah station to Patna station and to deliver the same to the plaintiff at the last named station.

3. In breach of the said agreement the defendant failed to deliver the said goods to the plaintiff and has lost the said goods during transit.

4. By reason of the premises the plaintiff has suffered damage.

Particulars of claim:

Value of .... bags of vests on ...., i.e. when they should have been delivered	...	...	₹ ....
Railway freight paid by the plaintiff	...	...	₹ ....
Net amount due		...	₹ ....

5. On .... 20........, the plaintiff caused a notice under s. 106 of the Railways Act 1989 in writing dated .... 20........., to be served on ...., the General Manager of the Railway claiming ₹ .... as the damage suffered by the plaintiff aforesaid.

6. On ...., the plaintiff also served a notice on the General Manager of the .... Railway under s. 80 of the Code of Civil Procedure.

The plaintiff claims—

(*a*) ₹ ....; and

(*b*) Costs

Verification

Affidavit

403. Suit against Railway Administration for short delivery, non-delivery, destruction, damage or deterioration to Railway Claims Tribunal

In the Railway Claims Tribunal

.... Bench

Between

A.B. ... *Applicant*

And

C.D. ... *Respondent*

PART-I

Application under s. 16 of the Railway Claims Tribunal Act in respect of claims for compensation for loss, destruction, damage, deterioration or non-delivery of goods.

Title of the case:

PART-II

S. No.	*Description of documents attached*	*Page No.*
1.	....	....
2.	....	....
3.	....	....
4.	....	....
5.	....	....
6.	....	....
7.	....	....
8.	....	....
9.	....	....
10.	....	....
11.	....	....
12.	....	....

Signature of the Applicants

For use in Tribunal's office

Date of filing

or

Date receipt by post

Registration No. ...

Signature for Registrar

PART—III

1. Particulars of the Applicant:

   Name and Address:

2. Particulars of the Respondent/Respondents:

3. Value of Claim and details of application fee:

   (1) Value of Claim:

   (2) Details of Application Fee:

4. (*i*) Name and address of the Bank on which the Draft/Pay order is drawn:

   (*ii*) Demand Draft/Pay order No. and the Branch at which payable.

5. Full booking particulars of the consignment

Date of Booking	*Railway Receipt or Parcel Way Bill*	*Station From To*	*Description of consignment*	*Value of consignment*	*Any other particulars*
(1)	(2)	(3)	(4)	(5)	(6)

6. Date on which notice served on the Rly. Administration under s. 106 of the Railways Act 1989.

7 (*i*) Facts of the case:

(*ii*) (*a*) Nature of relief sought;

(*b*) Grounds of relief.

8. Matters not previously filed or pending with any other court: NIL

9. Jurisdiction of the Bench.

10. List of enclosures:

(*i*)

(*ii*)

(*iii*) etc.

Affidavit

Before the Railway Claims Tribunal .... Bench

Original Application No. ....

Title ....

Affidavit of .... son of/daughter of/wife of .... aged .... years .... occupation .... resident of ....

I, the above named do hereby solemnly affirm and declare as under:

(State all relevant facts of first person in paragraphs numbered consecutively).

Place:

Date: Deponent

Verification

I ....(the above named) further declare that para No. .... to .... are true and correct to my personal knowledge and para No. .... to .... are true and correct on the basis of information derived from available records and para No. .... to .... are believed to be true on the legal advice received from my legal practitioner. No part of it is false and nothing relevant has been concealed therein.

Place:

Date: Deponent

NOTES: 1. See Railway Claims Tribunal Act 1987 and the Railway Claims Tribunal (Procedure) Rules 1989.
2. For Carriage of Goods—See Chapter IX of the Railways Act 1989.
3. Responsibilities of Railway Administrations as Carriers—See Chapter XI of the Railways Act 1989.
4. Section 200 of the Railways Act 1989 repeals the Indian Railways Act 1890.
5. Review of the Order of the Tribunal, from which no appeal is allowed, is permissible.
6. Order of a Tribunal shall be executed as a decree of Civil Court, CP Code shall apply.

404. Suit against a Railway Administration for refund of overcharges

See s. 13(1)(*b*) of Railway Claims Tribunal Act

In the Court of .... at ....

or

Before the Railway Claims Tribunal

Suit No. .... of 20 ....

(Set out cause title)

PART I

Title of the case

PART II

Index

Sl. No.	*Description of documents attached*	*Page No.*
1.		
2.		
3.		
4.		
5.		
6.		

Signature of the Applicant

For use in Tribunal's Office
Date of filing
or
Date of Receipt by post
Registration No.
Signature for Registrar

PART III

In the Railway Claims Tribunal

.... Bench

Between

A.B. .... *Applicant*

And

C.D. .... *Respondent*

1. Particulars of the applicant:
   Name and address:
2. Particulars of the respondent/respondents
3. Value of claim and details of application fee—
   (*i*) Value of claims
   (*ii*) Details of Application Fee
4. Particulars of Bank Draft/Postal Order in respect of Application Fee:
   (*i*) Name and address of the Bank on which the Draft is drawn;
   (*ii*) Demand Draft No. and the Branch at which payable

   or

   (*i*) Number of Indian Postal Order(s)
   (*ii*) Name of issuing Post Office
   (*iii*) Date of issue of Postal Order(s)
   (*iv*) Post Office at which payable.
5. Full Particulars of payment of fare/freight.
   (*i*) Claim for refund of freight.

Date of Booking	*Railway Receipt or Parcel Way Bill*	*Station*		*Description of consignment*
		From	*To*	
1	2	3		4

Freight paid	*Amount Refund of Claims or other payment particulars*	*Money Receipt/Credit Note*
5	6	7

(*ii*) Claim for refund of fare.

Date of journey	*Train No.*	*Class of travel*	*Class actually travelled*
1	2	3	4

Ticket or Ticket Deposit Receipt/ Excess Fare Ticket etc., Guards or Conductors, Certificate	*Fair Paid Rs.*	*Refund Claimed Rs.*
5	6	7

6. Date on which notice served on the Railway Administration under s. 78B of Indian Railways Act, 1890 (in respect of claims for refund of freight)—attach proof.
7. (*i*) Facts of the case:

   (Give here a concise statement of facts in a chronological order, each paragraph containing as nearly as possible, a separate issue, fact or otherwise).

   (*ii*) (*a*) Nature of relief sought; and

   (*b*) Grounds of relief.
8. Matters not previously filed or pending with any other court.

   (State whether the applicant had previously filed any claim, writ petition or suit regarding the matter in respect of which the present application has been made).

   In case the applicants had previously filed any claims, application, writ petition or suit, indicate the stage at which it is pending, and if decided, attach a certified copy of the Order.
9. Jurisdiction of the Bench (indicate the facts on the basis of which the Bench to which application is made, has the jurisdiction).
10. List of enclosures:

1.	
2.	
3.	
4.	
5.	

Verification

Affidavit

I, ... (Name of the applicant) S/o, D/o, W/o, ... age .... resident of .... do hereby verify that the contents of paragraphs .... to .... are true to my personal knowledge, and paragraphs .... to .... are believed to be true to the best of my knowledge or the legal advice given to me, and that I have not suppressed any material fact.

Date: Signature of the applicant

Place: Full Address:

To
The Registrar,
Railway Claims Tribunal
.... Bench
....

405. Claim against railway for shortage in delivery

[Form I, Appendix XXVII of the Railway Claims Tribunal (Procedure) Rules 1989]

1. Particulars of the Applicant
   Name and address :
2. Particulars of the Respondent :
3. Value of claim and details of application fee—
   (*i*) Value of claim :
   (*ii*) Details of application fee :
4. (*i*) Name and address of the Bank on which draft is drawn :
   (*ii*) Demand Draft No. 1 and Branch at which payable :
   or
   (*i*) Number of Indian Postal Order(s) :
   (*ii*) Name of issuing Post Office :
   (*iii*) Date of issue of postal order(s) :
   (*iv*) Post Office at which payables :
5. Full Booking particulars of the consignment—

Date of Booking	*Railway Receipt or Parcel Way Bill*	*Station From To*	*Description of consignment*	*Value of consignment*	*Any other particulars*
(1)	(2)	(3)	(4)	(5)	(6)

6 Date on which notice served on the Railway Administration under s. 106 of the Railways Act 1989 :
   (Attach proof)
7. (*i*) Facts of the case :
   (Give here a concise statement of facts in a chronological order, each paragraph containing as nearly as possible, a separate issue, fact or otherwise)
   (*ii*) (*a*) Nature of the relief sought :
   (*b*) Grounds of relief :

8. Matters not previously filed or pending with any other court :
(*State whether the applicant had previously filed any claim, writ petition or suit regarding the matter in respect of which the present application has been filed*).

In case the applicant had previously filed any claim, application, writ petition of suit, indicate the stage at which it is pending, and if decided attach a certified copy of the order.

9. Jurisdiction of the Bench :
(*Indicate the facts on the basis of which the Bench to which application is made, has the jurisdiction*).

10. List of enclosures :

    1. Copy of notice under s. 106 of the Railways Act 1989.
    2. Copy of invoice
    3. Copy of open delivery memo.
    4. ....
    5. ....

Verification

Affidavits

406. Suit against a railways for damages for injuries sustained in a collision

Application under section 16 of the Act in respect of claims for compensation arising out of accident to a train.

PART I

Title of the case:

PART II

Index

Sl. No.	*Description of documents attached*	*Page No.*
1.		
2.		
3.		
4.		
5.		
6.		

Signature of the Applicant

FOR USE IN TRIBUNAL'S OFFICE

Date of filing

or

Date of Receipt by post

Registration No.
Signature for Registrar

PART III

(*See* rule 5)

Application for compensation under section 16 of the Act in respect of claim for compensation for death, injury, etc., in a train accident

To
The Railway Claims Tribunal
....
....

I, ..., son/daughter/wife/widow of .... residing at .... having been injured in accident to train or untoward incident hereby apply for the grant of compensation for the injury sustained.

I, ..., son/daughter/wife/widow of .... residing at .... hereby apply as dependent for the grant of compensation on account of the death/injury sustained by Shri/Kumari/Shrimati .... son/daughter/wife/widow of Shri/Shrimati .... who died/was injured in accident to train or untoward incident referred to hereunder.

Necessary particulars in respect of the deceased/injured in the accident or untoward incident are given below:

1. Name and father's name of the person injured/dead (husband's name in the case of married woman or widow).
2. Full address of the person injured/dead.
3. Age of the person injured/dead.
4. Occupation of the person injured/dead.
5. Name and address of the employer of the deceased, if any.
6. (*a*) Brief particulars of the accident indicating the date and place of accident and the name of the train involved—

   (*b*) Brief particulars of the untoward incident indicating the date and place of the untoward incident.
7. Class of travel, and tickets/pass/platform ticket number, to the extent known ....
8. Nature of injuries sustained along with medical certificate.
9. Name and address of the Medical Officer/Practitioner, if any, who attended on the injured/dead and period of treatment ....
10. Disability for work, if any, caused.
11. Details of the loss of any luggage on account of the accident to the train ....
12. Has any claim been lodged with any other authority? If so, particulars thereof ....
13. Name and permanent address of the applicant ....

13A. (*i*) Bank Account Number of the claimant ....

(*ii*) Name of the Bank and Branch ....

(*iii*) Type of Account ....

14. Local address of the applicant, if any ....
15. Relationship with the deceased/injured ....
16. Amount of compensation claimed ....
17. Where the application is not made within one year of the occurrence of the accident, to the train or untoward incident the grounds thereof ....
18. Any other information or documentary evidence that may be necessary or helpful in the disposal of the claim ....
19. Mention the documents, if any, filed along with application.

I, ... solemnly declare that ....

(*a*) the particulars given above are true and correct to the best of my knowledge and

(*b*) I have not claimed or obtained any compensation in relation to the injury/death/loss of luggage which is the subject-matter of this application.

Date ....

Place ....

Signature or left thumb-impression of the applicant

Name of witness and his address in case Left Thumb Impression is put by applicant.

Verification

I, ... (Name of the applicant) S/o, D/o, W/o, ... age .... resident of .... do hereby verify that the contents of paragraphs .... to .... are true to my personal knowledge, and paragraphs .... to .... are believed to be true to the best of my knowledge or the legal advice given to me, and that I have not suppressed any material fact.

Date:

Place:

Signature of the applicant

Full address

To

The Registrar,

Railway Claims Tribunal

....

NOTES: 1. Railway accident—claim application.

Civil Court's jurisdiction not totally barred.

The Claims Tribunal under the Railway Claims Tribunal Act is a Tribunal of limited and specified jurisdiction. It can exercise jurisdiction and power as conferred upon it under the said Act only. Section 19(1) of the Claims Tribunal Act provides for jurisdiction power and authority of the Claims Tribunal and by virtue of the express provisions contained in s. 15 thereof, the jurisdiction of the Civil Court or any other authority is barred only in regard to the matters specified in said s. 13(1). Therefore, in regard to the matters other than matters covered by s. 13(1) of the said Act the Civil Court will have a jurisdiction to entertain a Civil Suit—*Ratnakar Tanbaji* v *Union of India* AIR 1994 Bom 132.

2. The claim petition arising out of an accident in which the passenger fell out of the bogie of the train and died on being caught between the platform and the running train in not cognisable by the Claims Tribunal as the accident in question is not an 'accident' to the train within the meaning of s. 82A of the Indian Railway Act 1890 and does not fall under sub-clause (*ii*) of cl. (*a*) of s. 13(1) of the Railway Claims Tribunal Act. The claim also does not either fall under s. 13(1)(*a*)(*i*) of the Claims Tribunal

Act—*Ratnakar Tanbaji Itankar* v *Union of India* AIR 1994 Bom 132 (See Railway Act—ss. 82A, 80 of the Act 1890 and Railways Act—ss. 124, 125 of the Act 1989).

3. For principles of assessment of damages in personal injury due to accident—AIR 1970 Mys 13.
4. Railway level crossing—gates open while train approaching is *prima facie* evidence of negligence on the part of Railway Administration—AIR 1978 All 303.
5. Railway Accident Compensation (Amendment) Rules 1974

   For each and every injury sustained by the victim claimant, the amount of compensation shall have to be payable and the amount of compensation shall have to be determined for each such injury after taking into consideration all the circumstances of the case by the Claims Commissioner for determination of reasonable amount of compensation—*Sailendra Nath Banerjee* v *Union of India* AIR 1988 Cal 333.
   (*Union of India* v *Ad hoc Claims Commissioner* AIR 1977 Cal 393; (1977)1 CLJ 456 Relying on) [case under the old Act of 1890].
6. Railway Act 1890—s. 82C.

   Railways Act 1989: Application for compensation under s. 124 is to be made to Railway Claims Tribunal—See s. 125 of the Railways Act 1989.
   Jurisdiction—Railway Claims Tribunal, s. 109.
   Notice of Accident—s. 113.
   Inquiry by Commissioner—s. 114.
   Inquiry by Railway administration where the Commissioner pleads inability—s. 115.
   Extent of liability—s. 124.

(a) Carriage by air

407. Suit against an air company for damages for loss of goods

In the Court of .... at ......

Suit No. .... of 20.......

(Set out cause title)

The above-named plaintiff states as follows:

1. That the defendant M/s. .... has had a carrier service by air for reward (or that the defendants are and were at all material times carrying on the business of an air transport undertaking under the trade name of M/s. ....) and is governed by provisions of the Carriage by Air Act 1934.

2. That the plaintiff had delivered to the defendant on .... three hundred baskets of black grapes for carriage by their airship (aircraft, kite) from Kolkata to Bagdogra, Consignee being M/s. .... of Bagdogra.

3. That the defendant had realised charge of carriage (or, way bill) from the plaintiff on .... and issued to the plaintiff a Consignment Note No. .... dated ....

4. That the defendant failed to deliver the consignment to the consignee and either the same slipped off the plane while in air or misdelivered to any other airstrip. Anyway, the same was lost to the plaintiff.

5. That the defendant and or his employees were thoroughly negligent and have been guilty of breach of duty as common carriers, of breach of conditions in the said Consignment Note, or alternatively, of breach of their duty as bailees for reward and did not take proper care of the consignment to avoid the loss.

6. That the consignment of three hundred baskets of grapes was valued at ₹ ....

7. That the cause of action for this suit arose on .... when the consignment was delivered to the defendant for carriage at .... within the jurisdiction of this court.

The plaintiff claims:

(1) ₹ .... as compensation/damages for loss of the consignment.

(2) Costs.

Verification

Affidavit

NOTES: 1. Carriage of goods by air is governed by the provisions of the Carriage by Air Act (Act XX of 1934).

2. Either the consignor or the consignee may sue—see Rule 14 of the First Schedule (Part III, Chap. 2).

3. Suit may be filed either at the booking station or at the destination.

4. Limitation—three years from date of the loss or injury *vide* Art. 10 of the Limitation Act 1963.

408. Suit against carriers by air for damages due to delay in carrying goods

In the Court of .... at ......

Suit No. .... of 20.......

(Set out cause title)

The above-named plaintiff states as follows:

1. That the defendant carries by air for reward by his aircraft goods from.................... .... to ...., amongst other places.

2. That the plaintiff had delivered on .... to the defendant, 300 baskets of grapes on .... valued at ₹ .... to be carried by the defendant's aircraft to Cooch Behar and paid the charge therefor. The defendant issued a Consignment Note No. .... dated .... to the plaintiff and agreed to deliver the consignment to the consignee within seven days of booking.

3. That the defendant failed to deliver the consignment to the consignee at Cooch Behar within the stipulated period and the consignment was not delivered until after 20 days from the said date.

4. That for the delayed delivery of the consignment, the grapes suffered deterioration and the plaintiff has suffered loss of ₹ ....

5. That the cause of action for this suit arose on ....

6. Suit valuation.

The plaintiff claims a decree for ₹ .... as compensation as per account in the Schedule below.

Account of claim

Value of 300 baskets of grapes	...	...	...	₹ ....
Air charge	...	...		₹ ....
Add profit @ ....% over the value		...		₹ ....
			Total	₹ ....

Verification

Affidavit

NOTES: 1. Jurisdiction—Place of booking or destination—Rule 28, Chap III, Part III of Schedule V.

2. Consignor or consignee—any of them may sue.

3. Three years—*vide* Art. 11 of the Limitation Act 1963.

409. Claim by a consignor against carriers by air for damages for loss of goods

In the Court of .... at .....

Suit No. .... of 20......

(Set out cause title)

The plaintiff states as follows:

1. That by an Air Consignment Note dated ...., duly signed, the defendants, for consideration, mentioned therein, agreed, to carry in their aircraft ...., 250 packets containing tea from Delhi to Calcutta, subject to the rules relating to liability contained in the First Schedule to the Carriage by Air Act (XX of 1934).

2. That on execution of the Consignment Note the plaintiff had delivered to the defendant the said consignment for carriage and the defendant accepted the same.

3. During the carriage, 110 packets slipped off the plane in mid-air and were consequently lost.

Particulars of Goods lost and their value

The plaintiff claims

₹ .... damages.

Verification

Affidavit

410. Suit by executor against carriers by air for the benefit of dependents of a deceased passenger

In the Court of .... at .....

Suit No. .... of 20......

(Set out cause title)

The plaintiff states as follows:

1. The plaintiff is the executor of the Will of A.B., deceased, and brings this suit for the benefit of the widow and the children of the said A.B.

Particulars of the persons on whose behalf the suit is brought:

C.D.	...	...	Widow.
E.F.	...	...	Son aged ....
G.H.	...	...	Daughter aged ....

2. At all material times the defendants were carriers of passengers by air.

3. On or about .... the defendants received the said A.B. on board the aircraft .... as a passenger for reward from .... to ....

4. On .... at about ...., while the said A.B. was on board the said aircraft as such passenger, an accident occurred to the said aircraft in consequence of which the said A.B. was killed.

Particulars of the accident

5. The said A.B. was forty years of age and was employed in .... at a salary of ₹ .... per month. By his death his widow and children have been deprived of all means of living.

Particulars of damage

The plaintiff claims—

₹ .... damages.

Verification

Affidavit

(b) Carriage by sea

411. Suit by shipowner against charterer for failure to load

In the Court of .... at ......

Suit No. .... of 20......

(Set out cause title)

The plaintiff states as follows:

1. By a charterparty dated .... it was mutually agreed between the plaintiffs, owners of the screw steamer called the .... of .... tons gross and .... tons net register, and the defendant, charterer, that the said steamer should after arrival at .... and after discharge of her inward cargo, if any, proceed under steam to Karachi *via* Suez Canal and there receive from the defendants or his agents a full and complete cargo of cotton in full pressed bales, seed and/or wheat in bags and/or maize and/or other lawful merchandise and being so loaded should with all reasonable speed therewith proceed under steam *via* Suez Canal to .... or so near thereto as she could safely get and there deliver the cargo in accordance with the custom of the port for steamers on being paid freight at the rate of .... *per* ton, English weight. It was also thereby agreed that the defendant should have .... working days to be computed from 24 hours (if berthed alongside the wharf, otherwise 48 hours) after receipt by the charterer a written notice from the master or agents that the vessel was clear of her inward cargo, in seaworthy condition and ready to load, and should the steamer be detained beyond the time stipulated for loading and discharging, demurrage should be paid at .... *per* day and *pro rata* for any part thereof.

2. The said steamer arrived at Karachi on .... and the next day the master gave notice in writing to the defendant that the vessel was clear of her inward cargo, in seaworthy condition and ready to load and was lying alongside the wharf.

3. No reply was received to the said letter until .... when the defendant by letter wrongfully repudiated the said agreement.

4. By reason of the premises the plaintiffs have suffered damage.

Particulars

Freight payable on a full and complete cargo (.......... tons) at .... *per* ton	...	₹ ....
Demurrage for $4^1/_2$ days from .... to .... at .... *per* day	...	₹ ....
Net amount due	...	₹ ....

The plaintiff claims—

(1) ₹ ....; and

(2) Costs.

Verification

Affidavit

412. Suit for realisation of freight against a shipper

In the Court of .... at ......

Suit No. .... of 20......

(Set out cause title)

The plaintiff states:

1. The plaintiff is a shipping company with its registered office at .... and runs a business of common carriers by sea.

2. The defendant has on the .... day of .... 20............. shipped .... tons of wheat on board the plaintiff's ship S.S. *Ganga* for carriage ex .... to .... The said carriage is covered by a bill of lading bearing No. .... of the date the .... day of .... 20............. and is signed by the master of the ship and by the defendant-shipper.

3. The plaintiff carried the cargo to the defendant at the destination on the .... day of .... 20.............

4. The defendant has refused to pay the freight. The plaintiff is entitled to recover the freight as agreed in the said bill of lading.

5. Cause of action.

6. Suit valuation.

Particulars of the claim

Freight at the rate of ₹ .... per	₹ ....

The plaintiff claims:

(*a*) a judgment and decree for ₹ ....

(*b*) Costs.

Verification

Affidavit

NOTES: 1. For absence of cause of action plaint is rejected under Or. 7, r. 11(*a*), CPC. Suit against Carrier by Sea for damage caused to goods transported. Carrier by Sea not being common carrier, suit could not be founded under s. 180 of the Contract Act. The plaintiff was neither a consignee nor endorsee under bill of lading. Provisions of Carriage of Goods by Sea Act are attracted—*Dadsal (P) Ltd.* v *Narmada Seaways* AIR 1989 Bom 96.

2. The period of one year prescribed under Art. III, r. 6 for filing suit for short delivery of goods cannot be extended by agreement between parties in absence of any provision in the rule for contracting out of statute—*Mineral & Metals Trading* v *Shipping Corporation of India* AIR 1987 Cal 276; AIR 1960 SC 1058; AIR 1972 SC 1405 and AIR 1981 Cal 298.

413. Suit for realisation of freight against a consignee of bill of lading

In the Court of .... at ......

Suit No. .... of 20.......

(Set out cause title)

The plaintiff states:

1. That the plaintiff is a shipping concern carrying on business of carriers by sea under the trade name of .... by his ship *S.S. Ganga*, amongst others.

2. That the defendant A.B. as consignor had shipped on board the plaintiff's ship *S.S. Ganga* .... (name the cargo) consigned to self ex .... to .... under a bill of lading dated the .... day of .... 20......... Freight was 'to pay' as recorded in the bill of lading.

3. That on arrival of the said (name the cargo) at the destination the defendant/ his agent took delivery of the (cargo) under the said bill of lading.

4. The defendant is liable to pay the freight to the plaintiff in terms of the said bill of lading for carriage of the (cargo) in the plaintiff's said vessel.

Claim

Freight
at the rate of ₹ .... per ....
for ....
₹ ....

The plaintiff claims:

(*i*) Freight of ₹ ....

Verification

Affidavit

414. Suit in admiralty jurisdiction

In the High Court at Calcutta

Admiralty Suit No. ...... of 20...

M/s. P & Co. Ltd., a company registered under the Companies Act 1956 (now 2013) and carrying on business, *inter alia*, at.......... Kolkata

.... *Plaintiff*

versus

M/s. X & Co. Ltd. a company registered under the Companies Act 1956 (now 2013) and carrying on business, *inter alia,* at .... Kolkata

...... *Defendant*

The plaintiff states as follows:

1. The plaintiff is a company registered under the Companies Act 1956 (now 2013) and carries on business, *inter alia*, as the exporter and importer of goods.

2. The plaintiff purchased certain plant and machinery from the defendant having an office in Kolkata. The said plant and machinery items were shipped on the Vessel "SWIFT" belonging to the defendant. The said Vessel issued a bill of lading being No. .... dated .... in acknowledgement of receipt of the said plant and machinery from the exporter to the plaintiff and the cargo was covered by terms and conditions contained in the bill of lading. A copy of the said bill of lading is annexed hereto marked "A". The goods were to be carried from a Port in England to Port of Calcutta. The freight on the cargo of the said goods was prepaid at the time of shipment.

3. The said bill of lading guaranteed delivery at the Port of Calcutta of specified packages of plant and machinery on carriage to the Port of Calcutta and delivery thereof to the plaintiff at Kolkata.

4. The said vessel was due to arrive at the Port of Calcutta on or about 15th September 20 ....

5. The voyage of the said vessel was undisturbed by any bad weather or otherwise.

6. On production of the bill of lading, the said vessel of the defendant failed to deliver the agreed items of plant and machinery covered by the said bill of lading on its arrival.

7. The plaintiff took delivery of the balance items of plant and machinery duly recording its protest in writing regarding shortage of goods covered by bill of lading over which freight has been paid.

8. The plaintiff duly informed and protested about short delivery of goods covered by the said bill of lading. A copy of the letter recording the said shortage of goods covered by the said bill of lading is annexed hereto marked 'B'

9. The said short delivery of cargo covered by the said bill of lading resulted in plaintiff suffering loss and damages the amount being assessed at ₹ ....

PARTICULARS

Cost of plant and machinery undelivered out of the full quantity indicated in bill of lading	...	₹	....
Proportionate freight paid on the said undelivered items of plant and machinery	...	₹	....
Interest at 12% per annum	...	₹	....
Expected profit from the sale of the non-delivered plant and machinery	...	₹	....
	Total	₹	....

10. The plaintiff demands compensation for the said loss and damages directly caused by the breach of contract to carry goods and deliver the same to plaintiff.

This loss has been suffered during the voyage of the said Steamship in the High Seas, the vessel in registered in Calcutta and the defendant has an office in Calcutta. In the premises, this Hon'ble Court has the jurisdiction to entertain, try and determine this suit.

11. The plaintiff's cause of action for this suit arose on or about .... on which date the goods should have been delivered and in spite of demand, the same has not been delivered in breach of terms and conditions of the said bill of lading.

12. In spite of demands, the defendant has failed to give any valid reasons for such short delivery of the goods covered by the said bill of lading.

13. In spite of demands the defendant has failed to pay the plaintiff's claims herein.

14. The plaintiff claims a decree for payment of ₹ .... with interest and costs by the defendant. The defendant being owner of the said vessel who had issued the said bill of lading is liable to pay the plaintiff's claims herein.

15. No part of the plaintiff's claims herein is barred by Law of Limitation.

16. For the purposes of jurisdiction and court-fees, the suit is valued at ₹ .... on which court-fees in stamps have been duly paid.

The plaintiff, therefore, claims:

(*a*) A decree for payment of ₹ .... with interest at 12% per annum till the date of decree and thereafter on decretal amount till realisation;

(*b*) Costs;

(*c*) Injunction restraining defendant from creating any charge on the said Vessel or disposing of the same or in any way encumbering the said vessel till the claims of plaintiff arc paid.

(*d*) Further and other orders be made as this Hon'ble Court may deem fit and proper to afford complete relief to the plaintiff.

Verification

Affidavit

415. Suit by a shipowner against charterer for freight due under a charter-party

In the Court of .... at ......

Suit No. .... of 20......

(Set out cause title)

The plaintiff states:

1. That the plaintiff is a shipping concern carrying on business of common carriers by sea under the business name of ....

2. Under a charter-party dated the .... day of .... 20...................... between the plaintiff and the defendant charterer, the plaintiff ship *S.S. Ganga* was chartered by the defendant for carriage of the defendant's goods (name cargo) from .... to ....

3. The plaintiff carried the said goods on board the ship *S.S. Ganga* and delivered the same to the defendant on the .... day of............... 20 ..... at the destination.

4. The plaintiff is entitled to freight of ₹ .... under the said charter-party, as per claim below, which remains unpaid as yet.

5. Cause of action.

Claim

Freight
at the rate of ₹ .... per Qls
for .... Qls ₹ ....

The plaintiff claims:

(*i*) Freight of ₹ ....

Verification

Affidavit

416. Suit by shipowner against cargo-owner for freight, demurrage and expenses

In the Court of .... at ......

Suit No. .... of 20.......

(Set out cause title)

The plaintiff states as follows:

1. The plaintiffs at all material times were and are the owners of the steamer .... which traded between the ports of L. and H.

2. On ...., the defendant, a merchant dealing in petroleum, oils and chemicals, delivered 750 barrels of petroleum (hereinafter referred to as 'the goods'), on board the said steamer in port L. to be sent to port H. and the Captain gave the defendant a bill of lading, the material terms whereof were the following—

(*a*) The defendant to take out the goods within 24 hours of the steamer's arrival, or pay ...., per day as demurrage.

(*b*) The goods to be delivered in good order and condition at port H. on payment of freight at the rate of .... in accordance with the charter-party dated ....

3. The steamer, with a general cargo, sailed from L. on .... and arrived in the port of H. at .... p.m. on ....

4. On the following morning, the authorities of the port of H. compelled the master of the steamer to take her away in consequence of the petroleum being on board.

5. Thereafter the master took the said steamer to the neighbouring ports of .... and .... but was compelled by the authorities for the same reason, to leave those ports.

6. On .... the steamer returned to port of H. and obtained permission to enter the outer harbour and discharge the goods into a lighter vessel there. The goods remained in the harbour under the master's control until .... when the steamer discharged the rest of her cargo at the quay and was ready to sail on her return voyage. During this time the bill of lading had not been presented, nor had any request been made by the defendant or any holder of it for delivery of the goods.

7. The master under those circumstances, reshipped the goods which had been lying in the harbour between .... and .... and brought them back to port of L., giving notice in writing to the defendant of its arrival.

Particulars of claim

Outward freight ....

Back freight ....

Demurrage ....

Expenses for storage at port of H. ....

8. The defendant has not paid the aforesaid sum or any portion thereof in spite of demand made in writing on ....

The plaintiff claims—

₹ .... for freight, demurrage and expenses.

Verification

Affidavit

417. Suit by a shipper against a shipowner on a bill of lading for damage to goods and/ or for short delivery

In the Court of .... at .....

Suit No. .... of 20......

(Set out cause title)

The plaintiff states:

1. The defendant owns a ship S.S. *Ganga* and is a common carrier for reward.

2. The plaintiff had shipped on the .... day of .... on board the defendant's ship S.S. *Ganga* .... Qls. of rice for carriage ex .... to .... and a bill of lading was duly signed by the master of the said ship for and on behalf of the defendant bearing No. .... dated ....

3. The defendant's agent/servants delivered to the plaintiff at the destination (...........) .... Qls. of rice in water-damaged condition and .... Qls. .... Kg. were not delivered at all.

4. Such damage and short delivery was due to failure to take reasonable care and diligence by the defendant and his agents and/or employees concerned.

5. The plaintiff has suffered loss and damage.

6. Cause of action.

7. Suit valuation.

The plaintiff claims:

(*i*) Compensation of ₹ .... for damage.

Account of claim

Value of ....Qls. of rice (damaged) ₹ ....

Value of .... Qls. .... Kg. of rice (delivered short)— ₹ ....

Verification

Affidavit

NOTES: 1. Carriage of Goods by Sea Act—Schedule, Art. 3.
For loss of goods suit is filed against owner of vessel and his agent. Causes of action pleaded in the plaint were firstly on basis of contract and secondly on basis of liabilities arising out of alleged tortious acts of owner of vessel and his agent. Suit against agent also *held*, is maintainable—*Nepal Food Corporation* v *U.P.T. Import etc.* AIR 1988 Cal 283.

2. Schedule, Art. III, r. 6—Suit for short-delivery of goods. The suit being filed beyond the period of (1) year either from date of delivery or date of departure of vessel, the Carrier and the ship were discharged from their liability in view of Art. III, r. 6 of Schedule to the Act—*National Insurance Co.* v *Navron Constantza* AIR 1988 Cal 155.

3. Article III, r. 6—Limitation for statutory discharge of liability—Goods delivered short and short delivery certificate was issued. Limitation must run from date of delivery and not from date when balance goods should have been delivered—*Jugolinija Rajea* v *Fab Leathers Ltd.* AIR 1985 Cal 193.

4. The material clause, i.e. cl. (*vi*) of Art. 3 of Hague Rules adopted by India provides that the Limitation for the statutory discharge of liability is expiry of a year after delivery of the goods or the date whether goods should have been delivered. In a case where the shipper delivers the goods acknowledging the loss by way of short delivery and a short delivery certificate has been issued the second alternative can have no application—*Jugolinija Rajea* v *Fab Leathers Ltd.* AIR 1985 Cal 193 at p. 196.

418. Suit by an indorsee of a bill of lading against shipowner for short/non-delivery and damage to the consignment

In the Court of .... at ....

Money Suit .... of 20...........

(Set out cause title)

Valued at ₹ ....

The plaintiff states:

1. That the defendants named herein are owners of a Steamship (Name and description).

2. That the defendants received on board the said steamship on ....(date) from one A.B. .... upon receipt of ₹ .... lump freight, ... cases chests of tea weighing .... Kg. in good order and condition for carriage to .... upon the terms and conditions stated in a bill of lading dated 20.............. signed by the master of the said steamship for and on behalf of the defendants, whereby the defendants agreed to deliver the said goods in good order and condition at .... to the order of the shippers or their assigns. The plaintiff will refer to the said bill of lading for its terms.

3. On .... 20 ...., the said bill of lading was endorsed for value by the said A.B., to the plaintiff to whom the property in the goods vested by such endorsement.

4. That out of the said consignment .... chests/cases were delivered in a wet and damaged condition on .... and .... cases were not delivered at all, for such damage to the consignment in part and for non-delivery in part the plaintiff has suffered damage.

5. The said damage was caused by the carelessness and gross negligence of the defendants their servants and/or agents.

6. The plaintiff has become entitled to a sum of ₹ .... as damages, particulars of which are given below:

Particulars of claim

Value of .... chests of tea	...	₹ ....
Estimated value of .... chests of damaged tea	...	₹ ....
Total		₹

7. Cause of action etc.

8. Suit-valuation etc.

The plaintiff claims:

(1) A decree for ₹ .... as damages;

(2) Costs.

Verification

Affidavit

419. Suit by an endorsee of a bill of lading against shipowner for non-delivery of goods

In the Court of .... at ......

Suit No. .... of 20.......

(Set out cause title)

The plaintiff states:

1. That one Sri .... of .... had shipped on the .... day of .... 20.................., on board the defendant's ship (name the ship) .... tons of rice for carriage ex. .... to .... upon a bill of lading bearing No. .... dated .... signed by the master of the said ship, consignee being self.

2. That the plaintiff paid to the said Sri .... the value of the goods and became the owner thereof and the bill of lading was endorsed to the plaintiff by the said Sri .... on the .... day of .... 20.......

3. That the goods were not delivered to the plaintiff even after expiry of normal period of transit, and the same is consequently lost to the plaintiff.

4. Such non-delivery is due to wilful negligence, gross carelessness and misconduct of the defendant, his agents and/or employees concerned.

5. The plaintiff is entitled to compensation of ₹ .... for non-delivery of the ....

6. Cause of action.

7. Suit-valuation.

The plaintiff claims:

₹ ....

Verification

Affidavit

420. Suit by an endorsee of a bill of lading against shipowner for damage to goods

In the Court of .... at ......

Suit No. .... of 20......

(Set out cause title)

The plaintiff states:

1. That one Sri .... of......................... had shipped on the .... day of .... 20................, on board the defendant's ship (name the ship) .... tons of rice for carriage ex. .... to .... upon a bill of lading bearing No. .... dated .... signed by the master of the said ship, consignee being self.

2. That the plaintiff paid to the said Sri .... the value of the goods and became the owner thereof and the bill of lading was endorsed to the plaintiff by the said Sri .... on the .... day of .... 20.......

3. That the defendant failed to exercise reasonable care and diligence while carrying the goods and failed to deliver the (cargo) in its condition as when shipped. The (cargo) has suffered damage in the manner as follows:

(Specify here the nature and extent of damage)

4. The plaintiff entitled to damages suffered for damage done to the cargo.

The plaintiff claims:

(*i*) Damages of ₹ ....

(*ii*) Costs.

Verification

Affidavit

421. Suit against common carrier (by inland navigation) for damages for injury to goods

In the Court of .... at ......

Suit No. .... of 20 ....

(Set out cause title)

The above-named plaintiff states as follows:

1. That the defendant is a common carrier by inland navigation with its office at .... and owns a steamship 'Ganga' plying in the river Ganges and the Brahmaputra for hire.

2. That the plaintiff had delivered to the defendant on .... at his aforesaid office at Kolkata 250 bales of jute for carriage from Kolkata to Gauhati on the steamship 'Ganga' on the said rivers.

3. That the defendant had issued to the plaintiff a Consignment Note No. .... bearing date .... and accepted the said consignment for safe carriage to Gauhati.

4. That on the occasion of delivery of goods at Gauhati on .... it was noticed that jute in 80 bales of the consignment was badly water-damaged and stained. The

plaintiff was granted a damage certificate by the branch office of the defendant at Gauhati on..............

5. That such injury to the goods was due to carelessness and negligence of the defendant and/or their agents and employees concerned.

6. That the plaintiff has served by registered post with A/D a notice dated .... under s. 10 of the Carriers Act 1865, on the defendant.

7. That the cause of action for this suit arose on .... at Kolkata Jurisdiction is restricted to Kolkata by a condition on the back of the Consignment Note when the goods were delivered in damaged condition.

The plaintiff, therefore, prays for a decree of ₹ .... as compensation.

Verification

Affidavit

NOTE: Goods carried by inland navigation are governed by the Carriers Act (Act III of 1865) while on sea by the Carriage of Goods by Sea Act (Act XXVI of 1925) and while on air by the Carriage by Air Act (Act XX of 1934).

POST AND TELEGRAPHS

422. Suit against Post & Telegraphs Department for misdelivery of a parcel

In the Court of .... at ......

Suit No. .... of 20......

(Set out cause title)

The plaintiff states as follows:

1. That the plaintiff had sent on .... a registered parcel, containing a .... valued at ₹ .... from the .... Post Office at .... to Defendant No. 2, at .... Street under the .... Post Office, Dist. .... in West Bengal.

2. That the plaintiff was granted a Registration Coupon No. .... dated .... by the staff concerned of the .... Post Office, payment of charge therefor.

3. That the said registered article was not delivered to the addressee even on expiry of normal transit period and a communication from the defendant No. 2 to that effect was received by the plaintiff on ....

4. Thereafter the plaintiff entertained correspondence with the Superintendent of Post Offices .... Division and only on .... the Superintendent of Post Offices .... Division intimated the plaintiff that the said registered article was delivered to defendant No. 2 on receipt. The plaintiff immediately made a reference to defendant No. 2 who denied to have received the article on .... or on any date and stated that if any receipt was found the same was not genuine.

5. That the plaintiff is entitled to recover from defendant No. 1 a sum of ₹ .... for misdelivery of the aforesaid registered article or, alternatively, from defendant No. 2, if it is proved that defendant No. 1 delivered the article to defendant No. 2 duly.

6. That the plaintiff has served a notice dated .... under s. 80 of the Code of Civil Procedure on the Chief General Manager, Department of Posts and Telegraphs, New Delhi, by registered post with A/D through his authorised lawyer Sri .... Advocate.

7. Cause of action.

8. Suit valuation.

The plaintiff, therefore, prays:

(*a*) For a decree of ₹ .... from defendant No. 1 or, alternatively, from defendant No. 2 if it is proved that the article was delivered by defendant No. 1 to defendant No. 2 duly.

(*b*) Costs.

Verification

Affidavit

423. Suit by sender for failure on the part of postal authorities to collect value of a Value Payable Parcel

In the Court of .... at ....

Suit No. .... of 20.......

A.B. residing at ....

... *Plaintiff*

versus

Union of India ....

... *Defendant*

The plaintiff states:

1. On ...., the plaintiff delivered a parcel containing silver jewellery of the value of ₹ .... to the Postmaster of the .... Post Office, for transmission to one K.C. of Delhi, as a value payable article. The plaintiff also registered and insured the parcel for ₹ .... and duly paid the fees and obtained a receipt, and the said Post Office took charge of the said parcel.

2. The Post Office delivered the said parcel to the said addressee without collecting its value from him and failed to pay the money or return the article to the plaintiff in spite of demands in writing made on .... and ....

3. On ...., the plaintiff caused a notice in writing under s. 80 of the Code of Civil Procedure to be served on .... a Chief General Manager, claiming the said sum of ₹ .... posts.

The plaintiff claims—

₹ ....

Verification

Affidavit

RECTIFICATION

424. Suit for rectification of a sale deed

In the Court of .... at ......

Suit No. .... of 20.......

(Set out cause title)

The plaintiff states as follows:

1. That the defendant had agreed to sell and the plaintiff agreed to purchase three acres of land appertaining of Khatian No. 112 of Mouja .... P.S. .... District .... and accordingly the defendant executed on .... a Bainanama promising to sell the said land for a total consideration of ₹ .... at ₹ .... per acre.

2. That pursuant to aforesaid contract of sale, the defendant had executed in favour of the plaintiff a sale deed on .... against receipt of the agreed consideration.

3. That on .... the plaintiff got the sale deed from the office of the Sub-Registrar of .... and found that the number of Khatain was by mutual mistake not recorded correctly in the sale deed. In the sale deed, the Khatian No. was given as 212.

4. That the sale deed mentioning Khatian No. 212, did not correctly reflect the intention of the parties hereto.

The said deed of sale, therefore, requires rectification to confirm the agreement of sale.

5. That the plaintiff has requested the defendant to take steps for rectification of the said deed, particulars of which are—

Deed of sale (Kobala)

Date of execution ....

Date of registration ....

No. .... pages .... to .... in Vol. No. ....

The defendant received the said notice on .... but did not comply with the request made therein.

6. That the cause of action for this suit arose on .... when the deed of sale was executed at .... within the jurisdiction of this court.

7. Suit valuation.

The plaintiff, therefore, prays:

(*a*) For a judgment and decree for rectification of the deed of sale dated .... executed by the defendant by substituting the figure '112' in place of the figure '212' (State here particulars of rectification).

(*b*) For costs of suit.

(*c*) Further and other reliefs.

Verification

Affidavit

NOTES: 1. See s. 26 of the Specific Relief Act for a remedy of this nature when mistake is mutual or through fraud. For unilateral mistake no rectification is permissible—26 CWN 36. A suit of this type may be brought for rectification of a decree (14 IC 407) for rectification of a compromise decree—AIR 1928 Mad 1097.

2. Limitation—three years will govern from the knowledge of fraud or mistake— Art. 113 of the Limitation Act 1963—AIR 1940 Bom 321.

3. Either party to the deed or their representative in interest may bring like suit—ILR 31 Cal 614.

4. Court-fees to be assessed on the value of the subject-matter of the suit.

425. Suit to have a wrong description in a sale deed rectified

In the Court of .... at ......

Suit No. .... of 20.......

(Set out cause title)

The plaintiff states as follows:

1. By an agreement in writing dated ...., the defendant agreed to sell and the plaintiff agreed to purchase 8 acres of land situate in Mouza .... Khatian No. .... Plot No. ....

2. In the sale deed which was executed by the defendant on .... pursuant to the said agreement, it was by mutual mistake recorded that the property sold was in Mouza .... Khatian No.................... Plot No. ....

3. On ...., the plaintiff applied to the Revenue Court for mutation of his name in respect of the said 8 acres of land but, on the objection of the defendant that there had been no sale in favour of the plaintiff of Plot No. .... the said application was dismissed on ....

4. The said sale deed in so far as it purports to record that the property sold was entered in respect of Plot No. .... does not truly express the common intention of the parties thereto, who were under a common mistaken supposition that their intention was rightly expressed in the said instrument. The said sale deed ought therefore to be rectified in order to bring it into conformity with the prior agreement.

The plaintiff claims—

That the said sale deed be rectified by substituting the words and figures Plot No. .... in place of Plot No. ....

Verification

Affidavit

REGISTRATION

426. Suit for enforcing registration of a document

In the Court of the Civil Judge (Junior Division) at ....

Other Class Suit No. .... of 20..........

(Set out cause title)

Suit for registration of document under s. 77 of the Registration Act. Valued at ₹ ....

The plaintiff states as follows:

1. That the defendant, after negotiations and talks of sale, had executed on .... a deed of conveyance, in favour of the plaintiff, on receipt of consideration of ₹ .... in respect of certain immovable property situated at vill. Bara Simulguri, P.S. Mathabhanga, fully described in Schedule "A" below, in presence of some gentlemen whose names appear on the said Kobala deed as attesting witnesses.

(That defendant made over delivery of possession of the lands so sold to plaintiff on .... and the plaintiff is in possession thereof as the case may be).

2. That the defendant deferred registration of the said deed on .... on the plea of his occupation in Fouzdari Court in connection with a .... case then pending against the defendant. Thereafter, the defendant was requested to register the deed but he avoided registration on various pleas and then on .... the defendant flatly refused to register the document.

3. That the plaintiff, therefore, had presented the said deed before the Sub-Registrar, ... on .... who issued a notice upon the defendant calling upon him to register the document. The defendant did not appear before the Sub-Registrar, ... in response to the notice. His non-appearance before the Sub-Registrar was considered as a denial of execution. (Or the defendant appeared before the Sub-Registrar but denied execution of the deed—as the circumstances may be). The Sub-Registrar, ... accordingly passed orders on .... refusing registration of the said deed.

4. That the plaintiff thereafter filed an application under s. 73(1) before the District Sub-Registrar, ... whereupon a Registration Appeal Case No. .... of 1967 was started and registered. The District Sub-Registrar, ... upon enquiry passed an order of refusal on ....

5. That the said enquiry and findings thereof are perverse and untenable in facts or law.

6. That the plaintiff in the circumstances of the case seeks relief in this court for getting the said sale deed registered.

7. That the cause of action for the present suit arose on .... when the District Sub-Registrar .... dismissed the plaintiff's said application under s. 73(1) of the Registration Act and refused to register the document at .... where the Registration office is situated within the jurisdiction of this court.

8. Suit valuation—(value of the interest, i.e. amount of consideration in the deed).

The plaintiff accordingly prays:

(*a*) That a decree be passed declaring that the defendant executed the document in question and that the said deed is fit for registration according to law and directing the registration of the document in the office of the Sub-Registrar, ...

(*b*) Costs.

SCHEDULE 'A'

Verification

Affidavit

NOTES: 1. On refusal under s. 72 or s. 76 of the Registration Act by the Registrar, a suit lies under s. 77 of the Indian Registration Act by any person claiming under the document, or his representative, assign or agent. (Also see AIR 1970 All 221). Dismissal of application under s. 73—Remedy of civil suit under s. 77 is available—AIR 1977 Pat 295.

2. AIR 1970 Ker 261—Suit for registration of sale deed though also asking for possession and *mesne profits* is not barred.

3. Limitation 30 days (*vide* s. 77 of the Registration Act) after the making of the order of refusal.

4. For court-fees—See AIR 1970 Bom 109.

5. Suit for direction for registration—conditions for success—AIR 1971 Raj 181.

6. Section 71 applies to re-registration (200 IC 632) and to documents registration of which is optional—ILR 16 Cal 509.

7. No claim other than registration of the document can be claimed in a like suit (AIR 1933 Cal 196) but see AIR 1970 Ker 261.
8. Only the executant should be made a defendant. The Registrar or the Government is not a party.
9. Suit-Valuation—For the purposes of jurisdiction the suit is to be valued at ₹ .... (consideration amount) with fixed court-fees of ₹ ....

427. Petition under s. 73 of the Registration Act 1908 for registration of a document

Before the District Registrar at.........

Regn. Appeal No. .... of 20.........

A.B. .... *Petitioner-Vendee*

versus

C.D. .... *Opposite Party–Vendor*

The above-named petitioner most respectfully sheweth:

1. That the opposite party, on receipt of a consideration to ₹............ from the petitioner has executed a deed of sale on .... in favour of the petitioner, at .... within the jurisdiction of the Registrar at.........

2. That the said deed was written by one .... and the signature of the executant opposite party was attested in the deed by Sri .... and Sri .... on .... (date of execution).

3. That after execution the opposite party did not present the deed for registration. Thereupon the petitioner filed the said deed before the Registrar at......... on......... for registration. A notice was issued to the opposite party but he did not turn up before the Registrar at ....

4. That non-appearance of the executant was treated as denial of execution and the Registrar has on .... refused to register the said deed.

5. That the petitioner files herewith:

(*i*) the said deed, executed by the opposite party on .... (Annexure 'A').

(*ii*) Copy to the reasons for refusal under s. 71 of the Registration Act; and prays that the said deed be registered .... (Annexure 'B').

The petitioner asserts his right to have the document registered.

(ANNEXURES 'A' & 'B')

Verification

Affidavit

NOTES: 1. Oral application before Registrar under s. 73 is not permissible. It must be in writing and verified under Or. VI, r. 15 of the Code (see s. 73(2) of the Act).
2. District Registrar has jurisdiction to entertain an application under this section—AIR 1956 Pat 129. Refusing Registrar must be subordinate to the District Registrar.
3. Application must be made within 30 days "after the making of the order of refusal" by a Registrar. Date of the order of refusal for computing the 30 days, is the date of communication of the order—*Swaminathan* v *Lakshmanan* AIR 1930 Mad 490. Also see *Ramautar Sah* v *State of Bihar* AIR 1977 Pat 295.

4. Copy of the reasons of refusal under s. 71 must be submitted along with the application. Section 73 does not speak of document has to be filed with the application. It is advisable so to do.

SALE OF GOODS

428. Suit by buyer for damages for non-delivery of an instalment of goods

In the Court of .... at .....

Suit No. .... of 20.......

(Set out cause title)

The plaintiff states as follows:

1. By a contract in writing, dated .... 20....., the defendant agreed to sell, and the plaintiff agreed to buy, ... bags of ...., each bag weighing .... kg., in three equal instalment deliveries in May, June and July, 20......, such deliveries to be deemed as those under three separate contracts and to be separately paid for at the rate of ₹ .... *per* bag.

2. The defendant has not delivered the first instalment and the plaintiff has thereby suffered a loss of ₹ ...., being the difference between the contract rate and the market rate on 31st May 20........., the date of the breach in respect of the said instalment.

The plaintiff claims—

₹ .... damages.

Verification

Affidavit

429. Suit for price of goods sold at a price fixed and delivered

In the Court of the Civil Judge (Senior Division) at......................

Money Suit No. .... of 20............

M/s. Jormal Harakchand, a firm registered under the Indian Partnership Act with its principal place of business at Cooch Behar town, P. S. Kotwali, District—Cooch Behar.

.... *Plaintiff*

versus

.... Large-sized Co-operative Agricultural Marketing Society Ltd. having its registered office at .... P.S. .... District ....

.... *Defendant*

Suit for price of goods sold on credit together with damages. Claims laid at ₹ ....

The above-named plaintiff states as follows:

1. That the plaintiff is a registered partnership firm.

2. That the plaintiff firm deals in fertilisers having its business place at Cooch Behar.

3. That the defendant is a registered co-operative society and a body corporate registered under s. 14 of the West Bengal Co-operative Societies Act 2006, with perpetual succession and a common seal.

4. That on request of the defendant the plaintiff firm had supplied to the defendant on credit fertilisers on different dates from .... to .... valued at ₹ .... only. The defendant took delivery of the same by signing credit memos of the plaintiff firm agreeing to pay the value thereof at the *'guddee'* of the plaintiff firm at Cooch Behar.

5. That after such purchases from the plaintiff firm, the defendant had opened an account in the plaintiff firm in their name and made payments in their running account within the period from .... to .... as per account in the Schedule below, of a sum of ₹ .... leaving a balance of ₹ .... only due to the plaintiff firm.

6. Meantime, the plaintiff firm became entitled to damages over the dues unpaid whereupon the defendant sought to meet the claim of the plaintiff by issuing two cheques No. .... Dated .... for ₹ .... and the other No. .... dated .... for ₹ .... drawn on the .... Bank.

7. That both the cheques were presented to the bank by the endorsee of the plaintiff but those cheques were dishonoured. The factum of dishonour was made known to the defendant by the plaintiff by the latter's letter No. Nil dated .... In the said letter, the plaintiff firm had demanded from the defendant a sum of ₹ .... outstanding balance plus damages up to .... making a total of ₹ .... only.

8. That in spite of repeated *takids* the defendant did not pay up the plaintiff's dues. The plaintiff is entitled to recover from the defendant a sum of ₹ .... as per account in the Schedule below. The plaintiff has served a notice dated .... by registered post with A/D through their authorised lawyer on the Chairman of the defendant society. The Chairman received the notice on .... in his office.

9. That the plaintiff submits herewith extract of accounts maintained by the plaintiff firm in the regular course of their business.

10. That the cause of action for this suit arose first on .... and on each subsequent date of transaction at Cooch Behar within the jurisdiction of this court.

11. That for the purpose of jurisdiction and court-fees the suit is valued at ₹ .... and *ad valorem* court-fees are paid thereon.

The plaintiff, therefore, prays:

(*i*) For a judgment and decree for ₹ .... against the defendant as per account in the Schedule of claim below together with damages at .... (rate) till realisation.

(*ii*) Costs.

SCHEDULE OF CLAIM

Verification

Affidavit

430. Suit for price of goods sold and delivered but price not fixed

In the Court of .... at ....

S.C.C. No. .... 20 ....

(Set out cause title)

The above-named plaintiff states as follows:

1. That the plaintiff is a wholesale trader in mustard oil whereas the defendant runs a grocery and deals in retail sale of edible oil.

2. That at the request of the defendant, the plaintiff sold and delivered to the defendant on .... 50 (fifty) tins of Cawnpore mustard oil on credit.

3. That on the occasion of sale the goods were, as per market rate, worth ₹ .... at the rate of ₹ .... per tin. The said price was reasonable and as per prevailing wholesale market rate.

4. That the plaintiff had requested the defendant to pay the price thereof amounting to ₹ .... but the defendant has not paid.

5. That the cause of action for this suit arose .... (date of sale and delivery of oil) at .... within the jurisdiction of this court.

6. Suit valuation—(value of oil).

The plaintiff claims:

(*a*) a decree for ₹ ....

(*b*) a decree for ₹ .... as interest on the above sum @ 12.5% per annum from .... to ....

Verification

Affidavit

NOTES: 1. Limitation—three years from the date of delivery of the goods *vide* Art. 14 of the Limitation Act 1963.

2. Quantum of interest—See s. 61, Sale of Goods Act 1930.

3. Where no price fixed—reasonable price should be the price—See s. 9 of the Sale of Goods Act.

431. Suit by a seller for damages for non-acceptance of goods purchased

In the Court of .... at ......

Suit No. .... of 20.......

(Set out cause title)

The above-named plaintiff firm states as follows:

1. That the plaintiff firm is a registered partnership with its principal place of business at .... P.S. .... District ....

2. That the defendant by an order in writing dt. .... agreed to purchase from the plaintiff firm 35 bags of Chhati masoor dal to be delivered to the defendant at .... within 21 days from the date of order. The defendant agreed further to pay the price of the goods at ₹ .... per bag on delivery of the same.

3. That the plaintiff firm accordingly despatched a consignment by railway ex .... to .... under R/R. No. .... Dt. .... That the said consignment reached the destination on .... but the defendant did not accept the goods.

4. That the plaintiff firm was not paid the price of the said consignment.

5. That the plaintiff is entitled to damages as detailed in the statement of claim below.

The plaintiff, therefore, prays:

For a decree of ₹ .... as damages.

Statement of claim

Difference of price (—between contract price of ₹ .... per bag)	₹ ....
and	
(market price of ₹ .... per bag at the destination)	₹ ....
(Rupees .... in words)	
Total	₹ ....

Verification

Affidavit

NOTES: 1. See s. 56 of the Sale of Goods Act.
2. Difference of price should be claimed—See s. 73 of the Contract Act.

432. Suit for damages by a seller for loss on resale of goods

In the Court of .... at ......

Suit No. .... of 20......

(Set out cause title)

The plaintiff states as follows:

1. That the defendant had placed an order on .... with the plaintiff firm for purchase of 20 Qls. of sugar. Accordingly, the plaintiff firm had despatched by the carrier service of M/s. .... Transport Co., Kolkata, the said 20 Qls. of sugar under a Consignment Note No. .... date ....

2. That on arrival of the consignment on .... at the destination, the defendant refused to accept the consignment or to pay price thereof.

3. Thereupon the plaintiff firm was constrained to issue a notice dt. .... to the defendant by registered post with A/D that unless the defendant accepted goods and paid price thereof to the plaintiff firm within seven days from the date of receipt of the notice, the plaintiff firm shall be constrained to resell the same in the local market and if there was loss on such resale the defendant shall be liable for the loss for breach of contract. The defendant received the notice on .... but did not comply with the notice. The plaintiff firm has resold the said 20 Qls. of sugar on .... and suffered damage of ₹ .... in the said transaction, besides costs of resale.

4. Cause of action—(on the date of refusal and then, on the date of resale).

5. Valuation—loss in terms of money.

6. That the plaintiff firm is entitled to damages of ₹ .... account of claim appended below and prays, accordingly, for a decree .... as per account appended below:

Account of claim

Difference between contract rate of ₹ .... per Qls.	₹ ....
and less	
Market rate when resold at ₹ .... per Ql.	₹ ....
Add costs incurred in advertisement, conduct of sale.	₹ ....
Total	₹ ....
(In words)	

Verification

Affidavit

NOTE: See s. 73 of the Contract Act. For damages for breach of contract—See AIR 1971 Del 120—measurement of damages. Also see *American Pipe Co.* v *State of U.P.* AIR 1983 Cal 186.

433. Suit by buyer for damages for breach of implied warranty of fitness

In the Court of .... at ......

Suit No. .... of 20......

(Set out cause title)

The plaintiff states as follows:

1. The plaintiff, an ink and sealing wax manufacturer, wished to start the manufacture of carbon-paper, and, with that object in view, he consulted the defendant, an import merchant dealing in machinery for making paper, on 9th August .... as to the suitable plant and machinery for that purpose.

2. On the advice of the defendant, the plaintiff, by an agreement in writing, dated ...., agreed to buy from the defendant for the purpose aforesaid a machine for winding and cutting paper and also a low pressure steam and hot water boiler "Perfekt" No. 2 with accessories as *per* prospectus handed to the plaintiff, delivery 'in one lot as quick as possible', shipment to .... through ...., payment 60 days after delivery, price 850 RM. net, including package f.o.b. Continental port.

3. The machineries together with the boiler were delivered to the plaintiff in ...... and were taken by him to the works at .... and thereafter installed so as to form part of the plant for making carbon-paper.

4. The plaintiff paid the defendant for the machine and the boiler, ₹ .... in two instalments, the first, on ...., and the second, on ....

5. The boiler was worked for three days and was found to be not physically fit for the purpose for which it was supplied (here set out defects), and the authorities under the Indian Boilers Act also refused to certify it as fit for use under the Act, because the seam were welded and the boiler plates were too thin. The said defects were latent or hidden and were not discoverable by the plaintiff before the boiler was worked as aforesaid.

6. On .... the plaintiff wrote to the defendant rejecting the said boiler and demanded back the price paid for it. In reply the defendant refused to take back the boiler and to refund the purchase money.

7. On .... the plaintiff placed an order for another boiler with .... and the said boiler was received on .... and thereafter fitted upto the plant and was found satisfactory.

8. The plaintiff sold to one .... the boiler supplied by the defendant, on ...., for ₹ ....

9. The plaintiff has suffered damage by reason of the defective boiler supplied by the defendant.

Particulars of damage:

(*a*)	Expenses incurred in removing the boiler supplied by the defendant	...	₹ ....
(*b*)	Expenses incurred in installing the new boiler	...	₹ ....
(*c*)	Difference between the price of the new boiler and the price for which the first boiler was resold	...	₹ ....
(*d*)	Estimated overhead charges in respect of the carbon-paper plant, during the time necessarily taken up in removing the first boiler and installing the new one	...	₹ ....
(*e*)	Loss of profit on the manufacture of carbon-paper from ...., the date of supply of the first boiler,to ...., the date when the second boiler was installed	...	₹ ....
	Total	...	₹ ....

The plaintiff claims—

₹ .... damages.

Verification

Affidavit

434. Suit by a purchaser for delivering goods not according to sample

In the Court of .... at .....

Suit No. .... of 20 ....

(Set out cause title)

The above-named plaintiff states as follows:

1. That the defendant had contracted to supply to the plaintiff within the period from .... 20......... to .... 20.......... 25 Qls. of Chaati Masoor dal @ ₹ .... per Ql. and on the occasion of contract had shown sample of the dal which he contracted to supply.

2. That the defendant thereafter supplied to the plaintiff 25 Qls. of Chhati Masoor dal on .... The plaintiff paid to the defendant the price of the consignment on .... at the agreed rate.

3. That the masoor dal so supplied by the defendant was not as per sample and was of inferior quality and of lower price.

4. That the plaintiff had to undersell the said masoor dal and sustained damages, as per account below.

5. That the cause of action for this suit arose on .... when the defendant supplied goods not according to sample at .... within the jurisdiction of this court.

The plaintiff, therefore, claims:

₹ .... as damages.

Account of claim

Difference of value paid for the consignment and the prevailing market value @ ₹ .... per k.g.	₹ ....
Difference of value paid and market rate at which sold @ ₹ .... per k.g.	₹ ....
Total	₹ ....

(In words ....)

Verification

Affidavit

NOTES: 1. Sale of Goods Act, s. 59.

2. Once the goods are accepted the plaintiff cannot recover price but can sue for damages (100 IC 548). Buyer accepting goods though not strictly conforming to agreed specifications and consuming for its own use-amounts of waiver of condition. He is not entitled to claim breach of warranty—*City & Industrial Dev. Corporation v Nagpur Steel* AIR 1992 Bom 55.

435. Suit for specific performance of contract to sell goods

In the Court of .... at .....

Other Suit No. ...... of 20 ....

A.B. .... *Plaintiff*

versus

C.D. .... *Defendant*

The above-named plaintiff states as follows:

1. That the defendant owned an oil-painting of .... drawn by .... and the said oil-painting is rare and can hardly be purchased from the market.

2. That the defendant agreed on .... verbally to sell to the plaintiff the said oil-painting for a sum of ₹ .... on .... the plaintiff had tendered the said sum of ₹ .... and requested the defendant to deliver the oil-painting but the defendant withdrew his offer by refusing to sell the same to the plaintiff.

3. That the said oil-painting being rare and of a special value to the plaintiff, the plaintiff is entitled to specific performance of the contract dt. ....

4. That the cause of action arose on .... at .... within the jurisdiction of this court.

5. That the suit is valued at ₹ ....

The plaintiff, therefore, prays for a judgment for:

(*i*) Specific performance of contract dt. .... of sale of the said oil-painting to the plaintiff on payment of a sum of ₹ .... to the defendant.

(*ii*) Alternatively, damages of ₹ .... for breach of contract.

Verification

Affidavit

NOTE: Specific performance of contract to sell movables is permissible under situations contemplated in s. 12 of the Specific Relief Act.

436. Suit in respect of articles prepared to defendant's order

In the Court of .... at ......

Suit No. .... of 20.......

(Set out cause title)

The plaintiff states as follows:

1. That the plaintiff is a tailor and owns a tailoring shop wherefrom shirtings (or, shirt lengths) are sold as well.

2. That on .... the defendant agreed with the plaintiff that the latter would stitch a shirt for the defendant within seven days and shall supply the shirting required for the purpose and that the defendant on the occasion of taking delivery of the shirt shall pay to the plaintiff the value of cloth together with sartorial (tailoring) charges.

3. That the defendant selected three metres of shirting valued at ₹ .... The defendant was told that the entire cost would come to ₹ .... The defendant agreed.

4. That the plaintiff had stitched the shirt on .... and got the same ready for delivery but the defendant did not turn up even after expiry of a reasonable period to take delivery of the same.

5. That the plaintiff has suffered damage to the tune of ₹ ....

6. Cause of action.

The plaintiff, therefore, claims:

₹ .... as damages.

Verification

Affidavit

437. Suit for damage for breach of express condition and also for breach of warranty

In the Court of .... at ......

Suit No. .... of 20......

(Set out cause title)

The plaintiff states as follows:

1. The plaintiffs are shipbuilders. The defendants are makers of ship propellers and other articles of manganese-bronze manufactured in accordance with a special process belonging to them. The defendants are known as propeller experts.

2. On .... 20........, the plaintiffs contracted to build a single screw motor-ship for the ...... Company, hereinafter referred to as 'the owners', for ₹ .... lump sum. The ship which was numbered 972 was to be fitted with main propelling Diesel engines

of "North-Eastern" type with 2300 shaft horse-power at 110 revolutions *per* minute. It was to be completed and handed over to the owners not later than .... calendar months from December 20..... It was to be classed as Lloyd's 100 A1, for carrying .... and all things necessary to obtain the classification were to be done by the plaintiffs.

3. On .... 20........, the defendants contracted with the plaintiffs in writing to provide a propeller of special manganese-bronze of 16 ft. diameter, with a pitch of 11 ft. and maximum B.H.P.— 2150 at 105 revolutions *per* minute for the said ship manufactured in accordance with a working drawing supplied by the plaintiffs and to be to the entire satisfaction of the plaintiffs and of the representative of the owners.

4. The propeller was delivered by the defendants on .... It was fitted to the ship which then underwent trial on .... During the trial a noise of severe character occurred when the engines were running at revolutions below 100 *per* minute and after a number of trials and experiments the source of the noise was ascertained to be in the propeller. Accordingly, the ship was not passed and classed as Lloyd's 100 A1 for carrying .... and the propeller was rejected.

5. The defendants then provided a first replace, without prejudice to the rights of the parties, on ...., but that also on trial, which took place on ...., proved unsatisfactory for the same reason and was rejected.

6. The defendants, without prejudice to the legal position, provided a second replace on .... and that proved satisfactory and was accepted and the ship was passed and classed as Lloyd's 100 A1, on ....

7. By reason of the above facts, the plaintiffs could not complete the ship before .... and have thereby suffered loss.

Particulars of damage

The plaintiffs claim—

₹ .... damages.

Verification

Affidavit

SALE OF LAND

438. Suit by a vendee for specific performance of contract for sale of land

In the Court of the Civil Judge (Senior Division) at ....

Other Suit No. .... of 20.............

Sri A.B. son of late .... by faith Hindu, by occupation—agriculturist, residing at ...., District ....

.... *Plaintiff*

versus

Sri C.D. son of .... by faith Hindu, by occupation—agriculturist, of village ...., District ....

..... *Defendant*

Suit for specific performance of contract.

Valued at ₹ ....

The above-named plaintiff states as follows:

1. That the defendant, while owning and occupying the property, had entered into a contract in writing on .... agreeing therein to sell to the plaintiff the land, described in the Schedule below, at a consideration of ₹ .... and received from the plaintiff a sum of ₹ .... as earnest money.

2. That it was agreed therein that the defendant would sell the said property to the plaintiff by executing a proper sale deed and registering the same on receipt of the balance sum of ₹ .... within six months from the date of the 'Bainanama' referred to above.

3. That the plaintiff has been always ready and willing to pay to the defendant the balance of consideration money and as a matter of fact, the plaintiff offered to the defendant the said balance of consideration by a notice dated ...., served by the plaintiff on the defendant by registered post with A/D through his lawyer Sri ....Advocate.

4. That in the said notice the defendant was requested for compliance with the terms in the notice within 15 days from the date of receipt of the plaintiff's notice. The defendant received the notice on .... but did not comply with the request made therein.

5. That the plaintiff is entitled to specific performance of the said contract dated ....

6. That the cause of action for this suit arose first on .... (the date fixed for performance of the contract) and thereafter on ...., after expiry of 15 days' period after receipt of notice by the defendant at Mouja .... P.S. .... within the jurisdiction of this court.

7. That for the purpose of jurisdiction and court-fees, the suit is valued at ₹ .... and *ad valorem* court-fees of ₹ .... are paid.

The plaintiff, therefore, prays:

(1) that the suit be decreed directing the defendant to execute and register the sale deed in question in favour of the plaintiff in respect of the property in the Schedule below, on accepting the contracted purchase money less the amount already paid as an earnest money;

(2) that the defendant be directed to execute and register the sale deed within a time specified by the court, failing which the said deed be executed and registered according to the provisions of Or. 21, r. 34(5) and r. 34(6)(*a*) of CPC;

(3) Costs.

SCHEDULE

Verification

Affidavit

NOTES: 1. The plaintiff (when vendee) may sue for specific performance of contract of sale. With such a claim, he may, alternatively, claim for the refund of purchase money, when already paid with interest—AIR 1940 All 41. The plaintiff (when vendor) shall sue for directing the purchaser to pay the balance of consideration and obtain conveyance.

2. AIR 1970 Guj 145—valuation of suit must be made on averments and allegations made in the plaint.
3. Court-fees—*Ad valorem* court-fees on the amount of consideration agreed—See s. 7(*x*)(*a*) of the Court-fees Act.
4. Limitation—for specific performance of contract three years under Art. 54 of the Limitation Act 1963, from the date fixed for the performance or if, no such date is fixed, when the plaintiff has notice that performance is refused.
5. Plaintiff must prove continuous readiness and willingness to perform his part from date contract till date of hearing—*P.G. Sinha* v *Commodore, K.C. Chatterjee* AIR 1991 Cal 327 (s. 16 of the Specific Relief Act 1963). But averment in plaint that the plaintiff has been and always ready to perform his part of contract—the absence of expression 'willing' is not fatal on basis of pleading as a whole and conduct of the plaintiff—*Nambarukandi* v *Nattithadi* AIR 1991 Ker 1.
6. Whether the time is of essence on contract—the real test in the intention of parties, Generally in the context of immovable property time is not of the essence of contract. But this general principle is subject to the exceptions as may arise on the facts of a given case wherein the parties may make time to the essence of contract even in cases relating to immovable property. The intention of the parties has to be found out, on the basis of the materials on record—*Nanak Builders* v *Vinod Kumar* AIR 1991 Del 315.
7. Sale of Land Agreement not containing stipulation for amount of consideration. There is no separate agreement or understanding between parties about the same. Agreement is void and not enforceable—*Rabindra Nath Sahu* v *Maya Devi* AIR 1991 Pat 192.
8. See s. 22(1) of the Specific Relief Act—decree for specific performance of contract. Decree is silent as to delivery of possession, defendant in exclusive possession of the property. Decree-holder is entitled to claim possession in execution of the decree [In consonance with s. 55(1)(*f*) of the Transfer of Property Act 1882]—*Gyasa* v *Smt. Risalo* AIR 1977 All 156.

439. Suit by a vendor for specific performance of a contract of sale of land

In the Court of .... at ......

Suit No. .... of 20.......

(Set out cause title)

The plaintiff states as follows:

1. That the defendant had agreed, by a written agreement entered into by the parties hereto on ...., to purchase certain immovable properties mentioned in the said agreement and specifically described in the Schedule appended below for a consideration of ₹ .... within the month of .... 20.................

2. That the plaintiff had requested the defendant by a notice in writing dated ...., sent to the defendant by registered post with A/D, to complete the purchase by payment of the agreed consideration and was warned in the said notice that in case the defendant did not perform his part of the contract within 15 (fifteen) days from the receipt of the notice, the plaintiff would sue him for specific performance of the contract.

3. That the defendant received the notice on .... but did not complete the purchase till now.

4. That the plaintiff has been always and is ready and willing to perform his part of the agreement.

5. That the cause of action for this suit arose on .... at .... within the jurisdiction of this court.

6. That the suit is valued at ₹ .... (value of consideration) for the purposes of jurisdiction and court-fees.

The plaintiff claims for:

(*a*) a decree of specific performance of the contract of purchase by the defendant on payment of ₹ .... to the plaintiff;

(*b*) in the alternative, damages for ₹ ....

(*c*) costs.

SCHEDULE

Verification

Affidavit

NOTES: 1. A notice for performance of the contract within a definite time must be given by the vendor—AIR 1971 Mys 217.

2. Suit by *A* against *B* for specific performance of contract. Property agreed to be sold only for a sum of ₹ 17,000. *B* from time to time paying ₹ 12,000. *B* was also in possession of property. *A* calling upon *B* to pay the full amount of purchase price. *B* failed.

A's suit for possession and, in alternative, for the balance amount of purchase price and interest thereon. Held, that it could not be said that they by reason of ss. 39 and 55 *A* was not competent to maintain the suit—*Ranchhoddas Chhaganlal* v *Devaji Supdu Dorik* AIR 1977 SC 1517.

3. In a suit for specific performance against a purchaser with notice of a prior agreement of sale, the vendor is a necessary party—AIR 1973 SC 655.

4. Decree in a suit for specific performance of the contract for sale of immovable property calling upon the purchaser to deposit balance of consideration within the time stipulated in the decree. Orders extending time to deposit would not result in amending the decree—AIR 1978 SC 537.

5. Suit under s. 58(*c*) of the Transfer of Property Act—

Q. Whether document was a mortgage by conditional sale or was an outright sale accompanied by an agreement for reconveyance?

Once the condition is incorporated in the same document and the terms of the document are covered by s. 58(*c*) of the Transfer of Property Act, the transaction will be considered to be a mortgage only unless the person who asserts it is not a mortgage is able to prove, either from the language contained in the document or from the attendant circumstances that the transaction was intended to be an outright sale.

The same can be shown by two means: one, by establishing that there are express words in the document itself which will be indicative of the character of the document not as a mortgage by conditional sale and establish it to be an outright sale; and, secondly, by establishing the attendant circumstances which will necessarily lead to the inference that the transaction was meant to be an outright sale only—AIR 1978 Mad 75; AIR 1954 SC 345 foll. Also see AIR 1978 Cal 4; AIR 1978 Cal 443; (1964) SCR 239; 70 CWN 139; 70 CWN 982.

440. Suit against a vendor for refund of purchase money for defect of title

In the Court of the Civil Judge (Senior Division) at................

Money Suit No. .... of ....

Plaintiffs:

1. A.
2. B.
3. C.

sons of Sri "D" all by faith Hindu, by occupation agriculturist, residing at village .... P.S. .... District ....

versus

Defendants:

1. A.B.
2. C.D.
3. E.F.

All residing at village .... P.S. .... Date ....

Suit for recovery of consideration money with damages.

Valued at ₹ ....

The above-named plaintiffs states as follows:

1. That defendant No. 3 held vast landed properties and owned, amongst others, a land measuring .... acres at Mouja .... P.S. .... District .... more particularly described in Schedule "A" below.

2. That the said defendant No. 3 had retained the property by a Return in Form 'B' and sold to defendant No. 2 a portion thereof measuring 3 bighas more particularly described in Schedule "B" below, by executing a registered kobala dated .... 14 .... B.S. (corresponding to ....) and made over delivery of possession of the same to defendant No. 2 after sale.

3. That defendant No. 2 owned and possessed the land in Schedule B and thereafter sold the said property in Schedule B to defendant No. 1 by instalments by executing two registered kobalas dated .... defendant No. 2 made over delivery of possession of the land in Schedule B to defendant No. 1 after such sale.

4. That defendant No. 1 while owning and possessing the property in Schedule B has sold the same to the plaintiffs, on receipt of a consideration of ₹ .... by executing a kobala (registered) in favour of the plaintiffs on the ...., B.S. (corresponding to ....) and made over delivery of possession of the property in Schedule B to the plaintiffs.

5. That the plaintiffs had been possessing the property in Schedule B in their right till middle of .... 20........, when the plaintiffs were dispossessed by 15/16 families of .... claiming that the land in Schedule B was a land vested in the State.

6. That after so dispossessed from the land in Schedule B, the plaintiffs were led to make shifting enquiries here and there. It then transpired that defendant No. 3 originally retained the land in Schedule B but he retained land in excess of retainable ceiling. He was asked in Case No. .... under s. 47 of the West Bengal Estates

Acquisition Act to surrender the excess land whereupon defendant No. 3 at the back of the plaintiffs had without jurisdiction and fraudulently surrendered the land in ....Schedule B in favour of the State on the basis of which surrender the property Schedule B vested in the State.

7. That the plaintiffs took out certified copy of the judgment dated .... of Case No. .... on ...., and came to know precisely the facts stated in para 6 herein above.

8. That the said property in Schedule B is the suit property.

9. That because of the aforesaid subsequent conduct of defendant No. 3, defendant No. 3 could not, and had no right, to sell the suit property to defendant No. 2. Defendant No. 2 did not acquire any right, title or interest in the property in Schedule B on the basis of the void kobala executed by defendant No. 3, in favour of defendant No. 2. Similarly the kobalas executed by defendant No. 2, in favour of defendant No. 1 and that executed by defendant No. 1 in favour of the plaintiffs are void.

10. That the plaintiff-transferees are entitled to benefits of contract of sale entered into by defendant No. 3 and his transferees and are entitled to recover from defendant No. 1 a sum of ₹ .... being refund of consideration money plus costs of stamp for conveyance and registration cost a sum of ₹ .... plus damages of ₹ .... making a total of ₹ .... as per account in Schedule C below.

11. That the cause of action for this suit arose on ...., when the plaintiffs purchased the property in Schedule B on payment of consideration of ₹ ...., and incurred other incidental expenses and thereafter on ...., when the plaintiffs took out certified copy of the judgment of Case No. .... under s. 47 of the West Bengal Estates Acquisition Act and came to know that the property in Schedule B vested in the State, as stated in para 6 hereinabove.

12. That for the purpose of jurisdiction and court-fees the suit is valued at ₹ .... and *ad valorem* court-fees are paid thereon.

The plaintiffs, therefore, pray:

(*a*) For a decree of ₹ .... against defendant No. 1 or, in the alternative, if admissible, against defendant No. 3 as per account in Schedule C below.

(b) For damages .... ₹ ....

(*c*) For costs of the suit.

SCHEDULE A

(State here particulars of land)

SCHEDULE B

(State here particulars of land)

SCHEDULE C

Consideration money	...	...	₹ ....
Stamp for conveyance	...	...	₹ ....
Registration cost	...	...	₹ ....
			₹ ....
Add damages on ₹ .... for the period from			
.... to	...	...	₹ ....
			₹ ....

(Rupees in words)

Verification

Affidavit

NOTES: 1. See AIR 1970 Ori 89—suit by vendee against vendor for refund of consideration—sale found to be void for want of subsisting interest in vendor (Limitation under the old Act six years under the Act 1963—three years).

2. Contract for purchase of land—purchaser by such purchase will have land exceeding the ceiling—contract is not void, specific performance can be decreed—AIR 1968 SC 1358.

3. Court-fees—in a suit for refund of purchase money—*ad valorem* court-fees under s. $7(x)(a)$ of the Court-fees Act.

4. Reg: Deposit of earnest money and forfeiture thereof—see AIR 1970 SC 1955; AIR 1970 SC 1986.

441. Suit for refund of baina money with damages

In the Court of .... at ......

Suit No. .... of 20......

(Set out cause title)

Suit for return of baina (earnest) money with damages.

Valued at ₹ ....

The plaintiff states as follows:

1. That the defendant being impelled by necessity of money had represented to the plaintiffs that he had saleable interest in the land in Schedule "A" below and wanted to sell the same to the plaintiffs at a consideration of ₹.................... (in words) and executed an agreement for sale of the land in Schedule "A" below on .... in favour of the plaintiffs on taking from the plaintiffs the same day a sum of ₹ .... (in words) as part of the agreed consideration as 'Baina' promising *inter alia* to execute and register a deed conveying the property in Schedule "A" to the plaintiffs within the month of .... on receipt of balance of the consideration.

2. The said Bainanama is filed herewith and may be treated as part of the plaint.

3. That the plaintiffs acted on the representation of the defendant and entered into the transaction in good faith.

4. That the plaintiffs have been always ready and willing to perform their part of the contract in respect of the said transaction.

5. That only the other day in ...., the plaintiffs have learnt that the defendant had no saleable interest in the land in Schedule 'A' below and he had taken the Baina of ₹ .... on false representation.

6. That it is impossible for the defendant to perform his part of the contract and the Bainanama is a void document.

7. That, in the circumstances of the case, the plaintiffs have no necessity or reason to offer the balance of the consideration or to seek completion of the transaction.

8. That the plaintiffs are entitled to refund of the Baina money, i.e. a sum of ₹ .... together with damages at 10% per annum thereon. The plaintiffs claim a sum of ₹ .... as per account in Schedule "B" below.

9. That the cause of action for this suit arose at Mouja .... P.S. .... District ...., within the jurisdiction of this court on .... when the plaintiff paid to the defendant the Baina of ₹ .... only.

10. That for the purpose of jurisdiction and court-fees the suit is valued at ₹ .... and *ad valorem* court-fees are paid thereon.

The plaintiffs, therefore, pray:

(*a*) for a judgment and decree for ₹ .... as per account in Schedule 'B' below (after setting aside the Bainanama deed in question, if necessary—*void document does not require setting aside*),

(*b*) Costs.

SCHEDULE 'A'

SCHEDULE 'B'

Verification

Affidavit

NOTES: 1. See s. 64 of the Indian Contract Act. When a contract for sale of land comes to an end by frustration, the vendor is entitled to get back earnest money and not to compensation and/or damages—AIR 1968 Assam 26.

2. For refund of earnest money—(Also see s. 22 of the Specific Relief Act 1963). In a suit for specific performance of the contract for the transfer of immovable property, a plaintiff may in an appropriate case ask for any other relief including the refund of earnest money, in case specific performance is refused. The plaintiff must in his suit claim such a relief. Failure gives the plaintiff compensation under s. 21 of the Act.

442. Suit for refund of earnest money, in the alternative, for specific performance of contract

In the Court of .... at ......

Suit No. .... of 20......

(Set out cause title)

The plaintiff states as follows:

1. That the defendant executed on the .... of ...., 14 .... B.S. corresponding to ...... an agreement for sale of the property mentioned in Schedule 'A' below for a consideration of ₹ .... (in words) and took ₹ .... (Rupees in words) as *baina* on the same date promising *inter alia* to execute a kobala deed within .... of .... 14 .... B.S. and register the same on taking the balance of the agreed consideration. The consideration was reasonable with reference to the value of the property and the plaintiff entered into the transaction in good faith.

2. That the plaintiff repeatedly offered the said balance of the consideration, i.e. a sum of ₹ .... (Rupees in words) to the defendant on .... and asked him to execute and register the intended sale deed at the plaintiff's cost, but the defendant neither took the balance of the consideration nor did execute and register the sale deed in favour of the plaintiff.

3. That thereafter the plaintiff gave notice dt. .... through registered post with A/D to the defendant through his Advocate .... stating *inter alia* that

the plaintiff was ready and willing to pay the balance consideration and asked the defendant to complete the transaction, i.e. to execute and register the sale deed in respect of property mentioned in Schedule 'A' within .... of .... 14 .... B.S. on taking the balance of the consideration. That the defendant received the notice on ...., but did not perform his part of the contract and, as such, the plaintiff is entitled to sue for specific performance of the contract.

4. That on enquiry the plaintiff has learnt that the defendant has had no marketable interest in the said property in the Schedule below. Even if the sale materialised the plaintiff could acquire no right, title and interest therein by such sale.

Or

(That on enquiry the plaintiff learnt that the property in Schedule 'A' is partly under occupation of persons other than the defendant and the defendant may not be in a position to deliver peaceful vacant possession of the entire property after the sale).

In the above circumstances, the plaintiff prays for refund of earnest (or, *baina*) money of ₹ .... (Rupees in words) only.

5. If, however, the defendant be agreeable and willing to execute the sale deed as per aforesaid agreement, the plaintiff reserves his right to pay the balance of the agreed consideration and pay additional court-fees in the suit, and to pray for specific performance of the contract of sale.

6. That the cause of action for the present suit arose at .... (the place of transaction) within the jurisdiction of this court on .... (date of payment of earnest money).

7. That for the purpose of court-fees and jurisdiction the suit is valued at ₹ .... and court-fees are paid accordingly.

The plaintiff prays:

(*a*) for a decree of ₹ .... (Rupees in words) only against the defendant.

SCHEDULE 'A'

Verification

Affidavit

443. Suit for refund of price of auction, judgment-debtor not having saleable interest

In the Court of .... at ....

Money Suit No. .... of 20.............

(Set out cause title)

The plaintiff states as follows:

1. That the defendant was a judgment-debtor in an Other Suit No. .... of 20............. in the court of the .... of the district of ....

2. That one A.B. brought an Other Execution proceeding No. .... of 20 .... against the defendant for not satisfying decretal dues to the said O.C. Suit in the Court of .... at ....

3. That on .... the under-mentioned property of the defendant was put to court-sale by auction in the said execution proceedings and the plaintiff purchased the said property on ...., on payment of ₹ ....

4. That one C.D. had brought a Misc. Case No. .... of the year. .... in the said court against the defendant and obtained a decree on .... to the effect that the said auction sale on .... in respect of the property in the Schedule below was void inasmuch as the judgment-debtor had no saleable interest in the said property.

5. That the plaintiff is entitled to recover from the defendant a sum of ₹ .... which the plaintiff had to pay for purchase of the land in the Schedule below.

6. Cause of action (on the date of sale and thereafter on .... when the sale was declared void).

The plaintiff claims—

₹ ....

SCHEDULE

Verification

Affidavit

444. Suit by a vendee for unpaid purchase money

In the Court of .... at ....

Money Suit No. .... of 20 ....

(Set out cause title)

Suit for money claim laid at ₹ ....

The above-named plaintiff states as follows:

1. That the plaintiff has sold to the defendant on .... a piece of land measuring .... kathas at .... town, P.S. .... District .... more fully described in the Schedule appended below by executing a kobala the same (registered on ....) day for a consideration of ₹ .... only.

2. That on the date of sale, the defendant paid to the plaintiff a sum of ₹ .... agreeing to pay the balance of ₹ .... the next day.

3. That the defendant did not pay the said sum of ₹ .... on the following day and has not paid even now despite the plaintiff's request therefor.

4. That the plaintiff is entitled to recover from the defendant the said sum of ₹ .... together with interest $6^1/_2$% per annum till realisation.

5. That the cause of action for this suit arose on .... when the plaintiff executed the sale deed and completed the sale at .... within the jurisdiction of this court.

6. That for the purpose of jurisdiction and court-fees, the suit is valued at ₹ .... and *ad valorem* court-fees are paid thereon.

That the plaintiff, therefore, claims:

(*i*) a decree for ₹ .... as per account in Schedule 'B' below.

(*ii*) Costs.

SCHEDULE 'A'

(State here particulars of the land)

SCHEDULE 'B'

(Account)

Verification

Affidavit

NOTES: 1. Allegation that the deed recited falsely that price had been paid—Art. 111 and not Art. 116 applies—*Marni Veeranna* v *Kanumuri Lakshminarayana Rao* AIR 1977 AP 405.

2. See s. 55(5)(*b*) of the Transfer of Property Act 1882.

445. Suit for damages by a vendor for breach of agreement to purchase land

In the Court of .... at ......

Suit No. .... of 20 ....

(Set out cause title)

The plaintiff states as follows:

1. That the defendant contracted to purchase and the plaintiff to sell a piece of land measuring 10 acres at Mouja .... P.S. .... District ...., more particularly described in the Schedule below under a Bainanama (or, agreement as the case is) dated. .... for a consideration of ₹ .... only.

2. That on the occasion of execution of Bainanama the defendant paid to the plaintiff a sum of ₹ .... as earnest money and promised to pay the balance of the consideration within three months from the said date and to complete the contract of purchase within the said period.

3. (*Where time is of essence of the contract*)—

That the defendant did not pay to the plaintiff the balance of consideration and did not complete the purchase depriving thereby the plaintiff of the benefits of the said contract.

(*Where time is not of the essence of contract*)—

That the defendant did not complete the purchase on payment of the balance of the consideration within the stipulated date. Thereupon the plaintiff has served a notice dated .... on the defendant by registered post with A/D. requesting the defendant to complete the purchase within one month from the date of receipt of the said notice. The defendant received the notice on .... In the said notice the defendant was intimated that in case of non-compliance the contract under the said agreement dated .... should be intended by the plaintiff to be considered at an end. The defendant has not complied with the request made in the said notice.

4. That the plaintiff has suffered damage for the non-performance of the contract by the defendant.

5. That the cause of action arose on ...., on expiry of the said period of three months, at .... within the jurisdiction of this court.

6. That for the purpose of jurisdiction and court-fees the suit is valued at ₹ .... (amount of damages claimed).

The plaintiff claims a decree of ₹ .... as damages.

SCHEDULE

(State here particulars of the land)

Verification

Affidavit

NOTES: 1. See s. 21 of the Specific Relief Act 1963. In a suit for specific performance of the contract the plaintiff may also claim compensation for its breach either in addition to, or in substitution of, such performance. Under s. 21(5) the plaintiff must claim compensation in the plaint. Standard of compensation to be governed by s. 73 of the Indian Contract Act.

2. Transfer of property by natural guardian of minor. Transfer was made without permission of the court and without legal necessity. The minor, within 3 years after he attained majority can file a suit to set aside sale by minor's guardian—*Amirhan* v *Savnam* AIR 1991 SC 1256.

3. Court-fees—Court-fees is payable on the value of the relief

(*i*) damages when claimed.

4. Limitation—for breach of contract—three years

(*ii*) damages when claimed under s. 73—three years *vide* Art. 54 from the date fixed for performance of the contract.

5. When the contract is for the sale of immovable property, the vendor must give reasonable notice regarding the performance within a definite time—AIR 1971 Mys 217.

446. Suit for possession of land

In the Court of Civil Judge (Senior Division) at Diamond Harbour

Suit No. .... of 20...

Mr. P. residing at .... Alipore, Kolkata

... *Plaintiff*

versus

Mr. X residing at .... Diamond Harbour, Kolkata

... *Defendant*

Suit for possession of land valued at ₹ ....

The plaintiff states as follows:

1. The plaintiff is the owner and occupier of three acres of land in the Diamond Harbour as shown and indicated in a map annexed hereto marked 'A'.

2. A portion of such land measuring about one acre was submerged by the river along with portion of defendant's land adjacement to the plaintiff's land.

3. After about 15 years, the river started to recede and the said submerged land appeared again on surface and the plaintiff was entitled to take possession of and make proper use thereof.

4. The defendant, however, has wrongfully taken possession of the said one acre of land which was submerged and reappeared after river has receded.

5. The plaintiff states that the defendant is wrongfully claiming the said land as will appear from the particulars of land and the map or plan showing the location of plaintiff's land belonging to defendant.

6. The defendant has wrongfully taken possession of plaintiff's land surfaced after the river receded and legally belong to the plaintiff.

7. The defendant wrongfully and illegal has taken possession of plaintiff's land which was earlier submerged but subsequently surfaced.

8. The plaintiff claims a declaration that the said land as marked in the plan a copy whereof is annexed hereto marked 'B', actually belong to the plaintiff and the defendant has no right, title or interest therein.

9. The plaintiff also claims damages by way of compensation for the wrongful and illegal occupation by the defendant of plaintiff's said land and depriving the plaintiff from useful cultivation and raising crops.

10. The plaintiff claims that the damages due to wrongful acts of the defendant is assessed at ₹ .... as being estimated price of crops that the plaintiff expected to grow on such land which is being wrongfully occupied by defendant.

11. The plaintiff is entitled to claim and recover the said loss and damages and also recovery if possession of the said land now under the control of defendant.

12. In spite of demands, the defendant has not paid the said sum of ₹ .... and has not vacated the said land and the plaintiff has been kept out of possession of said land thus causing loss and prejudice to the plaintiff.

13. For purposes of jurisdiction and court-fees, the suit is valued at ₹ .... on which court-fees in stamps have been paid.

14. This learned court has the jurisdiction to entertain, try and determine this suit inasmuch as the defendant resides within the jurisdiction of this learned court and the land is situated within the territorial limit of this learned court.

15. The plaintiff has valued the suit at ₹ .... on which court-fees in stamps have been paid and undertakes to pay further court-fees if this learned court so directs after ascertaining the quantum of loss and damages suffered by the plaintiff or value of land wrongfully taken possession of by defendant.

The plaintiff, therefore, prays for and claims:

(*a*) A declaration that the defendant has no right, title or interest in the said land and the plaintiff is the sole and lawful owner thereof;

(*b*) Decree for ₹ .... with interest a 16% per annum from the date of the suit till date of decree and on decretal amount till payment;

(*c*) Cost;

(*d*) Further and other orders be made as this learned court may deem fit and proper to afford complete relief to the plaintiff.

ANNEXURES

SCHEDULE 'A' (MAP)

SCHEDULE 'B' (PLAN)

Verification

Affidavit

TORTS AND OTHER MISCELLANEOUS CAUSES

447. Suit for damages for assault (without battery)

In the Court of .... at

Suit No .... of 20 ....

(Set out cause title)

The plaintiff states:

1. That on or about the day of March, 20 .... when the plaintiff was cycling back to his residence from the market place, the defendant stopped the plaintiff and, without the slightest provocation, raised his fist threatening to strike the plaintiff. The plaintiff fell down from his cycle and sustained injuries.

2. The plaintiff as a result thereof could not attend to his business. The plaintiff has suffered damage, as detailed below.

3. Cause of action.

4. Suit valuation

Nature of injuries sustained

(*i*) One lacerated injury on right forearm.
(*ii*) Echymosis etc.

Special damage

Loss of business—for the period from .... to .... (both inclusive) causing loss in terms of money ₹ ....

The plaintiff prays for:

a decree of damages amounting to ₹ ....

Verification

Affidavit

448. Suit for damages for assault

In the Court of .... at ....

Suit No .... of 20 ....

(Set out cause title)

The plaintiff states as follows:

1. The plaintiff is a licensed medical practitioner or ....

2. On .... 20 ...., at about .... p.m., the plaintiff was lawfully walking along .... Road when the defendant who was following the plaintiff overtook him and assaulted him by pointing a revolver at him and repeatedly threatening to shoot him therewith if he moved a single step forward, by reasons whereof the plaintiff was prevented from walking along the said street as aforesaid and suffered from a nervous shock and was unable to do any work for a week.

3. By reason of the premises the plaintiff has suffered damage.

Particulars of special damage:

The plaintiff claims—

₹ .... damages.

Verification

Affidavit

449. Defence to a claim for assault

In the matter of ....

(Set out cause title)

The defendant states as follows:

1. The defendant denies that he assaulted the plaintiff as alleged in the plaint at all.

2. Further, the defendant denies that the plaintiff suffered from the alleged assault or any shock or has suffered the alleged or any damage by reason of the alleged or any assault by the defendant. In any case, the damages claimed are excessive.

3. The suit be dismissed.

Verification

Affidavit

Libel and Slander

450. Suit for libel

In the Court of .... at ....

Suit No. .... of 20 ....

(Set out cause title)

The plaintiff states as follows:

1. That the defendant No. 1 is the proprietor of a Bengali weekly entitled ".................", which is published from .... and is circulated throughout the district of .... The defendant No. 2 is the printer and publisher of the said weekly.

2. That the plaintiff is the Executive Officer of .... in the District Headquarters at .... and is a respectable citizen with his friends and relations in the district.

3. That the defendants has printed and published in the issue of the said journal dated .... a news item under the caption "Apakirti" which reads as follows:

(State the exact language and expression).

4. That the defendants in printing and publishing the same acted falsely and maliciously to injure the reputation of the plaintiff. As a matter of fact, by the publication of the same, the plaintiff has been injured in his credit and reputation. The plaintiff has suffered mental pain and has been lowered down in the estimation of the public, brought into scandal and contempt.

5. Cause of action—(on the date of publication of the libel).

The plaintiff claims damages of ₹ .... as per account in the Schedule below.

SCHEDULE

(Account of damages)

Verification

Affidavit

NOTES: 1. Exact words which are defamatory should be averred in the plaint.
2. Pleading special damages is not required.
3. Limitation–one year from the date of publication of the libel.
4. Editor, printer, proprietor, publisher may be sued jointly in one suit.

451. Suit for slander

In the Court of .... at ....

Suit No. .... of 20 ....

(Set out cause title)

The above-named plaintiff states as follows:

1. That the plaintiff is and was at all material times an assistant teacher in English in the .... School at .... P.O. .... District ....

2. That on the .... day of .... 20............ the defendant, a member of the Managing Committee of the aforesaid school, spoke to A.B.C. and D., residing at .... guardians of their wards reading in the said school regarding/concerning the plaintiff that:

> "Sri .... (plaintiff) was a man of bad character. He did not obtain Degree in Honours and is not a fit person to be retained as a teacher in any school."

3. That the said words were meant to disparage the plaintiff in his profession as a school teacher and in so saying the defendant acted falsely and maliciously. The plaintiff, in consequence, has suffered mental pain and has been greatly injured in his credit, character and reputation.

The plaintiff claims:

₹ .... as damages.

Verification

Affidavit

NOTES: 1. Slander is libellous statement made orally.
2. In a suit for slander special damage may be pleaded, but no compulsion.
3. Limitation–one year under Art. 76 of the Limitation Act 1963 from the date when the words are spoken.

452. Suit for damages for slander of goods

In the Court of .... at ....

Suit No. .... of 20 ....

(Set out cause title)

The plaintiff states:

1. That the plaintiff is the owner of a baby food known as............. which is manufactured by the plaintiff. The same has a large market throughout the State of West Bengal.

2. That the defendant has liberated in the said market only recently a tinned baby food under the style '.....................'. The said baby food is packed in cartons on which is printed qualities of the food in contrast with similar articles and, specially, there is an oblique reference to the plaintiff's baby food '.....................' stating that the plaintiff's said baby food "contains nothing but wheat and is likely to harm babies, if taken."

3. That said remarks by the defendant are deliberate false statements, calculated to do harm to the plaintiff. The '....................' does not contain wheat and the same cannot do any harm to babies.

4. That the plaintiff has suffered in his trade as sale of the baby food "....................." went down appreciably after such publication.

(State here extent of loss)

... ...

The plaintiff claims:

(*a*) ₹ .... as damages.

(*b*) Order of injunction restraining the defendant from further publishing comments as to plaintiff's baby food, as mentioned in para 2 above; and

(*c*) Appropriate order for destruction of all cartons of the defendant containing above-mentioned comments.

Verification

Affidavit

453. Suit for damages for malicious prosecution

In the Court of the Civil Judge (Junior Division) .... at ....

Money Suit No. .... 20.............

A.B. .... *Plaintiff*

versus

C.D. .... *Defendant*

Suit for damages
claim laid at ₹...............

The above-named plaintiff states as follows:

1. That the plaintiff is a respectable citizen, a medical practitioner, and is .... (state the status).

2. That the defendant had filed before the Additional Chief Judicial Magistrate of .... a complaint against the plaintiff on .... charging the plaintiff with an offence of criminal breach of trust in respect of a sum of ₹............., allegedly deposited by the defendant with the plaintiff on.............

3. That in so doing the defendant acted maliciously and without reasonable or probable cause.

4. That the defendant got a non-bailable warrant issued by the said court against the plaintiff and as a consequence the plaintiff was arrested on .... and detained in jail hajat till .... when he was released on bail.

5. That the plaintiff was tried for an offence of criminal breach of trust under s. 406 of the Indian Penal Code and was acquitted on ....

6. That the plaintiff in consequence suffered professional loss, and was injured in his reputation and had incurred huge costs for defending himself as per account below.

7. That the cause of action for this suit arose on .... when the plaintiff was acquitted at .... within the jurisdiction of this court.

8. That for the purpose of jurisdiction and court-fees, the suit is valued at ₹............. and *ad valorem* court-fees are paid thereon.

Account of claim

Injury in reputation	...	...	...	₹...............
Professional loss	...	...	...	₹...............
Legal costs	...	...	...	₹...............
			Total	₹...............

The plaintiff, therefore, prays:

(*i*) For a decree of ₹............ as damages.

(*ii*) Costs.

Verification

Affidavit

NOTES: 1. Malice—malice in its legal sense means malice such as may be assumed from the doing of a wrongful act intentionally but without cause or excuse or for want of reasonable or probable cause—AIR 1979 SC 49.

2. Essential elements of malicious prosecution—AIR 1997 Cal 356.

3. The plaintiff has to prove—

(*i*) that he was prosecuted by the defendant;

(*ii*) that the prosecution terminated in his favour;

(*iii*) that there was absence of reasonable or probable cause for initiating the prosecution; and

(*iv*) that the prosecution was malicious, i.e., the defendant was actuated by malice—AIR 1970 Ker 229; AIR 1970 Ori 91; AIR 1971 All 109.

See AIR 1939 PC 225; AIR 1969 Pat 102; *R.K. Soni* v *S. Singhara Singh* AIR 1992 Del 264; *C.M. Agarwalla* v *Halar Sait* AIR 1977 Cal 356; *Sova Rani Dutta* v *Debabrata Dutta* AIR 1991 Cal 186.

4. Limitation—Art. 74 of the Limitation Act 1963—one year from the date of actual or otherwise termination of prosecution.

5. See AIR 1970 Ori 91—on the question of onus of proof, and ingredients of a malicious prosecution.

6. Forum—Part of cause of action, in a like suit, arises where summons of criminal court is served on the plaintiff. Issue of summons, a necessary consequence of complaint—court at the place of service of summons can entertain the suit—AIR 1961 Mys 188; AIR 1970 Mad 330.

7. Malicious arrest and false imprisonment—Nature of proof in malicious arrest explained in *Rusi Sahu* v *Debaraj Biswal* AIR 1991 Ori 30.

8. In an action of malicious prosecution, the damages would represent first the general damages, a solatium for injured feelings and reputation. The second would be special damages incurred by the plaintiff as a pecuniary loss—*R.K. Soni* v *S. Singhara Singh* AIR 1992 Del 264.

454. Suit for damages for malicious arrest

In the Court of .... at ....

Suit No. .... of 20.............

(Set out cause title)

The above-named plaintiff states as follows:

1. That the defendant has lodged an FIR with the .... P.S. of District on .... alleging that the plaintiff had committed rape on his wife in the night of .... 20..........

2. That in so doing the defendant acted maliciously and without just and probable cause.

3. That the plaintiff was arrested on .... and produced before the Judicial Magistrate of .... on .... on a charge under s. 376 of the Indian Penal Code when he was sent to judicial custody.

4. That the plaintiff was acquitted on .... by an order of the said Magistrate.

5. That the plaintiff, as a consequence, has suffered in his reputation and money.

6. That the cause of action for this suit arose on .... when the plaintiff was acquitted.

7. Suit valuation.

The plaintiff claims ₹.............. as damages as per account below.

Account of claim

(*i*)	Loss of reputation	... ...	₹ ....
(*ii*)	Legal costs	... ...	₹ ....
		Total	₹ ....

Verification

Affidavit

NOTE: Article 72 of the Limitation Act 1963.

455. Suit for damages for false imprisonment

In the Court of .... at ....

Money Suit No. .... 20............

(Set out cause title)

Claim laid at ₹............

The above-named plaintiff states as follows:

1. That the plaintiff is a respectable citizen of the town and is a .... (state the status).

2. That the defendant had lodged an FIR, with the .... P.S. on .... against the plaintiff alleging commission of an offence of cheating by the plaintiff in respect of a cheque and caused the plaintiff to be arrested next morning and detained in police lock-up till 3 p.m. of the same day when he was produced before the Judicial Magistrate .... and remanded to judicial custody till ...... when he was released on bail.

3. That a trial ensued in G.R. Case No. .... of 20 .... under s. 420, IPC and the plaintiff was found not guilty and was honourably acquitted.

4. That the defendant caused the plaintiff to be wrongfully imprisoned and deprived of his liberty for .... days and in so doing the defendant had no just and probable cause.

5. That by reason of the matters aforesaid, the plaintiff suffered mental shock and anguish and has also suffered loss and damage in reputation.

6. That the cause of action arose on .... when the plaintiff was released from imprisonment.

The plaintiff prays for a decree of ₹............... as damages for false imprisonment.

Particulars of special damage

Verification

Affidavit

NOTES: 1. Limitation—One year from date when imprisonment ends—vide Art. 73 of the Limitation Act 1963.

2. For principles of assessment of damages—See AIR 1969 Pat 194; AIR 1979 AP 31.

3. For wrongful imprisonment—Essentials—See AIR 1971 All 162.

4. Unlike the case of malicious prosecution, for false imprisonment it is not necessary for imposition of liability that the arrest should have been malicious. It is enough that it was without reasonable or probable cause. The burden of proving the existence of reasonable and probable cause is on the defendant—*Rusi Sahu* v *Debraj Biswal* AIR 1991 Ori 30.

456. Suit for damages for false imprisonment (Another Form)

In the Court of .... at ....

Money Suit No. .... 20............

(Set out cause title)

The above-named plaintiff states:

1. That at all material times the plaintiff was employed as a cashier of the defendant company at its office at ....

2. That on .... the defendant Company through their Managing Director, lodged an information before the Officer-in-Charge, of P.S. .... Kolkata, charging the plaintiff with criminal breach of trust in respect of some cheques (state particulars) totalling to ₹............ and caused the plaintiff to be arrested on .... whereupon the plaintiff was detained in the police lock-up at .... for .... hours.

3. That on the following day the plaintiff was brought in custody before the Chief Judicial Magistrate at .... There a charge was preferred against the plaintiff and the Magistrate remanded him in police custody.

4. That the plaintiff was committed by .... to face the trial but the Judicial Magistrate, 2nd Court at ....

5. That the said trial commenced on .... and lasted till .... ultimately the plaintiff was found not guilty and acquitted honourably.

6. That the cause of action arose on .... when the plaintiff was acquitted following his imprisonment.

The plaintiff claims—

₹............... damages for false imprisonment.

Verification

Affidavit

NOTES: 1. Suit valuation on the claim.
2. AIR 1979 AP 31.

457. Suit for damages for injuries caused by negligent and rash driving of a vehicle

In the Court of .... at ....

Suit No. .... 20............

(Set out cause title)

The plaintiff states as follows:

1. That the plaintiff had been walking on .... at about .... p.m., along the .... Road. At about the same time a motorcycle bearing No. ...... driven rashly and negligently by the defendant, hit the plaintiff. The plaintiff in the impact fell down and sustained severe injuries all over his body, as detailed in Schedule 'A' below.

2. That the plaintiff had to remain hospitalized for about a month from .... to .... in the .... Hospital.

3 That the plaintiff is a medical practitioner. His daily earning is about ₹............. The plaintiff lost his earning for the period he was in the hospital. Besides, the plaintiff had to defray medical expenses to the tune of ₹.................. as per account in Schedule 'B' below.

4. That the plaintiff has suffered other damages in addition to special damage, as detailed in Schedule 'B' below, his physical and mental sufferings as detailed in Schedule 'C' below.

5. That the cause of action for this suit arose on .... (when the plaintiff was hit by the motorcycle by the defendant's rash and negligent driving) at .... within the jurisdiction of this court.

6. Suit valuation (total of amounts in Schedules 'B' and 'C').

The plaintiff, therefore, prays:

(*i*) For a decree of special damage of ₹.............. as per account in Schedule 'B' and for other damages of ₹............. as per account in Schedule 'C' below.

(*ii*) Costs.

SCHEDULE 'A'

Details of injury sustained by the plaintiff
(State here nature of injuries)

SCHEDULE 'B'

Special Damages

(*i*)	Loss of earning at the rate of ₹............ per diem from .... to	₹ ....
(*ii*)	Medical expenses.	₹ ....

SCHEDULE 'C'

Other Damages

(*i*)	Compensation for physical and mental sufferings.	₹ ....

Verification

Affidavit

NOTE: Instead of suit—see proceedings under ss. 92A and 110A of the M.V. Act 1939 and now ss. 140, 166 of 1988 Act in Motor Accidents Claims Tribunal.

458. Suit for damages for negligence of a doctor

In the Court of .... at ....

Suit No. .... 20............

(Set out cause title)

The plaintiff states as follows:

1. That the defendant is a medical practitioner and is known as a surgeon. The defendant runs a Nursing Home where he carries on his practice of surgery.

2. That on or about the .... day of .... 20............. the plaintiff's father, aged about .... was admitted to said Nursing Home for operation of prostrate gland. The same day the defendant carried on the job of operation on the plaintiff's father who died on the table in the operation theatre in the said Nursing Home.

3. That the death of the plaintiff's father in the above circumstances was due to negligence of the defendant. [Explain brief the circumstances and acts amounting to negligence].

4. That the plaintiff is the only legal representative of the deceased and is entitled to bring this action.

5. That plaintiff, by reason of the matters aforesaid, has suffered mental shock and the loss to him is irreparable, besides loss of expenses.

The plaintiff claims:

(*i*) damages;

(*ii*) an order for reference to the appropriate authority for cancellation of the defendant's licence; and

(*iii*) any other relief.

Verification

Affidavit

NOTE: Remedy is also available under Consumers' Disputes Redressal Forum.

459. Suit for trespass to the plaintiff's fishery

In the Court of .... at ....

Suit No. .... 20............

(Set out cause title)

The plaintiff states as follows:

1. That the plaintiff is a *bona fide* fisherman. The State Government of West Bengal through the District Fishery Officer, Cooch Behar, leased out to the plaintiff the fishing right on Jari Torsha between 'A' and 'B' points for the year 14 .... B.S.

2. That on the .... day of .... 20...... (equivalent to the day of............. 14 .... B.S.), the defendant surreptitiously fished in the said fishery for about four hours, caught fish, took away and converted the same to his use and/or benefit.

3. The plaintiff has suffered loss of ₹................

(State here: Nature, class and quantity of fish caught and converted—value thereof).

4. Cause of action.

5. Suit valuation.

The plaintiff claims:

(*a*) Damages of ₹................

(*b*) Costs.

Verification

Affidavit

460. Suit for damages for trespass by cattle

In the Court of .... at ....

Suit No. .... 20............

(Set out cause title)

The plaintiff states as follows:

1. That the defendant owns a dairy at .... P. S. .... District .... within the jurisdiction of this court whereon he has had a herd of cattle.

2. That to the East of the defendant's dairy is situate the plaintiff's peanut farm.

3. That on or about the .... day of .... 20 ...., the defendant's cattle trespassed into the plaintiff's farm, grazed on the farm land and caused damage to the plantation. The extent of damage is mentioned below.

4. That defendant was negligent in keeping his cattle and by reason of the matters aforesaid, the plaintiff suffered loss and damage.

Particulars of loss and damage

The plaintiff claims:

(*i*) Damages of ₹........................

(*ii*) Costs.

Verification

Affidavit

461. Suit for compensation for digging plaintiff's land

In the Court of .... at ....

Suit No. .... 20............

(Set out cause title)

The plaintiff states as follows:

1. That the plaintiff owns, amongst others, three kathas of land, in Plot No. ....of Mouja .... P.S. .... District .... within the jurisdiction of this court, described more specifically in the Schedule appended hereto.

2. That the defendant has had his homestead land to the contiguous south of the plaintiff's aforesaid land.

3. That the defendant, while raising his homestead on his land had dug the plaintiff's land in the Schedule during the period from .... to .... of the year .... and removed earth therefrom measuring .... cu.m.

4. That for such digging of the plaintiff's land, considerable earth was washed away, besides earth removed by the defendant. (State measurements of earth).

5. That the plaintiff has suffered damages.

The plaintiff claims ₹................ as compensation.

SCHEDULE

Verification

Affidavit

462. Suit by an individual for damages for polluting water and for injunction

In the Court of .... at ....

Suit No. .... 20............

(Set out cause title)

The plaintiff states as follows:

1. That there is a *pucca* well situated in the plaintiff's land at Mouja .... P.S. .... within the district of .... The plaintiff and members of the public of Mouja .... draw their drinking water from the said well.

2. That of late the defendant has been cherishing ill-feelings against the plaintiff and the defendant and his men polluted the water of the well by allowing sewage to escape thereinto.

3. That the plaintiff and others have been constrained to draw water from a distance of three miles every day since about ...., 20 ...., as water in the well has been rendered unwholesome.

4. That the cause of action arose in ...., 20 .... when the defendant and his men began polluting water of the said well.

The plaintiff, therefore, prays:

(*a*) for a judgment and decree for damages of ₹................

(*b*) for a decree of injunction restraining the defendant and his men to allow escape of sewage into the well.

Verification

Affidavit

NOTES: 1. Limitation for the relief of injunction—three years *vide* Art. 113.
2. See also Easements Act for riparian ownership.

463. Suit for damages for tortious act

In the Court of Civil Judge (Sr. Division) at ....

Suit No. .... of 20...

Mr. P. residing at .... Alipore Road, Kolkata

.... *Plaintiff*

versus

Mr. X son of Mr. Z residing at ...., Alipore Road, Kolkata

.... *Defendant*

The plaintiff states as follows:

1. The defendant stays at the house next to the plaintiff's residential accommodation as mentioned above.

2. The defendant had kept a dog in his premises .... mainly unchained all the time of the day. The said dog sometimes attacked and bit the passers-by unaware. On 6th January, 20........, while the plaintiff was entering his house, the dog unknowingly came near him and bit him.

3. The said dog was of a ferocious nature and is in the habit of attacking and biting passers-by.

4. By reason of the said attack by the dog, the plaintiff had to take costly injections and undergo medical treatment under a doctor for several months as a result of which he had to remain on leave and could not attend his job for a month. Due to wrongful act of the defendant in not keeping his dog in chains, the plaintiff suffered the said dog-bite, had to undergo medical treatment apart from physical and mental agony and suffering.

5. The plaintiff states that due to wrongful act of the defendant, the plaintiff had to physically suffer and suffered mental agony and further damages by way of monetary loss in medical treatment and further loss in his monthly earnings from his job. The plaintiff assesses such loss as follows:

(*i*) Mental agony valued at ₹.................

(*ii*) Cost of medical treatments valued at ₹................

(*iii*) Loss in monthly earnings from job valued at ₹...............

and thus claims a total amount at ₹............. from the defendant by way of compensation and damages due to the dog bite, with interest and costs.

6. The plaintiff's cause of action for the present suit arose at ...., Alipore Road, Kolkata, on 6th January 20.... For the purposes of jurisdiction and court-fees, the suit is valued at ₹.................... on which court-fees in stamps have been paid.

7. In the premises this learned court has the jurisdiction to entertain, try and determine this suit.

The plaintiff, therefore, prays for and claims:

(*a*) A decree for payment of ₹............... by the defendant with interest at 16% per annum till realisation;

(*b*) Costs;

(*c*) Further and other orders/reliefs be granted as the plaintiff is entitled to in law and in equity.

Verification

Affidavit

464. Suit for compensation for damages to goods

In the City Civil Court at Calcutta

Suit No. .... of 20...

Mr. P., carrying on business at .... Strand Road, Kolkata

...... *Plaintiff*

versus

M/s. X & Co. Ltd., carrying on business *inter alia*, at ...... Strand Road, Kolkata

.... *Defendant*

The plaintiff states:

1. That the defendant is the owner of a vessel M.V. 'Z' and is carrying on business, *inter alia*, for carriage of cargo by sea.

2. That the plaintiff carries on business in textile goods and other miscellaneous consumer goods.

3. That in course of its business, the defendant as owner of Steamship M.V. 'Z' and carrier of goods on hire received textile goods for a shipment in Hong Kong and issued a bill of lading No. 6 dated 4th January 20......

4. That the said bill of lading No. 6 dated 15th December 20...... was endorsed to the plaintiff by the holder of the said bill of lading for consideration whereby the plaintiff became the holder of the said bill of lading for value and was entitled to delivery of the said goods covered by the said bill of lading.

5. That the said Vessel of defendant arrived at Port of Kolkata on 6th February 20.......... and your petitioner duly tendered the said bill of lading for obtaining the goods covered by it from the said vessel of the defendant.

6. That at the time of taking delivery of said goods covered by the said bill of lading it was observed that there were shortages of three packages and that two packages were badly damaged in transit by sea water and/or rain water.

7. That at the time of taking delivery of the goods, the said fact of short delivery as also delivery of some damaged goods were duly noted and recorded by the parties.

8. That in view of the said short delivery of goods and damage caused to a portion of the said goods, the plaintiff suffered loss and damages which plaintiff assesses at ₹.............. Copies of the said bill of lading duly endorsed in favour of the plaintiff and the documents evidencing short delivery and damage to the goods duly signed and recorded by parties are annexed hereto and collectively marked 'A'.

9. That the said short delivery and damage to the said goods covered by said bill of lading were duly surveyed and assessed by a Government Licensed Surveyor who did the survey in the presence of the duly authorised representatives of the defendant. A copy of the Survey Report is annexed hereto marked 'B'.

10. That the defendant could not offer any reasonable explanation as to the reason for shortage of goods and also damage to goods covered by the bill of lading.

11. That in the premises for breach of obligations covered by bill of lading to carry the cargo and deliver the same to the bill of lading holder in good and perfect condition, and also in full quantities, the plaintiff has suffered loss and damages as mentioned above.

12. That in the premises the defendant is liable for such negligence and for also breach of the contract contained in the said bill of lading and should duly compensate the plaintiff for the same.

13. That by reasons of defendant's breach of contract and breach of its duties and obligations as a Carrier of Goods by Sea, as also breach of terms and conditions of bill of lading covering the said goods the plaintiff has suffered loss and damages which the plaintiff assesses at ₹................ The plaintiff, therefore, claims the said sum of ₹............. with interest at 16% per annum from the defendant for negligence and breach of the contractual obligations and duties as Carrier of Goods by Sea.

14. That in spite of several demands, the defendant has failed to compensate the plaintiff for the loss and damages suffered by him due to short delivery of goods and delivery of damaged goods. (The particulars of loss/claim be mentioned).

15. That the plaintiff, therefore, demands the payment of a sum of ₹............. from defendant by way of damages due to short delivery of goods and for delivery of damaged goods in breach of the conditions of the contract as contained in the bill of lading. The plaintiff claims interest at 16% per annum on the said sum till realisation.

16. That the defendant carries on business within the jurisdiction of this Hon'ble Court and as such, this Hon'ble Court has the jurisdiction to entertain, try and determine this suit.

17. That in spite of requests and demands, the defendant has not paid the aforesaid claims of the plaintiff which was payable at the said address of the plaintiff within the jurisdiction of this Hon'ble Court.

18. That no part of the claims of the plaintiff is barred by Law of Limitation.

19. For the purposes of jurisdiction and court-fees, the suit is valued at ₹.......... on which *ad valorem* court-fees have been paid.

The plaintiff, therefore, prays for and claims:

(*a*) Decree for loss and damages suffered by the plaintiff valued at ₹..............;

(*b*) Interest at 16% per annum from till payment;

(*c*) Costs;

(*d*) Further and other orders be made as to this Hon'ble Court may deem fit and proper so as afford complete relief to the plaintiff.

SCHEDULE 'A'

SCHEDULE 'B'

Verification

Affidavit

465. Suit for damages for assault and battery

In the Court of .... at ......

Suit No. .... of 20.......

(Set out cause title)

The plaintiff states as follows:

1. That the plaintiff is a Professor in History in the .... College for the last .... years.

2. That on .... at about .... p.m. while the plaintiff was returning home from the college by the .... road the defendant suddenly appeared there and shouted: "You were the invigilator yesterday and for your detection of copying I was expelled" and so saying the defendant hit the plaintiff on his head with an iron rod. The plaintiff cried for help when two men on the road came running to the place of occurrence. The defendant ran away at the sight of those men.

3. That the plaintiff received severe injuries on his head and was in the .... Hospital for 21 days from .... to ....

4. That the plaintiff has suffered damages as under:

(State here particulars of damage)

5. Cause of action—(date of occurrence).

6. Valuation of the suit—

The plaintiff claims:

(*i*) ₹ .... as damages for pain and humiliation.

(*ii*) ₹ .... as special damages for medical treatment.

(*iii*) Costs.

Verification

Affidavit

NOTES: 1. Conviction in a criminal court will not bar defendant's civil liability but acquittal in a criminal court is likely to influence the result of the civil suit.

2. See AIR 1936 Nag 231; AIR 1931 Lah 648.

3. Limitation—three years under Art. 113 of the Limitation Act 1963.

4. In a suit for damages in tort, the tortfeasor dies during pendency of suit. Maxim *'Actio personalis moritur cum persona'* applies. The suit as against the tortfeasor abates. His L.R.'s cannot be brought on record—AIR 1977 AP 20.

466. Suit for damages for wrongful attachment

In the Court of .... at ......

Suit No. .... of 20.......

(Set out cause title)

The plaintiff states as follows:

1. That the defendant as plaintiff in a Money Suit No. .... of 20............. got a decree for ₹ .... against one 'A'.

2. That later, it is learnt reliably, the defendant brought a Money Execution Case No. .... of 20............. and through process of court got attached on .... the .... (name goods attached) in the house of the plaintiff. The defendant had represented to the Court Officer at the time of attachment that the said goods were of the judgment-debtor 'A'.

3. That the plaintiff pointed out to the defendant as well as to the Court Officer that the said goods did not belong to 'A', but to no purpose.

4. That the plaintiff has suffered damages for wrongful attachment of the same which the plaintiff values at ₹ ...., (Better, state here how damage was sustained).

5. That the cause of action for this suit arose on .... when the said goods were attached wrongfully at .... within the jurisdiction of this court.

6. That for the purpose of jurisdiction and court-fees, the suit is valued at ₹ .... (same value as estimated).

Particulars of goods attached

.... value

The plaintiff prays:

(*i*) For release of the said goods from attachment after finding those goods to belong to the plaintiff;

(*ii*) For a decree of ₹ .... or for such sum as may be found admissible as damages.

Verification

Affidavit

NOTES: 1. Limitation for compensation for wrongful seizure of movable property under legal process is one year from the date of seizure under Art. 80 of the Limitation Act 1963. No separate provision for attachment of immovable property—period of limitation is the same.

2. Attachment may not be malicious—13 IC 799. It may result in no damage to the plaintiff; nevertheless if the attachment is wrongful the plaintiff is entitled to bring the suit.

3. Order 38, r. 5—attachment before judgment—applicant must state grounds. Claim by applicant on basis of mere conjectures and imagination is not tenable—*UCO Bank, Madras* v *Sukra Shoe* AIR 1992 Mad 293.

4. Order 38, r. 6—Appendix Form No. 6. Furnishing of security by defendant—nature of security contemplated under r. 6 is not qualified. It may be even of a third party—*Adauru Dasaratha* v *Vani Reddy* AIR 1992 AP 307.

5. Where 'A' merely obtains an order of attachment against 'B' and nothing more is done in furtherance thereof, 'B' cannot complain in a suit for malicious attachment that he has been damnified. But if something was done in furtherance of the order of attachment, such as the bailiff going to the place of attachment, 'B' would get a cause of action for damages, even though the amount was paid to avoid actual attachment—AIR 1975 Mad 108.

467. Suit for damages for attachment before judgment

In the Court of .... at ......

Suit No. .... of 20.......

(Set out cause title)

The plaintiff states as follows:

1. That the defendant had brought a Money Suit No. .... of 20............ in this court against this plaintiff for a decree for ` ....

The said suit is pending.

2. That on the date of filing of the said Money Suit on .... the defendant filed a petition under Or. 38, r. 5 in this court, supported by an affidavit, for attachment of the plaintiff's house property, described in Schedule 'A' below. In the said petition and affidavit the defendant stated falsely and maliciously that the plaintiff intended and/or attempted to dispose of his property in Schedule 'A' below to defeat the possible decree of the plaintiff of the Money Suit.

3. That on the strength of the said petition and supporting affidavit, the defendant obtained from this court an order of attachment before judgment and the plaintiff's house property in Schedule 'A' below was attached by the court on ....

4. That the defendant obtained the said order of attachment maliciously on false allegations (here explain want of reasonable and probable cause as averred by the defendant). The plaintiff has suffered damage for such attachment.

5. That the cause of action arose at .... on .... (date of attachment) within the jurisdiction of this court.

The plaintiff claims:

(*a*) Release of the house property in Schedule 'A' from attachment.

(*b*) A decree for ₹ .... as damages.

(*c*) Costs.

SCHEDULE 'A'

(Description of house property).

Verification

Affidavit

NOTES: 1. Attachment in a like case is not *per se* justiciable. Such attachment must be malicious, i.e., without just and probable cause—13 IC 507.

2. Notice and want of reasonable and probable cause in setting the court in motion should be averred in the plaint (but see 16 IC 443)—absence of reasonable and probable cause need not be proved.

3. It is doubtful, in the face of provision of s. 95 of the Court-fees Act, providing a summary remedy and almost without Court-fees, whether a regular suit will at all be filed.

4. Limitation—three years under residuary Art. 113 of the Limitation Act 1963.

5. Attachment before judgment:

The remedy of an attachment before judgment is certainly extraordinary. If granted, it casts an obligation on the party against whom it is made, even before he is heard in defence of the suit. The court has, therefore, to act with utmost circumspection before issuing such an order to avoid it becoming a weapon of oppression in the hands of unscrupulous plaintiffs. In such an application it is incumbent upon plaintiffs to state the ground on which he entertains the belief or apprehension that the defendant would dispose of or remove the property, or to give the source of his information and belief in the matter. A verbatim copy of the provisions of the Code in the affidavit in support of the application, or a mechanical repetition of the language of the Code without an iota or substratum of truth underlying the allegation is merely colourable and constitutes an abuse of process of the court. The court must insist upon strict proof of the said allegations. Any order of the court without a proper investigation whether the allegations are well-founded or not constitutes a gross dereliction of duty—*V.K. Nataraja* v *S.A. Bagam* AIR 1965 Mad 212.

Inadequate materials and absence of valid grounds in the application for attachment. Relief of attachment before judgment cannot be granted—*L.V. Bhujanga Rao* v *Ch. Venkataswar* AIR 1993 Mad 246.

6. Right, title and interest of a partner in firm can be attached before judgment—*Raja Theatre* v *Selvan Financiers* AIR 1992 Mad 227.

Interest of a partnership in the partnership property is movable property. Order 21, r. 46(1), CPC is attracted—*Narayanappa* v *Bhaskara Krishnappa* AIR 1966 SC 1300.

468. Suit for conversion of goods entrusted to defendant

In the Court of .... at ......

Suit No. .... of 20.......

(Set out cause title)

The above-named plaintiff states as follows:

1. That the plaintiff had a milch cow. Prior to his transfer to .... the plaintiff had entrusted his cow to the defendant to keep the same in the latter's custody, maintain the same as needed and appropriate to himself milk and to re-deliver the same when demanded on the plaintiff's return.

2. That the plaintiff returned on .... and demanded back from the defendant on .... his cow, but the defendant failed to return as he, in the meantime, sold the cow for ₹ .... and converted the sale proceeds to his own use.

3. That the defendant by his act of conversion has caused a loss of ₹ .... to the plaintiff.

4. That the plaintiff is entitled to recover from the defendant a sum of ₹ .... for such conversion.

5. That the cause of action for this suit arose on .... when the plaintiff learnt of the conversion at .... within the jurisdiction of the court.

6. That for the purpose of jurisdiction and court-fees the suit is valued at ₹ .... and *ad valorem* court-fees are paid.

The plaintiff claims:

₹ .... as damages.

Verification

Affidavit

NOTES: 1. Only in cases of bailment, pledge, etc., the owner has the right to sue.
2. If the plaintiff is not entitled to immediate possession, if lent for a term the plaintiff is not entitled to sue.
3. Damages is the value of the articles on the date of conversion.
4. Limitation three years under Art. 68 of the Limitation Act from the date of conversion.

469. Application for compensation

Before the Commissioner, Employees' Compensation, WB

Suit No. .... of 20 ....

1. Mr. P., son of late Mr. M.
2. Mr. Q, being the widow of the deceased Mr. M.
3. Mr. R. being the minor son of deceased Mr. M.
4. Mr. N. being the minor daughter of the deceased Mr. M.

The aforesaid plaintiffs Nos. 3 and 4 are duly represented by their next friend the plaintiff No. 1, and all are residents at .... Kolkata.

.... *Plaintiffs*

versus

Mr. X, son of Mr. Y. working for gain at .... Kolkata

... *Defendant*

The plaintiff states as follows:

1. Mr. M. was working as a mason and employed by the defendant, Mr. X for construction of a two-storeyed building at Kolkata at a fixed remuneration of ₹ .... per diem.

2. The said Mr. M. while working as a mason during construction of the first floor of the said building accidentally fell down from the scaffolding down to the ground on 10th September, 20................ at 12.0' noon when he was immediately removed and rushed to the nearest hospital but was ultimately declared "brought deed".

3. The deceased was a young man of 45 years only at the time of his death and he left behind plaintiffs No. 1 to 4 as his natural heirs and dependants.

4. Due to the untimely and premature death of Mr. M, his dependants being the plaintiffs No. 1 to 4 have been deprived of their survival and maintenance and also education of minor children being the plaintiffs No. 3 and 4 above named.

5. In spite of demands by the plaintiffs advocates, on 17th September 20 ...., and duly received by the defendant, the defendant has failed and neglected to comply with the demand of the plaintiffs to pay adequate compensation to the plaintiffs as per provisions of law within 15 days from the date of receipt of the said demand letter.

6. The defendant, however, received the said demand letter of the plaintiffs and was liable to pay the claims of the plaintiffs as the Employer of the said deceased Mr. M. but the defendant has failed to comply with the demand.

7. The plaintiffs are entitled to claim and they are claiming from the defendant adequate compensation in regard to their said demands in accordance with provisions of law applicable to such cases.

8. The plaintiff's cause of action for this suit arose within the jurisdiction of this learned court and is continuing from day to day.

9. In spite of demands, the defendant has failed to pay the plaintiff's claims herein for compensation of ₹ .... or any portion thereof.

10. The plaintiff's cause of action for this suit arose within jurisdiction of this learned court and is still continuing from day to day.

11. For the purposes of jurisdiction the application is valued at ₹ ....

12. The plaintiffs state that in the premises, this learned court has jurisdiction to entertain, try and determine the present suit.

The plaintiffs, therefore, pray for and claim:

(*a*) Compensation for ₹ .... against the defendant;

(*b*) Costs;

(*c*) Further orders be issued and directions be given as this learned court may deem fit and proper to afford complete relief to the plaintiffs.

Verification

Affidavit

470. Suit for damages for trespassing on land

In the Court of Civil Judge (Senior Division) at Alipore

Suit No. .... of 20......

Mr. P., residing at .... Alipore, Kolkata

...... *Plaintiff*

versus

Mr. X, residing at .... Alipore, Kolkata

...... *Defendant*

Suit for damages for trespassing on land valued at ₹ ....

The plaintiff states:

1. The plaintiff is the owner and occupier of premises No. .... of 'Z' Road, Alipore, Kolkata. The said premises of the plaintiff consists of about 2 bighas of land of which a part is the residential portion. The plaintiff has cultivated different varieties of costly flowers which the plaintiff regularly sells in the market to dealers at the best available price.

2. The defendant is occupying the land adjacent to plaintiff's structures and is residing therein with his family. The defendant has three grown-up sons.

3. The defendant with his sons has trespassed into the adjoining land and flower gardens of the plaintiff and took away the flowers and has sold them in market from .... 20 .... to .... 20 ....

4. In spite of requests, the defendant did not pay any heed but continued to trespass into the premises of the plaintiff off and on and plucked the flowers and sold them. The garden covers a huge area and as such, the plaintiff could not physically prevent the defendant from entering into and plucking flowers and selling them.

5. By reason of the aforesaid wrongful trespass and taking away the flowers, the plaintiff has suffered loss and damages which the plaintiff assesses at ₹ ....

6. In spite of requests, the defendant has not paid the said sum or any portion thereof to plaintiff.

7. In spite of requests, the defendant has not desisted himself from trespassing into the land of the plaintiff and from plucking flowers and selling the same and appropriating the sales proceeds thereof.

8. The plaintiff is entitled to and claims damages for the wrongful trespass by defendant and plucking the flowers growing therein and selling the same without making payment for the same to the plaintiff.

9. The plaintiff's cause of action for this suit arose on 17.1.20 .... and such cause of action is continuing from day to day.

10. The plaintiff claims a decree for ₹ .... with interest and an injunction restraining the defendant, his son and agents from entering the flower garden of plaintiff or plucking the flowers therein or selling the same in market.

11. The plaintiff's cause of action for this suit arose within the jurisdiction of this learned court and the defendant is residing at the said address within jurisdiction of this learned court.

12. The plaintiff's cause of action for this suit arose on or about .... and the same is continuing from day to day.

13. For purposes of jurisdiction and court-fees, the suit is valued at ₹ .... on which court-fees in stamps have been paid.

The plaintiff, therefore, claims:

(*a*) Decree for payment of ₹ .... against the defendant with interest at 16% per annum till payment;

(*b*) Injunction restraining the defendant, his sons and agents and servants from trespassing into the premises, land and garden of plaintiff and/or plucking flowers from the same;

(*c*) Costs;

(*d*) Further and other orders and/or reliefs as the plaintiff is entitled to in law and equity.

Verification

Affidavit

471. Suit for damages for slander

In the Court of Civil Judge (Senior Division) At Alipore

Suit No. .... of 20 ....

Mr. P. residing at ...., Alipore, Kolkata

...... *Plaintiff*

versus

Mr. X, residing at..........................., Alipore, Kolkata

...... *Defendant*

Suit for damages for slander valued at ₹ ....
on which court-fees in Stamps have been duly paid.

The plaintiff states as follows:

1. The plaintiff carries on business in various articles of domestic necessities including all groceries and has many valued customers from his locality and also from distant places. The plaintiff has acquired a reputation and good will for the good quality of all articles sold from his shop.

2. The defendant was a regular customer of plaintiff and he used to purchase goods from the plaintiff from time to time mainly on credit. For some months the defendant made regular payments to the plaintiff but subsequently the defendant was not making such payments in spite of demands.

3. Being unable to realise the price of goods sold and delivered to defendant, the plaintiff ultimately on 15th January, 20 .... stopped giving defendant further articles on credit basis.

4. Thereafter falsely and maliciously the defendant on 15th February 20 .... made derogatory statements as regards the plaintiff's goods and articles sold from the shop and in relation to the plaintiff's trade and conduct of business. False and malicious statements were made to one Mr. Z regarding the articles dealt with by the plaintiff that the same were of inferior quality and edible oils and other similar goods were adulterated.

5. In consequence of false and malicious statements made by defendant the plaintiff's reputation was injured and his creditworthiness as a trader in grocery goods was spoiled due to which some of his regular customers refused to purchase any oil or other articles from the petitioner's shop.

6. By reason of the defendant's wrongful acts and slanderous statements the plaintiff has suffered reduction of turnover of sales of several products and suffered loss of reputation and damage which the petitioner assesses at a sum of ₹ ...., which the defendant is liable to compensate to the plaintiff.

7. The plaintiff has suffered loss and damages as a direct result of the slanderous and derogatory statements and wrongful conduct of the defendant, and the plaintiff is entitled to claim damages for ₹ .... plus interest from defendant and cost of the proceedings.

8. The plaintiff's cause of action for this suit arose within the jurisdiction of this learned court on 5th January 20 .... and on subsequent dates till 5th June 20 .... and is continuing from day to day.

9. For the purposes of jurisdiction and court-fees, the suit is valued at ₹ .... on which court-fees in stamps have been paid.

The plaintiff, therefore claims:

(*a*) Decree for payment of ₹ .... by defendant for loss and damages along with loss of business and good will thereof;

(*b*) Injunction restraining defendant from making any slanderous or derogatory statements against plaintiff;

(*c*) Cost;

(*d*) Further orders be made and other reliefs be granted as the plaintiff is entitled to in law and equity.

Verification

Affidavit

TRUST

472. Suit under s. 92 of the CPC for administration of a charitable trust

In the Court of .... at ....

Suit No. .... of 20............

1. A. B.

2. C. D. .... *Plaintiffs*

versus

1. XY.

2. (name the trustees with their description and places of residence).

3. Trustees in respect of the trust known as ....

.... *Defendant*

Suit for administration of trust and for other reliefs.

The plaintiffs state as follows:

1. That one A.B. dedicated, by a deed of trust executed on ...., the properties, described in the Schedule appended below, for charitable purposes, to wit.

(*a*)

(*b*)

(*c*)

The plaintiff's crave leave of the court to submit a copy of the said deed at the trial.

2. That the defendants were constituted trustees for administration of the said trust by the terms of the said deed of trust.

3. That the defendants have, in violation of the terms of the trust deed, committed

(*i*)

(*ii*)

Further they omitted to do—

(*i*)

(*ii*)

and thus failed to carry on the objects of the said trust.

(State acts of commission and omission).

4. That plaintiffs have .... and are thus interested in proper administration of the said trust.

(State here how the plaintiffs are interested in the trust).

5. That the plaintiffs have obtained consent of the .... in writing on .... for institution of this suit. The said fiat (Order of Consent) is submitted herewith and may be treated as a part of the plaint.

6. That the cause of action for suit arose on .... at .... within the jurisdiction of this court.

7. That for the purpose of jurisdiction and court-fees, the suit is valued at ₹ ....

The plaintiffs, therefore, pray:

(*i*) for a declaration that acts referred to in para 3 above are null and void;

(*ii*) for removal of the defendants from the office of trustees;

(*iii*) for appointment of new trustees and for administration of the trust under a scheme;

(*iv*) such other and further reliefs as may be admissible.

Verification

Affidavit

NOTES: 1. Limitation—Three years.

2. Court-fees—₹10 under Art. 17, cl. (*vi*) of the Court-fees Act.

3. A like suit should be brought by the Advocate-General (or, by his substitute—see s. 93, CPC) in writing (see s. 92 of the CPC) or by not less than two persons with leave of the court.

4. Section 92 does not apply if reliefs claimed do not fall within the section—AIR 1972 SC 246.

5. Private wakf—suit for removal of a *mutawalli* and appointment of a new *mutawalli*. Forum—As s. 92 does not apply to a private wakf suit need not be filed in the District Court. Suit filed in the Court of a Civil Judge under s. 9 read with s. 15 of the Code of Civil Procedure is in order—AIR 1974 All 382.

473. Suit under s. 14 of the Religious Endowments Act

In the Court of .... at ....

Suit No. .... 20............

(Set out cause title)

The above-named plaintiff states as follows:

1. That one A.B. had built a temple at .... P.S. .... District .... and installed therein Sri Sri .... and by executing a deed of endowment on .... had dedicated to the said idol movable and immovable properties, described at the foot of the plaint, for expenses and upkeep of the said temple.

2. That by the said deed of endowment the said A.B. constituted the defendant as the sole trustee of the temple and the defendant since then is functioning as the sole trustee of the said temple.

(Or, state here the process of devolution of the office of the trustee as mentioned in the deed of endowment).

3. That the defendant, in violation of the scheme of the trust, has committed:

(*i*) (State here acts of misfeasance, abuse of power),

(*ii*) (in breach of trust).

4. That the plaintiff is the *Pujari* of the said temple and is, therefore, interested in the said trust.

(State the interest of the plaintiff—see s. 15 of the Act).

5. That the plaintiff has been granted leave of court for institution of this suit.

6. That the cause of action for this suit arose on .... at .... within the jurisdiction of this court.

7. That for the purpose of jurisdiction and court-fees, the suit is valued at ₹ .... and court-fees of ₹................ are paid.

The plaintiff, therefore, prays:

(*i*) For an appropriate order for removal of the defendant from the office of trustee of the said trust;

(*ii*) For appointment of a trustee and for administration of the trust.

Details of properties

Verification

Affidavit

NOTES: 1. Court-fees ₹10 under Art. 17(*vi*) of the Court-fees Act.

2. Leave of court prior to institution of suit is necessary—See s. 18 of the Religious Endowments Act.
3. Forum—Principal court of original civil jurisdiction in a district.
4. Test of private and public temple—criteria—AIR 1970 SC 2025; *Radhakanta Deb* v *Commissioner of HRE, Orissa* AIR 1981 SC 798. Civil Court has jurisdiction to frame scheme for management of private temple as well—AIR 1970 SC 532. Public and private trust—AIR 1973 All 238.
5. Section 92 will not be attracted if there is no trust, express or constructive, for public purposes of a charitable or religious nature. The beneficial interest in the trust of a permanent character must be shown to have vested in an uncertain and fluctuating body of individuals—AIR 1973 All 238.
6. A suit by some of the devotees in a representative capacity for possession of properties belonging to the deity against a person who is not a trustee does not come under s. 92—AIR 1973 Mys 280. Some of the devotees of a deity can maintain a suit on behalf of the entire body of devotees with the leave of the court under Or. 1, r. 8 against an alienee of the temple property alleging that the alienation is not binding on the deity (ibid).
7. Family deity—Worshipper has right to institute suit to protect the interest of the deity—AIR 1978 Ori 199.
8. Religious Endowment—Essentials—AIR 1978 Ori 203.
9. When the property dedicated to the deity is large, and the religious ceremonies which are expressly prescribed by the settlor cannot exhaust the entire income, some portion of the beneficial interest may be construed as indisposed of and cannot but vest as secular property in the heirs of the settlor—AIR 1978 SC 1329; AIR 1937 PC 185 Rel. on.

474. Suit for removal of trustee

In the Court of Civil Judge (Senior Division) at Alipore

Suit No. .... of 20......

Mr. P., residing at .... Alipore, Kolkata

... *Plaintiff*

versus

Mr. X. residing at ...., Alipore Road, Kolkata at the Trustee

..... *Defendant*

Suit for removal of the Trustee valued at ₹................ on which court-fees in stamps have been paid.

The plaintiff states as follows:

1. A temple at Chetla Road, Alipore, Kolkata was built and the deity "Sri Durga Mata" was installed thereat at Chetla Road, Alipore, Kolkata by Mr. Q by transferring immovable property and movable assets to and for seva puja of the deity.

2. By a deed of trust, the said Mr. Q appointed Mr. X the defendant as trustee for the said deity for the seva puja of the deity. It is a Public Trust and the temple is open to public for seva, worship and prayers.

3. The plaintiff has the right to attend the functions of the said deity at the said temple and regularly attended the performance of sandhya puja of the deity.

4. The plaintiff is an interested person and entitled to offer regular prayers and attend arati and other daily functions for the said deity.

5. The plaintiff has further noticed for the last six months that the said Devi prayers, sandhya arati and other normal functions are being performed in a haphazard manner, and in slip-shod way causing annoyance to attending devotees during the said puja of the deity.

6. The plaintiff made the defendant aware of the careless manner of performing the various pujas of the deity causing serious prejudice to the devotees who attend the same.

7. The plaintiff states that the defendant is incapable of performing seva puja of the deity and also discharging his normal functions at the temple.

8. In the premises, the plaintiff claims immediate removal of the defendant from the post of Trustee of the said temple and appointment of another suitable person as the Trustee to look after the interest and welfare of deity and to arrange for regular performance of the seva puja and other functions at the temple.

9. The plaintiff's cause of action for the suit arose within the jurisdiction of this learned court on or about 10th October 20 .... and the same cause of action is still continuing.

10. The suit is valued at ₹................ on which court-fees in stamps have been paid.

11. In the premises, this learned court has the jurisdiction to entertain, try and determine this suit and grant the required reliefs as prayed for.

The plaintiff, therefore claims:

(*a*) Decree removing the defendant as the Trustee of the said temple deity.

(*b*) Appointment of a suitable person as the Trustee to perform the seva puja of the said deity and to look after the interest and welfare of devotees attending the prayers at the temple;

(*c*) Cost;

(*d*) Further and other reliefs as the plaintiff is entitled to in law and equity.

Verification

Affidavit

SUCCESSION

475. Application for appointment of a curator (ss. 192 and 195)

In the Court of District Judge/District Delegate at ....

1. That A.B. of .... District .... died on the .... day of .... 20.......... at .... within jurisdiction of this court.

2. That your petitioner is the widow of the deceased and as such, is the only heiress of the deceased.

3. That the said A.B. at the time of his death left the properties described in Schedule 'A' below. Besides, the said A.B. carried on a business of manufacture of mustard oil under the name and style of .... at .... within the jurisdiction of this court.

4. That one C.D., of late, claiming himself as one of the legal heirs of said A.B. has taken wrongful possession of the immovable property, described in item No. (1) of Schedule 'A' below and has further threatened to take forcible possession in other properties listed in Schedule 'A'.

5. That the said C.D. entered on the .... day of ...., 20........, in the premises of the said .... Mills, took over possession of the mill's premises with plants, machinery, stock-in-trade and has reportedly removed some costly machinery from the premises, all account books, vouchers etc. from the office of the mills.

6. That unless a curator is immediately appointed, your petitioner would be prejudiced and may not get relief in a suit.

7. An affidavit in support of this petition is annexed herewith.

It is, therefore, prayed that a curator be appointed to the estate of A.B. deceased.

SCHEDULE 'A'

Verification

Affidavit

NOTE: Appeal does not lie (AIR 1953 All 707; AIR 1958 All 663). Revision lies (AIR 1938 Lah 753; AIR 1933 Cal 17).

476. Petition for grant of probate of a Will

In the Court of the District Judge/District Delegate at ....

Act 39 of 1925 Case (Or. Misc. Judicial Case)
No. .... of 20..............

A.B. son of C.D.
(State here description and address)

.... *Petitioner*

In the matter of grant of a probate of the Will of E.F., deceased, under s. 276 of the Indian Succession Act.

The above-named petitioner states as follows:

1. That E.F., since deceased of .... P.S. .... District .... died at his residence at .... on .... (date of death) and the writing annexed, in sealed cover, is his last Will, duly executed by the deceased on ....

2. That the petitioner was named as the executor in the said Will.

3. That the amount of assets which is likely to come to the petitioner's hand is estimated at ₹................ as described in Schedule 'A' below (*when necessary* and the amount of debts are shown in Schedule 'B' below).

4. That the said deceased left behind the following relations, besides the petitioner:

(*i*)	G .... Son of .... (State residence)	Brother	of the deceased
(*ii*)	H .... widow of (State residence)	Widow	
(*iii*)	M .... Daughter of (State residence)	Daughter	

5. That at the time of his death the deceased had his fixed abode at .... (or the deceased had his immovable properties at village .... P.S. ...... District ....) within the jurisdiction of this court.

6. That to the best of the petitioner's belief no application has been made to any other court for a probate of the said Will or for letters of administration in respect thereof.

7. (Where necessary) That the petitioner has paid off Estate Duty on the estate of E.F. .... deceased.

The petitioner, therefore, prays that the court may be pleased to grant to the petitioner probate of the said Will of the deceased.

SCHEDULE 'A'

(State here assets likely to come to the hand of the executor)

SCHEDULE 'B'

(State here liabilities, debts, if any—where necessary)

Verification

Affidavit

NOTES: 1. Application for probate, for letters of administration, for revocation of both should be treated as Misc. Judicial case—until the date upon which it is contested. It should be treated as a suit from that date (see Rule 775 of Civil Rules & Orders, Vol. 1, Calcutta High Court).

2. Provisions in Or. 23, r. 1 of CPC applies to probate proceedings. The court cannot refuse permission. In matters of procedure, CPC applies—AIR 1971 Ori 102. Provisions of Or. 9, r. 9 are applicable in view of s. 141 of CPC and ss. 268, 295 of the Indian Succession Act—*Bimala Kanta Sen Gupta* v *Sarojini Konar* AIR 1985 Cal 275.

3. Jurisdiction of the District Judge (s. 264) vested with all powers of Civil Court (s. 266). Appointment of District Delegates by High Court—Only in non-contentious cases (s. 265).

4. For difference in power between the District Judge and the District Delegate— See ss. 270, 272 and 276 of the Indian Succession Act 1925.
5. Testamentary capacity in a testator—*a sine qua non* for a valid will, Registration simpliciter cannot be regarded as a talisman casting away all suspicion at once —75 CWN 63.
6. For contents of an application for probate or for letters of administration with the Will annexed—See ss. 276, 279, 280 and 281 of the Indian Succession Act 1925.
7. For West Bengal—In uncontested proceedings under the Indian Succession Act 1925, it shall be competent to the court of the Judge exercising jurisdiction therein to permit or direct, except when otherwise provided by any law or rule for the time being in force that any particular fact or facts may be proved or evidence upon any application may be given by affidavit—Rule 301 of the Civil Rules and Order, Vol. I, Calcutta High Court.
8. Loss of Will—AIR 1979 SC 145.
9. Application for probate or letters of administration is to be for entire Will or estate—AIR 1979 AP 144.
10. Schedule of property should not form part of probate—AIR 1980 Del 57.
11. Who can oppose—AIR 1977 Cal 496. For modes of proof of a Will—see *Alok Aich* v *Asoke Aich* AIR 1982 Cal 599.
12. Proof of a Will as well as the onus of proof is on the propounder—*K. Venkatachala* v *Thimmajamma* AIR 1959 SC 443. If suspicious circumstances appears to be there attending the execution of the Will, then the propounder must remove the doubts by clear and satisfactory evidence and if the propounder succeeds in removing the doubts then the court would grant probate—*Rani Purnima Devi* v *Kumar Khagendra Narayan Deb* AIR 1962 SC 567. A propounder of the Will has to prove the due and valid execution of the Will and if there are suspicious circumstances surrounding the execution of the Will, the propounder must remove the said suspicions from the mind of the court by cogent and satisfactory evidence—*Anath Nath Das* v *Bijalibala Mondol* AIR 1982 Cal 236. Relied upon in *Bishnupriya Mohapatra* v *Bata Krishna Mohapatra* AIR 1933 Ori 218; *Niranjan* v *Mrudula* AIR 2007 SC 614.

    Will, more than 30 years old. Executing and attesting witness not alive. The mode of proof as required under s. 69 is not possible. No suspicion as to unnaturalness of or tampering with the document. Court may raise presumption in favour of it—*Haradhan Mahatha* v *Dukhu Mahatha* AIR 1994 Pat 129; *M.B. Ramesh (Dead by LRs.)* v *KM Veerajee (Dead by LRs.)* AIR 2013 SC 2088.

    All attesting witnesses are dead. A plain perusal of s. 68 of the Evidence Act shows that the requirement of examining at least one attesting witness is to be fulfilled 'if there be an attesting witness alive'. Where the attesting witness are dead the will can certainly be proved in the manner provided for proof of document—*Balwant* v *Maina Bai* AIR 1991 MP 11.
13. Article 137 of the Limitation Act would not apply to proceedings filed for grant of probate or Letters of Administration with or without the Will annexed. Though the proceedings filed for grant of probate or letters of administration may not come within the mischief of Art. 137 of the Limitation Act, yet the delay aspect is relevant to test of genuineness of the will propounded. Delay in taking steps gives rise to suspicion; the longer the delay the stronger the suspicion—*In the matter of S. Krishnaswami* AIR 1991 Mad 214; *Balwant* v *Mainabai* AIR 1991 MP 11.
14. Administrators General issuing Certificate under s. 29 of the Administrator General Act—Court can grant decree on strength of certificate in a fit

case. Held s. 213 of the Indian Succession Act is not a bar to matters under s. 29 of the A.G. Act. Even without a probate having been issued in favour of the plaintiff—*Thresia* v *Kohcuthommen* AIR 1991 Ker 337.

Article 137 of the Limitation Act would not apply to proceedings filed for grant of Probate or Letters of Administration with or without the Will annexed—*In the matter of S. Krishnaswami* AIR 1991 Mad 214. No period of limitation for applications for the grant of probate—*S. Vatsala* v *K.S. Mohan* AIR 2016 Mad 59; *State of Meghalaya* v *Bimal Deb* AIR 2015 Meg 48.

15. Application for Probate, Letters of Administration or Succession Certificate. Right to apply accrues when it becomes necessary to apply and may not necessarily be within 3 years from date of death of deceased. Delay beyond 3 years must be satisfactorily explained—*Vasudeb Daulatram* v *Sajni Prem* AIR 1983 Bom 268.
16. Appeal against an order for grant of Probate or Letters of Administration. Order is not a decree. Formal decree is not required to be drawn. Hence failure to supply copy of decree along with Memorandum of Appeal cannot render the Appeal incompetent—*Balai Lall Banerjee* v *Debaki Kumar Ganguli* AIR 1984 Cal 16.
17. Misc. Appeal to High Court against order dismissing application for grant of probate is maintainable—*Balwant* v *Mainabai* AIR 1991 MP 11.
18. Sections 275 to 283 of the Indian Succession Act provide special rules for evidence and would have to be followed irrespective of any conflict between these provisions and provisions of the Evidence Act.
19. Indian Succession Act [s. 63(*a*)]—Expression 'sign or affix his mark'. Even if the testator is capable of writing but on account of weakness he is unable to put his signature, he can execute the will by affixing his mark—*Sushila Bala Saha* v *Saraswati Mondol* AIR 1991 Cal 166.

477. Petition for revocation of probate of a Will

In the Court of District Judge/District Delegate at ....

Case No. .... of 20 ....

(Set out cause title)

The petitioner states as follows:

1. That the opposite party has been granted by this court on .... a probate in respect of a Will, allegedly executed on .... 20 .... by one A.B.—deceased. The O.P. has suppressed the mateiral facts which if disclosed, would have disentitled him from oftaining the probate/letters of administration.

2. That the petitioner is the son of the said A.B. who died on ....

The material facts are as follows:

The petitioner was all along with the deceased during his last days. The deceased did not execute the said Will of which probate was obtained by the opposite party as aforesaid.

3. That no notice from any court or this court was served on the petitioner in respect of aforesaid probate proceedings.

4. That the petitioner has lastly known of the said probate proceedings (state here the source of knowledge).

5. That the petitioner being the only legal representative and heir of the said A.B., is interested in the estate of the said deceased.

It is therefore, prayed that the probate granted to the O.P. may please be revoked.

Verification

Affidavit

NOTES: 1. See s. 263 of the Indian Succession Act. The grant of probate or letters of administration may be revoked or annulled for just cause [Just cause—enumerated in Explanation and (Illustrations to Expl. under s. 263)].

2. The applicant for revoking probate must show that he is interested in the alleged will (AIR 1933 Bom 370) in the estate of the deceased—AIR 1917 Pat 532; AIR 1959 Cal 277; AIR 1950 Cal 179.

3. Forum—application should be filed in the court granting probate or letters of administration—AIR 1929 Lah 483.

4. Section 263 contemplates a case for revocation based on the single ground that the will in respect of which the grant in question was obtained was a forged one. In such a case, whether or not the will was a forged one would be the only question to be canvassed before the court before the order of revocation could be made out (AIR 1978 MP 201; AIR 1955 SC 566 relied on). When Will is held genuine probate cannot be revoked—*Biphuti Bhuson Mayur* v *Bhabash Bhuson* AIR 1982 Cal 374.

5. Absence or non-service of citation is not always a just cause under s. 263—AIR 1940 Cal 296; AIR 1978 MP 201.

6. Clauses and illustrations under s. 263 provide guidelines, revocation of grant only on strict proof of presence of any of the stated circumstances—AIR 1978 Mad 265.

7. No period of limitation, no time-limit has been fixed for application for revocation—AIR 1931 Cal 717; AIR 1924 Mad 578.

8. Provisions of Or. 23, r. 1 applies to probate proceedings. The court cannot refuse permission. In matters, of procedure CP Code applies—AIR 1971 Ori 103 contra 49 CWN 636. Also see AIR 1970 All 382.

9. Burden of proving revocation—AIR 1979 SC 145; 18 CWN 527.

478. Petition for Letters of Administration (without Will annexed)

In the Court of the District Judge/District Delegate at ....

(Act 39 of 1925)

Case No. .... of 20 ....

In the matter of grant of Letters of Administration to the estate of A.B.—deceased.

1. That A.B., lately of .... P.S. .... District .... died on .... at .... within jurisdiction of this court.

2. That the deceased left behind him the following near relations or next of kin besides the petitioner.

(*a*) ....

(*b*) (Name and residence) .... (State relationship with the deceased).

3. That the petitioner being the only son is entitled to grant of letters of administration to the estate of the said A.B.—deceased.

4. That the amount of assets which are likely to come to the petitioner's hand is ₹ .... as shown in Schedule 'A' below and the amount of (on the property) liabilities of the deceased is shown in Schedule 'B' below.

5. That the deceased has his fixed place of abode at .... within the jurisdiction of this court.

6. That the deceased died intestate and to the best of the petitioner's belief no application has been made for letters of administration to the estate of the deceased.

Your petitioner, therefore, prays that letters of administration to the estate of A.B. may be granted to the petitioner.

SCHEDULE 'A'

(State here particulars of property)

SCHEDULE 'B'

(State here particulars of assets)

Verification

Affidavit

NOTES: 1. Probate can be granted only to an executor appointed by the Will. Whereas letters of administration can be granted to anybody, excepting a minor, a person of unsound mind, a Christian married woman without the previous consent of her husband.

2. Also see Form No. 479 below.

3. In a proceeding for grant of letters of administration, it is not for the court to decide the question of title. The court's duty is precisely to consider whether the Will had been genuinely made by the testator out of his free volition and it had been properly executed and attested in accordance with the law and the testator had testamentary capacity to execute it.

(A Will may not be permissible under the Muhammedan law and valid title may not pass because of some infirmity in the Will under the Muhammedan law, but such contention is foreign to the scope of probate proceeding or a proceeding for grant of letters of administration)—AIR 1935 Cal 154; AIR 1978 Cal 399.

4. Particulars of debts due to the estate.

479. Petition for Letters of Administration (with Will annexed)

In the Court of the District Delegate/Civil Judge (Senior Division) at ....

Case No. .... 20 ....

Applicants:

(1) A.B. son of E.F. of ....
P.S. .... District ....

(2) C.D. son of S.T. of ....

In the matter of grant of Letters of Administration with the will annexed, of the estate of G.H.—deceased, under s. 276 of the Indian Succession Act.

The above-named applicants beg to state as follows:

1. That G.H. died at her residence at .... Town on the .... day of .... 20…, and that the writing annexed is her last Will and testament, which was duly executed by her.

2. That by the said Will, G.H. made a scheme for worship of an idol 'Sree Sree Radha Govinda Vigraha' and bequeathed properties in Schedule 'A' below to the deity and by the said Will constituted the applicants as joint shebaits of the said deity. The applicants since after death of the said G.H. have been discharging their duties as shebaits.

3. That by the said Will the said G.H. bequeathed her dues, from the State of West Bengal, as compensation for vesting of her intermediary rights in equal shares to her three daughters P.W. and R.

4. That the amount of assets, which are likely to come to the applicants' hands is ₹......... as shown in Schedule 'B' below.

5. That the deceased left no debts.

6. That the applicants are sons of the deceased. That no executor having been appointed by the said Will, the applicants apply for letters of administration with the Will annexed.

7. That the testatrix left behind her the following near relations, besides the applicants:—

(1) M
(2) N } Sons.
(3) O

(State here description and address).

(4) P
(5) Q } Daughters and Legatees.
(6) R

(State individual description and respective address).

8. That the deceased, at the time of her death, had her fixed residence at .... within the jurisdiction of this court.

9. That to the best of applicants' belief, no application has been made to any other court for letters of administration of the said estate.

The applicants, therefore, pray that the court may be pleased to grant to them letters of administration with the will annexed to the estate of the said deceased.

Annexure—Will

SCHEDULE 'A'

SCHEDULE 'B'

Verification

Affidavit

480. Petition for Caveat against Grant of Probate or Letters of Administration

In the Court of the District Judge at

Misc. Case No. .... of 20.........

In the matter of the estate of A.B ...... *Deceased*

And

In the matter of C.D. .... *Petitioner*
for grant of probate.

And

In the matter of E.F. .... *Caveator*

Notice is hereby given that nothing should be done in the matter of the estate of A.B.—deceased without notice to the objector, as the caveator is interested in the said estate.

E.F.

Objector,

of Vill. .... P.S. ...... District ....

Or,

Let nothing be on done in the matter of the estate of A.B., late of .... P.S. ...... District ...... who died on the .....day of .... at ...... without notice to E.F. of .... (place or residence).

E.F.

Verification

Affidavit

NOTES: 1. The form given above is according to Form in Schedule V of the Code of Civil Procedure, under s. 284(4) of the Indian Succession Act.

2. Caveats against the grant of probate or letters of administration may be lodged with the District Judge or a District Delegate.

3. No proceeding shall be taken on a petition for probate or letters of administration after a caveat against the grant thereof has been entered with the Judge or District Delegate to whom the application has been made or notice has been given of its entry with some other Delegate, until after such notice to the person by whom the same has been entered as the court may think reasonable (s. 285).

4. Entry of a caveat must be made by a person who wishes to oppose the grant of probate—AIR 1940 Oudh 16. Caveator must be interested in the estate of the deceased. Any interest, however slight, and even the bare possibility of interest is sufficient to entitle a person to enter caveat in a probate proceeding—49 CWN 713. Caveator cannot challenge the title of testator to the disputed property—AIR 1911 Ori 95; AIR 1954 SC 280.

5. Since the judgment debtor is not a party who has a right to be heard or is ordinarily heard in applications under Or. 21, r. 24, the provisions of s. 148A are not attracted to such execution application. The defendants are not entitled to file a caveat in such an application for execution of a decree passed against them. Caveat is directed to be taken off the file—*Nara Digvijoy Co-op.* v *Sadhana Builder* AIR 1984 Bom 114.

6. In an application for probate or letters of administration if a caveat is entered and the application is registered as a suit then court-fees will be one half the scale of fee prescribed in Art. I of Schedule I on the market value of the estate less the fee already paid on the application.

7. Creditors of heirs at law can ask for revocation of probate and enter caveat during probate proceedings in response to general citation—AIR 1944 PC 11; AIR 1971 Ori 95.

8. Contents of caveat—Right under which caveator claims to appear before the court must be stated—AIR 1978 Cal 492.

9. For caveat under s. 148A of the Code of Civil Procedure 1908 see Form under CPC.

481. Petition for succession certificate

In the Court of ....

Testamentary and Intestate Jurisdiction

Petition for Succession Certificate in respect of certain $\frac{\text{securities}}{\text{debts}}$

belonging to .... *Deceased.*

... *Petitioner*

Sheweth:

1. That the above-named .... died at .... on or about the .... day of .... 20 ....

2. That the said Deceased ordinarily resided and left his property within .... (state place).

3. That the said Deceased died intestate and that due and diligent search has been made for a Will but none has been found.

or

The said Deceased died leaving a Will dated .... and executed at .... a copy of which is hereto annexed and marked "A".

4. That the said Deceased at the time of his death left him surviving as his next-of-kin according to law .... (*a*) ....

5. That the Petitioner as .... (*b*) .... of the Deceased claims to be entitled to a .... share of the estate.

6. That there is no impediment under s. 370 of the Indian Succession Act 1925, or under any other provision of this Act or any other enactment to the grant of the certificate or the validity thereof if it were granted.

7. That the petitioner has truly set forth in Schedule No. 1 hereto the securities in respect of which the certificate is applied for. The Succession Certificate is required for the purpose of .... (*c*) .... The said assets in respect of which the Succession Certificate is required are under the value of ₹..............

8. That no application has been made to any District Court or Delegate or to any court for Probate of any Will of the said Deceased or for Letters of Administration with or without the Will annexed to his property and credits.

9. That no application for Succession Certificate in respect of any debt or security belonging to the estate of the Deceased has been made to any District Court or Delegate or to any court.

Your petitioner therefore prays that a Succession Certificate be granted to the Petitioner in respect of the debts and securities set forth in Schedule I hereto.

Verification

Affidavit

482. Petition for a succession certificate to the estate of a Hindu deceased

In the Court of the District Judge, at......................

Misc. Case No. .... of ....

In the matter of Succession Certificate under Act XXXIX of 1925 to estate of .... deceased.

The humble petition of:

(1) A etc.

(2) B etc.

(3) C etc.

all by faith .... residing at ....

P.S. .... District ....

Most respectfully sheweth:

1. That one 'X' by faith Hindu .... of .... P.S. .... District .... died on .... where he was taken for treatment 10 days prior to his death.

2. That the deceased ordinarily used to reside at the time of his death at .... P.S. .... District .... within the jurisdiction of this court.

3. That the near relations left surviving by the deceased with their respective addresses are given below:

(*a*) 'D' son of late E residing at .... P.S. .... District ....

(*b*) Brother of the deceased.

4. That the petitioners and their ancestors are guided by the provisions of the Hindu Succession Act in the matters of succession and inheritance. The petitioner No. 1 is son of the deceased, the petitioner No. 2 is the daughter of the deceased and the petitioner No. 3 is the widow of the deceased and all are fit and proper persons to be entitled to the grant of a certificate as prayed for.

5. That there is no impediment under s. 370 or any other provision of Act XXXIX of 1925 to the granting of a certificate to your petitioners.

6. That the deceased did not make any Will and no letters of administration or probate of any Will in respect of the estate of the deceased has been taken or applied for by anybody.

7. That the debts in respect of which the certificate is applied for are mentioned in the Schedule below.

8. That the petitioners have deposited a sum of ₹.............. with the State Bank of India, ... on .... to cover the cost of stamp for the certificate. The challan thereof No. .... dated .... is enclosed herewith.

Your petitioners, therefore, pray that a certificate may be granted to them for collection of debts and securities mentioned in the Schedule below with interest due thereon.

SCHEDULE

	Debtor	How debt secured	Amount
(1)	Union of India P. & T. Deptt. .... Post Office, P.S. .... District	P.O. Savings Bank A/C. No.	₹ ....
(2)	Union of India P. & T. Dept.	National Savings Certificate No.	₹ ....
(3)	United Bank of India .... Branch. Dt.	A/C. No.	₹ ....
			Total ₹ ....

Verification

Affidavit

NOTES: 1. See Rule 301 of C.R.O. Vol. 1 Calcutta High Court—"In uncontested proceedings under the Indian Succession Act 1925, it shall be competent to the Court or Judge exercising jurisdiction therein" to permit or direct, except when otherwise provided by any law or rule for the time being in force, that any particular fact or facts may be proved, or evidence upon any application may be given by affidavit.

2. Payment of court-fee along with application is not a pre-condition. Court-fee can be paid at the time of Issue of Certificate—*Smt. Usha* v *State* AIR 1993 MP 41.

483. Petition for revocation of a succession certificate

In the Court of the District Judge at.................

Misc. Judicial Case No. .... of 20...................

A.B. ....

...... *Petitioner*

versus

C.D. ....

...... *Opposite Party*

Petition for revocation of the Succession Certificate under s. 383 of the Indian Succession Act 1925.

The plaintiff states as follows:

1. That on the petition of C.D. before this court, a Succession Certificate was granted by this court to C.D. on .... in Succession Certificate Case No. .... of .... for collecting debts and securities due to one .... deceased.

2. That the said .... deceased, at the time of his death, left your petitioner as one of his heirs besides the opposite party. The opposite party on the occasion of filing application for grant of the Certificate deliberately suppressed the name of the petitioner and claimed himself as the sole heir of the deceased.

3. That your petitioner being a daughter of the deceased is entitled, under the Hindu Succession Act, to 8-annas interest in the estate of the deceased.

4. That the opposite party obtained the said Certificate on false pleadings and affidavit and by fraudulent suppression of the claim of your petitioner.

It is, therefore, prayed that the Certificate granted to the O.P. be revoked forthwith.

Verification

Affidavit

NOTES: 1. See s. 383 of the Indian Succession Act for grounds of revocation of a Certificate. In the above Form ground in cl. (*b*) of s. 383 has been taken.

2. There cannot be partial revocation. Section 383 provides for the revocation of a Succession Certificate in its entirety—AIR 1960 Cal 578.

3. No suit lies for annulment of the Certificate.

4. Order refusing revocation—Appeal against it does not lie. Revision, held, is maintainable—*Chintamoni Devi* v *Upendra Nath* AIR 1981 Cal 263.

484. Petition for extension of a succession certificate

In the Court of the District Judge/District Delegate

Act 39 (Succession Certificate) of 1925 Case No....... of 20.......

In the matter of extension of Succession Certificate under Act 39 of 1925.

And

In the matter of the estate of XY ..... *Deceased.*

And

In the matter of A.B. S/o C.D.

.... *Petitioner*

(residence)

1. to 3. See Form No. 483 (adopt as far as practicable).

4. That the petitioner was granted by this court a Succession Certificate dated ...... in the estate of XY in Succession Certificate Case No. .... of 20....

5. That the petitioner prays that the said Certificate may be extended to the following debts, mentioned below.

6. That the petitioner has deposited with the .... Treasury a sum of ₹ ...... on .... by challan No. .... dt. .... to cover the cost of the stamp for the Certificate. A copy of the challan is enclosed herewith.

PARTICULARS OF DEBTS

Sl. No.	*Name of debtor*	*Amount due*	*How secured*

It is, therefore, prayed that an order of extension be made with reference to the Succession Certificate granted on ....

Verification

Affidavit

NOTES: 1. The petition shall be signed and verified by or on behalf of the applicant conforming to provisions of Or. 6, rr. 14 and 15 of the Code of Civil Procedure.

2. According to s. 383(*b*) revocation of Succession Certificate can be claimed on two grounds, i.e. first when it is obtained fraudulently by making a false suggestion and secondly by concealment from the court of something material to the case—*Brij Balai Mishra* v *Vijai Shankar* AIR 1991 All 236.

3. Order refusing to revoke Succession Certificate—Appeal against is not maintainable—vide s. 384, Indian Succession Act—*Brig Balai Mishra* v *Vijai Shankar* AIR 1991 All 236 at p. 238.

4. Application to recover a portion of the debt to the deceased is permissible—ILR 42 Cal 10.

5. See s. 376 of the Indian Succession Act 1925. Extension of Certificate can only be applied for by the person who has been granted a Certificate. If he dies application shall be for a fresh Certificate and not for an extended Certificate.

485. Form of valuation

In the Court of............................

Re: Probate of the Will of.................(or administration of the property and credits of..............) deceased.

1. I .... of .... solemnly affirm (or make oath) and say that I am the executor (or one of the executors, or one of the next-of-kin) of.........deceased, and that I have truly set forth in the Annexure 'A' to this affidavit all the property and credits of which the above-named deceased died possessed or was entitled to at the time of his death and which have come, or are likely to come, to my hands.

2. I further say that I have also truly set forth in Annexure 'B' all the items I am by law allowed to deduct.

3. I further say that the said assets, exclusive only of such last mentioned items, but inclusive of all rents, interests, dividends and increased values since the date of the death of the said deceased are under the value of ₹ ....

ANNEXURE 'A'

Valuation of the movable and immovable property of .... deceased

	₹..................
Cash in the house and at the banks, household goods, wearing apparel, books, plate, jewels etc.	₹ ....
Property in Government securities transferable at the Public Debt Office	₹ ....
Immovable properties consisting of	₹ ....
Leasehold property	₹ ....
Property in public companies	₹ ....
Policy of insurance upon life, money out on mortgage and other securities, such as, bonds, mortgages, bills, notes and other securities for money	₹ ....
Book debts	₹ ....

Stock in trade	₹ ....
Other property not comprised under the foregoing heads	₹ ....
Total	₹ ....
Deduct amount shown in Annexure B not subject to duty	₹ ....
Net Total	₹ ....

ANNEXURE 'B'

Schedule of debts etc.

Amount of debts due and owing from the deceased, payable by law out of the estate	₹.....................
Amount of funeral expenses	₹.....................
Amount of mortgage-incumbrances	₹.....................
Property held in trust not beneficially or with general power to confer a beneficial interest	₹.....................
Other property not subject to duty	₹ ....
Total	₹ ....

486. Application for grant of Succession Certificate

In the Court of District Delegate at Alipore

Case No. .... of 20...

In the matter of:

An Application for the grant of a Succession Certificate under section 372 of the Indian Succession Act 1925

And

In the matter of:

1, Mr. P, son of Mr. Z residing at ...., Alipore Road, Kolkata

.... *Petitioner*

The humble petition of Mr. P. the petitioner above-named, most respectfully sheweth:

1. Your petitioners state that Mr. Z, died at his residence at ...., Alipore Road, Kolkata on the 10th day of November 20........

2. The ordinary place of residence of the said deceased at the time of his death was at ...., Alipore Road, Kolkata within the jurisdiction of this learned court.

3. The said deceased left behind his properties mentioned in Schedule 'A' within this jurisdiction of this learned court.

4. Your petitioners state that the said deceased left behind him the following surviving relatives:

(*a*) Smt. W, the widow of the said deceased;

(*b*) Mr. S, being the son of petitioner Mr. P.

5. Your petitioner states that being the only son of the late deceased, your petitioner claims to be entitled to a Succession Certificate under provisions of the Indian Succession Act 1925.

6. Your petitioner states that there is no impediment under s. 370 of the Indian Succession Act 1925 for the grant of Succession Certificate to your petitioner.

7. Such a Succession Certificate, if granted, the validity thereof cannot be questioned.

8. The said deceased did not make any Testamentary Will and hence no application has been made to any other court for grant of Probate of any Will or for any Letter of Administration to the Estate of the said deceased.

9. Your petitioner states that the particulars of debts and securities in respect of present application is contained in a Schedule annexed hereto marked 'B'.

10. For the purposes of the present application and the issue of a Succession Certificate, the properties left behind by the said deceased are valued at ₹.......... on which necessary court-fees in stamps have been paid.

11. In the facts and circumstances of the case your petitioner has made this application *bona fide* and in the interests of justice for protection and preservation of the assets and properties left behind by the said deceased.

Your petitioner, therefore, most humbly prays Your Honour for the following orders:

(*a*) A Succession Certificate be issued in favour of your petitioner authorising him to collect the debts and assets mentioned in Schedules being the annexures 'A' and 'B' hereof and to appropriate the same in accordance with the rights of the successions of the deceased;

(*b*) Costs of this application do come out of the Estate of the said deceased;

(*c*) Further and other orders be made and directions be given as this learned court may deem fit and proper so as to afford complete relief to your petitioners.

And your petitioners as in duty bound shall ever pray.

SCHEDULE 'A' (Assets)

SCHEDULE 'B' (Debts)

Verification

Affidavit

CONSUMER PROTECTION

487. Applications for deficiency of service

In the District Consumer Disputes Redressal Forum
Darbhanga Collectorate, Darbhanga
Consumer Complaint No. ...... of ......

In the matter of:
A complaint under ss. 11 and 12 of the Consumer Protection Act 1986 and the Rules made thereunder

And

Mr. X residing at ....
....
...... *Complainant*

versus

Machinery Company Limited, a company incorporated under the Companies Act 1956 and carrying on business at ....
...... *Respondent*

To
The Hon'ble President and His Companion Member of the District Consumer Disputes Redressal Forum

The complainant above-named most respectfully sheweth:

1. The respondent is a manufacturer of electrical goods including Washing Machines and carries on business in ....

2. The claim of compensation and/or redressal of grievances of the complainant does not exceed ₹ ....

3. The complaint relates to the malfunctioning of the Washing Machine purchased by the complainant from the respondent about 18 months ago. This Application is being made within 2 years from the date of cause of action for making this application.

4. On 15th June 1998 the complainant purchased one Automatic Washing Machine from the respondent at ₹ ....

5. The complainant paid the price, took delivery of the machine and the respondent issued a cash memo and a Guarantee/Warranty Card guaranteeing the proper functioning of the machine. The guarantee was valid for 3 years.

6. After about 7 days of running the said machine in accordance with the printed instructions given by the respondent the machine did not work properly. The complainant by his letter dated 25th June 1998 complained to the respondent setting out the malfunctioning of the Washing Machine including the non-working of the spinning mechanism.

7. The respondent sent its mechanic who apparently repaired the defect. But after some time again there was the malfunctioning of the machine since its water pump was not properly functioning. Its spinning mechanism also did not work.

8. After several reminders the respondent sent its mechanic who tried to repair the machine and ultimately made the machine workable but stated that the defect was a manufacturing one and therefore the same could not be fully repaired.

9. The complainant requested the respondent by a letter dated 10th December 1998 to replace the said machine as there was a manufacturing defect and in spite of best efforts the respondent's mechanic could not repair the defects. The respondent

received the said letter but neither replaced the machine nor repaired the defect nor replied to the said complaint. A copy of letter and copy of the receipt are annexed hereto marked "A" and "A-1".

10. Copies of the Cash Memo and the Guarantee Card are annexed hereto marked "B" and "C" respectively.

11. Copies of the previous complaints are annexed hereto marked "D".

12. By reasons of the breach of the agreement, breach of the Warranty and negligence of the respondent, the complainant has suffered loss and damages which the complainant assesses at ₹ ....

In the facts and circumstances of the case the complainant prays for the following reliefs:

(*a*) Refund of ₹ .... paid to the respondent for the purchase of the said Washing Machine;

(*b*) Interest from date of purchase on ₹ .... at 18% per annum;

(*c*) Damages for harassment, physical injury and mental agony assessed at ₹ ....;

(*d*) Costs of the present proceeding;

(*e*) Further and other reliefs as the complainant is entitled to.

And the complainant as in duty bound shall ever pray.

Place: ....
Date: ....

Signature of Complainant

ANNEXURES:

1. Cash Memo
2. Guarantee Card
3. Letters of complaint

Verification

Affidavit

488. Applications for deficiency of service (Another Form)

In the Bihar State Consumers Disputes Redressal Commission
12 North Srikrishnapuri, Patna, Bihar

Original Jurisdiction
Consumer Complaint No. .... of 20........

In the Matter of:
A complaint under section 17 of the Consumer Protection Act 1986 and the Rules made thereunder

And

Mr. X residing at 2 North Shrikrishnapuri, Patna, Bihar

... *Complainant*

versus

Computer Limited a company registered under the Companies Act 1956 and carrying on business at 5 North Srikrishnapuri, Patna, Bihar

... *Respondent*

To
The Hon'ble President and his Companion
Members of the State Commission

The humble complaint of the complainant above-named most respectfully sheweth:

1. The respondent is the manufacturer of and dealer in Computers both Hardwares and Softwares and is carrying on business, *inter alia*, at Patna and New Delhi.

2. The claim of the complainant is less than ₹ .... but more than ₹ ....

3. The complainant's cause of action for this complaint arose on and after 30th December 1998 within two years of the present application.

4. The complainant purchased a Computer from the respondent on 10th July 1998 at ₹ .... on terms and conditions contained in the Guarantee Card given by the respondent.

5. Under the terms and conditions of the said sale of Computer by the respondent the respondent undertook to render free service for one year in relation to the said Computer.

6. Within six months of its installation at the office of complainant at 2 North Srikrishnpuri, Patna there was malfunctioning of the said Computer.

7. The complainant by a letter dated 15th December 1998 requested the respondent to replace the Computer as in spite of repairs by the respondent's mechanic, the Computer was malfunctioning and was of no use to the complainant.

8. The respondent again sent its mechanic who attended the Computer but could not repair it or remove the defect and the machine continued to malfunction.

9. The complainant by its letter of 5th January 1999 made a detailed complaint to the respondent about the machine and requested respondent to replace the said Computer.

10. The respondent by its letter of 28th January 1999 denied any defect in the Computer or that it was malfunctioning.

11. The complainant contacted an expert Mr. Z from Patna who was the Principal of Patna Computer College and got the Computer examined by him and received a certificate/report of his examination of the Computer.

12. According to the expert opinion there was a manufacturing defect in the Computer and it could not be repaired by any mechanic and required substantial replacement of certain parts of the Computer and reassembly thereof. A copy of the expert's report was sent to the respondent. In spite of this, the respondent did not take any effective steps. A copy of the expert's report is annexed hereto marked 'A'.

13. The complainant by a letter of 5th February 1999 requested the respondent to take back the Computer and refund the price paid therefor. A copy of the letter is annexed hereto marked 'B'.

14. The respondent in reply stated that there was no defect in the Computer and that the complainant is not entitled to any refund of the price for the Computer. A copy of letter is annexed hereto marked 'C'.

15. Copies of the receipt given by the respondent for purchase of the Computer and Guarantee Card are annexed hereto marked 'D' and 'D-1' respectively.

16. The complainant states that the contention of the respondent is untenable and unwarranted and in spite of several attempts the respondent has not been able to make the Computer function properly. The expert opinion is also to the effect that there was a manufacturing defect in the Computer.

17. In view of the aforesaid the respondent is bound to take back the Computer and refund the purchase price thereof and pay the costs and expenses incurred by the complainant in taking the expert opinion and incidentals thereto.

18. The respondent shall also pay the compensation due to the complainant for the harassment, troubles, loss of business, physical inconvenience and mental agony arising directly out of the breach of warranty, breach of the agreement and breach of duty on the part of the respondent. The complainant assesses such loss and damages at ₹ ....

19. Without prejudice to the aforesaid the complainant states that an enquiry be made as to the loss and damages the complainant has suffered due to the defective and malfunctioning Computer sold and delivered by the respondent to the complainant and its inability to repair the same and depriving the complainant of any use of the Computer and putting the complainant to harassment and mental agony and loss of business.

In the facts and circumstances of the case the complainant prays for the following reliefs:

(*a*) Refund of ₹........ paid as consideration for the said Computer;

(*b*) Interest from the date of payment of the said consideration money till realisation at 18% per annum;

(*c*) Payment of ₹ .... by the respondent to the complainant by way of compensation for the loss and damages caused to the complainant by the wrongful acts of the respondent;

(*d*) Alternatively an enquiry into the loss and damages suffered by the complainant due to wrongful acts of the respondent and malfunctioning of the Computer and payment by the respondent to the complainant the amount so found due on such enquiry;

(*e*) Costs of the present complaint and proceeding be paid by respondent to complainant;

(*f*) Further and other reliefs that the complainant is entitled to.

And the complainant as in duty bound shall ever pray.

Place ....

Date ....

ANNEXURES:

1. Receipt
2. Guarantee Card
3. Expert Report
4. Copies of correspondence

Verification

Affidavit

489. Complaint before National Commission

In the National Consumers Disputes Redressal Commission
5th Floor, Janpath Bhawan, New Delhi
Original Jurisdiction
Consumer Complaint No. .... of .....

In the matter of:
A complaint under s. 21 of the Consumer Protection Act 1986 and the rules made thereunder.

And

Mr. X residing at ....
....

... *Complainant*

versus

Computer Limited a company registered under the Companies Act 1956 and carrying on business at .... within the said jurisdiction

... *Respondent*

To
The Hon'ble President and His Companion
Members of the National Commission

The humble complaint of the complainant above-named most respectfully sheweth:

1. The respondent is the manufacturer of and dealer in Computers both Hardwares and Softwares and is carrying on the business, *inter alia*, at Patna and New Delhi.

2. The claim of the complainant exceeds ₹ 20 lakhs.

3. The complainant's cause of action for this complaint arose on and after 30th December 1998 within two years of the present application.

4. The complainant purchased a Computer from the respondent on 30th December 1998 at ₹ 26 lakhs on terms and conditions contained in the Guarantee Card given by the respondent. The said Computer was sold and delivered by the respondent from its New Delhi Office.

5. Under the terms and conditions of the said sale of Computer by the respondent the respondent undertook to render free service for one year in relation to the said Computer.

6. Within six months of its installation at the office of the complainant at 2 North Srikrishnapuri, Patna there was malfunctioning of the said Computer.

7. The complainant by a letter dated 15th January 1999 requested the respondent to replace the Computer as in spite of repairs by the respondent's mechanic, the Computer was malfunctioning and was of no use to the complainant.

8. The respondent again sent its mechanic who attended the Computer but could not repair it or remove the defect and the machine continued to malfunction.

9. The complainant by its letter of 5th February 1999 made a detailed complaint to the respondent about the Computer and requested the respondent to replace the said Computer.

10. The respondent by its letter of 28th February 1999 denied any defect in the Computer or that it was malfunctioning.

11. The complainant engaged an expert Mr. Z from Patna who was the Principal of Patna Computer College and got the Computer examined by him and received a Certificate/report of his examination of the Computer.

12. According to the expert opinion there was a manufacturing defect in the Computer and it could not be repaired by any mechanic and required substantial replacement of certain parts of the Computer and reassembly thereof. A copy of the expert's report was sent to the respondent. In spite of this, the respondent did not take any effective steps. A copy of the expert's report is annexed hereto marked "A".

13. The complainant by a letter of 5th March 1999 requested the respondent to take back the Computer and refund the price paid therefor. A copy of the letter is annexed hereto marked "B".

14. The respondent in reply stated that there was no defect in the Computer and that the complainant is not entitled to any refund of the price for the Computer. A copy of the letter is annexed hereto marked "C".

15. Copies of the receipt given by the respondent for purchase of the Computer and the Guarantee Card are annexed hereto marked "D" and "D-1" respectively.

16. The complainant states that the contention of the respondent is untenable and unwarranted and in spite of several attempts the respondent has not been able to make the Computer function properly. The expert opinion is also to the effect that there was a manufacturing defect in the Computer.

17. In view of the aforesaid the respondent in bound to take back the Computer and refund the purchase price paid therefor and to pay the costs and expenses incurred by the complainant in taking the expert opinion and incidentals thereto.

18. The respondent is also liable to pay compensation to the complainant for the harassment, troubles, loss of business, physical inconvenience and mental agony suffered by and arising directly out of the breach of warranty, breach of the agreement and breach of duty on the part of the respondent. The complainant assesses such loss and damages at ₹ ....

19. Without prejudice to the aforesaid the complainant states that an enquiry be made as to the loss and damages the complainant has suffered due to the defective and malfunctioning of the Computer sold and delivered by the respondent to the complainant and its inability to repair the same and depriving the complainant of any use of the Computer and putting the complainant to harassment and mental agony and loss of business.

In the facts and circumstances of the case the complainant prays for the following reliefs:

(*a*) Refund of ₹ .... paid as consideration for the said Computer;

(*b*) Interest from date of payment of the said consideration money till realisation at 18%;

(*c*) Payment of ₹ .... by the respondent to the complainant by way of compensation for the loss and damages, harassment and mental agony caused to the complainant by the wrongful acts of the respondent;

(*d*) Alternatively an enquiry into the loss and damages suffered by the complainant due to wrongful acts of the respondent and malfunctioning, costs of expert opinion and payment by the respondent to the complainant the amount so found due on such enquiry;

(*e*) Costs of the present complaint and proceeding be paid by respondent to the complainant;

(*f*) Further and other reliefs that the complainant is entitled to be granted.

And the complainant as in duty bound shall ever pray.

Place: ....
Date: ....

ANNEXURES:

1. Receipt
2. Guarantee Card
3. Expert report
4. Copies of correspondence

Verification

Affidavit

490. Application against bank for damages for loss of valuables from the locker

Before the Hon'ble State Commission, WB

Consumer Complaint No. ..... of 20......

Mr. P. residing at .... Alipore Road, Kolkata
...... *Complainant*

versus

X Bank, having its branch office at ....
Alipore Road, Kolkata

.... *Respondent*

The humble petition of Mr. P., the complainant most respectfully sheweth:

1. The petitioner .... complainant is an individual and resident of........... Alipore Road, Kolkata and a "Consumer" within the meaning of s. 2(1)(*d*)(*ii*) of the Consumer Protection Act 1986, having dealings and transactions with the respondent, a Banking Company which carries on business of Banking within the meaning of the Banking Regulations Act 1949. The respondent provides banking services within the meaning of the s. (2)(1)(*o*) of the Consumer Protection Act 1986. There has been deficiency of service as stated hereinafter by the respondent Bank and as such, the present complaint is within the provisions of the said Act of 1986.

2. The complainant is having a Current Account with the respondent and maintains Fixed Deposits by way of investment and has hired a Locker in the said Branch of .... Bank.

3. The complainant has been depositing his moneys in the Current Account and creates Fixed Deposits on the terms and conditions of the respondent Bank.

4. The credit balance in the Current Account and a Fixed Deposit are being utilised by the complainant for expansion of his business and the respondent is earning profits

by way of interest and banking charges. The complainant is, therefore, a consumer and has hired the services of the respondent within the meaning of the Consumer Protection Act 1986.

5. The complainant hired a Locker from the respondent Bank in which from time to time the complainant kept ornaments and other valuables including Fixed Deposit receipts and title deeds of the complainant's residential house. The complainant regularly paid the hiring charges of the Locker. To meet emergency the complainant also kept in the Locker Currency Notes for ₹.............. so that in case of emergency, and urgent need of money, the same could be had from the Locker.

6. The complainant did not operate the Locker for about ten months.

7. There was urgent need of some money and complainant went to Bank on 10th January 20..., and opened the Locker but was surprised to find that the Locker was empty. Immediately the complainant called the Bank's Officers who examined the said Locker but did not find any sign of breaking open the Locker and the complainant got the impression that with the duplicate keys in possession of the Bank, some unauthorised persons in collusion with Bank's staff must have opened the Locker and took away the contents therein. The Officers of Bank were unable to explain the unauthorised opening of Locker and taking away of jewellery, valuable documents and the cash from Locker. There has been deficiency of service by the respondent Bank.

8. By virtue of the said unauthorised opening of the Locker apparently, with the duplicate keys kept by the Bank, in collusion with the officers of the Bank's staff, the assets of the complainant were taken out as a result of which the complainant has suffered loss and damages to the extent of ₹.................. particulars whereof are given in a Schedule annexed hereto marked 'A'.

9. The complainant states that the contents of Locker have been unauthorisedly taken away and the complainant has been deprived thereof due to the deficiency of service by the respondent Bank and its officers and claims compensation of ₹............. with interest at 12% per annum since this is due to deficiency of service by the respondent Bank.

10. The complainant further claims by way of compensation for mental strain, humiliation, harassment, and legal expenses involved including the advocate's fees the details whereof are given in a Schedule annexed hereto. This is due to deficiency of service by Bank.

11. This complaint is being filed within the period of limitation.

12. The complainant has valid cause of action for deficiency in service of the respondent. The cause of action of the complaint arose at Alipore Road, Kolkata at the Branch of the Bank and the amount of the claim is within the jurisdiction of this Hon'ble Commission.

The complainant, therefore, humble prays before the Hon'ble Forum for the following orders:

(*a*) An order be passed directing the respondent Bank to pay ₹............... by way of damages for loss of valuables from the Locker and for damages with interest as claimed;

(*b*) Cost of present proceedings;

(*c*) Such further and other orders be made as this Hon'ble Forum may deem fit and proper to afford complete relief to the complainant for his mental strain, harassment etc.

And the complainant, as in duty bound, shall ever pray.

Complainant

Verification

Affidavit

491. Complaint for deficiency of service by the Housing Board

In the Consumer Dispute Redressal District Forum at ....

Consumer Complaint No. .... of .... 20........

Mr. AB ....

... *Complainant*

versus

Popular Housing Board at ....

... *Opposite Party*

To
The Hon'ble President and His Companion
Members of the District Forum
Sirs,

The complainant above-named respectfully submits as follows:

1. The opposite party advertised a Housing Scheme and invited purchasers of the houses to be constructed. A copy of the advertisement is annexed hereto marked "A".

2. Pursuant to the said advertisement and invitation to offer the complainant made application for purchase of a house of specified area and at a price of ₹.............. In the application the complainant also made reference to the opposite party's scheme to provide in the building complex roads, schools, parks and other amenities under the said scheme.

3. On completion of the houses the opposite party allotted a small house to the complainant which the complainant took delivery of though the scheme of the opposite party was not completed so far as roads, schools, parks, etc. were concerned.

4. The complainant with his family started residing at the newly purchased house and after the rainy season it was found that the iron bar in the roof of the house became visible and developed crack in the wall due to use of sub-standard material in the building. The complainant in writing stated the facts to the opposite party and requested for taking necessary steps. A copy of the letter is annexed hereto marked "B".

5. After the lapse of a year it was found that the opposite party has failed to provide suitable roads or to establish schools or to provide parks as originally promised in the scheme published by the opposite party. The complainant also made a complaint in this respect to the opposite party and a copy of the complaint is annexed hereto marked "C".

6. Further, after the opposite party informed that the particular house allotted to complainant was ready for occupation and wanted the complainant to pay the balance price for the said house and as requested by the opposite party the complainant paid the balance consideration price for the said house. A copy of the receipt granted by the opposite party is annexed hereto marked "D".

7. In spite of receiving the full consideration money for the said house the opposite party delayed for a year delivery of possession of the said house to the complainant.

8. In view of the aforesaid the complainant states that there has been deficiency of service within the meaning of Consumer Protection Act 1986. The complainant claims damages for deficiency of service by the opposite party and such compensation is assessed at ₹................

9. The complainant states that in the facts and circumstances of the case and considering the misrepresentation by the opposite party and its inability to make constructions according to the published plan and using inferior materials and inefficient labour, an order be passed directing the opposite party to pay compensation to the complainant which the complainant assesses at ₹................

10. No part of the complainant's cause of action herein is barred by the law of limitation in view of the facts and transactions stated in the documents, copies whereof are annexures hereto.

11. No part of the claim or cause of action of the complainant is barred by the law of limitation.

12. For the purposes of jurisdiction the value of the subject matter of the complaint is ₹................ plus interest.

13. This application is made *bona fide* and for the redressal of genuine grievances of the complainant, a consumer.

The complainant, therefore, prays for the following reliefs:

(*a*) Decree or direction for payment of ₹................ by the opposite party to the complainant with interest from the date the complainant paid the entire consideration money to the opposite party;

(*b*) Receiver;

(*c*) Injunction;

(*d*) Costs;

(*e*) Further and other reliefs.

Place: Complainant in person
Date: or through Advocate

ANNEXURES

(1) Advertisement of the opposite party "A".
(2) Complainant's letter to the opposite party regarding the defect in the building "B".
(3) Complaint of the complainant to the opposite party "C".
(4) Receipt of the opposite party in respect of receipt of balance money from the complainant "D".

Verification

Affidavit

492. Complaint regarding defective construction of house

In the State Consumer Disputes Redressal Commission at ....

Consumer Complaint No. .... of .... 20 ....

(Set out cause title)

To
The Hon'ble President and His Companion
Members of the State Commission

Sirs,

The complainant named-above respectfully submits as follows:

1. The complainant is the owner of a plot of land situate at .... within the jurisdiction of this Hon'ble Forum.

2. The complainant entered into an agreement with the opposite party on .... for the construction of a four-storied building according to specifications given to the opposite party on the said plot of land of the complainant. A copy of the specifications is annexed hereto marked "A".

3. The opposite party inspected the plot of land and made enquiries and tested the soil and satisfied himself of the legal and physical viability of such proposal for construction of the multistoried building on the said land.

4. The opposite party entered into a contract with the complainant for construction of the multistoried building at a price of ₹ .... lakhs all inclusive. A copy of the contract is annexed hereto marked "B".

5. The contract provided detailed specifications of the building to be constructed and provided that the opposite party will prepare a plan and obtain sanction of the Municipality concerned and observe and comply with all formalities and requirements for the commencement and completion of the said building and after completion obtain certificate from the concerned authority to the effect that the construction has been made according to the law applicable and that the house is fit for residence.

6. The complainant paid from time to time the entire contracted amount of ₹ .... lakhs to the opposite party for the construction and completion of the said building. The claimant took possession of the building and entered occupation with family members. There were intermittent rains for two or three days and it was found that the roofs were leaking and there were damps indicating soaking and leaking of water from several walls of the building visible from inside as also outside the rooms. A complaint was lodged with the opposite party and by mutual consent an Engineer-expert was appointed to look into the matter. A copy of the appointment letter issued to the Engineer-expert is annexed hereto marked "C".

7. There were joint inspections of the building for two days and the expert tested here and there of the building as to the mode and manner and material of construction and submitted his report. A copy of the report dated .... is annexed hereto marked 'D'. From the report it will be apparent that there were defective workmanship in the construction of the house apart from the fact that sub-standard material were used in the construction and proper steps were not taken to prevent leakage of water from the ceiling roof and walls. The materials were of inferior quality and the proportion of cement and quality thereof were not according to the required norms. The opposite party therefore committed breaches of the agreement, violated the rules of the Sanctioning Authority and did not conform to the normal practice of the trade to make the building water-proof as is required both under the law and practice. The opposite party committed breaches of the agreement as also the statutory requirement for construction of buildings.

8. Due to the aforesaid wrongful acts of the opposite party the complainant a consumer has suffered loss and damages which the complainant assesses at ₹ .... lakhs.

9. The complainant prays for an order directing the opposite party to pay to the claimant ₹ .... lakhs plus interest at 15% per annum thereon and costs of this proceeding.

10. This complaint is made within the period of limitation, that is, within three years of the breach of contract by the opposite party.

11. The subject matter of this complaint and cause of action for this complaint and the claims made herein are all within the jurisdiction of this Hon'ble State Commission.

12. This application is made *bona fide* and for the redressal of genuine grievances of the complainant consumer.

Complainant therefore prays for the following reliefs:

(*a*) Order be made directing the opposite party to pay to the complainant ₹ ...... lakhs plus interest at 15% per annum till realisation.

(*b*) ....

(*c*) ....

And the complainant as in duty bound shall ever pray.

Place: (Complainant in person or through Advocate)
Date:

Annexures:

1.
2.
3.
4.

Verification

Affidavit

DEFAMATION

493. Suit for damages for publication of defamatory matter

In the City Civil Court at Calcutta

Suit No. .... of 20........

Mr. P. residing at .... Kolkata

.... *Plaintiff*

versus

1. X prop. of Newspaper Upright carrying on business at ...., Kolkata.

2. Mr. Y, Printer & Publisher of the Newspaper X, from ...., Kolkata

.... *Defendants*

The plaintiff states:

1. The plaintiff is a well-qualified medical practitioner and is owner of a medical shop known as Medical Store. As a medical practitioner the plaintiff has considerable income ranging from ₹............ to ₹........... per year. The plaintiff has a surplus of profit from the medical shop to the extent of ₹............. per year. The defendant No. 1 is a limited company, owns newspaper 'Upright'. Defendant No. 2 is the Printer & Publisher of the said daily newspaper 'Upright'. This paper has a large circulation in the neighbourhood where the plaintiff resides and carries on his practice.

2. In the issue of the said newspaper dated 16th September 20..... the defendant falsely, maliciously and with a view to causing pecuniary loss and damages to goodwill of the plaintiff published several comments concerning the plaintiff as a doctor and his medical shop as lower him in the estimation of the public.

3. The said newspaper published defamatory words .... and incorrect imputations both against the plaintiff as doctor and against the said Medical Store, the particulars whereof will appear from a cutting of the said newspaper published on 16th September 20...... is annexed hereto marked "A".

4. By the publication of the said objectionable and false words and allegations the plaintiff has suffered injury in his credit and reputation as a medical practitioner and his income from profession has substantially been reduced. As a result of such defamatory words, the plaintiff has suffered injury in his credit and reputation and suffered damages which the plaintiff assesses at ₹............. per month from his profession and ₹.................... per day in his business, the said medical shop.

5. The plaintiff has suffered the said damages as a direct result of the publication of the defamatory statement in the said newspaper by the defendants and that the defendants had no justification whatsoever to publish the said defamatory statements in the newspaper.

6. The plaintiff claims the said sum of ₹............ by way of compensation for damages suffered due to wrongful and malicious publications of defamatory statements in the said newspaper, a copy whereof is annexed hereto.

7. The plaintiff's cause of action arose on 16th September 20..... when the said defamatory statements were published and on subsequent days when as a result of the said publication the plaintiff suffered the said loss and damages mentioned hereinabove.

8. The plaintiff demanded payment by his letter dated 20th September 20..... which the defendants received by signing on a copy of the said letter, copies whereof are annexed hereto collectively marked "B".

9. The plaintiff's cause of action for his suit arose at the addresses of the defendants and also in Kolkata, both within and outside the jurisdiction of this Hon'ble Court as the paper has circulation outside Kolkata also and the plaintiff suffered loss and damages at his address from where he carries on his practice and where the plaintiff has the medicine shop, all within the jurisdiction of this learned Court.

10. For the purposes of jurisdiction and court-fees the suit is valued at ₹............... on which court-fees in stamps have been paid.

11. No part of the plaintiff's claims is barred by the Law of Limitation. The defendants have not issued any notice in the newspaper that the said defamatory publication in the newspapers on the 16th September 20.......... was incorrect and false.

The plaintiff, therefore, prays for and claims:

(*a*) Decree for ₹............. against the defendants jointly and severally by way of damages;

(*b*) Interest at 12% per annum on the amount claimed from the date of filing of the suit till the date of the decree and on the decretal amount till realisation;

(*c*) Injunction restraining the defendants from repeating defamatory statements against the plaintiff as practitioner or as owner of the medical shop;

(*d*) Costs;

(*e*) Further and other orders be made so as to grant complete relief to the plaintiff.

ANNEXURE 'A'

ANNEXURE 'B'

Verification

Affidavit

FAMILY COURT

The State Government after consultations with the High Court has by notification established for every area in the State comprising a city or town whose population exceeds 1 million, a Family Court. In consultation with the High Court the extent of jurisdiction may be increased or reduced. The State Government will appoint with the concurrence of High Court the Judges of a Family Court.

Section 7 of the Act deals with jurisdiction of the Family Court. It provides that a Family Court shall—

(*a*) have and exercise all the jurisdiction exercisable by any District Court or any subordinate civil court under any law for the time being in force in respect of suits and proceedings of the nature referred to in the explanation, and

(*b*) be deemed, for the purposes of exercising such jurisdiction under such law, to be a District Court, or, as the case may be, such subordinate civil court for the area to which jurisdiction of the Family Court extends.

Explanation. The suits and proceedings referred to in this sub-section are suits and proceedings of the following nature, namely:

(*a*) a suit or proceeding between the parties to a marriage for a decree of nullity of marriage (declaring the marriage to be null and void, or as the case may be, annulling the marriage) or restitution of conjugal rights or judicial separation or dissolution of marriage;

(*b*) suit or proceeding for a declaration as to the validity of a marriage or as to the matrimonial status of any person;

(*c*) a suit or proceeding between the parties to a marriage with respect to the property of the parties or of either of them;

(*d*) a suit or proceeding for an order or injunction in circumstances arising out of a marital relationship;

(*e*) a suit or proceeding for a declaration as to the legitimacy of any person;

(*f*) a suit or proceeding for maintenance;

(*g*) a suit or proceeding in relation to the guardianship of the person for the custody of, or access to, any minor.

2. Subject to the other provisions of the Act, a Family Court shall also have and exercise—

(*a*) the jurisdiction exercisable by a Magistrate of the First Class under Chapter IX (relating to order for maintenance of wife, children and parents) of the Code of Criminal Procedure 1973; and

(*b*) such other jurisdiction as may be conferred on it by any other enactment.

Section 8, *inter alia*, provides that where a Family Court has been established for any area—

(*a*) no District Court or any subordinate civil court shall in relation to such area, have or exercise any jurisdiction in respect of any suit or proceeding of the nature referred to in the explanation to sub-sec. (1) of s. 7.

(*b*) no Magistrate shall, in relation to such area, have or exercise any jurisdiction or power under Chapter IX of the Code of Criminal Procedure 1973;

(*c*) every suit or proceeding of the nature referred to in the explanation to sub-sec. (1) of s. 7 and every proceeding under Chapter IX of the Code of Criminal Procedure 1973—

(*i*) which is pending immediately before the establishment of such Family Court before any District Court or subordinate court referred to in that sub-section or, as the case may be, before any Magistrate under the said Code; and

(*ii*) which would have been required to be instituted or taken before or by such Family Court if, before the date on which such suit or proceeding was instituted or taken, the Family Courts Act 1984 has come into force and such Family Court has been established,

shall stand transferred to such Family Court on the date on which it is established.

Section 10 provides that the Code of Civil Procedure and any other law would be applicable to the Family Court and the Family Court shall be deemed to be a Civil Court having all the powers of such court. The provisions of Chapter IX of the Code of Criminal Procedure 1973 shall also apply to the proceedings before the Family Court. The Family Court may also lay down its own procedure. The proceedings shall be in camera and also in exceptional cases lawyers and experts assistance may be taken. From the decision of the Family Court appeal will lie to the High Court except against an interlocutory order.

Section 20 provides that the Family Courts Act 1984 shall prevail over any other Act. The High Court, Central Government and the State Government may make rules to carry out the provisions of the Act.

In the case of *Mary Sheila* v *Vincent Thamburaj* AIR 1991 Mad 180 it has been held that in respect of matters mentioned in Explanation to section 7, the Family Court as well as the High Court in its original jurisdiction will have concurrent jurisdiction. Family Court will have no power to issue a Succession Certificate or to grant relief in respect thereof. Reference be made to ss. 372 and 373 of the Indian Succession Act 1925. In spite of the wide provisions of the Family Courts Act 1984, in particular cases the question of jurisdiction has to be specially considered. An application under s. 3 of the Muslim Women (Protection of Rights on Divorce) Act 1986 is maintainable before a Magistrate and the Family Court will have no jurisdiction unless specifically authorised. Reference may be made to *Amjum Hassan Siddiqui* v *Salma* AIR 1992 All 322.

A Family Court cannot dismiss an application for maintenance filed under s. 125 of the Code of Criminal Procedure for default or non-appearance of the applicant in exercise of its inherent powers—*Aruna Kar* v *Sarat Bhas* 1993 CrLJ 1506. A Family Court will have jurisdiction under the Hindu Marriage Act to decide disputes relating to properties of the parties to the marriage as also the property of either of them. A petition filed by wife against her husband for partition of specified property and separate possession will be maintainable in a Family Court. However, the Family Court will have no jurisdiction to appoint a guardian or manager in respect of the property of a minor—*Susila Nail* v *Judge Family Court* AIR 1998 Ori 61.

An appeal would lie from the order of the Family Court to the High Court. Further, the High Court may of its own motion or otherwise call for and examine the record of any proceeding in which the Family Court situate within its jurisdiction passed an order under Chapter IX of the Code of Criminal Procedure 1973 for the purpose of satisfying itself as to the correctness, legality or propriety of the order not being an interim order and as to the regularity of such proceedings. The appeal would be heard by a Division Bench.

The provisions of the Act shall have effect notwithstanding anything inconsistent therewith contained in any other law in force or in any instrument having effect by virtue of any law other than Family Courts Act 1984.

MARRIAGE, DISSOLUTION, DIVORCE AND RESTITUTION

494. Suit for damages for breach of contract to marry

In the Court of .... at ....

Suit No. .... 20............

(Set out cause title)

The plaintiff states as follows:

1. That the plaintiff is a respectable citizen of the town and has had a large acquaintance and a host of friends and relations all over the district.

2. That the defendant after negotiations has agreed to give his daughter Srimati A.B. in marriage with the plaintiff on the .... day of ...., 20.......

3. That the plaintiff was willing to marry the said Srimati A.B. on .... but the defendant, in violation of his agreement, declined to give her daughter in marriage with the plaintiff and did not forget to allege falsely that the plaintiff was having connection with other women.

4. That the plaintiff in consideration of the proposed marriage had offered Srimati A.B. customary presents worth about ₹............. and incurred expenses to the tune of ₹............... making a total of ₹................ as per account below.

5. That the plaintiff has also suffered mental pain and insult as a result of the breach.

6. Cause of action.

The plaintiff claims:

(*a*) A decree for (*i*) ₹........ as damages for mental suffering and insult.

(*ii*) ₹........ as special damages as per account below.

(*b*) Costs.

ACCOUNT OF EXPENSES

Presents offered to the bride — one pair of gold Bauti	₹....................
Preliminary expenses for the marriage (State here details)	₹....................
	₹....................

Verification

Affidavit

495. Application for dissolution of a Hindu marriage by a decree of divorce

Before the Family Court at ....

Matrimonial Suit No. .... 20...

A.B. .... *Petitioner*

versus

C.D. .... *Respondent*

The above-named petitioner states as follows:

1. That the petitioner was married to the respondent on the .... day of Aghrayan, 14 .... B.S. corresponding to .... 20 .... at the petitioner's father's residence at .... P.S. .... District .... within the jurisdiction of this court.

2. That thereafter the petitioner and the respondent lived together as husband and wife last at .... P.S. .... within the jurisdiction of this court till..........

3. That the respondent had committed rape on other woman in the month of .... and was convicted and sentenced to R.I. for 7 years [*vide* s. 13(2)(*ii*)].

Or, that the respondent has been living in adultery with one .... since .... and up till now [*vide* s. 13(1)(*ii*)].

Or, that the respondent embraced Islam on .... [*vide* s. 13(1)(*ii*)] or, that the respondent developed insanity soon after marriage with the petitioner was solemnized and has been incurably of unsound mind since early ...., 20............... [*vide* s. 13(1)(*iii*)].

4. That the petitioner is, in the facts stated above, entitled to dissolution of her marriage by a decree of divorce.

5. That no issue was born of the wedlock.

6. The petition is not presented or prosecuted in collusion with the respondent.

7. Cause of action.

8. That for the purpose of jurisdiction and court-fees, fixed court-fees of ₹............ are paid.

The petitioner claims dissolution of her marriage with the respondent by a decree of divorce.

Verification

Affidavit

NOTES: 1. [See change in law by the Marriage Laws (Amendment) Act]. No petition for divorce to be presented within one year of marriage—see s. 14 of the Hindu Marriage Act.

2. Forum—Court of the District Judge—see s. 19 of the Family Courts Act 1984.
3. When the petition is filed under s. 13(1)(*i*)—The petitioner should aver "that the petitioner has not in any manner been accessory to or connived at or condoned the respondent's adulterous living."
4. Inference of impotency—AIR 1971 Cal 1.
5. For proof of adultery—AIR 1971 Del 208. Standard of proof of adultery—see AIR 1970 Cal 38.
6. Hindu Marriage Act, s. 7—Customary marriage—Custom not pleaded—nature of ceremonies performed not brought out. Living together as husband and wife—that by itself would not confer status of husband and wife—*Surjit Kaur* v *Garja Singh* AIR 1994 SC 135.

   If the marriage is not a valid marriage, it is no marriage in the eye of law. The bare fact of a man and a woman living as husband and wife does not, at any rate, normally give them the status of husband and wife even though they may hold themselves out before society as husband and wife and the society treats them as husband and wife—*B.S. Lokhandi's* case AIR 1965 SC 1564 at p. 1565.

496. Appliaction for dissolution of a Muslim marriage (by a wife)

In the Family Court at ....

Matrimonial Suit No. .... of 20.............

A.B. Khatun, daughter of late Ashu Mahmud Mistri, by faith Muslim, residing in care of Reaz Mia, Vill. .... P.S. .... District ....

...... *Plaintiff*

versus

C.D. Hossain, son of late Aineuddin Fakir, of Vill. .... P.S. .... District ....

...... *Defendant*

Suit for dissolution of marriage.

Valued for jurisdiction at ₹100.

The above-named plaintiff states as follows:

1. That the plaintiff lost her father in her infancy and was reared up by her uncle 'A' at his residence at Mouja ...., P.S. ...., District .... where she was given in marriage with the defendant in .... B.S. The plaintiff was then a minor aged 12 years only.

2. That the plaintiff, after her marriage with the defendant, lived with her guardian but for occasional visits at husband's place till she attained majority in .... B.S.

3. That the defendant is a landless fellow. He was unable to maintain the plaintiff and discharge his minimum marital obligations. Being anxious of the welfare of the plaintiff, the defendant was asked by the guardians of the plaintiff to come over to the plaintiff's house as domesticated son-in-law and live there and work upon the plaintiff's uncle's lands.

4. That the defendant turned out to be an worthless fellow and was found to be incompetent to discharge marital obligations. He would not work and often left home for couple of weeks together without intimation to the plaintiff or anybody of her house.

5. That the plaintiff while living in the house of her uncle has had a daughter by the defendant aged three years and odd, born in early part of Bhadra, 14 .... B.S. After birth of the daughter the plaintiff had requested the defendant to be practical and to mind household work, so that he could be of some use to the family and maintain his wife and daughter. The defendant appeared not to have moved. On the contrary, as usual he deserted the plaintiff within nine days of the birth of the daughter in the month of Bhadra, 14 .... B.S. Since then the defendant has not returned uptill now.

6. That before such desertion by the defendant the plaintiff and defendant were living as husband and wife at ...., P.S. ...., District .... at the residence of the plaintiff's uncle...............

7. That the defendant has neglected and has failed to provide for the maintenance of the plaintiff as well as the daughter for a continuous period of more than two years from Bhadra, 14 .... B.S. Besides, the defendant has failed to performs, without reasonable cause, his marital obligations for a period of more than two years from Bhadra, 14 .... B.S., by his wilful desertion of the plaintiff. The defendant by his such cruel conduct has made the life of the plaintiff miserable.

8. That the plaintiff in the aforesaid circumstances is entitled to a decree of dissolution of her marriage with the defendant on grounds mentioned above as contemplated in s. 2(*ii*)(*iv*) and (*viii*) of the Dissolution of Muslim Marriage Act 1939.

9. That the cause of action for the present suit arose on expiry of Bhadra, ... B.S. that is on completion of two years after desertion and on his failure to maintain the plaintiff at .... within the jurisdiction of this court.

10. The suit is valued at ₹............ for jurisdiction of the court and fixed court-fees of ₹............ are paid.

The plaintiff, therefore, claims:

(*a*) a decree against the defendant dissolving the marriage between the plaintiff and the defendant;

(*b*) costs;

(*c*) a decree for other relief to which the plaintiff may, in law and equity, be entitled.

Verification

Affidavit

NOTES: 1. Court-fees Hindu (*i*) Petition for restitution of conjugal rights
(*ii*) Judicial separation .... ₹5
(*iii*) Divorce
in West Bengal under the West Bengal Court-fees Act 1970.
(*i*) Plaint when presented under the Dissolution of Muslim Marriage Act 1939. .... ₹10
For West Bengal under the West Bengal Court-fees Act 1970.

2. Muslim wife staying away from husband without justifiable ground—No ground for dissolution under s. 2(*ii*)—AIR 1971 Cal 218.

3. Desertion as a ground of divorce—Petition by husband before completion of two years of marriage is premature. Time spent after filing of petition could not be considered for computing period of desertion—*Madanmohan Manna* v *Chitra Manna* AIR 1993 Cal 33.
4. Muslim Women (Protection of Rights on Divorce) Act, s. 3. Maintenance—Divorced woman leading adulterous life. Entitled to claim maintenance from her former husband—*M. Alavi* v *T.V. Safia* AIR 1993 Ker 21.
5. Under the Divorce Act (Act 4 of 1869)—*Ramish Francis Toppo* v *Violet Francis Toppo* AIR 1989 Cal 128; (1988)1 CLJ 294.

497. Application for dissolution of marriage under the Special Marriage Act 1954

Before the Family Court at................

In the matter of Special Marriage (Act XLII of 1954)

Matrimonial Suit No. .... of 20..........

(Set out cause title)

1. That the petitioner is Indian by birth is a school teacher by profession.

2. That respondent No. 1 is also an Indian by birth is a nurse of the .... Government Hospital at ....

3. That respondent No. 1 was married to the petitioner in the month of .... 20... at .... within the jurisdiction of the district court of .... and the petitioner and respondent No. 1 last resided together at .... within the local limits of jurisdiction of this court.

4. That no issue was born of the wedlock or, that out of the wedlock 2 sons were born whose particulars are given below.

Name	*Date of birth*	*Male or female child*
....	....	....
....	....	....

5. That the respondent No. 1 has been living in adultery with the co-respondent No. 2 A.B. [Mention details as far as practicable].

6. That the petitioner has not in any manner been accessory to or connived at or condoned the adultery of the respondent No. 1

7. That the petitioner is entitled to a decree of divorce.

8. That the cause of action for this petition arose on .... from when the Respondent is living in adultery with said co-respondent at .... within the jurisdiction of the learned court where the petitioner respondent No. 1 also last resided together.

The petitioner, therefore, prays:

(*i*) For a judgment and decree of divorce of the petitioner's marriage with respondent No. 1.

(*ii*) For custody of the children of the marriage, referred to above (if any).

Verification

Affidavit

NOTES: 1. Under Calcutta High Court Rules in a petition for divorce on the ground of adultery, the alleged adulterer shall be impleaded as a co-respondent—See CRO Vol. I. Rule 340 (1-28).

2. Court-fees—Fixed ₹5 under the West Bengal Court-fees Act 1970 in West Bengal.
3. For meanings of 'desertion', 'cruelty', 'adultery' (Special Marriage Act, s. 27)—See AIR 1970 Cal 266.
4. Relief under the Special Marriage Act is available only after compliance with Cal HC Rules and Orders—AIR 1970 Cal 266.

498. Application for judicial separation of a Hindu couple (Ground of desertion)

In the Family Court at..........

Matrimonial Suit No. .... of 20..........

(Set out cause title)

Suit for judicial separation under s. 10(1) of the Hindu Marriage Act.

The above-named petitioner states as follows:

1. That the petitioner, a Hindu female aged 21 years, was married to the respondent, at the petitioner's father's place at Mouja .... P.S. .... District .... within the jurisdiction of this Court on the 21st Falgoon, 14................ B.S. according to Hindu rites.

2. That the respondent after his marriage with the petitioner took the petitioner to his house at .... where the petitioner stayed for a week. Then she returned to her father's place and lived with parents till the end of ...., 14 .... B.S. By the first week of ...., 14........ B.S. the respondent took the petitioner at his house at .... where the petitioner lived with the respondent as husband and wife till ...., 14.........B.S.

3. That the respondent has no source of income of his own and has had no means to maintain his wife (petitioner). The respondent plainly confessed to the petitioner during her stay at husband's place in the period from ...., 14............ B.S. to........ 14............... B.S., that he could not maintain the petitioner and the petitioner should go back to her parents. As a matter of fact, during the aforesaid period the respondent neglected the petitioner as to food, wearings etc. and the petitioner was subjected to all sorts of ignominy.

4. That in ...., 14.......... B.S., the respondent having pressed hard, the petitioner was compelled to go to her father's place. The respondent then promised that he would seek some job and take her back within a month. The respondent, on expiry of a month or thereafter, did not bring her back. The petitioner through her relations requested the respondent to take the petitioner back, but to no result. That the petitioner has been living at her father's place since ...., 14......... B.S.

5. That the respondent has deserted the petitioner for more than two years continuously from Sravan, 14 .... B.S. when from the respondent is living separately intending to bring co-habitation permanently to an end. The plaintiff did not consent to such desertion.

6. That for continuous desertion by the husband for more than 2 years preceding the suit the petitioner is entitled to judicial separation from the respondent.

7. That the petitioner has no issue of their wedlock.

8. That this petition is not presented in collusion with the respondent.

9. That the cause of action for this petition arose at Mouja .... P.S. ....within the Jurisdiction of this Court in the month of ...., 14 .... B.S. ....

corresponding to ...., 20............., on completion of 2 years of continuous desertion by the Respondent.

10. That for the purpose of jurisdiction the suit is valued at ₹............ and fixed court-fees of ₹............ is paid.

The petitioner, therefore, prays:

(*a*) For a decree of judicial separation from the respondent;

(*b*) Costs.

Verification

Affidavit

NOTES: 1. Order 22 of CPC applies to suits and appeals under the Hindu Marriage Act—AIR 1971 Bom 183.

2. Desertion—For the offence of desertion so far as the deserting spouse is concerned two essential conditions must be there namely—(1) the factum of separation and (2) the intention to bring co-habitation permanently to an end and similarly two elements are also essential so far as the deserted spouse is concerned, namely—(1) the absence of consent and (2) absence of conduct giving reasonable cause to the spouse leaving the matrimonial home to form the intention aforesaid—*Bipin Chandra* v *Prabhabati* AIR 1957 SC 176. The burden of proving desertion and without just cause is upon the petitioner.

If a spouse is forced by the conduct of the other spouse to live separately or to stay away, in such a case there is no legal desertion to constitute a ground for divorce—*Toppo* v *Toppo* (1988)1 CLJ 294; *Elokeshi Chakraborty* v *Sunil Kumar* AIR 1991 Cal 176.

3. Hindu Marriage Act, s. 13(1)(*ib*)—Desertion.

If the spouses could not live together, do not live together and they swear that they would no longer live or be able to live together then we have no doubt that desertion by the one or the other is complete whoever might have given the initial cause, because all the three elements that generally go to constitute 'desertion', namely the factum of separation, the *animus deserendi*, i.e. the intention to live apart and the *animus non-revertendi*, i.e. the intention not to revert to matrimonial home stare at the face—*Apurba Mohon Ghosh* v *Manashi Ghosh* AIR 1989 Cal 115. Also see *Rohini Kumari* v *Narendra Singh* AIR 1972 SC 459.

Desertion is the intentional permanent forsaking and abandoning of one's spouse by the other without that other's consent and without reasonable cause—*L.U. Kripalani* v *Mana* AIR 1964 SC 40. The law is well settled that for the offence of desertion so far as the deserting spouse is concerned, two essential conditions must be there, namely—(1) the factum of separation and (2) the intention to bring co-habitation permanently to an end and similarly, two elements are also essential so far as the deserted spouse is concerned namely, (1) the absence of consent and (2) absence of conduct giving reasonable cause to the spouse leaving the matrimonial home to form the intention aforesaid—*Bipin Chandra* v *Prabhabati* AIR 1957 SC 176.

499. Application for restitution of conjugal rights (Muslim)

In the Family Court at ....

Matrimonial Suit No. .... 20............

(Set out cause title)

The plaintiff states as follows:

1. That the defendant was married to the plaintiff in the month of .... in the year 20 .... The said marriage is still subsisting and the defendant is still the wife of the plaintiff.

2. That the defendant left the care of, and deserted, the plaintiff since .... and the defendant has been living with her brother at .... since then.

3. That the plaintiff has requested the defendant through plaintiff's agent Md. A.B., on .... to come and live with the plaintiff but to no effect.

4. That the plaintiff is entitled to restitution of conjugal rights.

5. That the cause of action for this suit arose on .... at .... within the jurisdiction of this Court.

6. That the suit is valued at ₹.................... for the purpose of jurisdiction and court-fees and fixed court-fees of ₹............ are paid.

The plaintiff prays for:

A decree directing the defendant to live with the plaintiff and allowing the plaintiff to exercise conjugal rights.

Verification

Affidavit

NOTES: 1. Restitution of conjugal rights of a Hindu can be had by a petition under s. 9 of the Hindu Marriage Act 1955. Remarriage cannot, stand in the way of a decree for restitution—AIR 1971 J&K 31. In a husband's suit for restitution of conjugal rights the wife cannot be compelled to live with the husband if she has a reasonable apprehension that her life with the husband is impossible or dangerous to her—AIR 1971 Bom 166.

2. Marriage of the defendant with the plaintiff and her desertion of plaintiff should be averred and proved.

3. In a suit like this an injunction may be claimed against relations of the wife if they prevent the wife from going to her husband.

4. Court-fees—

For restitution under Hindu Marriage Act	....	₹ 5
Restitution of Muslim	....	₹ 10
Restitution under the Special Marriage Act	....	₹ 5

5. Limitation—Formerly old residuary Art. 120 providing 6 years; —now Art. 113 providing 3 years.

500. Application for divorce by a Muslim wife on ground of impotency of the husband

In the Family Court at ....

Matrimonial Suit No. .... 20............

(Set out cause title)

The plaintiff states:

1. That the parties hereto are Muslims by faith.

2. The plaintiff was married to the defendant on the .... day of .... 20........ at the plaintiff's father's house at village .... P.S. .... within the District of ....

3. The plaintiff lived with the defendant at the latter's house until the month of .... 20......... as husband and wife when the plaintiff returned to the house of her father.

4. That while so living with the defendant the plaintiff found that the defendant was impotent. He was so at the time of his marriage with the plaintiff and is so and has failed to consummate the marriage.

5. The plaintiff is entitled to dissolution of her marriage with the defendant by the reason aforesaid.

6. Cause of action—date of knowledge.

7. Suit—valuation (Fixed court-fees of ₹.......... under the West Bengal Court-fees Act 1970).

The plaintiff claims:

(*a*) dissolution of her marriage with the defendant;

(*b*) maintenance;

(*c*) cost of the suit;

(*d*) other relief (if necessary).

Verification

Affidavit

501. Petition for divorce by mutual consent

In the Court of .... at ....

Matrimonial Suit No. .... of 20............

AB (Name, description and address)

.... *Petitioner No. 1*

CD (Name, description and address)

.... *Petitioner No.* 2

Petition under section 13B of the Hindu Marriage Act 1955

The petitioners states as follows:

1. That the petitioners were married to each other on .... according to Hindu rites and ceremonies within the jurisdiction of this court.

2. That owing to incompatibility of temperaments between the petitioners they could not pull on well in matrimonial life. They have also not been able to live together.

3. That the petitioners have been living separately for more than one year.

4. That there is no issue of the petitioners.

5. That the petitioners have mutually agreed that their marriage should be dissolved.

6. That this court has jurisdiction and the court-fees have been paid according to law.

It is therefore prayed that a decree of divorce dissolving the marriage of the petititoners be granted.

Guardians and Wards

502. Petition for appointment of a guardian of a minor

In the Court of the District Judge at ....

Misc. (Guardianship) Case No. .... of 20 ....

or

Act VIII Case No. .... of 20 ....

In the matter of appointment of Guardian of

(A)
(B) } Minors.
(C)

Under s. 10 of the Guardians and Wards Act1890

And

In the matter of

'M', widow of late D by faith Muslim, residing at village......... P.S. .... District ....

.... *Petitioner*

The humble petition of the aforesaid petitioner respectfully sheweth:

1. That A, B and C are the sons of late "D" who are ordinarily residing at Vill. .... P.S. .... District .... within the jurisdiction of this court, were born respectively in .... B.S. .... B.S. and .... B.S. and by faith are .... and by sex are.............

2. That the said minors are entitled to certain property; nature, situation and approximate value of which are:

Locality	*Khatain No.*	*Area*	*Approx. value*
Mouja			
Plot No. & Khation No.			
J.L. No.			
P.S.			
District			
		Total	₹...............

3. That the said property is in the possession of one 'P', grandfather of minors, residing at Vill. .... P.S. .... District ....

4. That M the mother of minors, has the custody of the person of the said minors.

5. That the minors have the following near relations:

(*i*) P son of late Q. — Grandfather of minors residing at Vill. .... P.S. .... District ....

(*ii*) son of T. — Maternal grandfather of minors, residing at Vill. .... P.S. .... District ......

(*iii*) E.
(*iv*) F.
(*v*) G. } Sons of Z—Maternal uncles of minors residing at Vill. .... P.S. .... District ....

6. That no application has at any time been made to this court, or to any other court, with respect to the guardianship of the person and property of the said minors.

7. That no guardian of the person or property of the said minors has been appointed by any authority.

8. That this application is for the appointment of a guardian to the person and property of the said minors.

9. That your petitioner is the mother of the minors. The minors were so long living in the same mess along with their mother with grandfather P. The said P was neglecting the welfare of the minors and appropriated to himself all the returns from minors' properties. Of late he stopped payment of tuition fees of private tutor of minors A and B. In last......... B.S. the said P managed to transfer minors' .... bighas of land in the name of his daughter .... by a fraudulent and forged kobala after the death of minors' father. Besides, he is selling the produce of the lands of the minors and appropriating proceeds to himself. He has kept the revenue in arrear for .... years for which minors' properties are liable to be sold for Certificate Proceedings. To recover possession of the land, to manage properties, for the welfare of minors the situation requires that the mother petitioner be appointed guardian for minors without further delay.

(Or, that the appointment is necessary for sale of a portion of minor's property for meeting debts left by the deceased father of minors).

That your petitioner, therefore, prays that an order appointing the petitioner a guardian for the person and property of minors be issued under s. 7 of the Guardians and Wards Act 1890.

And your petitioner, as in duty bound, shall ever pray.

Verification

Affidavit

NOTES: 1. See the Form (J) 62 prescribed by the Calcutta High Court, C.R. and for West Bengal Orders Vol. II.

2. See Rule 296 (C.R.O. Vol. 1 of Calcutta High Court).
No. 296(2) where the father of the minor is living, and is not proposed as guardian, the application shall also state any facts relied on as showing that he is unfit to act as guardian of the minor, or that he consents to the application.

3. The declaration of the willingness of the proposed guardian to act may be inserted at the foot of or annexed to, or exhibited with the petition.

4. Particulars required in the application are to be found in s. 10 of the Guardians and Wards Act.

5. See s. 8 of the Guardians and Wards Act—for persons entitled to apply.

503. Petition for custody of child

In the Family Court at ....

Matrimonial Case No. .... of 20 ....

A.B. .... *Petitioner*

versus

C.D. .... *Respondent*

Petition under s. 26 of the Hindu Marriage Act 1955, for custody of child.

The petitioner states as follows:

1. That the petitioner has commenced in this court the above proceeding against the respondent praying for a decree of judicial separation from the respondent under provisions contained in s. 10 of the Hindu Marriage Act. The said proceeding is pending.

2. That the petitioner and the respondent have a son Sriman E.F. born of the wedlock on the .... day of ...., 14 .... B.S. and the boy is now aged 6 years 11 months and odd.

3. That the said boy is now living at the father's place in a very wretched condition as if a charity boy. The boy is not receiving any proper education and he is being neglected. That for the welfare of the boy he should be reared up by his mother. The boy also intends to put up with the petitioner.

It is, therefore, prayed that Your Honour may be pleased to pass necessary order on the respondent:

(*i*) for handing over custody of Sriman E.F. to the petitioner till disposal of the proceeding;

(*ii*) for an interim order in the light of the above prayer.

Verification

Affidavit

NOTES:
1. See Guardians and Wards Act. Words 'care' and 'custody' in s. 4 are different though they may also be used synonymously—*Hasmat Ali* v *Suraya Begum* AIR 1971 All 260.
2. Section 6 of the Hindu Minority and Guardianship Act shall apply having overriding effect—74 CWN 690.
3. Welfare of minor to be paramount consideration. Mother declared entitled to guardianship and custody of a child 11 years old—*Smt. Mohini* v *Virender Kumar* AIR 1977 SC 1359.
4. Where the minor is not ordinarily resident within the jurisdiction of the District Court concerned, it will have no jurisdiction to proceed under the Act (Guardian and Wards Act)—AIR 1979 Raj 128.
5. Section 17 conversion to a different faith cannot be regarded as a disqualification for the custody of the minor so long as the guardian is capable of providing a congenial, comfortable and a happy home for the minor—*Sheila Umesh Tahiliani* v *Soli Phiroj Shaw* AIR 1981 Bom 175.
6. Father though a natural guardian, welfare of ward is of paramount consideration. Looking to the status in life of parties, availability of educational at facility, mother having permanent home, sufficient earning and her parents to look after the child in her absence, the custody of child was directed to remain with her—*Jayant Bavar* v *Smt. Deepa Bavar* AIR 1994 NOC 269 (MP).
7. Meaning of the expression 'Child's Welfare'—*Tarun Ranjan Majumder* v *Siddhartha Dutta* AIR 1991 Cal 76.

504. Petition for custody of child (Another Form)

In the Family Court at ....

(Matrimonial Jurisdiction)

Matrimonial Suit No. .... of ....

AB (Name, description and address)

.... *Petitioner*

versus

CD (Name, description and address)

...... *Respondent*

Petition for custody of child

The petitioner states as follows:

1. That your petitioner has filed a petition for divorce against the respondent *inter alia* on the ground of cruelty and the same is pending in this Court.

2. That a female child named .... was born to the parties to the proceeding on .... and she is now aged .... years.

3. That the respondent is neglecting up bringing of the child according to status and does not look after her education, full and harmonious development of her personality, in a word, the respondent is not looking after the welfare of the child.

4. That before now the petitioner tried to bring the child to her custody for her welfare, but the respondent has been forcibly resisting the said child to come and live with the petitioner.

5. That the petitioner is now appointed as an assistant teacher of XY Institution and drawing salary of ₹.................. per month. Accordingly she is now capable enough to maintain the child, including its proper educational expenses.

6. That in the above premises your petitioner is entitled to custody of the said child for the benefit and welfare of the child.

It is, therefore, prayed that the court may be graciously pleased to pass

(*a*) an appropriate order for custody of .... the female child to the petitioner;

(*b*) interim order in terms of prayer (*a*);

(c) costs.

Verification

Affidavit

NOTES: 1. See the provision of s. 7(1) jurisdiction—Explanation 'G' of the Family Courts Act 1984.

2. Interest of the child is of paramount consideration in deciding grant of custody of a minor child—*Veena Kapoor* v *V.K. Kapoor* AIR 1982 SC 792.

505. Suit by father for custody of minor from the maternal grandmother

In the Family Court at ....

or

In the Court of .... at ....

Misc. Case No. .... of 20 ....

(Act VIII of 1890)

(Set out cause title)

Petition for seeking order under s. 12 of the Guardians and Wards Act 1890

The humble petition of the above-named petitioner most respectfully sheweth:

1. That the petitioner is the father and natural guardian of the minor X.

2. That on .... (date) .... petitioner's wife and the mother of the minor X, died when she was being operated upon in the .... Hospital.

3. At that time X, the minor was one and half years old.

4. After death of the petitioner's wife, the petitioner became the only person in his family. There was no other person to look after X, the minor. However, the maternal grandmother took the minor to her family on ....

5. After completing the rituals, the petitioner made arrangement for the minor and asked the maternal grandmother to return the minor to him, but she paid no heed.

6. Both the petitioner and the maternal grandmother of the minor are living within the jurisdiction of this learned court.

7. The suit is not barred by law of limitation.

It is, therefore, prayed that the maternal grandmother of the minor be directed to return the minor to the father.

Verification

Affidavit

506. Petition for permission for sale of minor's property

In the Court of the District Judge .... Family Court at ......

Misc. Judicial Case No. .... of 20 ....

Petitioner:

A.B. widow of late .... by caste .... residing at village .... P.S. .... District ....

The above-named petitioner states as follows:

1. That one C.D., husband of the petitioner held properties described in the Schedule "A" below.

2. That the said C.D. died on the ................B.S. leaving as his heirs his three sons and his widow.

(*i*) P.

(*ii*) Q.

(*iii*) R.

(*iv*) A.B. widow of C.D.

each of whom inherited the said properties in equal shares. The said P, Q and R are minors and they are living in the care and custody of the petitioner.

3. That the said minors have following near relations:

(*a*) (State here name, description, place of residence of the

(*b*) relatives and their respective relationship with the

(*c*) minors—See Note 3 below).

4. That the petitioner's husband incurred a debt of ₹ .... from one Sri .... son of .... of .... P.S. .... District .... during his life-time. The debt was not liquidated and the minors are liable to pay the debt. The said creditor is threatening the minors with suit for realisation of his dues. That minors have no fund to liquidate the debt. The debt can be liquidated only by sale of 50% of the property in the Schedule below.

(Or, state the reason necessitating sale of minor's property).

5. That the petitioner has entered into talks of sale of 50%, of the said property with one .... (state name, description and address of the proposed vendee) and the price has been tentatively fixed at ₹.................... The fair market value of the said 50%, property would be ₹............. only.

6. That such transaction will be to the benefit and welfare of minors (or, would be beneficial to the minors' interest).

It is, therefore, prayed that Your Honour would be pleased to accord necessary permission for sale of minors' 50%, share in the property in Schedule "A" below for ₹................ and to apply the sale proceeds towards liquidation of the aforesaid debt.

SCHEDULE

(Here describe the property)

Verification

Affidavit

NOTES: 1. Under s. 27 of the Guardians and Wards Act (Act VIII of 1890), a guardian of the property of a ward, subject to provisions of Chapter III of the Act, may do "all acts which are reasonable and proper for the realisation, protection or benefit of the property". Section 28 speaks of the power of testamentary guardian and s. 29 of the Act impose limitation of the powers of guardian of property appointed or declared by the court. Under s. 30 a transfer in contravention of provisions of ss. 28 and 29 is voidable at the instance of any other person affected thereby.

2. Section 8 of the Hindu Minority and Guardianship Act 1956, prescribes additional restrictions on the power of a natural guardian of a Hindu minor. Under provisions in s. 8(2) of this Act, the natural guardian shall not, without the previous permission of the court, mortgage, or charge or transfer by sale, gift, exchange etc. Again permission shall not be granted to the natural guardian "except in case of necessity or for an evident advantage to the minor." (cf. s. 29 of the Guardians and Wards Act). Under s. 8(5) of the Hindu Minority and Guardianship Act, it is enjoined: "The Guardians and Wards Act shall apply to and in respect of an application for obtaining the permission of the court under sub-sec. (2) in all respects as if it were an application for obtaining permission of the court under s. 29 of the Act..........." No form of petition has been prescribed by the Act VIII of 1890. Permission under s. 29 shall not be granted except in case of necessity or for an evident advantage to the ward. Therefore, an application shall contain materials sufficient to justify the transaction promoting benefit of the minor—See ILR 6 Cal 161.

3. Under s. 31(4) of the Act VIII of 1890, the court may cause notice of the application to be given to any relative as friend of the ward—11 IC 946. The court is not bound to issue notice.

507. Application for production of minor and interim protection of the person and/or property of the minor

Petitioner:

X, widow of late .... by caste .... residing at village .... P.S. .... District ....

* * *

In the matter of ....
.... An application seeking order under section 12 of the Guardians and Wards Act.

The humble petition of X most respectfully sheweth:

1. That on .... the petitioner has filed the above application for appointment of a guardian of the person and/or property of minor A.

2. That in the meantime things have come to such a pass that the welfare and interest of the minor's person and/or property have been placed at great stake inasmuch as the present guardian of the person, in whose custody the minor and/or his properties is/are, is not taking any interest whatsoever with respect to safety, health, education, maintenance and upkeep of the minor and/or proper management of his properties.

(Here mention details of such acts and omissions in separate paragraphs).

3. ....

4. ....

5. That unless immediate order for the production of the minor before this court is passed and interim arrangement for his protection is made the safety of the minor *vis-a-vis* his welfare and interest will be in great jeopardy.

Or

That unless immediate orders are passed placing the properties of the minor under an interim guardian, the entire/a large portion of the property of the minor will be lost to the minor.

6. That the welfare and interest of the minor demand immediate appointment of an interim guardian for the protection of the person and/or property of the minor.

Under the circumstances it is prayed that Your Honour may be pleased to pass orders—

(*i*) directing ...., the present guardian/the present custodian to produce the minor before this court and to produce all papers relating to the properties of the minor before this court, and

(*ii*) on such production appoint an interim guardian/custodian for the protection of the person of the minor and management of his properties or to pass such other or further orders as Your Honour may deem fit and proper.

And your petitioner as in duty bound shall ever pray.

Verification

Affidavit

508. Petition for having back the custody of the minor when the minor was removed

In the District Court at ....

(Minority, Guardianship and Custody Matter)

Misc. Case No. .... of 20............

(Under Act VIII of 1890)

In the matter of ....

An application under s. 25 of the Guardians and Wards Act 1890;

And

In the matter of ....

A ...., son of .... of P.S. ...., District ...., A minor

And

In the matter of ....

B ...., son of ..... of P.S. ....., District ....

.... *Petitioner*

versus

C ...., son of .... of ......, P.S. ..... District

..........*Opposite Party.*

The humble petition of petitioner above-named most respectfully sheweth:

1. That ...., the aforesaid minor, is at present aged .... years and has not as yet acquired sufficient intelligence to express any choice about his guardianship and custody and to understand what will be to his welfare and best interest.

2. That the said minor is my son and for all purposes I am his natural guardian.

Or

That the said minor was since his birth completely neglected by his father ...., the opposite party, who has never taken any interest whatsoever in the minor and because of the same and the minor being my own sister's son, both the minor and my sister are residing under my care and I have maintained them so long in proper way and have made all arrangements for the education of the said minor, who is now reading in class .... in the PQ Institution at .... My nephew, the said minor, was thus in my care and custody since about a year after his birth.

3. That during my absence from my home, my wife had been to her brother's .... place at .... to visit them taking my said minor son with her and when on .... I went to bring back my wife and the said minor son to my own home, while my wife came with me, the opposite party, who is my brother-in-law, did not allow by said minor son to return on the plea that as he has been admitted in a school there

and is having his education there, he cannot be allowed to have a break in the progress of his education.

Or

That on ...., during my absence, my said brother-in-law, the opposite party, came to my place, and without waiting for my arrival has taken away my sister as also the minor to his place.

4. That this act on the part of the opposite party has been tantamount to removal of the said minor from my lawful custody.

5. That the best interest and welfare of the minor demands that the said minor should be placed under my custody immediately (IN CASE OF THE FATHER BEING THE PETITIONER—ADD). I being the natural guardian of the minor I am entitled to have the custody of my minor son.

Under the circumstances the petitioner humbly prays that Your Honour may be pleased to direct the opposite party to produce the minor before this court and to pass necessary orders enabling me to have custody of the minor or to pass such other or further order or orders as Your Honour may deem fit and proper.

And your petitioner as in duty bound shall ever pray.

Verification

Affidavit

509. Petition for discharge of a guardian appointed by the court

In the Court of the District Judge at..............

Misc. (Guardianship) Case No. .... of 20...

In the matter of:

1. A.B. minor sons of late .... residing at .... P.S. .... District ....
2. C.D.

And

In the matter of E.F. .... Certificated Guardian—

.... *Petitioner*

Petition for discharge under s. 40(1) of the Guardians and Wards Act 1890.

The plaintiff states as follows:

1. That the petitioner was appointed guardian of the person and property of aforesaid minors by this court by orders dated .... in Misc. .... (Guardianship) Case No. .... of 20 ....

2. That the petitioner has been suffering from various ailments for the last .... months and cannot attend to his normal work. It has been impossible for him to look

after the interest of the minors any further and or to discharge responsibilities of his office.

3. That the petitioner seeks to resign his office with effect from the date when Your Honour would be pleased to accept resignation.

4. That your petitioner has submitted in the court an up-to-date accounts of the minors' properties which was also audited by the competent officer of the court and there was no objection.

It is, therefore, prayed that the petitioner may kindly be discharged from office as also from liabilities.

Verification

Affidavit

NOTES: 1. Discharge from office (s. 40) does not guarantee discharge from liabilities (s. 41).
2. Refusal is appealable under s. 47 but appeal shall lie to the High Court.
3. The court may remove a guardian (s. 39) on application by any person interested or *suo motu* on grounds in cls. (*a*) to (*j*) of s. 39.

MENTAL HEALTH CARE

510. Petition for inquisition under the Mental Health Care Act

In the Court of Shri .... M.A., LL.B. etc.

District Judge..............

Misc. (Lunacy) Case No. .... of 20 ....

A.B. etc. .... *Petitioner*

Prayer for appointment of manager of the properties of .... of unsound mind and for custody of his person under the Mental Health Act 1987

The above-named petitioner respectfully submits:

1. That C, son of D, ordinarily residing at vill. .... P.S. .... District .... was born on .... B.S./A.D. and is by religion .... and by sex .... He is Indian by domicile and an agriculturist.

2. That the said C since the month of .... B.S./A.D. has become unsound in mind and incapable of managing his property and taking care of his person.

3. That the said C, is married but his wife had deserted him under the machinations of some interested persons nearly .... years back.

4. That the said C, is entitled to certain property within the jurisdiction of this court, to wit.

Sl. No.	*Situation*	*Nature*	*Approximate value*
....	....	....	....
....	....	....	....

5. That the annual income of the said property is ₹...................... approximately.

6. That the said property is in the custody of A.B., the petitioner named above, residing at vill. .... P.S. .... District .... and is being cultivated by another son of your petitioner.

7. That one .... son of late .... and .... son of .... of vill. .... P.S. .... District .... has taken away the said C.D. .... at the residence of .... at .... year .... months back against his mother's consent with a motive of getting his property transferred in the name of the said...................... That the said C.D. is at present in the custody of .... and .... within the jurisdiction of this court. That there is a criminal case pending in the court of .... for recovery of the said C.D.

8. That the said C.D. has the following near relations:

(*a*) A.B. widow of late ....
of vill. .... P.S. .... District ....
Mother of the mentally ill person.

(*b*) E.F. etc.

(*c*) G.H. etc. both of village .... P.S. .... District ....
Mothers' brothers of the mentally ill person.

9. That there was no prior application in any court for appointment of manager of the mentally ill person's property or guardian for his person.

10. That reasonable apprehension of alienation of the mentally ill person's property by the said .... referred to in para 6 above has given occasion to this application. The petitioner is the mother of the mentally ill person and she intends to save the property of the mentally ill person from apprehended fraudulent transactions of .... and .... referred to above.

11. That the mentally ill person is not violent but he understands nothing and has no control over his intelligence. Since the mentally ill person C.D. is incapable of managing his property and taking care of his person, this application is being filed by the mother of the mentally ill person.

12. An affidavit in support of the petition and two medical certificates, issued by registered medical practitioners are enclosed and may be treated as part of this petition.

Your petitioner, therefore, prays that Your Honour would be pleased to order for service of notice of application upon the alleged mentally ill person and upon his relations and direct an inquisition under s. 54 of the Mental Health Act 1987, as to his lunacy and when satisfied, order for appointment of your petitioner as the manager of the mentally ill person's estate and guardian for his person may please be passed.

Verification

Affidavit

NOTES: 1. For proceedings within the State of West Bengal, see Rule 328 (1-8) of the Civil Rules & Orders, Vol. I, published by the Calcutta High Court.

2. Every such application shall set forth the following particulars, namely:
   (*a*) Name, age and residence of the alleged mentally ill person (if a minor, name of person acting as guardian), also his position in life and domicile.
   (*b*) Whether the alleged mentally ill person is married or unmarried or a widow or widower.
   (*c*) Names and addresses of all near relatives of, and persons interested, in the alleged mentally ill person.

(*d*) Concise description of the property of the alleged mentally ill person and the income thereof.

(*e*) A statement of the interest of the applicant in making the application.

(*f*) A concise statement of the facts on which the application is based, stating, where possible, the nature of the alleged lunacy and the time during which it is alleged that he has been of unsound mind.

(*g*) Name of persons (if any) proposed for appointment as manager of the alleged mentally ill person's estate and/or guardian of his person vide Rule 328/2.

3. "Every such application, unless made by the Government pleader, shall be supported by an affidavit; and every such application, whether made by the Government pleader or by any other person, shall be accompanied by the certificate of two registered medical practitioners who had reasonable opportunity of seeing and observing the alleged mentally ill person. Such certificates shall be to the effect that in the opinion of the writers the person in question is insane or incapable of managing himself or his affairs. Such certificates shall also state whether or not, in the opinion of the medical practitioners, service of notice of the proceedings on the alleged mentally ill person would be ineffectual by reason of his state of mind and whether or not if it is undesirable on medical grounds that he should be required to attend for the purpose of being personally examined"—*Vide* Rule 328/3 of C.R.O. Vol. 1.

PUBLIC DEMANDS RECOVERY

Section 3(2) of the Act defines the "Certificate Holder" which means Government or person in whose favour a certificate has been filed under the said Act and includes any person whose name has been substituted later on or added subsequently or credited by the Certificate Officer concerned.

Certificate Officer is a Collector or Sub-district Officer or an authorised officer to perform the functions of the Certificate Officer.

Section 4 of the said Act provides that a Certificate Officer may issue a Certificate stating that a demand is due.

Section 6 of the said Act provides that if the Certificate Officer is fully satisfied that the said demand is recoverable and that a suit is not barred by provisions of any law then he will sign the Certificate which is to be filed in his office.

Under section 7 of the said Act the Certificate Officer issues a notice on the Certificate debtor, and the Certificate Officer under ss. 13 and 14 may execute the Certificate issued by him.

Under ss. 17 and 20 of the said Act the Certificate Officer may attach and sell the properties in question.

Section 23 provides for an application to be made to set aside the sale.

511. Petition under s. 23 of the Bengal Public Demands Recovery Act 1913 for setting aside a sale

Before the Certificate Officer

Land Reforms Office (Sadar South Circle)............

Misc. Case No. .... of 20.............

A.B. etc. ....

.... *Applicant*

versus

1. C.D. etc. ....

.... *Auction Purchaser*

2. E.F. etc. ....

.... *Certificate Debtor*

The humble petition of the above-named applicant most respectfully sheweth:

1. That the sale of the property, described in the Schedule below, in the Certificate Case No.......... of .... of the Certificate Officer of .... on .... should be set aside on the following amongst other grounds:

(*a*) That G and H, sons of M of village .... P.S. .... District .... held in equal shares in a land measuring .... plot No. .... khatians .... The said land is described in the Schedule below .... G, having died unmarried and intestate his 8 anna interest in the land devolved on his brother H said .... possessed 16 anna of the chukani and died leaving .... (O.P. No. 2) as his only heiress/heir who then came to acquire 16 anna interest in the land. Landuri sold the holding to one .... by a registered kobala dated .... B.S. .... possessed the holding and thereafter died leaving .... and only .... while possessing the land sold the holding to the applicant A.B. by a registered kobala dated .... B.S. The applicant since then had been in possession of the said property in the Schedule below under his own right, title and interest till the possession was delivered on .... to O.P. No. 1 ....

(*b*) That in the current settlement the said property stands recorded in the names of .... and .... in Khatian No. .... of Mouja .... P.S. .... for .... acres. Said Khatian is erroneous. That though mutation of name of the applicant was not effected the applicant's interest in the property will be materially affected in the event of the sale not being vacated.

(*c*) That the Certificate Proceedings No. .... of .... have been void *ab initio* as

(*i*) the proceedings were initiated against the deceased .... and .... who died .... years and .... years back respectively,

(*ii*) that the notice under s. 7 of the Bengal Public Demands Recovery Act has not been served lawfully,

(*iii*) that even if there be any service return, the same is forged and not genuine,

(*iv*) the sale proclamation has not been lawfully published on the land and all processes have been fraudulently suppressed and the whole of the Certificate proceedings is tainted with fraud and is nothing better than a paper transaction,

(*v*) that the notice served on .... under s. 43 is illegal.

(*d*) That the property is valued at present at ₹......... only. That for the aforesaid acts of fraud and fraudulent suppression of all the processes the property has been sold at a very low price and as a result the applicant has been put to much loss.

(*e*) That the present state of things has been brought above by the collusive suppression of processes, etc., at the instance of the opposite parties, the certificate debtors and the auction-purchaser. Your petitioner has sustained substantial injury by reason of such fraud and irregularity.

(*f*) That the whole transaction of the sale being tainted with fraud, your petitioner had not the least knowledge of the same or of his right to set aside the sale.

(*g*) That on .... when the auction-purchaser attempted to take possession your petitioner came to know about the sale and consequently the present petition, reckoned from date of knowledge, is not barred by limitation. This petition is within two months from the date of his knowledge.

Your petitioner accordingly prays that Your Honour would be graciously pleased to pass orders setting aside the sale and allowing costs to your petitioner.

SCHEDULE

Verification

Affidavit

512. Petition under s. 22 of the Bengal Public Demands Recovery Act 1913

(Bengal Act No. III of 1913)

Before the Certificate Officer at...................

Misc. (Cert.) Case No. ... of 20..................

A.B. ....

.... *Petitioner (Certificate Debtor)*

versus

1. C.D. ....

......*Opposite Party (Certificate Holder)*

2. E.F. ....

.......*Opposite Party (Auction Purchaser)*

Petition for setting aside a sale of immovable property under s. 22 of the Bengal Public Demands Recovery Act 1913.

The above-named (A.B.) petitioner states as follows:

1. That in the Certificate Proceedings No. .... of .... the immovable property of the petitioner, described in the Schedule below, has been sold in execution of the Certificate and the Opposite Party No. 2 purchased the same on .... on payment of ₹ .... only.

2. That the petitioner hereby deposits with this office/court—

(*i*) a sum of ₹ ...., the amount specified in the proclamation of sale with interest therein at $12^1/_2$% per annum, calculated from the date of the Certificate to the date of deposit;

(*ii*) a sum of ₹ .... (the sum should be equal to 5% of the purchase money) for payment to the purchaser (Opposite Party No. 2) as penalty;

(*iii*) a sum of ₹ .... for payment to the Collector .... as outstanding charges due to the Government (where the Certificate is for a public demand payable to the Collector, the sum should be what the Collector certifies to be payable by the Certificate debtor).

It is, therefore, prayed that the said sale in respect of the property, in the Schedule below, be set aside after notice to the Opposite Party.

SCHEDULE

(State here particulars of the property)

Verification

Affidavit

NOTES: 1. Certificate debtor or the Certificate holder or any person whose interest is affected by sale can apply.

2. Application and deposit must be made within 30 days from the date of sale. Mere deposit is not sufficient—ILR 43 Bom 735. Calcutta view otherwise—ILR 25 Cal 216 under s. 12(1) of the Limitation Act, the day of sale is to be excluded in calculating 30 days.

3. Period of limitation is 30 days. The court cannot extend 30 days—16 CWN 736.

4. No appeal lies from an order s. 22 of the Act.

MATRIMONIAL CAUSES

The Family Courts Act 1984 in s. 20 therein provides that the provisions of the said Act will have an overriding effect.

The provisions of the said Act shall have effect notwithstanding anything inconsistent therewith contained in any other law for the time being in force.

Section 21 of the said Act provides that the High Court by issuing a Notification may make Rules for carrying out the purposes of the Act.

Section 7 of the said Act provides for jurisdiction to be exercised under the Act. A Family Court shall have all jurisdiction exercisable under the said Act by any District Court or by any Subordinate Civil Court. The Family Court should be treated for all practical purposes as a District Court under the said Act. The Family Court provides for deciding the nullity of marriage, judicial separation, divorce, restitution of conjugal rights, or declaration as to the validity of a marriage, matrimonial status of a person, for settlement of a dispute as to property between a husband and his wife, injunction proceeding related to matrimonial relationship, legitimacy of a person, prayer for maintenance allowance, appointment of a guardian, custody or having access to any minor, and a Magistrate of First Class shall have the power to order for maintenance of helpless children by defaulting parents under provisions of the Code of Criminal Procedure 1973 and other such legal proceedings or powers that may be conferred. The Family Courts shall have all the powers of a Civil Court in general. In all the cases, the provisions of the Code of Criminal Procedure 1973 and the Rules framed thereunder shall apply to the legal proceedings included in Chapter IX of the Code of Criminal Procedure 1973 before a Family Court.

The Family Court shall also lay down its own procedure and rules with a view to arriving at a settlement in respect of subject-matter of the suit or proceedings to arrive at the truth of facts as alleged by one party as against the other.

Section 19 of the said Act provides for appeal or revision. Such an appeal shall lie from the judgment and order of a Family Court to the High Court both in facts and on law except from an Interlocutory Order.

Such an appeal has to be normally filed within a period of 30 days from the date of such judgment or order passed by the concerned Family Court. The High Court may also *suo motu* call for and examine the relevant records of the proceedings held before the Family Court. Further, against an order under provisions of the Code of Criminal Procedure 1973, an appeal has to be heard by a Bench of two or more Judges except as provided under s. 19 of the said Act. No appeal or revision shall lie to any other Court from any order or judgment or decree passed by Family Court.

513. Petition for judicial separation under the Hindu Marriage Act 1955

(By a wife on the ground of desertion)

In the Hon'ble Family Court at ....

Matrimonial Case No. .... of 20 ....

A.B. .... *Petitioner*

versus

C.D. .... *Respondent*

Petition for judicial separation under s. 10 of the Hindu Marriage Act 1955

The above-named petitioner states as follows:

1. That the petitioner was married to the respondent on .... at the residence of your petitioner's father at .... P.S. ...., District .... according to Hindu rites and ceremonies within the jurisdiction of this court.

2. That after her marriage with the respondent, the petitioner and the respondent lived together as husband and wife at .... until ...., 20.........

3. That your petitioner and the respondent have a son born of wedlock. He is now aged 3 years (Or, that no issue was born to the petitioner and the respondent out of their marriage).

4. That on the said date (........., 20.........) the respondent deserted the petitioner and left the matrimonial home and since then the respondent is continuing the act of desertion for a period more than two years.

5. That this petition is not presented in collusion with the respondent (where necessary add: "There has not been unnecessary delay in instituting the proceeding").

6. That the cause of action for this petition arose at .... within the jurisdiction of this court on ...., 20........., when desertion for two years was completed.

The petitioner prays:

(*i*) a decree of judicial separation between your petitioner and the respondent,

(*ii*) costs.

Verification

Affidavit

NOTES: 1. Petition has to be filed in the Family Court. For definition of 'District Court'— see s. 3(*b*) of the Hindu Marriage Act 1955. See also s. 19 for jurisdiction.
2. The petition shall be verified as required by law (Or. 6, r 14 of CPC) for verification of a plaint.
3. For what amounts to 'desertion'—see s. 10. In addition—AIR 1970 Cal 266; AIR 1970 Mys 59; AIR 1964 SC 40.
4. Delay in filing petition may disentitle a petitioner to relief—it has to be shown that delay was both unnecessary and improper—AIR 1970 MP 36.
5. Order 9, r. 9 provisions are applicable—AIR 1978 Punj 150.
6. Demand for dowry by itself amounts to cruelty entitling the wife to get a decree for dissolution of marriage—*Sobha Rani* v *Madhukar Reddi* AIR 1988 SC 121.

514. Petition for restitution of conjugal rights under the Hindu Marriage Act (by a wife)

In the Court of the District Judge at ....

Matrimonial Case No. .... of 20.........

A.B. .... *Petitioner*

versus

C.D. .... *Respondent*

Petition for restitution of conjugal rights under s. 9 of the Hindu Marriage Act 1955.

The above-named petitioner states as follows:

1. That the petitioner was married to the respondent on .... at the residence of your petitioner's father at .... P.S. ...., District .... according to Hindu rites and ceremonies within the jurisdiction of this court.

2. That after her marriage with the respondent, the petitioner and the respondent lived together as husband and wife at .... until ...., 20.........

3. That your petitioner and the respondent have a son born of wedlock. He is now aged 3 years (Or, that no issue was born to the petitioner and the respondent out of their marriage).

4. That the respondent, without reasonable excuse, withdrew himself from the society of the petitioner on .... and since then the respondent has been living out of her society and has been denying the petitioner conjugal rights.

5. That your petitioner is entitled to restitution of conjugal rights and there is no legal bar to the grant of such decree.

6. That the cause of action for this petition arose on .... when the respondent withdrew himself from the society of your petitioner at .... within the jurisdiction of this court.

The petitioner, therefore, prays for:

A decree directing the respondent to receive the petitioner and live with her and render her conjugal rights.

Verification

Affidavit

NOTES: 1. Regular suit for restitution of conjugal rights is inconsistent with provisions of s. 9 of the Hindu Marriage Act (AIR 1959 MP 410) and the right has been taken away by s. 4 of the Act.

2. Court-fees—₹ 1—AIR 1958 AP 340. In West Bengal ₹ 5 (Vide item 20 of Schedule II of the West Bengal Court-fees Act).

3. Withdrawal of Society—Burden of proof—AIR 1979 MP 15. But see the Explanations to s. 9 of the Hindu Marriage Act 1955.

4. Delay in bringing a suit—AIR 1980 Raj 35.

5. Jurisdiction—Court of the District Judge under s. 19 of the Hindu Marriage Act. District Court means City Civil Court where there is one.

6. Husband, on facts, proved to have withdrawn from society of his wife without reasonable excuse. Wife would be entitled to decree for restitution of conjugal rights. Permanent alimony—Decree for restitution of conjugal rights, Court has jurisdiction under s. 25 to order payment of permanent alimony to her—*Sandhya* v *Gopinath* AIR 1983 Cal 161; AIR 1963 Cal 428 relying on.

515. Petition for restitution of conjugal rights under the Hindu Marriage Act (by a husband)

In the Court of the District Judge at ....

Matrimonial Case No. .... of 20.........

In the matter of the Hindu Marriage Act 1955

In the matter of ....

A.B. ....*Petitioner*

versus

C.D. .... *Respondent*

Petition for restitution of conjugal rights under s. 9 of the Hindu Marriage Act 1955.

The above-named petitioner states as follows:

1. That the respondent was married to the petitioner at former's father's place at .... P.S. .... District .... within the jurisdiction of this court on ....

2. That the petitioner and the respondent lived as husband and wife, until .... at your petitioner's place at .... dated .... when the respondent quite unexpectedly and without any reasonable cause withdrew herself from the society of your petitioner. She has been living at her father's place at .... since .... and has been denying the petitioner conjugal rights.

3. That no issue of their marriage was born to the parties hereto.

4. See Form No. 514 (page 687)

5. See Form No. 514 (page 687)

The petitioner, therefore, prays for a decree directing the respondent to come to live with the petitioner and render him his conjugal rights.

Verification

Affidavit

NOTES: 1. Husband has to prove want of reasonable excuse for withdrawal from society—AIR 1970 Mad 434—Contra: wife has to prove reasonable excuse for withdrawal—AIR 1970 Punj 284. The addition of Explanation to s. 9 of the Hindu Marriage Act now puts the burden of proving reasonable exercise on the person who has withdrawn from the society of the spouse.

2. Reasonable excuse—meaning of—AIR 1970 MP 36.

516. Defence by wife to husband's claim for restitution of conjugal rights

In the Court of .... at ....

Suit No. .... of 20 ....

(Set out cause title)

[The respondent may take one or more of the following defences]

1. The respondent was not validly married to the petitioner. The following ceremonies which are the most essential ingredients in the marriage of the............................ caste to which the parties belong, were not performed: (Give particulars).

2. At the time the respondent left the petitioner's house the petitioner was suffering from venereal diseases and he is still suffering from the same.

3. The petitioner after the marriage habitually treated the respondent cruelly by beating her at regular intervals and keeping her confined in a room without providing her with any food and the respondent cannot return to his house without endangering her personal safety.

4. The petitioner kept a low caste woman as his mistress in the house to live with him as a member of the family and thereby made it impossible for the respondent to live with the petitioner. The petitioner still keeps and maintains the said mistress in his house.

The respondent therefore prays to the learned court to dismiss the suit with costs.

Verification

Affidavit

517. Suit for annulment of marriage

In the court of.................................

In the Family Court at........................

Matrimonial Suit No.........................

In the matter of:

The Hindu Marriage Act 1955

And

In the matter of:

AB........... ...... *Petitioner*

versus

CD........... .... *Respondent*

Petition under section 12 of the Hindu Marriage Act

The petitioner states as follows:

1. That the petitioner and the respondent CD were married according to Hindu rites and customs on.................at....................within the jurisdiction of this court.

2. That after the said marriage between the parties herein the petitioner has discovered that the respondent is impotent and consequently the marriage was not consummated.

3. That the petitioner and the respondent are living separately from each other and there is no collusion between them.

4. That the cause of action in the case arose on..............when the petitioner discovered that the respondent is impotent.

5. That there is no unnecessary delay in instituting this case.

6. That this court has jurisdiction to entertain, try and determine the suit.

It is therefore prayed that the marriage between the parties herein be annulled by a decree of nullity.

Verification

Affidavit

518. Petition for divorce under the Hindu Marriage Act

In the Court of.......................at...............

Matrimonial Case No.........of 20.........

AB (Name, description and address)

...... *Petitioner*

versus

CD (Name, description and address)

...... *Respondent*

Petition under section 13 of the Hindu Marriage Act 1955

The petitioner states as follows:

1. That the petitioner was married to the respondent on.........at.........within the jurisdiction of this Court according to Hindu rites and ceremonies and they are governed by the Hindu Marriage Act 1955.

2. That both the petitioner and the respondent lived together immediately after solemnization of their marriage at the matrimonial home at..............as man and wife. They last resided at...............from...........to............

3. That a male child was born of their lawful wedlock on....................

4. That the respondent has renounced the world by entering into a religious order and has become a sanyasi by leaving the matrimonial home permanently on ....

5. That there is no collusion between the petitioner and the respondent.

6. That the cause of action arose on.................when the respondent had permanently left the matrimonial home on entering into the religious order as aforesaid.

7. That this court has jurisdiction to entertain, try and determine this matter.

8. That a court-fee of ₹..............has been paid in accordance with law.

The petitioner therefore prays that a decree of divorce be granted to the petitioner against the respondent by dissolution of their marriage.

Verification

Affidavit

NOTES: 1. Section 5(*ii*)(*b*)—ground of mental disorder—degree of proof of mental disorder in avoiding marriage under s. 5(*ii*)(*b*) is lighter as compared to degree of proof of mental disorder for seeking divorce under s. 13—*Alka Sarma* v *Avhinesh Sarma* AIR 1991 MP 205.

Mental disorder—A few stray instances indicating a short tempered nature and somewhat erratic behaviour is not sufficient. Alleged mental disorder must be of such a kind and to such on extent that one spouse cannot reasonably be expected to live with the other—*Nirmala Monohar Jogesha* v *Manohar Shivram Jogesha* AIR 1991 Bom 259; *Ram Narain* v *Ramaswami* AIR 1988 SC 2260 relied on.

2. Declaration of nullity—Long delay in institution of proceedings is no ground for refusing declaration—*Harendra Barman* v *Suprobha Barman* AIR 1989 Cal 120. Petition filed after 8 years of marriage is apparently barred by time—*Sarlabai* v *Komal Singh* AIR 1991 MP 358.
3. Divorce Act (4 of 1869)—Divorce petition by wife on the ground of adultery. Wife did not name mention specifically woman with whom husband had illicit relations, Held, adultery not proved—*Urmila M. Ram* v *Patras Masih* AIR 1993 P&H 121.
4. Unfounded allegation of adultery by one spouse against the other—constitutes mental cruelty of gravest character to warrant divorce—*Harendra Barman* v *Suprobha Barman* AIR 1989 Cal 120.
5. Divorce Act, s. 19—A widower father of children in his first marriage undergoing vasectomy. Non-disclosure of fact of vasectomy to second wife on the occasion of remarriage. It amounts to fraud of such nature as to vitiate consent for marriage—*P.J. Moore* v *Valsa* AIR 1992 Ker 176.
6. Section 15 proviso of the Hindu Marriage Act—A marriage contracted in contravention of or violation of the proviso to s. 15 is not void but merely invalid not affecting the core of marriage and the parties are subject to a binding tie of wedlock flowing from the marriage. The woman cannot be denied the status of wife, the widow in that capacity is an heir to him—AIR 1978 SC 1351; AIR 1971 Cal 307 overruled.

519. Petition for divorce under the Hindu Marriage Act 1955 (by a wife)

In the Hon'ble Family Court at ....

Matrimonial Suit No. .... of 20.........

A.B. .... *Petitioner*

versus

C.D. .... *Respondent*

Petition for dissolution of marriage by a decree of divorce under s. 13 of the Hindu Marriage Act 1955.

The above-named petitioner states as follows:

1. That the petitioner was married to the respondent on .... at the residence of your petitioner's father at .... P.S. ...., District .... according to Hindu rites and ceremonies within the jurisdiction of this court.

2. That after her marriage with the respondent, the petitioner and the respondent lived together as husband and wife at .... until ...., 20.........

3. That your petitioner and the respondent have a son born of wedlock. He is now aged 3 years (Or, that no issue was born to the petitioner and the respondent out of their marriage).

4. That the petitioner got a decree for restitution of conjugal rights with the respondent in the Court of the District Judge at .... on .... the Matrimonial Suit No. .... of 20 .... within the knowledge of the respondent. Since after the decree one year and a half elapsed but the respondent failed to comply with the said decree for restitution of conjugal rights.

The petitioner craves leave of the court to produce a certified copy of the said decree at the trial.

5. That the petitioner is entitled to dissolution of her marriage with the respondent by a decree of divorce under s. 13(1-A) of the Hindu Marriage Act.

6. That this petition is not presented in collusion with the respondent.

7. That the cause of action for this petition arose on .... when failure of compliance with the decree completed one year at .... within the jurisdiction of this court where the parties hereto last resided as husband and wife.

The petitioner, therefore, prays for:

(1) A decree of dissolution of marriage of the parties hereto by a decree of divorce.

(2) Costs.

Verification

Affidavit

NOTES: 1. Suit was decreed *ex parte*. Wife filed a petition to set aside the *ex parte* decree. Subsequently the husband died. Proceedings would not abate. Application under Or. 22, r. 4 by the wife to bring on record legal representatives of deceased husband is maintainable. Principle of *actio personalis cum moritur persona*— does not apply—*Vadala Setti* v *V. Nagamma* AIR 1994 AP 13.

2. Appeal against decree of divorce—death of respondents pending appeal. The appeal does not abate—*Kamalabai* v *Ramdas* AIR 1981 Bom 187.

3. Section 13(1)(*ia*)—divorce on the ground of cruelty. Term cruelty has not been defined in the Hindu Marriage Act. Connotation of cruelty as defined in s. 498A of the Indian Penal Code or s. 2(*viii*) of the Dissolution of Muslim Marriages Act, should not be imported into the scheme of the Hindu Marriage Act, as these definitions are for the limited purposes of those Acts only—*Sebaprasad Basu* v *Gouri Basu* (1994)1 CHN 324.

   Cruelty—See *Yosada Bai* v *Krishna Moorthy* AIR 1992 Kant 368; *Bipin* v *Sukomal* AIR 1979 Cal 87 relying on.

4. Section 13(1)(*i*)—on ground of adultery—proof of single act of adultery by wife is sufficient to grant of decree of divorce—*Rajendra Agrawal* v *Sharada Devi* AIR 1993 MP 142. Divorce being a civil proceeding, the standard of proof cannot be on the analogy of criminal law—*Dr. Saroj Kumar Sen* v *Dr. Kalyan Kanta Roy* AIR 1980 Cal 374.

5. Marriage has irretrievably broken down—is no ground for divorce. Filing of false and scandalous case by one spouse against other amounts to cruelty. It is now not necessary to prove that cruelty has caused reasonable apprehension that it would be harmful or injurious for a spouse to live with the other—*Rajinder Bhardwaj* v *Mrs. Anita Sharma* AIR 1993 Del 135.
6. Unauthorised and unfounded allegations of adultery in Written Statement—such allegation itself amounts to cruelty. It forms basis for a decree of divorce—*Jaisree Mohon* v *Mohan Govind* AIR 1987 Bom 220.

520. Petition for a decree of divorce by mutual consent under the Hindu Marriage Act

In the Court of the District Judge at ...../... Family Court
Matrimonial Suit No. .... of 20.........

AB wife of CD ....

.... *Petitioner No. 1*

CD son of XY ....

.... *Petitioner No. 2*

Petition for a decree of divorce by mutual consent (under s. 13B of the Hindu Marriage Act 1955).

The above-named petitioners state as follows:

1. That the petitioners were married to each other at .... on the .... day of .... 20......... according to Hindu rites and ceremonies within the jurisdiction of this court.

2. That the petitioners are not pulling on well in respect of their marital relationship and that the petitioner No. 1 has been living in her father's house since February 20......... continuously separated from the petitioner (*or for more than one year, which ever is applicable*) No. 2 (*or that petitioners are not living together for more than one year*).

3. That the parties hereto have consented in the month of .... 20......... to a dissolution of their marriage by mutual consent and such consent was not obtained by fraud or undue influence. There was no mutual connivance in the matter.

4. That this court has had jurisdiction and the petitioners submit this petition with fixed court-fees of ₹ ....

5. That the cause of action for this petition arose in the month of .... 20......... when parties hereto mutually agreed to seek a divorce.

The petitioners, therefore, pray for:

(*a*) a decree of divorce dissolving the marriage of the petitioners,

(*b*) any other relief.

Verification

Affidavit

NOTES: 1. No harm if a joint petition is filed. Law is silent as to the procedure.
2. Unless in the joint application under s. 13B(2) of the Hindu Marriage Act it is specifically stated that mutual consent to divorce was not obtained by fraud or undue influence within the meaning of s. 23(*bb*) & (*c*) of the Act, the decree of divorce cannot be granted even if the other conditions of s. 13B of

the Act are present. The time-limit envisaged in s. 13B(2) of the Act is mandatory and not directory—*Pranab Hazra* v *Ratna Hazra* (1994)1 CHN 360.

3. A party to petition for divorce by mutual consent can unilaterally withdraw consent. It is not irrevocable. Mutual consent must continue till divorce decree is passed. For contrary view—see *Joysree Ramesh Londha* v *Ramesh Vikaji* AIR 1984 Bom 302.
4. Expression 'living separately' occurring in s. 13B connotes not living like husband and wife. It is immaterial whether spouses live under same roof or in different houses—*Sureshta Devi* v *Om Prakash* AIR 1992 SC 1904.
5. Decree of divorce solely on basis of compromise—not valid. A decree of divorce solely on the basis of compromise, without any advertence as to the existence of any of the permissible grounds is not permissible under the law. Even a decree for divorce under s. 13B labelled as 'divorce by mutual consent' cannot be granted by the court on mutual consent alone, without being satisfied that the parties are living and could not but live separately for one year or more and things have come to such a pass that they cannot cohabit together—*Apurba Mohan Ghosh* v *Manasi Ghosh* AIR 1989 Cal 115.

521. Petition for divorce by mutual consent under the Special Marriage Act

(By mutual consent under s. 28 of the Act)

In the Court of the District Judge/Family Court at ....

Matrimonial Suit No. .... of 20.........

In the matter of the Special Marriage Act (XLIII of 1954)

And

In the matter of:

(1) A.B. wife of C.D.

Indian by birth and by occupation .... residing at ....

.... *Petitioner No. 1*

(2) C.D. son of Sri E.F. Indian by birth, by occupation .... residing at village......

.... *Petitioner No.* 2

And

In the matter of a petition under s. 28 of the Special Marriage Act 1954, for divorce by mutual consent.

The joint-petition of the above-named petitioners sheweth:

1. That the petitioners were married to each other on the (date of marriage) at .... (place where marriage solemnized) within the local limits and jurisdiction of this court under the Special Marriage Act 1954, and a record thereof was made in the Marriage Certificate Book under s. 13 of the said Act on ....

A certified copy of the Certificate of Marriage is attached herewith.

2. That prior to the marriage petitioner No. 1 was a maiden.

3. That soon after the marriage on .... it was found that temperaments and ways of life of the petitioners were different and in spite of their best efforts there was such incompatibility of temperaments that there were constant quarrels between them and the life of both became unbearable.

4. That friends and relations of both the petitioners also tried to intervene at times but their efforts to effect reconciliation proved abortive although more than three years elapsed since the date of marriage and the date of entering the Certificate of Marriage in the Marriage Certificate Book.

5. That the petitioners last resided together at .... P.S. .... District .... till .... (date).

6. That petitioner No. 1 is living separately at .... (place), since .... (date), petitioner No. 2 is also living separately at .... (place), since .... and even now for a period of more than one year.

7. That for such strained relationship the parties have not been able to live together. That the petitioners have agreed orally (or, in writing) in May .... that the marriage should be dissolved by mutual consent.

(Where there is agreement in writing—the said agreement is filed herewith and may be treated as a part of this petition).

8. That no child was born of the wedlock [or, in appropriate case, the petitioners should state whether there is any living issue or issues of the marriage, and, if so, the name, the date of birth or age of such child or each of such children, and also that the parentage of any living child or children of the wife born during the marriage is in dispute. If such be the case—see Calcutta High Court Rules 340-A(3)(*iii*).

9. That there is no collusion between the petitioners in presenting this petition.

10. That the cause of action arose in early May 20 ...., when divorce was agreed upon orally (or, in writing).

11. The petitioners have paid requisite court-fees of ₹ ....

It is prayed that on a motion being made therefor after the expiry of six months from the date of presentation of this joint petition, the court may be pleased to grant a decree for divorce of the said marriage dated ...., and dissolve the marriage with effect from the date of the decree.

Verification

Affidavit

NOTES: 1. In West Bengal before presenting a like petition Calcutta High Court Civil Rules and Orders, Vol. I containing the Special Marriage Act [Calcutta High Court Rules 1955 should be read carefully for instruction (Rule 340-A)].

2. In West Bengal: Court-fees ₹ 5 see Schedule II 'Fixed fees' Item No. 19 of the West Bengal Court-fees Act 1970.

522. Petition for declaration of nullity of marriage

In the Hon'ble Family Court* at ....

Matrimonial petition No. .... of 20...

---

* Where there is no Family Court the petition is to be made to the civil court having jurisdiction.

In the matter of:

Proceedings under s. 11 read with s. 5 of the Hindu Marriage Act 1955

And

In the matter of:

Smt. P., residing at ....

.... *Petitioner*

versus

Mr. X, residing at ....

.... *Respondent*

The humble petition of Smt. P. the petitioner above- named most respectfully sheweth:

1. Your petitioner is the wife of Mr. X.

2. The marriage between the petitioner and respondent was preceded by negotiations between the senior members of both the families who met frequently and the petitioner and respondent were allowed to mix freely so as to know each other fully before their proposed marriage.

3. The senior members of the respondent's family and the respondent himself represented that the respondent was not married earlier and that they were looking for a suitable bride for the proposed marriage of respondent.

4. The senior members of the petitioner's family and also petitioner had no previous independent knowledge that the respondent was already married and some time after marriage his previous wife was forcibly driven out by the respondent and his family members on the ground that his first wife's parents failed to pay the agreed dowry to the father of the respondent.

5. The marriage between petitioner and the respondent took place on .... at .... Kolkata according to Hindu religious rites and customs. But soon after such marriage your petitioner came to know from some of the family members of respondent that the respondent had already a wife living and that the first marriage was still subsisting between the respondent and his first wife and this fact was deliberately concealed by the respondent from petitioner and other family members of petitioner.

6. Your petitioner further states that the marriage between your petitioner and respondent is null and void under provisions of section 5(*i*) of the Hindu Marriage Act 1955, for the fraudulent conduct of the respondent and his family members. Your petitioner states that it is necessary that this learned court will be pleased to declare the said marriage between respondent and your petitioner as null and void.

7. Your petitioner also prays Your Honour for leave of this learned court to sue the respondent and some of his family members for damages caused for the loss suffered by your petitioner for fraud practised by respondent and his family members, inasmuch as your petitioner also suffered mental agony and also social ignominy due to such marriage.

8. The petitioner's cause of action for this application arose at .... Kolkata where the marriage took place within the jurisdiction of this learned court.

9. For purposes of jurisdiction and court-fees, the present application is valued at ₹......... on which court-fees in stamps have been paid.

10. Your petitioner further declares that there is no collusion between the parties or otherwise.

11. Your petitioner states that it is not a case where the petitioner is taking advantage of her own fault.

12. There is no plausible reason or ground for not allowing the present petition of your petitioner and prayers made therein.

13. This application is made *bona fide* and in the interest of justice.

Your petitioner, therefore, humbly prays Your Honour for the following orders:

(*a*) Declaration that the marriage which has taken place between the petitioner and respondent on .... is null and void;

(*b*) Such reliefs be granted as to this learned court may deem fit and proper in the facts and circumstances of the case;

(*c*) Leave be given to your petitioner to take proceedings against the respondent and his family members for damages;

(*d*) Costs of the proceedings;

(*e*) Further and other orders be made as this learned court may deem fit and proper so as to afford complete relief to your petitioner.

And your petitioner, as in duty, bound shall ever pray.

Verification

Affidavit

523. Petition for a decree of nullity of marriage under the Hindu Marriage Act (Another Form)

In the Court of the District Judge at ....

Matrimonial Suit No. .... of 20.........

A.B. .... *Petitioner*

versus

C.D. .... *Respondent*

The above-named petitioner states as follows:

1. That your petitioner was married, in fact though not in law, to the respondent, on .... at .... at the father's place of the petitioner.

2. That no issue was born of the said pretended marriage of the parties hereto.

3. That the petitioner has learnt on .... that on the date of the petitioner's pretended marriage with the respondent, the respondent had his another wife living and on suppression of the said fact he married the petitioner.

4. That the marriage of the petitioner with the respondent contravened the condition contained is s. 5(*i*) of the Hindu Marriage Act and such a marriage is void *ab initio*.

5. The cause of action for this petition arose on the (date of marriage) .... and thereafter on .... when the petitioner came to know of the fact of the respondent's first marriage at .... within the jurisdiction of this court.

The petitioner, therefore, prays that Your Honour would declare that the marriage between the parties hereto is null and void.

Verification

Affidavit

524. Petition for judicial separation under s. 10 of the Hindu Marriage Act 1955

Application No. .... of 20..........
In the Hon'ble Family Court at ....

Smt. P. wife of Sri Z, residing at ....
Alipore, Kolkata

.... *Petitioner*

versus

Mr. X, son of Mr. Y, residing at ....
Alipore, Kolkata

.... *Respondent*

The humble petition of Mrs. P. the petitioner above-named, most respectfully sheweth:

1. Your petitioner was married to the respondent on 7th January 20..... according to Hindu Marriage Rites at Alipore Road, Kolkata.

2. Your petitioner states that from such wedlock one son was born to the petitioner on 9th June 20......

3. Your petitioner states that since marriage the petitioner and respondent lived as husband and wife at Alipore Road, Kolkata until 5th January 20..... and finally have resided together at Alipore within jurisdiction of this learned court.

4. Your petitioner states that the respondent (husband) started misbehaving with the petitioner without any reason or cause whatever and ultimately deserted her and the said minor child on 15.12.20...... and there have been negotiations for payment of maintenance of your petitioner and minor son.

5. Your petitioner does not have sufficient means or income of her own to maintain herself and her minor son and your petitioner including her minor son has been forced to stay with her father at .... Alipore, Kolkata.

6. Your petitioner has her father, family friends and other well wishers who have been making sincere efforts again and again to send her back to her matrimonial home at Alipore but the respondent refused to take back your petitioner and their minor son. Further, the respondent has been abusing your petitioner, her father and friends who are still negotiating with the respondent for taking back the petitioner and her minor son. In the premises, the question of petitioner living with the respondent does not arise.

7. In the facts and circumstances of the case, your petitioner is entitled to live separately and receive maintenance allowance for such separate living with her minor son.

8. Your petitioner does not intend to trouble her father as it will be burdensome for her father to maintain her and the child as he has already other dependants.

9. Your petitioner states that the respondent is gainfully employed in the .... at a monthly remuneration of ₹................

10. Your petitioner states that in the acts of desertion of your petitioner by respondent your petitioner has not in any way been an accessory to or connived at or condoned the aforesaid wrongful acts and ultimate desertion and cruelty by the respondent. Further, there is no collusion between your petitioner and the respondent and that

there is no valid ground as to why the petitioner's prayers should not be granted by this learned court.

11. Your petitioner, by a letter dated 15th December, 20...... stated the various acts of cruelty of the respondent, the factum of negotiations and failure thereof and the adamant attitude of the respondent not to pay any maintenance to the petitioner and her minor son. But the respondent though received the said letter, kept quiet. A copy of the said letter is annexed hereto marked 'A'.

12. The petitioner's cause of action for this application arose on 15.12.20...... when the respondent actually deserted your petitioner and the petitioner had to take shelter at her father's place with her minor son.

The same cause of action is still continuing due to the continued wrongful acts of the respondent.

13. The cause of action for this application for judicial separation arose on 15.12.20...... when the respondent deserted your petitioner and the cause of action is continuing from day to day *inter alia* for the failure of the respondent to maintain your petitioner and her minor son.

14. For the purposes of jurisdiction and court-fees, the suit is valued at ₹............. on which the necessary court-fees in Stamps have been paid according to provisions of law.

15. Your petitioner states that there is no other proceeding pending in any other court in relation to the said marriage and/or desertion either by petitioner or by respondent.

16. This application has been made *bona fide* and in the interest of justice.

17. Unless orders are made, as prayed for, your petitioner will suffer irreparable loss and prejudice.

Your petitioner, therefore, humbly prays Your Honour for the following orders:

(*a*) Decree for judicial separation of petitioner with respondent.

(*b*) Decree direction for payment of maintenance allowance by respondent at ₹............. per month for petitioner and ₹............. per month for her minor child.

(*c*) Cost of ₹.............. in lump sum be paid by respondent to your petitioner.

(*d*) Further and other orders be made and other reliefs be granted as this learned court may deem fit and proper to afford complete relief to your petitioner.

And your petitioner, as in duty bound, shall ever pray.

ANNEXURE 'A'

Verification

Affidavit

NOTES: 1. For cruelty—See AIR 1970 Cal 266.

2. In a wife's application for dissolution of marriage, the husband's allegation about the wife's disinclination to reunite did not amount to misconduct grave enough to disentitle the relief the wife asked for—AIR 1977 SC 2218.

525. Plaint for claim by Mahomedan wife for prompt and deferred dower

In the Court of.......................at...........

Matrimonial Suit No.................of 20........

(Set out cause title)

The plaintiff states as follows:

1. That the parties were and are Sunni Mahomedans.

2. That the plaintiff was married to the defendant on...................

3. That at the time of the marriage, it was verbally agreed between A.B., father and natural guardian of the plaintiff, acting for the plaintiff, who was then a minor, and C.D., father and natural guardian of the defendant, acting for the defendant, who was also then a minor, that the plaintiff's dower should be ₹...............out of which half was to be prompt and half was deferred.

4. That the marriage was duly consummated.

5. That by a Talaknama dated...................., made in the presence of witnesses and duly registered, the defendant who was then a major declared that he divorced the plaintiff as from that date.

6. That the plaintiff came to know of the said divorce on.............................

When the defendant sent a copy of the said Talaknama to her.

7. That the plaintiff had made no demand for dower before the said date.

8. That the defendant has not paid the said dower or any part thereof to the plaintiff in spite of demand in writing dated.............

The plaintiff claims—

(1) ₹......................

(2) Interest by way of damages.

Verification

Affidavit

PUBLIC INTEREST LITIGATION

The court found that the poorest of the poor, deprived, the illiterate, the unorganised labour, women, children, persons handicapped by ignorance, poverty, or illiteracy, down-trodden people having no access to justice, had been denied justice. For redressal of their grievances a new branch of proceeding now known as Public Interest Litigation (PIL) has been evolved. For justice any person on behalf of the aggrieved person belonging to any of the said categories, may by a Writ Petition under Art. 226 of the Constitution of India or even by a letter in special cases, approach the court for redressal of grievances of the deserving aggrieved person. The court will not permit abuse of the process, or use of such process for oblique purpose.

The broad principles for entertaining a Public Interest Litigation and the principles required to be followed are, *inter alia*, as follows:

(*a*) Any interested person may make an application under Art. 32 and/or Art. 226 of the Constitution of India for the welfare of a person who is in a disadvantaged position and cannot approach the court, when the court may direct the State to fulfil its constitutional promises.

(*b*) Such an application can be made by a writ petition or in special circumstances, by a letter or a telegram. Issue of public importance, enforcement of fundamental rights of large number of public against the constitutional duties and functions of the States can be agitated by the writ petition and in exceptional cases by a letter or a telegram and the court will relax the rules of the pleadings.

(*c*) If injustice is meted out to a large number of people the court will provide reasonable and fair trial in view of Arts. 14 and 21 of the Constitution of India and the International Conventions on Human Rights.

(*d*) The rule of *locus standi* is relaxed and anybody is allowed to make such an application and the court will look into the grievances complained of on behalf of the poor, deprived, illiterate and the disabled who cannot approach the court for any violation of their constitutional or legal rights.

(*e*) The court being satisfied about violation of any constitutional rights of a group of people belonging to the disadvantaged category may not allow the State or the Government to raise the question of maintainability of the petition.

(*f*) Normally, the procedural law will apply in PIL cases and depending on the nature of petition, the facts and circumstances of case, the principle of *res judicata* or principles analogous thereto may be applicable.

(*g*) The disputes between two rival groups in the domain of private laws will not be allowed to be agitated as a Public Interest Litigation. But even in such a case, the court may treat, if necessary, the same as Public Interest Litigation, if the facts of the case justify that the litigation is in the nature of justice of those disadvantaged people.

(*h*) The court in special circumstances may appoint a Commission or other Bodies for investigating into the allegations to find out facts. The court may also direct to take over the management of a Public Institution by a Committee appointed by it.

(*i*) The court would ordinarily act within the scope of judicial review. The High Court may pass an order for doing complete justice to parties but such powers are not as extensive as provided in Art. 142 of the Constitution of India.

(*j*) Ordinarily, the High Court will not entertain a writ petition by way of Public Interest Litigation questioning constitutionality or validity or a Statute or a Statutory Rule—AIR 2004 SC 280 and 561.

(*k*) It was held that Public Interest Litigation should not be entertained if it is for "Publicity Interest Litigation" or "Private Interest Litigation" or "Political Interest Litigation" or "Paise Income Litigation". It is not available for furtherance of the petitioner's personal grudge or enmity. A person acting *bona fide* and having sufficient interest in the Public Interest Litigation will alone have a *locus standi* and can approach the court to redress violation of fundamental rights and genuine infraction of statutory provisions but not for personal gain, of private profits, or political motives or for any oblique consideration.

Original Public Interest Litigation Sometime near about 1970 some Judges innovated Public Interest Litigation as there was a need for it. PIL was intended to vindicate public interest where fundamental and other rights of poor, ignorant or socially or economically inadvantageous position and were unable to seek legal redress were required to be assisted. PIL is a litigation in the interest of the public.

The court will exercise jurisdiction under PIL, *inter alia*, in the following cases:

(*a*) Where the concerns in the petition are not individualised but are shared widely by large number of people, such as, bonded labour, under-trial prisoners and prison inmates.

(*b*) Where the affected persons belong to the disadvantageous sections of society, such as women, children, bonded labour, unorganised labour, etc.

(*c*) Where judicial law-making is necessary to avoid exploitation, such as, inter-country adoption, education of the children of prostitutes, etc.

(*d*) Where judicial intervention is necessary for the protection of sanctity of democratic institutions, such as, independence of judiciary, existence of grievances redressal fora.

(*e*) Where administrative decisions related to development are harmful to the environment and jeopardise people's right of access to natural resources such as air, light and water.

PIL is essentially meant to protect basic human rights of the weak and disadvantaged. It is a procedure which was innovated by public spirited persons by filing petitions, in effect, on behalf of persons who on account of poverty, helplessness or economic and social disabilities could not approach the court for relief. The court is also aware that there should not be abuse of this process.

Public Interest Litigation is not maintainable in all cases where the petitioner feels the court should be approached for relief. The court has discretion to entertain petition by way of Public Interest Litigation and in many cases the court rejected such petitions as not coming within the parameters of Public Interest Litigation. In the following cases the court entertained Public Interest Litigation and granted relief:

(*a*) Where there was deprivation of basic requirement and right of villagers to have access to water storage by natural source. PIL was maintainable where there was violation of right to reach natural water by an act of State. It was held that pendency of civil suit filed by some members of the village will not affect the right of other members to invoke the extra-ordinary jurisdiction of the court by way of PIL.

(*b*) Where Government land was given on lease for 88 years subject to deposit of balance premium within 90 days but the premium was never paid but the Chairman of the Standing Committee completed the lease in spite of adverse note and adverse legal opinion. On a Writ Petition filed as Public Interest Litigation High Court quashed the Government order and Supreme Court held that substantial justice was done by the High Court—*Bahudursinh Lakhubhai Gohil* v *Jagdishbhai M. Kamalia* AIR 2004 SC 1159.

(*c*) Public Interest Litigation was commenced alleging sale of public property at a throwaway price. It was pointed out that a public body had thrown public interest to the winds in selling its properties.

(*d*) In a Public Interest Litigation concerning prisoners detained in lunatic asylum despite medically fit certificate the High Court took a serious view of the criminal lapse on the part of some institutions and jail authorities in not responding to the shift of the inmates from lunatic asylum to jail.

(*e*) Municipal Corporation passed a resolution at a Standing Committee after it being rejected earlier. The notice convening the meeting of the Standing Committee did not contain Agenda for consideration of grant of vacant land.

The grant of vacant land was done in undue haste. The public interest was given a go-by and valuable public property was attempted to be doled out at the behest of those who were bound to protect the interest of the Municipal Corporation.

(*f*) Land was allotted for the purpose of Primary School but thereafter at the behest of the Revenue Minister proceedings were taken for cancellation of the allotment. The sole motive of such attempt for cancellation was to benefit some individuals who were unsuccessful litigants in respect of the said land. The action was taken on behalf of the authorities at the cost of interest of the public in getting school functioning and as such it was held that the action suffered from legal malice.

(*g*) Public Interest Litigation was initiated for the alleged usurpation of public largesse by legislatures by the representative of the people. Defence was taken that the petition was belated. The court held that the PIL could not be dismissed on the ground of delay because of the importance of the matter and the far reaching effect of the orders that might be passed by the authorities.

PIL not maintainable In the following cases, the court held that PIL was not maintainable or did not pass any order as prayed for:

(*a*) A petition was filed by an MLA along with 11 others. The court held that no fundamental rights of the petitioner were infringed, they were not aggrieved persons as none of them was buyer or seller of properties, and not affected by increase in valuation of stamp duty upon the sale or transfer of land by concerned authorities. Further, the MLA could raise the point before the Government.

(*b*) Petition was filed challenging decision of Govt. of India Ministry of Home Affairs for deployment of Intelligence Wings of various Border Guarding Forces in various parts of States bordering neighbouring countries was taken.

The court held that Public Interest Litigation against the policy decision of the Government was not maintainable regarding re-location of Special Service Bureau from the State of Assam to Indo-Nepal Border.

(*c*) Public Interest Litigation filed directly for repair of village roads, was not entertained as the issue could be raised before the Panchayat.

(*d*) The petitioner based his petition on a copy of a representation sent by Mr. R. to the President of India and other Constitutional Functionaries that Mr. J is not a suitable person to be appointed as a Judge. Petitioner has no personal knowledge. He is defendant on newspaper reports also. No element of Public Interest was involved. The petition was filed with oblique motives—*B. Singh* v *Union of India* AIR 2004 SC 1923.

(*e*) The scope of judicial review has been limited to want of consultation with the named constitutional functionaries or lack of any condition of eligibility. The petition was filed with oblique motive and was dismissed.

(*f*) The PIL challenging setting up of a new company by Government was dismissed as the Government fulfilled technical requirements of Parliamentary Approval when the new company was set up.

(*g*) Public Interest Litigation challenging validity of contracts, was dismissed as the court found that the petitioner was not truly Public Spirited person and, as such, prosecution of Public Interest Litigation by such a person was not proper.

(*h*) On a petition the court directed petitioner to deposit security amount which the petitioner did not deposit. The court directed deposit of security so that the person who is involved in the litigation unnecessarily and without justification could be compensated by court at the end of such litigation, if necessary. The petitioner failed to deposit the security amount and the court dismissed the petition.

(*i*) A petition should not be treated as Public Interest Litigation if the dispute raised therein was purely a personal litigation or a contractual litigation, even though a prayer for the investigation by the CBI was made.

(*j*) A petition raised the question regarding the date of birth of Kolkata and its Founder. An Expert Committee had already been appointed to go into the said question. The Expert Committee report showed that Kolkata did not have a "Birth Date" but its origin was part of general process of Rural Settlement and there was no "Founder". And this was accepted by the state. The High Court directed the State Government to proceed in accordance with the findings given by the said Committee and the PIL stood dismissed.

(*k*) Public Interest Litigation is not meant for serving political purposes, or solving political problems.

The petitioner prayed for ban on proposed "Gaurav Yatra" by a political party. The court held that there was no wrong or legal injury to the petitioner or any class of people and the petition was an abuse of judicial process.

(*l*) The Minister concerned issued directions to grant water connection to Hotel after examining the public interest. The petition to restrain the grant of water connection to the Hotel was dismissed as the Minister had passed such an order after examining the public interest.

The complaint was not within the domain of Writ Court.

(*m*) A Public Interest Litigation was dismissed in respect of allegations of irregularities, corrupt practices, maladministration and mismanagement of a temple governed by self-contained statutory enactments.

(*n*) A writ petition for performing Puja in Public Temple and for refusal of such a right by the State is not maintainable.

(*o*) A writ petition against order for the shifting of petrol pump to another location was dismissed as the petitioner corporation did not challenge the recommendations of the Committee appointed by a High Court. The petitioner did not raise any objection that the location should not be shifted on account of traffic hazards.

(*p*) The petition should not be merely a cloak for attaining private ends of a third party or of the party filing the petition. The court can only examine the previous records of public service rendered by the said organisation which filed such a petition. Even when a Public Interest Litigation is entertained, the court must be very careful to weigh conflicting public interests before intervening as such an intervention may ultimately result in delay in execution of the project, and as such, the court must carefully weigh conflicting public interests. Only when the court comes to a conclusion that there is an overwhelming public interest involved in entertaining the petition, it should so intervene—*Raunaq International Ltd.* v *IVR Construction Ltd.* AIR 1999 SC 393.

(*q*) A petition was filed complaining that iron ore mine was transferred to private sector without calling global tenders. The court held that such transfer was neither *mala fide* nor against industrial policy of the Government, and not calling of Global Tenders had not vitiated the transaction.

(*r*) The court will have no jurisdiction in interfering if there be no arbitrariness or unreasonableness in the decision-making process involving revival of a company.

(s) On a petition filed by a contractor it was held that the power of the State to cancel contract could not be curtailed on the basis of individual interests.

(*t*) A petition is not maintainable for settling disputes between individual parties. PIL is not available to further personal interests or to satisfy any grudge or enmity.

(*u*) Such a petition is not maintainable for a direction for investigation by CBI in respect of a Government Contract.

(*v*) It was held that a PIL was not maintainable where the authorities established Electronic and Video Games Complex, Amusement Park on Sea Beach Lines after taking proper precautions against pollution, and on environmental aspects, the PIL was dismissed as not maintainable.

(*w*) A PIL was dismissed as not maintainable because it claimed conversion of death sentence into life imprisonment due to prolonged delay in execution of the death sentence.

(*x*) In respect of a Government Contract, it is the tenderer whose tender had been rejected to make grievance. The petitioner who was neither a resident of the territory nor submitted any tender could not make the petition.

(*y*) A Public Interest Litigation was dismissed where the allegations were malpractices and atrocities committed by the self-proclaimed caste Panchayats and its Panchas on weaker sections specially on women, it was held that the court could not provide cover to every citizen against all wrongs done to him by other members of society. As the order would be futile and unexecutable the court dismissed the petition.

(*z*) The jurisdiction of PIL should be invoked very sparingly and also in favour of vigilant litigant and not for the persons who invoked the jurisdiction for publicity or for serving private ends. The extraordinary powers under PIL should be used sparingly and absolutely in necessary matters involving downtrodden people—*R and M Trust* v *Koramangala Residents Vigilance Group* AIR 2005 SC 894.

526. Public interest litigation in Supreme Court to prevent continuance of water and air pollution

In the Supreme Court of India

Constitutional Writ Jurisdiction

Matter No. ... of 20.....

In the matter of:

A Public Interest Litigation under Art. 32 of the Constitution of India

And

In the matter of:

Writs in the nature of Mandamus and Prohibition and orders and directions in relation thereto

And

In the matter of:

Water and Air pollution

And

In the matter of:

A Society for Protection of Environment and Atmosphere

And

In the matter of:

Welfare Society having its office at Connaught Circus, New Delhi

.... *Petitioner*

versus

1. Union of India represented by Secretary to the Department of Environment, Government of India having his office at New Delhi.
2. State of West Bengal represented by the Secretary to the Department of Environment of the Government of West Bengal having his office at ....

.... *Respondents*

To
The Hon'ble Mr. ...., Chief Justice of India
and His Companion Justices of the said
Hon'ble Supreme Court of India

The humble petition of the petitioner above-named most respectfully sheweth:

1. Your petitioner is an Association formed for environmental protection and the Society is registered under the Societies Registration Act.

2. Your petitioner states that both sides of the river Ganges upto 100 Kms. in length are highly congested. The people of the State of West Bengal consider the water as sacred and take their bath and perform Puja in the river or in the banks of the river.

3. Your petitioner states that on both sides of the river covering the length of about 100 Kms. there are Jute Mills, Paper Mills, Cotton Mills, Engineering concerns and other manufacturing units and also the Howrah Station. These units discharge their waste materials and effluents into the river Ganges.

4. These practices to use the river Ganges as a drain to dispose of their unusable and disposable waste materials including effluent from manufacturing processed septic tanks in the river Ganges. These reckless acts have made the water of the Ganges polluted and unhealthy. Bad smells come out of the river to the extent that normal people cannot stand by it and cannot have stroll on the banks.

5. With a view to ameliorate and prevent such pollution the Ganga Action Plan was established but the same has not been able to do much and has been remaining inactive and idle.

6. Your petitioner states that the river Ganges has been treated by the people having a particular sanctity and this has been so right from the Himalayas, the source of Ganges to the Bay of Bengal where it meets the sea. The river Ganges need to be kept pollution-free apart from other consideration for the believers that its water is required by the Hindu community for Puja purposes and actually Pujas are performed at homes and on the banks of the Ganges.

7. In spite of the aforesaid, due to neglect of the authorities the water of river Ganges has become so polluted that it has become a national hazard and disgrace.

8. Under the provisions of Art. 21 of the Constitution of India people have a right to live and stay in a pollution-free decent atmosphere. If the water of the Ganges is allowed to be polluted in the manner as it has been and is being done, it will be a threat and menace to the public.

9. Several Associations including your petitioner have made several representations to the respondents as also the factories on the banks of the Ganges for the purpose of preventing from using the river Ganges as a drain and to discharge their waste and disposable articles and effluents. In spite of best efforts your petitioner could not succeed to improve the situation and change the habits of the factories on the banks of the river Ganges.

10. Being aggrieved by and dissatisfied with the inactivity and gross apathy of the respondents your petitioner has been compelled to make the present application, *inter alia*, on the following:

GROUNDS

I. For that it is obligatory on the part of the respondents to take suitable measures for preventing the wrongdoers from polluting the water of the river Ganges.

II. For that it is widely admitted fact is that the water of the river Ganges has become unusable, unhealthy and emitting bad smell and the respondents are oblivious of this fact and remain inactive in this matter of grave and national importance.

III. For that the people have a right to use the water of river Ganges as before and to have pollution-free water of the Ganges as guaranteed by Art. 21 of the Constitution of India.

IV. For that the factories on the banks of the river Ganges cannot have any right to discharge their effluents in the Ganges using the same as a drain.

V. For that the people have a right to use the river Ganges having the normal flow of water originating from the nature without being polluted by any act of factories and business houses without proper licence to pollute the water of the Ganges.

11. Your petitioner has made this application for the purpose of protecting the health of the people and to make the river Ganges free of pollution.

12. Your petitioner states that unless appropriate orders are made and directions be given to make the river Ganges pollution-free it will be dangerous for the health and lives of the people.

13. Your petitioner states that the factories and other establishments have no right to use the Ganges as their drains for their effluents.

14. This application is made in the interest of the large number of public to protect the health of the people beginning from the Himalayas to the Bay of Bengal.

15. Your petitioner states that several complaints were made to several appropriate authorities in respect of the pollution on the banks of the river Ganges but no proper steps have been taken and the pollution continues unabated.

16. In the premises, an order of this Hon'ble Supreme Court of India is essential to save the river Ganges from pollution and to protect the health of the people on the banks of the Ganges and people using the Ganges for their business, pujas and taking baths. The river Ganges as it is now used has been converted into canals for discharge of effluents of the factories and mills situate near the banks of the Ganges.

17. This application is made *bona fide* and in the interest of the public.

Your petitioner, therefore, humbly prays your Lordships for the following orders:

(*a*) A Writ in the nature of Mandamus be issued commanding the respondents to take suitable measures for making the water of the river Ganges pollution-free.

(*b*) A Writ of Prohibition be issued preventing the wrongdoers including factories, mills and other concerns discharging their effluents in the Ganges and preventing them from polluting in any manner whatsoever the river Ganges.

(*c*) Orders and directions be issued to redress the grievances as to pollution of the river Ganges by appropriate order.

(*d*) Further and other orders be made as this Hon'ble Supreme Court of India will deem fit and proper.

And for this act of kindness the petitioner as in duty bound shall ever pray.

Verification

Affidavit

NOTE: Normally the petition contains an Index, a list of dates and points of law involved in the matter separately prefixed to the petition.

527. Petition for prevention of environmental pollution

Matter No. .... of 20...

In the High Court at Calcutta

Constitutional Writ Jurisdiction

ORIGINAL SIDE

In the matter of:

A Public Interest Litigation under Art. 226 of the Constitution of India;

And

In the matter of:

A Writ or Writs in the Nature of Mandamus and/or Prohibition and/or Orders or Directions;

And

In the matter of:

Environmental Pollution;

And

In the matter of:

A Registered Society for Prevention of Environmental Pollution;

And

In the matter of:

Environmental Pollution Society having its Registered Office at Netaji Subhas Road, Kolkata within the said jurisdiction.

...... *Petitioner*

versus

1. State of West Bengal represented by the Chief Secretary, Government of West Bengal having his office at Writers' Buildings, Kolkata
2. Chairman of Commissioner of Kolkata Municipal Corporation having his office at S.N. Banerjee Road, Kolkata within the said jurisdiction.

.... *Respondents.*

To
The Hon'ble Mr. .... the Chief Justice and His Companion Justices of the said Hon'ble Court

The humble petition of the petitioners above-named most respectfully sheweth:

1. Your petitioner is a Registered Association for Environmental Pollution and a Society registered under the Societies Registration Act 1860.

2. The entire city of Kolkata is highly congested comprised of schools, Nurseries, Nursery to Secondary and Higher Secondary Levels, Nursing Homes and Hospitals which are functioning in different parts of the city.

3. There are several small stalls cooking food stuff and such stalls are numerous and situate around and very close and nearby to such schools and hospitals.

4. Such cooking stalls cater to general public openly on the roadside and waste parts of animals the and vegetables are strewn all over and also stored by the side of stalls.

5. There are blood stains of animals which cause mental depression not only to children but also patients and passers-by.

6. The feathers of animals and waste parts of animals and vegetables cause environmental pollution and are very displeasing not only to eyes but also to health of children and patients.

7. The respondents claim to work for a decent environment free from pollution and are entitled to do something for treating patients in hospitals suffering from any pollution.

8. The petitioner has made several representations to respondents but respondents have not responded favourably and the nuisance caused by such cooking stalls is still continuing.

9. Being aggrieved by and dissatisfied with the non-cooperation of respondents, apathy and noninterference in alleviating the miseries of school and college children and also ailing patients due to such nuisance and pollution created by the stalls, the petitioner begs to move the present application on, *inter alia*, following:

GROUNDS

A. For that it is obligatory on the part of respondents to take suitable remedial measures for protection and control of environmental pollution so that particularly children and patients may live in decent and pollution-free atmosphere.

B. For that apparently the chickens and vegetables are cut in open public view and the insanitary conditions prevailing in the stalls cause horror in the minds of children also to patients suffering from diseases who come to nearby hospitals inasmuch as the respondents cannot be mere idle spectators.

C. For that particularly the children and patients ailing and going to hospitals have a moral right to live and stay in a decent pollution-free environment which right has been validly guaranteed by Art. 21 of the Constitution of India and such denial of right to live in a healthy and pollution free atmosphere will be denial of rights guaranteed under Art. 21 of the Constitution of India and the respondents have certain legal and moral obligations to take suitable measures to prevent and control the said pollution.

10. This petition is made to request the respondents to take suitable measures for control and prevention of such pollution as aforesaid.

In the facts and circumstances of the case, the petitioners pray for and claim:

(*a*) A Writ in the Nature of Mandamus be issued commanding respondents to take suitable measures to prevent and/or control the environmental pollution by cutting chickens and vegetables in public view and storing feathers and waste materials;

(*b*) An order be issued directing the respondents to take suitable measures to prevent such environmental pollution;

(*c*) Such further orders be made or directions be given as this Learned Court may deem fit and proper to afford complete relief to petitioner.

And for this act of kindness, the petitioner, as in duty bound shall ever pray.

Verification

Affidavit

CODE OF CIVIL PROCEDURE

528. Application for stay of suit (s. 10, CPC)

In the Court of .... at ....

Suit No. .... of 20 ....

(Set out cause title)

The defendant states as follows:

1. That the plaintiff has instituted the instant suit for declaration of his title in and for khas possession of the suit-property, described in the Schedule appended below the plaint of the above suit.

2. That in the said suit the plaintiff claims his title on the strength of a deed of gift allegedly executed in his favour by one A.B. on the .... day of .... 20 ....

3. That the said deed of gift is fraudulent and was not executed by A.B. The defendant as the only heir of the said A.B. since deceased has right, title and interest in the property mentioned in the said deed of gift and has had possession therein.

4. That the defendant, as plaintiff has instituted a Title Suit No. ..../20........ in this court on .... for declaration that the deed of gift allegedly executed by A.B. in favour of the plaintiff of the above suit is fraudulent and prayed for setting aside the deed.

5. That the matter in issue in the present suit is directly and substantially in issue of the Title Suit No. .... of .... filed by the plaintiff.

6. That unless the hearing of the suit brought by the plaintiff is stayed there is reasonable apprehension of conflicting decisions in two suits between the same parties over the same subject-matter.

7. That in the interest of justice, the suit brought by this defendant should be heard and disposed of first as that would settle the question of the plaintiff's title as well.

8. By reasons aforesaid, the above-numbered suit brought by the plaintiff should be stayed till disposal of the Title Suit No. ..../20.........

It is, therefore, prayed that Your Honour would be pleased to stay further proceedings of the Title Suit No. ..../ 20......... till disposal of the Title Suit No. ..../ 20.........

Verification

Affidavit

NOTES: 1. Orders staying suit. Appellate Court set aside its order. Decision, though improper, cannot be interfered with under s. 115, CPC—AIR 1978 Cal 305.

2. Court has inherent power to stay suit where s. 10 does not strictly apply, for ends of justice—AIR 1978 Del 221; [AIR 1979 Del 1 under s. 151, CPC].

3. Principles stated—AIR 1976 Cal 18; AIR 1977 Cal 451.

4. Similarly, the plaintiff may also pray for stay of trial of the subsequent suit in which the matter in issue is also directly and substantially in issue in a previously instituted suit between the same parties.

5. Also see AIR 1972 Cal 128; AIR 1974 Del 95; AIR 1976 Cal 18: AIR 1973 Mad 476. One of the tests of the applicability of s. 10, CPC to a particular case is whether, on the final decision being reached in the previous suit would operate as *res judicata* in the subsequent suit—*O.P. Steel Traders* v

Steel Strips AIR 1992 P&H 217. Applicability of s. 10—Test: if decision in previous suit does not operate as *res judicata* in subsequent suit, subsequent suit cannot be stayed. Expression 'Matter directly and substantially in issue' means whole of subject-matter in both suits should be identical—*R. Srinivasan* v *Southern Petrochemical Industries* AIR 1992 Mad 363.

6. Subject-matter in controversy between two suits same. Reliefs claimed, however, are based on different causes of action. Held, latter suit should be stayed—*Challapalli Sugars* v *Swadeshi Sugar* AIR 1983 Cal 199.
7. Merely because one of the questions in issue is same as in the other suit, it would not make subject-matter identical—*Mahesh Ch. Sinha* v *Hindusthan Gas & Industries* AIR 1985 Cal 154.

529. Application for transfer of suit (s. 24, CPC)

In the Court of District Judge at ....

Misc. Judicial Case No. ..../20.........

(for transfer to Title Suit No. ....

of .... of the third Court of Civil Judge (Junior Division) at ....

(Set out cause title)

The defendant above-named states:

1. That the plaintiff has instituted the above title suit which is at its preliminary stage. The plaintiff is a lawyer of this court and is the Secretary of the local Bar Association.

2. That the defendant approached several lawyers of this court, but all lawyers of repute refused to accept the brief of the defendant on this or that plea and some of them candidly confessed their inability to accept brief against the plaintiff.

3. That the above suit involves intricate questions of law and it is apprehended that the defendant will not be able to contest the claim with an able lawyer.

4. That the defendant's witnesses also live outside the ordinary jurisdiction of this court. The defendant may not be able to bring his witnesses before this court in time and without much expense.

5. That the plaintiff has his hearth and home at X. It is believed that the plaintiff's witnesses, if any, also reside at X.

6. That in the interest of justice and for convenience of the parties hereto the above suit should be transferred to Mr. .... Civil Judge (Junior Division) at......... from the file of thrid court to sixth court.

It is, therefore, prayed that Your Honour would be pleased to pass:

(*i*) Orders transferring the above-numbered title suit to the file of the Civil Judge (Junior Division) at .... from the file of thrid court to sixth court; and

(*ii*) such other order or orders as deemed proper.

Verification

Affidavit

NOTES: 1. Rule 15(1) and (2) of Or. 18 of the CPC.

2. The convenience of parties concerned is one of the criteria for the purpose of transferring the suit—AIR 1977 Mad 27.
3. Also see AIR 1972 Cal 29; AIR 1972 Ker 263.

4. Suit by husband for dissolution of marriage. Wife leading life of destitute with aged parents at other place. Transfer of suit to that place is permissible—*Smt. Nanda Kishri* v *S.B. Shivaprakash* AIR 1993 Kant 87.
5. Wife's application pending in one court. Husband instituting suit in court at another place. Wife filed an application for transfer. Nature of both proceedings is such that they should be heard by same court. Prejudice to husband cannot be assumed from mere fact that he would have to undertake journey. Suit filed by husband is transferred—*Ms. Sakuntala Modi* v *Om Prakash Bharuka* AIR 1991 SC 1104.
6. Transfer of suit under s. 22—Balance of convenience of parties should be examined. Fact that one suit was instituted earlier is immaterial—*Seeta Mahalakhmi* v *Rajesh Trading Co.* AIR 1983 Bom 486.

530. Application for award of compensatory costs

(Under s. 35A of the CPC)

(I) *Application by the plaintiff of the suit:*

In the Court of .... at ....

Suit No. .... of 20 ....

(Set out cause title)

The plaintiff states as follows:

1. That the contention put forward by the defendant to the effect .... in para .... of his written statement is false to the knowledge of the defendant.

2. That the said defence of the defendant was held false by the court and was disallowed.

(or, that the defendant abandoned his said defence).

The plaintiff petitioner, therefore, prays for an order for payment to him by the said defendant a reasonable sum as costs by way of compensation.

(II) *Application by the defendant of the suit:*

After the main contention in the W.S. to be added:

1. That the plaintiff's said claim in para .... of the plaint was false (or vexatious or false and vexatious) to the knowledge of the plaintiff. The plaintiff has subsequently abandoned his said claim (or, the plaintiff withdrew his said claim) in writing.

2. The court was pleased to hold the said claim of the plaintiff as false (or vexatious or false and vexatious).

3. The defendant, therefore, claims special costs by way of compensation.

Verification

Affidavit

NOTES: 1. The prayer for compensatory costs may be made in a separate petition.
2. Before awarding costs by way of compensation the court has to record its reasons for holding claim or defence as false or vexatious.

531. Application for transfer of decree for execution to another Court

In the Court of the .... at ....

Title Ex. No. .... of ....

A.B. ....

.... *Decree-holder-Petitioner*

versus

C.D. ....

.... *J. Dr. Opposite Party*

The above-named petitioner states as follows:

1. That the applicant has obtained a decree against the Opposite Party in Title Suit No. .... of 20 .... of this court.

2. That the Opposite Party has had no property within the local limits of the jurisdiction of this court but he has property within the jurisdiction of the Court of the Civil Judge (Senior Division) at ....

SCHEDULE

It is, therefore, prayed that the decree, referred to above, be sent to the Court of the Civil Judge (Senior Division) at ....

Schedule of property

Verification

Affidavit

NOTES: 1. Section 39 of CPC—On the application of the decree-holder the court, which passed a decree, may send it for execution to another court under any of the circumstances in cls. (*a*) to (*d*) mentioned in s. 39(1) of the Code. The above form contains the ground in cl. (*b*) of the said section.

2. The court may *suo motu* send a decree for execution to any subordinate court of competent jurisdiction.

3. An application for transmission of a decree under s. 39 is not required to be in any particular form—AIR 1953 SC 65. A mere clerical error in writing the application will not invalidate it—AIR 1937 All 397.

4. Also see provisions of Or. 21, r. 6 of CPC.

5. Execution proceedings—During pendency of proceedings decree-holder dies. Substitution application by legal heirs is not necessary in view of Or. 22, r. 12 for continuation of proceedings. Bar of limitation under Art. 137, Limitation Act is not attracted—*Chhotey Lal* v *The District Judge* AIR 1991 All 214.

6. Order of court is executable as a decree—*Hungerford Investment Trust* v *Turner, Morrison Co. Ltd.* (1994)1 CLJ 500.
Section 36 of CPC—The provisions of this Code relating to the execution of decrees (including provisions relating to payment under a decree) shall, so far as they are applicable, be deemed to apply to the execution of order (including payment under an order).

7. Execution of Decree—Court can refuse to execute decree if the decree is a nullity or decree-holder loses right to execute it on account of a subsequent change in law or some subsequent development—*Radhi Dei* v *Lalit Behari* AIR 1991 Ori 36.

8. Transfer of decree to another court of competent jurisdiction. Expression "competent jurisdiction" relates only to pecuniary jurisdiction and not to jurisdiction over the subject-matter—*Prem Raj* v *3rd Addl. Dist. Judge* AIR 1992 All 332; AIR 1978 All 428.
9. Injunction Decree is inexecutable. But it can be implemented by seeking Police aid or by seeking necessary directions from either civil court under s. 151 or High Court under Art. 226—*Matha Gavareeyya* v *District Collector* AIR 1993 AP 103.
10. Death of decree-holder during pendency of Execution Proceedings—Succession Certificate by legal heirs under s. 214 of the Indian Succession Act is not necessary for continuation of proceedings. Substitution application by legal heirs also not necessary—*Chhoteylal* v *D.J.* AIR 1991 All 214 (s. 214(2) of the Indian Succession Act).
11. In case of Execution of a decree when decree-holder died it is mandatory that the legal representatives of the deceased decree-holder must obtain Succession Certificate before realising the decretal amount due to deceased decree-holder in an execution proceedings irrespective of the fact whether the legal representatives initiate execution proceedings at first instance or they come on record during the pendency of execution proceedings initiated by decree-holder by virtue of Or. 21, rr. 10, 11. Order 22, r. 12 and s. 217 read with s. 146 of CPC—*Sri Kaviyamma* v *Asst. Commr. Land Agr. Officer* AIR 1993 Kant 321.

532. Application for leave of the court for bringing a suit without serving notice under s. 80, CPC

In the Court of the Civil Judge (Junior Division) at ....

Title Suit No. .... of 20...

A.B. .... *Plaintiff*

versus

C.D. .... *Defendant*

Petition for court's leave under s. 80(2) of the Code of Civil Procedure.

The above-named plaintiff states:

1. That the plaintiff is the Branch Post Master of the ....

2. That the Inspector of Post Offices .... Sub-division, an officer of the defendant Government, issued a notice on .... inviting applications within .... for appointment to the post the plaintiff is holding. This is illegal and without jurisdiction.

3. That the plaintiff has had information that the defendant proposes to finalise fresh appointments within the month of .... 20.........

4. That the plaintiff intends to sue the Union of India for declaration of plaintiff's status, legal character and for injunction restraining such appointment. The reliefs are urgent and immediate.

The plaintiff, therefore, in view of the urgency of the matter and/or for obtaining immediate relief prays that leave be granted to the plaintiff to file the instant suit without serving notice under s. 80(1) of CPC.

Verification

Affidavit

NOTE: Leave granted under s. 80(2) of CPC for dispensing with provisions of s. 80(1)—Filing of Written Statement and taking of all steps and others passed in presence of Counsel for State. Formal notice thereafter under s. 80(1) is not mandatory—*Kailash Chandra Jain* v *State of M.P.* AIR 1992 MP 242.

Return of plaint as envisaged by proviso to s. 80(2)—*De hors* provision of Or. 7, r. 10—is revisable and not appealable.

533. Application for leave of the court for bringing a suit by two or more persons against public nuisance or other wrongful act [s. 91(1)(*b*), CPC]

In the Court of the Civil Judge (Junior Division) at ....

O.C. Suit No. .... of 20 ....

1. Dr. S. Sarkar
2. 'X' ...... *Plaintiffs*

versus

1. State of West Bengal represented by the Sub-Divisional Officer at .... under s. 91(1)(*b*) of the Code of Civil Procedure.
2. 'Z' ...... *Defendants*

The above-named plaintiffs state:

That the plaintiffs intend to institute this suit for injuncting the Government and the Defendant No. 2 to refrain from allowing and/or causing public nuisance affecting the public of the locality, mentioned in the accompanying plaint.

Your petitioners pray for leave of the court to bring a suit in this court.

Verification

Affidavit

534. Application for leave of the court for bringing a suit by two or more persons regarding public charities [s. 92 (1), CPC]

In the Court of .... at ....

Title Suit No. ..../20.........

1. A.B. son of .... residing at .... etc.
2. C.D. son of .... residing at .... etc.

.... *Plaintiffs*

versus

O.P. son of .... residing at ....

.... *Defendant*

Petition for leave of the court under s. 92(1) of the Code of Civil Procedure.

The above-named plaintiffs state:

1. That the plaintiffs intend to bring a suit against Mr. .... sole trustee of .... trust for his removal.

2. That for institution of such suit leave of the court is necessary.

3. That the plaintiffs have a *prima facie* case.

Your petitioners pray for leave of the court to bring the suit (plaint of which has been filed separately this day).

Verification

Affidavit

NOTE: Suit under s. 92 against public trust is not similar to a representative suit under Or. 1, r. 8 of C.P. Code in all respects. Leave of court is a condition precedent for institution of suit under s. 92 whereas permission to sue under Or. 1, r. 8 can be granted even after the institution of suit.

Leave of court. Whether can be implied. Application seeking leave is pending before the court— Leave cannot be presumed to have been granted by implication—*N. Anandam* v *Ayyanna Gounder* AIR 1994 Mad 43.

535. Application for compensation for obtaining attachment on insufficient grounds under s. 95 of the CPC

In the Court of the Civil Judge (Senior Division) at ....

Misc. Judicial Case No. .... of 20 ....

A.B. .... *Petitioner*

versus

C.D. .... *Opposite Party*

Application for compensation under s. 95 of the Code of Civil Procedure.

The petitioner states as follows:

1. That the opposite party as plaintiff commenced a Money Suit No. .... of .... in this court against the petitioner and on an application before this court on .... obtained an *ex parte* order of attachment before judgment in respect of the properties of the petitioner, under orders of attachment dated .... 20 ....

2. That the opposite party stated in his application for attachment that the petitioner was about to dispose of the whole of his property with intent to obstruct or delay the execution of the decree that might be passed against him. Such a statement was false and the affidavit sworn by the opposite party in support of his application was equally false (where necessary) that the plaintiff had no reasonable or probable ground for instituting the said Money Suit (see s. 95(1)(*b*) of the CPC).

3. That the petitioner never intended to dispose of any property, not to speak of the whole of it. The said application of the opposite party was made on insufficient grounds to harass the petitioner and injure him in his reputation and to cause him incur unnecessary expenses.

4. That subsequently on an application by the petitioner the court was pleased to release the properties of the petitioner holding that there was no sufficient ground for attachment before judgment.

5. That for such attachment of properties without just cause the petitioner has suffered loss (*State: nature of loss*) to the extent of ₹...........

The applicant, therefore, prays for an award of compensation of ₹............ or for such other sum as deemed proper.

Verification

Affidavit

NOTES: 1. "Insufficient grounds" in s. 95(1)(*a*) means without sufficient and probable cause—AIR 1953 MB 90.

2. Humiliation and/or injury to reputation will be included in the term "injury" in s. 95—AIR 1955 Mad 552; AIR 1953 MB 247.

3. Circumstances under which compensation can be granted are enumerates in sub-clauses (*a*) and (*b*) of cl. (1) of s. 95. The above form is an illustration of sub-clause (*a*) of cl. (1).

4. Compensation shall not exceed the pecuniary jurisdiction vested in the concerned court.

5. An application under s. 95 can be made even without getting the order of attachment set aside—1939 MWN 1084.

6. Special damages as well as general damages can be awarded—AIR 1963 Raj 177.

536. Application for compensation for obtaining injunction wrongfully (Another Form)

In the Court of .... at ....

Misc. Judicial Case No. .... of 20.........

A.B. ....*Petitioner*

versus

C.D. ......

.........*Opposite Party*

Application for compensation under s. 95 of the CPC.

The above-named petitioner states:

1. That the opposite party as plaintiff had instituted a Title Suit No. .... of 20 .... in this court and on .... had applied for an order of injunction to restrain the petitioner to .... The opposite party on false pleadings and by suppression of facts succeeded in obtaining an *ex parte* order of *ad interim* injunction by which the petitioner was restrained from ....

2. That the petitioner had entered his appearance in the suit and had shown cause against orders of *ad interim* injunction and against opposite party's prayer for temporary injunction.

3. That on hearing both the parties on .... the suit of the opposite party was dismissed and it appeared that there was no reasonable or probable ground for instituting the said suit.

4. That the petitioner has suffered unnecessary expenses and has been injured in his reputation by the said suit and orders of injunction.

The petitioner, therefore, prays for an award of compensation of ₹.......... or such other sum as may be deemed proper.

Verification

Affidavit

NOTES: 1. An application is to be made only after the suit is heard and not before—AIR 1923 Mad 352. The right arises when the order of injunction is vacated or dissolved either by the court granting it or by the Appellate Court on appeal—AIR 1971 Mys 178.
2. See s. 95(2)—An order determining any such application shall bar any suit for compensation in respect of attachment, injunction etc.
3. In an action for damages for wrongful injunction order, it is incumbent on the plaintiff to prove malice as also that the defendant acted without reasonable and probable cause—AIR 1978 Cal 259.
4. Section 95 applies where in any suit in which an arrest or attachment has been effected or a temporary injunction granted under s. 94 of the CPC.
5. Where the goods of a person, who was not liable under the decree in execution, were attached when the warrant of attachment did not authorise the seizure of goods of that person nor did it specifically authorise the seizure of goods lying in the premises of such person, the seizure being wrongful the judgment-creditor was liable to the owner of goods seized for damages caused to him in consequence of such tort—such wrongful attachment being a tort, all other persons who aided and abetted the judgment-creditor in the commission of such tort, or who acted as accessories in its commission or who acted in concert in its commission, would also be jointly and severally liable, as well as the judgment-creditor as joint tortfeasors—AIR 1974 Mys 24.

537. Application for review of court's earlier order (s. 114, CPC)

In the Court of .... at ....

Suit No. .... 20 ....

(Set out cause title)

The plaintiff states:

1. That on the application of the plaintiff dated .... in the above title suit, the court was pleased to pass orders to the effect.

....

....

2. That the said order suffers from inherent defect and is palpably wrong on the face of it which Your Honour may like to review with a view to advancing the cause of justice.

It is, therefore, prayed that the court would be pleased to review the order dated ...... if necessary after hearing the parties.

Verification

Affidavit

NOTES: 1. Interlocutory orders do not operate as *res judicata*.
2. The section does not confer on the court general power to review its earlier order *suo motu*—AIR 1967 Bom 355; AIR 1978 Mad 221.

3. Trial Court returning plaint for filing in proper court. There could be no review against the same. Appeal is maintainable—*Pratibha* v *Dr. Kamlesh* AIR 1992 MP 199.

538. Application under s. 115, CPC for revision

In the High Court at ....

Civil Revision No. .... of ....

In the matter of:

An application under s. 115 of the Code of Civil Procedure 1908

And

In the matter of:

Order No. .... dated .... passed by Mr. .... Judge .... in Title Suit No. ...... of 20........

And

In the matter of:

AB.........

(Name, description and address of the petitioner).

.... *Plaintiff*
Petitioner

versus

CD.........

(Name, description and address of the O.P.'s)

.........*Defendant*
Respondent

To
The Hon'ble Mr. .... Chief Justice
and His Companion Justices of the said
Hon'ble Court.

The humble petition of the above-named petitioner most respectfully sheweth:

1. That your petitioner filed a Title Suit being No. .... against the Respondent on the pleadings.

(State in a nutshell the case of the plaint)

2. That the defendant had entered appearance on about .... and filed a written statement on .... Its defence in brief is—(State defence in a nutshell).

3. That after lapse of 6 years the defendant made an application before the learned court below praying for amendment of written statement for the purpose of—(state here amendments sought for) which was not stated in the written statement. In spite of objection in writing the prayer for amendment has been allowed on contest by an order dated.........

A certified copy of the said Order is annexed hereto.

4. That being aggrieved by the said order dated......... your petitioner begs to move this petition on the following amongst other.

GROUNDS

1. For that ....
2. For that (state the grounds)
3. For that
4. For that

5. That your petitioner submits that if the impugned order be allowed to stand, that would occasion a failure of justice (or, if the impugned order be allowed to stand that would cause irreparable injury to your petitioner).

6. That this application is made *bona fide* and for the ends of justice.

Your petitioner therefore humbly prays that—

(*a*) Your Lordships be graciously pleased to call for the records of the case and issue a Rule calling upon the Respondent to show cause as to why the order complained of should not be set aside and after hearing the cause shown or if no cause is shown, to make the Rule absolute.

(*b*) To stay further proceedings of the Title Suit No. .... till disposal of the Rule or this application.

(*c*) And to pass such other order or orders and/ or directions as Your Lordships consider fit and proper.

And Your Petitioner, as in duty bound, shall ever pray.

Verification

Affidavit

NOTES 1. Revision Petition cannot be filed against on Order under s. 115, CPC, Revision would not lie even against the Order passed on review application in respect of the same Revision Petition—*Ratan Singh* v *Tarabai* AIR 1992 MP 59.

2. A Revision Petition under s. 115, CPC is a separate and distinct proceeding from a petition under Art. 227 of the Constitution and one cannot be identified with the other—*Vishesh Kumar* v *Shanti Prosad* AIR 1980 SC 892. Revisional proceedings cannot be converted into proceedings under Art. 227—*Ratan Singh* v *Tarabai* AIR 1992 MP 59.

3. Sufficiency of cause under s. 5 of the Limitation Act is a mixed question of law and fact—can be gone into in Revisional Jurisdiction—*Home Secretary, P&H* v *Sarwan Singh* AIR 1992 P&H 143.

4. Revision lies where no appeal lies.

5. See Explanation to sub-see (2)—Any case which has been decided—vide CPC (Amendment) Act 1976.

539. Application for restitution under s. 144, CPC

In the Court of .... at ....

Misc. Judicial Case No. .... of 20 ....

A.B. .... *Petitioner*

versus

C.D. .... *Opposite Party*

The above-named petitioner states as follows:

1. That the opposite party obtained a decree of khas possession of the properties, described in the Schedule below, against this petitioner in Title Suit No. .... of 20 .... of this court, together with costs of the suit.

2. Thereafter by a Title Execution No. .... of 20 .... of this court, the opposite party, obtained possession of the said properties on .... through process of the court. The petitioner also deposited with the court on .... a sum of ₹ ....as costs of the suit and of execution proceedings.

3. That the petitioner preferred an Appeal No. .... of 20 .... in the court of .... at .... against the said the judgment and decree of the Title Suit No. .... of 20 .... of this court and the judgment and decree were set aside by the Appellate Court. Certified copics of the judgment and the decree of the said appeal are filed herewith.

The petitioner, therefore, prays by way of restitution—

(*i*) Possession of the properties described in the Schedule below.

(*ii*) Refund of ₹ .... with interest at 6.5% from .... (date when deposited) till realisation.

(*iii*) Damages of ₹ .... for deprivation of use and occupation of properties in the Schedule below.

SCHEDULE

Verification

Affidavit

NOTES: 1. See s. 144 of CPC. The court may make any orders, including orders for the refund of costs and for the payment of interest, damages, compensation and *mesne profits* which are properly consequential on variation or reversal of a decree.

2. An application for restitution should be made in all cases to the court of first instance, that is, the primary court that passed the decree in the suit.

3. Application under s. 144 are not proceedings in execution—AIR 1956 Nag 129; AIR 1958 Punj 132; ILR 2 Cal 315; AIR 1932 Cal 308. Application under s. 144 are proceedings in execution—AIR 1921 Bom 67. An application under this section is to be treated as a Miscellaneous Judicial case—ILR 2 Cal 315; AIR 1958 Punj 132—Application for restitution is an application in execution—AIR 1934 Pat 246; AIR 1977 Pat 204.

4. Eviction decree against tenant set aside in appeal—third person inducted by the landlord as tenant during pendency of appeal being representative of the landlord is liable to restore possession—AIR 1976 All 250. *Ex parte* decree for eviction is set aside. Party dispossessed in pursuance of such *ex parte* decree. He is entitled to restitution. Person entering in possession through party obtaining *ex parte* order cannot resist restitution—*Chanda* v *Jamshed Khan* AIR 1993 Kant 338. Restitution is available even where decree is set aside in proceeding under Or. 9, r. 13 (s. 144 as amended by Amending Act 1976)—*Mst. Fatima Khatoon* v *Swaraj Singh* AIR 1984 Cal 257.

5. Section 144 is not exhaustive; the court can grant restitution under its inherent power—AIR 1975 All 102 (FB).
6. Right to claim restitution can be enforced against a party or his transferee or assignee even if he is not a party to the application for restitution—AIR 1974 All 82.
7. On reversal of a decree, the law imposes an obligation on the party to the suit who received the benefit of the erroneous decree to make restitution to the other party for what he has lost. The court may refuse restitution where it does not appear to be in consonance with the real and substantial justice of the case—AIR 1973 MP 6.
8. Limitation—Art. 137 of the Limitation Act 1963 to be reckoned from the date of reversal of the decree—AIR 1965 SC 1477.
9. Possession obtained forcibly, unauthorisedly and not pursuant to orders of court—Restitution cannot be ordered by invoking s. 144. However, to meet ends of justice. Court can restore possession under s. 151—AIR 1993 AP 292.

540. Application for enlargement of time under s. 148, CPC

In the Court of .... at ....

Money Suit No. .... of 20 ....

A.B. .... *Plaintiff*

versus

C.D. .... *Defendant*

The above-named plaintiff states as follows:

1. That the plaintiff filed the above suit on .... with insufficient court-fees and under orders of the court the plaintiff was to pay deficit court-fees by ....

2. That the plaintiff was incapacitated due to his illness (state here cause) to collect necessary money for requisite court-fees and was unable to pay deficit court-fees by the said date.

It is, therefore, prayed that the time for payment of court-fees be extended by another week from.........(date)

Verification

Affidavit

NOTES: 1. Where any period is fixed or granted by the court, s. 148 of the CPC applied.
It does not apply when a period is fixed by law, e.g.—
(*i*) Supply of deficient stamp paper—AIR 1958 Ker 58.
(*ii*) Time for filing written statement, Additional W/S.
(*iii*) Production of documents etc.
2. A court has power to extend time under the section even after the time fixed by decree or order had expired (AIR 1961 SC 882; AIR 1971 Cal 243: AIR 1965 Cal 354, held not good law; AIR 1977 J&K 36; AIR 1976 Bom 369) irrespective of whether the application for extension is made before or after the expiry of the period—AIR 1972 All 246.
3. Time fixed by consent decree. Court has power to extend time—*Periyakkal* v *Dakshyani* AIR 1983 SC 428.

541. Application for a caveat (s. 148A, CPC)

In the Court of .... at ....

In the matter of caveat

P.Q., son of M.N. residing at ....

.... Caveator-Petitioner

The caveator submits:

1. Let nothing be done in the following matter touching upon properties of the petitioner without notice to the petitioner.

2. The necessary particulars are:

(*a*) (Name and full postal address of the person lodging the caveat).

(*b*) (Name of the applicant in respect of whose application the caveat is intended to be lodged and the full-postal address of such applicant).

(*c*) (The court by which the decree or order referred to in the caveat was passed together with the number and the year of the suit or proceeding in which the decree or order was passed).

(*d*) (Particulars of the suit or proceeding in case the caveat is lodged in a pending suit or proceeding).

(*e*) (A statement that the notice of the caveat had been served on the person by whom the application in respect of which the caveat is being lodged has been or is expected to be made).

Date: ....

....
Signature

NOTES: 1. See Rule 40A of the Civil Rules and Orders, Vol. I of Calcutta High Court.
2. Fees for caveat—₹10 for West Bengal under Item No. 13 in Schedule II (fixed fees) of the West Bengal Court-fees Act 1970.
3. Nature of caveat—20 CWN 787; 36 IC 38.
4. 'In the caveat the name of the person who is expected to file or has filed the application, the nature of the application and the right under which the person lodging the caveat claims to appear before the court have to be stated'—AIR 1978 Cal 492 at p. 494.
5. In a pending Title Suit caveators appearing by caveat apprehending that opposite party would file petition for injunction—Rejection of caveat without affording opportunity of hearing to caveators—Rejection not proper. Court has to give opportunity of hearing the caveator if it has to pass an order against them—*Ranjit Kumar Malo Das* v *Khanindra Nath Gayan* AIR 1994 Gau 34.

542. Application for amendment of a decree (s. 152, CPC)

In the matter of .... at ....

Suit No. .... of 20 ....

AB of .... *Petitioner*

versus

CD of .... *Respondent*

The above-named petitioner states as follows:

1. That the above suit was decreed on .... by a judgment of the court. The decree was drawn up and signed by the court on ....

Case of clerical mistake

2. That the plaintiff's title to properties in items No. (1) to (3) of the Schedule to the plaint was declared by the judgment of the court. In the decree the property in item No. (2) of the Schedule has been misdescribed through inadvertence as ....

Case of arithmetical mistake

That the plaintiff has been awarded costs of the suit of ₹......... inclusive of pleader's fees of ₹......... Rate of fees of a pleader has since undergone change by orders of the Hon'ble High Court at Calcutta under Notification No. .... dated .... Pleader's fees would be ₹......... as per rate as revised. The decree, so far as it relates to pleader's fees, contains an arithmetical mistake.

Case of accidental slip

That by the judgment in the said suit, the decree was for ₹25,500 but due to presumable accidental slip of pen, the decree was drawn up for ₹500 only.

Case of omission

That by the judgment the plaintiff has been awarded costs of suit. Through inadvertence the direction as to costs has not been mentioned in the operative part of the judgment.

It is, therefore, prayed that the decree may be amended in appropriate manner to conform with the judgment.

Verification

Affidavit

NOTES:

1. Inadvertently recording order of dismissal instead of order decreeing suit or appeal can be corrected under s. 152—AIR 1915 All 323.
2. The court has inherent power to amend the decree when it is at variance with the judgment—AIR 1953 VP 2; AIR 1932 All 587; AIR 1967 SC 1440. When the decree does not correctly express what was really decided and intended by the court, the court has an inherent power to amend the decree so as to carry out its directions—AIR 1931 PC 104; AIR 1944 PC 46.
3. There is no limitation for an application for amendment under this section—AIR 1953 All 485; AIR 1958 MP 307. A consent decree may be corrected by the court under s. 152—AIR 1953 Ajmer 1.
4. Suit for dissolution of Partnership—Preliminary decree not stating shares of parties as required by Or. 20, r. 15 and Appendix D, Form 21—mistake can be rectified under ss. 151 and 152—AIR 1977 Mad 140.
5. The judgment declared the successful party to be entitled to costs. An application was made for including some items as costs incidental to the proceedings. Held, that the application can be construed to be an application for amendment of decree—AIR 1978 Mad 163.
6. Decree for specific performance of sale not fixing date for completion thereof. Decree can be amended—AIR 1976 AP 50.
7. Issue 'whether plaintiff was entitled to possession' was decided in plaintiff's favour. Relief of possession not incorporated in judgment and decree. Omission being due to accidental slip can be amended under s. 152—AIR 1975 Kant 107.

8. Where clerical and arithmetical errors creep in the plaint and as a consequence in the decree as well, they can be rectified at any time even after a final decree. But where the error related to a mistaken identity of the property but not a misdescription thereof, proceedings under s. 152 of CPC cannot be resorted to—AIR 1963 SC 1879; AIR 1974 AP 201.
9. Decree in accord with the judgment is silent on future interest—constitutes no accidental error/omission attracting rectification under s. 152—AIR 1973 Raj 307.
10. Accidental mistakes in decree pertaining to description of suit-property can be corrected by court in exercise of its powers under ss. 151 and 152—AIR 1973 All 116.
11. Accidental error ought to be rectified—AIR 1979 Mad 14; AIR 1979 Punj 47.
12. Correction of clerical errors in judgment. Decree passed by trial court affirmed by the Appellate Court. Only Appellate Court can correct errors therein—AIR 1979 Pat 5.

543. Petition for amending defects in proceedings under s. 153, CPC (Suit filed against dead sole defendant)

In the Court of the Civil Judge (Senior Division) at ....

Money Suit No. .... of ....

A.B. .... *Plaintiff*

versus

C.D. .... *Defendant*

The above-named plaintiff states:

1. That the plaintiff has instituted the above-numbered suit for realisation of money on a handnote executed by the above defendant on ....

2. That from the report in the writ of summons on the said defendant, it transpires that the defendant died on the .... day of .... 20 .... at Kolkata, 25 days ahead of the date of institution of the above suit.

3. That the fact of death of the defendant was not known to the plaintiff-petitioner at the time of the institution of the above suit. Your petitioner came to know of the defendant's death for the first time on .... when the said report on service-return came to his knowledge.

4. That the plaintiff petitioner has filed this day in the court separately a petition for substitution of legal heirs/representatives of the deceased defendant.

5. That the suit will be within the period of limitation after the substitution is made.

It is, therefore, prayed that Your Honour would be pleased to pass necessary orders allowing the plaintiff petitioner to remove defects in the above suit and to proceed with the suit, after substitution, against the legal representatives of the said deceased defendant.

Verification

Affidavit

NOTE: The section confers a general power to amend defects in a proceeding and so, when a suit is filed against a dead person, the plaint can be amended to substitute the legal representatives of the deceased. Therefore, when a money suit is filed against a dead sole defendant and the death is known only subsequently, the suit is not void *ab initio* and can be continued against the legal representatives of the deceased if their substitution is made within the limitation period for the suit. It cannot be said that the section does not apply when there is a sole defendant since on his death before the suit there is 'no proceeding in a suit' within the meaning of the section—AIR 1976 AP 65.

544. Application under Or. 1, r. 8, CPC

In the Court of .... at ....

Title Suit No. .... of ....

(Set out cause title)

Petition under Or. 1, r. 8 of the CPC.

The above-named petitioners submit:

1. That the petitioners belong to .... community residing at .... P.S. .... in the District of .... and there are about 500 people of the said .... community at ....

2. That the petitioners intend to commence, as plaintiffs, a suit as suit of all the persons of the said .... community of the village .... for vindication of their common right (state here the rights).

The petitioners, therefore, pray for necessary permission for the same.

Verification

Affidavit

NOTES: 1. Under Or. 1, r. 8 same suit may be a representative one both as regards plaintiffs and as regards defendants—AIR 1935 Mad 542.
2. See under heading 'Representative suit' supra.
3. Community of interest is an essential condition precedent for bringing a suit in representative character.
4. On death of defendant (permitted to defend under Or. 1, r. 8 by the court)—his legal representatives need not be brought on record—AIR 1939 Lah 572.
5. Even in the absence of a formal order granting permission under Rule 8, the direction to publish notice is sufficient to infer permission being granted—AIR 1972 Ker 269.

545. Application for intervening in a suit (Or. 1, r. 10, CPC)

In the Court of .... at ....

Money/Title Suit No. .... of 20.........

A.B. .... *Plaintiff*

versus

C.D. .... *Defendant*

E.F. .... *Petitioner*

Petition under Or. 1, r. 10 of CPC for intervention as a co-defendant.

The above-named petitioner states as follows:

1. That the plaintiff has instituted the above mortgage suit praying for .... (state here substance of reliefs prayed).

2. That the petitioner has had interest in the said mortgaged property and intends to challenge the binding nature of the mortgage on this petitioner.

3. That the petitioner in the facts of the case should be allowed to intervene in the suit as a co-defendant.

4. An affidavit in support of this petition is attached herewith.

It is, therefore, prayed that the court may be pleased to permit the petitioner to intervene directing the plaintiff to add the petitioner as a co-defendant.

Verification

Affidavit

NOTES: 1. Under Or. 1, r. 10 the court is empowered to add parties at any stage of the suit *suo motu* or on application of a person seeking to be made a party, or on application of parties on record. "Intervenors are third persons, not originally parties to a suit, who claim an interest in the matter and right to interpose at any stage of the suit in defence of their own interest, whenever affected as to person or property"—Wharton's *Law Lexicon*, pp. 413-432.

2. For fuller treatment see Chapter VIII, Note 2(*c*) "Intervenor" *supra.*

546. Application for addition or substitution of plaintiff (Or. 1, r. 10(1), CPC)

In the Court of the .... at ....

Title Suit No. .... of 20 ....

A.B. .... *Plaintiff*

versus

C.D. .... *Defendant*

E.F. .... *Petitioner*

The above-named petitioner states as follows:

1. That one A.B. as the plaintiff has commenced the above Title Suit against C.D. in this court praying for (state here the substance of relief).

In case of addition of plaintiff [under Or. 1, r. 10(1)].

2. That the petitioner is also a co-sharer with the said A.B. in respect of the suit property shown in the Schedule to the plaint of the above suit. The plaintiff alone cannot get full reliefs without joinder of this petitioner as a co-plaintiff.

3. That the addition of this petitioner as a co-plaintiff is necessary for full and final determination of the matter in dispute.

In case of substitution of plaintiff [under Or. 1, r. 10(2)].

2. That the said A.B. is the agent of this petitioner. The aforesaid suit was instituted through *bona fide* mistake in the name of the agent.

3. That the petitioner is the real owner of the suit property, shown in the Schedule to the plaint and substitution of his name as plaintiff against the said A.B. is necessary for the determination of the matter in dispute.

It is, therefore, prayed

In case of addition

that Your Honour may be pleased to pass orders for addition of the petitioner as co-plaintiff in the suit.

In case of substitution

that Your Honour may be pleased to direct substitution of the name of the petitioner against the name of the present plaintiff.

4. An affidavit in support of the petition is furnished herewith.

Verification

Affidavit

NOTES: 1. See AIR 1957 Cal 688 for further discussion.
2. On the death of a party application for substitution of his L.R.'s after setting aside abatement was rejected. Application under Or. 1, r. 10 for bringing the L.R.'s as necessary parties is not maintainable—AIR 1978 Cal 344.
3. Application of this nature should be supported by an affidavit.

547. Application for substituted service (Or. 5, r. 20, CPC)

In the Court of .... at ....

Suit No. .... of 20 ....

(Set out cause title)

The plaintiff states:

1. That before now the plaintiff has tried to serve summons on the defendant through the court in the ordinary way but to no purpose.

2. That the defendant is ordinarily a resident of the place where the summons was directed to. There is reason to believe that the defendant is keeping out of the way for the purpose of avoiding service.

3. An affidavit in support of the petition is furnished herewith.

It is, therefore, prayed that an order be passed for substituted service of summons on the defendant in a manner as the court thinks proper.

Verification

Affidavit

NOTE: The application is to be supported by an affidavit stating reasons leading to the conclusion that the defendant was keeping out of the way.

548. Application for permission to verify a plaint through an agent

In the Court of the Civil Judge (Senior Division) at ....

S.C.C. No. .... of 20 ....

A.B. .... *Plaintiff*

versus

C.D. .... *Defendant*

Petition under Or. 6, rr. 14 &15 of the CPC

The above-named plaintiff states:

1. That the plaintiff has been living at his native place in Rajasthan and is unable to sign and verify the pleadings.

2. That Sri .... is the agent and constituted attorney of the plaintiffs. He is conversant with the facts of this suit, which is being filed this day. The said .... is competent under the power of attorney to bring the suit and sign and verify pleadings.

It is, therefore, prayed that the said .... may please by permitted to act for the principal plaintiff.

Annexure (power of attorney)

Verification

Affidavit

The statements made above are true to my knowledge and I sign this verification this the .... day of ...., 20........ at ....

549. Application for permission to sign a plaint by an agent (Or. 6, rr. 14 & 15, CPC)

In the Court of the .... at ....

Money Suit No. .... of 20 ....

A.B. .... *Plaintiff*

versus

C.D. .... *Defendant*

Petition under Or. 6, r. 15 of the CPC.

The plaintiff petitioner states as follows:

1. That the plaintiff has been living away from .... and is unable to sign and verify the plaint.

2. That one XY is the agent of the plaintiff. He is conversant with the facts of the Money Suit that is going to be filed by the plaintiff and the said XY is competent to sign and verify the pleadings and is duly authorised by the plaintiff in that behalf.

3. That the plaintiff intends filing of the plaint by the said XY after signature and verification by the said XY.

It is, therefore, prayed that the said XY may be permitted to sign and verify the pleadings in the plaint.

Verification

Affidavit

NOTES: 1. See Or. 6, r. 15—Every pleading shall be verified at the foot by the party or by one of the parties or by some other person proved to the satisfaction of the court to be acquainted with the facts of the case.

2. Order 6, r. 14 where a party pleading by reason of absence or for other good cause is unable to sign himself, it may be done by any person duly authorised by him to sign the same.

550. Application for striking out pleadings (Or. 6, r. 16, CPC)

In the Court of .... at ....

Title Suit No. .... of 20........

A.B. .... *Plaintiff*

versus

C.D. .... *Defendant*

The above-named defendant states as follows:

1. That the plaintiff has commenced the above suit against the defendant which is pending.

2. That the plaintiff has made an averment in para 3 of the plaint, to wit, ... (State here the averment).

The said allegations are scandalous and irrelevant for the purpose of this suit.

(Or, that the plaintiff has made an averment in para 4 of the plaint, to wit).

(State here the averment).

The said allegations are wholly unnecessary for determination of the issues relating to this suit and those are embarrassing to the defendant.

The petitioner, therefore, prays that the said averments in paras 3 and 4 of the plaint may be ordered to be struck out from the plaint.

Verification

Affidavit

NOTES: 1. Pleadings include a plaint as well as a written statement. Unnecessary or scandalous pleadings may be struck out both from the plaint and the written statement.

2. Application of this type may be filed at any stage of the suit.

3. The court can *suo motu* or on application by the plaintiff or the defendant compel striking out of pleadings which may be unnecessary or scandalous or which may tend to prejudice, embarrass or delay the fair trial of the suit.

551. Application for amendment of plaint (Or. 6, r. 17, CPC)

In the Court of .... at ....

Suit No. .... of 20 ....

(Set out cause title)

The plaintiff states:

1. That the above-numbered suit stands posted on .... for preliminary hearing and for framing of issues.

2. That inadvertently an error has crept in the averment in para 2 of the plaint. In place of .... in line 3 of para 2 the plaintiff wrote.........

3. The plaintiff intends to remove the said statement by amendment in the plaint in the manner shown below.

4. That the proposed amendment if allowed will not change the nature and character of the suit.

It is, therefore, prayed that Your Honour would be pleased to allow the amendments prayed for in the interest of justice.

Amendments prayed for

In line 3 of para 2 of the plaint the words "..........." should be deleted and be substituted by "........."

Verification

Affidavit

NOTE: Amendment adding time-barred claim not permissible—AIR 1978 Cal 298.

552. Application for restoration of a suit dismissed for default (Or. 9, r. 9, CPC)

In the Court of the .... at ....

Misc. Case No. .... of 20 ....

A.B. .... *Petitioner*

versus

C.D. .... *Defendant Opposite Party*

Petition under Or. 9, r. 9 of the CPC 1908 for restoration of Title Suit No. .... of 20.... of this court after setting aside orders of dismissal.

The above-named petitioner states as follow:

1. That the petitioner had instituted a Title Suit No. ..... of 20 .... against the Opposite Party in this court and was diligently prosecuting the said suit.

2. That the aforesaid Title Suit No. .... of 20 .... stood fixed on .... for peremptory hearing.

3. That the petitioner was lying bed-ridden with ....for the period from .... to .... both inclusive and, therefore, could not attend the court when the said Title Suit was called on for hearing.

4. That the petitioner's absence in the court on .... was not wilful and he was prevented by his illness from attending the court when the said Title Suit was called on for hearing.

5. A medical certificate in respect of the illness of the plaintiff petitioner is annexed.

6. That the petitioner has suffered hardship due to dismissal of the said suit.

It is prayed, therefore, that the said Title Suit No. .... of 20 .... be restored to its file and number after setting aside the order of dismissal.

Verification

Affidavit

NOTES: 1. Where the dismissal is under Or. 17, r. 3 or under Or. 11, r. 21 or where the plaint is rejected under Or. 7, r. 11 this application does not lie.

2. Misc. case under Or. 9, r. 9 dismissed for default. Misc. case under Or. 9, r. 9 against such dismissal is maintainable (contra AIR 1970 MP 199—s. 151 applies).

3. When an appeal is dismissed for default under Or. 41, r. 17 or r.18 this rule does not apply. The proper course is by prayer for readmission of appeal under Or. 41, r. 19 of the CPC.

4. Application under s. 10, Hindu Marriage Act, dismissed for default but not restored. Subsequent application under s. 13 of the Act on the same cause of action is barred—AIR 1978 Punj 150.

5. Order dismissing suit for default passed due to mistake of court. The Court can recall it *suo motu* under its inherent power—AIR 1977 Del 7.

553. Application for setting aside an ex parte decree (Or. 9, r. 13, CPC)

In the Court of .... at ....

Misc. Judicial Case No. .... of 20.........

A.B. ....

.... *Petitioner-Defendant*

versus

C.D. ....

.... *Opposite Party-Plaintiff*

The above-named petitioner states as follows:

1. That the Opp. Party as plaintiff had instituted a Title Suit No......... of 20 .... in this court against the petitioner and obtained on .... an *ex parte* decree in the absence of the petitioner.

2. That the petitioner entered his appearance in the said Title Suit and was diligently contesting the claim.

3. That the said Title Suit was fixed for peremptory hearing on .... Your petitioner suddenly fell ill on .... and was lying bed-ridden for a period of .... days from .... to .... and was unable to appear when the said Title Suit was called on for hearing.

4. That the petitioner has suffered hardship for the said *ex parte* decree. A medical certificate in support of the petitioner's illness is attached herewith.

It is prayed that Your Honour would be pleased to set aside the *ex parte* decree passed against the petitioner upon such terms as the court deems proper.

Verification

Affidavit

NOTES: 1. Submission as in para 4 not required always.

2. Order 9, r. 13 does not apply to appeals. It does not apply to summary suits (for summary suits see Or. 37, r. 4), but the provision is applicable to orders by the Small Cause Court.

3. No fresh Vakalatnama is required if application is filed by the lawyer who was conducting the suit—AIR 1944 All 238.

4. Any one of several defendants against whom the decree is *ex parte* can apply—8 CWN 621; when a defendant dies after *ex parte* decree is made against him his legal representatives can apply—AIR 1954 Mys 32.

5. No appeal when petition is allowed; but appeal lies when there is rejection of the petition either on merits or on default—AIR 1948 Mad 416; AIR 1954 Ass 1; AIR 1970 Cal 229.

6. Mere non-service of summons is not enough to find a cause of action for setting aside a decree—AIR 1978 Cal 177.

7. A court can pass a conditional order on an application under the rule for setting aside an *ex parte* decree and where such order is passed and the condition is not fulfilled within the time specified therein, the application automatically stands dismissed—AIR 1972 All 166.

8. Suit dismissed for default—application for restoration was filed beyond 30 days. Application was dismissed for default stating it was time-barred application; to set aside order of dismissal under s. 151 is maintainable—AIR 1978 Pat 253.

9. Application under Or. 9, r. 13 to set aside *ex parte* decree. Also appeal preferred. During the pendency of application for restoration, the memo of appeal is rejected as barred by limitation. This tantamounts to dismissal of appeal. Court passing *ex parte* decree has no jurisdiction thereafter to entertain restoration application—AIR 1956 SC 367; AIR 1978 Cal 392.

10. Relief claimed under wrong provision of law. Application was wrongly made under Or. 9, r. 7 to set aside an *ex parte* order. Application can be treated under Or. 9, r. 13 from its substance—AIR 1978 AP 395.

11. Where the defendant appeared but did not file written statement after being granted many adjournments and the judgment followed by a decree was passed, it could not be called an *ex parte* decree within the meaning of Or. 9, r. 13 in view of the amended provision of Or. 8, r. 10. Therefore, the application under Or. 9, r. 13 for setting aside an *ex parte* decree would not be maintainable as the decree passed was not an *ex parte* decree—*Satyanarain Sha* v *Brijgopal Mundra* AIR 1991 Pat 60. Contra—Provisions of Or. 9, r. 13 can be invoked—*Innovation Apartments* v *Innovation Associates* AIR 1991 AP 69.

554. Application for leave to deliver interrogatories (Or. 11, r. 12, CPC)

In the Court of .... at ....

Suit No. .... of 20 ....

(Set out cause title)

The petitioner states as follows:

1. That the petitioner is the plaintiff of the above-numbered title suit.

2. That your petitioner prays for leave of the court to deliver interrogatories, appended below, for examination of defendant No. 2, within........ days (or within the time specified by the court).

Interrogatories:

(On behalf of the plaintiff A.B. for examination the above-named defendant C.D.)

1. Did not etc.
2. Has not etc.

Verification

Affidavit

NOTES: 1. See Or. 11, r. 1. The plaintiff as also the defendant may deliver interrogatories in writing by leave of the court.

2. Interrogatories must be as to questions of fact and not of law.

3. Interrogatories shall be in Form No. 2 in Appendix C of the Code, with such variations as circumstances may require—See Or. 11, r. 4.

4. The court has no power to strike out the defence of the defendant or dismiss the plaintiff's suit *suo motu* under Or. 11, r. 21—AIR 1977 Cal 187.

Questions that may be relevant during cross-examination are not necessarily relevant as interrogatories. The only questions that are relevant as interrogatories are those relating to 'any matters in question'. The interrogatories served must have reasonably close connection with 'matters in question'—AIR 1972 SC 1302.

5. Objection regarding vagueness of the W.S. was taken. No attempt to amend the W.S. by supplying particulars was made.

555. Application for discovery of documents (Or. 11, r. 14, CPC)

In the Court of .... at ....

Suit No. .... of 20 ....

(Set out cause title)

The plaintiff states:

1. That the defendant has alleged in paragraphs .... and .... of his written statement that ....

2. That for fair disposal of the case and to minimise costs of litigation discovery of documents relating to those allegations in the written statement is necessary.

The plaintiff, therefore, prays:

An appropriate order directing the defendant to make discovery on oath of the documents lying in his custody, possession or power relating to the said matters in paras .... of the written statement.

Verification

NOTES: 1. The other party of the suit is bound to disclose all documents in his affidavit—AIR 1962 Cal 325.

2. Application for production is to follow application for discovery of documents—AIR 1961 J&K 20. Application by defendant for discovery of documents. Plaintiff has filed all requisite documents on which he relies with copies thereof. No specific document relating to controversy in suit is available with the plaintiff. Question of discovery does not arise—*Canara Bank* v *Steron Castings* AIR 1991 Del 211.

3. Discovery of documents/letter—Mere confidentiality is not sufficient to resist production of letters exchanged between parties to the suit—*Kamatia Bros.* v *State of Gujarat* AIR 1992 Guj 138.

556. Application for summoning a record (Or. 13, r. 10, CPC)

In the Court of .... at ....

Suit No. .... of 20 ....

(Set out cause title)

The plaintiff states as follows:

1. That the defendant has submitted a written statement in the above suit denying the plaintiff's right, title and interest in the suit property.

2. That before now the defendant by submitting a written statement in Title Suit No. .... of 20 .... of the Court of Civil Judge (Junior Division), at .... admitted plaintiff's title in the suit property.

3. That the plaintiff files herewith a certified copy of the written statement dated .... filed by the defendant in the said Title Suit No. .... of 20 ....

4. That the plaintiff intends to prove the contents of the said written statement, by calling for the original, which is absolutely material for disposal of this suit.

Particulars of the Record to be sent for:

Title Suit No. .... of 20 ....
of the Court of Civil Judge (Junior Division) at ....

A.B. ... versus C.D. ...

Date of disposal— ....

The Record is now lying in the District Record Room of .... (Place).

5. An affidavit in support of this petition is attached herewith.

It is, therefore, prayed that the court may be pleased to call for the record of the aforesaid Title Suit No. .... of 20 .... containing the written statement, dated ....

Verification

Affidavit

NOTES: 1. The court from which a document is sent for need not necessarily be a civil court. But it must be a court.

2. An application without setting forth the necessary grounds satisfactorily in the affidavit will be rejected—AIR 1931 Lah 119.

557. Application for summoning witnesses (Or. 16, r. 1, CPC)

In the Court of .... at ....

Title Suit No. .... of 20 ....

A.B. ....

.... *Plaintiff*

versus

C.D. and two other ....

.... *Defendants*

The defendants sheweth:

That for proving the defendant's case in the above suit evidence of the undermentioned persons will be material.

It is, therefore, prayed that necessary orders for issue of summonses on the undermentioned persons be passed. Dated .... the day of .... 20 ....

Names and addresses of witnesses to be summoned:

(1) ......
(2) ...... etc.

Verification

Affidavit

NOTE: Application cannot be refused on the ground that such an application is too late, though it is within the discretion of the court to refuse an adjournment of the hearing on ground of want of diligence of the party—AIR 1950 Cal 326; AIR 1958 Pat 458.

558. Application for issue of warrant of arrest against absentee witness (Or. 16, r. 10, CPC)

In the Court of .... at ....

Suit No. .... of 20 ....

(Set out cause title)

The defendant submits:

1. That one A.B., son of late C.D. of .... P.O. .... Dt. .... is a witness for the petitioner and was duly summoned through the court.

2. That the said witness, in spite of due service of summons, failed to appear in the court on .... without lawful excuse.

3. That the said absentee witness, is a material witness of the defendant and through him the defence version of adjustment of the plaintiff's claim will be proved.

4. An affidavit in support of this petition is attached herewith.

It is, therefore, prayed that necessary orders of production on the next date of hearing of the suit of the said A.B. by issue of warrant of arrest may please be passed.

Verification

Affidavit

NOTES: 1. Conditions precedent laid down in sub-rule (2) of Or. 16, r. 10 must be satisfied before any coercive action is taken.

2. 'Without lawful excuse'—See AIR 1952 Pat 243 at p. 244.

559. Application under Or. 21, r. 2(2) for a certificate

In the Court of .... at ....

Money Execution Case No. .... of 20 ....

A.B. ....

..... *Judgment-debtor—Petitioner*

versus

C.D. ....

..... *Decree-holder—Opposite Party*

The above-named petitioner states:

1. That your petitioner is the judgment-debtor in Money Suit No. .... of 20 .... of this court.

2. That after filing of the above execution case by the aforesaid decree-holder, your petitioner has paid to the decree-holder Opposite Party a sum of ₹ .... on .... towards decretal dues and has been granted a receipt therefor.

It is, therefore, prayed that the said payment on .... be recorded in the relevant Register after notice to the decree-holder.

Verification

Affidavit

NOTES: 1. Order 21, r. 2 applies when money is paid out of court or the decree is otherwise adjusted in whole or in part to the satisfaction of the decree-holder. No distinction between voluntary and non-voluntary payments—AIR 1978 SC 118.

2. Provisions of this rule are not confined to money decree but apply to every kind of decree—AIR 1952 All 814; AIR 1928 Cal 715, contra: AIR 1951 Mad 853; AIR 1958 AP 705.

3. An agreement not to execute the decree is an adjustment of the decree within the meaning of the rule—AIR 1957 Cal 308.

4. On filing of an application by the judgment-debtor, the court shall issue a notice to the decree-holder—AIR 1923 Nag 20.

5. Under Or. 21, r. 1 the correct method is to appropriate the payments made by judgment-debtors first towards costs and interest payable under the decree and the balance, if any, towards the discharge of the principal amount—AIR 1922 PC 233; AIR 1970 SC 171 and AIR 1973 Mys 86.

560. Application for a claim under Or. 21, r. 58, CPC

In the Court of .... at ....

Misc. Case No. .... of 20 ....

Arising out of Money Execution Case No. .... of .... 20 ....

A.B. ....*Claimant (Petitioner)*

versus

1. C.D. .... *Plaintiff*

.........*Opposite Party*

2. E.F. .... *Defendant*

The petitioner states:

1. That Opposite Party No. 1 had instituted a Money Suit No. .... of 20 .... in this court against the Opposite Party No. 2 and under orders dated......... of the court in Money Execution Case No. .... of 20 ...., attached the properties described in the Schedule below.

2. That the said property in the Schedule below belongs to the claimant-petitioner and the claimant is in exclusive possession thereof. The Opposite Party No. 2 has no interest or possession in the said property.

It is, therefore, prayed that necessary orders may be passed—

(*i*) releasing the property in the Schedule from attachment;

(*ii*) granting costs to the petitioner.

SCHEDULE

(State here particulars of property)

Verification

Affidavit

NOTES: 1. See Or. 21, r. 58—Investigation of claims to, and objections to attachment of, attached property. A claimant may file an objection or he may straightway file a suit for the appropriate relief—AIR 1948 Sind 24. Third party objector cannot prefer an appeal against orders of attachment—AIR 1937 Lah 313.

2. Petition lies only when there is an attachment and after such attachment. Petition does not lie after sale of attached property. Rule applies to attachment before judgment as well.

3. All persons who, at the date of attachment, have some interest in or are possessed of the property can prefer a claim under this rule. A transferee after attachments is not entitled to benefits of this rule, but when attachment is subsequent to transfer such transferee can prefer a claim.
Objection should be on the basis of possession—AIR 1971 Bom 94. Complicated question of title not to be decided.

4. An application under Or. 21, r. 58 when dismissed for default cannot be restored under Or. 9—AIR 1934 Mad 699 nor a second petition lies when the first application is dismissed for default—AIR 1953 Pat 223; when claim is allowed *ex parte* restoration by setting aside is not admissible. Remedy of the decree-holder is by a separate suit.

561. Application for substitution of heirs/legal representatives of deceased plaintiff (Or. 22, r. 3, CPC—In case of death of one of several plaintiffs or sole plaintiff)

In the Court of .... at ....

Suit No. .... of 20 ....

(Set out cause title)

The above-named petitioner most respectfully sheweth:

1. That one A.B. of village......... P.S. .... District .... filed a Misc. Judicial Case No. .... of 20 .... in this court. The said A.B. was the plaintiff of the said case.

2. That the said A.B. died intestate on the .... leaving his only widow, the present petitioner and the right to proceed with the said suit survives.

3. That the petitioner seeks substitution of her name against the name of said A.B. deceased.

Substitution prayed for:

In the Cause Title of the Title Suit No......... of 20........., the substitution will be as:

C.D. widow of late A.B.

4. This petition is within time.

It is, therefore, prayed that Your Honour may be pleased to substitute the name of the present petitioner, as petitioner, in place of deceased A.B. and to proceed with the said suit.

Verification

Affidavit

NOTES: 1. Order 22, r. 3 of the Code. In order that this rule may apply, the right to sue must survive to a legal representative—AIR 1936 Pat 123—Rule applies to appeals—AIR 1953 Nag 12; AIR 1935 All 640.

2. Limitation for substitution—90 days under Art. 120 of the Limitation Act 1963, Aid of s. 5 of the Limitation Act may be invoked for a delayed application when there was 'sufficient cause' for delay. If the plaintiff brings on record all the heirs then known to him and leaves out one of whom he had no knowledge, his application to implead the latter can be made within three years under Art. 137 of the Limitation Act 1963—AIR 1945 Nag 53.

3. The court cannot act *suo motu* under this rule. An application has to be filed to invoke the aid of the rule.

4. When the legal representatives of a deceased plaintiff or appellant are already on the record, though in another capacity, an application to bring them in as legal representatives is unnecessary—AIR 1943 Nag 13 but this should be brought to the notice of the court at any stage of the suit.

5. Death of plaintiff—Parties substituted not amending basis of suit nor reliefs. No change of cause of action either claim of being legal representative based on settlement and will. No ground to deny substitution—*Ambalika Padhi* v *Radhakrishna Padhi* AIR 1992 SC 431.

6. When substitution is prayed for it should be stated in the petition that the deceased died intestate and applicants are *sui juris*.

562. Application for substitution of legal representative of the deceased defendant (under Or. 22, r. 4, CPC—In case of death of one of several defendants or of a sole defendant)

In the Court of .... at ....

T.S. No. .... of 20.........

(Set out cause title)

The plaintiff states as follows:

1. That one A.B., one of the defendants of the above numbered Title Suit died on ....

2. That the right to sue does not survive against the surviving defendants alone.

3. The said A.B. died leaving his legal representatives:

(*a*)
(*b*) (State here names and addresses)
(*c*)

4. That the plaintiff seeks substitution of the said legal representatives of the deceased defendant.

5. That this petition is within time.

The petitioner, therefore, prays for orders of substitution of the persons, mentioned in para 3 above, as defendants in place of A.B. deceased, and to proceed with the said suit.

Verification

Affidavit

NOTES: 1. Under the rule it is open to any person interested to apply for the addition of the proper representative—AIR 1923 Mad 679; where legal representatives of the deceased defendant are already on record no application is necessary when some of the legal representatives are impleaded the suit does not abate—AIR 1970 Mys 84.

2. When no substitution was made within the time, the remedy is to file an application for setting aside abatement of the suit. Application should be:
   (*i*) That the defendant A.B. died on ....
   (*ii*) Legal heirs of A.B. not having been brought on record the suit abated.
   (*iii*) The petitioner was prevented by sufficient cause (state the cause) from praying for substitution.
   (*iv*) Pray (*a*) abatement of the suit be set aside, (*b*) legal representatives be substituted, (*c*) to proceed with the suit.
   (*v*) Petition should be supported by an affidavit.

   No particular form is prescribed. Such an application may be in any form, e.g. an application for amending the plaint consequent on the death of a party. It might be a prayer for expunging the name of the deceased on the allegation that his legal representative was already on record—AIR 1961 AP 112; AIR 1973 Pat 289.

3. Limitation—90 days under Art. 120 of the Limitation Act 1963, from the date of death of the defendant.

4. Appeal will not abate if all legal representatives impleaded are on record except one for want of his particulars. He can be subsequently impleaded—AIR 1971 SC 673. Appeal from a suit under s. 92 of the CPC plaintiff-

respondent dying pending appeal—personal heirs cannot be brought on record as legal representatives—AIR 1971 All 207.

5. For petition beyond limitation—s. 5 of the Limitation Act 1963, is unnecessary. 'Sufficient cause' within Or. 22, r. 9(2) to be considered—AIR 1971 Mys 79. But delay in petition under Or. 22, r. 3—s. 5 of the Limitation Act was applied—AIR 1971 Ass 97.

563. Application for substitution of legal heirs of deceased/defendant [Or. 22, r. 4(1)]

In the Court of .... at ....

Suit No. .... of 20 ....

(Set out cause title)

The plaintiff states as follows:

1. That defendant No. 3 in the above suit No. .... of 20 .... died on the .... day of ...., 20.........

2. That the right to sue in this suit does not survive against the surviving defendants alone.

3. That names and respective addresses of the legal representatives of the said defendant No. 3 are furnished below.

4. This petition for substitution is within time.

It is, therefore, prayed that the legal representatives named below be substituted in place of the deceased defendant No. 3.

Names and addresses of the legal representative to be substituted

(*a*) ....
....

(*b*) ....

(*c*) ....
....
....

Verification

Affidavit

NOTES: 1. Abatement of appeal—an application for substitution may in substance be treated as an application for setting aside an abatement—AIR 1977 Del 38; AIR 1971 P&H 243 and AIR 1930 Cal 422 relied on.

2. *Ex parte* decree against defendant. Defendant was not contesting the suit despite service and abstained from filing w.s.—Defendant died. Substitution of legal representatives of deceased defendant in such situation is not necessary. Passing of *ex parte* decree against defendant is proper—*Badanilal* v *Harshvardhan* AIR 1994 Raj 9.

3. Abatement of appeal—Defendant died before appeal was filed, No valid appeal is existing. There is no question of bringing legal representatives on record. Remedy is not under Or. 22, CPC. The appellant was directed to file fresh appeal against legal representative if within time or apply for condonation of delay in filing appeal against legal representatives—*Mohamed Ibrahim* v *Chellammal* AIR 1991 Mad 309.

4. When appeal abates for non-substitution it does not imply adjudication on merits. As such when appeal abates there is no decree. Second appeal against such order is therefore incompetent—*Madan Naik* v *Hansubala* AIR 1983 SC 676.
5. Court has no inherent power to set aside abatement—*Morasa* v *Kondragunte* AIR 1993 AP 156 (AIR 1960 Cal 291 held no longer good law in view of *Union of India* v *Ramcharan* AIR 1964 SC 215).

564. Application for setting aside an abatement (Or. 22, r. 5, CPC) (in cases of death of defendant/s)

In the Court of .... at ....

Suit No. .... of 20 ....

(Set out cause title)

The plaintiff states:

1. The above-numbered suit is posted for steps on ....

2. That defendant No. .... in the above suit died on the .... day of .... 20......... His heirs were not brought on record within 90 days and the suit abated on the .... day on expiry of the said period.

3. That the petitioner was not aware of death of the said defendant and was thus prevented from praying for substitution of legal heirs of the deceased defendant in time.

4. An affidavit in support of this petition is enclosed.

It is, therefore, prayed that the said abatement be set aside. A separate petition for substitution of the legal representatives of the deceased defendant No. .... has been filed in the court this day.

Verification

Affidavit

NOTES: 1. Exemption—Under Or. 22, r. 4(4). Death of defendant—Suit does not abate as a whole as regards surviving defendants—*Nanigopal Nanda* v *Badal Kumar Giri* AIR 1991 NOC 59 (Cal).

2. Application for setting aside of abatement is provided for under Or. 22, r. 5. Provision for consideration of s. 5 of the Limitation Act.

3. Order refusing to set aside abatement. Order 43, r. 1(*k*) applies—Order is appealable. Revision not maintainable—*Nanigopal Nanda* v *Badal Kumar Giri* AIR 1991 NOC 59 (Cal).

565. Petition under Or. 22, r. 9, CPC

In the Court of .... at ....

Suit No. .... of 20 ....

(Set out cause title)

The plaintiff states:

1. That defendant No. 3. .... died on the .... day of .... 20 .... and his heirs not being brought on record, within the prescribed period, the suit abated on ....

2. That the fact of death of the said defendant No. 3 was not known to this defendant as he was at all material times living in Bangladesh until the .... day of .... 20 ....

3. That on the .... day of .... 20 ...., the plaintiff could know of defendant No. 3's death on perusal of the report of the service-peon made on the reverse of the writ to summons.

4. A petition for substitution of heirs of the said deceased defendant has been filed separately this day.

5. An affidavit in support of this petition is furnished herewith.

The plaintiff-petitioner, therefore, prays:

(*i*) that delay in making the application be condoned and abatement of the suit be set aside;

(*ii*) for other order/orders as deemed proper.

Verification

Affidavit

1. That A.B. as plaintiff instituted the above suit. The said A.B. died on .... As heirs of the late A.B. were not brought on record the suit abated on the .... day of .... 20 ....

2. That the plaintiff was unmarried and died intestate. The petitioners are the only legal successors to the said A.B. and are *sui juris*.

3. That your petitioners were not aware till .... that A.B. instituted the above suit. The petitioners knew of the suit only on .... (State here source of knowledge).

(*Add* Affidavit and prayer).

NOTES: 1. In an application by a party for setting aside abatement—separate and formal application under s. 5 of the Limitation Act is not necessary—*Sm. Sakuntala Devi* v *Banwari Lal* AIR 1977 All 551.

2. Suit against a person who was dead at the time of its institution—not void *ab initio*, Legal representative can be impleaded even after expiry of limitation for filing the suit if the omission to implead then was due to *bona fide* mistake—AIR 1976 AP 65; AIR 1978 AP 279.

3. Application for substitution may in substance be treated as an application for setting aside abatement—AIR 1977 Del 38; AIR 1973 Del 262.

4. Application for substitution of deceased respondent was filed. It was later found that the respondent had died earlier and the appeal had abated. First application can be treated as application for setting aside abatement and bringing on record legal representatives of the deceased respondent—AIR 1977 All 551.

5. Setting aside abatement of appeal—'sufficient cause'—AIR 1976 Cal 299. Expression not to be construed strictly—AIR 1978 Cal 505.

6. Proceedings to bring legal representatives on record are distinct and separate from proceedings to set aside abatement—AIR 1973 Raj 332.

566. Application for substitution on assignment/creation/and/or devolution of interest during pendency of suit (Or. 22, r. 10, CPC)

In the Court of .... at ....

Suit No. .... of 20 ....

A.B. .... *Plaintiff*

versus

C.D. .... *Defendant*

The plaintiff states as follows:

1. That the plaintiff has filed the above title suit against the defendant for a decree of khas possession of the suit property after finding the plaintiff's title thereto.

2. That the defendant has, by executing a sale-deed on .... (registered on ....) transferred his entire right and interest in the suit property to one E.F. during the pendency of the suit and has delivered possession thereof to the said E.F.

3. That the defendant has had no interest in the suit property.

4. That the said E.F. whose name and particulars are given below, be substituted in place of the defendant.

Name and particulars.
E.F. son of P.Q. by faith ....
by occupation .... residing at .....
.........P.S. .... District ....

It is, therefore, prayed that the name of E.F. be substituted in place of the defendant.

Verification

Affidavit

NOTES: 1. An application under this rule can be made at any time when the suit is pending (AIR 1930 Cal 267) but not after a final decree has been passed—AIR 1931 Cal 51. Delay or laches will be a ground for refusing permission under this rule—AIR 1933 Cal 696.

2. The rule contemplates the substitution of a new party and not the addition of a new party—42 CWN 1183.

3. The rule applies to appeals and second appeals.

4. In order that this rule may apply, there must be an assignment, creation or devolution of an interest in the subject-matter of the suit—AIR 1930 Cal 113; AIR 1930 Pat 145.

5. Suit by partner "A" in name of firm to evict tenants. Firm dissolved and premises assigned to other partner "B"—A can continue suit—*Sajjan Singh* v *Nadeali and Bros.* AIR 1978 NOC 218 (MP).

567. Petition under Or. 22, r. 11 of the CPC to set aside abatement of an appeal by reason of the appellant's death

Before the District Judge of ....

Title Appeal No. .... of 20 ....

A.B. .... son of ....residing at ....
.... *Appellant*

versus

C.D. .... son of .... residing at ....
.... *Respondent*

And

1. E.F. widow of late A.B. residing at ....
2. G.H. son of late A.B. residing at ....

.... *Petitioners*

The above-named petitioners state:

1. That one A.B., husband of petitioner No. 1 and father of petitioner No. 2 was the appellant in the above Title Appeal pending Your Honour's court.

2. That the said A.B. having died intestate on the .... day of .... 20 .... and his heirs not having been brought on record, the appeal abated on the .... day of .... 20 ....

3. The petitioners were prevented by sufficient cause.

The petitioners, therefore, pray that the said abatement of the above Title appeal be set aside and your petitioners be substituted in place of the deceased appellant A.B.

Verification

Affidavit

NOTES: 1. Appellant dying when appeal was pending, legal heirs can be substituted in spite of recording of abatement—AIR 1961 Mys 197; AIR 1978 NOC 167 (Cal).

2. Several suits are decided by common judgment. Separate appeals were preferred; if there be abatement of one of them remaining appeals thereby do not become incompetent—*Tata Chemicals* v *Sadhu Singh* AIR 1994 All 66.

3. Order 22, r. 11—All three Appellants died. Diligent steps were taken in bringing L/R's of two on record. This is fit case for condoning delay in bringing L/R's of the third Appellant on record—*Piara Singh* v *Natha Singh* AIR 1991 SC 1529.

4. Defendant died before appeal was filed. No valid appeal is there; question of bringing legal representatives on record does not arise. No remedy is under Or. 22, CPC. (The Appellant was directed to file fresh appeal against legal representatives, if within time or apply for condonation of delay in filing appeal against legal representatives)—*Mohamed Ibrahim* v *Chellammal* AIR 1991 Mad 309.

568. Application for withdrawal of a suit under Or. 23, r. 1, CPC

In the Court of the .... at ....

Suit No. .... of 20 ....

(Set out cause title)

The (plaintiff) petitioner states as follows:

1. That the petitioner has instituted the above suit. Inadvertently there have been some formal defects in the plaint, to wit.

(*a*) ....

(*b*) (State the nature and particulars of formal defects: See Note 5 below).

2. That the suit is likely to fail owing to above-noted formal defects in the plaint.

It is, therefore, prayed that the plaintiff petitioner be permitted to withdraw the suit with liberty to sue afresh on the same cause of action.

Verification

Affidavit

NOTES: 1. Provisions in Or. 23, r. 1 applies to appeals—AIR 1951 Hyd 70 to insolvency proceedings (ILR 17 All 156) but not to probate proceedings—49 CWN 636 nor to execution proceedings—ILR 18 Cal 635. In probate proceedings court permitting withdrawal but refusing permission to file fresh proceedings such splitting is not permissible—AIR 1970 All 382. Applies to probate proceedings—AIR 1971 Ori 103.

2. At any time the suit/appeal can be withdrawn but before judgment is passed—AIR 1931 Cal 336. The power can be exercised by the Appellate Court which can allow withdrawal of the suit with liberty to file a fresh suit. Also see—*Dinabandhu Sahoo* v *Budhi Devi* AIR 1991 Ori 215. But at the appellate stage no absolute right. Plaintiff may withdraw with leave of the court—AIR 1971 All 41. A plaintiff can always withdraw from a suit even at an appellate stage and the Appellate Court has power to allow withdrawal under Or. 23, r. 1 even where the suit had been dismissed by the trial court—AIR 1973 All 466. Order 23, r. 1 confers an unqualified right on the plaintiff—AIR 1972 All 143.

3. Until order is passed a petition for withdrawal of a suit may be withdrawn—AIR 1958 Bom 28; AIR 1923 Mad 246.

4. Withdrawal by lawyer is permissible when so authorised in the Vakalatnama—14 IC 190. Where there are several plaintiffs in a suit, the suit cannot be withdrawn without the consent of all the plaintiffs—AIR 1956 Mad 115; AIR 1943 Cal 437. But one of several plaintiffs or appellants may withdraw from the suit or appeal so far as his own interest is concerned—AIR 1943 Cal 437.

5. Formal defect is the 'defect in form' which is prescribed by rules of proceeding—AIR 1956 Ori 77. The formal defect need not be in pleadings—AIR 1931 Cal 268.

Illustrations of formal defects.

(*a*) Misjoinder of parties or causes of action—AIR 1956 Ori 77; non-joinder—AIR 1977 HP 91.

(*b*) Failure to disclose cause of action in the suit—AIR 1956 Ori 77.

(*c*) Plaint by incompetent person—AIR 1957 Cal 688.

(*d*) Erroneous valuation of the subject-matter of the suit—AIR 1950 All 489.

6. A suit can also be withdrawn under Or. 23, r. 1(2)(*b*) on 'other sufficient grounds' as well. "Other sufficient grounds" should be construed *ejusdem generis* with 'formal defect' in cl. (*a*) of the sub-rule (2).

7. Withdrawal and withdrawal with liberty to file afresh—for distinction see AIR 1970 Mys 155.
8. The words 'subject-matter' appearing in Or. 23, r. 1 of the CPC cannot be equated with the property in respect of which the parties quarrel. It includes the cause of action also. It, therefore, follows that unless the cause of action for the two suits is the same, the bar of Or. 23, r. 1(3) of the Code cannot be applied. Where in a suit the cause of action is the service of notice under s. 106 of the T.P. Act, which was not served before the filing of earlier suit which is withdrawn, it cannot be said that the cause of action of the two suits is common. The subsequent suit cannot be barred under Or. 23, r. 1—*Kaloot Sao* v *Mostt (name not known) wife of Munni Sao* AIR 1977 Pat 90; AIR 1970 SC 987.
9. Withdrawal of suit with liberty to file fresh suit—permission granted on terms. Fresh suit filed without complying with terms. Fresh suit not *ab initio* void. Non-compliance with the terms will be an irregularity, for which the suit will not proceed further until the irregularity is cured, *i.e.*, until the terms are complied with—*Raja Traders* v *Union of India* AIR 1977 MP 54.
10. The court cannot split up application under sub-rule (2) of Or. 23, r. 1, CPC into two parts, one for withdrawal of the suit and the other for permission to file a fresh suit and allow the former and refuse the latter—AIR 1977 Raj 131. Also see AIR 1951 Mad 715; AIR 1975 Kant 101. An order whereby the suit stood withdrawn without such liberty is erroneous—AIR 1974 Bom 39. Effect—When plaintiff's prayer for liberty is not refused the order has the effect of granting permission to sue afresh—AIR 1982 Cal 17.
11. Withdrawal of suit—Application allowed. Subsequent application for withdrawal of application for withdrawal of suit. *Held,* court can allow such application in exercise of its inherent powers—*Rameswar Sarkar* v *State of West Bengal* AIR 1986 Cal 19.
12. In a partition suit cause of action is recurring. Dismissal or withdrawal of suit for partition—subsequent suit is not barred as long as property is not partitioned effectively—*S. Jaswant Singh* v *S. Darshan Singh* AIR 1992 Del 80.

569. Application for abandonment of a part of claim (Or. 23, r. 1, CPC)

In the Court of .... at ....

Suit No. .... of 20 ....

(Set out cause title)

The plaintiff states as follows:

That the plaintiff hereby abandons his claim to partition in respect of the property in item (3) of the Schedule appended to the plaint inasmuch as all the defendants are not co-sharers in respect of the said property and have no community of interest therein.

It is, therefore, prayed that necessary orders may please be passed for withdrawal of the suit accordingly with liberty to institute a fresh suit for partition hereafter in respect of the said property.

Verification

Affidavit

NOTE: No appeal lies from an order allowing withdrawal (AIR 1928 Mad 416; AIR 1939 Lah 472; AIR 1969 Ker 78)—Revision—AIR 1922 Cal 58.

570. Application for examination of a witness on commission (Or. 26, rr. 2 and 4, CPC)

In the Court of .... at ....

Suit No. .... of 20 ....

(Set out cause title)

The plaintiff respectfully sheweth:

1. That the plaintiff's witness A.B., wife of C.D., residing at .... P.S. .... District .... is a '*pardanashin*' lady and she does not come out in the public.

(Or, that the plaintiff's witness, Sri A.B., son of late C.D., is a resident of .... P.O. .... District .... beyond the local limits of this court's jurisdiction).

(Or, that the plaintiff's witness Sri A.B., son of late C.D. of village .... P.O. .... District .... has been lying bed-ridden with .... since .... and is unable to attend court on ...., the day fixed for peremptory hearing of the above suit).

2. That the said A.B. is a material witness of the plaintiff and will prove (state what such witness is likely to prove or how the witness is material).

3. That in the circumstances, evidence of the said A.B. should be recorded on commission.

4. An affidavit in support of this petition is enclosed.

5. That execution of the writ of commission may require .... hours and cost is likely to be ₹......... or so.

6. The petitioner undertakes to bear the costs of the commission as may be ascertained by the court.

It is, therefore, prayed that necessary orders may please be issued appointing a Commissioner for recording evidence of the said A.B. at his or her residence at.........

Verification

Affidavit

NOTES: 1. Section 132 of the Code recognizes, the right of '*pardanashin*' ladies to claim the privilege of being examined on commission—AIR 1951 Mad 311; AIR 1942 Cal 143.

2. Application made on grounds of illness and old age, supported by Medical Certificate. Court has to record its satisfaction as to existence of sickness/ infirmity and that because of sickness witness is unable to come to court. *Held*, order passed without recording such satisfaction is illegal. Court directed to hear application afresh in revision—*Adhir Chandra Banerjee* v *Sm. Lilabati Mokherjee* AIR 1994 Cal 226.

3. If sickness or infirmity is alleged, the court will consider the character and gravity of sickness—AIR 1924 Cal 971. In case of illness commission ought not to be refused—AIR 1923 Mad 321.

4. Under Or. 26, r. 2 commission may issue for the examination of any person including a defendant—AIR 1955 Mad 210 a plaintiff—AIR 1935 Pat 220, contra AIR 1949 Mad 468. But the evidence of a plaintiff in a case ought not to be taken on commission except for very strong reasons—AIR 1935 Pat 220.

5. 'Expenses of Commission' does not include the expenses to be incurred by the other party. Where there is a right in a person not to be compelled to

appear in court for the purpose of his examination as a witness but a commission has to be issued for his examination, it would neither be legal nor proper to add another limitation to the exercise of that right by an order for payment of costs to the opposite party—AIR 1973 Pat 155.

6. No affidavit filed to support the petition, no other evidence—the application should not be granted—AIR 1978 NOC 57 (Pat).

571. Application for issue of a commission for local investigation (Or. 26, r. 9, CPC)

In the Court of Civil Judge (Junior Division) at ....

T.S. No. .... of ....

A.B. .... *Plaintiff*

versus

C.D. .... *Defendant*

The above-named plaintiff states as follows:

1. That the land in suit appertains to Mauja .... P.S. .... in Hal plot No. .... and is owned by the plaintiff petitioner and that the disputed land (in Schedule 'C' of the plaint) does not appertain to defendant's holding as alleged by the latter in his written statement.

2. That the said point cannot be ascertained unless the disputed land in Schedule 'C' is measured by a pleader-Advocate commissioner and is relayed with reference to survey maps of Mauja. Besides, there is a dispute about the area of the suit-land and for this purpose survey of the land is necessary.

In the above circumstances, your petitioner prays that the court be pleased to pass an order for appointment of a Commissioner who should be directed to—

(*i*) measure the disputed land and prepare its plan showing the area of the disputed land with plots No. to which the suit land appertains;

(*ii*) measure respective holdings of the plaintiff and of the defendant and report whose holding the disputed land appertains to and whether the disputed land is covered by the plaintiff's deed of gift dated.........

Be it stated that the suit is valued at ₹......... The Commission shall be executed at .... within half a mile from the court premises and shall not take more than a day and the cost is likely to be ₹........... or so.

An affidavit in support of this petition is enclosed herewith.

Verification

Affidavit

NOTES: 1. Where the report of the Commissioner appointed for local investigation substantially complied with the requirements of the Writ of Commission issued to him and *prima facie* there was no possibility that new Commissioner can do anything more, order of the court observing necessity of the fresh

Commissioner for local investigation would be liable to be set aside especially when it was cryptic and was not showing what was the real difficulty faced by him so far as the report of the Commissioner was concerned—*Budhia Dhobia* v *Nokholal Mahato* AIR 1991 NOC 64 (Cal).

2. Order 26, r. 10, CPC—Appointment of second Commission without superseding first Commissioner's Report and proceedings deprecated.

   When both parties to a litigation agree to take out a second Commission for obvious reasons the evidentiary value of the first report is automatically demolished. In that case the court need not pass separate orders setting aside the fresh Commission report because it is implied when the order for appointment of second Commission is passed. What is necessary under sub-rule (3) of r. 10 is that the courts shall be dissatisfied 'for any reason' and not 'for reasons to be recorded'—*Balakrishna Menon* v *Padmavatty Amma* AIR 1993 Ker 218.

3. Order 26, r, 9—Petition praying for appointment of Commissioner for localising site in dispute with reference to documents of title. Order of dismissal of petition is 'case decided' and is revisable—*Chintaputta* v *Balakistamma* AIR 1992 AP 300. Revision lies—*Vijaya Bank* v *C. Srinivasa Raju* AIR 1991 NOC 41 (Kant).

572. Petition for Commission (Or. 26, r. 11) for examination of accounts

In the Court of ....

Title Suit No. .... of 20 ....

A.B. .... son of .... *Plaintiff*

versus

C.D.......... son of .... *Defendant*

The plaintiff states:

1. That the plaintiff has instituted the above suit for dissolution of partnership now subsisting in between the plaintiff and the defendant and for accounts.

2. That under cl. .... of the deed of partnership, the defendant was to maintain and has been maintaining accounts of the partnership business.

3. That the defendant has submitted in the court accounts with vouchers, etc. examination of which is necessary.

4. That such examination of accounts should be made by appointment of a Commissioner.

5. The execution of the writ of Commission may be done at the office of the partnership firm or at such other place as the court may be pleased to direct and is likely to be completed in 3/4 sittings of 4 hours each.

6. An affidavit in support of this petition is enclosed herewith.

Your petitioner, therefore, prays for appointment of a Commissioner for the purpose of examination of accounts and adjustment if necessary.

Verification

Affidavit

NOTES: 1. The Commissioner does not take over the functions of the court in the matter of summoning witnesses and recording evidence as such. He has to go into the accounts and deal with such questions as incidentally arise in the course of scrutiny or examination of the accounts—AIR 1973 Raj 271.

2 Though Or. 26, r. 12(2) makes the report submitted by the Commissioner to be evidence in the case, the same value cannot be attached to that part of the report in which the Commissioner draws his conclusions—AIR 1973 Raj 271.

573. Application for appointment of a guardian ad litem for minor defendants (Or. 32, r. 3, CPC)

In the Court of .... at ....

Suit No. .... of 20 ....

(Set out cause title)

Petition for appointment of a guardian *ad litem*.

The plaintiff states as follows:

1. That defendants No. 2 and 3 of the above suit are minors.

2. That summonses were duly served on the said defendants through their natural guardian and father A.B.

3. The said defendants No. 2 and 3 have no guardian appointed by the court.

4. The said A.B. has interest adverse to the interest of the said minor defendants.

5. That the mother C.D. of the said minors has had no interest adverse to that of the said minor defendants in the matters in controversy in the suit.

6. That the said C.D. is a fit person to be appointed as the guardian *ad litem* of the aforesaid minor defendants No. 2 and 3.

7. An affidavit in support of the petition is attached herewith.

It is, therefore, prayed that the said C.D. be appointed guardian *ad litem* of the aforesaid minor defendants No. 2 and 3.

Verification

Affidavit

NOTES: 1. An application for making appointment of a guardian *ad litem* can be made after the expiry of the period of limitation for filing the suit—AIR 1978 Punj 100.

2. An order for the appointment of a guardian for the suit may be obtained upon application in the name and on behalf of the minor or by the plaintiff—see Or. 32, r. 3(2). The court is bound to appoint a guardian for the minor defendant, even though the managing member of the family of which such minor is a member is a co-defendant—AIR 1931 All 136.

3. An application for the appointment of a guardian should be supported by an affidavit stating the fact of minority of the defendant and that the proposed guardian is a fit person to be appointed as guardian. But the absence of such an affidavit is an irregularity and cannot render the decree invalid—ILR 2 Cal 73; ILR 24 All 383.

4. Appointment of person other than natural guardian. Order does not prohibit such appointment—AIR 1970 Mad 179.
5. Suit against X as major—X really a minor. Application by father of minor to represent X as his guardian—order refusing, is illegal and is a failure to exercise the jurisdiction vested in the court by law—AIR 1977 Cal 171.

574. Application for leave to proceed with a suit by a minor on attaining majority (Or. 32, r. 12, CPC)

In the Court of .... at ....

Suit No. .... of 20 ....

(Set out cause title)

Sri A.B., late a minor by C.D., his mother and natural guardian, but now having attained majority sheweth:

1. That the above suit was filed during minority of the petitioner through his mother and natural guardian. The petitioner was born in .... and has attained majority on ....

2. That the petitioner elects to proceed with the said suit as one of the plaintiffs.

It is, therefore, prayed that Your Honour may be pleased to pass necessary orders—

(*i*) discharging his next friend/guardian,

(*ii*) granting the petitioner leave to proceed with the said suit in his own name, after issue of notice to the next friend and guardian the said C.D.,

(*iii*) amending the cause title of the suit in the manner as indicated in Or. XXXII, r. 12(3) of the Code of Civil Procedure 1908.

Verification

Affidavit

NOTES: 1. The rules does not apply where the suit has been filed in the name of an alleged minor who is really a major at the time—AIR 1940 Mad 522.
2. Suit filed by minor, plaintiff attaining majority during pendency of suit. Suit held could be disposed of according to law—AIR 1976 Mad 235.
3. Minor not making election whether to continue suit on his becoming major—Or. 32, r. 12 does not require that suit should be dismissed—*Smt. Vidyawati* v *Hansraj* AIR 1993 Del 187.

575. Application to sue as an indigent person

In the Court of the Civil Judge (Senior Division) at ....

Misc. Judicial Case No. .... of ....

Title Suit No. .... / 20 .... (New)

A.B. .... *Plaintiff*

versus

C.D. .... *Defendant*

Suit for title and khas possession valued at ₹..........

The above-named plaintiff states as follows:

(Here insert the pleadings)

Then add:

The plaintiff petitioner is an indigent person. He is not possessed of sufficient means to enable him to pay the said court-fees of ₹......... prescribed by law for the plaint of the above suit.

(Or, where no such fee is prescribed—The plaintiff petitioner is an indigent person. He is not entitled to property worth ₹.......... other than the subject-matter of this suit).

The petitioner has not entered into any agreement with anybody in respect of the subject-matter of the suit. He has not transferred any of his property within two months next before presentation of this application, either fraudulently or in order to be able to apply for permission to sue as an indigent person.

The properties owned and possessed by the petitioner, with estimated value thereof, are specified below.

List of properties with value thereof.

(*a*)	....	₹ ....
(*b*)	....	₹ ....
Total		₹..........

(In words ....)

It is, therefore, prayed that the plaintiff petitioner may be permitted to sue as an indigent person.

Verification

Affidavit

NOTES: 1. See State amendments to provisions in Or. 33, r. 1 (of Andhra Pradesh, Bombay, Kerala, Madras and Orissa).

2. Such application shall be signed and verified in the manner prescribed for the signing and verification of pleadings (Or. 33, r. 2).

3. A plaint duly signed and verified may be annexed to a petition for permission to sue as an indigent person or the application may be in the body of the plaint itself as above.

4. Order 33, r. 2 is not to be meticulously interpreted against the petitioner. A substantial compliance with the rule is sufficient—AIR 1957 J&K 15; AIR 1942 Oudh 239. Where there is omission in the application, it should be returned for amendment—AIR 1954 Cal 89; AIR 1957 Pat 562.

5. Ornaments which a woman ordinarily wears should be regarded as being in the nature of wearing apparel—AIR 1927 Cal 309; AIR 1950 Ori 234, contra AIR 1949 All 631.

6. 'Sufficient means'— The possession of sufficient means refers to the possession of sufficient realisable properties which will enable the plaintiff to pay the court-fee on the plaintiff—AIR 1978 Pat 129.

7. Courts are duty bound to ensure that the cause of a litigant does not fail merely because of genuine incapacity to pay requisite court-fees. Despite earnest efforts a plaintiff, even having some interest in immovable property, may be unable, in the ordinary course and without undue hardship and

delay, to convert his possession, if any, into liquid cash for purposes of paying the requisite court-fees. In such a case, leave to sue in *forma pauperis* must be granted—AIR 1973 Ker 19.

8. Pauper application finally disposed of after refusing leave. Amounts to rejection of plaint and not dismissal of suit for default. Applicant whose appeal against rejection of pauper application was dismissed without granting time to pay court-fees, applying under ss. 151, 152 for grant of time—application cannot be dismissed for quoting wrong provision of law and can be treated as one filed under correct provision of law—AIR 1972 AP 55.
9. Order 33, r. 7—Date of application to sue in *forma pauperis* and not the date on which the application was allowed would be deemed as date of institution of the suit—AIR 1978 All 264.
10. Pauper application can be filed by a Company. Word 'person' in Or. 33, r. 1 includes juridical person, and not limited to natural person—*Union Bank of India* v *Khaders International* AIR 1993 Ker 31.
11. When applicant dies his L.R's cannot take advantage of the indigency of their predecessor—*Chayamoni Tripathy* v *Dharmananda Panda* AIR 1993 Ori 23.
12. Dismissal of application to sue in *forma pauperis*—Rules 15, 15A of Or. 33 apply whether dismissal is on merit or for default—*Makaruj Krishanji* v *Sadashiv Vithal* AIR 1990 Bom 159.
13. Word 'person' in Or. 33, r. 1 includes juristic as well as natural person. Deity, a juristic person, is entitled to sue as pauper—*Jogesh Chandra Bera* v *Iswar Braja Raj* AIR 1981 Cal 259.
14. Application to sue in *forma pauperis*—Rejection or refusal of. Court is bound to grant time to applicant to pay requisite court-fee—*Mavji* v *Pranji* AIR 1992 Guj 147.

576. Application for making a preliminary decree for partition final

In the Court of .... at ....

Title Suit No. .... of 20 ....

(Set out cause title)

The plaintiff petitioner states:

1. That a preliminary decree for partition was granted by this court on .... in the above title suit directing the parties to partition the suit property amicably within six months from the date of the said preliminary decree.

2. That the defendants did not comply with the instructions in the preliminary decree, though repeatedly requested.

3. That in the circumstances, the plaintiff is entitled to final decree of partition by...........

4. That the subject-matter of the suit is valued at ₹.........

5. That survey work will require two days at an approximate cost of ₹.........

The petitioner, therefore, prays that the final decree for partition be passed in the said suit by engaging a Commissioner.

SCHEDULE

Verification

Affidavit

NOTES: 1. Order 34, r. 3 provides for application for making preliminary mortgage decree absolute (final decree in foreclosure suit).

2. Preliminary decree in an Administration suit, in a suit for dissolution of partnership and the taking of accounts can be made final.

3. Order 34, r. 5, *ex parte* steps for preparation of final decree. Notice to non-appearing parties is necessary—AIR 1961 Cal 534; AIR 1974 Pat 244.

4. A suit continues even after the preliminary decree and it is only after the final decree that the suit can be said to be terminated. It is, therefore, open to the courts to amend the plaint and decree Schedules at any stage before the passing of the final decree under s. 152 of the CPC—AIR 1974 AP 201.

5. Where only a money decree has been passed initially, a final decree under r. 5 is not necessary although the decree may authorise the decree-holder to realize the decretal amount by sale of judgment-debtor's property—AIR 1972 Del 118.

577. Application for making a preliminary mortgage decree absolute (Or. 34, r. 3, CPC)

In the Court of .... at ....

Suit No. .... of 20 ....

A.B. ....

.... *Plaintiff-Decree-holder*

versus

C.D. .... *Defendant*

The above-named plaintiff submits:

1. That the plaintiff was granted a preliminary mortgage decree in the above suit on.........

2. That under the decree the defendant was to pay to the plaintiff decretal dues within.........

3. That the defendant not having satisfied the decree, the said decree has to be executed.

It is, therefore, prayed that necessary orders may please be passed for making the preliminary decree absolute.

Verification

Affidavit

NOTES: 1. See Notes under Form No. 576 *supra*.

2. Notice of an application for final decree for foreclosure must be served on the defendant before a final decree is passed—AIR 1964 Tri 60; AIR 1959 All 251.

3. Dismissal for default of an application for a final decree does not preclude a fresh application—AIR 1927 Andh 49. An *ex parte* final decree can be set aside under Or. 9, r. 13, CPC—ILR 32 Cal 253, contra AIR 1949 Pat 68.

578. Application for a final decree for sale (Or. 34, r. 4, CPC) (in suits relating to mortgages of immovable property)

(See Form No. 577)

NOTE: Order 34, Rule 4(1) enjoins:

"In a suit for sale, if the plaintiff succeeds, the court shall pass a preliminary decree to the effect mentioned in clauses (*a*), (*b*) and (*c*) (*i*) of sub-rule (1) of rule 2, and further directing that, in default of the defendant paying as therein mentioned, the plaintiff shall be entitled to apply for a final decree directing that the mortgaged property or a sufficient part thereof be sold ...." etc.

579. Application for attachment before judgment (Or. 38, r. 1, CPC)

In the Court of .... at ....

Suit No. .... of 20 ....

(Set out cause title)

The plaintiff states as follows:

1. That the plaintiff has instituted the above Money Suit against the defendant on ....The plaintiff has a fair chance to get a decree.

2. That the defendant has had only property described in the Schedule below.

3. That the defendant after receipt of summons of the above Money Suit, is trying to dispose of his said property and has entered into negotiations with one ....of village .... P.S. .... District ....

(Or, the defendant is about to remove the whole/or a substantial part of his said property from the local limits of the jurisdiction of this court) with the intent to delay (or obstruct) the execution of the possible decree that may be passed against him.

4. That the defendant is left with no other property, movable or immovable, by which the decree can be satisfied.

It is, therefore, prayed that the defendant be directed by the court—

(*i*) to furnish such security as the court deems proper within a time specified by the court,

(*ii*) on failure to comply, the property of the defendant, described in the Schedule below, be attached conditionally pending final order of the court and/or till disposal of the suit.

SCHEDULE

(State here particulars of the property sought to be attached).

Verification

Affidavit

NOTES:
1. There must be definite evidence and not merely vague allegations—AIR 1953 MB 90; AIR 1934 Cal 694.
2. Mere disposal or removal will not do. The court must be satisfied that the defendant's object in so doing is to obstruct or delay the execution of any decree that may be passed against him—AIR 1934 Cal 694.
3. Attachment before judgment would not become ineffective after passing of decree permitting the judgment-debtor to pay decretal amount in instalments—AIR 1977 Mad 339.
4. Also see Or. 38, r. 5(4).

580. Application for orders of injunction with prayer for ad interim orders

In the Court of the Civil Judge (Junior Division), at.........

Other Class Suit No. .... of 20.........

A.B. and others

.... *Plaintiff-petitioners*

versus

C.D. and others

.... *Defendants Opposite Party*

Petition under Or. 39, rr. 1 and 2, CPC.

The above-named plaintiff-petitioners state as follows:

1. That the petitioners have filed the above suit praying for declaration of title of the plaintiffs to the suit property and for perpetual injunction restraining the defendants from dispossessing the plaintiffs from the suit property.

2. The defendants' father held 2.19 acres of land at Mouja Haribhanga, P.S. Kotwali, District Cooch Behar, recorded in Hal Settlement Khatian No. 43.

The said Khatian is marked Annexure 'A'.

3. That Debendra Nath Barman died leaving his widow, Defendant No. 1, 5 sons, Defendants No. 2 to 6 and 2 daughters, Defendants No. 7 and 8, who inherited the above property in equal shares.

4. That the defendants sold to the plaintiff .... by a kobala dated .... and 2.2 acres by another kobala dated .... The said kobalas dated ...., and .... are annexed herewith and marked with letters, 'F' and 'G', respectively.

5. That in each case the vendors of the plaintiffs delivered possession of kobala purchased lands by the plaintiffs which measure 1.87 acres, as more specifically described in Schedule C appended to the plaint.

6. That the said lands as described in Schedule C comprise full dags and are in exclusive possession of the plaintiffs and are well defined by boundaries.

7. That the plaintiffs are being threatened by the defendants since the last week of ...., 14 ...., B.S. alleging that the property in Schedule C belonged to minors and were sold to the plaintiffs by the defendants' guardians without legal necessity or without the permission of the court having jurisdiction. Not only the minors sold their shares even the Defendant No. 1 and Defendant No. 2 sold their shares as well by the aforesaid kobalas.

8. That no court of law held so far that sales effected by minors were void.

9. The plaintiff are being threatened with dispossession or suit property or otherwise with injury in relation to property in suit.

10. That the plaintiffs are law-abiding citizens. If the defendants be not restrained, the plaintiffs would suffer irreparable injury and there will be multiplicity of suits.

11. An affidavit in support of this petition is enclosed herewith.

It is, therefore, prayed that Your Honour would be pleased to grant temporary injunction till disposal of the suit restraining the defendants from dispossessing the plaintiffs from the suit property in Schedule "C" to the plaint.

It is further prayed that an interim order may please be passed in the light of the above prayer.

SCHEDULE 'C'

Verification

Affidavit

NOTES: 1. Such an application shall be supported by an affidavit.

2. The rule that before the issue of a temporary injunction order the court must satisfy itself that the plaintiff has a *prima facie* case does not mean that the court should examine the merits of the case closely and come to a conclusion that the plaintiff has a case in which he is likely to succeed. This would amount to prejudging the case on its merits. All that the court has to see is that on the face of it, the person applying for an injunction has a case which needs consideration and which is not bound to fail by virtue of some apparent defects. The balance of convenience also has to be looked into—AIR 1972 Ker 181.

3. See Or. 39, r. 1(*c*).
In circumstances not covered by Or. 39, the court can issue injunction in exercise of its inherent powers.

4. A *prima facie* case implies the probability of the plaintiff obtaining a relief on the materials placed before the court at that stage. Every piece of evidence produced by either party has to be taken into consideration in deciding the existence of a *prima facie* case to justify issuance of a temporary injunction—AIR 1968 Ker 179; AIR 1977 Raj 196.

5. A defendant can move for a temporary injunction against the plaintiff without filing a counter-claim only when and where the relief claimed arises out of the plaintiff's cause of action or is incidental to it—AIR 1975 Kant 137.

6. Order of interim injunction—At least *prima facie* discussion of documents and affidavits filed is a must. Mere reference would vitiate the order—AIR 1974 Mad 87.

7. Order 43, r. 1(*r*)—Appeal lies against an order refusing to grant *ad interim* injunction—AIR 1974 Cal 119.

8. Where a court grants temporary injunction without considering the question of irreparable or serious injury and balance of convenience, its order is vitiated by material irregularity—AIR 1973 HP 42.

9. Main factors to be considered are the question of balance of convenience and the question of *prima facie* case—AIR 1972 Cal 105—Decisive factors—AIR 1972 All 418.

10. 'Balance of Convenience'—Where injunction, pending suit, if issued, is likely to cause irreparable loss to the opposite party, while loss, if any, that may cause to the plaintiff is agreed to be re-imbursed, the balance of convenience lies in refusing the injunction—AIR 1972 Cal 105.

581. Application under Or. 39, r. 2A for breach of order of injunction

In the Court of .... at ....

Suit No. .... of 20 ....

(Set out cause title)

The petitioner states:

1. That by an order dated .... in the above suit, the defendant was restrained by an injunction from trespassing on the land in suit vide Schedule appended below the plaint.

2. The said order of injunction was served on the defendant on the .... day of .... 20 ....

3. That the defendant in disobedience of the said injunction trespassed on the suit land on the .... day of .... 20 .... and tried to raise on a portion thereof an unauthorised structure.

Your petitioner, therefore, prays:

For attachment of the properties of the defendant described below; Alternatively, (or/and) order the defendant to be detained in civil prison for a term as deemed proper.

SCHEDULE

Description of properties
of the defendant to be attached

(set out details)

Verification

Affidavit

NOTES: Contempt of Courts Act (ss. 2 and 14). Contempt of Court—

1. Deliberate disobedience of order of court is necessary—*Jiwan Kumari Parekh* v *Satyabala Chakravorty* AIR 1991 SC 326. Wilful disobedience of order of court by Govt. official. No lenience in court's attitude should be expected from court as a matter of course merely on the ground that an order of conviction would damage service career of the concerned officer—*Tapan Kumar Mukherjee* v *Heromoni Mondal* AIR 1991 SC 281.
2. Proceedings under Or. 39, r. 2A can be proceeded against defendant even though he was neither personally present at the time of disobedience nor was a party to suit— *K.L. Virmani* v *3rd Addl. D.J.* AIR 1992 All 326. Stranger to order of court can be held guilty—*Vidyacharan Sukla* v *Tamil Nadu Olympic Asson.* AIR 1991 Mad 323.
3. Party taking possession in breach of injunction. Court has inherent power under s. 151 to restore possession in the decree—AIR 1978 Cal 499.
4. No attachment made under this rule shall remain in force for more than one year, at the end of which time, if the disobedience or breach continues, the property attached may be sold and, out of the proceeds, the court may award such compensation as it thinks fit to the injured party and shall pay the balance, if any, to the party entitled—Order 39, r. 2A(2) of the CPC.
5. Criminal Contempt—Consent of Advocate-General is necessary. High Court cannot issue Rule without such consent—In re *Mukunda Chandra Halder* (1994)1 CHN 291.
6. Power of the Supreme Court and High Court to punish contempt is not restricted or trammelled by ordinary legislations. Summary procedure is to be followed. Power is to be used sparingly—*Pritam Pal* v *High Court of M.P.* AIR 1992 SC 904.
7. Where an appeal is filed against the order of the learned Single Judge to a Division Bench the statutory right of appeal gets exhausted and there is no further right of appeal to the Supreme Court—*Purushottam Das Goel* v *Hon'ble Justice B.S. Dhillon* AIR 1978 SC 1014; *Md. Idris* v *Rustam Jehangir* AIR 1984 SC 1826.
8. It would be a travesty of justice if the courts were to allow gross contempt of court to go unpunished without an adequate sentence—*Balram Singh* v *Bhikam Chand* AIR 1985 SC 1726.

9. Interim order of injunction obtained in earlier suit by suppressing correct facts. More comprehensive suit filed by other party subsequently—Principles of *res judicata* do not apply—*Abhi Prasad Sen* v *Puspa Doshi* AIR 1984 Cal 250.

582. Application for appointment of a Receiver (in a partition suit) (Or. 40, r. 1, CPC)

In the Court of the Civil Judge (Senior Division) at ....

Title Suit No. .... of 20............

A.B. .... *Plaintiff*

versus

C.D. and 10 others .... *Defendants*

Petition under Or. 40, r. 1 of the CPC

The above-named plaintiff states as follows:

1. That the plaintiff is the owner of three acres of land (vide Schedule "C" of the plaint) by purchase by a registered Kobala from Defendant No. 2, a co-sharer of the holding, on .... 20 ....

2. That the said land in Schedule "C" is separated from the rest of the holding by clear and defined boundaries and is so mentioned in the plaintiff-petitioner's title deed.

3. That the plaintiff has since been in possession thereof. All the defendants excepting Defendants No. 5 to 8 have submitted a joint written statement confirming plaintiff's possession over the "C" Schedule land.

4. That Defendants No. 5 to 7 are denying the plaintiff's possession. The plaintiff has sought for relief of partition in the above suit.

5. That for undue interference by Defendants No. 5 to 7, the plaintiff apprehends breach of peace and molestation if cultivation by the plaintiff is resorted to. On the contrary, the plaintiff would lose crops if the land is not cultivated and tilled immediately.

6. That in the circumstances of the case, a Receiver should be appointed for bringing the land in Schedule 'C' under cultivation and to reap and harvest the future crop under the court's orders, even if the said Defendants No. 5 to 7 claim falsely possession over the land in Schedule 'C'.

SCHEDULE 'C'

Verification

Affidavit

NOTES: 1. For West Bengal—see Rule No. 253 of the Civil Rules & Orders, vol. 1.

2. First application for appointment of Receiver rejected. Fresh application is not barred if new facts are alleged to have arisen in new circumstances—AIR 1973 Gau 74.

3. Act done by a Receiver is subject to directions and order of court appointing Receiver—*Krishna Kumar Khemka* v *Grindlays Bank* AIR 1991 SC 899.

4. Order appointing *ad interim* Receiver appealable under Or. 43, r. 1(*s*)—*BDA Ltd.* v *Central Bank of India* AIR 1995 Bom 14.

583. Application for readmission of an appeal dismissed for default

In the Court of the District Judge, ... at ....

1. A.B. ....
2. C.D. .... *Appellants*

versus

E.F. .... *Respondent*

Application under Or. 41, r. 19 of the CPC for readmission of Title Appeal No. .... of 20 .... dismissed for default.

The above-named appellants state as follows:

1. That the appellants preferred a Title Appeal No. .... of 20 .... against the judgment and decree of Title Suit No. .... of 20 .... of the Court of Civil Judge (Junior Division) at.........

2. That after several adjournments, the appeal was fixed for peremptory hearing on.........

3. That Appellant No. 1 is the elder brother of Appellant No. 2 and is looking after the appeal. Appellant No. 2 is a college student. That the Appellant (No. 1)'s wife had been suffering for long. She had to be hospitalised and she underwent a major operation at the material time. For the above situation, the appellants could not meet their lawyer Sri .... Advocate of this court.

4. That on .... Sri .... was out of the station in connection with a part-heard hearing of a suit in the Court of Civil Judge (Junior Division) at .... and he failed to attend this court when the above appeal was called on for hearing.

5. That the appellants in view of circumstances stated in para 3 could not come to .... and did not know the situation. He necessarily could not engage any other lawyer.

6. That the appeal was called on for hearing and was dismissed for default under Or. 41, r. 17 of the CPC.

7. That in view of the position the appellants were not at fault and they were prevented by the above circumstances from appear or getting the appearance of their lawyer when the appeal was called on for hearing.

8. That the appeal has had merits and the petitioners have suffered much hardship and will suffer so if the appeal be not readmitted for hearing.

It is, therefore, prayed that Your Honour would be pleased to readmit the appeal and grant your petitioners hearing in the matter.

And for this act of kindness, your petitioners as in duty bound shall ever pray.

Verification

Affidavit

NOTES: 1. Date not fixed for hearing but for some other purposes—court cannot dismiss appeal in the appellant's absence—AIR 1957 Punj 80; AIR 1971 Manipur 17.

2. Readmission of Appeal dismissed for default. *Bona fide* mistake of Counsel. Mistake should be condoned—*Oil & Natural Gas Commission* v *Tridib Sanyal* AIR 1983 Cal 124.

584. Application for production of additional evidence (Or. 41, r. 27, CPC)

In the Court of the .... at ....

Title Appeal No. .... of 20 .....

A.B. .... *Appellant*

versus

1. C.D.

2. E.F. .... *Respondents*

Application for production of additional evidence.

The above-named appellant states as follows:

1. That the appellant has preferred the above appeal against the judgment and decree in Title Suit No. .... of 20 .... of the Court of the Civil Judge (Senior Division) at .... and the said appeal is pending for hearing.

2. That during trial of the said Title Suit No. .... of 20 .... in the court below, the plaintiff had filed an unregistered partnership deed which was admissible in evidence for collateral purposes. The learned court below refused to admit the said document in evidence and the same was improperly rejected.

(Or, that the appellant had produced copies of certain documents in the court below but failed to produce the originals within the time specified by the court. The court rejected the said documents. The Appellate Court requires those originals to enable it to pronounce judgment).

(Or, that the evidence in the said Title Suit was taken by the court below imperfectly).

3. That the plaintiff-appellant has suffered hardship for such improper rejection of the document/for such imperfect recording of evidence.

It is, therefore, prayed that Your Honour may be pleased to allow additional evidence of the said document by calling witnesses,

(or, production of the said document with opportunity to prove the same by calling witnesses,

or, allow witnesses to be examined to prove the plaintiff's contention).

Verification

Affidavit

NOTES: 1. The words 'additional evidence' imply that some evidence has already been given—AIR 1957 Cal 59.

2. The Appellate Court may admit additional evidence if it was tendered in the lower court but was improperly rejected—AIR 1955 Ass 110; AIR 1924 Cal 578. Party unable through no fault of his to produce evidence in trial court—additional evidence may be allowed—AIR 1949 All 173. Evidence

taken by the lower court imperfectly—Appellate Court unable to pass satisfactory judgment—additional evidence may be admitted—AIR 1940 Mad 707.

3. Mere insufficiency of evidence is no ground for allowing additional evidence—AIR 1931 PC 143; AIR 1977 Cal 3.
4. Documents neither original nor proved by anybody cannot be accepted at the appellate stage—AIR 1978 Cal 332.

585. Application for permission to prefer an appeal as an indigent person

In the Court of the District Judge at ....

Misc. Judicial Case No. .... of ....

Title Appeal No. .... of ....

A.B. ....

.... *Petitioner-Appellant*

versus

C.D. ....

...... *Opposite-party-Respondent*

Application under Or. 44, r. 1 of the CPC

The above-named petitioner states as follows:

1. That the petitioner brought a Title Suit No. .... of 20 .... in the Court of Civil Judge (Junior Division) at .... as an indigent person. The said suit was dismissed on contest. The petitioner is entitled and intends to prefer an appeal against the judgment and the decree of the said Title Suit.

2. That the petitioner is an indigent person. He is not possessed of means sufficient to enable him to pay the court-fees required for the memorandum of appeal.

3. That the petitioner has not entered into any agreement with anybody in respect of the subject-matter of the appeal nor has transferred any of his property within two months next before presentation of this application either fraudulently or in order to be able to apply for leave to prefer an appeal as an indigent person.

4. That the properties, movable and immovable, owned and possessed by this petitioner, valued at about ₹......... are shown in the Schedule appended below.

5. The petitioner encloses the Memo of Appeal and certified copies of the judgment and decree appealed against.

The petitioner, therefore, prays that he may be permitted to prefer the appeal as an indigent person.

List of properties	Value
(1)	......
(2)	......

₹ .... (In words)

SCHEDULE

Verification

Affidavit

NOTES: 1. Only when a person is entitled to prefer an appeal that he can apply for leave to appeal as a pauper. The application, therefore, should state that he is entitled in law to prefer an appeal.

2. Appeal filed in *forma pauperis* not presented by the Appellant herself. The appeal was admitted earlier but subsequently dismissed on the ground that it was not preferred by party herself. Dismissal of Appeal, held, was not proper—*Smt. Dipo* v *Wassam Singh* AIR 1983 SC 846.

3. This application should be accompanied by the memorandum of appeal. Application for leave and memorandum of appeal are two distinct documents.

4. Granting of leave to appeal as an indigent person is subject to provisions relating to suits by indigent persons as provided in Or. 33, CPC.

5. Such an application shall have to be signed and verified in the manner prescribed for the signing and verification of pleadings (see Or. 44, r. 1 read with Or. 33, r. 2 of the CPC).

6. Application for dispaupering—Application is maintainable on proof of active concealment of declaration of assets—*State of Bihar* v *Ramlakhan Prasad Sinha* AIR 1977 Pat 44.

586. Application for review of a judgment (Or. 47, r. 1, CPC)

In the Court of .... at ....

Suit No. .... of 20 ....

A.B. ....

.... *Plaintiff*

versus

1. C.D.

2. E.F. .... *Defendants*

The above-named defendants most respectfully sheweth:

1. That the plaintiff instituted a suit against the petitioner-defendants in this court and obtained a judgment and decree in his favour on.........

2. That no appeal is allowed against the said judgment/decree by law.

(Or, no appeal has been preferred against the said decree/judgment).

3. That the defendants are aggrieved with the said judgment/decree and pray for review of the said judgment/decree on the following, amongst other.

GROUNDS

(*a*) Discovery of new and important matter or evidence.

(*b*) Discovery of some mistake or error apparent on the face of the record.

(*c*) Any other sufficient reason.

It is, therefore, prayed that Your Honour may be pleased to—

(*i*) set aside the judgment;

(*ii*) re-hear the suit and pass judgment accordingly.

Verification

Affidavit

NOTES: 1. The expression "any other sufficient reason" should be interpreted as meaning a reason sufficient on grounds at least analogous to those specified immediately previously—AIR 1949 PC 112; AIR 1954 SC 526; AIR 1973 Ker 285. Plaintiff alleging his inability to place before the court certain facts owing to death of his solicitor—Review allowed on ground of "any other sufficient reason"— AIR 1970 Cal 231. But omission to argue a ground is not a ground for review—AIR 1976 Ori 64. It includes misconception of fact or law by Advocate. Inherent power could be used to correct erroneous view of Advocate—In re *Mahamaya Banerjee* AIR 1989 Cal 106. Counsel's failure to explain legal position cannot be a ground for Review—*Hem Narain Singh* v *Ganesh Singh* AIR 1995 Pat 5.

2. Admissible against a compromise decree—AIR 1915 Cal 622; contra AIR 1970 Punj 176 against *ex parte* disposal—AIR 1957 Pat 575; AIR 1929 Cal 322. Rule applies to all decrees and others under the Code, under the circumstances mentioned in the Rule—AIR 1940 Lah 276; ILR 44 Cal 850. Court can review even an interlocutory order—AIR 1971 Manipur 28.

3. Power of review is not an inherent power—AIR 1970 SC 1273.

4. Mistake or error mentioned in Or. 47, r. 1, should be so manifest and clear that no court would stand it being retained on the record. An erroneous view of the law or a wrong exposition of the law cannot be considered as a mistake or error apparent on the face of the record—AIR 1971 Mad 28; AIR 1978 All 270. Erroneous application of law cannot be a ground for review—*Raj Kumar* v *Mathew* AIR 1984 Bom 458.

5. Review—application can be filed by a party to *lis*. Third party cannot prefer a review application—AIR 1978 Del 122.

6. Power of the court to review is not limited to discovery of a new document after the judgment, but the court has wide discretion to do justice by granting review for any other sufficient reason—AIR 1949 PC 112; AIR 1973 P&H 236. Review should be granted in case of error apparent on record, though the point was not urged before—AIR 1973 P&H 265.

7. That a decision is erroneous in law is no ground for ordering its review—AIR 1973 Ori 93; AIR 1977 Kant 193. But the decision of a court by overlooking a decision of the Supreme Court, which is binding on all courts in India, constitutes an error apparent on the face of the record and justifies review of the decision contrary to the decision of the Supreme Court—AIR 1972 Mys 44.

8. A plaint rejected for non-payment of court-fees can be restored on application under Or. 9, r. 4 or s. 151, as well as on review of the order of rejection. The order allowing restoration under Or. 9, r. 4 or s. 151 can be deemed to be one under Or. 47, r. 1—AIR 1972 Pat 289.

9. Application for review is not maintainable merely on the ground that the case should have been argued differently—AIR 1977 All 163.

10. Court-fee. Review of judgment in original suit sought—One half of fee payable on plaint would be payable—*Kannegolla* v *L.A. Officer* AIR 1993 AP 209.

11. Maintainability—On date of filing review application no appeal was pending. Appeal was filed subsequently. *Held*, dismissal of review application as not maintainable on that ground cannot be sustained—*Kannegolla Nagabhushanam* v *L.A. Officer* AIR 1993 AP 209.

12. If the party is aggrieved by the judgment of the Single Judge sitting in Second Appeal the appropriate remedy for the party is to file an appeal against that judgment. A remedy by way of an application for review is entirely misconceived—*Debarajan Pillai* v *Sellayya Pillai* AIR 1987 SC 1160.

13. Review is not permissible on the ground that decision is erroneous on merits. That would be the province of a Court of Appeal. A power of review

is not to be confused with appellate power which may enable an Appellate Court to correct all manner of errors committed by the Trial Court—*Chandmull Chopra* v *State* AIR 1986 Cal 111.

14. Indigent plaintiff or Appellant filing review petition—need not pay court-fee—*Mathai Brijitha* v *Thankappan Nair* AIR 1993 Ker 79.
15. Discovery of new evidence on question of fact is no ground for review of decree of second Appellate Court—*Horilal* v *Chawan Kumar* AIR 1993 Del 85; *Mariam-un-Nissa* v *Babu Ram* AIR 1923 All 541; *Saila Bala* v *Gadadhar Hazra* AIR 1922 Cal 165; *Bhyrab Nath Toee* v *Kally Chander Chowdhuri*, referred to in AIR 1922 Cal 165.
16. Dismissal of suit on statement by Counsel that plaintiff does not want to proceed against Defendant. Restoration of suit by review of judgment is not permissible—*Chilyoda Corporation* v *National Fertiliser Ltd.* AIR 1993 Del 134.
17. Order allowing review is appealable—*Harendra Prasad* v *Parshottama* AIR 1995 All 30.

587. Memo of Appeal from a decree of a lower court (Original Decree)

In the Court of the District Judge ....

Title Appeal No. .... of 20 ....

.... *Plaintiff-Appellant*

versus

.... *Defendant-Respondent*

The appellant appeals to the Court of the District Judge, ... from the judgment and the decree passed by Mr. .... Civil Judge (Senior Division) at .... in Title Suit No. .... of 20......... dated the .... day of ...., 20......... dismissing the appellant's suit on the following grounds of objection:

1. Because the findings of the lower court.........
2. Because.........
3. Because.........

Value of the appeal—₹..............

Relief: To set aside the decree of the lower court and to decree the plaintiff's suit with costs of both courts.

....

Advocate for the Appellant

Verification

Affidavit

NOTES: 1. See s. 96 and Or. 41(1) of the CPC.

2. When an appeal is presented after the expiry of the period of limitation specified therefor, it shall be accompanied by an application under Or. 41, r. 3A(1). If application under r. 3A(1) is not filed the appeal cannot be dismissed summarily—*M. Dasgupta* v *Prakash Sha* AIR 1984 Bom 390.
3. Appealable Order under Or. 43, r. 1—In case of an appealable order, the order should be a speaking order so that the validity or otherwise of such order can be examined by the Appellate Court in the appeal before such court—AIR 1978 Cal 379.

4. Admission of appeal as to part and rejection as to other part is wholly illegal. Appeal can be admitted wholly or rejected wholly—*Ramji Bhagala* v *Krishnrao Bagre* AIR 1982 SC 1223.
5. Order 43, r. 1—Dismissal of Appeal for default of Appellant's Counsel. *Held*, party should not suffer for misdemeanour or inaction of his counsel. Dismissal set aside by Supreme Court—*Rafique* v *Manshilal* AIR 1981 SC 1400.

588. Memo of Appeal (in a District Court)

In the Court of the District Judge at ....

Title Appeal No. .... of 20 ....

A.B. .... *Appellant*

versus

C.D. .... *Respondent*

Appeal valued at ₹..............

Being aggrieved with the judgment and decree passed by Sri .... Civil Judge (Junior Division) at .... in Title Suit No. .... of .... the above-named appellant begs to prefer this appeal on the following, amongst others.

GROUNDS

1. For that ....
2. For that .... etc.

Certificate

Verification

Affidavit

NOTE: In West Bengal the memo of appeal is to bear at its foot a certificate under r. 255(1) of the Calcutta High Court Civil Rules and Orders, vol. 1.

589. Memo of Appeal (in a District Court) from judgment and decree of a Court of Civil Judge (Junior Division)

In the Court of the District Judge.........

Title Appeal No. .... of 20.........

A.B. .... *Appellant*

versus

1. C.D.

2. E.F. etc. .... *Respondents*

Appeal against the judgment and decree in other Class Suit No. .... of 20 .... valued at ₹...........

Being aggrieved by the judgment passed by Sri .... Civil Judge (Junior Division) at ...., ... on .... and Decree signed on .... in other Class Suit No. .... of 20 .... the appellant before Your Honour begs to prefer this Memo of appeal, enclosing certified copy of the judgment and the decree appealed against, within the period of limitation, on the following, amongst others.

GROUNDS

1. For that the learned court below could not appreciate the facts of the case and erred in law.

2. ....

3. ....

It is, therefore, prayed that Your Honour would be pleased to admit the appeal, call for the records of the lower court and after hearing set aside the judgment and the decree appealed against by decreeing the suit with costs.

*Certificate**

I certify that I have examined the papers supplied to me and that, in my opinion, there are good grounds, as set forth above, for this appeal; and I undertake to appear and support the appeal before the Appellate Court.

....
Advocate

Verification

Affidavit

NOTE: *Certificate at the foot of the memoradum of appeal is required under r. 255(1) of Civil Rules and Orders, vol. 1 (Calcutta High Court).

590. Memo of a cross-objection to an appeal under Or. 41, r. 22, CPC

In the Court of the District Judge at ....
Memo of cross-objection .... of 20 ....

(Arising out of Money Suit No. .... of 20 .... in the Court of Civil Judge (Senior Division), ... decreeing the suit on .... for ₹ .... and

In respect of Money Appeal No. .... of 20 .... in this Court).

A.B. .... *Plaintiff-Appellant*

versus

C.D. .... *Defendant-Respondent*

The plaintiff-appellant instituted in the Court of the Civil Judge (Senior Division) .... a Money Suit No. .... of 20......... praying for recovery of ₹ ...... from the defendant-respondent. The suit was decreed in part on .... of ₹.........

The plaintiff-appellant has preferred the above Money Appeal against judgment and decree in said Money Suit No. .... of 20 ....

The respondent received the notice of the said Money Appeal No. .... of .... on .... of 20 .... and submits the cross-objection on the following, amongst other.

GROUNDS

(State here grounds of objection)

Relief

That the amount of the decree be reduced to ₹.........

Certificate

Verification

Affidavit

NOTES: 1. A memo of cross-objection should bear at its foot a certificate by the counsel—see Civil Rules and Orders, vol. 1 (Calcutta High Court).

2. Decree in favour of respondent some finding against respondent though not incorporated in decree. Cross-objection by respondent is maintainable—AIR 1979 Cal 30.

3. Cross-objection filed before service of notice is maintainable—AIR 1979 Cal 152.

4. Filing of cross-objection is permissible if substantial question of law is raised therein—*Palasseri Velayudhan* v *Palasseri Ithayi* AIR 1994 Ker 267.

591. Memo of First Appeal in High Court

In the High Court of Judicature at Allahabad

First Appeal No. .... of 20 ....

(District: Allahabad)

(Under s. 96 of the Code of Civil Procedure)

A.B. ....

...... *Opposite Party-Appellant*

versus

C.D. ....

...... *Applicant-Respondent*

The above-named Appellant appeals to this Hon'ble High Court of Judicature at Allahabad against the decree passed by Sri ..... 1st Additional District Judge, Allahabad dated .... in Civil Reference No. ....

BETWEEN

C.D. .... *Applicant*

versus

A.B. .... *Opposite Party*

The relief sought by this appeal is that this Hon'ble Court be pleased to allow the appeal and to set aside the decree passed by the Court below with costs in both the Courts and grant such further and other reliefs as the Court may deem fit and proper.

Valuation of the appeal is ₹.........

Court-fees paid ₹.........

The grounds of objection to the said decree are as follows:

1. Because ....
2. Because ....

....

Counsel for the Opposite Party-Appellant

Verification

Affidavit

NOTE: See s. 100(1) of CPC.

592. Memo of First Appeal in a High Court (Another Form)

In the High Court at Calcutta
(Civil Appellate Jurisdiction)

Memorandum of appeal from original decree

First Appeal No. .... of 20 ....

A.B. ....

.... *Opposite Party-Appellant*

versus

C.D. ....

..... *Petitioner-Respondent*

(Court-fees paid)

The above-named Opposite Party-Appellant being dissatisfied with the judgment dated .... and decree signed on .... by Sri .... District Judge, ... in Matrimonial Suit No. .... of 20 .... begs to prefer this appeal before the Hon'ble High Court on the following, amongst others.

GROUNDS

1. For that ....
2. For that ....

I, ..., Advocate for the above-named Appellant do hereby certify that in my judgment each of the grounds of appeal in the above petition presented by me on behalf of the said Appellant is a good ground of appeal.

....

(Advocate)

List of papers

1. Memo of Appeal
2. Certified Copy of Judgment
3. Certified Copy of Decree

4. Hon'ble 2nd Judge's Copy
5. Vakalatnama

Total 5 Dated ....

593. Application for leave to appeal

Appeal No. .... of 20.........

In the Hon'ble Supreme Court of India

Appellate Jurisdiction

In the matter of:

An Appeal under Art. 132 of the Constitution of India;

And

In the matter of:

An Order dated 2nd December 20… passed by Hon'ble High Court at Calcutta

And

In the matter of:

Mr. P. residing at ...., Alipore Road, Kolkata

...... *Appellant*

versus

1. Land Acquisition Collector having its office at ...., Alipore Road, Kolkata

2. Government of West Bengal through Secretary, Land and Land Reforms Department, Writers' Buildings, Kolkata

.... *Respondent*

Appeal from Order dated 2nd December 20…, passed by the Hon'ble High Court at Calcutta in Matter No. 5 of 20….

To
The Hon'ble Mr. .... Chief Justice
of India and His Companion Justices
of the said Hon'ble Supreme Court

The humble petition/appeal of the Appellant most respectfully sheweth:

1. The appellant-petitioner filed a Writ Petition No. .... of 20....... on 2nd June 20......, under Art. 226 of the Constitution of India, against the respondent praying for writs of Mandamus, Certiorari and Prohibition on the grounds of violation of the appellant's fundamental rights guaranteed by the Constitution of India.

2. In the said proceedings the respondent appeared, filed an affidavit-in-opposition and contested the said petition.

3. After hearing the matter, the Hon'ble Judge dismissed the petition. From the said Order of Dismissal, your petitioner preferred an appeal before a Division Bench of the Hon'ble High Court but the said appeal was dismissed on 2nd December 20....

4. The appellant being aggrieved by and dissatisfied with the Order of Dismissal dated 2nd December 20............ begs to move Your Lordships, *inter alia*, on the following.

GROUNDS

I. For that reasonable opportunity was not given to the appellant of being heard.

II. For that the Hon'ble Judges should have held and erred in not doing so that the appellant's rights as guaranteed under the Constitution of India have been defeated.

III. For that the appellant's fundamental rights have been infringed upon.

IV. For that the appellant's writ petition has been wrongly dismissed in violation of the provisions of Art. 311(1) of the Constitution of India.

V. For that the Hon'ble Judges failed to appreciate and erred in doing so that the appellant's fundamental rights should be protected under Art. 311(1) of the Constitution of India.

VI. For that the appellant's petition has been wrongfully dismissed in violation of the provisions of Art. 311(1) of the Constitution of India.

VII. For that the Hon'ble Judges failed to consider and appreciate and to give effect to the scope and meaning of Art. 311 and violation of the said provisions or any other provisions of the Constitution of India.

VIII. For that the Hon'ble Judges failed to appreciate and erred in doing so that the respondent acted in breach of the fundamental rights of the petitioner guaranteed by the Constitution of India.

IX. For that the Order appealed from is otherwise bad in law and cannot be sustained and the same be set aside.

5. The appellant states that the respondents wrongfully acquired the appellant's property and are in wrongful possession without any justification under any of the provisions of law.

6. This appeal is being preferred *bona fide* and in the interests of justice and to enforce the appellant's fundamental rights.

The appellants, therefore, humbly prays Your Lordships for the following orders:

(*a*) Granting leave to prefer the appeal against the said appellate order dated 2nd December 20..., in matter No. 5 of 20... passed by the Hon'ble High Court at Kolkata a copy of which is annexed hereto;

(*b*) Injunction restraining the respondent from transferring, encumbering, or in any way dealing with the property in the proceedings;

(*c*) Further and other orders be made as this Hon'ble Court may deem fit and proper to afford complete relief to the appellant.

Verification

Affidavit

594. Memo of Appeal from a High Court's (Original Side) decree

In the High Court at Calcutta

Appeal No. .... of 20 ....

Suit No. .... 20 ....

A.B. ....

.... *Appellant-Plaintiff*

versus

C.D. ....

.... *Respondent-Defendant*

The appellant above-named prefer this appeal against the Decree/Order of the Hon'ble Mr. Justice .... in the No. .... of 20 .... passed on .... on the following amongst other.

GROUNDS

1.
2. State here grounds of appeal
3.

The appellants, therefore, humbly prays Your Lordships for the following orders:

(*a*) Granting leave to prefer the appeal against the said appellate order dated 2nd December 20..., in matter No. 5 of 20... passed by the Hon'ble High Court at Kolkata a copy of which is annexed hereto;

(*b*) Injunction restraining the respondent from transferring, encumbering, or in any way dealing with the property in the proceedings;

(*c*) Further and other orders be made as this Hon'ble Court may deem fit and proper to afford complete relief to the appellant.

And the appellant as in duty bound shall ever pray.

Verification

Affidavit

595. Memo of Second Appeal in a High Court

In the Hon'ble High Court of Judicature at ....

Second Appeal No. .... of 20 ....

(Under s. 100, CPC)

1. A.B. (State names and addresses)
2. C.D.

.... *Plaintiff-Appellants*

versus

1. E.F. (State names and addresses)
2. G.H.

.... *Defendant-Respondents*

To
The Hon'ble Chief Justice and His
Companion Judges of the aforesaid
Court

The appellants above-named beg to prefer this Second Appeal against the decree and judgment of Sri .... Additional Civil Judge, at .... dated .... in Civil Appeal No. .... between E.F./G.H. and A.B. and others allowing the appeal and setting aside the decree and judgment dated .... of Sri .... Civil Judge (Junior Division), ..., District Aligarh decreeing the plaintiff-appellant's Suit No. .... of 20 .... between A.B. and others versus E.F. and others.

The relief sought by this second appeal is that the Court be pleased to allow the appeal with costs and set aside the decree and judgment of the lower appellate court and restore the decree of Civil Judge (Junior Division), ... decreeing the plaintiff-appellant's suit and grant such other and further relief as the Hon'ble Court may deem fit and proper.

The valuation of appeal is ₹ ....

The court-fee paid is ₹ ....

The grounds of objection to the aforesaid decree are as follows:

1. Because the decree of the learned lower court is contrary to law.
2. Because ....
3. Because ....

I certify that the above grounds are
good grounds for Second Appeal

....

Advocate

Dated .... Counsel for the Appellant

NOTES: 1. Section 100, CPC. Consideration of a disputed document raising question of law. Question directly and substantially affecting right of parties. It can be considered as a substantial one between parties—*Pankaj Bhargava* v *Mohinder Nath* AIR 1991 SC 1233.

2. High Court has no jurisdiction to entertain a second appeal even on the ground of erroneous finding of fact however gross the error may seem to be—*Sinha Ramanuja* v *Raya Ramanuja* AIR 1961 SC 1720.

3. In a second appeal the court cannot reappreciate the evidence unless the judgment is perverse or the judgment is based upon evidence admitted illegally or the finding is without evidence or there has been wrong construction of documents or misreading of evidence—*Surendra Mohon Das Bhowmick* v *State of West Bengal* AIR 1979 Cal 3.

596. Memo of a Mandamus Appeal

District ....
In the High Court at ....
(Civil Appellate Jurisdiction)

Mandamus Appeal No. ..... of 20 ....

Appeal from the final order dated the .... 20 .... passed by His Lordship the Hon'ble Mr. Justice .... dismissing *in limine* a writ petition under Art. 226 of the Constitution of India.

A.B. .... *Petitioner-Appellant*

versus

1. State of West Bengal through the Secretary, Department of Health, Swasthya Bhavan, Kolkata
2. Director of Health Services, Government of West Bengal, Swasthya Bhavan, Kolkata
3. Chief Medical Officer of Health

.... *Respondents*

Being aggrieved by and dissatisfied with the order dated .... passed by His Lordship Hon'ble Mr. Justice .... dismissing *in limine* the petition moved under Art. 226 of the Constitution of India, the Appellant begs to file this appeal on the following, amongst other.

GROUNDS

1. For that the Hon'ble Judge was wrong to dismiss the petition *in limine* without assigning any reason.

2. For that the Hon'ble Judge dismissed the petition without entering into the merits of the petition.

3. For that the Hon'ble Judge has acted in the exercise of his jurisdiction illegally and with material irregularity in not considering the grounds taken in the petition under Art. 226 of the Constitution of India.

4. For that the Hon'ble Judge should have found, in the facts and circumstances of the case, that the impugned order of dismissal from service was illegal, without jurisdiction, motivated and was liable to be set aside.

5. For that the Hon'ble Judge ought to have held that the purported order of dismissal, during pendency of the Criminal Appeal before the Hon'ble High Court, was violative of the rules of natural and procedural justice and on that count alone the said order was liable to be struck down.

6. For that the Hon'ble Judge, in the facts and circumstances of the case, ought to have held that the disciplinary authority failed to act objectively in passing the impugned order inasmuch as it was incumbent upon the said disciplinary authority to consider pros and cons of the entire case and after such consideration to come to a determination in consonance with the provisions of the West Bengal Civil Services (Classification, Control and Appeal) Rules 1971.

7. For that the Hon'ble Judge ought to have held that there was violation of principles of natural justice as no opportunity of being heard was given to the Petitioner-Appellant before the penalty of dismissal was imposed on him and that the impugned order violated the provisions in Art. 311(2) of the Constitution of India.

8. For that the Hon'ble Judge should have found that the order of dismissal said to be issued pursuant to the judgment passed by the Additional Sessions Judge .... was wholly bad in law.

9. For that the Hon'ble Judge should have, in the facts and circumstances of the case, issued the appropriate Rule.

10. For that the order and judgment appealed against is otherwise bad in law.

List of papers

1. This Memorandum of Appeal.
2. Judgment impugned.
3. Hon'ble 2nd Judge's Copy.

Verification

Affidavit

597. Petition for Revision (Civil) under s. 115, CPC

District ....

In the High Court at ....
(Civil Revisional Jurisdiction)

In the matter of:

An application under s. 115 of the Code of Civil Procedure

And

In the matter of:

An Order No. .... dated .... passed by Sri .... Civil Judge (Senior Division) .... in Money Suit No. .... of 20 .... imposing a cost of ₹.................

And

In the matter of:

A.B. son of C.D. residing at .... P.S. .... District ....

... *Defendant-Petitioner*

versus

1. E.
2. F.
3. G.

... *Plaintiff-Opposite Party*

To
The Hon'ble Mr.................. Chief Justice and His Companion Justices of the Hon'ble Court.

The humble petition of the petitioner named above most respectfully sheweth:

1. That ....

2. That .... (State facts leading to the impugned order).

3. That being aggrieved by the aforesaid order dated .... passed by the Civil Judge (Senior Division) .... in Money Suit No. .... of 20 .... Your petitioner begs to move Your Lordships on the following, amongst other.

GROUNDS

(*i*) For that the learned Civil Judge (Senior Division), ... acted in the exercise of his jurisdiction illegally and with material irregularity in holding—

(*ii*) ....

(*iii*) ....

(*iv*) For that the impugned order dated .... is otherwise illegal and ought to be set aside.

Your petitioner, therefore, prays that Your Lordships would be pleased to call for the records of the case and issue a Rule on the opposite party to show cause as to why .... after setting aside the impugned order; And, after perusal of records and hearing Your petitioner's Advocate to make the same absolute and/or to pass such other order or orders as Your Lordships deem fit and proper.

And, pending the hearing of the Rule, operation of the impugned order and further proceedings in the suit be stayed.

Verification

Affidavit

I, ...

1. ....

2. ....

NOTES: 1. Section 115 proviso—order should either cause irreparable injury or cause failure of justice. Order need not cause both irreparable injury and failure of justice. Word 'Or', in cl. (*b*) of the proviso should not be read as 'and'—AIR 1978 Cal 264.

2. Decision of lower court is erroneous in fact or law. Errors, however, not having relation to jurisdiction. Decision cannot be interfered with in Revision—*R.S. Cambray* v *Bishnu Banerjee* AIR 1988 Cal 400.

3. *Ex parte* decree of eviction—Revision petition filed. One of the co-owners dies during pendency of Revision petition. LR's are not substituted. Right survives to other co-owners on record. Revision would not abate—*Ram Gopal Sharma* v *1st Additional D.J., Meerut* AIR 1993 All 124.

598. Petition for Revision (Civil) under s. 115, CPC (Another Form)

In the High Court of Judicature at ....

Under s. 115, CPC

District ....

A.B. aged about .... years son of .... resident of .... Thana .... Pargana .... Tahsil .... District ....

.... *Applicant*

versus

1. C.D. aged about .... years wife of ....
2. E.F. aged about .... years son of .... residents of .... etc.

.... *Opposite-Party*

The applicant above named prefers this Civil Revision in this Hon'ble High Court of Judicature at .... against the decree and order of Sri ...., Additional District Judge .... dated .... in Misc. Appeal No. .... of 20 .... in original suit No. .... of 20 .... of the Court of Civil Judge (Junior Division) ....

BETWEEN

C.D. and another ....

.... *Plaintiff-Appellant*

And

A.B. ....

...... *Defendant-Respondent*

The relief sought by this revision is that the Hon'ble Court be graciously pleased to allow the revision, to set aside the judgment and order of the court below allowing the plaintiff-appellant's appeal with costs throughout or the Hon'ble Court may grant such other relief as it deems just and proper.

Valuation of the suit and revision is ₹...........

The court-fee paid is ₹...........

The grounds of objection to the said decree and order are as follows:

1. Because the Civil Court had no jurisdiction decide suit of the plaintiff-opposite party No. ....

2. Because ....

3. Because ....

Dated:

....

Counsel for the Applicant

Verification

Affidavit

NOTES: 1. There is no specific provision for the conversion of an appeal into a revision or *vice versa*. Consequently, the exercise of power has to be only under the provisions of s. 151. The inherent powers of the Court permit the Court to make such orders as may be necessary for the ends of justice.

There is nothing like a period of limitation for making an application for conversion of an appeal into a revision or *vice versa*. All that is required to be seen is if the appeal, or the revision had been filed within the time prescribed for the filing of the appeal, or the revision, as the case may be. Even otherwise, there would be very few cases where the conversion would be sought before the expiry of the period of filing of the appeal. In most cases the point would emanate after an objection has been filed or made by the other side.

Where the District Judge declined to convert revision into appeal only on the ground that the prayer for conversion was made after the expiry of the period for filing appeal but was otherwise disposed to do so in the interest of justice the refusal to convert was not correct—AIR 1978 All 299. Also see AIR 1978 Goa 44.

2. Failure of lower court to consider records and relevant facts—not only illegal or erroneous decision but material irregularity committed—interference in revision justified (AIR 1978 Cal 505). Order suffering from an infirmity arising out of illegal exercise of jurisdiction—Revision maintainable—AIR 1978 Goa 44.

599. Petition for Review of judgment (under Or. 47, r. 1) in the High Court

District ....

In the High Court at Calcutta

(Civil Appellate Jurisdiction)

In the matter of:

An application for review of judgment under Or. 47, r. 1 read with ss. 114 and 151 of the CPC

And

In the matter of:

Second Appeal No. .... of 20 ....

And

In the matter of:

Sri ....

.... *Plaintiff-Appellant Petitioner*

versus

1. State of West Bengal
2. State Transport Corporation

...... *Defendants-Respondents Opposite Party*

To

The Hon'ble Mr. ...., Chief Justice and His Companion Justices of the Hon'ble Court

The humble petition of the aforesaid petitioner most respectfully sheweth:

1. That Your petitioner's case *inter alia* is that ....

2. That against said decision Your petitioner filed a Second Appeal before the Hon'ble High Court being Second Appeal No. .... of 20 .... The appeal was heard by Mr. Justice .... who held .... and allowed the appeal on ....

3. That His Lordship Hon'ble Mr. Justice .... while passing the judgment on ....observed ".." which is apparently wrong on the face of the record.

4. That being aggrieved by the aforesaid remark in the judgment dated .... in Second Appeal No. .... of 20 .... Your petitioner begs to file this application for review of the judgment on the following, amongst other.

GROUNDS

I. For that His Lordship Hon'ble Mr. Justice .... was wrong in making the said observations in his judgment without having any materials before him.

II. ....

III. ....

IV. For that having regard to the fact that His Lordship set aside the decree passed by the lower Appellate Court he ought to have restored the decree of the trial court in its entirety without said observations.

Your petitioner, therefore, prays that Your Lordships would be pleased to issue a Rule on the opposite party to show cause why the application for review, on the grounds set forth above, should not be granted.

And, after perusal of the record and hearing the parties, would make the same absolute.

And/or pass such other order or orders as deemed proper.

Verification

Affidavit

600. Application for setting aside High Court order

In the Hon'ble Supreme Court of India

Appellate Jurisdiction

Appeal from the Order of Hon'ble High Court at Calcutta

Appeal No. .... of 20 ....

In the matter of:

An application under Art. 133 of the Constitution of India;

And

In the matter of:
Mr. P., residing at .... Kolkata
...... *Appellant*

versus

Mr. X., residing at .... Kolkata
.... *Respondent*

To
The Hon'ble Mr. Chief Justice of India and His Companion Justices of the Hon'ble Supreme Court

The humble appeal of the appellant abovenamed most respectfully sheweth:

1. That the appellant instituted on .... a suit against the respondent being the Suit No. .... of .... in the court of ...., claiming, *inter alia*, that she was the natural guardian of her minor son aged about 10 years.

2. That the facts disputed in filing of the said suit are briefly as follows:

(*a*) the appellant and respondent were married according to the Hindu rites on .... at the appellant's father's residence;

(*b*) out of the said wedlock, a son was born to them on ....;

(*c*) the marriage between the parties was dissolved subsequently by a decree of divorce on the ground of the respondent's adultery and cruelty to the appellant;

(*d*) the appellant's said suit was dismissed on contest by ....;

(*e*) against the said order of dismissal, the appellant preferred an appeal vide appeal No. .... of 20... in the High Court at Kolkata which appeal was also dismissed.

3. That the Hon'ble High Court at Kolkata on an application of the appellant granted a certificate under Art. 132 of the Constitution of India to the effect that the case involved substantial questions of law and facts.

4. That the appellant being aggrieved by and dissatisfied with the said judgment and order of the Hon'ble High Court dated .... begs to prefer this appeal, on, *inter alia*, the following amongst other.

GROUNDS

I. For that the Hon'ble High Court should have held that in the case of a dissolved Hindu Marriage, where the husband is found guilty of adultery and or he has remarried, the guardianship of minor child should be given to the mother of the child.

II. For that the Hon'ble High Court failed to appreciate and erred in doing so that the said minor child would be well looked after by appellant being the mother than the respondent father.

III. For that the Hon'ble High Court should have held and erred in not doing so that the respondent does not stay in Kolkata most of the time and he has no regular time of hours of work and as such, he will not be able to pay sufficient attention to the minor child.

IV. For that the Hon'ble Judge failed to appreciate and erred in doing so that for the health and education of the minor child, constant attention was required to be given and that the respondent was unable to do so as he had to go out of Kolkata very often and he was away from Kolkata for about 20 days in a month and as such he was incapable of paying proper attention to the welfare of minor child.

V. For that the Hon'ble Judge is otherwise wrong both in facts and in law that the sole custody of the child being minor could not be given to the respondent inasmuch as the minor child will not be properly looked after by the respondent by virtue of his preoccupation and the nature of work he is engaged in and as such, constant attention was required to be given to minor child and giving custody to the respondent was wrong both in facts and in law and against the interest of the minor child and the said order be set aside and quashed.

5. The appellant's suit was dismissed on contest and the decision was given in favour of respondent and custody of child was given to the respondent.

6. Against the said dismissal of the appellant's suit the appellant preferred an appeal being No. .... of .... in the High Court at Kolkata which was also dismissed.

7. The appellant will refer to and rely on the provisions of different statutes stated in the appellant's present case at the time of hearing of the present appeal.

8. This application has been made *bona fide* and in the interest of justice.

The appellant, therefore, humbly prays Your Lordships for the following orders:

(*a*) Your Lordships be graciously pleased to set aside the Appellate Order dated .... passed by the Hon'ble High Court at Calcutta after hearing the petition;

(*b*) Further and other orders be made as this Hon'ble Supreme Court of India may deem fit and proper to afford complete relief to appellant.

And the appellant, as in duty-bound, shall ever pray.

Verification

Affidavit

601. Application for leave to appeal against order of High Court

In the Supreme Court of India

Appellate Jurisdiction

SLP No. .... of 20............

In the matter of:

Mr. P. residing at ...., Alipore Road, Kolkata

.... *Petitioner*

versus

Mr. X. residing at .... Kolkata
.... *Respondent*

To
The Hon'ble Mr. ...., Chief Justice
of India and His Companion Justices
of the Hon'ble Court

The humble petition of the petitioner above-named most respectfully sheweth:

1. Your petitioner filed a Title Suit No. .... of 20....... in the Court of Civil Judge (Senior Division) at Alipore against the respondent for a declaration that the property mentioned in Schedule was the absolute property of the deceased being Mr. Y. Mr. Y purchased the property in the *benami* of respondent. The suit against the respondent is for declaration that the said property in the Schedule was the absolute property of the deceased Mr. Y.

2. The said deceased was governed by the Dayabhaga School of Hindu Law, and died intestate on the 4th June 20... leaving behind and surviving the petitioner and respondent being his two sons as the heirs and legal representatives.

3. In the said suit, the petitioner claimed that he inherited half share in the said property held in *benami* by respondent though he did not and could not pay the full consideration money for purchase of the said property.

4. The Ld. Trial Court dismissed the suit on contest relying on the provisions of s. 4 of the Benami Transactions (Prohibition of Rights to Personal Property) Act of 1988.

5. Against dismissal of the said suit the petitioner preferred an appeal before the Hon'ble High Court at Calcutta and the Appeal Court admitted the appeal being F.A. No. 61 of 20....

6. By an order dated 7th July 20... the Hon'ble High Court was pleased to dismiss the said appeal upholding the said decision of the Hon'ble Trial Court.

7. The petitioner prayed for a Certificate under Art. 134A of the Constitution of India which was rejected.

8. Substantial questions of law are involved concerning the Appeal before the Hon'ble Supreme Court a draft of which is annexed hereto marked with letter 'A'.

9. The petitioner states that all formalities as required under law have been completed and complied with.

10. The petitioner submits that he will suffer irreparable loss and prejudice unless the proposed appeal be heard on merits.

11. An order of injunction is required restraining the respondent from encumbering or in dealing with the said property in any manner. An order of the Hon'ble Supreme Court of India is necessary to set at rest the controversial legal questions of Benami Transactions particulars of which are given in the Schedule hereunder.

In the circumstances your petitioner prays Your Lordship for the following orders:

(*a*) Necessary orders be passed granting leave for preferring this appeal against the appellate order passed by the Hon'ble High Court at Calcutta, a draft of Grounds of Appeal is annexed hereto and marked with letter 'A'.

(b) An order of injunction be passed restraining respondent from encumbering or dealing with the said *benami* property in any manner whatsoever, pending this appeal.

(c) Further and other orders be made as the Hon'ble Supreme Court of India may deem fit and proper, to afford complete relief to the petitioner.

And your petitioner, as in duty bound, shall ever pray.

SCHEDULE

Verification

Affidavit

COMPANY LAW

The power of a Court to grant relief in certain cases under s. 463 of the Companies Act 2013 (corresponds to s. 633 of the Companies Act 1956). The said section provides that:

(1) If in any proceeding for negligence, default, breach of duty, misfeasance, or breach of trust against an officer of a Company, it appears to the court hearing the case that he is or may be liable in respect of the negligence, default, breach of duty, misfeasance or breach of trust, but that he has acted honestly and reasonably, and that having regard to all the circumstances of the case, including those connected with his appointment, he ought fairly to be excused, the court may relieve him, either wholly or partly, from his liability on such terms as it may think fit:

Provided that in a criminal proceeding under this sub-section, the court shall have no power to grant relief from any civil liability, which may attach to an officer, in respect of such negligence, default, breach of duty, misfeasance or breach of trust.

(2) Where any such officer has reason to apprehend that any proceeding will or might be brought against him in respect of any negligence, default, breach of duty, misfeasance, or breach of trust, he may apply to the High Court for relief and the High Court on such an application shall have the same power to relieve him as it would have had if it had been a court before which a proceeding against that officer for negligence, default, breach of duty, misfeasance or breach of trust had been brought under sub-section (1).

(3) No court shall grant any relief to any officer under sub-section (1) or sub-section (2) unless it has, by notice served in the manner specified by it, required the Registrar and such other person, if any, as it thinks necessary, to show cause why such relief should not be granted.

602. Application to be relieved of liability

C.P. No. .... of 20................

In the High Court at Calcutta

Original Jurisdiction

In the matter of:
An application under s. 463 of the Companies Act 2013.

And

In the matter of:

1. Mr. P. residing at ...., Alipore Road, Kolkata

2. M/s. X Co. Ltd. of ...., Alipore Road, Kolkata

.... *Petitioners*

versus

Registrar of Companies, West Bengal, Deptt. of Company Affairs, having his office at ...., Acharya Jagadish Chandra Bose Road, Kolkata 700 020

.... *Respondent*

To
The Hon'ble Mr. .... Chief Justice and His Companion Justices of the Hon'ble Court

The humble petition of the petitioners above-named most respectfully sheweth:

1. The address of the petitioners for the sake of all notices processes, etc. is that of the Advocate-on-Record Mr. Z, ..., Old Post Office Street, Kolkata 700 001.

2. Petitioner No. 2 M/s. X. Co. Ltd. was incorporated as a Public Company Limited by shares on 5th day of March 20... under the provisions of the Companies Act 2013, and obtained Certificate of Commencement of Business on 10th May 20........

3. The Authorised Share Capital of the Company is ₹10,00,000 divided into 1,00,000 equity shares of ₹10 each fully paid-up.

4. The object of the Company for which it was incorporated are contained in the Company's Memorandum of Association. The main objects of the Company are, *inter alia*, as follows:

(*a*) to carry on the business of manufacturers, importers, exporters, and distributors of Teas;

(*b*) to acquire and purchase land, to cultivate and grow teas and other produce, and to sell them in the manner convenient to the company.

The said and other objects will appear from the Company's Memorandum of Association.

5. There was crop failure and agitations by the workers, and some outside elements and the company could not carry on its business in the usual manner, suffered heavy losses, and there were widespread discontent and agitation by the employees which hampered the usual work of the company. The accounts could not be prepared and filed with the respondent being the Registrar of Companies.

6. The Registrar of Companies issued notices reminding non-filing of final accounts such as Profit & Loss Account and Balance Sheets for 3 years and threatened to take action against the petitioner for non-compliance of the provisions of the Companies Act 2013. A copy of the said notice is annexed hereto marked 'A'.

7. The petitioners replied to the respondent stating the agitation and stoppage of work by the workers including the office staff of the petitioner. A copy of the said letter duly received by respondent is annexed hereto marked 'B'.

8. The petitioners state that the petitioners have acted honestly and reasonably and in the circumstances even if there be technical breach of obligations of duty to file the Final Accounts in time according to the respondent, there has been no actual breach of duty in fact and the petitioners ought fairly to be excused and this Hon'ble court would be pleased to relieve them from their liability, the petitioners having been charged under ss. 92, 96 and 137 of the Companies Act 2013 (corresponds to ss. 159, 166 and 220 of the Companies Act 1956 respectively).

9. Your petitioners gave due reply to the show-cause notice issued by the respondent. The respondent, however, has not given his final reply even though several weeks have passed and the petitioners are apprehending that the respondent may take steps to give effect to the notice and institute legal proceedings against petitioners in respect of the matter referred to in the said notice.

10. Your petitioners state that if the respondent takes proceedings against petitioners undue hardship would be caused to the petitioners even though the petitioners have acted honestly and reasonably. There has been no wilful or deliberate default on the part of petitioner. There has been no negligence or breach of duty or breach of trust or misfeasance, by the petitioners and they have acted honestly and reasonably and having regard to the circumstances of the case ought fairly to be excused and be relieved from any liability on account of the default alleged.

11. Your petitioners state that in the facts and circumstances of case, Your petitioners be relieved from any liability on account of any default in filing accounts with the Registrar of Companies and in the meantime, an interim order be passed restraining the respondent, from initiating any legal proceedings, against the petitioners.

12. Unless orders are made as prayed for, your petitioners will suffer irreparable loss, injury, damage and will be seriously prejudiced. Your petitioners have a strong case for orders as prayed for being granted. The balance of convenience is also in favour of passing the orders as prayed for.

13. This application has been made *bona fide* and in interest of justice, and the notice of this application has been served on respondent.

Your petitioners, therefore, humbly pray Your Lordships for the following Orders:

(*a*) Petitioners be relieved from liability on account of any default in filing the Accounts mentioned in the notice of the respondent on such terms as this Hon'ble Court may deem fit and proper;

(*b*) Injunction restraining the respondent, from taking any further action pursuant to the notices issued by the respondent;

(*c*) *Ad-interim* orders in terms of prayers (*a*) and (*b*) above;

(*d*) Costs of this application be paid by respondent;

(*e*) Further and other orders be made as to this Hon'ble Court may deem fit and proper.

Any your petitioner as in duty bound shall ever pray.

Advocate-on-Record
for the petitioners.

Verification

Affidavit

603. Application to be relieved of liability for default (Another Form)

C.P. No. ...... of 20...

In the High Court at Calcutta

Original Jurisdiction

In the matter of:

The Companies Act 2013;

And

In the matter of:

An Application under section 463 of the Companies Act 2013;

And

In the matter of:

1. Mr. P. residing at ...., Alipore Road, Kolkata;
2. Mr. Q. residing at ...., Alipore Road, Kolkata;
3. Mr. R. residing at ...., Alipore Road, Kolkata;
4. M/s. PQ & R. Co. Ltd., a Company within the meaning of the Companies Act 2013 having its Registered Office at ...., Netaji Subhas Road, Kolkata 700 001 within the aforesaid jurisdiction.

........*Petitioners*

versus

The Register of Companies, West Bengal, Department of Company Affairs, having his office at Nizam Palace, II, MSO Building, (2nd floor), 234/4/, AJC Bose Road, Kolkata 700 020.

...........*Respondent*

To
The Hon'ble Mr. .... Chief Justice and His Companion Justices of the Hon'ble Court

The humble petition of the petitioners above-named most respectfully sheweth:

1. The address of the petitioners for service of all notices, processes, etc. is ...., Netaji Subhas Road, Kolkata 700 001.

2. PQ & R. Co. Ltd., was incorporated as a Public Company Limited by shares on 17th August 20…, under provisions of Companies Act 2013 as a Public Limited Company.

3. The Registered Office of the Company is at ...., Netaji Subhas Road, Kolkata 700 001 within the aforesaid jurisdiction of this Hon'ble Court.

4. The Authorised Share Capital of the company is ₹10,00,000 divided into 1,00,000 equity shares of ₹10 each, fully Paid-up.

5. The objects for which the company was incorporated are set out in Clause III of the Memorandum of Association of the Company. The main objects of company, are, *inter alia*, the following:

(*i*) to carry on business as Exporter and Importer, Buyer and Seller and supplier of all kinds of food grains;

(*ii*) to acquire agricultural land, gardens and any Estate; and buildings for the purpose of carrying out business of the company;

(*iii*) to raise capital by issue of Shares and Debentures and by borrowings from Banks and Financial Institutions against securities of assets of company and in that connection to execute requisite banking documents.

The said and other objects are to be found in Memorandum of Association of the Company a copy whereof is annexed hereto marked 'A'.

6. Due to recession in the market conditions of export trade, the petitioners had to suffer heavy losses and the petitioners were very much preoccupied to take necessary steps to save the company from going into liquidation. In this process, the petitioners could not pay attention to preparation of Company's accounts and filing the same with Registrar of Companies, West Bengal.

7. In the meantime, the Registrar of Companies had issued notices for default and breach in filing of the necessary Returns under provisions of the relevant sections of the Companies Act 2013, for the years ending on 31st March 20… and 31st March 20…. Copies of the said notices of Registrar of Companies are annexed hereto marked 'B'.

8. On behalf of the petitioners, the company by a letter dated 15th April 20… duly replied to the said notices of the respondent, Registrar of Companies, West Bengal. A copy of the said letter is annexed hereto marked 'C'.

9. Your petitioners are apprehensive that the Registrar of Companies may take legal proceedings against the petitioners for the said non-filing of the balance sheets and returns. From the said notices issued by the Registrar of Companies, it appears that the Registrar of Companies intends to charge your petitioners for violation of ss. 92, 96 and 137 of the Companies Act 2013 (corresponds to ss. 159, 166 and 220 of the Companies Act 1956) and to start proceedings thereunder.

10. Further the petitioners apprehend that on just and *bona fide* grounds the respondents will seek to institute criminal proceedings against petitioners in respect of the alleged default mentioned in the said notices issued by Registrar of Companies.

11. Your petitioners state that if any legal proceedings are instituted by the respondent, Registrar of Companies, they will suffer undue hardship in spite of the fact that they have all along been acting honestly and reasonably having regard to circumstances of the case and they ought fairly to be excused from charges against them in the said notices, copies of which are annexures hereto.

12. Your petitioners state that at all material times, they had acted diligently and honestly in the best interests of shareholders of the company, the company as a whole and all concerned and there has been no wilful or deliberate default or breach on the

part of the petitioners inasmuch as there has been no negligence or breach of duty or misfeasance or breach of trust by the petitioners, as they have acted honestly and reasonably and having regard to circumstances of the case they ought fairly to be excused and to be relieved from any liability on account of default on such terms and conditions as to this Hon'ble court may seem fit and proper.

13. In the facts and circumstances of the case, your petitioners state that it is also necessary for issue of interim orders restraining respondent from instituting any legal proceedings until the disposal of the present application.

14. Unless orders as prayed for are made, your petitioners will suffer irreparable loss, injury and damage.

15. This is a case of urgency in the matter and *ad interim* orders as prayed for are necessary in the best interests of justice and equity.

16. If the notice of this application is given to the petitioner before making an interim order the respondent will act overnight to render the present application infructuous and as such, an order be passed *ex parte* restraining the respondent from instituting any proceeding in any court of law against petitioners till disposal of this present application.

17. This application has been made *bona fide* and in the interest of justice.

Your petitioners, therefore, most humbly pray Your Lordships for the following Orders:

(*a*) The petitioners be excused and/or be relieved from any liability on account of any default or breach by the petitioners under provisions of ss. 92, 96 and 137 of the Companies Act 2013 as has been alleged in the notices being annexures hereto on such terms as this Hon'ble Court may deem fit and proper;

(*b*) *Ad interim* Orders in terms of the prayer (*a*) above;

(*c*) Cost of this application be paid by the respondent;

(*d*) Such further and other orders and directions be issued as this Hon'ble Court may deem fit and proper, to afford complete relief to the petitioners.

And your petitioners, as in duty bound, shall ever pray.

Advocate-on-Record
for the petitioners.

Verification

Affidavit

Right to Information

1. *Competent Authority* means the Speaker in the case of the House of the People or the Legislative Assembly of a State or a Union territory having such Assembly and the Chairman in the case of the council of the States or Legislative Council of a State; The Chief Justice of India, Chief Justice of all the High Courts, the Hon'ble President of India, Governor of a State and the administrator appointed under Art. 239 of the Constitution of India [section 2(*e*) of the Right to Information Act 2005].

2. The right to information includes inspection of any work, documents, records, taking notes, extracts, certified copies of the documents, records and also the certified material sample and such information may be given in the form of diskettes, floppies, tapes, video cassettes or in any other electronic mode or through printouts where such information is stored in a computer or in any other device (section 2(*j*) of the Act).

3. Public Information Officer shall be appointed by every Public Authority in all the Administrative Units or Offices and designated as Information Officer. An application for information has to be forwarded to the Information Officer of the particular area in respect of which Unit the information is sought for.

Normally, within 30 days of such a request, the information has to be furnished to the person but in case of such information asked for actually concerns the life or liberty of a person, the same shall be furnished within 48 hours thereof by Information Officer.

4. A request for access to the information sought for may be summarily rejected where such a request is for providing access to the information involving the copyright of a person other than the State and if the information asked for is severable, then the portion of information which does not directly infringe the copyright shall be furnished.

5. The Chief Information Commissioner and the Information Officers of States shall be appointed by the President of India on recommendation of a Cabinet Committee consisting of Prime Minister, Leader of the Opposition in the Lok Sabha and a Union Cabinet Minister appointed/nominated by the Prime Minister of India for the purpose.

The State Information Commission shall be appointed by the concerned State Government consisting of the State Chief Information Commissioner and the Information Commissioners not exceeding ten in total. They may be appointed by the Governor of the concerned State on recommendation of a Committee of the Chief Minister, Leader of opposition in the State Assembly and a Cabinet Minister.

6. *Power and functions of the Information Commission.* The Central or State Information Commission shall receive and enquire into the complaints of any person who has been unable to submit a request to the Public Information Officer because of its refusal to accept the application for furnishing such information or any appeal for forwarding the application to the Public Information Officer or the Senior in Rank to the Officer of the Commission or person who has been refused access to information or who does not receive any response to his application for information within a specified time or who has been asked to pay an unreasonable fee or who has been given incomplete or misleading or false information. If such application appears to be reasonable, then the Information Commission should initiate an enquiry and hear his grievances and make appropriate orders thereon.

A person aggrieved by or dissatisfied with decision of the Public Information Officer within 30 days may prefer an appeal to the Officer senior in Rank to the concerned Public Information Officer who will hear the aggrieved party and give his verdict.

7. *Protection of action taken in good faith.* No suit, prosecution or any other legal proceeding shall lie against any person for anything done in good faith or is intended to be done under the said Act or Rules framed thereunder.

8. *Exclusion of jurisdiction of courts.* No court shall ever entertain any suit, application or proceeding in respect of any order made under the said Act and no order shall be called in question other than by way of an appeal under this Act.

9. *Programme.* The appropriate Government subject to availability of financial and other resources develop and organise educational programmes, encourage the Public Authorities to participate in development of such programmes with a view to promoting the timely and effective dissemination of any accurate information by the Public

Authorities about their activities, to train the officers and make arrangements for giving timely and effective accurate information asked for by the applicants.

10. *Exemptions.* Section 24 of the said Act of 2005, in 2nd Schedule to the Act provides that it shall not apply to the following Intelligence and Security Organisations:

1. Intelligence Bureau.
2. Research and Analysis Wing of the Cabinet Secretariat.
3. Directorate of Revenue Intelligence.
4. Central Economic Intelligence Bureau.
5. Directorate of Enforcement.
6. Narcotics Control Bureau.
7. Aviation Research Centre of the Cabinet Secretariat.
8. Special Frontier Force of the Cabinet Secretariat.
9. Border Security Force.
10. Central Reserve Police Force.
11. Indo-Tibetan Border Police.
12. Central Industrial Security Force.
13. National Security Guards.
14. Assam Rifles.
15. Sashtra Seema Bal.
16. Directorate General of Income-tax (Investigation).
17. National Technical Research Organisation.
18. Financial Intelligence Unit, India.
19. Special Protection Group.
20. Defence Research and Development Organisation.
21. Border Road Development Board.
22. National Security Council Secretariat.
23. Central Bureau of Investigation.
24. National Investigation Agency.
25. National Intelligence Grid.
26. Strategic Forces Command.

The main object of the said Act of 2005 is to provide access to the information under the Control of the Public Authority, the setting-up of Central Information Commission and the State Information Commission.

The Right to information includes the Right to Information of work, documents, records, taking notes, extracts or certified copies thereof, or taking certified samples of all materials. This information may be provided in Diskettes, Floppies, Tapes, Video cassettes, printouts, etc. etc.

Every Public Authority shall maintain all its records duly catalogued and indexed, so as to facilitate the Right to Information under the said Act and wherever possible such records should be duly computerised. The Public Authority shall publish the requisite particulars mentioned in section 4, publish all relevant facts while formulating the important policies or announcing the decisions which affect the public interests.

It should also provide proper reasons for its administrative or quasi-judicial decisions to affected persons.

Every Public Authority shall provide information to general public at regular intervals so that the there may not be too many applications to obtain such information from such Public Authority. Such information should be disseminated widely and in such form and manner which is easily accessible to the general public.

A person may make his request in writing or through electronic means in English or Hindi, as the case may be, being the Official Language of the area or locality concerned with the prescribed fees, to the Central Public Information Officer or the State Public Information Officer, as the case may be, or the Central Assistant Public Information Officer or the State Assistant Public Information Officer. However, if such request cannot be made in writing to the Central Assistant Public Information Officer, they shall render all reasonable assistance to the person making such a request orally to reduce the same in writing. Further, if the application is made to an authority which is not the appropriate authority, then it shall transfer such complaint to the appropriate authorities for disposal, which should be done within 5 days thereof.

Such an application should be disposed off within 30 days by either providing the information or rejecting such request on the ground or grounds mentioned in ss. 8 and 9 of the said Act of 2005, regarding the information asked for. If the information asked for concerns the life or liberty of a person then such information shall be provided within 48 hours from the date of such a request.

If the concerned Information Officer fails to give any decision on such request for information within 30 days thereof, or 48 hours as the case may be, it should be deemed to have been refused.

Where the officer concerned decides to provide such information it should inform the applicant to pay the requisite fees, being the cost of providing such information. The Officer concerned should inform the applicant about his right to apply for review the decision as to the amount of fees charged or to be charged or the form of access provided including particulars of appellate authority, time-limit, process or any other form.

Where the applicant is sensorily disabled the concerned officer should provide necessary assistance to enable the applicant access to such information.

The applicant has to pay the necessary fees for providing information through electronic media, and the procedure to be followed by the officer concerned is given in s. 7 of the said Act.

No obligation. The Officer or the authority shall have no obligation to give any information for any citizen in respect of the information enumerated in s. 8 of the Act. However, if the public interest so demands this reservation shall not be applicable. The Right to obtain Information relating to any occurrence, event or matter which took place more than 20 years ago shall be provided to the applicant but this will be subject to the usual appeals provided under the said Act.

Where the information sought for relates to a third person then the Information Officer shall give an opportunity to such third person to make his submissions and inform him about the decision. Such third party shall have the usual right to prefer an appeal from decision of the concerned Public Officer under s. 19 of the Act against the decision to disclose any information regarding him.

Central Information Commission or State Information Commission may receive or enquire into any complaint and shall have the same powers or authority as are vested in a Civil Court for summoning and enforcing the attendance of persons and compelling them to give evidence and direct the discovery and inspection of documents, receive evidence-on-affidavit, request for disclosure of public records, or certified copies thereof from any court or office, issue regular summons for examination of witnesses or the documents or records. The Commission may also examine any records to which the said Act of 2005 applies and which is in the control of a Public Authority and no such records may be withheld from the Commission on any ground. An aggrieved person may prefer an appeal from such decision within 30 days before the officer senior in rank to the concerned Public Information Officer. When the disclosure of any information regarding a third party is involved any appeal filed by the aggrieved third party shall be filed within 30 days.

A second appeal against the decision of the concerned Information Officer shall be filed within 90 days from the date of such decision. Such appeal to the Central Information Commission or State Information Commission, as the case may be, may admit the appeal after the expiry of 30 days if it is fully satisfied that the applicant was prevented by sufficient cause for filing such appeal in time. In the appeal, the public authority shall have to justify the denial of the request to provide the required information.

The Information Commission concerned has the power to direct the concerned Public Authority to comply with the provisions of the said Act of 2005 by providing information, publishing certain information by making necessary changes to the usual practices in relation to maintenance, management and destruction of records or documents. An Annual Report should also be published. The Commission shall follow the usual procedure.

Public Authority. The term means any authority, body, or Institution, of Self-Government established or constituted by the Constitution, Central Act, State Act, by Notification issued or order made by Central or State Government and includes a Body owned, controlled or substantially financed, a Non-Government Organisation, substantially financed directly or indirectly, by funds provided by the Central or State Government.

Obligation of Public Authorities. Every Public Authority shall maintain proper Index of all its records, publish the specified particulars and provide information *suo motu* to the public at regular intervals in an appropriate manner, and designate some of its employees as Central Public Information Officers in case of Central Government, or State Public Information Officers in case of State Government, so that they could furnish information to the persons requesting for such information under the said Act.

Immunity. No suit, prosecution or legal proceeding shall lie against any person for anything which is in good faith done or intended to be done under the Act of 2005 or any Rules framed thereunder. The immunity would be available in respect of the provisions under the Official Secrets Act 1923, or any other law or any other instrument. No court shall entertain any suit, application, or any other proceeding in respect of any order made under the provisions of the Act of 2005 and no such Order shall be called in question otherwise than by an appeal preferred under the said Act of 2005 as provided in s. 21.

Information not available, Act of 2005 not applicable. The Act shall not apply to the Intelligence and Security Organisation, established by the Central Government.

A public authority shall have no obligation to give to any citizen:

(*a*) Information which would prejudicially affect the sovereignty and integrity of India, the security, strategic, scientific or economic interests of the State, relation with foreign State or lead to incitement of an offence;

(*b*) Information which has been forbidden to be published by any Court or Tribunal;

(*c*) Information which would cause breach of privilege of Parliament or Legislature;

(*d*) Information including commercial confidence, trade secrets, or intellectual property, the disclosure of which would harm the competitive position of a third party or information available to a person in his fiduciary relationship unless Competent Authority is satisfied that the larger public interests warrant the disclosure of such information;

(*e*) Information received in confidence from a foreign Government;

(*f*) Information the disclosure of which would endanger the life or physical safety of any person or identify the source of information or assistance given in confidence for law enforcement or security purposes;

(*g*) Information which would impede the process of investigation or apprehension or prosecution of offender;

(*h*) Cabinet papers, records of deliberations of the Council of Ministers, Secretaries, and other Officers;

(*i*) Personal information the disclosure of which has no relationship to any public activity or interest or which would cause unwarranted invasion of the privacy of the individual unless Public Information Officer or Appellate Authority is satisfied that the larger public interest justifies such disclosure and the information which cannot be denied to Parliament, or Legislature, shall also not be denied to any person;

(*j*) A public authority may allow access to any information if public interest in disclosure outweighs the harm to the protected interests;

(*k*) In spite of Official Secrets Act 1923, and provisions of sub-sec. (1) of s. 8 a Public Authority may allow access to information if public interest in disclosures outweighs the harm to the protected interests;

(*l*) Information regarding an event, which occurred 20 years before the date of application shall be provided. As to the date from which the 20 years will be computed the decision of Central Government shall be final subject to appeal under the Act of 2005.

Form. No particular form is mandatory for complaint or application or appeal under the said Act but the requisite particulars and fees are to be given. The Government concerned will constitute the Appellate Authority, but it is intended that the court will have no jurisdiction under the said Act of 2005.

Assistant Public Information Officer. At each sub-divisional level or other sub-district level, every Public Authority shall designate an Officer to receive the application for information or appeals, for forwarding the same forthwith to the Public Information Officer, Central or State, as the case may be, or to the specified senior officer or to Information Commission, State or Central, as the case may be.

Note. Section 18 of the Act of 2005 provides that it shall be the duty of the Central Information Commission or the State Information Commission, as the case may be, to receive and enquire into the complaint from any person who has been unable to submit a request to the Public Information Officer or who has been refused the Information asked or who has not been given a response to a request for information or who has been asked to pay an unreasonable fee or who feels that he has been given incomplete, misleading or false information. The Information Commission concerned may also initiate a detailed enquiry in respect of such a complaint and for this purpose may exercise the necessary powers vested in it and as enumerated in the said section.

Section 19 of the said Act of 2005 gives the Information Commission the Status of an Appellate Authority. A person who has been dissatisfied with the conduct or decision of the concerned Information Officer may prefer an appeal to the Officer Senior in Rank and position to the concerned Public Information Officer. The said appeal has to be preferred within 30 days but the Senior Officer has the sole discretion to admit the said appeal after the expiry of a period of 30 days if the appellant was prevented by sufficient cause from filing the said appeal in time. A third party who has been asked to disclose information by the Information Officer, may also prefer an appeal within a period of 30 days before the Officer Senior in Rank to the concerned Information Officer.

A Second Appeal may be preferred within 30 days to the Information Commission (State or Central, as the case may be). The third party who has been asked to furnish information may also prefer the appeal and he should be given a reasonable and fair opportunity of being heard by the concerned Information Commission.

Onus. Section 19(5) of the Act of 2005 provides that the onus to prove that a denial of a particular request was quite justified shall be on the Public Authority which denied to comply with the said request. The Information Commission (Central or State) has been vested with wide powers to make orders on the appeal against the order of refusal following the usual procedure.

604. Application for seeking information

To,

The Authorised Person,

....

....

1. Full name of the applicant
2. Address
3. Particulars of information required—
   (*a*) Concerned department
   (*b*) Particulars of information required—
      (*i*) Details of information required
      (*ii*) Period for which information asked for
      (*iii*) Other details
4. I state that the information sought does not fall within the restrictions contained in section of the Right to Information Act and to the best of my knowledge it pertains to your office.
5. A fee of ₹ .... has been deposited in the office of the authorised person *vide* Receipt No. .... dated ....

....

Signature of the Applicant

Place .... E-mail address ....

Date .... Telephone No. (Office) ....

Residence ....

NOTES: (*i*) Reasonable assistance can be provided by authorised person in filling up the Form.

(*ii*) Please ensure that the Form is complete in all respect and there is no ambiguity in providing the details of information required.

605. Application for obtaining information under the Right to Information Act 2005

To,
The State Public Information Officer,
(Name of the office with address)

(1) Full name of the applicant

(2) Address

(3) Particulars of information required.

(*i*) Subject-matter of information*

(*ii*) The period to which the information relates**

(*iii*) Description of the information required***

(*iv*) Whether information is required by post or in person (The actual postald shall be included in additional fees)

(*v*) In case by post

(Ordinary, Registered or Speed)

(4) Whether the applicant is below povery line

(If yes, attach the photo copy of the proof thereof).

Place ....

Date ....

....

Signature of the Applicant

NOTES: * Broad category of the subject to be indicated (such as Grant/Government land Service matters/Licenses, etc.)

** Relevant period for which information is required to be indicated.

*** Specific details of the information is required to be indicated.

606. Acknowledgment of application

Dated ....

1. Received an application from Mr/Mrs. .... Resident of .... under section of the Right to Information Act 2005.

2. The information is proposed to be given normally within fifteen days and in any case within thirty days from the date of receipt of application and in case it is found that the information asked for cannot be supplied, the rejection letter shall be issued stating reason thereof.

3. The application is advised to contact the undersigned on the .... day of .... between 11.00 a.m. to 1 p.m.

4. In case the applicant fails to turn up on the scheduled date(s), the authorised person shall not be responsible for delay, if any.

5. The applicant shall have to deposit the balance fee, if any, with the authorised person before collection of information.

6. The applicant may also consult Web-site of the department from time to time to ascertain the status of his application.

....
Signature and Stamp of
the Authorised person
E-mail ....
Web-site ....
Telephone No. ....

Dated ....

607. Appeal

I.D. No. ....
(For Official use)

To,
Appellate Authority
....
Address ....
....

1. Name of the applicant
2. Address
3. Particulars of the authorised person
   (*a*) Name
   (*b*) Address
4. Date of submission of application
5. Date on which thirty days from submission of application is over
6. Reasons for appeal
   (*a*) No response received within thirty days of submission of application
   (*b*) Aggrieved by the response received within prescribed period (Copy of the reply receipt be attached)
   (*c*) Grounds of appeal
7. Last date for filing the appeal
8. Particulars of information—
   (*i*) Information requested
   (*ii*) Subject
   (*iii*) Period
9. A fee of ₹ .... for appeal has been deposited with the authority *vide* Receipt No............ dated....................

Place ....
Date ....

....
Signature of Appellant
E-mail address ....
Web-site ....
Telephone No. ....
Dated
....

I.D. No ....

Received an Appeal acknowledgment from Mr./Mrs. .... resident of .... under section .... of the Right to Information Act, 2005.

....
Signature of Receipt Clerk,
....
Appellate Authority
E-mail Address ....
Web-site ....
Telephone No. ....

608. Second appeal

From:
....
(Appellant's name and address)

To,
....
....

(1) Full name of the appellant

(2) Address

(3) Particulars of the State Public Information Officer

(4) Particulars of the First Appellate Authority

(5) Date of receipt of the order appealed against

(6) Last date for filing the appeal

(7) The grounds for appeal

(8) Particulars of information—

(*i*) Nature and subject-matter of the information required.

(*ii*) Name of the Office or Department to which the information relates.

Place ....

Date ....

....
Signature of Appellant

Enforcement of Orders of Information Commission

Where a Public Authority fails to comply with an Order or Notice of an Information Commission, the Information Commission may certify in writing, to the High Court or Supreme Court, that the Respondent Public Authority has failed to comply with its Notice or Order. On such a reference the court may enquire into the matter and after the hearing any witness who may be produced against or on behalf of the Public Authority and after hearing any statement that may be offered in defence deal with the Authority as if, it has committed a contempt of the court.

The writ jurisdiction of the High Court or the Supreme Court is not intended to be ousted in relation to the proceedings under the Right to Information Act 2005.

In this connection, s. 23 of the said Act of 2005 should also be considered. The said section provides that

> "No court shall entertain any suit, application, or other proceeding in respect of any order made under this Act and no such order shall be called in question otherwise than by way of an appeal under this Act."

In view of the s. 23 of the said Act, it appears that the order of Information Commission is final.

However, the rights guaranteed by the Constitution of India cannot be taken away by Central or State Legislation. For protection of fundamental rights of a citizen, the recourse to proceedings under Arts. 226 and 227 of the Constitution of India will still be available in spite of the provision of s. 23 of the said Act of 2005.

609. Invocation of writ jurisdiction against the order of State Information Commission

In the High Court at Calcutta
Civil Revisional Jurisdiction
Civil Revision No. .... of 20...

In the matter of:

An Application under Art. 227 of the Constitution of India;

And

In the matter of:
An Order dated .... passed by the State Information Commission, Calcutta dismissing the appeal of the petitioner in violation of the ss. 18 and 19 of the Right to Information Act 2005;

And

In the matter of:

Mr. P. son of Mr. Q, residing at .... Kolkata

..... *Petitioner*

versus

1. State Information Commission, having its office at .... Kolkata.

2. X. Co. Ltd., a Public Authority, having its office and carrying on business at Kolkata

......*Respondents*
Opposite Parties

The humble petition of Mr. P. the petitioner above-named, most respectfully sheweth:

1. That the petitioner is a citizen of India and carries on business as a Contractor and supplier of all kinds of goods and also undertakes to procure orders and collection of all payments for Public Bodies and Authorities from their customers at a Commission and/or on remuneration.

2. At the request of the respondent No. 2, your petitioner sold and delivered diverse goods from time to time pursuant to orders placed by the respondent No. 2. Further at the request of the respondent No. 2, the petitioner also procured orders for supply of goods and produce of the respondent No. 2 to its various customers at a specific rate of commission to be paid to petitioner. The petitioner also realised the bills raised by respondent No. 2 on its customers on which the commission was payable by respondent No. 2 to your petitioner at a specified rate.

3. In respect of the goods sold and delivered by the petitioner to the respondent No. 2 which goods were duly received and appropriated by the respondent No. 2 there became due from and payable by respondent No. 2 to the petitioner a sum of ₹......... as on ....

4. In respect of orders procured by your petitioner from different parties on behalf of the respondent No. 2 and payments collected for the goods supplied by respondent No. 2 to its various customers and the payments duly handed over to the respondent No. 2, there became due from and owing by the respondent No. 2 to the petitioner, a sum of ₹............. in respect of commission as on ....

5. In spite of demands the respondent No. 2 failed to pay the said aggregate sum of ₹............. or any portion thereof and the respondent raised frivolous incorrect and untenable contentions and practically denied that there was any transaction by and between the petitioner and respondent No. 2 and asserted that the respondent No. 2 had no obligation to pay any amount of money to your petitioner.

6. The proceedings taken by your petitioner under the provisions of the Right to Information Act 2005, were unsuccessful. Ultimately your petitioner preferred an appeal before the State Information Commission on ....

7. In the said appeal your petitioner prayed for an order directing the respondent No. 2 to give inspection to your petitioner the books of accounts and other records of the respondent No. 2 for the relevant period in order to ascertain the genuineness of the transactions between your petitioner and respondent No. 2 and the amount of claim payable by respondent No. 2 to your petitioner. Such claim was in accordance with the provisions of the Right to Information Act 2005.

8. At the said hearing before the learned State Information Commission, the respondent No. 2 denied that any transaction took place by and between your petitioner and respondent No. 2 and as such, your petitioner was not entitled to inspect the books of accounts and other records maintained by respondent No. 2.

9. After hearing both the parties, the respondent No. 1 by a cryptic judgment dismissed the appeal filed by your petitioner. A copy of the said judgment order dated .... in annexed hereto marked 'A'.

10. Your petitioner states that the said judgment and order of the respondent No. 1 is contrary to the provisions of law and facts and violative of the fundamental rights of your petitioner as also violative of your petitioner's rights under the Right to Information Act 2005 and the said impugned order be set aside on, *inter alia*, the following:

GROUNDS

I. For that the State Information Commission acted arbitrarily without applying its mind to the facts and circumstances of the case in dismissing the said appeal;

II. For that the learned State Information Commission, respondent No. 1, failed to appreciate and erred in doing so that the respondent No. 2 is a Public Authority and is bound to give the information asked for, and also allow inspection of the relevant documents and records in its possession to your petitioner who is a member of public and a citizen of India.

III. For that the learned State Information Commission erred in not directing the respondent No. 2 to give inspection of relevant documents, Books of Accounts and other records relating to its business transactions for the relevant period on payment of the prescribed fees.

IV. For that the learned State Information Commission should have directed the respondent No. 2 and erred in not doing so to make available all the relevant documents being a Public Authority to your petitioner being a member of the public, a citizen of India and interested in the respondent No. 2 Public Authority and that your petitioner was entitled to inspect the Books of Accounts and records maintained by respondent No. 2 to ascertain the transactions of respondent No. 2 with your petitioner during the relevant period.

V. For that the rejection of the appeal by the learned State Information Commission was contrary to facts and law and without any valid reasons and the same is, therefore, invalid and contrary to law and be quashed and appropriate orders be made in conformity with the provisions of the Right to Information Act 2005.

11. In the facts and circumstances of case, and in view of the provisions of and objects and purposes of the said Right to Information Act 2005, respondent No. 2 being a Public Authority and the petitioner being a citizen of India and a person interested in the functioning of the respondent No. 2 a Public Authority, the respondent No. 1, should have directed the respondent No. 2 to give the information and inspection asked for by the petitioner.

12. Your petitioner states that respondent No. 2 in the proceedings before the Respondent No. 1, failed to controvert the facts and stated in the appeal and consequently the presumption should have been as to the correctness of the statements made by your petitioner.

13. Your petitioner states that the first respondent failed to consider the evidence and records and the presumption arising out of the records and pass the impugned order which your petitioner submits is not in accordance with the facts and documents-on-record and the law and as such, is liable to be quashed.

14. Your petitioner states that respondent No. 2 be directed to give inspection of its records and documents to your petitioner on payment of prescribed fees within a specified period.

15. Your petitioner states that the respondent No. 2 be directed to compensate your petitioner for its wrongful acts by payment of ₹...........

16. The present petition is being made *bona fide* and in the interests of justice and in accordance with the purposes and objects of the Right to Information Act 2005.

Your petitioner, therefore, humbly prays Your Lordships for following orders:

(*a*) Rule *Nisi* be issued on the respondent to show cause as to why the order complained of should not be set aside and the respondent No. 2 be directed to give inspection of its records and documents to your petitioner;

(*b*) A diretion upon the respondent No. 2 to pay ₹ .... as damages to the petitioner;

(*c*) Upon hearing the parties, and perusal of records and the cause shown, if any, the order dated .... passed by State Information Commission be set aside and the rule be made absolute;

(*d*) Such further and other orders be made as this Hon'ble Court may deem fit and proper to afford complete relief to your petitioner.

And your petitioner, as in duty bound, shall ever pray.

Verification

Affidavit

Writ Petition

610. Writ petition under Art. 227 of the Constitution of India

District ....

In the High Court at Calcutta

(Civil Revisional Jurisdiction)

Writ petition No. .... of 20 ....

Appellate Side

Civil Rule No. .... of 20 ....

In the matter of:

An application under Art. 227 of the Constitution of India

And

In the matter of:

An order dated .... passed by ....

restoring land to Bargadar

And

In the matter of:

A.B. .... *Petitioner*

versus

1. C.D.
2. E.F.
3. G.H.

.... *Respondents*

To
The Hon'ble Mr. .... Chief Justice
and His Companion Justices of this Hon'ble Court

The humble petition of the petitioner above-named most respectfully sheweth:

1.
2. State the facts and circumstances leading to the impugned order.
3.
4. That being aggrieved with the aforesaid order dated .... passed by Mr. .... in (State Case/proceedings No.) Your petitioner begs to move Your Lordships on the following, amongst others.

GROUNDS

(*a*) ....
(*b*) ....
(*c*) ....

In the premises aforesaid Your petitioner prays to Your Lordships for an order:

(*a*) to issue a Rule upon the Respondents to show cause why the order dated .... passed by Mr. .... in .... No. .... be not set aside;

(*b*) to make the Rule absolute on perusal of records and of the cause being shown by the Respondents;

(*c*) to grant an *ad interim* stay of all further proceedings (as is required in the circumstances of the case); and

(*d*) to pass such other order or orders as deemed proper.

Verification

Affidavit

NOTES: 1. Order without jurisdiction ought to be set aside despite misrepresentation or concealment of material facts by the petitioner—AIR 1977 NOC 237 (Del).

2. A finding as to whether circumstances justify the exercise of a discretion or not, unless clearly perverse and patently unreasonable is, after all, a finding of fact only, which could not be interfered with either under Art. 226 or under Art. 227 of the Constitution—AIR 1975 SC 1297; AIR 1978 SC 955.

611. Petition under Art. 227 of the Constitution of India

In the High Court at ....

District ....

(Civil Revisional Jurisdiction)

Writ petition No. .... of 20 ....

Appellate Side

Civil Rule No. .... of 20 ....

In the matter of:

An application under Art. 227 of the Constitution of India;

And

In the matter of:

Order No. .... dated .... passed by Mr. .... Judge .... Court in Case No. ....

And

In the matter of:

A.B. (Name, description and address)

.... *Petitioner*

versus

1. C.D. (Name, description and address)

2. E.F. (State of West Bengal)

.... *Respondents*

Application valued at ₹ ....

(Being money value of the Suit)

To
The Hon'ble Mr. ....
Chief Justice and his companion justices
this Hon'ble Court

The humble petition of the petitioner above-named most respectfully sheweth:

1. :
2. (State the facts leading to the passing of impugned order dated ....)
3. :
4. :
5. That being aggrieved by the said order dated .... passed by the Respondent No. .... Your petitioner begs to move this petition before Your Lordships on the following, amongst other.

GROUNDS

(i) For that

(ii) (Set out the grounds)

(iii) (Set out the grounds)

(iv) (Set out the grounds)

6. This application is made *bona fide* and for the ends of justice.

Your petitioner, therefore, humbly prays that Your Lordships would be graciously pleased to:

(a) Call for the records of the case and issue a rule upon the Respondents to show cause why the impugned order dated .... passed by ...... in Case No. .... of 20 .... should not be set aside;

(b) In case the Respondents fail to show cause or sufficient cause, to make the rule absolute on perusal of the records and of the cause being shown by the Respondents;

(c) Grant an interim stay of all further proceedings of the Case No. ..... of .... 20... in the court below till disposal of Rule;

(d) Pass such order or orders or directions as Your Lordships may deem fit and proper.

And for this act of kindness, your petitioner, as in duty bound, shall ever pray.

NOTE: No question of limitation for a petition under Art. 227 of the Constitution of India.

612. Writ-petition under Art. 226 of the Constitution of India

District ....

In the High Court at Calcutta

(Constitutional Writ Jurisdiction)

Appellate side

Writ Petition No. .... of 20 ....

In the matter of:

An application under Art. 226 of the Constitution of India

And

In the matter of:

A writ of and/or in the nature of Mandamus

And

In the matter of:

A writ of and/or in the nature of Certiorari and/or Prohibition and/or any other writ

And

In the matter of:

Judgment and/or Order dated............ passed by Sri............, District Judge in Estates Acquisition Appeal No. .... of 20 .... under s. 44(3) of the West Bengal Estates Acquisition Act 1953 reversing thereby the judgment and order dated .... of Sri .... A.S.O. & R. O. of .... in case No. .... of 20 .... under s. 44(*2a*) of the said Act.

And

In the matter of:

State of West Bengal through the Collector, ...

.... *Petitioner*

versus

1. A.B.
2. C.D.

.... *Respondents*

To
The Hon'ble Mr. ....,
Chief Justice and His Companion
Justices of the Hon'ble Court

The humble petition of the petitioner named above most respectfully sheweth:

1. That .... (State the facts) ....

2. That .... and the learned District Judge allowed the appeal being aggrieved whereby your petitioner begs to move Your Lordships under Art. 226 of the Constitution of India on the following, amongst other.

GROUNDS

I. For that ....

II. For that ....

III. For that the judgment is otherwise bad in law and is fit to be set aside.

3. That the petitioner has no other alternative remedy and the remedy sought for would give the petitioner complete relief.

4. That the records of the case are lying in the office of the A.S.O./R.O., ... District .... within the appellate jurisdiction of this Hon'ble Court.

5. (Add, where necessary) that your petitioner states that although there is no time-limit to move an application under Art. 226 of the Constitution of India yet by way of caution it is stated that the delay, if any, in moving this petition is due to (State the reason).

6. That this application is made *bona fide* and for the ends of justice.

In the circumstances stated above Your petitioner prays that Your Lordships may be pleased to issue:

(*a*) A writ in the nature of Mandamus directing the Respondents to show cause why the impugned order dated............ passed by the District Judge of .... in Estates Acquisition Appeal No. .... of, being Annexure 'A' should not be set aside;

(*b*) A writ in the nature of Mandamus restraining the Respondents from giving effect to the impugned order dated .... passed in the said Estates Acquisition Appeal being Annexure 'A' to the petition.

(*c*) A writ in the nature Mandamus commanding the Respondents including the District Judge (Tribunal) to cancel or rescind the impugned order;

(*d*) A writ in the nature of Certiorari directing the Respondents including the Tribunal to transmit the entire records relating to said Estates Acquisition Appeal No. .... of .... so that the same may be quashed and conscionable justice be done;

(*e*) A writ in the nature of Prohibition prohibiting the Respondents and each one of them to enter into the property till the hearing of the Rule;

(*f*) Interim order of injunction in terms of prayer (*e*); and

(*g*) Costs incidental to this application;

(*h*) Any other direction or writs as Your Lordships deem fit and proper.

And Your petitioner, as in duty bound, shall ever pray.

Verification

Affidavit

NOTES: 1. Issue of Rule Nisi—Court must be satisfied that arguable issues are raised—AIR 1980 Cal 95.

2. Writ petitions are decided on pleadings. Petitioner not to resort to *suppressio veri* or *suggestion falsi*. Courts to discourage attitude of taking interim orders on suppressed facts—AIR 1980 HP 5. But concealment or facts having no bearing on the main point in the petition—Petition cannot be dismissed on the ground that the petitioner tried to mislead or that he did not come with clean hands—AIR 1979 Raj 58.

3. (See in connexion with pleadings in para 5 of the application)—No satisfactory explanation for delay. High Court, held was justified in dismissing petition summarily—AIR 1977 SC 1979.

4. Writ sought without annexing copy of impugned order. *Held*, on facts that writ could not be issued in anticipation only—AIR 1978 Cal 405.

613. Writ petition under Art. 226 of the Constitution of India (writ in the nature of mandamus and certiorari)

In the High Court of Judicature at Allahabad
Constitutional Writ Jurisdiction
Writ petition No. .... of 20 ....

Sri A.B. son of .... resident of .... District ....
.... *Petitioner*

versus

1. The Assessing Authority under the U.P. Large Land Holding Tax Act in the District of ....
2. The Collector of the District of ......
.... *Opposite-Party*

To
The Hon'ble the Chief Justice and his companion Judges of the aforesaid Court

The humble petition of the petitioner above-named most respectfully sheweth:

1.
2. State facts
3.

4. That the petitioner has no equally efficacious alternative remedy except by way of a writ under Art. 226 of the Constitution.

5. That the impugned assessment order and the demand for and recovery of the amount are *ultra vires* and liable to be quashed on the following, among other:

GROUNDS

I. Because the ....
II. Because the ....
III. Because the ....

It is, therefore, respectfully prayed that this Hon'ble Court may be pleased

(*i*) To issue a writ in the nature of certiorari and quash the impugned assessment order annexed with the affidavit as Annexure 'A';

(*ii*) To issue a writ in the nature of mandamus commanding the Respondent/O.P. not to recover from the petitioner the amount of ₹ .... or any part thereof by way of tax under the impugned assessment order;

(*iii*) To issue an *ad interim* order staying recovery of any amount of tax under the impugned assessment order from the petitioner during pendency of this petition;

(*iv*) To issue such other writ, direction or order as this Hon'ble Court may deem proper in the circumstances of the case; and

(*v*) To award to the petitioner the costs of this petition.

Dated ....

....

Counsel for the petitioner

NOTE: Other remedy open. Not absolute bar. High Court may interfere in exceptional cases—AIR 1979 Raj 5. But see AIR 1979 NOC 78 (Raj). Other remedy open. High Court should be satisfied that the normal statutory remedy is likely to be too dilatory or different to give reasonable quick relief—AIR 1979 SC 1889. Alternative remedy—AIR 1977 SC 1132.

614. Writ in the nature of mandamus, certiorari and prohibition

In the High Court at Calcutta

Constitutional Writ Jurisdiction

Appellate Side

Writ Petition No. .... (W) of 20...

In the matter of:

An application under Art. 226 of the Constitution of India for issue of Writ or Writs in the nature of mandamus, certiorari and prohibition

And

In the matter of:

Memorandum of Agreement/National Coal Wage Agreement/Joint Bipartite Committee for Coal Industry

And

In the matter of:

Premature unnatural death of petitioner's father and refusal of respondents to give appointment on compassionate ground

And

Mr. P, son of late Q, residing at ...., Alipore Road, Kolkata

...... *Petitioner*

versus

1. Eastern Coalfields Ltd. having office at ...., Alipore Road, Kolkata
2. The Chairman-cum-Managing Director of Eastern Coalfields Ltd., 24-Parganas, Kolkata

.... *Respondents*

To
The Hon'ble Mr. .... Chief Justice and
His Companion Justices of this Hon'ble Court

The humble petition of Mr. P, the petitioner above-named, most respectfully sheweth:

1. Your petitioner is a citizen of India, aged about 25 years, keeping sound health and at present unemployed.

2. Your petitioner's father, Mr. Q, during his life-time was an employee in the colliery of the respondents in the district of Burdwan.

3. Your petitioner's father died on 5th January 20... while he was on duty leaving his wife, W, daughter V and his son, your petitioner. A copy of the Death Certificate is annexed hereto marked "A".

4. Your petitioner applied for appointment under the respondents on compassionate ground under the provisions of the said Memorandum of Agreement, National Coal Wage Agreement and Joint Bipartite Committee for the Coal Industry as your petitioner's father died in harness.

5. Your petitioner states that your petitioner is entitled to get service under the respondent on the compassionate ground and also the death benefits, such as, Gratuity, Provident Fund and Family Pension arising on of the death of the petitioner's father.

6. Your petitioner states that in spite of requests and application made the respondents have not given appointment to your petitioner. Your petitioner and the dependent members of the deceased's family have been facing financial hardship and it has become impossible for them to meet the day-to-day expenses, specially, in view of the facts that they have not received any monetary benefits consequent upon the death of your petitioner's father.

7. In spite of best efforts your petitioner did not get any reply from the respondents to the several letters and representations made by your petitioner. Copies of the letters are annexed hereto collectively marked "B".

8. Being aggrieved by and dissatisfied with the arbitrary, unjust, wrongful and unfair, motivated conduct of the respondents by not giving employment to your petitioner on compassionate ground, your petitioner begs to move this petition under Art. 226 of the Constitution of India on the following among other:

GROUNDS

I. For that the petitioner has the requisite qualification to get employment under the respondents on compassionate ground.

II. For that the respondent wrongfully and in breach of the agreement and understanding failed to consider the petitioner's application for giving appointment by the respondents on the compassionate ground.

III. For that the respondents failed to consider the financial hardship of the family members of the said deceased and are wrongfully withholding payment for maintenance of the dependent members of the deceased employee.

IV. For that the respondents have failed to act in accordance with the provisions of the agreement and law and to observe the principle of natural justice and further violated the fundamental rights of your petitioner guaranteed under Arts. 14, 16, 19(1)(*g*) of the Constitution of India.

9. Your petitioner has demanded justice but no reply has been received and further demand of justice will be idle formalities.

10. In the premises your petitioner prays for an order directing the respondents to give appointment to your petitioner on compassionate ground in place of his deceased father and to make payment of death benefits.

11. There is no alternative adequate efficacious remedy available to the petitioner. The orders prayed for herein, if granted, will afford complete relief to your petitioner.

Your petitioner, therefore, humbly prays Your Lordships for the following orders:

(*a*) A Writ of or in the nature of Mandamus be issued directing the respondents to honour their commitment to give appointment to the petitioner on compassionate ground in place of his deceased father;

(*b*) A Writ in the nature of Certiorari be issued directing the respondents to transmit their entire records in relation to the petitioner's case to enable this Hon'ble Court to do conscionable justice;

(*c*) Rule *Nisi* in terms of prayers above;

(*d*) Interim orders be made for payment of the death benefits arising on the death of his father to the petitioner and the family members.

(*e*) Direction to the respondents to give particulars of the death benefits payable to the members of the family of the deceased employee;

(*f*) Costs;

(*g*) Further and other orders be made and directions be given as this Hon'ble Court may deem fit and proper.

And your petitioner as in duty bound shall ever pray.

ANNEXURE A

ANNEXURE B

Verification

Affidavit

NOTE: List of Annexures
List of Dates
List of law points involved should prefix the petition

615. Writ petition to enforce equitable distribution of advertisement in newspapers

In the High Court at ....

Constitutional Writ Jurisdiction Original Side

Writ petition No. .... of 20.............

In the matter of:

An application made under Art. 226 of the Constitution of India;

And

In the matter of:

Violation of freedom of speech as guaranteed under Art. 19(1)(*a*) of the Constitution of India;

And

In the matter of:

A Writ of and/or in the Nature of Mandamus and/or Certiorari and/or Prohibition and/or Writ or Writs and/ or Order or Orders and Directions thereunder;

And

In the matter of:

Mr. P. residing in the State of 'X';

..... *Petitioner*

versus

State of X .... *Respondent*

Complaint against undue discrimination.

To
The Hon'ble Mr. .... Chief Justice
and His Companion Justices of this
Hon'ble Court

The humble petition of Mr. P., the petitioner above-named, most respectfully sheweth:

1. The petitioner is the Editor and also the Proprietor of a newspaper 'N' being a Bengali Daily newspaper published from Agartala in the State of Tripura. The petitioner has invested large sums of money in modernising the press for publication and printing of the said newspaper.

2. By a Notification dated 16th August 20..., the State Government through its Department of Information, Cultural Affairs and Tourism notified its current advertisement policy which states that the Director of Information, Cultural Affairs and Tourism would issue its advertisements to the approved newspapers or magazines. The newspapers are divided into three separate categories, (*i*) 'A', (*ii*) 'B' and (*iii*) 'C'.

3. A daily newspaper having minimum of 4 pages daily and having a minimum size of not less than 45 x 7 cms. standard column width or equivalent printing space and having a paid circulation of more than .... copies was categorised as 'A', category newspaper.

4. Your petitioner states that it was further declared in the Advertisement Policy that for equity of an Advertisement in a newspaper a proper rotation would be maintained to ensure that the newspaper belonging to category 'A' would get 40% of total quantum of advertisement, newspaper in 'B' category would get 32% of the total advertisement and the newspaper in category 'C' would get 28% of the total advertisement to be published. Subsequently, on account of increase in the number of newspaper of 'A' category and decrease in the number of newspapers in the categories of 'B' and 'C' 100 point Roster. was modified by the State Government and as per the modified 100 point Roster, 60% of the total quantum of advertisement were to be allotted to category 'A' newspapers, 22% to 'B' category newspapers and 18% to 'C' category newspapers.

5. The petitioner states that the newspapers belonging to the petitioner, namely, 'N' and 'CD' have been categorised as 'A' category. The said 'N' and 'CD' category newspapers were therefore entitled to their due share out of 60% of the total quantum of advertisement issued by the said Department. The petitioner, however, has not been given to the extent of his share of total advertisement for the last 11 months prior to filing of the present writ petition.

6. Your petitioner gives in a chart details of the State Government's advertisements issued to various newspapers in the State and from this chart it will be apparent that during the last 11 months, newspaper 'S' gets advertisement to the extent of 500 cms. and 'T' newspaper gets advertisement to the extent of 700 cms. while a daily 'EF' gets advertisement to the extent of 700 cms.

7. Your petitioner states that the State Government is showing undue favour to the newspaper 'EF' as it was the chief media organ of the ruling party which is in power in the State.

8. Your petitioner further states that your petitioner's newspaper has been criticising the policies and action of the State Government run by the party in power, openly expressing its weakness of the administration in interests of the general public and to get rid of the said severe and fair criticism made by the petitioner, the respondents are trying to restrict the publication and circulation of petitioner's newspapers by encouraging the advertisement and wide circulation of its newspaper 'EF' in the State.

9. In the premises it should be noted here that by wrongful act and conduct of the State Government, as aforesaid, your petitioner's fundamental right as guaranteed under the relevant provisions of the Constitution of India has been infringed.

10. Your petitioner states that if the respondent is allowed to continue with the allotment of 24% of the total quantum of advertisements to the daily newspapers 'C', Om and "Poli" as compared to only 6% of the total quantum of advertisements given to 'A' category newspapers the views expressed in those dailies 'C' and Poli will have a total sway in the minds of more and more public and general community and will affect the functioning of a healthy public opinion necessary for a good and fair democracy.

11. Your petitioner states that the said impugned memorandum dated .... issued by the State Government is violative of freedom of speech and expression as guaranteed under the Art. 19(1)(*a*) of the Constitution of India, as well as Art. 14 of the Constitution.

12. In the premises, your petitioner states that the said impugned order be set aside and quashed and respondent be directed not to discriminate in issuing advertisement in their newspapers in the State.

13. Your petitioner states that the respondent is acting arbitrarily, and wrongfully and contrary to the provisions of the Constitution of India. Further such discriminatory act of the respondent is arbitrary, *mala fide* and against the interests of the general public as also the newspapers in State.

14. Your petitioner states that being aggrieved by the wrongful and discriminatory acts of the respondent in not treating all the newspapers in the State on equal footing, this application under Art. 226 of the Constitution of India has been made, on *inter alia*, the following:

GROUNDS

I. For that the respondent has been wrongfully, illegally and arbitrarily not allotting fair quota of advertisements in the newspapers of the petitioner.

II. For that the respondent has discriminated against petitioner's newspapers in allocation of advertisements to the prejudice of your petitioner's newspapers.

III. For that the respondent has wrongfully, arbitrarily, *mala fide* and illegally shown undue favour to the newspaper published by the ruling party members in the State.

IV. For that the respondent in issuing advertisements to different newspapers in the State has acted wrongfully, arbitrarily, *mala fide* and in a discriminatory manner to favour unduly a newspaper dealing with the policies of the party in power with a view to misleading the general political opinion in the State.

15. For such wrongful act on the part of respondent in not giving advertisements on equality basis, and acting wrongfully, *mala fide*, illegally and discriminatory manner and thereby violating the fundamental rights of the petitioner enshrined in Arts. 14 and 19(1)(*a*) as well as Art. 226 of the Constitution of India along with its statutory rights therein.

16. Your petitioner states and submits that in the circumstances aforesaid an interim order of injunction is necessary in directing the respondent not to continue to discriminate in giving advertisements to the different newspapers in the State under each separate categories as aforesaid.

17. There is no other alternative or equally efficacious remedy readily available to your petitioner and the reliefs, if granted, as prayed for will provide adequate remedy to your petitioner.

18. By a letter dated .... Your petitioner's Advocate-on-record demanded Justice from the respondent but in vain. A copy of the said demand letter is annexed hereto and marked 'A'.

19. Unless orders are made as prayed for herein your petitioner will suffer irreparable loss, prejudice and injury.

20. This application is made *bona fide* and in the interest of justice and equity and in the interests of large number of people and the public in general.

In the premises, your petitioners most humbly prays Your Lordships for the following orders:

(*a*) A Writ and/or in the nature of a Mandamus do issue commanding the respondent to give advertisements in equal proportion to the newspaper as given to the category mentioned therein.

(*b*) The respondent be directed to release advertisement to your petitioner in the same proportion as it has been issuing to other category "..........." of Newspaper belonging to the ruling party in the State.

(*c*) A Writ of and in the nature of Certiorari do issue directing respondent to produce all previous records pertaining to the present case of your petitioner for due consideration by this Hon'ble Court so that conscionable justice can be done.

(*d*) Rule *Nisi* in terms of prayers (*a*) and (*c*) above.

(*e*) An order of mandatory injunction do issue commanding the respondent to release advertisement to the petitioner's newspapers at par with the newspapers in 'EF' category belonging to the party in power in State.

(*f*) *Ad-interim* orders in terms of prayer (*e*) above.

(*g*) Such further and other orders and/or directions be issued as this Hon'ble Court may deem fit and proper to afford complete justice to your petitioner.

And your petitioner as in duty bound shall ever pray.

ANNEXURE 'A'

Verification

Affidavit

616. Writ petition challenging order of disciplinary authority

In the High Court at Calcutta

Constitutional Writ Jurisdiction Original Side

Writ Application No. .... of 20...

In the matter of:

An application under Art. 226 of the Constitution of India;

And

In the matter of:

A Writ in the Nature of Mandamus, Prohibition and Certiorari; and Orders and Directions in relation thereto;

And

In the matter of:

A charge-sheet issued under Memo No. 5 dated 30th December 20... by the Disciplinary Authority;

And

In the matter of:

A Report of the Enquiry Officer dated 5th November 20...;

And

In the matter of:

An order dated 15th January 20... passed by Disciplinary Authority dismissing the petitioner from service;

And

In the matter of:

Appellate Order dated 16th March 20.......... rejecting the petitioner's appeal against his dismissal;

And

In the matter of:

Mr. P., son of Mr. X residing at .... Alipore Road, Kolkata

........*Petitioner*

versus

1. M/s G. Co. Ltd., a Government of India Undertaking having its Registered Office at 6 Lyons Range, Kolkata within the jurisdiction of this Hon'ble Court.
2. Mr. H, being a Director of the respondent No. 1 company having office at Alipore Road, Kolkata.
3. Mr. M. the Manager of the respondent No. 1 having his office at .... Alipore Road, Kolkata.
4. The Union of India, represented by Secretary Home Department, Government of India, having his office at .... Alipore Road, Kolkata.

...... *Respondent*

To
The Hon'ble Mr. ...., Chief Justice and His Companion Justices of the said Hon'ble Court

The humble petition of the petitioner abovenamed most respectfully sheweth:

1. Your petitioner is a Domiciled Citizen of India.

2. Your petitioner was appointed on 10th January 20..... by respondent No. 1 as an Accountant in the Accounts Department but was on probation for a period of one year.

3. Your petitioner's services were found to be satisfactory during the probation period. He was allowed to continue upto the year 20....

4. Your petitioner's service was found satisfactory. Your petitioner was confirmed in his services for the post of an Accounts Officer with effect from 15th January 20 ......

5. Your petitioner's superior officer being the Accountant took leave for 2 months from January 20... and your petitioner was allowed by respondent No. 2 to officiate in his place for the post of Accountant.

6. Your petitioner while going through the books of accounts of the department found that certain discrepancies have been committed in the ledger entries of books of accounts and brought such discrepancies to the notice of respondent No. 2.

7. Respondent No. 2 ordered the petitioner to pass the said discrepancies as correct to which petitioner did not agree.

8. In view of the petitioner's refusal a charge-sheet dated 10th January 20... was issued to petitioner by respondent No. 3 on the ground of gross dereliction of duties on the part of the petitioner and your petitioner was suspended from service. A copy of the charge-sheet issued against the petitioner is annexed hereto marked 'A'.

9. As directed in the said charge-sheet your petitioner submitted his written representation on 20th January 20... denying categorically the alleged charges levelled against him a copy whereof is annexed hereto marked 'C'.

10. In the enquiry proceedings held by respondent 3, some prosecution witnesses were examined behind the back of the petitioner and the petitioner was not given any opportunity to cross-examine those witnesses.

11. Your petitioner was examined by the enquiry officer but his statements were not allowed to be signed by him.

12. The enquiry officer submitted his report and finding that the petitioner is guilty of charges levelled against him. A copy of the Enquiry Report is annexed hereto marked 'D'.

13. Pursuant to the above finding by Enquiry Officer the respondent No. 2 by memo No. 5 dismissed the petitioner from his services. A copy of the said memo is annexed hereto marked 'E'.

14. Against the said order of dismissal your petitioner preferred an appeal before the respondent No. 1 which was summarily rejected without giving any specific reason and without the opportunity of being heard by the petitioner by Order dated 8th June 20....... copies of the appeal and the said Order of rejection of the said order are annexed hereto marked 'F' and 'G' respectively.

15. Being aggrieved by and dissatisfied with the Order of Rejection of the said appeal by the Disciplinary Authority your petitioner moves your Lordships on the following amongst other.

GROUNDS

I. For that no reasonable opportunity for being heard was given to the petitioner.

II. For that the respondents violated principles of natural justice in not allowing the cross-examination of the prosecution witnesses who were allowed to have deposed against him.

16. Further the wrongful acts of the respondents show the apparent high-handedness shown by them.

17. Further, the petitioner's right to hold his office as guaranteed by relevant Article of the Constitution of India has been violated and infringed upon.

18. Your petitioner demanded justice by his letter dated .... which has been denied to him without assigning any reason whatsoever. A copy of the said letter of the petitioner is annexed hereto and marked 'H'.

19. Your petitioner states that it is incumbent upon the respondents to act judicially and not violative of the principles of natural justice.

20. Your petitioner states that his dismissal from his services has been arbitrary, whimsical, capricious and *mala fide* in the facts and circumstances of the case.

21. Your petitioner states that unless the respondents are restrained from giving effect to the impugned order of dismissal your petitioner will suffer irreparable loss, prejudice and injury.

22. Your petitioner has not moved before any other Court for the self-same cause of action.

23. The cause of action for this petition arose within jurisdiction of this Hon'ble Court at Calcutta as stated hereinabove and records of this case are also lying within the jurisdiction of this Hon'ble Court.

24. The present application has been made *bona fide* and for the ends of justice.

Your petitioner, therefore, in the facts of the case, most humbly prays that Your Lordship will be graciously pleased to issue the following orders:

(*a*) A Writ in the nature of a Mandamus commanding the respondents to act judicially in the proceedings in accordance with provisions of law;

(*b*) A Writ in the nature of Prohibition be issued restraining the respondents from taking any steps or further steps with regard to the order of petitioner's dismissal;

(*c*) A Writ in nature of Certiorari be issued calling upon respondents to produce in court all records of the case so that impugned order may be quashed and justice be done to your petitioner;

(*d*) *Ad interim* order as per prayer (*b*) above;

(*e*) Further and other order be issued and directions be given as this Hon'ble Court may deem fit and proper so as to afford complete relief to your petitioner.

And your petitioner as in duty bound shall ever pray.

Verification

Affidavit

CONTEMPT OF COURT

617. Petition to punish for contempt of court

In the High Court at Calcutta
Special Civil Jurisdiction

Matter No. .... of 20...

In the matter of:

Contempt of Court Act 1971, and Art. 215 of the Constitution of India and a Writ Petition No. .... of 20....... (*P.S. Ltd.* v *State of West Bengal*).

And

In the matter of:

Contempt of Court committed by the respondents Nos. 4 to 8 by wilfully, or knowingly, deliberately and contumaciously interfering with the due administration of Justice by forcefully breaking open the locks and forcefully taking up possession of the room in the office premises at No. 3, Alipore Road, Kolkata in spite of direction to take recourse to law for obtaining possession of the Employees Union Office room by the Order passed on 16th January 20… passed by the Hon'ble Mr. Justice ....

And

In the matter of:

1. P.S. Ltd., carrying on business at ...., Alipore Road, Kolkata
2. Mr. P. working for gain at ...., Alipore Road, Kolkata

.... *Petitioners*

versus

1. The State of West Bengal, through the Secretary, Home (Police) Department, Government of West Bengal, Writers' Buildings, Kolkata 700 001
2. The Commissioner of Police, Kolkata having his office at Lal Bazar, Kolkata 700 001
3. The Officer-in-Charge, Park Street Police Station, Park Street, Kolkata 700 016
4. RCS
5. PLK
6. KS
7. HM
8. SP

All are employees of P.S. Ltd. of ...., Alipore Road, P.S. Alipore, Kolkata

.... *Respondents*

To
The Hon'ble Mr. ...., Chief Justice and His Companion Justices of this Hon'ble Court.

The humble petition of the petitioners above-named most respectfully sheweth:

The petitioners state as follows:

1. That your petitioner No. 1 carries on business as a manufacturer of and dealer in diverse goods and articles having its office in Bihar and a factory at ...., Alipore Road, Kolkata.

2. That the second petitioner is a citizen of India and is a shareholder of the first petitioner.

3. That owing to bad market conditions, the first petitioner suffered losses in its business and the Kolkata Office of the first petitioner had to be closed and all business operation and its factory were shifted to Bihar, and requisite notices were issued to the employees including the respondents Nos. 4 to 8, by offering them alternative employment opportunities in Bihar.

4. That respondents Nos. 4 to 8 thereafter had resorted to illegal, violent activities and threatened physical violence to the management, and serious apprehensions of breach of public peace and disturbance of public tranquility which might lead to an affray or even riots.

5. That in spite of asking for police help the situation did not improve and your petitioners made an application under Art. 226 of the Constitution of India in the Hon'ble High Court at Calcutta for an order of injunction and posting of police force and other reliefs.

6. That on the said application this Hon'ble High Court was pleased to pass on order directing the police authorities to arrange for police picket at the cost of the petitioners and to give liberty to respondents Nos. 4 to 8 to raise their alleged disputes before an appropriate forum.

7. That the petitioners also filed another suit in the Hon'ble City Civil Court at Kolkata on 4th January 20... and on such application being moved the respondents were directed to maintain the *status quo* in relation to the business activities of the petitioners at ...., Alipore Road, Kolkata.

8. That thereafter respondents Nos. 4 to 8 contested the said writ petition.

9. That some of employees gave up their possession of the Union office room to your petitioners and since that time, your petitioners are in lawful possession of the said Union room.

10. That on the respondents Nos. 4 to 8 through their authorised advocate requesting the police authorities that the interim order for police picket was vacated during the order remaining in force immediately thereafter respondents Nos. 4 to 8 went to the office premises of your petitioners, assaulted the security guards posted at the said office and beaten up them with iron rods, broke open the padlock and unlawfully occupied the said premises and stated that the Hon'ble High Court had authorised them to take possession of the Union office room in the premises. Such acts of the respondents Nos. 4 to 8 amounted to total contempt of the Hon'ble High Court by way of obstructing the normal course of justice affecting the public confidence in the functioning of Judiciary to uphold its dignity and honour and ability to prevent the wrongful and illegal acts of respondents Nos. 4 to 8 by wrongfully entering the premises and taking possession of the same.

11. That in the premises, the said respondents Nos. 4 to 8 and each one of them committed a gross contempt of this Hon'ble High Court and also the Judiciary in general and by wrongfully declaring that the said order dated 16th January 20... authorised them to forcefully enter the said premises with unlicensed firearms. In the process, respondents Nos. 4 to 8 assaulted the security guards and caused malicious damages to the assets and properties of your petitioners.

12. That your petitioners now state that the respondents Nos. 4 to 8 be called upon to show cause why they should not be sent to prison and fined for gross contempt of this Hon'ble High Court in particular and Judiciary in general or otherwise suitably dealt with for having illegally, knowingly, wilfully, deliberately, and contumaciously declaring that the order dated 16th January 20... authorised them to enter into the premises with unlicensed fire arms after breaking open the padlocks of the said premises and thereafter holding out threats and maliciously damaging the furniture, telephone and other assets of your petitioners.

13. That the said respondents Nos. 4 to 8 by their conduct committed wilful contempt of this Hon'ble Court and also of the Judiciary in general by wrongfully using force to interfere and to give respondents Nos. 4 to 8 unlawful possession of the said room in the premises by letter dated 7th January 20... during subsistence of the said order dated 3rd January 20... passed by this Hon'ble High Court in the petitioners said writ petition and by their wrongful acts the respondents Nos. 4 to 8 disregarded the said order of this Hon'ble High Court, with a view to obstruct the normal course of justice which wrongful acts tended to affect the public confidence in the Judiciary to enforce its order to maintain its dignity and majesty and to prevent usurpation of the jurisdiction and power by using physical force and holding out threats with dire consequences.

14. That in the premises, the orders prayed for be issued to uphold the dignity and majesty of this Hon'ble High Court and to maintain the public confidence and the confidence of the litigants in the functioning of Judiciary.

15. That this application is made *bona fide* and in the interest of justice and equity.

Your petitioners, therefore, most humbly pray Your Lordships for the following orders:

(*a*) Rule *Nisi* be issued calling on the respondents Nos. 4 to 8 to show cause why they should not be committed to Prison or suitably dealt with for having wilfully, or knowingly, deliberately and contumaciously interfering with the due administration of justice by shouting and declaring that the said order dated 16th January 20... authorised them to take possession of the premises in question in spite of the fact that the said respondents Nos. 4 to 8 were given liberty to approach the appropriate forum for recovery of possession of the said office premises and/or make any application in pending the Title Suit of the petitioners;

(*b*) Rule *Nisi* be issued calling upon the respondents Nos. 4 to 8 to show cause as to why they should not be committed to prison or otherwise be suitably dealt with for having committed contempt of this Hon'ble High Court by wilfully, knowingly, deliberately and contumaciously breaking open the padlocks of the petitioner's premises at .... Alipore Road, Kolkata along with their associates and brandishing unlicensed fire arms and shouting and declaring to have been acting under order of the Hon'ble High Court at Kolkata dated 16th January 20... and beating up security guards and causing intentional and malicious damages to assets and properties of the petitioners and wrongfully continuing to remain in the Company's premises with ulterior motive, in interfering with the course of justice and otherwise to make it impossible for the police authorities to render assistance to the victims of rowdyism and further to frustrate a fair and just adjudication of the disputes raised by the respondents.

(c) *Ad interim* orders be issued directing the respondents Nos. 4 to 8 to show cause as to why a Special Officer should not be appointed with direction to oust the said respondents Nos. 4 to 8 with police help and to restore the *status quo* as existing prior to 16th January 20....

(d) If respondents Nos. 4 to 8 do not show cause or show insufficient cause, the said Rule be made absolute and respondents Nos. 4 to 8 be committed to prison or be fined and/or be suitably dealt with and also a Special Officer be appointed to oust the respondents Nos. 4 to 8 and their associates from the said premises Nos. Alipore Road, Kolkata with the help of police authorities.

(e) A Special Officer be appointed to oust the said respondents and intruders with police help from the petitioners premises No. ...., Alipore Road, Kolkata.

(f) *Ad interim* orders in terms of prayers above.

(g) Costs.

(h) Further orders be made and directions be given as to this Hon'ble Court may deem fit and proper to meet the ends of justice and to uphold the dignity and majesty of Judiciary.

And for this act of kindness, the petitioners as in duty bound shall ever pray.

Verification

Affidavit

MISCELLANEOUS

618. Application for stay of execution proceedings

In the High Court at Calcutta

(Civil Appellate Jurisdiction)

Petition No. .... of 20 ....

In the matter of:

An application for stay of all further proceedings in Title Execution Case No. .... of 20 ....

And

In the matter of:

Second Appeal No. .... of 20 .....

And

In the matter of:

A.B.

.... *Defendant-Petitioner*

Appellant

versus

C.D.

..... *Plaintiff-Opposite Party*

Respondent

Application valued at ₹ ....

To
The Hon'ble Mr. .... Chief Justice and
His companion Justices of this Hon'ble Court

The humble petition of the above-named petitioner most respectfully sheweth:

1. ....

2. The learned lower Appellate Court was pleased to allow the appeal and ordered that the plaintiff do recover sum of ₹............ as compensation from the defendant petitioner together with costs of suit and of appeal.

3. That the plaintiff has filed the decree for execution on or about.................... 20 ...... and has claimed the decretal dues together with interest. The said execution proceedings is numbered T. Ex. No. .... of the year 20 .... and is pending in the Court of Civil Judge (Junior Division) at ....

4. That against the judgment and decree passed by the learned District Judge an appeal has been filed in this Hon'ble Court and the same was admitted for hearing on .... before the Hon'ble Mr. Justice .... and the Hon'ble Mr. Justice .... the said appeal has been numbered S.A. .... of 20..............

The appeal is pending decision/hearing/adjudication.

5. That the appellant-petitioner has been advised that there are fair chances of success in the Second Appeal.

6. That unless an order for stay of all further proceedings in the said Title Execution Case No. .... of 20 .... be granted, the petitioner shall be unable to recover the money and shall suffer irreparable loss and injury if the decree be satisfied pending the hearing of the appeal.

In the circumstances aforesaid the petitioner humbly prays that Your Lordships may be graciously pleased to issue a Rule upon the opposite party to show cause why all further proceedings in Title Execution Case No. .... of 20 .... pending in the Court of Munsif at .... shall not be stayed till the disposal of the Second Appeal No. .... of 20 .... pending in this Hon'ble Court.

And, pending the hearing to the rule the petitioner further prays that Your Lordships may be graciously pleased to grant interim stay of all further proceedings in Title Execution Case No...................... of 20 .... until hearing of the Rule.

Verification

Affidavit

NOTE: See provisions in Or. 21, r. 26(1) of the CPC for stay of Execution proceedings.

619. Application under s. 5 of the Limitation Act for condonation of delay in preferring an appeal

In the High Court at Calcutta

(Civil Appellate Jurisdiction)

In the matter of No. .... of 20 ....

Application No. .... of 20 ....

A.B. versus C.D.

And

In the matter of:

An application under s. 5 of the Limitation Act for condoning delay in filing the appeal

And

In the matter of

A.B. .... *Appellant-Petitioner*

versus

C.D.

E.F. .... *Opposite-Respondents*

Valued at ₹.................

To
The Hon'ble Mr. ....
Chief Justice and His companion Justices of this Hon'ble Court

The humble petition of the petitioner above-named most respectfully sheweth:

1. ....
2. ....

(State the facts of the case and subject-matter leading upto filing of the appeal on .....).

3. The appeal is out of time by .... days. Your petitioner has filed a petition under Or. 43, r. 3A(1), CPC along with memo of appeal.

4. That your petitioner could not prefer the appeal because of .... Your petitioner submits that there was sufficient cause namely .... for which the appeal could not be preferred in time.

In the premises aforesaid it is humbly prayed that Your Lordships would be pleased to issue a Rule on the Respondent to show cause why the delay in filing the appeal should not be condoned.

And, on hearing the cause shown, if any, to make the Rule absolute.

Verification

Affidavit

NOTE: After insertion of the provision in Or. 43, r. 3A(1) compliance with said rule s. 5 of the Limitation Act redundant.

620. Petition for grant of probate

In the High Court at Calcutta

Testamentary and Intestate Jurisdiction

Matter No. .... of 20...........

In the Goods of Mr. PQ (deceased) last residing at .... Ezra Street, Kolkata.

And

Mr. XY residing at .... Ezra Street, Kolkata

...... *Petitioner*

To
The Hon'ble Mr. ...., Chief Justice and His Companion Justices of this Hon'ble Court

The humble petition of XY residing at .... Ezra Street, Kolkata, appointed as Sole Executor of the Will of the said deceased PQ, most respectfully sheweth:

1. Your petitioner states that the said PQ is the father of petitioner and was residing at .... Ezra Street, Kolkata, and died on 5th December 20... leaving a Will written in English language made and attested on 5th June 20... appointing the petitioner as the Sole Executor of that Will.

2. PQ left behind the petitioner as the sole heir, PQ's mother and my mother having predeceased PQ and there was no other brother or sister of the petitioner.

3. The signature of the deceased in the said Will was duly attested by AB and CD who have proved the Will by two separate declarations made on 10th July 20.... The said declaration is annexed hereto.

4. The deceased above-named died leaving properties within the jurisdiction of this Hon'ble Court and your petitioner is desirous of taking Probate of the said Will.

5. The particulars of the estate of the deceased so far as the petitioner has been able to ascertain are set out in the affidavit of assets affirmed by your petitioner on 5th June 20.... The value of the assets after deducting the liabilities to the best of information of the petitioner amounts to ₹...........

6. Stamp Duty payable on the said estate amounts to ₹.......... which has been paid.

7. Your petitioner is desirous of obtaining grant of Probate of the said Will and Testament dated 5th June 20....... of the deceased under the seal of this Hon'ble Court in favour of your petitioner as the Sole Executor named in the said Will.

8. Your petitioner undertakes to pay additional court-fees if necessary.

9. This statement has been made *bona fide* and in the interest of justice.

Your petitioner, therefore, humbly prays Your Lordships for the following orders:

(*a*) That the Probate of the last Will and Testament dated 5th June, 20... of the deceased PQ above-named be granted to the petitioner as the Sole Executor named in the Will having effect throughout India;

(*b*) Your petitioner be given liberty to pay in the first instance out of the funds of the estate to come into his hands the costs and incidentals to this application;

(*c*) Such further and other orders be made and directions be given as may be deemed just and proper to this Hon'ble Court.

And your petitioner as in duty bound shall ever pray.

Verification

Affidavit

Index

Mitra's
Civil Reference

by
Sukumar Ray, LLM
West Bengal Judicial Service

A Virtual ENCYCLOPAEDIA on CIVIL LAWS

Key areas covered

- Constitution • Clinical Establishment
- Consumer Protection • Easement
- Electricity • Environment Protection
- Interpretation of Deeds & Statute
- Maintenance of Parents & Senior Citizen
- Marriage Laws including Child Marriage
- Specific Relief • Transfer of Property
- Land Law • Tort • Trust

Fifth Edition 2019
Hardcover ₹2850
ISBN 978-81-7177 345-9

Wills
Law and Practice

by
R.K. Bag
Judge, High Court at Calcutta

D.P. Dey
Judge, High Court at Calcutta

Key areas covered

- Presumption of will of 30 years
- Proof of Holograph will
- Suspicious circumstances
- Effect of slight discrepancy
- Will under Mahomedan Law

Edition 2018
Hardcover ₹875
ISBN 978-81-7177-336-7